The Peoples of Canada
A Post-Confederation History

The Peoples
of Canada
A Post-Confederation History

THIRD EDITION

J.M. Bumsted

OXFORD

UNIVERSITY PRESS

OXFORD
UNIVERSITY PRESS

70 Wynford Drive, Don Mills, Ontario M3C 1J9
www.oupcanada.com

Oxford University Press is a department of the University of Oxford.
It furthers the University's objective of excellence in research, scholarship,
and education by publishing worldwide in

Oxford New York
Auckland Cape Town Dar es Salaam Hong Kong Karachi
Kuala Lumpur Madrid Melbourne Mexico City Nairobi
New Delhi Shanghai Taipei Toronto

With offices in
Argentina Austria Brazil Chile Czech Republic France Greece
Guatemala Hungary Italy Japan Poland Portugal Singapore
South Korea Switzerland Thailand Turkey Ukraine Vietnam

Oxford is a trade mark of Oxford University Press
in the UK and in certain other countries

Published in Canada
by Oxford University Press

Copyright © Oxford University Press Canada 2008

National Library of Canada Cataloguing in Publication Data

Bumsted, J. M., 1938-
The peoples of Canada : a post-confederation history / J.M.
Bumsted. -- 3rd ed.

Includes bibliographical references and index.

ISBN 978-0-19-542341-9

1. Canada--History--1867-. I. Title.

FC500.B86 2007   971.05   C2007-905484-6
2 3 4 – 11 10 09

This book is printed on permanent (acid-free) paper ∞.
Printed in the United States.

CONTENTS

MAPS

Understanding History

Every experienced historian has at some point encountered someone from a totally different background who assumes that 'anyone can do history'. In the sense that anyone can research, write, and even publish historical work without specialized training, that assumption is correct. History is one of those fields—creative writing is another—where the standards of achievement can be flexible and intuitive, and where much of the methodology is based on plain common sense. History's accessibility to almost all of us, not simply as readers but as actual researchers, is one of its great charms and greater merits. And many people do engage in historical research without calling it by that name. Everyone who tries to trace her ancestry through the labyrinth of historical records (often called 'genealogy') is involved in a form of historical research. Everyone who tries to research the background to a business project as part of a report on its present status, or to explain how a sports team achieved a championship season, is in a sense 'doing history'. Every criminal trial (and almost every civil one) is at some level a historical reconstruction. The historical mode is one of the most common ways through which we attempt to understand the world we live in.

To say that nearly all of us engage in some form of historical reconstruction, often unconsciously, is not to say there are no fundamental rules to such activity. Most of us know instinctively that witnesses can be biased or mistaken, that human motivation is complex, and that in the chronological sequence of events—the establishment of which many non-professional historians regard as the centre of the enterprise—the cause must precede the effect. But history is not a laboratory science. Even the simplest rules of evidence and argument can be difficult to apply in specific situations, particularly if the researcher is operating intuitively. Understanding what causes these difficulties is important, and becoming sensitive to the problems of history is one of the chief benefits of formal historical study.

A good many Canadians (probably nearly as many as commonly read fiction or poetry) read history, for recreation and for information. Unfortunately, general readers often approach historical writing in much the same way they approach fiction, judging a work's value by its success in telling 'a good story'. But of course story-telling is only one of numerous ways in which history can be written. Although, as with fiction, there is great pleasure to be had from reading history simply at the level of entertainment, to remain at that level would be to miss much of the best modern historical writing. It is possible without training or formal critical tools to recognize that a Harlequin romance offers a far less complex view of the world than a Margaret Atwood novel; it is somewhat more difficult to appreciate a parallel difference in history. Readers who expect writers of fiction to have distinctive voices and world views still often assume that all historians participate equally in the effort to recover the truth of the past through application of some unspecified 'scientific' method: if history is about truth, then all historical writing must be more or less equally true, at least if the historian has 'the facts' right. The ordinary reader is frequently unable to distinguish between 'facts' and 'truth', failing to appreciate on one level that factual accuracy is in itself a complex issue and on another level that it has limited value as a critical test.

In addition, many readers fail to distinguish between history as everything that has happened before the present moment (also commonly known as 'the past') and history as the record (usually written) of the unfolding of some event(s) in that past. Yet the past can never be recovered, for reasons I shall discuss. All we can do is attempt to recreate and analyze discrete parts of it, refracted through the historian's prism. Only this history can be studied and investigated. As a further confusion, history can mean not only the historian's account of the past, but the systematic study of the past as a discipline or a craft. The study of either the work of individual historians or the discipline itself is often known as historiography. Just as filmmakers make a surprising number of movies about the process of making movies, so historians devote more of their energy to examining the making of history than they do to any other single project.

The processes of both reading and researching history can obviously be greatly enhanced by some understanding of the problems that engage historians as they pursue their craft. Before we turn to some of those problems, however, it might be well to consider the question of the value of history.

THE VALUE OF HISTORY

Once upon a time, especially in the nineteenth and earlier twentieth centuries, most people did not question the value of historical study or wonder how it was relevant to their lives. They did not doubt the value of the liberal arts or the humanities, much less debate the benefits of studying languages like Greek or Latin. There are really two separate but related issues inherent in the 'value of history' question. One is whether or not historical study has a sufficient grip on truth and meaning in our modern world to have any value at all, intrinsic or extrinsic. Ultimately, this question involves us in high philosophy and theory, but it also has a particular Canadian edge. The other question is whether or not historical work has a sufficiently attractive vocational payoff to justify its study at the university. Perhaps we should turn to the latter question first, since it is easier to answer and may be of more interest to the beginning historian.

For many centuries, the opportunity to attend a university was available only to those of outstanding intellectual abilities or privileged socio-economic standing. In a world that did not question the importance of religion, the original purpose of universities was to educate clerics. The university gradually became the centre of humanistic scholarship and enterprise generally, but so long as society valued education for its own sake—chiefly because it was something available only to the privileged few—its specific vocational role was quite insignificant. Universities turned out educated and 'cultured' men (not women until well into the nineteenth century) into a world that took for granted that such people were important to the society. Specific occupational training was not part of the university's function, and preparation even for such elevated professions as law or medicine was done outside its doors. Yet gradually the notion of vocational training did enter the cloistered world of the university, particularly in North America, and by 1940 it was possible to prepare for nearly any occupation through specialized studies at a university, although such opportunities were still limited to members of the elites. Despite the new vocational bent of the university, occupational studies were largely confined to the post-graduate level; most undergraduate students at universities (as opposed to acknowledged vocational centres such as teachers' training colleges) still expected An Education rather than A Vocation.

The great change in the nature of the university really came after 1945, when the idea took hold that all Canadians were entitled to attend university, and the number of university places was greatly expanded. A dynamic relationship has existed between the democratization of the university and the introduction of the idea that there should be some demonstrable economic value to a university degree. Thus specific occupational training now starts at the undergraduate rather than the graduate level. Today at many universities it is likely that the majority of students are enrolled in such programs, and even those who are not in such programs themselves commonly expect a university education to provide some kind of occupational entrée or advantage. In the new occupational sweepstakes, a field like history is of less obvious relevance than one like management or accounting or pharmacy or computers. Some historians would prefer to ignore the question of occupational relevance altogether, but the days of a simple liberal arts education for most university students are probably gone forever. History may not ever compete with accounting or pharmacy or medical school as preparation for employment, but it is still superb preparation for many professional programs (assuming that they do not insist on specialization from day one). And one can do more in the workforce with a history specialization than most students might at first think.

There are any number of history-related occupations besides teaching. They include work in archives, libraries, and museums, as well as in government service. 'Heritage' in itself is a major industry in Canada. Other occupations, such as law, journalism, and some branches of the civil service (the diplomatic corps, for example), have traditionally recruited heavily among history graduates, but any job requiring the ability to gather and analyze evidence and then communicate the findings is ideally suited to someone with a background in history. One individual with a graduate degree in history, Mike Smith, has become the general manager of several National Hockey League teams. What students have to do is learn to translate their historical training into the jargon of the contemporary job market. 'Researching term essays in history', for example, can be translated into 'using documentary resources to abstract and analyze complex information'. (At one recent 'interview' for a summer job with a government department, the student applicant was simply asked to summarize a complex document quickly and accurately.) To the extent that history is a discipline that teaches students both to think and to communicate, it should improve their qualifications for almost any job.

Beyond developing essential skills in research, analysis, and communication, what are the uses of history? Certainly few historians today believe—if they ever did—in the use of historical 'laws' of human conduct for predictive purposes. Most historians who have employed historical laws, such as Arnold Toynbee in *A Study in History*, Oswald Spengler in *The Decline of the West*, or Karl Marx in *Capital*, have done so on such an abstract level that it is difficult to translate those laws into specific terms. Toynbee's notion that civilizations pass through recognizable stages paralleling the human life cycle is attractive, but it does not tell us when our civilization will die. Employing the insights of Karl Marx, no reader could have concluded that the 'dictatorship of the proletariat' would come first in Russia, or that it would eventually lead not to a classless society but to the collapse of the Soviet Union. No discipline has worked harder than economics to achieve scientific status, but the whole world has come to appreciate that economists constantly disagree on even the most general level of prediction and analysis.

Yet if history cannot predict, it can help us to understand the difficulty of prediction. In the same way it can help us to recognize the recurrent and ongoing nature of many of society's problems. By and large, historians were far more sanguine about the outcome of the 1992 referendum on the Charlottetown constitutional accord than were the scaremongers on either side of the debate or many of the journalists covering the 'crisis'. Indeed, those with an understanding of Canadian history, constitutional and otherwise, were bound to find the very concept of a 'crisis' suspect, just as they would any other popular journalistic concept, such as 'conspiracy'. The historical record tells us that there have been crises and conspiracies, but equally that these terms have so often been used without justification that they have lost any real meaning.

History provides us not only with a social context but with a personal one as well. The genealogical search for 'roots' has become important for many Canadians seeking to trace their family backgrounds and to understand the circumstances that drove their ancestors across the ocean, or the ways their ancestors' lives changed as a result of the newcomers' arrival. Nor is the question of personal identity merely an individual matter. It is no accident that as minority groups in Canada work to develop themselves as collectivities, they need to establish and assert their historical experience. Over the past 30 or more years some Canadians have lost interest in the historical mode, adopting what we might call the 'irrelevance of history' position. But this has not been the case with collective 'minorities' such as women, Native peoples, blacks, and ethnic minorities. For these groups, establishing their rightful place in Canadian history has been an absolutely primary function. That these groups' interpretations of their histories have often run counter to the traditional versions of Canadian history does not render them any less consequential—or less historical.

THE ELUSIVE FACT

More than 50 years ago, a television series called *Dragnet* became famous for a catchphrase used by one of its characters, a police detective named Sergeant Joe Friday. When questioning witnesses, Friday always repeated the same request, delivered in an emotionless monotone: 'All I want is the facts, just give me the facts.' The monotone was intended to indicate Friday's objectivity and to extract from his witness a response devoid of personal bias and colouration. Of course he seldom got 'just the facts'—which from our perspective is exactly the point. Somehow, just as the popular mind in the 1950s associated Joe Friday with facts, so it has more recently come to think of historians as dealing in the same coin. The equation of facts and history has doubtless been assisted by the traditional way of teaching history in the schools, by marching out one name, date, event after another for students to commit to memory and regurgitate at the appropriate time in the course of an examination. Of course historians do rely on facts as their basic building blocks; but they do not think of them the way Sergeant Friday did, nor do they use them the way common opinion believes they do.

The *Canadian Oxford Dictionary* offers several meanings for 'fact'. The most familiar is probably number 1: 'a thing that is known to have occurred, to exist, or to be true', although number 4—'truth, reality'—is also very common. Facts, as *Dragnet* suggested, are true things, unsullied by any process of interpretation or conclusion. Such things may exist, but they are much harder to come by than one might expect, for several reasons. One problem is the language in which 'facts' must be stated. Another is the context in which they become significant.

Over the last century we have become increasingly aware that language is not a neutral instrument, but one that carries with it a heavy freight of cultural experience and usage. 'John Cabot discovered Newfoundland in 1497' may seem a straightforward statement of fact, but at least half of the words in it conjure up a whole host of meanings. One of those words is 'discovered'. The implication is that what Cabot found was previously unknown—but of course an Aboriginal population had been living in the area for millennia. Even qualifying the word 'discovered' with the phrase 'by Europeans' doesn't help much, since we now know that the Vikings had settled at L'Anse aux Meadows in the eleventh century, and even they may not have been the first Europeans to cross the Atlantic. 'Discovery' is a complex concept. The term 'Newfoundland' is equally problematic, since in modern geographic terms Cabot was not at all precise about his movements, and the land he sighted may not have been part of the island that we know as Newfoundland today. Indeed, Cabot called the land he saw 'the New-Founde Land', and it was only later that the label was applied to the island. Moreover, Cabot's sightings were not confirmed by anything other than vague self-declarations. To top matters off, there are questions about the identity of John Cabot himself, who started in Italy as Giovanni (or Zuan) Caboto and became John Cabot Montecalunya, a resident of Valencia, in the early 1490s, before he called himself John Cabot of Bristol. Almost all but the most simplistic statements are subject to the same difficulties. Philosophers have spent thousands of years trying to formulate 'true' statements, with very little success, and historians are unlikely to do much better. Almost any 'factual' statement worth making has to be expressed in a language heavily weighted with values and contexts. Language is only one of the challenges in the quest for the fact.

Even if facts could be expressed in a neutral language, such as numbers, we would still need to decide which facts are important. At any given moment there exists a virtual infinity of pieces of information that could be isolated and stated. Most 'historical facts' are simply labels of events and dates, names and movements, which by themselves do not tell us very much. They are not statements in which anything is asserted, and therefore they have no standing as facts. Only when their significance is implicitly or explicitly understood do they acquire any utility or susceptibility to truth. 'The Battle of Vimy Ridge' is not a fact, since it does not assert anything capable of being either true or false. 'The Battle of Vimy Ridge in 1917 was won by the Canadian army' is an assertion the validity of which can be assessed. Whether it is false or true (and hence 'a fact') is another matter entirely. The validity of the statement requires a detailed account of the battle in the context of the war.

One of the chief benefits of modern historical study is that it promotes a healthy skepticism about the neutrality and ultimate truth of the notorious fact. Taken by itself, in isolation, the fact has little meaning. It is only when facts are arranged into some larger picture—some sort of interpretive account—that they acquire significance. Those interpretive pictures themselves are subject to change over time. Anyone today who reads a Canadian history textbook written 40 years ago will be struck by the almost complete absence of any reference to women as important historical figures. Yet 40 years ago the majority of readers—even female readers—took that absence for granted. The apparent absence of women does not mean that women were not present. It simply means that historians of that generation did not regard their activities as worthy of attention. The historian can uncover whole constellations of new facts simply by asking a new question of the historical record, as happened when some scholar asked: 'What about the women?' History is not the study of something eternally fixed, of something that can be 'discovered', but rather the continual dynamic reinvestigation and re-evaluation of the past.

If historians can recover new facts, however, they are still limited to those facts that have been recorded in some way. The records need not be in written form; sometimes they take the form of oral history, sometimes of artifacts. Whatever form the evidence takes, it has to have been preserved. Preservation may be deliberate or serendipitous, but in either case certain biases may be observed. If we think about our own personal history, we realize that not every part of it has been recorded, let alone recorded with equal care; and much of the individual record that does exist has been preserved not through personal choice but to serve bureaucratic purposes. Not every society keeps public records, however, and even in the record-keeping societies, not everyone produces an equal quantity of evidence. Only a relative handful of historical actors, for example, have left behind their own written accounts. Personal evidence tends to be limited to those involved in self-consciously important activity, as defined by any particular society. Such recorders usually represent that society's elite, and what they record represents what the elites think needs recording. We know far more about taxation in the Middle Ages than we do about sexual behaviour, for example. Whatever their limitations, it is with the records that historians must start. They are the primary sources for historical investigation, as distinguished from secondary sources (usually other historians' research gleanings and interpretations). In working with primary sources, historians face two problems: the first one of authenticity, the second one of credibility.

For understandable reasons, historians have to be certain that the records they study are genuine. Historians thus prefer to work with original documents, the so-called 'manuscript' sources (although not all manuscripts are necessarily handwritten). The republication of such material often raises questions of accuracy, which become even more problematic when the documents have been translated from one language to another. Even the most scrupulous of editors may subtly alter the meaning of a document through changes in punctuation or spelling, and until our own time the editors of historical documents often intervened in other ways as well. A famous editor of Shakespeare named Thomas Bowdler expurgated material that he considered to be in bad taste (his name is now commemorated in the verb 'to bowdlerize'). Other editors silently rewrote texts to what they regarded as the advantage of their authors. Even the appearance of authenticity is no guarantee; many skilful forgeries have been designed to pass close inspection. The famous Shroud of Turin (supposedly showing the imprint of the body of Christ) is not necessarily a deliberate forgery, but recent scientific investigation has found that it could not be authentically associated with the crucifixion. As for the supposedly fifteenth-century 'Vinland Map', discovered in the 1960s, it still has not been satisfactorily authenticated, and many scholars think it is a forgery.

Even if we are dealing with an 'authentic' document, there are still many potential problems to face before we can use it as evidence. Many documents cannot be precisely dated or attributed to a specific author. But these questions must be addressed before the historian—acting all the parts in a court of law except that of witness—can determine the document's credibility. Was the author in a position to be authoritative? Are there reasons, obvious or subtle, for suspecting bias of some kind? Bias may appear in many forms. Authors may seek to justify themselves; they may place their interpretation of events in a context resulting from their place in society or from their ideological assumptions; they may report hearsay; they may adjust their accounts for literary reasons, or simply to tell 'a good story'. Evidence is best if it can be corroborated by more than one source; but supporting evidence is not always available, particularly for specific details. Like the 'facts' derived from them, the documents themselves are seldom unassailable as sources. Historians work with probabilities rather than certainties, and the more evidence is available, the more likely it is that there will be complications. In any event, students of history need to be both skeptical and critical of what they read, whether documentary evidence itself or interpretations of such material.

THE CONVENTIONS OF HISTORY

Historians have developed a series of conventions for dealing with their raw data. Historical information presented in its unexplicated form—as a series of unrelated facts—is not history as historians understand it, and insufficient attention to interpretation and context is one of the most common faults of beginning historians. Traditionally, the chief mode for historians has been narrative, the recounting of past events in the sequence in which they occurred. Like all aspects of historical work, narrative requires selection—cutting into the seamless web of the past to isolate a particular sequence of events involving a limited number of characters. Narrative deals with the passage of time, and—since it is axiomatic that cause and effect must be in the right sequence—chronology is critical to historical understanding. Many great historians of the past concentrated almost exclusively on narrative, appropriately embellished with description and context; an example is Francis Parkman, who wrote extensively on the early conflict of the French and British in North America. But most modern historians would agree with Arthur Marwick that 'the historian must achieve a balance between narrative and analysis, between a chronological approach and an approach by topic, and, it should be added, a balance between both of these, and, as necessary, passages of pure description "setting the scene", providing routine but essential information, conveying the texture of life in any particular age and environment.'[1] Some historians have even dropped narrative entirely, although the sequence of events remains implicitly crucial to their work.

Despite the common use of the term 'causation' in historical writing, particularly among beginners, philosophers of history have long emphasized that historians really do not deal much in the sort of cause-and-effect relationships usually associated with scientific work. The past is too complex to isolate factors in this way. Instead, historians talk about 'explanation', which is not quite the same as scientific causation. Explanation requires the inclusion of enough context and relevant factors to make it clear that the events in question were neither totally predetermined nor utterly capricious. As E.H. Carr has observed:

> . . . no sane historian pretends to do anything so fantastic as to embrace 'the whole of experience'; he cannot embrace more than a minute fraction of the facts even of his chosen sector or aspect of history. The world of the historian, like the world of the scientist, is not a photographic copy of the real world, but rather a working model which enables him more or less effectively to understand it and to master it. The historian distils from the experience of the past, or from so much of the experience of the past as is accessible to him, that part which he recognizes as amenable to rational explanation and interpretation, and from it draws conclusions.[2]

In their efforts at narrative and/or explanation, historians also use many other conventions. Among them, let us focus on periodization. The division of the past into historical 'periods' serves purposes beyond the organization of a teaching curriculum. By focusing attention on larger units of time, periodization serves to narrow and limit the range of material to be considered and helps to provide a structure for what would otherwise be a meaningless jumble of events and dates. The choice of beginning and end dates for larger historical sequences is hardly arbitrary, but it is still a matter of interpretation. Take, for example, the standard decision to divide Canadian history at 1867, the year of Confederation. This fundamental periodization reflects the assumption not only that political and constitutional development shaped everything else, but also that the creation of a national state called the Dominion of Canada was the critical point in that development. But it makes little sense for many other themes in Canadian history. Historians of Canada continually debate the question of relevant periods. The authors of the first survey of the history of women in Canada, for example, were forced to find a new way of periodizing their account, since the standard political and constitutional periodization reflected a chronology mainly masculine in emphasis.

NEW INTERPRETATIONS

Like all academic disciplines, history is constantly reinterpreting its subject matter. Some of the pressure for reinterpretation is a simple matter of growth: within the past quarter-century, the number of academic positions for historians in Canada has more than quadrupled, with the result that more individuals are now researching and writing within the field. At the same time, technological advances (in computers and photocopiers, for example) and the advent of the relatively inexpensive airline ticket have made it possible for historians to examine and process documentary materials in ways and quantities that would have been unthinkable at the beginning of the 1960s. Other pressures for revision, of course, come from changes in the social context, which is continually raising new questions for historians to explore, and shifts in the climate of opinion.

In history, revisionist movements usually arise out of new developments in three (often related) areas: subject matter, conceptual frameworks, and methodologies. A new development in any one of these areas may be enough on its own to provoke significant revision. When two or three come together (as is often the case), they can completely alter our understanding of the past.

Addressing new subject matter involves asking new questions about hitherto neglected aspects of the past. In Canadian history, with its traditional focus on the political and constitutional ways in which a national state was created, the opportunities for new questions have been quite substantial. Out of a variety of new subjects, we can perhaps offer three examples: women, Aboriginal peoples, and ethnic groups. While each of these subjects would today be regarded as central to any contemporary understanding of Canadian history, they were virtually neglected until recent years. As we have seen, lack of attention to women in the past did not reflect lack of information, but lack of interest on the part of historians. With the simple act of focusing attention on women, a new field of study was opened. In the case of Aboriginal peoples, the subject had not been entirely neglected, but it had virtually always been approached from the perspective of the developing national state. Thus many of the new questions raised today are aimed at understanding the First Nations' perspectives. As for ethnic groups, research has tended to involve scholars from a variety of disciplines, such as sociology and geography, and has been encouraged by the availability of grant money from governmental agencies at both the federal and provincial levels. Ethnic studies have proved to be politically popular within Canada.

New areas of study often suggest—if not require—new conceptual contexts. In general, all three of the new areas noted above fall under the rubric of 'social history'. As early as 1924, an article on 'The Teaching of Canadian History' advocated the study of the 'actual life of the Canadian people' in 'their efforts to secure a livelihood and then to provide for the higher demands of mind and spirit'.[3] Until recent years, however, much of the research in the social history area concentrated on the upper echelons of society in Canada, the so-called 'elites'. Broadening the social base to include individuals outside the ranks of those whose lives were normally documented (women, Aboriginal people, racial and ethnic minorities, ordinary working men) involved a substantial reconceptualization of the nature of Canada's past.

Studying those 'inarticulate' groups often required new methodologies as well. Perhaps the most important methodological innovation was quantification: generating new data sets by processing existing information not previously practicable for historical purposes out of data such as name-by-name census returns. At its worst, quantification could be little more than mindless number-crunching, but at its best it enabled historians to open up whole categories of hitherto unusable documentation. The information collected by the Dominion Bureau of the Census or the various provincial departments of Vital Statistics has provided much new insight into the way ordinary Canadians have lived (and loved) in the past. Computers have made it easier for historians to process large amounts of aggregate information—although the axiom 'Garbage In, Garbage Out' continues to apply. The complex processes of collecting and analyzing new categories of data have been contentious, and beginning historians should understand that the apparently simple act of producing a new set of information involves many steps and many disagreements. 'Hard' numbers and percentages are no more sacrosanct than information that appears 'softer'. Moreover, quantified data still require interpretation, and are subject to all the standard rules that apply to historical explanation.

Although explicit controversies do arise within the field of Canadian history, they are probably less common than controversies among historians of other nations, notably the United States and Great Britain. To some extent the profession has avoided confrontations by allowing each practitioner his or her own area of specialization (or 'turf'). This has made good sense because the number of questions not yet adequately explored in the history of Canada is considerable. Whatever the reasons for the muting of controversy, disagreements in Canadian historiography have had less to do with specific points and interpretations within a single tradition than with first principles and underlying assumptions. Thus Canadian historians tend to disagree only at the mega-level, as in the current debate over Canadian 'national history', which is really a debate among scholars with two totally different sets of assumptions about the role of narrative in the past. Those on the moving frontier of scholarship are in some ways far less embattled than those still working in older traditions, since they can simply add their 'new' interpretations onto the old ones.

Because history is a cumulative subject, students should not think that the latest books and journal articles are necessarily better simply by virtue of their dates of publication. Many older works of historical scholarship can still be regarded as the best treatments of their topics. This is particularly true in traditional areas of study that have not attracted much attention from modern scholars, such as the military history of the War of 1812. Earlier generations were fond of publishing editions of documents, which if well-transcribed, translated, and edited are just as valuable today as they were a century ago. The complete (and most commonly used) edition of the *Jesuit Relations* in English was published between 1896 and 1901. On some topics our only sources are earlier documents; for example, Richard Hakluyt's sixteenth-century accounts are still essential for any study of English overseas voyages.

By now it should be clear that both the writing and the reading of history are extremely complicated enterprises. Whole books with titles like *Understanding History* or *The Nature of History* have been devoted to introducing students to the complexities of the craft, and in the space of a few pages it is impossible to explore all the potential dimensions. In any case, readers of this book should understand that every work of history involves a series of decisions to hold various contradictions in dynamic tension. Among the most important issues held in tension in this book are the following:

1. *Interpretive complexity versus authority*. Virtually every sentence in this work (or any other work of history) could be hedged in with conflicting evidence and interpretation. The result would almost certainly be incomprehensible. I have chosen to favour readability over total academic accuracy. This is not to say that I do not recognize the issues of interpretive complexity. Rather, I have consciously addressed them in two ways: by introducing questions of interpretation into

the text on a regular basis, and by including three essays on historiography.

2. *Individual biography versus groups and forces.* One problem that all historians face (or ought to face) is how to make the material interesting to readers. As any newspaper editor will tell you, readers like their stories to have people in them. This work uses the experiences of individual people to represent and suggest the complex groups and forces that lie behind them. I do not subscribe to the Great Person theory of history, but I do believe in personalizing history as much as possible.

3. *Overarching master narrative versus the complex voices of social and cultural history.* Whether or not Canadian history has a single narrative is a hotly debated issue today, sometimes posed in the form of the question 'Is there a national history?' The single narrative is also related to the problem of authority, although the two are not the same. A coherent and connected single narrative could be based on the concept of the development of the nation, or on viewing events from the perspective of that nation, or on something quite different. The point is that any such narrative line represents an abstraction. Critics of the abstract, single-narrative approach associate it with the imposition of a hegemonic 'master principle' that in turn is often taken to represent the sequence of events preferred by the 'men in suits' or the 'ruling class' or the 'politicians in Ottawa'. Many groups are commonly left outside such a master narrative: workers, racial and cultural minorities, women, inhabitants of marginalized regions, inhabitants of alienated regions (e.g., Quebec for much of the twentieth century). Over the past 35 years, Canadian historians have concentrated on recovering the voices of these groups. But if those voices were all we heard, telling their own stories in their own tongues, the resulting cacophony would be unintelligible; and to establish chronology and meaningful periodization, we need a structure that will provide some common reference points. Hence a master narrative of some kind is still essential.

The master narrative around which this book is structured, into which all the other stories are woven, is a highly abstract one that may be labelled 'the history of Canada'. I hope this discussion will help readers to understand the chapters that follow.

J.M. Bumsted
Winnipeg, 2007

The Peoples
of Canada
A Post-Confederation History

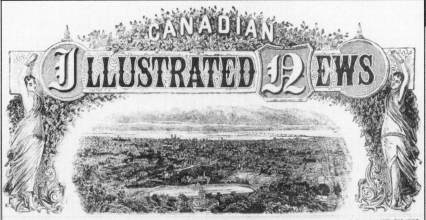

CANADIAN ILLUSTRATED NEWS

Vol. I.—No. 13.]   MONTREAL, SATURDAY, JANUARY 29, 1870.   [SINGLE COPIES, TEN CENTS. $4 PER YEAR IN ADVANCE.

"THE SITUATION."—See next page.

☐ 'The Situation', cover of the *Canadian Illustrated News*, 29 January 1870. Miss Red River must decide between the US Hotel, with its disreputable, apparently indifferent Uncle Sam, and the Hotel Canada, where a respectable lady offers a warm welcome. Library and Archives Canada (LAC), C-48653.

PART ONE

■ 1867–1885

■ When the Dominion of Canada began its formal existence on 1 July 1867, one of the main purposes behind the act of confederation—to separate the old united Canada (East and West) into two provinces—was achieved. The new country had little idea of its future direction beyond a general sense of a 'manifest destiny' to expand and create a new political entity stretching from coast to coast. In 1867, however, it was not at all clear that such a project could actually be carried out. Within six years Canada would gain three new provinces and a vast western hinterland. But Canadians had very little experience at continental empire-building, and they made some serious blunders in their efforts to take over and administer the vast territories that they purchased from the Hudson's Bay Company in 1868. They also blundered in their first efforts to bring in Prince Edward Island, and only financial pressures led the tiny Island to join Confederation in 1873. (Newfoundland would remain unpersuaded until 1949.)

By 1873 Canada in theory stretched from Atlantic to Pacific, but a vast expanse of the West was virtually uninhabited and lacked any sort of communication links with the East. The West would have to be settled, and a railway constructed to connect the country. The challenges were not merely physical. New policies had to be developed to accommodate the new provinces, and a sense of national identity needed to be encouraged that would be capable of transcending strong provincial loyalties. Nor did everyone agree on what sort of a nation Canada should become: centralized or decentralized, part of the British Empire or autonomous.

In November 1885, two events took place—within a few days of one another—that were to become powerful symbols for the young country: the last spike of the transcontinental railway was driven at Craigellachie, BC, uniting east and west; and the Métis leader Louis Riel was executed for 'treason', dividing not only Aboriginal and white but also French- and English-speaking Canadians.

CHAPTER ONE

The Completion of Confederation, 1867–1873

The first day of July 1867 certainly marked a beginning in the development of the Dominion of Canada. But in a larger sense it was only an interim point. The new union consisted of four provinces—carved from the three that had created it—and Sir John A. Macdonald's government was conscious that a lot of British territory on the continent had been excluded. The new government was also quite obviously the old Canadian coalition, with a few Maritime faces, organized into the old Canadian departments and using buildings erected in Ottawa for the old Union of the Canadas. Furthermore, several of the new government's first responsibilities involved 'old' rather than 'new' business. The malcontents from Nova Scotia would have to be pacified, the strays would have to be rounded up, and the promise of westward expansion would have to be fulfilled. Over the next half-dozen years three new provinces would be added, a fourth retained—and a fifth positively refused. Each situation was different, and few generalizations are possible. About the only thing the five provinces had in common was a singular lack of enthusiasm for the new union. By 1873 Canada would be a very different country, physically and demographically, than it had been in 1867. The possibilities for future development would be far more apparent.

THE ATLANTIC PROVINCES

NOVA SCOTIA AND NEW BRUNSWICK: PACIFYING THE ANTI-CONFEDERATES

When Joseph Howe returned from London in 1867, the anti-confederate movement in the Maritimes was stymied. A petition for reconsideration of Nova Scotia's membership in Confederation, although supported by John Bright (one of the leading Reformers in Westminster), was easily defeated in the British Parliament by a vote of 183 to 87. In September Nova Scotians elected pledged anti-confederates to all its seats, federal and provincial; but this was hardly a long-term solution. Like the provinces that had not joined, Nova Scotia (and New Brunswick) could only hope for 'better terms'. Howe led a repeal delegation to London in early 1868, but got no support from the British government and became disillusioned with British politics and politicians. Prime Minister Macdonald wrote Howe several times in the early autumn of 1868, emphasizing the government's dilemma: if he did not complete his cabinet and appoint officials, the government could not operate, and if he appointed unionists, he would be working against the public will.

TIMELINE

1865

Newfoundland assembly debates Confederation.

1866

British Columbia and Vancouver Island are united.

1867

The Dominion of Canada is proclaimed on 1 July. Parliament rejects petition for reconsideration of Nova Scotia's membership in Canada. William McDougall introduces resolutions for Canadian expansion.

1868

Joseph Howe leads repeal delegation from Nova Scotia to London.

1869

Howe reluctantly supports Confederation. Newfoundland debates prospective terms of union. This is the main campaign issue in 1869 election, which sees union candidates defeated. Howe joins Canadian cabinet. Governor Musgrave moves from Newfoundland to British Columbia. Métis led by Louis Riel organize resistance to Canadian takeover and set up provisional government.

1870

PEI rejects Canada's offer of 'better terms'. Execution of Thomas Scott. Debate over union in Legislative Council of British Columbia. Negotiations between BC and Canada over union. Red River admitted to Confederation as province of Manitoba. Wolseley expedition 'invades' Manitoba.

1871

British Columbia enters Confederation. PEI begins railroad construction.

1872

Responsible government comes to British Columbia. PEI opens union question.

1873

PEI delegation secretly negotiates terms with Canada. PEI joins Confederation.

Howe fully recognized the awkwardness of everyone's position. He was under pressure from some of the extremists to embrace independence or American annexation. In January 1869 Howe wrote Macdonald acknowledging his acceptance of the 'situation'. He then travelled to Ottawa (via Portland, Maine) to renegotiate Nova Scotia's debt and subsidies, thus providing 'better terms'. Howe's support for Confederation, however reluctant, was the key breakthrough in Nova Scotia. He could not prevent the formation of the Nova Scotia Repeal League and declarations (in the *Halifax Chronicle*) that 'We will not endure Union with Canada, we shall pay no taxes to the Dominion Government, except when we are forced to by the bayonets.'[1] But he could provide a conduit and a connection between the federal government and the province. Although he probably did not do his reputation much good—at the time or since then—by allying himself with Macdonald, his acceptance of the reality of the union and his refusal to engage in useless opposition were probably among his most important and statesmanlike acts.

In February 1869 Howe ran as a pro-confederate—in a hotly contested federal by-election—in Hants County. Despite a serious bout of bronchitis, which made campaigning difficult, he won with a comfortable majority and headed off to Ottawa. Within weeks he was sitting in the cabinet. In Ottawa, Howe's task was to attract the support of Nova Scotia MPs to the government, which he did gradually through local patronage. In 1871 he wrote a series of letters in support of confederation that were published in the course of the provincial elections, which substantially reduced the majority of the 'Nova Scotia Party' led by William Annand. In 1872 the Nova Scotia government started an active railroad building program, and after the Liberals under Alexander Mackenzie replaced the Tories in Ottawa in 1873, Nova Scotians increasingly spoke of a working alliance with the federal government. Gradually the Nova Scotia government abandoned its overt anti-confederate stance, and Nova Scotia MPs in Ottawa became allied with the two major federal parties, although residual resentment would surface from time to time over the years.[2]

PRINCE EDWARD ISLAND

THE LAND QUESTION

Most provinces had more than one reason for accepting Confederation. For Prince Edward Island an important motive was settlement of the long-standing land issue. As one Island newspaper put it, 'only let any government, legislative, federal, or mongrel, but offer 200,000 pounds sterling, to buy out the proprietors' claims, and give them [the people] free lands, and tell [them] their taxation will not be increased, and we believe the Islanders almost to a man would hold up both hands for the union.'[3] The Island's dele-

gates thought they had a commitment for that sum from the Canadians (chiefly George-Étienne Cartier). But when George Coles, the PEI delegate to the Quebec Conference, tried to write this condition into the Quebec Resolutions, his request was rejected; he then told the delegates 'they might as well strike Prince Edward Island out of the constitution altogether.'[4] Coles later declared himself against Confederation, and he was far from alone. In late 1864 the journalist Edward Whelen, one of union's main supporters, told A.T. Galt that the Island was totally against union; and the journalist Edward Reilly, denouncing the Quebec Resolutions as 'a scheme of spoliation for the Island', declared that resolution of the land issue was the *sine qua non* of the Island's entry into the union.[5]

Meanwhile, an organized movement of opposition to the proprietors called the Tenant League was becoming increasingly militant. In 1865 troops were required to quell sporadic outbreaks of disorder across the Island, and the British insisted the Island would have to pay for the troops itself. The Island government complained that the reason for the Tenant League's existence was the imperial government's failure to resolve the land question. When the House of Assembly and Legislative Council debated union again in May 1866, again most of the speakers opposed it. Among them was a farmer named Cornelius Howatt, who argued that Islanders 'would be such a small portion of the confederacy, our voice would not be heard in it. We would be the next thing to nothing. Are we then going to surrender our rights and liberties? It is just a question of "self or no self". Talk about a local Legislature. It would be a mere farce.'[6] In July the Island government bought the 212,885-acre (86,152-hectare) Cunard estate, initiating the policy of land purchase that would eventually prove to be the solution to the issue.

In London in August of 1866, at the imperial government meeting to finalize Confederation and prepare a final draft of the British North America Act, Premier J.C. Pope met privately with the Nova Scotia and New Brunswick dele-gates. Telling them that the Quebec terms were 'unjust, unfair and illiberal' to the Island, he added that, 'if they wished the people of Prince Edward Island to consider the matter at all, they must be prepared, in the first place, to enable us to extinguish Proprietary Rights, and to place us in as good a position as if our lands were crown lands.'[7] The delegates agreed unanimously that if the Island legislature would send delegates to arrange a plan that could be worked into the British North America Act, they would support the granting of whatever amount was necessary to purchase the proprietary rights, up to $800,000. The Canadian cabinet subsequently discussed this proposal and decided that the offer could be binding only if it were inserted in the BNA Act, which the cabinet had no power to do without legislative approval. If PEI joined, the land question could be discussed in a liberal spirit in London, and 'a strong representation to the first Government and Parliament of the United Provinces in favor of their granting com-pensation agreed upon by them'.[8] This response was seen by the Island government as unfavour-able, and in October the *Islander* newspaper printed a letter from former Premier Robert Haythorne mocking 'the paltry bribe of £3 cur-rency per head' and advising Islanders to reject the offer.[9] Lieutenant-governor George Dundas wrote to the Colonial Office that he thought a majority of the Island government would have accepted a proper offer. But that government was defeated in early 1867—partly because of the union question, partly because of its repression of the Tenant League—and the new government of George Coles voted to raise the cash required to buy out the proprietors on its own. In addition to this fundraising effort PEI proposed a reci-procity treaty with the Americans, who in August 1868 sent a committee to Charlottetown to dis-cuss the idea. The talks went very well—and when the Colonial Office learned of them it pan-icked, partly because a separate agreement might endanger a larger Canadian initiative with the

United States on reciprocity, and partly because such a deal might enable PEI to remain inde-pendent. A disapproving dispatch was sent accusing the Island of exceeding its authority. Many PEI legislators resented that interference, which they took as evidence that the British wanted to force the Island into union with Canada.

NEGOTIATING 'BETTER TERMS'

In the end, the Americans did not pursue the treaty, but the prospect was enough to galvanize the Canadian House of Commons into consider-ing the PEI issue. Action would probably have been taken had not Alexander Mackenzie, then a leading member of the opposition, been vehe-mently opposed. However, the Governor General of Canada and three Canadian cabinet ministers happened to visit the Island for a holiday in the summer of 1869, and they met with the provin-cial government. By now the Island had another premier, once again Robert Haythorne, who told them not only that 'the land question is the chief public question'[10] but that Canada would have to persuade Islanders that it did not intend to take more money from PEI than it spent there. As a result of those discussions, in December 1869 the Canadian government offered the Island gen-erous terms, including a per capita debt allow-ance of $25; a special subsidy to cover local gov-ernment; and an 'efficient Steam Service for the conveyance of Mails and Passengers' between the Island and the mainland, winter and summer, providing 'continuous communication'. It also promised that Canada would seek compensation from the imperial government for the Island's lack of Crown lands, and that if that request was refused, the Dominion itself would lend the Island $800,000 to help it deal with the land question.[11] Nevertheless, the Haythorne govern-ment summarily rejected the Canadian offer (always known as 'better terms') on the grounds that it did not resolve enough of the outstanding issues. Most observers agreed that union with Canada would require a full solution to the land question, not merely a loan to the Island government.

In 1871 the PEI legislature began on a course of active railway construction. The main objection to railway building was that it would lead to union with Canada. As one opposition legislator put it, 'the intention of the Government is to construct a railroad from one end of the Island to the other, saddle the Colony with a debt relatively heavier than that of the Dominion, then enter the Dominion and give up the Railroad.'[12] Between contracting overruns and the demands of every village for rail service, the province found that its debentures were unacceptable on the London market. Union with Canada was the only way to maintain the public credit, and the Dominion seized the opportunity when Premier Haythorne reopened the question of union late in 1872. In February 1873 a secret delegation headed by Haythorne stole off to Ottawa—in the night, by iceboat—and quickly agreed to a deal. The terms seemed generous on Canada's part. Not only did the Dominion assume the Island's debts and liabilities, but it agreed to pay a debt allowance, an annual grant, and a subsidy. Although all railroads under contract and construction became Dominion property, the Island would receive up to $800,000 in lieu of Crown lands to complete the purchase of proprietorial property, and continuous communication with the mainland was guaranteed. As Sir Leonard Tilley explained the Canadian offer in the House of Commons, 'the great local works there having been completed, there could never be any large local expenditure in the future, and it was in consideration of this fact that the Dominion Government had granted such liberal terms.'[13] All but one of the Island's legislators voted to accept the Canadian offer: the crusty old Cornelius Howatt refused to make the vote unanimous. (Over a century later, 'Cornelius Howatt, Superstar!' would become the symbol for an Island organization that questioned the positive rhetoric surrounding the centennial of PEI's entry into Confederation.)

On 1 July 1873, just before noon, the sheriff of Prince Edward Island, accompanied by some ladies and gentlemen, stepped forward on the balcony of the Colonial Building (where the Charlottetown Conference had been held nine years earlier) and read the proclamation of union. According to the *Patriot* newspaper, the audience below consisted of three people. After the reading, those on the balcony gave a cheer; the three persons below 'responded never a word'. Prince Edward Island settled down to become what it had known all along it would be: the smallest, least powerful, and poorest province within the Confederation.

NEWFOUNDLAND

In 1864 Newfoundland had in effect invited itself to the Quebec Conference, but the colony of 130,000 people scattered along the seacoast of a large island had found a decision on union too divisive to pursue. By the later 1860s, however, deteriorating economic conditions seemed to make the prospect of union more attractive. A series of bad years in the cod fishery,[14] mainly in the inshore areas, led the merchants to stop doing business on credit—'It is not our duty to maintain paupers', proclaimed one firm[15]—and the collapse of the truck system caused enormous suffering. Economic diversification was obviously essential, and those Canadian markets became increasingly inviting. Fearful of another Nova Scotia, Governor Anthony Musgrave and his Council agreed that it would be dangerous to pursue the project without 'a nominal reference to the body of the people'.[16] In 1869, therefore, the Assembly debated the proposed terms of union. None of the late applicants for entry would have any opportunity to alter the fundamental conditions of Confederation; all they could do was add 'terms'. Newfoundland's terms were fairly demanding (John A. Macdonald would later complain that they were far too great). In addition to the framework provided in the British North America Act, Newfoundland wanted the Dominion to pay the salaries of its leading officials; assume its public debt; provide subsidies for the support of local institutions; and pay $175,000 in return for the transfer of ungranted and unoccupied lands, mines, and minerals; as well as provide an exemption on export taxes, continuance of a garrison at St John's, special subsidies for the fishery, an annual subsidy to the government to replace lost income, and guaranteed steam communication with the mainland for both Newfoundland and Labrador. These terms were debated but then set aside pending 'an appeal . . . to the people at the next General Election'.[17]

An election is never ideal as a plebiscite, since other issues can intrude on the central question and influence the result. Other factors can also make a difference: for example, timing. Premier Frederick Carter delayed calling the election until after the spring fishery on the grounds that it would be unfair to hold an election when so many Newfoundlanders were away at sea; he wanted no charge of undue manipulation. Unfortunately, by the summer of 1869 the economy was looking up, and the opposition had had the benefit of five years (since 1864) to mobilize its forces. Turnout was unusually high—almost 10 per cent higher in most ridings than in the election of 1865. However, the Catholic vote was still firmly opposed to union— the confederate Ambrose Shea, running in a Catholic area, was greeted at Placentia by a priest and populace carrying pots of pitch and bags of feathers—and the Protestant vote split fairly evenly, as did the merchants'. In the end only nine confederates were elected, to 21 antis. Confederates blamed their defeat on the tactics of the opposition, which had predicted that the colony would surrender £618,000 to Canada in revenues in order to get £617,000 from Canada in subsidies and even spread rumours that Newfoundland children would be used as wadding for Canadian cannon. Perhaps the greatest argument against the scheme was fear of the unknown. Most contemporaries thought

intelligent people (read the elite) for the most part supported Confederation and the 'ignorant people' opposed it. Ultimately, however, it is impossible to tell whether the election reflected Newfoundlanders' true feelings about union. What is clear is that neither Canada nor the British government was sufficiently concerned about Newfoundland to seek to undo the conclusion reached in 1869; they were content to wait for Newfoundland to come around. The colony would from time to time show signs of a change of heart, but never quite managed one until 1949, and then under extraordinary circumstances.

THE CREATION OF MANITOBA AND THE NORTH-WEST TERRITORIES

CANADA MOVES TO EXPAND

On 4 December 1867, less than six months after the new Dominion of Canada had begun life as a nation, the MP from Lanark North (Ontario), William McDougall—one of the coalition Liberals who remained in the Confederation government—introduced seven resolutions into Parliament that were designed to set the stage for expanding the fledgling nation across to the prairies and out to the Pacific. The debate that followed was marked both by profound ignorance of the region and by extreme partisanship—and helps explain why the Canadian government would have so much trouble taking control of the West. Objections came from two separate quarters. One group, the opposition proper—the few remaining supporters of George Brown (who had failed to gain a seat in Parliament himself)—complained about the cost of expansion. The other, consisting of most of the Nova Scotia members and a number from New Brunswick, led by Joseph Howe, wanted relations between the Maritimes and the union government sorted out before embarking on a project of continental expansion that would make Maritime secession more difficult. Both groups agreed on the ultimate desirability of a continental nation. But not just yet.

The fact that a local population already existed in Red River was not completely ignored, either by McDougall in his resolutions or by the participants in the subsequent debate. But what was said about that population made it clear that Canada had no understanding of the local issues involved. Several supporters of the resolutions argued that the local people were entitled to liberation from the oppressive administration of the Hudson's Bay Company. Obviously they had read the *Nor'-Wester* newspaper's editorials, without realizing that these represented the opinions of only a small minority of Canadians resident in the settlement. Mr Chipman of New Brunswick used the occasion of the debate to remind the House of how the Maritimes had been dragooned into Confederation, posing a single rhetorical question—'were all the inhabitants of this territory willing to come into the Union, or were they to be dragged in against their will also?' and then sitting down. Dr Thomas Parker, a Tory representing Wellington Centre, Ontario, delivered a long, rambling speech in which he advocated taking possession of the territory on the sole principle of the 'right of a settler's spade' to cultivate the earth, arguing that the 'Indians' had been expelled from eastern Canada on that principle and that he saw no reason to treat the 'white savage'—apparently a reference to the mixed bloods—with any more consideration than the 'red' one. Parker had some qualms about purchasing the HBC charter, 'divorcing half a continent condemned . . . to sterility, unchristianity and barbarism', and many of his listeners agreed. On 11 December an opposition amendment was defeated by 104 to 41. The resolutions were then read and passed.[18] With expressions of ignorance and racism, the Canadian Parliament had endorsed westward expansion and the bringing of civilization to the Northwest.

In 1868 William McDougall accompanied Sir George-Étienne Cartier to London to negotiate the transfer of the region to Canada. The HBC bargained hard, but eventually agreed to sell the territory, including Red River, to Canada in return for £300,000 in cash, generous land grants—45,000 acres (18,210 hectares) around each trading post and what eventually amounted to 7,000,000 acres (2,832,800 hectares) scattered throughout the West—and the right of continued trade without hindrance. The negotiations were completed in March 1869, and the takeover was scheduled to take place on 1 December. Unfortunately, none of the parties involved—Canada, the British government, or the HBC—felt any need to consult formally or informally with either the Red River government (the Council of Assiniboia) or the residents of Red River at any point in this process. What the Canadians had in mind for the land acquired from the HBC (eventually divided into Manitoba and the North-West Territories) was a temporary colonial administration, to be run by a lieutenant-governor and an appointed council of seven to 15 members, with all previous functionaries and public officers continuing in their duties. The legislation prepared for the transfer was not very specific about details such as land policy. The Canadian government appointed McDougall the new territory's first lieutenant-governor and gave him a team of carpetbagging officials and councillors, none of whom had ever set foot in the West. The *Montreal Herald* described them as 'six Canadian adventurers . . . going there to try to make their fortunes in the scramble which is likely to take place for any good thing which might turn up, in the way of town lots, mines, or especially valuable agricultural territory'. Even the *Globe*, which had long supported western expansion, acknowledged that 'If William McDougall is sent to Fort Garry with a ready-made council composed of men utterly ignorant of the country and the people, the strongest feelings of discontent will be aroused.'[19] Naturally, the Canadian government did not bother to inform anyone in the West of the new arrangements.

The government proceeded to compound its

mistakes by dispatching in advance of the transfer a team of surveyors to prepare the way for an influx of settlement. Bishop A.-A. Taché of Red River, on his way to the Vatican Council in Rome, stopped in Ottawa to warn the Canadians of their errors. But Cartier brushed the warnings aside; as the Bishop later described their meeting, 'he [Cartier] knew it all a great deal better than I did, and did not want any information.' The survey team was officially welcomed by the local governor of the HBC in Red River, William Mactavish, who nonetheless warned that 'as soon as the survey commences the Halfbreeds and Indians will at once come forward and assert their rights to the land and probably stop the work.'[20] The leader of the team, John Stoughton Dennis, then made a difficult situation worse by attempting to survey occupied land in the settlement first. Nor was this the only provocation on the part of the Canadians: an earlier party, building a road from Lake of the Woods to the settlement, had been involved in a number of racial incidents, and some of the road crew were discovered trying to buy land from the Métis and Indians. By early September the American consul in Winnipeg was telling Washington that most of Red River was hostile to the plan for Canadian annexation. He thought an uprising unlikely, however, because the people had no political experience or talent for organization. At about the same time, McDougall ordered 100 Spencer carbines and 250 Peabody muskets to be sent to Fort Garry along with ammunition suitable for 'such Police and Volunteer Force as may be necessary'. Whether he had been warned by the leaders in Red River that trouble was brewing is not clear. By the early autumn of 1869, however, the Canadians were clearly perceived as a threat to the land, language, and religion of the local inhabitants, the Métis.

THE MÉTIS RESISTANCE

At this point Louis Riel emerged to lead the Métis. Born into a respected local family in 1844

and named after his father, who led a successful Métis protest against the HBC in 1849, the young Riel spoke out publicly against the surveys. Then in October 1869, while the surveyors were running their line south of Fort Garry through the land of André Nault, Riel led a party of neighbours to Nault's farm, where they stood on the surveyors' chain and told them to stop. This act was Riel's first resistance to Canada's acquisition of the HBC's territory. Soon after, Joseph Howe, the Canadian secretary of state for the provinces, arrived in Red River on an informal fact-finding expedition. Although Howe did not talk officially with any of the leading figures in the eventual uprising, he discovered that Red River already had a government (the Council of Assiniboia, created by the HBC in 1835) and a court system that had been functioning smoothly for years, and that many of the local people deeply resented Canada's interference.

In the meantime William McDougall was already on his way west to assume office. In late October, in the middle of a snowstorm, McDougall and Howe met as they were heading in opposite directions across the prairie, but Howe did not stop to brief the prospective lieutenant-governor. In Red River the newly formed National Committee of the Métis resolved that McDougall would not be allowed to enter the country, and sent him a message, which he received as he was approaching Pembina, on the American border: 'The National Committee of the Métis orders William McDougall not to enter the Territory of the North West without special permission of the above-mentioned committee.'[21] This warning—dated 21 October 1869 and signed 'Louis Riel, Secretary'—was Riel's second act of resistance to Canada. When the Council of Assiniboia summoned Riel to explain his actions, he replied that the Métis were 'perfectly satisfied with the present Government and wanted no other'; that they 'objected to any Government coming from Canada without their being consulted in the matter'; and that they 'would never admit any Governor no matter by whom he might be appointed, if not by the Hudson's Bay Company, unless Delegates were previously sent, with whom they might negotiate as to the terms and conditions under which they would acknowledge him'. Finally, Riel insisted that his compatriots were 'simply acting in defence of their own liberty', and 'did not anticipate any opposition from their English-speaking fellow countrymen, and only wished to join and aid in securing their common rights.'[22]

In early November Riel and a large party of his men walked into Upper Fort Garry, the Hudson's Bay Company fort, and took possession of it. The Métis then invited the anglophone mixed bloods to meet with them to 'consider the present political state of this Country and to adopt such measures as may be deemed best for the future welfare of the same.'[23] Delegates from the two groups would meet several times in November and debate subsequent actions. The English-speakers wanted to admit McDougall—who by now was marking time in a shabby residence at Pembina—and then negotiate with him, but Riel and his people insisted that negotiations must come first. On 27 November the Canadian government informed Britain that it would delay the transfer of the territory until the unrest died down. Prime Minister Macdonald understood perfectly well the consequences of any precipitate action, and on the same day wrote to McDougall warning him against any attempt to assume his position as lieutenant-governor, since that would automatically put an end to the authority of the Hudson's Bay Company:

> There would then be, if you were not admitted into the country, no legal government existing, and anarchy must follow. In such a case, no matter how the anarchy is produced, it is quite open by the law of nations for the inhabitants to form a government ex necessitate for the protection of life and property, and such a government has certain sovereign rights by the *ius gentium*, which might be very convenient for the United States, but exceedingly inconvenient to you.[24]

Unfortunately, communications with the Northwest still took a minimum of two weeks in winter, and this time lag would prove fatal.

Although he had been instructed to wait for an official warrant, on 1 December 1869 the impatient McDougall issued a proclamation extending the Queen's writ to Red River. When the Métis and mixed-blood delegates received this document, they decided to prepare a declaration of 'rights' as a preliminary to negotiations with Canada. The declaration was drafted by Riel, probably with the assistance of some Americans then in Winnipeg looking to encourage the Métis to negotiate with Washington. The list of rights began with the right of the people to elect their own legislature, with the power to pass all local laws, with a two-thirds majority overriding an executive veto. No act made by the Dominion Parliament would be binding on the territory without the consent of its legislature. All local officials were to be elected by the people. The document also called for a free homestead and pre-emption land law, providing cheap land for new settlers (a very American provision) and full bilingualism in both the legislatures and the courts, with 'all Public Documents and Acts of the Legislature' to be published in both French and English (very Canadian). Finally, the document demanded full and fair representation in the Canadian Parliament, and the continuation of 'all privileges, customs and usages existing at the time of the transfer'. The delegates of the two mixed-blood groups agreed that these were 'fair'. Where they disagreed was on the question of whether they could negotiate with Canada on the basis of this declaration. The anglophones were prepared to deal, but Riel and the Métis insisted that Canada had to come to the bargaining table with these rights embodied in an Act of Parliament as a preliminary to negotiation. When the mixed bloods refused to accept this position, Riel told them to 'Go, return peacefully to your farms. Rest in the arms of your wives. Give that example to your children. But watch us act. We are going to work and obtain the guarantee of our rights and of yours. You will come to share them in the end.'[25]

THE DECLARATION OF A PROVISIONAL GOVERNMENT

On 7 December Riel and his men surrounded the store owned by the leader of the 'Canadian party', Dr John Christian Schultz, where a number of Canadians had barricaded themselves. They took Schultz and 48 others to Fort Garry as prisoners, and the next day Riel issued a 'Declaration of the People', announcing the creation of a provisional government to replace the Council of Assiniboia. He, as president, offered to negotiate with Canada on the terms for Red River's entry into Confederation. A Métis flag—a fleur de lys and a shamrock on a white background—was raised over Upper Fort Garry on 10 December. Riel had done exactly as Macdonald had predicted. By now the Canadian press generally appreciated the extent of blundering involved, but the government could not bring itself to admit that it had been wrong in its approach to the transfer from beginning to end. Instead of sending emissaries fully empowered to negotiate with Riel, Canada sent a series of envoys with no authority to make any promises. On 27 December Donald A. Smith—the head of the Hudson's Bay Company in Canada, who had been appointed by Macdonald to explain to the people of Red River how Canada intended to govern the country and to report on the disturbances—arrived at the settlement and suggested a mass meeting of the inhabitants. Two such meetings were held, on 19 and 20 January 1870 —outdoors, in the bitter cold. Smith won over some of the crowd with his assurances that Canada would not interfere with the property, language, or religion of the people of Red River, but was forced by Riel to admit that he had no power to negotiate. Smith therefore agreed to take back to Canada a statement of what Red River regarded as essential to its acceptance of Canadian authority. Riel then proposed a convention of 40 representatives, equally divided

■ Louis Riel, a carte-de-visite studio portrait taken in Ottawa following his election as member of Parliament for Provencher, Manitoba, in 1873. LAC, 002048.

between the two language groups. At these meetings a new 'List of Rights' was debated, and Riel's provisional government was endorsed by the convention. In early February the remaining Canadian prisoners at Upper Fort Garry were released (some had already escaped), and three delegates were appointed to go to Ottawa to negotiate provincial status for Red River within Confederation.

Meanwhile, on 12 February 1870, a group of Canadian settlers, led by one of the surveyors, Major C.A. Boulton, and including several of the escaped prisoners, left Portage la Prairie to join a party led by Dr Schultz (another escapee) at Kildonan, a few kilometres from Fort Garry. The

■ Louis Riel at the centre of his provisional government, sometime in early 1870. Top row, left to right: Bonnet Tromage, Pierre de Lorme, Thomas Bunn, Xavier Page, Baptiste Beauchemin, Baptiste Tournond, and Thomas Spence. Middle: Pierre Poitras, John Bruce, Riel, John O'Donoghue, and François Dauphenais. Front: Robert O'Lone and Paul Proulx. LAC, PA-12854.

plan was to liberate the remaining prisoners, but Riel released them first, so the armed parties disbanded. However, on 17 February a small force of Riel's Métis arrested and imprisoned a number of the Canadians who were on their way back to Portage, including one named Thomas Scott.

Until now, Riel's strategy and tactics had been little short of brilliant. He had managed to keep the two mixed-blood groups, French- and English-speaking, together under the aegis of the provisional government, which was arguably necessary to maintain order in the settlement. Despite some talk about negotiating with the Americans—probably mainly for effect—Riel and his people clearly wanted Red River to be

admitted to Confederation, and had worked out their terms. In Ottawa, the Canadian cabinet agreed on 11 February to accept delegates from Red River and negotiate with them. But it was also agreed that if negotiations broke down, a military force would be necessary, and steps were taken with the British government to organize such a force, to consist of British regulars and Canadian volunteers.

THE EXECUTION OF THOMAS SCOTT

At this point Louis Riel made a mistake. When the prisoner named Thomas Scott became unruly, Riel allowed a Métis tribunal to conduct a

■ 'The Execution of Scott', 1870, from *Canadiana Military Events*, III, 429. This version of the event, in which Scott is casually dispatched with a pistol shot to the head, reinforces the Anglo-Canadian idea that his death was less a matter of formal execution than of cold-blooded murder. LAC, C-118610.

trial and sentence him to death.[26] Riel accepted the sentence, commenting that 'We must make Canada respect us.'

At the 1873 trial of Ambroise Lépine, who was charged with Thomas Scott's murder, Joseph Nolin under oath provided an account of Scott's trial on 3 March 1870. It is the only properly authenticated account in existence.

Scott was tried on the evening of the third of March; at the council that tried him Lépine presided; the other members of the council were Janvier Richot, André Nault, Elzéar Goulet, Elzéar Legemonière, Baptiste Lépine, and Joseph Delorme; I was secretary of the council; Scott was

not present at the beginning; some witnesses were examined to state what evil Scott had done; these witnesses were Riel, Ed Turner, and Joseph Delorme; don't recollect any other witnesses; do not recollect nature of the evidence; Scott was accused of having rebelled against the Provisional Government and having struck the captain of the guard; Riel made a speech, I think against Scott; after the evidence had been heard Scott was brought before the council; Riel asked me to read to Scott what had passed before the council; did not, as I had written nothing; Riel then explained the evidence to Scott, and he was condemned to death while he was there Riel explained the sentence to Scott, and asked him if he had any defence to offer? Scott said something but I forget what; Riel did not ask Scott whether he had any witnesses; there was no written accusation against Scott; the work of the Council was done in about three hours; the Council sat about 7 o'clock; took some notes of the evidence; wrote them out regularly, and gave them to the Adjutant General; Richot moved and Nault seconded that Scott deserved death; Lépine said he would have to be put to death—the majority want his death and he shall be put to death; that closed the business of the council; Riel explained to Scott his sentence; and asked him if he had any request to make or wanted to see a minister? I do not remember what answer Scott made; Riel said if the minister was at the Stone Fort he would send for him; Riel said he would send Scott up to his room, that his shackles would be taken off, and that he would have pen, ink, and paper to write what he wished to; Riel told Scott that he would be shot next day at 10 o'clock; I do not know what Scott said; he was then taken to his room; when the vote was taken Baptiste Lépine objected to taking the life of Scott; he said they had succeeded so far without shedding blood and he thought it better not to do so now; Ed Turner took Scott to his room; saw Lépine next morning about 8 o'clock; Lépine told me to write a verbal report of the proceedings of the Council; Riel came to see the report and said it was not formal; Riel then dictated the report; it was made from notes of the evidence; don't remember what Riel changed; gave it to Lépine when written. . . .[27]

On 4 March 1870, Scott was taken outside the gates of Fort Garry. His eyes were bandaged and he was shot by a firing squad. Riel apparently did not think much about this event, although it was the first fatality that had occurred in the course of Red River's resistance. But the execution of Scott was to have enormous repercussions in Ontario, which had apparently been searching desperately for an excuse to condemn Red River. When word of Scott's death reached Ontario, a secret society named 'Canada First'

undertook to orchestrate a public response. Inspired by the memory of D'Arcy McGee, who had been assassinated on the steps of the House of Commons on 7 April 1868, the members of Canada First believed in the need to inculcate a national spirit. They also believed in Canadian westward expansion and in the innate superiority of white Anglo-Saxon Protestants. Led by George Denison, the Canada Firsters—who included Charles Mair and John Schultz—organized their public campaign around the fact that Thomas Scott had been a member of the Orange Order. Soon all Ontario was up in arms about the murder of an innocent young Orangeman whose only offence was held to be his loyalty to Canada.

THE MANITOBA ACT AND THE WOLSELEY EXPEDITION

By the time the three-man delegation from Red River arrived in Ontario, the entire province was inflamed against Riel and the provisional government. Canada refused to meet officially with the delegates, led by Abbé Noel Ritchot, and negotiations were conducted in private. However, Ritchot was able to obtain the government's agreement to implement most of the 'List of Rights', and the Manitoba Act was quickly passed in May 1870—even if the Canadian government thought it had been forced to accede at the point of a gun. The Act granted provincial status to Manitoba (the name favoured by Riel), a province of only 1,000 square miles (2,590 square kilometres), with 1,400,000 acres (566,560 hectares) set aside for the Métis and bilingual services guaranteed. The Scott execution provided the Canadian government with an excuse to deny Riel and his lieutenants an official amnesty for all acts committed during the 'uprising'; although the Red River delegates who negotiated with Canada always insisted that such an amnesty had been promised as part of the unofficial settlement, there was nothing in writing. Instead of becoming premier of the province he had created, Louis Riel would go into long-term

AMBROISE LÉPINE
(1840–1923)

❖

Ambroise Lépine was born in St Boniface, the son of a well-to-do French-Canadian farmer and a Saskatchewan Métis woman. Educated at St Boniface College, he was hardly the illiterate 'savage' he was later made out to be by Canadians in Manitoba. In 1859 he married Cécile Marion, with whom he would have 14 children. The Lépines farmed a river lot (number 272) not far from the Riel family, but Ambroise also participated in the buffalo hunt. He was described as being 'of magnificent physique, standing fully six foot three and built of splendid proportion, straight as an arrow, with hair of raven blackness, large aquiline nose and eyes of piercing brilliance'.

In 1869 Lépine became an important figure in the uprising against the Canadian annexation of Red River, not surprising in view of his family position and hunting prowess, as well as his imposing size. He returned to the settlement around the end of October, just in time to be ordered to the border to make sure the Ottawa-appointed governor, William McDougall, did not cross it to assert Canadian control over the territory. Nobody knew who was in charge of this party, he later remembered, 'and I was made leader'. Lépine very nearly did not get his assignment right. He initially allowed McDougall to cross the border on 1 November, and then returned the next day to escort him back into the United States. Lépine continued to be associated with Louis Riel, and was the leader of the group who surrounded the Schultz house and store in early December. On 10 December he helped Riel and W.B. O'Donoghue raise the flag of the

■ Ambroise-Dydime Lépine, photographed in 1884. Glenbow Museum, NA-2631-3.

provisional government over Upper Fort Garry, and on 8 January he was named adjutant general of the provisional government, with the responsibility for the administration of justice—the equivalent of the chief of police in the settlement. He later represented St Boniface in the Convention of Forty, which met to formulate the demands to be made of the Canadian government, and chaired the Military Council of the convention.

It was Lépine who led the Métis forces out of Upper Fort Garry to confront the men from Portage la Prairie returning from a military gathering at Kildonan in February 1870. The Métis were on horseback and the Portage group on foot. The latter surrendered. Their captain, Charles Arkoll Boulton, was initially condemned to death by Riel, but was reprieved. Later, Lépine presided at the hearing that sentenced Thomas Scott to death, casting the deciding vote in favour of execution over the objections of his brother, Baptiste. The next day, he refused to listen to pleas for Scott's life and stood by stoically as the Canadian was shot by a firing squad.

When the Canadians took over Manitoba in late August of 1870, Lépine went on the run with Riel, whom he helped to raise a Métis militia force against a possible Fenian invasion in 1871. Later that year he was paid by the Canadian government to leave Manitoba with Riel, but he soon returned, and in 1873 he was arrested at his home for the death of Scott. His trial, which was really intended to test the government's case against Riel, ended in a conviction for murder by a mixed jury. Lépine did not testify at the trial, but issued a statement that denied the competence of the court to try him, insisting that his actions had been as a member of a de facto government; both assertions were dismissed by the court. He was sentenced to be hanged, but the Canadian Governor General commuted the sentence to two years in prison and permanent loss of civil rights. Lépine declined an amnesty conditional on leaving Manitoba for five years, and decided to serve his sentence. Released in 1876, he spent the rest of his long life in poverty and obscurity. He was conspicuous by his absence from the rebellion of 1885. In 1909 he helped A.-H. Trémaudan in the writing of a history of the Métis nation.

exile.[28] Whether Ottawa would uphold the land guarantees it made to the Métis remained to be seen, but the prospects were not good, for after passing the Manitoba Act it still dispatched a military expedition to Red River.

In August 1870 Riel was waiting at Fort Garry to hand over the government of the new province to Canada, but the leader of the expedition, Colonel Garnet Wolseley, insisted on entering the settlement as the commander of a conquering army. Realizing that they would be treated as rebels and murderers, Riel and several of his associates went into hiding. 'Personally,' Wolseley wrote, 'I was glad that Riel did not come out and surrender, . . . for I could not then have hanged him as I might have done had I taken him prisoner when in arms against his sovereign.'[29] Troops dragged some guns from the fort and fired a royal salute of 21 guns as the Union Jack was run up the flagpole. A small group of half a dozen spectators gave three cheers for the Queen. What followed was anticlimactic. In the end, the main function of Wolseley's volunteer troops was to protect the rebels from vengeful Canadians (among them some of the troops themselves). One of the volunteers brought with him a warrant for the organization of a new Orange Lodge; organized in September 1870, by February 1871 it claimed a membership of 110 'good men and true' opposed to Catholic 'bigotry' in 'this priest-ridden country'.[30] Also in September 1870 Adams Archibald was formally installed as lieutenant-governor of Manitoba. Whether this new entity, still occupied by the Canadian military, was a fully autonomous province was an open question.

THE NORTH-WEST TERRITORIES

Manitoba aside, the rest of the territory transferred to Canada by the Hudson's Bay Company—the North-West Territories—was initially administered under the legislation passed by the Canadian Parliament in 1869, before the Red River resistance. The lieutenant-governor of Manitoba also served as the lieutenant-governor of the Territories. The temporary legislation of 1869 was renewed without change in 1871. Not until 1872 was a territorial council appointed. Of its 11 members, only two resided in the Territories; the other nine lived in or near Winnipeg, where the council's initial meetings were held. Only in 1905 would the region achieve provincial status as Saskatchewan and Alberta.

BRITISH COLUMBIA

UNION WITH VANCOUVER ISLAND

The process by which British Columbia entered Confederation lacked some of the drama of the events in Red River–Manitoba, but it had its own complexities. The two colonies of British Columbia and Vancouver Island had been joined by the British government in 1866 in the hope of resolving some difficult economic and political problems.[31] As Governor Frederick Seymour had reported to the Colonial Office in 1865, 'separated it seems difficult for one Colony to flourish without inflicting some injury on the other.'[32] By the mid-1860s the gold rush along the Fraser River was over and the influx of miners and their money had dried up. Indeed, the movement was now in the other direction, making it difficult both to collect taxes on the mainland and to raise capital in Victoria, the population of which fell from as many as 10,000 to 3,000 by the mid-

1860s. The legislative assembly of Vancouver Island had battled for some time to gain control over finances, but without much success. As the economic recession deepened, the Vancouver Island Assembly found the possibility of legislative union attractive. A leading member of the Assembly, a Nova Scotia-born journalist calling himself Amor de Cosmos (William Alexander Smith), introduced motions in January 1865 for the union of the two colonies. The idea of union was quickly accepted in Westminster, but the Colonial Office chose to incorporate Vancouver Island into British Columbia and give the new colony, under Governor Seymour, a Legislative Council with a mix of elected and appointed members rather than an elected assembly. The debts of the two colonies at union were quite unequal; British Columbia owed more than $1,000,000, Vancouver Island less than $300,000. Seymour was known as a profligate spender, and many in Victoria feared for the future. On the day the union was proclaimed, the former governor, Sir James Douglas, wrote in his daughter's diary: 'The Ships of war fired a salute on the occasion—A funeral procession, with minute guns would have been more appropriate to the sad melancholy event.'[33]

DEBATING CONFEDERATION

The first contentious topic for the new Legislative Council was the location of the new capital. When Dr John Helmcken, the former speaker of the Vancouver Island Assembly, managed to steer through a motion choosing Victoria, Governor Seymour lost his temper at the vote, dismissing several members and disparaging Victoria as the home of 'a half alien, restless population, ill at ease with itself'.[34] Also at this first sitting of the Council, Amor de Cosmos—who found the union no improvement—introduced a resolution calling for the eventual admission of British Columbia into the Canadian Confederation. A full debate of the issue followed. Although most of the councillors cautiously refused to take any

■ Victoria, looking east along Fort Street from Langley Street, *c.*1862. Royal BC Museum, BC Archives, A-02999.

action, the proposal received additional impetus when, on 29 March 1867—coincidentally, the same day the British North America Act was passed by the British Parliament—the American government arranged to purchase Alaska from the Russians, touching off howls in the American press for the annexation of British Columbia.

Officially the colony was notified in November 1867 that no action could be taken on union with Canada until the HBC territory had been incorporated into the Dominion, an event that would take longer than anticipated. Early the next year, a committee appointed at a public meeting in Victoria composed a memorial to the government of Canada pointing out that the colony had no mechanism for determining the wishes of the people through the legislature, and calling on Canada to take immediate steps itself to bring British Columbia into the union.[35] The Canadian government replied through S.L. Tilley, Minister of Customs, who on 25 March 1868 wrote that 'The Canadian Government desires union with British Columbia, and have opened

communications with the Imperial Government on the subject of the resolutions, and suggests immediate action by your Legislature and the passage of an address to her Majesty requesting union with Canada.'[36] Although the Victoria memorial claimed that the only opposition to union with Canada came from a handful of American annexationists, many of the colony's officials—who had only just moved to Victoria from New Westminster and feared losing their appointments—were also unhappy about the idea. 'I suppose there is little doubt we shall have Confederation sooner or later,' wrote one such official, 'but it appears to me that our only chance is to work together, & battle against it until a satisfactory provision is made for us.'[37] On Dominion Day 1868, a large open-air meeting at Barkerville called for 'some organized and systematic mode of obtaining immediate admission into the Dominion of Canada', as well as the elimination of 'the present irresponsible autocracy'.[38]

At the meeting in December 1868, Dr Helmcken made an effort to reform the Legisla-

■ 'The Hurdies, German Dancing Girls at Barkerville', 1865, photo by Charles Gentile. Brought to Canada by a contractor who then had to be paid back for their passage, these 'hurdy-gurdy girls' were not prostitutes, but were hired out to dance with lonely men and persuade them to buy drinks. Royal BC Museum, BC Archives G-00817.

tive Council by increasing its elective members and by regulating official salaries. The officials sitting on the Council resisted, and also supported a resolution postponing discussion of union with Canada. Back in Ottawa, Prime Minister Macdonald was annoyed by this obstructionism; suspecting a Yankee conspiracy, he talked of replacing Governor Seymour. Conveniently, however, Seymour died in June 1869. He was replaced by Anthony Musgrave, the former Governor of Newfoundland. For years Musgrave had tried unsuccessfully to steer Newfoundland towards union with Canada, and he was discreetly ordered by the Colonial Office to bring his new colony into Confederation: in particular, Lord Granville told him to use 'no expressions which would indicate intention . . . to overrule the wishes of the community', but at the same time to recognize the importance attached 'to the early adhesion of British Columbia to the North American confederation' by the British government, which therefore 'would wish your language and polity to be such as are likely to conduce to that end'.[39] Musgrave arrived in British Columbia in August 1869, having travelled mainly by rail from Halifax to New York to San Francisco and then by steamer to Victoria. His journey was a suitable demonstration of the utility of a transcontinental railroad.

The colony that Musgrave was to govern consisted of some 10,500 settlers (6,000 white males, 2,600 white females, and 1,900 Chinese, mostly men) and roughly 50,000 Aboriginal people. Most of this population clustered around Victoria, which was the only substantial town: New Westminster had fallen from over a thousand to only about 600 people after the government had moved to the island, and a thin line of settlement along the Fraser River up into the Cariboo was becoming thinner. The colony was expected to support itself without financial aid from Great Britain—it got only about £1,200 in naval charges and other funds from the British in 1868—and it had cut its budget substantially. Its economy was in transition: the official yield of gold was down from over $4 million in 1863 to $2.5 million in 1868, but the value of forest product exports rose from $3,416 in 1861 to $252,154 in 1869, and the value of coal exports went up to $119,820 in 1869.[40] Farming and fishing had also expanded. Still, the economy continued to depend heavily on the extraction of raw materials.

Musgrave's Legislative Council had 22 members, 13 chosen by the Governor (five government officials and eight magistrates) and nine elected by the inhabitants. Although this was hardly government by the people, a variety of approaches—petitions, public meetings, newspaper debates, and private lobbying—served to make public opinion known to the government. Musgrave thought this arrangement well suited to the colony, but the elected representatives wanted responsible government and favoured union with Canada in the hope that, in Musgrave's words, 'it may be possible to make fuller representative institutions . . . part of the new arrangements'.[41] A convention of 26 delegates meeting at Yale in September 1868 had urged immediate union with Canada and the establishment of representative and responsible government. In early 1870 the Legislative Council passed a motion calling for union with Canada, providing satisfactory financial terms could be arranged, and began another round of debates on the subject in March.

Like the debates held by other late entrants into Confederation, these were quite different from the ones that had preceded the drafting of the British North America Act. British Columbia could not hope to influence the shape of the union; all it could determine was the terms on which it would join. The debate was in some ways odd. The leading spokesman for union was the Attorney General, Henry Crease, who had earlier opposed it, while the opposition to the plan was led by former supporters. The reasons for this inversion were connected with internal politics. In fact, those who now argued against union did so because they wanted the questions of popular elections and responsible government settled beforehand, whereas those who now argued in favour of union were members of the government party who were satisfied with the local status quo. One speaker successfully moved for postponement, saying:

> We are told that we are not fit for Representative Institutions or Responsible Government. Then we shall go into the Dominion as a Crown Colony—bound hand and foot. The few Members that will represent us at Ottawa, will not have the power to do anything for us. I do not trust the Politicians of Ottawa. . . . I would rather remain as we are, with some Change and modification in our Government.[42]

A similar point was made by Dr Helmcken: 'We are a Colony of England; and I don't know that many people object to being a Colony of England; but I say that very many would object to becoming a Colony of Canada.'[43]

THE REMINISCENCES OF
DR JOHN SEBASTIAN HELMCKEN

In 1892 Dr John Sebastian Helmcken (1824-1920) of Victoria wrote a lengthy memoir of his experiences. The manuscript ended up in the Provincial Archives of British Columbia in Victoria, and was edited for publication by Dorothy Blakey Smith, appearing in print in 1975. Here Helmcken discusses the election of 1868, fought over the issue of Confederation.

. . . [A] general election was ordered; Confederation being the burning question, everyone rampant on one side or the other; of course the American element being against the Union. At this time no distinct terms had been proposed, but if I recollect rightly De Cosmos and the colored man Gibbs and [John Norris] had been to the 'Yale Convention'; a Convention for the purpose of an organization for Confederation purposes. The Convention was ridiculed and lambasted by opponents—the colored man [Gibbs] having a good share. By the bye I had been a means of getting the coloured man elected to the House of Assembly and really he was in some measure a superior man and very gentlemanly withal. I think he claimed being a West Indian.

I came out against Confederation distinctly, chiefly because I thought it premature—partly from prejudice—and because no suitable terms could be proposed. The tariff was a sticking point: although we had at this time a tariff but could change it to suit ourselves. Our income too would be diminished and there at this time appeared no means of replenishing it by the [British] North America Act. Our population was too small numerically. Moreover it would only be a confederacy on paper for no means of communication with the Eastern Provinces existed, without which no advantage could possibly ensue. Canada was looked down upon as a poor mean slow people, who had been very commonly designated North American chinamen. This character they had achieved from their necessarily thrifty condition for long years, and indeed they compared unfavourably with the Americans and with our American element, for at this time and previously very many liberal-handed and better class of Americans resided here, many in business—some on account of the Civil War necessitating their remaining even after the frightful internecine killing had ceased. Our trade was either with the US or England—with Canada we had nothing to do. Of course my being an Anti-confederationist, led to my being dubbed an Annexationist, but really I had no idea of annexation, but merely wished the Colony to be let alone under HM Govt and to fight her way unhampered. I had nothing whatever to do with annexation petitions, and so not know who signed them—tho I have heard that some who now hold or have held official positions have done so. This petition doubtless went to the President of the US but no one has ever been able to see a copy of it since, altho it is said to exist in Victoria somewhere. There is no doubt the Americans had a contempt for Canada and this feeling extended to the colonists.

I suppose the election was one of the fiercest ever fought in Victoria, everyone seemed crazy, I among the number—these were the days of great excitements. I had the British and American elements and Jewish element on my side and after a time the election came on. Numberless ladies wore my colours, red, white and blue, in shape according to their taste, the men likewise. Ladies were at the windows waving their handkerchiefs, every hack in the place was frightfully busy. The polling went actively on, but there were no rows, or if there were, they were insignificant. Various committees had districts under control; they had to get the voters up and were responsible therefore. The cry went round that both sides had a number of voters locked up and were feeding them with whisky, to get them into proper trim; altho this accusation was not strictly true, still voters came to the polling place, where the Courts of Justice now stand, in files. Notwithstanding all this there were no rows outside the polling places, the matter was too serious for this. At length 4 o'clock struck—the polls closed; everyone tired—thirsty, hoarse and expectant. The Anti-confederates had won handsomely. . . .

SOURCE: Dorothy Blakey Smith, ed., *The Reminiscences of Doctor John Sebastian Helmcken* (Vancouver: University of British Columbia Press, 1975), 246-8.

■ Described by Dr Helmcken as 'a superior man and very gentlemanly withal', Mifflin Gibbs was born to free parents in Philadelphia in 1823 and arrived in Victoria from California in 1858. A successful businessman, by 1867 he was chairman of the finance committee of the Victoria City Council. Royal BC Museum, BC Archives B-01601.

On 14 March the debates turned to the admission terms proposed by Musgrave and the Executive Council. Everyone agreed that Canada should be liable for the debts of the colony and grant it a large subsidy. The first real question was over land communication with the East. While the government wanted a railway begun within three years of union, some members wanted a section between Yale and New Westminster to be constructed within three years, and an amendment to this effect was carried. Governor Musgrave subsequently reported to Britain that 'If a Railway could be promised, scarcely any other question would be allowed to be a difficulty',[44] but he may have overstated the case. In fact, the greatest debate concerned a seemingly innocuous Clause 15, according to which 'The Constitution of the Executive authority and of the Legislature of British Columbia shall, subject to "The British North America Act, 1867", continue as existing at the time of Union, until altered under the authority of the said Act.' A motion calling for the introduction of representative institutions and responsible government irrespective of Confederation failed, as did a proposed amendment calling for a constitution based on principles of responsible government to be introduced coincident with entry into Canada. Clause 15 was eventually passed as read. Interestingly, the question of administrative responsibility for the colony's Aboriginal population never arose in the debates.

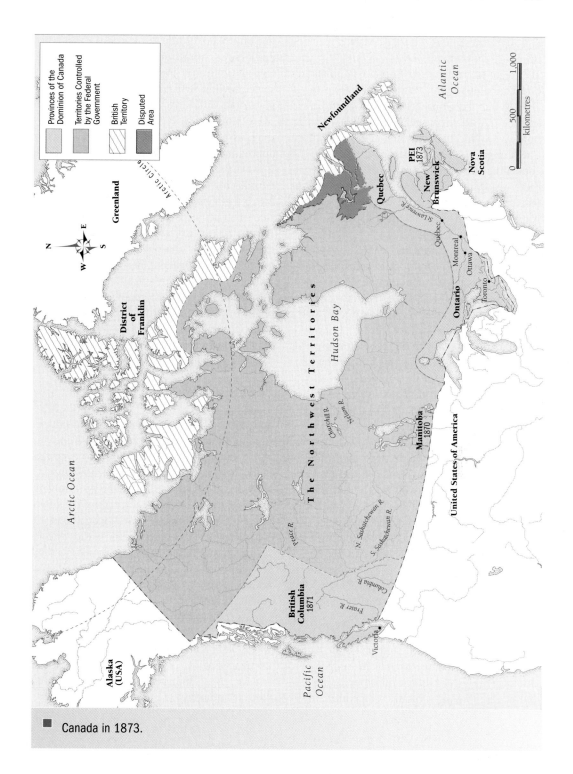

Canada in 1873.

ENTERING CONFEDERATION

The negotiations between British Columbia and Canada took place in Ottawa in the late spring of 1870.[45] The Manitoba Act had just been passed and the Canadian government's military expedition was setting out for the Red River territory. The Canadians were generous to a fault. Of course the debt could be wiped out. Of course there would be subsidies and grants, as well as federal support for the naval station at Esquimalt. Naturally British Columbia would get responsible government. Clause 15, as amended by the joint delegations, stipulated that although the existing constitution would continue until altered, it was understood 'that the Government of the Dominion will readily consent to the introduction of Responsible Government when desired by the inhabitants of British Columbia, and it being likewise understood that it is the intention of the Government of British Columbia under the authority of the Secretary of State for the Colonies, to amend the existing constitution of the Legislature by providing that a majority of its members should be elective.'[46] And of course the province would have a rail link with Canada—to be begun within two years and completed within 15. Governor Musgrave was astounded at the generosity of the terms. 'And then the Railway, Credat Judaeus! is guaranteed without a reservation! Sir George Cartier says they will do that, or "burst".'[47] The promise was certainly audacious (and in the end BC had to promise that it would not insist on the terms, especially regarding the railway, to the letter), but it was hardly surprising. For a variety of reasons, some political and some economic, Canada needed a transcontinental railroad to match the lines being rapidly constructed across the United States. As predicted, the railway guarantee wiped out most of the remaining opposition to union—but not all: 'We are a conquered country,' wrote one official on 19 July 1871, '& the Canucks take possession tomorrow.'[48] The following day British Columbia entered Confederation as the sixth province with Joseph Trutch as lieutenant-governor. Trutch had opposed the introduction of responsible government and continued to drag his heels on constitutional change, actually appointing the first premier himself. Finally, however, on 23 December 1872 Amor de Cosmos formed the first ministry fully responsible to the legislature.[49]

In most respects the new province would remain largely isolated from Canada until after the railway was completed in 1885. Nevertheless, Confederation did have several effects for British Columbia. One was the development of a new land policy that opened the province up for massive pre-emption rights for those who had 'squatted' on land, as well as free land grants. Another was the transfer to the Dominion of responsibility for 'Indian policy'.

CONCLUSION

By 1873 Canada was—at least on paper—a transcontinental nation. A number of provinces had been added to the union, however reluctantly, and at least one had already sought to leave and been pacified. Had the government in Ottawa not succeeded in extending the original union of the Canadas, Nova Scotia, and New Brunswick as expeditiously as it did, the new nation's future might have been in serious doubt. Today most Canadians are happy to celebrate the events of 1867, but the next few years were equally important.

At the same time, the Canadian government had demonstrated a marked clumsiness in the way it went about its westward expansion and in its treatment of the inhabitants of the western regions. This clumsiness was to haunt the new nation for many years to come

SHORT BIBLIOGRAPHY

Beck, J. Murray. *Joseph Howe*, vol. 2, *The Briton Becomes Canadian, 1848–1873*. Montreal and Kingston, 1983. The standard biography of Joseph Howe, judicious and well-balanced.

Bescoby, Isabel. 'A Colonial Administration: An Analysis of Administration in British Columbia, 1869–71', *Canadian Public Administration* 10 (1967): 49–104. The fullest and most detailed account available of the public history of British Columbia in the years 1869–71.

Bolger, Francis. *Prince Edward Island and Confederation, 1863–1873*. Charlottetown, 1964. The standard account of the Island and Canada.

Bumsted, J.M. *The Red River Rebellion*. Winnipeg, 1995. A study of the troubles in Red River that does not always put Louis Riel at centre stage.

Debates on the Subject of Confederation with Canada. Victoria, n.d. Transcripts of the BC legislative debates on union.

Hiller, James. 'Confederation Defeated: The Newfoundland Election of 1869', in James Hiller and Peter Neary, eds, *Newfoundland in the Nineteenth and Twentieth Centuries: Essays in Interpretation.* Toronto, 1980. The only detailed analysis of the 1869 Newfoundland election in which Confederation was defeated.

Morton, W.L., ed. *Alexander Begg's Red River Journal and Other Papers Relative to the Red River Resistance of 1869–70.* Toronto, 1956. A contemporary view of the Red River business.

————, ed. *Manitoba: The Birth of a Nation.* Winnipeg, 1965. A collection of contemporary documents, including Father Ritchot's journal of the actual negotiations with Canada.

Shelton, W. George, ed. *British Columbia and Confederation.* Victoria, 1967. A useful collection of essays on various topics connected with Confederation and the Pacific province.

Stanley, George F.G. *Louis Riel.* Toronto, 1963. The standard biography, well-researched and balanced in its interpretation.

STUDY QUESTIONS

1. In the end, did the antis in Nova Scotia have any choice but to accept Confederation?
2. Why did PEI change its mind about Confederation in 1873?
3. Why were Newfoundland merchants not enthusiastic about Confederation?
4. Why did the Newfoundland Irish oppose union?
5. What reasons lay behind the uprising in Red River in 1869?
6. What did Riel and the provisional government in Red River want from Canada?
7. What issues were involved in British Columbia's entry into Confederation?

CHAPTER TWO

Envisioning the New Nation, 1867–1885

In addition to completing the takeover of the northwestern part of the continent, the governments of Sir John A. Macdonald and Alexander Mackenzie gradually developed some national policies with which to govern the new Dominion. Before 1867, a good deal of energy had been devoted to arguments in favour of the union, but few attempts had been made to spell out the specifics of a vision for the new nation. Indeed, it turned out that there were several visions floating around, none of them acceptable to everyone. At the same time, most of the new nation's concrete policies were naturally carried over from the earlier Canadian system, with occasional adjustments to accommodate the other provinces. Among the most important developments were the emergence of a system of national political parties and the smooth transition, in 1873, from Macdonald's bipartisan coalition government to the Liberals under Mackenzie within the constitutional traditions of responsible government. Cultural developments in this period were significant as well.

THE QUEST FOR NATIONAL POLICIES

Sometimes, of course, the interests of the new nation's parts had to be sacrificed to larger concerns, one of which was Anglo-American entente. After the reciprocity agreement had been abrogated in1866, both Nova Scotia and the new Canadian government after 1867 tried to keep American fishermen outside a three-mile offshore limit. However, since there were other tensions with the US, the imperial government was unhappy about this additional strain on relations with the US. One problem concerned a raiding vessel built by Britain for the southern states during the Civil War: in return for the losses the *Alabama* had inflicted on the North, the Americans were only half-facetiously demanding the cession of British American territory. Another concerned the Fenian raids launched from American soil into Canada in 1866 and 1870. Accordingly, in 1871 the British government made John A. Macdonald a member of an international joint commission set up in 1870 to deal with the fisheries question and advised the Canadians to give up their claim to a three-mile limit—though only 'in return for an adequate consideration'. Sir Charles Tupper, representing Nova Scotian interests, argued that fishing rights should not be sold only for a 'money consideration', but the British were eager to settle their differences with the Americans (or at least have them brought to international arbitration), and were quite willing to sacrifice Canadian (really

TIMELINE

1868

Canadian National Series of readers introduced into Ontario schools.

1870

Dominion Notes Act passed.

1871

Canada signs the Treaty of Washington. Bank Act passed.

1872

Ontario Society of Artists formed. Passage of Dominion Lands Act.

1873

Pacific Scandal. Macdonald government resigns. Alexander Mackenzie leads new Liberal government. North West Mounted Police established.

1875

Supreme Court of Canada established.

1876

Treaty Six signed at Fort Carlton. Indian Act of 1876 passed by Canadian Parliament.

1878

Macdonald's Conservatives returned to power.

1880

Royal Canadian Academy of Arts and National Gallery of Canada established.

1881

John Bourinot publishes *The Intellectual Development of the Canadian People*. First western real estate boom, in Winnipeg.

1882

Royal Society of Canada established. *Picturesque Canada* published.

1883

Qu'Appelle Settlers' Rights Association calls for reform.

1884

Mercier tables resolutions on federal encroachments on provincial power. First Nations hold Thirst Dance in Saskatchewan on Poundmaker's reserve. Louis Riel invited back to Canada. Riel sends long petition to Ottawa.

1885

Battle of Duck Lake (March). Battle of Batoche (May). Treason trial of Louis Riel (July). Eight Aboriginal warriors executed for their part in the uprising (November). Public gathering in Montreal protests Riel execution. Last spike in CPR line driven at Craigellachie, BC, on 7 November. Riel executed nine days later.

Maritime) interests to that end. The British view prevailed, and Macdonald signed the Treaty of Washington, seeing his signature as recognition of Canadian diplomatic autonomy and the treaty itself as marking the Americans' recognition of Canada as a separate entity.

On the domestic front, the new country's banking system grew rapidly after Confederation, from 123 chartered bank branches in 1868 to 279 in 1879 and 426 by 1890, representing some three dozen banks. The two most important pieces of banking legislation were the Dominion Notes Act of 1870 and the Bank Act of 1871. The former allowed the government to issue circulating notes of small denominations only partly backed by gold and silver, while the latter established central control over the banking system, specifying the capital requirements for banks, prohibiting new foreign-owned banks, and providing general regulations, including standards for the issuing of bank notes. High capital requirements together with federal policy restricted the number of bank charters granted and encouraged the acquisition of new branches rather than the creation of new banks. Canada was integrated into the international gold standard, but the government would share responsibility for the issuing of currency (and control of the creation of money) with the banks until well into the twentieth century. Canada did not create a central bank until 1934.

Confederation suggested an economic future that was generally encouraging to foreign investment. From its inception, Canada was able to import large amounts of capital to help create its economic infrastructure, including $166 million (7 per cent of the gross national product) in the years 1871–5.[1] Between 1865 and 1869, Canada raised $16.5 million in Great Britain, a figure that rose to $94.6 million in 1870–4, $74.7 million in 1875–9, and $69.8 million in 1880–4.[2]

One of the principal economic arguments for Confederation had been the opportunity for further railway expansion, and railroads were a prime target of foreign investors. Construction of the Intercolonial Railway through New Brunswick began in 1867, but the Macdonald government was slow to move on the greatest of all, the transcontinental line, mainly because of the enormous expense involved in building it so much in advance of population needs. The prob-

lem was that the railway was essential to improve communications with the West, and to some extent the railway promise made to British Columbia was intended to cast the die. Following the usual scuffling, Parliament awarded the charter in 1873 to Sir Hugh Allan's Canadian Pacific Railway Company. Then the Pacific Scandal broke. Allan had provided the government with money—more than $350,000—for its 1872 election campaign, and Macdonald was unable to avoid the charge of corruption.

In November 1873 his government resigned and was replaced by a Liberal government headed by another Scot, a former stonemason turned building contractor named Alexander Mackenzie. Canada's first government had been bipartisan, and the British North America Act had not formalized either responsible government or political parties within the Constitution. Earlier parties were provincial rather than national. In the early 1870s Mackenzie therefore had to construct a federal opposition party from the bottom up, gathering in those who dropped gradually away from the governing party of Sir John A. Macdonald. Once in office, Mackenzie took a more gradual approach to building the transcontinental line. In addition to using public funds, he was prepared to encourage private interests to hook up with American western lines, and trains began running from Minnesota to Winnipeg late in 1878. By that time Mackenzie's dour earnestness had worn thin with the voters, and the probity of his government was not enough to save it in the 1878 election. Nevertheless, he had made a genuine contribution to national politics by insisting that his Liberals were a national alternative to Macdonald's Conservatives, and proving it by governing for five years without having the country fall apart. Moreover, the Mackenzie administration had finished much of the agenda begun in 1867. Federal administration of justice was functioning. The Maritimes had become part of the nation. The Mounted Police were introducing Canadian sovereignty into the western interior. A Supreme Court was in place, although perhaps not the Court envisioned by Sir John A. Macdonald.

ESTABLISHING A SUPREME COURT

The Macdonald government introduced a bill for a higher Dominion Court over the winter of 1868–9, apparently as a trial balloon. It was based on the American Supreme Court, provided for extensive original jurisdiction not involving appeals as well as a mechanism for appeal, and was intended as another centralizing institution for the new confederacy. However, as Oliver Mowat, the vice-chancellor of Ontario, pointed out to Macdonald later in 1868, 'You have the power of disallowing provincial statutes; you appoint the Provincial Governors, and you appoint also the Provincial Judges. The reasons therefore for which it was necessary in certain cases to have original jurisdiction to the Supreme Court in the United States are entirely inappropriate to our nation.'[3] Mowat doubted whether section 101 of the British North America Act authorized such a court, or whether it was appropriate that such a court could rule on provincial law 'which is not the *law of Canada*'. Other critics insisted that only provincial legislation could establish authority over the provinces. Even with a restricted jurisdiction, judges in the various provinces, especially Quebec, were dubious. Macdonald dropped his scheme, but it was picked up again by the Mackenzie government in 1875.

Instead of imposing a court on the nation, the Liberals sought to find a legitimate place for it within Canada's political institutions. They focused on the current need to appeal Canadian constitutional disputes to the Privy Council in England, which was not in keeping with a truly independent nation. A bill creating the Supreme Court carried in 1875 by a vote of 112 to 40 despite increasing hostility from the Colonial Office. Clause 47 ended appeals to the Privy Council based on statute, but not those based on the royal prerogative, and the latter were by far

the most common and contentious; Edward Blake, in England to plead the case for the Court, acknowledged that clause 47 was not important. The Liberals had trouble staffing the new Court, both because of partisanship among the judges and because of their known hostility to the institution of such a court. In the end, the Liberals had pressed for a new national identity but had accepted something considerably less. Sir John A. Macdonald allegedly quipped that he 'would rather be a dead premier than a live chief justice.'[4]

MACDONALD'S NATIONAL POLICY

On his return to power, Macdonald recognized the nationalist temper of the times and worked very hard to re-establish a direct connection in the public mind between his party and the process of nation-building. A certain decisiveness and flamboyance were all part of the Tory image. Even before the election, Macdonald had found his platform, introducing into the House of Commons a resolution 'That this House is of the opinion that the welfare of Canada requires the adoption of a National Policy, which, by a judicious readjustment of the Tariff, will benefit and foster the agricultural, the mining, the manufacturing and other interests of this Dominion.'[5] Macdonald invented neither the policy nor the term used to describe it. Both went back well into the traditional economic policy of the Province of Canada, which had begun using a tariff as an instrument of both protection and revenue in the late 1840s. Nor did Macdonald ever articulate the version of the National Policy later described by some economic historians and textbook writers. He certainly recognized connections between tariffs, manufacturing, employment, and 'national prosperity'. He also wanted a transcontinental railway and the western settlement necessary to make it a reality. But all these were traditional elements of Canadian economic expansionism.[6]

What Macdonald achieved was masterful,

nonetheless. He succeeded in persuading a large number of Canadians that policies strongly driven by the economic interests of some individuals were in the best interests of the nation as a whole, and he identified the party he led with the successful construction of that nation. The fact that many in the opposition party had quite a different vision of the meaning of Confederation, based on provincial rights, certainly helped in this identification.

PROVINCIAL RIGHTS

The development of nationhood in the years after 1867 did not mean that all Canadians shared the same vision of the new state.[7] To put it simply: was Canada an indissoluble new entity or was it the product of a compact among the provinces that they could modify or even withdraw from? Since the time of the debates over Confederation in the 1860s, many had disagreed over the nature of the union. While most Canadians in 1867 saw Confederation as creating a strong central government, the legislatures of the provinces had not been eliminated, and they would quickly reassert more than a mere 'local power'. As early as 1865 the arch-critic of Confederation, Christopher Dunkin, had prophesied that 'In the times to come, when men shall begin to feel strongly on those questions that appeal to national preferences, prejudices and passions, all talk of your new nationality will sound but strangely. Some older nationality will then be found to hold the first place in most people's hearts.'[8] Even John A. Macdonald had admitted in Parliament in 1868 that 'a conflict may, ere long, arise between the Dominion and the States Rights people.'[9]

The movement to support a 'provincial rights' interpretation of the new nation was spearheaded by Ontario, but it could have begun anywhere—including in Nova Scotia among those who wanted out of the Confederation deal. In any event, as early as 1869 Ontario became distressed at 'the assumption by the Parliament

of Canada of the power to disturb the financial relations established by the British North America Act (1867), as between Canada and the several provinces'.[10] Not surprisingly, it was the old Reform party of Canada West, in the persons of George Brown, Edward Blake, and Oliver Mowat, that took the lead in demanding—as Blake put it in 1871—'that each government [dominion and provincial] should be absolutely independent of the other in its management of its own affairs'.[11] The Rouges of Quebec soon made similar demands, calling for recognition not only of Quebec's 'provincial' rights but of 'national' rights for French Canadians. Before long, Liberals in most provinces—many of whom had either opposed Confederation or been lukewarm about it—had embraced provincial rights as a way of expressing their discontent with the prevailing vision of the union.

The provincial rights movement often seemed interchangeable with Ottawa-bashing for local political advantage, motivated by nothing more than the desire to pressure the federal government into fiscal concessions. In time the movement would obviously come to be dominated by Quebec and issues of cultural nationalism. This was not the case in the beginning, however. In 1884, for example, the Honourable Honoré Mercier tabled resolutions in the Quebec legislature stating merely that 'the frequent encroachments of the Federal Parliament upon the prerogatives of the Provinces are a permanent menace to the latter.'[12] Expressions of cultural nationalism in the ensuing debate went no further than one backbencher's assertion that 'Le Québec n'est pas une province comme les autres.'[13] As we shall see, the Riel affair of 1885 would push Quebec towards arguments of cultural distinctiveness, and when Mercier—by this time Premier of Quebec—invited the provinces to the Interprovincial Conference in 1887 to re-examine the federal compact, the five provinces in attendance could reach broad agreement on demands for better terms and constitutional change.

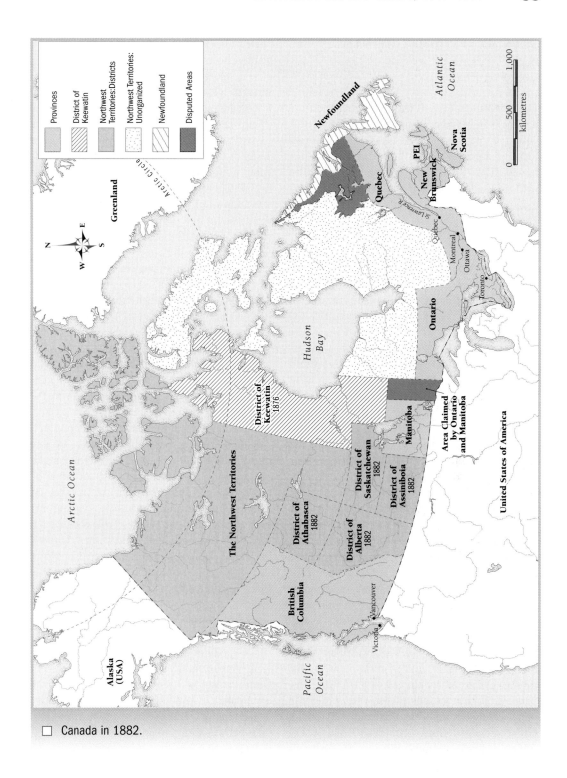

Canada in 1882.

SEEKING NATIONAL IDENTITY

CANADA FIRST

The identification of the emerging cultural nationalism, in the years immediately after 1867, with the movement that called itself 'Canada First' is in many ways unfortunate, for the Canada Firsters did not have a monopoly on national sentiment. Nor was their version of nationalism a very attractive one. One of the group's founders, Robert C. Haliburton, was an early exponent of the idea that Canadians were heirs to the glorious destiny of the 'Aryan' northmen of the Old World, and the Canada Firsters' position in the Red River controversy, for example, was plainly racist. They looked down their noses not only at Aboriginal people and Métis but at the French as well, seeing them as a 'bar to progress, and to the extention of a great Anglo-Saxon Dominion across the Continent'.[14] While these notions went together with Canadian westward expansion, they were fortunately not totally typical of the conscious development of Canadian nationalism. The French-Canadian poet Octave Crémazie, for example, lamented ironically that Canada's major literary languages were of European origin, arguing that 'if we spoke Huron or Iroquois, the work of our writers would attract the attention of the old world. . . . One would be overwhelmed by a novel or a poem translated from the Iroquois, while one does not take the trouble to read a book written in French by a native of Quebec or Montreal.'[15]

The major problem with most of the early expressions of a larger Canadian nationalism, even when they were not openly racist, was that they tended to visualize the new nation as seamlessly uniting the old colonies of British North America in a single entity—and to forget that those old colonies contained several quite disparate cultural traditions. Those who thought in pan-Canadian terms were almost entirely anglophone assimilationists. Manitoba's Chief Justice Edmund Burke Wood told the St Andrew's Society in Winnipeg in 1874 that 'Here we wanted no race, nationality, church, sect or religion to be dominant or in the ascendant; but we wanted all to be British subjects; all to be Canadians, all to be Manitobans, whatever his origin, language, race or pedigree.'[16] But Wood himself was not particularly sympathetic to the Métis or the Franco-Manitobans, and his underlying notion of Canadian identity was firmly British. The place of French Canada in the nation was an interesting question. In one draft letter to the press, probably written in 1870, Charles Mair virtually exploded on this subject:

> Ontario and the English-speaking people of Quebec have been milked long enough. . . . Thank God there is such a thing at last as a purely national feeling in Canada. There is a young and vigorous race coming to the front, entirely in earnest, and which is no longer English, Scotch or Irish, but thoroughly and distinctly Canadian. . . . It means strict justice to the French and nothing more—a fair field and no favour.[17]

The French language, claimed Mair, stood in the way of Canadians ever becoming a 'homogeneous people'. For these early nationalists, the condescending English represented more of a threat than did the Americans, whom they considered weak and 'effeminate' compared with their manly northern neighbours. They also saw the United States as the home of the 'grab' and a hotbed of political corruption.[18]

INTELLECTUAL DEVELOPMENT

JOHN BOURINOT

Politicians were not alone in endeavouring to create a sense of Canadian nationality. There were no guarantees that political unification would create a nation, particularly given the competing interpretations of the meaning of Confederation. Intellectuals and artists played their parts as well, providing rhetorical flourishes as well as the more mundane service of creating national institutions in which the arts could flourish. In 1881, for example, the chief clerk of the House of Commons, John Bourinot, published a book entitled *The Intellectual Development of the Canadian People: An Historical Review*, the first of his many works on history and Canadian government. Born in Sydney, Nova Scotia, in 1837, he was educated at the University of Toronto and then founded the *Halifax Herald* in 1860, becoming chief reporter of the Nova Scotia Assembly in 1861. In 1868 he moved to Ottawa to join the Hansard staff of the House of Commons, attracted—like many other intellectuals—by the economic opportunities and wider horizons that Canada seemed to offer after Confederation. In his book Bourinot sought to counter the tendency to deprecate the intellectual efforts of Canadians at home and abroad. Canada had moved 'beyond the state of mere colonial pupilage', he argued, implying that the cultural products of the new nation were just as worthy of respect as its political achievements.

Bourinot argued chiefly from advances in education and literacy. He began by writing in glowing terms of the free and accessible public education available in most provinces, and of the country's 21 colleges and universities. He pointed out that $64 million had been spent on public schools across the Dominion since 1867, adding that in 1839 about one in 13 young British North Americans had been attending school, while the proportion of young Canadians in school in 1881 was one in four. Newspapers were another sign of intellectual development, increasing from 65 in all British North America in 1840 to 465—56 of them dailies—in 1880. Fond of argument from sheer numbers, Bourinot wrote that in 1879, 4,085,454 pounds of newspapers at one cent per pound 'passed through the post offices of the Dominion', and over 30 million copies of newspapers were circulated annually in Canada through the mails.[19] He concluded with a chapter on literature, which catalogued a number of French-Canadian historians and poets—including Léon-Pamphile Lemay, Octave

Crémazie, Benjamin Sulte, and Louis-Honoré Fréchette, whose elegy 'Les Morts' he compared favourably to Victor Hugo's work—and offered a handful of English-Canadian writers, mainly from the Maritime region. The 'firm, broad basis of general education', Bourinot concluded, meant 'a future as full of promise for literature as for industry'.

Some of Bourinot's comments, especially about French Canada, sound extremely patronizing to the modern ear. He noted the 'greater impulsiveness and vivacity of the French Canadians' and was pleased to remind his readers that they were descendants of Normans and Bretons, 'people [who] have much that is akin with the people of the British Islands'. The idea of similarities between the French and the British was in the air in Bourinot's day, as Canadians attempted to define a new national identity after Confederation. At the same time he insisted on the existence of 'a national French Canadian sentiment, which has produced no mean intellectual feats'. On balance, 'in the essential elements of intellectual development, Canada is making not a rapid but certainly at least a steady and encouraging progress, which proves that her people have not lost, in consequence of the decided disadvantages of their colonial situation, any of the characteristics of the races to whom they owe their origin.'[20] In many ways Bourinot's book reflects the Victorian worship of Progress. Yet the very fact that in 1881 someone should have attempted to trace the intellectual development of the Canadian people indicates some of the distance covered in what the author himself saw as the movement from raw frontier colonies to civilized nation. That development, however, was hardly the simple progression that Bourinot sought to document.

EDUCATION

As Bourinot's comments suggest, if Canadians of his time had been asked to comment on their cultural accomplishments, they would surely have pointed with pride to their school systems—in particular, their accessibility and uni-

ISABELLA VALANCY CRAWFORD
(1850–1887)

❖

Isabella Valancy Crawford was born on 25 December 1850 in Dublin, Ireland. Her father, a surgeon who also studied the law, appears to have been a scapegrace member of a well-to-do family. Probably a heavy drinker, he migrated with his family to Wisconsin around 1854, and later moved first to Paisley and then to Lakefield, Canada West. In Lakefield young Isabella grew up as a companion to Catharine Parr Traill's daughter Katherine and was educated at home by her parents. Her father was convicted of the misappropriation of funds while serving as township treasurer in Paisley in the mid-1860s, and the ensuing stigma appears to have weighed heavily on his family, especially Isabella. In 1869 he set up a medical practice in Peterborough.

Local legend described his daughter as 'eccentric' before the death of her father in 1875. Like many another gentlewoman of the time, she managed to establish a modest career as a writer, mainly for Toronto newspapers, in order to support her mother and sister. Eventually the family moved to Toronto, where Isabella found more outlets for her writing, publishing prose and poetry in newspapers under a variety of pseudonyms and moving from one lodging house to another. Virtually all her life would be spent in genteel poverty. In 1884 she collected 43 of her poems in a volume entitled of *Old Spookses' Pass, Malcolm's Katie and Other Poems*, of which she published 1,000 copies at her own expense. Despite a number of positive reviews in British journals, only a handful of copies were ever sold. Nevertheless, she continued writing, mainly fiction of the women's romance variety for American popular magazines, and one of her novels was serialized in the *Evening Globe* in 1886.

Isabella Valancy Crawford died in 1887 after catching a bad cold. Not until well after her untimely death was she recognized as one of Canada's most important poets. Transferring the Tennysonian tradition of narrative poetry to pioneer Canada, she was extremely sensitive to Aboriginal legends, and had a highly developed sense of Canadian identity, which has led to her association with the 'Confederation Poets'. In a poem entitled 'The Camp of Souls', she wrote:

> White are the wigwams in that far camp,
>   And the star-eyed deer on the plains
>   are found;
> No bitter marshes or tangled swamp
>   In the Manitou's happy hunting-
>   ground!
> And the moon of summer forever rolls,
>   Above the red men in their "Camp of
>   Souls."

Much of her poetry was concerned with the role of suffering in life. A complete edition of her work is still not available. For a biography based on the limited material available, see Elizabeth McNeill Galvin, *Isabella Valancy Crawford: We Scarcely Knew Her* (Toronto, 1994).

CHARLES G.D. ROBERTS'S 'CANADA'

In 1886 Charles G.D. Roberts published a small volume of verses in Boston entitled *Divers Tones*. The following is one of the first poems in the book.

Canada

O Child of Nations, giant-limbed,
    Who stand'st among the nations now
Unheeded, unadorned, unhymned,
    With unanointed brow,—

How long the ignoble sloth, how long
    The trust in greatness not thine own?
Surely the lion's brood is strong
    To front the world alone!

How long the indolence, ere thou dare
    Achieve thy destiny, seize thy fame—
Ere our proud eyes behold thee bear
    A nation's franchise, nation's name?

The Saxon force, the Celtic fire,
    These are thy manhood's heritage!
Why rest with babes and slaves? Seek higher
    The place of race and age.

I see to every wind unfurled
    The flag that bears the Maple-Wreath;
Thy swift keels furrow round the world
    Its blood-red folds beneath;

Thy swift keels cleave the furthest seas;
    Thy white sails swell with alien gales;
To stream on each remotest breeze
    The black smoke of thy pipes exhales.

O Falterer, let thy past convince
    Thy future,—all the growth, the gain,
The fame since Cartier knew thee, since
    Thy shores beheld Champlain!

Montcalm and Wolfe! Wolfe and Montcalm!
    Quebec, thy storied citadel
Attest in burning song and psalm
    How here thy heroes fell!

O Thou that bor'st the battle's brunt
    At Queenston, and at Lundy's Lane,—
On whose scant ranks but iron front
    The battle broke in vain!—

Whose was the danger, whose the day,
    From whose triumphant throats the cheers,
At Chrysler's Farm, at Chateauguay,
    Storming like clarion-bursts our ears?

On soft Pacific slopes,—beside
    Strange floods that northward rave and fall,—
Where chafes Acadia's chainless tide—
    Thy sons await thy call.

They wait; but some in exile, some
    With strangers housed, in stranger lands;—
And some Canadian lips are dumb
    Beneath Egyptian sands.

O mystic Nile! Thy secret yields
    Before us; thy most ancient dreams
Are mixed with fresh Canadian fields
    And murmur of Canadian streams.

But thou, my Country, dream not thou!
    Wake, and behold how night is done,—
How on thy breast, and o'er thy brow,
    Bursts the rising sun!

SOURCE: Charles G.D. Roberts, *Divers Tones* (Boston: Lothrop, 1886), 2–5.

■ 'Lock no. 1, new Welland Canal', from *Picturesque Canada* (1882). LAC, C-083047.

versality. British North America's first Free Public Education Act, under which schools were fully financed by the state, was passed in Prince Edward Island in 1852, but in the post-Confederation period all the provinces moved to public funding and schooling became increasingly universal. Public financing allowed the colonial governments and their provincial successors to provide centralized control over education. These small bureaucracies were part of the administrative state that began to develop in the 1840s and continued growing through the Confederation period. Attempts by these centralized agencies to control denominational schools in the same way that they did public ones would lead to much controversy over the next years.

The greatest issue in education in the period immediately after Confederation arose in New Brunswick and involved not control over denominational schools but an effort by those schools themselves to gain some privileges. Section 93 of the BNA Act guaranteed educational rights to Ontario Catholics and Quebec Protestants, but in the Maritime provinces allowed only those privileges sanctioned by law before unification. In a famous court judgement in New Brunswick in 1873, Chief Justice Ritchie declared that the privileges of local Catholics before 1867 did not exist by law. The remedy, said Ritchie, was within the power of the legislature, not the courts. But the legislature was in the control of English-speaking Protestants. Following serious riots in the Acadian community of Caraquet in 1875, an attempt was made to find a remedy in the Canadian House of Commons. But to amend section 92 of the British North America Act, under which education was left to the provinces, would have set too dangerous a precedent. And there the matter stood.

Indeed, education was one of the most divisive issues in the new nation, and educational diversity was still the norm. Canada East had been somewhat slower than Canada West to move towards universality, and most of its schools continued to be dominated by both clerical teachers and clerical values, although Protestants were able to establish their own institutions in Quebec, particularly after education was reorganized in 1875. In Ontario a Canadian National Series of Readers was introduced as early as 1868, based on the Irish National Readers but 'greatly improved and Canadianized'.[21] Of course, using material published in Canada and adapted for Canadians was not the same as promulgating a strident or even standard Canadian nationalism in the schools. In the short run, English-Canadian educators tended to Canadianize by emphasizing 'the rich heritage of British history . . . reflected in our national escutcheon'.[22]

CULTURAL DEVELOPMENT

In various fields of the arts and letters, stirrings of cultural nationalism could be observed as Canadians attempted to break through the hard ground of the new nation's traditional colonial mentality, which tended to look to Great Britain and the United States for cultural models and directions.

THE CONFEDERATION POETS

The search for an essential 'Canadian-ness' went on in many corners of the new Dominion, but nowhere did it meet more success than in the somewhat remote New Brunswick town of Fredericton, home of the University of New Brunswick. There the rectory of St Anne's Parish (Anglican) produced Charles G.D. Roberts, while not far down the road lived his cousin Bliss Carman. Along with Ottawa's Archibald Lampman and Duncan Campbell Scott, William Wilfrid Campbell, and Isabella Valancy Crawford, these individuals made up the 'Confederation Poets', a designation invented by modern literary critics for the first 'school' of Canadian poets to wrestle with Canadian themes—notably the local or regional landscape and sometimes its deterioration—with some skill and sensitivity.[23] The Confederation poets were internationally known (in their day), familiar with American and European literary traditions, and not always much concerned with Canadian identity. Both Roberts and Carman eventually moved to the United States, and Roberts, in 'The Poet Is Bidden to Manhattan Island' (1886), explained why: 'Your poet's eyes must recognize / The side on which your bread is buttered!'[24]

THE ROYAL ACADEMY OF ARTS

Curiously enough, it was the painters rather than the writers who took the lead in organizing national groups to maintain professional standards and publicize Canadian art. The Ontario Society of Artists, formed in 1872 and incorporated in 1877, took the lead in this effort. It was instrumental in the formation of the Royal Canadian Academy of Arts in 1880—in collaboration with Governor General Lord Lorne—and in the establishment that same year of the National Gallery of Canada. The Academy not only held an inaugural exhibition in Ottawa, but planned others in

Toronto, Montreal, Halifax, and Saint John. As one of the founding academicians wrote, 'We are bound to try to civilize the Dominion a little.'[25] The year 1880 was doubly important in art circles, for in that year the Canadian Society of Graphic Art was also founded.

The first president of the Royal Canadian Academy, the painter Lucius O'Brien, was art director of an elaborate literary and artistic celebration of the young nation, *Picturesque Canada* (1882), which was based on the highly successful books *Picturesque America* and *Picturesque Europe*. It was the idea of two Americans, the Belden brothers, who had established themselves in Toronto. The editor of the project—George Monro Grant, the principal of Queen's University—stated in the Preface: 'I believed that a work that would represent its characteristic scenery and history and life of its people would not only make us better known to ourselves and to strangers, but would also stimulate national sentiment and contribute to the rightful development of the nation.' The two large volumes of *Picturesque Canada*—which can sometimes be found in second-hand bookshops—contained 540 illustrations. They included wood engravings based on paintings and, for the West, engravings of photographs of serene vistas, fulfilling the promise of the title. The descriptive texts by Grant, Charles G.D. Roberts, and others presented an idealized, complacent view of the cities, towns, and regions of Canada, praising the present and pointing to their glorious future. *Picturesque Canada* was a monument to the optimism of the time.[26]

THE ROYAL SOCIETY OF CANADA

The Royal Society of Canada was founded in 1882 to promote research and learning in the arts and sciences.[27] Again Lord Lorne provided much of the impetus, replicating a British institution to establish the importance of cultural accomplishments in creating a sense of national pride and self-confidence. He was the first of several governors general to make significant contributions to Canadian cultural nationalism; in

1936, for example, John Buchan (Lord Tweedsmuir) would help to introduce the Governor General's awards for literature. Lorne himself was an intellectual who painted and wrote poetry. The society was to be self-selective, with membership by invitation only, and bicultural, with a separate section for 'Littérature française, Histoire, Archéologie', although the scientific sections had 'no distinctions of race or language'. Its first president, J.W. Dawson, principal of McGill University, emphasized in his presidential address a sense of national purpose, especially 'the establishment of a bond of union between the scattered workers now widely separated in different parts of the Dominion'. At an early meeting Thomas Sterry Hunt, a charter member and later president, spoke of 'a new departure in the intellectual history of Canada' and added that 'the brightest glories and the most enduring honours of a country are those which come from its thinkers and its scholars.'[28] However romantic that statement may be, what is important is Hunt's emphasis on the country as a whole. Like the Royal Canadian Academy, the Royal Society had its headquarters in Ottawa.

THE NORTH-WEST TERRITORIES

Despite efforts to encourage a sense of nationhood that might transcend the barriers of cultural difference and geographical distance, the fact remains that the new Canadian nationality remained fragile, more than a little precious, and very racist. In addition, at least outside French Canada, it mainly expressed the prejudices and ideology of British Ontario. Many believed that the crucible for the new Canadian nationality, and the nation itself, was in the vast unsettled expanse of territory west of the Great Lakes that had been obtained from the Hudson's Bay Company. Here Canada had insisted from the beginning on controlling both the land and the natural resources, subject only to negotiations over the rights of the Aboriginal inhabitants. Here Canada would govern its own colony and make its own policy, free of the compromises required to bring older provinces into Confederation. And here its limitations would be most clearly evident.

The interests of the Canadian government in the Northwest, particularly under Sir John A. Macdonald, were focused on agricultural settlement, both as an outlet for excess eastern population and as a stimulus to the development of a truly transcontinental nation. Several problems faced the Dominion in the Northwest, however. In the first place, the government did not have the money to develop the territory as quickly as it, and the incoming settlers, would have preferred. The attempt to finance the building of a transcontinental railway had helped to push the Macdonald government out of office. Finding the large number of surveyors necessary to survey the land in advance of settlement, and the money to pay them, proved extremely difficult. Paying the compensation required to extinguish Aboriginal title to the land was almost impossible. In the second place, at the time of the transfer of the western territory to the Dominion in 1870, Quebec had assumed that western expansion was mainly Ontario's business. It was therefore surprised to discover that the West had a significant French-speaking Roman Catholic population: the Métis. As the government struggled with the Riel insurrection in Red River and then the new province of Manitoba, Quebecers became increasingly protective of the rights of French Canadians, including the Métis, in the region. The federal government's treatment of Riel became a major issue for Quebec, where it was widely believed that Riel was persecuted for being a French Canadian. The interpretation of Riel's career is still contentious today, and the arguments have not changed much since the nineteenth century.

WESTERN LAND AND SETTLEMENT POLICY

In 1872 the Canadian Parliament passed the Dominion Lands Act, based in large measure on the American Homestead Act. The insistence on a homestead act had been one of the 'rights' demanded by the people of Red River in 1869 and 1870. The legislation also regularized the Dominion Lands Survey, which had been in operation since 1869. The survey system continued the 640-acre square section that set the pattern for the landscape of the Prairie provinces. Under the Lands Act, any male farmer could obtain a quarter-section, 160 acres (65 hectares) of land, for $10 upon his agreement to cultivate 30 acres (10 hectares) and construct a permanent dwelling house within three years of registration. The law also allowed the farmer an additional quarter-section for an additional $10. This was designed to compensate the farmer for lack of rainfall and other drawbacks in much of the West. The homestead arrangement was not very important for settlement before 1890, because most of the best arable land on the prairies was initially held by the CPR, the HBC, and in reserve for the Métis.

In its eagerness to get the prairies populated, Canada also encouraged the settlement of various ethnic communities from Europe, usually through promises to immigrant leaders to provide blocks of land for self-contained ethnic settlement. The first successful negotiations along these lines were carried out with Russian Mennonites beginning in 1872 and 1873. These Mennonites, members of a Protestant pacifist sect founded in the sixteenth century, were from Prussia and Poland. They had left their homes because of military conscription in the eighteenth century. Catherine the Great of Russia offered them generous terms of resettlement, including land, freedom of religion, their own separate schools, and permanent exemption from military service. By the 1870s, however, Russian nationalism was threatening the Mennonite independence and communal lifestyle.

The Canadian government offered similar inducements to the earlier Russian ones: exemption from military service, religious liberty, control of education, free homesteads of 160 acres, and the right to purchase additional land at one dollar per acre. Canada set aside two blocks of townships for the Mennonites in southern Manitoba: one block of eight townships was on the east side of the Red River southeast of Winnipeg, and another block of 12 townships (the 'West Reserve') was along the international boundary west of the Red River. The blocks of reserves made plain to the Mennonites that they could live in their own village communities (and hold land in common) apart from their neighbours. About 8,000 Mennonites settled in 1874 in Manitoba.

The other ethnic group allowed by the Canadian government to establish itself as an autonomous community before 1885 was that of the Icelanders. People from Iceland had begun drifting to Canada in substantial numbers in the early 1870s, motivated both by volcanic eruptions and land shortages in their homeland. The first immigrants settled in Ontario and Quebec but were dissatisfied with their situation. In the spring of 1875 a party of Icelanders travelled west to find satisfactory land for a block settlement they had been promised by the Canadian government. The land they chose was on the west side of Lake Winnipeg, stretching from present-day Selkirk to Hecla Island and including the modern town of Gimli. This territory was north of the boundary of the province of Manitoba and was thus in the relatively ungoverned North-West Territories of Canada, where the newcomers were able to establish the Republic of New Iceland, an autonomous settlement with its own laws and judicial system. The Canadian government accepted a provisional council set up by the Icelanders and allowed them to produce a fully articulated system of self-government with four districts (*byggdir*), each governed by a council of five people headed by a reeve, culminating in a governing council (*Thing*). This republic became part of Manitoba when the boundaries of the province were expanded in 1881, but self-government remained in effect until 1887. Schools

were established in New Iceland only months after arrival of the immigrants, with instruction being conducted in Icelandic.

Although the territory chosen for New Iceland was ideal for access to fishing on Lake Winnipeg, it was some of the poorest agricultural land in the region. Moreover, the Icelanders were struck with a devastating smallpox epidemic in 1876, transmitted by Aboriginal peoples to Icelanders who also lacked immunity to the disease. Spring flooding on Lake Winnipeg occurred between 1876 and 1880. When a major religious dispute among the settlers emerged in the late 1870s, outward migration began. Many Icelanders went either to North Dakota or to the burgeoning city of Winnipeg.

THE MOUNTIES

The North West Mounted Police, based on the Irish constabulary, were established in 1873 to act as a quasi-military agency of the Canadian government in the West. Its officers, drawn from the elites of eastern Canada, were committed to the notion of public stability that associated crime and violence with the 'lower orders' and Native people. Red coats were chosen for uniforms because the Native people still held a traditional respect for the British Army. The 'Mounties' moved into the West ahead of the settlers and have always symbolized a peaceful process of westward expansion, in contrast to the violence of the 'wild' American West. Certainly in Canada there was less individual violence, but peace was often imposed through state intervention and control.

THE ABORIGINAL PEOPLE

On the surface, Dominion policy concerning the Native inhabitants of the North-West Territories was simple and sensible. Canada acknowledged the Aboriginal rights to land of the 'Indians'—though not the Métis—and was prepared to negotiate treaties extinguishing those rights in

STEPHEN LEACOCK'S 'MY REMARKABLE UNCLE'

The first real estate boom in the new Canadian West began in Winnipeg in 1881. It was the harbinger of many similar phenomena in the ensuing years, and was treated later with affectionate humour by Stephen Leacock, who wrote of his uncle, a man who truly behaved much as his nephew described. E.P., as he was known, couldn't really be much exaggerated.

The most remarkable man I have ever known in my life was my uncle Edward Philip Leacock, known to every so many people in Winnipeg fifty or sixty years ago as E.P. His character was so exceptional that it needs nothing but plain narration. It was so exaggerated already that you couldn't exaggerate it. . . . all the talk was of Manitoba now opening up. Nothing would do E.P. but that he and my father must go west. . . . They hit Winnipeg just on the rise of the boom, and E.P. came at once into his own and rode on the crest of the wave. . . . In less than no time he was in everything and knew everybody, conferring titles and honours up and down Portage Avenue. In six months he had a great fortune, on paper; took a trip east and brought back a charming wife from Toronto; built a large house beside the river; filled it with pictures he said were his ancestors, and carried on in it roaring hospitality that never stopped.

His activities were wide. He was president of a bank (that never opened), head of a brewery (for brewing the Red River), and above all, secretary-treasurer of the Winnipeg and Hudson Bay and Arctic Railway that had a charter authorizing it to build a road to the Arctic Ocean, when it got ready. They had no track, but they printed stationery and passes, and in return E.P. received passes all over North America. . . .

Naturally E.P.'s politics remained conservative. But he pitched the note higher. Even the ancestors weren't good enough. He invented a Portuguese Dukedom (some one of our family once worked in Portugal)—and he conferred it, by some kind of reversion, on my elder brother Jim who had gone to Winnipeg to work in E.P.'s office. This enabled him to say to visitors in his big house, after looking at the ancestors—to say in a half-whisper behind his hand, 'Strange to think that two deaths would make that boy a Portuguese Duke.' But Jim never knew which two Portuguese to kill.

To aristocracy E.P. also added a touch of peculiar prestige by always being apparently just about to be called away—imperially. If some said, 'Will you be in Winnipeg all winter, Mr. Leacock?' he answered, 'It will depend a good deal on what happens in West Africa.' Just that; West Africa beat them.

Then came the crash of the Manitoba boom. Simple people, like my father, were wiped out in a day. Not so E.P. The crash just gave him a lift as the smash of a big wave lifts a strong swimmer. He just went right on. I believe that in reality he was left utterly bankrupt. But it made no difference. He used credit instead of cash. He still had his imaginary bank, and his railway to the Arctic Ocean. Hospitality still roared and the tradesmen still paid for it. Any one who called about a bill was told that E.P.'s movements were uncertain and would depend a good deal on what happened in Johannesburg. That held them another six months.

SOURCE: Stephen Leacock, *My Remarkable Uncle and Other Sketches* (Toronto: McClelland & Stewart, 1965 [1942]), 15–17.

■ Inspection of NWMP lancers at Fort Walsh, Cypress Hills, 1878. LAC, C-18046A.

exchange for reserves, often located on the most marginal and least fertile land. These treaties not only freed the more desirable land for settlement, but enabled the Canadian government to continue to pursue its pre-Confederation policy of settling First Nations people on the land as farmers in the hopes of eventually assimilating them into mainstream Canadian society. In 1876, for example, the Plains Cree of central Saskatchewan gathered at Fort Carlton to consider the terms of the government's Treaty Six. Their chief, Poundmaker (Pitikwahanapiwiyin), objected to the terms, arguing that the government should be prepared to do more than provide small plots of land, livestock (especially oxen), and farming implements. If Ottawa expected his people to become good farmers, it should also provide training and other forms of assistance, particularly after the buffalo disappeared. Lieutenant-Governor Alexander Morris, who had presented the terms for the treaty, considered this suggestion as an example of pure greed, and it was pushed aside.[29] Nevertheless, Poundmaker signed the treaty, and three years later accepted a reserve on the Battle River. Another important Plains Cree leader, Big Bear (Mistahimaskwa), held out for six years. But by December 1882 his people were starving, and he agreed to sign.

After most of the Aboriginal bands on the prairies had signed the numbered treaties, the government consolidated the laws regarding Aboriginals into one omnibus piece of legislation, the Indian Act of 1876. This Act made Aboriginals wards of the state and regulated the sale of their land. The Aboriginal peoples of the West were caught in an inexorable process of change. The buffalo were rapidly disappearing, the victims of over-hunting, the arrival of settlement and new technology, and probably some sort of bovine disease epidemic. Whatever the reasons, most Aboriginal leaders knew that their traditional way of life was disappearing forever. But the Department of Indian Affairs expected them to become self-sufficient virtually overnight. It did not supply the reserves with enough food to prevent starvation and disease, and it complained when the desperate people slaughtered their livestock for something to eat. The reserve lands tended to be marginal, the assistance supplied was inadequate, and the attitude of many of the Indian agents (the government's representatives on the reserves) was basically unsympathetic. By the early 1880s, the West was a virtual powder keg of Aboriginal discontent. Cree leaders in what is now Alberta sent a letter to Sir John A. Macdonald (who was Minister of the Interior and head of Indian Affairs as well as Prime Minister) telling him they were destitute and that their motto was, 'If we must die by violence let us do it quickly.' The winter of 1883–4 was particularly severe, and many were starving. Some Indian agents wrote to Ottawa, but nothing was done. In June 1884 Big Bear and his followers, with many others, travelled to Poundmaker's reserve for discussions, after which some 2,000 people took part in the religious ritual known as the Thirst Dance.

■ The Plains Cree leader Poundmaker (Pitikwahanapiwiyin; 1842–86) was named for his skill at constructing the pounds (pens) used to trap bison. LAC, C-001875.

THE MÉTIS

Like the First Nations, the Métis were systematically pushed to the margins. The Macdonald government had created Manitoba as a province only under duress, and the Prime Minister regarded the mixed-bloods as needing merely to be 'kept down by a strong hand until they are swamped by the influx of settlers'.[30] And swamped they were. As thousands of new settlers, mainly from Ontario, arrived in the province, the land rights that had been guaranteed to the Métis were gradually whittled down, and much of the land itself—about 2 million of the 2.5 million acres (809,370 out of 1,011,715 hectares) promised the Métis in 1870—ended up in the hands of speculators. By 1885 Ontario-born settlers outnumbered Métis five to one in Manitoba, and only 7 per cent of the province's population was of mixed-blood origin. The extent to which deliberate government policy was responsible for the plight of the Métis has been one of the most bitter historical controversies ever seen in Canadian historiography, and

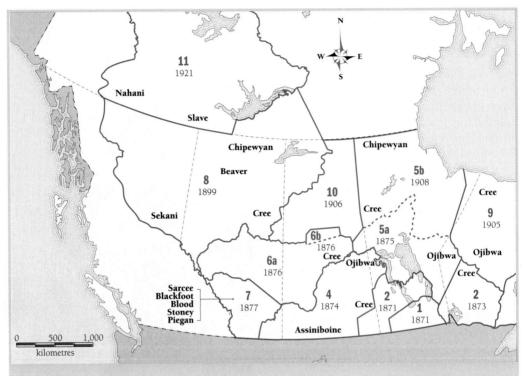

☐ The numbered treaties, 1871–1921. Adapted from J.R. Miller, *Skyscrapers Hide the Heavens: A History of Indian–White Relations in Canada*, rev. edn (Toronto: University of Toronto Press, 1991), 166.

the last word has not yet been written on the subject.

Many Métis headed farther west, often to the Saskatchewan Valley, where they formed several mission settlements, including Qu'Appelle, Batoche, and Duck Lake.[31] But the buffalo were becoming scarce. French, English, and Scottish mixed-bloods in the region demanded grants similar to those given to the mixed-bloods under the Manitoba Act. As in Red River a decade before, the arrival of government surveyors sparked fear and uncertainty as to whether the river lot holdings of the Métis would be allowed to survive in a square survey system. Part of the problem was that the surveying was not happening fast enough, not just for the Métis (who sought exemptions from it), but for the European

settlers as well. By the early 1880s, the Europeans in the region were becoming as restive as the First Nations and the Métis, although for different reasons. Their concerns were more political. In March 1883 the Qu'Appelle settlers' rights association passed resolutions calling for parliamentary representation, land law reform, proper legislation for settlers, and government assistance for immigrants. In December of that year a Manitoba and Northwest farmers' union was organized in Winnipeg. A motion for repeal of the BNA Act and the formation of a 'new confederacy of the North-West Provinces and British Columbia' was only barely defeated. A Bill of Rights was drawn up, which was summarily rejected in Ottawa.

In the late spring of 1884 the despairing

■ Big Bear trading at Fort Pitt, an HBC post on the North Saskatchewan River, 1884. In the same year the post was taken over by the North-West Mounted Police. In April 1885, in the course of the uprising, Big Bear's band attacked the fort, which they evacuated and then burned. LAC, PA-118768.

Métis turned to their old leader, Louis Riel. He had apparently put his life back together after several years of exile in the United States and institutionalization for mental disturbance in Quebec asylums between 1876 and 1878. Riel had become an American citizen and was teaching in St Peter's, Montana—where he had married and started a family—when a delegation from the Saskatchewan country visited him on 4 June. They told him of all the grievances that were burdening the peoples of the region, explained that agitation was developing against the Canadian government, and pleaded with him to return and lead them. Within a month, Riel and his family were in Batoche and he was initiating a peaceful movement of protest against Canadian policies.

By December 1884 Riel and W.H. Jackson (secretary of the North-West Settler's Union) had drafted a long petition, with 25 sections, which they sent to Ottawa. The document concluded by requesting that the petitioners 'be allowed as in [1870] to send Delegates to Ottawa with their Bill of rights; whereby an understanding may be arrived at as to their entry into confederation, with the constitution of a free province'.[32] Ottawa acknowledged receipt of the petition, but made no other response. Riel was mistaken in thinking the tactics that had worked—under special conditions—in 1869–70 could be repeated 15 years later. He was equally mistaken in believing that he had the support of all the people in the region. As soon as signs of armed confrontation appeared, the European settlers quickly dissociated themselves from Riel's movement, and the First Nations moved in their own direction, attacking European settlements in several places.

THE NORTH-WEST REBELLION

Events took a menacing turn on 18 March 1885, when Riel and some of his men strode into the Walters and Baker store in Batoche. Riel announced, 'Well, gentlemen, it has commenced.' 'What has commenced?' asked Walters. 'Oh, this movement for the rights of the country', was the reply.[33] The visitors then helped themselves to ammunition and provisions. On 21 March Riel sent a letter to Superintendent L.N.F. Crozier of the North West Mounted Police at Fort Carlton, which was manned by a force of Mounted Police and volunteers. The missive demanded that the fort surrender, on pain of attack by Riel and his men. Crozier refused. On 26 March, Gabriel Dumont, Riel's military 'general', intercepted a small detachment from Fort Carlton near Duck Lake. When Crozier heard of this action he left the fort with as many men as he could muster. This force met Riel and 300 Métis on horseback before it reached Duck Lake. Startled, Crozier gave an order to fire. Thirty minutes of gunfire exchanges followed, during which lives were lost on both sides.

The Métis, who outnumbered Crozier's men, forced them to retreat. Gabriel Dumont later recalled this confrontation in vivid detail:

> They had to go through a clearing so I lay in wait for them, saying to my men: 'Courage, I'm going to make the red coats jump in their carts with some rifle shots.' And then I laughed, not because I took any pleasure in killing but to give courage to my men.
>
> Since I was eager to knock off some of the red coats, I never thought to keep under cover and a shot came and gashed the top of my head, where a deep scar can still be seen. I fell down on the ground and my horse, which was also wounded, went right over me as it tried to get

away. . . . When Joseph Delorme saw me fall again, he cried out that I was killed. I said to him, 'Courage! As long as you haven't lost your head, you're not dead!' . . .

> While we were fighting, Riel was on horseback, exposed to the gunfire, and with no weapon but the crucifix which he held in his hand.[34]

Riel wrote a letter to Crozier blaming him for the battle. 'A calamity has fallen upon the country yesterday', he insisted. 'You are responsible for it before God and man.'[35] He then appealed to the Cree to assist him. He got more than he had anticipated. Poundmaker's men broke into buildings in Battleford, terrifying settlers, and the Cree warrior Wandering Spirit (Kapapamahchakwew) led a band that attacked Frog Lake, killing nine.

Prime Minister Macdonald was determined to crush this uprising quickly[36] and sent a military force under Major-General Frederick Middleton—by way of the new Canadian Pacific Railway—to put it down. Many of the troops came from Winnipeg militia units composed of ex-Ontarians.[37] Lieutenant-Colonel William Otter relieved Battleford, but was fired on by Aboriginal warriors at Cut Knife Hill and had to withdraw. A battle with the Métis at Fish Creek delayed the march on Batoche, where Middleton intended to confront Riel. But on 9 May the Canadian force of 800 men arrived at Batoche, where they quickly defeated Riel, Dumont, and about 200 armed Métis. The uprising was over by 12 May. Dumont fled to the United States and Riel was arrested.

THE AFTERMATH OF REBELLION

A formal charge of high treason, carrying the death penalty, was laid against Riel on 6 July. Even though Riel was now an American citizen, the Canadian government insisted that his activities had been treasonable and made the charge stick.[38] The trial began on 28 July at Regina.[39] Many Canadian historians have characterized it as a political trial, infamously coloured by the

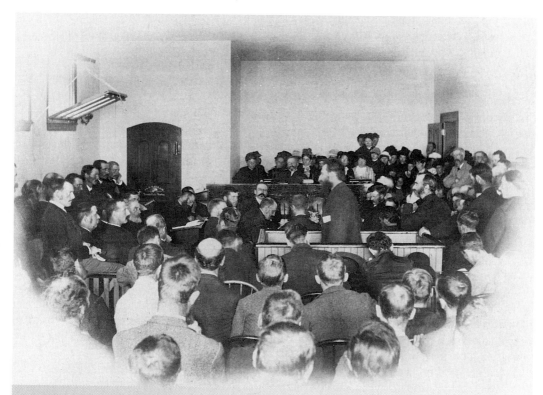

■ Riel in the prisoner's box. He addressed the court twice during his trial, once after all the evidence had been presented (when he spoke for more than an hour) and once before sentence was pronounced. LAC, C-1879.

government's determination to see Riel found guilty and executed (on the other hand, Thomas Flanagan, in his book *Riel and the Rebellion: 1885 Reconsidered*, argues that the government behaved quite properly[40]). In any case, Riel passionately denied a plea of insanity proposed by his lawyers, who failed to present the defence argument that Riel himself insisted on: that the uprising was justified. The jury found him guilty, in effect rejecting the insanity plea, but recommended mercy. Ottawa dismissed two appeals, and Riel was hanged on 16 November 1885. A number of other leading rebels received lesser sentences.

If Riel was treated without sympathy by the Canadian government, the punishments meted out to the First Nations, who were regarded as having joined Riel's resistance rather than acting on their own initiative, were equally severe.[41] The Macdonald government used the rebellion and the violence committed by the leaders of the First Nations as pretexts to crush the protests against the failure to observe the negotiated treaties. Eight warriors were executed in late November 1885, and before the courts were finished, more than 50 others were sentenced to imprisonment. Among the leaders, Poundmaker stood trial for treason and was sentenced to three years in prison. Released after a year, he died four months later. Big Bear received a similar sentence, but was released after a year and a half. Wandering Spirit was hanged. The trials were conducted in a highly improper manner. Few of the accused were properly represented in court, and translation was inadequate for people who understood little English and less of Canadian law. Most First Nations leaders and people tried to remain clear of the Métis uprising, but this did not save them from a campaign of repression, in the late 1880s and after, mounted by Assistant Indian Commissioner Hayter Reed, who maintained that the rebellion had abrogated the treaties and proceeded to introduce a series of policies that made the First Nations totally dependent on the largesse of Canada.

At the time of his death Riel was already one of the most controversial figures in the nation's history. Contemporaries argued over whether he was a murderous traitor or a martyr, the saviour of his people. For French Canadians as well as Métis he symbolized resistance to Anglo-Saxon domination, and later generations would see him as symbolic of still other values, including a general resistance to the imperialism of central Canada. The execution of Riel had a lasting impact on Canada, particularly in Quebec, where it served to strengthen French-Canadian nationalism and turn voters away from the Conservative Party. On 22 November 1885, at a huge gathering in the public square in Montreal called the Champ de Mars, Honoré Mercier, the Liberal leader in Quebec, joined Wilfrid Laurier in denouncing the government action. 'In killing Riel,' Mercier said, 'Sir John has not only struck at the heart of our race but especially at the cause of justice and humanity which . . . demanded mercy for the prisoner of Regina, our poor friend of the North-West.'[42] Laurier added rhetorically, 'Had I been born on the banks of the Saskatchewan . . . I myself would have shouldered a musket to fight against the neglect of governments and the shameless greed of speculators.' But when Mercier proposed that French Canadians leave the two major parties and form one of their own, Laurier disagreed: 'We are a new nation,' he said, 'we are attempting to unite the different conflict elements which we have into a nation.

Shall we ever succeed if the bond of union is to be revenge?'[43] Laurier argued that Mercier's proposal would destroy Confederation.

THE COMPLETION OF THE CPR

The defeat of the Métis and the public execution of Louis Riel were only two of the reasons the year 1885 was so significant in the history of Canada, especially the West. On 7 November 1885, nine days before Riel's death, the last spike was driven at Craigellachie in eastern British Columbia, marking the completion of the Canadian Pacific Railway. The CPR had been resurrected in 1881 as a hybrid corporation controlled by private capitalists and financed chiefly by the state—which, along with public subsidies, gave it about 25 million acres (more than 100,000 square kilometres) of land along its right-of-way, as well as other concessions. The wisdom of rail construction in advance of settlement—building what T.C. Keefer had called 'colonization lines'—was actively debated at the time, particularly given the inducements needed to convince hard-headed businessmen to proceed, but the Macdonald government defended the railroad on the grounds of national interest. Since this concept is not measurable in quantitative terms, it is impossible to know whether the financial price was too high.

What we can say with certainty is that the construction of the CPR was a spectacular feat, attributable in part to the engineers in charge and in part to the managerial skills of William Van Horne. The actual construction, however, was carried out chiefly by the 6,500 Chinese labourers who were specially imported for the job. Many died, and those who survived were summarily discharged when the work was completed. Macdonald had defended Chinese immigration in 1883, arguing that it would 'be all very well to exclude Chinese labour, when we can replace it with white labour, but until that is done, it is better to have Chinese labour than no labour at all.'[44] With the completion of the CPR,

MEMORANDUM ON 'THE FUTURE MANAGEMENT OF INDIANS', JULY 1885

In 1885, a number of Indian bands in the North-West violently attacked post and forts at the same time as the Métis were engaged in battle with Canadian troops. The Canadian government responded to this violence in kind, both in terms of formal court action against the offenders, and in terms of a tougher policy. This memorandum was written by the Assistant Indian Commissioner, Hayter Reed, to his superior from Regina in July. It became the basis for the new policy.

Regina
July 20th/85

Memorandum for the Honourable the Indian Commission relative to the future management of Indians

1. All Indians who have not during the late troubles been disloyal or troublesome should be treated as heretofore; as they have not disturbed our treaty relations, and our treatment in the past has been productive of progress and good results.

2. As the rebellious Indians expected to have been treated with severity as soon as overpowered, a reaction of feeling must be guarded against. They were led to believe that they would be shot down, and harshly treated. Though humanity of course forbids this, unless severe examples are made of the more prominent participants in the rebellion much difficulty will be met with their future management, and future turbulence may be feared. It is therefore suggested that all leading Indian rebels whom it is found possible to convict of particular crimes, such as instigating and citing to treason, felony, arson, larceny, murder, etc., be dealt with in as severe a manner as the law will allow and that no offences of their most prominent men be overlooked.

3. That other offenders, both Halfbreed and Indian, who have been guilty of such serious offences as those above mentioned should be punished for their crimes in order to deter them from rebellious movements in future.

4. That the tribal system should be abolished in so far as is compatible with the treaty, e.g., in all cases in which the treaty has been broken by rebel tribes; by doing away with chiefs and councillors, depriving them of medals and other appurtenances of their offices. Our instructors and employees will not then be hampered by Indian consultations and interferences, but will administer direct orders and instructions to individuals; besides by this action and careful repression of those that become prominent amongst them by counselling, medicine dances, and so on, a further obstacle will be thrown in the way of future united rebellious movements.

5. No annuity money should be now paid any bands that rebelled, or any individuals that left well disposed bands and joined the insurgents. As the Treaty expressly stipulated for peace and good will, as well as an observance of law and order, it has been entirely abrogated by the rebellion. Besides this fact, such suggestion is made because in the past the annuity money which should have been expended wholly in necessaries has to a great extent been wasted upon articles more or less useless and in purchasing necessaries at exorbitant prices, entailing upon the Department a greater expenditure in providing articles of clothing, food

and implements, not called for by the terms of the Treaty, than need have been entailed if the whole of the annuity money had been well and economically applied to the purchase of such necessities. All future grants should be regarded as concessions of favour, not of right, and the rebel Indians be made to understand that they have forfeited every claim as 'matter of right'.

SOURCE: Blair Stonechild and Bill Waiser, *Loyal till Death: Indians and the North-West Rebellions* (Calgary, 1997), 250–3.

the Canadian government moved swiftly to limit Chinese immigration.

Despite the high costs, the positive aspects of the CPR far outweighed the negative for most Canadians at the time. On 4 July 1886 the first through passengers from Montreal arrived in Port Moody, British Columbia. A journey that only a few years before would have taken several months—sailing around the southern tip of South America or travelling overland by Red River cart—had taken just seven days. The railroad became the physical symbol of a transcontinental nation that now existed in fact as well as in the abstract.

■ The first transcontinental passenger train arrives at the foot of Howe Street in Vancouver, 23 May 1887. City of Vancouver Archives, CAN.P.78, N.52.

CONCLUSION

The West was to be an anglophone colony of Canada. Not only were First Nations, Métis, and Chinese cast aside as quickly as possible, but French Canadians were not supposed to move there in any substantial numbers. Most Quebecers in the years after Confederation considered the West important mainly in commercial terms, or as a better destination than the United States for Quebec migrants. As *L'Opinion Publique* (Montreal) stated in 1879: 'For five years English emigration has flooded Manitoba, and French emigration has been pretty well nil. . . . The North-West, founded and settled by the French, is destined, like the rest of North America, to be English.'[45] The francophone response to the execution of Louis Riel, however, was hardly so fatalistic. By 1885 Quebec public opinion was prepared to believe in theories of anti-French conspiracies.[46] National consolidation was arguably completed in 1885, but much Canadian 'nationalism' still bore the distinctive mark of the Ontario WASP. Two cultures, French and English, were being firmly set in opposition to each other. Trying to satisfy the country's two major components was the most challenging task facing the Canadian government.

SHORT BIBLIOGRAPHY

Beal, Bob, and Rod MacLeod. *Prairie Fire: The 1885 North-West Rebellion*, 2nd edn. Toronto, 1994. The best overview of the 1885 rebellion.

Berger, Carl. *The Sense of Power: Studies in the Ideas of Canadian Imperialism, 1867–1914*. Toronto, 1970. A pioneer work in Canadian intellectual history, still not superseded.

———. *Honour and the Search for Influence: A History of the Royal Society of Canada*. Toronto, 1996. A useful account of the development of a crucial national institution.

Bumsted, J.M. *Louis Riel v. Canada: The Making of a Rebel*. Winnipeg, 2002. A recent attempt at a balanced view of Riel.

Cook, Ramsay. *Provincial Autonomy, Minority Rights and the Compact Theory 1867–1921*. Ottawa, 1969. The standard study of the alternative vision of Confederation.

Lamb, W. Kaye. *History of the Canadian Pacific Railway*. New York, 1977. The best overview of the CPR currently available.

Neufeld, Edward P. *The Financial System of Canada, Its Growth and Development*. Toronto, 1972. The standard study of a complex subject.

Pór, Jonas. *Icelanders in North America: The First Settlers*. Winnipeg, 2002. An account of the early settlement of Icelanders in America.

Reid, Dennis. *Our Own Country Canada: Being an Account of the National Aspirations of the Principal Landscape Artists in Montreal and Toronto, 1869–1890*. Ottawa, 1979. An interesting piece of art history, relating the art to larger political and intellectual currents.

Sprague, D.N. *Canada and the Métis, 1869–1885*. Waterloo, Ont., 1988. A controversial account of the way in which Canada treated the Métis.

Stonechild, Blair, and Bill Waiser. *Loyal till Death: Indians and the North-West Rebellions*. Calgary, 1997. A superb analysis of the First Nations and the 1885 rebellions.

Swainger, Jonathan. *The Canadian Department of Justice and the Completion of Confederation*. Vancouver, 2000. A fine study of a much neglected topic.

Warkentin, John. 'The Mennonite Settlement of Southern Manitoba', Ph.D. thesis, University of Toronto, 1960. A thorough scholarly study of a complex question.

STUDY QUESTIONS

1. What was the National Policy?
2. What was the basic thrust of the provincial rights movement?
3. Comment on John Bourinot's arguments concerning 'the intellectual development of the Canadian people'. Do they really address the question?
4. Why was it difficult to develop a sense of Canadian nationalism?
5. Was the West treated fairly by the Canadian government after Confederation?
6. Is there a difference between being commissioned by the Canadian government to write a study of the military events of 1885 and being commissioned by the Canadian government to help prepare a brief in a court case regarding land claims?
7. What was the secret of E.P. Leacock's success?

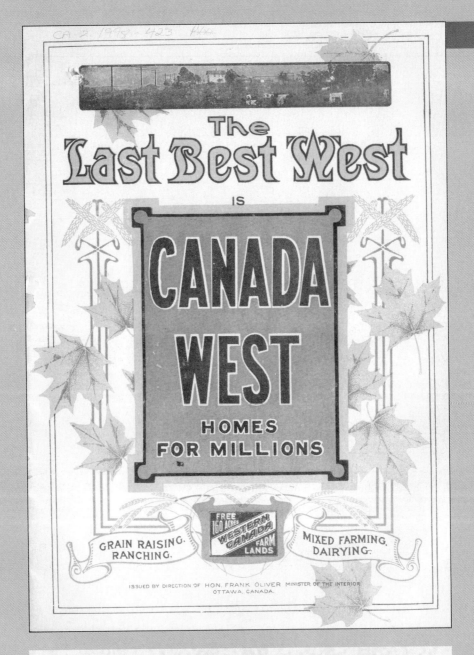

□ A 1907 poster exhorting immigrants to settle in western Canada. LAC, C-30621.

PART TWO

■ 1885–1914

■ From the start, Canada possessed rich natural resources, and by 1885 a burgeoning industrial sector was exploiting them so successfully that the young country was among the world's top 10 industrial nations. Industrialization was concentrated in Ontario and Quebec, where urban growth produced serious social and economic dislocation. A vibrant labour movement began to develop, along with recognition of the need for social reform. In this period, reform activity was largely the preserve of private citizens, generally from the middle classes; paternalistic at best, in many cases the reformers were openly racist in their attitudes. At the same time, urban growth made it possible to develop the infrastructure necessary for a new cultural sophistication, and in the performing arts particularly, Canadians began to make their way onto the world scene.

Despite the migration of many rural dwellers to the industrializing cities of the young country, the majority of Canadians in the years before 1914 still made their living from agriculture or natural resources. The settlement of the West was essentially completed in this period. Many of the settlers were new immigrants, and after 1896 many of them came from outside the British Isles. By 1914, however, large amounts of prime uncultivated land were no longer available, and rural Canada entered a long decline that would last for most of the twentieth century.

Political developments in this period were complex. Despite the potential for conflict, the domestic political system worked quite well, largely because political parties concentrated on patronage rather than ideological differences. On the other hand, Canada's position in relation to the British Empire remained the subject of national debate for many years. Not all Canadians, English- or French-speaking, embraced the implications of an imperial Canada with equal enthusiasm. Some even suggested that Canada would be better off aligning itself with the United States.

CHAPTER THREE

■ The First Triumph of Industrialism, 1885–1914

■ All things are relative. Compared with the economies of the United States and Britain, Canada's economy in the years before World War I seems weak. Yet when measured in terms of gross national product and per capita income, Canada was among the richest nations in the world.[1] According to one estimate, Canada led the world between 1870 and 1913 in real gross domestic product, real GDP per capita growth rate, and real GDP per labour hour.[2] From the late 1870s to the end of the Great War, Canada managed to maintain its position of relative wealth, if not power, despite the industrial development of such nations as Japan and Germany and the substantial economic growth of many other countries. The extent of Canada's technological and financial expertise was reflected in the success with which Canadian businessmen were able to invest in Latin America and the Caribbean. However weak the Canadian economy may have appeared at home, from the standpoint of most of the world Canada was not only rich and powerful, but highly industrialized and 'progressive'. Its advantages in agriculture and natural resources aside, much of its success could be attributed to its industrial development and success in creating a self-sustaining internal economy and dynamic foreign trade. In addition, Canada was able to export its entrepreneurial expertise to less developed neighbours.

Continuing the process of industrialization that had begun in the mid-nineteenth century involved more than the simple construction of new and larger factories. Transportation facilities had to be extended and rationalized, investment mobilized, resources exploited, and a labour force recruited. Despite the National Policy and the introduction of the protective tariff, Canada did not succeed in retaining total control over, or ownership in, its economy. Moving onto the international stage increased the extent to which the economy was affected by world economic conditions and economic cycles. Thus, Canada's growth rate was limited by the poor international economic conditions from the late 1870s to the mid-1890s and benefited from an international boom between 1900 and 1913. Moreover, industrial development was extremely uneven, with industrial growth above the national average only in Ontario. Through the period before 1914, Quebec remained steady at the national average, but the Maritimes fell further and further below it, and the West never became a serious player. Industrial disparities developed within provinces as well as between them. Between 1880 and 1920, for example, industrial growth in larger urban centres such as Montreal and Toronto expanded constantly, while smaller communities—particularly in central Canada—fell steadily behind.

TIMELINE

1869
T. Eaton Company founded.

1872
First Dominion Land Act.

1878
Alexander Graham Bell invents telephone.

1881
Geological Survey of Canada moves to Ottawa.

1882
Founding of Scotia Steel and Forge Company.

1884
First Eaton's catalogue published.

1885
CPR completed.

1886
Dominion Experimental Farms established.

1892
Thomas Ahearne showcases electric stove at Ottawa Exhibition.

1895
Nova Scotia Steel Co. founded.

1896
Gold discovered in Yukon on Rabbit Creek (renamed Bonanza Creek), a tributary of the Klondike River, leading to Klondike gold rush of 1897–8.

1898
Ontario government requires that resources taken on Crown land be processed in Ontario.

1899
Founding of Dominion Iron and Steel Corporation (Disco). Construction begins on Shawinigan Dam. Thomas Ahearne introduces electric auto in Ottawa.

1900
Cuba Company founded.

1901
Nova Scotia Steel and Coal Co. founded.

1904
Canadian investors organize Rio de Janeiro Tramway, Light and Power Co. Socialist Party of Canada organized in BC.

1906
Ontario Hydro incorporated by provincial legislature.

1907
Max Aitken leaves Halifax for Montreal.

1910
Aitken creates Steel Company of Canada and moves to England.

1911
Reciprocity debate of 1911.

FOREIGN INVESTMENT

In all sectors, one of the keys to Canadian economic growth during the three decades prior to World War I was the influx of foreign investment. Few nations have relied so heavily on foreign capital to fuel economic growth as Canada has throughout its history, but such investment was particularly significant in the boom years from 1900 to 1913. Like other countries, Canada used much of its imported capital to finance large development projects, such as railways and hydroelectric generation. In the grossest terms, imports of capital came in two forms—indirect (portfolio) and direct investment—which could be roughly identified with Canada's two largest financial partners. Much of the portfolio investment came from Great Britain, much of the direct investment from the United States. The latter form of investment always implies greater foreign involvement in the host economy. But at the time few Canadians worried much about either the extent or the origin of foreign investment. (Foreign control would not become a serious issue in Canadian economic theory or public life until the late 1950s.) Almost all would probably have agreed with American entrepreneur Frank Clergue, who declared in 1901 that 'foreign money injected into the circulating medium of Canada' would 'remain forever to the everlasting blessing of thousands of its inhabitants'.[3]

INDIRECT INVESTMENT

The differences between indirect and direct investment are symbolic of the different economic strategies preferred by the two imperial powers with which Canada had the most direct contact. Portfolio investment represents money borrowed against securities—mainly bonds in the period before 1914. Most bonds are issued for limited periods of time and do not carry the same management involvement as stocks; nevertheless, they are regarded as 'safer' than stocks because they have first claim on the assets of any

company and pay a predetermined interest off the top of revenue. That the British by and large chose portfolio investment in Canada had more to do with Britain's economic needs than with any desire to let Canadians retain management control. Growing prosperity in Britain had produced thousands of middle-class citizens eager to 'clip coupons' in their old age, and Canada was a relatively secure place in which to invest. Most of Canada's borrowing in Britain was done by government (federal, provincial, and municipal) and the railways. The money went to finance transportation networks and public works: little was available for private enterprise and almost none for 'venture capital'. Canada was one of the major borrowers in the British money market, the sale of its securities between 1865 and 1914 representing about 10 per cent of foreign issues in London. Some British capital came with immigrants or was subsequently sent to them, such as the investments in fruit growing in the Okanagan Valley of British Columbia or the cattle industry in Alberta. But only a relatively small percentage of British investment was direct, and an even smaller proportion (less than one-tenth) of British direct investment was in manufacturing. More typically, British direct investment went to businesses like the Hudson's Bay Company as it moved into retailing operations, or to the British Columbia Street Railway Company, which operated the tramlines in the Lower Mainland of the province and was the silent partner in tramway development in the interior of the province. British management of these enterprises was often charged with being conservative, and indeed did tend to be paternalistic.

In the years immediately before the Great War, Canadian entrepreneurs exploited the complexities of the British investment market, chiefly by merging smaller companies to create industrial giants and then issuing bonds. Such mergers were common across most of the industrialized world in this period as successful companies sought to reduce competition, rationalize, and modernize their particular industries. In Canada,

TABLE 3.1

PERCENTAGE CHANGE IN MANUFACTURING OUTPUT, 1870–1890

Industry	Nova Scotia	New Brunswick	Quebec	Ontario
All factories	128	42	104	116
Farm production (butter, cheese, and cloth)	60	67	50	34
All manufacturing	120	44	101	113
Consumer goods	160	95	100	119
Durable goods	30	-10	83	61
Intermediate goods	214	50	120	162
Chemical products	210	03	149	410
Clothing	224	49	125	277
Coal & petroleum products	164	321	365	-5
Food & beverages	361	292	122	82
Iron & steel products	142	21	92	90
Leather & fur products	-1	-12	50	41
Non-ferric metal products	348	204	191	854
Non-metallic mineral products	114	121	186	215
Printing	54	111	86	177
Paper products	48	-52	313	254
Rubber goods	na	na	202	4311
Transport equipment	3	-38	154	26
Tobacco products	-78	64	162	263
Textiles	505	443	406	150
Wood products	213	2	64	153

SOURCE: Kris Inwood, 'Maritime Industrialization from 1870 to 1910', *Acadiensis* 21, 1 (Autumn 1991): 147.

no one was more successful at merging than William Maxwell Aitken. The son of a New Brunswick Presbyterian minister, 'Max' Aitken (later Lord Beaverbrook) built on his success as a securities broker to consolidate Canadian manufacturing.[4] His greatest success came with the

TABLE 3.2

INDUSTRIAL MERGERS, CONSOLIDATIONS, ACQUISITIONS, AND
FIRM DISAPPEARANCES, 1885–1918

Year	Mergers	Consolidations	Acquisitions	Firm Disappearances
1885	3	2	1	3
1886	0	0	0	0
1887	1	0	1	1
1888	1	1	0	1
1889	6	2	4	9
1890	3	2	1	14
1891	7	4	3	14
1892	6	4	2	10
1893	6	4	2	8
1894	0	0	0	0
1895	4	2	2	4
1896	0	0	0	0
1897	0	0	0	0
1898	2	1	1	6
1899	4	4	0	11
1900	7	3	4	10
1901	7	4	3	25
1902	3	2	1	51
1903	3	1	2	24
1904	4	1	3	5
1905	10	7	3	26
1906	8	5	3	14
1907	6	1	5	11
1908	3	3	0	7
1909	12	10	2	52

TABLE 3.2 (CONTINUED)

Year	Mergers	Consolidations	Acquisitions	Firm Disappearances
1910	22	20	2	69
1911	16	12	4	37
1912	13	8	5	21
1913	8	5	3	17
1914	1	0	1	2
1915	3	2	1	4
1916	1	0	1	1
1917	3	2	1	5
1918	1	1	0	3
Total	174	113	61	465

SOURCE: Gregory P. Marchildon, *Profits and Politics: Beaverbrook and the Gilded Age of Canadian Finance* (Toronto: University of Toronto Press, 1996), 255.

Steel Company of Canada, created in 1910, the bonds of which his Royal Securities firm sold in London on the pre-war boom market. 'I created all the big trusts in Canada', Aitken told Winston Churchill in 1911,[5] after moving to England in 1910 in search of greater challenges. The statement was a typical exaggeration, for he was only the sharpest and most visible operator in a movement that saw 58 giant corporations created in Canada between 1909 and 1912.

DIRECT INVESTMENT

Throughout most of the period before World War I, the US itself was a major importer of British capital and had little available for portfolio investment. The Americans always tended to direct investment as part of an aggressive strategy to gain access to Canadian raw materials and the Canadian market. Much US investment in Canada went to the resource sector, either to take advantage of potential profit in newly developing areas (such as mining) or to control the supplies and prices of raw materials needed for American industries (such as pulp and paper to supply newsprint for American newspapers and books). The other important American strategy was to invest in the Canadian manufacturing sector in order to gain maximum access to the Canadian market. Less than half of all American direct investment was in Canadian manufacturing, but the total amounts involved were still impressive—well over $100 million by 1910. The protective tariff and the National Policy played an important role in encouraging American 'branch-plant' investment.

It is important to remember that the establishment of American branch plants was almost universally regarded as a desirable consequence of protectionism in the years before the Great War. If tariffs on manufactured goods are set sufficiently high, of course, foreign firms cannot

MAX AITKEN (1879–1964)

❖

William Maxwell Aitken, first Baron Beaverbrook, was born in Maple, Ontario, in 1879, the fifth of 10 children. In 1880 his family moved to Newcastle, on the New Brunswick resource frontier, where his father was minister of the Presbyterian church. Young Max grew up in comfortable middle-class surroundings, and although obviously bright, was unable to apply himself at school. At the age of 16 he went to work as a clerk in the law firm of Richard B. Bennett in neighbouring Chatham, but he was too impatient to make a career as a lawyer. His obvious métier was in selling and promoting, and before his twenty-first birthday he had become successful as an insurance salesman in Saint John. He soon moved into selling private company bonds, and in 1903 founded the Royal Securities Corporation in Halifax, which he used as a springboard for modernizing and rationalizing a number of business enterprises in the Maritime region. By 1907 he was a multimillionaire.

Not satisfied in Halifax, in 1907 he moved to Montreal, where he had purchased the Montreal Trust Company and took advantage of a long-lasting Canadian boom to expand his business consolidations. He would buy small, outmoded companies and combine them into larger corporations with more up-to-date machinery and business practices. His first great success came in 1910 with the consolidation of several cement companies into the Canada Cement Co. In the same year he created Stelco, which brought together a number of smaller companies responsible for various stages in steelmaking into a single vertically integrated producer. Aitken's operations did add genuine value to the companies he consolidated and modernized, although some

of his dealings in the stock and bond markets at the very least sailed close to the edge of illegality. In 1910 he and his family moved to England, where he was persuaded by fellow New Brunswicker Andrew Bonar Law (leader of the British Conservative Party) to enter politics, winning a parliamentary seat in the autumn of 1910. Within a year he was knighted, and he continued to pursue industrial consolidation in Canada while sitting as a Tory MP in Westminster until the Great War. During the war he served as Canadian Military Representative in England, introducing the scheme of Canadian War Artists in 1916 (in which Canadian artists painted scenes of the military in action, including on the battlefield) and becoming Minister of Information in the war cabinet in 1917 as Lord Beaverbrook.

Aitken wrote and published several military histories during the war, one of which—*Canada in Flanders*—was widely circulated and helped publicize the heroic actions of the Canadian Expeditionary Force. In London he bought a bankrupt newspaper, the *Express*, in 1917, and after the armistice he put most of his considerable energy into building a media empire, starting with the *Daily Express*, which reached out to all sectors of English society and became the first popular newspaper in the country. He followed this success with the *Evening Standard* and the *Sunday Express*. During the dark days of World War II he served as Churchill's Minister of Aircraft Production, bullying the industry into a greatly increased pace of production that helped save Britain in 1940. After the war he wrote extensively while presiding over his media empire, frequently visiting New Brunswick. He died in 1964.

■ Workers at looms, c. 1908. City of Toronto Archives, Fonds 1244, Item 137.

compete with domestic ones. But early protectionism was really less concerned about ownership than it was about employment. As one protectionist Liberal argued in the Reciprocity debate of 1911: 'I want the American manufacturers to be forced to establish plants on this side of the line and provide work for our Canadian workmen if they want to have the advantage of supplying our home markets.'[6] Supporters of the tariff boasted in 1913 that 450 American branch plants represented a total investment of $135 million. Protectionism was therefore not anti-American before 1914, but rather a form of mercantilism that in part encouraged investment. There was no concern about the outflow of profits or the influx of foreign managers. 'That a portion of the profits made on the development of our latent resources has to be paid out in interest

is no hardship,' commented one business magazine in 1908, 'since without the capital there would have been no profits at all.'[7]

All Canadians, including Quebecers, understood that American investment meant prosperity. Far from endangering the Canadian—or French-Canadian—identity, American investment protected it, for the alternative was to lose Canadian workers to the United States. As one woman with two sons working in the US wrote in a letter to a Montreal weekly in 1903, supporting the tariff, 'I want my boys to come home because I think Canada is a purer and better country. They will be better men here. I don't mean that they are not good now. They are both good boys, but I am afraid for the future.'[8] Since the costs of production in Canada offered little incentive for American manufacturers to locate

■ Clothing manufacturer's shop, Québec City, c. 1905. Archives Nationales du Québec, N79-12, 43. In this shop, as in the textile factory, mechanical jobs were performed mostly by women working under the supervision of men.

their operations in Canada, the tariff was regarded as a necessary step to force most of them to open for business in this country. The majority of American branch plants went to southern Ontario, perhaps because such plants were more common in the heavy industries of Ontario than in the lighter ones (such as food processing and textiles) located in Quebec. Not until the 1920s was any attention paid to the extent of foreign ownership of Canadian industry, and it would be another two generations after that before its implications were seriously considered.

CANADIAN INVESTMENT OVERSEAS

Those Canadians who remember Sir William Mackenzie at all usually do so in connection with the building of the Canadian Northern Railway—Canada's second transcontinental line, taken over by the Canadian government in 1918 and turned into the Canadian National Railways. Born at Kirkfield, Canada West, the son of Scottish immigrants from the Highlands, Mackenzie became a successful railroad contractor and in the early 1890s was a pioneer in street-railway electrification in Winnipeg and Toronto. His most successful operation, however, was not in Canada but in Brazil, where the Ontario-based São Paulo Railway, Light and Power Co. Ltd had the concession to build a street-railway system and supply electricity to Brazil's second-largest city. The company was so successful that it repeated the performance in Rio de Janeiro through the Rio de Janeiro Tramway, Light and Power Co., founded in 1904. In 1912

TABLE 3.3

MANUFACTURING VALUE ADDED PER CAPITA, RELATIVE TO CANADA AS A WHOLE

Region	Year						
	1870	1880	1890	1900	1910	1915	1926
Quebec	0.97	1.03	0.98	1.06	1.03	1.04	1.11
Ontario	1.11	1.16	1.18	1.20	1.45	1.53	1.52
Rest of Canada	0.92	0.81	0.84	0.74	0.52	0.43	0.37

NOTE: Canada as a whole equals 1.

Mackenzie's various Brazilian utility companies were consolidated in one great holding company, Brazilian Traction Limited, for many years the largest single corporation in Brazil.[9]

Mackenzie and his various associates in Brazil were not the only Canadian entrepreneurs active in Latin America. Following the conquest of Cuba by the US in 1898, William Van Horne —the man largely responsible for Canada's first transcontinental railway, the Canadian Pacific— came to terms with a rival group of American entrepreneurs, some of whom were involved in the Brazil operations, and led a syndicate of 160 capitalists from the US and Canada who invested $50,000 each to found the Cuba Company, which intended to build a railway between Santiago and Havana—a 10-day ride by horseback.[10] This venture was centred in a company incorporated in New Jersey (a state with little regulation or supervision of its corporate citizens, and hence a popular place to incorporate in this period) under Van Horne's presidency. Other Canadians, including New Brunswick's Max Aitken, were active in utility development in Cuba, Puerto Rico, and various British colonies in the Caribbean. What seems most striking, however, is the extent of overseas adventuring by Canadian entrepreneurs in the less developed parts of the Americas.

INDUSTRIALIZATION AND THE GROWTH OF REGIONAL DISPARITY

If few Canadians worried much about the dangers of foreign investment, a good many more were concerned about the difficulties of attracting it, particularly in regions that were falling behind in the industrial sweepstakes. One of the more revealing economic statistics for this period is the index of the manufacturing value added per capita in three regions relative to Canada as a whole, as shown in Table 3.3.[11] A related index, outlining per capita manufacturing output of regions as a percentage of the Canadian average, provides a more detailed regional breakdown (see Table 3.4).[12] These tables clearly illustrate the growing disparity in manufacturing between central Canada (especially Ontario) and the remainder of the country. While Quebec remained near the national average, Ontario was gradually gaining at the expense of everybody else.

CENTRAL CANADA

Central Canada's industrial growth after 1881 is one of the great success stories of the country's history, and also one of the most controversial. Much of the political conflict that the nation has experienced since Confederation has its origins

TABLE 3.4
PER CAPITA MANUFACTURING OUTPUT OF REGIONS AS
PERCENTAGE OF THE CANADIAN AVERAGE

Region	1870	1880	1900	1915
Ontario	112	115	123	153
Quebec	101	107	103	100
Maritimes	69	65	59	61
Prairies	–	40	40	38
BC	–	80	132	86

in that growth, which accelerated in the late nineteenth century and continued throughout the twentieth century. While central Canada has explained its development as a product of the region's rich resources of goods and people, combined with its access to markets, other regions have seen that growth as coming at their expense, ascribing much of the expansion to government policies and private actions directed by central Canadians in their own interest. In any event, after 1881 manufacturing replaced commerce as the chief propellant of urban growth in Ontario and to a lesser extent in Quebec, and much of that industrial development involved sophisticated technological applications.

Ontario was the centre not only of iron and steel production but of the secondary manufacturing of iron and steel (i.e., for the machine-tool industry) that played such an important role in transferring technology from one industry to another. The transformation of the iron industry into the steel industry was typical of the process that was occurring. Coke replaced charcoal as the source of heat, but the big changes had less to do with the blast furnace than with the way pig iron was refined into wrought iron. The refining process was turned into two steps, involving first open-hearth furnaces and then a steam-driven rolling mill. The result was a product with a slightly higher carbon content, called steel. Then mechanization was added to each step in the manufacturing process. Raw materials were unloaded and moved by machinery; coke was prepared without being touched by human hand; the blast furnace was loaded by machinery that quadrupled output. 'Gigantic automation' was the watchword at huge installations like Stelco's Hamilton plant and Algoma's Sault Ste Marie operation. In the years before the Great War, the major Canadian steelmakers expanded both to control their own raw materials and to diversify their output. Nevertheless, mechanization worked best when a standard product could be manufactured for a steady demand, and in this period steel rails were the most common product of this type.[13]

Quebec manufacturing relied far less on heavy industry (and vast capitalization) than Ontario, and far more on industry that depended on skilled labour and fussy mechanization, such as clothing, wood products, textiles, and food processing. One reason for the difference may have been the nature of the labour force in each region, and another—especially after 1900—the cheap hydroelectric power available to Quebec. Ontario's marginal early advantage in secondary over primary manufacturing (the province had more than 42 per cent of its total manufacturing in the secondary sector by 1870, while Quebec had only 29 per cent) was eliminated by 1915, when Quebec outstripped Ontario with 77.5 per cent secondary manufacturing, to Ontario's 74.6. While Ontario's manufacturing continued to grow in a number of smaller urban centres, much of Quebec's output was concentrated in Montreal, which by 1900 employed about half of the province's manufacturing workers. Nevertheless, it is easy to overemphasize the notorious 'lag' between the two central Canadian provinces, which were certainly more like one another industrially than they were like the rest of the country. The financial power of Montreal was critical, particularly for the Maritime region.

THE MARITIMES

Before World War I the Canadian West was for the most part too recently settled to move into an active industrial phase, but this was hardly the case with the Maritime provinces. Here the hemorrhaging of population that had begun in the 1860s as a result of rural stagnation was aggravated in the 1870s by a crisis in the shipbuilding industry, which had represented a substantial proportion of the region's export production. Part of the problem for shipbuilding was the growth of new technologies that rendered the wooden sailing ship obsolescent, if not quite obsolete. The real failure, however—in terms of the future development of the region—was probably that of the Maritime shippers, who suffered a collective entrepreneurial failure of will as the sailing vessel went into decline. The owners tended to see their ships merely as instruments of trade, and instead of reinvesting their capital in a modern shipbuilding industry, they (with the business community of the region) finally broke with their transatlantic mentality and looked inward to the continent for markets for industrial production. As a result, the region accepted the National Policy and made increasingly serious efforts to work within it,

although the competition from central Canada was tough and all the Maritime experience and connections were transatlantic in nature.[14] The new continentalism started well in the 1880s. In particular, Maritime businessmen expected to be able to develop textile and iron-and-steel industries, the latter based on regionally available deposits of iron. Up to 1885 they succeeded in competing with Canadian and other producers. But success soon turned to failure. The reasons for that failure remain uncertain.[15] However, it seems that Maritime entrepreneurs lacked the financial resources to withstand falls in the economic cycle, and by 1886 they were blaming too many of their problems on high railroad freight rates. 'How can the National Policy succeed in Canada where such great distances exist between the provinces', wrote one businessman, 'unless the Government who controls the National Railway meets the requirements of trade?'[16] While the region's business community was concentrating on railway rates, outside capital moved in and began buying up locally based companies. Much of the damage was done by Montreal capital, which took over and dismantled a good many burgeoning industries. Maritime entrepreneurs, convinced that they were at a geographical disadvantage in competing with central Canada, ceased trying in most sectors after 1895. One of the chief Montreal raiders was Max Aitken, who had left Halifax for Montreal in 1907 and taken the management of his capital with him.

Instead of pursuing a variety of activities across the economy, the region focused on iron and steel, believing that the presence of local raw materials would make this industry a competitive one. In the short run the strategy appeared successful, with the emergence of the Nova Scotia Steel and Coal Corporation ('Scotia') as a major industrial player, to be joined in 1899 by the Dominion Iron and Steel Corporation ('Disco'). Disco was the creation of New England-born Henry Melville Whitney, who had begun rationalizing the Nova Scotia coalfields in the 1890s and went on to create a new steel company, financed partly by Nova Scotia interests but chiefly with Toronto and Montreal capital. Its new plant at Sydney opened in 1902 at a cost of $15 million and was supposed to put Canada in the big leagues of steelmaking. Although the *Canadian Mining Review* complained in 1903 of the company's 'kaleidoscopic changes, of extravagance, vacillation and blundering', not least in its labour relations, the company survived and in 1910 was merged by Max Aitken with the Dominion Coal Company as the Dominion Steel Corporation. But spinoff industries, such as the Rhodes, Curry Company of Amherst, which manufactured railroad cars, were subject to buy-outs and mergers by Montreal interests.

One of the problems faced by Maritime industry was its inability to use protective tariffs against the outsiders, most of whom were Canadians. The conflict between local and central Canadian capitalists reached its peak in 1910, when Aitken attempted to include the Scotia corporation in his Dominion Coal and Steel merger and was only just beaten off. Nevertheless, Montreal interests owned or dominated much of the region's industrial enterprise by 1911, replacing Halifax as its dominant financial city. Meanwhile Toronto interests were moving into the Maritime region in wholesale and retail marketing, particularly after 1911. Between 1901 and 1921, the number of regional businesses that were branches of central Canadian enterprises based in Montreal or Toronto more than doubled, from 416 to 950. The loss of regional economic autonomy meant that capital was siphoned away from the Maritimes—and that when times got tough, stores and factories would close. The region was systematically deindustrialized and decommercialized, and would never recover its economic vitality.

BANKING AND FINANCIAL SERVICES

In 1914 the American 'muckraker' Gustavus Myers, in his book *History of Canadian Wealth*, argued that the process of centralization of wealth and capital was a major component of Canadian economic development, particularly since 1879, when railway amalgamation had begun. Canadian banking had always been highly centralized, Myers added: 'perhaps nowhere in the world can be found so intensive a degree of close organization as among the bank interests of Canada.'[17] He contrasted the US, which in 1914 had 18,000 separate banking institutions, with Canada, where 26 banks had 2,888 branches and some of the larger banks (the Royal Bank, the Bank of Commerce) had more than 300 branches each, extending over vast territories.[18] Certainly the control of capital through chartered banks headquartered chiefly in Montreal and Toronto was one of central Canada's great advantages.

How the banks had come to be controlled in those cities is an interesting question. Part of the answer can be found in the fact that the Canadian banking system had its origins in the centralized commercialism of English banking. In British North America, the chief task of the newly chartered banks was not to serve local customers or provide local credit, but to facilitate the transfer of commodities and funds from one place to another. The first Canadian Bank Act of 1871 guaranteed that banks everywhere in the nation would follow this model. Banks had to be chartered by Parliament. They could not issue notes in excess of their paid-up capital plus reserves, and a failed bank's notes were paid up before any other liabilities. The result was a constraint on the extension of credit in the outlying regions of the nation. According to the general manager of the Bank of Toronto, the 1871 Banking Act had been written by the bankers in close co-operation with members of Parliament. In 1913, Sir Edmund Walker, president of the Bank of Commerce, insisted that no changes in banking legislation had ever occurred since 1871 that had not been instituted by the industry itself. Moreover, Walker boasted that the Canadian banking business was dominated by a handful of men,[19] most of whom lived in central Canada. Although in 1913 Montreal-based banks held just over half of the assets of all Canadian banks ($788 million of $1,551 million), Quebec at the time had considerably fewer bank branches per capita than the rest of Canada. To fill the gap, the Quebec journalist Alphonse Desjardins established the system of 'caisses populaires' (credit unions), many of which were run by local *curés* in association with Catholic parishes.[20] Quebec Catholicism could be quite innovative in some areas of economic activity.[21]

Despite sporadic efforts to create competing financial institutions—including government savings banks, local savings banks, and mortgage companies, as well as caisses populaires—the financial power of the chartered banks combined with their control over banking legislation to ensure that the chartered banks continued to grow, not only by opening new branches but by controlling subsidiary financial institutions such as trust companies. Often, especially in the Maritimes, they would wait for the competition to collapse, then open new branches, and were able to drain money from the local community. Banks with head offices in central Canada refused to make local loans, and they set local interest rates (including those in Halifax) at higher levels. In 1913 the president of the Bank of Commerce dismissed complaints from the Maritimes as 'local grievances against what we regard as the interests of the country as a whole'.[22]

NATURAL RESOURCES

Financial centralization and growth in industrial capacity, particularly the shift from the processing of primary goods into secondary manufacturing of finished goods, were not the only economic developments in Canada in the years 1880–1914. Manufacturing for the domestic market (and occasionally, in certain primary industries, for the American one) was not enough on its own to propel the nation into the international marketplace. If Canada was to avoid the kind of international balance-of-payment deficits that have plagued Third World countries in more recent years, it needed commodities to export. It found many such commodities in the natural resource sector. To a considerable extent, Canada's resources were the old 'staples' of the colonial economy, produced in different places, under different conditions, and often in different guises. Not only did the staples earn money abroad, but they also encouraged manufacturing, for those who extracted the resources needed finished goods, such as machinery, that they could not make themselves.

MINERAL EXTRACTION

In 1890 mineral production in Canada had not yet taken off; the fact that the leading mineral producer was Nova Scotia—although it did have rich coal resources and considerable surface gold—says a good deal about the relative stage of development.[23] After that year three factors encouraged a new emphasis on mineral extraction. One was the development of new technologies with respect to methods of extraction and to the production of new metals containing minerals that Canada had in good supply. Iron ore, for example, was not something that Canada had in abundance, but nickel—which could harden steel—was commonly available; so was copper, increasingly favoured for electrical uses because of its conductive properties. A second important factor in mining, as in agriculture and almost every other resource enterprise, was the increasing availability of railway transportation to open remote areas to exploitation. But most important of all was the growth in international demand as technology and heavy industry expanded everywhere.

Almost overnight, Ontario and British Columbia outpaced Nova Scotia in mineral production. In both provinces the focus before 1919 was on the extraction of high-grade ores at minimal cost, which offered great returns to investors. The most famous mining 'rush' of the

■ Government assay office, Cobalt, Ont., 1907. LAC, PA-56054.

period took place in the Klondike district of the Yukon, but Klondike gold was atypical because —at least in the beginning—it did not depend on industrial machinery and chemical processing.[24] More important than Dawson City were the mining towns that suddenly sprang up (and just as rapidly closed) in British Columbia's Kootenay Mountains over a few years at the end of the century, when the international price of precious metals was at its peak. The most important of these towns was Rossland, just southwest of Trail. As with most Canadian mines, it took machinery and expertise well beyond the resources of individual operators to open the Kootenay mines, and most were estab-

lished by well-capitalized corporations. Most of the technology, capital, and management for mining were American in origin, and most of the large mine owners initially came from the US. In the Kootenays, however, Canadian capital quickly took over from the Americans.[25] In Quebec, the most buoyant segment of the mineral industry after 1900 was in asbestos fibre, used mainly in construction material consumed in the United States.

FORESTRY

In forestry, the harvesting of eastern white pine— most of which was sold to Britain as squared timber—reached its peak in 1881 and then declined rapidly because this 'renewable resource' had not been renewed. With the permanent depletion of the white pine forests, the centre of the timbering industry shifted rapidly west to British Columbia, with its vast expanses of Douglas fir and cedar. As eastern Canada had done earlier, British Columbia concentrated initially on harvesting from the coastal regions closest to water. But the province was vast, and the increase in production prodigious. From 350 million board feet of lumber in the period 1871–80, BC's production increased to more than 4.3 billion board feet between 1901 and 1910, most of it destined for the American and Canadian markets.[26] The softwood forests of northern New Brunswick and Quebec also became much more important in the early 1900s as the new pulp and paper industry burgeoned, driven by insatiable American demand for inexpensive newsprint. By 1915 wood pulp and paper accounted for one-third of the value of all Canadian exports, virtually equal to wheat and grain in the overseas markets. Quebec produced nearly half of Canada's wood pulp and paper. Wood products continued to represent a major part of Quebec's manufacturing output, although the nature and location of the industry changed: timbering shifted from the pine forests of the Ottawa Valley to the spruce and fir stands in the St Maurice and Saguenay regions, where cheap hydroelectricity was available for manufacturing products such as furniture.

■ A lumberman in BC's coastal rain forest. LAC, PA-40959.

OTHER ECONOMIC DEVELOPMENTS

RAILROAD EXPANSION

Transportation was of course essential to resource development in this period. As during the first railway boom of the 1850s, railways were seen as both means of development and fields of investment in the subsequent boom periods of the 1880s and 1910s. Rail construction was a constant in this era; but costs were high and no line was built without substantial public subsidy, often in the form of land grants along the right of way. The debate over costs has long raged in Canadian academic journals, centring on the economic profitability of the roads and the necessity of the public subsidies provided to get them built quickly.[27] For example, the federal government gave the CPR two complete rail lines—from Fort William, Ontario, to Selkirk, Manitoba, and from Kamloops to Port Moody in British Columbia—as well as a cash payment of $25 million, 25 million acres (more than 100,000 square kilometres) of land 'fairly fit for settlement', and protection of its monopoly.

The land concessions, which were typically taken in a checkered pattern along the CPR's right of way, not only disrupted prairie settlement for years but limited the tax base of many prairie communities. Either cash subsidies or public construction, which the Liberals under Alexander Mackenzie had undertaken, would probably have been less expensive and caused less trouble. But such policies would have resulted in a much slower pace of construction and hence of western settlement.[28]

The Canadian Pacific was not the only railway so favoured. Literally dozens of lines were incorporated in Canada during these years, and not exclusively in the West.[29] Many of these railways were promoted by 'boomers' for speculative purposes, a process depicted by Stephen Leacock (whose own uncle, E.P. Leacock, was an inveterate railway promoter) in his sketch 'My Remarkable Uncle', excerpted in Chapter 2. But local communities as well as regions and provinces also fought desperately for railroads, occasionally trying to raise funds for the lines themselves. Any town knew that its future depended on its access to rail. Not only were the railroads essential for getting goods to market, but passenger travel was swift and relatively cheap. Railroads also continued to contribute to manufacturing, an indirect but tangible economic benefit. From 1890 to 1910, for example, railway industries contributed more than 21 per cent to Quebec's manufacturing employment growth.[30] By 1910, railway-related industries accounted for 7 to 10 per cent of Quebec's total manufacturing output and 2 to 4 per cent of Ontario's. Nationally, railroads contributed about 16 per cent of manufacturing growth from 1890 to 1910.

ENERGY

Canada before 1914 was richly endowed with potential energy resources, although it did not always take full advantage of them. Coal, for example, was essential for the iron and steel industry as well as for domestic heating and driving steam engines for trains and ships. In 1914, 44 per cent of the coal produced in Canada came from Cape Breton alone, and 57 per cent from Nova Scotia. Yet in that same year Canada imported 57 per cent of the coal it used from the United States: it cost far less to transport Pennsylvania anthracite to the homes and factories of central Canada than it cost to transport coal from Nova Scotia—let alone coal from British Columbia. The Ontario iron and steel industry flourished, ironically, on both imported coal and imported iron.

Central Canada may have lacked coal, but it did have abundant water power, which had been used to run gristmills and sawmills since colonial days. Here, too, changing technology came to the fore at the end of the nineteenth century.[31] Some major natural waterfalls were harnessed and artificial falls were created using dams. The West Kootenay Power & Light Company Ltd was chartered by the British Columbia legislature in 1897, and electrical current began passing through its lines from a dam on the Kootenay River in July 1898. Of the three original founders, two were Americans active in the development of mines in the region.[32] Within a year, the first street railway car rode down the Main Street of Nelson, BC, on a line built by a company owned by the British Electric Traction Co. The dam at the falls in Shawinigan, Quebec—begun in 1899 by the Shawinigan Water and Power Co.—began supplying Montreal with electricity in 1903; Niagara Falls was first developed for hydroelectric purposes in 1905 and 1906. The heavy and rapid flow of the Winnipeg River in northwestern Ontario and eastern Manitoba was initially dammed for hydroelectric power in 1892, with a first hydroelectric station constructed at Pinawa Falls in 1902 to supply Winnipeg. No province was better placed for hydroelectric generation than Quebec, which thereby found a use for hitherto wasted water resources along the St Lawrence River system. Six private companies gained control of most of the province's water rights and were able to keep domestic rates higher than in Ontario.

The process of harnessing electricity, both for lighting and for motive power, was one of the great technological developments of the age. Once technical problems in the transmission of electric energy were resolved, early in the twentieth century, water power could be used as an alternative to fossil fuel to generate large volumes of electrical power, at extremely low cost, that could be transmitted over great distances. The engineer T.C. Keefer was one of the early prophets, as he had been with railroads, telling the Royal Society of Canada in his 1899 presidential address that the future belonged to hydroelectricity. Cheap hydroelectric power was soon recognized as one of the few advantages that Canadian industry possessed. One Toronto journalist described his excitement at discovering that 'a source of energy as vast as the entire coal deposits of Pennsylvania had by some miraculous process been transferred to Canadian soil and by another miracle made not only clean but inexhaustible.'[33] Hydroelectric power was also used to light Canadian homes at relatively low cost (although electrical appliances other than lights did not become common until after the Great War), and fostered the growth of electric-powered public transportation in the form of the trams and trolleys that connected city centres and suburbs in all of the larger urban conglomerates in Canada. Electric transit was cheap and efficient, and cities were never so well served by mass transportation as they were before 1920, when the gasoline engine began to overtake the trolley car.

THE POLITICS OF RESOURCE DEVELOPMENT

Resource development in Canada between 1880 and 1920 reflected a variety of agendas. In the first place, the older provinces fought hard to prevent their natural resources from falling under the control and regulation of the federal government. A major western grievance was that western provinces did not have control over Crown lands. When Saskatchewan and Alberta gained provincial status in 1905, the federal government retained its control over Crown lands and natural resources. At the same time, Ontario—which had led the way to Confederation and an integrated national economic pattern—insisted that it had the right to control its own natural resources against federal pretensions. Ontario liked to believe that it had within its own borders all the requirements of a self-sufficient industrial polity. Manufacturing in the province was to be encouraged not by protective tariffs but by control of natural resources.

The result was the so-called 'manufacturing condition' of development, by which Ontario required that resources taken on Crown land be processed in Ontario. This policy was first introduced in British Columbia in 1891, and was adopted in Ontario in 1898 with an amendment to the provincial Crown Timber Act that prevented the export of timber cut on Crown land. Such a provision was the provincial equivalent of the protective tariff: 'Debarred from the opportunity of cutting logs for export, it is an absolute certainty that the American lumberman, in default of other sources of supply, will transfer his sawmill enterprises to Canadian soil.'[34] In 1900 the principle that Crown resources should be kept at home was extended first to spruce pulpwood and then to nickel. In the latter case the federal government disagreed, and Ontario—facing royal disallowance—withheld proclamation of the legislation that would have prohibited export out of the province. But users of the province's natural resources were clearly being pressured to manufacture within Ontario. At the same time that Ontario was using protectionist measures to assist both resource extraction and industrial development, it was also seeking to encourage development by offering virtually free access to the province's natural resources provided they were processed in the province, along with strong technical assistance where needed; mining schools and forestry courses were

■ The Toronto Power Generating Station, Niagara Falls, Ontario, designed by E.J. Lennox (1904–12), was closed in 1973 and remained unused for more than 30 years. Renovations were begun in 2006. Future use of the building is still undetermined. Niagara Falls (Ont.) Public Library, Ontario Power Generation Collection, 250664.

encouraged. Many of the most energetic speculators were Americans.

The provincial involvement in resource development inevitably extended to hydroelectric power. Ontario had initially pursued the standard utility model for hydroelectricity, parcelling out charters to syndicates of industrialists, many of whom had been impressed with the Canadian development of hydroelectric power in Latin America. But the new companies unwisely tried to deal with the Canadian people as if they were Brazilians or Cubans. In response to this treatment a public power movement emerged that reflected the reforming spirit of the time. As the *Toronto Daily Star* observed as early as 1900:

[T]he twentieth century will be kept busy wrestling with millionaires and billionaires to get back and restore to the people that which the nineteenth century gave away and thanked the plutocrats for accepting. . . . The nineteenth century shirked its duty, humbugged and defrauded the common people, played into the hands of the rich, and left the twentieth century with a host of perplexities.[35]

The manufacturing community saw inexpensive, regulated power as essential to its growth and development, and the result was the establishment of the Ontario Hydro-Electric Commission in 1906, under the chairmanship of Sir Adam Beck.

SIR ADAM BECK (1857–1925)

❖

Adam Beck was born into a Loyalist Mennonite family that settled in Upper Canada after the American Revolution. He was educated at Dr Tassie's boarding school at Galt, where his schoolmates regarded him as a 'dunce'. His life was greatly altered when his father lost all his money in 1879. Adam and his brother William soon thereafter went into business together as manufacturers of cigar boxes, substituting canvas strips for the hinges earlier employed in construction. The business prospered, but Beck's political aspirations were not successful. In 1898, as a 41-year-old bachelor, he met and married Lillian Ottaway of Hamilton. By 1902 he became a successful mayor of London and soon entered provincial politics as a Conservative.

Within a year he found himself caught up in the 'cheap power' movement of Ontario spearheaded by a number of the larger municipalities of the western part of the province. At a meeting of 16 municipalities in Toronto on 12 August 1903, Beck became a member of the Ontario Power Commission appointed to develop Niagara Falls water energy. Two years later, the newly elected government of James Pliny Whitney appointed a commission to investigate the power question. Most of its findings reflected evidence collected by Adam Beck's Ontario Power Commission. Beck himself introduced in 1906 the bill into the Ontario legislature creating the Hydro-Electric Power Commission of Ontario, and he served as its chairman until his death.

Like many another appointed public servant, Beck became increasingly impervious to criticism. For many years, Beck continued to be the most visible public advocate of a publicly owned power system in Ontario. Much of his public life was spent fending off attacks to public power from various quarters. He was prepared to use almost any tactics to defend his position. In 1909 he produced the formal reply of the Ontario government to the application for disallowance of the Power Act of 1909 organized by the province's private power companies. This reply insisted that the royal veto was not justified by the circumstances, because Ontario's legislature had full power over property, a legal position confirmed by the federal government in 1910. In 1913 he had to defend Ontario Hydro against an attack mounted by a joint committee of the New York legislature that was based on inadequate data. In 1914 he became a proponent of a centrally controlled telephone system under the aegis of Ontario Hydro.

Increasingly, Beck became persuaded that he knew best, adopting a dictatorial manner in his public and private dealings that did not go down well with many politicians. Despite his Germanic heritage, Beck had no doubt of the righteousness of the Canadian position in the Great War. Because of his experience with horse breeding, he was put in charge of supervising the purchase of horses for the war effort between Lake Superior and the Atlantic Ocean. After the war, Beck came under increasing attack from Premier Ernest C. Drury because of his dictatorial manner, and his final years were spent in much controversy.

In Quebec the provincial government was unable to develop any resource policy, selling off most of its water rights before 1907, when it adopted a long-term leasing system. In 1910 the administration of Sir Jean-Lomer Gouin joined Ontario in embargoing the export of raw pulpwood from Crown lands, but the ban was not extended to minerals before the Great War.

Along with public monopoly (at least in Ontario) came a more general public regulation of utilities, which by the turn of the century included telephone and water as well as electric light and power companies. For the most part, commissions of regulation were not intended to break up the private monopolies, but simply to prevent them from becoming too exploitative for the general public.

CANADIAN BUSINESS

The Canadian business mentality, always agile in its quest for profit, was particularly flexible in this era. But there were some general principles. One was the insistence on government involvement in large public development schemes, such as railways. Another was acceptance of government's use of its power to grant monopolies of public service through charters, or access to Crown lands through advantageous leases. A third principle was to minimize competition wherever possible, even at the cost of accepting public regulation. Small businesses that could not combine institutionally to restrain trade—such as the small retailers—fought hard for early closing hours and price-fixing. Rhetoric about competition focused not on extolling the virtues of the free-enterprise system but on complaining about unfair competition. The business community insisted that what it wanted was a 'living profit', a reasonable return on investment of time and capital. Sensing the value of professionalization in areas such as medicine and the law, which had become in effect self-defining guilds, Canadian businessmen wanted something similar for themselves.

Canadian nationalism was a variable commodity among businessmen. Although most supported tariff protectionism ('the National Policy') and resource regulation ('the manufacturing condition'), they did so not in the hope of keeping Americans out of Canadian business but in order to lure the Yanks, with their energy and their capital, into the country. At the highest levels of financial wheeling and dealing, Americans and Canadians could work together quite amicably. But it was also commonly accepted that Canadian businessmen and investors were not very adventurous, preferring familiar fields. 'In grain and real estate people will invest their money whether they gain or lose,' reported the *Monetary Times* in 1892, 'and they will continue to do so in a most persistent manner; while even one loss in mining operations seems to discourage them for a lifetime, so they will not touch the thing again.'[36] A few years later, in 1905, the same journal commented that 'The best sections both of agricultural and mineral-bearing lands in Canada are falling into the hands of our enterprising neighbours, while we ourselves are waiting Micawber-like to see how things will turn out.'[37] While Canadian business often envied the Americans, it sought neither to emulate nor to exclude them.

The backgrounds of businessmen in this era are interesting, particularly since the mythologies of success in Canada, as in the US, tended to preach hard work rather than advance advantages. Most successful businessmen were immigrants or sons of immigrants, with Scots farmers over-represented in both categories. Few leading businessmen had actually begun at the bottom, although there were exceptions, such as Alexander Gibson of New Brunswick, who began as a humble axeman in the lumber industry and ended at the head of a major industrial empire. French Canadians were seriously under-represented among larger-scale businessmen and industrialists even within their own province, although again there were exceptions, such as the stockholder and politician Sir Joseph-David Forget, who became actively involved in the

Montreal Street Railway Co. and in local power and navigation companies. Most French-Canadian businesses remained small in scale, family-oriented, and content to operate within the confines of Quebec. They were regionally, but not nationally, well integrated.[38]

Although most of the leading Canadian businessmen were either industrialists or resource developers, one of the most interesting changes in business occurred at the retail end of commerce. The reshaping was most observable in shopkeeping, particularly in the expanding cities. In 1840, retail establishments had been relatively small, concentrating for the most part on supplying products within some specialized range such as dry goods, groceries, or drugs. Those goods were generally carried in bulk, and doled out by the shopkeeper in small quantities. Beginning around 1870, general merchandising underwent a revolution in which goods were specially packaged in smaller amounts under recognizable brand names. The retail establishment altered as well, with the first development of the 'big-box' retailer—the department store—which offered a multitude of packaged goods, segregated into appropriate departments, under a single roof. Timothy Eaton opened his Toronto store in 1869, and his competitor Robert Simpson followed suit in 1872. In the West, the Hudson's Bay Company virtually abandoned the fur trade and moved into general retail merchandising in the early 1880s.[39]

The department store was characterized not only by the variety of packaged goods it carried, but by two other features. One was the mail-order catalogue, which was first issued by Eaton's in a 32-page format in 1884. Intended to promote sales in rural areas, it depended on the cheap and efficient delivery of mail by the Canadian post office, and was the first large-scale catalogue in North America.[40] The other distinctive feature of the department store was its increasing employment of women as shop clerks, often at relatively low wages. As in most other areas where women found employment, the sub-

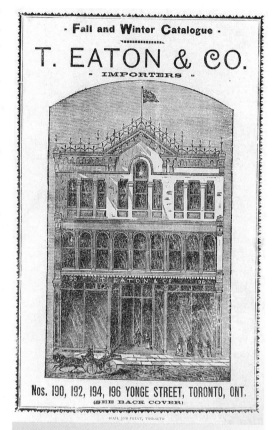

■ The first Eaton catalogue, 1884. According to a prefatory note, it was published in response to an 'immense increase in our Mail Order Department'. Metropolitan Toronto Reference Library.

stantial wage differentials between males and females encouraged the hiring of the latter. In a department store a large number of relatively inexperienced and poorly paid women could be supervised by a few men. Women could also handle the filling of mail orders.

TECHNOLOGY

The years between 1880 and 1919 were a great period for science and technology throughout

■ 'Starting a bicycle race', Manitoba, c. 1895. Photo by H.J. Woodside. LAC, PA-016114.

the Western world. In most fields of scientific endeavour the basic theoretical assumptions were transformed out of all recognition and an astounding variety of practical inventions altered how people lived and worked. Timekeeping became more sophisticated, and standard time zones were introduced; firefighting equipment was improved; the telegraph was introduced in 1847 and the telephone in 1878.[41] In pure science Canada produced no world leaders, although several world-class scientists, such as Ernest Rutherford in physics and Otto Hahn in physics and chemistry, passed through on their way to international recognition. Science was taught at most Canadian universities, but with virtually no laboratory experimentation, and—except in engineering and medicine—the number of programs beyond the elementary level was relatively small. The record was even less prom-

ising in Quebec, probably as a result of the traditional emphasis on a classical education. In science generally, Canada tended to lag behind Great Britain and the US. In some fields of applied science, however, Canada played an important role. The Geological Survey of Canada, founded in 1842, did not grow much until after its move to Ottawa in 1881 to become part of the Department of the Interior.[42] Parliament was willing to fund the GSC because of its obvious utility in surveying the vast land mass of the nation. Although a few GSC geologists, such as George M. Dawson, became well known for their exploration, the bulk of the work was slow, time-consuming, and extremely technical.

Despite the growing sophistication of pure science, many of the technical advances of the period were made by laymen, or at least by individuals who were not employed as researchers and made their discoveries without the assistance of fancy, publicly financed laboratories or equipment.[43] Such institutional support was still in the future. Notable among the few men who did enjoy professional careers as inventors was the Scottish-born Alexander Graham Bell, who worked with deaf people in Brantford, Ontario, and in the early 1870s produced a series of inventions to assist them. The culmination of his work, the telephone, came in the mid-1870s while he was employed in Boston, Massachusetts. The invention made Bell rich, and he moved to Washington, DC, to supervise his patents, spending the remainder of his life in the laboratory and financing the research of others. He would also make important breakthroughs with the phonograph. Although he summered at his home, Brinn Bhreaugh ('Beautiful Mountain'), in Cape Breton after 1890 and occasionally carried out experiments at Baddeck (including the flight of an early aircraft in 1907), Bell was essentially part of the American research world.

More closely identified with Canada than Bell was the Scottish-born engineer Sir Sandford Fleming, who designed Canada's first postage stamp, in 1851, and later became the chief engineer of the Canadian Pacific Railway. In 1884 he helped organize a conference at Washington, DC, at which his system of international timekeeping—involving a mean time (set at Greenwich in England) and a series of 24 one-hour time zones stretching around the world—was adopted.[44] Less well known was the Ontario-born Thomas Ahearne, head of a firm of electrical engineers and contractors from 1882, who invented a number of important electrical devices, including an electric snow-sweeper to clear tram tracks (1891), an electric stove (1892), and an electric automobile (1899).

Canadian industry has long been criticized for its tendency to lag behind other nations in its development of new technology and for its inclination to borrow heavily from Great Britain and the United States. While these charges are not unjustified, it must be emphasized that the problem was not necessarily a lack of inventiveness or technological infrastructure. Although Canada never developed a proper automobile industry, for example, it played an active role in popularizing the bicycle and manufacturing it on a large scale. The machine tools for automobile manufacturing—drills, grinders, boring machines—were in place by the turn of the century. What Canada had difficulty finding was the venture capital required to develop an expensive technology into a final product.[45]

CONCLUSION

Almost from the establishment of the Dominion, Canada was a major economic player in the world, highly industrialized and capable of exporting entrepreneurial skills—even technology—to less developed places in the Caribbean and Latin America. The nation had a rich supply of natural resources and an inventive and adaptable people. What it lacked was capital. No highly industrialized nation in the world depended more heavily than Canada on foreign investment.

SHORT BIBLIOGRAPHY

Babcock, Robert. *Gompers in Canada: A Study in American Continentalism before the First World War*. Toronto, 1974. An important study of the most prominent figure in the mainstream labour movement in Canada, a fitting counterpart to the great businessmen of the age.

Bliss, J.M. *A Living Profit: Studies in the Social History of Canadian Business, 1883–1911*. Toronto, 1974. Some of the essays in this volume are showing their age, but many remain fundamental to our understanding of the subject.

Brown, Robert Craig, and Ramsay Cook. *Canada*

1896–1921: A Nation Transformed. Toronto, 1974. A synthetic overview now more than 30 years old, but still not superseded.

Heron, Craig. *Working in Steel: The Early Years in Canada, 1883–1935*. Toronto, 1988. Perhaps the best introduction to the history of the key industry of the period.

Linteau, Paul-André, et al. *Quebec: A History 1867–1929*. Toronto, 1979. Older, but still the best general treatment of the era.

Marchildon, Gregory P. *Profits and Politics: Beaverbrook and the Gilded Age of Canadian Finance*. Toronto, 1996. A first-rate analysis of the Golden Age of the robber barons in Canada, seen through the eyes of one of its key figures.

Nelles, H.V. *The Politics of Development: Forests, Mines & Hydro-Electric Power in Ontario, 1849–1941*. Toronto, 1974. A detailed study of industrial development in Canada's largest and richest province.

Paterson, Donald. *British Direct Investment in Canada, 1890–1914*. Toronto, 1976. The best analysis of foreign investment available for the pre-war period.

Sager, Eric W., and Gerald E. Panting. *Maritime Capital: The Shipping Industry in Atlantic Canada, 1820–1914*. Montreal, 1990. A useful study of an important industry, which goes a long way towards explaining the economic problems of the Atlantic region in the period following Confederation.

Spector, David J. *Agriculture on the Prairies, 1870–1940*. Ottawa, 1983. A superb introduction to the agricultural sector.

Waite, Peter B. *Canada 1874–1896: Arduous Destiny*. Toronto, 1971. Still the best overview of the period.

STUDY QUESTIONS

1. What can we learn about the Canadian economy from the Tables 3.1 and 3.2?
2. Why did the Maritime provinces lag in industrial activity?
3. How did Canadian banks differ from American banks?
4. What was 'the manufacturing condition'?
5. Was Canada technologically backward?
6. What was the greatest weakness of the Canadian economy between 1880 and 1914?

CHAPTER FOUR

Urban Canada, 1885–1914

In 1881 Canada had a population of 4,325,000, of whom 3,349,000 lived outside urban centres. Forty years later, of the nation's 8,788,000 inhabitants, only 4,811,000 resided in non-urban areas. A full 1,659,000 lived in cities with populations over 100,000. In other words, while the non-urban population had increased substantially (from 3,349,000 to 4,811,000), the number of city-dwellers had burgeoned from 974,000 to 3,977,000. As Canada's cities grew, so too did the complexity of their problems. The relative proportions of residents above and below the poverty line (an arbitrary standard designating the minimum income required to secure the necessities of life) might not have changed much since the middle of the nineteenth century, but the total numbers of people below it had doubled or tripled. After about 1880, as Canada's largest cities began to develop middle-class suburbs, different residential districts became increasingly associated with specific income levels and ethnic backgrounds. Cultural and physical amenities grew in tandem with movements to reform the appalling disparities between rich and poor that were observable almost everywhere.

At the same time, the process of Canadian urbanization indicated more than simply the development of some very large metropolitan centres with some very big problems. If 1,659,000 Canadians lived in cities of over 100,000 in 1921, another 2.3 million lived in smaller centres, with 1,058,000 in towns of between 5,000 and 29,999 people, and 765,000 in towns of 1,000 to 4,999. In some ways small towns tended to merge into the rural countrysides for which they served as shopping and cultural centres, with shops and services beyond their own local requirements; but many of these towns, especially in rapidly growing western Canada, aspired to a greater status. The market town developed many urban characteristics that made the lifestyle of its inhabitants substantially different from that of people living in the countryside.

EASTERN AND CENTRAL CANADA

As with most other aspects of Canadian development in this period, urban growth was not equally distributed across the regions, or even the provinces. Maritime cities grew fairly sluggishly, and none was able to establish a position of regional dominance; Halifax actually lost ground as its financial institutions were siphoned off to central Canada. In Quebec, Montreal continued on its trajectory to the status of the Dominion's premier city, with Quebec

TIMELINE

1873
Winnipeg incorporated as a city.

1875
Fort Calgary established at confluence of Bow and Elbow rivers.

1882
Regina founded.

1883
Regina made capital of the North-West Territories.

1884
Toronto Board of Health inspects and reports on sanitation problems.

1886
William Howland elected on reform platform as mayor of Toronto.

1892
Edmonton incorporated as town.

1897
Herbert Brown Ames's *The City Below the Hill* published in the *Montreal Star*.

1898
C.S. Clark publishes *Of Toronto the Good*.

1901
Montreal creates Board of Control to govern city.

1903
Non-partisan government advocated in Montreal election.

1904
Assiniboine Park established in Winnipeg.

1906
Three villages incorporated as city of Saskatoon.

1910
City Improvement League (CIL) triumphs in Montreal election.

1913
Passage of Ontario Housing Act.

1914
Thomas Mawson publishes a grand scheme for planning in Calgary. Stephen Leacock publishes *Arcadian Adventures of the Idle Rich*.

City and other places lagging far behind. In Ontario, Toronto was plainly the 'Queen City', although a number of smaller centres (Hamilton, London, Kingston) were also vibrant. Ottawa inhabited a world of its own as the nation's capital, as it always would. The most spectacular urban growth rates were found in the West, which in this era gave rise to two major cities, Winnipeg and Vancouver, and two contenders for such a rank, Edmonton and Calgary. Indeed, while western settlement is usually associated with farms and agriculture, urban development in the West was strong from the outset, with land speculation driving local pretensions and many communities aspiring to become major centres.

THE MARITIMES

Most of the growth in Maritime cities came in the first decades after Confederation, during the period of rural depopulation and rapid industrialization spurred by the National Policy. Thereafter they stabilized—perhaps even stagnated—as deindustrialization set in and central Canada established its primacy in the early years of the twentieth century. Saint John continued to be dominant in New Brunswick even though it had been hit by various calamities: a disastrous fire that destroyed most of the city in 1877; a drop in the demand for wooden ships; the end of the British market for Maritime timber; and the arrival of the Intercolonial Railway, which brought trade goods from central Canada into competition with goods produced in Saint John. In Nova Scotia, late-Victorian Halifax was dominated by the Citadel. Just below the massive fortifications—built between 1828 and 1856 and manned by British troops until 1900—ran the notorious Barrack Street, about which one wag in 1883 commented that, despite its elevated location, it was 'the lowest street of the city'.[1] More than 40 per cent of the city's population was Irish and 3 per cent black; together these people made up the bulk of the poor and the casual labour force. Halifax was spared major fires in the 1800s only to be devastated in 1917, when the collision of two ships in the harbour sparked a massive explosion. As for Charlottetown—still hardly more than a village in the last quarter of the nineteenth century—it was nonetheless by far the largest community on Prince Edward Island. No Maritime city grew large enough to expand beyond its central warehouse core, and in the larger centres the early years of the new century brought serious losses of employment, especially in the skilled artisan trades. Much of the urban growth that did take place in the Maritimes went to the smaller industrial centres. Around the turn of the century, Moncton in New Brunswick added factories and briefly flourished, as did Yarmouth, New Glasgow, Amherst, Truro, and Sydney in Nova Scotia.

Perhaps no town developed more rapidly or extensively than Amherst, located not far from the New Brunswick border on the main line of the Intercolonial Railway. Visitors to Amherst can still see the baronial stone mansions of the local business elite and the row cottages of the workers, located on different streets, but not at all far, geographically, from one another. The distance from cottage to mansion was psychological as much as physical. By the early 1900s Amherst employed more than 4,000 workers in a variety of industries, especially in the metal trades, and was one of the largest manufacturing centres in Canada. The year 1910 was the high point of Amherst's industrial and urban development, however, and as local industrialists were displaced by executives from central Canada, Amherst's industrial capacity was gradually reduced by plant consolidations that favoured central Canadian over Maritime operations. Many Maritime towns were increasingly dominated by single industries, and were thus particularly susceptible to downturns in the economic cycle. World War I would bring a final glow of prosperity to Nova Scotia's coal and iron towns, but it was an artificial flame.

MONTREAL

Montreal had always been the commercial and financial capital of the St Lawrence region, and with increasing industrialization it continued to flourish. By the end of the nineteenth century it had a population of 328,000, which at the conclusion of the Great War had nearly doubled, to 618,000. Ethnically, the city remained divided between French (about 60 per cent of the population) and English speakers (about half of them Irish), although increasing numbers of immigrants from Eastern Europe were making the city the centre of Jewish culture in Canada. Economically and socially, Montreal was divided between the working-class districts below Mount Royal and the prosperous suburbs that climbed the hill. The city's wealth was exemplified by the

■ Dominion Square, Montreal, *c.* 1901, composite photograph used in a calendar. LAC, PA-028938.

mansions of its business elite. As in many cities in Canada (and in North America), there was a direct correlation between social status and physical elevation. Most of the working classes lived in overcrowded tenements with substandard services and amenities. Sanitary conditions were so bad that at the turn of the twentieth century an infant's chance of surviving its first year was better in Calcutta or Shanghai than in Montreal.

Just before the hill was Sherbrooke Street—'Plutoria Avenue' as satirized by Stephen Leacock in his *Arcadian Adventures of the Idle Rich* (1914). Here, in 'the very pleasantest place imaginable', lived steely-eyed capitalists and thoughtful uni-

versity professors, almost all of British origin. Just below Plutoria, wrote Leacock,

> . . . and parallel with it, the trees die out and the brick and stone of the city begins in earnest. Even from the avenue you can see the tops of the sky-scraping buildings in the big commercial streets, and can hear or almost hear the roar of the elevated railway, earning dividends. And beyond that again the city sinks lower, and is choked and crowded with the tangled streets and little houses of the slums.

In fact, if you were to mount to the roof of the Mausoleum Club itself on Plutoria Avenue

HERBERT BROWN AMES
(1863–1954)

❖

Herbert Brown Ames was born in Montreal in 1863. His parents came from the United States, and he was educated at Amherst College in Massachusetts, receiving a BA in 1885. He then spent some time studying French literature in France before joining the family firm—Ames-Holden Ltd, a major shoe wholesaler in Montreal. He also acquired a number of other corporate directorships. Ames quickly tired of industry, however, and in 1893 he left Ames-Holden to devote himself to public service. Even before his retirement, Ames had helped to organize the Volunteer Electoral League, which was dedicated to rooting out municipal corruption in Montreal. He always assumed that if elections were fairly conducted, the 'good' politicians would win. With the League he canvassed widely to make it possible for those in working-class districts to vote, and in 1894 they achieved considerable success. In a famous article—'The Machine in Honest Hands'—published in the *Canadian Magazine* in June 1894, Ames insisted that it was possible to beat the corrupt machines at their own game. He became increasingly involved with municipal politics and reform, being elected to the Protestant section of the Council of Public Instruction in 1895 (serving until 1920) and president of the Montreal YMCA in 1896.

That same year Ames supervised a detailed investigation of two working-class districts of Montreal, which was published first in the Montreal Star and then as a book enti-tled *The City Below the Hill*. This work, based on more detailed and extensive studies outside Canada, demonstrated that the districts he had investigated housed a 'submerged' population of working poor, most of whom were not of the 'undeserving' sort. Many of the people he studied worked for Ames-Holden, and Ames was instrumental in unionizing the family firm. But he was not an advocate of radical reform. Instead, he spent much of his energy building model housing for a few families in the district he had studied.

In 1898 Ames entered municipal politics, serving as alderman for St Anthony until 1906. In 1904 he was elected to represent the federal district of Montreal–St Antoine in Ottawa, where he served until 1920. Before the Great War Ames was an active imperialist and a supporter of imperial trade, serving as a delegate to the 1909 Imperial Commercial Congress. In 1914 he was one of the organizers of the Canadian Patriotic Fund, and he was elected as a Union candidate in the 1917 federal election. After the war he became involved with international affairs, serving as a financial director of the Secretariat of the League of Nations and then as Canada's delegate to the League's Seventh Assembly. He also helped to organize the League of Nations Society in Canada and after 1930 became a lecturer for the Carnegie Endowment for International Peace. An excellent example of a progressive businessman/reformer, Ames died in 1954.

you could almost see the slums from there. But why should you? And on the other hand, if you never went up on the roof, but only dined inside among the palm trees, you would never know that the slums existed—which is much better.[2]

Montreal was becoming not only a large city—it annexed 22 suburbs between 1883 and 1918—but a great one, with correspondingly great economic and social problems. When a Montreal syndicate, backed by the powerful Bank of Montreal, financed the building of the CPR, the city became the centre of the nation's railway network, and in the early years of the twentieth century it also housed the largest stock exchange in Canada.

In 1897, a Montreal businessman named Herbert Brown Ames produced a pioneering sociological study entitled *The City Below the Hill*.[3] Initially published serially in a Montreal newspaper, it eventually appeared as a book. Ames was a member of a wealthy Montreal family, and like some of his class in Britain, the US, and Canada at the end of the nineteenth century, he had a social conscience. In 1894 he organized the Volunteer Electoral League to assist the urban reform movement in Montreal. Familiar with a number of American and British studies of the working poor, some dating back to the mid-1800s, Ames attempted to describe working-class Montreal to those who lived 'on the hill'—people who likely knew more about Europe than about their own city of residence. In comparison with works such as Henry Mayhew's multi-volumed *London Labour and the London Poor* (1851), Charles Booth's *Life and Labour in London* (1893), or the many studies by the Fabian reformers Beatrice and Sidney Webb, Ames's study was sketchy and incomplete. But he used maps to describe visually the statistics he had collected personally on the working-class districts, and his findings would undoubtedly have been a revelation for any of his wealthy intended readers. What Ames documented was a population inhabiting a world of poverty, disease, and overcrowding. He did not offer many long-term solutions to

these problems. Nevertheless, he revealed an important insight when he insisted that 'philanthropists' who sought to ameliorate the lives of the poor needed to understand them better: for example, there was no point in constructing housing for the poor that they could not begin to afford. In emphasizing the importance of understanding how poverty worked before trying to fix it, Ames was well ahead of his time.

TORONTO

Toronto did not dominate Ontario to the extent that Montreal dominated Quebec (and the Maritimes, and to some extent eastern Ontario), but it expanded rapidly once it became the hub and commercial centre of the region. In addition to sending small railroads fanning out into the province, Toronto was the terminus of the Grand Trunk Railway. The CPR brought its tracks into the city and connected Toronto with Buffalo, and thus with Detroit and New York City. As a financial centre Toronto was second to Montreal, but it was an increasingly strong rival. Its business district was dominated by splendid bank buildings that were consciously designed to emanate wealth and power, solidity and prestige. The banks' shareholders were drawn from Toronto's elite, who lived in a style befitting merchant princes. Like Montreal and most North American cities in the late nineteenth century, Toronto grew geographically mainly by annexing communities adjacent to the urban centre, which in 1882 had measured a mere 7,900 acres. Thirteen communities were gobbled up between 1883 and 1893, and another 18 were annexed between 1903 and 1912, for a total land area of more than 20,000 acres. The city sloped gently upward from Lake Ontario, with the wealthier northern suburbs, such as Rosedale, on higher ground than the tenements of the poor. Toronto continued to be a British city. In 1901, out of a total population of 208,040, the city had 94,021 inhabitants claiming English origin and 96,070 of Scottish and Irish origin. A few thousand French Canadians and some Germans were the only substantial non-British elements at the turn of the century. Before the Great War, however, many Eastern Europeans would arrive, and by 1921 the population would reach over half a million.

THE WEST

The fastest-growing cities in Canada were in the West, especially after 1900. In the Prairie provinces between 1900 and 1916 the urban population grew from 103,000 to 606,000, and city-dwellers, who made up 25 per cent of the region's population in 1901, had increased to 35 per cent 10 years later. By 1921 Vancouver (117,217) and Victoria (38,727) accounted for one-quarter of British Columbia's population.

WINNIPEG

Winnipeg's tiny population of 241 in 1871, the year after the Riel uprising, expanded over 50 years to 179,087. Unlike Montreal or Toronto, Winnipeg at this time grew not by annexing adjacent communities but by immigration. Although commonly perceived as being a predominantly ethnic city, Winnipeg began as a British city; in 1881, fully 83.6 per cent of its inhabitants were of British origin. It would end its great period of growth in 1921 with 67.1 per cent of its people claiming British roots. Although the percentage of British stock gradually declined between 1881 and 1911, it actually increased during the decade of the Great War. The Eastern European population of the city never exceeded 20 per cent of the total, while the Franco-Manitoban presence had stabilized by 1901 at just over 2 per cent. Not blessed with many higher elevations, Winnipeggers used complex river and railroad systems to divide the city into socio-economic/ethnic sections, and by 1914 it was perhaps the most thoroughly segregated city in Canada. The immigrant poor, mainly from Eastern Europe, were largely confined to the north-central sector of the city (the notorious 'North End'), sealed off from

■ The Canadian Bank of Commerce building at 25 King Street West, designed by R.A. Waite and erected in 1889-90, was one of several new office buildings in Toronto that had some claim to architectural distinction and even grandeur. At seven-and-a-half storeys, it soared over neighbouring three- and four-storey buildings, and reflected the influence of the first skyscrapers in New York and Chicago. City of Toronto Archives, Micklethwaite Collection, SC 1497 #21.

members of the business and professional community, who increasingly moved south of the Assiniboine River (which flows east–west) and west of the Red River (north–south) into the southwest quadrant of the metropolitan area, mostly outside the city limits.

C.S. CLARK ON
SUNDAY IN THE CITY

In 1898 the reforming journalist C.S. Clark published *Of Toronto the Good: A Social Study: The Queen City of Canada as It Is*. The book was inspired by the world conference of the Woman's Christian Temperance Union, which was held in Toronto in 1897. Clark spent many years crusading against what he regarded as the immorality of his city.

Sunday in the City

In Toronto, like all cities of any pretensions, Sunday is a day of rest, but practically it is the very reverse. The morning is usually devoted to church going, and the churches are pretty well filled, for as I mentioned there is a halo of respectability surrounding him who goes to church, which nothing else can give. But those who are impervious to the refining influences of church attendance, if it be summer time, hie themselves down to their boat houses, and prepare for the afternoon sail; or others again to the island, there to remain during the day.

Some afternoons in the spring time, the Queen's Own Rifles have a regular parade to some one of the churches, and if the weather is fine, and it usually is, the streets are thronged with the youth and beauty of both sexes. . . . In the afternoon, the park and gardens are open in the summer and those who are intellectually inclined will find a rich treat in store for them if they go to the park. The Salvation Army holds forth in all its glory and beauty, distinguished by sacred words adapted to the tunes of different waltzes, bar-room songs, and any class you can think of, while the partakers therein are ever and anon, moved by the spirit to give vent to their holiness and happiness, by yelling, 'Glory be to God,' 'Praise be to God,' and various other expressions too numerous to recollect. . . .

At night the streets are crowded with people of both sexes, especially Yonge and Queen, and the promenade is kept up until nearly eleven when the streets become entirely deserted.

By a recent decision sacred concerts at the Island or in the city or elsewhere are as lawful on the Sabbath as on a work day. Chief Justice Armour and Mr. Justice Street having so held and as a result quashed Magistrate Denison's conviction of Bandmaster John Bayley of the Q.O.R, for playing sacred music at Hanlan's Point on a Sunday afternoon in August last. Magistrate Denison held he was guilty of a violation of the Lord's Day Act, that he was pursuing 'his worldly calling' unlawfully and fined him $1 and costs. But with all due deference Mr. Bayley differed as did the counsel, in their interpretation of the 'act to prevent profanation of the Lord's day' from that of the Court street judiciary, and obtained a reserved case, which was argued with the above result in the Divisional Court to-day. The argument was brief, the court at the outset favouring the appeal against the conviction, and holding the act was no more intended to apply to a bandmaster than to an organist in a church. The Appeal allowed with costs. B.B. Osler, Q.C., appeared for Mr. Bayley, and Mr. Moss, Q.C., for the Crown. The concerts were free and were provided by the Toronto Ferry Co.

And now, horror for horrors! the populace of Toronto have decided by a substantial vote that they desire street cars on Sunday and they have them.

SOURCE: C.S. Clark, *Of Toronto the Good: A Social Study: The Queen City of Canada as It Is* (Montreal: Toronto Publishing Company, 1898), 62–4.

Winnipeg's municipal government was dominated by promoters and real estate developers to an even greater extent than most cities in the East. Those interests saw the administration of the city chiefly in terms of growth and expansion. Members of the western urban business elite have always tended to be incorrigible 'boosters', but developers had particular axes to grind, for outlying land could not be properly improved without an extension of services at municipal expense. The city government—especially during the boom years between 1900 and 1913—amounted to little more than a contest between rival groups of promoters for control of local improvements. Even the city's great public space, Assiniboine Park—established in 1904 and designed by a major firm of American landscape architects—was little more than an excuse for speculators to run tramlines and other services into what was then a remote area of the suburbs in the southwest section, far removed from the poor who were supposed to benefit from the facility.

The (famously windy) intersection of Portage and Main had by 1885 become the centre of Winnipeg's commercial and financial district, and one of Canada's best-known street corners. The surrounding blocks were dominated by buildings of the Grain Trade (designed chiefly by Chicago-trained architects), many of which still remain as reminders of the city's heady early history. The Legislative Building was constructed between 1912 and 1920; designed in the grand classical manner, it features a high central dome and a circular rotunda and stands at the end of an impressive boulevard. Most provinces in the nation had already built, or were building, similar legislative monuments.

Winnipeg overcame its climatic disadvantage as literally the world's coldest major city—at least during a long winter—and countered its lack of natural scenery with a tree-planting program along its wide streets and boulevards; by 1905 it had already planted 12,072 trees. The summer profusion of trees and green grass astounded visitors to the 'bare Prairies'. Labelled by its civic boosters 'the Gateway City' and 'the Chicago of the North', Winnipeg justified these claims because of its role as a transportation hub, with rail lines radiating out in all directions. The railways made the city a nexus for the financial aspects of grain marketing, the centre of the nation's largest livestock market, and the wholesale supplier for the entire prairie agricultural hinterland.

VANCOUVER

The railway was also the key to Vancouver's development.[4] The CPR, after a flirtation with Port Moody, had decided to terminate its transcontinental line at the banks of False Creek. The city's rapid population growth—from a mere handful of people in 1881 to 117,217 by 1921—was fuelled chiefly by immigration. Even more than in Winnipeg, the bulk of the newcomers were of British origin and arrived after the turn of the century; in 1911, one of every three Vancouverites had been born in the 'old country'. Vancouver was also even harder on non-British immigrants than was Winnipeg, partly because many of the newcomers came from Asia rather than Eastern Europe. The city saw a series of anti-'oriental' riots, and in May–July 1914 largely approved when a group of East Indian Sikhs aboard the *Komagata Maru* was refused entry to Canada by intrepid members of the Canadian Immigration Service. To some extent, Vancouver's growth came at the expense of Victoria, reflecting a shift in the emphasis of BC's economy from Vancouver Island to the province's mainland. While coal and salmon declined in importance, the quantity of lumber cut in the province more than tripled between 1901 and 1910. Most of this lumber was shipped to the booming Prairie provinces via Vancouver.

OTHER WESTERN CITIES

Calgary and Edmonton in Alberta, and Regina and Saskatoon in Saskatchewan, had their beginnings well before their respective provinces were formed in 1905. Fort Calgary was established by the North West Mounted Police in 1875 at the confluence of the Bow and Elbow rivers. In 1884 the CPR laid out the townsite, west of the Bow and south of the Elbow, and Calgary was incorporated as a city in 1893, becoming the chief transportation centre in Alberta and—until the harsh winter of 1906–7, which killed most of the cattle on the open range—thriving as the centre for the meat-packing industry. Calgary also benefited from cash-crop farming after the turn of the century, and the first oil strike, in 1914 at Turner Valley, a few miles southwest of the city, presaged another source of revenue that would develop over the next decade. Between 1891 and 1921 the population rose from 3,876 to 63,305. Fort Edmonton had been a centre for the western fur trade, but permanent settlement outside the fort did not begin until the 1870s. Edmonton, on the North Saskatchewan River—with access both to the farmlands of central Alberta and to the northern hinterland—was incorporated as a town in 1892 and a city in 1904; it became the capital of the new province in 1905, the same year that the arrival of the Canadian Northern Railway gave it a transcontinental rail connection. Its population grew slowly; it had only 50,000 people during World War I.

Like Calgary, Regina was located and laid out by the CPR. It was founded in 1882 and made the capital of the North-West Territories in 1883 (and was therefore the site of Louis Riel's trial in 1885). Its growth, which did not really begin until it was named the provincial capital in 1905, was determined by its location in the heart of the wheat-growing plains and its role as a distribution and service centre for southern Saskatchewan. The northern prairies and northern Saskatchewan were served by Saskatoon on the South Saskatchewan River, some 120 miles (about 190 kilometres) northwest of Regina. Made up of three villages that were combined and incorporated as a city in 1906, Saskatoon became a hub of western railways and a major

distribution centre. Edmonton and Saskatoon were made the seats of provincial universities in 1906 and 1907 respectively.

FACTORS CONTRIBUTING TO URBAN GROWTH

Generalizations about urban growth are difficult, given the variety of economic conditions and stages of economic development found across a country as vast and as regionalized as Canada. Nevertheless, some factors and patterns cut across geography.

TRANSPORTATION

The first and most important factor was transportation, which in the period from 1880 to 1914 meant railways. No urban centre could expect to prosper unless it was on a main line. This reality was clearly recognized, and during the several bursts of rail expansion—particularly between 1906 and 1915, when more than 14,000 new miles (22,540 kilometres) of track were added to the network, mainly in western Canada—aspiring communities made prodigious efforts to become main-line (or even branch-line) depots or junction points. At the same time, rumours of new railroad construction were sufficient to create new villages where none had previously existed. The extremes to which communities would go to publicize themselves and attract rail service were usually expensive and occasionally ludicrous. When funds were in short supply, the boosters mounted publicity campaigns—sometimes in the form of catchy slogans ('New York may be Big, but this is Biggar'; 'You'll Hear from Champion')—in local newspapers that in some cases were created for the purpose. Agricultural fairs, town bands, and sports teams also helped to publicize communities. A brass marching band was regarded as one of the best advertisements a town could have.

But nothing succeeded like money. 'Bonusing'—financial inducements offered to railways

■ British Empire Day parade, Gladstone, Man., 23 May 1915. False fronts such as the one on the third building from the right created the illusion of a second storey. Provincial Archives of Manitoba: Gladstone 3 (N1258).

and business entrepreneurs alike—was a way of life in this period. In 1883 the little community of Minnedosa, Manitoba, located well north of the CPR main line, contributed $30,000 as a bonus to the Manitoba and North-Western Railway, and the surrounding country added another $100,000 in inducements. Once it acquired its railroad, Minnedosa rejoiced. 'In no distant day,' exulted one resident, 'the little town in the valley will seem more like an eastern town of Ontario than the newly discovered, just put together town on the Little Saskatchewan.' Descriptive pamphlets proudly proclaimed Minnedosa to be 'the most important grain and stock centre on the Manitoba and North-Western Railway'.[5] Although Minnedosa did not continue

to grow—partly because neighbouring Neepawa was able to connect with both the Canadian Northern and the Manitoba and North-Western—its population of 1,100 by 1911 was fairly substantial. Across Canada, for every Minnedosa there were dozens of villages that never got past the stage of yearning for greatness, when some optimistic land speculator would build a general store in the middle of nowhere and advertise lots for sale. Main-line was better than branch location, main-line junction was better than simple main line, and railhead was the best of all. But in the early twentieth century, as automobiles gradually became more common, roads replaced railways as the subject of intense lobbying efforts. Towns bypassed by provincial highways often built connector roads to the main road at their own expense.

LAND SPECULATION

Most urban growth in this period was carried out in a context of blatant land speculation: the holding of land for future profit. In western Canada, every attempt—successful or not—to create a new city began with a land boom, and the first stage of development usually ended with a collapse in land prices that would require several years for recovery. The collapsed land boom of Winnipeg in the early 1880s was only the most notorious of hundreds of similar economic disasters. Many small businessmen in the West made a decent living by selling out in one community just before it went bust and moving to a new townsite farther down the rail line. The false fronts on western small-town stores (and not a few eastern ones as well) were symbolic of the transitory nature of local commitment. But speculation in land was hardly confined to businessmen. Almost all segments of the local community would join in real estate speculation whenever they could. The hope of turning a profit by investing in undeveloped land must surely be one of the most enduring features of Canadian business.

SUBURBANIZATION

In the larger metropolitan centres, land speculation and development—the subdivision of land (often acquired at bargain prices) into sites for houses or factories, at an immediate profit—were inseparable from the process of suburbanization. Although we often associate suburbs with the later twentieth century, in Canada they were really a creation of the late nineteenth century, when cities were beginning to expand away from their commercial cores. The growth of suburbs (often with longer commuting times to place of work) required substantial changes in public transportation systems, and the electric tramlines

introduced towards the end of the century helped to open up new territories to residential populations. There were basically three distinct motives for suburban expansion, and different types of suburbs grew up in response to them.

THE SOCIAL MOTIVE

Members of the prospering business and professional classes often moved to the new suburbs to escape the undesirable living conditions of the central city—everything from horse droppings on city streets (a major sanitary problem) to noise, bustle, and crime. Some suburbanites, of course, also sought to put physical distance between themselves and the growing slums of the industrializing city. They were attracted by the possibility of large lawns and landscaped gardens, by the opportunity to build proper carriage houses for horses and equipment—and later to construct garages to house large automobiles. The houses built for the suburban elites, in the years around the turn of the century, tended to be substantial both inside and out, surrounded by large lots. The architectural style most closely associated with these houses grew out of the English Arts and Crafts movement, which was dedicated to the revival of traditional building forms and practices in a modern context. It became known as the English Domestic Revival, of which three noted practitioners were Eden Smith (Toronto), Percy Nobbs (Montreal), and Samuel Maclure (Victoria). There was no shortage of variation, however. In Vancouver, for example, both California bungalows and Tudor Revival houses were common.

Internally, suburban elite housing featured large formal rooms on the first floor and smaller rooms with lower ceilings in the upper storeys, with a servant's bedroom somewhere.[6] The employment of household servants—particularly 'live-ins'—continued to distinguish the wealthy from the ordinary householder. Not until after the Great War did fireplaces become mostly ornamental, as central heating became more and more common—usually using some form of hot water, hot air, or steam heat, which was delivered only to the first floor on the principle that hot air rises. The author's house in Winnipeg, built in 1906 for a marble dealer, has one of the city's first forced hot-air systems. Electrical service became available in the 1880s, supplied by privately owned facilities, but for some time its use was mostly limited to lighting. Although the electric range was beginning to make some inroads by 1914, most cooking continued to be done on gas, wood, or coal stoves until after the war, and large appliances like washing machines remained luxuries even in the 1930s. Nevertheless, electrical service, along with indoor plumbing and servants, helped to distinguish the well-to-do from the rest of society at least until the Great War, and would continue to distinguish urban from rural Canada until after World War II. Every town aspiring to urban standards introduced water and sewer systems, as well as an electricity plant of some kind. Larger centres often also had gas service. By the 1900s these amenities had reached as far north as Dawson City in the Yukon Territory.

THE COST OF LAND

Another set of motives for suburban growth had to do with the cost of land and rising taxes in the central city, which drove certain businesses—especially those requiring considerable amounts of land, particularly for large industrial operations—out of the urban core. The result was the development of a number of industrial suburbs, such as Montreal's Maisonneuve, that flourished outside the city but within its orbit. Especially after 1910, lower land costs and lower taxes also attracted better-paid members of the working classes into working-class residential suburbs, usually consisting of rows of virtually identical small cottages. In fact, the sameness that we associate with the large post-1945 subdivisions actually had its counterpart in many suburbs constructed before the Great War. In these districts

the lots were smaller than in middle-class subdivisions, but most houses were intended for single families and included some space for a garden at the front and the back. The presence of a front lawn, however tiny, distinguished suburban housing of this period from the earlier urban housing that tended to front directly on the street (and now contained poor working-class tenants).

PROXIMITY TO WORK

The third factor that contributed to the creation of new suburbs had to do with proximity to work. On one hand, developments in urban transportation enabled people to work farther away from their homes. The upper and middle classes could afford to commute fair distances on newly constructed tramlines—and as the automobile grew in popularity (the Ford Motor Company of Canada was founded in 1904), more people began to drive into the central city. Unlike horses, which had to be stabled, fed, and watered, automobiles required nothing but parking space. Among the working classes, who already toiled for 55 to 60 hours over a six-day week, long-distance commuting was considerably less popular. Thus, as industrial development moved outside the downtown urban core, which tended to become financial and commercial in its emphasis, workers were forced to follow their jobs into (often inadequate) new housing. Slums were soon created by absentee landlords who discovered that their houses were more profitably employed as rental units for people who needed to be relatively close to their work.

THE TOWNS

Suburban service towns were, almost by definition, not completely independent of the larger metropolitan centres, although the modern concept of the metropolitan area had not yet been developed. As we noted earlier, both Toronto and Montreal grew in large measure by incorporating outlying communities, and—given the inclination of industry and workers alike to keep moving beyond municipal taxation boundaries—this process was continual. The genuine Canadian 'small town' tended to fit one of three models: a community serving a surrounding agricultural region; a community, often located in some remote area, formed around some single resource operation, such as a mine or paper mill; or a community based on a single factory or industry, such as a textile plant. Many resource towns—though not all—were company towns.

THE SERVICE TOWN

The typical service town consisted of several banks, a post office, stores, a hotel or two, churches, schools (including the only secondary school for the surrounding area), professional offices (doctors, dentists, lawyers), a barber, a funeral parlour, and the inevitable railroad depot. In older established towns of eastern Canada, religious, ethnic, or political divisions—the first two often producing the third—resulted in parallel establishments for the different clienteles. The most familiar division was between Protestant and Catholic. A larger town might have a small hospital or library—amenities rarely seen in smaller communities before the Great War. Few towns of any substance were without at least one newspaper, usually a weekly, and almost all had a Chamber of Commerce or Board of Trade dedicated to boosting the town into greater prominence and prosperity. By 1910 even the smallest community was at least giving serious thought to an electrical plant and a public water system, although the costs of such facilities would increase the mill rate substantially. Amateur sports were thought to build the appropriate character for young men, and most towns had some kind of sports facility, usually a baseball field and occasionally, after 1890, an unheated building that served as a combination hockey and curling rink. Specific sports often reflected social differences among the middle classes; lacrosse teams tended to recruit players of a higher social standing than baseball, for example.[7]

A simple catalogue of facilities, however, cannot convey the importance of the town as the centre of social and recreational life for the surrounding area. Before the advent of the radio and television, the social life of small-town Canada was especially bustling. Organizations of all kinds flourished. Most towns had a variety of fraternal lodges (Masons, Elks, Moose, Odd Fellows), church- and school-related organizations, and an endless round of meetings, dances, suppers, and 'occasions' ranging from concerts and plays to sermons by visiting evangelical preachers to lectures on such diverse subjects as temperance or art in China. Lectures were often accompanied by lantern slides or, after 1910, motion pictures. By the end of the Great War, most towns had at least one 'movie house', or at least a hall where films could be shown on a regular basis, and city newspapers were available for sale in the local stores. Although some towns had bars in the hotels, or in the halls of fraternal organizations, many exercised the local option permitted by provincial liquor legislation and 'went dry'.

THE RESOURCE TOWN

Unlike the agricultural service town, the resource town was isolated. Places such as Glace Bay (Nova Scotia), Black's Harbour (New Brunswick), Murdochville (Quebec), Snow Lake (Manitoba), and Rossland (British Columbia) were surrounded by wilderness, difficult to get to, and inhabited mostly by single men. Such towns were often centred on a single industry, and in fact many were created by the particular companies involved. Only in Nova Scotia (particularly Cape Breton) and Quebec did resource towns develop with relatively normal family life and institutions, and even those towns were usually dominated by the 'company', which provided everything from credit at the local store

■ 'Steel mills at Sydney, Cape Breton', oil on canvas, 1907, by the railway magnate Sir William Cornelius Van Horne. Built between 1900 and 1905, these two plants attracted hundreds of workers, creating an instant city. The Montreal Museum of Fine Arts, gift of the artist's grandson, William C. Van Horne. Photo Brian Merrett.

(which it operated) to the sermon preached on Sunday morning. Eastern resource towns drew most of their population from the surrounding region, and thus tended to have a more balanced social structure than their counterparts in the West, where women were worshipped as idealized figures—mothers, sisters, sweethearts— capable of saving 'wicked men from a hardness scarcely less than that of the rocks they crushed'.[8] In 1897 a rare 'Working Girl' in Rossland told the local newspaper how she found work there by dressing in men's clothes:

In three days after I had donned male attire I had secured a job at $2.50 per day, and have a steady engagement. I have my own clothes locked up in my trunk and will resume the wearing of them when I return to Toronto with a stake. . . . My advice to other young girls, who are strong, hearty, and young is to do as I have done if they wish to get on in life.[9]

In most regions, particularly on the mining frontiers of northern Canada, retail stores were limited in number, and churches and schools were rare. With few sources of entertainment other than booze and gambling, social life in most resource towns centred on bars and brothels. In many cases the men lived in huts or barracks, working long hours for relatively short periods, perhaps six to 10 weeks.

Many resource workers were recent immigrants, and some were 'sojourners' intending to return to their country of origin when they had accumulated enough savings. Such communities could be restless and violent. Men alienated from their work were easily persuaded by the arguments of radical labour organizers, who often provided the only social cohesion in the resource districts. Mine owners seldom resided in towns like Sudbury, Cobalt, and Timmins in Ontario, or Flin Flon in Manitoba, or in the Cape Breton coal-mining communities; instead, they were represented by tough local managers. A few planned or 'model' towns—such as Brûlé and Nordegg in Alberta—were created before or during the Great War, particularly in the coal districts of Alberta, but conditions there were better only in a physical sense. Naturally susceptible to the boom-and-bust cycle of resource industries, a mine or smelter could shut down virtually overnight, putting an entire community out of work—as happened in Dominion, on Cape Breton Island, when the Dosco steel plant closed, or in Cadomin, Alberta, when the local coal mine shut down. A whole series of 'ghost towns' in the mountainous country of British Columbia document the brief fluorescence of silver mining at the turn of the century.[10] Under the circumstances, labour–management relations in these communities were seldom satisfactory, and a good many bitter strikes and lockouts occurred.

Single Industry and Factory Towns

Towns dominated by a single industry or factory were most common in southern Ontario, but also were present in Quebec and the Maritimes, and these towns reflected complex patterns of gender and class relations. In some towns, such as Paris, Ontario, the principal workers were women, while in others, such as Hanover, Ontario, they were men. Women tended the knitting mills of Penman's in Paris, while men trod the furniture-making shop floors of Hanover. The gender differences produced unionization differences. Like most industries dominated by female workers, the knitting industry had great trouble unionizing; many women thought of themselves as employed only until marriage, and they were less militant than men, as well. The furniture industry, on the other hand, saw men fight successfully for 'breadwinner unionism'. Employment in the knitting industry may have offered to women a slight edge in power and autonomy in their own families and households. Factories provided more stable employment than did service or resources, and the towns housing them had evolved social structures of voluntary organizations, including churches and fraternal groups, operating just beneath the surface.

Urban Social Problems

'Urban Canada' was far more than the country's relatively few large cities. Yet it was naturally the cities—the largest concentrations of population—that exposed most clearly the social problems of the later Victorian and subsequent Edwardian eras. Of these, the most important was—as it always has been—poverty. There were now far more Canadians living in the cities, so inevitably there were far more urban poor. People below the poverty line tended to live in the worst housing conditions, to suffer from the most serious health problems, and to present the greatest challenges for all urban institutions, including the educational system. Income data are sketchy before 1921, but existing evidence suggests that perhaps up to half the Canadian urban working class lived around the poverty line. In 1912, for example, a child welfare committee in Montreal stated that the typical unskilled labourer earned

TABLE 4.1

WEEKLY SHOPPING LIST FOR FOUR PEOPLE, 1906

Bread at 14 cents a loaf	.85
Oatmeal	.25
Milk at 6 cents a quart	.42
Sugar	.10
Butter	.20
Lard	.12
Meat	.25
Potatoes	.15
Currants	.06
Coal oil	.10
Soap and salt	.10
	$2.60

SOURCE: Gregory Kealey, *Hogtown: Working Class Toronto at the Turn of the Century* (Toronto, 1974), 25.

$1.75 per day or $550 per year, adding that, 'To get this much . . . a man must have continuous work (six days a week, 52 weeks a year) with no sickness, no changes in jobs, and he must not waste his money on drink or dissipation. Granted all this he can give a family of five a mere existence. . . . No allowance is made here for sickness, recreation, church, house furnishings, lectures and savings.'[11] Such a family would have to 'live in unsanitary quarters, sometimes below street level', and would not have sufficient nourishment even if meals were prepared according to strict domestic science methods. Table 4.1 shows a weekly shopping list from 1906 for one Toronto working girl—intended to feed herself, her mother, and two sisters.[12]

A diet based on such a list—heavy on starch and light on fresh vegetables—was not likely to provide adequate nourishment. Little wonder that most working-class families were glad to supplement the income of the principal wage earner with the small earnings of spouse and children in menial occupations. Nor is it surprising that many sought release from the grinding conditions of their lives in alcohol, to the displeasure of middle-class reformers.

HOUSING

For those living near the poverty line, an unbalanced diet or even malnutrition was only the start of their problems. Working-class housing was not merely overcrowded but often unsanitary. No city in Canada provided adequate inexpensive housing. Despite concern and discussion about housing in Toronto, no system existed for dealing with it. The idea of government-subsidized housing was not well recognized and in any case the city fathers were well aware that the public would not stand for the increase in taxes required to provide sewers, electricity, and running water in parts of the city where there were still water pumps on street corners. Toronto, for example, was much readier to build libraries, hospitals, parks, and playgrounds, and to improve public transportation, than it was to pay for more basic urban infrastructure and housing. The city core did not get amenities such as sewers until the 1920s, when the public had become accustomed to wartime taxation and was willing to accept a hike in rates to pay for them. The entire Western world lacked inexpensive working-class housing, although in Toronto a few enlightened employers—the Gooderhams (of the Gooderham distillery), Sir Joseph Flavelle (president of the William Davies Co., pork packers, and vice-president of Simpson's), and two of the Masseys—subsidized workers' housing near their factories from the 1880s.

Some efforts to create working-class housing were made just before the Great War. In 1907 the Canadian Manufacturers' Association sponsored a plan to produce small houses that could be sold at reasonable prices while still providing a profit. There was a recession in 1912, but in May of that year the Association—together with the Toronto Board of Trade, the Toronto City Council, the Guild of Civic Art, and the local Council of Women—conceived the Toronto Housing Company to provide acceptable low-cost accommodation. The Ontario Housing Act, passed in 1913, gave municipalities the power to guarantee bonds for a housing company of up to 85 per cent of its working capital, as long as the remaining 15 per cent was invested by the public. In 1914 this initiative produced two sets of 'Cottage Style' flats—apartments with their own front doors to the street—in Toronto: Spruce Court in Cabbagetown, and Riverdale Courts on Bain Avenue, east of the Don River. Very well designed, both complexes are still in use. Originally the rents were $14.50 to $16 a month, including heat and utilities—still too much for the very poor, but within the reach of more comfortable working-class families, who paid it gladly. Such

developments were not common, but they showed what could be done.

Driven by demand, rents in the tenement areas of the central cities went inexorably upward, while only the most thrifty and skilled of workers could afford to buy a house, even in a distant suburb. Home ownership was difficult even for middle-class people, because mortgages were hard to obtain and had to be paid off in no more than three or four years. In Toronto, single-family dwellings in St John's Ward (more or less where the present City Hall stands) were turned into multiple-family tenements in the 1870s. 'The intensive use of land', reported one Toronto observer in 1914, 'has lent itself to the creation of slums, and the scarcity of small houses has resulted in a doubling up of families in houses, so that two, three, and in some cases even five families are housed in a building constructed for one family only and with but one set of sanitary conveniences.'[13]

Intensive land use and large populations did not necessarily produce slums, as the Annex in Toronto demonstrated. But demand led to overcrowding in all cities, even a young one like Winnipeg, where one health inspector reported in 1911:

> A house of ten rooms was found occupied by five families, also roomers—26 adults and two children. Three of the families had only one room each. There were eight gas stoves, and none of these had hoods or pipes for carrying of the products of combustion and the odors of cooking. Two girl boarders occupied a portion of the cellar. . . . There was one water closet, one sink, a bath, and a wash basin. Two faucets had been fitted on the water-service pipe, and buckets placed under same in lieu of sinks.[14]

Sanitation was one measure of the problem. In 1884 the Toronto Board of Health inspected 5,181 Toronto houses, finding '201 foul wells, 278 foul cisterns, 814 full privies, 570 foul privies, 739 cases of slops being thrown into privies,

■ A slum interior, October 1913. Presumably the younger woman's husband was out at work—or looking for a job. City of Toronto Archives, Series 372, Sub Series 32, Item 243.

668 cases of slops in the streets, 1207 cases of no drainage whatsoever and 503 cases of bad drainage'. A mere 873 of the 5,181 houses had water closets, and the Board recommended earth closets because the sewer system was inadequate. It subsequently reported that in one block 67 by 200 yards (61 by 183 metres) in extent, 14 to 18 tons of 'solid excreta' were dumped annually.[15] As late as 1905, Winnipeg had 6,153 box-closets and 186 earth-pits still in use.

Poor nutrition and evil housing conditions combined to produce high mortality rates in Canada's largest cities. Montreal's overall death rate peaked at 24.81 per thousand in 1895, and declined very slowly. Equally significant were the wide differentials between poorer and better-off districts, ranging from 35.51 deaths per thousand in 1895 in one working-class ward in Montreal, to less than 13 per thousand 'above the hill'. In Winnipeg a death rate that had fallen to 11.4 per thousand in 1896—just before the surge of immigration into the North End from Central and Eastern Europe—climbed as high as 23.2 per thousand in 1906. Statistics for infant mortality were even more appalling. In Montreal, between 1899 and 1901, 26.76 per cent of newborn children died before their first birthday. In Winnipeg in 1912, the figure was just under 20

■ Riverdale Courts, Toronto. This complex of 204 apartments (some on two floors, with four bedrooms) was designed by Eden Smith around three-sided courtyards on both sides of Bain Avenue in the Riverdale neighbourhood, east of the Don River. Intended as low-cost subsidized housing, it is now run by tenants as a co-op. City of Toronto Archives, Fonds 1018, File 4, Item 1.

per cent, with 1,006 deaths for 5,041 live births. Such disasters could be traced to impure water and milk, and failure to take advantage of vaccinations against smallpox and diphtheria, in addition to generally debilitating conditions.

EDUCATION

Education was yet another measure of the effects of poverty on Canada's cities. In working-class districts it was extremely difficult to keep chil-
dren in school beyond the early elementary grades. In Montreal in 1905, for example, the Montreal Catholic School Commission reported that it had 3,442 students in grade one and only 426 (with an average age of 13) in grade five. Ten years later, Montreal Catholic schools had 25,792 students in grade one and 2,848 in grade five, while Montreal's Protestant schools (almost all 'above the hill') had 1,187 in kindergartens (which did not exist in Catholic schools), 4,197 in grade one, and 2,761 in grade five. In 1917,

■ Slum district, Winnipeg, c. 1912, from F.J. Billiarde, *Annual Report of the Superintendent of Neglected Children for the Province of Manitoba, 1912*. LAC, C-30953.

secondary schools accounted for fewer than 25 per cent of the total enrolment in Montreal—a figure inflated by the Protestant Anglos above the hill. The comparable figures were 33 per cent in Toronto and 37 per cent in Ottawa—and only 5 per cent in Winnipeg. Pressures for compulsory education were, as we shall see, strenuously resisted by the poor in all Canadian cities.

URBAN GOVERNMENT AND POLITICS

GOVERNANCE

The extent of the growth of urban Canada between 1880 and 1914 was largely unanticipated, and it presented many challenges for a society that in many ways remained traditional and rural. Towns were comprehensible, huge cities were not. Because of the unplanned,

unconsidered nature of this growth, the institutions of urban government were not well integrated into the overall Canadian political system. The 'Fathers of Confederation' had conceived of provincial governments as the equivalent of British municipal corporations, and had produced a constitution that left little room for city governments of any size to operate—much less the governments of cities such as Montreal, Toronto, and Winnipeg, which would have budgets and revenues almost as large as those of the provinces in which they were located. The result, especially after 1885, was continual friction between provincial legislatures—which tended to be dominated by rural politicians—and the cities, which were usually under-represented at the provincial level, partly because their populations were growing faster than legislative seats could be added to represent them.

At the start of this period, towns and cities

were governed by councils, those in the larger urban centres elected on a ward-by-ward basis. The major source of revenue was a land or real property tax, and cities were slow to abandon property qualifications for voting. Few places went so far as Winnipeg, which allowed property owners to vote in any voting district in which they paid taxes, so that the wealthier inhabitants were over-represented. In many towns and cities, tenants were excluded from voting (Montreal tenants gained the right to vote only in the 1960s) and in those places that did allow everyone to vote, there were efforts to correct the many voting abuses that a democratic franchise supposedly created.[16] By and large, Canadian history has traditionally concentrated on those levels of government and politics sanctioned by the British North America Act, and as a result has neglected the municipal arena, but in fact that is where much of the action has always occurred.

POLITICS

As urban government tended to operate outside the structures of Confederation, so did urban politics. Provincial and federal politics represented separate levels of operation, and the use of the same party labels federally and provincially often led to confusion, since parties had relatively independent federal and provincial wings with distinct policies, though there was some connection and overlap in personnel and party administration. Municipal politics, however, was quite removed from the national and provincial party systems, and municipal politicians seldom aspired to political office at the senior levels of government. Municipal politics had not only its own agendas but distinct local party labels, though these generally disappeared in the course of efforts at non-partisan city government, such as those undertaken in Montreal in the elections of 1903 and 1910 (when the City Improvement League was elected). The ward system—particularly in cities with democratic franchises, such as Toronto or Halifax or Saint John—was heavily

criticized for its tendency to produce 'ward-heeling' municipal politicians whose efforts to curry favour with the electorate through patronage and services were seen as 'corrupt'. That certain people were drawn into urban politics out of economic self-interest became a major problem in most Canadian cities. Businessmen saw the success of the city as intimately connected to their livelihoods, with the result that city councils tended to be dominated by local merchants and real estate promoters. The businessmen shamelessly 'boosted' their city, and equally shamelessly took advantage of the boosting.

THE CONTINUING DEVELOPMENT OF CULTURAL INFRASTRUCTURE

As Canadian cities got bigger, larger numbers of people and greater collective wealth made possible an increasingly rich and varied cultural life. The larger the city, the greater the opportunities for resident professional artists, although before 1914 culture-making of all kinds in Canada continued to be dominated by amateurs. Certainly urban growth facilitated the creation of cultural infrastructure in the form of both organizations and buildings.

Many museums, for example, were built in the late Victorian and Edwardian periods. A new museum era began after 1890, partly because of the emergence of wealthy merchant princes who could afford to collect expensive things. Some specialized in art, mainly European Old Masters. Others collected antiques, or artifacts such as rare coins and stamps. Because it had the most and longest established merchant families in the country, Montreal also had the best museums before 1914. In 1892 the Montreal Museum of Fine Arts, a small institution of limited collections, received a major bequest from John W. Tempest in the form of an art collection and money for further acquisitions. Other gifts and bequests soon followed, from the collections of the Learmonts (Dutch masterworks), Lord Strathcona, and Sir William Van Horne. The Art

Museum of Toronto was founded in 1900, and in 1911 Goldwin Smith and his wife Harriette (whose first husband had been a member of the Boulton family) bequeathed their home, the Grange, to the museum, which became the Art Gallery of Ontario in 1919. An art gallery in Winnipeg opened in 1912, with many exhibits borrowed from the National Gallery of Canada in Ottawa. Founded in 1880, the National Gallery itself acquired a full-time director, Eric Brown, in 1910, and in 1913 was incorporated, with funding provided by Parliament for administration and acquisitions.

In its early years the National Gallery benefited greatly from the patronage of Sir Edmund Walker, president of the Bank of Commerce and himself a collector, who became the second chairman of the Gallery's Council in 1910. Walker was a sterling patron of the arts. He played a central role in the founding of other cultural institutions, such as the Champlain Society, established in Toronto in 1905 to republish editions of rare books and manuscripts related to Canadian history, was active in the organization of the Mendelssohn Choir, and was a keen alumnus of the University of Toronto. Walker was also a founding patron of the Art Museum of Toronto and the first chairman of the board of the Royal Ontario Museum (founded in 1912). His magnificent house in Toronto, Long Garth—built in 1882 on the east side of St George Street—was demolished in 1969 to make way for a parking lot.

Equally characteristic of the age was the formation of artistic organizations such as the Canadian Art Club, founded in 1907 in Toronto but intended to be national in emphasis (although its founders had no idea how to achieve this goal). The club exhibited new Canadian painting and provided a place for artists and prospective patrons to meet. The first formal art schools were established around this time. Such schools were not confined to eastern Canada. In Winnipeg, an interest in art had been present from the beginning, reflecting the conviction that

a city's standing was closely connected to its patronage of cultural activities that 'elevated humanity'. The Manitoba Society of Artists was founded in 1903, and was greeted enthusiastically by the *Manitoba Free Press*:

> For years Toronto has made and modified the artistic standards of the West, just as for years it controlled and governed much of its commerce. Western artists have long felt the limitations of Eastern standards hampered the development of Western initiative, and the formation of the Society of Artists is a step towards the establishment of Western ideals of artistic excellence, which, while drawing inspiration from all centres of art, may in process of time evolve essential and individual characteristics.[17]

In 1911 a Free Art School was opened to give lessons in drawing and painting 'from draped models and portraits', and in 1913—with the support of the merchant-oriented Winnipeg Industrial Bureau—the Winnipeg School of Art was opened, shortly after the creation of an art gallery called the Winnipeg Museum of Fine Arts. The sponsors of these two institutions frankly hoped that they would be good advertising for a city that billed itself as 'the Chicago of the North'.

CONCLUSION

Cities provided showcases for the best and the worst features of Canada in the years between 1885 and 1914. As they got bigger, the tradition of face-to-face community that had characterized much of British North America before 1870 disappeared. As we shall see later, the new cities provided the basis for a much richer and more varied cultural life than had been possible earlier. They also provided irrefutable evidence of poverty and social disadvantage, the gulf between rich and poor, and consequently gave rise to a reform impulse and efforts to improve society that will be considered in more detail in Chapter 7.

SHORT BIBLIOGRAPHY

Artibise, Alan F.J. *Winnipeg: A Social History of Urban Growth, 1874–1914.* Montreal and London, 1975. A careful picture of the spatial and social development of western Canada's major city before the Great War.

Bradbury, Bettina. *Working Families: Age, Gender, and Daily Survival in Industrializing Montreal.* Toronto, 1993. An insightful study of the family lives of the industrializing working classes in Montreal.

Copp, Terry. *The Anatomy of Poverty: The Condition of the Working Class in Montreal, 1897–1929.* Toronto, 1974. One of the classics of Canadian urban social history, still a useful study.

Doucet, Michael, and John Weaver. *Housing the North American City.* Montreal and Kingston, 1991. An important synthesis of the problem of housing.

Fingard, Judith. *The Dark Side of Life in Victorian Halifax.* Porter's Lake, NS, 1989. A rich study of the 'underclasses' in the Maritime city.

Kaplan, Harold. *Reform, Planning, and City Politics: Montreal, Toronto, Winnipeg.* Toronto, 1983. An important comparative study of the connections and inter-relationships of reform, planning, and politics in Canada's three major cities before World War I.

Linteau, Paul-André. *The Promoters' City: Building the Industrial Town of Maisonneuve, 1883–1918.* Ottawa, 1979. A study of the process of suburban industrialization in Quebec.

McDonald, Robert J. *Making Vancouver: Class, Status, and Social Boundaries, 1863–1913.* Vancouver, 1996. A detailed analysis of the way in which urban growth in Vancouver affected and reflected social matters.

Mouat, Jeremy. *Roaring Days: Rossland's Mines and the History of British Columbia.* Vancouver, 1995. An important account of the growth and development of one of British Columbia's major mining communities.

Parr, Joy. *The Gender of Breadwinners: Women, Men, and Change in Two Industrial Towns, 1880–1950.* Toronto, 1990.

Rutherford, Paul, ed. *Saving the Canadian City, the First Phase 1880–1920: An Anthology of Early Articles on Urban Reform.* Toronto, 1974. A rich collection of primary material on the urban reform movement.

STUDY QUESTIONS

1. Did urban development proceed at a regular pace across Canada?
2. What factors were most responsible for the rapid growth of Toronto and Montreal between 1883 and 1914?
3. What factors accounted for the rapid growth of suburbs in this period?
4. What is the difference between a service town and a resource town?
5. What were the most serious problems for the poor in Canadian cities?
6. Why could cities be said to grow 'outside the framework' of Confederation?

CHAPTER FIVE

■ Rural Canada, 1885–1914

■ Despite the growth of the towns and cities, most Canadians in the years 1885–1914 still lived in rural areas, either in small communities or on isolated farms, and agriculture was the dominant economic enterprise. That rural life no longer exists anywhere in Canada, and it was always subject to a good deal of mythologizing. Still, we cannot understand Canada before the Great War without examining its rural roots. The great region of Canadian agriculture was the Prairie West, just opening up in these years. Although homestead land was free to male settlers (married women could not even apply for homesteads), successful farming still required considerable capital investment. Conservative estimates of the costs of 'farm-making' ranged from a minimum of $300 (the annual wage for an unskilled labourer) to $1,000. Most settlers brought money with them from the sale of land back east. The western farm was a market operation. Although the family grew as much food as possible for personal consumption, the farmer's instinct was to keep increasing the acreage under production. Before World War I, mechanization was limited mainly to harvesting. Animals (horses and oxen) did most of the ploughing and cultivation. Nevertheless, individual farmers managed to cultivate large expanses of land, limited mainly by the size of their labour force.

Beginning in the 1890s, open and aggressive immigration policies at both the federal and provincial levels brought new settlers to Canada, especially to the prairies. Many came from the United States, which no longer had an unsettled frontier of its own. Others came from Eastern Europe, where grain cultivation was a long-standing tradition. Moving into the great dry-belt area of Saskatchewan and southern Alberta, the new immigrants initially experienced some very good luck with rain and moisture. Farming in the East tended to be less specialized, but the importance of the farm and the farmer was obvious in every province. In all regions, rural success depended on the labour of family members, particularly the women.

THE WEST

The settlement of the West was undoubtedly a major event of the years between 1885 and 1914. Manitoba grew from 25,228 inhabitants in 1871 to 461,394 in 1911, and whereas the entire North-West Territories counted only a few thousand people in 1881, by 1911—six years after Saskatchewan and Alberta gained provincial status—the total for the two new provinces alone was 876,375 (492,432 and 373,943 respectively).

TIMELINE

1882
Cannington Manor established in southeast-ern Saskatchewan.

1885
Aboriginal people pressured to become farmers.

1886
Dominion Experimental Farms are estab-lished. Dower rights abolished in the North-West Territories.

1891
Massey-Harris established to manufacture farm implements.

1898
A.J. Cotton of Treherne, Manitoba, harvests 17,000 bushels of number one hard.

1900
Shift to mixed farming begins in eastern Canada. Fruit-growing develops in Annapolis Valley, Niagara Peninsula, and Okanagan Valley.

1906
Marquis wheat is developed.

1908
The *Grain Growers' Guide* established.

1910
Farmers establish their own system of grain elevators.

1912
Opening of Abitibi region.

1914
Georgina Binnie-Clark publishes *Wheat and Woman*.

1916
Robert J.C. Stead's *The Homesteaders* pub-lished. Louis Hémon's *Maria Chapdelaine* published.

The Canadian agricultural staple had always been grain, chiefly wheat. As if on some master schedule, once the western prairies were opened to agricultural settlement, the centre of the wheat economy merely shifted from southwestern Ontario to Manitoba, and slightly later to the North-West Territories. Between 1870 and 1890, thousands of farmers, mainly from Ontario, poured into the West. The total of occupied land went from 2.5 million acres (1,011,700 hectares) to over 6 million (2,428,100 hectares) in the years 1881–91 alone; improved land under cul-tivation went from 179,000 acres (72,438 hectares) to 1,429,000 acres (578,295 hectares) in the same 10-year period. Not until the open-ing of the CPR, and the subsequent development of branch lines north and south, could the pro-duction of western wheat really take off. The early years saw considerable experimentation with new wheat strains less susceptible to frost than Red Fife (which had been popular in Upper Canada) and more capable of maturing in the short prairie growing season. By 1921 over 44 million acres (almost 18 million hectares) of prairie were under cultivation. According to one set of calculations, the wheat economy between

■ The interior of a CPR colonist railway car as drawn by Melton Prior for the *Illustrated London News*, 24 Nov. 1888. Glenbow Archives, NA-978-4.

1901 and 1911 contributed more than 20 per cent of the growth in per capita income in Canada, and other estimates run as high as 30 per cent.[1]

WESTERN AGRICULTURE

Before the mid-1890s the typical prairie settler was an experienced Ontario-born farmer who had come to feel thwarted by shrinking productivity, limited access to land, or both. Often a younger son of a farm family, he headed west—sometimes alone, sometimes with a wife and young children—to make a new start on virgin prairie land. Although homestead land was available under the first Dominion Land Act (1872), most farmers preferred to purchase their land from companies set up by the great corporate beneficiaries of government policy, particularly the Hudson's Bay Company and, later, the railways. It was commonly believed that government-provided homestead land was less likely to enjoy nearby rail facilities than was land owned and sold by the railways themselves. Nearly all settlers established themselves within a few miles of a railroad, for transporting bulky crops by wagon over long distances was difficult and expensive. Even on homestead land, which was free (except for the small legal costs of registration), the capital investment required to build

THE DOMINION EXPERIMENTAL FARMS SYSTEM

Begun in 1886, the experimental farms system was founded to provide a scientific basis for agricultural improvement. Various experimental operations preceded the formal establishment of five experimental farm stations, the one for Ontario and Quebec to be the central station, located just outside the city boundary of Ottawa. William Saunders, whose work had focused on improving apples for prairie conditions, was named the first director. As in most other areas of cultivation, priority was always given to the question of hardiness, and many varieties of early-maturing plants saw their first development on federal experimental farms. Gradually the system expanded to all the provinces, with particular stations devoted to research in local problems. The research reflected the expansion of Canadian agriculture into mixed farming. The central station rapidly entered into livestock development with the goal of raising dairy herd standards through the introduction of proven sires; Ayrshires and Holsteins were the original breeds emphasized. Later work was done on draft horses, breeding sheep, and swine. The first apiary was established at Morden, Manitoba, in 1889. A division of botany was established in Ottawa in

1909, charged with research on the destructive diseases facing plants of all kinds. Its first task was to limit the introduction of wart disease in potatoes imported from Newfoundland, and it subsequently undertook the breeding of rust-resistant varieties of potatoes.

In 1889 the branch began the search for the ideal wheat for prairie conditions. Seventy-four varieties of spring wheat were imported into Canada for experimental use by 1889. They were not only grown but crossbred. The first crossbreeds were not very successful, but a cross of Hard Red Calcutta from India and the previously popular Red Fife produced Marquis wheat, introduced for trial in the Prairies in 1907. Marquis ripened three to 10 days quicker than Red Fife, a major advantage given the shortness of the growing season on the Prairies.

The Great War sparked much new research, especially into the cultivation of flax. Substantial attention was paid in the years before the war to improving soil-moisture retention. From the beginning, agricultural research was one of the jewels of the Canadian research and development crown.

houses and barns, dig wells, string fences, and acquire livestock was considerable. By 1890, mechanized harvesting equipment was common, but until World War I most farmers still used horses and oxen to do most of the ploughing, cultivation, and hauling. In 1898, with mechanized harvesting equipment but no internal combustion engine, Ontario-born Almon J. Cotton harvested more than 17,000 bushels (618,270 litres) of top-grade wheat at Treherne, Manitoba.[2] The government actually contributed to the development of more productive wheat farming.

Following the establishment of the Dominion Experimental Farms system by Ottawa in 1886, director William Saunders (1836–1914) set up the Central Experimental Farm at Ottawa and four other similar farms across the nation, in imitation of American practice. The great achievement of Canadian agricultural research in this period was the creation of Marquis wheat in 1907 by Charles Edward Saunders (1867–1937), the son of William. Maturing early and giving excellent yields, Marquis wheat took the West by storm. Less successful were attempts in

■ Ranching near Calgary, 1880. Provincial Archives of Alberta, Ernest Brown Collection, B.114.

the experimental stations to discover ways of farming with low moisture in the dry-belt areas of the West. The scientists may even have misled a generation of settlers into believing that the new techniques could substitute for rain and snow, thus encouraging the over-cultivation of the dry belt.

Wheat, of course, was the big prairie crop, but under certain conditions other crops were possible.[3] Almost every wheat farmer before 1914 grew oats as well, mainly to feed his draft animals and other livestock. And before the grain farmers arrived, much of southern Alberta and southwestern Saskatchewan was the domain of ranchers, who grazed thousands of cattle on open range leased from the federal government.[4] Capital costs ran high—a herd of 400 cattle was conservatively valued at $10,000 in 1889—but so did profits, estimated at 33.3 per cent per

annum on investment. Much of the money came from Britain, as did a number of ranchers who sat on English saddles and played polo in their spare time.[5] At the height of the cattle boom, in 1898, ranchers exported 213,000 live head. After the turn of the century, the industry was greatly constrained by the influx of farmers and by new restrictions in the primary markets of the United Kingdom. Although ranchers insisted that water shortages made much of the range land unsuitable for agriculture, their obvious interest in maintaining an open range tended to undermine their argument. Some of the land could be cultivated, particularly after 1905, when incoming farmers began digging large irrigation ditches. Nevertheless, water was to prove a major problem across much of the West.

The Canadian West differed from eastern and central Canada in that it was a new society,

BAR U RANCH

The Bar U Ranch (a.k.a. the North West Cattle Company) was one of the first and largest corporate ranches established in the Canadian West. It was founded in 1882 in a frenzy of investment in a 'beef bonanza' during the 1870s and 1880s, based on the Canadian government's decision to lease large amounts of pasture land in the North-West for grazing. Its first manager was Fred Stimson, who ran the outfit for 20 years. Stimson was an experienced stock raiser from the Eastern Townships of Quebec who understood that an early priority was to acquire a herd, which he did in Montana in 1882. The herd, a mixed one of 3,000 head with a number of breeding cows, was driven 700 miles north to Alberta with little loss of life, where it joined up with a number of purebred bulls purchased in Chicago in 1881. In 1890 the Bar U claimed 10,140 cattle and 832 horses, probably a somewhat inflated total. Observers commented on the good condition and the fatness of the cattle, grazed on the 'free grass' of open range.

Unlike the Americans, the Canadians promoted the range cattle industry by regulating grazing. Leases were set at $10 per thousand acres, a figure that met with the approval of the industry. The North West Cattle Company acquired 59,000 acres along the Highwood River and added another 88,000 acres adjacent to the core. Leases had little reality on the spot, since animals initially roamed the open range without regard for land boundaries, but the leases encouraged capital to invest in livestock, and in 1896 were converted into deeded land at low prices. In the early years, most markets were found among local Native bands, and only in 1887 did the ranches begin shipping cattle overseas, into Great Britain. The North West Cattle Company shipped 700 finished steers to Britain in 1887, and this market became the premium one until the end of the century. The ranch headquarters was established on the middle fork of the Highwood River, and consisted of a number of buildings housing a substantial labour force. The work was seasonal and highly specialized. Branding was especially tricky. The Bar U used a number of brands, and identification of the ranch with the brand occurred only after 1902, when the company was purchased by George Lane, an American, who owned and managed it until 1927 in partnership with Gordon, Ironside and Fares.

Lane worked closely with Clifford Sifton in the early years of the twentieth century, ending up with two townships of lease land and substantial deeded holdings. He was hard hit by the killing winter of 1906–7, which forced ranchers to shift into stock farming rather than more open grazing. With this shift, George Lane found a new business enterprise for the Bar U: the breeding and sale of purebred Percheron horses, which commanded premium prices among farmers needing draft horses.

In 1927 the Bar U Ranch was purchased by Pat Burns and converted into part of an integrated food-processing system. By adjusting to the changing demands of the livestock industry, the Bar U Ranch remained viable until well into the twentieth century. Today it is a showpiece for Parks Canada.

composed of immigrants from Europe as well as eastern Canada. The emphasis was on creating new institutions, not maintaining old ones. Moreover, the concentration on grain, particularly wheat, set western agriculture apart, and not only in the sense that western farmers tended to focus on a single crop. Wheat culture allowed many farmers to become more prosperous than

■ Doukhobor women pulling a plow near Swan River, Manitoba, 1899. LAC, C-681.

they could have as mixed farmers in the East. In addition, the rhythm of wheat farming freed them from drudgery not only during the long winter months but also for long periods during the summer. Together, the potential prosperity and the relative freedom from year-round daily labour compensated to some extent for the climate and the isolation of individual homesteads. After the initial hard years of settlement, westerners were able to become sociable. Much of their life, as in eastern Canada, revolved around church and school.

THE MYTHOLOGY OF THE PIONEER FARM

The popular image of farming in western Canada, as presented both in immigration litera-

ture and in fiction by best-selling writers such as 'Ralph Connor'—the pen name of the Reverend Charles W. Gordon of Winnipeg—was largely utopian, emphasizing the opportunities that free land offered for making a fresh start—in every sense of the expression. The West was egalitarian and neighbourly, and offered an unparalleled chance to succeed even for those beginning with very little. As A.J. Cotton, a farmer in Swan River, wrote in 1903 to relatives in eastern Canada:

Many a one have come to Manitoba with no capital and today are in easy circumstances. Farmers all over Manitoba say they are prospering and they look it, and if one prospers, can't another try, and where one meets with success, why can't another? This is true that Manitoba has advantages to offer the farmer that no other country has and there is

CANADA WEST

THE LAST
BEST
WEST

160 ACRE
FARMS IN
WESTERN
CANADA
FREE

RANCHING
DAIRYING
GRAIN RAISING
FRUIT RAISING
MIXED FARMING

ISSUED BY DIRECTION OF HON. FRANK OLIVER, MINISTER OF THE INTERIOR, OTTAWA, CANADA

■ This recruitment poster from the Department of the Interior promised that immigrants to the Canadian West, in exchange for hard work, would have the best of all possible worlds: mountain scenery, modern railways and thriving factories, productive fields, and idyllic homesteads. LAC, C83565.

no other country under the sun where farmers have and can do so well as in our Canadian North West. Prosperity reigns throughout and I like to see everyone come and take a share in it.[6]

Though clearly a booster, Cotton was not unrealistic. He warned a family member:

> You cannot be promised ease or luxury. There will be a certain amount of hardship to endure, obstacles to contend with, and privations to overcome. Your first four years would be your greatest worry. After that you would be into shape to go ahead.

Of course, the more capital you can put into it, the easier you can get through. Pioneering now is not what it used to be.[7]

Nevertheless, Cotton—like other prosperous farmers—saw 'industry and good management' as the keys to his success. And like most successful people, he tended to recall the hardships of earlier days through a golden haze, persuaded that though they had tested his physical and spiritual endurance, his triumph over them marked the end of a great quest, which Stephen Leacock once described as the Canadian equivalent of the search for the Holy Grail. Also, like many other farmers, Cotton had little to say about the contributions the women of his family had made to his success.

UTOPIANISM

Another popular theme in the mythology of the West was the association of nature with the 'Promise of Eden', a primordial garden of paradise. Four decades later, in 1931, W.C. Pollard rhapsodized about opening the West in his autobiographical *Life on the Frontier*:

> Did humanity ever set for itself a nobler task than that of pioneering in a new and virgin country, there the work of Nature can be seen on every side, and there avarice and selfishness are unknown, and all are engaged in Man's primitive occupations: tilling the soil, guarding the flocks and herds, fishing in the waters, hunting in the wilderness and mining in the ground. There the brotherhood of man is amplified and common interests cement together social ties and friendships and there the works of the Creator are seen before man makes any contributions or contaminations.[8]

Such utopianism was not simply rhetorical. In fact, many communities such as Steinbach, Manitoba, and Thunder Hill, Saskatchewan, were founded by men and women seeking to create ideal new societies in the new environment. Cannington Manor, in southeastern Saskatchewan, was founded by an idealistic Englishman, Captain Edward Michell Pierce, who wanted to establish a self-contained farming community. He attracted roughly a dozen English families, who emigrated in 1882 with their servants, racehorses, and grooms. But they were not seriously interested in farming, and by 1902 the experiment had collapsed. Other new communities, however, did succeed, especially those founded by dissenting Christian sects from Central Europe and beyond. Among the groups that found a haven in the West were German-speaking Hutterites and Mennonites, and some 7,400 Russian-speaking Doukhobors—followers of a pacifist religious leader named Peter Verigin—who arrived in Saskatchewan in 1899 and registered for homesteads. Verigin, who had been exiled to Siberia, finally joined them in 1902. In 1905, when the Doukhobors refused to swear an oath of allegiance, their homestead rights were cancelled, and Verigin led them to southern British Columbia, where a community of some 6,000 was founded. Over time, the mountains of British Columbia would become home to many people seeking a refuge from modern society.

PASTORAL CAPITALISM

Utopians aside, the norm for western farmers before and during the Great War was pastoral capitalism, and it is in this context that their early efforts at organization and co-operation need to be understood. Although tenant farming increased over the years, the basic unit of production throughout this period continued to be the family farm, usually producer-owned. Farmers operated as individual entrepreneurs, coming together in co-operative organizations for the moving and marketing of their crops, as well as the purchase of consumer goods through the power of increased consumer organization. Farmers tended to see eastern capitalists as their enemies, and wanted to develop new marketing

mechanisms as alternatives to the old systems that they felt had abused them. In economic terms there was little difference between French- and English-speaking farmers.[9] Not surprisingly, the most successful aspect of agrarian co-operation in the West was the farmer-controlled system of grain elevators used to store grain along the railway lines until it could be shipped to market. After 1910 this system grew rapidly, pledged to guaranteeing fair treatment for farmers through open competition with the private elevators dominated by the great railroads. But the co-operative in no way altered the free-enterprise system to which farmers themselves were committed.

THE POSITION OF WOMEN

The family farm depended to a large extent on the principle of deferred expectations and the exploitation of family members who could not expect to inherit any substantial share of the farm property. This system was particularly hard on women, who usually did not share in the ownership of the farm and whose labour was seldom remunerated (or indeed recognized as having monetary value; even the Canadian Bureau of the Census persistently refused to consider farm women as workers). Western farmers were particularly hostile to 'anachronistic' legal concepts such as the dower rights that protected women's inheritances, which were abolished in the North-West Territories as early as 1886. Furthermore, the homesteading system was generally unsympathetic to women who wanted to farm. Georgina Binnie-Clark, whose account of farming in Saskatchewan without a male partner was published in 1914 as *Wheat and Woman*, was unusual, if not unique. In the West, as everywhere in Canada, women's daily responsibilities tended to be much more demanding than men's, including not only the kitchen garden and small livestock (like chickens) that needed more regular tending than grain fields did, but care of the family itself. Harvest time was especially hectic, for a substan-

GEORGINA BINNIE-CLARK
(1871–1947)

❖

Georgina Binnie-Clark was born in Dorset, England, the daughter of a prosperous businessman. She first travelled to Canada in 1905 to visit her brother, who had set up a homestead at Lipton, Saskatchewan, and for the next three years she worked to establish herself as a wheat farmer. Thereafter, she published two fictionalized accounts of her experiences: *A Summer on the Canadian Prairie* (1910), essentially a travel book intended to introduce British readers to the Canadian West, and *Wheat and Woman* (1914). The latter book, obviously written for genteel women like herself, detailed her experiences, including the mistakes she made on the way to becoming a successful prairie farmer.

She had begun by purchasing a farm fully planted and ready to be harvested. As a woman she was not entitled to a homestead grant, but beginning her farming career on unbroken land probably would not have suited her plans anyway. Although she was probably wise to purchase a fully planted farm, she then made the first of many mistakes in allowing the vendor to keep the hay he had not yet cut, leaving herself short for the winter. Then she had hired a crew for the harvest and purchased her animals. Many of the problems she faced could beset any beginning farmer, even one with some capital. Farm buildings, for example, cost far more to construct than the builder had estimated, but she had no estimate in writing. All her expenses were more than she had anticipated, and she quickly discovered that hired hands had to be fed no matter how little work they did.

She also discovered that certain problems were specific to female farmers. One was the government's refusal to grant homestead land to a woman. The other was the labour problem. 'The best system of all for the woman-farmer', she wrote, 'is to train herself to do all her own chores and hire her field labourers at special seasons by the day.' By the end of the book, Binnie-Clark was able to record a profit of $700 on her operation for the year 1908, and was heading off for Ottawa 'to claim the right of women to their share in the homestead land of Canada'. She was subsequently joined by her sister Ethel, and the two women farmed together until the 1930s, when Georgina apparently returned to England—probably because of ill health—and left her sister in Saskatchewan, where Ethel remained until her death in 1955. Georgina died in 1947.

tial farm required many extra helpers, whose feeding was the responsibility of the women. What pioneer women complained most about, however, was the isolation they experienced, since farmhouses were a couple of kilometres or more apart.

THE FARM LABOUR PROBLEM

All farms had a potential labour problem because at peak production times the farmer's family was seldom large enough to handle the necessary

■ 'Hot Meals Served at all Hours': threshers take a lunch break, c. 1910. Saskatchewan Archives Board, R-A8634-1.

tasks. The situation in the West became particularly difficult in the summer, and thousands of temporary workers were recruited in eastern Canada to help with the harvest. In addition, however, few farm families had enough sons to do all the work needed throughout the year, and so the 'hired hand' became a fixture in many operations. A farmhand was usually required to board at the farm, and many farmhands were treated like family members, but this could be a mixed blessing. The typical farmhand was a young man temporarily filling a job, either to earn enough money to get a farm of his own or to gain experience as a sort of apprentice. Exploitation could work both ways. One farmer in 1907 complained, 'Last spring I hired a man for $210.00 for seven months. He is with me yet, but he feels just like he were in jail. He knows he

could get $3.00 a day if he were free, and he reminds me of that fact quite often. He is the boss and I am the roust about. . . . He does just as he likes and knows I have to put up with it.'[10]

The unequal treatment of women also contributed to the labour problem. Young women whose fathers did not or could not provide adequately for them often left the farm for the city, where the work expected of them might be less onerous and more remunerative. Back on the farm, their places were filled by 'servant girls', who were often hired from among recent immigrants stranded in the western cities. But although such workers were usually in short supply, they were not treated generously. While male hired hands usually worked specified hours, female employees—like the wives who supervised them—were expected to work around the clock.

LIFE ON A CHICKEN RANCH

In 1912 English journalist Ella Sykes, who in 1901 had published *Through Persia on a Side-Saddle*, visited Canada to explore the opportunities for educated Englishwomen in the American colonies. This is her account of a chicken ranch in British Columbia.

My host was emphatically a 'man of his hands,' and I never ceased admiring his energy. . . . Mrs. Bent was almost as fully occupied as her husband. Her house was beautifully clean and well kept, her stove brightly polished, and she had to prepare four meals a day, afternoon-tea being included in their menu, and also make her own bread. Once a week she scrubbed out her large kitchen and pantry (probably she will have recourse to covering the floor with linoleum later on, or painting it), on Monday she did the household wash, and Tuesday was ironing-day.

Most women would consider that her house gave her occupation and to spare, especially as she was dainty in her table appointments and always had flowers in the pretty living room, but she did almost as much on the ranch as her husband. The stock had to be fed, and needed water at frequent intervals, this being mixed with a few grains of permanganate of potash as a disinfectant, and clover had to be gathered daily at some little distance from the house to provide green food for the hens which were shut up in runs. The fowls were fed three times a day, twice with grain, and their 'balanced ration' (a mixture of grain, meal, powdered green food, and ground-up bone), was given to them in the evening, while the chickens required five meals. She also washed and packed the eggs for market, put the chickens into 'brooders' for the night, and lit the lamps to keep their shelters up to the right temperature, and on occasion she would chop up logs to feed the insatiable stove, wielding an axe with skill, and making me feel ashamed that I never got much beyond splitting up kindling wood with this weapon, so dangerous in unaccustomed hands.

Though she never grumbled, yet to me her life seemed lacking in relaxation. She and her husband could not leave the ranch together, unluckily she had no congenial neighbours close at hand (they were of the English labouring type), and as her chief friends lived at a distance, she did not care to go and see them by herself—in fact, I believe that during my visit she went farther afield than she had done since her marriage.

To balance this, she was young and full of hope, there was the possibility that people of her own class might settle near them later on, and more than all, the encouraging sense that she and her husband were making their way in the world together, and that their efforts had every prospect of being crowned with success. . . .

SOURCE: Ella C. Sykes, *A Home-Help in Canada* (London: G. Bell & Sons, 1912).

After 1900, farmers turned increasingly to other sources of labour, including young children brought over from Britain by charitable institutions hoping to give them a fresh start. More than 50,000 of these 'home children' were imported into Canada before the Great War. Some were orphans; others were encouraged to emigrate by their impoverished parents; and others still were literally seized from their families and sent overseas 'for their own good'. The results were mixed. In general, the worst experiences were suffered by children—male and

A LETTER TO THE GRAIN GROWERS' GUIDE, 1915

From 1908 to 1928, the *Grain Growers' Guide* was the official organ of organized grain growers of western Canada. From the beginning, it included pages for women, and through its correspondence pages (both edited by Frances Beynon from 1912 to 1917) gave a voice to farm women right across the Prairies. The following letter, signed 'Bluebell', was a response to a letter from one 'Helen Maloney' (the correspondent may not have been a woman at all) criticizing farmwives.

8 September 1915

With your permission I will take the opportunity to say a few things in answer to Helen Maloney. I do not know whether she is country or city bred, but somehow I gather that she does not belong to the country. If she did, I think she would be able to sympathize more with the country women; and find less room to criticize. How easy it is to sit at a desk in some city office and make copy out of the things that are not as they should be in the country.

I am a farmer's wife, the mother of four children, and have, at present, a family of nine to look after. I have seen something of life in three provinces, in the country, in town, in city, in villages, and I don't think any place could lay claim to a monopoly of dirty, nagging, childless women. You may find some of these wherever you go. Of course, you will not likely find any screaming chickens in the city, nor yet a cow to milk. That same cow might be the reason why the farm woman cannot put on her Sunday frock of an afternoon; for where is the woman who can milk cows without getting some spots on her clothes? And perhaps that same Sunday frock has to last more than the year she speaks of.

We get criticized for that, too; our old-fashioned clothes and our lack of a fluffy pompadour, and our hats set on our ears &c. &c. &c. It is easy to see the unlovely side of anything; but sometimes we must strain our eyes to discern anything worthy, especially about the country and the folks in it.

Now, I am not saying that the things which have been written in this page at times are not true; but, while written about the country women the same could be said about plenty of women in the city or town. All the clean folks do not belong to the city; nor all the dirty ones to the country. But anyone who gives the matter a thought knows how much easier housekeeping is in town than it is on the farm. Not one woman in a dozen or a hundred in the city does as much work as the average farmer's wife. She has bread to bake, butter to make, and has her own washing, ironing, cooking, canning, paperhanging, sewing, &c. to do, besides gardening and poultry raising, and no woman who is not skilled in all these fine arts should think of making a home in the country. It takes a smart woman to be a successful farmer's wife.

Well, perhaps I have said enough, but I believe the majority of childless mothers, or those with but one child, belong to the city. The women there want to get out to bridge parties, or afternoon teas, or to see the sights. For that reason it ought to be easier for them to wear the necessary smile, for out here there is no diversion or recreation.

We certainly find it hard enough to live up to all the dictates of arm-chair farmers; even if it were possible to do so. Some of those should be transported to actual farms, and then we would see what kind of a fist they would make of it.

SOURCE: Barbara Kelcey and Angela Davis, eds, *A Great Movement Underway: Women and The Grain Growers' Guide, 1908-1928* (Winnipeg: Manitoba Record Society, 1997), 137–8.

female—sent into rural homes. While some farm families in effect adopted such children—as Matthew and Marilla did with Anne Shirley in L.M. Montgomery's *Anne of Green Gables*—many others treated them as nothing more than a source of labour to be exploited.

CHANGING PATTERNS OF WESTERN LIFE

Except in the more isolated districts, life in the West became much less adventurous after the turn of the twentieth century. Schools and churches had been built, the land had filled up with settlers, and the prosperity created by the wheat boom of 1895–1914 made conditions considerably less harsh than they had been a generation earlier. Enough surplus was now left over to provide some amenities for farm women, particularly in the kitchen. Although electrification and indoor plumbing were slow to make their way in rural Canada before 1919, some farmers constructed their own electrical generators, and all got telephones as quickly as they could organize the stringing of the lines. Many of the more prosperous wheat farmers began to visit friends and relatives back east during the winter months, and some even began wintering in warmer climes to the south. In towns and villages across western Canada, organized social activities increased. Farmers travelled long distances by horse and buggy—or in winter by horse and sleigh—to participate in dances, church socials, and cultural activities in the community nearest them. As in eastern Canada, the closest village or town became an integral part of the rural environment. 'A working day . . . was from about 4:30 a.m. to 11 o'clock at night,' reported one farmer, 'but this was only in seeding and harvesting time. In the winter we used to really have fun.'[11] Social gatherings lasted well past midnight, since people who had travelled from remote farmsteads wanted to make the most of the outing. Social events were planned and publicized well in advance, and even afternoon teas were organized.

THE RISE OF SPECIALIZED FARMING

If the Prairie West, particularly after 1900, was quite similar to the rest of Canada in its social activities, it remained quite distinctive in its focus on the grain monoculture. For most of western Canada, the only other significant farm businesses had to do with horses (raising them and growing grain to feed them) and the beginning of fruit growing in British Columbia. In other regions much of the movement was to 'mixed farming' as the solution to holdings not large or fertile enough to grow a commercial crop. Specialization was the order of the day wherever possible.

One ironic effect of the shift into specialized farming, such as dairying, was that parts of the business previously left to the women—which often provided them with a small income independent of their husbands—were taken over by the males. Almost every farm (and many an urban household) kept a cow and some chickens; even a fishing family in Newfoundland or the Maritimes would have a cow. So long as the animals were part of the subsistence economy they were the women's responsibility, and surplus production was frequently sold or bartered in the community in return for 'egg money'. Once this sideline became the business of the farm, however, the woman lost this small bit of autonomy. She might still assist with the cows, but not with the milking if it became a large-scale operation.[12]

Not all regions were able to move easily to specialized farming. In the Maritime provinces, for example, the agricultural sector peaked in importance and size in 1891, with strong concentrations in PEI, north-central Nova Scotia, and southeastern New Brunswick. Some farmers found new crops in which to specialize, such as potatoes and fruit. But between 1891 and 1921, the Maritimes lost 22,000 farms and 630,000 hectares of farmland under cultivation. Farms continuing in operation still had less than half as much investment as central Canada in equipment and livestock, and large-scale commercial agriculture was on the decline almost everywhere except on Prince Edward Island.

Substantial changes in agriculture occurred in central Canada. In Ontario farmers shifted from wheat to specialized high-quality consumer production, becoming increasingly dependent on off-farm processing, particularly of butter and cheese. By 1900 Ontario had 1,200 cheese factories and had captured over half the British market, so that the value of cheese exports from the province exceeded that of wheat. The production of meat—both beef and pork—for the dinner table at home and abroad also grew substantially. Similar shifts occurred in Quebec, although the relative poverty of many Quebec farmers and the marginality of much of their land inhibited the process. In Quebec, dairy products accounted for less than 20 per cent of agricultural production in the years 1900–10, and field crops still made up the largest proportion of farm income. While the production of wheat steadily declined in Ontario and Quebec, the acreage under cultivation in these provinces continued to expand; much of the increase went to grazing for livestock and the hay and grain to feed them. Districts around the larger cities generally profited most from the changes in farm production in both provinces, although the St Lawrence Lowlands around Montreal suffered a dramatic rural exodus. Some districts—like Quebec's Eastern Townships, where French Canadians had virtually overwhelmed the anglophones by the close of this period—were very stable. In many parts of Quebec subsistence agriculture remained resilient.

Specialty farming was profitable for those in a position to pursue it. Few Maritime farmers were able to respond to changing circumstances as well as those in the Annapolis Valley, where the development of an apple industry to serve the British market was encouraged in the 1880s by improved steamship service and reduced freight rates. By 1911–12 the Valley was producing more than a million barrels of apples, and had introduced co-operative marketing. Another fruit-growing district developed in the Niagara Peninsula, and a third in British Columbia's Okanagan Valley, where land speculators found purchasers among Britain's landed aristocracy and wealthier commercial classes. At the peak of the boom, land planted with maturing fruit trees was selling at prices of up to $1,000 per acre (0.4 hectares). Apart from the fruit growers, the aristocrats of Canadian farming outside of the Prairies were the dairy farmers, whose success was inextricably connected with the growth of the cities. Dairying had begun in earnest in the 1860s, producing butter and cheese for export. By the 1890s dairy farmers in most provinces were also supplying milk (and products such as ice cream) to nearby cities. Successful dairy farming increasingly involved substantial capital investment—in herds, barns, and machinery—and it was quite labour-intensive.

NEW TECHNOLOGY

Between 1880 and 1914, technological change was as powerful a force in rural districts as it was in urban ones, but it had more impact in some aspects of farming than in others. The pace of agricultural mechanization, particularly in the time-consuming and labour-intensive harvest process, had increased. Mechanical hay mowers, introduced in the 1880s, enabled a man to cut 10 acres (4 hectares) of hay a day. In the 1890s the reapers, mowers, drills, and threshing machines of the 1880s were supplemented by a variety of other equipment—all horse-drawn—that would serve Canadian farming until well into the tractor era. Hart Massey acquired most of the American patents for farm equipment in the 1860s. In 1870 he had incorporated the Massey Manufacturing Company, which in 1891 merged with its chief rival, A. Harris Son and Co., to become Massey-Harris, the leading farm implement manufacturer in the British Empire.

Technology separated the successful farmer

■ Breaking land with a steam tractor, Pincher Creek, Alberta, *c.* 1910. Glenbow Archives, NA-2382-9.

from his less successful fellows. New labour-saving technology enabled one man in 1900 to produce a bushel (over 35 litres) of wheat in less than one-hundredth of the time required in 1870. The centrifugal cream separator, introduced at the turn of the century, revolutionized dairy farming. Another important development came in the processing and shipment of foodstuffs, particularly the use of canning as a means of preservation. The use of refrigeration for shipping and new processes for the production and preservation of dairy products were equally influential. Probably no new technology was more welcomed by farmers than the telephone, which made it possible for farm dwellers to talk on a regular basis with their neighbours. Social

activities could be planned, advice solicited, business transacted, and gossip—the heart of rural life—exchanged.

RURAL PATRIARCHY AND THE INHERITANCE PROCESS

In this period, the organization of Canadian rural society continued to be inherently patriarchal. Men owned the land and usually made the decisions—including the decision to uproot and resettle—often against the wishes of their wives. Edna Jacques, the daughter of a Saskatchewan pioneer, described what happened when her father received a visitor in January 1902, while the family was still living in Ontario: 'They were

■ Mr Rogerson's old and new homesteads, north of Morden, Manitoba, September 1905. LAC, PA-11445.

in the parlour talking and laughing together. . . . Suddenly the folding doors between the two rooms opened and dad stood in the doorway (I can see him yet) and loudly announced to my mother, "We're leaving Collingwood [Ontario]". Taking a long breath, he said, "We're going homesteading in the Northwest Territories. . . ." My mother fainted.'[13] Such a scene could just as easily have been played out in Quebec, where the destination might have been the Laurentian or Appalachian Highlands, or the Clay Belt on the Canadian Shield in northwestern Quebec. By 1910 the Lac Saint-Jean district was fully settled, and the Outaouais and Témiscamingue districts were rapidly filling, as was the Baie-des-Chaleurs coast of the Gaspé Peninsula. The Abitibi region

in the Clay Belt was opened in 1912, while the National Transcontinental Railway (later part of the Canadian National system) was being built (between 1906 and 1914) in northern Quebec and Ontario, chiefly in an effort to develop an empty wilderness. The colonization movements into these regions were led by the clergy; the government provided little assistance beyond access and road construction. For the most part the land was marginal, and settlement was closely tied to nearby resource industries—usually lumbering, but sometimes fishing or mining.

The figure of the rural patriarch as a land-hungry, if self-righteous, tyrant became a common motif in Canadian fiction of this period and slightly later, especially from the Prairie region.[14]

Patriarchy meant something quite different for sons, who would inherit the land, than for daughters, who would not, but the very family-oriented nature of the typical farm meant that its operation and ultimate disposition had to be intensely practical. In fairness to the acquisitive patriarch, his greed for land usually had its roots in a desire to provide security for his sons, who would have to support their own families, whereas his daughters would be taken care of by their husbands.

By and large, those who succeeded in making the shift to specialized agriculture did so on land they had inherited; those who had to buy land on the open market or start a farm in some remote district could rarely afford to specialize right away. The emergence of highly specialized agriculture also increased the distinction between prosperous farmers and those who subsisted on the economic margins—although all wished to provide some patrimony for their sons. Wheat farmer A.J. Cotton moved from southern Manitoba much farther north to the newly opening Swan River Valley in 1901 in order to provide for his sons; he managed to carve out farms for four of them from his property.

The quantities of arable land available were declining—and prices were rising—in this period, but entry into agriculture was still possible. Hence the rush to districts like the Swan River Valley in Manitoba, the dry belt of southern Alberta, and the Peace River districts of northern Alberta and British Columbia, as well as the continued movement into northern Ontario and Quebec. French Canadians, however—encouraged by the Quebec government and the Church to perpetuate French Canada, and perhaps discouraged by the hostility to their culture on the Prairies—were virtually excluded from the 'Last Best West'. The most famous French-Canadian novel of this period, Louis Hémon's *Maria Chapdelaine* (1916), reflected the choices facing traditional Quebec society in this period: set in the remote Lac Saint-Jean region, it tells the story of a young woman who sacrifices a chance to

marry a man who would take her to the United States—at a time when the migration of Québécois to the northern states was again becoming heavy—and gives herself to another in order to safeguard her family and community.

The inheritance process in Quebec was not all that different from that in the remainder of rural Canada. Basically, one of two strategies could be adopted. One possibility was to send the older boys off to establish new farms; this strategy—more common in the earlier period, when land was still available—overturned the traditional right of primogeniture, as one observer in French Canada of the 1860s described:

> In certain parishes, it is almost always the youngest who inherits the paternal estate. Canadians marry young and these marriages are productive. When the oldest boy reaches the age of settling down, his father and mother are still in possession of all their strength and do not even think of giving up work; they are satisfied with providing their son with the means of starting a farm in the parish not far from their own but settled later, where land is therefore cheaper. The same plan is adopted with regard to the second, third, and each following boy; by the time the last one is in a position to manage a rural estate, the father is approaching old age and feels the need to retire; if the youngest is intelligent, he becomes the owner of the property, in return for a life annuity assured his parents by a contract signed before a notary.[15]

As arable land disappeared, however, farmers had to rely on different strategies. The same observer described one alternative approach:

> It is not customary to break up landed property as is done in France. The head of the family works hard at economizing and acquires a piece of land for each of his sons who is old enough to cultivate. If his resources do not allow him entirely to accomplish this task, to which he attaches an

extreme importance, he bequeaths the patrimonial estate to his most intelligent son, delegating to him the responsibility of helping his brothers and sisters and, little by little, setting them up properly. . . . The patrimonial estate remains intact in the midst of the ups and downs undergone by the family, which becomes divided without the property itself being broken up; the successive emigrations which leave to populate neighbouring parishes radiate from this traditional center.[16]

This strategy—which was also employed in the Maritime region and to some extent in Ontario as well—would become a veritable recipe for rural depopulation when adjacent districts no longer had available land.

RURAL DISPLACEMENT

In the process of agricultural development, families that persevered were rewarded. But not many newcomers were able to gain entry into the community of prosperous specialized farmers in the established agricultural regions of eastern Canada. The farmers who, for one reason or another, did not move west, or who did not inherit decent land near a market (and they were extremely numerous), had to adopt other strategies for survival. Some farmers, especially in French Canada and in the more marginal districts of the Maritimes, were forced either to leave the farm for part of the year in search of additional income, or to move into newly colonized districts with dubious soils and climatic conditions.

The history of rural Canada in this period continued to be one of constant mobility and family fragmentation. Few farmers could provide separate farms for all their sons. Even if they had the money, the farms were not available to be purchased. Those sons who would not inherit moved on, with or without financial assistance from their parents. Even those who did inherit were not necessarily safe. One such son was Félix Albert, born in the old seigneury of L'Île Verte on

the St Lawrence, northeast of Rivière-du-Loup. His parents owned an 84-arpent (29-hectare) farm, of which less than one-fifth was under cultivation. The land could not support many children, much less provide for their futures. In 1857 Félix joined his father and one brother in colonizing land in St-Éloi, a newly established parish to the east. Through hard work the family survived and even prospered. Félix married and came into sole possession of the family farm. But bad harvests, caused by drought and frost, demoralized him, and in 1880 he went off to Maine to work for the winter. He never returned to Quebec. In 1909 he dictated his autobiography and hawked it on the streets of Lowell, Massachusetts.[17]

URBAN MIGRATION

A growing rural population was arguably the most important surplus that Canadian agriculture produced in this period. Some young people left the farm with the express purpose of finding work in the city, but others ended up there less intentionally. Many of the eastern migrants, for example, probably moved west to become farmers, but ended up in the cities. As one commentator in 1915 pointed out:

> The cities were bright; there were people, moving picture shows, taverns, music halls, churches, life and electric light. . . . The city seemed happier. There was work in the city at good wages; and the hours of such work were regular,—just so many hours per day. Evenings and Sundays were for pleasure and self-indulgence. And like seafaring men, farm hands acquire a faculty enabling them to shape well in many branches of labor: Therefore, they had little difficulty in doing well in our cities.[18]

Permanent residence in the city, however, was not the only possible response of those forced off the farm by inheritance patterns or economic marginality. Three others were possible.

AGRO-FISHING AND AGRO-FORESTRY

One survival strategy for displaced farmers was to work part-time in a local resource industry, usually fishing or lumbering. Along the coasts of the Maritime provinces, for example, the emergence of new markets (particularly for shellfish, such as lobster, which could now be canned and sent long distances) encouraged many farmers to supplement their agricultural income with fishing during relatively short seasons. Until a generation ago, in New Brunswick and Prince Edward Island, it was common to see a fishing boat sitting next to a potato field. On Tancook Island, off the south coast of Nova Scotia, the residents—descendants of Lunenburg Germans—grew cabbage and manufactured sauerkraut, which they transported to Halifax and beyond in their distinctively designed fishing vessels, the 'Tancook schooners'. In the interior of New Brunswick and Quebec, men continued to farm on marginal holdings during the summer and go to work in the woods during the winter. Local folksongs attest that many young Maritimers worked in Maine as well as Canada. While agro-fishery and agro-forestry were not very lucrative, those who engaged in them were probably better off than full-time fishermen in places like the Gaspé or Grand Manan Island who lacked access even to a subsistence farm.

AGRO-INDUSTRY

Industrialization permitted another pattern to develop, perhaps most strikingly in the Maritimes: agro-industry. The rise of factories designed to process farm produce or resource products (such as fish and shellfish) offered opportunities for part-time employment. Like the products they processed, most of these factories were seasonal in their operations. The cheese and butter plants of central Canada were unusual in the length of their seasons, but even they had times when the lactation period of the animals meant less milk. More typical were the fish-packing plants on both coasts, especially those involved in the new processing technology of canning. Geared to the 'run' and the season, whether salmon or lobster or herring, such plants would spring into operation for a few weeks each year, usually hiring female workers from the surrounding community who were eager to supplement their family income. In 1902 in British Columbia, for example, nearly 100 plants packed a total of more than 1,200,000 cases of canned salmon. Fruit-packing warehouses in regions like the Annapolis Valley and the Niagara Peninsula similarly employed seasonal workers at harvest time. In some areas men were able to work in nearby mines and mills while their families struggled to keep a subsistence farm going.

THE IMPLICATIONS OF OCCUPATIONAL PLURALISM

Rural occupational pluralism—combining agriculture with fishing, lumbering, manufacturing, or (later) service employment in the tourist industry—had several important implications and consequences. It was a survival strategy for the less prosperous members of the rural community, whether unsuccessful members of an otherwise flourishing farming community or typical residents of a region that was generally marginal and depressed. Consequences were both positive and negative. On the plus side, occupational pluralism enabled families to remain together by providing extra income to supplement limited agricultural production. It was an alternative to migration, and in many regions it was seen as preferable to full-time urban or industrial employment. Such a strategy, usually geared to the seasons, left time for hunting in the autumn and provided a break from the drudgery of regular work, particularly for men. On the negative side, rural occupational pluralism was associated with inferior agricultural practices and work attitudes. Since income was derived less

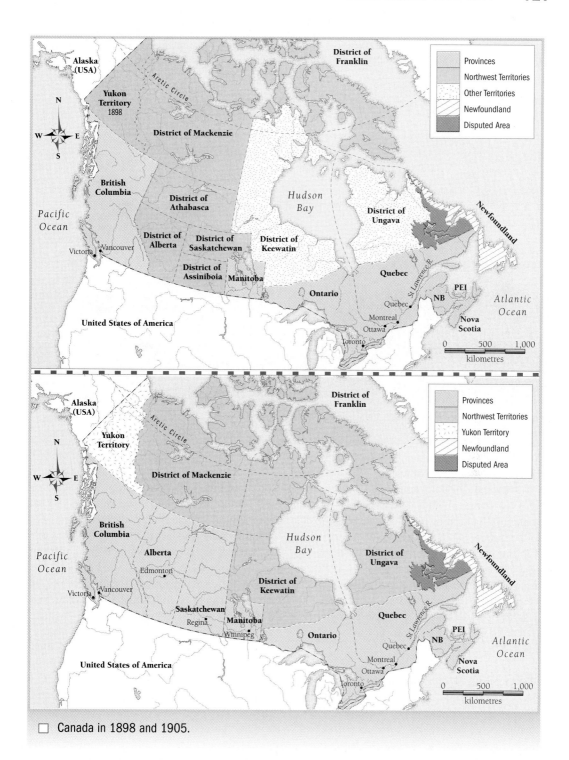

☐ Canada in 1898 and 1905.

■ The first school in Edmonton, built in 1881. LAC, C-003862.

from farming than from other work, the land did not have to be efficiently and expertly cultivated. Moreover, marginal lands could be kept in cultivation and the farm owner did not have to make hard economic decisions. Finally, occupational pluralism contributed to the difficulty of labour organization in rural sectors of the economy, which was rarely attempted before 1919. Occupational pluralism did not end with the Great War, and in some regions it may even have become more common later in the twentieth century.

RURAL HIERARCHIES AND INSTITUTIONS

Canadian rural society was not only patriarchal, but intensely hierarchical. Even the basic unit—

the family farm—was organized in hierarchical layers, with the father on the top, the male children favoured over the female, and a considerable gap between 'family' and the 'hired help'. On the larger scale, the fact that landownership was not limited to the wealthy—and that different sorts of farms were often separated by large distances—fostered illusions of social equality. The extent to which an individual rural family was aware of its socio-economic position depended on the extent of its involvement in the community. Residents of the local village or town—merchants, schoolteachers, clergymen, as well as the occasional doctor or lawyer—were perhaps more status-conscious. Obviously, one factor that helped to stratify rural society was prosperity, but another—particularly in older, settled regions—was persistence. Those families with roots going

■ 'A Meeting of the School Trustees', oil on canvas, 1885, by Robert Harris. National Gallery of Canada, Ottawa. Purchased 1886, #6.

back to the period of first settlement had claims to status and importance—whatever their material circumstances—that no newcomer could ever hope to enjoy. Cities and larger towns may have cared little about such things, but local history mattered in rural Canada.

THE SCHOOL

Across vast regions of rural Canada, a school was the only evidence of a local community (and a school district the only sign of political organization). The one-room rural schoolhouse was the

focal point of the community, providing space for meetings, dances, and suppers as well as the classes taught by a series of young schoolmarms and older schoolmasters. The school year was commonly geared to the agricultural season, and girls attended both more regularly and for longer periods of time than boys. L.M. Montgomery's response to her first such school as a newly appointed teacher, in 1895 at Bideford, Prince Edward Island, was probably typical:

This morning Mr Millar drove me up to the school and I went in, feeling forty ways at once and rather frightened into the bargain. The school is rather big and bare and dirty. There were about twenty children there, from six to thirteen years, and I called them in, said a few words to them and took down their names, feeling as idiotic and out of place as I ever did in my life.[19]

Schoolmistresses were expected to take a certain cultural lead in the community, both in school and outside it. They faced numerous challenges, from finding suitable lodging, to disciplining young men at least as large as themselves and sometimes nearly as old, to negotiating salary and working conditions with patriarchal school trustees. Robert Harris's well-known painting, 'The Meeting of the School Trustees' (see p. 129), captures the tension of one such meeting, with the young teacher facing down a collection of grizzled men twice her age. Conditions were much the same in rural areas across the country, whether French- or English-speaking. In Quebec, according to the 1913 census, the typical school was built at a cost of $1,200 and consisted of one room, with a young female teacher paid less than $200 annually and pupils ranging in age from age 6 to 14.[20]

THE CHURCHES

In addition to a school, many villages in rural Canada had at least one church. Since members of the same ethnic group tended to cluster together, the range of denominations within a given area was usually small. Most Protestants were content to attend the church of whichever denomination was predominant, and all Catholics could attend the same mass. Language could be a problem, however, especially where pastoral care was concerned. In the West, particularly, clergymen tended to be in short supply. Low salaries, harsh living conditions, and inadequate supervision were reflected in high rates of turnover. In many regions, clergymen would travel a 'circuit', conducting services in various places over the course of a season or year. Among Protestant denominations many rural preachers were actually laymen working towards ordination, and in rural Quebec, priests often maintained an iron grip on their congregations. Everywhere, the local clergyman typically represented contact with the wider world, perhaps the only such contact a farm family would experience.

NATIVE PEOPLE AND FARMING

Various efforts were made, particularly between 1850 and 1914, to turn Aboriginal people into 'peaceable agricultural labourers'.[21] For government bureaucrats and reform-minded private citizens alike, conversion from wandering hunters to settled agrarians appeared to be a simple solution for all the troubles that First Nations faced. Towards the end of the nineteenth century, Hayter Reed—the deputy superintendent of Indian Affairs who advocated a policy of repression after the uprising of 1885—explained the civilizing effects of an agrarian lifestyle:

> Corn precedes all civilization; with it is connected rest, peace and domestic happiness, of which the wandering savage knows nothing. In order to rear it nations must take possession of certain lands; and when their existence is thus speedily established, improvements in manner and customs speedily follow. They are no longer inclined for bloody wars, but fight only to defend the fields from which they derive their support. The cultivation of corn, while it furnishes man with a supply of food for the greater part of the year, imposes upon him certain labours and restraints, which have a most beneficial influence upon his character and habits.[22]

This agrarian ideology played a double role in Canada's Indian policy: as the justification for dispossessing First Nations of their hunting grounds in the first place, and then as the solution to the question of what those people would do after they gave up their lands. But this ideol-

■ Aboriginal farmers, *c.* 1906–10. Archives of Manitoba, Edmund Morris Collection. G11-510 (N15364).

ogy was also central to Canadian society in general. Before the Great War, most Canadians regarded agriculture as 'the mainspring of national greatness' and farming as a way of life that uplifted one 'morally and emotionally'.[23] Scientists (and others with scientific pretensions, such as anthropologists) saw agriculture as a crucial step on the ladder of progress. As a result, other ways of using the land, such as mining or lumbering, were regarded as inferior—and the people who engaged in such enterprises as somehow tainted. The fact that occupations like mining or timbering were not conducive to a settled family life only added to their disrepute.

Aboriginal people could be uprooted by treaties, removed to reserves, and encouraged to farm. But encouragement was not synonymous with practical assistance. First Nations needed help to make the transition from a nomadic life based on hunting and gathering to a settled agri-

cultural life, and they did not always receive it, although the situation improved after 1885. Government aid was the subject of considerable public debate in the years immediately after 1885. Although the Department of Indian Affairs defended its assistance program as more than was required, it did provide more working oxen and tried to deliver seed in a more timely fashion. Nevertheless, equipment—especially threshing machinery and grist mills—tended to be in short supply in many places. At the end of the nineteenth century, the Department of Indian Affairs devoted much attention to breaking down tribal and communal systems of agriculture and to encouraging subdivision of reserves and individual ownership of farm lots. Officials pressed bands to sell reserve lands to European settlers while encouraging 'peasant' agriculture on small allotments. According to Hayter Reed, an acre of wheat, an acre in vegetables, and a cow were sufficient to support a First Nations family—and with such a small acreage, they would have no need of expensive machinery; as he explained, 'our policy is to make each family cultivate such quantity of land as they can manage with such implements as they can alone hope to possess for long enough after being thrown upon their own resources.'[24]

The Plains Cree of the Treaty Four territory, in what would become southern Saskatchewan, began the conversion to farming in the 1870s, but their enthusiasm waned as quickly as the government's subsidies. When they resisted in the early 1880s, they were quickly suppressed militarily. Aboriginal resistance to government policy became unfortunately merged with the second Riel uprising, as we have seen. The Treaty Four First Nations were among those defeated at Batoche—and this, according to one observer, 'knocked the bottom out of every Indian on the Reserve, leaving them "completely subdued and quite tractable ever after"'.[25] After 1885, repression rather than subsidization was the federal government's major weapon in its efforts to impose agriculture on the reserves. Not surprisingly, the policy failed.

CONCLUSION: THE CULTURE OF SMALL-TOWN CANADA

Despite the rapid growth of Canada's cities, the vast majority of Canadians before 1914 continued to hold rural values and to think of the nation in essentially pastoral terms.

In April 1899 the 25-year-old Lucy Maud Montgomery sat down at her desk to take stock of her life over the preceding winter. Like many ambitious young women of her day, Montgomery had studied to be a teacher, first at Prince of Wales College in Charlottetown and then at Dalhousie University in Halifax. She had spent several years as a 'schoolmarm' in small communities on her native Prince Edward Island, but in 1898 had been called home to Cavendish to care for the grandmother who had brought her up— much as her fictional orphan, Anne of Green Gables, would care for her beloved foster parent, Marilla. Montgomery found the years in Cavendish difficult: 'In a way,' she wrote, 'I have been having quite a nice time this winter. I say "in a way" because in reality the gayety was all on the surface and away down underneath my new inner consciousness was coiled up, brooding like a snake in its den and every once in a while darting a pang into my soul's vitals.'[26]

Across Canada, winter was the time when rural social life really came alive, partly because farm families had more time, partly because travelling was much easier on ice and snow than on rough or muddy roads. Thus Montgomery, in late January 1897, travelled by sleigh to a distant village for a concert and supper. She and her friends left for home at about 11 p.m. in three sleighs: 'It was fine and calm all the way down to the ice but we had scarcely driven a mile on the latter when suddenly there came up a blinding snow-squall. In the twinkling of an eye we were enveloped in a white whirl so thick that we could not see from one bush to another.'[27]

However troubling she may have found the superficial aspects of the social round, historians can be grateful that Montgomery was a natural observer, for her journals can tell us a lot about small-town life in this period. 'The Literary Society has been in a flourishing condition this winter and I owe to it the few books that have delighted my soul.' She also attended several concerts and 'socials': 'I had to recite at most of them and as a rule enjoyed them.' As the last comment suggests, such events were participatory rather than spectator-oriented. Then there was the 'sewing circle' organized in aid of the new church building fund, which was time-consuming but had its amusing aspects 'in our pleasant afternoons of work and gossip—strictly harmless and clarified gossip, of course, patented for the use of church sewing societies!—and our evenings of fun when the boys came in and we play games of the same brand as the gossip.' As Montgomery recognized, gossip was at the heart of rural entertainment:

We are losing our minister. He has accepted a call to Tryon and Hampton, and is 'flitting' today. I do not think he will be much regretted. He was a fairly good preacher but no pastor and his wife and family were certainly fearful and wonderful creatures—whole reams of description could not do them justice. What Cavendish will find to talk about when Mrs Robertson is gone I really do not know. Her sayings and doings quite usurped the place of the weather in current greetings. 'Have you heard Mrs Robertson's latest?' or 'What will Mrs R. do next?' being standard questions.[28]

The culture of the Canadian small town before the Great War was more complex than the mythology—at the time or later—would suggest. All of the successful writers of the period were at their best writing about the values of rural and small-town Canada, and their work tended to be more representative of popular culture than of elite culture in Canada.

It is true that most people in a given area belonged to the same church—Roman Catholic in French Canada and Protestant everywhere else. It is also true that most people accepted the same middle-class values—because the middle class dominated the society and worked hard to ensure that those values prevailed.[29] But the supposed homogeneity was never complete, and by the late nineteenth century even small-town Canada was beginning to change.

Church attendance was starting to decline, especially among males, who increasingly looked to fraternal organizations and sports teams for their associational life. The homogeneity of earlier Protestantism, particularly in Ontario, was now breaking down (to some extent it was being recreated in the West), although the long-standing tensions between Protestants and Catholics showed no sign of abating. At the same time,

since the development of railways had begun bringing industry to small towns in eastern and central Canada, social relations were becoming strained between the middle classes and the factory workers who were increasingly in evidence in many small towns. And in the West class conflict began to emerge between prosperous farmers and hired hands or the crews of threshing contractors. The possibility of violence was never far away.

Yet even by 1900, rural areas of Ontario, Quebec, and the Maritime provinces were all experiencing depopulation. As the *Farmers' Advocate* remarked in 1911, the most important issues of the day were not 'those touching important practical problems of soil culture and stock husbandry, but the ones aroused by disputatious views on matters of social and business relationships, . . . the perennial debates as to "Why the Boys Leave the Farm"'.[30] One newspaper compared the progress of this population loss to consumption:

> At first there is a slight cough, a little weakness, but no serious symptoms to cause alarm. Then the cough gets worse. Spasmodic attempts are made to check the disease, but neither the patient nor his friends are seriously alarmed. But if the disease is not resolutely taken in hand at this stage, it is almost certain to result in suffering later and perhaps death.[31]

In the years before 1914, farmers in western Canada joined their fellows elsewhere in the nation to call for political reform aimed at preventing urban concentrations of wealth and power from destroying their way of life. Although overshadowed by the Great War, their campaign would be renewed after it by the Progressive Party.

SHORT BIBLIOGRAPHY

Carbert, Louise. *Agrarian Feminism: The Politics of Ontario Farm Women*. Toronto, 1995. A careful examination of women and politics in rural Ontario.

Carter, Sarah. *Lost Harvests: Prairie Indian Reserve Farmers and Government Policy*. Montreal and Kingston, 1990. A case study of Canadian attempts to turn First Nations people into prairie farmers.

Courville, Serge, and Normand Séguin. *Rural Life in Nineteenth-Century Quebec*. Ottawa, 1989. The best general overview and synthesis of a complex subject.

Evans, Simon. *The Bar U and Canadian Ranching History*. Calgary, 2004. A fascinating study of one of the large ranches of the Alberta cattle culture.

Harris, R. Cole, and Elizabeth Phillips, eds. *Letters from Windermere, 1912–1914*. Vancouver, 1984. A fine collection of letters from well-to-do British agricultural immigrants in the West Kootenays, British Columbia.

Jones, David. *Empire of Dust: Settling and Abandoning the Prairie Dry Belt*. Toronto, 1987. The tragic story of the attempt, mainly by Americans, to farm in Palliser's Triangle.

Owen, Wendy, ed. *The Wheat King: The Selected Letters and Papers of A.J. Cotton, 1888–1913*. Winnipeg, 1985. A collection of letters from one of Canada's leading farmer-capitalists in the years before the Great War.

Parr, Joy. *Labouring Childen: British Immigrant Apprentices to Canada, 1869–1924*. London, 1980. A pioneering study of the British children brought to Canada by philanthropy in the half-century after Confederation.

Rubio, Mary, and Elizabeth Waterston, eds. *The Selected Journals of L.M. Montogomery*, 4 vols. Toronto, 1985. A wonderful first-hand view of rural life by one of Canada's best-loved novelists.

Sylvester, Kenneth. *The Limits of Rural Capitalism: Family, Culture and Markets in Montcalm, Manitoba, 1870–1940*. Toronto, 2000. An important study of what happened to the French-Canadian family farm on the Prairies.

Voisey, Paul. *Vulcan: The Making of a Farming Community*. Toronto, 1988. An evocative micro-study of one Alberta small town and its service connections with a rural hinterland.

STUDY QUESTIONS

1. What was the mythology of pioneer farming?
2. Why do we characterize farmers as capitalists?
3. Why was 'Bluebell' so vehement in her 1915 letter to the *Grain Growers' Guide*?
4. What was unusual about the seasonal rhythms of grain farming?
5. What were the possibilities for occupational pluralism in the farming communities of rural Canada?
6. Why has Canadian rural society in this period been described as patriarchal?
7. What do the careers of A.J. Cotton and Georgina Binnie-Clark tell us about the agricultural society of western Canada?

CHAPTER SIX

Immigration Policy, Immigration, Ethnicity, and Racist Exclusion, 1882–1914

Just as British North America before Confederation had developed as a result of massive European immigration between 1815 and 1860, so the young nation of Canada flourished because of massive international immigration between 1882 and 1914. According to official statistics, between 1882 and 1914 approximately 4 million newcomers arrived in Canada, nearly 3 million of them after 1900. At its height, in 1913, the annual flow into the country reached 400,000. Not all of them stayed. Many passed on to the United States, but increasingly smaller numbers left the country after 1896, partly because the Americans sought to regulate their immigration and partly because free or cheap land in the United States was gone. Nearly two-thirds of these immigrants to Canada came from the British Isles, but increasing numbers did not. Many came from other parts of the world besides Europe. Beginning in the early 1880s, considerable numbers of people were recruited elsewhere as temporary contract labourers rather than as permanent settlers.

Immigration was the key element not only in the settlement of the West, but also in the promotion of industrial growth. Nevertheless, the numbers before 1892 were fairly disappointing. Between 1867 and 1892 perhaps one and one-half million foreigners entered Canada. Although we do not have precise numbers, contemporaries recognized that many if not most of those newcomers passed on to the United States, and they were joined by large numbers of Canadian residents as well. Indeed, before 1900 more people departed Canada than entered it. Part of the problem was intense competition from other nations with large amounts of free land, such as the United States, Australia, New Zealand, South Africa, Brazil, and Argentina. Many of these nations had more temperate climates and could offer incoming settlers a less heroic opportunity for success than western Canada, with its long, cold, winters, early frosts, and various other obstacles to settlement, including rebellion and vast distances.

The focus of early Canadian immigration policy was to attract newcomers to settle the Canadian West. The Canadian government preferred immigrants from Britain with agricultural experience, ignoring that knowing how to farm intensively in the temperate climes of Western Europe was not the same as being able to farm on the vast expanses of the Canadian steppes. After 1874 the federal government, by dominion–provincial agreement, was responsible for recruiting immigrants in Europe. It had to face both European hostility to losing citizens and competition from other recruiting nations,

TIMELINE

1881–4
Over 15,000 Chinese admitted to work on railway.

1882
240 Jews leave London for Manitoba and the North-West. CPR begins selling large land blocks to settlers.

1885
North-West Rebellion suppressed. Métis and First Nations moved to the margins. Chinese immigration restricted and regulated. Stiff head tax of $50 later raised.

1887
Small community of Mormons led by Charles Card comes to Alberta. Emigrants' Information Office established in London under control of Colonial Office.

1888
Passenger warrant system discontinued. First Scots crofter settlers arrive under crofter settlement schemes.

1892
Federal immigration, previously under the Department of Agriculture, administered to 1917 under the Department of Interior.

1896
Clifford Sifton appointed Minister of Immigration.

1898
Sifton orders Italian labourers deported. Doukhobor immigration agents arrive in Canada.

1899
North Atlantic Trading Company (a syndicate of steamship agents based in Antwerp) organized to send agricultural settlers from Europe to Canada. Bloc settlements encouraged in Canada; 7,500 Doukhobors arrive between January and July.

1900
Sifton encourages American farmers to migrate. Japanese begin to arrive in northern BC. Organized labour opposes inundation by non-English speaking aliens.

1901
CPR imports Italian workers through Montreal-based agent Antonio Cordasco. BC mining companies import Italian strike-breakers.

1902
Salvation Army immigration office opened in London. Barr colonists organized in Britain to come to Saskatchewan.

1903
Federal immigration office opened in London.

1904
Sikhs arrive in BC in 1904.

1905
Frank Oliver appointed Minister of Immigration. Canadian immigration policy becomes more selective.

1906
Immigration Act of 1906 consolidates immigration legislation.

1907

One hundred immigration agents appointed for Britain, to receive $2 bonus for every farm labourer recruited. Vancouver Branch of Asiatic Exclusion League organized. Oriental riots in BC. Pressure for immigrant navvies mounts for railroad construction. Canada sends mission to Japan, which reaches an agreement that while all immigrants could come, the Japanese government would limit Japanese labourers to 400 a year.

1908

Continuous journey regulation introduced. Border inspection service established on American border, beginning with border from Toronto to Sprague, Manitoba.

1909

J.S. Woodsworth publishes *Strangers within Our Gates*.

1910

Another restrictive Immigration Act passed.

1911

Petitions against blacks lead to Order-in-Council prohibiting black immigration.

1914

The *Komagata Maru*, a Japanese-registered ship carrying over 350 emigrants from the Indian subcontinent, is denied landing at the Port of Vancouver and eventually returns to Asia.

---

notably the United States. Canadian agents in Europe insisted that the Americans misrepresented their own advantages and the rigours of life in Canada, although most immigrants probably had a pretty good idea of the comparisons between the two countries. Canada did its best to downplay the immigration statistics, especially the outflow of people from Canada into the United States.[1]

IMMIGRATION POLICY, 1896–1914

After a succession of undistinguished Ministers of the Interior before 1896—including Sir John A. Macdonald, who was in the post at the time of the Riel uprising of 1885—Canada got two dynamic ministers in the portfolio under Sir Wilfrid Laurier. The first was Clifford Sifton (1861–1929).[2] Like many of the early settlers of Manitoba, Sifton was born in Ontario and was very much opposed to the principle of separate schools. He was instrumental in implementing the Manitoba government's unilingual schools

policy in opposition to the Laurier government from 1891–6, and then joined Laurier to settle the West, in which he instinctively believed. Sifton's policy was many-stranded, but was anchored by the belief that the West needed farmers above all else, regardless of their origins. In his search for new strategies, Sifton swept away previous Dominion Lands policy, simplifying the homestead procedures and attacking the railroad's land grant system. The railroads, especially the CPR, had been awarded millions of acres of land along its right of way in the 1880s but had not selected most of them. Sifton forced the railroad to take its acreage, thus opening the remaining land for general settlement. He advertised aggressively for new settlers in Britain, the United States, and Continental Europe. Recognizing that many Americans understood agriculture in the Canadian West, he also appreciated that many Europeans—especially those from the steppes of Central and Eastern Europe—were experienced at dry farming of large acreages. He publicly encouraged the settlement of 'stalwart

■ Minister of the Interior Clifford Sifton, c. 1901. Archives of Manitoba, 3 (N19971).

Belgium, Holland, and northern Italy, reflecting Sifton's prejudices and political agenda. He also returned to the group/bloc settlement ideas of the 1870s, encouraging such groups as the Doukhobors, the Mormons, and the Barr Colony settlers. Two thousand British immigrants with virtually no agricultural experience, led by clergyman Isaac Barr, received a block of land in remote Saskatchewan. The colony was successful despite the best efforts of the founder, who was headstrong and eccentric, to undermine it. And Sifton wholeheartedly supported child immigration from the slums of Britain in defiance of the attacks on the program from many quarters. Under Sifton's administration, a number of immigrants also arrived from places and races the minister was not fond of as sources of Canadian newcomers. Like most Anglo-Canadians, he was not keen on arrivals from Asia and the Indian subcontinent. Nor did he want blacks from the United States or unskilled Italians from southern Italy. In the end, the vast majority of immigrants in the Sifton years went into industry and transportation rather than into agriculture, partly because they lacked both farming skills and the capital to prosper on newly settled farms created from 'wild' land in the Canadian West.

Under Clifford Sifton, the Canadian door was opened to immigration, and very little was done to regulate the flow. Frank Oliver's approach was different. Like Sifton, who owned the *Manitoba Free Press*, Oliver (1856–1933) was a transplanted easterner and successful newspaper publisher.[4] Despite his constant criticisms of Sifton's policies, Oliver was recommended by Sifton to succeed him when he broke with Laurier over separate schools in Alberta and Saskatchewan in 1905. Although both Sifton and Oliver were ostensibly Liberals, their views were quite far apart. Oliver insisted that newcomers to Canada had to be assimilable into English-Canadian society, helping to build up 'a Canadian nationality so that our children may form one of the great civilized nations of the

peasants' in sheepskin coats, 'born to the soil, whose forefathers have been farmers for ten generations'.[3]

Sifton's reforms stretched in a variety of directions. To counter the hostility of many European governments to emigration advertising, he made a private arrangement with European shipping agents to encourage agricultural immigrants to Canada in return for special bonuses. The agents were active in Russia, Germany, Austria, Switzerland, Rumania, France, world and be one of the greatest forces in that civilization.'[5] He preferred British and American settlers of any description to experienced farmers from Central and Eastern Europe. Oliver moved quickly to end his predecessor's free-entry policy, supervising the passage of the Immigration Act of 1906, which emphasized 'selective' immigration and the denial of admission to 'undesirables', including those with health handicaps and those without capital. The new Act barred large categories of people: prostitutes and pimps, the mentally retarded, those with contagious diseases, the insane, epileptics, the deaf and dumb, and the blind. A larger immigration service to monitor the border was created, and prohibited immigrants who had managed to get into Canada and those who became public charges within two years were deported. The Department of Immigration also gained the power to control the amount of landing money required of immigrants. In addition, Oliver cancelled the North Atlantic Trading Company contract and raised bonuses for British immigrants. Many of the provisions of the 1906 Act echoed legislation passed in the United States, which had become concerned with the quality of its newcomers about 10 years earlier. The Act greatly widened the categories eligible for deportation, and permitted immigration officers to expel both foreign-born residents of Canada and those who were naturalized Canadian citizens with little more than an informal hearing, without any guaranteed rights for the deportee. Selective entry implied some sort of procedures at the point of entry. These were nothing new for immigrants entering by sea, but represented a total change in the process for crossing the long Canadian–American border. Throughout the nineteenth century, people had wandered across the border in both directions without papers and without being counted. Formal border crossings were now established in both directions, maintained by immigration officers who had the power to deny admission virtually arbitrarily to anyone who did not satisfy their standards. By 1908 the Immigration Branch

staffed 37 points of entry between Toronto and Sprague, Manitoba. That same year, an amendment to the Immigration Act had provided that all immigrants from Asia had to travel directly to Canada on a through ticket from the country of origin. This 'continuous journey' requirement was intended to make it more difficult for immigrants, especially from the Indian subcontinent, to travel by steamship to Canada.

In 1910 a further piece of restrictive legislation—'An Act Respecting Immigration'—was passed by the Canadian Parliament at Oliver's initiative. The new law went much further than earlier legislation in permitting the Governor-in-Council (i.e., the cabinet) to exercise discretionary powers to regulate immigration, subject to virtually no checks. It came from the same stock of thinking that brought Canada the War Measures Act in 1914. The principle being developed was the right of the state to take what steps it deemed necessary to protect itself. Section 38 authorized the cabinet to proscribe the entry of 'immigrants belonging to any race deemed unsuited to the climate or requirements of Canada' and enlarged the 'prohibited classes' to include those assisted to immigrate by charitable organizations; a subsequent Order-in-Council insisted that every immigrant have $25 in cash as well as a ticket to a destination in Canada. The 1910 Act also allowed for deportation if the individual was politically or morally undesirable. Section 41 defined political undesirability as advocating 'in Canada the overthrow by force or violence of the government of Great Britain or Canada'.

THE BROADENING OF THE MOSAIC

Despite the restrictive legislation and a variety of informal strategies for keeping 'undesirables' out of Canada, the nation experienced a substantial addition of non-British and non-Northern Europeans between 1882 and 1914. The temptation has always been to assume that Canadian immigration history was like that of the United

■ Kindergarten class of the All Peoples' Mission in North End Winnipeg, 1904. J.S. Woodsworth served as superintendent for the Mission, which sought to alleviate the living conditions and life trajectory of poor immigrants in this working-class area of the city. Archives of Manitoba, 3 (N13261).

States, except that it involved smaller numbers. In many respects the Canadian story did sound much like the American one, with its increasing exclusionism and racism. But in the details of the arrival of the immigrants and their history, there were substantial differences.[6] Canadians should not assume that their ancestors were more tolerant and less racist than their American cousins. Scholars still debate whether racism in Canada was caused primarily by socio-economic pressures or some inherent prejudice and hostility against those who were different from the majority.[7] On the whole, the Canadian pattern often led to less assimilation and greater retention of culture than was the case in the United States, although assimilation was the official goal.

THE CHINESE

Some Chinese had arrived in British Columbia with the gold rush in 1858 and others were brought to the province by mine owners as contracted labourers in the 1860s and 1870s.[8] But a major immigration of Chinese did not begin until the early 1880s, when Andrew Onderdonk, the contractor responsible for the construction of the British Columbia section of the Canadian Pacific Railway, began importing Chinese workers to

ASSIMILATION

James Shaver Woodsworth, who would later become an Independent Labour MP (1921) and the first leader of the Co-operative Commonwealth Federation (1933), worked with immigrants in the inner city of Winnipeg and expressed mixed feelings about their acculturation and assimilation.

It is not in the school, however, but on the street and in the shop that the foreigners acquire their knowledge of Canada. . . . What are the first lessons the foreigner receives in the government of our country? A thoroughly disreputable fellow, who is useful because he can speak several languages, is engaged to secure voters. He 'rounds up' as many as he can, and enters their names on the voters' lists. . . . This is the way voters are made. Their qualifications? They are supposed to have been resident in the country for three years. And the vote of one of these foreigners 'kills' the vote of the most intelligent Canadian!

When the election comes, the services of the aforesaid disreputable fellow are again required. With his knowledge of English and the foreign tongues he commands the situation. The party must have him and must depend upon him. Big promises and a little money will go a long way. He 'fixes' a few of the leaders in the settlement. Then, on election day, the beer and whiskey flow freely. The election is won! This is no fancy picture and no isolated case. How can the foreigner have any regard for our institutions? How can our free institutions be maintained?

Peoples emerging from serfdom, accustomed to despotism, untrained in the principles of representative government, without patriotism—such peoples are utterly unfit to be trusted with the ballot. . . .

Our democratic institutions are the outcome of centuries of conflict by which to some extent we have been fitted for self-government. It is as absurd as it is dangerous to grant to every newly arrived immigrant the full privilege of citizenship. Just what qualifications should be required cannot be discussed here. The next reform should look to the restriction rather than the extension of the franchise.

Several considerations are essential if we are to assist our immigrants to become Canadians. In the first place we must divest ourselves of a certain arrogant superiority and exclusiveness, perhaps characteristic of the English race. Our untravelled Canadian despises all foreigners alike. We must remember that many of the world's greatest and best men were from the very countries which our immigrants call home. . . . We must in many ways meet these people half way—seek to sympathize with their difficulties, and to encourage them in every forward movement. Only those who in time can take their place as worthy fellow citizens should be admitted to our Canadian heritage.

SOURCE: James S. Woodsworth, *Strangers within Our Gates or Coming Canadians* (1909, reprint edn Toronto: University of Toronto Press, 1972), 238–41.

perform heavy labour on what was generally agreed was the most difficult part of the building of the CPR. The workers were transported to railway camps along the line at Yale, Port Moody, and Savona. It has been estimated that approximately half of the 15,701 Chinese who entered Canada between 1881 and 1884 were employed directly on labour crews for the CPR, and a number of the others worked in industries that supported the construction. Sir John A. Macdonald

■ Chinese CPR workers in camp, Kamloops, 1886. LAC, C-2880.

protected the Chinese during the building of the CPR, telling the Canadian House of Commons in 1883 that 'It will be all very well to exclude Chinese labour, when we can replace it with white labour, but until that is done, it is better to have Chinese labour than no labour at all.'[9] As soon as the railroad construction was completed, Macdonald gave in to pressures from British Columbia and elsewhere to 'do something' about the Chinese, who were regarded as the source of a variety of social and economic evils. A Royal Commission on Chinese immigration in 1885 recommended restrictions, and Macdonald legislated a head tax of $50 on every Chinese entering the country. The law also restricted the number of Chinese who could be carried on individual vessels entering Canadian ports. This federal legislation joined numerous provincial statutes limiting the rights of the Chinese in Canada. Despite various attempts to stem the immigration of Chinese to Canada, by 1921 there were almost 40,000 Chinese living in the country. One of the major effects of the various restrictive regulations was a gender-skewed Chinese population—in 1921 there were 1,533 males for every 100 females.

THE JAPANESE

Several thousand Japanese immigrated to Canada, often as contract labourers brought by immigration companies, especially in the first 10 years of the twentieth century.[10] Many of these immigrants were using Canada as a back door into the United States. Unlike most nations, Japan actually collaborated with the Canadian government on several occasions to limit immigration, apparently in order not to lose 'face' through restrictive policies on the part of the host country. Those who remained in Canada were often male sojourners who intended eventually to return to Japan. But saving enough money for a triumphal return to a Japanese village was not always possible, and many of the sojourners instead turned to importing brides through photographs and arranged marriages. These were the so-called 'Picture Brides', brought into Canada between 1908 and 1928.[11] Children inevitably followed, and as they became acculturated to Canadian society it was harder to return to the home country. Because of the short time spans involved, a clear distinction among first generation immigrants (Issei), second generation Canadian-born (Nisei), and third generation (Sansei) was possible. Faced with innumerable obstacles to obtaining full Canadian citizenship, many Japanese remained under the informal dominance of the Japanese consul in Canada and made few demands on public services. Most Japanese settled in coastal British Columbia and were employed in fishing, timbering, and agriculture.

THE JEWS

Very small numbers of Jews arrived in Canada before the 1880s.[12] They came initially as individuals, via Britain or the United States, and were mainly of Sephardic origin. A wave of Jewish immigration to America began in the late 1840s from Germany and Eastern Europe; most of these migrants before 1900 ended up in the United States. The early Jews were affluent and successful, numbering only 2,456 in 1881. Eastern European Jews entered Canada in substantial numbers a generation after their arrival in the United States, beginning only after 1900. The Canadian Jews tended to be more influenced by Zionism and Bundism (a form of Jewish nationalism) than the American Jews, who had been subject to substantial assimilationist pressures. As a result, the Jews in Canada were more resistant to assimilation and more likely to retain aspects of their culture, especially traditional languages. Initially they mainly gathered in ghettos in cities like Toronto, Montreal, and Winnipeg, which further preserved their culture by recreating the Eastern European shtetl. By 1921 the Jewish population of Canada was 126,201, and it was rapidly becoming a population highly educated and highly skilled.

THE UKRAINIANS

In the later nineteenth century the Ukraine, a vast territory on the central and southern steppes of Eastern Europe, was part of the Russian (85 per cent) and Austrian Empires (15 per cent). The first settlers from this region had come to Canada in the early 1890s, where they joined Mennonites and Hungarians as early arrivals from these two vast empires. In 1895, Dr Joseph Oleskiw, a Ukrainian academic who taught agriculture, visited Canada and proposed an extensive Ukrainian immigration to the Canadian West, which Clifford Sifton did his best to implement.[13] Between 1896 and 1914, about 170,000 Ukrainians—chiefly from the overpopulated Austrian provinces of Galicia and Bukovyna—entered Canada, settling mainly in the prairie region. These peasants were experiencing increasing subdivisions of their land and a declining productivity because of lack of capital caused primarily by heavy taxation. By 1900, half of the landholdings in the provinces of Galicia and Bukovyna were less than two hectares in extent, and many small landholders were heavily in debt. These conditions, not appreciably different from those of Scottish crofters of the same period, provided a ready-made incentive for immigration to North America. The Ukrainians probably would have preferred the United States, but they faced increasing immigration restrictions and, if they were able to get into the US,

■ A Ukrainian family harvesting wheat, 1918. LAC, PA-88504.

they often were met by a hostile reception from the Americans, who no longer had any unsettled agricultural land to distribute to newcomers. Many of the newcomers came to Canada because of a secret agreement between the Canadian government and the North Atlantic Trading Company, which directed immigrants to Canada in return for under-the-table payments on a per capita basis. Indeed, steamship and railway companies were probably more active recruiters of agricultural immigrants outside of the British Isles than the Canadian government.

Canada may have been a second choice, but at least it encouraged Ukrainian immigration and could make land available to them. Most Ukrainian immigrants were poor but not destitute. They had sold their land and possessions to purchase their passage. Like all immigrants of this period, they found the transatlantic passage in steerage to be a difficult experience. As their historians have emphasized, the situation the Ukrainians entered in Canada was little different from that at home: bare survival on the land and

an early death for those who failed. But they were stubborn and hopeful. Many new arrivals found the quarter-section homestead conceptually beyond their comprehension, partly because there was too much land, partly because the size of the homestead meant there could be no compact village communities as they had at home. The first Ukrainians typically emigrated without many of their natural leaders, especially parish clergymen, and were assisted by men like Joseph Oleskiw, Kyrolo Genik, and the Reverend Nestor Dmytriw, who were members of the Ukrainian intelligentsia employed by the Canadian government as 'overseers' and advisers. All three produced a substantial body of writing to assist the new arrivals. This advice emphasized the need for capital to establish a farm, the adoption of Western dress, and the acquisition of free land. Canadian society received the Ukrainians with considerable suspicion, chiefly because they were obviously non-British 'foreigners' who spoke an alien language and practised different customs. Those who settled in the cities (espe-

THE FOREIGNER

In his 1909 novel *The Foreigner*, Presbyterian clergyman C.W. Gordon, writing as 'Ralph Connor', suggests that assimilation allows his young heroine to free herself from the clutches of predatory fellow-immigrants.

'Pretty gay girl, our Irma has come to be,' continued the cheerful Samuel, who prided himself on his fine selection of colloquial English. 'She's a beaut now, ain't she? A regular bird!'

Rosenblatt started. At his words, but more at the admiration in Samuel's eyes, a new idea came to him. He knew his clerk well, knew his restless ambition, his insatiable greed, his intense selfishness, his indomitable will. And he had good reason to know. Three times during the past year his clerk had forced from him an increase of salary. Indeed, Samuel Sprink, young though he was and unlearned in the ways of the world, was the only man in the city that Rosenblatt feared. If by any means Samuel could obtain a hold over this young lady, he would soon bring her to the dust. Once in Samuel's power, she would soon sink to the level of the ordinary Galician wife. True, she was but a girl of fifteen, but in a year or so she would be ready for the altar in the Galician estimation.

As these thoughts swiftly flashed through his mind, Rosenblatt turned to Samuel Sprink and said, 'Yes, she is a fine girl. I never noticed before. It is her new dress?'

'Not a bit,' said Samuel. 'The dress helps out, but it is the girl herself. I have seen it for a long time. Look at her. Isnt she a bird, a bird of Paradise, eh?'

'She will look well in a cage some day, eh Samuel?'

'You bet our sweet life!' said Samuel.

'Better get the cage ready then, Samuel,' sug-gested Rosenblatt. 'There are plenty bird fanciers in this town.'

The suggestion seemed to anger Samuel, who swore an English oath and lapsed into silence.

Irma heard, but heeded little. Rosenblatt she feared, Samuel Sprink she despised. There had been a time when both she and Paulina regarded him with admiration mingled with awe. Samuel Sprink had many attractions. He had always plenty of money to jingle, and had a reputation for growing wealth; He was generous in his gifts to the little girl—gifts, it must be confessed, that cost him little, owing [to] his position as clerk in Rosenblatt's store. Then, too, he was so clever with his smart English and his Canadian manners, so magnificent with his curled and oily locks, his resplendent jewelry, his brilliant neckties. But that was before Irma had been brought to the little mission, and before she had learned through Margaret Ketzel and through Margaret's father and mother something of Canadian life, of Canadian people, of Canadian manners and dress. As her knowledge in this direction extended, her admiration and reverence for Samuel Sprink faded.

The day that Irma discarded her Galician garb and blossomed forth as a Canadian young lady was the day on which she was fully cured of her admiration for Rosenblatt's clerk. For such subtle influence does dress exercise over the mind that something of the spirit of the garb seems to pass into the spirit of the wearer. Self-respect is often born in the tailor shop or in the costumer's parlor.

SOURCE: Ralph Connor, *The Foreigner: A Tale of Saskatchewan* (Toronto, [1909]).

cially Winnipeg's North End) in ethnic communities bordering on slums were most visible. But the willingness of most new arrivals to work hard was in their favour, at least before the arrival of the Great War. After 1914 Austria–Hungary joined Germany as the enemy, and many Ukrainians in Canada became enemy aliens.

Usually considered as separate from the Ukrainians—although originating in the Ukraine—were the Doukhobors, a sectarian movement that broke away from the Russian Orthodox Church in the eighteenth century.[14] The Doukhobors (the term means 'spirit wrestlers') in the nineteenth century became a Quaker-like pacifist group emphasizing the brotherhood and sisterhood of all men and women and the validation of their beliefs not in books but in the 'book of life'. With the aid of the Russian novelist Leo Tolstoy, the Doukhobors sought refuge from Russian persecution in western Canada. They were granted recognition as conscientious objectors by the Canadian government on 6 December 1898. Over the next few years, more than 7,500 Doukhobors arrived in Canada to settle on tracts reserved for them in what would become Saskatchewan and Alberta. They were joined by their leader, Peter Verigin (1859–1924), in 1903. In 1907 the Canadian government backed away from an earlier promise that the Doukhobors could live and work communally, insisting instead on individual homesteading and an oath of allegiance. As a result, under the leadership of Verigin, communal Doukhobors bought land in the interior of British Columbia and moved into the Kootenay region. Many of the Doukhobors subsequently struggled with the Canadian authorities over the issue of compulsory education, oaths of allegiance, and participation in the body politic.

THE AMERICANS

Although the Canadian press would occasionally complain about the 'Americanization' of the West, most Americans had always been regarded as desirable settlers who 'understand the ways of this continent and its institutions'.[15] Many Americans, of course, had at one time resided in British North America. Some exceptions to the favourable attitude towards Americans existed, however. Many Canadians objected to the polygamous marriage practices of the Mormons, who were one of the earliest groups of immigrants into Alberta in the 1880s, and few Canadians showed any enthusiasm for the admission of American blacks. As well as the Mormons, a few American cattle and sheep ranchers arrived before the 1890s. But after the well-publicized 'closing of the frontier' in the United States after 1896, the Canadian government made a real effort to recruit American farmers of European origin for what became known as 'The Last Best West'. Canadian agents openly sought wealthy immigrants, and the most common form of recruitment was through personal correspondence from existing settlers. Much of the settlement in Alberta and Saskatchewan occurred in the so-called 'Palliser's Triangle', a dry-belt region with marginal rainfall. American farmers were alleged to be the best settlers of such land, since they were familiar with techniques of dry farming. In a series of land rushes, thousands of American farmers settled the dry belt in the years between 1906 and 1914. They prospered because there was adequate rainfall in this period. When drought conditions resumed, beginning during the Great War, the Americans rapidly abandoned the region and returned to the United States.

The Canadian reaction to the threatened arrival of hundreds if not thousands of black Americans from Oklahoma, driven out of the state by a combination of segregation and disenfranchisement in the early years of the twentieth century, is illustrative of the ways in which exclusionism worked in Canada. By the spring of 1910, enough blacks had arrived in Alberta to lead the Edmonton Board of Trade to pass a resolution calling the federal government's attention to the marked increase in black immigration to

Canada. The blacks were a most undesirable element, said the Board, and something needed to be done quickly.[16] The Canadian immigration service responded by attempting to use rigorous health examinations at the border to repel the new arrivals, but they were perfectly healthy. The successful arrival of several parties of blacks in western Canada led to an outburst of negative editorial opinion in the newspapers, as well as a concerted campaign by the Edmonton Board of Trade. Interior Minister Frank Oliver, whose newspaper supported the Edmonton initiative, recommended at the end of May 1911 that the cabinet by Order-in-Council bar black immigration to Canada for a period of one year. After initial reluctance, the cabinet passed such an order on 12 August 1911, claiming the Negro race was 'deemed unsuitable to the climate and requirements of Canada'.[17] The order was never enforced and was repealed several months later after a Canadian advertising campaign in Oklahoma had stilled the flow to the north.

THE HOME CHILDREN

Canadians were generally more willing to accept immigrants from the British Isles than from any other place, although there was some resentment against those who looked down their noses at the 'colonial cousins'. On the other hand, some Canadians objected to the activities of British philanthropists and philanthropic institutions in using Canada as a dumping ground for unwanted children of the urban poor. These children were recruited as cheap labour, chiefly for Canadian farms. The majority were young boys, but there was a substantial minority of girls as well. More than 50,000 of these 'home children' were imported into Canada before the Great War, most of them recruited in British slums. Many were encouraged to go by their parents; others were literally seized from parents and sent overseas 'for their own good'. The results were rather mixed, with the worst experiences suffered by children—both male and female—sent into rural

homes, where they were often treated cruelly by their supposed benefactors.

Perhaps the most colourful of the philanthropists involved in this child rescue venture was Thomas John Barnardo (1845–1900), who was personally responsible for sending more than 30,000 youngsters to Canada. Barnardo, a Dubliner by birth, had been rejected for missionary service in China because of his idiosyncrasies, and thus he poured his energy into child-saving near his mission house in East End London, according to legend sending his first boy to Ontario in 1871. Barnardo, always known as 'Doctor' Barnardo, actually scoured the streets of London for waifs and collected thousands of pounds for his charity work. He did not use the money to improve existing care, but constantly expanded his activities. In 1877 Barnardo's Homes for Destitute Girls and Boys were formally vindicated from accusations of abuse and mistreatment by a blue-ribbon committee of charity leaders after a summer of hearings. A few years later, in 1882, he decided to concentrate on sending the children to Canada, and in 1884 he established a huge (14 square miles) industrial farm at Russell, Manitoba, and an urban residence in Toronto. Despite a continual low level of complaints of abuse and victimization, he carried on with his work until his death in 1900.

OTHER NEW ARRIVALS

EUROPEAN CONTRACT WORKERS

Despite the emphasis on agricultural settlement and the assimilability of new immigrants, a number of Canadian corporations insisted on the need for willing workers. For these companies, headed by the railroads, British and Western European immigrants were not desirable because they complained about wages and working conditions; farmers left their jobs at harvest time. The CPR turned increasingly after 1901 to contract workers, often Italians, who could 'live for a year on the wages they earn in six months'.[18] These workers were supplied by labour agents in Europe. The railroads also liked Bulgarians and Poles for the same reason, claiming they were 'peculiarly suited for the work'. A massive national railway construction program between 1900 and 1914 by Canadian Pacific, Grand Trunk Pacific, and Canadian Northern was sustained basically by between 50,000 and 70,000 immigrant navvies per year. Mining corporations were equally attracted by Slavic and Italian workers. Over 110,000 Italians entered Canada before World War I, most of them contract labour. How many actually returned to Italy is not known. By 1913 over 300 labour agencies were recruiting over 200,000 workers abroad for labour in Canada per year. The majority of them were construction navvies. Several foreign governments protested the treatment of their nationals by labour agencies and Canadian employers, claiming that workers were being exploited by high agency fees and kickbacks, as well as by bad working conditions in construction camps. Undoubtedly, more Asian workers would have been recruited except for the extent of the public hostility to Asians. Both organized labour and nativist groups opposed the contract labourers as scabs and put enormous pressures on the Canadian government for exclusionist policies.

THE LEBANESE

The Chinese and the Japanese were not the only visible minorities to come to Canada in the years before the Great War. A small but constant stream of immigrants arrived from the Near East after 1900. Most came from Lebanon, which was officially under Turkish rule as a part of Syria before 1920. Thus these people usually appear as 'Syrians' in the early official records. The overall Lebanese diaspora was a substantial one, with over 15,000 people per year departing the country in the early years of the twentieth century for a variety of foreign destinations, including Canada, the United States, and Australia. The bulk of the Lebanese were Coptic Christians and Eastern Orthodox Christians and felt persecuted by the Ottoman Muslim authorities. These people also were searching for better economic opportunities. Those who came to Canada, at the rate of a few hundred a year, settled mainly in small numbers right across the Canadian provinces. Many did not choose to come to Canada, but instead were transported to North America by immigrant contractors who decided destinations according to the availability of ships. One of the curious footnotes to the sinking of the *Titanic* in 1912 was that the bulk of Canadian-bound steerage passengers on board the ill-fated liner were 'Syrians'. Once Lebanese immigrants had established themselves in a destination, they wrote home for their relatives. In Canada, the newcomers tended to become small businessmen. Many began life as itinerant peddlers pushing handcarts and wheelbarrows and worked their way up into small stores. Because there were not enough people or clergymen to establish Coptic or Orthodox churches, most of the arrivals gravitated to the churches with rituals closest to those which were familiar. For Coptic Christians this was often the Anglican Church; for Eastern Orthodox, frequently the Roman Catholic Church. The 1921 Canadian census showed 4,134 persons in Canada who had been born in Syria, distributed as follows:

PEI	27
NS	419
NB	233
Quebec	1,416
Ontario	1,467
Manitoba	122
Sask.	227
Alberta	146
BC	82

The Syrians were one of the few visible minorities that did not congregate in British Columbia; many went to the Atlantic region instead.[19]

■ Sikh sawmill workers in Burnaby, British Columbia, *c.* 1904. Royal BC Museum, BC Archives D-04655.

THE SIKHS

East Indians did go to British Columbia. Substantial East Indian immigration to British Columbia began only in the early years of the twentieth century. It occurred against the background of a growing movement for 'Oriental' exclusion in the province, with repercussions across Canada and, indeed, across the continent. However, the East Indian diaspora, while in Canadian terms directed chiefly to British Columbia, was both a continental and an international phenomenon. Economic conditions in India were leading large numbers of Indian workers to seek new sources of employment, and political conditions in India were leading a smaller but active number of Indian nationalists to look both for politi-

cal refuge and a new audience for their critique of the Raj. Most of the early East Indian immigrants to British Columbia were male Sikhs from the Jat Sikh community in the rural Punjab, chiefly from six districts of the central Punjab: Hoshiarpur, Guraspur, Jullundur, Ferozepur, Amritsar, and Ludhiana. As was usually the case, the path-breakers among immigrants came from an energetic community of peasant landholders who were well prepared for a highly calculated immigration. The males came to Canada as 'sojourners' seeking employment and intending to return to the Punjab when the remittances home from their labour had sufficiently improved the economic status of their families. Most were between the ages of 20 and 29. According to official Canadian statistics, the number of East

Indian adult females entering Canada over the period 1904–7 was 14, and the number of children 22, out of a total East Indian immigration of more than 5,000. This initial sojourning pattern was typical for immigration to Canada from Asia and was quite common among immigrants from other places, such as Italy and the Balkans.

By the 1890s, the Sikhs had begun spreading through the British Empire in search of employment. Their dispersal was to some extent facilitated by the British Empire itself, which employed Sikhs as show troops. One contingent of Sikh soldiers travelled via Vancouver to and from the coronation of Edward VII in 1902. Whether or not this incident publicized British Columbia as a possible destination, numbers of Sikhs began arriving in the province beginning in 1904. Sikh immigration was given a double boost by the introduction of a new Canadian head tax of $500 in 1904 on Chinese immigrants. The head tax both increased the job prospects for Sikhs and made available a carrying capacity aboard vessels from Asia that had previously dealt mainly with the Chinese. Local employers found them to be 'energetic workmen with a keen desire to learn'. Soon the white workers of British Columbia became concerned about the Sikhs, who readily found employment with lumber companies and railway contractors at wages substantially lower than that demanded by the natives.

Most of the more than 5,000 immigrants from India who arrived in British Columbia in the years between 1904 and 1907 came in 1906 and 1907. American evidence suggests that, almost without exception, Indians arriving in the United States in this period paid their own way. There is no reason to doubt that the situation in Canada was any different. Immigrating East Indians, therefore, were among the most prosperous members of their communities, a typical situation for immigrants to Canada. At the same time that the Canadian government was moving firmly towards exclusion, the East Indian community was beginning to become both organized and articulate. A Khalsa Diwan Society was organized

in Vancouver in 1907. A Committee for the Management of Sikh Gurdwaras and Temples was established by well-educated East Indians—not all of them Sikhs—soon afterwards. Equally important, Indian revolutionary agitators had begun their work, initially in the United States but soon extending to Canada. Separating the activities of Indian nationalists into those directed at abuses at home and those concerned with treatment of immigrants abroad is not easy and perhaps futile. An inability to rouse the local Sikhs was characteristic of the agitators, who often complained of the subservience or apathy of the immigrant community. But in the emergence of even the threat of violence involving the immigrant community, the Sikhs had introduced something new into Canada. For the most part, immigrants before this had left their domestic agitations behind when they came to Canada.

The Swadesh Sevak Home was begun by Guran Dittar Kumar in Vancouver in 1909. It was alleged to be a rendezvous and residence for revolutionaries. Kumar's periodical, 'Swadesh Sevak', published in Vancouver, was banned by the Indian government. The 'United India House' was opened in Vancouver in 1910; its leaders were interested in protesting the new immigration regulations. The Vancouver Sikh temple in 1912 agreed to send a deputation to Victoria, Ottawa, London, and India to take up the case of Indians in Canada. This delegation presented its arguments to the Indian National Congress and, when they returned to Vancouver, the government attempted unsuccessfully to deport them. The battle for Canadian Sikhs had become part of the Indian nationalist agitation. Much of our knowledge about the nationalists comes from information collected by police undercover agents such as William Charles Hopkinson in Vancouver, and must be understood in this context. Hopkinson was convinced that the leading revolutionaries were advocates of violence, prepared to employ terrorism in support of their goals. He was responsible for the attention given by government to the revolutionary agitator Har Dayal in 1913.

THE HINDUS

In 1914 W.D. Scott, formerly federal Superintendent of Immigration, contributed a chapter on immigration to *Canada and Its Provinces: A History of the Canadian People and Their Institutions.* This excerpt comes from this chapter.

One of the different immigration problems which from time to time have faced the Dominion, that of the influx of Hindus appeared for a time to be possibly the most serious. This movement commenced in 1905. The arrivals up to the close of the fiscal year 1911–12 were 5,203. British Columbia, the nearest province to the Orient and the one possessing the climate most closely resembling that of their native land, was the ultimate destination of these unwelcome comers, and British Columbia was not slow in expressing her disapproval of them. 'A White Canada' was her cry. That these immigrants were British subjects; that many had fought for the Empire; that many expressed their willingness to do so again should occasion arise—all this in no way lessened the antipathy of the white race towards them.

True, there were some imperialists who, recognizing in the Hindus subjects of the same sovereign, argued that they were entitled to enter the Dominion as a matter of right, and that any action towards restricting their movements from one part of the British domains to another would endanger the existence of the Empire. But the counsels of the advocates of 'A White Canada' finally prevailed, and an order-in-council was passed providing that persons of Asiatic origin, other than Chinese and Japanese, must have in their possession $200 at the time of landing in Canada. This came into force in 1908, and the numbers arriving immediately dropped from 2,623 in that year to almost nothing.

The Hindus who came to Canada were largely from the Punjab and, physically, were a fine set of men. The term Hindu as here applied is a misnomer, denoting as it does a religious sect rather than a race of people. In religion they were divided, some being Hindus, other Buddhists and others Mohammedans. It is doubtful whether with their constitutions, suitable for the country and climate from which they came, they will ever become thoroughly acclimatized in Canada. Pneumonia and pulmonary troubles have already resulted in the death of no small numbers. Their bodies were disposed of by cremation, the burial method of their own country; possibly this is the only one of their customs which might with advantage be adopted.

Saw-mills and railway construction work offered employment to the Hindus. While they were able at most times to secure employment, it was at a lower rate than that paid to white men or even to Japanese or Chinese. They were unaccustomed to Canadian methods, and though able to speak a little English were slow to learn more. Their greatest disadvantage, however, is their caste system, which prevents them from eating and sometimes even from working with white men, or even with others of their own race who belong to a different social scale—for this is practically the meaning of caste. Now that the influx is checked the Hindu problem is ended.

In May of 1914 the Japanese vessel *Komagata Maru* arrived in Vancouver harbour with 376 passengers aboard. Of these, 165 had boarded at Hong Kong, 111 at Shanghai, 86 at Moji, and 14 at Yokohama; 340 of the passengers were Sikhs. The expedition had originated with a Punjabi-born contractor, Baba Gurdit Singh, supported by Indian nationalists from Hong

■ Sikhs aboard the *Komagata Maru*, 1914. Gurdit Singh is on the left in the light-coloured suit. Vancouver Public Library 623.

Kong. It was motivated by a mixture of humanitarianism, profit-making, and nationalism. The Canadian regulations to which Indian immigration were subject were patently exclusionist and inequitable. The head tax did not apply to European immigrants, and the 'continuous voyage' requirement could not ever be met since no vessels sailed directly from India to Canada. Singh expected that the Canadians would overlook the continuous voyage requirement when they were actually at the dock in Vancouver, and he thought that the local East Indian community would raise the money for the head tax and for the ship's charter. He was right on the second count but wrong on the first.

The voyage across the Pacific of the *Komagata Maru* (almost no one calls the vessel by the name

given it by Gurdit Singh—'Guru Nanak Jahaz') was long and difficult. The Canadian government—backed by Vancouver municipal authorities and the British Columbia government, both of which became quite hysterical over the entire business—refused to allow most of the passengers to land, conditions on board the ship deteriorated rapidly, and the incident quickly became an international one. The Canadian government seriously contemplated kidnapping the passengers to return them to India, while the passengers equally seriously contemplated a mass escape into Vancouver. The local courts refused to hear a test case and Singh refused to order the vessel to depart. Canadian immigration authorities attempted to storm the ship by force, but failed abysmally. Eventually the vessel sailed out of Vancouver harbour under naval escort and returned to India, a graphic symbol of a Canadian racially exclusionist policy that is still very powerful today.

The *Komagata Maru* has quietly entered into the textbooks and reference works in Canadian history over the past few years, becoming an incident familiar to at least some Canadians. But two significant aftermaths of the affair are almost totally unknown among Canadians at large: the riots at Budge Budge in India in 1914, and the execution of Mewa Singh in 1915. The Budge Budge affair appears to have originated in a heavy-handed attempt by the Raj government of Bengal to force the passengers of the *Komagata Maru* against their will back to their villages, where they would have found no employment. A committee of inquiry naturally laid all the blame for the riots on Gurdit Singh and the passengers, who were said to be heavily armed. The inquiry did provide a good deal of further evidence on the composition of the passengers, a subject hitherto shrouded in much mystery. The riots themselves provided a set of Indian martyrs to the oppression of British rule in India.

As for the execution in Canada of Mewa Singh, it came at the end of a long and complicated series of events. A police informer named Bela Singh was arrested in September 1914 for shooting several Sikhs in the gurdwara. While he was awaiting trial, fellow police informer William Hopkinson was shot in the provincial courthouse by a man named Mewa Singh, who immediately surrendered to police and confessed his guilt, saying that he had taken Hopkinson's life in order to publicize the spy's behaviour. Although Canadian officials doubted that Singh had acted on his own, he was summarily tried within 10 days of the shooting and easily found guilty; there was no defence. Soon afterwards, Bela Singh was acquitted by a judge and jury, while Mewa Singh was hanged on 11 January 1915. The date of his death was for many years commemorated in the Indian community of British Columbia.

The events of 1914 in one sense provided their own closure. But they were also quickly subsumed in the War to End All Wars. In any event, the death of Mewa Singh can be seen both as ending the first period of East Indian immigration to Canada and as exemplifying the ways in which the Sikh history in Canada was intertwined with violence.

RACIAL EXCLUSION

The growth of Canada before the Great War was not accomplished without considerable trauma. Disquieted Canadians might have looked almost anywhere for answers to the question of what had gone wrong. Many, however, focused on the growing number of newcomers to Canada as the main source of trouble. Immigrants and immigration policy became convenient scapegoats for the nation's woes.

'Race regeneration' was one of the central themes—often unspoken—of the reform movement to be discussed in detail in Chapter 8. A related theme was the call for social purity, sometimes through restrictions on the consumption of alcoholic beverages, but also through concerted campaigns against prostitution, venereal disease, and sexual exploitation of various kinds. The desire for racial regeneration and the restoration of social purity was one of the major links between racial attitudes in Canada and the introduction of restrictive immigration laws in this period. The policy of the Canadian government was to keep 'undesirables' out of the country. In 1914, former Superintendent of Immigration W.D. Scott summarized 'undesirability' under three heads:

1. Those physically, mentally or morally unfit whose exclusion is provided for by the immigration act.
2. Those belonging to nationalities unlikely to assimilate and who, consequently, prevent the building up of a united nation of people of similar customs and ideals.
3. Those who from their mode of life and occupations are likely to crowd into urban centres and bring about a state of congestion

which might result in unemployment and a lowering of the standard of Canadian national life.[20]

Not only federal action was involved with restrictions against the visible minorities from Asia, however. Provincial governments—especially in British Columbia—introduced their own restrictions. As early as 1884, Chinese were prohibited from acquiring Crown lands. In 1890 they were prevented from working underground in mines, and by 1897 they could not be hired on public works. In 1907, the British Columbia legislature disenfranchised nationals of China, Japan, and Imperial India. This effectively prevented such nationals from serving in municipal office, on school boards, and on juries, since such service was based on the provincial voters' lists. These restrictions were generally reaffirmed in 1920.

CONCLUSION

The Canadian record on immigration was, to say the least, a mixed one between 1867 and 1914.

Millions of newcomers were allowed into the country, mainly from the British Isles but also from a variety of other sources in Europe and Asia. For some peoples there was an 'open door' policy. But a tension always existed between the nation's need for immigrants to help develop the country and serve as a source for labour and its reluctance to accept immigrants without reference to their background or circumstances. Almost all Canadians wanted immigration, but few wanted to deal with immigrants whose language was strange, whose customs were different, whose education was deficient—and whose skin colour was not the same as that of the vast majority. British Columbia and Quebec led the way in opposing the open admission of large numbers of immigrants. Even J.S. Woodsworth, one of the major champions of a warm welcome for *Strangers within Our Gates*—as his 1909 study of immigration policy was called—insisted on the exclusion of 'essentially non-assimilable elements'.

SHORT BIBLIOGRAPHY

Avery, Donald. *Reluctant Host: Canada's Response to Immigrant Workers, 1896–1994*. Toronto, 1995. An important survey, most notably about contract workers.

Barrier, N. Gerald, and Verne A. Dusenbery, eds. *The Sikh Diaspora: Migration and the Experience Beyond Punjab*. Delhi, 1989. A useful study.

Johnston, Hugh. *The Voyage of the Komagata Maru: The Sikh Challenge to Canada's Colour Bar*. Delhi, 1979. A well-balanced account of this contentious affair.

Kelley, Ninette, and Michael Trebilcock. *The Making of the Mosaic: A History of Canadian Immigration Policy*. Toronto, 1998. Perhaps the best book on the development of immigration policy.

Knowles, Valerie, *Strangers at Our Gates: Canadian Immigration and Immigration Policy, 1540–1997*, rev. edn. Toronto, 1997. An important survey designed for the popular market.

Macdonald, Norman. *Canada: Immigration and Colonization 1841–1903*. Toronto, 1970. The best attempt to relate immigration to settlement.

Magosci, Paul Robert, ed. *Encyclopedia of Canada's Peoples*. Toronto, 1999. Not quite definitive, but irreplaceable.

Petryshyn, Jaroslav. *Peasants in the Promised Land: Canada and the Ukrainians, 1891–1914*. Toronto, 1985. A scholarly treatment.

Roy, Patricia. *A White Man's Province: British Columbia Politicians and Chinese and Japanese Immigration, 1858–1914*. Vancouver, 1989. The argument for socio-economic explanations of the rise of racism in BC.

Scott, W.D. *Canada and Its Provinces: A History of the Canadian People and Their Institutions by One Hundred Associates*, Adam Shortt and Arthur C. Doughty, general eds. Toronto, 1914, vol. 7. A survey of immigration to Canada before 1914 by the former Dominion Superintendent of Immigration.

Shepard, R. Bruce. *Deemed Unsuitable: Blacks from Oklahoma Move to the Canadian Prairies in Search of Equality in the Early 20th Century Only to Find Racism in Their New Home.* Toronto, 1997. An angry look at a minor episode.

Singh, Narindar. *Canadian Sikhs: History, Religion, and Culture of Sikhs in North America.* Ottawa, 1994. An important book.

Ward, W. Peter. *White Canada Forever: Popular Attitudes and Public Policy towards Orientals in British Columbia.* Montreal, 1990. Explains racism in terms of deep-seated colour prejudice.

STUDY QUESTIONS

1. Why was Canada so hostile to immigrants from Asia?
2. Was assimilation the only possible outcome of the immigration experience? Why?
3. Did W.D. Smith want Hindus in Canada?
4. Would you have supported an 'open door' policy towards immigration in 1900?

CHAPTER SEVEN

Politics and the National Question, 1885–1914

At least one observer of Canada's national political scene in the decades around the turn of the twentieth century saw it as oddly lacking in ideological issues and debates. These issues may not have been reflected in the platforms of the national parties, but in fact some of the most serious ideological questions ever to confront Canadians and their political culture were debated during those years. Chief among them was the so-called Canadian Question. Bearing in various ways on the future of the young nation, this question was in part a debate between those who sought to keep Canada within the British Empire and those who wanted it to assume full sovereignty. But it also involved some who did not believe that Canada could or should be a nation at all, and others who thought it should become part of the United States. Not surprisingly, these questions also surfaced during another round of massive immigration, discussed in Chapter 6. Among the related questions that made their way into the debate were the future of French Canadians within an evolving Anglo-American country and the attitude that Canada would take towards the admission of immigrants. At the same time, questions about the nature of the nation and its allegiances were reflected in Canadian military policy and behaviour. Debate and disagreement over imperialism,

Anglo-French relations, and immigration—the three strands were loosely if inextricably linked—kept political Canada bubbling from the late 1880s to the beginning of the Great War.

THE NATURE OF CANADIAN PARTY POLITICS

In 1906 a young French scholar named André Siegfried published a book that was translated the following year as *The Race Question in Canada*. A cogent study of the nation based on three visits—the most recent one during the election of 1904—it presented a revealing portrait of the country's two 'races', French and English, and political life, combining classically French lucidity and wit with anticlerical attitudes that only an outsider (in this case a French Protestant) could have expressed. Accustomed as Siegfried was to the complex politics of the Third Republic, in which ideologically based parties thrived, he found Canadian national politics difficult to fathom. Apparently without ideological foundation, Canadian parties seemed to be little more than machines 'for winning elections':

> In the absence of ideas or doctrines to divide the voters, there remain only questions of material interest, collective or individual. Against their

TIMELINE

1882

Privy Council Judicial Committee decides in favour of provinces in fight over provincial boundaries.

1888

Quebec Assembly passes Jesuits' Estate Act.

1889

Equal Rights Association founded in Ontario.

1890

Manitoba government abolishes public funding for confessional schools, beginning Manitoba Schools Question.

1891

Death of Sir John A. Macdonald. Goldwin Smith publishes *Canada and the Canadian Question*.

1896

Wilfrid Laurier becomes Prime Minister.

1899

Canada agrees to send volunteers to South Africa. Bourassa breaks with Laurier.

1904

Sara Jeannette Duncan publishes *The Imperialist*.

1906

André Siegfried publishes *The Race Question in Canada*.

1907

Borden presents 'Halifax Platform'. Fédération Nationale Saint-Jean-Baptiste founded.

1910

Naval debate in House of Commons.

1911

Laurier defeated in complex election; replaced by Borden.

1912

Regulation 17 passed in Ontario.

pressure the candidate cannot maintain his integrity, for he knows that his opponents will not show the same self-restraint. The result is that the same promises are made on both sides, following an absolutely identical conception of the meaning of power. Posed in this way, the issue of an election manifestly changes. Whoever may be the winner, everyone knows that the country will be administered in the same way, or almost the same.[1]

Only occasionally, according to Siegfried, when 'some great wave of opinion sweeps over the whole country', did Canadian politics escape 'its sordid preoccupations of patronage or connection'. Otherwise Canadian politicians seemed to do their best to avoid confrontations. Indeed, he wrote, 'the parties borrow one another's politics periodically, displaying a coolness in this process that would disconcert us Europeans.'

Perhaps part of the reason Canadian political leaders so assiduously sought consensus was the sheer magnitude of the potential for conflict in the new nation. In 1904 the Canadian educator James Cappon suggested as much. Discussing

the role of the party system as it currently operated, Cappon speculated on what would become
of Canada in its absence. Would not the result,
he asked, be

> the unchecked conflict of class interests, provin-
> cial interests, religious interests, the free play of
> jealousy and prejudice? At present all these antag-
> onisms are to a great extent modified and con-
> trolled by the party system of government and a
> certain amount of moderation and mutual under-
> standing. What other system could do that work
> at present? It is useful training for nations com-
> posed of heterogeneous elements; it has really cre-
> ated our national unity, and it produces probably
> the best and clearest expression of national opin-
> ion and will at which we could arrive. And it
> remains to be seen whether Canada is capable of
> making it a good deal better than it is at present.[2]

Although the Fathers of Confederation had
not written political parties into the Canadian
Constitution, by the mid-1880s a two-party system had evolved at both the federal and provincial levels (at least east of Manitoba) that would
survive virtually unchanged until World War I.
Indeed, this period was in many respects the
Golden Age of Canadian Party Politics, an era in
which party affiliations were taken seriously, and
being a 'Liberal' or a 'Conservative' was a lifetime
commitment passed on from father to son. The
seeming vitality of the two-party system disguised, to some degree, the extent of underlying
tensions within the expanding Canadian federation, but until 1914 the traditional parties
seemed flexible enough to contain the various
conflicting currents.

As Siegfried argued, both national parties
had developed consensual styles capable of holding a vast array of differing ideological opinions,
as well as various sectional and interest groups.
Reformers and Tories, regionalists and nationalists, farmers and businessmen could all coexist.
Individuals from all regions and all walks of life
could be found within each of the parties. The
key that allowed the parties to function—and
hold the allegiances of their widely varied members—was in large part to be found in the power
of patronage. The movement to reform government service along meritocratic lines was somewhat slow to develop in Canada, partly because
the process of industrialization lagged behind that
in Great Britain and the United States and partly
because the parties' supporters continued to see
them as sources of employment. Both national
parties were firmly committed, when in office, to
distributing honours and jobs to their leading
supporters, employing careful systems of appor-
tionment to adherents whose qualifications were
judged solely in terms of political service and loyalty. A 1907–8 Royal Commission on the public
service outside Ottawa concluded that, 'As a rule,
. . . politics enter into every appointment and
politicians on the spot interest themselves not
only in the appointments but the subsequent promotion of the officers. . . . [T]he politics of the
party is of greater importance in making appointments and promotions than the public interests of
the Dominion.'[3] The patronage system worked
similarly for both parties, with members of
Parliament making the actual decisions based on
recommendations from local party organizations.
Even those who did not seek patronage in the
form of appointments but merely wanted assistance of some kind from their MPs often invoked
party loyalty when making their requests. Only
on the very eve of World War I were serious questions raised about the efficacy of such a system.

The patronage system chiefly rewarded
those members of the Canadian business and
professional elites (most of whom came from the
upper reaches of the so-called middle class) who
ran the two political parties. It tended to diminish ideological and regional differences, offering
French Canadians their own opportunities for
advancement. Patronage thus encouraged a stable party system in which matters of principle
were less important than division of the spoils of
victory; in this way many festering problems
could be conveniently ignored.

Another aspect of Canadian politics in this period that was much the same for English and French Canadians was the complex relationship between the federal and provincial governments, and indeed between the federal and provincial wings of the two major Canadian parties. Sir John A. Macdonald's centralizing vision of the nation had met with opposition from the provinces, expressed initially by Sir Oliver Mowat, the Liberal Premier of Ontario from 1872 to 1896, who was determined that the provinces should remain important political units. Certainly his province was too rich and powerful to submit to federal domination. Seeking provincial control over economic development, Mowat successfully confronted the federal government in 1882 over the question of provincial boundaries, persuading the Judicial Committee of the British Privy Council (the court of last resort in Canada until 1949, when Canada's own Supreme Court, established in 1875, finally took on the role) to reject a federal proposal to turn the territory west of Lake Superior over to Manitoba. Exulting in his success in asserting provincial rights over a wide range of responsibilities and in extending provincial boundaries, Mowat told one audience in Niagara Falls: 'I rejoice to know that the one great cause, the principal cause of your enthusiasm, is that you love Ontario as I love it. The display that you have made this night shows that you are for Ontario, and that you are for those who maintain Ontario's cause.'[4] Such enthusiasm suggests an alternative nationalism based on identification with the province. Other provinces were forced to bargain with the federal government for 'better terms', as did W.S. Fielding's Liberal government in Nova Scotia in 1886 and 1887 in a search for some financial advantages for the province, but Ontario consistently held out for a constitutional arrangement in which the provinces would have a veto. In so doing, Mowat helped to elaborate the 'compact' view of Confederation, according to which each province was an equal partner with Ottawa in the constitutional arrangement. By and large, Canadian

■ Oliver Mowat, *c.* 1873. LAC, PA-28631.

historians over the years have been far more sympathetic to the centralist position. Nevertheless, after the constitutional debates of recent years, there is now considerably more support for the 'compact' view than there was in the past.[5]

Provincial parties of the opposite stripe to the party in power in Ottawa were often in a better position to confront the federal government because they were not tied to or associated with it. Canadians were not slow to appreciate this point and quickly established two enduring patterns in Canadian politics at the provincial level: first, voters complain about Ottawa, then they elect the provincial party that promises to defend provincial interests against the federal government. A succession of Ontario Conservative leaders complained that the patronage of the Macdonald government was not enough to compensate their party for the damage done by its

■ Sir Wilfrid Laurier campaigning, 26 Oct. 1908. LAC, C-932.

in 1905, they would only rarely relinquish it over the next century.

One of the great ironies of Confederation was that Quebec remained the cornerstone region upon which national political success had to be built. A national party had to win in Quebec while also picking up sufficient strength in the other provinces to put together a majority. Until the death of Macdonald in 1891, the Conservative Party had successfully appealed to French Canadians with a judicious combination of political patronage and continuing national leadership. But even before Macdonald's death, the beginnings of a shift had become evident— notably in 1885, when Louis Riel was executed for treason, despite fierce opposition from Quebec. The shift became definitive in 1896, when Laurier was selected as the national 'chief/chef'. Laurier carefully put together a coalition of provincial Liberal parties, and his notions of consensus were considerably more nuanced than those of Macdonald. His agonizing over the Manitoba Schools Question of the early 1890s—when his distaste for a unilingual language policy for Manitoba schools came into conflict with his support for the right of provinces to run affairs within their general mandate—was a pure reflection of the Laurier mind, which gravitated to conciliation. 'My object', he wrote in 1904, 'is to consolidate Confederation, and to bring our people, long estranged from each other, gradually to become a nation. This is the supreme issue. Everything else is subordinate to that idea.'[6] Laurier saw national unity in terms of national harmony and considered a bicultural state essential. He would manage to survive politically on the strength of a wave of national prosperity, until 1911, when his government was voted out of office by electors who apparently rejected his platform of establishing a Canadian navy and limited free trade with the United States. Even Quebec returned a minority of Liberals, and Ontario, in Laurier's word, 'went solid against us'.

identification with Ottawa. On the question of provincial rights, which Mowat had made into a crucial and ongoing issue, the Ontario Tories were disadvantaged. Mowat's Liberals left their provincial opponents the dubious choice of supporting the federal government or splitting the party. Moreover, the increasing hostility within Ontario to French Canada, exemplified by the Anglo-Protestant response to the Riel uprising of 1885, could not be harnessed by the provincial Tories while Macdonald's government relied on Quebec support. Only with the success of the Liberals under Wilfrid Laurier in 1896 were the Ontario Tories freed from the burden of a Conservative government in Ottawa, and they moved quickly to dissociate themselves from the national politicians; taking power in the province

Laurier's Liberals were succeeded in 1911 by the Conservatives under Robert Borden, who used traditional means (including bribery) to split the Quebec vote and almost swept Ontario. Borden's victory was a triumph for supporters of Canada's imperial connection and advocates of certain public reforms—in both cases, mainly the Anglo-Protestant middle class of Ontario. In short, Borden represented the 'progressive', reform-oriented forces of Anglo-Canadian society that had been marshalling strength since the mid-1880s. In this sense, Laurier's conciliatory policies had been a check on an important underlying current of Canadian public affairs in the 30 years before the war. Borden's victory began the process of the political isolation of French Canada.

CANADIAN IMPERIALISM AND ITS OPPONENTS

Years of internal and external crises had followed Confederation. Against a backdrop of continuing federal–provincial struggle for control of economic development, a series of well-publicized confrontations suggested an equally serious cultural struggle: the New Brunswick Schools Question of the 1870s, the Riel uprising of 1885, the rise of the anti-Catholic Equal Rights Association in Ontario (organized in 1889 in response to Quebec's Jesuit Estates Act[7]), and the notorious Manitoba Schools Question of the 1890s. The increasing power of the United States sparked increasing fear of what some Americans saw as its 'Manifest Destiny' to expand and take over the entire continent, especially after the Spanish-American War of 1898. A new flood of immigrants, particularly into the developing western region, brought a new infusion of 'British' sentiment to the nation, along with an 'alien' population that was neither French nor British in origin that settled mainly in the Prairie provinces.

As Britishness sought ways of expressing itself in Canada, 'Little England' sentiment in Great Britain itself began to fade. Anti-colonial attitudes gradually disappeared as the world's shopkeeper realized that it was impossible to guarantee raw materials and markets on the basis of economic relations alone. Simultaneously, British overseas adventurers found that windfall profits could be made by exploiting 'underdeveloped' regions, especially in Africa and in Asia. Great Britain would increasingly expect her major 'settlement colonies'—Canada, the Australian states (which would not federate until 1901), and New Zealand—to assist her militarily, and just before the turn of the century, Joseph Chamberlain at the Colonial Office would begin to advocate that these colonies be joined together in some pan-Britannic political and economic union, the so-called 'Imperial Federation'.

Against this backdrop of continuing internal dissension (among political parties, regions, and 'races') and growing imperial pressure, a number of Canadians from both the pro- and anti-imperialist camps were beginning to speak and write about the problems facing Canada. That the arguments presented by these journalists, pamphleteers, and editorialists tended to generate more heat than light will surprise no one who has lived through more recent discussions of free trade, constitutional change, and globalization. But the absence of careful argumentation did not mean that the questions discussed were not serious ones.

THE IMPERIALISTS

The standard imperialist view was promulgated by men from central Canada and the Maritime provinces. The leading spokesmen for the cause were George Denison, George Parkin, George Monro Grant, Charles G.D. Roberts, Stephen Leacock, and the Reverend C.W. Gordon (aka the novelist 'Ralph Connor'). Part of the impulse behind their efforts was simply conservative, rooted in their desire to preserve the Loyalist traditions that were still strong in eastern Canada. They saw no inconsistency between promoting on the one hand Canadian nationhood and on the other the nation's membership in a larger British Empire. 'I am an Imperialist', argued Stephen Leacock in 1907, 'because I will not be

GREATER CANADA: AN APPEAL

In 1907 Stephen Leacock wrote passionately about imperialism in the McGill *University Magazine.*

. . . To many people in Canada this imperialism is a tainted word. It is too much associated with a truckling subservience to English people and English ideas and the silly swagger of the hop-o'-my-thumb junior officer. But there is and must be for the true future of our country, a higher and more real imperialism than this—the imperialism of the plain man at the plough and the clerk in the counting house. The imperialism of any decent citizen that demands for this country its proper place in the councils of the Empire and in the destiny of the world. In this sense, imperialism means but the realization of a Greater Canada, the recognition of a wider citizenship.

I, that write these lines, am an Imperialist because I will not be a Colonial. This Colonial status is a worn-out by-gone thing. The sense and feeling of it has become harmful to us. It limits the ideas, and circumscribes the patriotism of our people. It impairs the mental vigor and narrows the outlook of those that are reared and educated in our midst. The English boy reads of England's history and its glories as his own; it is his navy that fought at Camperdown and Trafalgar, *his* people that have held fast their twenty miles of sea eight hundred years against a continent. He learns at his fireside and at his school, among his elders and his contemporaries, to regard all this as part of himself; something that he, as a fighting man, may one day uphold, something for which as a plain citizen he shall every day gladly pay, something for which in any capacity it may one day be his high privilege to die. How little of this in Canada! Our paltry policy teaches the Canadian boy to detach himself from the England of the past, to forget that Camperdown and Copenhagen and the Nile are ours as much as theirs, that the navy of the Empire is ours too, ours in its history of the past, ours in its safe-guard of the present. . . .

Thus stands the case. Thus stands the question of the future of Canada. Find us something other than mere colonial stagnation, something sounder than independence, nobler than annexation, greater in purpose than a Little Canada. Find us a way. Build us a plan, that shall make us, in hope at least, an Empire Permanent and Indivisible.

SOURCE: *The University Magazine* 6 (June 1907): 132–4.

a Colonial. This Colonial status is a worn-out, by-gone thing.'[8] What Leacock sought, he said, was 'something other than mere colonial stagnation, something sounder than independence, nobler than annexation, greater in purpose than a Little Canada'. This sort of pan-Britannic nationalism was common to all the 'white-settlement' former colonies of the British Empire. It expressed itself concretely in the form of demands for Imperial Federation, which George Monro Grant, the principal of Queen's University, defined in 1890 as 'a union between the Mother Country and Canada that would give Canada not only the present full management of its own affairs, but a fair share of the management and responsibilities of common affairs'.[9]

The imperialists were committed to the idea of a single national identity emerging initially out of Confederation and continuing to develop in the process of westward expansion, and they hoped that their banner would be one under which Canadians could unite. Canada Firster Charles Mair expressed this idea as early as 1870: 'Thank God there is such a thing at last as a

GERMANS　ICELANDERS　SCOTCHMEN　ENGLISHMEN　AMERICANS　FRENCHMEN　SCANDINAVIANS
BELGIANS　RUSSIANS　AUSTRIANS　IRISHMEN

THE MAPLE LEAF　FOR EVER

CANADA

"NOW THEN, ALL TOGETHER"!

■ 'Now Then, All Together!' In this cartoon from the Liberal election pamphlet *Laurier Does Things* (1904), Jack Canuck conducts a chorus of stereotyped immigrants. Among the groups not represented are Asians, blacks, Italians, and women. Saskatchewan Archives Board, R-A 12402.

purely national feeling in Canada. There is a young and vigorous race coming to the front, entirely in earnest, and which is no longer English, Scotch or Irish, but thoroughly and distinctly Canadian.'[10] The three 'old' nationalities that Mair referred to indicate how profoundly anglocentric his vision of Canada remained. Newcomers were acceptable, so long as they were prepared to assimilate to the English-speaking and Protestant norm. Not only did most imperialists support the concept of English-only schools for western Canada, but many secretly admired the Americans for their displays of nationalism. In his 1917 novel *The Major*, Ralph Connor allowed one of his Canadian characters to advocate 'flag-flapping' because it promoted a common identity

for 'foreigners, Ruthenians, Russians, Germans, Poles'. Here the narrator describes a 'flag-saluting' ceremony he witnessed in Oregon:

A kid with Yiddish written all over his face was chosen to carry in the flag, attended by a bodyguard for the colours, and believe me they appeared as proud as Punch of the honour. They placed the flag in position, sang a hymn, had a prayer, and then every kid, at a signal, shot out his right hand toward the flag held aloft by the Yiddish colour-bearer and pledged himself, heart, and soul, and body, to his flag and his country. The ceremony closed with the singing of the national hymn, mighty poor poetry and mighty hard to sing, but do you know that listening to those kids and watching their foreign faces I found myself with tears in my eyes and swallowing like a darn fool.[11]

The racism in this passage is as clear as the nationalism.

Philosophically, Anglo-Canadians born in the first half of the nineteenth century generally tended towards either utilitarianism ('the greatest good for the greatest number') or social Darwinism' (Darwin's theory of natural selection—or 'survival of the fittest'—applied to human society). By the latter part of the century, however, many thoughtful people throughout North America and Europe were embracing a more idealistic philosophy centred on duty and responsibility and emphasized the needs of the community over those of the individual. The prevailing philosophy in both Canadian and British universities in the last quarter of the nineteenth century, idealism was the perfect underpinning for a generation of paternalistic imperialists who exalted British civilization and political progress and believed that every member of that Empire had a duty to promote its principles. As George M. Grant wrote in 1890:

> The Empire to which we belong is admittedly the greatest the world has ever seen. In it, the rights of all men are sacred and the rights of great men are also sacred. It is world-wide and therefore offers most opportunities for all kinds of noblest service to humanity, through the serving of fellow-citizens in every quarter of the globe. . . . Of the few great nations of the future the English-speaking people is destined, if we are only true to ourselves, to be the greatest, simply because it represents most fully the highest political and spiritual life that humanity has yet realized.[12]

How could one be satisfied with less?

THE ANTI-IMPERIALISTS

Unfortunately for the imperialists, a good many Canadians were not convinced by their arguments. Of several anti-imperialist positions in existence in Canada around the end of the nineteenth century, one was the pro-American stance advocated by the British-born political journalist (and former Regius Professor of History at Oxford) Goldwin Smith, who had settled in Canada in 1871. Smith was an anti-statist liberal, a proponent of free trade with utilitarian leanings and no sympathy for the British Empire. He was a great admirer of the United States, however, and after a brief flirtation with Canada First he became persuaded that Canada's future lay in a continental union with the Americans. A firm believer in the 'invisible hand' of the market, Smith opposed not only economic regulation but any interference with natural processes. In 1878 he argued that four forces would ultimately lead to the severance of the political connection between Canada and Britain: 'distance, divergence of interest, divergence of political character and the attraction of the great mass of English speaking people which adjoins us on this continent'.[13] His most famous formulation of his position, however, came in *Canada and the Canadian Question* (1891). Arguing on the one hand that Canada had little in common with other members of the British Empire (such as 'an Asiatic dominion extending over two hundred and fifty millions of Hindoos [and] a group of West Indian Islands full of emancipated negro slaves'[14]) and on the other that the geography of North America meant that the continent was Canada's natural market, he concluded by advocating 'Commercial Union' with the United States. Smith has always been labelled an 'anti-imperialist', but a persuasive case could be made for his being merely an anti-British imperialist—one who would simply prefer to see Canada absorbed into the American empire. Certainly his arguments were pragmatic rather than abstract, and quite different from those of the mainstream of anti-imperialists, who emphasized the need for Canada to mature in the direction of eventual independence and sovereignty. Many Canadians were troubled by the idea of annexation to the

JOHN S. EWART ON THE 'KINGDOM OF CANADA'

In 1908 the Manitoba lawyer John S. Ewart wrote with reason and, at times, a touch of passion on the subject of Canada's independence. In the following passage he employs both semantic and geographical arguments.

I claim independence of the Parliament of Great Britain; and I object, therefore, to Canada being called a 'dominion,' for the word implies subjection. Further, I object to being called a 'British dominion,' for I assert that Canada belongs, not to the British, but to Canadians (saving always allegiance to the King). And I resent being lumped with Trinidad, and Guiana, and Barbados, as 'British Dominions beyond the Seas.' Canada, I desire to remark, is on this side of the seas—of the two largest seas in the world, and it stretches across, a few thousand miles or so, from one of them to the other. Secondly, I claim the word 'kingdom,' because the assertion of political equality necessarily involves the assumption of an equal title. Until we have that, we shall be thought of, and shall probably be, subordinate, and colonial, and somebody's dominions, some thousands of miles in more or less definite direction, beyond the seas.

SOURCE: John S. Ewart, *The Kingdom of Canada* (Toronto: Morang, 1908), 27-8.

US, but no group found the prospect more frightening than the Quebec clergy, who, according to André Siegfried, 'realize[d] that on the day the province should be swept into the American vortex there would be an end to its old isolation, and it would be overwhelmed by the torrent of new ideas. It would mean the end of Catholic supremacy in this corner of the world, perhaps a deathblow to the French race in Canada.'[15]

Among the Anglo-Canadian advocates of full Canadian sovereignty was the lawyer John S. Ewart. Born in Canada West in 1849, he was largely self-educated before entering Osgoode Hall Law School in the late 1870s, and moved to Manitoba in 1881. There he abandoned his Presbyterian roots for the Anglican Church, to which he was attracted by its tolerance and lack of doctrinal rigour. Ewart rejected moral absolutes and had little patience for abstract arguments. In the 1890s he made a public reputation as the leading lawyer for Manitoba's French-speaking Catholic minority in their constitutional appeals connected with the Manitoba School Question. His arguments for independence, as he presented them in 1908, tended to be legalistic, based on the constitutional provisions of the BNA Act. Like Stephen Leacock, he found colonial status degrading, for 'Colony implies inferiority—inferiority in culture, inferiority in wealth, inferiority in government, inferiority in foreign relations, inferiority and subordination.'[16] He did not advocate a violent breaking of the imperial connection, but envisioned a gradual evolution through which the government in Ottawa would eventually gain equal standing with the one in Westminster.

In contrast to the idealistic imperialists, Ewart did not believe that Canada had any responsibility to shoulder the burdens of Empire. It had ceased in 1867 to be a subordinate state, and all that remained was 'the semblance and appearance of subordination'.[17] Insofar as

Henri Bourassa, July 1917. LAC, C-9092

ated by the chief French-Canadian opponent of imperialism. Henri Bourassa was a Liberal member of Parliament when he came to national attention in 1899 for resigning his seat in protest against Laurier's decision to permit Canadian volunteers to assist Britain in South Africa without parliamentary approval. Re-elected (unopposed), he was unsuccessful in his insistence that only the Canadian Parliament had the right to declare war, but would eventually help defeat Laurier in 1911 over the issue of naval assistance to Britain in time of emergency. Unlike Ewart, who seldom addressed linguistic or cultural issues, Bourassa stood for a fully articulated bicultural Canadian nationalism:

> The only possible basis for the solution of our national problems is one of mutual respect for our racial characters and exclusive devotion to our common land. . . . We are not asking our neighbours of English extraction to help us develop a political reconciliation with France, and they have no right to use their strength of numbers to break the rules of the alliance, forcing us to shoulder new obligations towards England, even if these were completely voluntary and spontaneous.[19]

Canadians had a duty, it was to cut the final tie and become truly independent. Like most other nationalists, Ewart felt that artificially created feelings for the Empire stood in the way of the development of a genuine homegrown Canadian consciousness:

> Our unofficial orators have held up to us, not Canadianism, but Imperialism, and their failure to achieve success is similar to that of those who endeavour to love God and yet remain out of sympathy with their fellow men. How can Canadians love the British Empire which they have not seen when they do not love their own country which they have seen?[18]

Coming from the prosaic Ewart, this argument for Canada amounted to a transcendent vision.

A different perspective entirely was enunci-

Although Bourassa emphasized that 'My own people . . . are the French Canadians', he did not see English-speaking Canadians as foreigners: 'My native land is all of Canada, a federation of separate races and autonomous provinces. The nation I wish to see grow up is the Canadian nation, made up of French Canadians and English Canadians.'[20]

Bourassa saw his vision of Canada as the only viable alternative to national disintegration and chaos. In his ultimate insistence on full Canadian sovereignty he was in agreement with Anglo-Canadian nationalists like Ewart, but he reached that point only in 1917, at the time of the conscription crisis. Bourassa's bicultural vision was not the only version of nationalism current among French Canadians in this period. There was also a more traditional nationalism

HENRI BOURASSA
(1868–1952)

❖

Henri Bourassa was born in 1868 into a prominent Quebec family, the grandson of Louis-Joseph Papineau. He attended Holy Cross College in Worcester, Massachusetts, for a year before taking over the management of his grandfather's seigneury, Montebello. Elected mayor of the community at the age of 22, he acquired a newspaper, *L'Interprète*, and used it to support Wilfrid Laurier. In turn, Laurier urged the young man to run for Parliament in 1896, and he was easily elected. Three years later, in October 1899, Bourassa joined a few other Liberals in refusing to approve Canada's participation in the Boer War. When he returned to Parliament he explained his position by describing himself as 'a Liberal of the British school', one of the 'Little Englanders' who opposed the idea of empire. He argued that only Parliament could declare war and moved a resolution to this effect, which was defeated.

Increasingly distrustful of Britain, Bourassa became more involved with French-Canadian institutions. In 1903 his younger followers formed the Ligue Nationaliste, a political movement that called for autonomy from Britain, maximum freedom for the provinces within Confederation, and a policy of economic and intellectual development. Bourassa supported the Ligue and began developing his ideas of a bicultural nation. In 1907 he left Parliament, and the following year he was elected to the Quebec Assembly, where he would serve until

1912. Meanwhile he created a new daily newspaper committed to his version of Quebec nationalism: the first issue of *Le Devoir* appeared in January 1910, and Bourassa would continue as its editor until 1932. By now Bourassa represented the leading counterweight to Laurier within Quebec. He opposed Laurier's naval bill in 1910 because it involved extra-parliamentary actions, and used the issue in 1911 to help cut into Laurier's Quebec strength. After toying briefly with the victorious Conservatives, he became an outspoken opponent of Regulation 17 (limiting the use of French in Ontario's public schools) in 1912 and after. During the Great War he opposed Canadian involvement.

In the 1920s Bourassa successfully defended his moderate bicultural nationalism when more extreme nationalists like the Abbé Lionel Groulx began to advocate a separate French-Canadian state. By now, however, he was more concerned about the influence of American big business in Quebec. Devoting himself to the defence of Catholic values, he became increasingly close to the Catholic hierarchy in Quebec. Bourassa lived until 1952—long enough to see Canada adopt many of the policies he had advocated. However, perhaps because his ideas had become so much a part of the mainstream, the public no longer listened to him very attentively in his last years.

'A FRIENDLY REPLY TO MR BOURASSA'

In April of 1904, the editor of *La Vérité*, J.-P. Tardivel, opened a debate with Henry Bourassa by announcing in an anonymous article the nature of his disagreement with Bourassa's Nationalist League. Bourassa sought a development of 'a Canadian feeling that is not concerned with questions of origin, language, or religion', wrote Tardivel, while *La Vérité* believed in French-Canadian nationalism. In the course of the subsequent exchange, the following piece appeared in the newspaper.

Those who cherish the idea of creating a great, unified Canada, homogeneous, stretching from Atlantic to Pacific, and taking in all the British possessions in North America, are also proposing an aim that has attractive aspects. However, this plan frightens and terrifies us, because, as we see all too clearly, it will come about only to the detriment of the French-Canadian nationality.

Mr Bourassa distrusts colonial ties because the imperialists make use of them to build up the empire they dream of. We agree with this distrust, but does he agree with the distrust we feel for the interprovincial ties that serve as instruments in the hands of those who dream of creating a great, unified Canada by slowly strangling the autonomy of the French-Canadian nationality? We dare not answer this question, but we do feel the need of clearly defining our position and feelings . . . .

We are neither revolutionaries nor dreamers. We do not want to resort to violence in any way to break these interprovincial ties; the danger that we see for our nationality in the existence of these ties is very real; we wish these ties had never been formed, yet we know they exist and we must take them into account in all our dealings.

But it is only to prevent them from harming us French Canadians that we must take them into account. And we must know how to proclaim at the top of our voices: may these interprovincial ties perish rather than allow the French-Canadian nationality to be injured by them! . . .

This plan [of Bourassa, for a duality of the races]—or should we say this dream—could have perhaps been put into effect if we had confined ourselves to the original plan of federation; that is, if we had been content to unite the four provinces of Quebec, Ontario, New Brunswick, and Nova Scotia under one federal government. Such a confederation would have had a certain geographical symmetry and sufficient uniformity of general material interests to keep itself going. Moreover, the two races would have been sufficiently equal in power to preserve the desired equilibrium and keep the governmental machine in good working order, based on 'the duality of the races and the special traditions this duality imposes'.

But from the beginning, megalomania and the mania for constant growth have laid hold of our politicians, and they introduced Prince Edward Island into the confederation—which could have been tolerated if really necessary—and then British Columbia and all the Northwest.

This was obviously too much; and wishing to erect a colossal edifice, we sinned against the laws of stability.

SOURCE: *La Vérité*, 15 May 1904, as quoted and translated in Ramsay Cook, ed., *French-Canadian Nationalism: An Anthology* (Toronto: Macmillan, 1969), 150–1.

that had its origins in earlier times, but had been considerably sharpened by Quebec's experiences since 1867. It was most clearly expressed by Jules-Paul Tardivel in his newspaper *La Vérité* in 1904:

> Our own brand of nationalism is French-Canadian nationalism. We have been working for the last twenty-three years toward the development of a French-Canadian national feeling: what we want to see flourish is French-Canadian patriotism; our people are the French-Canadian people; we will not say that our homeland is limited to the province of Quebec, but it is French Canada; the nation we wish to see founded at the time appointed by Providence is the French-Canadian nation.[21]

This nationalism was simultaneously defensive and aggressive: French Canada had a mission to uphold the Roman Catholic faith and the rights of French Canadians, not only within Confederation but everywhere in North America. In its own way, this vision even had imperialist overtones, for it saw Quebec as a 'mother country' for francophones across the continent.

EARLY MILITARY ACTIVITIES

Canadians in the late nineteenth century were not notably militaristic, but neither were they without military activity and organization. The Canadian militia had joined British regulars under Colonel Wolseley in 1870 to assume possession of Manitoba. Fourteen years later, when Wolseley was to lead a British military expedition up the Nile River to relieve General Charles Gordon at Khartoum, he remembered the Canadian boatmen who had made possible the movement of his troops from Lake Superior to Winnipeg over the summer of 1870, and asked the Canadian government to find volunteers to man the boats carrying the troops. More than 300 were recruited, mainly from the First

Nations reserves around the Great Lakes but also from western Canada.[22] Ten of these boatmen died in Egypt, the first Canadian foreign casualties in a military conflict. The following year, Winnipeg units—made up in large part of militiamen who had travelled west with Wolseley in 1870—went into battle in Saskatchewan against Louis Riel and the Métis.[23] The North-West campaign of 1885 was Canada's first war, and would not be its last.

British imperial adventuring brought Canada into the world in the latter years of the nineteenth century. The most common public confrontations over Canada's role in the Empire occurred in the context of imperial defence. The British Colonial Secretary, Joseph Chamberlain, used the occasion of Queen Victoria's Jubilee celebration in June 1897 to assemble the leaders of the various 'colonies'. He saw to it that Wilfrid Laurier was knighted, and pressed 'for some adequate and regular system of contributions to sea-power' and exchange of troops. The colonies were largely cool to Chamberlain's proposals, concluding that political relations were 'generally satisfactory under the existing condition of things'.[24] The question of Canadian assistance to Britain rose again in concrete terms in July 1899, when the mother country requested Canadian troops for the forthcoming war in South Africa against the Boers. Laurier temporized, but the issue would not go away, particularly when the shooting began on 11 October 1899. The popular press in English Canada responded enthusiastically to the idea of an official Canadian contingent, while their counterparts in French Canada opposed involvement in Britain's overseas adventures; as *La Presse* put it, 'We French Canadians belong to one country, Canada; Canada is for us the whole world; but the English Canadians have two countries, one here and one across the sea.'[25]

The government compromised by sending a force of 1,000 volunteers and insisting that it was not setting a precedent. The thousand untrained infantrymen, who sailed from Quebec on 30 October 1899, were followed by 6,000 more vol-

■ Men of the Winnipeg Field Battery asleep in a special railway car taking Louis Riel from Swift Current to Regina to stand trial for treason, 22 May 1885. Photograph by O. B. Buell. Saskatchewan Archives Board, B2298.

unteers in Canada's second contingent, and later by another thousand men—all equipped, transported, and partially financed by the Canadian government. Another contingent, Lord Strathcona's Horse, was supported entirely by Lord Strathcona (Donald A. Smith), Canada's High Commissioner in Britain. The Canadians took part in 29 engagements before the war ended on 11 May 1902, and suffered heavy casualties in several of them.[26] When Henri Bourassa asked, in the Liberal caucus in 1899, whether Quebec's opinion had been taken into account in the decision to send volunteers, Laurier answered, 'My dear Henri, the Province of Quebec has no opinions, it only has sentiments.'[27] Laurier rode out the storm of objection, but the experience did not incline him towards supporting imperial entanglements, much less imperial federation.

He continued to attend imperial conferences called by the British. But, conscious of the growing anti-imperialist sentiment in Quebec—where people were beginning to talk about organizing a new nationalist party—he firmly resisted any movement to institutionalize Canada's relations with the Empire through, for example, imperial leagues.

The defence issue emerged again in 1909, this time over naval policy. Britain had been pressing the colonies since the mid-1890s for naval contributions that would be integrated into the Royal Navy. At a naval conference in 1909, Canada finally agreed to provide a unit of five cruisers and six destroyers, having been assured that the Admiralty would not insist on a unified command structure (except, of course, in time of war). When the Laurier government introduced its Naval Service Bill in January 1910, the results were predictable. While English Canadians—especially Tories—sneered at this 'tin-pot navy' and complained that the legislation did not go far enough towards assisting the British, in Quebec nationalists and the Conservatives joined forces to fight for its repeal. These conflicts helped to defeat Laurier in 1911, and the Conservative government of his successor, Robert Borden, was much more sympathetic to the Empire. It would therefore not be quite true to say that Canada had no share in the buildup to the Great War, for its support of the Empire undoubtedly led the British to count on Canadian support as they weighed their options in the summer of 1914. They would not be disappointed. Canada was among the first dominions to follow Britain into war, quickly raising and transporting an army to Europe. It hardly needs to be said that Canadians had no conception of the war's ultimate length or essentially futile savagery. Among the early volunteers who flocked to recruiting stations, especially in English-speaking Canada, the main worry was that the fighting would be over before they got action.

THE DEBATE OVER 'RACE'

Today, of course, use of the term 'race' raises questions under any circumstances—including the question of whether the idea of racial difference among humans means anything at all. The term is all the more problematic in the context of Canada around 1900, when 'French Canadian' was regarded as a racial category and the relationship between French- and English-speaking Canadians was commonly referred to as 'the race question'. One problem was obvious to many people at the time: as John Macdougall, author of *Rural Life in Canada*, wrote in 1913, 'It is unfortunate that this matter has to be referred to in terms of race, inasmuch as it is not racial in essential character. There is absolutely no racial barrier to preventing our French and English people commingling.'[28] Nevertheless, English-

speaking nationalist-imperialists had no doubt about the superiority of their own 'Anglo-Saxon race'.

'RACE' AND FRENCH CANADA

Behind the condescending attitude of English Canadians towards French Canadians, their fellow citizens, were generations of suppressed mutual antagonism, as André Siegfried recognized:

> The English Canadians consider themselves the sole masters of Canada; they were not its first occupants, admittedly, but it is theirs, they maintain, by right of conquest. They experience, therefore, a feeling of indignation at the sight of the defeated race persisting in their development instead of fusing or being submerged. And to the classic cry of the mother country—'No Popery!'—they add another of their own—'No French Domination!' English Protestants and French Catholics thus find themselves face to face every day in the political arena; and the English obstinately make it a point of honour not to allow themselves be surpassed by adversaries whom they judge backward and inferior.
>
> An attitude frequently adopted in Anglo-Canadian circles is that of ignoring deliberately the very presence of the French. From their whole bearing and conversation, you might suppose that the French element in Canada was quite insignificant. You might spend many weeks among the English of Montreal without anyone letting you realize that the city is two-thirds French. Many travelers never suspect this.[29]

Some English-Canadian intellectuals pointed out that French Canadians, too, had 'northern' origins, and that Quebec had grown and developed politically under British influence; according to George Monro Grant, French Canadians were politically 'British and their Hearts are all for Canada'. Others, however, made no effort to hide their contempt for what they generally perceived to be a peasant mentality encouraged by the Roman Catholic Church. Goldwin Smith dismissed French Canadians as 'tractable, amenable', though 'neither cultivated nor aspiring'.[30] According to George Parkin, 'One has no hesitation in discussing frankly this question of race inertia in Quebec. The most clear-sighted men of the province admit and deplore it.'[31] The French-Canadian people were 'simple and docile', and needed to be saved from their 'narrow, bigoted, and isolated ways'. The poet Wilfred Campbell saw French Canada as 'useless, despotic, intolerant, and ultra-conservative in her body politic and her social ideas'.[32]

Such judgements were not confined to intellectual circles, as the newspaper debate over Louis Riel demonstrated in 1885. 'The masses of the French-Canadian people are simple and ignorant', declared the *Toronto Weekly News* in May of that year. In July the *Toronto Mail* published a more thoughtful editorial: 'In Quebec there is a caricature Ontario, and in Ontario a caricature Quebec, both invented by politicians; and until those wretched figments are replaced by more truthful and intelligent conceptions, we cannot hope to become an united Canada.' The *Mail* went on to say that the problem was not simply a tendency on the part of English Canadians, particularly in Ontario, to disparage the ordinary French Canadian, but a tendency for French Canada to emphasize its own distinctiveness.

Much of the emphasis on the distinctiveness of 'the French race in North America' could be attributed to the clergy, who since 1840 had preached to their flocks about the providential mission of French Canada. Mgr L.-A. Paquet described that mission in 1902, on the simultaneous occasion of the fiftieth anniversary celebration of Laval University and the sixtieth of the Saint-Jean-Baptiste Society in Quebec:

We are not only a civilized race, we are the pioneers of civilization; we are not only a religious people, we are the messengers of the religious idea; we are not only the submissive sons of the Church, we are, we ought to be, numbered among its zealots, its defenders, and its apostles. Our mission is less to manipulate capital than to change ideas; it consists less in lighting the fires of factories than to maintain and to make shine afar the luminous fire of religion and thought.[33]

Of course this was rhetorical excess, but the sort of excess employed in such a context can be instructive. Earlier expressions of these ideas had often used the term 'people' instead of 'race', but after the turn of the century, French-Canadian writers commonly used the latter word, not always in an anthropological sense. Henri Bourassa, for example, in a published speech of 1912 entitled 'La Langue française et l'avenir du notre race' ('The French language and the future of our race'), referred to the 'Irish race, which has continued to exist and preserve its ethnic character, although it lost its language a long time ago'. He went on to discuss the 'Scottish people' who, 'by losing their language and being intellectually assimilated into the Anglo-Saxon race, . . . have furnished England and the British Empire with a moral and intellectual factor of undeniable value.' Bourassa concluded, 'When a race ceases to express its thought and feelings in its own language, the language that has grown with it and has been formed along with its ethnic temperament, it is lost as a race. The preservation of language is absolutely necessary for the preservation of a race, its spirit, character, and temperament.'[34] This French-Canadian definition of 'race' was chiefly homegrown, based on historical experience. It is particularly interesting for the importance it attaches to language.

We can perhaps give André Siegfried the last word on what he called 'The French-Canadian Programme for the Future'. From his perspective in 1906, French Canada seemed to be hoping that, over time, numerical increase would enable them to overwhelm the English and take Canada back. Siegfried thought that hope was futile: 'Canada will not become French again.'[35] Rather,

■ Sikh mineworkers wait on the CPR platform at Frank, Alberta, 1903. NAC, PA-125112.

he thought, French Canadians should concentrate on 'establish[ing] themselves strongly and for all time in the province of Quebec'.[36] In the larger scheme of things, Siegfried was more interested in the future of Canada in North America than in the future of Quebec in Canada. Here he saw three possibilities: 'Either the present state of things will continue indefinitely, Canada remaining a British colony; or this link will be broken and she will become independent; or, finally, she will be annexed by the United States.'[37]

THEORIES OF RACE

George Parkin once claimed that one of the Anglo-Saxons' great assets was their 'special capacity for human organization' and stability. Never before had 'any branch of the human family been so free to apply itself to the higher problems of civilization'.[38] The historical development of Great Britain, the United States, and

Canada demonstrated that special genius. But Canada had advantages over both the United States and Britain. Many imperialists believed that Canada's 'strenuous climate' would attract principally immigrants 'belonging to the sturdy races of the North'. Although Canada's population would therefore increase only slowly, 'quality would be balanced against quantity'.[39] Immigrants from 'the vagrant population of Italy and other countries of Southern Europe' might be able to live out of doors all year round in parts of the United States, but such undesirables could never survive the inhospitable Canadian climate. Other arguments for Canada's eventual superiority pointed to its wholesome rural way of life, by contrast to the debilitating effects of industrialization and urbanization in the United States and Britain. The anti-imperialist Goldwin Smith, who shared in these assumptions, argued that continental union would ensure the continuation of the Anglo-Saxons in North America and shore up the American system of democracy, which was 'hard pressed by the foreign element untrained to self government'.[40] When, after Canada broadened its immigration policy in 1896, those same 'foreign elements' began entering Canada in large numbers—from Italy and Eastern Europe, even Asia—the imperialists were greatly troubled.

In 1883 Prime Minister Macdonald, in a debate over Chinese immigration, had told Parliament that he was 'sufficient of a physiologist to believe that the two races cannot combine and that no great middle race can arise from the mixture of the Mongolian and the Arian.'[41] Perhaps the reference to physiology was intended to suggest a scientific basis for that unscientific opinion. Certainly there was a widespread general interest in science, particularly natural history, at the time, and various theories were taken as 'evidence' for racial arguments. For example, the concept of natural selection, introduced by Charles Darwin in his *On the Origin of Species by Means of Natural Selection* (1859), was taken as the basis for various social theories, even though Darwin had proposed it only as a biological construct explaining how species evolved. Social Darwinism proposed not only a description of human society but a prescription: that the strong must take control of social development and eliminate the weak so that undesirable qualities are not passed on by heredity. By the turn of the century this line of thinking had developed into the 'science' of eugenics, whose chief spokesman was the British scientist Francis Galton. Opposing the eugenicists were another group who were equally convinced of the importance of heredity, but drew entirely different conclusions: these 'environmentalists' traced their intellectual ancestry back to the French scientist Jean-Baptiste Lamarck.[42]

NATURE OR NURTURE?

The principal issue in this debate, still with us in a different guise, was whether heredity (nature) or environment (nurture) was the key to human characteristics. Although the Lamarckians were as convinced as the eugenicists of the importance of heredity, they believed that characteristics acquired by one generation would be passed on to the next. Accordingly, they believed that if the environment of the less privileged members of society were ameliorated through reform, their children would grow up smarter and stronger. The eugenicists, on the other hand, insisted that reform would merely perpetuate the characteristics of the weak and 'degenerate'. Ethel Hurlbatt, a Montreal reformer, posed the question this way in 1907:

> Can we, by education, by legislation, by social effort change the environmental conditions and raise the race to a markedly higher standard of physique and mentality? Or is social reform really incapable of effecting any substantial change, nay by lessening the selection [selective?] death rate, may it not contribute to the very evils it was intended to lessen?[43]

Where eugenicists and environmentalists agreed was on the need to improve the society and prevent degeneracy. This concern would find expression in various movements of social reform, discussed in the next chapter.

CONCLUSION

Canadian politics between 1885 and 1914 may have been short on ideological debate, as André Siegfried noted, but the effort to achieve consensus was crucial to a young country in which the potential for conflict was great. Among the subjects of disagreement were underlying assumptions about the nature of the nation, its two founding peoples, and its role in the world. More than once, issues involving imperial defence raised questions about Canada's place in the Empire, to the distress of many in French Canada.

SHORT BIBLIOGRAPHY

Berger, Carl. *The Sense of Power: Studies in the Ideas of Canadian Imperialism, 1867–1914*. Toronto, 1970. The pioneering work of modern intellectual history in Canada, still not superseded.

Bernard, Jean-Paul, ed. *Les Idéologies québécoises au 19e siècle*. Montreal, 1971. A useful collection of studies of ideas in Quebec.

Brown, R.C. *Robert Laird Borden: A Biography*. Vol. 1, *1854–1914*. Toronto, 1975. An excellent biography of a critical politician in this period.

———— and Ramsay Cook. *Canada, 1896–1914*. Toronto, 1974. Older, but still the best general synthesis and survey of the period.

Crunican, Paul. *Priests and Politicians: Manitoba Schools and the Election of 1896*. Toronto, 1974. The standard account of a complicated topic.

English, John. *The Decline of Politics: The Conservatives and the Party System, 1901–20*. Toronto, 1977. One of the best books ever on politics in Canada.

Miller, Carman. *Painting the Map Red: Canada and the South African War, 1899–1902*. Montreal, 1993. A thorough discussion of the Boer War from a modern perspective.

Miller, James R. *Equal Rights: The Jesuit Estates Act Controversy*. Montreal, 1979. A detailed study of a complex and important subject.

Monière, Denis. *Ideologies in Quebec: The Historical Development*. Toronto, 1981. A historical study of the development of ideas in Quebec.

Moyles, R.G., and Doug Owram. *Imperial Dreams and Colonial Realities: British Views of Canada, 1880–1914*. Toronto, 1988. The view from the imperial centre.

Neatby, H. Blair. *Laurier and a Liberal Quebec: A Study in Political Management*. Toronto, 1973. A useful introduction to Laurier's Quebec.

STUDY QUESTIONS

1. Were there any significant differences between the Liberal and Conservative parties in this period?
2. What role did patronage play in Canadian party politics?
3. How could imperialism be viewed as an expression of Canadian nationalism?
4. What were the major alternatives to imperialism advocated in Canada? Did they share much in common?
5. What role did naval defence play in Canadian national politics?
6. Was the division between French and English Canada a 'racial' one?
7. What is the great fallacy in Stephen Leacock's argument for Empire?

CHAPTER EIGHT

The Era of Social Reform, 1885–1914

The years between the early 1880s and the Great War saw many changes in Canada— adding up to one monstrous Change: as transcontinental railways and telegraph lines began to link the old provinces to the Prairies and British Columbia, countless numbers of Canadians were able for the first time to conjure up the image of a nation. At the same time, rapid changes meant that many found the society in which they lived bewilderingly different from what they had known. The cities were much bigger, filled with recent arrivals from the countryside as well as overseas, and were difficult to govern. The rural regions were also experiencing transformation. On the Prairies and elsewhere, instability was built into the family farm. Almost all institutions had trouble functioning.

What was happening in Canada was not very different from what was happening in the United States, and it was possible in the smaller nation to learn from the experience of the giant. On both sides of the border, there was a general assumption that society was breaking down, or falling apart, and needed to be fixed. But not everyone agreed on what was breaking down or falling apart, or why. Many different solutions were proposed, and the vast array of reform movements that emerged became one of the chief characteristics of the age. Many of these reform efforts were initiated by the private sector for the private sector, but increasingly some reformers became convinced that major social alterations were going to require the power and revenue of the state at all levels. Because the British North America Act left most social matters to the provinces, the federal government was the least likely to feel pressure for reform. Many reforms were implemented at the municipal or provincial level, especially the latter. Looking back on this period, reformers in the mid-twentieth century would often assume that because there had been little or no national action, there had been little real change. The documentation and analysis of reform in the period 1885–1914 has become one of the major ingredients of the revolution in Canadian historiography since the 1960s. The literature is enormous, and we can examine only a sample of its themes here. In what follows, reform movements are grouped according to their major emphases.

REFORM AND THE CANADIAN CHURCHES

REFORM AND THE MORAL STATE

Every city and every part of the nation had periodic campaigns against 'vice', usually led by local

TIMELINE

1870

England passes Married Women's Property Act.

1870s

Knights of Labor spread to Canada from United States.

1874

WCTU founded in Owen Sound, Ontario.

1876

Emily Stowe creates first suffrage organization in Canada.

1883

Chinese 'coolies' arrive to build the Canadian Pacific Railway.

1886

Quebec Board of Health created.

1893

Montreal Local Council of Women founded. National Council of Women founded.

1894

Fred Victor Mission founded in Toronto.

1896

Clifford Sifton expands sources for Canadian immigration to include Southern and Eastern Europe.

1897

First Women's Institute founded. Clara Martin becomes first woman in the British Empire admitted to practise law.

1904

All Peoples' Mission founded in Winnipeg by J.S. Woodsworth.

1906

New Immigration Act passed to regulate immigration more carefully.

1907

Anti-'Oriental' riots in Vancouver. Fédération nationale Saint-Jean-Baptiste founded in Quebec. Moral and Social Reform Council of Canada organized.

1910

Cabinet is empowered to regulate immigration.

1912

Social Services Council established.

1914

Social Services Congress held in Toronto.

Protestant clergymen who were, in their own way, responding to a sense that the churches were no longer doing their jobs. The two favourite targets of this sort of reform were alcohol and prostitution. As one prominent Winnipeg minister wrote in 1910 in a pamphlet on 'The Problem of Vice' in the city:

> a minority who choose to degrade the sacred powers of generation, and by the use of aphrodisiacs, and the cultivation of filthy imaginations, bring themselves into a pathological debasement,

A posed photograph of mission workers delivering Christmas hampers to a home in Winnipeg's North End. Photographer unknown, c. 1910. The United Church of Canada Archives–Conference of Manitoba and Northwestern Ontario. J.M. Shaver fonds, PP53, No. 2484.

that seems to themselves a permanent institution of sexual vice, have no right, Divine or human, to maintain such an institution to the injury of the commonwealth.[1]

The trouble with such rhetoric—associating the struggle of one or another campaign against social evil with a holy war to ensure the purity of 'future generations'—was that it failed to distinguish among evils, or to search for causes beyond a fall from grace. Vice, crime, and poverty were commonly associated by the moral reformers, but often there was no clear idea of which of

these evils needed to be addressed first.[2] Even those reformers who concentrated on poverty seemed reluctant to attribute it to a failure of the economic system to distribute wealth equitably. Moreover, most efforts to address poverty had a definite class element, with a 'superior' class helping an 'inferior' one.

Moralistic reformers attempting to help the human victims of disastrous urban conditions tended to take a high-minded tone. The short mayoral term (1886–8) of William Holmes Howland is an early example of reform politics in Toronto. Born into a moneyed, well-established family in 1844—his father, Sir William Pearce Howland, was a Father of Confederation—Howland had a successful business career while still a young man, but as a serious evangelical Christian he came to focus his efforts on the temperance movement and philanthropic activities, especially in St John's Ward, a poor and vice-ridden district in the centre of the city. In 1884 he was one of the founders of the Toronto Mission Union, a non-denominational organization devoted to providing the poor with various forms of social assistance. Two years later, reformers bent on ridding the city of corrupt 'ward-heelers' joined with the prohibitionists to back Howland in his campaign for mayor. With the additional help of the city's newly organized labour movement and the property-owning women—spinsters and widows—who were allowed to vote for the first time in this election, Howland was elected on a platform of reforming the social and moral life of the city. Over the next two years he became embroiled in a strike against the Massey Manufacturing Co. and in a labour dispute with the Toronto Street Railway Co., in both cases backing the workers. He also reduced the number of liquor licences available and tried with limited success to end civic corruption and shut down both houses of prostitution and unlicensed liquor outlets.[3]

In his passion for moral reform, Howland provided a model for subsequent mayors, earning for his city the sobriquet 'Toronto the Good', but his actual accomplishments were less notable. The city had not changed much a decade later, when C.S. Clark published his ironically titled book *Of Toronto the Good: The Queen City of Canada As It Is* (1898), an anecdotal study of what he saw as the city's multiple evils, enumerated in chapters with titles such as 'The Social Evil' ('houses of ill fame'), 'Street Walkers', 'The Poor of the City', 'Gambling Houses', 'Drunkenness', 'Crooks', 'Thieves', and 'Swindlers'.

One of the principal concerns of the early reformers involved the single women working for wages in the larger cities, especially Toronto.[4]

This sector of the urban population was quickly identified as a 'moral problem' requiring a variety of new reform initiatives. What bothered society, of course, was what these women, living on their own away from their families, might do in their time off from work. It was assumed that they would stray into improper behaviour, frequenting dance halls and other places of amusement where they would be exposed to white slavers and all manner of rapacious villainy. Toronto was the centre of the social purity movement. To provide a safe home for young working women, these Protestant reformers founded agencies such as the Young Women's Christian Association. Ironically, however, it was not unusual for young women to be evicted from such residences, often for some petty transgression of strict regulations; a girl suddenly rendered homeless in this way really was exposed to the evils of the city. Of course, the principal fear of such reformers was the sexual danger facing innocent young women. But the major result of their efforts was to promote a general assumption that young single women were prone to promiscuity. The reformers were probably more successful when they turned to providing alternative amusements such as sports clubs. Not until after 1920 was the single working woman accepted as a regular part of urban society.

THE SOCIAL GOSPEL

In the 1890s a new movement to combat the ills of the new industrial society and to promote social reform grew out of the Protestant churches, beginning with the Methodists. Exponents of the 'Social Gospel' regarded work for social change as a spiritual activity inspired by God and the desire to establish the Kingdom of God on earth.[5] In the wave of social service activity that followed, city missions (such as Toronto's Fred Victor Mission, founded in 1894) and church settlement houses were established that offered various kinds of assistance for the poor. The All Peoples' Mission in Winnipeg concentrated on non-English-speaking people from Europe, providing financial assistance, educational opportunities, and relief in the form of food and clothing. In 1912 the churches joined to form Social Service Council of Canada. Perhaps the most famous Social Gospel reformer of the time was Methodist minister James Shaver Woodsworth, who as superintendent of All Peoples' Mission in Winnipeg from 1904 to 1913 devoted himself to the problems of urban slums and immigration, producing two important books: *Strangers within Our Gates: Or, Coming Canadians* (1909) and *My Neighbor: A Study of City Conditions, A Plea for Social Service* (1911).

In *Strangers* Woodsworth identified numerous 'evils' associated with the 'motley crowd of immigrants' to Canada, including 'Ignorance of the language, high rents, low standards of living, incompetency, [and] drunkenness'. Instead of further restrictions on immigration, however, Woodsworth recommended measures to help new immigrants integrate more quickly into Canadian society. In *My Neighbor* he discussed urbanization in terms of both 'menace to our . . . civilization' through problems such as vice, crime, and disease, and the 'hope of Democracy' through the new co-operative efforts to deal with those problems. While the earlier book clearly recognized that immigrants to Canada had special problems, it tended to associate the difficulties they faced with their ability to assimilate into Canadian society. *My Neighbor* was considerably more general and more sympathetic to new immigrants, particularly those from Eastern Europe. Combining secular analyses of urban problems with a spiritual call for a new Christianity in which traditional churches' concern for the individual soul would expand to include concern for broader social problems, Woodsworth wrote in his concluding chapter:

> We can hardly be accused of under-estimating the value of social settlements, institutional churches, and city missions, but more and more we are convinced that such agencies will never meet the great social needs of the city. They serve a present need; they bring us face to face with our problem; they point out the line of advance. Then by all means let us multiply them and extend the scope of their work. But the needs will remain until the community at large is dominated by the social ideal. This is surely the mission of the Church, and yet the Church itself is hardly awake to the situation, much less fitted to meet it. Will the Church retain—perhaps we should rather say, regain—her social leadership?

As this passage suggests, the Social Gospel was as much about regenerating the Protestant churches of Canada as it was about reforming society.[6]

URBAN REFORM

By the 1880s, most of Canada's principal cities had begun to produce groups of urban reformers who would gradually coalesce into reform factions. The arguments for municipal reform were fairly obvious, although the reformers often had difficulty agreeing on priorities, such as where to put the emphasis in planning. The earliest reformers were the humanitarians. They often became involved with the city through charitable work among the poor, or as professionals concerned with social and educational services; many of the former turned into the latter. They were interested in making the city clean, healthy, moral, and equitable in its treatment of its citizens—quite a different agenda from that of the 'corporatist' businessmen, who after the turn of the century would promote public ownership of city services, especially utilities, as a way of increasing revenue without increasing taxes, while at the same time eliminating greedy capitalists and permitting the extension of essential services to the less prosperous members of the community. Humanitarians and corporatists could agree on the need for urban planning, although they had different priorities.

Both reform wings were frustrated by the resistance to change among entrenched interests

■ Immigrant woman and children in front of the Winnipeg station, from J.S. Woodsworth's *Strangers within Our Gates*. United Church of Canada/Victoria University Archives, Toronto, Acc. No. 93.049 P/3111N.

in municipal government and politics, and they tried to address this problem as a first step. Thus 'good government' became the rallying cry for urban reformers of various persuasions.[7] Their platforms and activities suggest both the strengths and the weaknesses of urban reform in this period. The advocates of reform tended to be men from the business and professional elites, with their wives. These people saw the objects of their concern as victims to be helped rather than as citizens to be consulted or involved in the reform process. Indeed, some reformers saw the people in need of assistance as the principal obstacle to improved conditions—a classic case

of blaming the victims. The reformers failed to appreciate that many of the poor preferred help to promises of improved administration. Much of the reform advocated was structural or a matter of business practice: increasing efficiency and planning, for example, or adding more regulatory agencies. As G. Frank Beer, a city planner, wrote in 1914, 'Slums produce inefficiency— inefficiency begets poverty and poverty of this character means disease and degradation.' He went on to emphasize that, 'as population centralizes, the power of the individual to shape his environment lessens and the responsibility of the state increases'.[8]

■ 'The Civic Centre of Calgary as It May Appear Many Years Hence': the frontispiece of Thomas Mawson's scheme for Calgary, inspired by the City Beautiful movement. From 'The City of Calgary: Past, Present and Future' (1914) by Thomas H. Mawson & Sons, Town Planning Commission, Box 1, File 6, City of Calgary, Corporate Records, Archives.

The goal of the corporate reformers was structural change, and the model was usually sound business practice. City planning was one aspect of this project, and was strongly supported by professional architects, who combined an urge to 'plan the city as a whole' with aesthetic considerations of coherence, visual variety, and civic grandeur. The City Beautiful Movement reflected the idea that many of the city's ills could be overcome by a comprehensive plan combining social programs, new facilities, rational street and transportation planning, and overall beautification. The movement gained attention at the Expositions of 1876 and 1893 in Philadelphia and Chicago, respectively, and several Canadian cities were influenced by it. Toronto, after a

major downtown fire in 1904, funded a comprehensive plan the following year to create park areas on landfill along the waterfront, a system of parks and driveways encircling the city, and a series of diagonal avenues connecting the core of the city with the suburbs. Calgary, Ottawa, and Toronto all sponsored lavish books presenting plans, drawings, and textual descriptions of projects for remodelling the cities. An unusually fine example of bookmaking for the time—published in a limited edition 'under the auspices of the City Planning Commission'—is Thomas Mawson's *Calgary: A Preliminary Scheme for Controlling the Growth of the City* (1914), which included colour reproductions of many watercolour renderings of his grandiose proposals. Such grand plans had their opponents, however. In 1911 an article in the *Canadian Municipal Journal* commented: 'Magnificent avenues, leading to grand buildings, are desirable. Lovely and artistic parks should be in every city. But the dwellings in which those live who cannot get away from their homes the whole year long, really decide whether any city is to be healthy, moral and progressive. The common people are in the great majority, their proper accommodation is the greatest problem.'[9] None of the grand designs ever came to fruition, although every city in Canada shows traces of what was intended in the form of parks, railway stations, and, in provincial capitals, the imposing legislative buildings built before the Great War.

Political change at the level of municipal government was one goal on which reformers of almost all persuasions could agree. Efforts to elect reformers to municipal office often were frustrated by corruption of the electoral process, and many reformers combined the goal of 'throwing the rascals out' with implementing structural changes to limit the damage the rascals could do while still in power. Elimination of the ward system—the traditional source of local graft and corruption—was one popular proposal. The typical committee system, which allowed senior members of council to control critical sectors, was frequently criticized. Several cities, including Montreal after 1901, adopted the Toronto scheme of a board of control to administer the city as a sort of executive. The introduction of the commission system of government, run by professional bureaucrats, was attractive to many municipal reformers, although it tended to substitute the evils of bureaucracy for those of direct democracy.

Perhaps the fiercest battles were fought over the ownership of municipal utilities, with local corporatist leaders usually seeking to recover control of utilities from outside capitalists who siphoned profits from the local business community. While the utility barons complained of such attacks on private enterprise, the corporatists countered by arguing that utilities were intrinsic monopolies that should be operated in the public interest. Municipal ownership or control of transit lines, waterworks, electrical plants, and telephone systems reflected statist rather than socialist thinking.

THE PROFESSIONAL REFORMERS

Another wing of reform was associated with various professional groups that became involved in social problems through either their professional practices or work with private voluntary agencies. Thus, doctors were active in establishing a public health system and recommending ways of improving public health care. The Quebec Board of Health, for example, was created by the Public Health Act of the province in 1886, and its medical members pressed for inoculations, regulation of milk quality, and water purification, among other reforms. Doctors in French Canada had long attributed the high infant mortality rates in French Canada to mothers' weaning their babies too soon. Although they could not regulate mothers' nursing behaviour, they were able to improve the cows' milk provided to infants through grading and labelling, and making properly pasteurized milk available through milk depots (called Gouttes de Lait, 'drops of milk'). Doctors in Quebec and elsewhere also pressed for the establishment of public facilities to treat diseases such as tuberculosis and for a general commitment to publicly financed health facilities to replace the largely private institutions of the past. One of the most common public health recommendations made by the medical profession was compulsory inspection of school children. Boards of public health, staffed by early versions of social workers, were actively involved in reform in most cities in Canada.

EDUCATION

Not all children, of course, attended school. Teachers were often in the front lines of reform, since adequate schooling was recognized as one

■ Adelaide Hunter Hoodless and her children, 1887. Hoodless was first impelled to work for reform causes after the death of her infant son, in 1889, as a result of drinking impure milk. In addition to the Women's Institutes, she helped to found the National Council of Women, the Victorian Order of Nurses, and the national YWCA. LAC, PA-128887.

that the provinces one by one confirmed the principle of universal education by making school attendance compulsory to (usually) age 14. Such laws were in place everywhere in Canada by World War I. Regular school attendance would ensure a more suitable environment for children than roaming the streets or working in factories, help them to learn skills that would lift them out of their poverty, and—in the case of immigrants—enable them to assimilate the values of Canadian society. In most parts of the country, 'Canadian society' meant Anglo-Canadian society.

Educational reformers were confident they were doing the right thing. Thus, in 1911 the editor of the *Manitoba Free Press*, J.W. Dafoe, described 'the necessity of compulsory education as a self-evident truth, a law of right reason, an inescapable conclusion, a point of view that no intelligent citizen could oppose, a proposition that only the apathetic would fail to support'.[10] And when parents who insisted on schooling in some language other than English kept their children out of school, they were regarded as ungrateful members of the 'lower orders' who did not know what was good for them.

Teachers and educational reformers plainly believed that compulsory education and the use of the schools for social purposes were in the best interests of Canadian society. But these reforms benefited them as well. Compulsory education opened many more teaching jobs, particularly at the higher-paid senior levels, and completed the professionalization of teaching. With compulsory education (and all the intellectual freight it carried) came the teacher as social expert, as a professional who knew more about children than their parents, particularly the parents of disadvantaged children. Compulsory education, medical examinations, school nurses, and lunch programs were all part of a new type of social engineering, conducted in the name of 'right reason', which would become even more prominent after World War I.

of the best ways to prevent the children of the poor from following in their parents' footsteps, and the only way to assimilate the thousands of immigrants after 1896 who spoke neither English nor French. In this period, educational reformers pressed not only for improved schooling but for the schools themselves—especially in urban areas—to assume some of the responsibility for providing social services for their charges, in effect acting *in loco parentis* for the children of slum and ghetto dwellers. The greatest problem was school attendance, and it was in this period

Women's Institutes were a movement

founded in Canada in 1897 by Adelaide Hood-less at Stoney Creek, Ontario.[11] They eventually spread around the world. Women's Institutes were intended to promote appreciation of rural living and also to encourage better education of all women for motherhood and homemaking through extension of the principles of domestic science, a subject rapidly developing around the turn of the century at the university level. Hoodless had argued for 'a better understanding of the economic and hygienic value of food and a more scientific care of children with a view to raising the general standard of life of farm peo-ple'. By 1913 there were branches in every pro-vince; they were especially common in Ontario and Prince Edward Island. More radical women before 1914 felt that the Women's Institutes had been encouraged by provincial governments eager to defuse potential feminism, particularly in rural districts; Ontario's Department of Agriculture in 1904 had seven full-time staff pro-moting the institutes within the province.

In any event, once urban suffragists became involved in such organizations, many farm women regarded them with suspicion; urban and rural women saw the world quite differently. Both wanted the vote, but the reforms they sought were quite different. For example, farm women wanted to do something about rural depopula-tion, while urban suffragists wanted to improve working and living conditions in the nation's cities.[12] Manitoba branches focused much atten-tion on campaigns for public rest rooms in mar-ket towns in the province. In local branches, lec-tures and demonstrations responded to the needs of the community. Pamphlets were published for local branches to reduce their sense of isolation. During the war the Institute concept was intro-duced to Great Britain. In 1919 the Federated Women's Institutes of Canada was formed follow-ing a meeting in Winnipeg of a representative from each provincial WI. The motto adopted by the national organization, 'For Home and Country', reflected the desire to promote rural values in the context of national and international issues and work towards achieving common national goals. Judge Emily Murphy was selected as the first national president.

THE LABOUR MOVEMENT

THE RISE OF LABOUR

For many Canadians, the organization of labour was an attack on the right of individuals to run their businesses as they saw fit. The earliest suc-cesses in labour organization had come in the more skilled trades, and it was particularly hard to organize in the resource industries.[13] Although the growth of secondary manufacturing and a service sector created a working class (or prole-tariat) that clearly saw its interests as different from those of the 'bosses', actually persuading workers to organize was far from easy, in part because industrialization had reduced craft iden-tification, and in part because many semi-skilled workers—especially women—were not em-ployed on a full-time or long-term basis. In many cases, however, management pressure for greater efficiency, combined with mechanization, was a recipe for worker alienation. One showcase fac-tory, the Lumen Bearing Company of Toronto, had a 'staff boss' whose job it was to save time:

> He is on the floor all the time; he is corrective to slovenly practices. The stop-watch is his gauge. By careful and accurate observations a basis is arrived at for piece-work prices . . . In the Lumen Bearing Co.'s foundry a certain class of castings was for-merly made at the rate of twenty-eight a day. That was in the day work era. Today the average pro-duction per man of the same casting is sixty-five. The history of the change in output from twenty-eight to sixty-five daily is the story in concen-trated form of efficiency management.[14]

Sooner or later, such pressure was bound to lead to industrial conflict.

Even harder to organize than the factories were the many business operations that em-

■ Rolling-mill hands, Hamilton Steel and Iron Company, 1906. Photo courtesy of Labour Studies, McMaster University.

ployed women, usually at the lower end of the clerical scale. Gradually, as business structure and technology became more sophisticated, male clerks of the Bob Cratchit variety would be replaced by women who knew how to type. The invention of the typewriter (in the 1870s) and the telephone, together with the telephone exchange (in the 1880s), created occupational avenues for women in increasing numbers after 1885.[15] What did not change was the inequitable wage structure: women were paid between 50 and 60 per cent less than men until 1914, and the discrepancy did not begin to lessen significantly until the 1980s. The question of equal pay for equal work did not arise because in most cases women and men did different kinds of work, and under different circumstances. For example, women often did piece-work in the

home, or worked only until they married. Women could be kept on the bottom rung of any business on the grounds that they were not really making a career and hence did not require the sort of training that male workers did. At the same time, the lack of training kept women at the bottom, and underpaid, because they were unable to advance. Another factor that kept wages low for women working in clerical jobs and retail trade, and hindered their involvement in labour organizations, was the notion that those were 'respectable' white-collar occupations. The association of white-collar work with middle-class respectability helped reinforce bourgeois hostility to labour unions, which were invariably associated with blue-collar occupations.

Many of the labour organizations active in Canada in the late nineteenth century were foreign imports, often from the United States, although many Canadian labour leaders had British backgrounds. The railway brotherhoods moved into Canada with the expansion of the railroads in the 1870s and 1880s, and were joined in 1881 by the Noble Order of the Knights of Labor, a fraternal-industrial union that attempted, not very successfully, to bring unskilled and semi-skilled workers together under one umbrella. The American Federation of Labor (AFL), led for many years by the cigar-maker Samuel Gompers, concentrated strictly on craft organization in certain industries. In the early years of the twentieth century more radical industrial-type unions than the Knights of Labor emerged, particularly the Industrial Workers of the World (the IWW or 'Wobblies'), which concentrated on resource workers in western Canada. In Quebec, many unaffiliated Catholic unions emerged in the early 1900s. For Canada as a whole, the Canadian Labor Congress (CLC) was established in 1883 as a holding body for local trade councils, and in 1892 became the Trades and Labour Congress of Canada (TLC)—affiliated with the AFL. In 1902 the TLC expelled unions with connections to the Knights of Labor or AFL affiliations. Seventeen of the 23 unions involved were from Quebec, and they became the backbone of the National Trades and Labor Congress of Canada (NTLC), founded in 1903. Not until the 1940s was an indigenous Canadian industrial union formed.

There was no single factor that created labour unrest in Canada between 1880 and 1914. However, unionism was still trying to gain a permanent foothold, and most labour conflict revolved around the right to organize and the recognition of unions. The strike and the lockout were the two most common weapons of labour and management, respectively, and despite the work of labour 'arbitrators' and conciliators like the future Prime Minister, William Lyon Mackenzie King—who began his public career in 1900 as Canada's first deputy minister of labour —there were few alternatives to open industrial warfare. The leading provinces for labour unrest

were British Columbia and Quebec, although strikes became common everywhere after 1900. Except in the far West, most of the workers involved in labour confrontations were skilled rather than unskilled, but much depended on local conditions. In Ontario, for example— which in its 10 largest cities alone witnessed 421 strikes and lockouts, involving 60,000 workers, between 1901 and 1914—fewer than 10 per cent of strikers came from the ranks of the unskilled or semi-skilled. But Ontario was highly industrialized. In the Maritimes, 324 strikes occurred between 1901 and 1914. Unskilled workers were involved in 37 per cent of these strikes, skilled workers in 28 per cent, and miners in another 18.5 per cent.[16]

Socialists were to be found everywhere in Canada after 1900, although their political successes in local and municipal elections are still among Canada's best-kept secrets. One of the most successful was Arthur W. Puttee of Winnipeg, who became Canada's first labour member of Parliament in 1900 as a result of a by-election. The most militant socialists were in British Columbia, where socialism represented both a political and a labour movement, the two parts often colliding with one another. The Socialist Party of Canada was organized in 1904 in BC as the result of a merger of Marxists and the Canadian Socialist League. BC labour unrest was particularly strong among miners, for whom the common categories of skilled and unskilled held little meaning. In this kind of environment, syndicalists (who sought to transfer the means of production to the workers by means of industrial action) and radicals (such as the Wobblies, or the 'Impossibilists', who insisted that capitalism could never be reformed) did very well. The leading theoretician of the BC Socialists was the American-born E.T. Kingsley, who had lost both his legs in an industrial accident in California. Kingsley had left the United States in an internal struggle with Daniel De Leon in the Socialist Labor Party, and he was a fervent believer in 'Impossiblism'.

There were only too many occasions in Canada when the civil authorities (in the person of policemen and even militiamen) intervened in labour conflicts—usually in the name of public order and hence on the side of management. Nevertheless, the Canadian state was relatively receptive to the rights of labour to organize. Whereas in the United States public policy was almost universally hostile to labour organization, in Canada union activity was legalized fairly early (beginning in the 1880s). Thus, it is not surprising that in Canada the incidence of strikes and lockouts actually increased in comparison with the United States. By 1914, approximately 155,000 Canadians belonged to organized labour unions, many of them affiliated with American 'internationals'. Labour unrest was endemic in Canada before and even during the Great War.

LABOUR AND REFORM

The role played by organized labour in social reform was complex. Certainly the labour movement grew substantially in the reform years, consolidating its position in the larger industrial areas of the nation as industrialization expanded. Many labour leaders were sympathetic to reform of the larger society, but reluctant to spend energy pressing for change outside the immediate purview of the workplace. This certainly was the position of Samuel Gompers and the American Federation of Labor after 1896.[17] Gompers demanded 'more, more, more' for his membership, but showed little interest in the community. The Trades and Labour Congress of Canada had a reform wing and supported many initiatives, including the passage in 1906 of the Lord's Day Act, prohibiting most work and commercial recreation on Sundays. Other labour leaders, especially the more radical ones in western Canada, opposed social reform on the grounds that capitalism (and the society based on it) was incapable of reform and that attempts at improving conditions served to weaken the

class struggle—the only hope the proletariat had of bringing down the wage system. 'Do not think that a revolutionary socialist is opposed to reform as such', insisted Ed Fulcha of Brandon, 'he would gladly make things better for the working class were it possible; but he knows that nothing short of socialism can benefit the workers.'[18] Winnipeg's *Western Clarion*, a popular labour newspaper, editorialized in 1908 that 'to improve conditions under any system is surely to strengthen that system and to strengthen a system means to prolong its existence'.[19] Many socialists maintained that only when conditions became intolerable would the workers do what they had to do in order to overturn the system. At the same time, the association of labour organizations with strikes, violence, and even the advocacy of revolution, meant that many middle-class reformers were quite happy not to have the wholehearted support of a movement that they found suspect and distasteful.

Nevertheless, in the 1880s one of the major labour organizations in Canada was an important advocate of social change. The Noble and Holy Order of the Knights of Labor had been founded in Philadelphia in 1869 and soon spread across the continent, arriving in Canada in the 1870s.[20] Unlike earlier craft unions, the Knights were an all-inclusive body that excluded only bankers, lawyers, gamblers, and saloon-keepers; even women were welcomed as members. The Knights were less concerned with industrial action than with moral suasion and the establishment of fraternal bodies combining the functions of labour union locals, the secret societies so common in the period, and political reform clubs. The Knights sought—as one of their American declarations of principles put it—'to secure to the workers the full enjoyment of the wealth they create, sufficient leisure in which to develop their intellectual, moral, and social faculties: all of the benefits, recreation and pleasures of association; in a word, to enable them to share in the gains and honors of advancing civilization'.[21] As a consequence, they had a lengthy shopping list of reforms, including prohibition of child labour, preservation of the health and safety of workers, temperance, and equal pay for equal work for both sexes—as well as restrictions on immigration, especially from countries that today would be called 'underdeveloped'. The fraternal ritual of the Knights was typical of the age, and it was consciously employed to create a unified working class and working-class culture in Canada. Hundreds of supporters of the Knights established newspapers (often short-lived) and spoke from the hustings to advocate a more egalitarian and humanitarian society. The Knights of Labor ultimately failed in their aims, partly because their organization was localized, partly because their platform was so diffuse. But the movement certainly succeeded in educating many Canadians in a variety of radical ideas, many of which came under the general heading of social reform.

For labour, the question was always whether to stick tenaciously to workplace issues, or whether to join in larger reform movements. The problem with larger movements was that they often put labour on the same side as its enemies, and furthermore hopelessly confused goals. For example, while the Trades and Labour Congress had joined the Presbyterian and Methodist churches in supporting the 1906 Lord Day's Act because it legislated a day off for workers, the bill was basically sectarian in nature and had several weaknesses from labour's perspective. In the first place, it provided many exemptions for industries that could not be easily shut down for one day a week or that provided essential services. Moreover, it prohibited most of the recreations popular with the working classes, such as Sunday excursions and games charging admission fees. Yet sporting activities run out of private clubs—such as golf—which did not charge daily admission fees—were permitted to continue. The bill was also attacked by some French-Canadian members of the House as an attempt to impose the values of Ontario Protestants on all Canadians. The chief legacy of the bill was the

total Sunday ban on commercial activity, which remained in force throughout most of Canada until the 1960s. But it was relatively ineffectual in its efforts to close down industrial production on Sunday, and had only limited benefits for workers.[22]

WOMEN AND REFORM

Mainstream reform movements in English-speaking Canada were spearheaded by members of the middle and professional classes who shared the common assumptions of the age about moral regeneration and social purity. Women, because of their generally nurturing role in society, played critical roles in almost all aspects of reform, but particularly in the areas of temperance–prohibition, public health, education, reform of vice, and women's suffrage. Some modern scholars have argued that Canadian women were not seriously involved in the restructuring of gender roles in society, but concentrated on 'maternal' or 'social feminism', supporting movements that emphasized moral regeneration or the traditional Protestant middle-class virtues. Even potentially radical change, such as labour reform, was often approached from the point of view of motherly care. In urban and rural areas alike, existing women's organizations were harnessed to different reform causes.

THE SUFFRAGE MOVEMENT

An early proponent of women's rights and political activism was Emily Stowe, the first Canadian woman doctor and the founder, in 1876, of Canada's first suffrage organization. Born in 1831, Stowe obtained a degree from the New York Medical College for Women in 1867, after being refused admission to a Canadian medical school. She set up practice in Toronto, but initially was refused certification by the Ontario College of Physicians and Surgeons on the grounds that she had not attended one of the provincial medical schools—because, of course,

■ 'The Door Steadily Opens', cartoon by Dick Hartley, *Grain Growers' Guide*, 21 Sept. 1910. 'Special Privilege' still tries to keep her out, but the woman will soon use her suffrage broom to sweep him away, along with 'Monopoly', 'Drink', 'Corrupt Press', 'Graft', 'White Slavers', and 'Combines'. Saskatchewan Archives Board, R-A369-2.

none of them would admit her. She was not properly accredited until 1880 (her refusal to take provincial examinations allowed another woman, Jennie Trout, to become licensed before her). Like many of the early female activists, Stowe turned to political militancy as a result of personal experience.

Aimed at redressing women's lack of political power, the suffrage movement was dominated by well-educated, middle-class urban women who wanted the vote in order to bring about legislative change in other areas, especially to address the evils of a decadent society—such as prostitution and the liquor trade—and correct injustices against women, such as unequal pay, bad working conditions, and legal discrimination. Not all supporters of suffrage were women—in fact, about a quarter of its leaders in the late nineteenth and early twentieth centuries were men—but the suffragist elite of both sexes were almost exclusively Canadian- or British-born, members of the mainline Protestant churches. Fewer than 5 per cent of the leaders were Roman Catholics—even though Catholics made up nearly 40 per cent of the country's anglophone population by 1911. Significantly, well over half (60 per cent) of the female leaders in the early twentieth century were gainfully employed, mainly in middle-class occupations—at a time when only about 15 per cent of all Canadian women had jobs (the largest single concentration of employed women in the suffrage movement was in journalism and writing). More than 40 per cent of the suffragist women were single, and most of the rest were married to middle-class professional men. Well over half of this female elite had some form of higher education.[23] These women, first to gain the right to vote, did so in municipal elections. British Columbia led the way in 1872 as part of a legislative extension of the rights of property to married women, and Ontario followed 10 years later.

Gradually, around the turn of the century, the goals of the suffrage movement shifted, as did the composition of its leadership. As some of the barriers to careers for women were lowered slightly and more women entered professional life, the predominantly male society around them adjusted, at least superficially, to their presence, and discrimination became less blatant. But many women—perceiving how deeply rooted was male domination and how difficult to eradicate it would be—chose to get on with their work instead of pursuing the right to vote. They became skeptical about suffrage, and as a result the movement was taken over by women from the upper and middle classes who did not have to work for a living, and for whom social service—'volunteer work', as it was called—was extremely important. The key organization became the National Council of Women of Canada, founded in 1893. For many women, social reform took precedence over the vote itself; indeed, achieving the vote for women was increasingly justified in terms of its impact on recalcitrant governments, rather than on the grounds of the benefits to women that would follow in its wake. According to one women's journal in 1909, 'The hour is now come to call the women of Canada to redress the political, electoral and social evils from which the country suffers.'[24]

As the suffrage movement changed its emphasis, it lost whatever contact it might have had with working-class women. Suspicious of the class bias of both the suffrage and the reform movements, many working-class women refused to support either. As for farm women, their organizations could agree with the urban suffragists on the importance of gaining the vote so that women could use it to 'throw the rascals out' and elect new politicians with new policies. But they were unable to persuade their urban counterparts of the urgency of the particular concerns of the farm sector.[25] Many of the most active organizations among farm women were 'special-interest' branches of larger, male-dominated farmer groups, such as the United Farmers of Alberta and the Saskatchewan Grain Growers, or initiatives encouraged by provincial governments to address the particular problems of rural farm women.

WOMEN'S LEGAL STATUS

A much less publicized set of changes affecting women occurred between 1870 and 1914 as the old prescriptions of the English common law were gradually set aside, in many cases following changes in the legal status of women in England itself. Canadian women benefited greatly from the efforts of their sisters across the Atlantic. New Canadian legislation was based on British parliamentary precedents, notably England's first Married Women's Property Act (1870). By 1900 every common-law province had passed similar legislation. As already noted, these reforms often entailed granting the municipal suffrage to women, since the municipal vote usually was associated with property ownership. Many judges tended to give the new laws a narrow construction. In Ontario, for example, one insisted that the legislature could hardly have intended to give women absolute control over their own property, and the courts continued to maintain that women could not make binding contracts except with their separate property until 1897,

CLARA BRETT MARTIN
(1874–1923)

❖

Born in 1874, Clara Brett Martin decided to enter the legal profession after graduating from Trinity College in Toronto with high honours in mathematics in 1890. In 1891 she petitioned the Law Society of Upper Canada to be registered as a student. The petition was denied, and she was advised to 'remove to the United States', where more than 20 states were prepared to admit women to the bar. Instead of leaving the country, Martin found an Ontario legislator willing to introduce a bill into the provincial legislature that would explicitly define the word 'person' in the statutes of the Law Society as including females. This initiative was supported by Dr Emily Stowe, leader of the Dominion Woman's Enfranchisement Association, who gained the approval of Premier Oliver Mowat for new legislation. However, the legislation that was passed in 1892 was watered down so that women could become only solicitors (not barristers), and then only at the discretion of the law society. But once again the Law Society refused entry to Ms Martin. Only after Oliver Mowat himself moved her admission did the members of the Law Society agree—by the narrowest of margins. Although she was accepted as an articling student by one of the most prestigious law firms in Toronto, disapproval from within the firm forced her to change firms in 1893. She also was harassed in the lecture halls of Osgoode Hall, and missed as many lectures as she possibly could. She eventually completed her degree and easily passed the bar examinations. Martin also pressed for revision of the legislation that allowed women to be only solicitors. She won this battle, and then had to face the Law Society again. A final controversy came over the dress code for female barristers. Women were required to wear their gowns over a black dress. Martin was finally admitted as a barrister and solicitor on 2 February 1897, the first female in the British Empire to enter the legal profession. For most of her career she practised in her own firm in Toronto.

when unambiguous legislation was passed. By 1900 married women had full control of their own property and wages, could carry on business in their own right, and, except in Prince Edward Island, had the right to profits from their own businesses. The achievement of these reforms, however, probably had less to do with recognizing the rights of women than with serving the needs of a business-oriented society that could no longer operate under the old agrarian-based law.

Many of the other legal disabilities affecting women were much slower to change, including the prohibition on women's practising law. In 1874, the *Canadian Illustrated News* found the notion amusing: 'The idea of women mingling in public affairs . . . and exercising professions which necessarily banish all maiden mawkishness, is so novel, so contrary to all notion of feminine sweetness, modesty, and delicacy, that we are apt to be hilarious over it, even when most gravely advocated.'[26] Twenty years later, nothing

SPEECH BY
SARA ROWELL WRIGHT,
PRESIDENT, WCTU, 1914

The following is an excerpt from a speech delivered to the Social Service Congress of Canada in March 1914.

I wish I had time to tell you of the many departments of our work. Primarily we were organized for the abolition of the liquor traffic, and I can truthfully say that through the years we have faithfully followed the gleam. Some of you may have thought that we have been detracked by side-issues. Ah, not so, for we have learned with heartache that there were many streams, all tributary to the dark gulf stream of intemperance; and that is why we are agitating for the cigarette bill, and that is why our organization from coast to coast stands almost a unit for the enfranchisement of women. Why should we not? During all the time since ever liquor was introduced women have ever and always been its chief sufferers. Its sword has pierced her very soul, she has again and again seen the lord of her life, her husband, transformed into a veritable beast through its malignant spell; and if there be one thing harder than this I think it must be for a mother to see the idols of her soul, her own children, dragged down to the nethermost depths because of it. . . . Is it any wonder, then, that the wctu ardently desires the enfranchisement of women? Why? Not from such low aims as to add a little paltry power to their positions; ah, not so, but because we realize that the ballot in the hands of the women must mean eventually the outlawry of the liquor traffic. It will mean more than that. Olive Schreiner [a British feminist], in her admirable work 'Women and Labor', sounds a high clear, strong note when she enumerates the many things which she from her very soul believes will come to pass when the women of the world are enfranchised; and one of those things she predicts is that war will of necessity cease, and she adds, in pertinent fashion, 'I cannot think it can cease much before then, and its discontinuance cannot be much longer delayed.' And so you can understand how greatly we were encouraged by that resolution [of the Congress], that carried amidst tumultuous applause for the enfranchisement of women. As a woman—a mere woman, a voteless woman—I think I should have felt rather badly if you had seen fit to enfranchise your Indians—and you don't know how glad I was for that—without saying what you would have done for the women of Canada. You passed a resolution to enfranchise the Indians; and supposing your Federal Parliament did it, you would have left your mothers and wives and sisters alone with the criminals and idiots. Today we stand with the Indians, and criminals and idiots, but we will be so glad if the women and the Indians can be enfranchised by our friends—and then that will leave the criminals and idiots. But you know that you cannot be doing a better thing for your Indians than to enfranchise them. How can we expect them to develop into the full stature of perfect manhood while we deny them the rights of citizenship? It is our fault, not theirs, that they have fallen so far below the standard.

had changed. In 1896, the *Canada Law Journal* admitted that 'there is some reason for the admission of women to the medical profession', but insisted that:

we know of no public advantage to be gained by their being admitted to the bar, whilst there are many serious objections on grounds which are scarcely necessary to refer to. As a matter of taste it is rather a surprise to most men to see a woman seeking a profession where she is bound to meet much that would offend the natural modesty of her sex.[27]

Finally, after a five-year battle, Clara Brett Martin of Toronto in February 1897 became the first female lawyer in the British Empire. Despite this victory, women were otherwise barred from the legal system, unable to vote let alone to serve as jurors, judges, or legislators. Not many women were willing to follow Clara Brett Martin into the legal profession, and as late as 1930 there were fewer than two dozen women practising law in Canada. Moreover, the law continued to exhibit a double standard towards men and women in most of its dealings.

THE WOMAN'S CHRISTIAN TEMPERANCE UNION AND ITS FRIENDS

One reform organization was equally strong in urban and rural areas.[28] The Woman's Christian Temperance Union (WCTU) was an excellent example of the maternal, evangelical strain in women's reform organizations. Founded in 1874 in Owen Sound, Ontario, by 1900 the WCTU claimed 10,000 members, and its influence ranged far beyond its membership. Ultimately dedicated to preserving the family, especially children, against the dangers of degenerate modern society, the WCTU had its first great success in 1878 with the passage of the Canada Temperance Act (the Scott Act), which authorized prohibition of the sale of alcohol by 'local option' in counties and smaller jurisdictions within the provinces.

In fact, despite the 'temperance' in its name, the WCTU was from the beginning committed to prohibition, and soon came to see the elimination of alcoholic beverages as the solution to many of the ills besetting Canadian society, from the abuse and exploitation of women and children to crime, political corruption, and general immorality. But prohibition was not the only strategy for reform. The WCTU also organized children's play groups (the 'Little White Ribboners') and youth groups (the 'Bands of Hope'). A speech made in 1898 by Jessie C. Smith, called 'Social Purity', expressed the spirit of the WCTU:

What strength, what purity, what self-control,
What love, what wisdom should belong to her
Who helps God fashion an immortal soul.

That is the burden that rests on Christian Mothers, helping God fashion immortal souls, and our WCTU true to God, and Home, and Native land, sets itself to help Mothers, and Fathers too, in laying, as the hearthstone of every home, the foundation of Social Purity in Canada, let us, then, like charity, begin at home.[29]

The WCTU was only one of several members of the Dominion Alliance for the Total Suppression of the Liquor Traffic. Like most reform movements in Canada, prohibition required state intervention in order to be effective. The WCTU was unusual, however, in its ability to generate credible political candidates, who campaigned as independents (the two major parties generally tried to ignore the question) on a prohibition platform and appeared regularly on the ballot in most provinces. Inevitably the political goals of prohibition drew its supporters into women's suffrage. As the president of the WCTU explained in 1914, women were the chief victims of liquor, and therefore they realized that 'the ballot in the hands of the women must mean eventually the outlawry of the liquor traffic'.[30] For many women, this was a compelling argument.

As a movement, prohibitionism exemplified both the best and the worst features of reform. Strongly based in the Protestant churches, it had only limited support in Catholic districts and in Quebec, and none among the urban working classes, who regarded it with suspicion on several

■ A WCTU group in Regina, 1908. Standing at the right is Louise McKinney, who in the 1920s would be one of the 'famous five' behind the *Persons* case, as a result of which women gained the legal status of 'persons' eligible to serve in the Senate. Glenbow Archives, NA-1399-1.

grounds. Many urban workers were recent immigrants of Catholic background and felt personally attacked by the prohibitionists, who often attributed their political failures to an unholy alliance between the 'liquor interests' and the 'Catholic vote'. Other workers regarded prohibition as a class issue, an attempt by the middle classes to eliminate one of the few pleasures they enjoyed in a hard and otherwise impoverished life.

Anti-liquor organizations such as the WCTU were frequently overzealous in their desire to suppress what they saw as related 'vices'—such as public dancing, gambling, theatrical performances, and the reading of 'trashy novels'—that

were acceptable to most Canadians at the time. From the WCTU perspective, innocent children were entitled to protection against all abuses. Even when their campaigns were directed against social evils that most of society shared in condemning—such as prostitution—the moral fervour and single-mindedness of the prohibitionists turned many citizens against them. Its efforts to establish curfew laws for minors in several provinces were never universally popular and seldom successful. Much prohibitionist sentiment tended to be morally old-fashioned, even puritanical. Organizations like the WCTU were especially traditional in their attitudes towards women, exalting their role as moral guardians of society. In addition, many prohibitionists were unabashed eugenicists, despite a fundamental contradiction (if 'evil habits' were inherited, the effort to legislate them out of existence would seem pointless). For many Christian anti-liquor campaigners, the prohibition movement served as an outlet for energies that in earlier days might have found expression in religious revivalism.

In Quebec, the conditions for a social-reform movement certainly existed, and many French Canadians, male and female, were actively involved in addressing the consequences of urbanization and industrialization on a variety of fronts. But French-Canadian women were significantly underrepresented in most national reform movements, and had great difficulty creating viable organizations. Nevertheless, the bicultural Montreal Local Council of Women was founded in 1893, and in 1907 Marie Gérin-Lajoie created the Fédération nationale Saint-Jean-Baptiste (FNSJB). Her call for action could have been made by many of her anglophone sisters:

> Ladies, do you realize how important it is for you to vote in the municipal elections. . . . You will complain that your son dissipates his health and fortune in the neighbourhood bar, you will be overcome with sorrow at the sight of your daughter whose virtue is gradually being eroded by immoral theatre, you will condemn the death of a child, contaminated by the filth in the streets and still you do not attempt to remedy these evils.[31]

But the scope for action available to women, especially French-Canadian women, in Quebec was severely limited by the anti-feminist ideology of the traditional society and in particular the Roman Catholic Church. Religious women were allowed an active role outside the home, but most women were expected to live their lives inside the family, as mothers and homemakers.

The FNSJB distinguished between 'good' feminism, which did not challenge traditional roles, and 'bad' feminism, which searched for alternatives to tradition. It became actively involved in various social-reform movements, including the campaign against liquor, but instead of seeking prohibition sought only to reduce the number of liquor outlets in Montreal. It was able to co-operate with the WCTU in an Anti-Alcoholic League that ran candidates in municipal elections. For its part, the WCTU fought, not always successfully, to protect the limited voting rights enjoyed by women in the province, and in 1902, managed to prevent the City of Montreal from withdrawing the vote from women who paid property taxes. In general, however, women in French Canada faced insurmountable hurdles in the male-dominated attitudes of society and Church.

As the goals of reform shifted in the early years of the century—from the search for remedies to specific ills towards generalized efforts at moral regeneration—the opposition to reform became much more widespread and complex. Like the Lord's Day Act, prohibition met with criticism on the grounds of class and religious interests. Although the prohibitionists narrowly won the national plebiscite on prohibition in 1908, Prime Minister Laurier refused to implement national legislation because only 20 per cent of the total electorate had supported the principle. The prohibitionists turned to the provinces, where they succeeded in passing legislation in Prince Edward Island in 1900 and in Nova Scotia in 1910. Local option was even more effective, since it permitted local jurisdictions where prohibitionist sentiment was strong to have their way without requiring hard-to-obtain provincial majorities. Equally local were most of the victories for women's political rights, which often consisted in preventing the removal of existing rights in jurisdictions where votes were granted to women who paid taxes or held property.

THE SOCIAL SERVICE CONGRESS OF 1914

After the turn of the century, the various groups and organizations in Canada concerned with social reform began to recognize the need for co-operation and communication among themselves. Many private agencies—often set up as charitable operations by various churches—were conscripted into quasi-public roles under provincial legislation, serving as arms of the state in the intermediate period before the establishment of permanent government social services. Thus, private child-welfare programs were often made officially responsible for abandoned, abused, and delinquent children while continuing to operate as private charities. The result was an increasing tendency towards a professional approach, although still within the framework of assumptions about individual morality. Thus, women unable to provide for their children because of male abandonment were 'good' clients; women unable to care for their children because they worked as prostitutes were 'bad' clients.

In 1907 the Moral and Social Reform Council of Canada was established, and in 1912 it became the Social Service Council of Canada, which summoned a major congress to meet in Ottawa in March 1914. The report of the congress indicates that many different organizations with many different perspectives were interested in social reform; one basic division was between those who wanted to eradicate capitalism and those who wanted moral reform. Above all, how-ever, reformers generally agreed on the need for public programs of social insurance, mainly in emulation of advanced thinking in Britain, the US, and Germany.[32] Unfortunately, any agreement among reformers in early 1914 was to be rendered irrelevant within a few months, as the nation marched to war.

CONCLUSION

By 1914 the Canadian social-reform movement had many achievements to its credit, including a total overhaul of urban school systems and the introduction of new notions of child care (both public and private, within the family). Some inroads had been made in most areas of urban life and society. Since reform was mainly middle-class and professional in its orientation, it was most successful in areas where professionals held sway, such as the schools, and where its objectives were limited. In those areas where successful reform demanded state intervention—such as housing or poverty—the record was more mixed. The reformers themselves were convinced that most opposition to their endeavours came from corrupt politicians and businessmen. There is a good deal of evidence, however, that, for various reasons, a significant proportion of ordinary Canadians were simply never convinced that the reformers had the answers.

SHORT BIBLIOGRAPHY

Allen, A.R. *The Social Passion: Religion and Social Reform in Canada, 1914–28*. Toronto, 1971. The best study of the Social Gospel movement in Canada.

Bacchi, Carol. *Liberation Deferred: The Ideas of the English-Canadian Suffragists, 1877–1918*. Toronto, 1991. An important work that distinguished between a conservative brand of feminism ('maternal feminism') and more radical varieties.

Backhouse, Constance. *Petticoats and Prejudice: Women and Law in Nineteenth-Century Canada*. Toronto, 1991. A careful analysis of women and the law in the nineteenth century, including the various attempts at reform.

Carbert, Louise. *Agrarian Feminism: The Politics of Ontario Farm Women*. Toronto, 1995. A major and thorough study, confined to Ontario.

Cook, Ramsay. *The Regenerators: Social Criticism in Late Victorian English Canada*. Toronto, 1985. A fascinating introduction to Victorian social criticism in Canada, emphasizing some of the less familiar themes.

Cook, Sharon A. *'Through Sunshine and Shadow': The*

Woman's Christian Temperance Union, Evangelicalism, and Reform in Ontario, 1874–1930. Montreal, 1995. A thorough study, unfortunately confined to Ontario, of the major reform organization in prewar Canada.

Fraser, Brian. *The Social Uplifters: Presbyterian Progressives and the Social Gospel in Canada, 1875–1915*. Waterloo, 1988. The best study of the early Social Gospel.

Kealey, Gregory, and Bryan D. Palmer. *Dreaming of What Might Be: The Knights of Labor in Ontario, 1880–1890*. Toronto, 1982. A fascinating account of the Knights of Labor and working-class culture and reform in Ontario.

Strange, Carolyn. *Toronto's Girl Problem: The Perils and Pleasures of the City, 1885–1930*. Toronto, 1995. A useful study of the condition of women and its perception in Toronto during the period of the feminization of office work and shop services.

Valverde, Mariana. *The Age of Light, Soap, and Water: Moral Reform in English Canada, 1885–1925*. Toronto, 1991. An important general synthesis.

STUDY QUESTIONS

1. Would you have voted for William Howland for mayor in 1886?
2. What was the Social Gospel?
3. What was the difference between corporate reform and humanitarian reform?
4. What were the main divisions of feminism in this period?
5. Why was the WCTU so important?
6. Comment on the speech by the WCTU president to the Social Services Congress in 1914.
7. How many distinct strands of social reform can be identified for the period 1880-1914?
8. What were the principal weaknesses of social reform in Canada before the Great War?

Writing about Agriculture and Rural Society

Despite their importance throughout most of Canada's history, neither agriculture nor rural society received much attention from historians before the 1970s. A large part of the problem was that agricultural development was usually not perceived as central either to the nation's political and constitutional development or to the growth of the cities that for many years—in the 'metropolitan' school of history—were seen as the dominant force in Canada. True, wheat was one of the exportable commodities fundamental to the 'staples' theory of Canadian economic history that dominated the first half of the twentieth century. But agriculture in general was seen as subsidiary to resources and considered only in the context of what new settlers had to do to open up the country. Hence, most early agricultural and rural history focused on wheat and settlement.

Indeed, wheat and settlement were central components of Canadian history for the years between 1870 and 1914. With railway construction and tariff protectionism, the opening of the Prairie West was an integral part of the 'National Policy' by means of which Canada grew and expanded in that period. Most research on wheat production before 1870 was done in the context of political economy. Studies like George Britnell's *The Wheat Economy* (1939) and Vernon Fowke's *The National Policy and the Wheat Economy*

(1957) linked wheat to national and international political and economic issues. What was important was the movement of wheat out of western Canada, not the way it was grown and what that meant for western Canadian society. One exception was the series 'Canadian Frontiers of Settlement', a set of nine volumes researched and written during the 1930s, of which some—most notably Arthur S. Morton's *A History of Prairie Settlement* (1938)—actually dealt in detail with the process of agricultural settlement in the West. The title of the series reflected an attempt to import the major American metaphor of settlement—the frontier—to Canada. But the idea of the frontier never entirely caught on, and work on Prairie settlers and communities was thin on the ground.

Perhaps the most important early work of rural social history was produced by a sociologist in a series that sought to explain a political movement (Social Credit): Jean Burnet's *Next-Year Country: A Study of Rural Social Organization in Alberta* (1951). Considerably more was written by historians about farmers in politics than about farmers on the farm. A few historical geographers pointed the way to the future—particularly Andrew Hill Clark, a Canadian teaching at the University of Wisconsin, and his students. Clark's *Three Centuries and the Island: A Historical Geography of Settlement and*

Agriculture in Prince Edward Island appeared in 1959, and his *Acadia: The Geography of Early Nova Scotia to 1760* was published in 1968. One of Clark's students, R. Cole Harris, published *The Seigneurial System in Early Canada* in 1966. Focusing on the land and the way it was used, historical geography made important contributions to rural history in Canada in the years before social history became so dominant. However, most of the early work on everyday rural life and the actual processes of farming was done by local historians. Although such studies tended to be anecdotal rather than analytical, they were more valuable than is usually recognized. Among historians, both historical geography and local history were widely disdained, the former because it often worked with abstract models and the latter because it did not.

The shift towards a greater interest in farming, together with agricultural lifestyles and socio-economic structures, began during the 1960s as part of a larger movement in the writing of history, both in Canada and internationally. Many factors contributed to the new history. European historians, particularly those working on the medieval period, when political organization was primitive, took the lead. The French 'Annales' school—named after its leading journal, *Annales d'histoire économique et social* (founded 1929)—was extremely influential in its focus on total history (as opposed to political narrative), changes over long periods of time, and study of the relationship between structures and moments of crisis. So, too, was the new concern in the United States to learn more about the history of ordinary people ('history from the bottom up') and previously neglected groups, including women. Works in early American history that reconstructed local communities, particularly in Puritan New England, were important for highlighting a social unit larger than the individual farm. Nevertheless, agrarian history was somewhat

slow to gain a foothold in Canada, perhaps because so few of the new historians emerging in an increasingly urbanized country had much experience of rural life and society, and perhaps because other topics (the working class, the urban poor, racial minorities) seemed much more interesting and relevant. In the hope that Canadian historians might find new strategies for their work, an early issue of *Histoire Sociale/Social History* (founded in 1968) published an article (co-authored by this writer) about community studies in New England, but the journal published little else on rural history in its first 10 years. Gradually, however, new studies began to appear, and not all of them were about prairie wheat.

In many ways, the key works came from French Canada. Fernand Ouellet's *Histoire économique et sociale du Québec, 1760–1850* (1966) imported much of its conceptual approach from the Annales tradition. But the first full-blown application of European methodology to a Canadian historical situation was Louise Dechêne's *Habitants et marchands de Montréal au XVIIe siècle* (1974). At first glance, that title sounds like urban history, but in the seventeenth century the town and its adjoining countryside were inextricably interwoven. Dechêne was able to demonstrate that the region around Montreal looked a good deal more like a French peasant community than had previously been suspected. In addition to drawing on the French tradition, she tapped into the growing anglophone methodologies of quantification and family reconstitution (a sophisticated adaptation of genealogical work for the purposes of historical demography) that had developed out of the French models.

The first attempt to apply the new techniques to English-speaking Canada was made in the 1970s, when the Peel County Historical Project studied one Ontario county immediately west of Toronto for 20 years, from 1851 to 1871, collecting monstrous quantities of data and using both computer analysis and family reconstitution. The final results were explicated in David P. Gagan's *Hopeful Travellers and Social Change in Mid-Victorian Peel County, Canada West* (1981). In many ways, Gagan's use of complex methodologies based on historical demography proved less important than the context in which he put his findings. Gagan demonstrated that family farms were inherently unstable and exploitative, throwing off unwanted family members to seek land or employment elsewhere. Inheritance became an important consideration in which, of course, females were disadvantaged. Similarly, the Saguenay project, headed by Gérard Bouchard, investigated 10 rural parishes near Chicoutimi, Quebec. Its findings were reported by Christian Pouyez and others in 1983 in *Les Saguenayens: Introduction à l'histoire des populations du Saguenay XVI–XXe siècles*. Once again, inheritance proved a critical issue. Because of the enormous costs involved, neither the Peel County nor the Saguenay project was likely to be repeated in subsequent years, when competition for scarce financial resources became fierce.

While the research teams of Gagan and Bouchard were using sophisticated technology to collect and analyze their data, the historian Donald Akenson was taking a different approach to popularizing rural history. In 1978 he founded the journal *Canadian Papers in Rural History*, which provided a publishing outlet for scholars working in the field. Akenson also produced a rural history, *The Irish in Ontario: A Study in Rural History* (1984), that did not rely very much on the computer.

One of the major challenges of the new scholarship was to press beyond the generalizations familiar to Canadians from the Prairie literature. In most of Canada, settlement did not involve homesteading (getting free land from the federal government in return for building a house, cultivating the land, and living on the property). In all areas, carving a farm out of the wilderness was difficult and expensive, and many did not succeed. In a few regions, such as the fruit-farming districts of the British Columbia interior, large amounts of capital were imported to establish farms. In other regions, especially in eastern Canada, occupational pluralism became the only way to survive. Everywhere, scholars emphasized that the image of the independent farmer did not in fact describe those who worked the soil. In his *Empire of Dust: Settling and Abandoning the Prairie Rural Belt* (1987), David C. Jones discusses the rise and fall of a major western region that was unable to withstand decades of drought and bad crops. Historians also increasingly stressed the extent to which the structure of rural life was fundamentally patriarchal and hence ill-suited to the aspirations of women. The life of rural women remains under-investigated today.

Although modern rural history comes in various forms and studies a variety of topics, much of the most important work has focused on the study of particular communities, especially in western Canada. Community studies give historians the opportunity to integrate the various strands of rural life and agriculture. Perhaps the first of the new community studies was Paul Voisey's *Vulcan: The Making of a Prairie Community* (1988). In some ways (such as its nearness to Calgary), Vulcan was not a typical rural community, but Voisey was particularly successful at demonstrating the extent of social life and activity possible in the pre-electronic age. Lyle Dick's *Farmers 'Making Good': The Development of Abernethy District, Saskatchewan, 1880–1920* (1989) may have dealt with a more typical community, in which land consolidation was an important issue. More recently, Kenneth Sylvester has studied a mixed French- and English-speaking community in Manitoba. In *The Limits of Rural Capitalism: Family, Culture, and Markets in*

Montcalm, Manitoba, 1870–1940 (2001), he discusses the resistance of many residents to large-scale commercial agriculture and their willingness to distribute their land among their many offspring, in marked contrast to inheritance strategies farther east.

Almost all studies of rural history in Canada so far have dealt with the period before World War II. Canadian historians have not yet begun to explore the decline of agriculture and rural society after 1945, although this is obviously one of the most important themes for Canada in the post-war period.

A recruitment poster, lithograph, 1914–18. LAC, C-147822.

PART THREE

■ 1914–1945

■ The years between 1914 and 1945 began and ended with wars in which Canada was fully engaged as a loyal member of the British Empire. By the end of World War I it was ready to take an independent seat at the League of Nations; by the end of the second, a new American empire was on the rise, to which it became increasingly tied. The period between the wars saw a difficult period of readjustment, including severe labour unrest, followed by nearly a decade of international depression caused at least in part by the economic dislocation that was one of the costs of the Great War. In Canada the depression was characterized not only by unemployment and personal suffering, but by a retreat from the practice of strong central government that had developed during the war: governments, federal and provincial, seemed incapable even of addressing immediate problems, let alone finding long-term solutions. Unlike some European nations, however, Canada did not fall prey to the simplistic solutions offered by dictators.

Life expectancy increased between 1914 and 1945, as did divorce rates, while the birth rate steadily declined and population continued to shift from rural to urban areas. Although women had gained the federal vote in 1917, they still occupied a second-class position in the society. With increasing independence came an upsurge of nationalism and efforts to establish a distinctive Canadian culture, in which the movement towards 'realism' played an important part. However, a continuing tendency towards racism was highlighted by Ottawa's refusal to accept Jewish refugees from Nazi-dominated Europe in the 1930s.

At home, the war years saw the emergence of a new concern for social welfare. Demands for a new kind of social security would not be fulfilled until after the fighting ended, but the groundwork was laid—politically and ideologically—during the war. By 1945 Canadians would have deferred their expectations of a better life for more than three decades. Canada emerged from World War II, as it had from the previous war, on a note of increased central state power and enhanced national aspirations.

CHAPTER NINE

The Great War and Its Aftermath, 1914–1919

■ Canada's entry into World War I marked a triumph of sorts for Canadian imperialism. It also rejuvenated Canadian reformers. Canada had played very little direct part in the events leading up to the war. Nonetheless, the war was in many respects a watershed for Canadians. It introduced them to the realities—positive and negative—of the twentieth century. Canadian casualties were extremely heavy. At a time when the total population was only 8 million, 620,000 served in uniform, of whom 60,661 were killed in action and 172,000 wounded. Together, the patriotic fervour of the war and the eventual political isolation of French Canada, sealed by the Conscription Crisis of 1917, made possible a sweeping program of reform, much of which French Canadians had opposed. Reform has always required an active state, and wartime conditions encouraged the Canadian government to intervene in almost all areas of life and work.

MOBILIZATION FOR WAR

Canada officially went to war at 2045 hours (Ottawa time) on 4 August 1914, as an automatic consequence of the British declaration of war on Germany. Yet, if Canada had no say in the decision to go to war, it did have some control over the extent of its involvement. The Canadian Minister of Militia was Colonel Sam Hughes, who had long expected that Canadians eventually would meet Germans on the battlefield.[1] On 10 August, an Order-in-Council permitted him to call 25,000 men to the colours. By this time some militia units had already begun appealing for men. In Winnipeg, for example, Lieutenant-Colonel J.W. de C. O'Grady had mustered his unit, the 90th Winnipeg Rifles, in their drill hall and announced that he had promised that the regiment would turn out 'not only [in] full strength but one thousand strong. Who goes?'[2] The response was overwhelming, and on 9 August—the day before the Order-in-Council—the Rifles held a recruiting parade on the streets of Winnipeg. When formal sign-ups began after 10 August, one of the rules was that married men had to have the permission of their wives, many of whom dragged their spouses out of the ranks while brandishing their marriage certificates. These early volunteers had virtually no uniforms or equipment, and were sent for first training aboard trams.

By the time the Canadian Parliament met on 18 August the die was cast. Canadian volunteers would participate in the war on a massive scale. On 22 August Parliament passed 'An Act to confer certain powers upon the Governor in Council in the event of War, Invasion, or Insurrection'—

TIMELINE

1909

At imperial conference Canada agrees to create navy.

1910

House of Commons debates naval policy. In Ontario, battle over bilingual schools begins.

1911

Laurier government defeated, partly over naval question.

1914

Canada enters the Great War. War Measures Act passed.

1915

A revised Regulation 17 passed in Ontario.

1916

British launch first tank attack.

1917

National Wheat Board established to market wheat. Great War Veterans Association formed. Canada's first income tax introduced in July. Military Service Act becomes law in August. Wartime Elections Act passed in September. Union government created in October.

1918

Women get federal vote. Federal government introduces prohibition. Letter carriers strike post office. War ends.

1919

Exhibit of Canadian war art in London. Winnipeg General Strike and other sympathetic strikes. 'Soldier Settlement' schemes introduced.

1928

Canadian Legion organized.

---

the famous War Measures Act—enabling the government to act in the defence of the realm without consulting Parliament. Before August was over, Sam Hughes had created a vast training camp northwest of Quebec City at Valcartier—a tent city capable of housing 32,000 men. Before the end of September the first contingents of soldiers from Valcartier were boarding the passenger liners that would take them to Britain. The fleet sailed on 3 October and arrived at Plymouth 11 days later. 'Canada's Answer', as the British called the new arrivals, numbered 31,200. Sent to bivouac on Salisbury Plain, they were finally reviewed by King George V on 4 February 1915, and before the end of the month they were suffering their first casualties on the front lines in France. One of the advantages of the breathtak-ing speed with which Hughes had moved to create Canadian regiments was that Canadian troops were kept together as units rather than being broken up and integrated into the British forces.

WAR IN THE TRENCHES, 1914–1918

TECHNOLOGICAL CHANGE

Only a handful of military theorists in 1914 appreciated how long and horrible the war was likely to be; their predictions were based mainly on the American Civil War and the Boer War. New technologies—including machine guns, tanks, submarines, airplanes, poison gas, radios,

CECILY JANE GEORGINA FANE POPE
(1862–1938)

❖

Cecily Jane Georgina Fane Pope was born in 1862, the second youngest of eight children. Her father was William Henry Pope, one of Prince Edward Island's most powerful politicians, and her mother a Desbrisay, with roots dating to the early days of settlement. Raised in an atmosphere of Victorian respectability and genteel poverty, 'Georgie' joined several siblings in converting to Roman Catholicism in the 1870s. In 1885 she graduated from the Bellevue Hospital School of Nursing in New York City, and she soon became superintendent of nursing at Washington's Columbia Hospital for Women and then head of the nursing staff at St John's Hospital in Yonkers, New York.

In 1899 she was as one of seven medical staff—three doctors and four nurses—sent by the Canadian Militia Department to South Africa, where she was named to head the Canadian nursing staff. Complaining that the authorities would not allow the nurses anywhere near the battlefields, she was put in charge of the nurses at a 600-bed hospital near Cape Town, and soon was helping to care for hundreds of casualties there. At the end of 1899 she was transferred to another hospital near Rondesbosch, put in charge of the 'enteric fever' ward (a catch-all for various epidemic diseases). Later she and her fellow nurses were moved very near the battlefield at Kroonstadt before returning home early in 1901.

Pope returned for a second tour of duty early in 1902, and the following year was the first Canadian to be awarded a Royal Red Cross medal. Remaining active in the militia, she waited for the establishment of an Army Medical Corps (1904) and then a permanent Nursing Branch in 1906, which she quickly joined. By 1908 she was the head of Nursing, but although she designed the uniform for the Canadian Army Medical Corps nurses, she was apparently regarded as too old for active service when the Great War began. She spent the first three years of the war in Halifax training more than 3,100 nurses for duty in France and Flanders. Finally posted to France in late 1917, she soon came down with arteriosclerosis and, in June of 1918, was diagnosed with 'battle fatigue' and sent home. She retired on 1 March 1919 to Prince Edward Island. On her death in 1938 she lay in state at Government House before her burial with full military honours.

and telephones, in addition to an assortment of huge cannons—would make it possible to slaughter increasing numbers of soldiers and civilians alike. Canadians also served not only in the navy but in the air force (initially the RAF and later the Canadian Air Force), and a number of young Canadians became well-known as flying aces. The best-known of the group, Captain Billy Bishop, was the top-scoring Imperial pilot, claiming 72 aerial victories (although controversy would erupt in the 1980s over whether he had exaggerated his exploits).

The really important developments, however, were in the technology for defensive firepower—the repeating rifle, the machine gun, the big artillery, with barbed wire and concrete that made it increasingly difficult for offensive charges to overwhelm enemy positions, especially when the defensive forces (usually the Germans) were dug into permanent trenches along a line that extended 475 miles (765 km) across Europe from the North Sea to the Swiss frontier. The machine gun was the centrepiece of the defensive position, capable of spitting out a hail of fatal bullets at any charge. On one horrible day in 1916 at Beaumont-Hamel in the Somme, 684 Newfoundlanders were trapped by barbed wire and mowed down by German machine guns; 310 died. The British Army suffered 57,470 casualties and the Germans 8,000 on that day alone. Not an inch of ground was gained. By the time the Somme campaign had ended in November, the Allied forces had gained 10 kilometres of ground at a cost of approximately 600,000 casualties. Failure to comprehend how defensive firepower had changed the rules of war was endemic among leaders both civilian and military. For Canada, this lack of comprehension was perhaps best symbolized by the Ross rifle with which Sir Sam Hughes had equipped most Canadian troops. The Ross was a splendid gun for sharpshooting and sniping, but its repeat mechanism tended to overheat and jam, making it practically useless for rapid fire in mass assault situations. In 1915, when Canadian soldiers were first exposed to such conditions, they threw their Rosses away by the thousands and collected either Mausers (German) or Enfields (English) from those who fell on the battlefields. Hughes nonetheless waited for months before agreeing to replace the Rosses with Enfields.

Towards the end of the war, airplanes and tanks made some breakthroughs in the defensive stalemate on the Western Front. The first tank

attack, launched by the British in September 1916, succeeded in frightening the Germans, and although the early tanks were not very reliable, they were soon improved. In November 1917, at the battle of Cambrai, the British sent 400 tanks into 'No Man's Land', flattening barbed wire and crossing ditches. The attack was so successful at breaching the Hindenburg Line that the British did not have enough infantry at the spot to follow it up.

LIFE IN THE TRENCHES

The Germans began digging in from September 1914. Because they were the first to dig they were able to choose the best locations and possessed most of the higher and drier ground. The British and their allies quickly responded with entrenchments of their own paralleling the German ones, with a No Man's Land—varying in size from a few metres to several hundred—in between along the entire length of the line. Allied trenches, on lower ground, tended to be less permanent, often filling with mud and water. The trenches were not just long straight fortified holes in the ground, but zigzags and cul-de-sacs, including 'saps'—narrow passages leading only to isolated listening posts. As fully articulated, there would be a whole series of lines of trenches extending back from No Man's Land with connecting passages. These were inhabited by troops in various stages of combat readiness. Not everyone was on the 'front lines', but reserves might be called up at any time. Within the trenches were the dugouts, shelters against the weather and enemy artillery. For officers these could be quite elaborate, but most enlisted men sheltered under bits of wood or even in hollows dug into the walls of the trench.

The study of military history has altered substantially in recent years. Historians are no longer as concerned as they once were with command decisions or the strategic movement of troops (although these subjects are still taught at staff colleges). Rather, the influence of social his-

■ Canadian soldiers washing their feet in a flooded shell hole, June 1917. LAC, PA-1456.

tory has been reflected in the increasing attention paid to the experiences of the soldiers under battle conditions.[3] Life in the trenches—the experience shared by of the majority of the Canadian soldiers in World War I—was a nightmare, so hard to describe that most returning veterans did not really try. Those at home seldom heard about their loved ones' experience in the trenches, even in letters from the front. Although troops were rotated in and out of the front lines, periods of rotation were not standardized, and during times of crisis the time spent in the front line could be quite long. Artillery shelling was constant, and reserves in the secondary and tertiary lines of fortifications were even more likely than those in the front lines to come under fire from the big guns, since artillery crews always aimed at longer-range targets for fear of hitting their own men. Actual attacks and offensives were relatively rare, and many units sustained heavy casualties without ever engaging the enemy. Shells, snipers, sickness, and mud were the major culprits. Changing positions in the mud was particularly difficult. Most Canadian soldiers carried more than 60 pounds (27 kg) of equipment, and a mud-soaked army greatcoat could weigh another 50 pounds (23 kg).

Soldiers in the front-line trenches had to be constantly on the alert while employed on 'fatigues': moving rations, stores, and wounded

A Letter from Convalescence in England, 1915

William Gavin Johnston, from Morden, Manitoba, spent four years at the front in World War I, rising from private to captain with the Princess Patricia Regiment Canadian Light Infantry. Like many another soldier, he wrote home regularly. This letter to his sister is probably more frank than most.

June 4, 1915
Manor House Hospital
England

My Dear Sister Maud:

I received your letter after it had been to France and followed me back. I was very glad to hear from you. I was wounded by shell splinters on May 5 and was sent over here. I was not severely injured at all and will be out in a week or so.

Our regiment was nearly wiped out the day I was wounded. There were only 62 men and one officer left and I considered myself very lucky indeed to get off so lightly. We had to return two miles as the Germans tried to outflank us. There were 33 divisions of us holding trenches in a half circle when the enemy brought up reinforcements and nearly cut us off. So at night we retired back and dug ourselves in about 3 miles in front of the city of Ypres.

The Germans seemed particularly eager to capture that city, as there is a straight road from there to Calais. We were in a sort of half circle but somewhat diminished. The Germans could sweep in from both sides and the front with their artillery, and they sure opened up something awful with all kinds of big guns.

They even had heavy siege guns playing on our humbly made trenches, which knocked them practically to nothing. It was just murder. Men were buried alive, blown to pieces and we had to find shelter in shell holes, behind the dead, or any cover we could get. Reserves were constantly coming up but half of them were wiped out before they even got to us.

The German infantry made several attempts to advance but were driven back each time till we were ordered to retire to the support trenches, as there was nothing left of the firing line. At night our men regained the front line trench again after a desperate bayonet charge. I do not know what happened after that.

In fact I was wounded before the charge was made. The hospital behind the firing line is more like a slaughterhouse than anything else. Doctors are rushing around with sleeves rolled up, blood all over, giving the men their first dressing, digging the bullets and shell splinters out, or cutting off limbs that are hanging by the skin. They do not seem to be very gentle either, but when you consider the number that go through their hands, it is something remarkable how they go through so fast. Sometimes it is two to three thousand.

I had a piece of shell in my chest the size of a marble and I did not have time to holler before he had it cut out. . . . What is left of the regiment is coming back to England to reorganize. It is reported that they may be sent to the Dardanelles if the war lasts another winter. I would prefer going there, as the wet and cold in Flanders is something cruel. I have had more shivers run up and down my skin in some of the trenches in one hour in January and February than I have ever had in Canada. You can just imagine, say in Manitoba in November, getting into a ditch with water and slush over your knees for 48 hours with never a hot drink and only cold water and biscuit and corn beef. . . . It is surprising how the men keep up spirit. No one except those who have had the experience knows the terrible hardships that the troops have gone through. It is a great strain on a man as one is practically always under shellfire.

SOURCE: Phillip R. Giffin, 'A Family Memoir: The Men of #2 Company, Princess Patricia Canadian Light Infantry, 1915', *Manitoba History* no. 53 (Oct. 2006): 48–9.

men, and repairing the trenches. Sleep deprivation was the norm. Soldiers suffered from the heat in summer and the cold in winter, and from rain virtually year-round. Corpses lying outside and inside the trenches attracted vermin in great numbers, including what one Canadian remembered as huge rats, 'so big they would eat a wounded man if he couldn't defend himself'.[4] The trenches also stank, not only of decomposing bodies but of chloride of lime (a disinfectant), creosol (for the flies), human sweat, and excrement. Most soldiers were also constantly conscious of the noise of the guns, and some were able to distinguish the various weapons. In his diary Dr Andrew Macphail, who served with the 7th Canadian Field Ambulance, recorded how he would 'amuse' himself finding words to describe the sounds made by the various classes of guns:

The 18 pounders thud, thud. The 4.7s bark like an infinite dachshund. The howitzers smash. The machine-guns rat-tat like a wood-pecker or the knocker of a door. A single rifle snaps like a dry twig when it is broken. Rapid rifle fire has a desolating sound; it is as if a load of small stones was being dumped from a Scotch cart. A large shell sounds exactly like a railway train; and shrapnel bursts as if boiler-plate were being torn into fragments, or as if the sky were made of sheet-iron, and had been riven by a thunderbolt. The whistle of the passing rifle bullet is unmistakable.[5]

What many found most disturbing in the sound of gunfire were the vibrations and the 'solid ceiling of sound'. By 1918 soldiers were also exposed to attacks from the air. The Great War produced a new form of nervous affliction that at the time was called 'shell shock' but has more recently been labelled as a form of traumatic stress disorder.

The conditions of trench life may help to explain how the men were able to risk death in battle. Sleep-deprived and in a chronic state of shock, most troops fought in a numb, zombie-like state. Those in charge never knew what the war was like in the trenches. Convinced of the mystical value of moral fortitude, the British high command apparently never understood that a frontal assault could end in nothing but carnage. In April 1915, at Ypres, the Royal Winnipeg Rifles withstood one of the first poison gas attacks, using for protection nothing but handkerchiefs soaked in urine. After beating back the enemy at great human cost and with other units retreating all around him, the regiment's colonel, with the support of his junior officers, volunteered to hold the line. He telephoned divisional headquarters and reported modestly, 'The 90th Rifles can hold their bit.' And they did. The battalion's casualties in this one battle amounted to 20 officers and 550 men killed, wounded, missing, or gassed out of a total of 900.[6]

The dispatches spoke reassuringly of heroic stands, but the soldiers knew perfectly well that

■ A Canadian battalion going 'over the top', October 1916. LAC, PA-648.

their sacrifices were achieving little. Canada, like the other settlement colonies, including New-foundland, tended to experience greater casualties than the European allies. It has never been clear whether the reason had more to do with the colonials' relative lack of experience or with the fact that they were placed in the most dangerous positions. A sufficiently serious wound—a 'blighty'—might allow a soldier to be invalided back to Britain or even to Canada, but most of the Canadian troops sent to Europe either died on the battlefield or remained on the lines until the Armistice. In 1917 the Imperial Order Daughters of the Empire campaigned for home furloughs for the 'Old Originals'—those who had

been in the army since the early days of the war—but in the end only 838 men ever made it back to Canada on leave.

CONSCRIPTION

In Canada the greatest wartime debate concerned conscription. Canada had entered the war with an army made up entirely of volunteers whose enthusiasm was predicated on the prospect of a swift victory. By 1917, however, support for the war effort had come to be based on the sheer extent of the sacrifices that had already been made. Canada's military contribution was sub-stantial. Serving as the shock troops of the

■ The Newfoundland Regiment, D Company, near St John's, 1915. On 1 July 1916 the Newfoundlanders would see their first action in France. Of the 801 who fought that day at Beaumont-Hamel, in the first engagement of the battle of the Somme, more than 700 were killed, wounded, or reported missing. The Rooms Provincial Archives, E-22-45.

Empire, Canadians rapidly achieved a well-deserved reputation for bravery and fierceness. They were continually thrown into the most difficult situations and invariably performed well. The list of battles in which they fought heroically began with Ypres in 1915 and continued through to the Belgian town of Mons, where fighting ended for the Canadians at 11 a.m. on 11 November 1918.

The Canadian government had totally mobilized for victory; Secretary of State Arthur Meighen once declared in the Commons that he would bankrupt the country, if necessary, in support of the war effort. It also fought—ultimately successfully—for a say in imperial war policy and for the maintenance of separate Canadian units and command structures. But proving Canada's readiness for autonomy meant, in part, providing manpower. By the time of the Canadian triumph at Vimy in April 1917, Canada could no longer recruit enough volunteers to replace the mounting casualties and was finding it difficult to meet the military responsibilities it had agreed to shoulder. Conscription was seen as the only solution.

Conscription ran directly against the grain of French-Canadian attitudes towards the war—and towards the British Empire. In the words of Henri Bourassa: 'I find that Canada, a nation of America, has another mission to accomplish than

■ Prisoner of war and enemy alien train at Hearst, Ontario, en route to Kapuskasing Internment Camp. Glenbow Museum, NA 1098-19.

to bind herself to the fate of European nations and of despoiling empires.'[7] From the standpoint of Anglo Canadians, French Canadians had not borne their fair share of the war effort. In June 1917 the Minister of Militia told the Commons that fewer than 5 per cent of the more than 432,000 Canadian volunteers had come from French Canada, which had 28 per cent of the total Canadian population.[8] On the other hand, French Canadians did not identify with France in the same way that Anglo Canadians did with Britain and the Empire. Moreover, they had for years felt increasingly beleaguered by English Canada, and after 1915 were able to point to Ontario's limitation of French-language instruction as a symbol of their situation. The question of the use of French in Ontario's public schools had long been contentious. The notorious Regulation 17, which insisted that all students, in public and private schools, must be taught in English beyond the earliest grades, was first passed in 1912, and by 1915 was strongly supported by the English-speaking community on the grounds that French Canada was not pulling its weight in the war.

The debate over conscription split along ethnic lines. For English Canada, the war was an imperial obligation and Canada was falling short in its contribution; for French Canada, the restrictions on Ontario francophones justified resistance to supporting the war. Quebecers responded to the government's announcement of conscription in May 1917 with protest meetings across the province, some of which turned to violence; a crowd of 15,000 in Montreal on 24 May broke windows and assaulted soldiers.[9] Ignoring French-Canadian objections, the Borden government introduced the Military

■ Enemy aliens at Camp Petawawa sawing wood under armed guard, *c.* 1916. A.A. Chesterfield Collection, Album #2, Queen's University Archives.

Service Act into Parliament on 11 June. Declaring all male British subjects aged 20 to 45 eligible for military service—with broad exemptions for those engaged in war work and conscientious objectors—the bill became law in August 1917. Although virtually all French-Canadian members of Parliament opposed it, a federal election was approaching, and the government took advantage of Quebec's isolation to create a Union government out of the ruling Conservatives and those anglophone members of the Liberal Party who had broken with Laurier over his opposition to conscription.

THE WAR AND CIVIL LIBERTIES

As we have seen, one of the first steps taken by the government of Robert Borden after Canada entered the war was to pass the War Measures Act, according to which 'The Governor in Council may do and authorize such acts and things,

and to make from time to time such orders and regulations, as he may by reason of the existence of real or apprehended war, invasion or insurrection deem necessary for the security, defence, peace, order, and welfare of Canada.'[10] In effect, the Act was an unprecedented blank cheque allowing the government not only to censor writing and communications but to arrest, detain, and even deport those deemed to be obstructing the war effort. The Act had no mechanism for termination, and thus could be continued at the will of the government, who took full advantage of it during the war and afterwards. The government insisted that all 'enemy aliens' (residents of Canada born in the countries of the enemy) be registered and examined. Those who chose not to leave were to report monthly, and thousands of aliens were interned as dangerous to the security of the nation.

Under the War Measures Act, the government also censored communications.[11] By 1918,

THE WAR MEASURES ACT

War Measures Act, 1914
An Act to confer certain powers upon the Governor in Council in the event of War, Invasion, or Insurrection
Statutes of Canada (1914) Chapter 2.

short title.
1. This Act may be cited as the War Measures Act, 1914. . . .

EVIDENCE OF WAR.
4. The issue of a proclamation by His Majesty, or under the authority of the Governor in Council shall be conclusive evidence that war, invasion, or insurrection, real or apprehended, exists and has existed for any period of time therein stated, and of its continuance, until by the issue of a further proclamation it is declared that the war, invasion or insurrection no longer exists. . . .

POWERS OF THE GOVERNOR IN COUNCIL.
6. The Governor in Council may do and authorize such acts and things, and make from time to time such orders and regulations, as he may by reason of the existence of real or apprehended war, invasion or insurrection deem necessary or advisable for the security, defence, peace, order and welfare of Canada; and for greater certainty, but not so as to restrict the generality of the foregoing terms, it is hereby declared that the powers of the Governor in Council shall extend to
(a) Censorship and the control and suppression of publications, writings, maps, plans, photographs, communications and means of communication;
(b) Arrest, detention, exclusion and deportation;
(c) Control of the harbours, ports and territorial waters of Canada and the movements of vessels;
(d) Transportation by land, air, or water and the control of the transport of persons and things;

(e) Trading, exportation, importation, production and manufacture;
(f) Appropriation, control, forfeiture and disposition of property and of the use thereof.
2. All orders and regulations made under this section shall have the force of law, and shall be enforced in such manner and by such courts, officers and authorities as the Governor in Council may prescribe, and may be varied, extended or revoked by any subsequent order or regulation; but if any order or regulation is varied, extended or revoked, neither the previous operation thereof nor anything duly done thereunder, shall be affected thereby, nor shall any right, privilege, obligation or liability acquired, accrued, accruing or incurred thereunder be affected by such variation, extension or revocation.
10. The Governor in Council may prescribe the penalties that may be imposed for violations of orders and regulations made under this Act, and may also prescribe whether such penalties shall be imposed upon summary conviction or upon indictment, but no such penalty shall exceed a fine of five thousand dollars or imprisonment for any term not exceeding five years, or both fine and imprisonment.
11. No person who is held for deportation under this Act or under any regulation made thereunder, or is under arrest or detention as an alien enemy, or upon suspicion that he is an alien enemy, or to prevent his departure from Canada, shall be released upon bail or otherwise discharged or tried, without the consent of the Minister of Justice.
12. Section 3 of the *Immigration Act*, chapter 27 of the statutes of 1910, is amended by adding thereto the following subsection: —
'2. No resident of Canada, whether he is a Canadian citizen or not, and whether he has a Canadian domicile or not, who leaves Canada to perform any military or other service for any country then at

war with His Majesty, or for the purpose of aiding or abetting in any way, His Majesty's enemies, shall be permitted to land in Canada, or remain therein, except with the permission of the Minister. If any such person is also prosecuted for any offence of which he may have been guilty, he shall be liable to undergo any punishment imposed upon him under such prosecution before he is deported.'

13. Notwithstanding the provisions of section 8 of the *Royal Northwest Mounted Police Act*, Revised Statutes, 1906, chapter 91, the Governor in Council may from time to time authorize the appointment of such number of constables, supernumerary constables, scouts and boys, in addition to the numbers limited by the said section, as he thinks necessary.

nearly 200 publications were proscribed, most of them in German and printed in the United States. As well, the government greatly increased security forces during the war. Ironically, however, the government made the greatest use of its internment, deportation, and censorship powers under the War Measures Act after the war itself was over, as it moved to head off the 'Red Menace' of 1919.[12]

French Canada was not alone in becoming isolated by the war. People from Germany and the Austro-Hungarian Empire found themselves under severe attack. In 1914 the Canadian government attempted to distinguish between the 'German people' and the 'German government', but the distinction soon collapsed. Before the war Germans had been 'privileged' as an ethnic minority, considered superior to other minorities on account of their 'northern' qualities, but that privilege soon disappeared. Many towns changed their German names: Berlin, Ontario, became Kitchener, and Dusseldorf, Alberta, became Freedom. Tancook Island in Nova Scotia, populated almost entirely by people of German origin according to the census of 1911, had no people claiming German background among its population in the 1921 census. In the end, over 6,000 'aliens'—mostly Ukrainians recently arrived from the Austro-Hungarian Empire—were interned and the foreign-language press was severely restricted. Pacifist members of German and Russian sectarian groups, such as Mennonites and Doukhobors, also met with public hostility, and

when the Wartime Elections Act of September 1917 declared naturalized citizens ineligible to vote, English-speaking Canadians did not object.

THE WAR AND SOCIAL REFORM

During the war, several provinces (mainly in the West) had granted women the right to vote, and women had been arguing for general suffrage on several grounds, of which the most powerful was that they needed to vote in order to bring the war to an end and to have a voice in post-war reconstruction. Given the pacifist leanings of the pre-war women's movement, it was ironic that when Borden's government did extend the federal franchise to some women—specifically those with close relatives in the war—in the new Elections Act of September 1917, they used it to support the government and its conscription policy. The isolation of Quebec was completed when the Union government under Borden took office in October 1917. With a bipartisan government made up almost exclusively of English-speakers, it was now possible to implement another reform long advocated by Anglo Canadians: prohibition.

Like female suffrage, prohibition also triumphed as a result of the war. It was seen as necessary not only for the benefit of the soldiers, to ensure that the country they returned to would be a better place, but also for the war effort, to prevent waste and inefficiency. Earlier arguments about infringing personal liberty lost their cogency during wartime. As the popular writer and activist for women's rights, Nellie McClung, put it: 'We have before us a perfect example of a man who is exercising personal liberty to the full . . . a man by the name of William Hohenzollern.'[13] With many former opponents of prohibition effectively silenced, the provinces began introducing the measure, and many supporters of the Union government expected to see it implemented after the election of 1917. They were correct: the federal government introduced national prohibition by Order-in-Council on 1 April 1918.

THE ECONOMY AT WAR

The Great War both accelerated and distorted virtually every economic development that Canada had experienced over the previous 40 years, creating new conditions and altering old ones. The great stories of World War I have always concerned the appalling Canadian casualty rates, the maturation of Canadian independence and identity, and the Conscription Crisis of 1917. But in Canada itself the economic consequences of the war were almost equally dramatic—positive in the short run and negative in the long run because of the sudden quickening of earlier trends.

The sequence of events that began with the assassination of Archduke Ferdinand at Sarajevo in August 1914 took place against a backdrop of an international slump that had followed more than a decade of overheated boom. For Canada 1914 was not a good year. The western wheat economy had collapsed, unemployment rates in Ontario and Quebec reached 25 per cent before seasonal adjustment, and the per capita national income had shrunk by a full 10 percentage points. Thousands of the young Canadians who volunteered to enlist were motivated not only by loyalty but also by the absence of employment opportunities.

THE GAINS OF WAR

Canadian industrialists responded to the war with three successive strategies. First, they tried

to move into markets the Germans had abandoned, chiefly in the United States, without very much success. Then they tried a 'Buy Canadian' campaign. For the very first time in Canadian history they even encouraged the government to create an Advisory Committee on Industrial and Scientific Research to find some new technology to exploit. But real success came only when the Canadian government managed to convince the Imperial War Cabinet that it had the iron and steel capacity to churn out enough artillery shells to supply the entire Allied force. Since the Allies used over 150 million shells between 1914 and 1918, this was a considerable commitment. Initially the government allowed Canadian businessmen to contract directly with the British government for munitions, and by March 1915 over 200 firms, mainly in central Canada, had converted to munitions manufacture. Later in 1915 the government set up the Imperial Munitions Board, chaired by businessman Joseph Flavelle, and Canadian munitions production rose dramatically, raising the export of iron and steel products from $68.5 million in 1915 to $441.1 million two years later.

In the latter years of the war, nearly 40 per cent of Canadian manufacturing found export markets, and Canadian industry employed 200,000 people—men and women—in munitions production. By 1917 the Munitions Board alone had an annual budget three times that of the federal government in 1914. At one point 675 factories were operating full-time filling war orders. By 1917 Canadian industry was turning out ships, airplanes, and motor vehicles in record numbers. Throughout the war, Canadian soldiers were equipped with arms and kits manufactured in Canada and were fed by Canadian suppliers. Some firms profiteered, but most merely made huge gross profits on small margins and substantial volume.

Only central Canada and Nova Scotia saw much direct benefit from this bonanza, although the resource industries of the entire country—particularly the metals sector—also did well.

However, most of the raw materials of the munitions industry, especially iron and coal, were imported from the United States and Newfoundland. Iron-ore imports from the United States in 1918 were 1,392,000 short tons and from Newfoundland 754,000; only 93,100 tons of domestic iron ore were processed. In coal, 861,000 tons were imported and 561,000 produced domestically, mainly for use in Nova Scotia plants. Wartime demand for metals, of course, was highly artificial. Nickel production, which had reached a height of 46,300 short tons in 1918, had dropped back to 8,800 by 1922, and the post-war collapse in other metals was equally dramatic.

The war also led the Canadian government to take a number of steps that would have been unthinkable before 1914. In July 1917 the Borden government introduced the nation's first income tax, which the *Grain Growers' Guide* described as 'an adjunct of the conscription bill . . . the natural result of the demand for conscription of wealth as well as manpower'.[14] The following month Ottawa began nationalizing the railways, in response to the recommendations of a Royal Commission that had called for the immediate nationalization of all railways except the CPR and those owned by Americans. For some years the government had provided subsidies for these lines, and it would eventually insist that all the shares be handed over to it. The first line taken into the new Canadian National Railways was the Great Northern, in 1918. The process, which eventually involved the Grand Trunk, the Grand Trunk Pacific, the Intercolonial, and the National Transcontinental, was not completed until 1923.

No sector of the Canadian economy was more affected by the Great War than agriculture, especially western wheat production. From 1914 to 1919 in Canada as a whole, agricultural acreage cultivated and wheat exports both doubled, while the acreage under seed in the three Prairie provinces increased from 9.3 million acres (3.8 million hectares) in 1914 to 16.1 million acres (6.5 million ha) in 1918. Wheat and oats covered more than 90 per cent of the fields. 'Improved' land as a proportion of total land in these provinces increased from 40 per cent in 1911 to more than half in 1921. Wheat prices trebled, and the wartime boom helped the rural population of the Prairies to grow from 858,000 to 1,250,000, thus keeping pace with growth rates in Canadian cities. The number of Prairie farms rose during this decade by an astounding 28 per cent. Marketing during the years 1917–20 was carried out on a national basis, under the auspices of a Wheat Board.

THE COSTS OF WAR

AGRICULTURE

Other Canadians often regarded farmers as particularly favoured by the war. Their young men could gain exemption from conscription and, as Stephen Leacock once put it, the farmer's wartime profits were enough to sustain the purchase of 'pianos, victrolas, trotting buggies, books, moving pictures, [and] pleasure cars'.[15] But while farmers did benefit from high international grain prices, the war had its costs. By the time conscription was introduced in 1917, there were few farmers' sons left in the West to be exempt from it, for the region had outdone the rest of Canada in rates of volunteer enlistment in the first years of the war. Moreover, the cost of increasing production was high. More land often had to be acquired, and land prices rose substantially in the process. The CPR, for example, still a major source of land, charged $21.65 per acre (0.4 ha) in 1917, compared to only $13.55 just two years earlier. Labour costs increased commensurately, and farmers were forced to buy new and ever more expensive agricultural equipment. Farmers also bought automobiles in large numbers. However, most did not move to gasoline-powered tractors, partly out of conservatism and partly because satisfactory models were not yet available. Instead, the number of farm horses doubled between 1911 and 1921. Given the number of horses the military took overseas (tanks and other motorized vehicles were no substitute for a team of horses in the mud of France), it was no surprise that so many acres were sowed in oats. The cost of meeting external and internal demands was high, and many farmers—particularly the smaller ones—did so with borrowed money. Farm credit was easily available during the war, although at high rates of interest, and the rate of farm debt increased in proportion to everything else.

The land itself—or, more precisely, the way the land was used—was another potentially negative consequence of wartime expansion. High prices and the pressures for increased production emanating from the Canadian government encouraged farmers to expand marginal land and abandon most of the techniques of soil and moisture conservation. Farms got larger—the average farm size on the Prairies increased from 289.4 acres (117.1 ha) in 1911 to 335.4 acres (135.7 ha) in 1921—and, because of labour shortages, the land was often hastily cultivated. 'We have developed weeds to the extent that they are a very important factor', complained one farm journal. 'We have cultivated our land in such a manner that soil drifting has become a very serious problem.'[16] For a variety of reasons, therefore, western farmers would be in serious trouble when—as would inevitably happen—the price of grain fell, and when climate cycles produced moisture shortfalls, particularly in the dry-belt areas.

LABOUR

While farmers were encouraged to mortgage their futures, workers were required to defer their expectations during the war. Although organized labour made some gains in the early years of fighting, labour leaders remained convinced that the government was permitting wartime profiteering to benefit the industrialists at the expense of the workers. Constant inflation eroded the purchasing power of labour incomes—the cost of living in 1919 was 64 per cent higher than in 1913, and annual inflation

rates had reached double figures by 1916—while wages did not keep pace, particularly after the government began to control labour's ability to bargain effectively. The *Canadian Annual Review* in 1920 calculated that between 1914 and 1919 the cost of living in Canada had virtually doubled, with most of the rise coming in 1917–18. Removing hundreds of thousands of able-bodied young men from the workforce for the Canadian Expeditionary Force (CEF) was bound to produce a labour shortage, and by 1917 that shortage was estimated at 100,000 workers. Bringing women into the workforce helped to take up the slack, but was not enough. To control labour's enhanced bargaining power, the government introduced compulsory arbitration into all war industries in 1916, and in the crisis year of 1917 it announced its intention of outlawing strikes and lockouts.

The situation in 1917 was as desperate on the home front as in the trenches of Europe, with at least 148 work stoppages and over a million working days lost through labour unrest. While eastern workers called for reform, western radicals demanded general strikes and even revolution. As one Alberta miner argued in 1917, 'We want to be using some Russian methods—resolutions don't get us anywhere.'[17] In 1918 the Association of Letter Carriers went on strike—the first important strike in the public sector in Canadian history. By 1918 Canadian newspapers were warning that the 'climbing up and up of prices is having an unsettling effect upon the wage earning masses of the people.'[18] By the time the war finally ended, union membership and labour discontent were both on the rise. That discontent would culminate in violence on the streets of Winnipeg in 1919.

THE AFTERMATH OF WAR

THE CANADIAN WAR ARTISTS

Burlington House in London was the place to be on 4 January 1919, when more than 2,000 peo-

CANADA AND THE PEACE TREATY

Sir Robert Borden was in England in January 1919 because of his participation in the Treaty of Versailles. Only days after the Armistice was declared in November 1918, Borden had headed for Europe to head the Canadian delegation at the Peace Conference. Canada's participation at Paris beginning in January 1919 was less concerned with the disposition of European and international problems than it was with its own status in dealing with that disposition. This was a policy agreed on in advance by the Union cabinet in Ottawa, although much Canadian public opinion would have preferred to stay away from Versailles. Canada and the other dominions banded together to insist on being treated as independent nations at the Peace Conference, rather than as part of the British imperial delegation. The principal opponent to this change of policy was not the British government but the United States, backed by other participants, who insisted that autonomous dominions would enhance the British voice in the deliberations, which did not answer the dominions' claim that their commitment of manpower (and casualties) during the war entitled them to a separate say in the outcome.

Sir Robert Borden proved to have an influence on the conference greater than Canada's actual power in world affairs. The first breakthrough came in early January 1919, when President Woodrow Wilson conceded a representative from each dominion at the peace table. Sir Robert Borden responded by calling a meeting of the dominions, refusing to accept one representative and calling for two. Wilson agreed to two representatives from Canada, Australia, South Africa, and India, and one for New Zealand. Newfoundland would have to sit as part of the British delegation. The dominions subsequently got the right to separate membership on new international organizations coming out of the treaty, including the League of Nations, and a separate signature on the treaty and conventions. Membership in the League, of course, implied liability for any commitments undertaken by that organization. Canada had achieved a new status in world affairs. Whether that status justified the numbers of dead and wounded was another matter.

ple, including Sir Robert Borden, attended the opening of an exhibition of paintings depicting the Canadian army during the war that had just ended. Until then, few Canadians had known that a formal project to document the war had been undertaken through the Canadian War Memorials Fund, an official arts program founded by Lord Beaverbrook (Max Aitken) and Lord Rothermere in 1916. More than a hundred artists—British, European, and Canadian, including a handful of women—had been commissioned by the Fund to paint the Canadian troops on and behind the front lines. They were hardly the first war artists, but they were part of the first official arts program of any nation in any war. Successful applicants had received an officer's rank and the opportunity to produce paintings that might well be remembered by posterity. The works on exhibit covered a wide range of styles and a variety of topics. Most of them depicted the horrors of war in colours unavailable to the photographers who also accompanied the soldiers. A huge charcoal drawing by Augustus John—12 by 40 feet (3.7 by 12.2 m)—dominated the central gallery of Burlington House. Although the stars of the show were the British painters, two future members of the Group of Seven, A.Y. Jackson and F.H. Varley, had their careers advanced by their association with the project, particularly when the exhibit later travelled to leading Canadian cities. Perhaps more important, the outstanding visual record of Canada's participation was one of the war's few positive legacies.[19]

THE WINNIPEG GENERAL STRIKE

Given the extent of domestic unrest during the war, especially in western Canada, a post-war reaction of some kind might have been expected. It arrived in 1919 in the form of radical strikes in a number of Canadian cities. Many factors contributed to the most famous of them, the 'confrontation at Winnipeg'. Among those factors was the Bolshevik Revolution of 1917, which had showed radical labour leaders—some of whom came from the same Eastern European cauldron that had given rise to a number of revolutionary theorists, including Karl Marx—what could be done against a repressive capitalist system. That same revolution, however, had shown Canada's government and business leaders what could happen if popular unrest were permitted to get out of hand.

Most of the demands that led to the Winnipeg strike in the spring of 1919 were traditional ones exacerbated by the war: recognition of union rights to organize, higher wages, better working conditions. But there were also some underlying issues. One was the public hostility to enemy aliens during the war. Another was the sudden return of demobilized veterans to a city that had no jobs for them and no plans to help them readjust to civilian life. Still another was the agitation of a small number of radicals who were hoping to provoke social change. Most important of all was the mindset of the Canadian government, which feared revolution and was prepared to repress any signs of its public emergence.

A walkout by workers in the city's metal trades and building industries was quickly joined by other malcontents in a general sympathy strike, and on 15 May the strikers voted to close down the city's services. Most Canadian historians have taken the line that these actions were nothing more than familiar labour tactics, although couched in the rhetoric of radicalism.[20] Certainly the leaders of the strike were British- and Canadian-born labour activists, not revolutionaries—though many had flirted with radical ideas and may have hoped that the strike might lead to a more general reform of society.[21] To some (understandably worried) businessmen, placards on wagons allowing essential deliveries by permission of the strikers became a symbol of the breakdown of public authority. Workers in cities such as Toronto and Vancouver declared their support, and the Canadian authorities were easily persuaded that 'the revolution was nigh'. As usual, the Canadian government's response to anything that smacked of popular uprising was to repress it as quickly as possible.

A delegation of Canadian cabinet ministers headed by Justice Minister Arthur Meighen (MP for Portage la Prairie, Manitoba) recommended bringing in militia and Mounted Police to maintain order, since the Winnipeg police force refused to promise that it would not join the strikers. The postal workers were ordered back to work, and in early June the Canadian Naturalization Act was amended to allow for the instant deportation of foreign-born radicals who advocated revolution or belonged to 'any organization entertaining or teaching disbelief in or opposition to organized government'.[22] The bulk of the city's police force of 200 men was dismissed on 9 June, to be replaced by local militia units, the Royal North West Mounted Police, and 1,800 special constables recruited and paid by the Citizens Committee of 1,000, which represented the city's business and professional elite. The meetings of this committee were held in secret, and no list of its members was ever published. Some of the constables were recently demobilized servicemen—although the war had ended in November, it had taken the government many months to organize ocean transport to bring the soldiers home—who accepted the offi-

■ Anti-strike veterans' rally at Winnipeg's City Hall, 4 June 1919. Archives of Manitoba, 5 (N12296).

cial assessment that the best way to end the strike was, as *Winnipeg Free Press* editor J.W. Dafoe put it, 'to clean the aliens out of this community and ship them back to their happy homes in Europe which vomited them forth a decade ago.'[23] But many ex-servicemen refused to join the forces of law and order, and instead began marching in support of the strikers. Other veterans soon responded by marching in opposition to the strike.

Open violence between special police and the demonstrators erupted on 10 June. A few days later, 10 strike 'leaders' (six actual leaders of British background and four radical 'foreigners') were summarily arrested. This action probably broke the back of the actual strike, although a group of strikers and returned soldiers marched towards the Winnipeg City Hall to show their solidarity with the arrested leaders on 21 June ('Black Saturday'). The mayor read the Riot Act

and the Mounted Police charged the march on horseback. In the ensuing melee many were injured, two marchers were killed, and a number of 'foreign rioters' were arrested. The militia cleared the streets of troublemakers, and two days later a rump of the Strike Committee, with many of its leaders in jail, offered to end the strike if a Royal Commission would investigate the underlying causes.

The aftermath of the Winnipeg General Strike was anti-climatic and is often overlooked or forgotten. But it reveals a lot about Canada in 1919. The Royal Commission found that much of the labour unrest in Winnipeg was justified, and that the strikers' principal goal had been the introduction of collective bargaining, an ambition that the tribunal supported. Separate deportation hearings, held in July 1919 against some of the 'foreign' strikers under arrest, also suggested that these men were concerned with local issues

■ Strikers tipping a streetcar, 21 June 1919. Archives of Manitoba, 1696 (N2762).

rather than with radical revolution. Most of the 'foreigners' arrested on 21 June were summarily sent to an Ontario internment camp and were ultimately deported in secret. Hugh John Macdonald, the police magistrate who interned these men, explained to Arthur Meighen:

> As Police Magistrate I have seen to what a large extent Bolsheviki ideas are held by the Ruthenian, Russian and Polish people, whom we have in our midst. . . . it is absolutely necessary that an example should be made. . . . If the government persists in the course that it is now adopting the foreign element here will soon be as gentle and easily controlled as a lot of sheep.[24]

The government charged most of the arrested British strike leaders with sedition and obtained several convictions, but juries refused to convict in several cases.

Thus, a strike that began with local industrial conditions, exacerbated by the Great War and involving a fringe of political radicals, ended as a concerted campaign that reached far beyond Winnipeg to suppress radicalism and 'foreign agitation'. The use of the civil arm to deal with radicalism was given a new meaning in post-war Winnipeg. Equally important, the fragility of the nation's social compact was exposed.

DEALING WITH THE VETERANS

Canada was no better prepared for peace after 1918 than it had been for war in 1914. Its failure to plan thoroughly in advance for the reintegration of more than half a million veterans into post-war society was particularly marked, and in a number of well-publicized instances the returning soldiers were let down. Two points need to be emphasized about the post-war situation, however. One is that no nation that had participated in the Great War did much better than Canada at dealing with its returning soldiers. The seeds of World War II were thus sown, especially in Germany, France, and Italy. The second point is that Canada did gradually develop some policies for dealing with returned soldiers, policies that would serve as the basis for expanded social welfare during and after World War II. Some of these policies were forced on the government after returned soldiers began forming veterans' organizations and demanding that they be treated not as objects of charity but as a group entitled to social benefits as a matter of right. The Canadian Association of Returned Soldiers, formed in the midst of the war, became the Great War Veterans' Association in 1917 and eventually the Canadian Legion, which by 1928 had 55,000 members in 594 branches with 179 ladies' auxiliaries.[25] The Department of Pensions and National Health was created mainly to deal with veterans' issues. In 1933 more than 75,000 former Canadian soldiers received disability pensions worth more than $30 million, and veterans' benefits (at $55 million) constituted 16.9 per cent of federal revenue.[26] Although the policy was cheese-paring, benefits for veterans constituted around 15 per cent of federal revenue throughout the 1930s, and were obviously a major charge on the public purse. As we shall see in Chapter 11, the nation did provide land for thousands of veterans after the war.

CONCLUSION

The Great War was a traumatic experience for Canada. Casualties were high, and the fissures revealed by the war were merely papered over by politicians and repressive policies. At least as much happened on the home front as on the battlefield, including a substantial increase in the centralization of power and the fulfillment of some of the reform agenda advanced before the war. As the American pacifist Randolph Bourne put it in 1917, war certainly was 'the Health of the State'.

SHORT BIBLIOGRAPHY

Bercuson, David. *Confrontation at Winnipeg: Labour, Industrial Relations, and the General Strike*, rev. edn. Montreal, 1990. The most detailed analysis of the Winnipeg General Strike, it argues that the strikers were not really very radical.

Granatstein, J.L., and J.M. Hitsman. *Broken Promises: A History of Conscription in Canada*. Toronto, 1977. A useful study of the conscription issue in both wars.

Greenhous, Brereton. *Canada's Air Forces, 1914–99*. Montreal, 1999. A reminder of the importance of the Canadian air force in the Great War.

Gutkin, Harry, and Mildred Gutkin. *Profiles in Dissent: The Shaping of Radical Thought in the Canadian West*. Edmonton, 1997. An excellent discussion of radical thought in Western Canada, central to understanding the Winnipeg General Strike.

Miller, Carman. *Painting the Map Red: Canada and the South African War, 1899–1902*. Montreal, 1993. An important study of Canada's major military involvement before the Great War.

Milner, Marc. *Canada's Navy: The First Century*. Toronto, 1999. A book that reminds us that not all Canadians fought in the CEF.

Morton, Desmond. *When Your Number's Up: The Canadian Soldier in the First World War*. Toronto, 1993. A brilliant social history of the Canadian soldier in the Great War.

Rawling, Bill. *Surviving Trench Warfare: Technology and the Canadian Corps, 1914–1918*. Toronto, 1992. A vivid picture of life in the trenches.

Thompson, John Herd. *The Harvests of War: The Prairie West, 1914–1918*. Toronto, 1978. The best single book on the economic effects of the war, focusing chiefly on agriculture in the Prairie provinces.

Tippett, Maria. *Art at the Service of War: Canada, Art, and the Great War.* Toronto, 1984. An important study of the official art produced during World War I.

STUDY QUESTIONS

1. Why was Billy Bishop criticized during and after the war?
2. Why was life in the trenches so horrible?
3. What was a 'blighty' and why did soldiers welcome the prospect of one?
4. What was the Conscription Crisis of 1917?
5. Who were the 'enemy aliens'?
6. In what ways did the Great War fulfill the demands of Canadian social reformers?
7. What happened in Winnipeg in June 1919?
8. In what respects might war represent 'the health of the state'?

CHAPTER TEN

Economy, Polity, and the 'Unsolved Riddle of Social Justice', 1919–1939

Once the war had ended, most Canadians did their best to put it behind them and—in the phrase popularized south of the border—'return to normalcy'. But 'normalcy' would not be easy to achieve. The prosperity of the 1920s was somewhat artificial—based on an unprecedented use of credit—and was unevenly distributed across the nation; it certainly did not reach the average western farmer or eastern miner. The Great Depression, which followed the inevitable crash, was deeper and longer than any ever previously experienced in Canada. The scope for government intervention to deal with the consequences was circumscribed by the Canadian constitution, which gave the provinces most of the social powers but did not provide them with the necessary revenue. Economic and social conditions encouraged movements of political protest, but they remained regional rather than national, and most Canadians drew back from extreme action—although government also did its part to suppress radicalism. In any event, the Great Depression was an experience that most Canadians would not choose to repeat.

STEPHEN LEACOCK AND THE UNSOLVED RIDDLE OF SOCIAL JUSTICE

The process of demobilization was slowed by the most devastating pandemic of modern times, the Spanish flu outbreak of 1918–19. The situation was so desperate that the Canadian government actually tried—without success—to postpone public celebrations of the armistice for fear of spreading infection. Canadian deaths from the flu ran ultimately to 50,000, only a few thousand short of the number of deaths in battle.[1] Fatalities had shifted from the front to the home front.

Many thoughtful Canadians understood the potential difficulties of the return to peace, but few expressed them as articulately as Stephen Leacock, who wrote a series of articles for the *New York Times* that he published a year later as *The Unsolved Riddle of Social Justice*. Setting aside his well-established role as a humorist and writing instead as an economist, the head of the Department of Economics and Political Science at McGill University, he stated:

> These are troubled times. As the echoes of the war die away the sound of a new conflict rises on our ears. All the world is filled with industrial unrest. Strike follows upon strike. A world that has known five years of fighting has lost its taste for the honest drudgery of work. Cincinnatus will not back to his plow, or, at the best, stands sullenly between his plow-handles arguing for a higher wage.[2]

Neither a social revolutionary nor a reactionary,

TIMELINE

1918

Spanish flu pandemic begins. McLaughlin Motor Co. sells out to General Motors.

1919

Leacock writes 'The Unsolved Riddle of Social Justice'. United Farmers of Ontario form minority government.

1921

Progressive Party wins 64 seats in House of Commons, while Mackenzie King becomes Prime Minister. Growth of Maritime Rights movement.

1922

Labour unrest peaks in the coal fields. Lionel Groulx publishes *L'Appel de la race*.

1925

William Aberhart begins Prophetic Bible Institute broadcasts on CFCN.

1929

Stock market crashes in New York and Toronto.

1930

R.B. Bennett's Conservatives defeat King's Liberals in federal election. Communist Party creates a National Unemployed Workers' Association.

1931

Depression really begins; 741,000 unemployed in Canada. League for Social Reconstruction formed.

1932

First credit union established by Antigonish Movement.

1933

Maurice Duplessis becomes leader of Quebec Conservative Party. CCF supports Regina Manifesto. Duff Pattullo elected in British Columbia.

1935

R.B. Bennett announces a 'New Deal' and is defeated at polls. Social Credit sweeps to power in Alberta. On-to-Ottawa Trek ends in riot in Regina. Riots in downtown Vancouver.

1936

Union Nationale wins 1936 Quebec election.

1937

'Padlock Act' in Quebec against communism. Royal Commission on Dominion–Provincial Relations appointed. Oshawa strike at General Motors.

Leacock wanted desperately to make sense of the future, for himself and for his readers. Technology, industrialization, and war had profoundly altered the modern world, he wrote, and there was no turning back:

With all our wealth, we are still poor. After a century and a half of labour-saving machinery, we work about as hard as ever. With power over nature multiplied a hundred fold, nature still conquers us. And more than this. There are many senses in which the machine age seems to leave the great bulk of civilized humanity, the working part of it, worse off instead of better.[3]

■ Stephen Leacock in 1914. 11-202933
Notman Photographic Archives, McCord
Museum, Montreal.

Despite the immense destruction of war, in which 'some seven million lives were sacrificed; eight million tons of shipping were sunk beneath the sea; some fifty million adult males were drawn from productive labour to the lines of battle', the 'productive machine' had never ceased to function. Industrial society, obviously, did not normally employ its full potential.

Leacock could only hope that the destructive energy of war would be harnessed for peacetime use in ensuring for every child 'adequate food, clothing, education and an opportunity in life'. Writing for an international audience, Leacock did not discuss Canada specifically; however, towards the end of his extended essay he did refer to the wartime issue of conscription, emphasizing that it was seen as part of a democratic obligation. 'But', he added, 'conscription has its other side. The obligation to die must carry with it the right to live.' Unemployment should become a 'social crime', said Leacock, for states capable of waging total war should also be

capable of eliminating such a scourge. His traditional liberal economics offered no solutions, but at least Leacock recognized the problem.

The development of Canada over the next two decades demonstrated how hard it was for Canadians in peacetime to come to terms with the paradox of poverty in the midst of plenty. One point that Leacock might have emphasized more forcefully was the need for a unified body politic to implement the new society he envisaged. While Leacock understood the importance in wartime of creating a public consensus, and was correct in his assertion that the war had demonstrated the immense power of the state, for both destruction and construction, he failed to observe the extent to which the war—at least in Canada—had mortgaged the future.

REGIONAL PROTEST IN THE 1920S

The war had set off and perpetuated economic trends—unsustainable agricultural expansion and regional industrial disparities—that would trouble the nation in its post-war readjustment. The decade of the 1920s is usually associated with prosperity, but in truth the years immediately after the armistice were difficult economically. The boom of the twenties did not begin in earnest until 1924, and it was not shared in equally by all sections of the country or by all sectors of the economy. After an initial round of strikes in reaction against inflation and the deferral of expectations in the war, industrial unrest remained high through 1925, when it collapsed in the face of the boom. By 1921, labour candidates sat in seven of nine provincial legislatures, and in the election of that year over 30 federal constituencies had labour candidates of some description, although only four were actually elected. Labour unrest continued to be most prevalent at the two ends of the country, with notable strikes in Cape Breton, Alberta, and British Columbia, particularly in the coal fields. In August 1922, 22,000 coal miners were on strike, and a number of unions were broken in some of the bitterest labour disputes Canada had ever seen.[4]

Much of the social and economic unrest of the 1920s found expression in movements of regional protest. The collapse of the international wheat market in 1921, and the beginning of a serious drought in parts of western Canada, meant that Prairie farmers would never fully share in the prosperity of the decade. And in the Maritimes, economic conditions that had been poor during the war failed to improve with the peace. Both regions responded with movements of political protest directed against central Canada. Quebec, also, was unhappy, though for reasons more cultural than economic, and it developed its own protest movement in the form of Quebec nationalism. Only in Ontario, which by 1921 was the only province with a self-sustaining economy, was regional protest muted.

Buoyed by a major resource boom in pulp and paper, mining, and hydroelectricity, Ontario's economy recovered from post-war problems more quickly than its counterparts elsewhere in Canada and adjusted far more smoothly. The early Canadian demand for automobiles had been met by the Ford Motor Co. of Canada in Windsor, formed in 1904 soon after Henry Ford began production in Detroit, as well as Canadian manufacturers including the McLaughlin Motor Co. (1907) of Oshawa, which produced the McLaughlin-Buick and later the McLaughlin-Chevrolet. The business was sold to General Motors in 1918 and became General Motors of Canada, with R.S. McLaughlin as president. By the 1920s no independent Canadian company survived, and the growing market for cars was controlled by American branch plants—Ford, Chrysler, and General Motors— encouraged by a preferential tariff on the entry of parts from Detroit into Canada and by the easy entry of finished cars into all British countries. Detroit manufactured in Canada to sell to the Empire. Henry Ford's assembly line and philosophy of plant organization and labour management had even led to the elaboration of a new industrial strategy, commonly called 'Fordism'.

THE PROGRESSIVE PARTY

Western farmers, whose post-war problems were the most serious, had long been convinced that protective tariffs were not in their best interests. Yet, both the Liberal and Conservative parties had accepted protectionism while in office. This suggested that there was no significant difference between the two parties and encouraged western farmers to look for an alternative to both. In the United States, similar agrarian discontents had found expression in the 'populist' movement, which provided not only rhetoric and some policies for Canadian farmers but a number of leaders (in the form of American immigrants) who called for a new political organization, free from the influence of the 'eastern capitalists' and committed to truly democratic principles.

Farmers everywhere in English-speaking Canada were displeased with the governments in power, especially after Ottawa revoked its exemption in the spring of 1918, making their sons eligible for conscription after all, and provincial governments failed to sympathize with their grievances. In Ontario the United Farmers formed a minority government in October 1919, and in both Nova Scotia and New Brunswick farmers elected half a dozen MLAs in provincial elections in 1920.

Nevertheless, the pressure for a new national party came mainly from the West. Despite western farmers' relative prosperity during the Great War, they remained convinced that they were at the mercy of central Canadian profiteers and protectionists. The isolation of French Canada and the achievement of the Union government in 1917 momentarily dampened Prairie discontent. But the farmers had high expectations of the new government, and not all of them would be met. Two issues of economic policy remained crucially important: restoration of the national wheat marketing program discontinued after the war and a reduction in the tariff on manufactured goods. But the Union government temporized, and as a result, in 1919, the Liberal Thomas A. Crerar

■ Progressive Party supporters, Moose Jaw, December 1921. Moose Jaw Public Library, Archives Department, 73-96.

resigned as Minister of Agriculture. The following year, with the backing of Prairie and Ontario farmers on the Canadian Council of Agriculture and other dissident Liberals, Crerar founded the Progressive Party and became its first leader.[5]

In the 1921 election the Progressives won 64 seats—37 on the Prairies, 24 in Ontario, one in New Brunswick, and two in British Columbia. With 50 Conservatives and 117 Liberals in the House of Commons, the Progressives held the balance of power, finally breaking the two-party tradition that had been greatly weakened during the war by the coalition government and the isolation of Quebec. Whether the Progressives could make anything of their success remained

an open question, however, for they were deeply split. Former Liberals such as Crerar wanted to reform the existing Liberal Party and bring about freer trade by lowering tariff rates. But farmers' representatives such as Henry Wise Wood wanted to create a more radical party by adopting an essentially occupational ideology centred on farm grievances. The only point the two wings could agree on was their refusal to become the official opposition, which would have required a coherent program.

The most divisive issue was the idea of forming a coalition with the Liberals. Once the Progressives had rejected this idea, their position was hopelessly compromised. Refusing to behave

■ The 'dust bowl' south of Regina in the 1930s. Saskatchewan Archives Board, R-A 15077-1.

as a distinct party of opposition and unable to achieve coalition with a minority government, the Progressives took the blame from both traditional parties for the problems of the Fourteenth Parliament. In the elections of 1925, 1926, and 1930 they gradually were reduced to a small 'ginger group' that would merge eventually with the Co-operative Commonwealth Federation (CCF) in 1932.

The Progressives' failures in Ottawa were not paralleled at the provincial level in Alberta and Manitoba, where farmer parties controlled the governments, or in Saskatchewan, where farmers dominated the ruling Liberal Party. Nevertheless, the collapse of progressivism as a phenomenon of national importance coincided with the farmers' own decline during the 1920s. Two disasters struck almost simultaneously. First, in 1921 the bottom fell out of wheat prices, which dropped from over $2 per bushel to less than $1 for the 1922 crop. Second, drought conditions, which

had begun in the later years of the war, did not go away. The situation in the dry-belt region of southern Alberta and western Saskatchewan became desperate. Average rainfalls of less than 10 inches (about 25 centimetres) were accompanied by above-average temperatures, and no matter how much care the farmers took, crop failure was virtually guaranteed. The result was a widespread inability to meet mortgage payments, resulting in a wave of foreclosures. Farmers lost their property and mortgage companies lost their investments.

Much of the land in the dry-belt region reverted to the provinces for unpaid taxes, and the farm families occupying it moved elsewhere. Credit facilities in the region virtually dried up, and one farm journalist reported in 1925 that it had become 'impossible to negotiate a desirable farm loan in the west'.[6] The spillover effect on towns and villages in the western farm country was substantial, and many previously prosperous places began to look like ghost towns. After the virtual collapse of the federal Progressive Party in the 1926 election, many farmers were simply too disheartened to continue the fight, and some turned to less confrontational approaches, such as the co-operative movement.

THE MARITIME RIGHTS MOVEMENT

A similar fate befell the Progressive Party's eastern protest equivalent, the Maritime Rights movement. The economic slump that followed the end of the war was a disaster for the three Maritime provinces, since they had been relying heavily on resource industries—such as lumber and coal— that no longer had markets. Immediately after the war, farmers and workers in the region both saw their economic positions deteriorating under runaway inflation, and the two groups formed a series of coalitions at the provincial level that achieved some brief success, if not power. But the general international economic collapse of 1921 greatly weakened the unions, leading many Maritimers to believe that gaining effective representation in Ottawa, especially in the cabinet of the governing party, was more important than creating new political alliances. The farmer-labour parties found it difficult to make common cause with the westerners. The two were badly divided over tariff policy, eastern labour tending to support protectionism because it meant jobs. The government in Ottawa in the early 1920s deliberately exploited these incompatibilities between the eastern and western peripheries, and it would continue to play one region against the other throughout the century.[7]

The Maritime region was acutely conscious of its increasing disadvantages within Confederation. Part of the problem was its lack of political clout. As the region's population base stagnated, and even declined in proportional terms, central and western Canada continued to grow. Early in 1920 the legislatures of the three Maritime provinces agreed that joint action was required, particularly on the contentious issue of freight rates. When Ottawa sought to make the Intercolonial Railway—which it now owned— pay its own way by increasing rates, Maritimers protested that they could 'no longer successfully compete in the markets of Central and Western Canada, which they are obliged to do to market their surplus production'.[8] In retrospect, we can see that freight rates were only the visible symptom and not the cause of Maritime economic problems, but by the end of 1921 farmer-labour support had drifted into the camp of the newly organized Maritime Rights movement, which combined a drive for equitable freight rates with various specific provincial demands, producing widespread public agitation. Unfortunately, farmer-labour allies never were able to agree on a tariff policy. In the 1921 election the Liberals under William Lyon Mackenzie King did extremely well in the East, mainly because they alone sought to mobilize regional sentiment. Yet the Maritime Liberals, once elected, found themselves unable to influence their party's policies; instead, they saw their interests sacrificed to King's need to appease the Progressives—who in turn saw themselves sacrificed to eastern Canada.

Eschewing the third-party route taken by western farmers, the Maritime Rights leaders decided in 1923 to appeal to the remainder of the country over King's head. Efforts were made to persuade Canadians through advertising and public relations campaigns that the Maritimes represented more than economic backwardness and old-fashioned political corruption. This program would eventually have some success, but it was not nearly enough. Maritimers would have to abandon the Liberal Party and begin voting Conservative. This they did, starting with by-elections in Halifax and in Kent, New Brunswick, late in 1923. Instead of publicizing the region's grievances, however, this voting pattern merely annoyed the Prime Minister, who continued to tailor government policy to meet the demands of the moderate Progressives and refused to deal with Maritime needs. By the 1925 federal election, the shift to the Tories was virtually complete (23 of 29 seats). The King government responded by offering the Maritimes a Royal Commission to investigate regional grievances. It then proceeded to buy off the region as cheaply as possible through concessions on freight rates, subsidies, and port development. In the end, working through the two-party system achieved even less for the Maritimes than creating a third-party movement did for western Canada. The Maritimes simply did not have a large enough population to elect enough members of Parliament to make a difference. The worst fears of the anti-confederates in the 1860s were now fully realized. Perhaps the inability of eastern and western protestors to find common ground was a contributing factor. But neither side was able to see beyond its regional interests. And regional political protest—especially when kept divided—was unable to achieve very much.

QUEBEC 'NATIONALISM' IN THE 1920s

While the West and the Maritimes protested with little success on the federal level, Quebec turned increasingly inward in pursuit of a narrow nationalism (or provincialism) as a reaction against the sense of isolation from the rest of Canada that had grown during the war. The chief outlet for the new nationalism was the journal *L'Action française*, founded in 1917 (on the eve of the Conscription Crisis) by the Ligue des droits du français—a movement that started out to save the French language but gradually shifted to broader-based agitation.[9]

The inspiration for both movement and journal was the Abbé Lionel Groulx. Born in 1878 at Vaudreuil, Quebec, to rural parents, Groulx had begun his education in village schools and then was sent on to the seminary in Ste-Thérèse. He punctuated a career as a young schoolteacher and an ordained priest with three years (1906–9) of graduate study in France, where he imbibed most of the intellectual ideas

■ Abbé Lionel Groulx. LAC, C-16657.

of the time. A self-taught historian, Groulx was appointed in 1915 to the first chair of Canadian history at the Université de Montréal. His 'nationalism' was heavily tinged with racism, both in its attitude towards French Canada itself and in its sweeping hostility to alien influences. 'It is this rigorously characterized French type,' Groulx insisted, 'dependent upon history and geography, having ethnical and psychological hereditary traits, which we wish to continue, on which we base the hope of our future; because a people, like all growing things, can develop only what is in itself, only the forces whose living germ it contains.'[10] To nurture this 'living germ', Groulx undertook to refashion the history of French Canada. The subordination of Quebec by a 'beneficial' British presence could no longer be accepted; the Conquest had become a disaster and the history of French Canada a constant struggle to survive in the face of oppression. Groulx's novel *L'Appel de la race* (1922)—which was published anonymously and was notorious at the time for its racist arguments—centres on Jules Lantagnac, a French-Canadian lawyer in Ottawa, educated at McGill, and his wife, Maud Fletcher, an Anglican who has converted to Catholicism to marry Jules and is a stereotype of the rigid Anglo-Saxon 'dominated by ethnic pride'. The novel reflects the tensions aroused by Ontario's Regulation 17, which leads to the breakup of the marriage (of the four children, two go to each parent). As a historian, Groulx was responsible for some of the excesses of French-Canadian historiography in the interwar period, including the cult that made the seventeenth-century soldier-adventurer Adam Dollard des Ormeaux into a nationalist symbol.[11]

Like many French Canadians—and many other Canadians, too—Groulx wanted to ensure the survival of traditional culture in the face of an increasingly alien and materialistic environment located in 'the middle of an immense Anglo-Saxon ocean'.[12] In the 1920s—when he shared in the sense of a post-war crisis—he denied advocating separatism, but his arguments did point in that direction. Groulx led the way in calling for a commitment to build the Quebec economy, using French-Canadian capital and skills to prepare for a future in which Confederation would be seen to have failed. He may have wanted only to be prepared for a political collapse resulting from many regional pressures; nevertheless, he did suggest that the British Empire might have 'become artificial, an outworn political formula, unable to sustain the shock of approaching realities'.[13] During the later 1920s, Groulx's monthly journal *L'Action française* lost the support of many French Canadians as prosperity and Quebec's return to federal power with the victory of the King Liberals in 1925 bled off much of the radical discontent in the province. Instead of commanding large crowds at public gatherings,

Groulx was reduced to the status of an ordinary professor lecturing to relatively small classes at the university. On the other side of the city, Stephen Leacock 'saved the empire three times a week' in his introductory political economy classes, and was regarded by many McGill students as an increasingly old-fashioned 'fuddy duddy'.

AN ARTIFICIAL BOOM AND A DEPRESSION

THE 'ROARING' TWENTIES

The wave of economic prosperity of the later 1920s was in large measure an artificial boom based on speculative activities in real estate, the stock market, and commodity futures. It was encouraged by a substantial increase in new housing construction (mainly in the suburban areas of larger cities) and a great wave of consumer spending on automobiles and various electrical appliances for the home, including radios, vacuum cleaners, washing machines, and phonographs. A newly expanded advertising industry was now promoting not only houses (and the goods to go in them) but also automobiles. And if the banks were reluctant to advance the purchase price of an automobile, the automobile manufacturers were not. They created their own finance companies and used them to add to their profits.

Just as the nation had mortgaged its collective future in the Great War, its citizens now mortgaged their individual futures by borrowing substantial sums of money to buy consumer goods and by 'selling short' (selling stocks one did not own) in the market. Between 1926 and 1928, one company of Canadian stockbrokers—Solloway, Mills and Co. Ltd, specializing in penny resource stocks—expanded from one small office in Toronto to 40 offices across the country, with more than 1,500 employees.[14] The newly minted millionaire became a folk hero. British Columbia alone could boast 83 millionaires, not one of whom, we are told, gave anything to a university or sponsored a major civic enterprise.[15] Some of the newly rich had made their money in the shadowy business of producing alcoholic beverages in Canada and distributing them south of the border.[16] Gambling became big business, particularly on sports—from boxing to baseball to horse racing.

BLACK TUESDAY

But the good times could not last. Canadians, like Americans, have generally associated the beginning of the Great Depression with the stock market crash of October 1929, when Wall Street led the way in a record meltdown of stock prices that encompassed every North American exchange, including those in Canada.[17] The stock market was badly regulated, with a number of dubious practices. The best-publicized was the process of buying 'on margin'—in effect, on credit—in the expectation of further increases in prices of already overvalued stocks. Many speculators (including the present author's grandfather) lost their shirts—and their paper fortunes—in the overnight collapse that reached panic proportions when orders to sell could not be executed swiftly enough. But businessmen at the time did not regard the violent market readjustment of 'Black Tuesday'—29 October 1929—as necessarily related to the overall economy. Some had won and some had lost in the 'speculative orgy', but it had quickly sorted itself out, and the economy as a whole was fundamentally sound. Perhaps. But just as the boom of 1925–9 had reflected an upsurge of consumer and business confidence, the economic collapse reflected, at least in part, a loss of confidence.

The Depression that followed Black Tuesday was hardly a distinctive Canadian or even North American phenomenon. It was one of those periodical international economic turns, or cycles, that can be properly analyzed only in terms of worldwide conditions. Though Canadian activity was not responsible for the downturn, Canadians certainly felt its effects because the Canadian economy was so closely tied to international resource and raw-material demands. In difficult economic times, resources are the first commodities to be affected and the last to recover. The worldwide fall in prices—which had not readjusted from the inflation of the wartime and post-war periods—could not be arrested by conventional national economic policies, and in its wake demand for the specialized goods produced by Canada fell off. An international failure to buy left Canada and other major resource producers—such as Argentina and Australia—with a serious problem. Trade deficits mounted, and nations that owed Canada money were unable to pay. The dollar fell, and in 1931 so did a number of major Canadian financial institutions, brokerage agencies, and insurance companies. The country would not fully recover until after another world war erupted, in 1939.

UNEMPLOYMENT

For most Canadians, the economic downturn of the 1930s was always the Great Depression, the Big One. People would live in its shadow for decades to come. What the Depression meant, first and foremost, was unemployment. Official statistics are meaningless as a measure of unemployment's extent, much less its significance. According to the *Historical Statistics of Canada* (1983), unemployment in Canada rose from 116,000 in 1929 to 741,000 in 1932 to 826,000 in 1933, ultimately declining to 411,000 in 1937 and then increasing to 529,000 in 1939. It is virtually impossible to cast these figures as percentages of the total numbers of employable persons, not least because no farmers, or fishers—or their wives—were tabulated among the ranks of the unemployed during the decade. Non-agricultural unemployment was something over 27 per cent in 1933, in the depths of the Depression, but when underemployment and the scarcity of jobs for women seeking to enter the workforce are taken into consideration the rate was probably closer to

■ Jobless men lining up at a 'soup kitchen' in 1934. City of Toronto Archives, Fonds 1244, Item 1683.

some land on which to grow food. In the 1930s, many members of farm families who had gone off to the cities returned to the family farm, and the decade was the first—and the last—since the 1880s in which the rural population grew at about the same rate as the urban one.

THE DEPRESSION ON THE FARM

Farmers in the 1930s were in serious trouble. The slump in international grain prices, which had begun long before the Depression, did fundamental harm to the agricultural economy, while continued drought and related dust-bowl conditions meant that many farm families could not harvest a crop. Omnipresent dust became the desolate symbol for the Depression on the Prairies. At the same time, because farm problems predated the current crisis, and because farm organizations and political movements were well established, provincial governments tended to be sympathetic at least to the farmers' plight, even if their responses were less active than the farmers might have wished.

THE DEPRESSION IN THE CITY

The poorest victims of the Depression were the urban unemployed, who found that their relief became the great political football of the thirties. Traditionally, municipalities and private charities had looked after the poor and the jobless, but the challenge became more than any city could handle. By 1933, 72 per cent of taxes levied in Burnaby, BC, were in arrears; the rates in neighbouring North Shore municipalities stood at 64 per cent for North Vancouver City, 60 per cent for West Vancouver, and 44 per cent for North Vancouver District.[18] Tax sales of houses proved impossible for want of buyers. Most municipalities distinguished unemployment rolls from relief rolls, regarding the latter as more permanent (and managing them more stringently). As one member of Parliament pointed out in 1930: 'Unemployment is created by conditions over

50 per cent. Regarded by the Canadian government as self-employed businessmen, farmers and fishers (and their families) merely lost money (and sometimes their 'businesses') during the decade. Nevertheless, a farmer whose expenses exceeded his income was probably better off than an urban resident who had no job and whose expenses similarly exceeded his intake. Farmers had at least

■ Workers on Relief Project No. 27 inside their hut at Ottawa, March 1933. LAC, PA-35133.

which the municipality has no control whatever. [It is] merely the victim of circumstances.'[19] If municipalities were victims, so were the recipients of their assistance. As James Gray recounts in his autobiographical account of life in Winnipeg during the Depression (see p. 267), municipal assistance was given grudgingly, almost always in the form of credit vouchers to be redeemed at local stores rather than as cash that might be spent on frivolities or worse. The relief lines were not called 'the dole' in jest. Gray recalled that the radio was the last material possession retained by many families, since it represented their principal enjoyment and contact with the outside world.[20] Single unemployed men looking for help were

usually advised simply to go elsewhere—perhaps to one of the work camps organized in the frontier districts of the West.

Family relationships were greatly affected by unemployment. But one study carried out in Montreal during the Depression emphasized that the determining factor for the family was the previous state of the relationship of the partners.[21] This study also suggested that working-class families, especially in Quebec, had considerable capacity to adapt and to find strategies for coping. Most families relied on the assistance of neighbours and relatives rather than on public financial support. Government assistance was dispensed to the husband, which, as one woman pointed out, meant that 'he went to collect it and if he spent it, then you had nothing.'[22] There was little fraud among relief recipients; most people were desperate to get off the dole. Certainly the Depression taught working-class families to avoid credit and view it with trepidation. According to one woman:

> We were never in debt. I never bought anything on credit because I told myself that if I didn't have the money today, I wasn't going to have it tomorrow. You mustn't go into debt. If we had, I don't know how we could have paid it. In our day, we always thought that maybe tomorrow we wouldn't have a paycheque. There wasn't anything to fall back on, you know. You couldn't count on anybody. You could only count on yourselves. That's why we often had to go without things we would have liked to have.[23]

The deferral of expectations—for material goods, marriage, children—was one of the most profound consequences of the Depression for many Canadians.

The fall in prices meant that costs were lower for the 50 per cent of Canadians who continued to work through the Depression. Wages also fell, of course, and many held their breath each time payday rolled around. But for those with secure jobs, life was good. Reported one Montreal woman, 'He had such a good job, I didn't worry.'[24] Homes could be purchased for a pittance (sometimes just the amount of back taxes) and rented or leased at advantageous terms everywhere in Canada. In Montreal, a private chef could be hired for $50 a month (plus room and board) at the height of the Depression, and laundresses who washed and ironed by hand in their own homes earned $2 a day.[25] While university professors took large cuts in pay—a typical pre-Depression salary was $3,000 per year—their households could still afford a servant.

In the industrial and resource sectors, the Depression meant layoffs, plant and mine closures, and general retrenchment. Canadian business corporations actually suffered losses (or negative profits) only in 1932, chiefly because they had not responded quickly enough to the slump by laying off employees and cutting back; in 1933—the lowest point on the economic curve—the corporations ended up collectively in the black. Retrenchment was relatively simple: excess workers were fired or laid off. Large corporations, such as those in the Ontario automobile industry, rebounded enough that by 1937 they were able to exceed 1929 production figures. Small businessmen were obviously not in the same favourable position as the larger corporations, however, and many went bankrupt.[26] The gradual recovery in the economy after 1935—with another minor slump in 1939—alleviated only some of the distress experienced in the first half of the decade.

REFORM AND RECOVERY

The relationship between the provincial and federal governments during the Depression was certainly not harmonious, and the constitutional wrangling over responsibility for assistance was irrelevant to those Canadians needing help. Mackenzie King's notorious remark about not giving a five-cent piece to help a Tory provincial government relieve unemployment—which some thought cost him the 1930 election—suggested the partisan tensions that existed between the two levels of government. King's successor as Prime Minister, R.B. Bennett, often responded to begging letters with assistance out of his own pocket.[27] But Bennett was a doctrinaire free-enterpriser, more concerned to end unemployment by manipulating tariffs than to relieve it by assisting the unemployed, whatever his campaign promises. A long-time opponent of the 'dole system', he resolutely balanced the federal budget and passed the buck to the provincial governments. They, in turn, passed it on to the municipalities, which had to balance declining revenue from property taxes against increasing expenditures on the unemployed and on relief assistance.

■ The Bennett buggy, named after Prime Minister R.B. Bennett, became a common conveyance during the Depression on the Prairies for those who could no longer afford gasoline and maintenance for their vehicles. University of Saskatchewan Archives, photo A-3412.

Throughout most of its term in office, Bennett's government kept tight controls on spending for unemployment relief, arguing 'constitutional limitations'. Not until an election loomed did Bennett listen to those within his own party who called for more action to be taken. What he apparently found persuasive was the popular success that Franklin Delano Roosevelt had achieved in the United States with more dynamic policies—though perhaps the defeat of the conservative Herbert Hoover was equally instructive. Influenced by his brother-in-law William D. Herridge, Canadian ambassador to Washington, Bennett converted to his own version of a 'New Deal'. He announced his new policy in a live radio address to the nation in January 1935, saying: 'I am for reform. I nail the flag of progress to the mast. I summon the power of the state to its support.' Echoing Stephen Leacock in 1919, the Prime Minister spoke of regulating working conditions, insuring against unemployment, extending credit to farmers. Like Leacock, Bennett in 1935 apparently had come to appreciate that only an active state intervening on behalf of the working people could save the system of capitalism and

free enterprise. Unfortunately, his radio proclamations ran well ahead of the practical legislative program he and his cabinet had ready for Parliament. Canadian voters rejected the Conservative Prime Minister in favour of Mackenzie King's Liberals, who had offered few rhetorical promises but had the solid backing of Quebec.[28]

Nevertheless, Bennett's 'conversion' to New Dealism symbolized the political desperation of more than one politician. It also represented a growing realization in large parts of the Canadian business and professional communities that stabilizing the economy of the nation was necessary to prevent a more serious upheaval.[29] Broad sectors of the business community had responded to the Depression by seeking to reduce competition—the aim of most businessmen within their own industries—through government regulation of the market. Many Canadian businessmen had looked favourably on the price-fixing schemes introduced in the United States under Roosevelt's National Recovery Administration (NRA) and advocated a similar agency in Canada. One speaker before the Canadian Pulp and Paper Association in 1934 argued:

Our government might do well to consider some such scheme for the stabilization of Canadian industry, which could be brought about by the vesting in industry of certain powers and authority which would enable it through trade associations to control itself in all its main phases, working hours, wages, manufacturing and marketing.[30]

Most mainstream reform policies advocated during the Depression found considerable support in the business community, which saw these proposals as stabilizing alternatives to economic and social chaos.

Some businessmen continued to oppose government intervention, but many leading businessmen and financiers were statist—providing that they could control the reforms and assuming that the policies adopted benefited their industries. As the economist A.E. Grauer explained in 1939:

> Since the Great War, the Great Depression has been the chief stimulus to labour legislation and social insurance. The note sounded has not been so much the ideal of social justice as political and economic financial expediency. For instance, the shorter working week was favoured in unexpected quarters not because it would give the workers more leisure and the possibilities for a fuller life but because it would spread work; and the current singling out of unemployment insurance for governmental attention in many countries is dictated by the appalling costs of direct relief and the hope that unemployment insurance benefits will give some protection to public treasuries in future depressions and will, by sustaining purchasing power, tend to mitigate these depressions.[31]

As Bennett himself had advised while he was Prime Minister: 'A good deal of pruning is sometimes necessary to save a tree . . . it would be well for us in Canada to remember that there is considerable pruning to be done if we are to preserve the fabric of the capitalistic system.'[32]

PROTEST MOVEMENTS

In fact, attacks on that system were increasing. Although all were in some senses 'radical', not all came from the traditional left of organized labour, socialism, or communism. Like Canadians generally during the Depression, most were regional rather than national in their outlook and organization, because the federal government was not considered responsive to public needs. One indirect consequence of the national government's loss of credibility in the 'Dirty Thirties' was a significant delay in the development of Canadian nationalism.

SOCIAL CREDIT IN ALBERTA

One successful radical movement not of the left was Social Credit. Farmers in the dry-belt region of the Prairies suffered severely from drought and the Depression. Although the provincial government run by the United Farmers of Alberta had tried to control the damage, Alberta farmers had been heavily hit by mortgage foreclosures throughout the 1920s and by the early 1930s were understandably hostile to banks and mortgage companies. They were strongly attracted, however, to the economic ideas proposed by William Aberhart, a fundamentalist radio preacher whose Sunday broadcasts over Calgary's CFCN for the Prophetic Bible Institute had a substantial following. In 1932 Aberhart added a secular dimension to his program following his conversion to an economic scheme devised by a Scottish engineer, Major C.H. Douglas.[33]

The most dynamic part of Douglas's philosophy was its monetary theory, according to which capitalism maintained a permanent deficiency of purchasing power among the masses and the credit system, in the hands of bankers, did not utilize the productive system to the fullest possible extent. To enable people to buy more of the goods and services produced, Douglas advocated distributing money, or 'social credit'. 'Poverty in the Midst of Plenty'—another version of Leacock's unsolved riddle—became a Social Credit slogan. Aberhart never understood all the details of C.H. Douglas's economic theories, and he assured his Alberta audiences that they need not, either. But from these theories he derived a practical plan for the state to make up the difference between the purchasing power of consumers and the total value of production by issuing a 'social dividend' (eventually set at $25 a month) to all citizens as part of their cultural heritage.

Early in 1935, with the assistance of a young associate, Ernest Manning, Aberhart organized the Social Credit Party. Attracting the attention of people with no previous political experience, the new party swept to success at the polls, taking 56 out of 63 seats and winning 54 per cent of the popular vote. It would maintain public support and credibility over the next few years despite

■ William Aberhart, July 1937. LAC, C-009339.

WILLIAM ABERHART
(1878–1943)

❖

William Aberhart was born in Perth County, Ontario, in 1878. His father's family was of Prussian origin. One of eight children, he grew up on a farm and was educated at Seaforth Collegiate Institute, the Chatham Business Institute, and the Ontario Normal School in Hamilton. He began teaching in Brantford in 1901 as head of the commercial form, at about the same time he became converted to a radical sectarianism known as 'dispensationalism', which united Biblical study with prophecy. As a teacher, he was a firm disciplinarian and organizer. By the time he had become interim principal of his school in 1905, he was bicycling on many Sundays to preach in outlying Presbyterian churches. He was much influ-

enced by Dwight L. Moody and other evangelical fundamentalists in style, although the substance was an individualistic dispensationalism diametrically opposed to the Social Gospel.

Aberhart took a university degree at Queen's University entirely by correspondence with a view to entering the Presbyterian ministry. In 1910, however, he was attracted to Calgary, becoming a school principal and entering actively into the life of the evangelically oriented religious community. His very popular Bible teaching met opposition from many traditionalists, and he left Grace Presbyterian Church in 1912, first, to join the Methodists, then, in late 1915, to preach at Westbourne Baptist Church. His Bible classes there were so popular that he established the Calgary Prophetic Bible Conference. Aberhart declined to become ordained, at least partly in order to maintain his independence of ecclesiastical authority. He taught with the Bible in hand, taking its text literally, yet striving constantly to reconcile its many contradictions as well as adding various 'charismatic' practices to the church. The Prophetic Conference made Aberhart's name well-known across Alberta before he added radio to his media in 1925 and began broadcasting ('Back-to-the-Bible') every Sunday afternoon on station CFCN, one of western Canada's most powerful transmitting stations. Using his position as principal of Crescent Height High School to provide for his family, he opened the Calgary Prophetic Bible Institute in 1927 and founded his own sect, the Bible Institute Baptist Church, in 1929. He kept his school life and religious life rigorously separated, but his religious activities attracted increasing attention from the Calgary School Board.

Aberhart first encountered the ideas of the British monetary reformer Major C.H. Douglas in 1932 in the pages of Maurice Colbourne's *Unemployment or War*. Like most Canadians, especially those in western Canada, Aberhart had been seeking an answer to the riddle of poverty, and he found it in the theory of 'social credit', which emphasized that the problem was an insufficiency of purchasing power in capitalist economies, which could be resolved by state control. He soon discovered that his fellow Albertans found the idea of social credit equally appealing, especially when combined with prophecy on the radio. Aberhart was a 'statist' who gave hope to Albertans that they could create a new social order. His economics were illogical, but he also took many ideas from western populism and left-wing ideologies; he was no democrat, since he believed in rule by experts. One connection between his religion and his politics was made in terms of conspiracy theories, but his political support did not come from religious fundamentalists. Attempting to place his political and economic teachings on a right–left/conservative–radical spectrum has been extremely difficult; much controversy remains over whether he was a radical or a right-wing authoritarian. In any event, Aberhart built a movement, the Alberta Social Credit League, to popularize his ideas, and converted the league into a political party in the 1935 Alberta election. His main campaign platform was a 'social dividend' out of the undistributed increment of $25 per month for every citizen. In office, Aberhart found he was unable to implement most of his electoral promises, at least partly because of objections from the federal government and the Supreme Court of Canada. He died in office in 1943.

vehement opposition to its program—particularly its mortgage, debt, and banking legislation from the Dominion government under Mackenzie King (a marked departure from King's generally cautious approach in Dominion–provincial relations) as well as the federal courts, which ultimately disallowed 13 Alberta statutes.

The Social Credit government in Alberta thereafter moved to more traditional (and conservative) fiscal practices, blaming Ottawa and eastern big business for its failure to enact its program. Under Aberhart and, following his death in 1943, under Ernest Manning, Social Credit won nine successive elections in Alberta and governed the province until 1971. It was much aided by the discoveries of oil and gas in Alberta, the revenues from which made the notion of a social dividend more plausible.

MAURICE DUPLESSIS AND THE UNION NATIONALE IN QUEBEC

The political movement that emerged in Quebec in response to the Depression was constructed out of distinctly French-Canadian elements, but its overall patterns were not appreciably different from some in English Canada, especially in Alberta and Ontario. A popular leader emerged —with all the trappings of a demagogue—to offer simplistic solutions within a highly paternalistic framework.

That populist leader was Maurice Duplessis, the son of a small-town lawyer in Trois-Rivières who was an active Conservative. Born in 1890, from the outset the young Duplessis had only one ambition: to be Premier of Quebec.[34] He trained as a lawyer and spent all his energies on politics and politicking. In 1933 he became leader of Quebec's minority Conservative Party without having committed himself to any particular position on the province's growing economic and social crisis. Recognizing that his party was too fragmented to win an election, he sought new directions and allies and found them in two burgeoning Quebec movements of the early 1930s: the Catholic social action of the École sociale populaire and the liberal radicalism of the Action libérale nationale (ALN).

Catholic social action offered an alternative to socialism that attempted to reconcile the need for reform with the teachings of the Church. It was critical of capitalism and supportive of government intervention to redistribute wealth, protect farmers and workers, and regulate large corporations in the public interest. As Father Louis Chagnon argued, capitalism needed to 'be subject to the Christian law of justice and charity, socially managed, and directed by government action and the organization of professionals'.[35]

From the ALN Duplessis took his program of economic nationalism, according to which the inferior status of French Canadians was a matter less of class than of foreign—i.e., British—ownership and colonial oppression. Most Quebec nationalists could agree on the need to preserve traditional rural virtues and to support Quebec industry through 'l'achat chez nous',[36] but the ALN merged that traditional Quebec nationalism with the new Catholic reform. It wanted agrarian reform, new labour legislation, and the promotion of small industry and commerce; but it also sought 'to destroy, by all possible means, the hold that the great financial establishments, the electricity trust and the paper industry have on the province and the municipalities'.[37] It sought banking regulation and a government not clandestinely linked through shareholding and directorates to the capitalist system.

Duplessis negotiated with the ALN (which won 26 seats in the 1935 Quebec election) an agreement to combine the ALN and the Conservatives in a new party, the Union Nationale. Campaigning on the ALN's reform platform, the new party swept to an easy victory in 1936, winning 76 seats and 58 per cent of the popular vote. Duplessis, now Premier of Quebec, quickly purged his government of ALN people and quietly abandoned most of the reform program that had brought him to power. What remained was a concern for provincial autonomy in federal–provincial affairs, anti-communism (expressed in Duplessis's infamous 'Padlock Act' of 1937, closing any place where it was suspected that communism was being propagated), and paternalistic handouts for the disadvantaged, carefully calculated to produce maximum electoral effect. Duplessis did not approve of the closed shop, and his labour legislation essentially imposed settlements from above if they could not be achieved through collective bargaining. Like Social Credit in Alberta, the Union Nationale in power was quite different from the party on the campaign trail. But, as in Alberta, once in power it was extremely difficult to dislodge.

THE ANTIGONISH MOVEMENT IN NOVA SCOTIA

A very different response to the Depression emerged in Nova Scotia, especially in Cape Breton and along the eastern shore. The people of these regions were mainly farmers and fishermen, small producers—many descendants of Catholic Scottish Highlanders—who had no control over the marketing and distribution of their commodities at the best of times. Their depression had started long before 1929, and they were as ripe as Albertans for some sort of social experimentation. It was provided by two extraordinary Roman Catholic priests at St Francis Xavier University in Antigonish: Father James J. ('Jimmy') Tompkins and Father Moses Coady. The underlying theory was supplied by Coady in his book *Masters of Their Own Destiny* (1939), in which he argued that the Industrial Revolution had taken economic power away from ordinary people. Capitalism was not to blame, but the system had a weak foundation and needed reconstruction. The solution was for small producers to regain power over their own production and consumption through economic co-operation. Building on example from the agricultural sector, the Antigonish Movement advocated co-operative banks, stores, and marketing agencies, and established its first credit union in 1932.

The Antigonish ideology, like western populism, was a curious mixture of radical rhetoric and conservative attitudes, well suited to a population of individualistic small producers. Thus, it criticized members of 'the bourgeoisie' as economic parasites, but insisted that it did not advocate class warfare. It was not socialistic and opposed labour unions, deriving much of its strength from principles of Catholic humanism, not all of which were shared by the Church's hierarchy at the time. Nevertheless, Coady insisted that the workers owned whatever they produced, and that any outside attempt to claim ownership was exploitation.[38] In its own way the Antigonish Movement—which swept across the Maritimes in the 1930s, joining already existing co-operatives—was wrestling with the unsolved riddle. Like Social Credit, it struck a chord with people seeking some kind of transforming solution to their problems. In its consciousness-raising transcendence of the existing capitalist system, the Antigonish Movement may have prepared the way for more radical measures among a very traditional population. But Antigonish did not advocate political activism, much less support parties to the left, such as the CCF.

THE CO-OPERATIVE COMMONWEALTH FEDERATION

The most important political response to the Great Depression based in the socialist tradition came from the Co-operative Commonwealth Federation. The CCF was founded in Calgary in 1932 as a coalition of farmers' organizations, labour unions such as the Canadian Brotherhood of Railway Employees, and labour-socialist parties in the four western provinces. Its platform, however, was provided by a group of socialist thinkers like F.H. Underhill, professor of history at the University of Toronto, who believed that mass unemployment and hardship presaged an economic breakdown. He received the support of many colleagues—including F.R. (Frank) Scott and Eugene Forsey, who taught at McGill; David Lewis, a law student there; and J. King Gordon, professor of Christian ethics at the United Theological College in Montreal and the son of C.W. Gordon (Ralph Connor). In 1931 they formed the League for Social Reconstruction (LSR), with the former Methodist minister J.S. Woodsworth (who had been involved in the Winnipeg General Strike) as honorary president and Frank Scott as president. The declaration of principles that was approved at the LSR's first convention in Toronto in January 1932 deplored the fact that 'In the advanced industrial countries [the present capitalist system] has led to the concentration of wealth in the hands of a small irresponsible minority of bankers and industrialists whose economic power constantly threatens to nullify our political democracy.' It stated that the League would work 'for the establishment in Canada of a social order in which the basic principles regulating production, distribution and service will be the common good rather than private profit'—by substituting 'a planned and socialized economy for the existing chaotic individualism'.[39]

The LSR was heavily influenced by British socialism, particularly the wing led before the Great War by Sidney and Beatrice Webb and Bernard Shaw, the leading exponents of 'Fabianism'. The Fabian Society (which took its name from Quintus Fabius Maximus, nicknamed 'the Delayer') was founded in England in 1884. Fabians believed in the gradual conversion of society to socialism through what Shaw called 'permeations' of the body politic by indirect influence. They were proudly non-Marxist and non-revolutionary, although vehemently committed to a welfare state and the takeover by the state of key industries.[40] These general goals were shared by the LSR, which considered itself to be an educational rather than a political organization.

The inevitable connection between the LSR and the CCF was made through individual LSR members who became active CCFers. Before the CCF held its first annual convention (in Regina in 1933), Underhill was asked to prepare a statement of principles and a program for the new party. He did so, in collaboration with some of his LSR colleagues, using the LSR manifesto as a model. The famous Regina Manifesto was the result. It promised a heady brew of political reform and action once the CCF came to power. All industry 'essential to social planning' would be nationalized, the former owners suitably compensated. A series of universal welfare measures—hospitalization, health care, unemployment insurance, pensions—would be introduced after amendments had been made to the British North America Act to remove constitutional impediments. The 'Co-operative Common-

CCF picnic poster, July 1939. Glenbow Archives NA 2629-10.

wealth' it defined as 'the full system of socialized planning'.[41] In its emphasis on the need to place social planning in the hands of 'public servants acting in the public interest and responsible to the people as a whole', the Regina Manifesto harked back to the days of the Progressives. (Indeed, the latter's 'ginger group' were among its founders.) In choosing the party's leader the Regina meeting compromised between its active and popular memberships—who were not entirely sympathetic to one another—by appointing Woodsworth, a pacifist, idealist, and moralist who since 1921 had led a small cadre of labour-supported MPs in Ottawa.[42]

The new party attracted over 300,000 votes in the 1933 BC provincial elections—more than 30 per cent of the popular vote. The *Vancouver Sun* described its platform in Sir John A.

Macdonald's phrase: 'Something to get in on—not to stand on.'[43] But while this support brought it seven provincial seats and made it the official opposition, the Liberals under Duff Pattullo took 34 seats and formed the government. On the national level, in the 1935 election the party obtained 8.9 per cent of the popular vote, which translated into seven CCF seats—including one held by T.C. Douglas of Saskatchewan. Woodsworth himself led the new MPs into the House, convinced that the CCF represented a 'distinctly Canadian type of socialism'. The party had high hopes after its early showings both provincially and federally, but in the later 1930s it would flourish only in BC and Saskatchewan.[44] Among the other provinces that might have helped the CCF to develop a national base, Quebec naturally refused to support anything that smacked of secularist socialism, while Alberta expressed its discontent through Social Credit at the provincial level and Nova Scotia had the Antigonish Movement.

THE COMMUNIST PARTY OF CANADA

The nation's politicians and businessmen took a dim view of the CCF as a movement on the radical left, but in fact the new party was middle-of-the-road compared with the genuinely radical Communist Party of Canada, which had become a legal party in 1924. At the outset of the Depression, only the Communists offered an organized outlet for Canadian popular discontent, creating in 1930 a National Unemployed Workers' Association that by the next year had attracted 22,000 members across the nation. The Communists operated under several serious disadvantages, however. One was the charge that they were 'un-Canadian' members of an international conspiracy. It was true that most of the party's leaders were strongly influenced by the Communist International operating out of Moscow. But it was equally true that the party was badly divided into a number of factions with varying attitudes towards the International.

Another disadvantage was the willingness of the Canadian government to repress the party in any way possible, using section 98 of the Criminal Code (introduced in 1919, at the time of the first 'Red scare', to outlaw the advocacy of revolution). Thus, when eight Communist leaders were arrested in August 1931, they were easily convicted and sentenced—although they were gradually released from prison after continuing public demonstrations on their behalf.[45]

The Communists eventually lost their momentum at the grassroots level in the course of their battles with the government and the courts. Nevertheless, they claimed credit for organizing, through the Workers' Unity League, a mass march on Ottawa in 1935 known as the On-to-Ottawa Trek. In fact, the trekkers were single young men who had taken refuge in the unemployment relief camps of British Columbia but found the conditions intolerable (for example, they were expected to work six and a half days a week for only 20 cents a day). Not even the Communists themselves claimed that the outbreak of trouble was anything but spontaneous. The trek began in Vancouver, and was halted by the RCMP at Regina. Eight trekkers were delegated to go to Ottawa and meet with Prime Minister R.B. Bennett, but the talks soon broke down. On the delegates' return to Regina a rally was held and the RCMP moved in, waving 'baseball bat batons'. The ensuing riot involved 500 Mounties, local police, and hundreds of trekkers. Downtown Regina was reduced to a shambles and 120 protestors were arrested. Most of the remainder accepted offers of passage back home. In 1937, many Canadian Communists were attracted into the European struggle between the Communist-supported Republican government and Franco's fascists in Spain.[46]

POPULAR VIOLENCE

The 1930s were regularly punctuated by outbreaks of popular discontent that turned to violence. Two points must be made about these

THE REGINA MANIFESTO, 1933

In 1933 a number of groups representing farmers, labour unions, and socialists met together in Regina. They adopted a social democratic platform that initially had been drafted by Frank Underhill, F.R. Scott, and the League for Social Reconstruction as the official program of the newly organized Co-operative Commonwealth Federation.

The CCF is a federation of organizations whose purpose is the establishment in Canada of a Co-operative Commonwealth in which the principle regulating production, distribution and exchange will be the supplying of human needs and not the making of profits.

We aim to replace the present capitalist system, with its inherent injustice and inhumanity, by a social order from which the domination and exploitation of one class by another will be eliminated, in which economic planning will supersede unregulated private enterprise and competition, and in which genuine democratic self-government, based upon economic equality will be possible. The present order is marked by glaring inequalities of wealth and opportunity, by chaotic waste and instability; and in an age of plenty it condemns the great mass of the people to poverty and insecurity. Power has become more and more concentrated in the hands of a small irresponsible minority of financiers and industrialists and to their predatory interests the majority are habitually sacrificed. When private profit is the main stimulus to economic effort, our society oscillates between periods of feverish prosperity in which the main benefits go to speculators and profiteers and of catastrophic depression, in which the common man's normal state of insecurity and hardship is accentuated. We believe that these evils can be removed only in a planned and socialized economy in which our natural resources and the principal means of production and distribution are owned, controlled and operated by the people.

The new social order at which we aim is not one in which individuality will be crushed out by a system of regimentation. Nor shall we interfere with cultural rights of racial or religious minorities. What we seek is a proper collective organization of our economic resources such as will make possible a much greater degree of leisure and a much richer individual life for every citizen.

This social and economic transformation can be brought about by political action, through the election of a government inspired by the ideal of a Co-operative Commonwealth and supported by a majority of the people. We do not believe in change by violence. We consider that both the old parties in Canada are the instruments of capitalist interests and cannot serve as agents of social reconstruction, and that whatever the superficial difference between, they are bound to carry on government in accordance with the dictates of the big business interests who finance them. The CCF aims at political power in order to put an end to this capitalist domination of our political life. It is a democratic movement, a federation of farmer, labour and socialist organizations, financed by its own members and seeking to achieve its end solely by constitutional methods. It appeals for support to all who believe that the time has come for a far-reaching reconstruction of our economic and political institutions.

SOURCE: D. Owen Carrigan, comp., *Canadian Party Platforms, 1867–1968* (Urbana: University of Illinois Press, 1968).

■ Strikers from the BC relief camps heading east as part of the 'On to Ottawa' trek; Kamloops, June 1935. LAC, C-029399.

events. The first is that most of the damage done to persons and property resulted from the efforts of the authorities to break up what were regarded as ugly but not yet destructive crowds. When the men from the relief camps gathered in Vancouver in 1935, they were orderly for days before starting a demonstration and breaking some showcases in the Hudson's Bay Company store. They then marched to city hall, where Mayor Gerry

McGeer—convinced that the city was 'being victimized by an organized attempt to capitalize, for revolutionary purposes, the conditions of depression which now exist'—read them the Riot Act, touching off street battles between police and protestors.[47] The second point is that much of the violence of the period resulted, as might be expected, from confrontations between organized labour and the authorities. These gained in intensity and frequency after 1937, when economic conditions had improved and workers attempted to organize industrial unions to represent those in large factories.

One particularly nasty series of incidents occurred in April 1937, when more than 4,000 workers in the large General Motors plant in Oshawa, Ontario, struck for an eight-hour day, better wages and working conditions, and recognition of the new union of United Automobile Workers (UAW). The union was an affiliate of the recently formed Congress of Industrial Organizations (CIO), which was organizing throughout the United States. Premier Mitchell Hepburn, who sided with General Motors in its refusal to negotiate with the CIO, clashed with the Prime Minister over King's refusal to send RCMP reinforcements for the local police. The Premier organized volunteers, labelled 'Hepburn's Hussars'. General Motors eventually agreed to most UAW demands, while not recognizing the CIO (though the settlement was widely seen as a CIO victory). Hepburn resigned as Premier in 1942.[48]

THE ROWELL-SIROIS REPORT

The difficulty of dealing with the economic and social consequences of the Depression was exacerbated by the division of powers set down in the BNA Act. Thus, in 1937 the federal government appointed a Royal Commission on Dominion–Provincial Relations chaired first by Newton Rowell of Ontario and then by Joseph Sirois of Quebec. Taking two and a half years to conduct extensive research, the Commission did not report until May 1940, by which time the nation was again at war and the Depression was over. It found that, although the BNA Act gave the responsibility for health, welfare, and social assistance to the provincial level, those governments could not be expected to carry out such expensive functions as providing for the unemployed. It recommended that the federal government take over certain taxation powers (including taxes on personal incomes) from the

provinces and relieve them of their debt burdens by providing adjustment grants. Although the restructuring proposed by the Commission would not be carried out until after the war—and Dominion–provincial relations would need a good deal more than fiscal reform—the Rowell-Sirois Report was a positive step towards more equitable constitutional arrangements.[49]

EXTERNAL RELATIONS BETWEEN THE WARS

Once Canada was admitted to the League of Nations as a full member, it became a regular if not influential participant, frequently lecturing Europe on its past and present failures. One Canadian delegate to the League Assembly in 1924, for example, observed that 'Not only we have had a hundred years of peace on our borders, but we think in terms of peace, while Europe, an armed camp, thinks in terms of war.'[50] Taking a position from such high moral ground became a durable characteristic of Canada's external relations, although it did not make the nation popular at the conference table. Canada's ambivalent attitude towards the League of Nations not only foreshadowed its ambiguous involvement in that organization over the next 20 years, but also illustrates the essential dichotomy and tension of Canadian external policy over that period and beyond it. On the one hand, Canada sought to give priority to its status as an independent nation. On the other hand, rights imply responsibilities and Ottawa was never convinced that its best interests were served by full involvement in the international world of crisis politics or in the maintenance of the military strength that such participation implied. Its isolationist instincts and its ambitions for sovereignty and international status were constantly at odds. Interwar external management concentrated on achieving full international sovereignty in several ways. First, the nation needed to develop an infrastructure for implementing Canada's role in the world apart from the British Empire. Second, there would have to be a foreign policy or policies, as well as a military establishment, capable of providing some response to the increasingly frequent international crises of the 1930s. Finally, Ottawa needed to complete the process of redefining the British Empire to reflect Canada's needs.

The process of redefinition came at the Westminster Conference in 1930. By this time, R.B. Bennett's Tories had replaced the Liberals, and Bennett himself headed the Canadian delegation to London. He was in no position to take a new direction, and he accepted the Statute of Westminster that had been agreed to at the conference, which would make six dominions (Canada, Australia, New Zealand, South Africa, the Irish Free State, and Newfoundland) legislatively independent. Although amendment to the British North America Act remained in the hands of the British Parliament, Canada became for all intents and purposes independent: a member of a 'Commonwealth of Nations that had no binding authority over anyone and was united mainly by allegiance to a single ceremonial monarch. As Bennett himself said immediately after the Statute of Westminster became law, with its adoption "the old political Empire disappears".'[51] Canada still had some hope in the 1930s for the economic empire, however.

In the later 1930s, Canadian isolationism was rapidly overtaken by events. Canada quietly supported the British policy of 'appeasement', of accepting an escalating series of aggressive moves by Germany—in the Rhineland, in Austria, in Czechoslovakia—as part of a legitimate quest for *lebensraum* and the consolidation of German-speaking peoples. However, by 1938, when Neville Chamberlain's Munich Agreement promised 'peace in our time', a vocal minority was arguing that appeasement was an immoral and futile policy.

CONCLUSION

The Great Depression obviously had an enormous impact on the people of Canada. Yet, it had surprisingly little effect on the political and constitutional system. Despite considerable provocation, Canadians refused to jump unreservedly on the bandwagon of any group advocating an extremist version of political reform. To some extent, regional fragmentation may have helped to prevent any extreme movement from gaining national popularity. The political and economic impact of the Depression would be felt most heavily in the years during and after World War II, when it led to a groundswell of demands for reform.

SHORT BIBLIOGRAPHY

Baillargeon, Denyse. *Making Do: Women, Family and Home in Montreal during the Great Depression.* Waterloo, Ont., 1999. One of the few books on the Depression that tries to understand the response of ordinary people through recreations of their stories.

Baum, Gregory. *Catholics and Canadian Socialism: Political Thought in the Thirties and Forties.* Toronto, 1980. A fascinating study of a much-neglected subject.

Black, Conrad. *Duplessis.* Toronto, 1977. The standard biography of 'le Chef'.

Fisher, Robin. *Duff Pattullo of British Columbia.* Toronto, 1991. An important study of British Columbia politics, especially in the 1930s.

Forbes, Ernest R. *The Maritime Rights Movement, 1919–1927: A Study in Canadian Regionalism.* Montreal, 1979. A useful analysis of the political view from the Maritimes in the 1920s.

Horn, Michiel. *The League for Social Reconstruction: Intellectual Origins of the Democratic Left in Canada.* Toronto, 1980. An intellectual history of the movement that made socialism respectable in Canada.

Pettigrew, Eileen. *The Silent Enemy: Canada and the Deadly Flu of 1918*. Saskatoon, 1983. A study of a much-neglected topic in Canadian history.

Safarian, A. *The Canadian Economy in the Great Depression*. Toronto, 1959. The most balanced and expert analysis of the Canadian economy in the 1930s.

Stacey, C.P. *Canada and the Age of Conflict: A History of Canadian External Policies*, vol. 2, *1921–1948*. Toronto, 1981. The most authoritative study of Canadian external relations between the wars and immediately after World War II.

Thompson, John Herd, with Allen Seager. *Canada 1922–1939: Decades of Discord*. Toronto, 1985. A wonderful general synthesis of the period.

Trofimenkoff, Susan Mann. *Action Française: French Canadian Nationalism in the Twenties*. Toronto, 1975. The best study in English of a contentious question.

Young, Walter. *Democracy and Discontent: Progressivism, Socialism and Social Credit in the Canadian West*. Toronto, 1969. A first-rate, middle-level synthesis of political protest in the Canadian West.

STUDY QUESTIONS

1. What was the 'unsolved riddle of social justice'?

2. Were the 1920s a period of prosperity?

3. What was the great weakness of the Progressive Party? What parallels and differences can you identify between the Progressives and the Reform Party and its successors, the Canadian Alliance and the Conservative Party?

4. Why did the Maritime Rights movement fail?

5. Where did Canadian business stand on state intervention in the 1930s?

6. Were any of the regional protest movements of the 1930s movements of the right?

7. Why was the Communist Party of Canada not more successful during the Depression?

CHAPTER ELEVEN

Canadian Society and Culture between the Wars, 1919–1939

Images of the period between the wars are dominated by drought and dust, soup kitchens and breadlines. But not all Canadians were unemployed, and the Depression years were only a part of the whole.[1] Moreover, Canadian society underwent enormous changes that had nothing to do with the Depression. It was during the inter-war period, for example, that Canada completed its demographic shift from an agrarian society to a modern industrial one. The 1920s saw an upsurge in immigration that was matched by a resurgence of racism in the form of nativist sentiment. During the 1920s, as well, prohibition (and reform generally) failed, and the main proponents of reform—the Methodist, Presbyterian, and Congregational churches—amalgamated. This era also saw vast technological changes with the general acceptance of the automobile and the radio, as well as the transition of the airplane from war machine to transportation vehicle. Although workers often suffered in these years, there were also some substantial gains for organized labour, especially during the Depression. Gains for women, however, were minimal. As for children, they began to come under the scrutiny of the new child-care 'experts'.

DEMOGRAPHIC TRENDS

For more than half a century before 1919, Canada had been involved in the gradual transition from developing frontier country to modern industrial nation. All Canadians were aware of the most obvious changes: the rapid growth of cities, the gradual decline of rural population, the establishment of factories. What they did not so clearly appreciate were the demographic changes occurring beneath the surface. The failure of the federal government to begin accurate national record-keeping until 1921 helped to keep the profundity of those changes from becoming too apparent, as did the enormous burst of immigration between 1896 and 1913. Even before the war, however, some commentators had begun to emphasize one of the major themes associated with the new society: the collapse of the family as the fundamental social unit. To some extent, the perceived change in the family unit was more a moral than a statistical point, and it was, of course, associated with significant alterations in the legal and practical status of women. The Great War removed more than half a million males from their homes, and the ensuing decades added their own particularities.

TIMELINE

1917

First Soldier Settlement Act passes Parliament.

1919

Soldier Settlement scheme revamped. Eighty-five radio stations operating in Canada. *Canadian Bookman* founded.

1921

Ku Klux Klan of the British Empire formed.

1922

Thirteen per cent of Canada's roads are surfaced. Insulin discovered at the University of Toronto.

1923

Final treaty, in northern Ontario, signed with First Nations. Three large ocean liners leave the Clyde with Scottish immigrants aboard. Canada is second-largest automobile producer in the world.

1925

Partial reform of federal divorce laws. United Church of Canada is formed. Institute of Child Study is formed.

1927

Temperance ends in Ontario. All-Canadian Congress of Labour formed.

1928

The Aird Royal Commission on Broadcasting is appointed.

1929

Privy Council declares that women are 'persons'. Grey Owl publishes *The Men of the Last Frontier*.

1931

First hockey game broadcast, with commentary by Foster Hewitt.

1932

Broadcasting Act leads to formation of Canadian Radio Broadcasting Commission (CRBC). First Dominion Drama Festival.

1934

Dionne quintuplets born.

1936

Canadians are only Commonwealth athletes to give Nazi salute at opening ceremonies of Olympics. CRBC becomes Canadian Broadcasting Corporation.

1937

Trans-Canada Airlines is formed. Oshawa strike of 1937. Governor General's Awards are launched.

1938

First Nations deaths from tuberculosis in British Columbia run at 8.1 per 1,000.

1940

10,000 British schoolchildren approved for admission to Canada.

1941

Census shows more Canadians living in urban than rural places. Birth rate begins recovering.

1945

Dr Henry Bruce Chown discovers the mechanism of RH hemolytic disease.

1946

Saskatchewan introduces no-fault auto insurance.

The 1941 census was the first to show more Canadians living in urban than in rural places, but there had been a substantial increase in urban population during the 1920s. The 1941 census was also the last one in which a pattern of continual growth in total rural numbers (as opposed to percentages of the population) was maintained. The 1951 census would document fewer rural dwellers than 1941, and the decline was even more significant for the farm population of Canada, which, having fallen slightly between 1931 and 1941, would drop substantially and continuously thereafter.

The Death Rate

For some time before 1921, death rates had been declining steadily, particularly for infants. But infant mortality took another major drop (after one in the nineteenth century) in the course of the 1930s, and the overall death rate drifted perceptibly downward throughout this period, with the standardized death rate (after controlling for age structure of the population) dropping from 12.9 per 1,000 in 1921 to 9.9 per 1,000 in 1946, and the median age at death rising from 41.3 for males and 43.5 for females in 1921, to 63.1 for males and 65.3 for females by 1946. As increasing numbers of people began to survive past the age when they could earn their own living, concern for old-age pensions increased. The difference in life expectancy between males and females in this era would only widen in subsequent years. The decreasing death rate (for both adults and infants) was associated with improvements in both the standard of living—which led to decreases in fetal as well as infant mortality—and medical treatment. Improvements in sanitation and control of contagious disease were also significant factors.

Related to changes in mortality were profound alterations in fertility patterns. Increased urbanization made large families less desirable. And by drawing married women into the workforce, industrialization created new challenges in the area of child care. Declines in infant mortality meant that couples no longer had to produce many babies to ensure that some would survive. As more women realized that there were alternatives to the traditional child-bearing function, more women began to practise some form of contraception, especially after the age of 30. Birth rates, which began to fall in Canada before 1919, continued to fall over the next two decades, recovering only in 1941 from an extremely low point in the mid-1930s.

Divorce Rates

Rates of mortality and fertility had begun falling in the nineteenth century, but substantial increases in divorce rates were a relatively new development of the period 1919–39. Before the Great War the total number of divorces in Canada in any given year was remarkably small. Pressure for reform of the divorce law had been increased by the social upheavals of the Great War. Immediately after the war, many suits were brought by wives on the grounds that their husbands had committed one or more abuses besides adultery (usually while serving overseas in the Canadian forces). For their part, husbands sued for divorce from wives who had established new relationships during their absence overseas. The year 1918 saw only 114 divorces in all of Canada, a rate of 1.4 per 100,000 people, but the number shot up suddenly in 1919 and 1920, and slowly but inexorably continued to grow thereafter. In 1925 a revision of the divorce laws made it possible for a wife to obtain a divorce on grounds of adultery alone, although the proof required was quite stringent. But other grounds such as insanity, desertion, or extreme physical cruelty remained unacceptable unless accompanied by adultery. Ontario courts obtained divorce jurisdiction in 1930. After that year, in cases of desertion a wife could bring a suit for adultery in the province of the husband's last residence, but if he hadn't deserted her, she could sue only in the province where the husband currently lived, regardless of her own residence. By 1929 the divorce rate had reached 8.2 per 100,000, and it rose to 18.4 per 100,000 in 1939. There were strong regional differentials, caused partly by the fact that divorce for Quebec residents required the consent of the Parliament of Canada. Throughout the period, and especially during the Depression, most marital dissolutions involved desertion on the part of the husband.[2]

THE EXCEPTIONS: THE FIRST NATIONS

Not all Canadians reflected the overall demographic trends, of course, but no group deviated from them to the extent that Aboriginal people did. While Ottawa could avoid taking responsibility for the plight of the unemployed by arguing that social welfare was a provincial charge, status Indians and Inuit were wards of the federal government. Many groups had signed treaties with the government by which they surrendered title (or at least control) of their lands in return for guaranteed assistance and protection. The final treaty was signed in 1923 in northern Ontario. The federal Indian Act (which first came into force in 1876 and was frequently revised) specified who was and who was not a status (or 'legal' or 'registered') Indian eligible for government support. Only about half of the Native population came under the Act and, hence, were subject to the supervision of the Department of Indian Affairs. The Métis, among others, were excluded completely. The Inuit (and to some extent status Indians) living in the Territories came under the separate jurisdiction of the Department of the Interior's Northwest Territories and Yukon branch. Together, the treaties and the Indian Act effectively isolated status Indians far away from the centres of population, keeping them on rural reserves located on marginal land. Many Métis and non-status Indians lived in urban areas, but the very structure of the Indian Act insisted, almost dictated, that status Indians live in bands on reserves, chiefly located in the north.

Until 1960 it was impossible to obtain sufficiently precise statistics about status Indians and Inuit to discuss their demographic characteristics in any useful way. The Bureau of the Census did not systematically record such data, and neither Indian Affairs nor the Department of the Interior routinely collected it. This vagueness in itself tells us something about the government's attitude towards First Nations between the wars. Not until the 1940s did government begin responding to pressure, mainly from Native people themselves, for more than token involvement with their affairs.[3] Between the wars, government's main activity—apart from administering the handouts guaranteed by treaties and legislation—had been to encourage the churches in their efforts to establish off-reserve boarding schools for Aboriginal children. In recent years the treatment of pupils in those schools has become a major public issue. At the time, however, the number of Native children enrolled in such schools was a matter of great pride at Indian Affairs, and the statistics were prominently displayed in the *Canada Year Books* for the period. Meanwhile, health care in the isolated northern regions, where most First Nations lived, was virtually non-existent, particularly during the Depression, when budgetary cutbacks affected all government departments.

Inadequate record-keeping makes it impossible to know precise figures, but modern scholarship has calculated the birth rate for status Indians in the inter-war period at something over 40 per 1,000, compared to overall Canadian rates closer to 20 per 1,000.[4] While Canadian fertility was that of a modern urban industrial nation, Aboriginal fertility was that of a developing nation: high by modern standards, and capable of going higher still at the first sign of improved living standards. The birth rate for Native peoples would jump to nearly 60 per 1,000 by the 1950s.

The other side of fertility was mortality. The death rate among Native people was astoundingly high, nearly four times that of the overall

■ Aboriginal parents camp by a residential school at Birtle, Manitoba, in 1904 in order to visit their children. Archives of Manitoba, 3 (N10264).

Canadian population in this period. In 1929, for example, when the Canadian death rate was just over 10 per 1,000, the figure for status Indians was 39.7 per 1,000. Infant mortality ran at more than twice the national average, with 200 deaths per 1,000 births among Native peoples in 1940, while in all of Canada infant deaths ran well under 100 per 1,000.[5] In addition, a large number of Native mothers died in childbirth; one study found that 21.8 per cent of all female deaths in this period were attributable to this cause.[6] Before 1940, less than 2 per cent of Native births in the James Bay region of Quebec were in hospital: more than half were delivered at home and more than 40 per cent in the bush.[7] In addition, First Nations suffered two to three times more accidental deaths (especially among

males) than non-Native Canadians, and had very high suicide rates. Accidents were second only to 'combined diseases' as the major statistical cause of death among status Indians.

Many Canadians took their impressions of Indian life from Hollywood movies or a few popular writers. Chief among the latter was Archibald Belaney, an Englishman adopted by the Ojibwa who called himself Grey Owl. His best-selling books about life in the bush—*The Men of the Last Frontier* (1929), *Pilgrims of the Wild* (1935), *Tales of an Empty Cabin* (1936)—stressed Aboriginal communion with nature. 'For we are Indian, and have perhaps some queer ideas,' he wrote in *Pilgrims*, 'yet who among you having a faith of any kind, will deny us our strange fancies and tell us we are wrong, or say us no.'[8] Grey Owl was not necessarily wrong about the Aboriginal people and the natural world—he was an exceptional naturalist and environmentalist—but his perspective was romantic and one-sided. The vital statistics told a different story about First Nations life.

SOLDIER SETTLEMENT AND IMMIGRATION

Some years after the war, efforts were made to find land for non-Canadian demobilized soldiers through the Empire Settlement Act of 1922, which replaced the earlier Soldier Settlement legislation. This Act brought 130,000 British immigrants, including many who were not ex-soldiers, into the country between 1925 and 1931 under various spinoff schemes. Contrary to the intent of Empire Settlement, less than 10 per cent of the newcomers were actually farmers.[9] Additional immigrants from the British Isles, notably the Scottish Highlands and islands also arrived in Canada during the 1920s, reflecting a significant shift in British immigration (before the war, the preferred destinations were Australia, New Zealand, and the US). One Scottish scholar has called this immigration a 'surprisingly neglected phenomenon'.[10] In March 1923 alone, the *Metagamia*, *Saturnia*, and *Marloch* all left the Clyde for Canada, with 1,100, 450, and 300 emigrants, respectively. Many of the British newcomers were young and single, marking a return to traditional immigration patterns from the British Isles. Most emigrated at their own expense; recently arrived Scottish agricultural settlers told Winnipeg immigration authorities in 1925 that they did not favour 'Government aided colonisation schemes', but preferred to save for the money required.[11] In 1925 the governments of Britain and Canada agreed with the transportation companies on a substantial fare reduction, which certainly encouraged individual immigrants. Another 185,000 Central Europeans were brought to Canada by the railroad companies in the mid-1920s. But public opinion, as

■ Grey Owl (Archibald Belaney) and his companion, Anahareo, at Squatteck, PQ, 2 Nov. 1929. LAC, PA-28198.

reflected in government policy, was not favourable to immigration in these years. Many Canadians felt that as agricultural land was now settled, new arrivals would simply increase the competition for jobs and opportunities while altering the ethnic composition of the population. Immigration dropped to an average of just over 124,000 per year during the 1920s—the lowest it had been in any decade during peacetime since Confederation—and then to around 20,000 per year during the 1930s.

The government discouraged all immigration during the Depression except that of farmers with substantial capital, and during the years 1930–3 it actually deported more than 23,000 residents it identified as 'undesirable', some for political reasons and others because they were held to be 'public charges'. There were Canadians who decided that the future held more promise outside Canada—especially in the United States. Canada actually had a net loss of population from migration during the decade 1931–41. The country's immigration policy operated on a 'preferred nation' basis, discouraging new arrivals from backgrounds other than British or French and demonstrating indifference if not hostility to immigrants from non-European nations. A rare indication of humanitarian sentiment came at the beginning of the World War II, when more than 10,000 British children between the ages of 5 and 15 were authorized to be admitted to the country under a government policy that included public money for their transportation and support, though in the end only about 1,500 'guest children' actually arrived (chiefly because of the risks to ships from German U-boats).[12] In 1940 Canada also agreed to intern several thousand German and Austrians who had been residing in Britain at the outbreak of the war. Many of these 'dangerous' people turned out to be quite harmless, often well-educated intellectuals and artists, and they were eventually released; nearly a thousand of them eventually chose to remain in Canada, among them the distinguished novelist Henry Kreisel.

One result of the minimal immigration in this period was that non-British, non-French immigrants who had arrived before 1913 were encouraged to assimilate into the two major linguistic-cultural groups (although this effect would become apparent only after 1950). The number of Canadians speaking languages other than English or French dropped off precipitously, and many surnames were adjusted to new cultural conditions. *Under the Ribs of Death*, a 1957 novel by John Marlyn, vividly evokes the effort to assimilate among the younger generation of immigrants in the 1920s. Furthermore, whereas immigration had added disproportionate numbers of males to the population, the reduction in immigration allowed the gender balance in most

provinces to level out. During this period of linguistic and cultural consolidation, the numbers of francophones outside Quebec declined everywhere except in New Brunswick. And far fewer anglophones than francophones were bilingual.

PROHIBITION, THE DECLINE OF REFORM, AND CHURCH UNION

Between 1920 and 1925 five provinces voted to repeal prohibition, and in 1927 Ontario replaced its temperance legislation with the Liquor Control Act. The failure of the prohibition experiment symbolized the decline of reform of the pre-war variety. The elimination of alcoholic beverages had made a demonstrable difference in society—the jails were largely emptied in most places, since alcohol-related offences had filled them in the first place. The Ontario Alliance for the Total Suppression of the Liquor Trade claimed in 1922 that the number of convictions for offences associated with drink had declined from 17,413 in 1914 to 5,413 in 1921, and drunkenness cases decreased in the province's major cities from 16,590 in 1915 to 6,766 in 1921. Nevertheless, in the public mind even these figures were not enough to compensate for the downside of prohibition. After the war, opponents of the law argued that too many people were prepared to ignore the law and drink illegally, and that prohibition actually contributed to the expansion of organized crime and vice. The new slogans were 'Moderation' and 'Government Regulation'. The possibility of new revenue led several provinces to introduce government control of the sale of alcohol. By the mid-1920s prohibition (and all that it represented) was fighting a losing battle. Protestantism was feeling more than a bit beleaguered by 1925, the year that the denominations of Presbyterianism, Methodism, and Congregationalism voted to merge, creating a much stronger 'liberal' voice in the nation.[13] Not everyone within the three denominations that became the United Church was prepared to water down doctrinal beliefs in the interests of ecumenism.[14] The battles over

■ Klansmen and burnt cross, Kingston, Ont., 13 July 1927. LAC, PA-87848.

church property and assets were bitter. In the end, 784 Presbyterian congregations and eight from the Congregational Church voted to remain as they were, while 4,797 Methodist, 3,728 Presbyterian, and 166 Congregational churches joined in the United Church of Canada. The new church was the largest Protestant communion in Canada, a national denomination generally committed to liberal theology and the Social Gospel.[15] The reaction against this consolidation of liberal theology expressed itself in various ways, one of which was through support for the Ku Klux Klan in Saskatchewan.

RACISM

Canada had a long history of exchanging people and ideas with the United States. One of the least desirable imports was the Ku Klux Klan, which experienced a revival in the US after World War I. The purpose of the original Klan, founded in the American South after the Civil War, was to use intimidation to prevent black people from voting and assuming their full rights as citizens. In the US, the revived Klan spread anti-black and anti-Catholic hate propaganda under the guise of a fraternal organization. In its secret rituals and social activities, the Klan appeared to some Canadians little different from a host of other Protestant secret societies. As with the original Irish Orange Order, Canadians were able to ignore the historical context of the organization. Like other American societies, the Klan in Canada assumed a Canadian face, posing as the defender of British nationality against the alien hordes and 'incorporating' as the 'Ku Klux Klan of the British

■ The executive of the Canadian Jewish Congress at the King Edward Hotel, Toronto, 27 Jan. 1934. Revived seven months earlier, partly to further plans for the relief of German Jews, the Congress included in its platform the following resolutions: 'To safeguard the civil, political, economic and religious rights of Jews' and 'To combat manifestations of anti-semitism in Canada by means of an intensive campaign of enlightenment and education among non-Jews as well as through legislative channels'. Courtesy the Canadian Jewish Congress Charities Committee National Archives, Montreal.

Empire'. Many of its outspoken supporters were conservative Protestant ministers.

Although the Klan had some success almost everywhere in Canada, it made particular headway in Saskatchewan, where by 1929 there were over 125 local chapters. Emphasizing conservative Protestantism and hostility to Catholics, the Klan in Saskatchewan was supported by a number of ministers who objected to the increasingly liberal leanings of the mainline Protestant churches, especially the ones that had joined to create the United Church of Canada.

A similar spirit of paranoid conservatism infused the anti-Oriental movement in British Columbia.[16] As the province through which im-

migration from Asia was bound to come, BC felt particularly threatened. Much of the criticism of the Oriental 'menace' was economic in nature, but underlying this objection was a general concern for the integrity of the province as a 'white' society. The Asian immigrants were anything but homogeneous, coming from three major countries with very different cultures: China, Japan, and India. As in the pre-1914 era, exclusion of new immigrants from Asia continued to be a major goal, but efforts also were made to limit the amount of land held by Asians, particularly in the agricultural sector, and the competition in retail trade, especially from the small Chinese groceries that were known for their long hours of opening. The federal government entered the picture on 1 July 1923 when it passed the Chinese Immigration Act (usually known as the Chinese Exclusion Act), which added to the head tax ($500) by restricting both immigration of Chinese people and their mobility once in Canada. During the 23 years that it remained in force, only 25 Chinese were admitted to Canada.

British Columbia's sensitivity to the possibility of Japanese expansion was the exception. Canadians as a whole in the 1930s were slow to appreciate that the peace of the world was threatened by the actions of Germany, Italy, Japan, and Russia. Indeed, Canada spoke sympathetically at the League of Nations in 1932 in support of Japanese claims to Manchuria, and many Canadians regarded German expansion in Europe as a legitimate effort to accommodate ethnic Germans living outside the country's borders. At the opening ceremonies of the Berlin Olympics in 1936, the Canadians gave Hitler a Nazi salute—a tribute that all the other Commonwealth teams refused, in protest against German policy, including the persecution of non-Aryans. It would be simple enough to blame the anti-Semitism of Mackenzie King and his advisors for Canada's failure to open its doors to Jewish refugees in the 1930s, but there was little public demand for a more liberal policy. In the event, the episode was one of the most disgraceful in the country's history: between 1933 and 1939 Canada accepted only 4,000 of the 800,000 Jews who had escaped from Nazi-controlled territory.[17]

NEW TECHNOLOGIES

Despite the nation's uneven economic record between 1919 and 1939, the pace of technological change continued to increase, and now much of the new technology was moving into individual households. The two major innovations adopted en masse were the internal combustion engine and the radio. As well, the airplane became a factor in Canadian transportation.

THE AUTOMOBILE

Before 1910 automobile ownership had been almost entirely an urban phenomenon in Canada, but by 1920 it had become more general. In 1904 there were fewer than a thousand motor vehicles in Canada; in 1918 there were half a million. From 1918 to 1923 Canadian manufacturers allied to American companies were the second-largest car producers in the world, and had made Canada a major exporter, especially within the British Empire. By 1930 only the United States had more cars per capita than Canada. One significant feature of the automobile was that it was individually owned and operated as an extension of a private household, representing private rather than public transportation. No product operated more directly than the automobile against the communal notion of the public good.

The automobile also had tremendous spin-off consequences, not merely in the industrialization required to manufacture it but in its secondary impact on the economy and the society. In the beginning, little thought was given to the potential for automobile accidents, but as litigation increased over damage to people and machines, it became increasingly necessary for drivers to carry insurance. By 1930, automobile insurance—not compulsory and sold by private insurers only—was a staple of the insurance industry, and gradually insurance coverage became mandatory across the country; in 1946 Saskatchewan introduced the first no-fault insurance system. The automobile also required roads, and provincial governments that had neglected road-building obligations during the railway era were forced to reassume them. Between 1922 and 1942 in Canada the total distance covered by roads of all kinds in Canada increased from 385,000 miles (roughly 620,000 km) to 565,000 miles (nearly 910,000 km) with much of the construction undertaken in difficult physical and economic conditions. The proportion of roads with some kind of surfacing also increased, from

■ A Toronto traffic jam, 1924: motorists out for a Sunday drive on the newly built Lakeshore Boulevard. City of Toronto Archives, Fonds 1244, Item 2530.

13 per cent in 1922 to more than 30 per cent in 1945, though even then nearly two-thirds of Canadian roads were still of earth construction, and gravel was regarded as an improvement. Only Australia had a larger road network per capita than Canada.

Gradually the extent of the road network cut into the railways' business—freight as well as passenger. Because cars, trucks, and tractors ran on petroleum products, they encouraged petroleum production (especially in Alberta) and created the gasoline station and the garage as new service industries. In addition, because people travelling by car needed to eat, drink, and sometimes even sleep, restaurants and primitive motels began to appear along the roads, and over time every city in Canada developed a 'strip', usually just outside the city limits, where people arriving in cars could eat, drink, and be merry. Door-to-door mobility—rather than the station-to-station kind that had characterized the railroad-streetcar era—made a new round of suburban expansion possible. It also greatly reduced the isolation of farm families, who despite the financial problems of the 1920s and 1930s began not only to buy cars but to replace their workhorses with tractors. The automobile also provided an important source of tax revenue for both federal and provincial governments: Ottawa imposed a 1 per cent sales tax on automobiles in 1922, as well as an excise tax, often stepped from 5 per cent to 10 per cent depending on the price of vehicle; and the provinces collected roughly 20 per cent of their total budgets from gasoline taxes and various fees. Apart from issuing licences and creating some fairly minimal traffic regulations, neither level of government made any serious effort to set safety standards for motor vehicles. The PEI legislature actually attempted to prevent the introduction of passenger motor vehicles to the Island in 1908, but the legislation was partially revoked in 1913, and the effort was significant mainly for its uniqueness. By the 1920s Canada had joined the United States in driving on the right and generally integrated into the American automobile network. The car quickly became the potent symbol of North American independence and individualism—as well as status and sex.

RADIO

Radio probably was the single most important household appliance of the inter-war period, providing both entertainment and information. The transmission and reception of sound via radio waves had been developed as a technology before the Great War, initially as an aid to ships at sea. The war spurred improvements, and radio began to take off after the armistice. In 1919 the federal Department of Marine and Fisheries attempted to license radio sets, most of which could be used to transmit signals as well as receive them. By then 85 broadcasting stations were operating in Canada under various ownerships. The Canadian government regulated wavelengths to prevent interference between transmission signals, but did not initially attempt to control broadcasting itself. It eventually became involved in the broadcasting end—federal jurisdiction was confirmed by the Supreme Court in 1932—mainly because Canadians spent much of their time listening to more powerful American stations. By the late 1920s the American stations were organized into networks with national programming originating from the entertainment capitals of New York and Los Angeles. Private radio broadcasting in Canada in the 1920s was not all bad, but it was not well financed, and the quality of the programming was uneven.[18]

In 1929 a Royal Commission on broadcasting under Sir John Aird recommended that radio be nationalized to foster national unity, and that the new system be financed by listener licences, parliamentary grants, and indirect sponsorship. Its advice was not immediately taken. Private broadcasters lobbied against the Aird report until the Canadian Radio League, a citizens' lobbying group organized by Graham Spry and Alan Plaunt, persuaded the government of R.B. Bennett to introduce the Broadcasting Act of 1932, which led to the formation of the Canadian Radio Broadcasting Commission (CRBC) to establish a national network and to supervise private stations. There were two models of radio broadcasting on which Canada could have based its own system. The American model allowed unrestricted private enterprise, while the British model carefully controlled all aspects of broadcasting under the government monopoly, the British Broadcasting Corporation. Perhaps characteristically, Canada chose a mixed system, half like the American and half like the British. In 1936 the CRBC became the Canadian Broadcasting Corporation, with extensive English and French networks operating alongside private broadcasters.[19]

■ Johnny Wayne and Frank Shuster performing in a CBC radio broadcast of *The Army Show*. Canadian Department of National Defence/LAC, PA-152119.

The CBC had to contend with nearly insuperable obstacles, ranging from limited financial resources to American competitors offering far more popular entertainment from New York and, increasingly, Hollywood. Most of these popular shows were broadcast by the private radio stations. Only the CBC's hockey broadcasts and current-events programming—such as the 1936 abdication speech of Edward VIII and wartime news broadcasts—drew truly impressive audiences.

THE AIRPLANE

The airplane entered the Great War as an interesting gadget and came out of it a major weapon.

Hundreds of Canadian pilots returned to civilian life, and many of them continued flying. During the 1920s some Canadian pilots dusted crops and performed in daredevil exhibitions, while others specialized in flying people and equipment into the remote northern bush. The airplane was ideal not only for the North, but for the vast distances of the entire nation, reducing travel time from many weeks by boat or overland to mere hours in the air. By 1930 one of the most important airports in Canada was in the Ontario mining town of Red Lake. Out of this bush-pilot tradition came the beginnings of organized aviation in Canada. The bush pilots joined to create small commercial aviation companies, and in

JAMES GRAY ON
THE DEPRESSION

In the early 1930s, the journalist James Gray experienced first-hand the unemployment and poverty associated with the Depression. He later wrote of that time in an award-winning book, *The Winter Years*, published in 1966. In this excerpt he recalls how a fellow patient in a tuberculosis hospital inspired him to take advantage of the opportunities for education that the Depression offered.

In the life of just about every living thing, there comes a time for a second look, and a momentary halt is called in the struggle with environment. . . . It happened to me when Johnny Timchuck wandered into my life in the King Edward Sanatorium. Though he was mortally ill, the nurses no longer tried to keep Johnny Timchuck in bed. He visited around from ward to ward during the day, and perhaps because I was new he frequently came to see me. He would sit on a chair by my bed for a few minutes and talk. Then he would return to his bed for an hour and come back for another short visit. In the course of the first week, he pieced together his view of the world. . . . The depression would get worse instead of better and would end in another world war, as had always happened.

But so what? People like us, he said, who had tuberculosis or were on relief, were living in Utopia. For the first time in history people like us could stop worrying about making our own living, because society was keeping us. Think of that! It was giving us a chance only the wealthy once enjoyed—to understand the world in which we lived. Why, he asked, was I so impatient to get well? The depression would still be there when I got out. The depression would have to run its course before there would ever again be jobs for men like me. So why weren't we all using the depression to further our education, to learn about life and what made the world go round! Everything a man needed to know about everything was in a book some place. The only trick was to locate the right books. . . .

When I left the hospital just before he died, I,

too, was afire with determination to make some sense out of the world while I waited for employment to find me, though when I hit the public library I scarcely knew where to begin. I approached the bookshelves almost like a drunk in a liquor store—eager to grab everything in sight. My batting average in selecting readable books was seldom over .500. To set against such palpable failures as Marx and Hegel were discoveries of delight—Thorstein Veblen's *Theory of the Leisure Class* and Alfred Marshall's development of the theory of marginal utility. . . .

The library on William Avenue not only did a thriving business lending books, it was a half-way house on the route to the Woodyard [where free firewood was distributed], a wonderful place in which to get warm on a cold day. Sometimes there were so many people soaking up heat that half the chairs in the reading room were occupied by non-readers. . . . All over western Canada, people were reading as never before. They may have fallen asleep over books and magazines that were beyond their understanding, but they were searching for a sign, a light to guide them out of their own personal wilderness. As they searched, the age of dogma came to an end in western Canada. The old ideas over which men had fought so bitterly less than twenty years before gradually disappeared. A new generation of dissenters was about to come into its own, with new heresies, and the leaders of the new radicalism would come from the groups who were once the epitome of orthodoxy and conformity—the teachers and the preachers.

SOURCE: James Gray, *The Winter Years: The Depression on the Prairies* (Toronto: Macmillan of Canada, 1966), 77–80.

1936 the federal government decided to create a national airline. In the process, it succeeded in disturbing the development of the private sector, particularly the emerging leader of the industry, Canadian Airlines.[20] In 1937, Trans-Canada Airlines was formed.[21]

THE PROBLEMS OF LABOUR

Although many workers suffered greatly in the years between the wars, whether because of unemployment or because of the state-supported repression of organized labour, there were some surprising gains, particularly in the area of large-scale industrial unionism. The basis for this development was the reorganization of Canadian industry into increasingly larger units, to which workers could respond with equivalent forms. Industrial unionism in Canada went back to the 1890s, and took a step forward in 1927 with the establishment of the All-Canadian Congress of Labour (ACCL). At least in theory, the ACCL was committed to both Canadianizing the US-based labour organizations active in Canada and breaking with the craft union traditions that still dominated the Canadian union movement. Not surprisingly, the Communists were active participants in the ACCL and later in the Workers' Unity League (WUL), which fought a series of bloody strikes in the mining industry in the early 1930s, including a notorious one at Estevan-Bienfait, Saskatchewan, in 1931. The main organizer for the WUL was Fred Rose, later one of the few Communists ever elected to Parliament.[22] The Communists claimed, with some legitimacy, that they led most of the strikes in Canada in the early 1930s.

Labour historians, however, disagree on the value of the Communists' contributions to the organized labour movement and the battle against the Depression in general.[23] The main lines of the debate echo the contemporary mud-slinging between the Communists and their opponents. One Communist called J.S. Woodsworth 'the main representative of the bourgeoisie

in the ranks of the working class', and Communists regularly labelled non-Communists 'social fascists'. In turn, the Communists were condemned for being abject slaves of the Comintern. In any event, the Communist-led unions faded after 1934, partly because of changes in the Communist Party line dictated from the USSR, partly because of the emergence of a new labour movement in the United States. Led by John L. Lewis, the Congress of Industrial Organizations was supported strongly by the Roosevelt administration. The main strength of the CIO was that it organized entire industries, such as the automobile industry, rather than just certain skilled sectors within it. Thus, the union appealed to workers across the spectrum of traditional skills and included the semi-skilled workers who previously had been left unorganized. In Canada, where the CIO did not officially exist, strikes in the automobile industry—especially the Oshawa strike in 1937—and advances in the steel industry in Cape Breton and elsewhere heralded the beginnings of a new union militancy. The CIO's actual victories were few before the re-emergence of war; fewer than 5 per cent of Canadian workers were affiliated with it in 1939. But the ground was prepared for greater gains in the 1940s.[24]

WOMEN

Canadian women emerged from the Great War with the vote in hand and great optimism for the 'New Day' to come. As some feminist critics had argued before the war, however, the achievement of women's suffrage was no panacea for the second-class position of women in Canadian society generally. Not until 1929 did the Privy Council determine, in response to a petition submitted by the 'Famous Five'—Emily Murphy, Henrietta Muir Edwards, Louise McKinney, Irene Parlby, and Nellie McClung—that women were 'persons' eligible for appointment to the Senate. Very few women between the wars ran for public office, and women generally did not constitute any rec-

SCALE OF WINTER AND SUMMER RATIONS APPROVED BY THE CITY OF MONTREAL, c. 1935

No.	Food (week)	Fuel (week)	Clothing (week)	Total (week)	Rent (month)	Total (month)	Total (year)
Winter Rations ($)							
1	1.65	0.00	0.15	1.80	6.00	13.80	165.06
2	2.50	0.90	0.30	3.70	7.00	23.03	276.40
3	3.15	1.15	0.45	4.75	7.50	28.08	337.00
...							
12	9.85	2.05	1.80	13.70	12.00	75.48	856.40
Summer Rations ($)							
1	1.65	0.00	0.15	1.80	6.00	13.80	165.60
2	2.50	0.60	0.30	3.40	7.00	21.73	260.80
...							
12	9.85	0.85	1.80	12.50	12.00	66.17	794.10

SOURCE: Montreal Unemployment Commission, *Renseignements à l'usage des chômeurs nécessiteux et des propriétaires*, as reprinted in Denyse Baillargeon, *Making Do: Women, Family and Home in Montreal during the Great Depression* (Waterloo: Wilfrid Laurier University Press, 1999), 184.

ognizable voting block to which politicians needed to pay attention. Most women simply carried on in their traditional stereotyped roles. Although the 'flapper'—with her bobbed hair, short skirts, and spirit of independent adventure—was the symbolic 'New Woman' of the twenties, she was hardly typical. Most Canadian women did not smoke or sip cocktails or dance the Black Bottom. The 'gay young things' were relatively few, and existed only in the larger cities. The only thing most Canadian women had in common with the flapper was the fact that there was a good chance they worked outside the home. In 1921, 490,150 women were part of a labour force of 3,173,169. By 1931 women totalled 665,859 of a workforce of 3,927,230.[25] Although most employers tried to prevent women from rising to positions of authority, a few women even reached the top of their chosen occupations; the greatest gains were made in law, medicine, social work, and university teaching. But women were still only a small minority in any profession, and most were stuck in relatively dead-end jobs. Women still were expected to find their chief fulfillment as wives and mothers. They bought the new labour-saving appliances and used them whenever possible—only to find that they still had to work as hard as ever.

The Depression was particularly difficult for Canadian women. At first one common response to the economic crisis was to transfer the bread-winning responsibilities from the males to the females, who yet could find work for lower wages in service sectors of the economy. But, gradually, public opinion turned against women, particularly married women, who held jobs that could be done by men—although in several tra-ditionally female industries, such as garment-making, men in desperation worked for even lower wages than the women. Most relief pro-grams were geared to men, partly because they were seen as more likely than women to threaten the social order if they were not given help. Many radicals who opposed gender discrimination in principle still accepted the idea that married women should be supported by their husbands, and as a result women's access to unemployment benefits (introduced in 1940 and made opera-tional in 1941) was often limited. For example, traditionally female areas of employment—school teaching, nursing, domestic service per-formed in private homes—were excluded from UI coverage. And the administrative structure of UI was, of course, dominated by males.[26] Some women were deserted by their husbands, and when the family did remain together, it was the wife who did most of the patching and scraping required to make it work. As one working-class Montreal wife put it:

> Children came along, and wages went down but the cost of living went up. In the end [around 1936] my husband was earning forty-five dollars

every two weeks. I had four children and my hus-band always had to have his car. His car—that was really important. . . . I had a lot of things to be worried about.[27]

In the House of Commons in 1935, J.S. Woods-worth cited the case of a child murder and sui-cide in Winnipeg. The husband was unem-ployed, and he came home to find his wife and children dead. His wife's suicide note read, 'I owe the drug store 44 cents: farewell.'[28] The reminis-cences of women in Barry Broadfoot's oral his-tory, *Ten Lost Years, 1929–1939: Memories of Canadians Who Survived the Depression* (1973), are easily the most poignant in the book.[29] Nevertheless, by 1941 the number of women in a total workforce of 4,195,951 had risen to 832,840.

THE CHILD-CARE EXPERTS

The rise of the middle classes has been accompa-nied by the rise of experts to advise them on how best to satisfy their aspirations. Each generation sees its intellectual and technological break-throughs translated into new categories of profes-sionals with new skills and pretensions. To iden-tify the particular body of experts that becomes indispensable in a given historical period is of interest. Between the wars in Canada, the most respected experts were those who worked in child care or performed other services related to children: doctors, schoolteachers, guidance coun-sellors. Such people had been developing their territory since the 1870s, but after the Great War they really came into their own.

There were complex reasons for the empha-sis on children, and for the unquestioned respect, bordering on reverence, for those who dealt with them. One was the fact that medical breakthroughs were cutting deeply into infant mortality and childhood diseases. Declining numbers of births meant that each child received greater attention. Another factor was the much-discussed breakdown of the traditional family

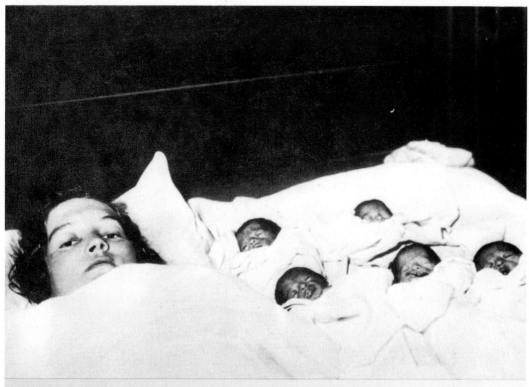

■ Mrs Elzire Dionne with her five baby daughters, 1934. LAC, PA-133260.

under the pressures of industrialization, new moralities, and—during the 1930s—economic hardship. Those professionals who addressed the problems caused by family disintegration were obviously performing socially useful work. A third factor was the heavy toll taken on the generation of young men who had died or been seriously injured in the trenches of the Great War. All Canadians hoped that the next generation would have a better chance at life than the classes of 1914–18, and saw those attempting to improve the odds, particularly under the trying conditions of the Depression, as peacetime heroes and heroines. In addition, the war had encouraged a sense of duty and responsibility to the state that also played a role here. In 1917 a British Columbia meeting of health officials was told by Dr Isabel Arthur of Nelson:

[T]he child is the asset of the State, and all conditions should be arranged as far as possible to get the best results from that child. . . . We do not want inferior products turned out that may or may not answer the purpose, but as perfect a thing as can be produced; something to be proud of; something with stability and quality, that can be used for the purpose of development and advancement and for protection, if need be, of the State to which it belongs.[30]

Undoubtedly the best-known triumphal child-care story, not just in Canada but in North America, was that of the Dionne quintuplets. In the warm spring days of 1934, the family of Oliva and Elzire Dionne made headlines around the world. The Dionnes were French-speaking Roman Catholic farmers with five children living in northern Ontario between Callander and Corbeil, just east of Lake Nippissing. Like many family farms during the Depression, theirs lacked plumbing and electricity, although the Dionnes were not as poor as their neighbours—they owned 195 acres (79 ha) as well as a car. Now, in one stroke, the Dionne children were doubled in number when Elzire gave birth to identical quintuplets—the third such set of infants recorded before hormonal tampering and the first to live beyond a few days. Curiously, the person acclaimed for this miracle was not Elzire Dionne, who bore the children, but Dr Allan Dafoe, the small-town physician who delivered them safely and kept them alive during their first precarious days. The Dionne parents, for their part, came to be seen as semi-villains, standing in the way of a better life for their children.[31]

Complex questions of benevolence, public responsibility, professional expertise, and private poverty soon swirled around the photogenic quints. The province of Ontario removed the children from the control of their parents, who were helpless in the face of media demands and crass commercialism. Ontario managed the quints as a major provincial asset and tourist attraction, putting nearly a million dollars aside in a trust fund built on strategically authorized commercial endorsements and moving them away from their family into a specially equipped hospital under the care of Dr Dafoe. By early 1935 the quints were declared wards of the Crown, although a horde of specialists would battle for years over control of their upbringing. Almost ignored in the sorry drama were the interests and concerns of the Dionnes themselves, both parents and children.

In a period when births were falling off, the arrival of five children at one time was a truly newsworthy event, providing a topic of universal interest and a welcome change from a child-related news sensation of two years earlier: the kidnapping and murder of the son of the American aviator Charles Lindbergh. At a time when poverty was so commonplace, it was also reassuring to know that the state might occasionally (if not regularly) intervene to rescue children. Yvonne, Émilie, Cécile, Annette, and Marie would soon join the ranks of the Depression's idealized moppets, headed by the Hollywood film star Shirley Temple. As a compelling mixture of 1930s hoopla and poverty, nicely seasoned with professional management, the Dionne story was hard to beat. It demonstrated the extent to which the entertainment media had taken over everyday life, in Canada as elsewhere.

Apart from Dr Dafoe, Canada's most famous medical figure of this era was probably Dr Frederick Banting, the leader of a research team at the University of Toronto. In the winter of 1921–2 Banting and his colleague, Dr Charles Best, discovered insulin as a treatment for diabetes mellitus, a disease that tragically affected young people as well as adults. Another renowned specialist was Dr Alan Brown, a pediatrician, who as chief physician at Toronto's Hospital for Sick Children halved the infant mortality rate there and was a co-developer of Pablum, the first pre-cooked vitamin-enriched cereal, which was marketed internationally in 1930 (with proceeds going to the hospital's Pediatric Research Foundation). In 1925 Dr William E. Blatz founded the Institute of Child Study, at the University of Toronto, to explore children's psychological development. The birth of the quintuplets, and their well-publicized supervision by Dr Dafoe, increased interest in child care and encouraged the establishment of pediatric units in the large hospitals of most cities. Indeed, first Brown, in 1935, and then Blatz, from 1936, became the determining authorities for the Dionne quintuplets in the first years of their lives. Finally, at the close of World War II, a research team led by Dr Henry Bruce Chown in Winnipeg discovered the mechanism of RH hemolytic disease and pioneered the blood transfusions to infants that eventually saved thousands of young lives.

Of course, Canadians were not the only ones interested in the 'appropriate' upbringing of children: so were the Soviets, the Italian Fascists, and the German Nazis. Around the world the inter-war years saw enormous public and private investments in the welfare of the young. Canadian society was not yet devoted to indulging young people—that breakthrough would come only after World War II—but it was heading in that direction. The experts had already identified a new stage of development, between puberty and full adulthood: adolescence. The Depression prevented the new adolescents from coming to full flower except in relatively prosperous families that could afford to keep them in school beyond the leaving age of 16 and later send them to university. During the 1930s, fewer than half of Canada's 16-year-olds were still in school, but as soon as times improved young people would be required to acquire more education.

Much of the ideological baggage of the emerging experts came from the newly respectable social sciences, particularly psychology. Attempts at formulating a science of the mind could be traced from Plato and the ancient Greeks through the Renaissance into the seventeenth-century psychology of the senses developed by John Locke, and on to a host of nineteenth-century notions such as mesmerism, spiritualism, and phrenology. Sigmund Freud added a whole new dimension with his 'discovery' of the unconscious level of the mind and his emphasis on the importance of sexuality in human behaviour. The Russian scientist Ivan Pavlov introduced the notion of conditioned learning through repetition of stimuli. The American philosopher John Dewey combined the long-standing concerns of education for the inculcation of moral virtues with the new psychology of personality development, arguing that educators needed to focus on teaching the 'whole child', not just the rote learning of academic subjects through memorization and intimidation.

Examples of these influences could be found everywhere in child-rearing advice and educational practice between the wars. Infant sexuality was seen as a normal part of the developmental process, not to be 'repressed'. Children could be toilet-trained at a very early age by methods adapted from the experiments of Professor Pavlov with his dogs. In schools the 'progressive' ideas of John Dewey conflicted with tradition, as a generation of reformist teachers reacted against the mechanical character of the earlier model. The problem was that in the hands of the unimaginative educator, even progressive approaches could become mechanical, and even insidious. According to the Alberta Department of Education's 'Programme of Studies for the Elementary School' in 1942, for example, 'the proper adjustment of the personality of the school child is another of our educational objectives. The school has a two-fold function—it holds before him the attitudes, standards, principles which have society's approval, and provides a supervised social situation in which these behaviour tendencies can be realized and undesirable patterns inhibited'.[32] The seeds of post-war 'conformity' were already being planted.

CANADIAN NATIONALISM

The divisions of the war made it quite impossible to pretend that Canada could manage a bicultural image. It was also clear that many English-speaking Canadians had become more conscious of their nation's distinctiveness. The painter Arthur Lismer once wrote: 'After 1919, most creative people, whether in painting, writing or music, began to have a guilty feeling that Canada was as yet unwritten, unpainted, unsung. . . . In 1920 there was a job to be done.'[33] That job was not only to write books and paint pictures that captured the Canadian spirit, but to create cultural organizations that would mobilize the new national consciousness.

By the 1920s it was clear that Canadian cultural nationalists, especially in English-speaking Canada, would have to confront American media culture, which was expanding its influence at a rapid rate. Canada had always imported much of its culture from abroad, but in the past it had usually achieved some kind of balance between the United States and Great Britain. That balance was now being broken in a number of areas, including periodical publications. By 1929 Canadians were spending $100 on American magazines for every dollar spent on British ones, and importing eight magazines from the US for every one printed at home. The combined circulation in Canada of the four leading Canadian magazines—*Maclean's*, *Chatelaine*, *Mayfair*, and *The Family Herald and Weekly Star*—was less than half that of the four leading American magazines, although in 1929 *Maclean's* had the largest circulation of any magazine in Canada, at 160,000 copies per monthly issue.[34] In their effort to stem the American tide, Canadian periodical publishers lobbied unsuccessfully in 1922 in support of low postal rates on second-class mail. A year later the House of Commons agreed unanimously that 'measures should be adopted to encourage the publication of Canadian magazines and periodicals', but the politicians could not agree on how to implement such a vague policy.

Within the universities, the 1930s saw a sort of debate over the meaning of Canada between two groups of North Americans working in the newly developing field of the social sciences. One group, led by Canadian-born academics teachings in the US, worked (with the support of the Carnegie Endowment for International Peace) to establish Canada as a North American nation with a friendly working relationship with the United States; in effect, they were the heirs of Goldwin Smith. The North Americanists were supported by a number of Canadian academics and journalists. The other, smaller group consisted of Canadian academics still resident in Canada (mainly in Toronto) working to establish the integrity of Canada's territory as both naturally and historically determined. This latter cluster developed the outlines of a Canadian 'national history'. Then, as now, the writing of Canadian history was a contentious enterprise, rife with political significance.

POPULAR CULTURE

Between the wars Canada's love affair with American popular culture continued to flourish. During the 1920s, radio, motion pictures, and the great expansion of professional sports all represented Yankee incursions into the Canadian consciousness. In sport the loudest critics of creeping Americanization usually preferred the 'gentlemanly' British tradition of amateurism in sport, and terms like 'commercialism' and 'professionalism' became pejorative code words for Americanism. The foes of American popular culture did not concede without a fight, but they had trouble finding ground to stand on and eventually tended to retreat into the rarified world of high culture. Undoubtedly the most important development in popular culture was a negative one—the failure within Canada to produce important indigenous traditions in many cultural arenas.

HIGH CULTURE

THE NOVEL AND POETRY

Books offered another avenue of escape. During the Depression, especially, many Canadians used their enforced leisure to read more; library memberships and circulation figures increased substantially. Between 1920 and 1940 over 750 Canadian novels were published, most of them escapist fiction in the form of historical romances or adventure, crime, and mystery.[35] A small number of strong, confident, realistic novels in this period formed the foundation of modern Canadian fiction. A notable example was Charles Yale Harrison's *Generals Die in Bed* (1930), which has been compared favourably with Hemingway's *A Farewell to Arms* and Remarque's *All Quiet on the Western Front*. The American-born Harrison worked for the *Montreal Star* before enlisting in the Royal Montreal Regiment and serving as a machine-gunner in the war. The short, direct sentences of his first-person narrative powerfully evoke the horrors of the trenches, where the ene-

■ Maple Leaf Gardens, Toronto, in 1932, the year after it opened. Metropolitan Toronto Library Board, T 10161.

mies included 'some of our officers'. One scene in which the narrator kills an enemy soldier with a bayonet has been read by thousands of Canadian schoolchildren in literature classes. Like many another writer, Harrison never replicated the success of his first autobiographical work.

Other novelists introduced Prairie realism to Canadian fiction. Manitoba was the setting not only for Martha Ostenso's *Wild Geese* but also for *The Viking Heart* (1923) by Laura Goodman Salverson, about the Icelandic immigrants who settled at Gimli and the three generations that succeeded them; and *Grain* (1926) by Robert Stead, who followed a series of popular romantic novels about pioneer life on the Prairies with this realist classic focusing on the spiritually impoverished

life of a farmer. Perhaps the greatest of the Depression-era Prairie novels, although not recognized as such until the 1950s, was *As For Me and My House* (1941) by (James) Sinclair Ross. Written in the form of a diary kept by 'Mrs Bentley' (we never learn her first name), the unhappy wife of a frustrated minister in a small Saskatchewan town during the Depression, it portrays the pressures not only of drought, dust, and bad economic times but of social conformity and intellectual and spiritual isolation. A realistic Quebec novel of the time was Gabrielle Roy's *Bonheur d'occasion* (1945), set in Saint-Henri, the slum district of Montreal. With its English translation as *The Tin Flute* (1947), Roy was recognized internationally as a new writer of distinction. Depicting the

■ Gabrielle Roy in the 1950s. LAC, C-18347.

■ F.R. Scott, 1941. Photograph by John Steele, Toronto.

pathetic yearning of Florentine Lacasse to escape her squalid environment, the novel also portrays the gradual disintegration of the Lacasse family, torn by poverty and war, and throws a harsh light on aspects of Quebec life that were very far from the experience Hugh MacLennan reflected in his 1945 novel, *Two Solitudes*. *The Tin Flute* was the first modern novel by a French Canadian to be widely read in English Canada, where Roy's fiction remains popular to this day. It is perhaps significant that she was not a native-born Quebecer but a Franco-Manitoban, born in Saint Boniface, who also lived for some time in London and Paris before settling in Quebec City. She was the first Canadian writer to win France's prestigious Prix Fémina (for *Bonheur d'occasion*).

Canadian poetry between the wars ranged from the last remnants of Victorian romanticism to experimental new forms that downplayed metrical and other conventions, used modern language, and expanded subject matter. As A.J.M. Smith, one of the best of the new poets, put it in the *McGill Fortnightly Review* (1925–7), the poet's task was 'to bring the subject-matter of poetry out of the library and the afternoon tea-salon into the open air, dealing with the language of present-day speech with subjects of living interest.'[36] Also interested in the new trends in poetry and attentive to the social conditions of the time were Dorothy Livesay, F.R. Scott, and A.M. Klein. Livesay was from early life a feminist and a socialist, and was an active member of the

Communist Party in the 1930s. Her poems in *Day and Night* (1944) dealt with workers in wartime industry: 'One step forward / Two steps back / Shove the lever / Push it back.' Scott—a McGill law professor who was one of the founders of the LSR and CCF—believed in the power of poetry to change society.

THEATRE

Late in 1931, in the midst of the worst of the Great Depression, Vere Brabazon Ponsonby, the ninth Earl of Bessborough (an Irish title), the newly appointed Governor General, received a letter from Lillian D. Myers of the Saskatoon Little Theatre in which she suggested that he might wish to help the Canadian theatre in some way. Bessborough was known to have a strong interest in the theatre, and even had a private playhouse in his luxurious home in Hampshire. Before long, Vincent Massey in Toronto (having recently stepped down as Canadian High Commissioner in London after the Liberals had lost the 1930 election) heard that Bessborough was interesting in 'doing something for amateur dramatics' in Canada, and wrote offering his assistance. Bessborough responded with a plan for 'an annual Dominion of Canada Drama Festival' that would enlist the aid of the provincial lieutenant-governors, university heads, directors of little theatres, and representatives of the Boy Scouts and Girl Guides in producing a festival 'that would create national interest and be of educational value'.[37] The plan was quite comprehensive, including a national office in Ottawa. Bessborough wrote to Massey that he did not mean to proceed any further with the scheme at the moment because of the Depression, but he was soon making speeches about it. As he told the Empire Club in Toronto in 1932, 'I should like to see as a normal part of our life in this country, dramatic performances taking place of plays by Canadian authors with music by Canadian composers, with scenic decoration and costumes by Canadian artists, performed by Canadian players.' Out of this enthusiasm, and with the assistance of Vincent Massey, a 'white tie and tails' organizational meeting for the first Dominion Drama Festival was held in Ottawa on 29 October 1932. Massey himself moved at the meeting that such a festival be held, seconded by Mr Justice Arthur Surveyor of Montreal. For the moment, the competition would involve 'established amateur dramatic societies' and would not be confined to 'original Canadian plays'.

The first Dominion Drama Festival was held in 1933. The plays—selected by the groups presenting them—did not include a single Canadian work. The first prize-winning play by a Canadian did not come until 1936, when the London Little Theatre presented *Twenty-Five Cents* by Eric Harris. Canadian plays never were in the majority during the lifetime of the festival, which was often criticized for its traditionalism. What was most interesting about Lord Bessborough's scheme—apart, perhaps, from the fact that it represented an effort undertaken by the Crown in Canada through the person of the Governor General to create institutions of national culture in the Dominion—was the number of amateur theatrical companies extant in 1933. This vital grass-roots movement consisted of Little Theatre groups in most major cities and towns, hundreds of high school drama groups, dozens of university drama groups, and innumerable other drama organizations sponsored by fraternal organizations, church groups, and labour unions. During the darkest days of the Depression, Canadian theatre flourished as the hard times that discouraged some artists energized others, particularly those seeking a new social involvement and commitment. A theatre of the left emerged in the major cities, particularly Vancouver, Toronto, Winnipeg, and Montreal, and then spread to smaller places (like Timmins, in northern Ontario) where 'progressive' people were to be found.[38] Toronto had its Progressive Arts Club (PAC), which spawned the Workers' Experimental Theatre and later the Theatre of Action. Vancouver had the Progressive Arts Players, Winnipeg had its Workers' Theatre and New Theatre, Montreal had its New Theatre Group, and Timmins had its Workers' Cooperative Drama Group.

In all of these places there was a twin emphasis on creating theatre that spoke directly to audiences about what was going on in Canada and the world and on exemplifying the ideals of collective experience in theatrical production. The theatre of the left tended to promote amateur values and participation, as well as Canadian content. On its first tour, the Workers' Theatre presented seven short plays, including *Eviction* (written by members of the Montreal PAC), *Farmers' Fight* (by the Montreal PAC), *Joe Derry* (by Dorothy Livesay), and *War in the East* (by Stanley Ryerson). Interestingly, progressive theatre groups did not shun the establishment-oriented Dominion Drama Festival; in fact they competed frequently, putting the theatrical quality of their work to the test. The DDF adjudicators, for their part, were sympathetic to the productions but often disliked the doom and gloom of their themes, preferring lighter fare.[39] In 1937, a four-person play entitled *Relief*, written by Minnie Evans Bicknell of Marshall, Saskatchewan, and performed by the Marshall Dramatic Club, was one of the finalists at the DDF. The play was a domestic tragedy, performed in naturalistic style, dealing with matters that, as the critics noted in their reviews, were only too familiar to the performers in their daily lives. Toronto's Theatre of Action was particularly keen to seek out Canadian themes and Canadian playwrights. The thematic content of the drama preferred by the theatre of the left was undoubtedly one of the factors that limited its popular acceptance. By the end of the 1930s, however, left-wing American theatre groups taking up the cabaret theatre of Kurt Weill and Bertolt Brecht, and progressive theatre people in Canada, became more interested in musical theatre. Some of the cabaret productions actually featured songs commenting satirically on Canadian politics. This topical humour offered a lighter alternative to the heavy fare offered by the more earnest groups on the left.

Professional cultural production in Canada between the wars may often have seemed stodgy and dull, but at the grassroots level, amateur activity often was vibrant.

MUSIC

Serious musicians found a new form of employment during the 1920s, when the musical accompaniment for silent films was upgraded from a single piano player to a full-sized orchestra in the pit. But the boom was short-lived, since the introduction of 'talkies' made the pit orchestra obsolete virtually overnight. Displaced musicians found employment in hotel orchestras and on the radio, and in the later 1930s many ensembles regrouped under the auspices of the CBC, which became a major patron and consumer of all sorts of music. By 1940–1 the CBC was broadcasting 45 operas a year, more than 600 symphony orchestra concerts, over 2,000 programs of chamber music, and thousands of hours of 'light music'. Most of these programs were aired live, and until 1958 the CBC prohibited the use of recorded music during prime-time in order to continue to encourage live performance and provide employment for musicians.[40]

THE VISUAL ARTS

In painting, the 1920s were dominated by the popular successes of the Group of Seven. Franklin Carmichael, Lawren Harris, A.Y. Jackson, Frank Johnston, Arthur Lismer, J.E.H. MacDonald, and F.H. Varley consciously sought to create a Canadian iconography, and according to the catalogue for their first exhibition, in 1920, their vision was simple: 'An Art must grow and flower in the land before the country will be a real home for its people.' Although the members of the Group always emphasized their break with the European traditions of the past, in fact they were heavily influenced by Scandinavian landscape painting of the period, which approached a similar topography in a similar fashion, and

■ 'Emily Carr and the Group of Seven', c. 1927, charcoal sketch by Arthur Lismer. Participating in this imaginary meeting are Lismer himself, Frank Carmichael, A.J. Casson (a later member), J.E.H. MacDonald, A.Y. Jackson, and Lawren Harris, along with their fellow artist Bertram Brooker. Private collection. Photograph courtesy McMichael Collection of Canadian Art. Used by permission of the Lismer Estate.

they were solidly grounded in the classic European techniques.[41] 'New art forms are necessary if the artist would develop', said A.Y. Jackson before departing on a painting tour of the Arctic in 1927; 'I think I will find new art values in the far north.'[42] The Group of Seven stood out from other painters of the era partly because they all were based in the same place (more than one regional artist railed unsuccessfully against the tyranny of metropolitanism), and partly because they understood how to present their work in ways that would appeal to a general audience; most of the Seven had worked for

years as commercial artists, developing visual techniques that grew out of posters and advertisements.[43] Six of them had painted war subjects and several had made reputations as war artists. All reflected the influence of the bleak imagery associated with the Great War.[44]

Other Canadian artists continued to paint wartime scenes after the armistice. In 1919 the Winnipeg artist Mary (Riter) Hamilton left for Europe with a publisher's commission to 'reproduce the battlefields in paint' and she remained there until 1922, producing more than 300 paintings of the devastated landscape.[45] (The paintings are now in the collection of Library and Archives Canada.)

Probably the best-known regional artist of this period was British Columbia's Emily Carr. Born and brought up in Victoria, Carr studied art in San Francisco, London, and Paris, where she came into contact with the post-Impressionist style that she later applied to paintings of BC First Nations sites and artifacts. By combining French style with Aboriginal forms and bold colours, Carr gradually created a distinctive and powerful art. But she was known only locally until 1927 when, at the age of 57, she travelled east for an 'Exhibition of Canadian West Coast Art' at the National Gallery. Enthusiastically encouraged, and then influenced, by Lawren Harris and other members of the Group of Seven, Carr went on to produce some of her most famous paintings, many of them depicting sculptured forests and pulsating skies inspired by BC. Emily Carr also made her mark on Canadian literature with three books published in her lifetime; the first, *Klee Wyck* (1941)—a collection of stories based on her visits to Native villages— won a Governor General's Award. By the time of her death in 1945, she had triumphed not only over the disadvantages of Canadian geography but over the limitations faced by any woman who aspired to more than genteel 'dabbling' in art, especially in a town as conservative as Victoria.[46]

Although the Group of Seven assisted Emily Carr and a few other artists whose work seemed to fit with their vision, their success as national symbol-makers prevented other styles from making much headway with the Canadian public. Even so, a number of important painters managed to produce some excellent work during the Depression. Canada had no equivalent of the American Works Progress Administration (WPA) to provide employment for artists. Many painters found work in journalism and teaching, often at art schools. Their accomplishments reflected their drive to create, but also suggest that the Canadian cultural environment was not quite as philistine

as often has been made out. Two paintings may stand to sum up the mood of the time. In 1932 the Scottish-born Charles Comfort, who had worked as a commercial artist in Winnipeg and then Toronto, painted his fellow artist Carl Schaefer as a generic *Young Canadian* (1932). Against a rural background of barn and menacing sky (on the Schaefer farm in southwestern Ontario), the young man—his paint-box before him and a brush in his hand—is ready to take up work. The bleak expression on his face could be interpreted as that of a depressed artist having to pursue his vocation in an unreceptive period, or of a worker willing to start a job if only one were available. A few years later a pupil of Schaefer, Polish-Canadian Nathan Petroff (who soon moved to New York), painted a watercolour entitled *Modern Times* (1937), showing a young woman despondently leaning over the want-ad section of a newspaper searching for a job. Under the classified section is part of the paper's headline, 'SHELL MADRID'. Unemployment and the growing international crisis were here inextricably linked.

Many Canadian painters were sensitive to international trends. In 1926 Alfred Pellan left the École des Beaux-Arts in Quebec City to study in Paris on a scholarship. On his return he sought a job at his old school, but after expressing his interest in Picasso and Matisse he realized that 'with such ideas I could never be accepted'. He returned to Paris, coming home only when Hitler's armies overran France. At a Montreal exhibition in June 1940 of his Cubist-influenced work and abstractions, he was praised as a 'European painter . . . born in Quebec'.[47] In the meantime, Paul-Émile Borduas, who like Pellan had studied at the École des Beaux-Arts and in Paris, had become interested in surrealism, relying on his unconscious to produce a series of abstract gouaches that were exhibited in April 1941 to great acclaim in the French-Canadian press. Borduas would go on to become a leader of the post-war artists in Quebec, eventually achieving an international reputation. A few

■ 'Young Canadian', watercolour, 1932, by Charles Comfort. Hart House, University of Toronto.

English-Canadian painters were also attracted to abstractionism, most notably Lawren Harris, who by 1930 had found in the Arctic an almost geometric landscape. Harris, like most of the abstractionists, turned increasingly inward to spiritual values for his inspiration.

Canadian architecture before 1939 had more difficulty breaking with tradition—not surprisingly, given the need to satisfy clients who were seldom adventurous. There was no Canadian equivalent of Frank Lloyd Wright, for example, although Wright's 'Prairie Style' was imitated often in Canada. Perhaps the most distinctive style (though it was not particularly 'Canadian')

was found in the resort hotels of the Canadian Pacific Railway that were built immediately before the Great War to designs combining elements of the Swiss chalet, the English Tudor hall, and the classic French château. The chain eventually stretched from Quebec City (the Château Frontenac) to Ottawa (the Château Laurier) to Toronto (the Royal York Hotel) to the Rocky Mountains (the Banff Springs Hotel and Château Lake Louise) to Vancouver (the Hotel Vancouver) to Victoria (the Empress Hotel). Many architects were content to decorate neo-classical buildings, such as banks, with a vaguely Canadian vocabulary. The Bank of Nova Scotia building in Halifax,

EMILY CARR'S *KLEE WYCK*

In 1941 painter Emily Carr published a small book of essays describing her travels in British Columbia in search of subjects for her paintings, particularly of the totem poles for which she probably is best known. The book was extremely well-received by the critics and the public. The old village described in the following excerpt was located on the southern island of the Queen Charlotte group (Haida Gwaii).

Cumshewa

Tanoo, Skedans and Cumshewa lie fairly close to each other on the map, yet each is quite unlike the others when you come to it. All have the West Coast wetness but Cumshewa seems always to drip, always to be blurred with mist, its foliage always to hang wet-heavy. Cumshewa rain soaked my paper, Cumshewa rain trickled among my paints.

Only one house was left in the village of Cumshewa, a large, low and desolately forsaken house that had a carefully padlocked door and gaping hole in the wall.

We spent a miserable night in this old house. All our bones were pierced with chill. The rain spat great drops through the smoke-hole into our fire. In comfortless, damp blankets we got through the night.

In the morning Jimmie made so hot a fire that the rain splatters hissed when they dropped into it. I went out to work on the leaky beach and Jimmie rigged up a sort of shelter over my work so that the trickles ran down my neck instead of down my picture, but if I had possessed the arms and legs of a centipede they would not have been enough to hold my things together to defy the elements' meanness towards my canopy, materials and temper.

Through the hole in the side of the house I could hear the fretful mewings of the cat. Indian people and the elements give and take like brothers, accommodating themselves to each others' ways without complaint. My Indians never said to me, 'Hurry and get this over so that we may go home and be more comfortable.' Indians are comfortable everywhere.

Not far from the house sat a great wooden raven mounted on a rather low pole; his wings were flattened to his sides. A few feet from him stuck up an empty pole. His mate had sat there but she had rotted away long ago, leaving him moss-grown, dilapidated and alone to watch dead Indian

■ 'Self-Portrait', oil on paper, c. 1938, by Emily Carr. Photo Saltmarche visual communication—Toronto. Private collection.

bones, for these two great birds had been set, one on either side of the doorway of a big house that had been full of dead Indians who had died during a smallpox epidemic.

Bursting growth had hidden houses and bones long ago. Rain turned their dust into mud; these strong young trees were richer perhaps for that Indian dust. They grew up round the dilapidated old raven, sheltering him from the tearing winds now that he was old and rotting because the rain seeped through the moss that grew upon his back and in the hollows of his eye-sockets. The Cumshewa totem poles were dark and colourless, the wood toneless from pouring rain.

When Jimmie, Louisa, the cat and the missionary's daughter saw me squeeze back into the house through the hole and heard me say, 'Done,' they all jumped up. Curling the cat into her hat, Louisa set about packing; Jimmie went to prepare his boat. The cat was peeved. She preferred Louisa's hat near the fire to the outside rain.

The memory of Cumshewa is of a great lonesomeness smothered in a blur of rain. Our boat headed for the sea. As we rounded the point Cumshewa was suddenly like something that had not quite happened.

SOURCE: Emily Carr, *Klee Wyck* (Toronto: Clarke, Irwin & Co. Ltd, 1971), 20-1.

built in 1930, featured decorations—according to its architect, John Lyle—ranging 'from the small trailing arbutus—the floral emblem of Nova Scotia—to the sunflower, and from the seagull to the Canada goose, the bear, the silver fox, the codfish and crab'.[48]

During the twenties and thirties, a modern classical style became the most common mode for large public buildings such as banks or government offices. The only significant competition came from the art deco movement, which emphasized vertical lines and decorated flat surfaces. The archetypal buildings were Montreal's Aldred Building, built in 1929–31, and Vancouver's Marine Building, built 1929–30, although Vancouver's City Hall (1935–6) shows art deco influences as well. Art deco ornamentation was also used on the interiors of several Eaton's department stores built around 1930. Art deco became a popular domestic housing style for those who could afford to build in the period. The houses in this style are typically plain stucco or concrete structures, divided into rectangular planes. Canadian architects proved quite resistant to the modern or 'international' style exemplified by Walter Gropius. Their frequent use of

modernism for industrial buildings during the 1930s suggested their disdain for it.

EDUCATION

Education was considered an important aspect of the reintegration of the Canadian soldier into the civilian community after the Great War. The 'Khaki University of Canada', as it was called, was the product of a concerted effort to provide classes for soldiers in the overseas camps and to assist in the demobilization process; it continued for two years after the Armistice. A separate program provided vocational rehabilitation for disabled veterans. In fact, a new emphasis on vocational training was an important by-product of the war. Industrial and technical training had been deferred during the military crisis, and in 1919 the Canadian Parliament passed the Technical Education Act, which provided money for any kind of instruction that promoted industrial development or improved the lives of workers. The result was the creation of a number of vocational and technical schools in the various provinces in the inter-war period. Another consequence of the war was the effort to professionalize teachers through the creation of provincial teachers' organizations; in most Canadian provinces the teachers organized between 1916 and 1920, and the Canadian Teachers' Federation was established in 1919. Finally, the war also saw an effort to promote co-operation between parents and teachers through Home and School Associations, the first of which was formed in Toronto in 1916. The movement spread rapidly in the 1920s, as everyone recognized what a Manitoba commission described as the need 'for better educational facilities and for the better adaptation of the elementary and secondary schools to the needs of the communities they serve'.[49]

It was during the inter-war years that the junior high school was introduced, and it probably would have spread more rapidly had the Depression not limited the funding available for educational innovation. By far the most important educational developments of the period, however, were various efforts to extend formal education to people—often in remote and rural areas—ill-served by traditional schooling. Most provinces recognized that rural districts represented a problem for education, especially beyond the elementary level. One obvious solution was consolidation into larger units, but the necessary transportation facilities were not widely available. Several experiments were tried. One relied on correspondence courses, often at elementary grade level. Another focused on radio, although school broadcasts were generally used only for extras such as music education. As well, a number of efforts were directed at adults, and many people regarded these adult education programs as the most important new educational developments of the time. The Workers Educational Association, founded in England before the war, was extended to Canada in the 1920s and was successful in some areas. Meanwhile, the 'Frontier College' worked to offer education to individuals, often recent immigrants, in remote work camps and mines, which involved sending university students into the bush to tutor workers after hours. Frontier College had been established in 1899 but really flourished in the Depression. In 1937 it had 185 volunteers in the field teaching thousands of workers.[50] The Chautauqua movement, which flourished from 1915 to the mid-1930s, offered families the chance to take advantage of lectures, concerts, and various other uplifting experiences in a holiday atmosphere. In the same period travelling libraries were established in many provinces, often with the assistance of the Carnegie Corporation.

Canadian universities after 1918 were especially affected by the presence of returning veterans displaying what one of them described as 'the indefinite expression of a vague discontent, the restlessness of dying men'.[51] They were also badly hit by post-war inflation. An Ontario Royal Commission on university finances in 1921 recommended public grants for the three universities in the province. The numbers of women attending Canadian universities rose significantly in the 1920s, and undergraduates increasingly passed over the traditional humanities in favour of vocational training in areas such as commerce and accounting. The expansion of engineering, spurred on by the Great War, continued unabated into the inter-war period; electrical engineering was by far the most popular specialty. And medical education became equally important, especially after researchers at the University of Toronto discovered insulin in 1922. Everywhere in Canada the universities were forced to accept that the public they were supposed to serve by and large wanted practical education. Under the circumstances, it may be surprising that the liberal arts survived at all, but, of course, instruction in the humanities is far less expensive than training in the vocational specialties. Especially after 1930, most universities were strapped for cash, and although not many saw their chief financial officers abscond with all the endowment funds, as the University of Manitoba did in 1932, everyone pinched pennies.

Curiously, the Depression had much less

effect on enrolment and student life than might have been expected. Student numbers remained fairly constant throughout the inter-war period, although universities constantly cut their budgets. The number of women actually increased in many places. Student bodies remained resolutely middle class, as they had been for years. However, Canadian universities were for an elite. Only about 3 per cent of people between 20 and 24 years of age were attending Canadian universities in 1931—a much lower percentage than in the US, though greater than in Britain or Germany. Those without funds may have found it more difficult to attend university in the 1930s, but all evidence suggests that most students did not come from particularly affluent backgrounds, representing instead what Paul Axelrod describes as the 'modest middle class'.[52] And many students succeeded in maintaining a full extracurricular life during their undergraduate years.

CONCLUSION

The experience of the Depression would condition the mindsets of many Canadians for the rest of their lives, affecting attitudes towards many aspects of life besides money, credit, and consumption. On the other hand, the physical health of most Canadians improved substantially in this period, and a new concern for children made its appearance. The nation was transformed by the spread of new technology, and there were even a few gains for organized labour.

Canadian culture may not have flourished between the wars, but it did move forward. Leading Canadian artists began to articulate a sense of cultural nationalism, and institutions such as the Dominion Drama Festival, the CBC, and the National Film Board were established to lead the way. With the creation of the CBC and the NFB the federal government became a very important patron of Canadian cultural production. After 1937 the Governor General's Awards recognized excellence in Canadian literature. In a curious way, the Depression encouraged culture-making, particularly of the amateur variety. Canadian culture was still under-appreciated in Canada, and cultural leaders like Sir Ernest MacMillan railed against Canada's colonial mentality. The gains were greater at the elite level than in popular culture, but the shape of a Canadian culture, at least in 'the arts', began to be recognizable, and by 1939 the leading Canadian figures were able to establish international reputations while remaining in Canada.

SHORT BIBLIOGRAPHY

Abella, Irving. *Nationalism, Communism and Canadian Labour: The CIO, the Communist Party of Canada and the Canadian Congress of Labour, 1935–1956*. Toronto, 1973. An important study of the manoeuvrings of the various ideologies on the labour front.

Allen, A.R. *The Social Passion: Religion and Social Reform in Canada, 1914–1928*. Toronto, 1971. The best book on the decline of social reform in the 1920s.

Association for Canadian Studies. *Canadian Society and Culture in Times of Economic Depression*. Montreal, 1987. A collection of useful essays on society and culture in the Depression.

Axelrod, Paul. *Making a Middle Class: Student Life in English Canada during the Thirties*. Montreal and Kingston, 1990. A richly textured analysis of university life during the Depression.

Berton, Pierre. *The Dionne Years*. Toronto, 1977. An innovative study focusing on the Dionnes as symbols of the Depression years.

Billinghurst, Jane. *Grey Owl: The Many Faces of Archie Belaney*. Vancouver, 1999. An attempt to come to terms with one of the great imposters of Canadian history.

Broadfoot, Barry. *Ten Lost Years, 1929–1939: Memories of Canadians Who Survived the Depression*. Toronto,

1973. A wonderful collection of first-person stories, mostly involving ordinary Canadians.

Grant, John Webster. *The Canadian Experience of Church Union*. London, 1967. The best book on one of the most important developments in organized religion in twentieth-century Canada.

Lee, Betty. *Love and Whisky: The Story of the Dominion Drama Festival*. Toronto, 1973. A popular treatment of the festival, focusing mainly on the 1930s.

Mellen, Peter. *The Group of Seven*. Toronto, 1970. A fabulously illustrated account of Canada's best-known group of artists.

Peers, Frank. *The Politics of Canadian Broadcasting, 1920–1951*. Toronto, 1969. An important study of the complexities of Canadian cultural policy.

Pigott, Peter. *Flying Colours: A History of Commercial Aviation in Canada*. Vancouver, 1997. An account of the development of the airplane as an instrument of commerce and transportation.

Ryan, Toby Gordon. *Stage Left: Canadian Theatre in the Thirties*. Toronto, 1981. A sympathetic study of engaged theatre during the Depression.

Shadbolt, Doris. *Emily Carr*. Toronto, 1990. A straightforward biography of a not-so-straightforward artist.

Tippett, Maria. *Making Culture: English-Canadian Institutions and the Arts before the Massey Commission*. Toronto, 1990. An important account of the creation of cultural infrastructure in anglophone Canada demonstrating that cultural life did not begin with the Massey Commission.

STUDY QUESTIONS

1. Apart from mortality due to conflict, why did the death rate fall in Canada between the wars?

2. What does the increased incidence of divorces after 1918 tell us about Canada?

3. In what ways were the First Nations exceptions to general demographic trends in Canada in these years?

4. What sorts of problems could be associated with the growth of child care between 1917 and 1939?

5. What were the objectives of Canadian cultural nationalism in the 1920s?

6. What were the main subjects of Canadian realist fiction between the wars?

7. How did Canadian dramatists respond to the Depression?

8. Why did the work of the Group of Seven come to be considered quintessentially Canadian? How is Emily Carr's work related to the Group?

9. What was the most important development in Canadian education between the wars?

10. What were the bright spots in the Depression era?

11. Were there gains for women between the wars?

CHAPTER TWELVE

■ World War II, 1939–1945

■ Canada reluctantly entered World War II in 1939. Before it was over, nearly 50,000 Canadians would be killed in military service, and another 30,000 members of the merchant marine would lose their lives in combat situations. Most Canadians felt that they understood why they were fighting, and ultimately they would experience a sense of victory. The war did not appreciably alter Canada's long-term international position, although for a time the nation had one of the largest and best-equipped military forces in the world and behaved in some ways like a major power. What the war did change was Canada's domestic policies. War enabled the state to undertake many activities that politicians had said were impossible under the Canadian Constitution, and by its end the nation was on the verge of a major shift in social policy.[1]

CANADA AND INTERNATIONAL AFFAIRS BETWEEN THE WARS

As a result of both its geographical position and its colonial situation, Canada before 1914 had enjoyed relative isolation from the turmoil of international politics and had been able to concentrate on its own domestic development. Like Americans, most Canadians were relatively inward-looking, even isolationist, in their atti-tudes towards the wider world. Most French Canadians saw themselves as an autonomous people without close European or international connections, and although Canadians of British origin could identify with the mother country, the vast majority of citizens felt no particular tie to the British Empire. Beyond the ongoing relationship with the United States and a continuing interest in Britain or France, there seemed little need for Canadians to concern themselves with the domestic developments of other nations or play a role in international affairs. Whitehall looked after most such matters, and the government in Ottawa had some input into international issues when specifically Canadian interests were at stake.

After 1918 Canada's international position changed rapidly. It could even be argued that the nation has never enjoyed more autonomy than it did in the inter-war period, as it gradually broke its imperial ties, became an independent dominion in the newly organized 'Commonwealth' in 1931, and began seriously to construct its own foreign policy and diplomatic apparatus. As late as the 1920s the Canadian military thought of the US as a potential enemy against which the nation might need to be defended, and before 1939–40 direct American influence over Canadian foreign and defence policy was mini-

TIMELINE

1928
Canadian Institute of International Affairs (CIIA) is founded.

1937
Frank Underhill calls for Canada to avoid European involvement. Mackenzie King meets with Hitler.

1938
Germany and Allied powers sign Munich Agreement. Conference on the refugee problem held at Evian, France. Jewish delegation pleads with Canadian government to admit refugees.

1939
John Grierson becomes head of National Film Board. Canada declares war against Germany. British Commonwealth Air Training Plan (BCATP) agreed to by Britain and Canada.

1940
Roosevelt and King meet at Warm Springs, Georgia (April). C.D. Howe becomes Minister of Munitions and Supplies (April). Roosevelt and King meet at Ogdensburg, New York, and sign an agreement of co-operation (August). Americans send British 50 destroyers under 'Lend-Lease'.

1941
CBC News Service begins. Hyde Park Declaration issued. Concern is expressed over neglect of the humanities at Canadian universities. Federation of Canadian Artists is founded. Pearl Harbor is attacked and Hong Kong falls.

1942
Japanese are removed from the coast of British Columbia. Rationing is introduced. Conscription plebiscite held. Dieppe disaster occurs in August. First Canadian Army formed. Tories become 'Progressive' Conservatives with John Bracken as leader and adopt platform of social reform.

1943
Canadian cabinet discusses training female pilots. Canadians develop 'functionalism' policy. A Canadian is given command of the Canadian Northwest Atlantic Theatre. Debate in Canada over reconstruction after the war. General McNaughton resigns as Chief of Staff. UNRAA is formed. Canadian War Art Program is established.

1944
CCF wins in Saskatchewan. D-Day occurs on 6 June. Canadian cultural organizations meet in Toronto to prepare brief to the government.

1945
San Francisco Conference creates United Nations.

mal. External Affairs, like other departments of the federal state, developed under the leadership of a new class of professional civil servants, an elite cadre of 'mandarins'.[2] World War II both completed the process of Canada's withdrawal from the British Empire and initiated the process of its integration into a less formal but no less powerful American empire.

The years after 1936 saw the press take a greatly increased interest in international affairs, and a genuine public debate emerged over foreign policy. The Canadian Institute of International Affairs (CIIA), founded in 1928 by Sir Robert Borden and John W. Dafoe of the *Winnipeg Free Press*, was particularly active in pressing for more recognition of Canada's role in the world. The focus was mainly on Europe, although Japan had provided evidence of its own ambitions in its 1931 occupation of Manchuria, and continued to behave aggressively in the Far East. In 1936 Canada began a modest program of rearmament, less by increasing expenditures than by co-ordinating forward planning for the next five years. In 1937, for the first time in years, Parliament entertained a serious debate over external policy when the pacifist J.S. Woodsworth moved a resolution of strict Canadian neutrality 'regardless of who the belligerents might be'. The government responded that its hands should not be tied, and that 'with respect to participation and neutrality . . . parliament will decide what is to be done'.[3] Appeasement may have been pusillanimous, but it was arguably unavoidable, particularly for nations that were as ill-prepared militarily and as weak economically as the Western democracies were in the late 1930s.

THE JEWISH REFUGEES

Far less defensible was Canadian policy towards the victims of the Nazi program in Europe, particularly the Jews. The exodus of refugees from Nazi Germany had begun soon after Hitler's takeover of power. Some were radical political dissenters, like the novelist Arthur Koestler, but many left in response to the anti-Semitic policies of the new Nazi state. Canadian authorities displayed little interest in accommodating these refugees, and in 1938 actually began restricting Jewish immigration. Over the protests of Immigration Minister T.A. Crerar, Prime Minister

King himself declared that Canada's actions should be based not on 'humanitarian grounds' but on political 'realities'. Those realities included a general Canadian suspicion of Jews and, in Quebec, what appeared to be a positive hostility to their admission to Canada. 'Why allow in Jewish refugees?' asked *Le Devoir*; 'the Jewish shopkeeper on St Lawrence Boulevard does nothing to increase our natural resources.' The St Jean Baptiste Society presented a petition to the House of Commons protesting against 'all immigration . . . especially Jewish immigration' and signed by 128,000 of its members.[5] Another reality was a sense that the world community would be quite happy to resolve its economic and political problems (including the international refugee problem, which was quite serious by 1938) by dumping them in Canada's lap.

With great reluctance Canada agreed to attend an American-backed international conference on the refugee problem at Evian, France, in June 1938. The Canadian cabinet breathed a collective sigh of relief when the conference decided to do nothing but affirm existing national immigration policies. Even more pointedly, earlier that June a cabinet committee refused even to hear a proposal from the Jewish community that Canada take to the conference a plan to accept 5,000 Jewish refugees over the next four years (none of whom would be settled in Quebec), with all costs to be borne by Canadian Jews.

The most that can be said for the official Canadian attitude towards the Jewish refugees was that it was consistent with past national policy. Canada's immigration policy had never been strongly influenced by humanitarian considerations, and Canadian authorities had always been obsessed by the need for assimilable newcomers. As it turned out, the Evian conference on refugees did not force Canada to alter its policy. Instead, the delegates mouthed platitudes and resolved unanimously that they were 'not willing to undertake any obligations toward financing involuntary immigration'.[6] As the European situation worsened, Canada's Jews mounted a desperate series of public demonstrations to arouse support for a change of policy. On 23 November 1938 a delegation of Jews met with Mackenzie King and T.A. Crerar to plead for the admission of 10,000 refugees at no expense to the government. They were rebuffed. On the other hand, mounting pressure on the government did lead to some internal discussion among the mandarins; as Norman Robertson noted, 'We don't want to take too many Jews, but, in the present circumstances particularly, we don't want to say so.'[7]

On 13 December 1938, the cabinet agreed to keep existing immigration regulations but to interpret them 'as liberally as possible'. Since the existing system encouraged the immigration only of farmers with capital, such a concession was not very significant. Immigration officials themselves were convinced that few Jews wanted to farm. In 1939 Canada joined with the United States in rejecting as immigrants over 900 Jewish refugees who were passengers on the SS *St Louis*, which had sailed from Hamburg for Havana, Cuba, on 13 May. The Cuban government refused to accept their landing permits, and the vessel sailed the Atlantic for days hoping that either the US or Canada would take them in. Eventually the *St Louis* returned to Antwerp, where Belgium agreed to accept them temporarily. Canadian officials believed that refugees would say anything to be admitted, and systematically rejected highly skilled professionals and intellectuals (including doctors, scientists, and musicians) as 'inadmissible'.

For a nation as limited in world-renowned scientific, intellectual, and cultural talent as Canada, the result was a huge shortfall in relation to other countries, particularly the US and Great Britain, which benefited greatly from the arrival of Jewish refugees educated in fields as diverse as physics, medicine, theatre, music, and psychiatry. . Even in the crassest of terms, Canadian policy was a disaster. But it was inexcusable in a moral sense—particularly on the part of a country that at the League of Nations was constantly lecturing other countries about their shortcomings.

THE WAR BEGINS

The greatest value of appeasement, apart from buying a little time to reinvigorate long-neglected military establishments, was that it delayed war until only the most ardent pacifist or isolationist could deny its necessity. By 1939 the Canadian economy was recovering from 10 long years of depression, during which both its agricultural and industrial sectors had run at half capacity and more than half of the Canadian population was effectively unemployed. By the summer of 1939 no informed observer could doubt that the next German aggression would be met firmly by the allied governments. When Hitler invaded Poland on 1 September 1939, the Prime Minister summoned Parliament to meet a week later, and on 10 September Canada joined Britain and France in declaring war against Germany. Only four MPs—three from Quebec and J.S. Woodsworth—spoke against the action. Having learned its lesson in 1914, the Canadian government had no intention of shipping thousands of volunteers (much less conscripts) overseas right away; the first Canadian troops ('bold-eyed Canadians—with a slouch and a swagger', as the diplomat Charles Ritchie described them) did not arrive in Britain until 17 December 1939. Instead, Canada's first response was to offer economic support to its allies and concentrate on the air force under the British Commonwealth Air Training Plan. From the outset, Canada understood the importance of close ties with the US, which was to remain officially out of the international conflagration until December 1941. Despite the Americans' policy of neutrality, Canada found the Roosevelt administration receptive to mutual defence undertakings. When France fell to the Germans in 1940 and Britain stood virtually alone against the Nazi war machine, Canada simultaneously gave cautious support to the British in Europe and moved increasingly under the American military umbrella.

Virtually from the outset of the war it was obvious that Canada's connection with Britain

■ The 1st Division Canadian Active Service Force embarking at Halifax, December 1939. LAC, C-24717.

would be reduced as a consequence of the conflict. When the British asked Canada to assist in financing essential supplies, for example, some of this aid took the form of an exchange—the 'repatriation of Canadian securities held in London'—that would reduce British investment in Canada substantially by the end of the war. American neutrality encouraged the two governments to keep some distance from each other until 1940, although Congress extended the 1935 trade treaty with Canada. In late April 1940, Franklin Roosevelt and Mackenzie King met in Warm Springs, Georgia, and worried together about the possible collapse of the French and British without actually agreeing to anything. Within little more than a month, however, even the US came to realize that its European friends were in serious trouble. The Americans moved swiftly to rearm themselves and achieve a state of military readiness. They sought desper-

ately to prop up the tottering British, who after Dunkirk were left virtually alone to face a German air blitz that everyone feared was intended to soften them up in preparation for an invasion. Washington's recently formed friendship with its northern neighbour made it possible to use Canada to channel assistance to the British while still remaining officially neutral.

British historians often perpetuate the myth that Britain stood absolutely alone in 1940; there is a famous cartoon of a single British Tommy standing at water's edge with his fist raised high, the caption reading 'VERY WELL, ALONE'. As a result they tend not to acknowledge the role played by Canada, their one major ally in those dark days. This was not the first time, nor would it be the last, when Canada's significance internationally would be undervalued. For Canada, the European war was—as wars go—a 'good' one. Canadians knew what they were fighting for, and did their job with a minimum of grumbling. Moreover, virtually alone among the Allied powers, Canada pulled its weight unstintingly, often without ulterior motives or expectations of advantage. Canada's war aims were simply the liberation of Europe and the restoration of democracy. The nation had no expectation of territorial gain or an enhanced world role. Virtually alone among allied leaders, Winston Churchill understood the true nature of Canadian altruism. At the last Quebec conference in 1944, according to the diary kept by Mackenzie King, 'Churchill [spoke] eloquently . . . of our not desiring an acre of land, of not wishing anything in the way of additional power, but fighting simply for the maintenance of our honour and the preservation of freedom.'[8]

In the spring of 1939 King had opposed 'the idea that every twenty years this country should automatically and as a matter of course take part in a war overseas, periodically, to fight for a continent that cannot run itself'.[9] Although he never entirely lost his isolationism, he became a staunch supporter of the British and even wrote a book entitled *Canada at Britain's Side*. King was a professional labour conciliator, and compromise ought to have been his middle name. He was a one-man committee, constantly balancing opposing interests and obfuscating serious disagreements within the nation. Unlike Churchill or Roosevelt (and even Stalin), King was not blessed with charisma. Publicly, he was mostly dull and cautious, just like the nation. His loyalties British and his realities American, he saw himself and his country as a bridge between Britain and the US. What the Canadian people would have thought of his private life, full of dreams to be interpreted and mediums to be consulted, is an open question.[10]

CANADIAN–AMERICAN CO-OPERATION

In August 1940 Franklin Roosevelt, on his own initiative, invited Mackenzie King to Ogdensburg, New York, where the two leaders—according to

their joint statement to the press—'agreed that a Permanent Joint Board on Defence shall be set up at once by the two countries'. The Ogdensburg Agreement was the product of two converging factors. One was that the US, which was officially neutral, needed Canada as a conduit for assistance to Britain. The other was that the US needed the assistance of Canada—which was legally able to gear up for wartime production—to rearm. Shortly after Ogdensburg, the Americans sent the British 50 destroyers in return for long leases on military bases within the British Empire, including Newfoundland. Since the latter had surrendered its dominion status in 1933, when it was facing bankruptcy, and was now technically a British colony, its government was not consulted about the British concessions to the US. Canada tried unsuccessfully to get the Newfoundland deal considered separately, but had to settle for a discrete protocol recognizing its 'special concern' about the defence of Newfoundland (which was critically important to the Allies as a staging and refuelling base for aircraft incapable of flying the Atlantic non-stop). American military investment on the island helped to turn its economy around. At the height of the construction boom of 1941–2 more than 20,000 Newfoundlanders were employed in building bases, and the buoyancy of the job market was reflected in the upward direction of public revenue. Although the Americans were sometimes exasperated by the Newfoundlanders' 'slow methods of work and habits of quitting on numerous holidays and other trivial excuses', by and large they got on well with the locals.[11] Newfoundland also benefited from an international shortage of salt fish, which enabled it to export as much fish as it could produce for the duration of the war. By the end of 1945–6, the colony's government had built up a surplus of nearly $30 million.

The next stage in the new relationship between Canada (in its role as intermediary for Britain) and the still-neutral US was the Hyde Park Declaration of April 1941, according to which 'each country should provide the other with defence articles which it is best able to produce, and above all, produce quickly, and that production programmes should be coordinated to this end.' Britain's investments in Canada could not be converted into cash fast enough to keep up with her war purchases, which in turn required the importation of American materials in record amounts. The result of the production and sale to Britain of such items as ships and munitions was an even more unfavourable balance of trade with the US, which in 1948 led Canada to seek further economic integration. In the short run, Hyde Park meant that the Americans ordered military equipment made in Canada under the war-production program created by the Minister of Munitions and Supply, C.D. Howe, using American technology and money. Howe developed a new Crown company, War Supplies Ltd, to deal with the Americans. Until American industry was fully geared for war, the Canadian production would prove extremely useful.[12]

ECONOMIC RECOVERY

Canada's entry into World War II on 10 September 1939 began the final stage of the economic recovery that had started in 1935. The nation was not prepared militarily, but as in the Great War, it was able to mobilize resources quickly when war was the objective. The British Commonwealth Air Training Plan (BCATP) had been quickly accepted by Canada as its principal war commitment, and the details of the scheme were agreed to by Britain and Canada on 17 December 1939. The achievement of an agreement on air training, with negotiations beginning before the start of the war, had been fraught with early misunderstandings. Britain wanted British air personnel trained in Canada, while Canada wanted the program expanded to the Commonwealth to promote the development of 'distinctive Canadian, Australian, and New Zealand air forces'.[13] Prime Minister King liked

this idea, partly because—as he put it himself—'with concentration of Canadian energies on air training and air power there would be less risk of agitation for conscription.'[14] Within months, the BCATP's first graduates emerged from Camp Borden, in eastern Ontario; over the course of the war it would graduate 131,533 Commonwealth airmen, 72,835 of them Canadian, at a cost of $1.6 billion.

A nation of fewer than 12 million people would eventually put more than one million men and women into uniform. Using the War Measures Act, Canada succeeded in mobilizing its economic resources in a way that had seemed beyond its grasp during the Depression. The aim was the total management and regulation of the economy—as the CCF had advocated in the 1930s—so that by 1943 unemployment was well under 2 per cent—a level generally regarded as representing 'full employment'. Federal spending rose from 3.4 per cent of the gross national product (GNP) in 1939 to 37.6 per cent by 1944—a full $4.4 billion in that year. Industrial growth was marginally better distributed across the regions than in 1914–18, inflation was controlled, and consumption was regulated. Canada's total GNP rose from $5.6 billion in 1939 to $11.9 billion by 1945, and Canada became one of the world's major industrializing nations, producing 850,000 motorized vehicles and more than 16,000 military aircraft (more than half of this war production went to other countries of the Empire).[15]

Yet, we must not think of this magnificent achievement as totally successful. To finance it, the government had to raise taxes and borrow heavily, chiefly from its own citizens through war bonds. Furthermore, at least three weaknesses emerged in Canada's heavily managed wartime economy. One was the perpetuation of regional disparities. While central Canada prospered, for example, the Economic Advisory Committee chose to purchase American coal rather than to develop the Cape Breton mines, which would have required transportation subsidies and labour peace in order to be truly productive. Plate steel also was purchased in the US, while the Dominion Steel and Coal Corp., the Maritime region's largest employer, was badly neglected. Maritime shipyards received little support at the beginning of the war. In 1941, of the half-billion dollars allotted to capital expansion of industry in Canada, Prince Edward Island and New Brunswick got nothing and Nova Scotia received just $8,759,430, or 1.81 per cent of the total commitment. Skilled workers were drawn off to central Canada until 1945, and none of the 28 Crown corporations created during the war was located in the Maritime region. What industrial expansion did occur came in industries unlikely to continue in peacetime. The result was that instead of laying the groundwork for post-war Maritime prosperity, Ottawa's economic management prepared the way for Maritime economic stagnation.[16]

The second weakness was in industrial relations, which in the early years of the war were almost always handled to the benefit of management rather than the workers or the trade unions. This adversarial relationship produced an increased labour militancy and strikes for better wages and working conditions. Until 1944 the number of strikes, workers on strike, and days lost to industrial action increased annually, and by 1943 one in every three trade unionists was on strike at some point during the year. Throughout the war, however, the federal government sought to co-opt labour into the war effort, and with the provinces began the slow process of altering labour legislation to recognize and protect the rights to organization and collective bargaining. The key breakthrough came in 1944, when the federal government used an Order-in-Council, PCO 1003, to introduce the principles of compulsory recognition and collective bargaining recently adopted in the US.[17]

The third great weakness was in manpower mobilization. The National Selective Service—the agency in charge of controlling manpower—was accurately described by the opposition Conservatives in 1944 as 'Canada's greatest wartime muddle'. The agency was characterized by lack of co-ordination and firm regulation, as we shall come to see in the conscription crisis of 1944. Planning was often non-existent. In 1942 Prime Minister King decided against comprehensive mobilization strategies, and almost lost control of the war as a result. The NSS was run by typical 'Ottawa men' in cautious and ineffectual ways.[18]

The man most closely identified with Canada's wartime production was Clarence Decatur Howe, a ninth-generation New Englander who had moved to Canada in 1908, at the age of 22, to teach engineering at Dalhousie University in Halifax. Howe left the university in 1913 to design elevators for the Canadian Board of Grain Commissioners, and in 1916 formed his own successful engineering firm. In 1935 he entered federal politics and was elected to a Liberal seat for Port Arthur (Thunder Bay), Ontario. He was soon appointed Minister of Transport in the King cabinet. In November 1939 Howe took over the task of mobilizing defence production, and he became minister of the Department of Munitions and Supplies (DMS) in April 1940. Chiefly at Howe's instigation, DMS moved quickly into government manufacturing, in preference to private enterprise, developing a new entity—the Crown corporation—to do the job. Before the war was over, 28 Crown corporations had been created by Howe under DMS. Howe also insisted that Canada could produce any wartime commodity the nation needed, and encouraged private enterprise to bid on defence contracts. Howe's most notorious quips—'What's a million?' and 'Who would stop us?'—entered Canadian political lore. The exigencies of wartime allowed him to get away with autocratic and peremptory behaviour that would not otherwise have been acceptable. By 1943 Canada had achieved levels of mobilization that compared quite favourably with those in Britain and the United States—both imperial nations with much broader responsibilities (see Table 12.1).

TABLE 12.1

MOBILIZATION OF CANADA, THE US, AND THE UK IN 1942–1943

	Canada 31 Jan. 1943		US 1 Jan. 1943		UK Mid-1942	
	('000)	%	('000)	%	('000)	%
War employment industry	1,036	9.0	8,700	6.4	5,110	10.9
Essential non-agricultural industry	1,089	9.5	7,700	5.7	4,566	9.7
Less essential non-agric. industry	1,317	11.4	26,600	19.7	7,000	14.9
Agriculture	1,020	8.9	8,900	6.6	1,107	2.4
Total Industry	4,462	38.8	51,900	38.4	17,783	37.9
Armed forces (projected to March 1944)	778	6.8	10,800	8.9	4,500	9.6
Total ind. & forces	5,240	45.6	62,700	46.4	22,283	47.5
Population	11,500,000		135,000,000		47,000,000	

SOURCE: J.M. Hitsman and J.L. Granatstein, *Broken Promises: A History of Conscription in Canada* (Toronto: Oxford University Press, 1977).

If Canada's achievement was on one level a great economic success story, however, it strongly suggested that the challenge noted by Stephen Leacock in 1919—the 'unsolved riddle of social justice'—had not yet been settled. Canada appeared far more capable of using its productive capacity to fight external enemies than to battle the domestic demons of poverty and unemployment.

THE CANADIAN MILITARY CONTRIBUTION

The principal Allied partnership was between Franklin Roosevelt and Winston Churchill, and most of the time Mackenzie King and his advisors seemed reasonably satisfied with this arrange-ment. As in the Great War, Canada had great difficulty gaining information about many high-level decisions, much less gaining access to the corridors of power. Ottawa never pushed for membership on the high-level military planning committee, the Combined Chiefs of Staff, which was strictly an Anglo-American operation; but it did try to gain representation on such middle-level co-ordinating bodies as the Munitions Assignment Board, the Combined Production and Resources Board, and the Combined Food Board. Canada had more leverage with the British than the Americans because of its substantial financial assistance to Great Britain, and finally won representation on some of the less important of the civilian boards, although not the Munitions Assignment Board or the Food Board.[19]

■ 9th Canadian infantry brigade landing at Bernières-sur-Mer, France, on D-Day, 6 June 1944. G.A. Milne/LAC, PA-137013.

Also, as in the Great War, the Canadians fought well whenever called upon, and were often employed as shock troops, sustaining heavy casualty rates. In the disastrous landing of the 2nd Canadian Division at Dieppe in August 1942, more than half of the 5,000 Canadians who embarked were killed or captured. The Dieppe raid became a classic example of military bungling because the Canadian troops were sent into combat under circumstances that almost certainly guaranteed disaster. On the other hand, the eagerness of Canada's armed forces in Britain to get into the thick of things contributed to the failure of its leading officers to mount any effective protest against the British planning for Dieppe. A considerable literature has grown up analyzing Dieppe, attempting to sort out Canadian from British responsibility for the debacle and assess the importance of what was learned.[20] Apart from the Dieppe adventure, most Canadian troops remained in Britain from their arrival (beginning in early 1941) until early 1944, when they were finally deployed first in Italy and then in Northwestern Europe. By late 1943, there were over 300,000 Canadians stationed in the United Kingdom—a population about the size of Ottawa at the time—most of whom were abroad for the first time.

The first Canadian Army, formed in 1942 under the command of General A.G.L. McNaughton, was composed of five divisions that eventually were split between Italy and Northern Europe. Canadians were involved in the Allied invasion of

■ A Canadian Liberator patrol aircraft shepherding a convoy of ships crossing the Atlantic in 1944. The ship in the foreground should not have been belching smoke in daylight—this could alert the enemy. Department of National Defence.

Italy beginning in January 1944 and in the D-Day invasion of Europe in June 1944. On both fronts, casualties were heavy; over 18,500 Canadian soldiers were killed, wounded, or missing in Italy. On the other hand, this war was not one of trenches but of movement and mobility as beachheads were established and troops advanced to liberate places held by the enemy. McNaughton and his successor, General H.D.G. Crerar, consulted with Ottawa in deploying their troops, and although the grand strategy was not in Canadian hands, Canadian soldiers fought as Canadian units throughout the conflict. Apart from the heavy casualties, perhaps the greatest problem faced by Canadian soldiers was

CANADA'S MERCHANT MARINE

Paul Brick, a member of the Canadian merchant marine during World War II, here describes the merchant seaman's gripes.

Canadian merchant seamen were noted for their sense of humour, could laugh at themselves. We got shit. 'Where the hell were you doing the war? I never heard a thing about you. Where's that uniform? Where'd you lose your arm?' But we kept our sense of humour right to today. See, once we left a ship, we went off pay. The navy was on pay 365 days a year. He got free medicine, free dentistry, free uniforms, subsidy, the whole works. We didn't. The minute you were torpedoed, your pay stopped. Bingo! You weren't working, were you? You were in your lifeboat. Are you talking about a just society or something? When you got back to port, the quicker you got back to work the better. And if you wanted a little torpedo leave, which I think came to four days, it took me two days to get home and two days to get back, so you didn't bother with any of that crap, did you? The bullet or torpedo that sunk the ship and sunk the naval officer, the merchant naval officer, the crew member and naval A.B. [able seaman] was the same thing. But the navy, immediately that the husband was killed, or the father or son, the next of kin got their insurance allowance, the whole works. It was one full year before the next of kin of a merchant seaman, British and Canadian, could be told that he was even missing. And when they did, if the company that he was working for did happen to have torpedo or wartime insurance, the next of kin got pennies. . . .

One thing has to be remembered: the air force fellow, a hell of a good guy, got a lot of time for him. He had his four hours of flight, came home, had his three squares a day. Certainly, he had that four or five hours where he lived in terror. The Canadian naval fella on convoy work, sure he had one hell of a rough time, rough. Their ships were not that good, neither was their food all that good. But when they got to port they had time off, and when their ships went into refit they had their way paid home, had their dental bills, their clothes, their medical bills, everything, looked after. The army never really did a hell of a lot except the Dieppe raid until early 1943, when they went into Italy, then the D-Day landings. They distinguished itself [*sic*], there's no doubt about. But ordinarily the merchant seaman could be at sea and in danger for nine-tenths of your time. We had the terror all the time, night and day, night and day.

I was very lucky and I'm glad, touch wood, that nothing did happen to me. If anything did, it's not visible. I'm not bitter about it anymore, a bit disappointed in the government that they didn't recognize us as veterans. That's the thing to come, but it's almost too late. We're treated shabbily, I can't understand it.

SOURCE: Mike Parker, ed., *Running the Gauntlet: An Oral History of Canadian Merchant Seamen in World War II* (Halifax: Nimbus Publishing Ltd, 1994), 43–4.

the long absence from home and family. Unless he was invalided back to Canada, a soldier served overseas for the duration of the conflict and did not get home until the end of 1945. Many soldiers were away from loved ones for as long as five years.

The Royal Canadian Air Force (RCAF) and Royal Canadian Navy (RCN) were well integrated with their British counterparts. Most RCAF personnel joined British RAF units, although Canada eventually sent 43 squadrons overseas. Canadian

ANDREW GEORGE LATTA McNAUGHTON (1887–1966)

❖

Andrew McNaughton was born at Moosomin, NWT (Saskatchewan), in 1887 to parents who had moved there from Ontario. His father was a prominent merchant in the town. Young Andrew studied at Bishop's College School, and in 1905 enrolled at McGill University intending to study hydroelectrical engineering. He stayed at Queen's for an M.Sc. and then taught electrical subjects and engaged in research at the university. He also became an officer in the 3rd Field Battery of Montreal, receiving his commission in 1910. In 1914 his battery was immediately placed on active service. Wounded several times, McNaughton advanced rapidly because of his scientific knowledge and training, and by the end of the war he was commander of the Canadian artillery.

McNaughton remained in the army and by 1922 was deputy chief of the general staff, serving as chief from 1929 to 1935, when he became head of the National Research Council of Canada. Almost inevitably, when World War II broke out McNaughton became General Officer Commanding. He was an adequate staff officer and a decent paper-pusher who was relatively successful in the years before the Canadians began fighting on the front lines, and he initiated several breakthroughs on the technological side of warfare. But he was weak tactically, as his support of the Dieppe raid would demonstrate, and his obstinate refusal to allow the Canadian Army Overseas to be broken up for service in different theatres of war put him out of favour in both Ottawa and London. After a part of the Canadian force was assigned to the Sicilian invasion, McNaughton made himself unpopular with Generals Montgomery and Alexander in June 1943 by insisting (unsuccessfully) in North Africa that he be allowed to inspect his troops personally, to ensure that they were being properly employed. Alexander told General Eisenhower that if McNaughton had 'been a junior officer he would have placed him under arrest'. McNaughton also fought with the Minister of National Defence, J.L. Ralston, over the issue of detaching contingents of the Canadian Army. In ill health, he resigned in December 1943, only to be called back into service as Mackenzie King's Minister of National Defence in the hope that he could avoid instigating conscription. He could not.

After the war McNaughton served in a series of high-level civilian posts. He was on the UN Atomic Energy Commission, was president of the Canadian Atomic Energy Board, and served at the UN as delegate in 1948–9. He was chairman of the Canadian Section of the International Joint Commission from 1950 to 1962, during the years when American responsibility for flooding of the Red River Valley in Manitoba was an issue. He was also chairman of the Permanent Joint Board on Defence from 1950 to 1959, and he spent his last public years, 1962–4, opposing the Columbia River Treaty with the US, on the grounds that Canada could not afford to sell out its water to a foreign buyer. McNaughton was a bluff and autocratic old soldier with few political or public relations skills, but his two major stands—on Canada's right to make its own decisions regarding the disposition of its troops, and on the long-term implications of continentalism in the area of national resources—were at least as popular as they were contentious.

An Air Attack on Stuttgart

By common consent, one of the finest autobiographies by a Canadian in combat in World War II was D. Murray Peden's *A Thousand Shall Fall: A Pilot for 214*, from which the following excerpt is reproduced.

On July 28th [1944] Peden's crew were on the battle order again. This time Stan was back with us, his first trip since Gelsenkirchen, five weeks earlier. He had arrived on the station on that afternoon. The MO checked and cleared him for operations, although Stan later told me that he had been feeling decidedly shaky.

I felt pretty shaky myself when we got to briefing. The target was Stuttgart, and Main Force was attacking on a route that would keep us in the air close to eight hours. More accurately, I should say that the target was Stuttgart again. Bomber Command [had] already attacked the city twice in the preceding four days, on July 24th and July 25th.

According to the Intelligence officer, the routing on the first occasion had been very carefully worked out so as to avoid heavy flak and searchlights as much as possible. The second time out, July 25th, Bomber Command had run a double bluff on the Germans and used the identical route again. The double bluff had worked; the losses had been only 12 aircraft, a little over half the number lost on the first attack.

But tonight we were really going to fool them, the Intelligence officer told us proudly; we were going to use the same route for the third time in succession. The Germans would never believe that we would attack Stuttgart again, three times hand-running [sic], using the same route. Their chief controller would interpret it as a bluff, and the closer we got to Stuttgart the more convinced he would be that we were bluffing and actually intended wheeling sharply to attack Frankfurt or one of several other targets north of our route. To confuse him even further, Main Force was going to attack to the north as well, with 321 aircraft being dispatched

to strike Hamburg while our force of 498 bombers attacked Stuttgart!

I felt sick. I did not normally second-guess the routing laid on by the high brass; but this conception, too clever by half to suit me, struck me as an invitation to disaster. The German controller already knew that three nights earlier we had bluffed him on exactly the same play, and had greatly benefited from his discomfiture; my feeling was that lots of poker players preferred to call rather than be laughed at on a bluff, lots of good poker players.

Later that night, after we took off, I climbed M Mike [the bomber, a Flying Fortress; sic] to operational altitude with grave misgivings. Hardly had we crossed the French coast than I realized that my fears were well founded. Combats broke out on all sides in the darkness, and soon the terrible sight of aircraft blowing up in mid-air, or burning fiercely as they spun to earth, was being repeated time and again. It took us three hours and 55 minutes to claw our way to Stuttgart, and by the time we got there I had long lost count of the number of combats that had broken out in close proximity to us, all too many of them terminating in the usual dreadful way. It seemed that at any given moment along that route, one could look aside or ahead and see flaming debris somewhere on the ground below us. Time after time I called: 'On your toes, gunners, there are fighters right near us' as vicious exchanges of fire tore the blackness open. Stan kept reporting contacts every few minutes, and the night air seemed alive with prowling German fighters.

The return journey was equally grim. Combats were taking place all around us, and every second I kept expecting our turn to come. It was the worst night of the war as far as I was concerned. I sat at interrogation later feeling as though my stomach muscles would never come unknotted.

We lost 62 aircraft that night, the majority of them on the Stuttgart attack! It was one of the few times that our elaborate tactics backfired.

SOURCE: Murray Peden, *A Thousand Shall Fall: The True Story of a Canadian Bomber Pilot in World War Two.* (Toronto: Dundurn Press, 1988), 429-30, 439.

flyers became noted for their work in bombers rather than fighters, and for their heavy casualty rates. The RCN, which grew to 365 ships, spent the war mainly protecting convoys on the North Atlantic route, achieving such expertise in this duty that by May 1943 a Canadian, Admiral L.W. Murray, was given command of the Canadian Northwest Atlantic theatre. Many other Canadians and Newfoundlanders served in the Canadian merchant marine, a thankless task that left them ineligible for veterans' benefits for many years. Among Canada's allies the most common criticism of the Canadian military machine was the inadequate experience of its officers.

Canadian assistance to American and British efforts in the Pacific and Southeast Asia was quite limited; most of the action took place in the last few months of the war against Japan. In October 1941, however, two Canadian battalions set sail for Hong Kong to reinforce the British garrison there. Japan attacked Hong Kong on 7 December (the same day it attacked Pearl Harbor). When Hong Kong fell on Christmas Day, 290 Canadians were killed and twice that number later died in Japanese prison camps. The 1,421 who returned home were forced to fight for 23 years to win proper veterans' benefits from the Canadian government. Despite Canada's declaration of war against Japan in the wake of this disaster, its commitment until the end of the war was almost entirely in the Atlantic-European theatre in support of the British.

As in the Great War, casualties were heavy; 42,642 Canadians lost their lives in military service between 1939 and 1945. Since most of those losses occurred in the later years of fighting,

when it had become clear that the Allies were winning, the total casualties were perhaps a little easier to accept than those of World War I, when most deaths seemed to serve no purpose at all.

THE WAR AND DOMESTIC POLITICS

In six years Canada had gone from mass unemployment and general hardship to relative prosperity and a booming economy. With the third-largest navy, the fourth-largest air force, and an army of five divisions, it had also become something of a power in the world—a transformation that, sadly, had taken a global conflict to achieve. The internal politics of the war revolved around two major questions: first, conscription and French Canada, and second, social policy and post-war reconstruction.

CONSCRIPTION

As in the Great War, support for the war effort was not evenly balanced between English- and French-speaking Canadians. The differences were clearly revealed in a national plebiscite on conscription held in the spring of 1942. While the nation as a whole voted 2,945,514 to 1,643,006 to release the government from an earlier pledge not to conscript for overseas service, Quebec voted strongly against this option. Public-opinion polling (a recent import from the US) indicated that most French Canadians were willing to defend Canada against an invasion, but not to serve overseas. As Table 12.2 shows, Quebec's rate of participation in the armed forces ran at just over half the rates of the other nine provinces. Nevertheless, some 50,000 French Canadians

TABLE 12.2
INTAKE INTO CANADIAN ARMED FORCES BY PROVINCE, 1939–1945

Place of permanent residence on enrolment	Percentage of male population, 18–45, entering armed forces
PEI	48.18
Nova Scotia	48.31
NB	48.17
Quebec	25.69
Ontario	47.77
Manitoba	48.12
Saskatchewan	42.38
Alberta	43.11
BC	50.47

from across the country volunteered for the army, more than half of whom served in anglophone units. At the same time, considerable evidence exists that Quebec supported the war effort on the home front with some enthusiasm.[21]

The conscription issue re-emerged in 1944, when the military announced that (as in 1917) it had become necessary, after all, to ship overseas conscripts who had been drafted on the understanding that they would not be required to serve abroad. These were the so-called 'Zombies', the forces of the National Resources Mobilization Act (NRMA). Contrary to popular opinion, these soldiers—more than 60,000 in 1944—were not all of non-British origin, and their ethnic composition probably reflected that of the nation at large. Efforts to persuade these conscripts to volunteer for overseas service were not particularly successful, and they were the targets of much public opprobrium. A contemporary piece of doggerel sums up the feeling:

Seventy thousand Zombies, isn't it a farce,

Seventy thousand Zombies, sitting on their

———

Eating up the rations, morning, noon and night.
Squatting here in Canada while others go to
fight.

Seventy thousand Zombies, hear the buzzards
sing,
Here's our thanks to you Quebec and old
Mackenzie King.
Never mind our comrades, let them be the goats,
As long as the politicians protect their slimy
votes.[22]

In the end, nearly 13,000 Zombies went abroad and 2,463 served in combat with the First Canadian Army, of whom 69 died, 232 were wounded, and 13 became POWs. As a marker of his concern, Prime Minister King accepted the resignation of J.L. Ralston, the Minister of Defence who had ordered the NRMA conscripts overseas; then he allowed overseas service to go ahead when the new Minister of Defence,

■ An anti-conscription rally organized by the Defence of Canada League at the Maisonneuve Market in Montreal, March 1942. LAC, *The Gazette* (Montreal) PA-173623.

General A.G.L. McNaughton, was unable to find enough volunteers.

PLANNING FOR POST-WAR RECONSTRUCTION

Politically, the government of Mackenzie King probably saw conscription and the Quebec question as less urgent than the increasing threat from the left posed by the CCF. By 1941, two years into the war, the mood in much of English Canada was far different from the mood at a similar stage in the previous war. Many Canadians had apparently come to realize that during the inter-war period neither constitutional nor physical reasons had stood in the way of a more concerted assault on the 'unsolved riddle of social justice'. The problem was the essential unwillingness of politicians and governments to act, since they were now demonstrating in the wartime emergency how well they could mobilize resources if they so desired. The shift may have begun in British Columbia, where the Liberal government of Duff Pattullo was devastated in late 1941, and only a coalition of the two traditional parties prevented the province from falling into the hands of the CCF. But overall public support for the

CCF grew significantly in 1942. Though still weak in Quebec and the Maritimes, the party was very strong from Ontario westward.

In early 1942, Arthur Meighen attempted to return to Parliament after having been chosen leader of the Conservative Party for the second time. He ran as a strong conscriptionist in a by-election in York South, and was badly beaten by the CCF candidate, an obscure schoolteacher named Joseph Noseworthy, who ran on a platform of winning both the war and the subsequent peace. Between the federal elections of 1940, when the CCF had received 8 per cent of the popular vote, and September 1943, when it was supported by 29 per cent of the electorate in the polls, Canadian public opinion had obviously shifted. Even the Conservative Party sensed the shift and replaced Meighen as leader with John Bracken, the long-time Premier of Manitoba, who insisted that the party rename itself 'Progressive Conservative' and adopt a platform of social reform. Unfortunately, Bracken had no record as a social reformer in his home province.

The Progressive Conservative platform, adopted in Winnipeg in December 1942, had a lengthy section on 'reconstruction'. It called for 'full employment at fair wages under progressively improving standards—and for the welfare and development of society' through individual enterprise wherever possible, but it also advocated a social security program that would include 'in a unified system' unemployment insurance, maintenance of unemployables, retirement insurance, old-age pensions, pensions for the blind, and adequate mothers' and widows' allowances. In addition, the party insisted it was the government's obligation to provide adequate medical and dental care to every citizen, 'financed under a contributory system supplemented by government assistance'. All this was to be provided under the aegis of a new Ministry of Social Security and Reconstruction, with the state share of the cost of the social security system 'borne by the Dominion'.[23] The Tories per-

haps sought to leave more to private enterprise than the CCF, but the point remains that by the end of 1942 every one of Canada's major political parties had a very similar vision of the important components of the post-war reconstruction.

The climate of opinion became more favourable to reconstruction partly as a result of several reports that were issued in late 1942 and early 1943. In December 1942 Sir William Beveridge issued a lengthy report on the need for post-war social services in Britain; identifying the 'Five Giants on the Road to Recovery' as 'WANT, DISEASE, IGNORANCE, SQUALOR and IDLENESS', Beveridge proposed a comprehensive 'social service state' to defeat them.[24] By this time the Canadian Tories had issued their Winnipeg platform calling for a social security system. In February 1943, a Canadian social work expert teaching in California published a book entitled *Social Security & Reconstruction in Canada*. Harry Cassidy began his book by referring to a Gallup public opinion poll released in mid-1942, which indicated that most Canadians believed that the soldiers had to be guaranteed some form of social security when they finally came home after the war. He went on:

> [T]here is a great need, from the standpoint of war morale, to resolve these fears of the men in the fighting forces and the civilian population. They cannot be expected to give fully of their energies and even of their lives unless they have some assurance that their welfare will not be disregarded in the post-war world.[25]

Moreover, Cassidy added, without the provision of a large measure of social security for their citizens, the democratic countries would face a revival of the social struggles of the 1930s that had produced the totalitarian dictatorships against which they were fighting.

Harry Cassidy was only one of several people in Canada and outside who called for careful planning to prevent a repeat of the disastrous period that followed the Great War. When the

Heagerty Committee (named after its chairman, John Joseph Heagerty), appointed in early 1942 to look into health insurance, reported in March 1943, it pointed out that several nations, including Germany, were well ahead of Canada in the provision of social security, which it defined as 'the security that society provides through appropriate organization against certain risks to which its members are exposed'. It added that, since 'the state is an association of citizens which exists for the sake of their general well-being, it is a proper function of the state to provide social security'.[26] The report emphasized the unhealthy condition of many Canadians: by European standards, tuberculosis mortality was high, venereal disease incidence was high, the situation with mental illness was grave, the maternal death rate was high, the infant mortality was high, and physical defects were high. In one health study of rural Manitoba youth aged 13 to 30, the Heagerty Committee noted, 70 per cent had one or more 'remediable defects or conditions which require medical attention'.[27] People like Cassidy and Heagerty framed their arguments not only in terms of the war, but in comparison with the achievements of other nations in the area of social services. By implication, they were arguing for Canada's full integration into the international community.

More comprehensive than the Cassidy and Heagerty proposals was the well-known *Report on Social Security for Canada*, tabled in the House of Commons Special Committee on Social Security by the economist Leonard Marsh in 1943.[28] Marsh—one of many Canadian academics employed during and after the war to prepare policy documents for government use—went further than the King government would be prepared to go, calling for a scheme of national health insurance as well as the more traditional unemployment insurance, old-age pensions and retirement insurance, and children's allowances.

In a 1944 election in Saskatchewan, a long-serving Liberal government was wiped out and replaced by the CCF under Tommy Douglas, giv-

ing the party its first government ministry, albeit a provincial one. The election debate in Saskatchewan had centred on social services and federal policy that discriminated against ordinary Canadians. The result of the Saskatchewan election was enough to change Mackenzie King's thinking. Until then, he had held out against reformers within his own party who had advocated the wholesale introduction of social welfare measures. But now he understood the political urgency of such a policy. Most political pundits agreed that the CCF was for the first time successfully polarizing Canadian politics in ideological terms. They argued that the CCF was drawing much of its support from Liberal rank-and-filers who wanted some action on pressing social issues. The upstart party would have to be politically outflanked.

In theory, Mackenzie King had supported social welfare since the Great War, although his record showed few major initiatives before 1939. One of them, legislation on old-age pensions for Canadians over 70, had been achieved (in 1926) only because two labour members of the House of Commons, J.S. Woodsworth and A.A. Heaps —who held the balance of power in a closely divided house—insisted on it as the price of their support. Even so, the pension scheme required that provinces participate on a 50–50 basis. Beginning in 1939, King's government had finally accepted the need for deficit spending to promote economic recovery from the Depression, thus adopting the new orthodoxy put forward by the English economist John Maynard Keynes in his *General Theory of Employment, Interest and Money* (1936). King's Minister of Finance, Charles Dunning, in his defence of the new policy in the Commons, made clear that the government did not regard public spending as a 'substitute for private enterprise', but he also emphasized that if business would not spend then government must, as a matter of 'sheer social necessity'. In 1940 the government had introduced unemployment insurance, and King's program for post-war reconstruction included

■ 'Bren Gun Girl': Veronica Foster, an employee at James Inglis Ltd, Toronto, posing with a finished gun, May 1941. National Film Board of Canada/LAC, PA-119766.

family allowances and proposals for health insurance. But the time had not been regarded as ripe to introduce such measures; that is, there was not yet an overwhelming public demand. Now, in 1944, that time had come. In July King announced in the House of Commons 'a wholly new conception of industry as being in the nature of social service for the benefit of all, not as something existing only for the benefit of a favoured few'. The introduction of social reform was necessary not only to steal ground from the CCF, but also to prevent possible public disorder at the end of the war. The two matters, of course, were related, for the CCF had been gaining ground on the strength of its willingness to press ahead with 'post-war reconstruction'.[29]

Once the decision was made at cabinet level to implement social reform, there would be little trouble producing the necessary legislation. King and the Liberals introduced enough social security sizzle to regain power in 1945 and to save Canada from the 'turn to socialism' that Britain experienced that same year when a Labour government implemented the Beveridge Report.

Ottawa was finally addressing seriously the 'unsolved riddle of social justice', though whether the King government was prepared to go far enough fast enough remained unclear. Public pressure in the later years of the war for a comprehensive housing policy to curb speculation and provide quality accommodation for everyone was met by the passage of the National Housing Act of 1944 and the establishment of the Central Mortgage and Housing Corporation in 1945. The latter would have the power to discount mortgages and, according to one government officer, was intended to encourage 'private enterprise to serve as much of the need as it possibly can and to serve an ever-increasing portion of the need as time goes on, thus reducing the need to be covered by direct public lending and private participation in housing schemes.'[30] Essentially, both the NHA and the CMHC offered market-based solutions to the housing situation, which had deteriorated during the war when new construction had been discouraged. The King government thus ignored the recommendations of another committee of experts it had appointed to study post-war policy, this one dealing with land use and housing. The Curtis Subcommittee on Housing and Community Planning had recommended in early 1944 a series of planning boards with sweeping powers to regulate land use, and a major program of subsidized low-rental housing involving the construction of 92,000 new public housing units to be administered by municipal housing authorities. The latter recommendation was in response to a report on low-income families in Montreal and Toronto indicating that many low-income families in those cities could not afford 'rents which would make house building a commercial proposition'.[31] Instead, the King cabinet was persuaded that 'children's allowances on anything like an adequate scale' would make it possible to avoid 'municipally constructed and municipally managed low-rental housing projects'.[32] In short, the Liberals chose reform within capitalism as the alternative to socialism, and the results of the 1945 election suggested that most Canadians concurred.

WAR AND PUBLIC ATTITUDES

WOMEN

Canada's attitude towards its women, as towards so much else, changed rapidly after 1939, at least for the duration of the war. Women were expected from the outset to manage the home front, keeping track of rationing coupons and tending 'victory gardens' to supply extra food. They were exhorted to buy War Savings Bonds and write to their men overseas. After 1942, when military and industrial needs had exhausted the pool of unemployed Canadians, women were also expected to enter wartime industries on an emergency basis. By June 1943, 255,000 women were employed in war industry, and a year later more than 40,000 were engaged in munitions manufacturing in Quebec and Ontario. Some claimed that they were much better than men at tedious jobs because they were accustomed to the boredom of housekeeping.[33] At war's end, women constituted nearly one-third of the Canadian labour force (31.4 per cent).

By 1945 more than 43,000 women were serving in Canada's armed forces, 21,000 of them in the Women's Army Corps. Each of the Canadian services had its own women's branch. Each carefully trained its own officers and NCOs. Much attention was devoted to appropriate uniforms, which were designed by a Toronto designer, Jack Creed, assisted by a special DND committee, whose modifications reduced Mr Creed to tears. By the end of the war, the occupations for which women could be trained had expanded to well over 50. Most of them were low-level, humdrum service jobs, but as more and more men were required for combat and overseas service, women increasingly moved into previously 'male' roles as radio operators, precision technicians, butchers, and welders. In January 1943 the Canadian cabinet actually discussed the possibility of training female pilots. The proposal was rejected for the moment and never re-examined. Most women served in Canada, although some were sent abroad for service in the United Kingdom.[34]

Whether the war provided much impetus for long-term gains for women in Canadian society is another matter. A 1944 Gallup poll indicated that most Canadians, including 68 per cent of the women polled, believed that men should be given preference for employment in the post-war reconstruction. A report on the future of women active in Canadian war industry—reluctantly commissioned by the government in 1943—was ignored almost completely, and governments moved with unseemly haste at war's end to dismantle the infrastructure, including daycare centres, that had been created to encourage women to work in critical industries. Within a year of VE Day, women's share of the labour force was down to 22.7 per cent, close to pre-war levels. Although commercial advertisements during the war—a useful measure of public opinion—recognized the importance of the war for women and were directed to war workers and those in the military, their appeals were phrased mainly in traditionally feminine terms. By 1947, the commercial world of advertising would be suggesting that all women were homemakers.[35]

DISSENT

As in the Great War, dissent was met with persecution. Although Canada was fighting for democracy, many Canadians found it hard to understand that suppressing dissenters and freedom of speech was inconsistent with their other war aims. The Canadian government proved almost wholly insensitive to the beliefs of pacifists, such as the Mennonites, who since the nineteenth century had been promised government understanding of their doctrinal opposition to war. Canada had a very limited view of conscientious objection, with National War Service Boards (each of which operated autonomously) often insisting that the candidate for CO status meet strict religious criteria. More to the point, only some Mennonites were generally recognized as coming under the guarantees of the Order-in-Council in 1873 by which the government had promised the religious sect freedom from military service. From the beginning of war, pacifist groups pressed the government to make some provision for alternative service, and in 1940 it did officially recognize other forms of service. Yet

most pacifists spent much of the war incarcerated in isolated work camps in the interior of British Columbia, unable to persuade the authorities to let them do useful alternative work.[36] J.S. Woodsworth was forced to step down as leader of the CCF—not by the government but by the war's supporters within his own party—because he opposed the war as a matter of conscience. The War Measures Act was used to intern thousands of Canadians without trial, including many young German immigrants who stayed in Canada and later made highly successful careers. Some of those detained were enemy sympathizers. But others were merely outspoken critics of government policy. Among the latter was Camillien Houde, the mayor of Montreal, who objected to registration for national service. Even the universities were not untarnished defenders of free speech. In 1941 the University of Toronto seriously threatened to dismiss the history professor Frank Underhill for having expressed unpopular opinions. For example, in 1938—before the war began—Underhill had written that the poppies growing in Flanders Field were no longer of interest to the people of Canada, and the following year, after Canada had joined the war, he had told a public panel that the country was going to have to face up to a diminution of its British connection and an enhancement of its American one. Toronto newspapers went after Underhill for his disloyal and seditious statements. The public outcry was such that both the Ontario government and the university's Board of Governors were quite prepared to dispense with Underhill's services, and he was spared only because of the intervention of students and some federal politicians.[37] Two students at the University of Manitoba were less fortunate in 1944, when a student literary journal published a poem suggesting that the Canadian government was as bloodthirsty as the enemy; in response to public outrage both the author of the poem and the editor of the journal were summarily expelled.

But the most severe repression in World War

■ Japanese Canadians being relocated to camps in the interior of British Columbia, 1942. LAC, C-046355.

II was directed against the Japanese community in Canada. Centred in British Columbia, the Japanese Canadians had never been particularly welcome, and their position became increasingly difficult as Japan became more aggressive militarily in the later 1930s. By 1941 they consisted of three distinct socio-cultural groups: the Issei had themselves immigrated from Japan or Hawaii; the Kibei were Canadian-born but Japanese-educated; and the Nisei were both born and educated in Canada (only 5,000 of the 13,600 Nisei were over 20 years of age). Numbering 22,000 in all, most Japanese residents were scattered in farming and fishing communities throughout the province and were acculturating rapidly. But white British Colum-

bians were convinced that they would not assimilate and responded to the attack on Pearl Harbor with great anger, which was only heightened by reports of Japanese ill-treatment of the Canadian contingent among the British garrison at Hong Kong, which had surrendered in 1941.

When Pearl Harbor came, many British Columbians claimed to be convinced that—as they had preached for years—the Japanese community would form a fifth column of support for the enemy. In fact, like most minorities associated with an enemy during wartime, most Japanese Canadians wanted to remain neutral, and neither the Canadian military nor the RCMP perceived any danger on the Pacific coast: 'I cannot see that the Japanese Canadians constitute the slightest menace to national security', wrote Major General Ken Stuart to Ottawa in 1941.[38] RCMP investigators were never able to uncover more than a handful of Japanese even worthy of suspicion, and the passage of time has not revealed a single Japanese spy in Canada. Nevertheless, the press and many politicians in British Columbia called for action, mainly in the form of internment for all Japanese so as not to miss a few potentially dangerous ones. Although the King government did not believe for a moment that they represented the slightest military danger, it yielded to local pressure and, on the pretext of needing to protect them from the white majority, evacuated most of the Japanese Canadians living on the west coast and sent them to locations inland. Most were sent to internment camps in the BC interior, and others were scattered across the country, mainly to sugar beet farms in Alberta and Manitoba. Their land was seized and their property sold at auction. A few young Japanese men were permitted to serve in special units in the Canadian army in the latter stages of the war, but on grounds of 'national emergency' the Canadian government refused to acknowledge any injustice in its treatment of Japanese Canadians as a group.[39]

THE MANAGEMENT OF INFORMATION

The dissemination of state propaganda in wartime is as old as war itself, but World War II gave rise to a new sophistication in that effort. The effective propaganda of the Great War was crude by comparison with the operations of Canada's Bureau of Public Information and the Wartime Information Board. The dissemination of propaganda became the 'management of information' and responsibility for it was handed over mainly to academic social scientists, who used the findings of sociology, psychology, and political science to achieve the desired results. Reliance on experts came to characterize the government's entire wartime propaganda effort, but the academics did not achieve their influence without a struggle.

Politicians were at first reluctant to allow public opinion to be moulded by outside experts, preferring to rely on journalists who argued that it was enough merely to choose the right news to report; as the general manager of the Canadian Press Association put it in 1939, 'the most efficient propaganda lies in the selection of news.' Prime Minister King apparently believed that the right information would, as his personal secretary later reported, 'ooze out by osmosis untouched by human hands', and throughout the war he provided private unattributed briefings to journalists like Winnipeg's Grant Dexter in an effort to maintain hands-on control.[40] The government soon overcame its scruples, however, and journalists would contend with academics for mastery of the spin on news throughout the war.

Information management gradually replaced blatant editorial comment as the essence of the wartime approach. Citizens needed to be educated in order to maintain 'faith and hope' and to eliminate 'potential elements of disunity'. In 1939 Scottish-born John Grierson was appointed the first Government Film Commissioner of the National Film Board of Canada, where he introduced his philosophy of documentary filmmaking as an enterprise undertaken in support of the state that should in turn be supported by the state. Grierson also hated Hollywood and the feature film as a cultural form, seeing Hollywood movies as 'lazy, weak, reactionary, vicarious, sentimental and essentially defeatist'.[41] He made no effort to present Canadian culture in the popular cinema. As in other areas, the war and federal government management had a substantial impact on Canadian film. Regarding himself as an expert in 'mind-bending', Grierson recognized the opportunity that the war offered for mobilizing 'the loyalties and forces of the community in the name of positive and highly constructive ideas' through 'information services— propaganda if you like' and took deliberate advantage of it. On another occasion, Grierson wrote, 'I look on cinema as a pulpit, and use it as a propagandist.'[42] Typical of Grierson's approach was the NFB's *Canada Carries On* and *World in Action* series, narrated by Lorne Green in stentorian voiceover to an original orchestral accompaniment. He managed to persuade the Prime Minister, at least some of the time, of the political advantages of scientific information management. Even after his resignation in 1945, the NFB remained committed to the principles Grierson introduced, and began to use public-opinion polling as a way to find out what information the public needed.[43] Although those involved with the NFB found it difficult to reconcile the manipulation of public opinion with democratic principles, such manipulation continued throughout the war, and the principle of using polls to establish the direction of policy became entrenched.

The CBC spent the war in trouble with the politicians, especially the opposition, over the issue of partisanship. The Corporation recognized that its role, like that of the NFB, was 'to inspire the nation as a whole and every individual to greater effort. To put everyone in the proper frame of mind to accept willingly the inevitable sacrifices involved in the war effort. . . . To invigorate every listener with new courage, mentally and physically.'[44] But government generated many of the programs, and government voices were constantly heard. During the 1942 conscription plebiscite, the government ordered the CBC to broadcast talks by speakers from all political parties—but only if they backed the 'yes' side. The antis (in Quebec) were told to buy time on private stations. In 1942 Arthur Meighen accused the CBC of political favouritism after his Conservatives were denied airtime for addresses from their national convention. Eventually the Tories were given 30 minutes for a speech by their new leader—provided it was 'not of a political nature', but 'made in the spirit of a constructive and positive statement of policy rather than a negative attack upon the policies of other people'.[45] As Meighen told the Winnipeg Tory Convention, 'we . . . cannot be heard and we cannot pay to be heard. . . . The radio of Canada has been for years and is today, and Mr King intends it will continue to be, the effective monop-

■ John Grierson (right), chairman of the Wartime Information Board, meeting with Ralph Foster, head of Graphics, National Film Board of Canada, to examine a series of posters produced by the NFB, February 1944. Ronny Jaques/National Film Board of Canada. Photothèque/LAC, PA-179108.

oly, tool and instrument of a partisan Government headed by himself.'[46] A year later the CBC cancelled John Bracken's report on his first year as party leader, arguing that his speech—which had been submitted in advance—was 'obviously steeped in politics' and was nothing but 'political controversy'.

TECHNOLOGY

Modern war has long provided a spur to technological innovation, both in the creation of new weapons and in their practical deployment. The Depression had seen funding for the National Research Council cut to the bare bones, but the outbreak of war rejuvenated the Council and the scientific community in Canada generally. A homegrown Canadian breakthrough in scientific research was hard to achieve, however. The British and Americans tended not to think of Canada as capable of its own initiatives. The head of the NRC later recalled of the beginning of the war: 'We did recognize . . . that we are not a major power, that our Army, our Navy, and our Air Force cannot go to war as separately trained and equipped units but must fight with and use equipment adopted by our larger Allies.'[47] Moreover, Canada's allies were slow to share their secrets. As a result, Canada found it difficult to engage in innovative work. Much of the best Canadian 'research and development' during the war consisted of taking new technology developed abroad and adapting it to more general applications, as was the case with radar. Canada was active in nuclear research at the Montreal Nuclear Laboratory, but required American approval and British co-operation to achieve anything worthwhile. The Yanks were reluctant to let Canada do anything important, partly for security reasons (they were partly right—there was a spy in Montreal, though the real security leak was at Los Alamos), but mainly because they wanted to keep post-war industrial applications for themselves. The Americans were very nervous about security. D. Martin Kamen, the Canadian-born discoverer of carbon-14, experienced continual persecution as a potential security risk, although nothing was ever proved against him.[48] Eventually Canada was allowed to build a nuclear reactor at Chalk River, which put the nation in on the ground floor of nuclear energy generation. But the successful continuation of Chalk River and the Canadian atomic energy program after the war was a close call, particularly after the British decided to end their collaboration with Canada and go their own way. Canadian post-war nuclear policy was appar-ently first stated by C.D. Howe in the House of Commons when he announced off-the-cuff late in 1945 in question period, 'We have not manu-factured atomic bombs, we have no intention of manufacturing atomic bombs.'[49] But the findings of Canadian nuclear scientists were used by the Americans for the deployment of atomic bombs. Another area where Canada took the lead was in the development of jet engines, which gave it a leg up in jet fighter design in the 1950s. However, too much attention was devoted dur-ing the war to Project Habakkuk, which attempted to develop floating platforms of ice (man-made icebergs) as landing strips for transatlantic aircraft, and not enough to the Weasel, a tracked vehicle for use on snow and ice, developed in Alberta, which might have been developed into something like the snowmobile.

THE HOME FRONT AT WAR

For most Canadians, life during the war was mostly a matter of dull routine. Few people trav-elled far from home, since even those who pos-sessed cars faced shortages of fuel and parts, espe-cially tires. Wartime demands and international dislocations produced other shortages. Silk, for example, was urgently needed for parachutes, so for most of the war women in Canada, as else-where, were unable to obtain silk stockings, and supplies of nylon (invented in 1937) were very limited. Canadians rarely ate out in restaurants, and wartime food, though nutritious, was not very exciting. Between rationing and shortages, it was difficult to put a pleasing meal on the table. Between 1942 and 1944 sugar, tea, coffee, and butter all were rationed (although extra sugar was available for preserving fruit); meat rationing (roughly 1 kg per week was allowed) began in May 1943 and continued until March 1944. By 1944, however, most Canadians had access to a more nutritious diet than either Britons or Americans.[50] Wartime shortages and austerities produced some degree of economic levelling, at least temporarily, because money could not necessarily buy goods and services. Rents were carefully controlled after 1941 as part of the government's anti-inflationary policy, and by 1944 landlords were prevented from evicting well-behaved tenants. At the same time, although rationing worked fairly well, there was a 'black market' in hard-to-obtain articles, including alcoholic beverages and cigars.

Nightly entertainment was provided at home by the radio. Canada got its comedy and drama programs from the American networks, and its news, public affairs, and some of its music from the CBC. According to chief news editor Dan McArthur, the aim of the CBC news service, launched on 1 January 1941, was 'to present the significant news of the day's happenings, in Canada and abroad, in a straightforward manner, without bias or distortion, without tendentious comment, and in a clear and unambiguous style'.[51] The CBC maintained that it did not censor the news. Overseas communiqués were censored 'at source' and reports from enemy sources were presented as 'claims' unless confirmed by Allied sources. Initially, the national news was read at noon and at 11 p.m., but the evening edition was later moved up to 10 p.m. so that workers could get to bed earlier. The national news was read by the same Lorne Greene who narrated the NFB's propaganda films and who acquired the nickname 'the Voice of Doom' for his solemn tones. In 1944 the radio accounts of the D-Day invasion were presented to the nation by a team of newscasters on site, which included Americans, Britons, and Canadians. In the course of the war, Robert Farnon —one of the CBC's most gifted musicians— moved to Britain to lead a swing band made up of Canadian musicians called 'the Canadian Band of the Allied Expeditionary Force', which many British listeners thought better than the Glenn Miller band because of the quality of Farnon's arrangements.

Many Canadians went to the movies once a week. With a few exceptions early in the war, most of the fare at the motion picture theatres was produced by the Hollywood Dream Factory, which was in its prime. Films were made mainly by a small number of large studios with the star system in full flight. Technicolour musicals were easily the most popular fare among the consumers, although a number of war movies were made and exhibited. Except for occasional films produced by the National Film Board and the newsreels, Canadians had little reason to be aware of how heroically their boys were performing overseas.

However buttoned up most of the nation may have been after dark, the city of Montreal truly came to life at night. Prosperity, a general indifference to the war, large numbers of servicemen stationed in or near the city, and abundant alcohol meant that taverns, bars, nightclubs, 'blind pigs' (after-hours drinking joints), gambling places, and dance halls ran full tilt every night. According to one reporter, 'From dusk until the milkman starts his morning rounds, the town glows like a Roman candle.'[52] Jim Coleman of *Maclean's* magazine added:

> Demon rum may be rationed in other sections of the country, but there is enough medicinal spirits in Montreal to float the entire Atlantic Fleet up St Catherine Street. Cigar smokers in other cities may be haunting streetcar stops, waiting for some fortunate [smoker] to discard a butt, but in Montreal you can buy cigars by the handfuls.[53]

The city generated not only a good deal of venereal disease and vice, but also a number of highly successful big bands playing swing music. On any weekend as many as 10 bands could be heard swinging in various venues. Each band contained between 10 and 15 musicians. A few were professionals, but most were young white men who had regular jobs during the week. The bands provided employment for young jazz musicians, and produced two outstanding Canadian jazz performers in Oscar Peterson and Maynard Ferguson.

CANADIAN CULTURE AT WAR

THE WAR AND THE HUMANITIES

Since the 1920s Canadian universities had been under increasing pressure to concentrate on useful vocational subjects such as medicine and engineering rather than the 'frivolous' humanities. Before 1939 the federal government had not been involved in this issue because higher education was a provincial matter. In November 1941, however, Principal W.C. Graham of United College in Winnipeg told his Board of Governors that 'propaganda emanating from Dominion government agencies [was] encouraging students to take technical studies in preference to arts courses'.[54] He was particularly upset by suggestions from one Dominion bureau to the university's senate that the shift take place before students had even matriculated, which he described 'constituting an encroachment upon intellectual freedom' that was 'very close to being fascistic'. By October 1942 rumours were circulating that universities would soon drop arts subjects altogether to concentrate on technical training. President Sidney Smith of the University of Manitoba wrote an open letter to the government, arguing that 'Students graduating in Arts are just as valuable to the war effort as those taking Engineering, Science, Medicine, Dentistry, or any other technical course.'[55] Together, government directives regarding student exemptions from military service and the general climate of opinion led male students to shift from arts courses to 'approved' programs in fields such as science, medicine, and engineering. The federal government classified the universities as essential war industries in 1940 and provided loans for students enrolling in science and engineering. Students in these disciplines were subsequently prohibited from joining the armed forces without permission. Reactions to this aspect of government policy were so strong that Prime Minister King issued a statement early in 1943 that universities should continue to teach arts and that a few students should even be carried through the postgraduate stage in social science disciplines. Even so, enrolment in humanities courses continued to fall for the duration of the war, and most of the remaining students in those courses were women.

THE WAR AND THE MOBILIZATION OF CULTURE

University humanities departments were not the only cultural institutions on which wartime mobilization wreaked serious damage. The budgets of most federally funded cultural institutions, such as the National Gallery, were reduced. The CBC cut back on drama and music programming '[i]n order to provide more time for the Dominion's political leaders to speak to the nation, and for the spokesmen of the Government Departments to describe what is being done to prosecute the war'.[56] And the Carnegie Foundation cut back on its funding for the arts in Canada. Many Canadians felt that cultural activities—like humanities courses—were frivolities that could not be tolerated in the midst of a national emergency. On the other hand, many Canadians began to insist that the arts were, as Ernest MacMillan put it in 1941, 'symbols of the very things our brothers-in-arms are fighting for'.[57] The arts could also be useful in helping to keep up morale and highlighting the purpose of the war to Canadians—above all, the crucial differences between the cultures of the Allies and the enemy.

In 1941 a Conference on Canadian Art held in Kingston made several recommendations for public activity in the arts, including 'machinery for the creation of works of art recording the various phases of the Dominion's war effort'. As a result, a formal War Art Program was organized in 1943 in which 32 Canadian artists, including Lawren Harris, Charles Comfort, Molly Lamb Bobak, and Alex Colville, were employed. Of the more than 1,000 works they produced, many focused on the horrors of battle,[58] but some depicted scenes from everyday life; Bobak, for instance, made a fascinating series of sketches of the informal activities of women in uniform.[59] In addition, the 1941 conference recommended a national exhibition of Canadian drawings at the National Gallery and the establishment of a national organization 'to serve the cultural needs of the Canadian public'. One result was the founding, in the same year and with the support of the Carnegie Foundation, of the Federation of Canadian Artists. As Lawren Harris, its first president, argued, the time had come when 'the artists of this country should contribute consciously and designedly to the growth of a more highly socialized democracy' by forming an organization through which 'to serve the cultural needs of the Canadian public'.[60] The Federation in turn petitioned Ottawa to establish a war artists' program and an all-embracing arts council. In 1944 representatives of 16 major cultural organizations met in Toronto to prepare a single brief to the House of Commons Special Committee on Reconstruction and Re-establishment, pointing out the need for public financial support for the arts in Canada. The 16 groups were heavily concentrated in the visual arts in English-speaking Canada—14 of them based in Toronto—and there were many interests that they did not represent, including those of French Canada, women, popular culture, the media, and the regions.

Although the arts community, at least in English Canada, came out of the war far more conscious of itself than it had been in 1939, it produced no great statements of Canadian patriotism or nationalism; nonetheless, the war was certainly important in the writing of the time. No significant war poetry was written. Nor did Canadian intellectuals produce anything comparable to George Orwell's essay 'The Lion and the Unicorn', attempting to understand why Canadians were fighting or what they were fighting for.

■ Prime Minister Mackenzie King and Louis St Laurent at the San Francisco conference, April–June 1945. Nicholas Morant/National Film Board of Canada/LAC, C-22717.

CANADA AND THE PEACE

When, in 1942, the British began planning for the post-war rehabilitation of Europe, Canada argued that as a major potential contributor to such activity it should have full representation in any formal organization such as the United Nations Relief and Rehabilitation Administration (UNRRA), formed in 1943. In the spring of 1943 External Affairs developed a position on this issue that was to serve as the foundation of Canada's policy regarding international organizations. Of course, Canada had recognized that the Great Powers would make the major decisions until well into the 1960s. Focusing on the principle of 'functionalism', however, Canada argued that authority in world affairs should be neither concentrated in the hands of the superpowers nor equally distributed among all sovereign states; instead, 'representation on international bodies should be determined on a functional basis so as to permit the participation of those countries which have the greatest stake in the particular subject under examination'.[61] In the end, Canada did get to play a direct role in UNRRA—though a smaller one than it had hoped.

The UNRRA debate served as a dress rehearsal for the much more complex business of organizing the United Nations in 1945—what many Canadians considered the country's finest moment in international affairs. Out of Canadian self-interest came an effort to find a middle ground where the new organization could exist without either succumbing to superpower domination or deteriorating into a mere international debating body like the League of Nations. The Canadian delegation at the 1945 San Francisco Conference that drafted the United Nations Charter was a who's who of Canadian mandarins and diplomats, including Mackenzie King himself, External's Escott Reid, Lester Pearson, Louis St Laurent, Hume Wrong, and Louis Rasminsky. The Canadians played a major role in gaining acceptance for the Charter; above all, they fully supported the principle that economic and social issues were no less important than security concerns in establishing a new basis for world peace. Since Canada was one of the few nations in a position to make a financial contribution to global reconstruction, its opinion mattered. Canada was not enthusiastic about special agencies such as the United Nations Educational, Scientific, and Cultural Organization (UNESCO), but it did support the World Health Organization (WHO). Canada also was a principal figure at Geneva in 1947 when 23 nations signed the General Agreement on Tariffs and Trade (GATT).

For the Great Powers, Canada was the largest and most deserving of the 'lesser powers', and to involve her would set a precedent. The USSR, for example, objected to the Commonwealth nations having any independent role unless Soviet republics were similarly recognized. For its part, Britain wanted Commonwealth assistance, but only under the British umbrella; during the Berlin airlift it went so far as to offer to put British insignia on Canadian

planes. Whereas Australia complained bitterly and publicly about this sort of treatment, Canada remained silent, partly because it was committed to facilitating international reconstruction and partly because it was feared that public discussion of the issue might be divisive at home.

The termination of hostilities in Europe finally came on 8 May 1945 (VE Day). Canada made some effort to transfer some of its soldiers to the Far East, but the Americans brought the war with Japan to a screeching halt in August 1945 by dropping atomic bombs on Hiroshima and Nagasaki. Canada played virtually no part in the peace negotiations in either Europe or Asia because it had not been one of the Great Powers that had worked together to direct the war effort. Privately, Prime Minister King complained about being left out of the surrender agreement with Germany, the drafting of a statement ending the war, and the Italian surrender, but in public Canada held to its policy of avoiding public disagreement with the Great Powers. In 1947, however, Canada withdrew troops unilaterally from Europe because of the Dominion's lack of involvement in policy-making.

CONCLUSION

Achieving a balanced judgement on the impact of the war is difficult. On the one hand, there is no denying the damaged psyches, bodies, and families, as well as reduced moral expectations, among those surviving the war. On the other hand, in many ways World War II was, on balance, a unifying and positive experience for most Canadians, especially those on the home front. Full employment, after a decade of Depression, helped. So did the blatant brutality of the enemy's actions over many years. At home, rationing of foods like butter and sugar may actually have improved the diets of many Canadians. Limited leisure time and the absence of consumer goods in the stores, especially durable big-ticket items such as automobiles and household appliances, forced many people to save their money (often in the form of war bonds), which served as a powerful anti-inflationary force. By war's end, however, people had been deferring their expectations for 15 years. The pent-up desire for normal conditions and material comforts was powerful, and Canadians were about to rush joyously into a new era of affluent consumerism. War is, after all, about reclaiming the health of the state.

SHORT BIBLIOGRAPHY

Abella, Irving, and Harold Troper. *None Is Too Many: Canada and the Jews of Europe, 1933–1948*. Toronto, 1982. A brilliant if partisan account of Canadian policy towards the Jews, especially in the years before World War II.

Bothwell, Robert, and William Kilbourne. *C.D. Howe: A Biography*. Toronto, 1979. A first-rate biography of the man who directed the Canadian economy during World War II.

Durflinger, Serge, *Fighting from Home: The Second World War in Verdun, Quebec*. Vancouver, 2006. An important corrective to any picture of Quebec as totally uninterested in the war.

Gilmore, John. *Swinging in Paradise: The Story of Jazz in Montreal*. Toronto, 1988. A loving account of the nightclub scene in the only Canadian city that had one.

Granatstein, J.L. *The Ottawa Men: The Civil Service Mandarins, 1935–1957*. Toronto, 1982. A study of the modern Canadian civil service in its formative years, emphasizing the similarities in the backgrounds of the men.

Hatch, F.J. *Aerodrome of Democracy: Canada and the British Commonwealth Air Training Plan, 1939–1945*. Ottawa, 1983. The story of the BCATP, perhaps the single most important Canadian contribution to the war effort.

Holmes, John. *The Shaping of Peace: Canada and the Search for World Order, 1943–1957*. Toronto, 1979. A masterful analysis of the making of Canadian foreign policy in the crucial years.

Marsh, Leonard. *Report on Social Security for Canada*. Ottawa, 1943, repr. Toronto, 1975. A reprint of the report that in 1943 helped to touch off a new national debate over social insurance.

Neary, Peter. *Newfoundland in the North Atlantic World, 1929–1949*. Kingston and Montreal, 1988. An important study of the history of Newfoundland in the 1930s and 1940s.

Pickersgill, J.M., and D.F. Forster, eds. *The Mackenzie King Record*, vol. 2. Toronto, 1968. An edition of Mackenzie King's wartime diaries published in defiance of his wish that the documents be destroyed.

Pierson, Ruth Roach. *'They're Still Women After All': The Second World War and Canadian Womanhood*. Toronto, 1986. An important survey of the role of women in the war effort.

Stevenson, Michael D. *Canada's Greatest Wartime Muddle: National Selective Service and the Mobilization of Human Resources during World War II*. Montreal and Kingston, 2001. A recent analysis of national planning during World War II, which concludes that it was pretty much a mess.

Sunahara, Ann. *The Politics of Racism*. Toronto, 1981. A study of the wartime evacuation of Japanese Canadians, all the more powerful for its restraint.

Villa, Brian. *Unauthorized Action: Mountbatten and the Dieppe Raid*. Toronto, 1989. A study of the Dieppe raid that implicates Lord Mountbatten in its misguided planning.

STUDY QUESTIONS

1. Why was the Canadian government so reluctant to accept large numbers of Jewish refugees?
2. What role did Canada play in bringing the US into the war?
3. What were the problems with Canada's managed wartime economy?
4. How did conscription become part of the political agenda during the war?
5. Why did support build for a system of social insurance as part of Canada's post-war reconstruction?
6. Did women become fully integrated into the military during the war?
7. Was the evacuation of Japanese Canadians justified?
8. What was the government's record on management of information?
9. What became the pillars of Canadian foreign policy as the war ended?
10. In what ways can the period of World War II be said to be a 'good' one for Canadians?

Writing about War in Canada

■ Perhaps the best way to start a discussion of Canadian writing about war is with two observations. First, Canadians have never been a military people—a fact in which many today take pride. Second, however important the role played by Canada in World Wars I and II, it was a subordinate one, and in both cases military policy and strategy were in the control of other nations. As a result, war has not generally been regarded as a central feature of the Canadian experience, and academic historians have until recently paid relatively little attention to it—although the veterans' lobby has ensured that the record of Canada's soldiers is included in high school curricula.

Another reason Canadians are not more familiar with the nation's experience in war is that the authors of Canada's official and semi-official military histories have focused almost exclusively on the actual fighting, producing dry, often mind-numbing accumulations of detail regarding events that took place far from Canada. These works rarely addressed wartime political issues apart from the need for manpower, which in both wars led directly to the intensely political question of conscription. Military history has always had considerable input from non-academics, in many cases professional military experts, and many practitioners would claim that only those who have been tested in battle are capable of writing about it.

Military history has been expanded in recent years in several important respects. For one thing, far more attention has been paid to those Canadians who served in branches other than the army. Research into the navy, the air force, and even the medical units has shown that some of the most dangerous work was performed by groups that were either officially non-combatant or not officially part of the armed forces, such as the merchant marine. The role of women, particularly in World War II, has also been explored in greater detail recently. If the focus in the past was on combat, historians more recently have looked at the other aspects of military life. As a result we now have a particularly rich social history of life in the trenches during the World War I, and a number of first-person accounts of individuals' experiences, especially between 1939 and 1945. Arguably the most gripping of all the latter is Murray Peden's *A Thousand Shall Fall: A Pilot for 214* (1979), in which the author lays bare his emotions amid the chaos of the Allies' saturation bombing of Germany. In fact, the emotional consequences of battle have attracted considerable attention in recent years. A number of popular historians have found their niches writing about aspects of military history relatively neglected by the academy.

The existing research into the international implications of Canada's wartime experience now seems quite dated. Canada's role at Versailles in 1919 deserves to be reinvestigated, as does its lack of involvement in the post-1945 peace negotiations. Over the past generation neither war has seen much new research from the perspective of relations with the Empire or the United States. The best relatively recent study of Canada, the Empire, and the Great War, for example, is Philip Wigley's *Canada and the Transition to Commonwealth: British–Canadian Relations, 1917–1926* (1977)—now more than 30 years old. Over the years, considerable effort has been devoted to integrating military, diplomatic, and domestic political history in a single account, especially for World War II. The best of these synthetic studies is Charles P. Stacey's *Arms, Men, and Governments: The War Policies of Canada, 1939–1945* (1970). But most syntheses, including Stacey's, do not include social or cultural matters.

Perhaps the most important product of the trend towards a broader perspective has been the recognition that military and political events are only two dimensions of the wartime experience. War affects all aspects of the society, even the culture involved, and a number of Canadian historians have worked to situate war within the overall history and historiography of Canada. No Canadian scholar has done a better job of relating war to a particular segment of the Canadian economy and society than John Thompson in *The Harvests of War: The Prairie West, 1914–1918* (1978), which should serve as a model for other such accounts. Another useful regional study is John Cardoulis's *A Friendly Invasion: The American Military in Newfoundland, 1940–1990* (1990). Other studies have explored the ways in which wartime exigency has been used to justify mistreatment of minority groups. The best-known case of this kind, of course, was the evacuation of the Japanese from the British Columbia coast during World War II. But war has affected civil liberties in other ways as

well, through censorship, surveillance (for example, of labour radicals regarded as dangerous to the state), and various sorts of information management (and mismanagement). War has had implications for the arts, as demonstrated by Maria Tippett in *Art at the Service of War: Canada, Art, and the Great War* (1984), as well as various studies of John Grierson and the National Film Board. John Bryden's *Deadly Enemies: Canada's Secret War, 1937–1947* (1989) showed that restriction on access to certain research materials is one of the reasons why we do not know more about the role of Canadian science during wartime. Governments at war often behave in ways that governments at peace would rather forget, and official Canada has rarely been willing to admit the full truth. Certainly Canadian governments in both wars were not particularly sympathetic to those who opposed them on principle, as Thomas Socknat showed in his study of the peace movement, *Witness against War: Pacifism in Canada 1900–1945* (1987).

One of the most important historiographical developments of recent years has been the recognition of a 'home front' that at first glance may not have appeared to have much to do with the war, but that in fact was intimately connected. Here, too, World War II has done better than its predecessor. Stephen Kimber's *Sailors, Slackers and Blind Pigs: Halifax at War* (2002) has received a lot of attention for its discussion of the Halifax riot of 1945—an orgy of destruction in which bored sailors played an important role—but its real subject is the civilian history of a Canadian city that had a large military population stationed within it. John Gilmore's *Swinging in Paradise: The Story of Jazz in Montreal* (1988) is chiefly about the effects of war on the entertainment scene in Montreal. But the study of the home front is still in its infancy, and there is much work to be done on topics ranging from rationing to popular culture.

As is frequently the case in Canadian historical writing, for neither world war is there a modern full-length study that synthesizes the latest literature and integrates military, political, international, social, economic, and cultural aspects in a single volume.

☐ Highway 400 near Barrie, Ont., in the 1960s. In the background is Lake Simcoe. Archives of Ontario, RG65-35-1, 2-J-965.

PART FOUR

■ 1946–1972

■ The quarter-century that followed 1945 was a period of unparalleled prosperity for Canada. Production and consumption rose steadily, fuelled in part by bottled-up consumer demand and in part by the military needs of the Cold War. Economic policy was based on the model developed by John Maynard Keynes, who argued that to maintain full employment—the mark of a successful economy—government should spend money on public works. Labour relations were improved by building trade unions into the system, and both inflation and unemployment remained low, at least until the late 1960s.

The end of the war was the signal for rapid population growth, partly through natural increase (the baby boom) and partly through immigration, at first mainly of refugees and displaced persons from Europe. The expanding population required new housing, roads, and schools. Increasing prosperity enabled more and more Canadians to move from the cities into the spreading suburbs. More than a geographical location, suburbia was a way of life centred on material comfort and an ideal of the family—including the new age group known as 'teenagers'—encouraged by the media.

Federal politics was dominated by the Liberal Party for all but the six years of John Diefenbaker's Tory government. Among the many new or expanded social programs supported by all parties were a pension scheme and universal health care. The public service burgeoned. Huge strides were made in the area of culture, with governments developing deliberate cultural policies and helping to create an infrastructure that eventually would produce world-class artists in various fields. At the same time, by the mid-1960s things were becoming more complicated on the political, constitutional, and social fronts. With the Quiet Revolution in Quebec came a new sense of nationalism and demands for independence for that province. However, English Canada experienced an almost unheralded 'revolution' of its own, which saw it cut most of its ancient ties with the British Empire and achieve a sense of nationalism of its own. This accomplishment mixed well with Ottawa's efforts to satisfy Quebec without offending the other provinces, which had their own ideas for constitutional reform. Meanwhile, other groups—women, First Nations, blacks, gay people—were beginning to express their own aspirations for a more equal part in the nation's life.

CHAPTER THIRTEEN

■ Canada and the World, 1946–1972

■ Soon after the end of World War II, Canadians faced the world with a new identity. On 22 October 1945, a bill was introduced into Parliament redefining nationality and the process of naturalization. Paul Martin, the minister who introduced it, said at the time:

> For the national unity of Canada and for the future and greatness of this country it is felt to be of utmost importance that all of us, new Canadians and old, have a consciousness of a common purpose and common interests as Canadians; that all of us are able to say with pride and say with meaning: 'I am a Canadian citizen.'[1]

The Act was passed on 27 June 1946 and became law on 1 January 1947. The Canadian Citizenship Act created a class of Canadian citizenship separate from that of Great Britain. The new citizenship could be vested on immigrants, non-Canadian British subjects living in Canada for more than five years, and non-Canadian women who had moved to Canada and married Canadian citizens. It would take some years to clean up all the loopholes, but it was a good start.

In retrospect, we can see the new Citizenship Act as a symbol and marker of one of the major changes, executed in incremental pieces, of the post-war period in Canada: the Canadi-anization of the symbols of sovereignty and the accompanying growth in Canadian national sentiment and identity, especially in English-speaking Canada. It was followed two years later by the elimination of judicial appeals to the British Privy Council, in 1952 by the appointment of the first native-born Governor General, and in 1960 by the passage of a Bill of Rights.

Although Canada would gradually eliminate the symbols of historic colonialism after 1945, by the end of World War II the country was probably too deeply enmeshed with the United States ever to cast its ties aside. Great Britain was not likely to provide much of a counterweight, having only barely survived the war financially itself; as one British official laconically explained earlier in the war, 'Boys, Britain's broke.'[2] Canadian economic policy during the war had been to avoid choosing between the US and UK, although Ottawa found Britain's 'prolific . . . requests on Canada' annoying in light of its 'much less prolific . . . appreciation of what we have done'.[3] Canada tried to help Britain recover something of its international economic position after the war, chiefly to avoid a total reliance on bilateral trade with the US. 'Our hope of continuing markets in the U.K. lies in the speedy re-building of U.K. export potential and in a return to multilateral trade', explained one External official in 1946.[4]

TIMELINE

1945

Igor Gouzenko defects in Ottawa.

1946

Canada sells wheat to Britain at bargain prices.

1947

Canada supports the partition of Palestine. New Citizenship Act becomes law.

1948

Canada allowed to participate in Marshall Plan, but rejects North American free trade.

1949

Canada takes lead in creation of NATO.

1950

Korean conflict begins.

1954

Canada becomes involved in Indochina as one of three members of International Commission for Supervision and Control.

1955

DEW Line established in Canadian North.

1957

L.B. Pearson wins Nobel Peace Prize. Herbert Norman commits suicide in Cairo. Diefenbaker government agrees to NORAD.

1959

Diefenbaker terminates Avro Arrow project.

1963

Diefenbaker cabinet fractures over Bomarc missiles.

1965

Pearson advocates a pause in the US bombing of Vietnam.

1968

Trudeau tries to reinvigorate Canadian foreign policy.

1972

Trudeau government proposes 'Third Option'.

But the American economy was seductive, and Canadian involvement in the Cold War was probably inescapable. Canada attempted to balance the pull into the American orbit with an international policy of multilateralism, with varying degrees of success.[5]

THE COLD WAR

The alliance between the Soviet Union and the Western democracies had never been comfortable. There were numerous signs in the latter years of the war that the USSR and the US were the emerging world superpowers, each eager to stake out as large a sphere of influence as it could. There were equally strong signs that the British and the French were simply not strong enough any more to count for much, yet they were satisfied to be allowed to participate in some of the major decisions. As we saw earlier, countries like Canada were virtually excluded from the peacemaking process and most of the other significant diplomatic manoeuvring of the post-war years. Canada attempted to remain clear of commitments in cases where it had no part in the decision-making process, such as the occupation of Germany or the Berlin blockade. As a result of the war, Canada had substantially

PAUL MARTIN SR ON THE CITIZENSHIP ACT

In his memoirs, Paul Martin Sr described the parliamentary response to the Canadian Citizenship Act in 1946.

John Diefenbaker, the first speaker for the Conservative Party, agreed . . . with my claim that the bill symbolized our aspirations as a nation. He added that it had achieved a long dream of his. However, he proposed that, a citizenship act should be followed by a bill of rights. Diefenbaker criticized the section of the bill requiring a British subject from commonwealth countries to file a notice of intention with the citizenship court in the same way as others before becoming a citizen. Would, he asked, this provision not strike at the unity of British citizenship? I said that it would not.

The House divided on the bill much as I had expected. A substantial number of members worried that commonwealth relationships would deteriorate in the wake of the act. Diefenbaker's unjustified objection that it would split the commonwealth was taken over further by his colleagues such as Tommy Church, an old-style imperialist, who took a determined stand against it. On the other hand, Liguori Lacombe, MP for Laval-Deux-Montagnes, expressed the French nationalist position that urged the elimination of Canadians' status as British subjects in order to eradicate all evidence of inferiority. . . .

During the debate on second reading,

Diefenbaker reopened the question of a bill of rights and offered an amendment to the effect that a certificate of citizenship should be deemed to include certain rights (freedom of religion, freedom of speech, and the right to peaceable assembly; no suspension of *habeas corpus* except by parliament, and no compulsion to give evidence before any tribunal in the absence of counsel or other safeguards). This amendment, I argued, was unacceptable, since the law of the land included these rights in the common law, the Magna Carta, and the legal system. No act of one parliament could limit the freedom of action of its successors, and infringements of rights could be taken pursuant to the authority of any parliament. Therefore, the only means of providing greater guarantees than currently existed would be to enact an organic law that could not be changed by the Canadian parliament; this type of law did not exist in the British system of government. . . . A fundamental constitutional departure, I contended, should not be taken in a section of an act that prescribes conditions for the issuance of citizenship certificates; if anywhere, it should be in a bill by itself.

Diefenbaker's argument, however, gained considerable public support.

SOURCE: Paul Martin, *A Very Public Life*, vol. 1, *Far From Home* (Ottawa: Deneau, 1983), 450–1.

increased its overseas diplomatic contacts, with 25 posts abroad in 1944 and 36 by 1947, but its international position had hardly improved at all. Towards the close of the war Canada tried to establish some diplomatic distance from the Americans and their continual arm-wrestling

with the Russians. But the Gouzenko affair made it difficult for Ottawa to remain sympathetic with the Russians, and probably crystallized Canadian public opinion at the same time. The Gouzenko business (and the larger Cold War) also fit perfectly into the new Canadian nationalism, creat-

IGOR GOUZENKO

Igor Gouzenko was born in Rogachov, USSR, in 1919, in the turbulent aftermath of the Russian Revolution. In 1943 he was posted with his wife and son to the Soviet embassy in Ottawa, where—as a secretary, interpreter, and cipher clerk under the head of Soviet military intelligence in Canada—he had access to much specialized information. In August 1945 Gouzenko was recalled to the Soviet Union, but he and his wife already had determined to defect. Realizing that his reception by the Canadian authorities would be eased if he could provide secret documentation of some value to the West, on the evening of 5 September he returned to his office at the embassy and removed a collection of 109 documents that he had previously taken from the files. Arranging the papers around his body, he managed to leave the embassy building without detection and go to the *Ottawa Journal*, where the night editor advised him to take the documents to the RCMP. But when he did so, he was told to come back in the morning. The next day the entire Gouzenko family appeared at the Justice Building in Ottawa, but they were turned away. When they tried again at the *Ottawa Journal*, they were told politely that 'Nobody wants to say anything but nice things about Stalin these days.' Gouzenko went again to the Justice Building, then tried the Crown Attorney's office, where the family was met with sympathy but no assistance. Finally, they returned to their apartment, where Gouzenko managed to speak to an RCMP sergeant who was a neighbour. The family remained safely hidden in an adjacent apartment when a party from the Soviet embassy broke into their old apartment, where they were discovered by the police. Gouzenko himself was taken eventually to RCMP headquarters.

Meanwhile, his visit to the Justice Building was brought to the attention of Prime Minister Mackenzie King, who refused to deal with the mat-

■ Igor Gouzenko with a copy of his novel *The Fall of a Titan*, 15 October 1954. *The Gazette* (Montreal) LAC, PA-129625.

ter because it could jeopardize Canadian–Soviet relations. Interrogation by the RCMP indicated that Gouzenko's incredible stories were true. A spy ring was in operation in Canada. Prime Minister King delayed for five months before appointing a Royal Commission that took detailed evidence from Gouzenko and found it credible. The Canadian authorities gave Gouzenko a new identity, and thereafter when he appeared in public he wore a hood over his face.

Gouzenko's revelations did not always lead to

successful prosecutions. A few Canadians were convicted of spying, but no great fifth column was ever uncovered in Canada. He received little or no money from the Canadian government, but his disclosures in *Cosmopolitan Magazine* (February 1947) and his autobiography, *This Was My Choice*, (1948) made him a rich man. Unfortunately, despite the establishment of a trust fund, Gouzenko was not able to hold on to his wealth and was eventually reduced to soliciting interviews from the media to earn money. In 1954 he was interviewed by an American congressional subcommittee, and in the same year a novel was published under his name describing life in Stalinist Russia. Entitled *The Fall of a Titan*, it won the Governor General's Award for 1954. The former spy spent his later years living on a tax-free pension of just over $1,000 a month. He died in 1982, apparently of natural causes.

ing as it did the image of a nation besieged by foreign enemies, which would have to fight to preserve its freedoms.

THE GOUZENKO AFFAIR

Igor Gouzenko was an obscure cipher clerk in the Russian embassy in Ottawa in September 1945 when he defected, taking to the RCMP material that demonstrated how the USSR had organized a spy ring in Canada during the war.[6] A handful of Canadians had been recruited to provide the USSR with classified information from several government departments (including the National Film Board), which had little top-secret intelligence to disclose. From today's perspective, the revelations, made public in 1946, seem quite tame and unsurprising.[7] We now understand that foreign nations routinely 'spy' (the euphemism is 'collect intelligence') through their overseas embassies and that, inevitably, a few local individuals can be persuaded to pass on classified data, for either ideological or financial reasons. But at the time, Gouzenko's information and the subsequent arrests of Canadian citizens (including Fred Rose, a Labour Progressive member of Parliament from Montreal) were shocking to naive Canadians. Canada did not exchange ambassadors with the USSR again until after 1953, and in 1946 public opinion polls indicated that Canadians were far more willing than people in other nations to believe that the USSR sought to dominate the world. The Gouzenko affair also sent shock waves across the Western world, for as other nations pursued loose ends from his files it became apparent that spying had not been confined to Canada. The fact that some American citizens actually were prepared to assist a foreign power, often for ideological reasons, was one of the reasons behind the Communist 'witch hunts' in the US in the late 1940s and early 1950s.

One by-product of the Gouzenko affair was the recognition that the tight security concerning atomic research carried out in Montreal in connection with 'Project Manhattan'—the research that led to the creation of the atomic bombs dropped on Hiroshima and Nagasaki—had been breached. When the Soviets tested their own atomic bomb, in 1949, it became clear that the USSR had received most of the project's findings. As a result, the Americans became even more secretive and possessive about their atomic energy research, and while the Canadian government complained about this policy, it went along because it 'had no plans for military use of atomic energy'.[8] But Soviet nuclear capability meant that Canada was now geographically sandwiched between the two great superpowers that possessed atomic bombs capable of overwhelming destructive force. Neutrality was impossible, and so Canada was increasingly pushed into becoming a 'Cold Warrior', often having to choose between the US and the UK in the years immediately after the war. On the other hand, as many came gradually to recognize, the presence of two great powers holding a monopoly of nuclear bombs produced a 'balance of terror', in which neither combatant wanted to take the next step. One downside of the standoff was that both sides kept seeking comparative technological advantage, at considerable expense. Inevitably, an arms race ensued. Another downside was that other advanced industrial nations, such as France and Britain, managed to create their own bombs and become members of the nuclear club. Diplomats consoled themselves with the thought that France and Britain were responsible members of the world community. What would happen when one of the world's 'rogue states'—and there were many after the war—acquired nuclear capability? The only deterrent was the expense of the technology.

Until at least the late 1960s, the Soviet Union seemed a perfect example of a successful socialist economy. Only after its ignominious collapse years later did most observers come to appreciate fully the true bases of Russia's success after the war. It had plundered the defeated Germans for materials and technology in 1945, and it systematically looted the economies of the Eastern bloc nations for years thereafter. It had devastated its own natural resource base, particularly in Siberia, in its rush to achieve full industrialization. Moreover, while political repression kept the Soviet people relatively quiescent, the deferral of consumer expectations and the preaching of a warlike situation against the West could work for only so long.

FROM THE BRITISH EMPIRE TO THE AMERICAN EMPIRE

Inevitably, economic and diplomatic considerations impelled Canada in the direction of the US. Canada did its best to trade with the UK, selling wheat there in 1946 at bargain prices in a four-year contract that considerably disadvantaged Canadian farmers. But Britain had to be kept afloat as the only counterbalance to the

Americans. In late 1947, for example, the US and UK took diametrically opposed positions for and against the partitioning of Palestine to create the state of Israel. Canada supported partition, less to please the Americans than because it believed that only partition would be supported at the United Nations, and the UN had to be successful in its first serious international test. However, when the UN failed to achieve a peaceful accommodation, Mackenzie King returned Canada to a position closer to that of the British, who were not enthusiastic about the creation of the state of Israel. Canada quickly dropped any notion of an independent position on Palestine for the sake of unity within the North Atlantic Triangle and initially withheld recognition of the new state, although it eventually relented. The case of Israel is a perfect example of how difficult it was for Canada to establish a truly independent foreign policy, given the differences between its senior partners.[9]

As C.D. Howe, among others, had predicted, years of consumer deprivation had produced so much pent-up demand that Canadian industry alone could not meet it. But the Canadian exchange position in a world dominated by the American dollar was weak, and in 1947 the nation was forced to put strict controls on imports. Howe even attempted to limit Hollywood's free access to the Canadian market in an effort to preserve precious dollars. When, early in 1948, the American Congress approved the Marshall Plan, by which the US proposed to rebuild war-torn Europe with unrestricted gifts of money and goods, Canada was forced to do something. If the reconstruction of Europe was achieved solely through American money, Canadian trade there would shrink to nothing. Canada had no desire to provide any of the financial assistance, arguing that it was already doing its share in helping out the British. What it wanted was market access into the American program, permission for Europe to use the American money to buy Canadian goods. The US readily agreed, for the process further integrated

Canada into the North American economy dominated by the US.

The Canadian government, thanks to Mackenzie King's forebodings, also rejected a scheme initiated by the Americans for a return to the complete economic integration of wartime. This proposal was discussed by leading civil servants on both sides of the border, including Lester Pearson.[10] One American official described these free trade discussions as 'a unique opportunity of promoting the most efficient utilization of the resources of the North American continent and knitting the two countries together—an objective of United States foreign policy since the founding of the Republic'.[11] Canadian financial mandarins were equally enthusiastic, for by freeing itself from dependence on the 'uncertain markets of Europe', Canada would 'maintain, as far as could be maintained, the prosperity of this country'.[12] King did not think Canada was ready for peacetime 'reciprocity', and he was probably right. Nevertheless, after 1948 Canada and the US were closer economic partners than ever before because the bulk of Canada's trade was with the US, which increasingly was investing in Canadian industry and natural resources.

NATO

In 1948, at about the same time that the Finance people were in Washington discussing free trade, the diplomats were meeting there to talk about North American security. Neither Canadian contingent was aware of the other's presence until the Prime Minister saw in North Atlantic security a way out of continental free trade. King observed, 'I felt trade proposals might be made to fit as it were into the larger Atlantic Pact.' He elaborated:

> if, for example, the Atlantic Security Pact were agreed upon and were brought before Parliament and . . . passed as it certainly would be, we might immediately follow thereafter with trade agreement as being something which still further

helped to further the object of the Pact, namely, the removal of restrictions to trade within the area arranged by the Pact.[13]

Thus, by one of those cruel ironies that have always governed Canadian–American relations, Canada took the initiative in the creation of the North Atlantic Treaty Organization (NATO), which the Americans would dominate for decades. As Canada saw matters at the time, a security treaty would not only deflect reciprocity, but as a multilateral arrangement might provide an international counterbalance against American military domination of Cold War defence. According to Lester Pearson's memorandum to the Prime Minister, dated 1 June 1948, 'the joint planning of the defence of North America would fall into place as part of a larger whole and the difficulties arising in Canada from the fear of invasion of Canadian sovereignty by the United States would be diminished.'[14] Since King 'felt sure that the long objective of the Americans was to control this Continent . . . [and] to get Canada under their aegis', Pearson's argument was compelling.[15] With the British in earlier days and now with the Americans, Canadian policy was always to involve as many other nations as possible in international agreements, on the grounds that such multilateralism helped to correct the substantial imbalance that Canada would experience in a bilateral arrangement with an overly powerful partner.

In the case of North Atlantic security, the US was not so enthusiastic about the notion of a multilateral arrangement. Some of the American opponents of NATO argued that the American Senate (which had to approve all foreign treaties) would never accept it, while others (led by George Kennan and Charles 'Chip' Bohlen) insisted that it was not only a step unprecedented in American history but one that would draw Soviet attention to the weakness of Atlantic defences, while foreclosing on an unforeseeable future. But Canadian negotiators, motivated both by fear for Canadian sovereignty and by a desire to regularize the North Atlantic partnerships, pressed their case. From the Canadian perspective, the more nations were involved, the better; and there was even talk in Ottawa about admitting non-Atlantic members of the Commonwealth. Escott Reid, the deputy under the Secretary of State for External Affairs, whose vision of the treaty was the most generous, also insisted that it should transcend purely military arrangements and encompass social and economic issues as well, representing a 'spiritual mobilization' of the Western democracies.[16] Reid was unable to gain complete support for his views, even in Canadian circles, but the final treaty did pay lip service to Canada's insistence on what Reid later described as 'provisions on economic and social co-operation and on the promotion of democracy'.[17] From the perspective of the US, however, what mattered were the treaty's military and security provisions, particularly the centralization of command under what inevitably had to be an American general. The regular meeting of the North Atlantic Council, for which Canadians and others held such high hopes, quickly turned into a perfunctory diplomatic event.[18] Though Canada may not have had much choice, it had created and joined an American-controlled alliance. Perhaps symbolically, the United States Marine Band that serenaded the Washington signing ceremony for the North Atlantic Treaty in April 1949 played 'It Ain't Necessarily So' and 'I Got Plenty of Nothin' from George Gershwin's *Porgy and Bess*. Pearson found the choices 'regrettable', but they aptly summarized what Canada got from its handiwork.[19]

THE SEARCH FOR MIDDLE-POWER STATUS

THE KOREAN WAR

By the time NATO was established in 1949, the Cold War had spread out of Europe into Asia, where the pro-American National government of

China had plainly been superseded by a Communist government headed by Chou En-Lai. Communists had made great gains in many parts of Asia in the period between the defeat of Japan and the re-establishment of 'legitimate'— often European colonial—governments, usually by speaking up for national aspirations. In the process, places like Indochina and Korea had been partitioned between Communist and other regimes. The US always saw the Communist governments as mere extensions of international Communism emanating from the USSR, ignoring the nationalistic element that to other observers —including Canadians—appeared to be just as fundamental to them as their Marxist aspirations. The US refused to recognize any of these governments as legitimate and consistently vetoed their gaining seats at the United Nations. In 1950 Canada was on the verge of some form of recognition of the People's Republic of China—despite American objections—when North Korea invaded American-controlled South Korea.

The Korean crisis was a serious challenge to Canada's international aspirations. The Americans took advantage of a Soviet boycott of the UN Security Council to invoke the doctrine of collective security. The Council recommended that its member nations assist the Republic of Korea (i.e., South Korea) militarily, thus supporting the unilateral armed intervention already undertaken by the United States by order of President Harry S. Truman. The Canadian government was in a quandary. It had not yet really re-established its military forces after the post-war demobilization, and had never been enthusiastic about the principle of automatic collective security on which the Americans insisted. A collective UN response to most international crises certainly seemed unlikely. But the Americans expected Canadian support for the UN forces under General Douglas MacArthur, and public opinion in Canada agreed. When Ottawa offered three destroyers, calling such aid 'no mere token', one American official allegedly commented, 'Okay, let's call it three tokens.'[20] Canada continued to

■ Sherman tanks of B Squadron, Lord Strathcona's Horse, moving up a path by the Imjin River in Korea in 1952. CP/LAC.

drag its heels while desperately seeking 10,000 volunteers for a 'Canadian Army Special Force' that in the end included more than 3,000 from Quebec. Eventually 20,000 Canadians served in Korea, with 1,557 casualties and 312 fatalities.[21]

While Canada recruited and trained its troops, events in Korea took a series of startling turns. The allied army—mainly Americans and South Koreans, assisted by a single British brigade—commanded by MacArthur broke out of a defensive position and headed north across the 38th parallel to the Yalu River. There they unexpectedly met Chinese 'volunteers' who pushed the allies southward. The contending forces surged back and forth across the 38th parallel for months. When, to bring the war to a quick end, MacArthur advocated the use of

nuclear weapons if necessary, President Truman ordered him home, where he delivered his famous 'Old Soldiers Never Die' address to the American Congress. Canada had always favoured an armistice, on the grounds that the UN had made its point about aggression, and the intervention of China only strengthened the case for an end to the fighting. While Canadian diplomats hunted for a way to make peace, Canadian–American relations became badly strained. The key show of strength came over an American resolution in the UN condemning the Chinese as aggressors, and in the end—despite statements of reservations—Canada voted for it. In private Canada continued to disagree with the Americans about the eventual peace settlement, but in public it always ended up supporting them.

Korea offered many lessons to Canadian policy-makers, but above all it added to the pressure to build up the nation's military forces and rearm them appropriately. By 1953, the defence budget stood at nearly $2 billion, up tenfold since 1947. Public opinion in the 1950s consistently supported rearmament, and there were few internal critics of the policy in those years. When C.D. Howe presented his Defence Production Bill of 1951—which gave the governor-in-council extraordinary powers 'to control and regulate the production, processing, distribution, acquisition, disposition, or use of materials, or the supply or use of services deemed essential for war purposes'—opposition was directed more to Howe's arrogance than to the principle, and the bill passed easily after some unseemly exchanges in the House of Commons.[22]

PEACEKEEPING AND MIDDLE-POWER STATUS

The policy-makers at External Affairs did their best to create the semblance of an autonomous international presence, mainly through the development of a 'peacekeeping' role for Canada in Indochina and the Middle East. For the most part, that role involved small numbers of well-prepared and well-equipped Canadian soldiers acting for supervisory agencies set up internationally to monitor local conditions in particularly troubled corners of the world. The nation's standing as a peacekeeper reached its high point in 1957, when External Affairs Minister Lester B. Pearson won the Nobel Peace Prize for his proposal to the UN General Assembly that it create a special Emergency Force to supervise the end of hostilities during the complex Suez crisis of 1956. The tribute was well deserved, not only for that specific plan but also for the ingenious negotiations that permitted Britain and France to back out of the impossible situation resulting from their ill-conceived invasion of Egypt to protect the Suez Canal. Pearson had effectively created the modern concept of 'peacekeeping' and the

■ Mr and Mrs Lester B. Pearson receiving the Nobel Peace Prize, 1957. Duncan Cameron/LAC, C-094168.

machinery for it. That his efforts had the wholehearted support and approval of the US was not an unimportant factor in their success, although the British and French were equally grateful for the Canadian initiative, which was finally in Canada's best interest as well, because it was so necessary to maintaining the North Atlantic Alliance and the cause of international peace.

One of the many consequences of the ill-conceived Anglo-French intervention in Suez was the final dismantling of the British Empire. One British response to Suez in 1957 was a drastic reduction in military manpower and the testing of Britain's first thermonuclear bomb as an alternate defence. Another was an active policy of 'decolonization'. Although India and Pakistan had achieved independence in 1947, between 1957 and 1963 more than 20 colonies and protectorates gained independence, and another half-dozen were scheduled for decolonization whether they were 'ready' for it or not. Even had Canada wished to continue as a part of the British Empire, by 1960 there was no longer any significant Empire left to belong to.

Without a 'British Empire' as a historic lifeline to the past, Canadian governments soon enough discovered that being a nation of some consequence on the global stage brought with it certain consequences. Some of these consequences related to having to bow to the expectations of those (i.e., the Americans) who carried the biggest stick; others were tragic. One morning in April 1957 the Canadian ambassador to Egypt, Egerton Herbert Norman, took the elevator to the top storey of a Cairo apartment building, removed his glasses and wrist watch, and jumped, landing on the pavement far below. A friend of Mike Pearson and a well-known radical, Norman had been recruited into the Communist Party at Cambridge in the 1930s. He subsequently became Canada's leading Far Eastern specialist and in 1950 was actually suggested by Pearson as the liaison officer between the intelligence units of Canada and the US. Almost inevitably, Norman's name had come up in American investigations into Communists and Communist sympathizers in the US, and he was already of considerable interest to the FBI. The RCMP in 1950 gave Norman a top security clearance, but from the American perspective his earlier involvement with the Communist Party would be impossible to overcome, especially after the defections of fellow student Communists Guy Burgess and Donald Maclean in 1951. In 1957 a US Senate Subcommittee on Internal Security brought Norman under its scrutiny as a suspected 'mole'. The truth of the American suspicions about Norman's underground allegiances—many of which were shared by Britain's MI5—will probably never be established, and two full-scale studies of his life have come to diametrically opposed conclusions.[23] However, these studies agreed that Mike Pearson protected

his friend during his lifetime. The Norman affair remains the subject of controversy today. A National Film Board film broadcast on CBC television in the summer of 2000 presented Norman as an innocent victim of a witch hunt. The more recent CBC series *The Peoples of Canada* added that Pearson himself was regarded with suspicion by the US Congress.

By 1957 Canada had earned its place among the 'middle powers'—an epithet that became popular among aspiring Canadian international relations specialists. The trouble with being a middle power, of course, was that the role required a large and well-equipped military force, which was expensive. Here the story of the Avro Arrow is instructive. A.V. Roe Canada had developed an all-Canadian supersonic fighter plane at Malton, Ontario, that was brilliantly designed for Canadian conditions and needs, but was insufficiently specialized to meet the requirements of larger air forces, particularly that of the US. A.V. Roe had considerable early success with the Avro CF-100 Canuck, the first jet fighter designed and built in Canada, initially flown in 1950 and used extensively by NATO for 10 years. The Arrow, like the CF-100, was an all-purpose fighter, with advanced fire-control and missile systems. The success of the Arrow depended on the production of 600 aircraft, which would reduce the cost to $2 million each. But there were not enough orders, especially from the Americans, who had competitive airplanes that were more specialized and were also promoting a new missile system. Its very complexity made the Arrow unsuitable for military reservists to fly, and even the RCAF cut back on its orders. The decision of the Diefenbaker government to scrap the Arrow, in February 1959, was very unpopular at the time—and in later years, particularly in 1961, when the government was forced to purchase inferior American aircraft (with subcontracting) to handle northern defence. The debate on the Diefenbaker decision has continued for decades, both in the media and in the historical literature, some seeing it as a financial necessity and others as a disaster for the nationalist cause, which in many ways it was.[24] It is quite likely, however, that the decision was never really in Canada's control at all.

Pearson had conducted his triumphant negotiations to resolve the Suez crisis at the tail end of the Liberal Party's 20-year dominance of the federal government, including the leading public service officials within External Affairs. After Suez, Canada's status as a middle power came increasingly into question. Both the world and the Canadian–American relationship gradually changed after 1957.

THE RETREAT FROM INTERNATIONALISM

Part of the change in Canada's status was a result of technology. When, in 1953, the USSR added a hydrogen bomb to its nuclear arsenal, Canadians became even more conscious than before that their nation was on the flight path between the two nuclear giants and adjacent to many military targets in the US. Canada expanded the RCAF and began development of the famed CF-105 (the Avro Arrow). The US pushed for increased electronic surveillance in the Arctic, and in 1955 Canada agreed to allow the Americans to construct at their expense a series of northern radar posts called the Distant Early Warning (DEW) Line, which greatly altered the lives of Aboriginal residents of the North. The Americans also began pressing for an integrated bilateral air defence system, the North American Air Defence Command (NORAD), which the Diefenbaker government agreed to soon after taking office in 1957.

THE DIEFENBAKER DISASTERS

John Diefenbaker was, at once, a Cold Warrior and a Canadian nationalist, holding both positions with unquestioned moral fervour and integrity. Unfortunately, the two were mutually contradictory, and the Diefenbaker governments

■ An artist's drawing of the CF 105 Avro Arrow. LAC, PA-111546.

of 1957–63 never succeeded in sorting them out. As a result, Diefenbaker found himself involved in an ongoing series of dilemmas, particularly involving Canadian–American defence arrangements. His administration consistently 'sold out' the big principles to the Americans without much argument, and then balked over the details and consequences. American President John F. Kennedy once referred to the 'Chief' as one of the few men he had ever despised.[25]

Three related issues—the decision to scrap the Avro Arrow, the acceptance of American Bomarc missiles on Canadian soil, and the government's reaction to the Cuban Missile Crisis of 1962—illustrate Diefenbaker's approach. When he terminated the Arrow project early in 1959, he did so for the best of fiscal reasons. The plane had no prospective international market and it had turned out to be far more expensive to develop than expected—unnecessarily expensive for Canada's needs, unless it truly wanted an air arm independent of the Americans. The Prime Minister explained his decision in terms of changing military technology and strategy. An

US State Department
Meeting re Herbert Norman

On 20 March 1957 several lawyers for the Senate Subcommittee on Internal Security and State Department officials discussed the Norman case. Following is an excerpt from the minutes of the meeting.

O'CONNOR [Deputy Assistant Secretary of State for Congressional Relations, State Department]: Canada has taken the view for the last six years or so that our State Department should pass on their views to the Canadian Government. Our interest here is to work out a plan for State and the Subcommittee to cooperate in this. State should get the first crack at this kind of testimony which is derogatory information against foreign officials of a friendly government.

MORRIS [Counsel of the Senate Subcommittee on Internal Security]: Canada knew about our testimony concerning Norman and there has been an exchange of information. (Morris then read a secret memorandum to the group and subsequently read Elizabeth Bentley's testimony of August 14 1951 concerning [Lester] Pearson.) Bentley's testimony was executive [session testimony, behind closed doors]. What would you do with this? Release it?

O'CONNOR: I am sure that would blow us out of the water on our northern border. The release of that kind of testimony would get us into a terrific jam with our Canadian friends. Before you do anything with it, give our top people a chance to talk it over with the Chairman [of the Senate Judiciary Committee].

MORRIS: The second thing. Could you check with the FBI on the truth and the accuracy of our evidence on Norman?

O'CONNOR: The information furnished us recently from the FBI is nothing more than you have.

MORRIS: The third thing. What do you suggest about how to protect the United States security against Norman? The FBI knew about Hiss and Fuchs but nothing happened until it was brought out. In this case

Norman and Emmerson had what looked to us like an emergency meeting [in Beirut] and they got together. We still do not know what happened. Emmerson wants to change his testimony. What do we do about it? You tell us.

O'CONNOR: Not about our guy (Norman).

MORRIS: About Norman too. . . .

O'CONNOR: I don't know what liaison we have with security organizations of [the] Canadian Government. . . .

MORRIS: We are not interested in Canadian security. Our concern is American security. . . . What about Burgess and Maclean? Should we clear through the British Government? What is the standard?

O'CONNOR: I think what we are talking about are friendly allied governments. This is probably a test case for allied governments. . . .

CARTWRIGHT [Deputy Administrator, Bureau of Security and Counselor Affairs, State Department]: Is there any element in the Canadian Government which would be more sympathetic?

LISTER [Deputy Director, British, Commonwealth, and North European Affairs, State Department]: Pearson is a hero. Right now he is cooperating to the fullest extent with our government in defense contracts.

MORRIS: This is just what I mean. Look at the situation. There are many Americans frightened about Pearson. There are a good many Canadians in the US who are pro-Communists. Why, Pearson has even objected to Americans employed in the UN when they were called before the Subcommittee during our UN hearings.

O'CONNOR: Why can't we delete some of the materials from the executive session if it is published?

SOURCE: James Barros, *No Sense of Evil: Espionage, the Case of Herbert Norman* (Toronto, 1986), Appendix C, 203–6.

■ DEW Line, Pelly Bay, c. 1960. Photo by Brian (Simon) Jeffrey.

aircraft to intercept bombers would soon be obsolete, said Dief, and what Canada needed were missiles, obtainable from the American military-industrial complex. (Canada still needed some fighters, and settled for some very old F-101 Voodoos from the United States). By surrendering Canada's technological breakthrough in big military rearmament in return for an agreement whereby parts of equipment purchased by Canada from the American defence industry would be assembled in Canada, Diefenbaker further integrated the two nations both economically and militarily.

The Bomarc-B missile that Canada bought from the US was armed with a nuclear warhead, but it was Canada's policy that nuclear warheads ought not to be stationed on its territory. Diefenbaker thus refused to allow the Bomarcs to be properly armed, erroneously insisting that they could be equipped with non-nuclear warheads and still be effective. The question of military integration came to a head in 1962, after President Kennedy confronted the USSR over its installation of missile bases in Cuba. As Soviet ships carrying the missiles cruised westward towards Cuba and Kennedy threatened war if they did not turn back, NORAD automatically ordered DEFCON 3, the state of readiness just short of war. Neither Diefenbaker nor his ministers were informed of this decision, let alone consulted about it. The Prime Minister was furious that a megalomaniac American President could, in effect, push the button that decided Canada's future. In the end, Soviet President Nikita Khrushchev backed down in the fearsome game of nuclear chicken, and one of the turning points in the Cold War was passed.

The Cuban crisis changed Canadian public opinion, which had been tending against nuclear armament. It also provoked considerable media discussion of the government's prevarications and inconsistencies over nuclear and defence policy. NATO made it clear that Canada was part of its nuclear system, and Liberal leader Lester Pearson announced that his party would stand by the nation's nuclear commitments even if the government that had made them would not. There was obviously no point in housing nuclear weapons on Canadian soil in a state of readiness if they could not be instantly deployed in the event of crisis. Such blunders in defence policy certainly did Diefenbaker no good in the 1962 election, and by January 1963 they had reduced his cabinet to conflicting factions. The minority government fell shortly afterwards. Traditional Canadian nationalism as practised by John Diefenbaker simply was not compatible with the nuclear age.

LIBERAL WAFFLING

The Liberals regained power in 1963 under Pearson and spent much of the 1960s attempting to implement the integration of Canada's armed forces, chiefly on the ground that duplication of resources and command structures was a luxury the nation could not afford. A unified military would be leaner and meaner, capable of remaining within the nation's means. The British had downsized militarily by joining the military nuclear club, an option that was not really available to Canada given its long-time hostility to possession of the bomb. The country and its politicians continued their inconsistent and contradictory attitudes towards the Canadian military and its foreign obligations. Genuine independence in military and foreign affairs—the Swedish model, for example—was too expensive and awkward to contemplate seriously. It would require a larger and better-equipped armed force and a willingness to manufacture and sell arms abroad to anybody with the money to pay for them. To give up and move definitively under the American defence umbrella would be far cheaper, but would mean sacrificing any remaining Canadian dignity. Everyone therefore pretended that Canada could hold the line on defence spending and still honour its commitments through military rationalization. This pretense became increasingly difficult to maintain as the years passed.

Despite Prime Minister Pearson's earlier success as a world diplomat, his governments were not distinguished by any triumphs in the international arena. In fairness to Pearson, the world was changing in ways not sympathetic to Canada's self-proclaimed position as a middle power. After 1960 the UN General Assembly opened its doors to dozens of Third World countries, many of them recently emerged from colonial status and often quite hostile to Western democracies. The new complexities of politics and expectations at the UN and in its various collateral organizations worked against a highly developed and industrialized nation such as Canada—populated chiefly by descendants of Western Europeans—that also happened to be a junior partner of the US. Canadian diplomats found themselves in the embarrassing position of defending in UN bodies the country's internal policy—particularly towards Aboriginal peoples—against criticisms of racism and insensitivity to minority rights. Canada was not as bad as South Africa, but its record on human rights was mixed at best. At the same time, the success of the European Economic Community (EEC, established in 1958) made Western European nations more important as international players, while Japan had succeeded in restoring its industrial position. As a result, Canadian influence among the world's developed countries was greatly reduced.

The configuration of world politics was not the only thing that altered in the 1960s. So, too, did the policy of the United States—and therefore its attitudes towards Canada. President Kennedy and his successor, Lyndon B. Johnson, were actually more hard-bitten and confrontational Cold Warriors than their predecessors in Washington. President Eisenhower had been extremely embarrassed in 1960 when the Russians shot down an American U-2 spy plane, capturing its pilot, Francis Gary Powers, and confirming American secret surveillance of the Soviet Union. By contrast, Kennedy authorized the CIA to carry out 'dirty tricks' in foreign countries and never offered the slightest suggestion of an apology when they were exposed or went wrong. His only regret about the abortive 1961 Bay of Pigs invasion of Cuba by US-backed Cuban exiles, for example, was that it had failed. Most important, both Kennedy and Johnson allowed their governments to become ever more deeply involved in the quagmire of Indochina.

Like Korea, Indochina had been partitioned into Communist and non-Communist states after World War II. When the French government proved incapable of retaining its colonial control against armed 'insurgents' from the Democratic Republic of Vietnam (Communist North Vietnam, governed by Ho Chi Minh), Canada in 1954 became involved in attempts at international control as one of three members, with Poland and India, of an International Commission for Supervision and Control.[26] Canada was actually keen to participate, initially seeing such work as part of its middle-power role in world affairs. The 1954 Commission set the pattern for the next 20 years: one Iron Curtain nation, one Western ally of the US (usually Canada), and one neutral power, with votes often going against the US (and Canada). From the outset Canada had persuaded itself of the absurdity that it had a free hand to carry out its mandate without either upsetting the Americans or appearing to act merely as their lackey. As the American administration gradually escalated US activity in Vietnam after 1963, Canada's position became increasingly anomalous, both on the Commission and outside it. Pearson was still trying to mediate in April 1965 when he used the occasion of a speech in Philadelphia to suggest that the American government might pause in its bombing of North Vietnam to see if a negotiated settlement was possible. He was soon shown the error of his ways when, in a private meeting with Lyndon Johnson, the American President shook Pearson by his lapels and criticized Canadian presumptuousness with Texan profanity. Vietnam certainly contributed to a new Canadian mood in the later 1960s, both in Ottawa and on the main streets of the nation. Canadians now sought to distance themselves from the policies of the 'ugly Americans'—although not by open withdrawal from the American defence umbrella. Many Canadians, perhaps even a majority, adopted a moralistic position on the war, objecting to the 'complicity' of Canadian industry in the manufacture of the worst instruments of war employed by the Americans. Particularly criticized was the manufacture of 'agent orange' in Canada by the Dow Chemical Company. Agent orange was a defoliant, sprayed in the jungles to eliminate cover for the Viet Cong. It was carcinogenic and environmentally destructive.

TRUDEAU AND THE 'THIRD OPTION'

After Pierre Elliott Trudeau succeeded Pearson as Prime Minister in April 1968, an undeclared and unco-ordinated policy of retreat from middle-power pretensions was accelerated. Trudeau had long been critical of Canada's foreign and defence policies. Soon after his accession to power he initiated formal reviews, which the departments of National Defence and External Affairs found threatening. The Prime Minister was particularly eager to ask 'fundamental questions', such as whether there really was a Russian threat, or 'Will the US sacrifice Europe and NATO before blowing up the world?'[27] The bureaucrats were not eager to tackle such questions, nor were several of his cabinet colleagues. Trudeau had a reputation as an internationalist, but he disliked the military and ultimately proved much more concerned with domestic matters than external ones. He did shake up the military and foreign policy bureaucracies, but the result was fewer new initiatives rather than more. For Trudeau, protecting Canada's sovereignty was far more important than international peacekeeping. Defence budgets were cut, and active Canadian involvement in NATO was pared to the lowest limits of allied acceptability. The best-known action by the Canadian military was its occupation of Quebec during the October Crisis of 1970.

In 1972 the government produced a policy document on Canadian–American relations that advocated a 'Third Option'. Instead of the status quo (option one), or even closer relations with the US (option two), it recommended option three: less dependence on the Americans. But if Canada moved away from the Americans, where would it go for friends? The obvious answer was to Europe, which was growing stronger day by day through the EEC and was increasingly visualizing itself as a third force in the world, on a par with the US and the USSR. The trouble was that Canada had waited too long and had become too closely identified with the US. Closer ties with European nations might have been forged in the days before the Common Market and the resurgence of Europe, but during that period Canada had backed the American horse, and it could not change its bets now. In 1973 Canada did send a large military mission to Vietnam to serve on a revised International Commission for Control and Supervision—essentially to oversee the American withdrawal from that corner of the world. But the Commission was not able to act effectively, and the Trudeau government ordered the Canadian personnel home in mid-1973.

By the early 1970s Canada no longer was a self-defined middle power and no longer had a clear conception of its place or role in world affairs. The problem was simple. Canada's economic activity entitled it to major-league status, but its close relationship with the US had made it a minor-league subsidiary. Its image abroad was as perplexing as its policies. On the one hand, it continued its habit of preaching from on high to nations that did not regard themselves as morally inferior and that relished the opportunity to catch Canada out in hypocritical moral contradictions. On the other hand, Canada continued to be one of the most favoured destinations of immigrants around the world—which suggested that it was doing something right.

The fizzle of the 'Third Option' left Canada little choice, after 1975, but to return to closer ties with the US. By this time the Americans had succeeded in disengaging themselves from their manifestly unpopular war in Vietnam and, despite the disasters of Watergate, were back in favour with Canadians. The love-hate relationship with the Americans continued, but after the mid-1970s a Canada fully independent of American pressures was not often mooted as a serious possibility in circles of power—or most other places.

SHORT BIBLIOGRAPHY

Barros, James. *No Sense of Evil: Espionage, the Case of Herbert Norman*. Toronto, 1986. A full study of the Norman case, which doesn't fully exonerate Norman.

Eayrs, James. *In Defence of Canada: Vol. 4, Growing Up Allied*. Toronto, 1980. One volume in a magisterial study of Canadian defence policy.

Kristmanson, Mark. *Plateaus of Freedom: Nationality, Culture, and State Security in Canada, 1940–1960*. Toronto, 2003. A controversial work arguing that Canada's security needs contributed to the growth of state nationalism, especially in English Canada.

Levant, Victor. *Quiet Complicity: Canadian Involvement in the Vietnam War*. Toronto, 1986. An account critical of Canadian policy.

Reid, Escott. *Time of Fear and Hope: The Making of the North Atlantic Treaty, 1947–1949*. Toronto, 1977. A brilliant study of the origins of NATO by a scholar who was intimately involved in the proceedings.

Ross, Douglas A. *In The Interests of Peace: Canada and Vietnam 1954–1973*. Toronto, 1984. A study that assumes America's legitimate interests in Southeast Asia.

Sawatsky, John. *Gouzenko: The Untold Story*. Toronto, 1984. A full-length study of the Gouzenko affair.

Stacey, Charles P. *Canada and the Age of Conflict: A History of Canadian External Policies*, 2 vols. Toronto, 1977, 1981. Perhaps the best general survey

Stairs, Dennis. *The Diplomacy of Constraint: Canada, the Korean War, and the United States*. Toronto, 1974. An important analysis of Canadian involvement in the Korean War.

Stewart, Craig. *Shutting Down the National Dream: A.V. Roe and the Tragedy of the Avro Arrow*. Toronto, 1988. An impassioned analysis of the failure of the Arrow and its implications for Canada.

STUDY QUESTIONS

1. Why was the Gouzenko affair so important?
2. What were the major justifications for Canada's participation in NATO?
3. What were the lessons of Korea?
4. Why was middle-power status so difficult for Canada to maintain?
5. How did technology work against Canada militarily after 1953?
6. What was Canada's place in the world in the early 1970s?

CHAPTER FOURTEEN

Prosperity and Growth in the Post-War World, 1946–1972

The period between 1945 and the early 1970s was one of unparalleled economic growth and prosperity for Canada.[1] Of course there were valleys as well as peaks, slowdowns as well as booms, and even occasional recessions. But overall, Canadian production and consumption moved constantly upward, employment rose almost continuously (except in 1945, 1954, and 1958), inflation was steady but almost never excessive, and interest rates seldom rose into double digits. These economic characteristics came to be considered normal. Almost all planning in the public and private sectors alike was based on assumptions of constant growth, and that approach seemed to work. Between 1946 and the early 1970s, per capita income doubled. Even allowing for inflation, this meant a substantial rise in living standards. Unemployment remained reasonably low, never exceeding 7.5 per cent of the total workforce before 1976, and typically running well below it, despite the constant addition of new workers, who nearly doubled the ranks of the employed in the quarter-century after the end of the war. There was a major boom in the late 1940s, and another in the 1960s, both fuelled by export sales and investment in domestic physical plant. This was a world of plenty, seemingly without end.

THE AFFLUENT SOCIETY

The economy in the quarter-century from 1946 to 1972 may not have been perfect, but Canadians could be forgiven for believing that there were no limits to growth, that major economic depressions could be avoided, that standards of living could continue to rise forever. Both politicians and economists believed that governments had learned to manage economies, and could correct for negative movements almost as soon as they emerged. The operative economic wisdom was Keynesianism, named after the English economist John Maynard Keynes, whose writings provided much of its theoretical underpinnings. The Tremblay Commission on constitutional problems in Quebec (1953) provided a summary of Keynesian thinking when it observed of the economy:

> The objective envisaged was the maintenance of economic stability and full employment. . . . Both expenditures and investments, by individuals as well as by companies, should, therefore, be encouraged. Moreover, the government should take a part in this, and co-operate in stabilizing the economy and in ensuring full employment by its own expenditures and investments. This

TIMELINE

1944

PCO 1003 introduced.

1946

Exchange rate is $1.10 Canadian to $1.00 American.

1947

Imperial Oil brings in Leduc oil field in southern Alberta. First private synthetic rubber plant established at Sarnia. Canada supports the petition of Palestine.

1948

Canada is allowed to participate in the Marshall Plan, but rejects North American tree trade.

1949

Asbestos strike in Quebec.

1950

$5 billion set aside by Canadian government for rearmament with onset of Korean War. First flight of Avro CF-100 Canuck. Public struggle in BC with International Woodworkers of America.

1952

Atomic Energy of Canada Ltd established.

1953

Quebec establishes Tremblay Commission.

1954

Banks allowed to move into consumer credit and mortgages.

1956

More than 1,200 firms involved in western Canadian oil and gas. Fierce pipeline debate in House of Commons. Merger of TLC and CCL into Canadian Labour Congress (CLC).

1957

Gordon Commission reports. Foreign ownership becomes an issue.

1958

Royal Commission on Canada's Economic Prospects report published. Inco strike at Sudbury.

1959

St Lawrence Seaway opened.

1962

Official exchange rate for Canadian dollar set at 0.925 American. Trans-Canada Highway officially completed.

1963

Hydro-Québec created. CUPE organized. Royal Commission on Government Organization (the Glassco Commission) reports.

1964

46 per cent of Canadians tell Gallup poll there is enough American investment; 33 per cent want more.

1967

Public Service Alliance of Canada created.

1968

Task Force on the Structure of Canadian Industry issues its report.

1970

Kari Levitt publishes *Silent Surrender*.

would demand from it an appropriate fiscal and monetary policy, as well as a programme of carefully planned public works. . . . The new policy necessarily entailed a considerable number of social security measures regarded as indispensable for the correction of variations in the economic cycle.[2]

The resulting general pattern of affluence, however, was not attributable to government planning and management, nor was it unique to Canada. It was general across the Western industrial world. It started, in part, with the rebuilding of the war-torn economies of Europe and Asia, but continued on its own momentum after those systems had been put back in operation.

Foreign trade had always been an important component of the Canadian economy, and the post-war period was no exception. The volume of imports and exports increased. Indeed, after 1950 Canada began to run a trading deficit, mainly because prosperity encouraged Canadians to consume more than they produced; growth was financed both by borrowing capital from aboard and by encouraging a good deal of direct foreign investment, chiefly from the United States. The outstanding development of the first 25 years after the war was without doubt the entrenchment of Canada's integration into the American trading market and the corresponding decline of Britain as a trading partner. In 1946 Britain received 26 per cent of Canadian exports and provided 7.5 per cent of imports; the US took 38 per cent of exports and supplied 75 per cent of imports. By the early 1970s the Americans were still supplying over 70 per cent of imports, with Britain taking less than 5 per cent of exports. The shift resulted from the relative decline of Britain as an industrial power, and, after 1965, from a relatively open North American border in automobiles and parts. At the same time, the Communist countries (especially Russia and China), the European Common Market (a new customs union formed in 1957), and Japan all became important trading partners.

Sales of wheat to Russia and China were supplemented by sales of raw materials to much of the rest of the industrialized world.

The second most important change was in the relative importance of the various sectors of the domestic economy. Manufacturing and construction became marginally less important over the quarter-century, starting at just over 30 per cent of national output in 1946, rising to over 35 per cent by the early 1950s, and then gradually declining to under 30 per cent by the early 1970s. Agriculture's share of the gross national product (GNP) declined almost continually throughout the period, as did the fisheries' share, while mining held virtually steady and by 1970 was slightly more significant than agriculture. The real growth industry was the public sector, particularly public administration and service, both as a producer of GNP and as an employer. On the latter front, 1946 saw just over 15 per cent of Canadians employed in the public sector, while by the early 1970s that figure was close to 35 per cent. Many of the public-service employees were highly educated white-collar workers, and the rapid increase in this sector not only provided jobs for the constantly growing numbers of graduates of Canadian universities but helped to change the occupational structure of Canadian employment. In 1946 fewer than 40 per cent of Canadians were white-collar workers, about the same percentage were in blue-collar jobs, and the rest were employed in farming and various extractive industries. By 1972 more than 60 per cent of Canadians held white-collar jobs, and the proportion in farming had declined dramatically. Not all the increase in white-collar work came in the public sector; there was a steady growing need for skilled workers in almost every sector of the economy. There was also an increasing demand for service workers in areas such as the retail food industry and tourism.

Throughout the period, the Canadian government set the value of the Canadian dollar in terms of the American dollar. In 1946 the exchange rate was $1.10 Canadian for $1.00

American, and then it was at par until 1949. In 1950 the government floated the dollar, allowing the market to determine its value, and in 1962 officially set it at $0.925 American, where it remained until 1970, after which it again floated. Throughout this period there was no relationship between the Canadian dollar and any base metal, including gold. Although the Canadian government stocked gold in its vaults for exchange purposes, the dollar's value was always based on some combination of what the government said it was worth (expressed in American dollars) and what the world thought it was worth. The dollar floated because too many people thought there was a discrepancy between these two values, and it was too difficult for the government to maintain its official value. The Bank of Canada controlled Canadian foreign exchange and Canadian domestic banking, the latter through interest rates and the ratios between deposits and credit. It zealously protected Canadian banks from foreign takeovers. Not until 1954 were banks allowed to move into consumer credit and mortgage loans, and before 1967 they were limited to a maximum of 6 per cent interest. Consumer credit really opened up after 1967, when interest-rate restrictions were removed and the banks began to issue plastic credit cards in profusion. Canada's monetary policy increased the supply of money in circulation substantially faster than the rise in the GNP, thus contributing to inflation. This result was partly an international phenomenon: a gentle rise in prices of 2 to 4 per cent per annum was regarded by most economists of the time as an inevitable by-product of the economic growth that characterized the period.

In most years, Canadian inflation ran well under 10 per cent, which became a sort of magic figure above which everyone suddenly became concerned. 'Double-digit' inflation did not hit Canada until 1974—but the cumulative effect of gradual increases in prices was a major increase in the 'cost of living' over the period (the government was constantly changing the baseline year in order to disguise the extent of the rise). On the whole, the price index doubled between 1945 and 1970, and it would double again during the 1970s, when double-digit inflation became a reality. Inflation meant a perennial struggle for Canadians—yet it also tended to encourage consumer credit, since loans could be paid back in constant dollars that were, in reality, worth less than they had been when borrowed.

In April 1958 the long-awaited final report of the Royal Commission on Canada's Economic Prospects—the Gordon Commission—was made available to the public.[3] The opening sentence announced its major themes: 'What will be Canada's economic potentialities over the next twenty-five years and what must we do if they are to be realized?' The commissioners began by admitting the difficulties of 'fortune-telling' and disclaiming total accuracy or consistency. They maintained that their forecasting had sought to achieve scientific quality, however. No doubt the sheer audacity of attempting to look a full quarter-century forward was possible only in the optimistic air of the 1950s. Most of the commissioners' prognostications—like most forecasts of the decade—were based on taking existing trends and projecting the future, and on the whole they were bullish:

> The promise of the economic future as we foresee it is one to command enthusiasm. An atomic war would blast it. A deep depression would blight it. But failing either of those catastrophes, which we believe it should not be beyond the wit of man to avoid, the next two or three decades should bring great prosperity for Canadians.[4]

The Gordon Commission identified some existing and some potential problems, including the extent of foreign ownership of Canadian industry, but the prospects were generally very promising. Predicting great increases in both the size of the nation's labour force and its productivity, it envisaged a 1980 national income three times as large as that of 1955.

Royal Commissions are notorious in Canada

■ The first oil well in the Leduc field, 13 Feb. 1947. City of Edmonton Archives EA-88-170.

for putting forward innovative ideas that never move beyond the idea stage. Even if they never have any direct impact on public policy, however, their findings—including the evidence on which they are based—constitute a wonderful source for the historian because they reveal the conventional thinking on the subject in question at the time of investigation. The guiding assumptions of the Gordon Commission tell us much about the overall climate of opinion, economic and non-economic, at the time. The Commission

assumed that nuclear war could be avoided, for example, mainly because the consequences would be so devastating as to be unthinkable. It pointed out that a single 'old-fashioned' hydrogen bomb 'could contaminate with radioactive fallout an elliptical area 200 miles or more in length, stretching, for example, along Lake Ontario from Hamilton to Kingston or along the St Lawrence from Cornwall to Quebec.'[5] It also assumed that defence spending in Canada would continue to be high, since it foresaw no end to the Cold War.

The Commission did not foresee a major depression, and it held full employment to be the indisputable goal, requiring a 'deliberate intervention' by the central government that it regarded as both necessary and efficacious. Reflecting the gradual, rather than cataclysmic, inflation of the time, it assumed 'no change either in the general price level or in price relationships', explaining that such matters could not be forecast. It recognized technology as a mixed blessing, but associated its negative side with war and argued that its peacetime possibilities were unending. Indeed, many of the Commission's forecasts were based on the assumption that technological development would continue unabated and that peacetime applications of technology were fundamentally positive. Most important of all, the Commission assumed a continuation and even acceleration of existing trends in most aspects of Canadian life. Its chairman, Walter Gordon, would later boast that most of its forecasts were accurate and that many of its recommendations were ultimately accepted by government.[6] In all its optimism—that nuclear war could be averted, that economies could be centrally managed, that technology promised an unambiguously better life—the Royal Commission on Canada's Economic Prospects reflected mainstream Canadian thinking before the early 1970s.

NATURAL RESOURCES

In the resource-extraction sector of the economy, several developments occurred that helped it maintain a fairly steady profile. In 1946 only about 10 per cent of Canada's petroleum needs were being met by domestic production. But the untapped potential was enormous, and in 1947 Imperial Oil brought in the major oil field at Leduc, in southern Alberta. Most of the experts in oil exploration came from the US because Americans were more willing than Canadians to risk venture capital in seeking and drilling new wells.[7] In 1956, more than 1,200 firms, most of them American-financed, were involved in western Canadian oil and gas. The Alberta oil industry was rapidly taken over by multinational firms, and by the early 1970s seven such firms controlled more than half of the Canadian oil business and took in 90 per cent of petroleum revenues. One of the principal uses for Canadian oil after 1945 was in a rapidly expanding petrochemical industry, which was developing a host of new synthetic products for consumers, especially plastics and fabrics. Although the government had produced synthetic rubber in Sarnia in 1942, the first private plant in Canada was established at Sarnia only in 1947.[8] Most of the major oil wells might be located in Alberta, but petrochemical processing in Canada occurred mainly in Ontario and Quebec. The oil was carried east by pipelines without regard for the international border. The Interprovincial Pipe Line, for example, sent oil from Edmonton to Wisconsin in 1950, then on to Sarnia from 1952. Before the international oil crisis of the early 1970s, this arrangement seemed quite satisfactory.

Natural gas also required pipelines to travel from the West into the major centres of population and industry. Westcoast Transmission built the first one, to Vancouver, and tried desperately to extend it into the US, but American approval was not immediately forthcoming. Unlike Westcoast Transmission's Frank McMahon (a native British Columbian), Trans-Canada Pipe Line's Clint Murchison (a Texan) advocated the construction of a transcontinental pipeline on Canadian territory rather than integration into the American market. Not surprisingly, the Canadian government—chiefly in the person of the Minister of Trade and Commerce, C.D. Howe—supported the all-Canadian scheme for political reasons. Howe's insistence on a Crown corporation to construct part of the line, and on government loans for the remainder, led to the fierce debate in the House of Commons in 1956 that would eventually bring down the Liberal government.

Potash was found in Saskatchewan during World War II in the course of drilling for oil, and it began to be exploited on a large scale in the later 1950s. By 1970 the province was producing nearly half of the world's supply of potash—which was considerably more than the international market required—and the provincial government moved in to control production. Despite the limitations of the world market, potash (the main ingredient in fertilizers) was potentially even more important as a resource than uranium, the other mineral that Canada had in unusual abundance. The Eldorado mine in the Northwest Territories was at one point the only producer in Canada, and Canadian uranium had been the basis of the wartime Manhattan Project at Los Alamos, New Mexico, that produced the atomic bomb. After the war, many thought that atomic energy would be increasingly used as an alternative to hydroelectricity and fossil fuels, and private industry developed many new mines. By 1955 the Canadian uranium industry had moved into large-scale production, under government regulation, despite the difficulty of finding ore of commercial grade. The real problem became oversupply, since the mineral could be sold only under government licence to a few major purchasers, most particularly the American government.[9] After 1958 the Canadian government allowed mines to sell anywhere in the world, once they had fulfilled their military contracts to the major atomic powers of the United States and Great Britain. But the peaceful use of atomic energy failed to catch on to the extent predicted by the optimists of the 1940s and early 1950s, chiefly because of the cost and difficulty

■ A worker at the Chalk River plant putting on special footwear to protect against radioactivity, November 1947. The lockers are designated 'Active' or 'Inactive' according to the levels of contamination on the workers' clothes. LAC, PA-111377.

involved in building and operating nuclear reactors that offered any real degree of safety from nuclear radiation and because the disposal of nuclear wastes presents very serious and extremely long-range problems. The Canadian uranium industry ultimately failed to expand beyond its 1958 output.

Fossil fuels and nuclear power were the growth areas of the energy industry until the early 1970s. In 1950 hydroelectricity generation accounted for well over 90 per cent of Canadian electrical capacity, but it slipped to less than 60

per cent by the mid-1970s. The problem essentially was cost. The exceedingly low international price of oil before 1972, combined with the expense of transmitting power from remote sites to population centres, discouraged hydroelectric development in Canada. Nuclear power generation was developed by the federal government through Atomic Energy of Canada Ltd (AECL), established in 1952, which finally produced the CANDU (Canadian Deuterium-Uranium) reactor after several serious accidents at its research facilities at Chalk River, Ontario, that released significant amounts of radiation. In this period experts insisted that nuclear accidents (particularly the meltdown of a reactor core) were virtually inconceivable. Those that occurred were hushed up, and no serious attention was given to the disposal of the ever-increasing amounts of nuclear wastes that were being stored at reactor sites or buried nearby.

Environmental effects were not a serious consideration in any part of Canadian industry before the late 1960s. That was when the Canadian public first became aware of the dangers of 'pollution', a word that had just come into common usage. Petrochemical plants dumped waste into rivers, pulp and paper mills dumped poisonous mercury into water systems, and solid industrial waste was simply buried, often serving as landfill to create housing estates near large urban centres, as in the Love Canal area near Niagara Falls. Many inland rivers and lakes, particularly in the industrial regions of central Canada, had become cesspools of toxic industrial waste and human sewage. Acid rain was increasing continually, but was still almost unrecognized as an international problem. Farmers applied chemical fertilizers and weed killers to their soil with no thought for tomorrow, defiling the underground aquifers that provided much of the continent's water supply. Increasing productivity while reducing cost was the goal, and the handful of Canadians concerned with environmental pollution before 1965 were often regarded as a lunatic fringe of troublemakers, the modern equivalents of the Luddites who tried to destroy the new industrial machines in Britain at the beginning of the nineteenth century. By the time the mercury pollution of the English-Wabigoon River system by a pulp mill in Dryden, Ontario, became headline news in 1970—although the Aboriginal people of Grassy Narrows had been complaining since the fifties—pretty much all of the people in a liberal democracy who might be considered aware had become so.

Nor was conservation of non-renewable resources given much attention. In the Canadian fisheries, for example, the period from 1940 to the late 1960s saw an unremitting expansion of productivity. Fishing fleets used federal subsidies to expand and adopt new technology such as sonar radio or radar, which enabled them to take ever more fish, while improvements in home refrigeration and freezing allowed their markets to expand as well. Newfoundland's entry into Confederation in 1949 gave a huge boost to Canadian fishery statistics, of course, but in addition several new fisheries, especially in shellfish, were opened, and the numbers of large vessels in the Canadian fishing fleet grew significantly. Meanwhile, similar developments elsewhere meant that Canada was not the only nation exploiting the existing stocks ever more effectively. By the time the supply crisis was finally recognized, in the late 1960s, it was already too late.

The Gordon Commission, in its 25-year economic forecast, had discussed the environment strictly from the perspective of rational resource management. 'Pollution' was not part of its vocabulary. Its discussion of effluent from the pulp mills of the west coast is revealing:

> . . . considering a higher stage of manufacture, some 50 per cent of the raw material is lost in the waste liquor effluent from sulphite pumping. This waste has been referred to as 'a rich storehouse of chemicals'. Technically, so it is, but with present knowledge—and foreign tariffs on imports of chemicals—domestic demand imposes modern

limits on the extent to which the store-house can yet be tapped. Nevertheless, increased utilization of the raw material and greater by-product diversification are in the shape of things to come. The benefits could be very substantial.[10]

From the standpoint of the 1950s, the trouble with liquid effluent was not that it poisoned living things (including humans), but that it could not be profitably utilized.

SECONDARY INDUSTRY

The decline in the relative importance of manufacturing as an employer in Canada was very gradual, and most Canadians continued to regard industrial development as the key to a healthy economy. Central Canada, especially Ontario, was the chief growth area. During the war the Canadian government had tried to spread the manufacturing wealth around a bit, but with the peace Ontario resumed its place as the bellwether of Canadian industry and even increased its share of the total, producing as much as 54 per cent of the nation's total manufacturing value added in 1971. Moreover, in industries such as the manufacturing of durable goods and big-ticket consumer items Ontario had more than its share of production. In 1957 it turned out 98.8 per cent of Canada's motor vehicles, 90.7 per cent of its heavy electrical goods, 90 per cent of its agricultural implements, and 80.7 per cent of its major household appliances. In most industries Ontario workers were considerably more productive in terms of net value added by employee, and Ontario plants were significantly larger than those in the rest of the country, both in value of production and in numbers of employees. Not surprisingly, the average size of industrial plants in Ontario continued to grow, from 32.5 employees per establishment in 1939 to 65 in the early 1970s. Ontario plants employed 319,000 people in 1939, 598,000 in 1946, and 822,000 in 1972. The internal structure of Ontario's manufacturing sector did not change much in terms of the relative importance of primary and secondary manufacturing, or in rank of major industries. What did change considerably was management structure. In 1946 fewer than 40 per cent of Ontario manufacturing companies were incorporated. The majority were operated on a small-scale personal management basis. By 1957 over 85 per cent were incorporated, employing 99 per cent of workers. Equally important, foreign ownership increased substantially, encouraged by all levels of government. Most manufacturing development occurred in the long-established industrial centres of southern Ontario.[11]

One important component of the post-war manufacturing boom was the need for ongoing military readiness after the Germans and Japanese had surrendered. In fact, the end of World War II was almost indistinguishable from the start of the Third, in which the threat was not European or Japanese militarism but Communist expansion. The new confrontation quickly became known as the 'Cold War', a phrase popularized, if not coined, by Winston Churchill in 1946. It meant increased federal expenditures on what was euphemistically labelled 'defence'. The Canadian government managed to concentrate on peacetime reconstruction between 1945 and 1948, but increased international tensions led Canada to initiate a new alliance system with the creation of NATO in 1949, discussed in the previous chapter. Between NATO's needs and the conflict in Korea, Canada's armed forces were greatly increased in 1950, and $5 billion was set aside for rearmament, with most of the money to be spent on military hardware. American military manufacturers were more than willing to subcontract parts of Canadian orders to their branch plants, but Canada naturally wanted to produce its own equipment, as we saw in Chapter 13 in regard to the Avro Arrow.

The post-war boom certainly encouraged the growth of American direct investment in Canada and the rise of the multinational corporation—usually with headquarters in the US and a branch operation in Canada. By 1950 more than three-quarters of total foreign investment in the country was American, mainly through branch subsidiaries functioning in Canada. The chief areas of American investment were mining, manufacturing, and petroleum. By 1968 foreign-owned companies controlled more than 60 per cent of assets in Canadian mining, nearly 80 per cent of the oil and gas industry, and almost 60 per cent of manufacturing. In the latter sector American ownership was especially prevalent in the highly profitable consumer area, where production flourished on the strength of American technology and American promotion of both goods and brand names. American advertising and cultural values created the consumer demand on a continental basis, and Canadian subsidiaries fulfilled it within the Canadian market. Not until 1957, however, did American investment and the growth of multinationals become an important public issue. Most Canadians were happy to take advantage, as they always had, of the American technology and the jobs it created. Canadian branches were for the most part run by Canadians, and the extent of American penetration in some areas of the economy—transportation, communications, public utilities, banking and finance, and construction—was relatively unimportant.

PUBLIC ENTERPRISE

Growing alongside the American multinationals were Canadian public enterprises. Crown corporations, for example, were created by both federal and provincial governments, by which they were owned and financed; however, their management structures were modelled on private corporations and government usually had nothing to do with their administration. The extent to which Crown corporations were responsible to government was never entirely clear. According to the Federal Administration Act of 1951 they were 'ultimately accountable, through a minister, to Parliament, for the conduct of affairs', but mat-

■ During construction of the St Lawrence Seaway more than 500 dwellings were moved to the newly created towns of Ingleside and Long Sault, Ontario. Hydro One Archives SLA 162. Hydro One Inc.

ters have never been that simple for either level of government. In terms of ultimate policy, Crown corporations reflected the ambitions of the governments that controlled the appointment of their upper management and the parliamentary allocations that supported their expansion. But on a daily basis they were given a virtually free hand, and they had a reputation for operating with little regard for the needs of the public, even if they were accountable to the public's government in the end. Most Crown corporations were created to provide important services that could not be profitably offered by private enterprise: in other words, public enterprise—almost by definition—was called into existence wherever the private sector refused to

go. Increasingly, governments propped up unprofitable industries that, for political reasons, could not be allowed to fail by creating Crown corporations to operate them. The CCF–NDP government of Saskatchewan, for example, began creating Crown corporations almost from the time of its election in 1944, and the Quebec government created a number of them in the 1960s. In 1962 the Social Credit government of British Columbia, under Premier W.A.C. Bennett, discovered that it could go into debt and still claim a balanced budget by creating a Crown corporation—BC Hydro—to finance huge hydroelectric expansion.[12]

The first Crown corporation had been created in the Province of Canada in 1841 to build

■ Her Majesty Queen Elizabeth II and President Dwight D. Eisenhower at the opening of the St
Lawrence Seaway, 26 June 1959, Saint-Lambert, Quebec. Duncan Cameron/LAC, PA-121475.
© Library and Archives Canada. Reproduced with the permission of Library and Archives Canada.

a canal network, and many of the earliest large
Crown corporations were in the transportation
and communications sectors. The Canadian
National Railways (CNR) was founded in the early
1920s to resolve the financial troubles of much of
the nation's rail system, and the Canadian
Broadcasting Corporation was created in 1936 to
produce a national radio system. Trans-Canada
Airlines began in 1937 as a subsidiary of the CNR
and expanded rapidly as both a national and an
international carrier (it was renamed Air Canada
in 1965). Under C.D. Howe, TCA was used to
promote aviation manufacturing, particularly
Canadair Ltd at Cartierville, Quebec, which designed and built the North Star airplane. During
World War II, the government had expanded and
extended the use of the Crown corporation, par-

ticularly in manufacturing, and after the war
most of those enterprises were sold to the private
sector—an early example of privatization, before
the term was coined. Most of the Crown corporations in transportation and communications
did not have monopolies but shared their markets with private enterprise.

One of the largest public enterprises of the
1950s, the St Lawrence Seaway, was a monopoly
constructed and operated through a Crown corporation.[13] It was developed with reluctant
American co-operation—the US did not regard it
as necessary or profitable—but it completed
almost 200 years of development of the inland
waterways of eastern Canada, linking the lake-
head cities of Lake Superior with the Gulf of St
Lawrence by means of a series of new canals and

locks.[14] The opening ceremonies—attended by Prime Minister John Diefenbaker, Queen Elizabeth II, and President Dwight D. Eisenhower—on 26 June 1959 are perhaps most often remembered by Canadians present for Eisenhower's halting attempt to speak a sentence in French to the assembled crowd.

The Trans-Canada Highway was not associated with a Crown corporation,[15] but its completion in 1962 marked the achievement of another major public transportation project undertaken by the federal and provincial governments. Distinguished by federal involvement on a cost-sharing basis—since highway construction was normally the responsibility of provincial and municipal governments—it was the most visible effort on the part of Canadian governments to meet the demands of the motoring public and the business community for improved roads. It also served to unite the nation in a far more obvious way than the Seaway did, ultimately making it possible for Canadians to travel from eastern Newfoundland to Vancouver Island entirely on Canadian roads (and ferries). Between 1946 and 1966, the number of motor vehicles registered in Canada nearly quadrupled to seven million, and the total of paved highway outside urban areas expanded from less than 20,000 miles (about 32,200 kilometres) to nearly 100,000 miles (about 161,000 kilometres). Even so, many rural roads remained unpaved, and when the Trans-Canada Highway was officially opened in 1962, nearly half of its 4,849 miles (7,803 kilometres) were still gravel-covered. Nevertheless, road construction and improvement were major activities in the post-war period, with expenditures increasing from $103 million in 1946 to over $2 billion annually by the early 1970s, as rural districts acquired highways and urban centres came to be criss-crossed with multi-lane expressways and interchanges. By the late 1960s the destruction of urban housing for road development would be a major political issue in most of Canada's larger cities, and throughout the post-war period road construction (and especially paving) was a fundamental component of the patronage available from provincial governments.

For many rural Canadians the other great public development of the post-war period was the extension of electricity into all but the most remote corners of the country. Before the war most provincial electricity-generating systems had a mixture of municipal, provincial, and private ownership, but after 1945 many provinces consolidated their electric utilities into provincial Crown corporations in order to extend services into rural districts. The British Columbia Power Commission was created in 1945 to expand service, and by 1962 most of the province was served by BC Hydro and Power Authority. Manitoba Hydro was quietly organized as a Crown corporation in 1961. Hydro-Québec, initially created in 1944, was extended to the entire province in 1963 as part of the nationalization program overseen by the Liberal Natural Resources Minister, René Lévesque, becoming the symbol of the Quiet Revolution. Initially organized by the provincial governments to improve domestic service, the great publicly owned electrical utilities created massive hydroelectric projects to supply not only their own provinces, but other Canadian and American customers as well. The nationalization of Hydro-Québec was considered particularly significant as a step in the repatriation of the province's economy, and in most other provinces the organization of major provincial utilities did not carry quite such heavy ideological freight. But public ownership of electrical power through Crown corporations did come to be taken for granted by most Canadians as a birthright.

THE RISE OF ORGANIZED LABOUR

A growing role for organized labour accompanied the economic trends of the affluent society. Union membership increased and unions were organized in a number of industries. The strike became the major weapon in unions' battles first for recognition and then for improved working conditions. Organized labour was to some extent hampered by divisions within its own ranks, including some nasty ideological splits between Marxists and non-Marxists. On the other hand, great gains were made by labour organizers among women, French Canadians, and public-service employees. Not all unions or union members supported the CCF–NDP, but the association between labour and Canada's third party was sufficiently close to permit the two major parties to criticize the latter for being both leftist and labourist, effectively condemning it to a continuing minority role. At the same time, organized labour increasingly came to be seen as a counter-force to the Canadian capitalist free enterprise system that had dominated the nation since before Confederation.

World War II proved a major turning point for Canadian labour. It had fought a number of bitter strikes during the Depression in a search for recognition of an unfettered right to bargain collectively. It had lost most of these strikes, and had received precious little support from either level of government. The percentage of union members in the total civilian labour force actually declined slightly between 1929 and 1939, to 7.7 per cent in the latter year. Throughout the war, however, the federal government sought to co-opt labour into the war effort, and with the provinces it began the slow process of altering labour legislation to recognize and protect the rights to organization and collective bargaining. The key breakthrough came in 1944 when the federal government, by wartime Order-in-Council, introduced PCO 1003, adopting the principles of compulsory recognition and collective bargaining previously enacted in the US under the 1935 National Labour Relations Act (also known as the Wagner Act).[16] By 1946, 17.1 per cent of all workers and 27.9 per cent of non-agricultural workers belonged to unions.[17] With bargaining rights achieved, labour unions went on to hammer out working relationships with most of Canada's traditional industries, insisting

on what amounted to closed shops in many of them. Working conditions (including hours and days of work), as well as wages, were negotiated and improved. In 1956 the two largest Canadian umbrella organizations for labour—the Trades and Labour Congress of Canada and the Canadian Congress of Labour—merged into one consolidated body called the Canadian Labour Congress (CLC), as had their American counterparts, the American Federation of Labor and the Congress of Industrial Organization. Thus internal jurisdictional disputes at the top of the labour organizations were reduced.

The process of coming to terms with employers was not painless. In 1946–7, as soon as the wartime emergency had ended, almost all industries experienced major strikes. Throughout the 1950s there were never fewer than 159 strikes per year across Canada, involving between 49,000 and 112,000 workers annually. Some of the strikes became both nationally known and symbolically important, for either the regions or the industries involved. For example, the great strike that broke out in the town of Asbestos, near Sherbrooke, Quebec, in February 1949 polarized the province and closed most of its asbestos mines for four months.[18] It also marked the beginning of the end for Maurice Duplessis's Union Nationale government, which supported the US-based employers in their refusal to grant a first contract to the unions of the Confédération des Travailleurs Catholiques du Canada (CTCC).[19] Two aspects of the Asbestos strike were especially notable. The first was that it drew public attention to the appalling conditions under which the miners worked and the chronic lung disease that they suffered as a result of breathing asbestos dust.[20] The second was that the union involved was a Catholic one, which had the support not only of the traditional left in Quebec but also of priests, professionals, intellectuals, and even the archbishop of Montreal, Monseigneur Joseph Charbonneau, who declared that 'When the working class is the victim of a conspiracy, it is the duty of the Church to intervene.'[21] Although the workers finally returned to their jobs with their major grievances unsettled, the CTCC continued to grow throughout the 1950s under the leadership of Jean Marchand.

Perhaps the most prominent labour action of the 1950s was the Inco strike in Sudbury in 1958. Here, a union affiliated with the International Union of Mine, Mill and Smelter Workers was beaten by a large multinational corporation—the International Nickel Co. of Canada—which refused to budge. After several months of stalemate, the workers' wives organized to call for civic intervention to end the strike, claiming that the union leadership was not listening to their husbands. In good 1950s fashion, the interest of families took precedence over other issues, and the strikers capitulated. Nevertheless, strikes at Inco became a standard part of the labour picture over the next two decades, and the workers finally won a 261-day marathon in 1978–9.[22]

Not all union battles were against employers. There were innumerable jurisdictional disputes between unions, particularly those formed in one industrial sector seeking to enter into unorganized industries. In the period before 1960, however, many of the critical internal battles reflected the extension of the Cold War into the labour movement. The Communist Party had long been one of the mainstays of labour militancy in Canada, but after 1945 the issue of 'Communist domination' of crucial unions attracted much public attention because of the international situation, another round of 'red-hunting' in both the US and Canada, and the taint of Stalinism associated with the Canadian Communist Party (and its supporters). One highly publicized struggle occurred in 1950 in British Columbia, where the CCF and the CLC, assisted by public opinion and the provincial government, managed to drive out the Communist leadership of the International Woodworkers of America (IWA).

The forces of anti-communism were prepared to use any weapons at their disposal. The Canadian Seamen's Union (CSU) and its Communist leaders were replaced (with government connivance) by the American-based Seafarers' International Union (SIU) headed by Hal Banks, who had close connections with American gangsters. Longshoremen were a rough lot at best, but Banks introduced new standards of intimidation and corruption into Canadian unionism.[23] His struggle with the CLC led to a commission of inquiry that described Banks as a hoodlum, and after a criminal conviction he left the country. The Steelworkers and the United Automobile Workers were also 'purged' (or 'cleansed') of Communist links.[24]

In the 1960s conflict between 'international unionism' and Canadian nationalists replaced 'Commie-bashing' as the main internal issue for the union movement. In general, the nationalists were younger workers who were also discontented with traditional union leadership and organization, whereas the older union leaders had little interest in reform, except in the area of wages and working conditions, or in politics, apart from the relationship with the CCF–NDP. There were many wildcat strikes, aimed as much at the old leaders as at employers. One commentator on a strike at Stelco in Hamilton observed that 'neither the union nor the company could identify those behind it. Some attributed it to young hotheads, others to communists, and still others to a group of Canadian autonomists within the union.'[25] Younger workers often reacted against local branches of international (i.e., American-dominated) unions that were seen as collaborating with American multinational corporations in both 'selling-out' Canada and sustaining the 'military-industrial complex'. By the later 1960s, general expressions of discontent with American domination of international unions could be heard within many Canadian unions: the Americans took more money out of the country in dues than they returned in assistance; they failed to organize outside traditional industrial sectors; they often supported American military adventurism abroad (the American union movement was especially keen on Vietnam); and finally, they did not understand Canada and treated Canadian members with contempt. Withdrawal from international unionism began seriously around 1970 and would increase over the next few years, as wholly Canadian unions grew in numbers and membership.

The numbers of organized industries and union members in Canada rose steadily from the end of the war to the early 1970s. The major gains were among the traditional white-collar employees of the service sector, including teachers, health-care workers, civil servants, and even sales clerks. In 1945 only 86,000 of 711,000 union members were in the service sector, and fewer than 50,000 of these worked under some kind of collective agreement. Banks and department stores proved extremely difficult to organize: a prominent attempt in 1951 to organize Eaton's, the third largest employer in Canada at the time, failed by 800 of 9,000 votes cast. But a major breakthrough for public-sector unionism came at the end of the 1950s, when the postal employees organized and began demanding collective bargaining rights. In 1963 the Canadian Union of Public Employees (CUPE) was organized, and in 1967 thousands of civil servants repudiated staff associations and formed the Public Service Alliance of Canada. Outside the civil service but still within the public sector, unions were organized in both the teaching and health-care professions. Strikes by postal workers, teachers, and even policemen and firemen irritated large segments of the Canadian public, and would eventually lead to a backlash against strikes in the public sector.

Related to the growth in union organization in the service sector, both public and private, was a substantial expansion in the number of women union members. In 1945 Canadian unions reported just under 60,000 female members, or 9.9 per cent of the total union membership, although in 1943 more than 250,000 women had been employed in strategic industries that tended to be heavily unionized.[26] On Prince Edward Island in 1945 there were only five female members in three union locals. On the whole, these small numbers reflected the fact that, after the war, women tended to work in occupations that were not organized, and of course there was a structural discrimination against women in the workforce. The expansion of public- and service-sector organization in the 1960s greatly increased the numbers and proportions of women in the labour movement, although in 1972 women still represented only about one-quarter of union members. Among the new issues that women brought to the bargaining table were daycare, maternity leave, and sexual harassment, as well as equal pay for equal work. By the early 1970s the power and militancy of Canadian labour had reached the point where the succeeding years would witness a significant backlash against unions.

SCIENCE AND TECHNOLOGY

For the most part, the Canadian public did not perceive any fundamental conflict between public and private enterprise in the post-war period. The conventional wisdom was that modern capitalistic states had 'mixed' economies in which government took charge of activities that private enterprise could not or would not undertake, or that seemed particularly suited to public management. Among the areas staked out by the public sector in Canada was scientific research and development. The story of Canadian science policy after World War II encapsulates many of the trends and developments we have been discussing, including a fascinating internal debate within the scientific community over the question of pure versus applied research that had many other resonances across the broad spectrum of the Canadian economy.

Throughout the nineteenth century, the Canadian government had supported various scientific activities in the name of economic practicality, giving Canada an unusually high degree of government involvement compared to other nations. The first federal attempt at co-ordinating scientific activity was the Canadian Conservation Commission, formed in 1909 to advise on policy for Canadian natural resources.[27] In 1917 the National Research Council (NRC) was created to advise the Privy Council on matters relating to science and technology, and in 1932 (in the midst of the Depression!) it began to create its own laboratories, which by 1939 employed 300 scientists and staff. However, none of Canada's many wartime scientific breakthroughs ever turned into peacetime profits, partly because the plants utilizing them were rapidly shut down after 1945.

The NRC itself survived the war and managed both to influence university research and to assist private enterprise with industrial research. It continued to expand its laboratory facilities, and by 1959 its total personnel numbered 2,400. Its nuclear laboratories at Chalk River, Ontario, first developed during the war, were taken over by Atomic Energy of Canada, a Crown corporation created for this purpose in 1952. Much of the NRC's research still had military implications, or was expected to 'yield results of immediate practical value', presumably for the private industry that otherwise depended heavily on American technology (since many research-oriented businesses in Canada were run by American multinationals).[28] The NRC was also an active supporter of university scientific research in an era of great university expansion. But university scientists, who generally preferred 'pure' to 'applied' research, tended to think of their work more as part of a great international scientific effort than as a specifically Canadian enterprise, and to that extent the purpose of the NRC was effectively negated. Meanwhile, Russia had put a satellite into orbit in 1957, and the worldwide debate over the merits of Western versus Soviet science was well underway before Canadians began to recognize, in the early 1960s, that Canada lagged behind other industrialized nations in its investment in scientific, and particularly industrial, research.

Two aspects of Canada's efforts on behalf of science were especially criticized. One was that Canada spent a far smaller proportion of its science dollars on the development side of research and development than did other nations, such as the US and USSR. The second was that industry in Canada contributed a far smaller share of scientific activity (and the public sector a far greater one) than in any other Western industrialized country. In 1959, for example, industry was responsible for only 39 per cent of scientific research in Canada, as opposed to 58 per cent in Britain and 78 per cent in the US. (By this time the federal government was spending more than $200 million per year on scientific activity.)[29] When John Diefenbaker pulled the plug on the Avro Arrow, A.V. Roe dismissed his entire development team without making any plans for commercial operations. Equally striking is the fact that between 1957 and 1961, of 95 per cent of all Canadian patents involving foreign applicants, nearly 70 per cent of them were American.[30] This percentage was far higher than for other industrialized countries.

In 1963 the Royal Commission on Government Organization (the Glassco Commission), as part of a study of the federal bureaucracy, reported on science policy and science organization.[31] It was very critical of existing science policy, noting that there was virtually no government supervision of the NRC except by the Treasury Board, and that the lack of private-sector research was the responsibility of the NRC itself. Instead of supporting industrial research as a 'primary goal', argued the Commission, the NRC had relegated it to 'little more than a minor distraction—a desirable but rather difficult task, and certainly of less pressing urgency than other items on the program'. This report had two results: the creation in 1964 of a Science Secretariat in the office of the Privy Council, and in 1966 the parliamentary establishment of the Science Council of Canada 'to define and determine feasible long term objectives for science in Canada, to suggest appropriate paths for reaching them and to consider the responsibilities of the various segments of the industrial, academic and government communities in this field'.[32] Nonetheless, in 1968 Prime Minister Pierre Elliott Trudeau acknowledged that Canada was still deplorably backward in the area of applied science. The situation proved exceedingly difficult to change: encouraging the private sector to increase its role was not enough.

As in many other areas, Ottawa's involvement in scientific research went virtually unmentioned in the press. Few realized in the 1960s how many government departments had research roles, or what the issues at stake in scientific policy really were. Some Canadians knew that the nation lagged behind somehow in scientific activity, but most did not appreciate the nature of the lag. There was no shortfall in public spending on scientific research. The problems were that publicly supported scientists preferred not to serve the industrial sector directly, and that Canadian industry did not feel a sufficient need to encourage co-operation with the scientists or to initiate its own research. Whether Canadian science ought to become the servant of industry was not a question ever discussed at the political level, although the scientists (especially in the universities) had some strong feelings about the matter. The approved political line was that public financial support for science could be justified only in economic terms. To be awarded a Nobel Prize would be nice, but to create a new technology and see it succeed would be even nicer.

The controversy over pure versus applied research was particularly complex. It was true that many scientists, especially in the universities, were not interested in applying their findings, or asking questions that might lead to applications, but it was equally true that 'pure' research could lead to huge technological breakthroughs—capable of creating new products and even new industries—in a way that research focused on simply refining existing processes (to save money, for example) never would. The obvious example, of course, was the revolution in computers that began in the post-war era.

Canadian scientists co-operated with their American counterparts to produce the IBM 101 electronic statistical machine in time for it to analyze the 1951 Canadian census data. But Canada did not pursue that line of research. It was the Americans, among others, who developed the new technology, and Canadians were not in the front lines of the microchip revolution of later years.[33] As international competitive advantages came increasingly to depend on 'R&D', the failure of Canadian industry to invest in it became more critical. In 1965, only 356 of 6,367 scientists and engineers employed by Canadian industry were engaged in pure research; and in 1962 spending on R&D as a proportion of sales averaged 0.7 per cent among all Canadian manufacturers, as opposed to 2 per cent among American ones.[34] Many critics complained that the result would be continued Canadian dependence in an age of increasingly complex technology.

CONTENTIOUS ECONOMIC ISSUES

The expansion of the public-enterprise and public-service economy at federal and provincial levels—or its counterpart in science and technology—was not in itself a major political issue in Canada. Most Canadians accepted increased government involvement in the economy, approving public enterprise anchored by the great Crown corporations, increased public expenditure in the administration of various social service programs, and expenditures on intellectual and scientific activities. The contentious issues were somewhat different: the perpetuation of regional and occupational economic disparities; the partly related question of the relationship between federal and provincial public activity; and after 1957, the problem of foreign ownership.

OCCUPATIONAL AND REGIONAL DISPARITIES

Not all sectors of the Canadian economy (and not all Canadians) benefited equally from the affluence of the period 1946 to 1972. There were occupational disparities and regional disparities, inevitably with some overlap between the two. The most obvious occupational weakness in the Canadian economy was in the agricultural sector. One problem was the same one that had become obvious after World War I: Canadian farmers who could hardly meet demand during World War II found that demand for their produce fell dramatically after the war, although government attempted to cushion the blow by retaining the Canadian Wheat Board as the sole Canadian marketing agency and selling Canadian wheat to the USSR and China in the early 1960s. But other factors also affected Canadian agriculture. Increased mechanization and use of fertilizers meant that fewer farmers were needed to produce larger crops, while market agriculture became ever more capital-intensive. Farming marginal lands became less economic than ever, while overall agricultural productivity (both in Canada and abroad) continued to rise steadily. But increasing productivity meant sluggish prices; most increases in food costs to the consumer were caused by non-agricultural factors, such as transportation and processing, rather than increased returns to farmers. Indeed, consumer resistance to paying more for food (as opposed to consumer goods and services) was endemic. The cost of food relative to other expenses actually decreased in this period, and—since food represented the largest single item in the typical Canadian family's budget—the money freed up for other spending was substantial, to the frustration of farmers.

Similarly, when the fishing industry expanded, it was not the fishers who prospered. In fact, a growing fleet in a time of declining fish stocks reduced most fishers' incomes. The government response was not to address the overfishing but to extend unemployment insurance (on a seasonal basis) to the fishing industry, which kept many fishers in the business but did nothing to solve their problems. As in agriculture, mechanization bit deeply into the incomes

■ Men filleting fish at Job Brothers, St John's, Newfoundland, late 1950s. LAC, PA-111454.

of individual producers. In the Atlantic region especially, increasing numbers of large trawlers owned by major fish-processing companies indiscriminately sucked the fish out of the ocean. Consumers were happy to buy the inexpensive refrigerated and frozen fish and seafood made available in this way.

The importance of regional disparities was widely recognized by politicians and economists throughout this period. The most significantly disadvantaged area was held to be the Atlantic region—the Maritime provinces plus Newfoundland, which after 1949 pulled even lower the regional economic statistics that were already poor. The per capita average income in the region was persistently more than 30 per cent below the figures for the other provinces, the proportion of the population working in marginal primary

■ Waiting for the high tide to carry Mr Malcolm Rogers's house ashore, August 1961. The house had been floated to Dover, Bonavista Bay, from Fox Island as part of Newfoundland's relocation program. B. Brooks/National Film Board of Canada. Photothèque/LAC, PA-154123.

resource extraction was much larger than elsewhere, and unemployment (especially on a seasonal basis) ran very high. Although most econo-mists identified inadequate capital investment as the reason for lag in economic growth, finding a way to increase that investment was not easy.

People outside the Atlantic region (and often within it) had a tendency to 'blame the victims' for their economic woes. In 1957, for example, the Gordon Commission followed its comments on comparative income statistics by observing that such data were not necessarily 'a true reflection of the real standards of living in different parts of Canada'. It added, 'many people in the Atlantic region would not exchange on any terms their more peaceful way of life and comparative ease and quiet that goes with it for the noise and bustle and the tenseness which one associates with living in large metropolitan areas like Montreal, Toronto and Vancouver.'[35] By implication, the region's enviable lifestyle compensated, at least to some extent, for its poverty. Such comments naturally raised hackles in the Atlantic provinces, although in fairness an idyllic image of the region as contentedly backward-looking was commonly promoted by its own popular culture and tourist publicity. Over the following decades, artists like Stompin' Tom Connors and Stan Rogers would suggest a more complex picture, combining songs celebrating the region's independence and carefree lifestyle with others expressing sadness and even anger over its economic state.

Related to the notion that the people of the Atlantic region had deliberately rejected Mammon in favour of pleasant living conditions—the classic urban perception of rural life—was one that held subsistence farmers, fishers, and loggers with relatively low incomes to be largely responsible for their fate because they refused to abandon these traditional extractive industries for more remunerative employment. In the 1960s the government of Newfoundland undertook a controversial campaign to remove traditional fisherfolk from its isolated outports. Many people did leave the region to seek employment in other provinces, although when the Gordon Commission suggested that such people should receive 'generous assistance', newspapers blasted the recommendation as 'the second rape of the Acadians'.[36] Nonetheless,

'Newfie' jokes became common in central and western Canada, and not all those treated as objects of derision came from the Rock. The westward migration became the theme of fiction and of Don Shebib's classic film *Goin' Down the Road* (1970), which followed the sad descent of two young Cape Bretoners into crime and ultimate disaster in Ontario.

Meanwhile, northern Canada was equally disadvantaged, but whereas the Atlantic region was expected to continue as an economic laggard into the future, the North could still be regarded as full of undeveloped potential. In 1957 and 1958 Prime Minister John Diefenbaker evoked a stirring 'Vision of the North'—but neither he nor anyone else on the national scene had any comparable dream for Atlantic Canada. Not until the 1970s did neo-Marxist economic thought propose the concept of 'underdevelopment' to explain the situation of Canada's peripheries, seeing their condition as a direct product of the successful development of the nation's economic centre. But if the peripheries were unaware of the explanatory term, they plainly understood the problem of regional disadvantage and looked to the federal system for compensation.

FEDERAL–PROVINCIAL ECONOMIC CONFLICT

The issue of economic disparities among the provinces was a fundamental part of the ongoing battles over constitutional matters after World War II. The Canadian government had significantly centralized economic policy during the war, on the inarguable grounds that the emergency demanded federal control. On the taxation front, the federal government not only greatly increased revenue but even took over some fields of taxation hitherto regarded as provincial prerogatives. Canada 'shared' its revenue with the provinces, which were on the whole happy to be relieved of the debts carried over from the 1930s. The provinces quietly began to balance their budgets. During the war, provinces together had spent only a small fraction of what Ottawa had—only $200 million as against $4.5 billion in 1944, for example. After the war the federal government insisted that it alone could develop and implement the policies required to master the economy. By and large, the poorer provinces were happy to go along with that idea, but it was quite unacceptable to the larger and more dynamic provinces with more extensive resource bases: Ontario, Quebec, British Columbia, and Alberta. They quickly reasserted the dormant concept of provincial rights at the Dominion–Provincial Conference on Reconstruction that opened in Ottawa in August 1945. As a result, the emergency powers were discontinued and a complex system of tax-sharing under the guise of 'tax rentals' was adopted under which the provinces received grants and subsidies in return for not exercising their powers of taxation (see also Chapter 15). Ontario and Quebec rejected the arrangement, but the remaining provinces (and later Newfoundland) went along with it—at least for the moment.

The years that followed saw the re-emergence of tension between the federal government and the provinces over finances and economic development. The key period was probably the 1950s and early 1960s, when the provinces greatly expanded both the social services they provided and the civil services that administered them. In the past, large teams of highly trained and skilled Ottawa mandarins had gone up against small teams of provincial ministers supported only by a deputy minister, but now the confrontations involved conflicting teams of specialists, each with its own agenda. No province was happy. The poorer provinces wanted a greater share of revenue through increased equalization payments, while the wealthier provinces (led by Ontario) opposed such schemes and demanded greater autonomy for development of their own resources. In a sense, nothing had changed since Confederation. Quebec was particularly difficult to accommodate, since it sought to control various programs such as pensions and unemployment compensation that the

other nine provinces (including Ontario) were willing to leave in the hands of the federal government. Moreover, Quebec had a substantial historical case to support its position.

In 1953 Quebec established a Royal Commission of Inquiry on Constitutional Problems (the Tremblay Commission), which was still able to offer a traditional and conservative French-Canadian nationalist position on these matters. Its report, submitted in 1956, argued a view of Confederation in which provinces could opt out of particular federal programs. It saw the need for the protection of Quebec distinctiveness almost exclusively in cultural rather than economic terms: 'Because of the religion, culture and the history of the majority of its population, the Province of Quebec is not a province like the others.'[37] It also offered a view, which would become more fashionable a decade later, of Canada as a bicultural nation.[38] But the report's most interesting sections, from our present perspective, made an unfavourable analysis of what it called 'the new federalism', which had emerged only after 1940: 'a system characterized by the predominant place which the central government occupies (or seeks to occupy) in the life of the Canadian community, mainly on the grounds of national defence, social welfare and security, economic stability and the fiscal system'.[39] Quebec objected particularly to federal control of social and economic policy and openly sought a return to the pre-1940 period, concentrating its financial recommendations on different formulas of tax-sharing and fiscal equalization. Although the focus and particular emphasis of Quebec's constitutional position would change over the ensuing decades, the general historical outline on which that position was based would stay much the same.

Questions such as control of offshore oil resources, which emerged as an issue in 1961 in British Columbia and made its way eastward, also bedevilled federal–provincial relations. Similarly, the government of W.A.C. Bennett disagreed with Ottawa on the sale of power from the Columbia River basin to the US.[40] Debate on the Canadian

Constitution focused mainly on bilingualism-biculturalism and a satisfactory means of repatriating the British North America Act from the British Parliament. But a fundamental subtext in the debate was the fact that few provinces wished to give the federal government control over economic development, particularly as more and more provinces found they had bonanza resources (such as oil and gas) to protect. Indeed, one of the principal characteristics of the constitutional conflicts of the 1960s was the disparity between their apparent focus on cultural and political issues and the growing restiveness of the provinces over economic issues.

FOREIGN INVESTMENT

The underlying economic tensions in federal–provincial relations seldom made the newspaper headlines or the top spot on the national TV news. Ordinary taxpayers did not fully understand about equalization payments or oil pricing. They might not have appreciated the technicalities of foreign investment either, but by the late 1960s every Canadian knew that the issue was somehow important. Before 1957 the nation had for decades paid virtually no attention to foreign (especially American) direct investment in its industry and resources. As late as 1956, a well-reviewed textbook in Canadian economic history discussed foreign investment in Canada as 'one of the mainsprings of progress', without much distinction between direct and indirect strategies.[41] The man responsible for publicizing the problem was Walter Gordon, a partner in a leading Toronto accounting firm who occasionally did work for the government. A more unlikely candidate for economic prophet was at first glance hard to imagine, although, in retrospect, we can see the extent to which he defined the issues of the debates of the period.[42] A soft-spoken man not known for his charisma, Gordon lacked the liberal arts background of most mandarins and had been best known for his chairmanship of the Royal Commission on Administrative Classifi-

cations in the Public Service of 1946 and his part in the reorganization of the Canadian Department of National Defence in 1949. Although acquainted with many of Ottawa's top civil servants, including Mike Pearson, Gordon was a Liberal Party outsider who had for years chafed under C.D. Howe's economic czardom, which was so friendly to American business enterprise. He had refused a junior portfolio in the St Laurent ministry in 1954, after much deliberation and a conversation with Howe in which he had wondered aloud what the elder man's response would be if a new minister questioned one of his policies in cabinet. Howe, astonished, shouted: 'You'd do what, young man?'[43] By 1955 Gordon was advocating a Royal Commission to investigate Canada's economic future, and in the end he was appointed to chair it himself.

The Commission consisted of Gordon and four colleagues, with a research staff of 24 full-time and 15 part-time members, most of them well-known academic economists. (One of its senior staff members was Simon Reisman, who then was at the Department of Finance, but who in the 1980s would become Canada's representative in the free-trade negotiations with the US.) It began its work in the spring of 1955, started public hearings in November of that year, and finished its deliberations, including the study of 330 separate briefs, within 18 months. But the final report did not actually appear until April 1958 (although dated November 1957), well after John Diefenbaker's Tories had come to power in a minority government. With a federal election in the offing, the Commission had issued a preliminary report in December 1956 that was made public a month later to considerable press coverage and controversy. C.D. Howe was extremely angry with the Commission's conclusions; Prime Minister Louis St Laurent was equally hostile, and Gordon (with others) lamented the Liberal Party's inability 'to accept the conclusions as a broad outline for the future', which he later argued might have spared the party from defeat in 1957.[44] A new approach to

WALTER GORDON
(1906–1987)

❖

Walter Gordon was born into a wealthy business-class family in Toronto. During World War I he accompanied his mother to England to be near his father, who was fighting in France, and contracted polio at his boarding school, which partially paralyzed his face and forced him to wear thick glasses. Back in Ontario, he attended Upper Canada College and Royal Military College, then joined the family accounting firm and settled down to a professional life that included occasional work for government commissions. During World War II a serious case of gout kept him out of the military, and he served for a dollar a year in Ottawa, consulting on financial issues for the Bank of Canada.

After the war Gordon was asked to chair the Royal Commission on Administrative Classifications in the Public Service, but agreed to serve only on a part-time basis. The Commission's report was weak and not very influential. Gordon spent more time founding Canadian Management Company, which became Canadian Corporate Management Co. Ltd in 1949. A long-time friendship with Lester B. Pearson continued to grow, and because of his obvious organizational skills, Gordon was pushed to enter political life, but he remained out of the front line of politics. In 1955 he began advocating new economic policies for the Liberal Party. His insistence led directly to the Royal Commission on Canada's Economic Prospects (appointed over the objections of C.D. Howe) and he was named its chairman. Recruiting a stellar staff of researchers and assistants, Gordon himself prepared the agenda for the Commission, demonstrating a keen interest in foreign investment. Concern over American economic influence was on the rise everywhere in Canada, and the statistics collected by the Gordon Commission on the level of American investment proved startling. It was the Gordon Commission that first publicized the dangers of foreign investment, but it was Walter Gordon himself who helped make foreign investment a major issue, as part of a rethinking of Canadian economic purpose and Canadian nationalism.

Beginning early in 1960, Gordon argued that Canada had to halt its economic integration with the US if it was to remain an independent country. He soon had 'Mike' Pearson convinced, but he offered little evidence and was unable to carry the Liberal Party with him. Many economists doubted his conclusions. Gordon repeated his arguments in *Troubled Canada: The Need for New Domestic Policies*, published in the summer of 1961. Again the economists were critical. In 1963 Gordon was elected to Parliament and became Pearson's Minister of Finance. He remained in office for two and a half years, despite being forced to withdraw a proposed tax on foreign ownership of Canadian firms. After leaving the cabinet he pressed for an investigation of Canadian industry (the Watkins Task Force), and with Abraham Rotstein and Peter C. Newman founded the Committee for an Independent Canada in February 1970 as an alternative to the left-wing nationalism of the Waffle movement within the NDP. Over the years from 1955 to 1970, no Canadian did more than Walter Gordon to promote a new sense of Canadian nationalism.

KARI LEVITT ON DEPENDENCE

In 1970 the economist Kari Levitt published *Silent Surrender*, a book subtitled *The Multinational Corporation in Canada*. Levitt's concern was to show how new economic forces were undermining the Canadian nation.

While economic factors are quick to act on the orientation of the business class, the erosion of the value system, which was formed during the nation-building phase of Canada's history, is a slower process. Although branch-plant industry, branch-plant culture and branch-plant universities are undermining traditional Canadian values, yet these values persist. Respect for law and order, regard for civil rights, abhorrence of mob rule and gangsterism (whether practised at the bottom or the top of the social scale), and traditional respect for Ottawa as the national government of the country are still deeply felt in English Canada. These are the elements of English-Canadian patriotism and they define the English Canadian, as distinct from the American. This value system is as real as the branch plants. It is the source that nourishes English-Canadian nationalism, and it is reinforced by every action of the United States which violates these values.

Whereas these values were created by the older Canadian elite, which shaped the nation, the existing business class cannot give effective expression to Canadian nationalism because it has been absorbed into the world of corporate empire. It rejected John Diefenbaker because he is a nationalist; it rejected Walter Gordon for the same reason [George] Grant has observed, namely, that the power of the American government to control Canada lies not so much in its ability to exert pressure as in the fact that the dominant classes in Canada see themselves at one with continentalism.

The effect of the American corporate presence on relations between central and provincial governments is clear; the linear trans-continental axis, which once integrated the nation under an active and strong central government, has largely disintegrated. The new pattern of north–south trade and investment based on resource-development and branch-plant manufacturing, does not require a strong central government. The central government is left to manage the old infrastructure of communications and commercial institutions carried over from the previous era. However, new public expenditures are typically regional—hydro-electric schemes, highways, schools, hospitals, and the like. The system of fiscal redistribution conflicts with the economic interests of the richer and more fortunate provinces. The federal function of providing for the defence of the nation is not sufficiently urgent to offset the shift of so many other functions to the regional level. Furthermore, a considerable part of the prosperity of defence work originates from the United States government, and is strongly regional in its impact on employment and income.

Political fragmentation along regional lines serves the interests of the international corporations. . . . Recent efforts to launch regional development policies at the federal level have produced a bureaucratic structure whose organizational sophistication far out-distances that of the policies which have to date been announced in Ottawa.

In the absence of effective federal initiatives to provide the means of mobilizing and directing Canada's resources towards the elimination of regional disparities, the provinces will reinforce the continentalist trend by joining the competitive scramble for foreign investment. They opposed the rationalization of the fiscal structure proposed by the Carter Commission and the government White Paper on taxation; they pressured the federal government into begging exemptions from the US interest equalization tax. They may be expected to oppose each and every measure devised to control the terms on which foreign capital may enter Canada. In the absence of effective leadership by Ottawa they reinforce the continentalism of big business by dismembering the federal structure of Canada.

SOURCE: Kari Levitt, *Silent Surrender: The Multinational Corporation in Canada* (Toronto: Macmillan Canada, 1970), 144–6.

foreign investment was the report's most controversial 'conclusion'.

In the final report, the discussion of foreign investment constituted only a part of one chapter out of 20. It focused on the current situation, which it pointed out had become more extreme since the war with the decline of British investment. The commissioners recognized that Canada needed external capital for development, but emphasized that since the war, US investment had more than doubled, chiefly through the retention and reinvestment of earnings by companies already controlled by American interests. It observed the concentration of American investment in secondary manufacturing and resource industries and quoted from one of its commissioned studies: 'No other nation as highly industrialized as Canada has such a large proportion of industry controlled by non-resident concerns.'[45] Only a few pages were devoted to 'the dangers . . . in the present situation' and to the potential conflicts between Canadian interests and foreign ownership. The Commission admitted that precise evidence was not easy to obtain and that most foreign-controlled companies were good corporate citizens. Concerns were speculative rather than documented, and the report merely recommended that such companies employ Canadian senior personnel, make full disclosure of their Canadian operations, include independent Canadians on their boards of directors, and sell appreciable amounts of their equity stock to Canadians. Such a program was hardly very radical.

By the time the final report of the Gordon Commission was issued, the Diefenbaker government was able to consign it to official limbo. Although the new Prime Minister probably concurred with its suspicions about the multinationals, he rightly regarded Gordon himself as a card-carrying Liberal. At first, many professional economists complained that insufficient data were available to support even the mildest of the report's claims about foreign investment. But in the later 1960s, the issue of American ownership began feeding into a new wave of nationalism, concerns over maintenance of a distinctive Canadian identity,[46] anti-American feeling (or at least opposition to the Vietnam War), and the New Left movement, centred in the universities, which had a strong voice in the New Democratic Party in the latter part of the decade. Radical younger scholars such as Mel Watkins—who headed the Task Force on the Structure of Canadian Industry, and in February 1968 released its report entitled *Foreign Ownership and the Structure of Canadian Industry* (the 'Watkins Report')—wanted to go further than Walter Gordon had 10 years earlier. Public opinion reflected the growing concern over US investment in Canada. In 1964, only 46 per cent of Canadians thought there was enough American investment, and 33 per cent wanted more. By 1972, 67 per cent said 'enough now', and only 22 per cent wanted more.[47]

CONCLUSION

By the early 1970s, the Canadian economy had enjoyed an unprecedented quarter-century of growth and prosperity. Yet the problems it was about to face did not spring full-blown out of nothing. There was an undercurrent of dissatisfaction throughout the period, although much of it did not come to popular attention until the mid-1960s, when critics of the status quo found new strategic and ideological vehicles to carry discontent into the public arena. Many argued that economic questions could not be divorced from social, political, and constitutional ones, and the result, as we shall see, was a period of widespread questioning of prevailing policy. As the saying went, if you weren't part of the solution, you were part of the problem.

SHORT BIBLIOGRAPHY

Azzi, Stephen. *Walter Gordon and the Rise of Canadian Nationalism*. Montreal and Kingston, 1999. An important study of how Walter Gordon became the leading guru of post-war Canadian nationalism.

Bothwell, Robert. *Nucleus: The History of Atomic Energy of Canada Limited*. Toronto, 1988. The best study of the history of atomic energy in Canada.

———, Ian Drummond, and John English. *Canada since 1945: Power, Politics and Provincialism*, rev. edn. Toronto, 1989. A rich narrative of the post-war period, very sympathetic to the federalist position.

——— and William Kilbourn. *C.D. Howe: A Biography*. Toronto, 1979. A sensitive biography of the economic czar of Canada's wartime and post-war economy.

Canada. Royal Commission on Canada's Economic Prospects. *Report*. Ottawa, 1958. The Gordon Commission's report, one of the most fascinating economic documents ever produced in Canadian history.

Doern, G. Bruce. *Science and Politics in Canada*. Montreal and London, 1972. A useful introduction to the complex relationship of science and politics in Canada.

Jackson, Eric, ed. *The Great Canadian Debate: Foreign Ownership*. Toronto, 1975. A collection of different voices on the greatest economic issue of the post-war years.

Rea, K.J. *The Prosperous Years: The Economic History of Ontario, 1939–1975*. Toronto, 1985. A careful analysis of the prosperity of Ontario—the bellwether province—in the middle third of the twentieth century.

Safarian, A.E. *Foreign Ownership of Canadian Industry*. Toronto, 1966. A sober and non-sensational study of the problem of foreign ownership from the vantage point of the mid-1960s.

Trudeau, Pierre Elliott, ed. *The Asbestos Strike*. Toronto, 1974. Trudeau's first important appearance before the public, originally published in French in 1951, with an introduction by the editor well worth revisiting for what it tells us about the young thinker.

STUDY QUESTIONS

1. Why did the Canadian economy boom after World War II?
2. What were the guiding assumptions of the Gordon Commission?
3. Why was industrial pollution not regarded as more important before 1972?
4. How did the Avro Arrow come to symbolize the downfall of Canadian defence production in the late 1950s? How did technology work against Canada militarily after 1953?
5. Why was the Crown corporation such an important part of Canadian enterprise?
6. What victories did organized labour win in the post-war period?
7. What factors constrained Canada's research and development efforts?
8. What were the major economic issues debated in Canada between 1946 and 1972?
9. Why was Walter Gordon called the father of Canadian nationalism? Is the label accurate?

CHAPTER FIFTEEN

The Era of Liberal Consensus, 1946–1972

Between 1945 and 1972, politics and public policy were dominated by a small-'l' liberal consensus that reflected the same Keynesian thinking that—translated into North American terms by Canadian-born John Kenneth Galbraith—dominated economics and economic policy in the same period.[1] On the whole, the civil servants were more willing than the politicians to accept that full employment and an end to poverty—the twin goals of Keynes's thinking—required a thoroughly interventionist state that would restrict capitalist enterprise and, in many cases, establish public enterprise to replace it.

Like the liberal democrats of the late nineteenth and early twentieth centuries, the Keynesians believed in market capitalism, properly regulated. But the 'new liberalism', as Keynesianism has often been called, was both more interventionist and more oriented to the economy than the liberal-democratic school that preceded it. Most of the prominent Keynesians in the governments of Mackenzie King and his successors were more economic than social thinkers, and most served in economic capacities, usually in the Finance ministry.[2] Politicians and civil servants in the post-1945 era remembered both the Depression, when government had stood back and allowed citizens to suffer, and World War II, when government had taken an active role in

many areas, sometimes to the benefit of citizens. For them, government intervention to produce full employment was the centrepiece of state policy. While variations in commitment to state activity existed among Canadian political parties, there was a remarkable underlying consensus to the political debates of this period, regardless of the party in power. The years between 1945 and 1972 saw the gradual and piecemeal establishment—by fits and starts—of what came to be called the 'welfare state' in Canada, a ramshackle, unco-ordinated collection of federal and provincial programs that together provided social insurance for most Canadians.

POST-WAR POLITICAL CULTURE

LIBERAL HEGEMONY

The period between the end of World War II and the early 1970s was part of a longer era from 1935 to 1979 in which federal politics (and the administration of government in Canada) were dominated by the Liberal Party. Except for a six-year hiatus between 1957 and 1963, when the Progressive Conservatives under John Diefenbaker ran the nation, the Liberals were in power throughout the era of post-war prosperity—and beyond. Both the party and the political pundits

TIMELINE

1944
Family Allowances Act passed.

1945
Dominion–Provincial Conference on Reconstruction.

1947
35,000 veterans are enrolled in Canadian universities.

1949
The Supreme Court of Canada replaces the Judicial Committee of the Privy Council, in London, as the final court of appeal for Canadians. National Housing Act revised to discourage public rental housing. Newfoundland enters Confederation.

1951
Old Age Security Act and Old Age Assistance Act pass Parliament. Indian Act amended to extend provincial social benefits to Aboriginal people.

1954
Passage of new National Housing Act, intended to assist low-income families with housing.

1956
Pipeline debate in House of Commons. Unemployment Assistance Act passed.

1957
Tory minority government elected. Hospital Insurance and Diagnostic Services Act passes Parliament.

1958
Diefenbaker sweeps the country.

1960
Royal Commission on Government Organization (Glassco Commission) battles with reform of bureaucracy in federal government. Louis Robichaud in New Brunswick cements link between Acadians and Liberal Party. Passage of John Diefenbaker's Bill for the Recognition and Protection of Human Rights and Fundamental Freedoms.

1961
National Indian Council is formed.

1962
26 of 30 Social Credit MPs elected from Quebec. Doctors strike in Saskatchewan over public medical insurance.

1965
Pierre Trudeau first elected to Parliament.

1966
Passage of the Medical Care Act and Canada Assistance Plan. Committee on Equality for Women organized.

1968
Robert Stanfield and P.E. Trudeau chosen new party leaders. Federal election campaign is the first conducted largely via television. Canadian Métis Society and the National Indian Brotherhood emerge out of the National Indian Council.

1969
Student protestors occupy computer centre at Sir George Williams University in Montreal. White Paper on federal Indian policy causes major controversy. Criminal Code provisions on sexual offences are revised.

1970
White Paper on Metric Conversion. Demolition of Africville in Halifax. First national Abortion Caravan.

WRM-943

■ The Hon. C.D. Howe broadcasting on CBC Radio on the occasion of the completion of the first Canadian-built tank, the Cruiser Tank, at Angus Shops, Montreal Locomotive Works, 27 May 1941. National Film Board of Canada/LAC, PA-174503.

came to view Liberal government as natural and inevitable, considering the Liberals to be Canada's 'natural governing party'. The Liberal hegemony was based on a number of factors, some of which seemed so immutable that a permanent change in the national political tendency was nearly unthinkable.[3] The Liberals might sometimes fail to win an absolute majority, but they could continue to govern so long as they were the largest political party in the House of Commons. Only very occasionally could the opposing PCs hope to construct a majority themselves, and then only on the basis of a general rejection of the Liberals by the national electorate.[4]

The nature of the Canadian electoral system—particularly the 'first past the post' method of determining the winners—combined with the presence of other political parties beyond the two major ones to make the popular vote almost irrelevant in determining the relative strengths of the various parties in the House of Commons. In the entire period the Liberals never won more than 50 per cent of the popular vote in any election, although they came close to it in 1949 and 1953, and only the Diefenbaker government of 1958 was elected by more than 50 per cent of the votes cast. The correlation between popular vote and number of seats could be quite low for major

CLARENCE DECATUR HOWE
(1886–1960)

❖

Born in Waltham, Massachusetts, in 1886, Clarence Decatur Howe, who was always known as 'C.D.', attended the Massachusetts Institute of Technology (MIT), graduating in 1907. In 1908, Dalhousie University in Nova Scotia asked the head of his department at MIT to recommend a bright young man for an appointment as a full professor in civil engineering. He and another young lecturer tossed a coin to see who would take the job, and Howe won the toss. He was an enthusiastic and successful young teacher for several years, and then left Dalhousie in 1913 to become chief engineer of the Board of Grain Commissioners in Ottawa. He also became a Canadian citizen. Howe's principal job was to build grain elevators. Three years later he formed his own engineering and construction firm in Port Arthur, Ontario, and over the next 20 years his firm handled over $100 million worth of construction projects, specializing in grain-storage facilities.

In 1935 Howe accepted a personal invitation from William Lyon Mackenzie King and the Liberal Party to run for the House of Commons. Elected Liberal MP from Port Arthur, he headed a new Department of Transportation formed out of the amalgamation of the Departments of Shipping and Railways. Unlike King, who was caution personified, Howe had an engineer's mentality. He was frustrated by red tape and by parliamentary niceties, and told the Commons at the end of his political career, 'somehow I reach a point in the development of a project where I begin to think it is important, and if it is a serious

enough project, then I begin to think it is the most important thing in the world.' His first achievement was to reorganize and rationalize harbour administration across Canada over the objections of local interests. Howe quickly became notorious for blunt speaking, joined to unswerving and uncompromising commitment to his goals. He soon introduced a bill to produce a special committee to examine the operations of the Canadian Broadcasting Commission and another bill to restructure the Canadian National Railway. One of the by-products of the railway legislation was a bill to establish a national airline. The government had not originally intended that the airline would be publicly owned, but with the refusal of one of the railway companies it had hoped would share in the airline venture (Canadian Pacific Railway) to become involved, the establishment of a public monopoly was almost inevitable.

From the beginning of his parliamentary career, Howe became associated with Crown corporations, and the elaboration and expansion of the Crown corporation has often been regarded as his principal contribution to Canada, although his role in economic planning and administration during World War II has to run at least a close second. Howe ran the Department of Munitions and Supplies from 9 April 1940, using Canadian businessmen as his managers and working closely with the United States. In December 1940 a ship in which he was sailing to Great Britain was torpedoed, and Howe spent eight hours in a lifeboat before being rescued. In 1944 he became Minister of Reconstruction, charged with supervising the return of the Canadian economy to peacetime while not sacrificing prosperity. He instinctively understood that this would involve a shift to production for the consumer market. During the Cold War, he became Minister of Trade and Commerce, responsible for armament production during the Korean War. The justification for Howe's increasing refusal to brook any opposition or

criticism was the need for efficiency during national emergency. But Howe became increasingly oblivious to either parliamentary or public opinion, and eventually his 'arrogant' behaviour and 'lust for power' helped bring down the Liberal government of Louis St Laurent in 1957. His legacy was the public ownership culture of the Crown corporation, which has never been totally dismantled.

and minor parties alike. The system tended to translate any edge in the popular vote for a major party into a significantly larger number of seats and to dissipate votes for other parties. Third parties were much better off electorally if their support was confined to ridings in one region and not spread widely across the country, although that situation was devastating to their national aspirations. Local strength gave some clout to the Créditiste followers of Réal Caouette in the 1960s and advantaged Social Credit over the CCF–NDP. In 1953, for example, the Liberals had 48.8 per cent of the popular vote to 31 per cent for the PCs, 11.3 per cent for the CCF, and 5.4 per cent for the Social Credit Party. These percentages translated to 171 Liberal seats, 51 PC, 23 CCF, and 15 Social Credit.[5]

The Liberals held several advantages in the pursuit of continued federal power, of which two were absolutely critical. Above all was the ongoing support of Quebec, which held one of the largest blocks of seats in the House of Commons. Support from francophone Quebec had come to the Liberals in the 1890s, was solidified during the Conscription Crisis of 1917, and was further confirmed by Mackenzie King's management of the same issue during World War II. The Liberals did not lose a federal election in Quebec between 1896 and 1958, usually winning over 75 per cent

of the available seats. To triumph nationally without Quebec support, an opposition party needed to win the vast majority of seats in the rest of the country, including Ontario (where the two major parties were always more evenly matched than in other regions). The Tory victory of 1957, achieved in just that way, could produce only a minority government. The Diefenbaker sweep of 1958 was the exception that proved the rule. In all other elections the Liberals had been able to persuade Quebec's francophone voters that the other parties were unsympathetic to them. The apparent Liberal stranglehold on Quebec had its impact on the other parties, particularly in terms of the choice of leaders and in electoral strategies. During this period, neither the Progressive Conservatives nor the CCF–NDP ever seriously considered selecting a leader from Quebec, or even a fluently bilingual anglophone—let alone a French Canadian. Nor did the other parties make much of an effort to campaign in French Canada, except perhaps in 1958. The Liberals, therefore, continued their historic collaboration with francophone Quebec, and this association tended to polarize Canadian federal politics. The Liberals also did well with other francophone groups, particularly the Acadians in the Maritimes.

But the Liberals' political advantage was not confined to support from francophones, as the elections of the 1960s would demonstrate. In order to win power, all national political parties needed to appeal to a broad spectrum of voters across the nation, but only the Liberals consistently succeeded in this effort, chiefly by staking out their political ground outside French Canada slightly to the left of centre. Mackenzie King had specialized in co-opting the most popular goals of the welfare state, often lifting them shamelessly from the platform of the CCF (a practice his successors continued). In 1963 the *Ottawa Citizen* was able to describe the Liberal Party as 'a coalition in the Canadian tradition that embraces people of all classes and regions built around a programme and the solution of issues rather than a person', while maintaining that the Progressive Conservative Party was 'built around the personality of Mr Diefenbaker'.[6] Equally to the point, when the Liberals failed to obtain a clear-cut parliamentary majority in the elections of 1963 and 1965, they were kept in power by the third parties. The Diefenbaker Tories, during their 1962–3 minority government, were unable to agree on a legislative program that could win third-party approval, while the Liberals were always flexible (their critics said opportunistic) enough to be able to accommodate third-party issues.

There were, of course, other reasons for the Liberals' continued success besides general support from French Canada and a moderate left-of-centre position on the political spectrum. Many involved luck as much as skill, although opportunism and an instinct for power made their contributions. For example, the Liberals should have been in serious trouble in 1968, when the PCs finally replaced John Diefenbaker with a credible and apparently sympathetic national leader in the person of Robert Stanfield of Nova Scotia. Stanfield's unquestioned integrity and good sense seemed to make him a good match for Prime Minister Lester Pearson. The party had a few carefully worked-out policies, including a guaranteed annual income, designed to capture some of the left-centre ground. But in December 1967 Pearson announced his retirement, and in April

■ John Diefenbaker and Lester Pearson, 30 January 1958. Duncan Cameron/LAC, PA-117093.

1968 Pierre Elliott Trudeau, recently arrived in Ottawa and currently Justice Minister, was elected to succeed him. Not only was he thoroughly bilingual and likely to appeal in Quebec, but he was able to convince the electorate that he was far more of a reformer than either his electoral pronouncements or subsequent policies would indicate. In addition, with a French-Canadian father and English-Canadian mother, he comfortably straddled Canada's two solitudes.

The campaign leading up to the federal election of 25 June 1968 was the first one conducted largely through the media, particularly television, and only the Liberals had a leader who was able to project a positive and charismatic personality on the tube. Stanfield was a leader seemingly designed for yesterday's politics. One reason for Trudeau's success was his ability, at the height of the 1960s ferment, to appeal to urban and female voters as a swinging 'instant pop hero'.[7] The Liberal candidates grasped Trudeau's coattails and won a resounding victory. As Dalton Camp, the architect of Stanfield's leadership victory and 1968 campaign, ruefully admitted: 'When all goes well, you are . . . courted by good luck. The sun beamed down on Trudeau. The rain poured down on Stanfield.'[8] To which the Liberals might have responded, 'You make your own luck by your choice of candidate.'

The Liberal Party had long had an unofficial policy of alternating its leadership between French and Anglo Canada. Between 1887 and 1984—virtually a century—it was led by only five men: Laurier (1887–1919), King (1919–48), St Laurent (1948–58), Pearson (1958–68), and Trudeau (1968–84), all of whom served as Prime Minister. Their longevity as leaders was greatly assisted by the party's ability to remain in office. The Liberals selected for leaders urbane, well-educated men from the professional middle classes oriented to federal government and politics. Each had his own expertise. King was a professional labour consultant and negotiator who had studied economics at Chicago and Harvard and written a well-known book entitled *Industry and Humanity* (1918). St Laurent, a former law professor at Laval, was a highly successful corporation lawyer and president of the Canadian Bar Association who became a popular Prime Minister under the folksy sobriquet of 'Uncle Louis'. Pearson had begun as a history professor at the University of Toronto before joining External Affairs as a professional diplomat. Trudeau was educated at the Université de Montréal, Harvard, and the London School of Economics, and was serving as a law professor at the Université de Montréal when elected to Parliament in 1965. None of these men had earned a doctorate, but all held non-political appointments that in our own time would probably require such a degree.

The Conservative Party had gone through a good many more leaders, few of whom had ever had a chance to govern the nation. From John A. Macdonald's death in 1891 to Brian Mulroney's election as leader in 1985, the Tories were led federally by 14 different men. Only Robert Borden and John Diefenbaker lasted for more than 10 years. From 1945 to 1972 the Conservative Party (renamed the Progressive Conservative Party in 1942) was headed by John Bracken (1942–8), George Drew (1948–56), Diefenbaker (1956–67), and Robert Stanfield (1967–76). Apart from Diefenbaker, the other three had been popular and successful provincial premiers with little federal administrative experience. Diefenbaker's federal expertise was as an opposition member (later spokesman) in the House of Commons from 1940. Except for Bracken, who had been a professor of field husbandry at the University of Saskatchewan before becoming head of the Manitoba Agricultural College in 1920, they were all small-town lawyers before entering politics. All the Tory leaders after World War II were regarded as being to the left of their parties, and both Bracken and Stanfield had a major influence in moving PC policy towards a national centre. Diefenbaker was *sui generis*, a brilliant if old-fashioned political orator and a genuine western populist. All the PC leaders had strong sympathies for the ordinary Canadian, although only Diefenbaker had the public presence to be able to convince the electorate of his concerns. Significantly, none of these men spoke French very comfortably, and Diefenbaker's electoral victories in Quebec were largely achieved without his campaigning presence in the province.

COUNTERBALANCING LIBERAL HEGEMONY

After 1945, the federal dominance of the Liberals as the party of government was mediated by a number of countervailing factors in Canadian politics. The Americans had provided checks and balances within their central government—the Senate, the Supreme Court—that were not available in the same way within the Canadian parliamentary system of responsible government, under which Parliament (especially the House of Commons) was supreme. So long as the government in power held a majority in the Commons, it had the legal and technical ability to do pretty much as it wanted. Nevertheless, there were some clear limitations on this theoretical omnipotence.

One limitation that applied to any government was the increased size and scope of the apparatus of bureaucracy, including the mandarins and, especially, the civil service. The fact that government at all levels became Canada's largest employer had substantial implications. From 46,000 employees in 1939 and 116,000 in 1946, by 1966 the federal government had grown to 228,000 employees. But both provincial and municipal governments grew even faster, the provinces employing a total of 50,000 in 1946 and 257,000 in 1966, the municipalities 56,000 in 1946 and 224,000 in 1966.[9] The scope of bureaucracy had political as well as economic implications. The larger it got, the harder it was to manage. A host of popular commentators attacked governments at all levels for mismanagement and waste; however, as one pointed out, 'the initial motive for reforms may be the outsider's simple-minded belief that gigantic savings can be effected. But once set an investigation afoot and the economy motive gets quickly overlaid with the more subtle and difficult problems of improved service and inefficiency.'[10] A Royal Commission on Government Organization—created by the Diefenbaker government in 1960 to improve efficiency and economy in the departments and agencies of the federal government and chaired by J. Grant Glassco—found itself unable to recommend ways to downscale the scope of operations. All governments, including federal Liberal ones, increasingly found themselves trapped by the actions of their predecessors and by the difficulties of dismantling systems already in place.

Another important limitation was the force of public opinion. Federal politicians took their chances when they attempted policies that were well in advance of what the country found acceptable, but they ran even greater risks when they crossed an unwritten boundary of fair play in their use of power, particularly in Parliament. The Liberals under St Laurent were defeated in the 1957 election for many reasons, but one of the most critical was a public sense that they had become too 'arrogant'. John Diefenbaker got great mileage from the abuse of the rights of Parliament in the notorious pipeline debate in May 1956, when the Liberals invoked closure on a controversial measure. The event became a symbol of Liberal contempt for the democratic process. The Canadian public over the years consistently demonstrated that it would tolerate quite a lot from its politicians and political parties before it became persuaded of systematic abuse of power, but the risk of earning such public disapproval has always helped to curb excesses, particularly for governments with large majorities.

THIRD-PARTY INFLUENCE

Opposition in Parliament was another factor that to some extent affected the ways in which Liberal dominance was played out and became limited politically. The elections of 1957, 1962, 1963, and 1965 all returned minority governments, which meant that the government had to pay more attention to third parties. In fact, substantial proportions of the federal electorate did not vote for either the Liberals or the Conservatives in this period (see Table 15.1). In the post-war period, the two principal third parties were the CCF–NDP and the Social Credit/Créditistes.

The CCF emerged from the war with high hopes, gaining 15.6 per cent of the popular vote and 28 members of Parliament in the 1945 federal election. Its popularity waned in the ensuing elections, however, and in 1958 it was reduced

■ T.C. Douglas at the founding convention of the New Democratic Party, in July 1961, when he was selected as its first leader. LAC, C-36219.

former Saskatchewan Premier T.C. (Tommy) Douglas. The new party did better than its predecessor had, drawing 13.5 per cent of the popular vote and 19 seats in 1962, 13.1 per cent and 17 seats in 1963, 17.9 per cent and 21 seats in 1965, and 17.0 per cent and 22 seats in 1968. But it continued to do poorly in Quebec and the East, and its admitted association with organized labour replaced its former association with communism as the principal obstacle to its making a real national breakthrough.

Although the NDP was unable to increase its national base of support, as a voice on the left it exercised considerable influence in the election campaigns of the 1960s and real power during the minority governments of Pearson. In the 1963 campaign, for example, it was Douglas who advocated income distribution and improved social services, including universal medicare. These policies were far more specific than Pearson's made-in-America 'war on poverty', and they were translated into legislative commitments by the Liberals when faced with a minority situation in 1963. The CCF–NDP also had considerable success at the provincial level in this period, forming governments in Saskatchewan (1944–64, 1971–82), British Columbia (1972–7), and Manitoba (1969–77), and often forming the official opposition in these and other provinces. It was the Saskatchewan NDP government that first introduced medicare, in 1962, championing the plan through to acceptance over considerable opposition from the province's doctors.

The CCF–NDP was not the only important third party on the federal scene. The other was

to eight MPs and 9.5 per cent of the popular vote. Support for the party eroded chiefly because some people mistakenly thought that the CCF was associated with international communism, and many considered it too radical (socialistic and statist) and too doctrinaire. It failed to achieve any electoral success east of Ontario, in either Quebec or the Atlantic region, and had difficulty in presenting itself as a truly national alternative to the two major parties. After its 1958 defeat, the CCF remobilized, forming an alliance with organized labour (the Canadian Labour Congress) and in 1961 becoming the New Democratic Party under the leadership of

---

TABLE 15.1

PERCENTAGE OF THIRD-PARTY VOTE IN FEDERAL ELECTIONS, 1945–1968

Year	1945	1949	1953	1957	1958	1962	1963	1965	1968
Percentage	32.7	20.8	20.2	20.1	12.8	25.5	25.5	27.4	23.1

SOURCE: J. Murray Beck, *Pendulum of Power, Canada's Federal Elections* (Scarborough, Ont.: Prentice-Hall, 1968), passim.

THOMAS CLEMENT DOUGLAS (1904–1986)

❖

Born in Scotland, 'Tommy' Douglas emigrated with his family to Winnipeg in 1910, growing up in the city that was the home of the General Strike of 1919, the social gospel, and the labour church. Not surprisingly, he became an advocate of social reform as a Christian minister, serving his first church (Calvary Baptist) at Weyburn beginning in 1929. Douglas was active (although not a leader) in the establishment of the Co-operative Commonwealth Federation in 1933, and managed to become elected to the federal Parliament as a CCFer in 1935. His pugnacious evangelical oratory soon made him an important figure in the House of Commons, although the party's reputation was damaged by James S. Woodsworth's pacifism in 1939. Douglas returned to provincial politics in 1942 and became provincial Premier in 1944, virtually sweeping the province. As Premier, Douglas was a reformer, active in social welfare legislation, the use of Crown corporations as economic arms of the government, and public health care.

It was in health care that he made his greatest impact. The passionate and vitriolic opposition of the medical community to universal public health insurance, which led to the famous Saskatchewan doctors' strike of 1962, took place after he had returned to federal politics as leader of the newly organized New Democratic Party—an alliance of left-wing politicians and the labour movement. But Douglas had been the original architect of the medicare program in Saskatchewan, which was eventually implemented after the province and the doctors compromised on the terms of its administration in 1962. Douglas paid a price for his association with medicare. He himself was defeated in Regina in 1962 and was never again elected to public office in Saskatchewan, serving ridings in British Columbia for the remainder of his life. During the 1960s, Douglas was a prominent member of what was probably the most impressive collection of federal politicians ever assembled in Ottawa. For a number of years in a House of Commons without a majority, he forced federal policy to the left. His ideas outlived those of his medical opponents, and an unscientific CBC poll in 2003 declared him the nation's 'greatest Canadian'.

the federal Social Credit Party, which began as an effort by Alberta's Social Credit movement to introduce its ideas on the national level: in the election of 1935 Alberta elected 15 Social Credit MPs (with nearly 50 per cent of the vote). After the war the party won some seats in Alberta and British Columbia and it achieved more prominence in the early 1960s, when it was led by Robert Thompson with the assistance of Réal Caouette and had two distinct wings, of which the one based in Quebec, under Caouette, was the more successful; in the 1962 election, for example, 26 of the 30 Social Credit MPs elected were from Quebec. After the 1963 election, Caouette broke from Thompson to form his own Ralliement des créditistes, which elected 9 MPs in

1965 and 14 in 1968. Social Credit was particularly strong in rural and small-town areas, which liked its combination of federalism and economic reform based on hostility to both traditional capitalism and public enterprise. Along with the NDP, the Social Credit Party between 1962 and 1968 garnered enough votes (and parliamentary seats) to prevent either of the two major parties from achieving majority status and firm control of the House of Commons. Although many observers bemoaned the absence of stable government in the 1960s, a sizable number argued that minority status kept governments on their toes and more responsive to the people. Certainly the governments of Lester Pearson, while constantly teetering on the edge of defeat in the Commons (and even going over it on occasion), were among the most energetic and innovative ones that Canada experienced in the twentieth century. The Pearson governments had to deal simultaneously with the problems of national unity and increased social welfare, and did so with some difficulty.

While public opinion as expressed at elections did have some influence, as did third parties, a more important limiting factor on Liberal dominance was undoubtedly the historic division of powers between the federal and provincial governments, and the ensuing constitutional debates. Canadian voters had long sensed that the really effective opposition to a federal majority was to be found at the provincial level, and most successful provincial governments relied on 'Ottawa bashing' as an essential part of their political arsenal, since the electorate frequently voted for quite different parties (and principles) at the federal and provincial levels.

PROVINCIAL POLITICS AND FEDERAL–PROVINCIAL RELATIONS

In most provinces after 1945, one party controlled the government even more continuously and powerfully than the Liberals did at the federal level. In New Brunswick, Liberal control was broken in 1951–60 by the Tories, but the traditional alliance between the province's substantial Acadian minority and the Liberals was cemented by Louis Robichaud in 1960. In Newfoundland, Joey Smallwood parlayed strong federal Liberal support for confederation with Canada into an unbroken tenure as Premier from 1949 to 1971. Nova Scotia was run continuously by the Tories, while Prince Edward Island was able to maintain one of the few truly viable two-party political systems in the nation, perhaps because of its small size. In Quebec the Liberals under Jean Lesage did break through the long control of the Union Nationale in 1960 and held power until 1966, putting into effect major changes in Quebec society and politics that came to be known as the Quiet Revolution, but west of Quebec provincial Liberals held little ground. Ontario continued in the grip of the 'Big Blue Machine' that controlled the province throughout the post-war period, while both Alberta (1935–72) and British Columbia (1952–72) were governed for decades by Social Credit. The only provincial Liberal government west of Quebec between 1945 and 1972 was that of Ross Thatcher in Saskatchewan (1964–71), but his government was one of the most vociferous critics of federal Liberalism under Pearson and Trudeau. So, whatever the source of the federal Liberals' strength, it was not provincial parties and organizations. By the early 1970s the only provincial governments controlled by the Liberals were in PEI and Quebec. Certainly Pierre Trudeau's conception of Liberalism (and liberalism) did not accord with that of Robert Bourassa, who succeeded Jean Lesage as leader of the Quebec Liberal Party in 1970, and the two leaders (with their governments) were continually at loggerheads.

The disagreements of the Saskatchewan and Quebec Liberals with the federal Liberals suggest that party affiliation as such meant little in the ongoing controversies between Ottawa and the provinces. Such conflict, which had literally been built into Confederation by the terms of the

British North America Act in 1867, had never been resolved. The Dominion of Canada had been created as a federal state with a central government in Ottawa and local governments in the provinces. The framers of Confederation had intended to create a strong central government and weak provincial ones, but they had been forced by the provinces—particularly, but not only, Quebec—to maintain separate identities for the constituent parts of the federation. Separate provincial identities were specifically guaranteed through an explicit division of powers between the federal and provincial governments in sections 91 and 92 of the BNA Act. The division thus created, reflecting the political thinking of the 1860s, gave the federal arm the authority to produce a viable national economy and the provinces the power to protect what were at the time regarded as local matters of social and cultural concern. Some of the provincial powers, such as the control of education, were acquired because the provinces demanded them. Others, such as the control over the health and welfare of provincial residents, were not regarded as critical for a national government. (Lighthouses and post offices were more important than public medical care in the 1860s.) Over time the division of powers had made the provinces responsible, in whole or in large part, for many of the expensive aspects of government—including health, education, and welfare—while limiting their ability to raise the necessary revenue. Thus, many important responsibilities came to be shared between levels of government, and it became clear that the division of powers in sections 91 and 92 of the BNA Act was dated, ambiguous, and hence contentious.

Like most constitutional documents, the BNA Act had not been written to stand by itself. It was intended to be wrapped in a larger context of precedent, almost all of which was either British or British imperial. The concept of unwritten precedent, very British in nature, did provide a considerable element of constitutional flexibility. For example, the entire system of political parties

and leaders—including prime ministers, premiers, privy councils, and cabinets—that enabled the governments of both Canada and the provinces to function, was never once mentioned in the BNA Act: it was one of the unwritten conventions of the Constitution. The official powers of the Governor General were listed very precisely, but the document never stated that these were to be exercised only on advice from the Privy Council. Precedents, both those brought into Confederation and those evolved within it, allowed for the survival of the Canadian Constitution. Pierre Elliott Trudeau observed in 1961 that the Constitution was 'the eighth oldest written Constitution, the second oldest one of a federal nature, and the oldest which combined federalism with the principles of responsible government'.[11] But despite the miracle of its longevity, the BNA Act had been constantly strained. Then as now, critics of the existing system stressed the tensions inherent in it, while its defenders concentrated on its capacity for survival.

One of the main problems lay in the arrangements within the BNA Act for settling disputes over its interpretation. The Act provided for a judicature modelled on British principles, with a general court of appeal or Supreme Court at the top. But this court, established in 1875, was not always the court of final decision, particularly on constitutional matters. Until 1949 constitutional issues could still be appealed to a British imperial court, the Judicial Committee of the Privy Council of the United Kingdom, which in the years after Confederation had interpreted the Canadian Constitution in ways distinctly favourable to the provinces. Even with the elimination of this remnant of colonialism, amendment of the BNA Act was extremely difficult. Amending procedures were not described in the Act itself, and ultimately required an Act of the British Parliament. By the mid-twentieth century, when the Judicial Committee's authority was finally removed, Canadian political leaders had worked out a variety of informal non-judicial means for resolving constitutional questions,

■ Prime Minister Trudeau and the newly elected Premier of Quebec, Robert Bourassa, at the federal–provincial conference of September 1970, in Ottawa. Duncan Cameron/LAC, PA-117468.

particularly those involving federal and provincial matters. One of the most important informalities, sanctioned by pragmatic precedent, was the federal–provincial conference.

FEDERAL–PROVINCIAL CONFERENCES

Meetings between federal and provincial governments had been an ongoing feature of Canadian political life since Confederation, but organized and systematic conferences between the feds and their provincial counterparts—particularly formal meetings of all the first ministers—were not regularized until after World War II. King's Liberals led the way, calling a Dominion–Provincial Conference on Reconstruction in August 1945, when the federal government had prepared a

comprehensive program for a welfare state based on the tax system and the economic policy of a strong central government and sought the cooperation of the provinces to implement its plans. What was required was agreement that Ottawa could keep the emergency powers it had acquired to fight the war. The major provinces, led by Ontario and Quebec, were not enthusiastic. The conference adjourned for 'study', and when it finally met again, in April 1946, Quebec and Ontario, in tandem, denounced centralization while insisting on provincial autonomy. In the wake of this meeting, the federal government offered the provinces a 'tax rental' scheme whereby it would collect certain taxes (on incomes, corporations, and successions to estates) and distribute payments to the provinces. Ontario and Quebec went for their own schemes, but the remaining provinces (including Newfoundland after 1949) accepted tax rental.

The conference was important in several respects. First, it demonstrated that even under the best of circumstances—with a program of acknowledged public popularity and advantage—the provinces were not prepared to surrender their autonomy to Ottawa. The provinces' refusal to play dead meant that the federal government would need to bargain for their co-operation in order to achieve many of its ambitions. Second, it created an institution that, in the course of time, would become entrenched. Subsequent federal–provincial conferences would be called on an increasingly regular basis, initially to deal with financial matters, but gradually to address constitutional matters as well. It was at the federal–provincial conference of July 1960, called by Prime Minister Diefenbaker to discuss tax-sharing, that the question of repatriation of the BNA Act (i.e., its amendment in Canada without recourse to the British Parliament) was put on the table by Premier Jean Lesage. Diefenbaker responded with instructions to his Minister of Justice, E. Davie Fulton, to meet with the attorneys general of the provinces on the question. A whole series of federal–provincial conferences— on pensions, financial arrangements, constitutional issues—followed in the 1960s, and became part of the accepted political practice of the nation.[12] Such meetings drew public attention to the difficulties of achieving national unity in the face of opposition from Quebec (and usually at least one other province) to whatever reform or change was on the agenda.[13]

THE CANADIAN BILL OF RIGHTS

A whole new dimension was added to the post-war constitutional mix through John Diefenbaker's insistence on the introduction of a Canadian Bill of Rights. The Americans had produced a Bill of Rights for their Constitution (the first 10 amendments) as part of the process of ratification. But the Canadian founding fathers did not follow the American lead, chiefly because in the British constitutional tradition Parliament was supreme, and the courts automatically protected the people against abuse of power. Like the British Constitution, the BNA Act had enshrined group minority rights—mainly in the areas of education, religion, and language—but had displayed little interest in the rights of the individual that were so crucial to the American understanding of democracy. The introduction of specified rights—for individuals or collective groups—was a potentially profound change in the Canadian Constitution.[14] Diefenbaker's Bill for the Recognition and Protection of Human Rights and Fundamental Freedoms, fulfilling campaign promises made in 1957 and 1958, was passed by Parliament in 1960. As it was limited to the federal level, and the rights it enshrined could be overridden by national emergencies, it had little immediate impact. A full 10 years went by before the Canadian Supreme Court heard a case based upon it. But its implications for constitutional reform were considerable, particularly when combined with the growth, in the 1960s, of demands from minority groups for formal recognition and equal protection and treatment under the law.

Over the course of the post-war period, Canadians discovered that the problems of their Constitution were greater than mere disputes over sections 91 and 92 of the BNA Act, or even the larger question of dominion–provincial relations. They ought also to have become aware that neither constitutional nor federal–provincial problems were the product merely of the uneasy presence of Quebec in Confederation. Nevertheless, the issue of Quebec dominated federal–provincial tensions, and constitutional reform— for better or worse—came to be seen as the panacea for what seemed to ail the nation. A host of interpreters and experts offered to answer that seemingly unanswerable question: What does Quebec really want? (This issue will be discussed in the next chapter.)

NEWFOUNDLAND ENTERS CONFEDERATION

One uncategorizable and somewhat surprising event of the post-war period was the entry of Newfoundland into Canada. The story started in 1945 with several demands from Newfoundland—at the time governed by a Commission appointed by Britain—for restoration of the self-governing status it had surrendered during the Depression. A National Convention to address the issue was called late in 1945 and elected in 1946. One of its elected members was Joseph Smallwood, a former journalist, now running a pig farm, who undertook a private visit to Ottawa to scout out Canadian opinion on the possibility of confederation. When the Convention met in late October, it somewhat unexpectedly heard a motion from Smallwood calling for the opening of negotiations with Canada. The proposal sparked intense debate among the people of Newfoundland. Although most of the Convention delegates appear to have preferred the restoration of responsible government, within a few months union with Canada became a serious alternative. Following another Smallwood motion, a Newfoundland delegation went to Ottawa in the early summer of 1947. Not all Canadians were equally enthusiastic; the senior bureaucrats at External Affairs adopted a 'manifest destiny' attitude, while many politicians noted that Newfoundland could easily become a 'little Ireland'—that is, a huge political and economic problem—for Canada, especially without Labrador iron ore. Although Labrador was officially part of Newfoundland, the territory was disputed by Quebec, which might well reopen the question were Newfoundland to become part of Canada. Talks continued over the summer, while public opinion polls in Canada indicated that Canadians only barely supported the notion. Nevertheless, the delegation eventually returned to St John's with a generous offer from Canada. On 19 January 1948, a motion was introduced in the Convention that Britain should

determine with all possible speed the wishes of the people of Newfoundland, given a choice between responsible government and the status quo. Smallwood himself failed in his effort to get union with Canada added to any referendum ballot. But a grassroots campaign helped persuade the British to announce that the referendum should offer three choices: '1. COMMISSION OF GOVERNMENT for a period of 5 years; 2. CONFEDERATION WITH CANADA; 3. RESPONSIBLE GOVERNMENT as it existed in 1933.'[15]

The referendum campaign was as fiercely fought as the Newfoundland election of 1869 (discussed in Chapter 1), and was complicated by the emergence of a movement for economic union with the US. Responsible government received 69,400 votes, Confederation with Canada 64,066, and Commission government 22,311. A second ballot was announced for 22 July 1948, with Commission government dropped from the ballot. The level of advocacy became even more intense in the second vote, when the result was 78,323 (52.34 per cent) for Canada and 72,344 (47.66 per cent) for responsible government. Canadian Prime Minister King had to be persuaded that the margin of victory was sufficient, but Canada accepted the result as a mandate and proceeded to welcome Newfoundland into the union, allowing Smallwood to organize the first government.

THE DEVELOPMENT OF THE WELFARE STATE

No necessary link exists between the development of a social welfare state and socialism or radical politics.[16] Indeed, most international scholars for most jurisdictions would emphasize that the vast majority of social welfare measures have been proposed for other purposes by factions other than the left. In Canada more social protection has been designed and executed for conservative purposes—to forestall the left and prevent social revolution—than has ever been introduced by socialists. In a few jurisdictions,

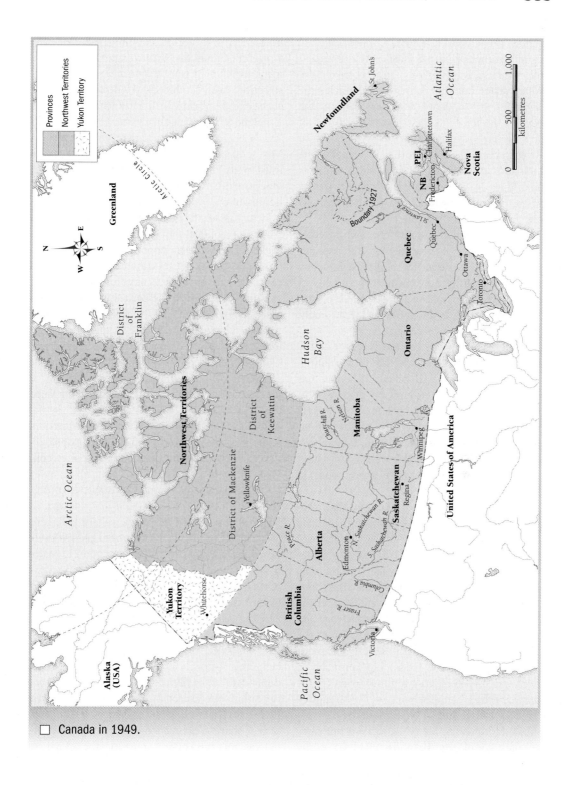

Canada in 1949.

such as Sweden and Great Britain, political parties calling themselves 'socialist' have dominated governments advancing social protection and the welfare state. But this is quite uncharacteristic internationally. A more common pattern has been for the left to see the statist expansion of social welfare as a mere palliative designed to prevent more radical reform, principally the elimination of capitalism and the substitution of some form of worker control. Certainly that is the position taken by much of the scholarly literature, often written from the left.

Another point that must be emphasized is that the main goal of those interested in expanding public social services has seldom been merely the humanitarian improvement of the quality of life for the recipients of those services. Lip service is always paid to the needs (or occasionally, rights) of those receiving the services, but typically other factors have been much higher on the motivational agenda. Perhaps the most common justification for increased welfare measures has been economic, through creation of new jobs, improvement of the economic climate, or raising the standards and productivity of the labour force. The intellectual ethos of those bureaucrats who created much of Canada's welfare legislation was a Keynesianism that saw government in highly interventionist economic terms.[17]

Among the schools of thought that promoted increased social protectionism in Canada were radicalism, social reform, professional social work, and statism. Canada was never exposed to a single dominant vision of a national system comparable to that of the Beveridge Report in Great Britain or the 'New Deal' in the United States. Indeed, the electorate rejected Prime Minister R.B. Bennett's 'New Deal' in the 1935 election.[18] The Marsh Report on social security, tabled in the House of Commons in 1943, was not taken very seriously even by the party that had commissioned it.[19] Although it produced a brief flurry of interest in the newspapers at the time, the Marsh Report did not carry the prestige of the Beveridge Report, partly

because it was not as comprehensive or well written. Neither the White Paper on Employment and Income nor the Green Book on Reconstruction, both produced by federal bureaucrats at the end of World War II, ever achieved a broad circulation.[20] Perhaps the closest thing to a well-known social reform document was the Regina Manifesto of 1932, although as the product of a third party it was never widely accepted as a blueprint for action.[21] The absence of a single dominant blueprint has meant that social protection in Canada never became associated with a particular political party or movement. Nor was social security the monopoly of a particular ideology. This helps to explain why social protection continued to grow over most of the twentieth century regardless of the parties in power either federally or provincially. It also helps explain why social protection arrived in piecemeal fashion and with different emphases in different places at different times. Although the public advocates of social security reform, especially in the 1930s and 1940s, all emphasized the need for planning and co-ordination, the actual process was one of unsynchronized accretion, with pressures exerted from a variety of directions, occasionally simultaneously and often contradictorily.

Canada emerged from World War II considerably behind both the US and Great Britain as far as the extension of social welfare programs was concerned. To some extent that lag was made up in the affluent years of 1945 to 1972. Major federal legislation included the Old Age Security Act (1951), the Unemployment Assistance Act (1956), the Hospital Insurance and Diagnostic Services Act (1957), and the Medical Care Act (1966). These measures were brought into existence in an era of unprecedented prosperity and economic growth for Canada. Most of them depended not only on federal–provincial co-operation but especially on substantial federal financial assistance to the provinces in the form of cost-sharing. Scholars disagree on whether the federal government was pressing the provinces forward or merely reacting to provincial pressures on a knee-jerk basis. What they do agree on is the absence at either level of government—and especially the federal one—of an integrated vision of social insurance. Moreover, the primary goal was to insure Canadians against adverse circumstances beyond their control, not to redistribute wealth or income. Three programs developed in those years stand out: the pension system, the unemployment program, and the health-care system. For the most part, these programs were established through bipartisan cooperation between political parties at both levels of government. But there were many more strands to social insurance.

FAMILY ALLOWANCES

A universal scheme of welfare payments for children had been the political choice of the Liberal government under Mackenzie King as the flag-bearer of its social insurance programs. Taking the form of the Family Allowances Act of 1944, it was intended to deflect public interest in more radical reform. By May 1946 more than 90 per cent of Canadian children under the age of 16 were receiving monthly benefits—through their mothers—at an average rate of $5.94 per child. The program was not intended to provide payments at a level that would eliminate the need for other allowances under public assistance programs. However, it did introduce the principle of universality, although children not born in Canada had to be residents for three years before becoming eligible. In 1949 the legislation was changed to reduce the payments for a family's children in excess of four.

VETERANS' BENEFITS

The process of preparing for the demobilization of Canadian veterans began as early as 1939. In 1941 the Liberal government announced a Post-Discharge Re-Establishment Order, which provided for benefits including the promise of free university education for demobilized soldiers. But the Department of National Defence established, through surveys and extracts from censored letters, that many soldiers believed that the government—especially Prime Minister King—would not live up to its promises. A poll of RCAF personnel in 1943 indicated that 40 per cent thought the CCF would do the best with veterans, and 37 per cent named the Tories, while only 12 per cent named the Liberals.[22] These revelations led the Liberals to improve the benefits package over 1944 and 1945. The showcase program was clearly the free university education, which was coupled with a living allowance. By 1947 almost 35,000 veterans were enrolled in university, and in the 1949–50 academic year veterans still accounted for more than 20 per cent of all university students in Canada. But the plan did not benefit all regions of the nation equally. The seven most popular universities for veterans were, in order, Toronto, McGill, British Columbia, Saskatchewan, Alberta, Manitoba, and Queen's. French-Canadian participation in the scheme, either by students or universities, was very low, and the figures from the Maritimes were only slightly better. Quebec's hostility to the federal government's involvement in higher education in the 1950s must be seen against the fact that the veterans' program did not significantly benefit French-language universities in Quebec, since relatively few veterans were francophone Quebecers. The government worked to look after all aspects of veteran welfare, from rehabilitation for those with disabilities, to help with re-establishment on farms, to pensions. By 1955, nearly $200 million had been spent on vocational and university training of veterans, including allowances, tuition fees, and supplementary grants.

HIGHER EDUCATION

One of the 'Five Giants on the Road to Recovery' included by Sir William Beveridge in his report on the welfare state was 'ignorance', which he insisted needed to be overcome through education. None of the Canadian equivalents of the Beveridge Report spoke about education, but access to education was obviously part of the package of post-war reconstruction, as the provision of higher education to veterans clearly indicates. In order to help the universities cope with the influx of veterans, a supplementary grant scheme was created that by June 1950 had funnelled over $16 million of federal funding to Canadian universities on the basis of veteran enrolment.[23] (These grants were in addition to payments to veterans for tuition.) Naturally, the universities wished to see such funding continue. Also in June 1950, F. Cyril James, principal of McGill University, told the National Council of Canadian Universities that national funding must continue if Canadian universities were to fulfill their obligations. The NCCU told the same thing to the Massey Commission on the Arts, Letters and Sciences, which recommended that the federal government make annual grants to the universities on the basis of the population of each province, to be given to each university proportionate to its student enrolment. In 1951 Parliament agreed, approving a total budget of 50 cents for each resident of Canada. Quebec's Premier Maurice Duplessis rejected the federal money, but the other provinces accepted it.[24] Until the later 1960s, the grants were distributed directly by the federal government to all degree-granting institutions of higher learning. The federal government provided only financial assistance and not planning, and each institution could use the funds as it desired, but eventually the provinces succeeded in clawing back control over the revenue, largely on the grounds that the existing scheme made educational planning almost impossible.

HOUSING

Despite a lack of enthusiasm within the Liberal government for low-cost public housing—which smacked of socialism—a wartime housing program begun in 1941 had built over 40,000 fam-

ily rental dwelling units by the end of the war. By 1948 the National Welfare Council (a lobbying group of professional social workers) was advocating that these housing projects be turned over to municipal governments to be managed under municipal housing authorities. The model was clearly public housing in the United Kingdom. Municipalities were still demanding wartime housing. In 1949 the federal government revised the National Housing Act to discourage public rental housing and to put it under provincial authority. Instead of having the federal government finance municipal projects, the federal and provincial levels would share the responsibility, paying 75 and 25 per cent, respectively. The informal calculation was that most provinces would pass responsibility for their share of funding on to the municipalities. The Act also transferred the management for housing to local authorities appointed by the province. This shift to provincial authority was supported by Ontario and Quebec, but opposed by Saskatchewan.[25] It provides an interesting example of a devolution of responsibility from the Dominion to the provinces initiated by the federal government in order to limit the spread of the welfare state. The major goal of the federal government, in terms of housing, increasingly became private home ownership, and the policies of the Central Mortgage and Housing Corporation, established in 1945 to provide mortgages for new houses, were directed towards stimulation of the private market. In 1954 another National Housing Act provided for housing for low-income families, but few dwellings were built under this program.

PENSIONS

Before 1951 Canadians were covered by the Old Age Pensions scheme of 1927, a shared-cost plan between the federal government and the provinces that paid to Canadians over the age of 70 a small monthly pension governed by a means test administered on the local level. This early scheme was extremely limited in a variety of senses. Many argued that the means test discouraged private saving and was variably administered (as late as 1949, fewer than half the pensioners in the Maritime provinces received the maximum amount, whereas 92.4 per cent of Newfoundlanders did).[26] Pension reform finally came in 1951, when the Old Age Security and Old Age Assistance Acts of 1951 created a two-tier system under which the federal government would pay a universal pension called 'old-age security' to those over 70, while retaining a cost-shared means-test scheme with the provinces for those between 65 and 69. This legislation also introduced the principle that pensions would be non-contributory (i.e., would not require contributions from recipients). The changing demography of Canada guaranteed that there would be continual pressures on the government to improve the system. Those who wanted better benefits could agree with those who sought to control costs on the superiority of a contributory scheme, which was added to the earlier arrangement in 1965 as the Canada Pension Plan (the Régime des rentes du Québec in Quebec). At the same time, the old-age security pension was linked to the consumer price index, although limitations on the amounts of increases meant that public pensions fell badly behind inflation in the 1960s and 1970s. Before 1971 the Canada Pension Plan had its own separate fund, but in that year contributions (and payments) were shifted to the federal government's general revenue account.

SPECIAL NEEDS

Less well publicized than pensions or education grants were a number of programs introduced in the 1950s to help those members of society who were regarded as having special needs. In 1951 the federal government passed the Blind Persons Act, which allowed it to agree with each province and territory on cost-sharing of allowances paid (following a means test) to the blind. That same year Canada (which had sole responsibility for

■ Postage stamp commemorating Judy LaMarsh, issued 26 September 1997. Designed by Kosta (Gus) Tsetsekas based on an illustration by Steve Hepburn. © Canada Post Corporation. Reproduced with permission.

Aboriginal people) amended the Indian Act to extend provincial social benefits to First Nations. In 1954 the Disabled Persons Act made the same provisions for severely challenged Canadians as it had for the blind. Although the estimates suggested that about half of the over 200,000 seriously challenged people in Canada had little or no income, means-testing meant that by 1956 the system was paying allowances to only 31,825. While the means test kept the lid on the payment of benefit allowances, it also necessitated continual supervision of those receiving assistance, which not only cost money but was regarded by many as demeaning.

JUDY LaMARSH (1924–1980)

❖

Julia (she always called herself 'Judy') Verlyn LaMarsh was born in Chatham, Ontario, in 1924 and educated in Niagara Falls. After graduation from Hamilton Normal School she served in the Canadian Woman's Army Corps from 1943 to 1946, translating Japanese documents. After the war she attended Victoria College and Osgoode Hall, and in 1950 she joined her father's law firm. LaMarsh first ran for Parliament in 1960, winning a stunning by-election in Niagara Falls. In 1963 she became head of the 'Truth Squad' that shadowed Prime Minister John Diefenbaker on his campaigns across the country, offering 'corrections' and 'constructive criticisms' to his comments and speeches. Although the squad gimmick backfired—Diefenbaker took full advantage of the opportunities it offered to ridicule the opposition—her part in it drew LaMarsh to the attention of the media. Upon re-election in 1963, she joined the Pearson cabinet and became Minister of Health and Welfare, a key portfolio that kept her in the headlines.

A member of the reforming wing of the Liberal Party, LaMarsh personally helped to draft the legislation for the Canada Pension Plan passed under her ministership, and oversaw the creation of the medicare system—although at the time she was probably better known for giving up smoking after her appointment to the Health portfolio. In 1965 she became Secretary of State, in which capacity she pushed for the creation of the Royal Commission on the Status of Women and took charge of Canada's Centennial celebration. Not a fan of Pierre Elliott Trudeau, at the 1968 leadership convention she made a negative comment about him that was caught on tape. Her retirement from politics left the incoming Parliament extremely short of women members.

In retirement LaMarsh wrote a humorous and abrasive account of her political career entitled *Memoirs of a Bird in a Gilded Cage* (1968). In it she pulled no punches about the cynicism of contemporary politics and politicians, presenting herself as the perennial isolated female outsider, never able to gain her colleagues' acceptance. Yet in so doing she may actually have done herself a disservice, since she was a major figure in the Liberal Party and governments of her time.

UNEMPLOYMENT COMPENSATION

The Unemployment Insurance Act of 1940 was based on British models in most respects, although it had followed the US in basing amounts in part on wages paid. Benefits were related to contributions. In 1956 the Unemployment Assistance Act provided for Ottawa to pay up to 50 per cent of the costs of various provincial programs of aid to the needy, particularly those unemployed who had exhausted or were not eligible for benefits. This legislation was intended to increase benefits for those who required them, but because of the budget-conscious attitudes of many provinces, it did not. To the surprise of many social planners, offering the provinces matching funds often led to lower rather than higher benefits. In many ways the most important change to unemployment assistance during the fifties came in 1955, when the plan was extended to include seasonal workers.

In 1966 the Canada Assistance Plan (CAP) made it possible for provinces to consolidate all federal–provincial assistance programs based on means and needs into a single benefit package. The federal government would pay half the cost of items shared. Under the CAP, for the first time the working poor could receive financial assistance, and provisions were made for clients to appeal unfair treatment. Between March 1956 and March 1974, the number of Canadians receiving aid under the Unemployment Assistance Act and the Canada Assistance Plan grew from 86,234 to 1,347,376.[27] Part of the increase was the result of changes in eligibility criteria, but part was attributable to larger numbers of unemployed and senior citizens in the late 1960s. The first total overhaul of unemployment insurance since 1940 did not take place until 1971. The Unemployment Insurance Act of that year extended coverage to nearly all workers, raised the amount of benefits, and shortened the waiting periods.

HEALTH CARE

During the 1930s, a number of doctors had begun to organize private health-care plans in order to make sure they would be paid for their services, and by the 1950s perhaps half of all Canadians were covered by private insurance, mainly under the aegis of Blue Cross and, in Ontario, Physicians Services Incorporated (PSI). Various provinces also had hospital insurance plans in place, most of them 'user pay' in one form or another, beginning with Saskatchewan in 1944. In 1956 the federal government offered to provide grants for a national hospital insurance scheme, on the condition that more than half of the provinces joined and more than half of the population would be covered. Within a year, eight provinces had agreed to join, and by 1961 every province had a hospitalization scheme. Virtually all Canadians were covered.

■ Supporters of striking Saskatchewan doctors symbolically hang CCF premiers Woodrow Lloyd and Tommy Douglas, Regina, 11 July 1962. The signs attached to the poles read 'Down with Dictators'. Saskatchewan Archives Board R-83980-2.

In regard to publicly funded out-patient health care, Saskatchewan again led the way, introducing a public medical insurance scheme in 1962. The Saskatchewan plan was opposed by the province's doctors, who went on strike for 23 days in the summer of 1962. Although they had supported the introduction of free hospitalization in 1947 and the establishment of a provincial health service in 1951, relations with the government became strained in the 1950s, partly because of the expansion of doctor-sponsored insurance schemes, partly because the composition of the medical profession was changing, with younger doctors who were more likely to live in the cities and towns. Basically, what was at issue in the early 1960s was control of the billing and payment process. Saskatchewan's compulsory health insurance plan emphasized universal coverage, known patient liability, and central administration. The doctors objected to all these principles as government coercion and were extremely well organized. Both sides became intransigent. The province was prepared to allow doctors to 'extra-bill' beyond the provincial reimbursement and even to work outside the Act so long as they accepted provincial payment. But it was also prepared to import doctors if necessary. In the end, the doctors conceded.[28] Contrary to the predictions of the medical profession, there was no evidence of a deterioration in the quality of care, and the number of doctors in Saskatchewan did not decline but actually increased between 1962 and 1964.

In 1965 Mr Justice Emmett Hall of Saskatchewan presented the report of a Royal Commission on Health Services that had been appointed in 1961. The Pearson government accepted its recommendation of universal public medical care and promised to have a medicare scheme in place by 1967. Not all provinces were equally enthusiastic about universal medicare. Manitoba joined with alacrity, but Ontario was reluctant to become involved and Quebec introduced its own scheme. By 1972, however, all provinces and territories in Canada had implemented medicare, with the general support of the Canadian Medical Association. Provinces vary in the services they cover and the opportunities they allow doctors for extra-billing. Although universality would become a major subject of public debate in subsequent years, once the principle was introduced, it would be difficult to remove.[29]

The piecemeal accretion of social insurance programs probably reached its high point in 1971, just as debate moved into new areas: the relationship between poverty and race and gender, and the possibility of alleviating poverty by establishing some sort of social minimum owing to every citizen as his or her right. What brought social insurance expansion to its knees, of course, was less the discussion of social minimums than major changes in the Canadian economy beginning in 1972. The rising costs of social insurance, which could be tolerated in an era of great prosperity, quickly became less acceptable. These economic shifts were accompanied, as we shall see in Chapter 20, by a sea change in public ideology.

METRIC CONVERSION

Another example of the Trudeau government's willingness to break with the past, to confront and change fundamental principles of Canadian life, came in 1970 when the White Paper on Metric Conversion in Canada was issued. Metrication did not seem to fit into any recognizable larger pattern of change, and its gradual adoption meant that it was difficult to associate with a single political party. The metric system had been authorized in Canada as early as 1871, but the imperial system of measurement continued in common use and was more or less in harmony with measurements used in the US (an imperial quart, for instance, was slightly larger than the US version). Shifting to metric would mean breaking with tradition, but Britain itself had decided to move to the metric system in order to be in step with Europe and the Common Market, so the change could not be challenged as 'anti-British'. In addition, several other former British colonies, including South Africa and Ireland in 1968, New Zealand and Rhodesia in 1969, and Australia in 1970, had decided to make the move—and the proposal was actually popular in Quebec. At the time of the White Paper, even the Americans were talking about converting, and it seemed likely that all of North America would go metric within a few years.[30] Canada appointed a preparatory agency, eventually called Metric Commission Canada, to co-ordinate a gradual conversion. The process was not easy, especially since the Americans ultimately decided against metrication, which meant that Canadian and American products would be based on different measurement systems. Canadian temperatures were changed to Celsius on 1 April 1975. Many westerners thought the change was part of a Liberal government conspiracy against the West, for the shift to Celsius meant that winter temperatures would almost always fall into the 'minus' figures, making the region seem much colder than it actually was. And, across the country, many people emotionally hostile to metrication argued that it was unwise for Canada to go out of step with the Americans and asked what would happen to the yard in Canadian football or square footage in real estate. As it turned out, most sports (apart from track and field) did not change. Real estate retained its old measurements as well, and the construction industry adopted a dual system.

From 1975 to the mid-1980s metric measurements were gradually introduced into Canadian usage. Road measurements changed to kilometres in 1977, and gasoline was pumped in litres beginning in 1979. Fabrics had to be sold in metric lengths after December 1980. Conversion of weighing scales in stores proceeded slowly and has never been totally successful. Proponents of the change were correct in asserting that, once the new system was taught in the schools, the nation's youth would become comfortable with it and see imperial measurements as hopelessly antiquated. But many Canadians who were adults by 1970 never did really grasp the new system. Many of those who continued to think in imperial terms saw metric measurement as one more example of unnecessary government interference. On the other hand, metric measurement did mark out a clear difference between Canada and the United States, one that was instantly recognizable as soon as the border was crossed in either direction.

NEW FORCES IN POLITICS

Although Quebec received the lion's share of press coverage and public attention during the

1960s, French Canadians were not the only minority in Canadian society demanding full recognition and full equality. The 1960s saw a number of other groups emerge with articulated positions and demands, including Aboriginal people, blacks, women, and homosexuals. To some extent all these groups shared a sense of liberation and raised consciousness in the heady days of the 1960s, as well as some common models and rhetoric. The several black movements in the US, especially civil rights and black power, were generally influential, and it was no accident that almost every minority, including French Canadians, found itself compared at some point with American blacks.[31] On one level, other emerging minorities could hardly avoid sympathizing with French Canada, but on another, Quebec's arguments and aspirations were in serious conflict with those of other groups. Of course, minorities within minorities often do face special problems, but there were additional issues. Perhaps the most important was the fact that other minorities relied on the federal power to control and influence provincial action. A brief examination of the growth of some of the other leading minority rights movements illustrates the complexities of simultaneously serving Quebec, French Canadians elsewhere in Canada, and everybody else.[32]

ABORIGINAL PEOPLES

Like so many other long-standing issues in Canada, that of Canada's Aboriginal peoples moved into a new activist phase in the 1960s. Native activists built on their own accumulated traditions of constructing organizations to speak for their concerns, but they were also able to take advantage of American models and Canadian federal policy, such as the 1960 Canadian Bill of Rights. Just as critically, the search for new sources of raw materials for exploitation in the Canadian North threatened indigenous peoples' way of life and forced them into the political mainstream. At the end of the 1960s, emerging

Native militancy ran head-on into a government effort to rethink the situation of Native people and their relationship to the federal government.

Before 1960, regional and provincial organizations representing the interests of Aboriginal peoples had gradually developed across Canada, often in response to particular situations or to organized investigations and commissions on either the provincial or federal level. Thus the Depression called into existence the Native Brotherhood of British Columbia in 1931, and in 1936 a strike gave rise to the Pacific Coast Native Fisherman's Association, which merged with the former in 1941. In Saskatchewan a number of groups merged into the Federation of Saskatchewan Indians at the end of the 1950s. National organizations were slower to take hold. In 1943 Andrew Paull tried to create a national organization, called the National Indian Brotherhood, but did not succeed, partly because he was seen to be linked too closely with the Roman Catholic Church. Finally, in 1960, the National Indian Council was formed 'to promote unity among Indian people, the betterment of people of Indian ancestry in Canada, and to create a better understanding of Indian and non-Indian relationship'.[33] The National Indian Council was organized mainly by urbanized Native people who hoped to combine the concerns of status and non-status Indians, including Métis. In 1968 political incompatibility led to the dissolution of the National Indian Council and the formation of two new groups: the Canadian Métis Society, which in 1970 renamed itself the National Council of Canada and would become the Métis National Council, representing Métis and non-status Indians, and the National Indian Brotherhood, which in 1982 would become the Assembly of First Nations, representing status Indians.

Before the late 1960s, consciousness-raising with regard to Native issues was a slow process. The granting of the franchise federally and provincially in 1960 seemed to have little initial impact. Then a sudden shift occurred, particularly among Native people themselves, that is still ongoing. In 1966 one government report complained of the difficulty of ascertaining Aboriginal opinion.[34] As late as 1971 one study, 'The Indian in Canadian Historical Writing', found that textbook surveys in particular regarded Native people as inferior beings who deserved what they got from Europeans and generally treated them more as 'obstacles to be overcome in Canada' than as integral parts of historical development.[35] The real explosion of Canadian academic interest in Native people did not come until the 1970s, when it coincided with a new awareness among Canadians generally that was sparked not by academics but by Native peoples' own political and legal efforts to fight for their rights in ways that drew attention to their situation. 'Aboriginal rights' existed as a concept in the 1960s, but had not yet produced the landmark court actions of later periods.[36]

One of the real catalysts for Native consciousness was the publication in 1969 of a White Paper on federal policy under Indian Affairs Minister Jean Chrétien.[37] The president of the Manitoba Indian Brotherhood, Dan Courchene, at the time observed, 'No single action by any Government since Confederation has aroused such a violent reaction from Indian people.'[38] The White Paper dealt with all aspects of First Nations policy, but its principal recommendations were threefold: abolition of the Indian Act (and the Department of Indian Affairs), which would mean an end to official 'Indian status'; the transfer of Aboriginal lands out of Crown trust into the hands of First Nations themselves; and the devolution of responsibility for Aboriginal matters to the provinces.[39] The White Paper touched off bitter criticism in all quarters, and it produced the first popular manifesto for Canadian Native people in Harold Cardinal's *The Unjust Society: The Tragedy of Canada's Indians* (1969), which argued for the re-establishment of special rights within the strengthened contexts of treaties and the Indian Act.

The White Paper, in broad outline, was consistent with federal policy towards all minorities, including French Canadians, at the end of the

1960s. It called for advancement of the individual rights of Aboriginal persons rather than the collective rights of Native people as a group:

> The Government believes that its policies must lead to the full, free and non-discriminatory participation of the Indian people in Canadian society. Such a goal requires a break with the past. It requires that the Indian people's role of dependence be replaced by a role of equal status, opportunity and responsibility, a role they can share with all other Canadians.[40]

The liberal philosophy of Pierre Trudeau is clear in this statement. The White Paper argued that treaties consisted of 'limited and minimal promises' and that the 'economic, educational, health and welfare needs of the Indian people' would be far better addressed by modern government policies. The government thought that allowing Aboriginal people full access to Canadian social services (many of which were provincially administered, especially in Quebec) would mark an advance over the paternalism of the existing arrangements, and—conveniently ignoring the White Paper's implications for treaty and Aboriginal rights—it seemed surprised that Aboriginal people responded so negatively. Defending the policy, Prime Minister Trudeau declared that the time had come 'to decide whether the Indians will be a race apart in Canada or whether they will be Canadians of full status. . . . It's inconceivable, I think, that in a given society one section of the society have a treaty with the other section of society. We must all be equal under the law.'[41]

Harold Cardinal, a member of Alberta's Sucker Creek band, had been elected president of the Indian Association of Alberta in 1968—and had read widely in the American activist literature of the 1960s. He condemned the White Paper as a 'thinly disguised programme of extermination through assimilation', adding that the federal government, 'instead of acknowledging its legal and moral responsibilities to the Indians of Canada and

■ In this photo, from June 1970, Harold Cardinal, president of the Indian Association of Alberta, tells Prime Minister Trudeau and cabinet members that treaty claims should be handled by a 'truly impartial' commission. CP Photo.

honouring the treaties that the Indians had signed in good faith, now proposes to wash its hands of Indians entirely passing the buck to the provincial governments.' Cardinal coined the term 'Buckskin Curtain' to refer to the separation between European and Aboriginal people in Canada, noting that 'while Canadian urbanites have walked blisters on their feet and fat off their rumps to raise money for underdeveloped countries outside Canada', Canadians generally did not 'give a damn' about the plight of their own Native people. He criticized 'Uncle Tomahawks' among his own peo-

■ In March 1967 former Africville residents returned for Easter Sunday services in the Seaview African Baptist Church, the heart of the community. Within weeks the church would succumb to bulldozers. Copyright CBC Digital Archives. http://www.cbc.ca/archives/africville

BLACK PEOPLE

By the mid-1960s there were an estimated 60,000 to 100,000 black people in Canada (nobody knew for certain, since accurate numbers would require a specific question on the census form). Many were descendants of early black immigrants to Canada, including the Loyalists of Nova Scotia and the fugitives from slavery in southwestern Ontario; others were among the increasing numbers of immigrants from the Caribbean who were entering Canada by the end of the decade. Canadian blacks faced a variety of discriminatory realities, both subtle and open, that often kept them on the margins of the society. They had learned to survive partly by stoic, uncomplaining endurance and partly by merging with the white community wherever possible. Except for a history of subtle oppression and the support of their churches, which tended to provide local leadership, there seemed little in their lives that could be identified as a distinctive heritage. When, in the mid-1960s, the city of Halifax decided to relocate the working-class community of Africville, on the grounds that it was a disgraceful slum, the 400 inhabitants protested but were unable to stop the expropriation, which was carried out between 1964 and 1970. When residents refused to leave their homes, the city cut off their water and electricity, and it paid them very little for their houses. (In July 2002 Africville was declared a national historic site.)

During the 1960s Canadian blacks, like other minority groups, underwent a transformation. The impact of various black movements in the US in raising black consciousness in Canada was substantial. Even the introduction of the term 'black' to replace 'Negro' was very significant, and was accompanied by an increasing sense of racial pride and identity. By the early 1970s the destruction of Africville had become a symbol of mainstream neglect, and systemic efforts were undertaken to recover the history of Africville and other black communities, lest they

ple who continually apologized for being Indian, and noted with some irony that indigenous people who wore their traditional clothing ran the risk of being confused with hippies. Cardinal also complained of the Canadian government's 'two founding peoples' concept, which did not recognize 'the role played by the Indian even before the founding of a nation-state known as Canada'. He pointedly denied that his people were separatists, arguing that they merely wanted their treaty and Aboriginal rights recognized so that they could take their place 'with the other cultural identities of Canada'. And he was not so much critical of the 'two founding nations' idea as he was insistent that his own people needed what he called 'a valid, lasting Indian identity'. Above all, Cardinal and other Aboriginal spokespersons made it plain that Native people did not want to be abandoned to the provinces, but wanted Ottawa to fulfill its fiduciary obligations to them.[42]

REPORT ON DIVORCE, 1967

In 1967 the Special Joint Committee of the Senate and the House of Commons presented its long-awaited report on divorce. It recommended the first wide-ranging changes in divorce legislation since Confederation, although many Canadians regretted it did not go further. It should be noted that while divorce is a matter of federal jurisdiction, collateral matters such as child custody are subject to provincial legislation.

Reconciliation and Marriage Counselling

While it is your Committee's opinion that a broadening of the grounds for divorce would not undermine the stability of marriage as an institution, it does believe that legislation seeking to rationalize the dissolution of marriage should not overlook the fact that dissolution is only the ultimate solution to a broken marriage and that an alternative is to try to mend it. Many witnesses before your Committee have stressed the desirability of an established reconciliation procedure to try to save as many marriages as possible. Some witnesses have urged that reconciliation attempts should be mandatory before divorce petitions are permitted to proceed. This has been suggested by the United Church of Canada, together with such organizations as the Catholic Women's League of Canada. Others have urged mandatory conciliation and counselling in certain cases and there has been considerable support for the establishment of marriage counselling services as adjuncts to the courts. Most witnesses would be satisfied, nevertheless, if provisions were made for counselling and reconciliation procedure in those cases where it might prove beneficial.

Two separate issues are really involved here. Firstly, the provisions of the actual law itself regarding reconciliation procedure, and secondly, the far wider implications of how much active interest the institutions of government should take in marriage guidance and counselling services.

To take up the first question, there is no doubt, that the law as it stands at the moment, does little to promote the reconciliation of couples contemplating divorce, and some of the provisions actually tend to discourage it. The existence of the absolute bars to divorce of collusion and condonation tend to keep the parties at arm's length. The law should be changed to ensure that any efforts a couple may make to save their marriage should not be held against them if they are unsuccessful in the attempt. In both the United Kingdom and in Australia, to cite but two examples, this problem has been recognized, and steps taken to obviate the difficulties. These provisions have been made to ensure that cohabitation for a limited period of time with reconciliation as its objective should not be considered as condonation and that reasonable negotiation between the parties should not be held as collusive. Such reforms are clearly necessary in Canada.

More can be done, however, than simply removing the legal obstacles to reconciliation. Steps can be taken to actively promote it. However, this is no easy task. Compulsory reconciliation procedure is not the answer. There are numerous objections to such a step.

In the first place, it must be realized that in the vast majority of cases, once the case has reached the divorce courts, the time for reconciliation in most cases has passed. Couples do not lightly rush into divorce actions without making sincere and strenuous attempts to save their marriages. Therefore, in the great majority of cases, compulsory arbitration would be futile.

In any case, marriage counselling is not a task just any person can do; it requires considerable training and skill and the number of persons so qualified is limited in Canada today. Counselling services would be swamped and in the vast majority of cases, their counsellors would be wasting time and talents that would be better spent trying to save those marriages that were salvageable. Compulsory marriage counselling is not a practical proposition. . . .

One fundamental obstacle to the introduction of elaborate reconciliation machinery as adjuncts to the divorce courts, is the sheer lack of personnel. Until there are ample numbers of trained people, any discussion of the desirability of such facilities must be academic.

SOURCE: Canada, *Report of the Special Joint Committee of the Senate and House of Commons on Divorce* (Ottawa: Queen's Printer, 1967), 152–4.

all suffer the same fate.[43] Some black militancy came from the US, but Canadian immigration trends were probably more important in encouraging protest against discrimination. In the 1960s, substantial numbers of decolonized Caribbean and African blacks settled in Canada, many of whom were highly skilled and educated professionals who were not accustomed to racism, however subtle. The most widely publicized incident of protest occurred at Sir George Williams (now Concordia) University in Montreal in January 1969 (see pages 453–4).

WOMEN

Like other groups that discovered a new voice in the 1960s, Canadian women had been quietly preparing for their emergence (or re-emergence) for many years. Whether or not one took a patient view of the lengthy period from the enfranchisement of women to the blossoming of 'women's lib'—and most modern feminists understandably did not—some things had changed, and some political experience had been acquired, particularly within the province of Quebec. The Committee on Equality for Women, which organized in 1966 to lobby for a Royal Commission on the Status of Women, consisted of experienced leaders from 32 existing women's organizations united by their feminism. When their first delegation to Ottawa was ignored,

Laura Sabia, president of the Canadian Federation of University Women and leader of the call for a national investigation, responded with a classic 1960s threat: she would lead a women's protest march on the capital. The Pearson government behaved equally characteristically. Although it was not convinced that women had many grievances, it agreed to hold an investigation 'to inquire and report upon the status of women in Canada, and to recommend what steps might be taken by the Federal Government to ensure for women equal opportunities with men in all aspects of Canadian society'.[44] One of the principal advocates of change was cabinet minister Judy LaMarsh. Unlike its contemporary, the Royal Commission on Bilingualism and Biculturalism, which literally had its recommendations spelled out in its terms of reference, the Royal Commission on the Status of Women, established in 1967, had a much more open-ended mandate, chiefly because the government had no preconceived position beyond a vague commitment to equality for everyone. It was the first Royal Commission chaired by a woman; Florence Bird was an Ottawa journalist and broadcaster. The Commission's investigation ranged far and wide, examining areas under provincial as well as federal jurisdiction. It made its recommendations based on four operating assumptions: the right of women to choose to be employed outside the home; the obligations of parents and society to care for children; the special responsibilities of society to women because of their maternal role; and, perhaps most controversially, the need for positive action to overcome entrenched patterns of discrimination. It provided the program that would occupy mainstream feminism in Canada for decades to come.

The investigations of the Commission coincided almost exactly with the emergence of the movement usually known as 'women's liberation'. This articulate and militant branch of feminism began in the US as an offshoot of the student movement, perhaps in response to the failure of male student leaders to take the women in their movement, or in the society at large, sufficiently seriously. Women's liberation shared its rhetoric with all leftist movements of decolonization. Woman 'realizes in her subconscious what [Herbert] Marcuse says', declared one manifesto: 'Free election of masters does not abolish the masters or the slaves.'[45] Not surprisingly, the liberationists found their organizing principles in issues of sexuality, particularly in the concept that 'woman's body is used as a commodity or medium of exchange'.[46] Liberation would come only when women were able to control their own bodies, especially in sexual terms. Thus, birth control and abortion became two of the central political issues, along with other matters such as daycare and equal pay for equal work. Such concerns brought feminists into conflict with what came to be known as 'male chauvinism' at all levels of society.

Although women's liberation shared some common ground with Quebec separatists in the form of decolonization theory, feminists in Quebec and English Canada did not always see eye to eye. The FLQ had little to say on women's issues. But the Front pour la libération des femmes du Québec refused to join the 1970 Abortion Caravan in its 'on to Ottawa' journey on the grounds that such protest legitimized federalism. And Quebec society apparently supported its politicians in a general hostility to abortion on demand. At the beginning of the 1970s the women's movement was poised on the edge of what appeared to be yet another 'New Day'.

THE OTHER WOMAN

MAY-JUNE '72   TORONTO   Vol.one No.one

25¢

A Revolutionary Feminist Newspaper

■ The first issue of *The Other Woman*, May–June 1972. Archives and Special Collections, University of Ottawa Library Network/CWMA Fonds.

HOMOSEXUALS AND LESBIANS: THE RISE OF 'GAY POWER'

Yet another minority group to emerge in the 1960s was composed of homosexuals and lesbians. The 'gays' (a term they preferred to more pejorative ones) focused their political attention on sexuality, particularly the sex offences enshrined in the

Canadian Criminal Code. After Confederation, Canada had largely replicated the various English statutes relating to sex offences, entrenching Victorian notions and definitions of 'unnatural' deviancy from approved heterosexuality in marriage, and when the Canadian Parliament later made changes in the legislation, it reinforced the notion of homosexuality and homosexual behaviour as criminal. Thus the term 'unnatural' was replaced by 'against morality' to cover a broad range of deviant behaviour when male offences such as 'indecent assault' (1886) and 'gross indecency' (1892) were added to the Criminal Code.[47]

Given the social stigma and even criminal sanctions attached to it, homosexual behaviour, male or female, was a distinctly underground business in Canada. It is impossible to estimate its prevalence. References to such behaviour were common in sociological texts about the impoverished and criminal classes, which were thought to be riddled with 'deviancy'. But homosexuality was never considered to be widespread before the 1960s. It had been among the medical grounds on which both males and females could be rejected for military service in both world wars, but it is impossible to pinpoint, among the many possible reasons for rejection, how many recruits were rejected because of sexual orientation. Certainly many recruits discovered their sexual inclinations through their wartime experience in the military.

The era after 1945 was one of rampant heterosexuality. Canadians joined Americans in expressing shock at the findings of American biologist Alfred Kinsey, who in two studies (1948 and 1953) reported that homosexual practices were regular and widespread among both males and females, although the number of full-fledged homosexuals was relatively small. The idea that heterosexuals—even married people, parents of children—could have, and act on, same-gender urges was revolutionary. Yet police raids on private clubs and bathhouses demonstrated that in fact, there were clearly defined homosexual communities and networks in most major Canadian cities. Now, however, such behaviour was gener-

ally regarded less as a criminal act than as a medical 'disorder' or a 'character weakness'. Thanks to the espionage and loyalty debates in the US and Britain, homosexuals were automatically regarded as security risks because of their vulnerability to blackmail, and when the RCMP created a special investigative unit called A-3 to identify homosexuals in the civil service, it claimed to find a good many in Ottawa. In 1959 the federal government commissioned research to ascertain whether all homosexuals represented potential security risks, which led to the development of the notorious, if ineffectual, 'fruit machine' to detect homosexuals within the civil service.[48] The Canadian Immigration Act had already been amended in 1953 to deny admission to homosexuals (defined as 'a status or type of person', not in terms of particular behaviour) as possible subversives.

The process of amending the Criminal Code in general began in the 1940s. In theory the revisions were intended to make the law more enforceable, but in the area of sexual activity they often expanded its coverage. Nevertheless, in the postwar era the law increasingly had to recognize new gender categories, and Canadian society gradually became more aware of the need for distinctions between gender and sexual orientation, and of the simultaneous blurring of such distinctions. The best-known examples of blurring were the transsexual ('sex change') operations, which were widely publicized, especially in the tabloid press. By the late 1950s more 'advanced' legal and medical thinking had come to recognize the importance of decriminalizing homosexual activity, at least between consenting adults. This view became more general in the 1960s, in part because of public lobbying by gay and lesbian organizations that emerged in this period, such as the Association for Social Knowledge (1964). Increasing numbers of gay newspapers and journals also appeared. Like other minority groups, gays began to concentrate on creating a positive rather than a destructive self-identity, as in the 'gay is good' campaign launched in 1968. Finally, in 1969 Parliament decriminalized sexual offences between consenting adults, making a distinction between private and public sex. Although the 1969 revisions to the Criminal Code did not actually legalize homosexuality and lesbianism, they did have a considerable effect on the gay community. It was now possible to become more aggressive in support of homosexual rights, and the first gay liberation organizations were formed in Vancouver, Montreal, Toronto, and Ottawa in 1970 and 1971. These groups led the way in advocating the protection of sexual orientation in any human rights legislation adopted by the government.

CONCLUSION

By the early 1970s gays had joined women, Aboriginal people, and black people at the fore-front of new demands for constitutional reform and political change. The political and constitutional agenda in Canada no longer focused exclusively on issues such as extending the welfare state, satisfying Quebec, or redefining the federal–provincial relationship. It now had to encompass a wide variety of organized and articulate collectivities demanding equality in law and in practice. In the 1970s the main item on the larger political agenda would be, as the historian John Saywell put it, 'a re-examination of fundamental attitudes, beliefs and values', challenging 'less the existence of the nation-state than the nature of the society within it'.[49] Canadian society had undergone profound changes during the quarter-century after the end of World War II, and to those changes we must now turn.

SHORT BIBLIOGRAPHY

Bacher, John C. *Keeping to the Marketplace: The Evolution of Canadian Housing Policy*. Montreal and Kingston, 1993. An important survey of Canadian housing policy, arguing that it was never really interested in public planning.

Bashevkin, Sylvia. *True Patriot Love: The Politics of Canadian Nationalism*. Toronto, 1991. A fascinating account of the uses of Canadian nationalism in the post-war period that views nationalism as a means, not an end.

Bell, David, and Lorne Tepperman. *The Roots of Disunity: A Look at Canadian Political Culture*. Toronto, 1979. Although older, this book still provides an excellent analysis of the major assumptions of Canadian politics.

Bryden, Kenneth. *Old Age Pensions and Policy-Making in Canada*. Montreal and London, 1974. The standard account of a complex problem.

Campbell, R.M. *Grand Illusions: The Politics of the Keynesian Experience in Canada, 1945–75*. Peterborough, Ont., 1988. A wonderful study of the importance of Keynesianism in post-war Canada.

Guest, Dennis. *The Emergence of Social Security in Canada*. Vancouver, 1980. The classic analysis.

Kinsman, Gary. *The Regulation of Desire: Sexuality in Canada*. Montreal, 1987. The first serious study in Canada of this important topic.

Neary, Peter, and J.L. Granatstein, eds. *The Veteran's Charter and Post-World War II Canada*. Montreal and Kingston, 1998. A collection of articles that demonstrates how important veterans' policy was in the post-war period.

Resnick, Philip. *The Politics of Resentment: British Columbia Regionalism and Canadian Unity*. Vancouver, 2000. One of the few studies that focuses on the politics of provincial–federal relations.

Simeon, Richard, and Ian Robinson. *State, Society and the Development of Canadian Federalism*. Toronto, 1990. An important analysis of the ways in which Canadian federalism has developed since World War II.

Weaver, Sally. *Making Canadian Indian Policy: The Hidden Agenda, 1968–70*. Toronto, 1981. A detailed study of the early years of the effort to reform the Indian Act.

STUDY QUESTIONS

1. What factors account for the Liberal Party's dominance in Ottawa from 1935 to 1979?
2. In what ways were the huge Liberal majorities deceptive?
3. How did Liberal and Progressive Conservative leaders differ in this period?
4. What were the checks on Liberal power during these years?
5. How did provincial politics provide a counterweight to federal power?
6. Why was the Canadian welfare state not better planned and co-ordinated?
7. What new collectivities emerged in Canadian politics during the 1960s, and what did they want?

CHAPTER SIXTEEN

Quebec and Confederation, 1945–1972

At 2:40 p.m. on 5 October 1970 the Honourable Mitchell Sharp, Minister for External Affairs, rose from his seat on the front benches to read a brief statement in the House of Commons. He began: 'Mr. Speaker, I regret to have to inform the House that Mr James Richard Cross, Senior Trade Commissioner of the British Trade Commission in Montreal, was abducted from his home early this morning by armed men. . . . the reasons for this act have not been conclusively established.' By the time of Sharp's cautious announcement, the governments in Ottawa and Quebec knew that the kidnapping had been carried out by the Front de libération du Québec (FLQ) as an act of political terrorism. In return for sparing the life of this 'representative of the ancient racist and colonial British system', the group demanded the release from prison of FLQ members; a 'voluntary tax' of $500,000 in gold bullion; the identity of the informer who had led police to the last FLQ cell captured; and the broadcasting as well as the newspaper publication of the communiqué itself, which included a lengthy statement of the organization's political position. Thus began the 'October Crisis', a series of events that eventually included the kidnapping and murder of a Quebec cabinet minister and the federal government's declaration of a 'state of apprehended insurrection' under the War Measures Act.[1] Peaceful Canada had joined the real world of political terrorism and violence.

Despite occasional bombs in mailboxes, Canadians had spent the 1960s largely as bemused observers of the era's most obvious discontents. The decade was probably no more violent than any other in recent history, but included the apparently senseless assassinations of public leaders (John F. and Robert Kennedy and Martin Luther King in the United States, for example) as well as deliberate acts of terrorism. In some cases, other governments' responses to terrorism seemed almost as brutal as the terrorist acts themselves. Canadians were astonished by the violence with which police repressed student demonstrators in Chicago, at the Democratic National Convention in 1968, in Paris that same summer, and at Kent State University in Ohio in 1970, where several students were shot dead by the US National Guard. Many Canadians were convinced that their country had escaped the worst of wanton violence and terrorism because, as Mordecai Richler put it in 1967, 'we are nicer'.[2]

Then suddenly, in October 1970, the worst features of other countries' 1960s were encapsulated in one set of events in Canada. On 2 October Prime Minister Trudeau declared that 'Canada is not a trap or a betrayal or a swindle. It is a hope, it is a promise, it is an ambitious challenge we can

TIMELINE

1949

Horace Miner reports dramatic changes in rural Quebec. Asbestos strike begins. First performance of *Tit-Coq*.

1950

Cité libre founded.

1954

Duplessis forces Ottawa to accept Quebec's separate collection of income tax.

1959

Le Devoir publishes letters on language by Brother Jean-Paul Desbiens. Maurice Duplessis dies and is succeeded as premier by Paul Sauvé.

1960

Liberals under Jean Lesage elected in Quebec. Louis Robichaud elected Premier of New Brunswick.

1962

Liberals win again on slogan '*Maîtres chez nous*' and promise to nationalize hydroelectricity in Quebec.

1963

Front de libération du Québec (FLQ) is founded.

1964

Bill 60 places education in Quebec under provincial administration. Paul Gérin-Lajoie becomes the first Minister of Education.

1965

'Three Wise Men' decide to become Liberals and stand for Parliament.

1966

Lesage Liberals defeated by Union Nationale under Daniel Johnson. Quebec Federation of Women founded.

1967

Expo 67. Charles de Gaulle declares '*Vive le Québec libre*'.

1968

First performance of Michel Tremblay's *Les Belles-soeurs*. Government of Quebec creates Radio-Quebec.

1969

Official Languages Act passes Parliament.

1970

Robichaud defeated in New Brunswick by Tory Richard Hatfield. James Cross is abducted on 5 October.

1971

Constitutional reform fails in Victoria.

1972

Gendron report recommends one official language and two national languages for Quebec.

meet if we believe in it, if we find within ourselves enough ardour, enough confidence, and enough energy to put an end to these quarrels and these secular animosities.'[3] Three days later, the FLQ succeeded in its goal of drawing 'the attention of the world to the fate of French-speaking Québécois'.

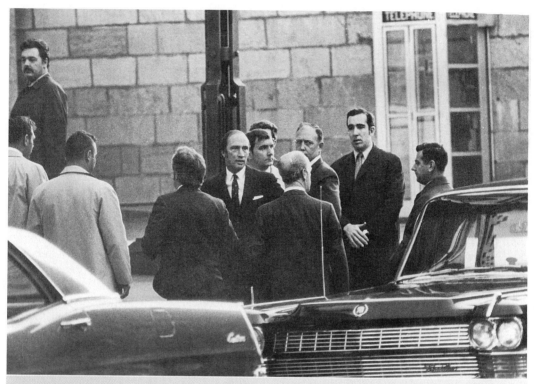

■ Prime Minister Pierre Trudeau arriving at the Notre-Dame basilica in Montreal for the funeral of Pierre Laporte, 20 October 1970. An FLQ cell had seized Laporte on 10 October, and his body was found a week later in the trunk of a car at the St-Hubert airport. His murder helped to justify the federal government in its imposition of the War Measures Act. *The Gazette* (Montreal) LAC, PA-113490.

As the drama unfolded, and commentators attempted to explain its origins and nuances, the rest of Canada was reminded that even though most Quebecers rejected the FLQ's terrorist tactics, the movement for Quebec's political independence had become much more than a sideshow for both Quebec and Canada. Perhaps equally important, Canadians everywhere discovered that their own governments were not necessarily better at handling radical discontent than those of other nations. The use of the War Measures Act, including the suspension of civil liberties and questionable repression of dissent in Quebec, in the long run proved far more controversial than the actions that had touched off the crisis. Prime Minister

Trudeau's television interview on 13 October, after the kidnapping of Pierre Laporte and before the proclamation of apprehended insurrection, sparked intense national debate, centring on the following exchange:

TRUDEAU: Yes, well there are a lot of bleeding hearts around who just don't like to see people with helmets and guns. All I can say is, go on and bleed, but it is more important to keep law and order in the society than to be worried about weak-kneed people who don't like the looks of . . .
INTERVIEWER: At any cost? How far would you go with that? How far would you extend that?
TRUDEAU: Well, just watch me.[4]

As the historian John Saywell put it shortly after the event, 'Whatever the future of the FLQ, the October crisis was a turning point in Canadian history.'[5] From it many Canadians felt that there could be no turning back.

QUEBEC AFTER THE WAR

THE FERMENT OF THE 1940S AND 1950S

The scope of social and economic change in Quebec, beginning in 1939, went largely unheralded in the remainder of the country until the 1960s, when the Front de libération du Québec (founded in 1963) began placing bombs in mailboxes to call attention to its critique of Quebec's 'colonial' status.[6] Most English-speaking Canadians refused to take the FLQ's campaign very seriously, thus contributing to what would eventually become the October Crisis of 1970. There was (and is) nothing unusual about this complacency on the part of the majority in Canada; around the world, terrorist violence was being used to dramatize issues. In English-speaking Canada during the 1940s and 1950s, the popular press was fascinated by Maurice Duplessis and his Union Nationale, which combined heavy-handed attacks on civil liberties and trade unions with far-sighted public works such as road-building and rural electrification. As a result, journalists generally ignored the changes underway in Quebec society,[7] and for English-speaking Canadians who depended on the press for their opinions, Quebecers remained the simple, priest-ridden rural folk of the old Anglo myth. For example, one of the most common names used by Anglos to refer to French Canadians in the thirties and forties was 'Pepsis'—a reference to Quebec's unfashionable preference for Pepsi-Cola, which offered 12 ounces for the same price that Coca-Cola charged for only six ('twice as much for a nickel too'). No doubt this reference to unfashionable consumer behaviour in

relation to a major symbol of North American popular culture was intended to suggest that Quebec was backward in other areas as well. But in fact it said more about English Canada than it did about Quebec. As *Le Devoir* pointed out in 1954, the socio-economic change taking place in Quebec was literally unparalleled in any other industrialized society.[8] At the same time, most Canadians equally failed to appreciate the extent to which English Canada had changed over the same period, particularly in terms of its sense of national identity.[9]

Outsiders could have discovered what was happening in Quebec if they had known where to look. For example, when anthropologist Horace Miner, who had studied the relatively self-contained rural parish of St-Denis (on the Richelieu River near Montreal) in 1936 and 1937, returned in 1949, he marvelled at the changes that had taken place.[10] In just over a decade the material culture of St-Denis had been transformed. The principal road, now paved, was in constant use by automobile traffic from outside the immediate area. With telephone and electric lines now installed, the parish had 40 telephones, and virtually every farm had electricity, making it possible to use radios, electric washing machines, refrigerators, and milking machines. As farm technology shifted from horsepower to electricity and gasoline, the focus of farm production had shifted from grain to dairy products and pork. The Canadian Family Allowances Act of 1944 brought cash income to every family, and made it possible for St-Denis farmers both to mechanize and to maintain their traditional large families. An unexpected development was the introduction of co-operatives, including a caisse populaire and a farmer-owned butter factory. The amount of mail had doubled between 1937 and 1949, and the number of daily newspapers subscribed to had grown by one-third. Women not only voted, but were rumoured in some cases to vote differently from their husbands. Demographic change was less visible than material change, but life expectancy

had increased, infant mortality had been reduced, and the numbers of marriages had gone
up. Miner attributed most of the material change
to 'the relatively sudden development of large
cash incomes in the parish' stimulated by new
policies of the Dominion government. He
thought the effect of mechanization on farm
women had been substantial and he predicted
an increase in the pace of integration into the
surrounding industrial life.

The rapidity with which Quebec caught up
with the rest of Canada was sensational and ultimately unsettling because it was not well understood. Certainly by the 1950s the province was
no longer behind in most social and economic
indicators. Hindsight can often trick us into fas-
tening onto those aspects of the past that find
confirmation in the future. But it can also lead us
to overemphasize the contrasts between the past
and a later time. In the case of Quebec, most
commentators from outside the province tended
to see the Quiet Revolution—which began in
1960 with the election of a Liberal government
under Jean Lesage—as establishing a new, progressive direction, in marked contrast to the supposed backwardness of the Duplessis era. In reality, however, conditions in Quebec had begun to
change well before 1960.

Symptomatic of the ferment that began
under Duplessis was the Asbestos strike of 1949
(see Chapter 14), when Quebec's other labour
unions joined the 5,000 workers of the
Confédération des Travailleurs Catholiques du
Canada (CTCC) in an unprecedented show of solidarity and—equally important—the archbishop
of Montreal himself, Mgr Joseph Charbonneau,
backed the strikers. In a sermon at Notre-Dame
Cathedral in Montreal, delivered on 1 May 1949,
Mgr Charbonneau proclaimed:

> The working class is a victim of a conspiracy
> which works to crush it, and when there is a con-
> spiracy to crush the working class, the Church has
> a duty to intervene. We want to have peace in our
> society, but we do not want to see the working

class crushed. We are more attached to man than
to capital. This is why the clergy decided to intervene. They want to see that justice and charity are
respected, and it is their wish that more attention
be paid to human beings than to the interests of
money.[11]

The bishops in many Quebec dioceses
requested that donations to assist the strikers be
left at the doors of their churches, and
$167,558.24 was collected over the next
weeks.[12] Since the industry was openly supported by the Duplessis government, the strike
became an unofficial confrontation between the
Church and the Union Nationale. Although the
union did not achieve all its demands, in the
end the most important results of the strike may
have been that it prompted opponents of
Duplessis and the Union Nationale to meet,
work together, and discover common ground,
and that it broke up the cozy relations between
Quebec industry and Quebec nationalism that
had prevailed before 1949.[13]

Outside Quebec there had been an unspoken assumption, dating back to the eighteenth
century, that when French Canadians finally
joined the modern world, they would assimilate
into the majority society in North America. Here,
too, the rest of Canada proved to be seriously
mistaken. Quebec's socio-economic transformation was accompanied by a series of ideological
shifts that shook the society to its foundations.
The patterns were probably recognizable to anyone familiar with what was happening elsewhere
in developing societies. The power and authority
of traditional defenders of traditional Quebec
nationalism, including the Roman Catholic
Church, were being swept away by a powerful
new secular nationalism that had already
become fully articulated in the years before the
demise of Maurice Duplessis. The main opposition to the new nationalism came not from the
old nationalism but from a renewed current of
nineteenth-century liberalism adapted to twentieth-century Quebec conditions. In the 1960s,

■ Premier Maurice Duplessis and Archbishop Joseph Charbonneau at a bridge opening in Ste-Thérèse, Quebec, August 1946. Three years later the two men would come into conflict over the Asbestos strike. Vic Davidson/Montreal *Gazette*/LAC, C-53641.

these two competing ideological currents would find popular labels in Quebec as 'separatism' and 'federalism'.[14]

THE NEW NATIONALISM

In its rhetoric the new Quebec nationalism often sounded quite similar to the old, but in fact its intellectual assumptions were radically different. In the first place, the new nationalists were profoundly anticlerical in their opposition to the entrenched role of the Church in Quebec society, although many of them continued to espouse Catholic values. In the second place, they accepted the industrial and urban realities of modern Quebec and had no desire to return to a Golden Age of agrarianism. They insisted that Quebec nationalism had to be centred on the interests of the growing French-Canadian working class; nationalists had to take the lead in the battle for socio-economic change. The new nationalists scorned international socialism because it was, by nature, insensitive to the particular cultural dimensions of French Canada;

however, they adopted a good deal of the Marxist vocabulary and economic analysis, including the essential concept of proletarian class solidarity and struggle. In their insistence on nationalism and cultural preservation they were hardly traditional Marxists, but similar efforts to reconcile Marxist categories with national decolonization were underway in many places after 1945. The new nationalists—particularly the younger, more militant ones—were able to find intellectual allies and models everywhere. The international neo-Marxist models most commonly cited in Quebec came from the former French colonies and Latin America, but the new nationalism also fitted easily into the North American 'New Left' movement and critique of the 1960s.[15]

The key to the new nationalists' program was an active and modern state. As Gérard Filion, publisher of *Le Devoir*, wrote in 1960:

> there are a certain number of accomplishments that only a modern state can fulfil, especially when it has the responsibility of seeing to the common good of an under-developed community. A system of natural resource exploitation, a policy of energy utilization, the protection of manpower, the participation of nationals at all levels of business and industry, the control over certain large areas of public service, respect for language and culture in the making of social choices and in public relations, these are some of the many functions that a state which recognizes its responsibilities and is convinced that it is there to govern and not to be tossed about should not hesitate in undertaking.[16]

A culturally homogeneous secular state represented the highest expression of the nation, and was the best means of liberating the people of Quebec. For the new nationalists, traditionalist forces in Quebec had historically collaborated with forces in the rest of Canada to keep French Canadians in their place. Not until the 1960s did the new nationalism openly advocate separatism, but the latter was always inherent in its position.

The chief opposition to the new nationalism came from a tiny but influential group of small-'l' liberals centred on the journal *Cité libre*, founded in 1950—at the height of Duplessis's power—by a group of intellectuals that included, among others, Gérard Pelletier and Pierre Elliott Trudeau. Born in Montreal in 1919, Trudeau was the son of a wealthy businessman and grew up fluently bilingual. He received a law degree from the Université de Montréal; later studied at Harvard and the London School of Economics; and began to practise law in Montreal in 1951, specializing in labour and civil liberties cases. Trudeau and his colleagues were as revisionist in spirit as the new nationalists, but also suspicious of what they regarded as simplistic ideology and committed to the secular rationalism of the new social sciences. As Trudeau wrote in a frequently quoted statement:

> We want to bear witness to the Christian and French fact in America. Agreed; but we must also throw everything else overboard. We must systematically question all political categories bequeathed to us by the intervening generation. The strategy of resistance is no longer useful for the growth and maturation of the City. The time has arrived for us to borrow from architecture the discipline called 'functional', to cast aside the thousands of past prejudices which encumber the present, and to build for the new man. Overthrow all totems, transgress all taboos. Better still, consider them as dead ends. Without passion, let us be intelligent.[17]

These liberals who evoked the ideas of the eighteenth-century French *philosophes* were even more anticlerical than the new nationalists, perhaps because they still believed in the need for a revitalized Catholic humanism and thus criticized the Church from within. They were equally critical of traditional French-Canadian nationalism, which they regarded as outdated, inadequate, and oppressive. They preferred to locate French Canada within an open multicultural and

multinational state and society. Not only traditional nationalism but all nationalism was unprogressive, undemocratic, and unmodern. *Cité libre*
insisted, moreover, that it was possible to be 'leftist' without being Marxist. The result was that its
vision of the state was quite different from that of
the new nationalists. The two groups could agree
on the goal of an active state, but the new nationalists were more inclined to see such a state as
the liberating embodiment of the Quebec collectivity, while the *Cité librists* wanted active intervention in the form of regulation and control.

By the mid-1960s it would be clear that the
differences between the new nationalists and the
Cité librists were serious, and separatism was at
the heart of the disagreement. Agreeing that a
more imaginative and flexible Canadian federalism was necessary to meet the challenge of separatism, in 1965 Pierre Trudeau and Gérard
Pelletier would join Jean Marchand in becoming
Liberals (they came to be called the 'Three Wise
Men') and successfully standing for election to
Parliament. Yet at an earlier stage, in the late
1950s, the two groups appeared to have arrived
at similar conclusions. Traditional nationalism in
Quebec had led nowhere. The Church had to be
removed from its remaining positions of dominance. And a modern state, secular and interventionist in nature, was needed to complete
Quebec's transformation. Whether that modern
state would be Quebec or Canada remained to
be seen.

THE QUIET REVOLUTION

The ground was well prepared for the famous
Quiet Revolution of the 1960s. The structural
changes in Quebec society had already taken
place. By 1960 it was an urbanized, industrialized, and secularizing province little different in
many respects from its neighbour, Ontario. At
the end of the 1950s traditional French-Canadian nationalism in Church and state, symbolized by the Union Nationale, still seemed solidly
entrenched. But the critique of tradition had

already been elaborated, and the reform program
was in place. All that remained was to fit the government of Quebec and popular aspirations
together. That task was begun by Paul Sauvé,
Duplessis's successor as leader of the Union
Nationale, whose slogan, '*Désormais*' ('hence-
forth'), was a clear signal of a change in direction.
But Sauvé died after just a hundred days as
Premier, and in the election of June 1960 the
provincial Liberal Party under Jean Lesage came
to power.[18] As usually happens in such cases, the
Liberals did not win the election so much as the
Union Nationale lost it. Following Sauvé's death,
the failure to find either a suitable replacement or
high-profile candidates did not help a party that
was more out of step with the province than
most analysts realized. The Liberals, by contrast,
had several well-educated and well-known stars,
including the television commentator René
Lévesque; in fact, keeping their strong egos in
line would be one of Lesage's major problems as
Premier. The party promised clean government
and progressive policies, but did not mention the
changes in education and energy policy that
would come to symbolize its success. Not even
the leading Liberal theorists in 1960 realized just
how ready Quebec was for change, and how easily the traditional institutions and ways would
crumble once they were confronted by an activist
government drawn from Quebec's new middle
and professional classes. The Quebec state
became the principal vehicle for the aspirations
of these classes, who would become particularly
militant politically in the 1970s, as they came to
feel blocked outside Quebec, especially within
the private sector.[19]

The new government's first major action
came in the area of hydroelectricity. The obstacle
that had to be overcome was Quebec's traditional
fear, nurtured for decades by the Union Nationale,
of anything resembling economic statism (or
'socialism' or 'communism'). To be *anti-étatiste* in
Quebec was not quite the same thing as to oppose
all government-led activity; under Duplessis the
provincial government had spent a good deal of

money on public services, including many local hydroelectric projects. What the Liberal Minister of Natural Resources, René Lévesque, proposed in February 1962—without consulting his colleagues—was the forced government takeover of all existing private hydroelectric companies into a massive Hydro-Québec (which had been created under Duplessis in 1944). Hydroelecricity was a good issue on which to fight the nationalization battle, partly because electrical generation and supply was a public enterprise in many parts of North America, partly because it directly touched the pocketbook of the rural Quebecers who were most likely to oppose state action. Lévesque acted unilaterally because he knew his colleagues were divided and he sensed the value of the surprise strike. Despite a famous '*Jamais!*' from Premier Lesage, nationalization (of hydroelectricity or other enterprises) was quickly accepted by the Liberal cabinet as a winning campaign issue, and the party took it to the province in 1962 under the slogan '*Maîtres chez nous*'. Led by Lesage and a compelling Lévesque, the Liberals managed to turn Hydro-Québec into a symbol of the economic liberation of Quebec from its colonial past, thus co-opting the new nationalism with a vengeance. Buying out the privately owned electrical utilities cost over $600 million, but this was only the beginning of the Liberal expenditures on public enterprise, which tripled the provincial budget in the early 1960s and saw some provincial government involvement in almost every economic and industrial activity in the province. The second Lesage administration (1962–6), unlike the first, was unabashedly nationalistic and statist.

The other great symbolic victory of the Quiet Revolution was the secularization and modernization of Quebec's education system. Since before Confederation schools had been in the hands of the Catholic Church, which staffed them mostly with priests and nuns teaching a curriculum that had been very slow to change from the nineteenth century. By 1960 the Church itself was in trouble, not just in Quebec but around the world. So it was perhaps not surpris-

■ Jean Lesage (1912–80). Assemblée nationale du Québec.

ing that the first telling shots in the campaign against its control of Quebec education were fired by a Catholic cleric, Brother Jean-Paul Desbiens, who in 1960 published a best-selling book called *Les Insolences de Frère Untel* (*The Impertinences of Brother Anonymous*, translated in 1962), based on a series of letters he had written to *Le Devoir* in 1959. Orchestrated by the paper's editor, André Laurendeau—perhaps the leading mainstream spokesman for the new nationalism in Quebec—the 'Frère Untel' debate boiled in the province for over a year.[20]

Frère Untel (literally, 'Brother So-and-So') attacked Quebec education not from the progressive left, but from an elitist position within the new nationalism. He equated the deterioration of French-Canadian culture with the success of an anglicizing North American popular culture and popularized the idea that *joual*, the everyday language of Quebec, was the product of British colonization. In a chapter entitled 'the Language of Defeat', he wrote:

> Our pupils speak joual, because they think joual, because they live joual, like everybody around here. Living joual means rock 'n' roll, hot dogs, parties, running around in cars. All our civilization is joual. Efforts on the level of language don't accomplish anything, these competitions, campaigns for better French, congresses, all that stuff. We must act on the level of civilization.[21]

In a nice piece of rhetorical simplification, Frère Untel blamed Quebec's cultural failings on *joual* and then found 'the only possible explanation for this lamentable failure' in the system of education, which, as a result of the authoritarian control exercised by the Church, was a sterile failure. The Church responded by ordering Desbiens to cease all public activity, subjecting him to an official letter of condemnation by the Sacred Congregation of Religious Orders and banishing him to Rome.[22] These actions were too late, of course, and only turned Desbiens into a martyr in the cause of freedom of speech.

Public responses to Frère Untel, which often took the form of letters to the editors of newspapers, demonstrated that he had struck a chord in the province. Lesage himself responded with a provincial commission of inquiry into education, chaired by the vice-rector of Laval University, Monseigneur Alphonse-Marie Parent. The Parent Commission's hearings produced a battery of complaints about the Quebec system, most of which it endorsed in its 1963 report. The Commission called not only for modernization along North American lines, but for administration by a unitary secular authority. Armed with this recommendation, the Lesage government in 1964 passed Bill 60, which for the first time placed education in Quebec under provincial administration. Thereafter, education in the province was rapidly brought up to national

standards. The Lesage government also recognized the importance of Frère Untel's call for the preservation and extension of French-Canadian culture and the French language. It had already created a cultural affairs ministry in 1961, which was soon presiding over a veritable explosion of French-Canadian art and writing. The Ministry of Cultural Affairs could not take credit for that explosion, of course. In that respect, it was typical of the Lesage government's role in the Quiet Revolution. The Liberal government was not so much the agent of change as its animateur, the beneficiary of years of preparation by others. The Liberals identified some of the key problems and liberated the new-found aspirations of Quebec—only to be defeated in 1966 by a rejuvenated Union Nationale under Daniel Johnson. The main reason for that defeat was that they failed to follow the logic of the revolution over which they presided to its separatist conclusion.

The events of the 1960s unleashed a Pandora's box of new energy in Quebec as many of the reform proposals of the province's labour organizations were taken up. The Confédération des syndicats nationaux (CSN) was both a supporter of the Lesage Liberals and a beneficiary of their restructuring of labour relations, which included legislation guaranteeing the right to strike in the public sector, except when essential services were jeopardized. The increasing importance of labour negotiations in the public sector, however, put the government and the unions on opposite sides of the bargaining table. The tendency to declare any area of the particular public sector essential quickly frustrated and radicalized the CSN. By 1970 the CSN, leaders and members alike, had come to believe that the state was on the side of the business community against the workers. Accordingly, this union turned to the left and to a Marxist analysis of society.[23] In 1972, an internal debate over strategy in public-sector negotiations led to the departure of the right wing—about one-third of the membership (70,000)—which founded a new union, the Centrale des syndicats démocratiques (CSD). The

FRÈRE UNTEL ON THE LANGUAGE OF DEFEAT

In 1960 a little book by a priest who called himself 'Frère Untel'—Brother Anonymous—first appeared in Quebec. The book was a savage attack on Quebec education in the context of French culture and quickly became a runaway best-seller.

In October, 1959, André Laurendeau published a short column in *Le Devoir* in which he qualified the speech of French Canadian students as 'joual talk'. He, not I, invented the name. It was well chosen. The thing and the name are alike, both hateful. The word joual is a summary description of what it is like to talk joual, to say joual instead of cheval, horse. It is to talk as horses would talk if they had not long since plumped for the silence and the smile of Fernandel.

Our pupils talk joual, write joual, and don't want to talk or write any other way. Joual is their language. Things have gone so far that they can't even tell a mistake when it is shown to them at pencil point. 'The man that I talk to', 'We are going to undress themselves', and the like do not bother them. In fact such expressions seem elegant to them. It is a little different when it comes to mistakes in spelling, and if a lack of agreement between noun and adjective or the omission of an s is pointed out, they can identify the error. But the vice is deeply rooted at the grammatical level, and on the level of pronunciation. Out of twenty pupils whose names you ask at the opening of school, not more than two or three will be comprehensible the first time. The others will have to repeat theirs. They say their names as if they were confessing a sin.

Joual is a boneless language. The consonants are all slurred, a little like the speech of Hawaiian dancers, according to the records I have heard. Oula-oula-oula-alao-alao-alao. They say *chu pas capable* for *je ne suis pas capable* (I am not able). I can't write joual down phonetically. It can't be fixed in writing for it is a decomposition, and only Edgar Poe could fix a decomposition. You know the story where he tells of the hypnotist who succeeded in freezing the decomposition of a corpse—it's a wonderful horror story.

Joual, this absence of language, is a symptom of our non-existence as French Canadians. No one can ever study language enough, for it is the home of all meanings. Our inability to assert ourselves, our refusal to accept the future, our obsession with the past, are all reflected in joual, our real language. Witness the abundance of negative turns of speech in our talk. Instead of saying that a woman is beautiful, we say she's not bad-looking; instead of saying that a pupil is intelligent, we say he's not stupid; instead of saying that we feel well, we say we're not too bad.

The day it appeared I read Laurendeau's comment to my class. My pupils realized that they spoke joual. One of them said, almost proudly, 'We've founded a new language.' They saw no need to change. 'Everybody talks like us,' they told me. Some said, 'People would laugh at us if we talked differently from the others.' One said—and it is a diabolical objection—'Why should we talk otherwise when everybody understands us?' It's not easy for a teacher, taken unaware, to answer this last proposition, which was made to me one afternoon.

Of course joual-speakers understand each other. But do you want to live your life among joual-speakers? As long as you want merely to chat about sports and the weather, as long as you talk only such crap, joual does very well. For primitives, a primitive language is good enough; animals get along with a few grunts. But if you want to attain to human speech, joual is not sufficient. You can make do with a board and some whitewash if you want to paint a barn, but finer tools are necessary for the Mona Lisa. . . .

> We speak two different languages, my class and I, and I am the only one who speaks both. What can we do? The whole French Canadian society is foundering. Our merchants show off their English company names, the billboards along our roads are all in English. We are a servile race; our loins were broken two hundred years ago, and it shows.

SOURCE: Frère Untel, *The Impertinences of Brother Anonymous*, trans. Miriam Chapin (Montreal: Harvest House, 1965), 27–30

remaining leaders of the CSN were fervent socialists. In the CSN and other Quebec unions, separatist sentiments spread rapidly, although formal support for separatism did not come before 1972.

Further changes were wrought by the rapid secularization of Quebec and the increasing availability of social programs beneficial to women. Between 1951 and 1971 the province's birth rate dropped from 29.8 to 14.8 per 1,000 as Quebec women gained the power and the means to limit the size of their families and embraced new cultural values.[24] Many more married women entered the workforce—usually still in traditionally 'female' jobs—and Quebec society in general learned to accept that women worked. The years after 1964 saw a new emphasis on organized feminism in Quebec. The Quebec Federation of Women was founded in March 1966, and nearly 400 women attended its first convention. A number of Quebec women's groups presented briefs to the Royal Commission on the Status of Women. In 1969 anglophone women in Quebec founded the Montreal Women's Liberation Movement, and by the early 1970s radical feminism was taking root in the province.

Finally, in 1968 the Johnson government appointed a commission of inquiry on the position of the French language and language rights (usually called the Gendron Commission). When it submitted its report at the end of 1972,[25] it called for one official language and two national languages for Quebec. To the surprise of many, it also established that most French Canadians did speak French in their working environment.

QUEBEC AND THE NATION

Between 1945 and 1972, Quebec succeeded in achieving virtual autonomy within the structure of Canadian Confederation. This result was not codified in formal constitutional terms, and Quebec did not have all the symbols of sovereignty, such as an independent armed force and foreign policy, but by 1970 it was an active player on the international stage and had full control of its internal affairs. It was in roughly the same position as the Dominion of Canada a century earlier. The extent of the practical freedom of action Quebec had achieved was disguised by demands for more explicit formulations of independence, and by a singular refusal on the part of English-speaking Canadians to recognize the political and constitutional realities within Quebec. Since almost all anglophones, at both the federal and provincial levels, spoke as if Quebec had yet to achieve autonomy, no one was really prepared to argue that it had already done so. Much of the constitutional agonizing of the post-1972 period would be about a *fait accompli*.

Three fundamental factors explain Quebec's achievement, however unacknowledged, during this period. In the first place, most Canadians, and certainly most Canadian politicians—especially among the federal Liberals—genuinely believed that Quebec was different and had some sort of special status within Confederation. Even those—perhaps especially those—who argued most strenuously against the various component parts of special status (such as the compact theory, or the 'two nations' concept) did so from some notion of Quebec's linguistic, cultural, and historic distinctiveness, as the writings of Quebec-based 'federalists' such as Pierre Elliott Trudeau made abundantly plain.[26] In 1954 Louis St Laurent had observed that Quebec could not become a province like any other. Only a relative handful of English-speaking Canadians were willing to speak out on behalf of a linguistically undifferentiated Confederation (although more may have silently believed in one). Such arguments were easily dismissible as out of date, or 'racist', or worse. In the second place, it was clear that few Québécois were happy with the province's place in Canada, past or present, and an increasing number advocated extreme solutions. Even fewer Canadians were able to conceive of a nation without Quebec, and so it became essential to respond at least to the province's 'legitimate' demands and aspirations. 'What does Quebec want?' began the jacket blurb of one English-Canadian paperback published in 1964. The blurb continued, 'Its grievances are desperate enough to threaten Confederation. English Canada, jolted from a state of comfortable indifference, is now forced to see and understand the plight of the Québécois.'[27] Quebec was unhappy, and most of English-speaking Canada was prepared to be sympathetic, at least to a point. That matters went further than many had anticipated was a product of the third factor: the support that Quebec's particular constitutional initiatives were able to attract from some of the other provinces, particularly Ontario, Alberta, and British Columbia. The political alliances between Quebec and other provinces against the federal government were constantly shifting in principles and particulars, but they were formidable.

Quebec's modern movement towards autonomy did not begin with the Quiet Revolution. Indeed, more than one expert has argued that the 'constitutional *coup d'état*' was delivered not by Jean Lesage or his successors but by Maurice Duplessis, who in 1954 forced Ottawa to let Quebec collect income tax itself, outside the tax rental system.[28] Prime Minister St Laurent had avoided any serious effort to repatriate the Constitution, and that issue would emerge as significant only after the Lesage victory. The Lesage Liberals had characterized Duplessis's constitutional policy as a negative one of 'defending our own', and offered instead 'positive autonomy' as 'the vision of our people'. At the 1960 dominion–provincial conference, Lesage called for action on the repatriation front and the subject was put back on the agenda.

The Lesage government made three distinct moves towards its declared ambition of 'positive autonomy'. First, it continued the Duplessis policy of opting out of centralized financial arrangements—a practice that after 1960 no longer entailed financial disadvantage (another specific federal concession to Quebec). The province successfully insisted on mounting its own versions of all the major social welfare programs, including unemployment compensation, pensions, and medicare. Second, it rejected proposed formal amendments to the BNA Act—the so-called Fulton (1961) and Fulton-Favreau (1965) formulas[29]—because it was not satisfied that key provisions could not be amended without unanimous consent of the provinces. Third, Lesage's government made tentative but increasingly ambitious moves into the international arena, establishing direct diplomatic links with francophone nations abroad that were not mediated through Ottawa's Department of External Affairs, although they were subsequently ratified by the federal government. On educational and cultural issues, Lesage's government dealt independently and bilaterally with nations like France, and Daniel Johnson's new Union Nationale would be prepared to go even further.[30]

THE NATION AND QUEBEC

The federal government, particularly during the minority ministries of Lester Pearson, tried a variety of responses to what was obviously a more aggressive Quebec. One was 'co-operative

■ The first raising of the Canadian flag, in Ottawa, February 1965. Standing at the far left are Prime Minister Lester Pearson and Governor General Georges Vanier. Murray Mosher Photography.

Quebec tensions, co-operative federalism reflected Pearson's own inclinations as a mediator and conciliator. If everyone truly tried to get along better they could do so, and the federal government was prepared to make concessions as evidence of its good faith. This strategy eventually ran aground because, as one political scientist put it, 'Quebec's demands for autonomy appeared to be insatiable.'[31]

Related to but independent of co-operative federalism were two other federal strategies developed under Pearson: one involved symbols of sovereignty, such as the flag, the national anthem, and anniversary celebrations; the other dealt with language and culture. Since 1867 the Canadian national flag had been Britain's Union Jack, although many English-speaking Canadians would have sworn in a court of law that it was the Red Ensign. In either case, the flag was a holdover from the days of the British Empire, symbolic of Canada's colonial status. Various efforts at reform had proved unsuccessful, but in 1963 Pearson raised the issue again, and several designs were vociferously debated in Parliament in June 1964. Diefenbaker's Tories were seriously divided (some Quebec MPs even broke with the Chief), but most preferred a version of the Red Ensign, while Pearson and the NDP wanted something with maple leaves. In the end, a special committee recommended the present design, which was finally adopted later in 1965—though only after the invocation of closure.[32] The baby boomers took to the new flag almost instantly, however, and Confederation Year (1967) offered the ideal opportunity to promote it. In the same year Canada acquired its own indigenous national anthem. For many English-speaking Canadians 'God Save the Queen' was good enough, but for others the objections were the same ones associated with the Union Jack. Some were quite fond of 'The Maple Leaf Forever', with its lilting tune, but its sentiments could not possibly be accepted by French Canadians ('In days of yore, from Britain's shore, Wolfe, the dauntless hero, came . . .'). 'O Canada' had the merit of

federalism', a concept exemplified in a series of agreements (1963–5) between Ottawa and the provinces that accepted the need for greater consultation and flexibility. Ostensibly designed to deal with federal–provincial rather than Ottawa–

having been written as a 'Chant nationale' by the composer Calixa Lavallée and Adolphe-Basile Routhier for a viceregal occasion in Quebec City in June 1880. The familiar English words (which have been the subject of frequent tinkering) were written by R. Stanley Weir in 1908. In 1967 Parliament approved 'O Canada' as the country's official national anthem, just in time for the Centennial celebrations. At first many Canadians were self-conscious about singing it, and sometimes it even met with public boos.

The Centennial Year bash was a bipartisan extravaganza. Plans for the hundredth anniversary of Confederation had begun under John Diefenbaker and continued under Pearson. Substantial amounts of money were spent by Ottawa (some of it naturally filtered through the provinces and municipalities) on public buildings intended as Centennial monuments, such as the National Arts Centre in Ottawa (which opened in June 1969). A national train toured the country, and various other manifestations included a catchy birthday song by Bobby Gimby ('Ca-na-da, We Love You'). Winnipeg hosted the Pan-American Games in the summer of 1967. The centrepiece of the Centennial, however, was the Canadian Universal and International Exhibition at Montreal, familiarly known as Expo 67, which had as its theme Man and His World (*Terre des Hommes*). The location of the exhibition in the province of Quebec was dictated by political considerations, and Montreal's Mayor Jean Drapeau used the 'Quebec card' to great effect in eliciting co-operation from Ottawa. Canadians surprised themselves and the world by surmounting a multitude of organizational complexities to create what many said was the greatest world's fair ever, with the participation of some 120 governments. Its magnificent displays in many buildings of architectural distinction (Buckminster Fuller's geodesic dome for the American Pavilion and Moshe Safdie's Habitat '67, an experimental housing project, were among the most talked-about), its World Arts Festival, and its excellent services and staff

attracted 50 million paid admissions. Though cost overruns and construction abuses were the stuff of legend, the tourist revenues generated by Expo were almost double the official $283 million cost, and all problems were easily dismissed in the euphoria and pride of having produced an undisputed world-scale triumph.[33]

During Expo an event occurred—brief, sensational, and unexpected—that shares an almost equal place in the history of the period and the memory of many Canadians. The occasion was the visit of French President Charles de Gaulle. From the outset Ottawa and Quebec had jostled over protocol for the visit. On 24 July de Gaulle stood on the balcony of Montreal's city hall with open arms, receiving the tumultuous applause of half a million Quebecers. It was an emotional moment. He spoke of cherished memories such as the liberation of France in 1944. Then, before the huge crowd and a television audience of millions, he concluded: 'Vive Montréal! Vive le Québec! Vive le Québec libre!' Whether de Gaulle had deliberately insulted the Canadian government and people (the official Pearson position) or had merely referred to Quebec's efforts to affirm its identity (the Johnson position) was irrelevant. The exclamation had been vociferously cheered, and the nation had been given yet another reminder of its deep division.[34]

The other policy initiative of the Pearson Liberals, involving language and culture, was the concept of 'equal partnership', or the right of French- and English-speaking Canadians to participate equally in the country's institutions. This concept, along with the notions of cultural dualism and 'two founding races', was enshrined in the Order-in-Council that in 1963 set up the Royal Commission on Bilingualism and Biculturalism. The Commission's terms of reference called for it:

> to enquire into and report upon the existing state of bilingualism and biculturalism in Canada and to recommend what steps should be taken to develop the Canadian Confederation on the basis

■ The Canadian pavilion at Expo 67, dominated by a huge inverted pyramid. LAC, E000990974.

of an equal partnership between the two founding races, taking into account the contribution made by the other ethnic groups to the cultural enrichment of Canada and the measures that should be taken to safeguard that contribution.[35]

Chaired by *Le Devoir*'s André Laurendeau and Davidson Dunton (the president of Carleton University), the Commission was plainly a response to the growing problems of Quebec. It was instructed to recommend ways of facilitating Canada's cultural dualism.

Two points about the work of the Commission and its eventual recommendations must be emphasized. The first is that its terms of reference stated almost all the conclusions that it was to reach; the Commission simply legitimized them in appropriate academic language. Second,

the members of the Commission made no attempt to dispute or broaden those terms of reference. Unlike most Royal Commissions, therefore, it served more to buttress already articulated public policy than to examine the issues or to analyze cherished beliefs. This distinction is important, for in the course of its hearings and investigations the B&B Commission discovered a good deal of evidence pointing to the limitations of its original terms of reference. If it had paid more attention to that evidence in formulating its eventual recommendations, it might have spared the nation some pain.

One major problem, of course, was that the concept of two founding peoples took no account of the First Nations. In its final report the Commission simply noted in its 'General Introduction' to 'Key Words of the Terms of

Reference' that those terms 'contain no allusion to Canada's native populations'. Nor were the First Nations included among the 'other ethnic groups' studied by the Commission. The volume of the report devoted to *Cultural Contributions of the Other Ethnic Groups* offered a potted history beginning with the statement: 'Canada, a vast territory inhabited in the beginning by Indians and Eskimos, was first colonized by the French, beginning early in the 17th century, and then by the British.'[36] A footnote to the word 'Eskimos' informed readers that 'Since the terms of reference contain no mention of Indians and Eskimos, we have not studied the question of Canada's native population.'[37] Instead, the Commission contented itself with an introductory 'reminder' to 'the proper authorities that everything possible must be done to help the native populations preserve their cultural heritage, which is part of the patrimony of all Canadians'.[38]

When the Commission moved its public hearings outside the central Canadian corridor, it heard from hundreds of groups and thousands of individuals, many of whom expressed doubts about its terms of reference. Most of the criticism came from spokesmen for ethnic communities that were not part of the cultural duality. The potential embarrassment associated with the Native peoples could be avoided through bureaucratic sleight-of-hand, but the issue of other ethnic groups was more complicated. The Commission's solution was to claim that other ethnic groups were too disparate to constitute a 'third force' in Canadian society:

> this 'third force' does not exist in Canada in any political sense, and is simply based on statistical compilations. All the available evidence indicates that those of other languages and cultures are more or less integrated with the Francophone and Anglophone communities, where they should find opportunities for self-fulfillment and equality of status. It is within these two societies that their cultural distinctiveness should find a climate of respect and encouragement to survive.[39]

Other ethnic communities were to be seen as individual cultural groups, argued the Commission, not a basic structural element equal to the French or the British (or English). As more than one scholar pointed out in essays submitted to the Commission at the time, however, there were serious doubts about the existence of an English-Canadian culture equivalent to that of French Canada. This question is one to which we shall return.

In the end—as the Commission recognized both in its opening remarks and in its recommendations—its principal concerns had to be language and bilingualism rather than culture. Most Canadians were prepared to accept that the nation should implement equality for the two languages it declared official, and it was perhaps unfortunate that the Commission strayed into the area of culture at all without challenging more directly some of the assumptions underlying its terms of reference. Its first recommendation was implemented by the Official Languages Act of 1969, which declared French and English to be official languages with equal status in all institutions under federal jurisdiction. This legislation did not resolve the language question in Canada, but it was all the federal government could do: most other recommendations, particularly those concerning language education, would require provincial co-operation and were more difficult to implement, although many were eventually followed, in whole or in part. The other recommendations also created much more controversy.

CULTURAL DEVELOPMENT

REINFORCEMENT OF THE FRENCH LANGUAGE

THE NEW QUEBEC THEATRE
The roots of the new Quebec theatre went back into the 1930s, when two quite distinctive theatrical directions emerged: on one hand, a popular theatre based on the revue or vaudeville

Gratien Gélinas (second from right) as Tit-Coq at the Monument National in Montreal, May 1948. Paul Henri/LAC, E000001167.

sketch, and on the other an avant-garde theatre that looked to Europe, especially France, for its inspiration. The most famous early revue was *Les Fridolinades*, written and produced by Gratien Gélinas.[40] Satirizing the Church and Quebec culture, it played in various updated versions in Montreal from 1938 to 1946, and one of its sketches found new life as *Tit-Coq*, the story of a returned soldier whose uneasy search for happiness is recounted in a series of monologues and dramatic encounters presented in working-class language (but not *joual*). Language was a frequent problem for plays of the 1940s and 1950s, which might have been more effective if they had used the *joual* that convention still banned from

the stage. Members of the avant-garde school were more willing to break with convention, particularly the constraints imposed by realism. One striking example was *Le Marcheur* (*The Walker*, 1950) by Yves Thériault, in which a dominant father, who never appears on the stage, controls the lives of the other characters, who are united in their hatred of him. Many who saw the play interpreted the father as representing the traditional French-Canadian paternal tyrant, or Premier Duplessis, or the Church.

The new theatre that emerged in the 1960s was the product of changes in Quebec society and the cultural patronage of both the Canadian and Quebec governments, which vied with one

RENÉ LÉVESQUE (1922–1987)

❖

René Lévesque was born on the Gaspé Peninsula (actually in Campbellton, New Brunswick) in 1922 and grew up in New Carlisle, Quebec. He was sent away to seminary school at the age of 11 and attended law school in Montreal. In 1943 he was recruited by the United States Office of War Information as a liaison officer, landing on D-Day and travelling as a war correspondent with American forces across Europe. In 1946 he joined the International Services of Radio-Canada as a general reporter; in 1950 he was sent by CBC radio to Korea; and two years later he was appointed to the radio-television news service of Radio-Canada International. In 1956 Lévesque became the host of an extremely popular weekly public affairs television program called *Point de Mire* (*On Target*). Working live, usually without much of a script, Lévesque was praised in *Le Devoir* for his ability to explain complex issues to his television audience. In 1959, however, he participated in a CBC producers' strike and spent several months out of work before running as a Liberal candidate for the Quebec assembly in an uncommitted Montreal riding.

Lévesque was one of the few media 'stars' in Canada who was able to take advantage of his exposure for political purposes, probably because his role as a journalist had made him a trusted voice in Quebec. To his surprise, he not only won his seat but was appointed to the new Lesage cabinet as Minister of Public Works and then of Natural Resources (1961–6). By his own admission, Lévesque sought to use Natural Resources as a power base for reform. It was he who proposed the nationalization of

■ René Lévesque as a Radio-Canada reporter interviewing Lester B. Pearson outside the Canadian Embassy in Moscow, c. 1955. Soviet/LAC, PA-117617.

hydroelectric power and encouraged Lesage to use it as the central election issue in the 1962 election. But the Liberal Party was neither sufficiently to the left nor sufficiently aggressive on the constitutional front for his taste, and he became increasingly restless. A brief term as Minister of Family and Social Welfare whetted his appetite for social reform, as he constructed a comprehensive package of family allowances for Quebec.

Finally, in 1967, Lévesque left the Liberals to sit as an independent member of the assembly. Later the same year he established the Mouvement souveraineté-association, inspired in part by the enthusiastic response of young Quebecers to de Gaulle's *'Vive le Québec libre'* speech. He entitled the manifesto for his new movement 'A Country that Must Be Made', insisting that Quebec must become a sovereign nation. Early in 1968 Pierre Elliott Trudeau, a man with whom Lévesque did not get along, became Prime Minister of Canada, and Lévesque soon after formed the Parti Québécois, bringing together most of the major groups advocating independence. The party won nearly a quarter of the vote in the 1970 provincial elections, although very few seats; Lévesque himself was defeated in his old riding. But by 1973 the PQ formed the official opposition in Quebec. Rene Lévesque was well on his way to becoming the nemesis of Pierre Elliott Trudeau, and would serve as the PQ Premier of Quebec from 1976 to 1985.

another throughout the period. With the creation of professional theatrical companies and experimental theatre groups, new audiences and performers were attracted to the theatre. The Centre d'essai des auteurs dramatiques was founded in 1965 to serve as 'a laboratory of dramaturgy, a place where a new form of dramatic discourse could evolve'.[41] On 14 August 1968 Michel Tremblay's *Les Belles-soeurs* was performed for the first time. Quebec theatre would never look back.[42] Set in the working-class neighbourhood of Plateau Mont-Royal, the play was presented entirely in *joual*, and many who saw it were offended (it was only a few years since Frère Untel had condemned *joual*, after all). But the very vulgarity of the language was part of the point of a play about how a group of friends, neighbours, and relations gather to help the central character, Germaine, deal with a windfall of trading stamps she has won and end up stealing them from her. By combining the techniques of Ionesco and Beckett with the common language of Quebec, Tremblay introduced a new kind of theatre to Quebec. Soon other dramatists would add to the use of *joual* a sense of political involvement in the affairs of the time.

In 1969 Françoise Loranger and Claude Levac wrote *Le Chemin du Roy*, in which the stage is a hockey rink and the actors divide into uniformed teams representing Ottawa and Quebec. A year later Loranger wrote *Médium saignant*, set against the context of the language legislation of Bill 63, in which the audience was invited to join in open expressions of hatred ('*Je les z'hais*'), first against immigrants and English Canadians, and ultimately against even Québécois themselves. Robert Gurik, on the other hand, employed socialist realism to dramatize situations of the time. Perhaps his best-known play was the Brechtian *Le Procès de Jean-Baptiste M* (1972), based on a real incident in which an everyman character shot three of the bosses who had fired him. The Quebec state increasingly used culture, especially the theatre, both to indicate the society's coming of age and to articulate the independentist aspirations of the province. Quebec theatre would reach its creative high point in the same time period that the Parti Québécois came to power. Most Quebec playwrights, like most creative people in the province, advocated separation. For Michel Tremblay, 'the only way for Canada and Quebec to be friends' was 'to be two countries'.[43]

FRANCOPHONES OUTSIDE QUEBEC

Although Quebec often behaved as if it were synonymous with French Canada, hundreds of thousands of French-speaking Canadians lived outside the province. The need to provide continuing sustenance and protection for this outlying population was an important federalist argument, and one that francophones outside Quebec fervently supported. Only in New Brunswick were francophones—the Acadians—sufficiently concentrated geographically, and sufficiently numerous, to regard themselves as a distinct people. After many years of effort to consolidate their position within New Brunswick, the 1960s saw a renaissance of Acadian culture and a new sense of political awareness. A contributing factor was the presence of Louis Robichaud as the first Acadian elected Premier of the province (1960–70), but more important was the general agitation over French rights and a growing awareness among New Brunswick politicians that the Acadians were a powerful political force who needed to be wooed. Robichaud's defeat in 1970 by the Tories, led by Richard Hatfield, owed much to Hatfield's recognition that Acadian interests had to be served. Thus both New Brunswick major parties supported bilingualism, French-language education (including a university at Moncton), and the institutional infrastructure of Acadian culture in the province.[44]

Outside Quebec, New Brunswick, and to a much lesser extent Ontario (where French-speakers were numerous but not so concentrated geographically), French Canadians began the 1960s as a linguistic and cultural population very much on the decline, especially in the West. The federal government's responses to the Quebec issue, especially its bilingualism and biculturalism policies, would have some spillover effect for these outlying francophones, almost all of whom were fluently bilingual. Not only did they gain advantages in obtaining federal employment in their regions, but their educational and cultural facilities received a good deal of financial assistance from Ottawa in one form or another.

To the extent that the Pearson government had hoped that bilingualism and biculturalism would defuse the explosive situation in Quebec—and relieve the pressure to develop a more appropriate federal language policy that would have benefits outside Quebec—the B&B

Commission was an abject failure. By the time bilingualism was formally adopted in 1969, Quebec had passed well beyond the stage where it might have been satisfied by such a policy. In fact, it had already begun moving towards its own version of unilingualism, in which all languages but French would be disadvantaged. Following the defeat of the Lesage government in 1966, all Quebec politicians and parties moved—with what appeared to be public opinion—towards a more militant view of autonomy. In 1960 the only significant party openly espousing separatism was the Rassemblement pour l'indépendance nationale (RIN). But in 1968 René Lévesque formed the Parti Québécois, and its platform of political independence and economic connection with Canada (sovereignty-association) quickly attracted significant support.[45] Moreover, even as the B&B Commission was conducting its inquiry, events in Quebec were rapidly advancing, and other forces in Canadian society were emerging to render obsolescent an obsession with language rights within the cultural context of a dual French–English society.

CONSTITUTIONAL REFORM

In 1971 the Trudeau administration made yet another effort to reach agreement on a formula for constitutional reform that would satisfy Quebec. The federal government offered the province's newly elected Liberal Premier, Robert Bourassa, a reform package that included some constitutional rights to be entrenched in a charter and an amending formula that gave Ontario and Quebec a perpetual veto. Bourassa insisted that the provinces would have to control social policy, and the federal government succeeded in persuading the have-not provinces that such a situation might well jeopardize national programs, which made them less than enthusiastic. After a premiers' conference held in Victoria in June 1971 failed to reach an agreement on a tentative understanding (which did not really provide a special status for Quebec), the participants were given 10 days to concur; otherwise, as Prime Minister Trudeau put it, 'That is the end of the matter.' Premier Bourassa faced a storm of protest and criticism of the arrangement when he returned to Quebec, and he refused to sign on until he saw the final text, which could hardly have been expected within 10 days. Although nothing concrete was accomplished, the 1971 constitutional negotiations did establish three points: first, that a charter entrenching certain rights could be used to reassure those who feared that the Constitution might be changed without an Act of Parliament; second, that Quebec did not achieve a sufficiently distinctive place in Confederation under this agreement to satisfy it; and finally, that if only Quebec and Ontario were given perpetual vetoes, the only way the other provinces could exercise a veto would be by co-operating using very complicated formulas. The question of constitutional reform was thus dropped in 1971, and was not picked up again until 1980, by which time many things had changed for both Canada and its provinces.

THE ENGLISH FACT

One seriously neglected aspect of the many changes that occurred in Quebec between World War II and the early 1970s was the effect they had on the province's anglophone community. Just as French Quebec represented a linguistic and cultural minority within Canada, Quebec's English-speakers were a linguistic and cultural minority within the province. Quebecers who spoke English as their first language—whether or not they were of British origin—were not a negligible part of the population, nor did they lack historic roots in the province. In 1971 there were 640,045 people of British origin in Quebec, compared to 4,759,360 of French origin, and 797,000 people whose mother tongue was English, compared to 5,060,000 whose mother tongue was French. The British presence in the province dated back to the 1760s. Not until the 1960s did the two communities dispute seri-

ously over language. Only two pieces of language legislation had been passed in Quebec before the 1970s, both designed merely to support the use of French in the province—not to give it supremacy. One sought to ensure that the two languages would be of equal importance for public utilities companies (1911), and the other to provide primacy (but not a monopoly) for French in laws and legislation (1937).

By and large, after 1960, the English-speaking population, particularly in Montreal, tended to blame French-Canadian nationalism for all its troubles, although a lot of the difficulty was caused by the anglophones' reluctance to adjust to the new power of the Québécois middle classes. Instead of trying to work with the majority, the anglophones turned themselves into an embattled community that became the very embodiment of the obstacles to the goals of the French collectivity. The English-language media of Montreal adapted a garrison mentality. Once most of the head offices of English-speaking multinational (or even Canadian) corporations had been pulled out of Quebec (starting long before the Quiet Revolution), English-speakers no longer had any substantial power base in the province. From there it was a short step to conceiving of Quebec as a French province and the rest of Canada as the English provinces. In this process, the English-speakers in Quebec became virtually isolated from the remainder of Canada.[46]

CONCLUSION

Quebec had been the outsider province in Canada since 1867, but not until after 1945 did nationalist sentiments turn it actively in the direction of separatism. A nationalism articulated by the highly traditionalist Roman Catholic Church before 1960 was unlikely to be very revolutionary. The Quiet Revolution was less a political movement orchestrated by politicians than an affirmation of an awakening by an entire society and the sudden integration of that society into the middle-class secular world of the twentieth century. The very speed of that social and economic assimilation helps to explain the direction taken by Quebec after 1960, as Quebecers strove urgently to prevent assimilation on the level of language and culture.

SHORT BIBLIOGRAPHY

Behiels, Michael. *Prelude to Quebec's Quiet Revolution: Liberalism versus Neo-Nationalism, 1945–1960*. Montreal and Kingston, 1985. An intellectual history of the background to the Quiet Revolution, identifying two major currents of thought in Quebec.

———, ed. *Quebec since 1945: Selected Readings*. Toronto, 1987. A useful collection of academic articles.

Cardin, Jean-François. *Comprendre Octobre 1970: le FLQ, la crise et le syndicalism*. Montreal, 1990. An important political analysis of the October Crisis.

Fournier, Louis. *FLQ: histoire d'un mouvement clandestin*. Montreal, 1982. An excellent study of the FLQ.

Godin, Pierre. *Daniel Johnson*, 2 vols. Montreal, 1980. A comprehensive biography of the Union Nationale leader and his times.

Igartua, José, *The Other Quiet Revolution: National Identities in English Canada, 1945-1971*. Vancouver, 2006. A fascinating study of the post-war cultural changes in English Canada that added up to another New Nationalism.

Quinn, Herbert. *The Union Nationale: Quebec Nationalism from Duplessis to Lesage*, 2nd edn. Toronto, 1979. A first-rate study of the progress of Quebec nationalism from the 1930s to the 1960s.

Thomson, Dale C. *Jean Lesage and the Quiet Revolution*. Toronto, 1984. A competent biography of Jean Lesage, focusing on his relationship to the Quiet Revolution.

Trudeau, Pierre, ed. *The Asbestos Strike*. Toronto, 1974. The English translation of a work published in French in 1956. Its contributors provide an engaged immediacy on the strike, one of the most important in Quebec history.

Vastel, Michel. *Bourassa*, trans. Hubert Bauch. Toronto, 1988. A useful biography of the man who opposed the PQ in Quebec.

Weiss, Jonathan M. *French-Canadian Theater*. Boston, 1986. An important study of theatre and its cultural implications in Quebec.

STUDY QUESTIONS

1. Why did the FLQ Crisis of 1970 come as such a surprise to most Canadians?
2. In what ways did Quebec play 'catch-up' before the Quiet Revolution?
3. What was so unusual about the asbestos strike of 1949?
4. What were the origins of the new ideas abroad in Quebec during the 1950s?
5. How did hydroelectricity become central to the Quiet Revolution?
6. Was *joual* a good choice to symbolize the cultural failings of Quebec?
7. Why did Canadians find it so difficult to establish what Quebec 'really wanted'?
8. How did the Pearson government attempt to deal with the new Quebec? Why did it fail?
9. How did the presence of francophones outside Quebec make it more difficult for the federal government to deal with Quebec?

CHAPTER SEVENTEEN

The New Suburban Society, 1946–1972

A major characteristic of post-war Canada was the trend towards suburbanization. There had been little new domestic building since the 1920s, and after the war a spate of young couples starting their lives together encountered a serious housing shortage. In response, the government, through the Canada Mortgage and Housing Corporation (CMHC), promoted suburban development, offering very cheap mortgages. The suburbs were built quickly by companies that had gained expertise during the war, and were often developed around schools. Meanwhile, the municipalities had to provide the necessary infrastructure, including roads to link these new communities to each other and to the city. Suburbia was a physical place of detached and semi-detached houses with yards and lawns around the outskirts of a city, but it was also a complex constellation of expectations and values centred on the home, the family, and a long-term economic affluence that encouraged consumer consumption.[1]

DEMOGRAPHIC FACTORS

THE BABY BOOM

Canadians emerged from World War II with virtually 20 years of disruption, deprivation, and deferral of expectations behind them.[2] Normal hopes for family life had been upset in a variety of ways. During the war few of those Canadians serving overseas had been able to see their families between their departure from Canada and their demobilization in the second half of 1945. Particularly during the Depression, marriage and birth rates had decreased, while the average age at marriage had risen. Marriage rates and average age at marriage change very slowly, over long periods, so that relatively small increases or decreases are very significant. The Canadian marriage rate, which had been under 8 per 1,000 during the Depression, jumped to 10.8 per 1,000 in 1939 (the prospect of war encouraged people to marry), and remained at over 9 per 1,000 until 1952, when it began a steady decline to well under 8 per 1,000 by 1966. Between 1967 and 1972 it rose again, reaching a high of 9.2 per 1,000 in 1972. Meanwhile, age at marriage initially dropped as the marriage rate for girls aged 15 to 19 doubled between 1937 and 1954.[3] The average age of bridegrooms fell from over 29 years during the Great Depression to just under 29 in 1940 and 1941; ran at 28+ between 1946 and 1956; and then stayed at 27+ until 1967. It dropped briefly to 26+ in 1967 and 1968, and then rose back to 27+. Over the longer period from 1921 to 1972, however, the drop in the

TIMELINE

1942

Quebec records 95,000 births out of a population of 3,400,000.

1945

Dr Benjamin Spock publishes his *Baby and Child Care*.

1946

War brides arrive in large numbers. Gallup poll indicates that most Canadians oppose large-scale immigration from Europe.

1947

Prime Minister Mackenzie King ties immigration numbers to Canada's 'absorptive capacity'.

1949

Norgate Shopping Centre (suburban Montreal) begun.

1953

Metropolitan Toronto formed. Hilda Neatby publishes *So Little for the Mind*.

1954

Yonge Street subway opens in Toronto.

1956

Hungarian rebellion brings large number of immigrants to Canada.

1960

'The pill' introduced.

1961

Publication of Jane Jacobs's *The Death and Life of Great American Cities*.

1962

Formal removal of racial bars from Canada's immigration policy.

1963

Construction of Toronto-Dominion Centre, designed by Mies van der Rohe, begins.

1965

Simon Fraser University opens in Burnaby, British Columbia. Student Union of Peace Action (SUPA) founded.

1967

Final report of Royal Commission on Bilingualism and Biculturalism. Publication of *The New Romans*.

1968

Living and Learning published in Ontario. René Lévesque founds Parti Québécois.

1969

Occupation of computer centre at Sir George Williams University. Criminal Code amended to exempt from prosecution 'indecent actions' by consenting couples over the age of 21.

1970

Commission of Inquiry into the Non-Medical Use of Drugs reports.

1971

One in every four Canadians reports an ethnic origin other than British, French, or Aboriginal. A coalition stops construction of the projected Spadina Expressway.

1972

'Waffle' faction purged from Ontario NDP.

average age of bridegrooms was more than two years. The average age of brides was more constant, running at 25+ between 1935 and 1956, and thereafter at 24+, although the age of brides at first marriage fell by three years (from 25.4 to 22) between 1941 and 1961.[4]

A number of small statistical variations combined with a constantly growing population attributable to natural increase, immigration, and, during the war, the perceived risks of waiting to increase the total number of marriages. In 1938, for example, 90,706 marriages took place in Canada, compared to 125,797 in 1940 and 130,786 in 1942. By 1945 the number of marriages had declined to 111,376, but in 1946 it jumped suddenly to 137,398, hovered between 124,000 and 132,000 from 1947 to 1964, and then began gradually increasing to 200,470 in 1972.

Meanwhile, the divorce rate was constantly accelerating from 6.8 per 100,000 in 1931, to 26.6 in 1942, and to 54.8 in 1967—the last year before federal reform—before jumping to 200.6 per 100,000 by 1973. But there were still many more family units being formed each year during and after the war than before. Most divorced people soon remarried. Combined with a much higher birth rate and post-war immigration, the result was the 'baby boom'. Several points need to be made about this extraordinary demographic phenomenon. First, a number of factors contributed to the increase in the numbers of children born, including trends towards earlier marriage and earlier decisions to begin having children, as well as increasing ability to afford more than two children. All these factors linked up with the values and expectations of the post-war years, which necessarily included the notion that mothers stayed at home. In addition, however, further declines in infant mortality rates, to the point where only slightly more than 1 per cent of infants who survived birth failed to live to their first birthday, had some impact, as did improvements in health care for older children. It is also important to recognize that this boom

occurred across the Western industrialized world, although it began earlier in North America than in most of the nations of war-torn Europe, and lasted a bit longer as well. Finally, the rise in births was a significant aberration from the pattern in the 'developed' nations since the last quarter of the nineteenth century. Nevertheless, the number of Canadian children below the age of 14 increased dramatically in each census period after 1941, until it levelled out in 1966 (see Tables 17.1 and 17.2).

What made the baby boom such an important phenomenon was not the number of children, but the challenge they presented to the society and economy that would have to educate and eventually bring them into the workforce. The baby boomers went through each stage of life in what journalists often called 'waves'—demographers call them cohorts—which in terms of sheer numbers put heavy pressure on social institutions (especially in the area of education).When birth rates began falling again, after 1960, Canadian population experts began worrying that significantly lower rates might not even allow for population replacement. This concern was felt deeply in Quebec, which had recorded 95,000 births in 1942 out of a population of 3,400,000, and the same number of births in 1967 in a population that had nearly doubled. Demographers joined French Canadians in fearing the cumulative effects of the change for the 'French fact' in Canada, and part of Quebec's fear concerning the future of its culture could be attributed to those numbers. But at the height of the boom those fears were still far in the future. Between 1951 and 1961 the annual rate of Canadian population growth averaged 2.7 per cent. Babies were not the only reason for the sudden expansion of the population after World War II.

IMMIGRATION

Another major factor in population increase was immigration. After the relatively low levels of the

TABLE 17.1

NUMBER OF CHILDREN UNDER 14 IN CANADA (BY AGE AND SEX GROUP, IN THOUSANDS), 1941–1966

YEAR	0-5		6-10		11-14	
	M	F	M	F	M	F
1941	534	518	529	517	556	545
1951	897	843	714	684	575	556
1956	1,012	972	920	887	732	703
1961	1,154	1,102	1,064	1,016	948	908
1966	1,129	1,069	1,173	1,128	1,071	1,022

SOURCE: Canadian census data.

TABLE 17.2

TOTAL CANADIAN POPULATION OF CHILDREN BY SEX AND TOTAL CHILDREN UNDER 14 BY SEX, 1941–1966

	ALL AGES		UNDER 14		UNDER 14
	MALE	FEMALE	MALE	FEMALE	TOTAL
1941	5,901,000	5,606,000	1,619,000	1,580,000	3,199,000
1951	7,089,000	6,921,000	2,168,000	2,083,000	4,251,000
1956	8.152,000	7,929,000	2,664,000	2,562,000	5,216,000
1961	9,219,000	9,019,000	3,166,000	3,026,000	6,192.000
1966	10,054,000	9,961,000	3,373,000	3,219,000	6,592,000

SOURCE: Canadian census data.

inter-war years, immigration to Canada shot up after the war. Between 1946 and 1972, more than 3.5 million 'new Canadians' arrived in the country, an average of about 135,000 per year. Even after emigration from Canada to other nations is subtracted (since people, especially recent arrivals, also left the country in substantial numbers), the net gain was well over two million. In relation to total population, this immigration was not as significant as in the periods

before Confederation and before the Great War, and the figures were lower than those for Australia in this period, but they were still impressive. Certainly in terms of the relative population bases, Canada was far more affected by new immigration than the United States, where immigration was very closely controlled. Net migration accounted for about 20 per cent of Canadian population growth in this period.

In general, patterns of immigration reflected

■ War brides and their children arriving at Pier 21 in Halifax. LAC, PA-47114.

both external and internal events. War brides were the first post-war arrivals. Almost 50,000 Canadian soldiers had found wives in Europe, mostly in the United Kingdom. There were 22,000 children of these marriages. The Canadian government admitted these dependants without question, and in addition facilitated transport (one-way only), documentation, and the transfer of their money and possessions.

Even before the war was over, the war brides were preparing to depart for Canada. The Salvation Army established war brides clubs, where Canadian military personnel offered crash courses on life in Canada. The process was facilitated in that many of the brides came from areas around major installations where Canadians had been based. In August 1944, a Canadian Wives' Bureau was set up just off Piccadilly Circus as a branch of Canadian Military HQ. It co-ordinated orientation for the women, distributing literature and other useful material. The European brides all were collected in London and then sent to Canada on the first available ship. Women planning to marry in Canada were assisted, so long as they paid their own passage. Newfoundland made similar arrangements for the dependants of its own military. Uprooting themselves was not easy for many of these women, but by and large they were welcomed enthusiastically by their husbands, families, and communities in Canada.

It should be added that the Canadian government did not regard the wives and children of servicemen as immigrants.

As many as 20 million Europeans were displaced by World War II. Eight million came from enemy territory. Most of these people were Volksdeutsche, ethnic Germans from Eastern Europe who had fled west ahead of the Russian advance into Germany in 1945 and been pushed into Allied-occupied Germany, where they joined large numbers of Germans who had also lost their homes. Nearly 12 million people came from countries occupied by the Germans. Many of these people had recently been released from prison camps and concentration camps. They joined former slave labourers, resistance fighters, and collaborators. When the Allied leaders meeting at Yalta discussed procedures for the repatriation of refugees, the Russians—concerned that the Eastern European exiles might easily form an anti-Soviet community—demanded that they be sent to the Soviet-occupied section and then sent them back to their homelands. By the end of 1945, perhaps two million refugees and displaced persons remained in Allied territory, mostly in Germany but also in Austria and Italy. Some lived in the countryside, but most were placed in refugee camps where agencies like UNRRA (the United Nations Relief and Rehabilitation Administration) could deal with them. Few of these people had proper documentation.[5] Canada was under considerably more pressure from the international community than from its own people to become a refuge for this displaced population; a Gallup poll in April 1946 indicated that two-thirds of Canadians opposed immigration from Europe. Nevertheless, after some fits and starts, Canada opened its doors to the refugees, and nearly 150,000 were admitted between 1947 and 1954.

The pace of immigration only increased after the war. British subjects in profusion came from the British Isles during the Suez Crisis of 1956, when Britain and France attempted to occupy the Suez Canal zone, and Hungarians flooded in after their country's abortive revolt of 1956. But the fact that, throughout the 1940s and 1950s, most immigrants came from Europe also reflected Canadian preferential recruitment and treatment. As late as 1960, nine of the 10 leading countries on the list of immigration sources were in Europe; at the top of the list was Italy, and the exception was the US. Beginning in the early 1960s, changes in Canadian immigration policy for the first time admitted larger numbers of non-European immigrants, and by 1973 Hong Kong, Jamaica, India, the Philippines, and Trinidad numbered among the 10 leading sources. It would take some time, however, for the shift in source countries to have any appreciable impact on the overall ethnic composition of the Canadian people.

By 1971 one in every four Canadians claimed an ethnic origin other than British, French, or Aboriginal. Unlike earlier arrivals, many of whom ended up on isolated farmsteads on the frontier, the new immigrants settled almost exclusively in urban areas, especially in Ontario, Quebec, and British Columbia. As a result, those cities were transformed. Toronto, for example, had been predominantly Anglo-Saxon before 1945, and languages other than English could be heard only in certain well-defined areas. By 1961, one observer wrote of the Toronto scene:

> Near Toronto's downtown area can be found the great unassimilated foreign communities, towns within a town, the bustling Jewish markets with their Kosher stores and Hebrew signs, the women in their shawls and aprons of eastern Europe, the Italian quarter with its pasta shops and multitudinous children; the Germans driving most of the cabs in Toronto; and most recently the sad faced Hungarians huddled together in disappointment, often despair. . . . Its new polyglot life is what gives Toronto a colour and fascination which it would not otherwise possess; but it is also what causes the native born (those outnumbered few) to exclaim in disgust, 'One never hears English on Yonge Street these days.'[6]

Montreal also received thousands of non-French (and non-English) speakers. By the 1960s almost all the larger cities of Canada west of the Atlantic region were attracting immigrants in large numbers. The urban concentration of the post-war immigration made for the emergence of cities with huge 'ethnic' populations. By 1971 urban areas with more than 100,000 people had received nearly three-quarters of the recent immigrants.

Canadian immigration policy has always been driven primarily by internal economic rather than humanitarian considerations. On the other hand, at least Canada has had a definite policy, something that cannot be said about several member nations of the European Community, which admit large numbers of 'guest workers' but have no system for allowing them to become citizens. When Canada has admitted refugees under special dispensations, it has usually attempted to select those candidates that best fit the nation's economic needs. (The principal exceptions to this rule were the war brides, who were treated as relatives of Canadian nationals.) In the period before 1960 Canada was seriously short of younger adults for the expanding economy, and healthy young immigrants from the Third World would have filled the bill admirably; yet before 1962 Canada did not welcome them. Canadian policy was influenced by a general perception, best expressed by Mackenzie King's 1947 statement on Canadian immigration, that no more immigrants should be accepted than could be absorbed into the Canadian population without disruption to the economy or 'the present character of our population'—King's euphemistic way of referring to racial or ethnic difference. He was mindful of public opinion among both founding peoples, for Quebec had its own concerns over immigration—chiefly that there were not enough French-speaking immigrants, and that large numbers of non-francophones would dilute French-Canadian culture in the province. Canada did broaden its categories of 'sponsored relatives' after the war, and in 1952 agreed to accept a handful of immigrants from

India, Pakistan, and Ceylon, but such concessions merely emphasized how restricted its immigration policy generally was.

Canada had long been under pressure from the international community to adopt a less restrictive immigration policy. It was able to ignore such pressure before 1945, because it did not regard itself as a significant player in the world. But new international ambitions and growing public concern for human rights (especially following the passage of Diefenbaker's Bill of Rights) led to the formal removal of racial bars from Canadian immigration policy in 1962. Five years later the Pearson government managed to combine Canada's desire to attract suitable immigrants to fill economic needs with a racially non-discriminatory policy when it introduced the 'points system' of immigration selection. Focusing on the education and skills of the applicant, the points system shifted the emphasis away from race or sponsorship and towards special training. Since the number of applications for immigration was greatly influenced by the availability of information and local processing services for applicants, Canada could still exercise some control over applications through the enthusiasm of its recruitment activities in any particular place. And of course, even if a Third World engineer or doctor might gain ready admission after 1967, a Third World peasant was unlikely to have the necessary credentials. Nevertheless, the door had been pushed ajar more than a mere crack, even if it was not opened wide.

MORTALITY

A final factor in population growth was a further decline in the death rate and a corresponding increase in the median age of death. By 1946 males could expect on average to live to 63.1 years, and females to 65.3. By 1971 life expectancy had risen to 68.5 for males and 74.7 for females. These relatively modest increases disguised the more important point that fewer Canadians were dying before the age of 40, as well as the fact that ever-increasing proportions were living well beyond the already high averages. Deaths from communicable diseases had been reduced for the population as a whole by 1946, and expanded government health-care services for Native people would make significant inroads in their patterns of death as well. The result was that for Canadians overall, the principal causes of death were reduced to four categories: cardiovascular disease, renal (kidney) disease, cancer, and accidents. The first three causes increased in incidence with age and had always been 'diseases of the old'. Accidental death was less discriminatory, but accidents had greatly increased as a cause of death between the early part of the century and the 1970s, chiefly because of the toll taken by the automobile, which became the principal weapon with which Canadians killed their fellows. Moreover, sharp increases in traffic accidents involving young (especially male) drivers did more than either heart disease or cancer to reduce overall life expectancy from avoidable causes.

The reductions in mortality rates were to a large extent a consequence of the new universal social-welfare coverage that was introduced into Canada during and after World War II and made health care more accessible to the less affluent. Family allowances, unemployment compensation, old-age pensions, and medical/hospital care together added up to a higher standard of living—always an essential ingredient of lower mortality—for most Canadians. (The lower standard of living for Aboriginal peoples typically kept Canadian living standards below those of the most advanced European countries.) Longer life expectancy brought with it new problems, in particular increasing numbers of people living for many years past the age of retirement. The full implications of caring for the older generation (not until later in the 1970s were they called 'senior citizens')—which would include not only increased demand for nursing facilities but the payment of old-age pensions far longer than the actuaries could have contemplated in the

1940s—had not struck the majority of Canadians. Only 'reactionaries' wondered whether the economy could afford to extend a helping hand to all Canadians.

ABORIGINAL PEOPLE

As in earlier periods, major differentials existed within the Canadian population. Native peoples were especially vulnerable. Improvements in medical care, which began when this responsibility was transferred from Indian Affairs to the Department of National Health and Welfare in 1945, narrowed the gaps but did not eliminate them. Infant mortality rates among Aboriginal people were greatly reduced during the first 28 days of life, but continued to run at four to five times the national average for the rest of the first year. A shift in causes of death from infectious to chronic diseases also occurred, but First Nations and Inuit mortality rates still ran at more than twice the national average, and the incidence of death from accidental causes and suicide only increased during this period. Accidental and violent death was third on the list of killers for all Canadians, but first for Native people, and automobile accidents were not a major factor in most Aboriginal communities. Alcohol probably was an important factor, less because of its long-term effects than because of the accidents and violence associated with drinking, neither of which could be effectively addressed simply by improving medical services. Native people drank for the same reasons as other socio-culturally dislocated and economically disadvantaged people around the world: out of frustration and the desire to escape a grim reality. While infectious diseases were virtually eradicated in southern Canada, they continued to stalk the northern regions, although at a lower rate; tuberculosis proved especially amenable to improved health care. But even as increased medical attention was bringing some traditional problems under control, increasing contact with the outside world was introducing a host of new ones, from tooth decay and obesity to ingestion of liquid solvents. As a solution to the problems facing Aboriginal people, health care had distinct limits.[7]

ETHNICITY AND LANGUAGE

The first quarter-century of immigration after the war wrought some changes in the ethnic makeup of the Canadian population. In 1941, just under half (49.6 per cent) of the Canadian population claimed origin in one of the four nations of the British Isles, with just over 30 per cent of French background and just over 20 per cent from other nations (almost all European). The most substantial population of non-European origin was the First Nations. By 1971 the British component had dropped to 44.6 per cent, the French to 28.6 per cent, and the 'others' had climbed to 26.7 per cent. While Canadians who originated in Europe beyond France increased markedly between 1941 and 1971, the most striking change was among those of Italian origin, who increased from 112,000 in 1941 to 730,000 in 1971. Most Italians were concentrated in southwestern Ontario, especially in and around Toronto. Other readily observable increases among less traditional sources occurred among Portuguese and Filipinos, both of whom settled chiefly in industrial and urban Ontario. In the first census after the official acceptance of the 'two founding peoples' principle (1971), both of those 'charter' groups saw their proportion of the total population eroded, if only slightly. French Canada especially found the downward trend ominous.

Immigrants of non-European origins (and some from Europe as well) complained frequently about the subtleties of Canadian racism and discrimination, and they were often joined in such criticisms by people of different skin colour who had been in Canada for centuries. The fact that Aboriginal people faced the same sort of discrimination indicated that the problem was not simply in the nature of being a newcomer. Ironically, Japanese Canadians were the group that experienced the least difficulty in the post-war period. This may be explained not only by Canadian guilt over their treatment during the war, but also by the fact that, as a result of their wartime experience, younger Canadian-born Japanese were determined to assimilate, and did so with striking success. The extent of Canadian racism would become a public issue only in the later 1960s, but complaints of discrimination were not confined to the recognizably different. In 1965 Canadian sociologist John Porter published a significant academic study, *The Vertical Mosaic*, in which he documented as fact what many Canadians long had known intuitively: Canadian elites were disproportionately dominated by people of British background.[8] French Canada took such analysis as further evidence of its disadvantaged status in Confederation.

Other disparities soon came to light. In 1967 the final report of the Royal Commission on Bilingualism and Biculturalism documented significant differences in income and occupational status among Canadians of various ethnic origins. In 1961 Canadian men of British origin earned on average nearly $1,000 more than those of French origin, and with the exception of Jews, other ethnic groups were also well below the British-Canadian average. As far as occupational discrepancies were concerned, the report again found 'substantial' differences between those of French and British origin, particularly at the professional and managerial levels, where the differences actually were widening. Equally striking discrepancies could, of course, be found for other ethnic groups.[9] Many of the data for such comparisons came from readily available Canadian census material, which was now being collected and analyzed in detail for the first time by Canadian social scientists.

Yet another aspect of ethnicity was language: specifically, the usage and protection of French. In his study *Languages in Conflict*, first published in 1967, Richard Joy observed:

> An extremely significant finding of the 1961 Census was that only 31 per cent of the popula-

tion claimed to be able to speak French, even after taking into account all those for whom it was merely a second or third language; this was hardly more than the 30 per cent who reported their ethnic origin as being French. In sharp contrast, 80 per cent of the population could speak English, almost double the number classed by the Census as being of British origin.[10]

Joy went on to demonstrate that the problem was not so much that most Canadians of non-French origin, including 95 per cent of recent immigrants, preferred to speak English rather than French as a first language, but that the use of French was becoming increasingly confined to Quebec and parts of New Brunswick; its use was rapidly declining in northern Ontario and the West, where there had previously been very concentrated French-speaking pockets of population. These findings may seem obvious from the perspective of the twenty-first century, but at the time they were regarded as highly significant, particularly as they substantiated or anticipated the results of the B&B Commission, which published other findings between 1967 and 1970. Though most non-English-speaking ethnic groups in Canada were concerned about the loss of language and the culture associated with it, the situation for francophones was freighted with political significance. Linguistic ghettoization and national socio-economic disadvantage together were held to constitute powerful grounds for protest in French Canada, especially Quebec. The growth of Quebec separatism probably was more a result of developments within that province than of the limitations of French language and culture elsewhere in Canada, but important issues clearly were connected with language use.

URBANIZATION, SUBURBANIZATION, AND RURAL DEPOPULATION

In general, the trends towards urbanization at the expense of rural residency, established in the early years of the century, continued unabated through the period 1946 to 1972. Urban population steadily increased, both absolutely and as a proportion of the total, while the number of rural inhabitants remained relatively constant. Within the rural population, however, the numbers of farm residents decreased dramatically, from 3,117,000 in 1941 to 1,420,000 in 1971. This national trend was most in evident in provinces still dominated by agriculture: Prince Edward Island, Manitoba, and Saskatchewan. On PEI, for example, the number of farms declined from 12,230 in 1941 to 4,543 in 1971, with the number of farm operators decreasing commensurately. Although there was no single cause, the continued inability of farmers to make a decent financial return on their labour and investment was undoubtedly one of the prime factors. Canadian farms became bigger and more mechanized as farmers tried to compensate for low rates of return per acre, and many farm families gave up and got out when the older generation died. Land anywhere near the cities became uneconomic to retain for farming, and by 1971 most of Canada's finest agricultural terrain—in the Fraser Valley of British Columbia and in southwestern Ontario—had been sold to speculators or cut into hobby-farm plots. The brighter lights of places with greater population density were powerfully alluring, particularly for those in the stage of family and career formation. Many former farm families discovered they did not even have to move to enjoy brighter lights, for the outskirts of cities were now expanding into adjacent rural areas.

While Canadian cities certainly grew in population, little of that growth took place in downtown areas or traditional residential districts. The trend in downtown cores was just the reverse. Rising land prices made it uneconomic for land there to be used residentially except for high-rise apartment blocks, which were less profitable than office blocks and thus were constructed only on the fringes of the downtown. Building upwards, the core of the business district produced those breathtaking skylines we associate with the modern city. Gradually, beginning in the 1960s, the skylines came to be dominated by buildings with vast expanses of tinted plate glass as the 'International style' of architecture made its way to Canada. One of the country's most famous monuments in this style was a complex of rectangular towers of black steel and dark bronze-tinted glass, the Toronto-Dominion Centre (1963–9), designed by the German-American architect Mies van der Rohe. Within the world of faceless skyscrapers came two fascinating developments: the virtual evacuation of downtown areas after working hours, and the tendency of the daytime inhabitants to spend the entire day inside their office complexes, most of which were connected to vast underground malls providing all necessary services. Canadians often forget the extent and rapidity with which the international or modernist style of architecture came to dominate our cities.

As might have been expected, the only real development strategies for Canadian cities in this period centred on greed, the market, and a vague belief that inevitable progress would triumph in the end. City development, like most aspects of Canadian life, had been put on hold by the Depression and the war, and when they were finally over, architects, planners, and developers were anxious to make new things happen, even at the cost of losing links with the cities' (mostly Victorian) past. The result was the destruction of many wonderful old buildings in order to make way for new ones that often were undistinguished. Such a trade-off was made in Toronto when the city's first skyscraper, the majestic Temple Building of 1895 at Richmond and Bay Streets, was demolished in 1970 to be replaced by two bland towers without any public character at all.[11] In Montreal there was much more indiscriminate destruction. For example, the handsome Georgian-style Prince of Wales Terrace of eight attached buildings—commissioned by Sir George Simpson and finished in 1860—was demolished in 1971, to be replaced by the ungainly juxtaposition of a tall hotel and a banal six-storey building to house a department of McGill University. Admittedly, Canadian cities did not go quite so far with their bulldozers as the urban 'renewal' projects in the United States and Great Britain, where hundreds of square miles of slum dwellings, as well as city cores, were razed and replaced with little concern for aesthetic or social sensitivity. In Canada the destruction tended to be piecemeal rather than wholesale. Eleven blocks adjacent to Vancouver's Chinatown disappeared in 1960, for example, but Chinatown itself was preserved.

After World War II, urban development throughout the Western world reflected impatience to demolish and relocate old slums and ghettos, and, in North America, a preference for suburbs. It is true that in the older cities many tenements, inhabited by recent immigrants and the permanently disadvantaged, were so badly deteriorated that brand new apartment blocks or bungalows seemed a considerable improvement. Not until the early 1960s—perhaps beginning with the publication of Jane Jacobs's influential *The Death and Life of Great American Cities* (1961)—was the case made publicly that destroying organic neighbourhoods and communities—however rundown—was retrogressive. Academics thereafter joined some politicians, young professionals, and citizens' groups in insisting that any city planning that ignored the needs of people and neighbourhoods was inviting negative consequences.

Toronto probably went furthest in its rush to modernize because of the speed and extent of its metropolitan growth. The model planned suburb of Don Mills was developed in the early 1950s, and in 1953 the city joined with 12 suburban municipalities to form Metropolitan Toronto. In 1954 the Yonge Street subway (north–south) was opened; in 1964 it was extended by the east–west Bloor Street line. Toronto also built a series of bypass highways—the 401, the Gardiner Expressway, the Don Valley Parkway—to enable people to get quickly from one end of the metropolitan area to the other. While not quite in the same league as Los Angeles or some other American cities—which were chopped into disconnected bits by freeways—Toronto was moving in that direction. With the ring roads done, the planners began conceiving the inevitable inner-city connectors, such as the Spadina Expressway, that would give every resident ready access to the freeway system. But there were two problems. One was 'freeway effect', in which superhighways multiplied new traffic as quickly as they relieved old bottlenecks. By 1972 bypass highways like the 401 were multi-laned traffic jams of bumper-to-bumper vehicles, at first during rush hours and eventually almost all day long. Improving connections between the city and its outskirts only prompted more people to move away or use the roads more frequently. The other problem was that building freeways in populated areas meant tearing down existing housing and devastating neighbourhoods. In Toronto a protracted opposition movement finally managed to stop construction of the projected Spadina Expressway in 1971, which brought a symbolic end to the period of unrestricted and unplanned urban expansion. In Vancouver at about the same time, proposals to extend the Trans-Canada Highway into the city's centre, demolishing many neighbourhoods—including the traditional Chinatown—were fought to a standstill. By the later 1960s citizens' coalitions were at work in every city, attempting to control the developers who influenced most city councils and departments.

Urban development was orderly by comparison with what went on outside the existing cities. New suburbs were created—usually where there were no zoning bylaws—by fast-talking developers who managed to convince rural municipal councils that population growth meant jobs and revenue (rather than new taxes and a totally changed community character). The principal attraction of the new suburbs was a lower cost per square foot of house, which meant that land costs were generally kept down by not providing amenities (especially costly sewers and buried power lines) in advance. The ubiquitous septic tank (and the exceptionally lush green grass that grew above it) became the symbol of the truly suburban bungalow. Leaving existing trees in a developing subdivision made construction more expensive, so down they came— although a few developers were willing to leave them standing in return for a premium price for the lot. In most suburban developments, planting new trees and shrubs (often in areas that had only recently been heavily forested) was the first outdoor task of the new homeowner. Only a handful of floor plans—with roughly identical floor areas, numbers of bedrooms, and maximum mortgage value—were drawn up for any new block, to save money and facilitate marketing. The number of amenities depended on price, and most builders were interested in the mass market at the lower end of the scale. The result was residential segregation based not on race or ethnicity but on number of children and ability to make mortgage payments.

Few developers regarded the creation of suburban infrastructure—schools, hospitals, shopping centres, churches, connecting roads— as their planning responsibility, and many buyers of the 1950s and 1960s would have shied away from any development whose community structure was predetermined by others. The trick was to sell houses to people who were either recent parents or newly affluent—often the same people. The typical first-time suburban buyers were a young couple with two children, attracted to a suburb partly by a love of green grass and open space, but mostly by cost. Marketers tried to attract buyers by giving fantasy names to the developments themselves (Richmond Acres, Wilcox Lake, Beverly Hills, Linden Woods) or to streets in them (Shady Lane, Sanctuary Drive, Paradise Crescent), but most newspaper advertisements concentrated on the price and down payment required. Few buyers did much research into the local amenities. According to one buyer in the 1960s:

■ In the middle of the prairie outside Calgary, a billboard announces the new 'engineered' suburb of Glendale Meadows in August 1958. Photo Rosetti's Studio. Glenbow NA-5093-558.

We chose this house because of the price. It was the best we saw for the money. We drove around on Sunday afternoons looking for a place and found this one. We wanted something out of the city—a good place to bring up children. . . . We may have come a little far out—I would prefer a place in closer, you know; what everybody wants: a place that has the advantage of both, all the conveniences of the city and plenty of room and good country air besides. That seems impossible around Toronto, except for a good price, and so it is impossible for us now.[12]

Few suburbanites had any idea that they were the advance guard of a new Canadian lifestyle.

Fewer newcomers had any real idea of what their living conditions would be, particularly those who were moving to developments lacking sewers, libraries, cultural facilities, shopping, and urban transit. They did not deliberately abandon the amenities of the city, but were forced by the need for space to move beyond them. The process of adjusting to the new conditions became a major part of the period's socio-cultural development.

The suburbs of the post-war period have attracted more than a little bad press, becoming exemplars of a vast identikit wasteland of intellectual vacuity, cultural sterility, and social conformity—'little boxes made of ticky-tacky' that

THE SHOPPING MALL

One of the most representative physical symbols of post-war suburban culture in Canada was the shopping mall, an enclosed collection of shops and services housed together and managed as a single unit, typically surrounded by acres of paved parking lot. Collecting shops and services together was not new—markets existed in ancient times, sheltered markets were part of the urban landscape in the Middle Ages, and enclosed markets (often called 'arcades') became popular in the nineteenth century in England. In many ways, the department store was really an enclosed market managed as a unit. The shopping mall after World War II was innovative for its suburban location and the insistence of its developers on adjacent free parking for large numbers of customers. The earliest department stores had usually been located in city centres, and even after the construction of parking garages beginning in the 1940s, these stores had only limited parking facilities.

A variety of styles of shopping centres and malls were developed in the post-war years, initially in the United States but with Canada not far behind. Most of the first shopping centres in Canada (Norgate Shopping Centre, suburban Montreal, 1949; Dorval Shopping Centre, suburban Montreal, 1950; Park Royal Shopping Centre, West Vancouver, 1950) were not actually malls—each store was entered directly from the parking lot. In a second stage of development, the shops usually faced an automobile-free courtyard rather than the parking lot; and finally, the Yorkdale Shopping Centre in North York (begun 1960) was a fully enclosed mall. One of the distinctive characteristics of the mall was the ability to control the internal space in all senses, thus producing a distinctive shopping culture within its walls. Physical climate could be controlled, emotional climate could be managed with soothing music ('muzak') and an absence of timepieces, and the extent of competition could be controlled by the choice of tenants and co-ordination of sales, advertising, and events in the enclosed space.

Shopping malls have been blamed for emptying the downtown cores of people, for the elimination of local merchants, and for the creation of a new style of consumer culture. They spawned, in turn, the ubiquitous 'strip mall', unsightly commercial development around the large regional shopping malls, and downtown redevelopment involving the use of underground tunnels and walkways to connect the commercial facilities in mall-like fashion.

'all look just the same', as the elderly American protest singer, Malvina Reynolds, described them. They could be and sometimes were all those things, of course; but they also were the spawning ground of much of the revolt and rebellion of the 1960s.

Part of the problem of understanding suburbs was the assumption of the post-war era (and beyond) that it should be possible to represent the movement from the urban core through the suburbs to the agrarian periphery by drawing a series of concentric circles. In the thinking of central-place theory (in the 1960s called 'metropolitanism', in the 1980s 'heartland–hinterland'), a suburb was an amenity-less satellite of a city rather than a distinct place in itself. But suburbia was not so much the simple projection of urban society as an imaginative recreation of the ideal world of aspiring middle-class Canadians with the adaptations required for new social conditions (including the Little League, the community hockey rink, the barbecue, and the shopping mall—all suburban features). Many people may never have achieved that goal, but most had

SAMUEL DELBERT CLARK
(1910–2003)

❖

S.D. Clark was born in Lloydminster, Alberta, in 1910. He studied history and political science at the University of Saskatchewan, where he worked with A.S. Morton and Hilda Neatby; he became a doctoral student at the University of Toronto in 1931, went to London as an IODE fellow at the London School of Economics in 1932, and after studying for an MA in sociology at McGill completed a Ph.D. in political science at the University of Toronto in 1938. Except for the year in London, Clark received all his academic training in Canada, a not uncommon experience among those who started their careers in the midst of the Depression. The direction of his training was largely historical, and he was much influenced by the thinking of the economic historian Harold Innis. He emerged from his graduate work in 1938 as an economic historian with a leaning towards sociological investigation and speculation. The connections he made between sociology and history were largely his own, as he married the political economy of Harold Innis to the sociology and anthropology of the Chicago School, particularly in its emphasis on the frontier as a source of social disorientation.

For almost all his career Clark was based at the University of Toronto. His first independent research project was his doctoral dissertation, a study of the Canadian Manufacturers' Association. He followed this work in 1942 with *The Social Development of Canada*, an early example of Canadian social history bearing a strong sociological interpretation. After World War II, Harold Innis selected Clark to direct a study of the Social Credit movement in Alberta financed by the Rockefeller Foundation. Clark's own contribution to the series of books published on this subject was *Movements of Political Protest in Canada, 1640–1840* (1959), a non-Marxist account of early protest.

In 1958 Clark responded to the new directions of post-war Canadian society by accepting a grant to study suburbanization in Canada. This work for the first time took him out of the archives and into the world of contemporary research, and resulted in his pioneering *The Suburban Society* in 1966. At the same time, his work became more sympathetic to the ideas of the mainstream pioneers of American sociology. He established the Department of Sociology at the University of Toronto in 1963, serving as its first chair. Clark never became thoroughly assimilated by American sociology, however. His work continued to have a strong historical bent, which was virtually anathema to the Americans. Moreover, throughout his career Clark continued to address the question of what was unique or distinctive about Canadian society, coming to focus increasingly on the subject of social change. Although he was respected in Canada as a pioneering sociologist, he was in later years criticized by many of his younger colleagues for lacking the 'methodological rigour' that characterized the leading American sociologists of his generation and—in a different way—their radical students. His work was seen as an ever-more conservative affirmation of Canadian society as seen from the vantage point of the University of Toronto.

probably never envisioned it in the first place. 'What was sought in the suburbs, by the vast majority who settled there,' wrote the sociologist S.D. Clark in 1966, 'was a home, not a new social world. . . . When the new social world developed, its development was a consequence of seeking a home, not the reverse.'[13] This had probably been the thinking of pioneers since the beginning of European settlement in North America. Nevertheless, in incremental ways another new socio-cultural world was in the making.

THE NEW SUBURBAN SOCIETY

Originating in eighteenth-century England, the suburb evolved gradually as 'the collective cre-

THE HOUSE AS HOME IN CRESTWOOD HEIGHTS

In 1956 a team of sociologists published a study of one of Canada's more affluent suburban communities, Forest Hill in Toronto. They gave it the fictional name of 'Crestwood Heights'. Following is an excerpt from their discussion of the Crestwood house.

The Crestwood home, must, ideally, provide ample space for separate sleeping and working quarters for each member of the family. There should be a desk or its equivalent in a well-demarcated area for each member of the family 'old enough.' These areas may be rooms, or merely corners, shelves, or drawers within a larger room; and little pressure is put on the individual to keep this area tidy. When occupying 'his' space, the individual should not be disturbed; when absent, his possessions are not to be rearranged. A place for the mother may be the entire kitchen with a still more private corner where she keeps household bills, personal correspondence, recipes, receipts, and money; the boy may have a lab, or a dark-room, and place for skates, skis, and other gear; the father will have a spot to keep his tobacco, pipes, golf clubs, bridge set, and he may possibly also have a workshop; the girl, similarly, will screen cherished items—letters, photos, diary, cosmetics—from the eyes of other family members. The bedroom is often the repository of most of these items of personal property around which the individual builds his own satisfactions, and which help to differentiate him from the other members of the inner circle of his life—indeed he will often reveal them more freely to a peer in age and sex than to a member of his own family. If he leaves home, he will take these possessions with him.

One Crestwood mother, contrasting the difference between the contemporary house and the house of her girlhood, which was of comparable size, said:

> When I was a girl, we all worked of an evening around the dining room table. We had a warm fire in the room and we all worked or read quietly in the same room. Now, we scatter throughout the house to follow our interests.

The hot stove and the oil lamp drew the family together; now, electric light and warmth, which are equally spread to all corners of the house, also disperse the members of the family. The description well underlines the difference between the activities of the Victorian family and the new individualistic pursuits of the family in Crestwood Heights, pursuits which the type of house encourages.

The material objects which fill the space

bought at such a price illumine another important facet of the Crestwood house as home. The Crestwood house, in this context, is not the home celebrated even to recent times in folklore and song, the 'home sweet home' which has a peasant meaning—a modest spot, fixed immovably in one locality through several generations, the only symbol of stability in a shifting cruel world, an abode that is always 'there' to 'come back to.' The dwelling-place does not have this traditional stability in Crestwood Heights, since the family takes for granted that its members will live in a succession of houses. The Crestwooder, therefore, cannot cherish a single image of home, a spot to which he may return at the moment, and an object of which he may be proud. The home image may change in the course of time; and it is confidently expected that to those who fashion it this image will become increasingly satisfactory. . . . Although members of the family may belong to clubs, own a summer cottage in the North, patronize a ski lodge, or vacation in Florida during the winter, a relatively permanent deposit of material goods remains in that house which at any particular time they call 'home'. Indeed, the presence of these objects in a succession of houses is probably the most important factor in the Crestwood concept of the home. It is really the movables which create the air of homeliness, and which are psychologically immovable, rather than the physically rooted house, which is there to be moved into, grown into, moved out of and left behind—an outmoded shell to be reoccupied by another mobile family.

SOURCE: John R. Seeley, R. Alexander Sim, Elizabeth W. Loosley, in collaboration with Norman W. Bell and D.F. Fleming, *Crestwood Heights: A North American Suburb* (Toronto: University of Toronto Press, 1956), 56–7.

ation of the bourgeois elite'[14] and extended to North America in the nineteenth century. Europe and Latin America, by contrast, remained committed to their central cities, as any visitor to Paris or Buenos Aires quickly realizes. By the twentieth century, the United States had become the international centre of suburbanization. Canada lagged somewhat behind, and at least before 1945 had never pursued the middle-class suburb with the single-mindedness of its southern neighbour.[15] Although many suburbs were established before World War II—including Westmount in Montreal, Lawrence Park in Toronto, Crescentwood in Winnipeg, and Shaughnessy Heights in Vancouver—in most cases they were not as clearly separated from the urban centre as their American counterparts.

Suburbia has always been less a geographical space than a mental and emotional one centred on family and emphasizing the home as a domestic space set apart from the workplace. When the trend towards domesticization began, early in the nineteenth century, it was confined to the middle and upper classes, but after 1945 it extended well into the ranks of the lower-middle and traditional working classes as well.[16] Suburbia was highly traditional with respect to gender roles, emphasizing the role of the female as child-bearer and nurturer to a degree that was almost retrogressive. In its consumer orientation and child-centredness, however, it was quite new.[17]

As might be expected, the resurgence of traditional domestic values was accompanied by a revival of religious commitment, at least in terms of formal church or synagogue membership and attendance. After World War II, attendance figures increased, as did enrolment in seminaries and convents, for both Protestants and Catholics. The Jewish faith experienced a similar resurgence. The religious upturn of post-war Canada, like the baby boom, was a temporary blip, and in time the deep-rooted problems of modern institutional Christianity—including its identification with an outmoded morality and the challenges

■ 'Modern Canadian living room', May 1956. Department of National Defence/NAC, PA-111484.

presented to it by secular thought—would be reflected in major declines for the traditional churches. But as long as that blip lasted, the mainstream Protestant denominations grew (Anglican membership by 10 per cent from 1951 to 1961, United Church membership by 25 per cent in the same period) and Catholics maintained a high level of church attendance, with a rate of 88 per cent in Quebec in 1957 and 75 per cent outside that province.[18] Not surprisingly, the revival in religious observance was largely a suburban phenomenon. Of the 600 new manses that the United Church built between 1945 and 1966—along with some 1,500 new churches and church halls—many were 'handsome rambling ranch houses'.[19]

Suburban houses became 'homes'. Some suburbanites devoted so much time, effort, and emotional energy to their houses that the latter often seemed to possess them. The modern avocation of 'do-it-yourself' home renovation was developed in the post-war period. The house focused the life of the nuclear family while at the same time permitting individual members to have some private space—often a separate bedroom for each child. A large 'recreation' or 'family' room in the basement provided a place for the children to play and for everyone to get together. (The kitchen, the traditional gathering spot, was now often too small for this purpose.) The replacement of coal with oil and gas furnaces governed by thermostats, and the introduction of automatic hot-water heating and air conditioning, insulated the inhabitants from the physical realities that in an earlier world had demanded hard work and constant vigilance. Now air temperature could almost be taken for granted—no mean accomplishment in the harsh Canadian climate. Those suburbanites who worried about 'getting soft' could assuage their consciences with summer camping trips and roughing it at the cottage.

Life in suburbia depended on a clear understanding of family roles. Husbands were the breadwinners, often working many miles from the home, while their wives were responsible for its daily functioning. After the war, most Canadian women had chosen to remain out of the workforce in order to enjoy marriage and child-rearing. They were reinforced in their decisions by advertising and articles in the women's magazines that exalted the roles of housewife and mother. Yet even as many women were making 'careers' of their domestic roles, the sociologist authors of *Crestwood Heights: A North American Suburb* (1956)—a study based on Forest Hill Village, a wealthy suburban residential area in Toronto—found a good deal of ambivalence over this decision and the values underlying it:

> The career of the woman in Crestwood Heights, compared with that of the man, contains many anomalies. Ideally, the man follows a continuous, if looping, spiral of development; the woman must pursue two goals and integrate them into one. The first goal has to do with a job, the second with matrimony and motherhood. The second, for the woman, is realized at the expense of the first; the man's two goals combine, since matrimony is expected to strengthen him for his work, and at it.[20]

Even younger women studying at university were confused. One confessed to an interviewer:

> Why I want to work—because I hope to express my personality through struggle and achievement. Why I want to get married—because my real role in society is that of wife and mother. If I don't get married, I will feel insecure—I will have no clearly defined role in society. I will probably sacrifice career to marriage if the opportunity comes up because the rewards of marriage are obvious, those of a career uncertain. In a way I envy those girls who only want to get married. They don't have to equate two conflicting desires.[21]

This conflict was certainly not unknown to many women living in suburbia.

The lives of parents increasingly revolved around their children. The baby boom children were brought up in a much more permissive environment than their parents had been. The new child-rearing attitudes were influenced by all sorts of factors, but found their popular expression in *The Pocket Book of Baby and Child Care*, by Benjamin Spock, MD, which outsold the Bible in Canada in the years after the war. Many Canadian and American mothers referred to Spock as 'God'. Canada had its own semi-official child-care manual, *The Canadian Mother and Child*, by Ernest Couture, MD—director of the Division of Child and Maternal Health of the Department of National Health and Welfare—which doctors distributed at no charge to pregnant women. It was a forbidding and austere book in a plain grey paper wrapper, illustrated with slightly out-of-date photographs and written in a prim, no-nonsense style. Couture's advice to prospective fathers was typical: they should accompany their wives on the first visit to the doctor, at the beginning of pregnancy, to understand what prenatal and postnatal care meant, and adopt a 'patient, kind, and forebearing' attitude, for pregnant women suffered from mood changes that they were 'quite unable to control'.[22] Otherwise, Dr Couture apparently thought that husbands should largely stay out of the way, perhaps undertaking a little home renovation, since 'Plumbing and drainage should be kept in good condition. Nothing is more destructive to a home, and to health, than leaky pipes and drains.'[23] Small wonder Canadian parents, at least in English Canada, preferred the folksy, conversational approach of the American expert—with its colour photograph of a smiling and obviously happy baby on the cover.

The triumph in Anglo Canada of Dr Spock over Dr Couture says a good deal about American versus Canadian style in the cultural realm of advice manuals. The Canadian approach was firmly elitist, with useful information generated at the top and trickling down to the potential client through semi-official channels. The American approach was frankly consumerist and user-friendly. The doctor came down fairly hard against the use of coercion—for example, in toilet training: 'Practically all those children who regularly go on soiling after 2 are those whose mothers have made a big noise about it and those who have become frightened by painful movements.'[24] Yet Spock was seldom categorical about any child-rearing strategy, taking a non-prescriptive position on breast-feeding versus bottle-feeding, for example. He also had more encouraging words for fathers than did Dr Couture, emphasizing that 'You can be a warm father and a real man at the same time' and noting that it was 'fine' for Dad to give bottles or change diapers 'occasionally'.

Spock may have gone too far in his opposition to structure and discipline, but post-war mothers came to rely on his commonsensical advice. He explained that children passed through stages, and that once parents recognized what stage their child had reached, they would be able to understand otherwise incomprehensible behaviour, and realize that seemingly exceptional problems were actually quite common. Spock's chapter on 'Puberty Development' emphasized the awkwardness that afflicts adolescents and devoted a full page to 'skin troubles', especially the pimples that the patent medicine industry labelled 'teen-age acne'.

The baby boom combined with the permissive attitudes of the Spock era and the new affluence to produce large numbers of adolescents with considerable spending power. In English-speaking Canada, teenagers became avid consumers—a recognizable market for fast food, popular music, acne medicine, and clothing fads. Melinda McCracken has explained that 'to be a real teenager you had to drink Cokes, eat hamburgers [known in Winnipeg as nips, because that was what the local Salisbury House chain called them], French fries [known in Winnipeg as chips, in the English tradition], go to the Dairy Queen, listen to the Top Forty and neck.'[25] The authors of *Crestwood Heights* found a central theme for their study in the 'difficulties experienced by the child in living up to the expectations of both parents and the school for "responsibility and independence"', adding that the problems were only amplified 'in an environment which largely eliminates necessity for striving in this direction'.[26] They labelled the stage between 16 and 19 'Dependent Independence'.

The term 'teenager'—an English-language neologism—had no equivalent in French. ('Adolescence'—used in both French and English—does not carry the same cultural freight.) French Canada has never had a 'teenage problem', but rather a *problème des jeunes*—with *les jeunes* generally being less alienated than anglophone teenagers from their elders. In his autobiographical *Nègres blancs d'Amérique* (1968; *White Niggers of America*, 1971), Quebec radical Pierre Vallières—who was jailed on charges connected with his FLQ activities and wrote his book in prison—suggests that men like his father had their own suburban fantasies:

'If only Madelaine [his wife] can agree to it,' he said to himself. He was marshalling his arguments and silently preparing his case. 'We'll be at peace. The children will have all the room they need to play. We'll be masters in our own house. There will be no more stairs to go up and down. . . . Pierre won't hang around the alleys and sheds any more. . . .' The owner was prepared to stretch the payments out over many years. . . . Life would become easier. . . . He would enlarge the house. A few years from now, Madeleine and the 'little ones' would have peace and comfort.[27]

And so in 1945 the Vallières family moved to Longueuil–Annexe: 'the largest of an infinite number of little islands of houses sprung up here, there, and everywhere out of the immense fields which in the space of a few years were to be transformed into a vast mushroom city'.[28]

EDUCATION

Education took on new importance for Canadians after World War II. The rapid expansion of Canadian schools and universities was a product of two overlapping trends. One, of course, was the baby boom. The other was a movement promoted by educators and parents alike for democratization of access to education. As a result, the 1960s saw enormous pressure on education budgets and increasing demand for the production of more—and better—teachers. School authorities attempted to ease some of their problems by consolidating rural schools—a process that continued until the early 1970s— and relying on the ubiquitous yellow school bus to transport students. Teachers acquired more formal credentials, began to earn more money, and organized themselves into a powerful professional lobby, often unionized. In most provinces schools were a public responsibility administered by provincial boards of education, but Quebec and Newfoundland struggled to reform denominational school systems that were holdovers from far less complicated times. In any event, education and its developments served as a mirror for the society as a whole, as trends that began in suburbs like 'Crestwood Heights' gradually found their way across the nation.[29]

Elementary school enrolment was the first to increase immediately after the war—a result of the rise in births during the war after years of decline; the average size of first-grade classes doubled between 1945 and 1965.[30] Before long secondary-school enrolments also began to rise. But not until the mid-1950s did it become obvious that a crisis was on the way, for in the decade after the war, class sizes in existing schools had simply expanded and only a few more teachers had been hired to deal with the additional students. Finally, however, the overcrowding became too obvious to ignore. Population shifts to the suburbs, combined with larger numbers of pupils and a heavier demand for a better education for a higher proportion of Canadians, made a real difference. The baby boom provided one level of pressure on the system, at least until 1966, but it was only part of the push for educational expansion. At the same time, Canadian educators began to press hard for the extension of universal education, at least through high school, with the campaign reaching full fruition by the later 1950s. The new insistence on a high-school education for all represented a profound social revolution and was arguably necessary, given the increasing complexity of technology and the need for skilled workers in a modern industrial country[31]—although, curiously, Canada lagged badly in terms of vocational and practical education, preferring to force the vast majority of its students into traditional academic endeavours. Many of the arguments for expanded education were imported from the United States, but they were increasingly accepted by Canadian parents and taxpayers— particularly after 1957, when the Russians put Sputnik into orbit and inadvertently gave rise to a concerted campaign for educational reform throughout North America.

As late as 1960, the numbers of children kept in school beyond Grade 6 or 7 showed substantial provincial variation, as did other major variables. In British Columbia, half of all possible candidates got through Grade 12, while in Newfoundland only 2 per cent graduated. Ontario retained 41 per cent from Grade 2 to Grade 11, double the rate for Quebec. In general, the retention rate before 1960 declined systematically as one moved from the Pacific coast to the Atlantic.[32] The 1960s were spent in attempting to achieve approximate national equality in terms of retention, with considerable success. By 1970 over 90 per cent of high-school age children were enrolled in school, most of whom went on to graduate, and by the 1980s it was hard to appreciate how recent a development the universal high-school education was.

The most powerful argument for keeping children in school was based on the enhancement of human capital. Statistics were trotted out to prove that it paid to go to school, showing a correlation between lifetime income and years of schooling. Now every penny spent on education was to be regarded as an investment. As a result, public spending on education rose from 2.5 per cent of the gross national product in 1950 to 9 per cent in 1970—the latter representing $8 billion[33] and nearly 20 per cent of all taxes levied by all three levels of government (federal, provincial, and municipal). Between 1950 and 1970 school enrolment in Canada nearly tripled, exerting profound strains on government budgets and teaching-training facilities. As with relief expenditure during the Depression, Canadian municipalities were in the front line when it came to financing educational expansion, although the federal government did increase its funding over the period. By 1970 one-third of the nation was in school, and teaching was easily Canada's largest single occupation. As teachers organized, into both professional organizations and labour unions, the late 1960s saw some major work stoppages, particularly in Ontario.

In 1956 the authors of *Crestwood Heights* observed that the flagship suburban community they had studied was 'literally built around its schools', with the 'massive centrality of the schools' representing 'the most immediate physical impact on any outside observer coming into the Heights'.[34] 'Crestwood Heights' was also an early exemplar of the new style of education, 'aimed primarily at preparing pupils for a middle-class vocation in a highly-industrialized cul-

ture'.[35] By 1970 this style had become accepted across the nation.

The 'progressive' ideals of Deweyism, which had begun to take hold before the war, now triumphed everywhere in Canada. No longer were children in school to learn facts by rote. The development of the 'whole child' was in vogue everywhere, and educators now emphasized socialization and co-operation, to prepare children for their roles in a more sophisticated technological society. In attempting to meet the needs both of the child and of society, the new system did create internal contradictions. As the authors of *Living and Learning*, an influential Ontario report on the aims and objectives of education, explained in 1968:

> The good school fosters a continuing desire to learn. It helps the individual pupil to feel secure and adequate within himself, encourages him to manage his own affairs, and helps him gain a measure of social competence. It gives all pupils an understanding of man and his world, encourages them to adopt positive attitudes toward change, and accustoms them to solving problems and overcoming difficulties. The good curriculum helps young people to acquire a purpose in life. It prepares them for the world of work and leisure.[36]

Living and Learning was the product of a commission co-chaired by Mr Justice Emmett M. Hall and Lloyd Dennis, a former school principal. It recommended continuous interdisciplinary education attuned to the needs of individual students: the abolition of grades, exams, and failure; streaming by ability or competence; centralized curricula; and liberal electives and pupil participation in choice of content. Many of its recommendations were accepted by the Ontario Ministry of Education, radically changing the school system in that province—and reaching farther afield.

In 1946 the typical teacher had spent a year or two at a special teachers' college; but by 1970 almost all teacher-training had moved into the universities. School boards across the country required that new teachers have university degrees that combined educational skills with subject-area background. Such teachers were therefore 'professionals' in a way that their predecessors never had been. Not all Canadians were convinced that enhanced education and professionalization improved what went on in the classroom. Thrown out along with the strap were provincial examinations and any tests that might evaluate the acquisition of traditional skills—or the performance of the teacher. Instead the emphasis was put on what the Hall-Dennis report described as the student's 'right to learn, to play, to laugh, to dream, to dissent, to reach upward, and to be himself'.[37]

Meanwhile, educational expectations continued to rise. The need for more and supposedly better-educated teachers combined with the general extension of the principle of universality to produce a demand for higher levels of university education. The same arguments used for high school universality were simply extended to the universities, with increased enrolments justified chiefly in economic terms.[38] For governments, the gains were to be general; for parents, they were individual. At first, substantial increases in university enrolments were met chiefly by existing facilities and teaching staffs, as the university student population doubled between 1945–6 and 1948, and then nearly doubled again by 1963.

By the later 1950s, existing facilities could no longer contain the human growth. Established universities began expanding and a number of new universities were founded. In some cases, existing colleges previously affiliated to universities were given independent status, in some cases new colleges were founded, and a number of new universities were chartered. The largest university in Canada, the University of Toronto, acquired two suburban campuses, Scarborough (1964) and Erindale (1966), and three colleges on the downtown campus: Massey (1960–3), a superb complex designed by Ron Thom; New (1962); and Innis (1964). There was much competition among the new universities for architectural distinction, but perhaps only Simon Fraser University, designed by Arthur Erickson, and Trent University, designed by Ron Thom, were truly impressive. In retrospect, most striking about these institutions is their frequent use of pre-stressed concrete and the similarity of architectural vision (or lack of it) across the nation. Although most universities built or expanded on spacious suburban sites, it seemed as if almost every campus had to have its own high-rise office complex.

New or expanding universities also competed for faculty. The Canadian higher education system had not looked ahead in the 1940s and 1950s, and hence failed to expand graduate training facilities to meet its undergraduate needs. The failure was especially marked in the humanities and social sciences, where the government's wartime concentration on science, technology, and medicine came back to haunt it. The result was that when the baby boomers hit the universities in the 1960s, it was far easier to construct buildings than it was to assemble faculties. Canada recruited over 20,000 new university faculty members in the 1960s, mostly from the US, Britain, and elsewhere in the Commonwealth. These new teachers quickly geared up to produce a generation of graduate students who were not always trained in a Canadian context. Indeed, there was some backlash within the universities against this massive intrusion of foreign teachers, chiefly because of their importation of non-Canadian approaches and general ignorance of Canadian society. Few economics departments, for example, discussed the Canadian economy except in advanced and specialized courses. The movement for Canadian Studies grew as a consequence, attempting to force departments to introduce Canadian content, particularly in the social sciences and humanities.

As with so much else in the post-war period, the educational system was expanded without appropriate planning or thinking, in an environment of unprecedented population growth, revo-

■ Simon Fraser University. Ron Long, SFU/LIDC.

lutionary changes in expectations, and general economic prosperity. Few were prepared to counsel a gradualist approach, or to warn of impending disaster when either the money or the new students ran out. By 1970 the demographic revolution had ended, and its demise was working its way through the schools. The result was obvious. The system began turning out large numbers of teachers (for all levels of education) at the very time the profession was contracting. Jobs became harder to find. Only the first of the baby boomers found employment prospects encouraging when they emerged with their qualifications. Later generations had to scramble for jobs.

Profound and even revolutionary changes in educational systems were underway before the early 1970s with a minimum of public debate. A handful of critiques of progressivism, such as

Hilda Neatby's *So Little for the Mind* (1953), seemed too old-fashioned to make much impression on a society that was impatient for the improved living standards that—rightly or wrongly—it associated with educational expansion. Neatby's work did stir up some discussion in the academy, but not much in ministries of education. In Quebec, as we have seen, Frère Untel's critique combining elitist condemnation of *joual* culture with criticism of the province's unprogressive educational system achieved far greater circulation. Outside Quebec (and to a lesser extent Newfoundland), one of the outstanding characteristics of the post-war educational revolution was the relative absence of public opposition. Part of the reason for the lack of controversy was the unwillingness of Canadians to challenge the 'experts' in education, a point observed by the authors of *Crestwood Heights* in 1956: 'The school, supported by the human relations experts and their institutions, has largely replaced the church as an ideological source.'[39]

Dramatic educational reforms were implemented in most provinces with a minimum of public objection. Only after the changes had been made did people begin to question their validity. Thus, a school consolidation program that was described by one educator as 'the most complete and socially significant transition to occur in Prince Edward Island since the Second World War'—it wiped out, virtually overnight, the small wooden schoolhouse, one of the most significant elements of village life and community identification in the rural districts of the Island—was implemented in the later 1960s and early 1970s without any significant local objection. Only after the centralization program had been virtually completed without achieving any of the improvements in cost efficiency or access to education promised by its proponents did parents and communities organize to object to it.[40] Other parts of the nation were equally slow to object to the general trend of rural school consolidation.

In Quebec, the political aspects of educational change focused on the refusal or inability of a traditionally oriented system, run by ecclesiastics, to respond to the new educational expectations or to an increasingly industrialized and urbanized society. Educational reform in Quebec became inextricably bound up with the 'Quiet Revolution'. In Newfoundland, the Smallwood government used educational opportunity as one of its main arguments in support of the policy of social modernization that included resettlement of the people in many isolated outports. Across Canada, most of the political objections were not so much to educational reforms per se as to broader social changes that they foreshadowed.

THE RADICAL SIXTIES

The usual picture of Canada in the quarter-century after 1945 presents a naive, optimistic, traditional, politically apathetic, and generally complacent society that suddenly, after 1960, began questioning virtually all its values (and overturning many of them), largely under the influence of trends in the United States. That view is reasonably accurate, but several important qualifications need to be emphasized at the outset. First, few 'revolutions' are truly sudden, and that of the 1960s was no exception: there was more ferment under the surface in 1950s Canada than is usually recognized. In many respects 1960 simply marked the shift to the public stage of ideas and behaviour that until then had been strictly private. Moreover, although on one level the 1960s involved a generational reaction by the maturing baby boomers against their suburban parents, that reaction itself was a product of the same romantic optimism and sense of general economic prosperity that had characterized the preceding decade. As is often the case, conflict often had more to do with impatience with the slow pace of change than with any desire to alter its ultimate import or even direction. The upheaval of the 1960s was a distinctly middle-class movement, particularly in Canada, and was fuelled by the rising expectations created by economic affluence. Finally, while American trends were extremely influential, one reason Canadians were able to pick up on them so easily was that they shared the American social critics' profound suspicions of the American system and establishment. Moreover, Canadians had a number of their own homegrown concerns.

The sixties were a complex period of currents and countercurrents, and no sketch of the major movements can do more than scratch the surface. Nevertheless, two of the period's most striking developments were a broad societal shift towards liberalization and the emergence of a youth-centred counterculture that scorned anyone over 30. Sixties rhetoric found a ready outlet on TV (at the very time when colour television became universally available), but only a few contemporaries were able to get beneath the rhetoric and come to terms with the substance of the counterculture's critique.

THE EMANCIPATION OF MANNERS

The 1960s have been credited with (or blamed for) a moral revolution in which the traditional values of our Victorian ancestors were overturned virtually overnight. But firmly held moral beliefs probably do not collapse quite so rapidly as the developments of the 1960s might suggest. Rather, a moral belief system that was already in an advanced state of deterioration and clearly out of step with the way people actually behaved finally was questioned in public. The temporary upsurge of formal Christianity in the post-war period collapsed just as suddenly as it had begun, and the churches found themselves divided internally at the very time when many Canadians were withdrawing from organized religion. The decline reflected both disagreement over fundamental doctrine and frustration with social attitudes that seemed increasingly irrelevant. The collapse was not limited to the Christian churches, for Judaism experienced similar problems. Again, the process of deterioration had been gradual, only temporarily disguised by the revival of traditional religion immediately after World War II.[41] Nevertheless, the decline in institutionalized religion did not necessarily indicate a widespread moral crisis, less a loss of Christian faith. More likely, fundamental moral principles remained largely unaltered: what changed were manners, including the willingness to talk openly about issues that in the past had not been discussed. These changes were international, and went much further elsewhere in the highly industrialized world. By comparison with Sweden or California, Canadian manners remained relatively stable.

The liberation of manners occurred on several levels, but some were particularly visible. The old taboos against sexual explicitness, obscenity, and graphic violence in the media virtually disappeared. Although television had attempted to maintain some kind of distinction between real life and the screen, between the movie theatre and the living room, TV news undermined that self-restraint, particularly with regard to violence. The 1960s were probably no more violent than any other period, but constant television coverage, increasingly in 'living' colour, brought violent events to everyone's living room. Memories of the period include a kaleidoscope of violent images: the assassinations of the Kennedy brothers and Martin Luther King; the Paris student riots of 1968; battle scenes in Vietnam. If the war in Vietnam was the most unpopular war in history, it was also the first in which the realities of the fighting were covered daily on colour television. Canadians liked to believe that most violence happened elsewhere, especially in the US. In 1970 the Guess Who, a Canadian rock group, had an international hit with 'American Woman', which alluded to Canada's relationship with the US in sexual terms—a common metaphor at the time.

As for sexuality, it became explicit in all sorts of ways. Canadians began to talk and write openly about sexual intercourse, contraception, abortion, premarital sex, and homosexuality. In place of the winks and nudges that had always accompanied certain 'unmentionable topics', a refreshing frankness was accepted. Many of these issues involved women's desire (hardly new) to control their own bodies and reproductive functions. The rapid spread in the use of 'Enovid', the oral contraceptive known as 'the pill', after its introduction in 1960, was part of the new development. The pill seemed far superior to earlier methods of contraception—one important advantage was that women did not have to rely on men to use it—and it became very popular before some of its side effects came to light. Although the birth rate had begun declining in 1959, before it was introduced, and would probably have followed a similar course in any event, the pill became a symbol of sexual freedom for women that gradually worked its way into the media. By the mid-1960s, popular women's magazines that until then had preached marriage and domesticity were now featuring lead articles on the possibility (if not the desirability) of premarital sex and extramarital affairs—options formerly regarded as available only to men.

Language, at least as the media used it, was equally liberated. Canadian writers—whether in fiction, poetry, drama, or film—had always used a sanitized and unrecognizable version of spoken English or French, which left out the vulgarities and profanities. Earle Birney's comical war novel *Turvey* (1949) had relied on dashes to suggest the profanities used by Canadian soldiers. (A year earlier, the American novelist Norman Mailer had used 'fug' repeatedly for the ubiquitous four-letter word in his war novel, *The Naked and the Dead*, which caused controversy but opened the floodgates for a greater laxity in what would become acceptable in written English.) But in everyday life, many ordinary Canadians, French- and English-speaking alike, drew heavily on a rich vocabulary of centuries-old vulgar slang that could not be found in standard dictionaries. The state played its own part in the reformation of manners in the 1960s. Pierre Elliott Trudeau achieved the reputation that helped make him Prime Minister by presiding over a reformist Department of Justice in 1967–8. He became associated with the federal reform of divorce in 1968, as well as with amendments to Canada's Criminal Code dealing with abortion and homosexuality (both in 1969). Trudeau was Prime Minister in 1969 when a Royal Commission was appointed to investigate the non-medical use of drugs. While its report, published in 1970, did not openly advocate the legalization of 'soft drugs' such as marijuana, its general arguments about the relationship of law and morality were typical of the period. The Commission insisted that the state had the right to limit the availability of harmful substances through the Criminal Code, but at the same time maintained that it was not necessarily 'appropriate to use the criminal law to enforce morality, regardless of the potential for harm to the individual or society'.[42]

The idea that it was not the function of the state to enforce morality, particularly a morality not held universally by Canadians, informed many of the other legal reforms of the late 1960s. Divorce reform was not opposed by many major elements of Canadian society. A number of Roman Catholic bishops, in a brief to a special joint committee of the legislature on divorce, stated in 1967:

> It will be up to the legislator to apply his principles to the concrete and often complicated realities of social and political life and to find a way to make these principles operative for the common good. He should not stand idly by waiting for the Church to tell him what to do in the political order. . . . The norm of his action as a legislator is not primarily the good of any religious group but the good of all society.[43]

Such liberated thought paved the way not only for a thorough reform of federal divorce legislation (making divorce easier to obtain) but for an amendment to the Criminal Code in 1969 that made abortions legal if they were carried out by physicians in proper facilities, and following a certification by a special panel of doctors that 'the continuation of the pregnancy of such female person would or would be likely to endanger her life or health'. Neither divorce nor abortion was made available 'upon demand', but these revisions went a long way towards meeting the demands of Canadians—especially women—for action on these fronts. The Criminal Code was also amended in 1969 to exempt from prosecution 'indecent acts' performed in private by consenting couples over the age of 21.

The reformation of manners, if not morals—including the ideas that the state had no place in the bedrooms of the nation (a view first enunciated by Trudeau) and that individuals were entitled to make their own decisions—was largely completed in principle by 1969. Since that time, Canada has witnessed a resurgence of demands for state intervention in areas where liberalization is thought to have had adverse consequences. Thus, many women's groups have come to advocate stricter legislation on obscenity and indecency, particularly in the media, in order to protect women and children from sexual abuse, and smoking has been subject to increasing restrictions in recent years, whereas cigarettes were freely sold—even to children—and smoked in the 1960s.

THE COUNTERCULTURE

One of the most obvious manifestations of the ferment of the sixties was the rebellious reaction of the baby boomers against the values of their parents and their attraction towards what came to be known as the 'counterculture'. Although they had their own issues to address, especially in Quebec, Canadian rebels of the decade took much of the content and style of their protest from the US, where the inconsistencies between the rhetoric of optimistic middle-class affluence and real life were even more apparent than they were in Canada. As in the US, youthful rebellion in Canada had two wings, never mutually exclusive: a highly politicized movement of active revolution, centred on the universities, and a less overtly political one of self-reformation, centred on the 'hippie'. Student activists and hippies were often the same people, and even when they were not, the culture was still the same, anchored by sex, dope, and rock 'n' roll. The participants in the two Canadian branches of youthful protest also had in common distinctly middle-class backgrounds, for this was not a movement of the disinherited.

The spiritual home of the sixties counterculture, in Canada and everywhere else in the world, was the American university. Americans had gone further than anyone else towards both suburbanization and universal education, and their rapidly expanding university campuses provided the ideal spawning ground for youthful rebellion. The Americans had also generated, in the civil rights movement, a model for subsequent agitation. The civil rights crusade focused attention on the rhetorical contradictions of mainstream American society that preached

equality while denying it to blacks, and mobilized youthful idealism. It also demonstrated the values of the protest march and civil disobedience, as well as the symbolic value of popular song. When some blacks left the movement, convinced that only violence could truly alter the status quo, they provided further models for urban guerrilla activity. In itself, the public concern for civil rights was an important element in the education of the sixties generation, and had some resonances in Canada. Nevertheless, what really touched off the revolt of American youth was the war in Vietnam.

Even in retrospect, the extent to which Vietnam dominated the period is not readily apparent. But the war was the perfect symbol of everything that was wrong with mainstream American society. Vietnam was certainly the wrong war for the 1960s. It required America's youth to fight overseas in a conflict with which they had no sympathy. Indeed, it was difficult for youth not to identify with the enemy, who were struggling for national liberation against a modern example of the worst features of imperialism. Vietnam was equally exportable as a symbol of American Evil, for it represented everything that the rest of the world most hated about the US, especially its arrogant assumption that it could do anything it pleased around the world. Vietnam was central to the Canadian counterculture in a variety of ways, and provided more than a mere symbol. Hostility to American policy in Vietnam was the central feature of a collection of opinions about the United States by Canadian writers edited by Al Purdy: *The New Romans: Candid Canadian Opinions of the U.S.* (1967). But it also connected many Canadians with the burgeoning American movements of protest. Many Canadian university faculty members recruited during the decade were Americans, most of them recent graduate students who were critical of American policy. They were joined in their sympathies by an unknown number of American draft dodgers—perhaps as many as 100,000 at the height of the Vietnam War—the majority of

■ Anti-Vietnam War protestors make their way to the US Consulate in Montreal, 19 February 1966. *The Gazette* (Montreal)/LAC, PA-173623, © Montreal *Gazette*.

whom sought refuge in communities of university students or hippies in Canada.

Post-war North American society—a product of capitalist prosperity—was full of imperfections that included a failure to allow everyone to share in the affluence and a largely unquestioned emphasis on material possessions. The baby boomers had been exhorted in their schools and homes to think for themselves, but they were really able to do so only after they had reached university age. By that time they felt alienated from the mainstream society that had nurtured them, because—some said—their parents had not provided them with a credible value system.

Perhaps it is inevitable that a younger generation will rebel against its parent, but in this case the search for alternatives was complicated by the fact that the parents themselves were not very clear about their values, apart from material success. It was also complicated by the fact that the traditional verities seemed to be collapsing around everybody's heads. Any rebellion against the materialism of the capitalist society was bound to turn to the alternative ideology of socialism—although, as the young liked to emphasize, their parents would have denied that capitalist materialism was simply a competing ideology. The youthful reaction was to advocate

■ Debris on Mackay St after the riot at Sir George Williams University, 11 Feb. 1969. *The Gazette* (Montreal)/LAC, PA-139986, © Montreal *Gazette*.

an eclectic kind of socialism—Marxist-influenced, democratically oriented, and idealistically romantic—usually referred to as the 'New Left'. This movement was much better at explaining what was wrong with the existing system than at proposing workable alternatives. It had no example of a large-scale society that operated successfully (or even unsuccessfully) on its principles. Nevertheless, Canadian student activists did rise to positions of power at a handful of universities, including Simon Fraser, York, Regina College, and the Université de Montréal, and established several national organizations, such as the Student Union for Peace Action (SUPA, 1965).[44]

Perhaps the best-known student protest in Canada occurred in February 1969, when the computer centre at Sir George Williams University (now Concordia) in Montreal was occupied for two weeks to protest racial intolerance and 'the military, imperialist ambitions of Canada in the West Indies'.[45] The student protestors completed their occupation on 11 February by smashing the computers and causing damage to the university's equipment and records, estimated in the millions of dollars, thus attracting the attention of Canadians everywhere. Ninety 'occupiers' were arrested, including 41 blacks, many of whom came from the Caribbean. The episode was a classic example of student radicalism, and it had little directly to do with American policy.

Student activism was not the same in Quebec as in the remainder of Canada. While young Québécois were no less alienated than their anglophone counterparts, their anger was directed less against their parents or their community than against the external colonial oppression of English Canada as expressed in Canadian federalism. English-speaking Canadian students spoke of 'the student as nigger' (a conceit imported from the United States), but French-Canadian students could compare their entire society with blacks. Only in Quebec could blacks protest as they did at Sir George Williams, since only in that province was there a well-developed concept of colonialism, summarized in Pierre Vallières's book *Nègres blancs d'Amérique*. Radical Quebec students were able to serve as the vanguard of a related series of movements of protest and reform, support for which cut across the age structure of Quebec society. They were not as isolated from the mainstream as many of their counterparts in English Canada were.

What did radicalized students in Canada in the 1960s believe? It is probably more useful to describe the ideology's component parts than to search for a philosophy. Typically, their Marxism was oversimplified, often derived from such other commentators as Herbert Marcuse or Chairman Mao (Mao Zedong). Students were persuaded that action and theory could not be divorced—the well-known concept that 'if you're not part of the solution you're part of the problem'. They also held that reform from within the existing system was impossible, since the system would either repress or co-opt any such efforts. They rejected study of the past as outmoded 'historicism'. Only the present moment (and perhaps the future) was 'relevant'. Most believed that they, as university students, could be the vanguard of a 'new working class'. They were no more sympathetic to communism than to capitalism, however, which helps explain why the Canadian philosopher George Grant, who criti-

cized both -isms from a Tory humanist perspective, was one of the leading Canadian heroes. Some of the less extreme student activists joined the 'Waffle' faction within the NDP, which tried to move the party in the direction of economic nationalism and social reform before it was expelled in 1971.

'The bureaucratic forms of organization shared by communism and capitalism', wrote American activist Murray Bookchin in 1971, 'were embodiments of insult to the ideals of individualism, spontaneity, mutual trust and generosity that are the dominant themes of the new sensibility.'[46] These were the ideals of the hippies, who accordingly dropped out. Earlier generations of middle-class Canadians had struggled dutifully up the ladder of success, and later ones would strive even harder, but many baby boomers seemed to lack any traditional ambition or direction. They were their parents' children, however, in their quest for personal self-fulfillment by any means possible. For some the quest led to vulgarized versions of Eastern mystical religions. For others it led 'back to nature', to communal living on subsistence farms. For the majority it meant experimentation with drugs, particularly cannabis, and a sexual freedom bordering on promiscuity that seemed to be danger-free at a time when sexually transmitted disease could be treated easily with antibiotics. Such experimentation was one essential feature of the sixties for many participants and observers alike. Another was the revolution in popular music. In the 1960s 'rock' came to incorporate everything from black rhythm and blues to traditional Appalachian folksongs to Indian ragas to medieval Gregorian chants to Bach organ music. For the young, rock was a symbol that both united them and set them apart from older generations.

It is impossible to define a precise moment when the bubble of the counterculture burst. Many of the characteristics and tendencies of the period continued in fragmented fashion into the following decades. But around 1970 the idealism of the era received a series of shocks when

American student activists were violently suppressed (Chicago, 1968; Kent State, 1970) and when rock festivals turned from peace and love to violence (Altamont, 1970). At the same time, the central rallying point—American involvement in Vietnam—was gradually coming to an end. In Quebec, the founding of the Parti Québécois in 1968 provided a place within the system for many student activists. Two years later the October Crisis had a profound impact, showing how far some activists were prepared to go in the use of violence, and how far the state was prepared to go in suppressing it. The purging of the 'Waffle' movement from the NDP provided a convenient symbol for the loss of momentum among activists in English Canada.

CONCLUSION

The period 1946–72 saw a revolution in Canadian lifestyle and manners as the implications of the baby boom were realized in a major emphasis on the young. When the counterculture collapsed, some observers explained its demise as the natural consequence of the baby boomers' becoming adults and needing to find jobs. Perhaps. In any event, by 1972 only memories of the 'good old days' remained for most of the 1960s generation. Not only had the bloom disappeared from the affluent optimism of the post-war period, but new circumstances and conditions had accumulated to produce a host of new reactions against it, in which all Canadians had to share.

SHORT BIBLIOGRAPHY

Axelrod, Paul. *Scholars and Dollars: Politics, Economics, and the Universities of Ontario, 1945–1980*. Toronto, 1982. A fascinating study of the ways in which university expansion was justified in the province of Ontario.

Canada. *Report of the Royal Commission on Bilingualism and Biculturalism*, 4 vols. Ottawa, 1967–70. A wonderful series of volumes that offers a glimpse of what the Canadian experts were thinking about bilingualism and biculturalism during the 1960s.

Clark, Samuel Delbert. *The Suburban Society*. Toronto, 1966. The classic analysis of Canadian suburbia by one of the founders of Canadian sociology.

Kettle, John. *The Big Generation*. Toronto, 1980. An early study of the baby boom generation and its impact on Canadian society.

Kovnick, Valerie. *Roughing It in the Suburbs: Reading Chatelaine Magazine in the Fifties and Sixties*. Toronto, 2000. A postmodernist essay on the messages sent out by Canada's leading women's magazine in the post-war era.

McCracken, Melinda. *Memories Are Made of This: What It Was Like to Grow Up in the Fifties*. Toronto, 1975. An autobiographical introduction to what it was to be young in the 1950s.

Owram, Doug. *Born at the Right Time: A History of the Baby-Boom Generation*. Toronto, 1996. A recent magisterial study of the baby boomers.

Porter, John. *The Vertical Mosaic: An Analysis of Social Class and Power in Canada*. Toronto, 1965. A classic text that demonstrated which variables mattered in Canadian society.

Seeley, John R., R. Alexander Sim, and Elizabeth W. Loosley, in collaboration with Norman W. Bell and D.F. Fleming. *Crestwood Heights: A North American Suburb*. Toronto, 1956. A classic text of Canadian sociology that saw its community as North American rather than distinctly Canadian.

Strong-Boag, Veronica. 'Home Dreams: Women and the Suburban Experience in Canada, 1945–60', *Canadian Historical Review* 72 (1991): 471–504. An exemplary journal article that details the role of women in the Canadian suburban experience.

Young, T. Kue. *Health Care and Cultural Change: The Indian Experience in the Central Subarctic*. Toronto, 1988. A useful study of health care—and its limitations—among First Nations in the Subarctic.

STUDY QUESTIONS

1. How would you define 'suburbia'?

2. What were the demographic dynamics of the 'baby boom'?

3. How did post-war immigration alter the makeup of Canadian society?

4. What do the post-war changes in mortality patterns tell us about Canadian society?

5. What disparities in income and occupational status were revealed by researchers in the 1960s?

6. Why was rural depopulation such an important trend of the post-war period?

7. From the standpoint of Canadian cities in the twenty-first century, was the success achieved by opponents of freeway construction a good thing?

8. What were the major characteristics of Canadian suburban society?

9. What was the single most important principle involved in the revolution of manners in the 1960s?

10. What did the counterculture believe?

CHAPTER EIGHTEEN

The Beginnings of Modern Canadian Cultural Policy, 1945–1972

Culture in Canada and Canadian culture—the two were not quite synonymous—emerged after World War II as major concerns for governments at all levels and for the private sector as well. Culture had not entirely been ignored before 1945, but it had always taken a back seat to political and economic matters, with Canada's performance (or lack of it) explained chiefly in terms of priorities: culture was a luxury that would come with political and economic maturity. That moment was now at hand. Four parallel and not necessarily related developments affecting culture occurred after 1945. One was the beginning of efforts at both federal and provincial levels to articulate and implement public cultural policy, usually in the interests of the enhancement of the state. Culture was increasingly recognized as the best way to promote Canadian identity and values, often as a strategy of resistance against the power of the United States. The second was an explosion of artistic activity and cultural industry that brought a significant rise not only in quantity and quality but also in the numbers of people who earned their living in the production or support of culture. The third development was a trend towards geographical decentralization and diffusion. Whereas in the past culture and cultural production were concentrated in a handful

of centres, now the entire nation became involved. Finally, definitions of 'culture' expanded to include a wide variety of new activities, and some new aesthetic approaches emerged in painting, music, and literature that helped to break down the old boundaries between high and popular. But with all these changes, a clear theoretical understanding of the meaning of 'culture' did not emerge anywhere, and popular culture (such as hockey) did not really become integrated into anyone's cultural policy until the end of the period.

THE MEANINGS OF CULTURE

The term 'culture' continued to be used in a wide variety of contexts, producing a 'general uncertainty of ideas respecting one of the major premises of socio-political thought in Canada'.[1] In its several guises, culture was the central subject of four federal Royal Commissions between 1949 and 1963: on the arts, letters, and sciences (the Massey Commission, 1949); on radio and television broadcasting (the Fowler Commission, 1955); on magazine publishing (the O'Leary Commission, 1961); and on bilingualism and biculturalism (the Laurendeau-Dunton Commission, 1963). It was also the subject of the crucial opening chapter of the report of the Quebec Royal

TIMELINE

1945
Canadian Arts Council established. Canada Foundation established.

1948
Saskatchewan creates the Saskatchewan Arts Board.

1949
Massey Commission established.

1950
Harold Innis publishes *Empire and Communication*. Federal assistance for Canadian universities begins.

1951
Marshall McLuhan publishes *The Mechanical Bride*.

1953
National Library established. Tremblay Commission established.

1955
Fowler Commission on radio and television broadcasting established.

1956
Branches of natural and human history created at the National Museum of Canada.

1957
Canada Council established.

1958
Broadcasting Act of 1958 creates Board of Broadcast Governors (BBG).

1961
The O'Leary Commission on magazine publishing established. Bill C-131 passed by the House of Commons to deal with fitness and amateur sport. Ministry of Cultural Affairs established in Quebec.

1963
The Royal Commission on Bilingualism and Biculturalism (Laurendeau-Dunton) established.

1968
Canadian Film Development Corporation (CFDC) founded. Social Sciences and Humanities Research Council hived off from Canada Council. Canadian Radio-Television Commission (CRTC) established.

1970
CRTC redefines Canadian content regulations. Winnipeg organizes Folklorama.

1972
Canada defeats USSR in final game of hockey series (September). Policy of multiculturalism is announced.

Commission of Inquiry on Constitutional Problems (the Tremblay Commission, 1953). The disparate subjects of these commissions suggest that culture was not only all-embracing, but freighted with political implications in these years.

As the topics of the Royal Commissions indicated, there were still three primary meanings to 'culture'. The Massey Commission concentrated on humanistic culture, the creative and intellectual aspects of civilization as manifested through such institutions as art galleries, museums, and libraries. There was also popular culture, which the Massey Commission avoided except in its discussions of television. The Fowler Commission never used the term 'culture' in relation to broadcasting, but culture was clearly its subject. Anthropological culture was the subject of both the Tremblay and Laurendeau-Dunton commissions, defined by the latter as 'a way of being, thinking and feeling. It is a driving force animating a significant group of individuals united by a common tongue, and sharing the same customs, habits, and experience.'[2] But Laurendeau-Dunton also used the word 'culture' in the humanistic sense when talking about other ethnic groups and the 'cultural enrichment of Canada'. Culture meant one thing in the context of 'biculturalism' and something else in the context of 'multiculturalism'. The Tremblay Commission was the only one that recognized a relationship between intellectual and anthropological culture, for although it distinguished between the 'culture of the elite' and 'a common culture which is that of the mass',[3] it found that between them there was 'such inter-dependence and constant inter-action that the problem of culture remains a single one'. The Tremblay Commission also tried to link mass culture and elite culture, claiming that mass culture was 'the culture of origin'.

Some critics after 1945 attempted to distinguish between a culture that was dispensed by the 'media' (itself a new term covering radio, television, and large-circulation journalism) and a culture that was intrinsic to the lives of ordinary people. In his later years, Harold Innis became fascinated with the manipulative power of the media. He became globally reflective, producing a series of books, articles, essays, and addresses under the general heading of one of his titles, *The Bias of Communication*.[4] For Innis, command of the media of communication was control of communication, and communication was a powerful influence on the development of political empires and societies. In every medium of communication, a monopoly or oligopoly of power was created. Radio and television were ideal media both for demagogues and for the dissemination of American commercial popular culture, in Innis's view. The effects on Canadian culture of American wartime propaganda and commercialism in the electronic media, he wrote,

> have been disastrous. Indeed they threaten Canadian life. The cultural life of English-speaking Canadians subjected to constant hammering from American commercialism is increasingly separated from the cultural life of French-speaking Canadians. . . . We are indeed fighting for our lives. The pernicious influence of American advertising reflected especially in the periodical press and the powerful persistent impact of commercialism have been evident in all the ramifications of American life.[5]

Innis's recognition of the relationship between technology and culture—and between culture and nation—in capitalistic societies was an important breakthrough. That relationship would become a major Canadian preoccupation in the post-war period.

Building on Innis, the Canadian scholar Marshall McLuhan became the chief international guru of 'media' culture. His first book, *The Mechanical Bride: Folklore of Industrial Man* (1951), examined comic strips, advertisements, and other promotional imagery of the American press to convey some insights into how 'many thousands of the best-trained individual minds have made it a full-time business to get inside the collective public mind'.

Three years later, in the journal *Explorations: Studies in Culture and Communications* (1953–9) —and itself one of the cultural landmarks of the fifties—McLuhan wrote a piece entitled 'Notes on the Media as Art Forms':

> The use of the term 'mass media' has been unfortunate. All media, especially languages, are mass media so far at least as their range in space and

MARSHALL McLUHAN
ON 'BLONDIE'

Marshall McLuhan was instrumental in making the study of popular culture, including all media, popular and trendy. His writing was glib, sometimes at the cost of precision, and in his later work tended be aphoristic. The following excerpt from his first book, *The Mechanical Bride*, illustrates all of these qualities.

It is not without point that Chic Young's strip is now misnamed and that popular use has long since changed its title to 'Dagwood.' This is because Blondie herself is of no interest. She is a married woman. It is only the sufferings, the morose stupidities, and the indignities of her husband, Dagwood Bumstead, which matter. These make up the diary of a nobody.

Blondie is cute. She started out as a Tillie the Toiler, a frisky coke-ad girl, supposed to be universally desirable because twice-bathed, powdered, patted, deodorized, and depilatorized. But the moment this little love-goddess is married, she is of little interest to anybody but to the advertisers and to her children. And to them she is conscience, the urgent voice of striving and aspiration. To them she apportions affection as reward for meritorious effort. She has 'poise and confidence,' know-how, and drive. Dagwood is a supernumerary tooth with weak hams and a cuckold hair-do. Blondie is trim, pert, resourceful. Dagwood is seedy, saggy, bewildered, and weakly dependent. Blondie lives for her children, who are respectful toward her and contemptuous of Dagwood. Dagwood is 'living and partly living' in hope of a little quiet, a little privacy, and a wee bit of mothering affection from Blondie and his son, Alexander. He is an apologetic intruder into a hygienic, and, save for himself, a well-ordered dormitory. His attempts to eke out some sort of existence in the bathroom or on the sofa (face to the wall) are always promptly challenged. He is a joke which his children thoroughly understand. He has failed, but Alexander will succeed.

Dagwood expresses the frustration of the suburban commuters of our time. His lack of self-respect

© King Features Syndicate.

is due partly to his ignoble tasks, partly to his failure to be hep to success doctrines. His detestation of his job is plain in the postponement of the morning departure till there comes the crescendo of despair and the turbulent take-off. Rising and departure are traumatic experiences for him, involving self-violence. His swashbuckling, midnight forays to the icebox, whence he returns covered with mayonnaise and the gore of catsup, is a wordless charade of self-pity and Mitty-Mouse rebellion. Promiscuous gormandizing as a basic dramatic symbol of the abused and the insecure has long been understood.

The number of suburban-marriage strips and radio programs is increasing. Each has the same theme —model mother saddled with a sad sack and a dope.

SOURCE: Marshall McLuhan, *The Mechanical Bride: Folklore of Industrial Man* (New York: Vanguard Press, 1951).

time is concerned. If by 'mass media' is meant a mechanized mode of a previous communication channel, then printing is the first of the mass media. Press, telegraph, wireless, telephone, gramophone, movie, radio, TV, are mutations of the mechanization of writing, speech, gesture. Insofar as mechanization introduces the 'mass' dimension, it may refer to a collective effort in the use of the medium, to larger audiences or to instantaneity of reception. Again, all of these factors may create a difficulty of 'feedback' or lack of rapport between 'speaker' and audience. There has been very little discussion of any of these questions, thanks to the gratuitous assumption that communication is a matter of transmission of information, message, or idea. This assumption blinds people to the aspect of communication as participation in a common situation. And it leads to ignoring the form of communication as the basic art situation which is more significant than the information or idea 'transmitted'.[6]

His later catchphrase, 'the medium is the message', echoed through the 1960s (and is still heard).[7] In later years, however, McLuhan's brilliant reconceptualizations were overshadowed by his own unexpected guru status and the hype of the media; in a sense, he became a victim of his own theories.

The distinction between media culture and received popular culture could be seen in popular music. Some songs were known only through the media, while others were part of a cultural heritage passed on orally. The production of folk culture received a substantial boost from the Royal Commission on Bilingualism and Biculturalism, which saw it as part of the cultural contribution of immigrants to Canada, and from the subsequent introduction of official multiculturalism in 1971.

Canada was hardly alone in discovering that culture in its various manifestations was a contentious matter in the post-war world, but no nation had more difficulties with culture, some obvious and some less so. It was a nation with-

■ Marshall McLuhan in Washington, DC, in the mid-1960s. Photographer unknown. © The Estate of Marshall McLuhan.

out a single unifying language and with at least two of what were increasingly referred to as 'founding cultures'. Moreover, although the word looks the same in both languages, French- and English-speaking Canadians often meant something quite different when they talked about 'culture'. Nobody doubted that French Canada had a distinctive culture. But defining the culture of English-speaking Canada was problematic. Unlike French Canadians, who happily looked to Montreal as their cultural capital, English-speaking Canadians outside Ontario (and perhaps within it as well) resented any suggestion that

Toronto was culturally dominant. Indeed, in many senses Toronto's claim to cultural pre-eminence did decline after the war as other cities became more important. Moreover, for historic reasons, most of the 'other ethnics' considered so culturally enriching by the Laurendeau-Dunton Commission resided in English-speaking Canada and were associated with it. Yet, if Canada lacked anything resembling a homogeneous national culture in either the humanistic or the anthropological sense, it was more exposed than most nations to external cultural influences, particularly from its behemoth neighbour to the south. The US purveyed first to Canada and then to the world a profoundly influential popular culture. If nations separated from the US by geography and history could be strongly affected by American popular culture, the situation for Canada was alarming, at least for those who worried about the integrity of Canadian culture. Certainly every one of the Royal Commissions that dealt with culture in its various forms began by referring to this problem, and most agonized over it.

The association of culture, in all senses, with the nation-state was a product of the nineteenth century, when many European states were created. At the time, one of the strongest arguments in favour of forming a nation was the cultural and linguistic homogeneity of a particular group of people; the very term 'nation' was associated with the possession of a common culture. The notion that political boundaries should follow those of language and culture had informed the deliberations, led by American President Woodrow Wilson, at the Versailles Peace Conference after the Great War, and the same notion was of course fundamental to Quebec nationalism. As the Tremblay Commission put it in 1956, 'the nation is a sociological entity, a community of culture which forms and renews itself down through the years by the common practice of a same general concept of life.'[8] Whether the rest of Canada had a parallel cultural identity was another matter. Much of the discussion about Canadian culture in this period involved attempting to ascertain what

was distinctive about Canadian culture—a task not very different from that of attempting to define the Canadian Identity.[9] Among cultural nationalists, those from Quebec and those from English-speaking Canada often had quite different definitions of culture and typically referred to quite different kinds of 'nations'. Furthermore, there were many on both sides who did not believe that a 'national genius' existed on either side—or that the state (provincial or federal) should attempt to encourage one.

At the same time, there was a growing international recognition that the older cultural categories and canons of taste had been extremely constricting. Artists, critics, and consumers all began to take seriously forms and styles that had previously been regarded as frivolous. The barriers that separated high culture, popular culture, and folk culture were in some fields reduced and in others totally demolished. Leonard Cohen, a well-regarded Canadian poet and novelist, became an internationally acclaimed pop-folk songwriter and performer. Paintings and sculptures by untrained artists of the past were brought out of the cupboards where they had been relegated for generations and were presented to a receptive public as fresh and attractive 'naive' or 'primitive' works of art.[10] Contemporary artists such as Jan Wyers, William Panko, and William Kurelek deliberately cultivated a naive style with considerable public success. Aboriginal, and especially Inuit, art was literally brought into existence through collaboration between European-trained and traditional Native artists, often with the assistance of government. Some critics sought the true Canadian content in folk art rather than high culture. In any event, older boundaries and canons were breached, to the pleasure of almost everyone except the traditionalists.

THE DEVELOPMENT OF CULTURAL POLICY

With respect to the development of cultural policy after 1945 it is important to remember that governments were not operating in a vacuum. As we have seen earlier in these pages, Canada's cultural life in 1945 (or for that matter at any point in its history) was considerably more vibrant than most Canadians would have thought at the time. One reason it was not recognized was that cultural critics and commentators were trapped by the categories imported from Europe and to a lesser extent the US. Art critics and historians who used European standards to guide their search for 'high art' in Canada naturally ignored significant achievements in folk art and crafts. In many fields, such as classical music, specialists did not even bother to investigate the Canadian past, since everyone believed that what little might be found would inevitably be derivative and second-rate. The general assumption was that only professionals—or at least appropriately trained amateurs—could possibly produce valuable work.[11] Much of Canada's cultural activity had taken place, and in 1945 was still taking place, outside the boundaries of what critics and experts regard as Culture with a capital 'C'. It consisted of arts practised by amateurs for their own pleasure—a tradition that offered fertile ground for growth but went unchronicled. One effect of the development of Canadian cultural policy after 1945 would be to encourage and support a professionalization of culture, which tended to play into the hands of the critics.

Theatre is a case in point. In the 1950s, the amateur dramatic societies that flourished in many places in the 1930s were partially supplanted by professional theatre companies with the founding of the Crest Theatre in Toronto and the Stratford Festival, both in 1953, the Manitoba Theatre Centre (the model for regional theatre in Canada) in 1958, and the National Theatre School in 1960—but only partially. In 1972 Samuel French Ltd, which supplied theatrical scripts for performance in Canada, calculated that the country had 500 active Little Theatre groups, 10 amateur children's theatre groups, 1,238 high school drama groups, 120 university drama groups, 200 college drama

groups, 100 fraternal drama groups, and an incalculable number of church drama groups. These organizations represented over 31,000 members and their productions were estimated to reach nearly 3,000,000 Canadians in the course of the year. In the same year, 1972, there were fewer than 60 professional and semi-professional theatrical companies.[12] Unfortunately, most amateur groups (and their audiences) were reluctant to experiment with new Canadian plays and playwrights until they had achieved international success. With the growth of professional theatre (and the expansion of television), the Dominion Drama Festival—which had flourished since 1933—lost its vitality. It changed its name to Theatre Canada, discontinued its annual competition, and collapsed entirely in 1978.

Similarly in music, professional choirs emerged in the 1950s and 1960s, although countless amateur choirs continued to flourish. To the established symphony orchestras in Quebec (1902), Toronto (1926), Vancouver (1930), and Montreal (1934) were now added orchestras in other cities, including Winnipeg (1948) and Ottawa (the National Arts Centre Orchestra, 1968), while many new community orchestras were organized and others continued to perform. The problem for Canadian composers was much the same as for Canadian playwrights, only worse. Whereas most playwrights still wrote in fairly traditional idioms, composers tended to avoid imitating the great masters and instead experimented with modern musical forms that were almost universally unpopular with audiences.

CULTURAL POLICY BEFORE THE MASSEY COMMISSION

The war had provided a focus for many cultural organizations and artists to organize in order to lobby for government recognition of the arts as an integral part of the battle for 'democracy'. In December 1945—six months after the birth of the British Arts Council—more than a dozen

■ Prime Minister Louis St Laurent, December 1953. LAC, PA-144069.

'music, literature, theatre and the visual arts did not really have a wide appeal in Canada—their place having been taken by the movies, the radio and the more popular magazines.'[13] In 1945—recognizing that the federal government was not likely to assist in the development of Canadian cultural life—an amateur playwright named Walter Herbert created the Canada Foundation to grant subsidies for such activities. Financed by tax-deductible contributions from the private sector, by 1947 it had raised only $45,000—a modest amount that suggests Canadian business-men were not yet greatly interested in Canadian culture.

By 1945 Canadian governments—particu-larly at the federal level with the Public Archives, the National Gallery, the National Film Board, and the Canadian Broadcasting Corporation—were already seriously involved in cultural activ-ities and institutions, although the extent of their involvement and the reasons for the funding were not clearly understood either by politicians or by the public. In 1947, when the vice-chair-man of the British Arts Council, B. Ilfor Evans, was invited to tour Canada, he pointed out that the government's reluctance to support cultural agencies like the Canadian Arts Council was sur-prising, given its involvement in other cultural undertakings.[14] Perhaps part of the reason was that whereas the wartime government had seen culture as a manifestation of the Western civiliza-tion that Canadians were fighting to preserve, in peacetime Canadian politicians saw culture more as a private business in which government should not intervene.

In cultural matters as in so many others, the CCF had a much more activist policy than other political parties. The CCF government in Saskat-chewan did not hesitate to found a provincial archive (1945) or a regional library system (1950), and in 1948 it established the first pub-licly authorized North American arts co-ordinat-ing organization in the Saskatchewan Arts Board, modelled on the British Arts Council. The Social Credit government of Alberta would follow

organizations (chiefly in the visual arts) formed the Canadian Arts Council. This umbrella group lobbied provincial governments to set up cul-tural facilities, and served as the official Canadian body for the International Olympic Committee. But it sought in vain to be accepted by the fed-eral government as the Canadian representative to UNESCO. In 1947 External Affairs Minister Louis St Laurent told the Council that there would be constitutional problems with the provinces—which were responsible for educa-tion—over setting up a national arts board under the UNESCO charter. Moreover, St Laurent argued,

Saskatchewan's lead, demonstrating that support for the arts could transcend political ideology. As the Arts Board was administered in Saskatchewan, however, it was quite different from its British inspiration. The particular vision of its administrators (and of the government that appointed them) and the nature of the task in a sparsely populated Canadian province made the Saskatchewan Arts Board more of a grassroots body fostering artistic activity on the local and individual levels than an umbrella agency.[15]

Louis St Laurent—who succeeded Mackenzie King as Liberal leader and Prime Minister in 1948—was told that in the 1949 election the Liberals might lose votes to the CCF from 'those Canadians who have a distinct national consciousness and feel that more should be done to encourage national culture and strengthen national feeling'.[16] Accordingly, the Throne Speech of the same year announced a Royal Commission on cultural issues to be headed by Vincent Massey, the former high commissioner. The Commission's scope was to include:

> All government agencies relating to radio, films, television, the encouragement of the arts and sciences, research, the preservation of our national records, a national library, museums, exhibitions; relations in these fields with international organizations, and activities generally which are designed to enrich our national life, and to increase our own consciousness of our national heritage and knowledge of Canada abroad.[17]

The federal government finally had decided to search for a national cultural policy.

THE MASSEY COMMISSION

The Royal Commission on National Development in the Arts, Letters and Sciences, or Massey Commission, was a landmark development in terms of elite culture. Like many such commissions, it was created because the time for it had come, and the fact that a cultural explosion fol-lowed did not mean that it was responsible for that explosion. Its recommendations were crucial in increasing government involvement in the arts, but they were precisely the ones envisioned in its terms of reference, which in turn were a product of considerable lobbying by well-established arts groups in the private sector. Although direct public patronage of the arts through national institutions and granting agencies was enhanced by the Commission's recommendations, indirect patronage in the form of full-time employment at universities probably was just as important. Moreover, although the Massey Commission has often been viewed as ahead of its time in advocating public support for the arts, in most respects it looked backward rather than forward. The vision it promoted came straight from the Victorian era in its separation of culture and the marketplace, and hence it never addressed some of the central problems of cultural policy in the middle of the twentieth century. It did establish a large part of the agenda for at least a generation to follow, but that agenda was narrowly conceived.

Assembling a committee of like-minded individuals—including Hilda Neatby, later the author of the controversial *So Little for the Mind*—Massey led his forces into a whirlwind of action that was carefully catalogued in his final report:

> . . . we have held public hearings in sixteen cities in the ten provinces. We have travelled nearly 10,000 miles, over 1,800 of these by air. In all the Commission has held 224 meetings, 114 of these in public session. We have received 462 briefs, in the presentation of which over 1,200 witnesses appeared before us. The briefs included submissions from 13 Federal Government institutions, 7 Provincial Governments, 87 national organizations, 262 local bodies, and 35 Private commercial radio stations.[18]

As these statistics demonstrated, cultural life in Canada already was active, with lobbying organizations eager to step into a new era.

VINCENT MASSEY
(1887–1967)

❖

The family into which Vincent Massey was born, in 1887, was the closest Canada came to an aristocracy. Having prospered in the Massey-Harris farm-implement firm, the Massey family became notable patrons. Vincent's grandfather, Hart Massey, set a precedent for patronage when he endowed the building of Massey Hall (1894) in Toronto; when he died he left the bulk of his estate—out of which the Massey Foundation was created—for philanthropic purposes. Vincent Massey himself, who had a strong interest in architecture, was much involved in the design of Hart House (1910–19) and Massey College (1960–3) at the University of Toronto. He was also an amateur actor, and helped organize the Dominion Drama Festival. He attended the University of Toronto and then Balliol College, Oxford, where he indulged an anglophilia that remained with him throughout his life. After teaching history at the University of Toronto, doing a stint as president of Massey-Harris, and receiving an appointment to Mackenzie King's cabinet in 1925 (he failed to win a seat in Parliament), he entered the diplomatic service at the ambassadorial level, serving as Canadian minister in Washington (1926–30) and High Commissioner in Great Britain (1935–46).

In England, Massey consorted with the aristocracy and cultivated a reputation as a connoisseur and collector of art, particularly English painting. He was a trustee of the National Gallery of Canada, advising it on the acquisition of Old Masters. More important, through the Massey Foundation he had assem-

bled a splendid collection of modern English painting that he presented in 1946 to the National Gallery of Canada. As a trustee (and chairman) of the National Gallery in London he served on several important British cultural committees. Massey was a cultivated amateur, a British-style 'gentleman of leisure', and an arts patron; both his cultural style and his aesthetic tastes were reflected in the Massey Commission's report. His closest connections with the world of popular culture came through his own interest in contemporary theatre and in the career of his famous brother Raymond, the actor. As Governor General (1952–9) he would be something of a paradox: in many ways staunchly Canadian, and the first Canadian to hold that office, he invested it with trappings that suggested an excessive reverence for Buckingham Palace.

Massey had in a sense prepared for his position as commission chair by writing a book *On Being Canadian* (1948). For him, Canada was the meeting ground between Britain and America, both a North American and a British Commonwealth nation. Admitting that in everyday life, 'our ordinary habits and equipment are little different from the Americans', Massey insisted that it was time that arts and letters should acquire a 'reasonable national flavour'. Because Canadian unity and the Canadian identity were spiritual and intangible, they required embodiment through the arts, letters, and intellectual life of the community. Massey set down a shopping list for a national culture, including an enhanced broadcasting system, film production, a national library, a national portrait gallery, a flag, a national anthem, and a system of non-titular honours. He thus provided the reform agenda for his own Royal Commission, the St Laurent government in the 1950s, and the Pearson government in the 1960s. While Massey was pleased that American–Canadian relations were good, he feared the increase of 'influences' across the border, particularly cultural and economic ones. 'We cannot afford to allow an erosion of our Canadianism', he emphasized.

The Commission indicated its biases in the opening chapters of its final report. It began by calling attention to the overall problem of American influence, and followed with a discussion of the media and popular culture that suggested both the intimate relationship of these matters to the US and the problems the commissioners had in getting a handle on them. But it disposed of these topics in 65 pages of a 515-page report, and then moved on to more congenial territory in the high arts. The Massey Commission was interested not only in elite culture itself, but in elitist ways of assisting and regulating culture. The first item in its terms of reference had required it to recommend the principles for a policy for radio and television broadcasting in Canada. Since television broadcasting had not yet begun in Canada, its recommendations—if adopted by the government—would set the path. With some reluctance, because of its controversial nature, and chiefly to counter the Americans, the Commission recommended that a national television service be created as quickly as possible; that direction and control of television broadcasting, as well as radio broadcasting, 'continue to be vested in the Canadian Broadcasting Corporation'; and that private television broadcasting be permitted only after the CBC had national programming in place in both French and English. The costs of television programming, which would be very high, were to be met from parliamentary grants and a licence fee on television sets. The main argument for giving a

monopoly to the CBC was that it would mean lower start-up costs, but it was also intended 'to avoid excessive commercialism and to encourage Canadian content and the use of Canadian talent'.[19] The Commission plainly approved of CBC's radio programming and condemned private radio for its excessive commercialism, its undervaluation of public taste, and its poverty of 'cultural offerings'—a phrase it did not define but that clearly meant serious, uplifting, and educational content. As the same time, it associated commercialism (the 'appeal to material instincts of various kinds') with Americanism, and Americanism with meretricious popular culture. These were classic Canadian assumptions of the time, particularly among those who, like Vincent Massey, were in a position to bemoan Canada's lack of a 'leisured class which may be expected to produce a few men in each generation devoted to the pursuit of learning and to the revelation of truth for its own sake'.[20]

Other issues addressed by the Commission fell broadly into two categories. One involved a series of recommendations to strengthen existing national cultural agencies and to create others. The Commission was supportive of the National Film Board, the National Gallery, the National Museum, the Public Archives, the Library of Parliament, and the Historic Sites and Monuments Board of the National Parks Service. It recommended more money and enlarged functions for these agencies, as well as the institution of new museums (one for history and one for sciences),

The Massey Commission: Dr Arthur Surveyer, the Most Reverend Georges-Henri Lévesque, the Right Honourable Vincent Massey, Dr Hilda Neatby, Dr Norman A.M. Mackenzie. LAC, C-16986.

national botanical and zoological gardens, and a National Library. Its other thrust involved federal aid for universities and scholarship, both through direct grants to the provinces and through the extension of the concept of the National Research Council (which supported scientific research) into the humanities and social sciences. It recommended graduate scholarships and advanced Canada Fellowships, as well as other grants to artists and scholars, all to be administered by a Council for the Arts, Letters, Humanities and Social Sciences. This 'Canada Council' would not only deal with grants and fellowships, but would co-ordinate Canada's relationship with UNESCO and 'promote a knowledge of Canada abroad'. While the Commission recognized the importance of the press and publishing to Canada and especially to Canadian culture—it called the content of the periodical press 'our closest approximation to a national literature'—it noted that it had no mandate for recommendations in this area. Nevertheless, it did observe that 'Canadian magazines, unlike Canadian textiles or Canadian potatoes, are sheltered by no protective tariff, although the growing extent of the Canadian market has attracted the interest of American advertisers and magazines so that competition from the south has become increasingly vigorous.'[21]

The cultural agenda laid out by the Massey Commission would engage the federal government for the next quarter-century and beyond. Its conception of culture was unabashedly traditional, elitist, and nationalistic. What must be preserved and encouraged was not simply a culture of excellence, but one that was 'resolutely Canadian'. Finally, in its centralist philosophy the report was well suited to the inclinations of federal governments of the era.[22]

CULTURAL POLICY AFTER THE MASSEY COMMISSION

Various federal governments acted on the Massey recommendations in piecemeal fashion over the next decade. Federal assistance for universities had begun in 1950; the National Library was established in 1953; branches in Natural and Human History at the National Museum of Canada were created in 1956. In March 1957, in the last days of the St Laurent government, the Canada Council, one of the principal recommendations of the Massey Commission, finally was adopted. Set up on a hands-off basis with an endowment fund (created out of windfall succession duties) to finance its operations and an autonomous board of directors appointed by the government, the Council had an initial budget of $1.5 million to cover all the expenses of supporting the arts, humanities, and social sciences. It began making two kinds of grants: one to individual artists and scholars, and the other to cultural organizations. Most of its assistance was directed to elite forms of culture and more professional organizations and individuals. Given the choice between protectionism and subsidies to producers as means of pursuing national aims, the Canadian government in 1957 chose subsidies, and the system achieved remarkable success, although the financial demands soon exceeded the endowment.

The Massey Commission also recommended that a new study of broadcasting be undertaken after the initial three-year trial period for television under CBC control. In 1955 a second Royal Commission on the subject was appointed, chaired by Robert Fowler of Montreal, which made its final report in 1957. The Fowler Commission faced a number of problems, of which the thorniest were the shift in the content of radio with the introduction of television, and the prevalence of American productions on both media. Television took over all the formats developed for radio—adding sight to sound on sitcoms, game shows, and drama, for example—

and turned radio into a vehicle mainly for news and recorded music. A detailed program analysis commissioned by the Fowler Commission attempted to document the change. The largest music category on the air had become 'popular and dance', chiefly from recordings. While CBC radio and Radio-Canada continued to broadcast some live music, the independent radio stations in both languages relied on recordings for over 98 per cent of their popular and dance programming. The study was unable to identify the 'nationality of source for any sound radio programs', but most popular recordings of the time clearly were American in origin.[23]

Similar results were found for television programming, particularly in the prime-time entertainment slots and especially in English-speaking Canada. Analyst Dallas W. Smythe found that 48.5 per cent of total program output on all Canadian television stations was produced in Canada, 47.9 per cent in the US, and only 3.6 per cent in other countries. French-language stations drew only 8.4 per cent of their programming from the US, producing 80.5 per cent at home. But in English Canada the programming was 53.1 per cent American, and the situation was even worse when categories of programs were considered. Canadians produced nearly all the programming in fine arts, dance, and 'serious' music; more than half of 'serious' drama; all the 'serious' children's programs; and most sports. But in the more popular categories—domestic drama, comedy, western and crime, romantic, musical comedy, and even total children's shows (including cartoons)—prime-time programming for English Canada came mainly from the US.[24] A major effect of the shift from radio to television was the raised cost of production. The CBC had been better able to compete with the Americans in prime-time entertainment during the radio era, when the production costs for shows like *Jake and the Kid* or *Anthology* were relatively low. But by the mid-1950s, Hollywood was producing most American programming on film for the American networks, and was able to sell its shows to Canadian stations at a fraction of the cost of Canadian production. Moreover, public viewing habits were even less Canadian than Smythe's programming data suggested. Many major Canadian cities were within reach of American television stations (some placed deliberately near the border), and Canadians in Toronto, Montreal, and Vancouver watched American programs on those channels as well as on Canadian ones.

The problems, as the Fowler Commission saw them, were serious:

> No other country is similarly helped and embarrassed by the close proximity of the United States. Much that is good and valuable can come from this closeness; there is an increasingly rich fare of programs on both radio and television available at relatively low cost from the United States. Much of this we cannot hope to duplicate and we would be poorer if we did not have it available as part of our total program supply. But as a nation we cannot accept, in these powerful and persuasive media, the natural and complete flow of another's culture without danger to our national identity. Can we resist the tidal wave of American cultural activity? Can we retain a Canadian identity, art and culture—a Canadian nationhood? . . . We may want, and may be better to have, a different system—something distinctively Canadian and not a copy of a system that may be good for Americans but may not be the best for us.[25]

The Commission repeated the standard Canadian wisdom when it responded to American integration by declaring:

> The Canadian answer, irrespective of party or race, has been uniformly the same for nearly a century. We are prepared, by measures of assistance, financial aid and conscious stimulation, to compensate for our disabilities of geography, sparse population and vast distances, and we have accepted this as a legitimate role of government in Canada.

While recognizing that such a policy would be expensive, the Commission believed that 'for Canada there is no choice', at least if the financial cost could be kept 'within reason'.[26] In so doing it implicitly acknowledged one given of Canadian cultural nationalism: that the Canadian public would never agree to paying very much more to have things 'made in Canada'.

To subsidies and protectionism the Fowler Commission added a third cultural strategy: regulated competition with a 'mixed system of public and private ownership'. While it accepted that the Federal Treasury should support the CBC, it argued that expansion of broadcasting hours and geographical coverage (especially for television) should be financed by private enterprise, which implied a second television network. Rather than permit the CBC to continue to control broadcasting, it recommended the creation of an independent regulatory agency. Such a board had been suggested by the private broadcasters to deal with their own activities, but the Commission instead opted for a single regulatory agency called the Board of Broadcast Governors (BBG), which would monitor all aspects of broadcasting performance, including program content, whether on publicly or privately owned stations.

The Diefenbaker government translated the Commission's recommendations into its Broadcasting Act of 1958, giving the new board responsibility for regulating 'the activities of public and private broadcasting stations in Canada and the relationship between them, . . . ensuring the continued existence and efficient operation of a national broadcasting system'. The BBG was also given a mandate to promote 'the greater use of Canadian talent by broadcasting stations', so that the service would be 'basically Canadian in content and character'.[27] After public hearings in 1959, the Board introduced 'Canadian content' regulations for television, a sort of quota system, to become effective 1 April 1961. However, the definition of Canadian content was so broad as to be operationally meaningless, and it applied only to television. A more significant action by the BBG was its licensing of new stations, including those that would constitute a second Canadian television network (CTV), which began operations in 1961. These private stations were allowed to confine their 'Canadian content' to certain categories of programming (sports, news, children's shows, and other less expensive programs) shown mainly out of prime time. The CTV network thus became even more dependent on American production than the CBC.

Publicly committed to principles of Canadian nationalism, the Diefenbaker government in 1961 took up the challenge—left dangling by the Massey Commission—of investigating the problems of Canadian magazine publishing, a central ingredient of nationalist concerns since the 1920s. Under the chairmanship of Ottawa journalist Grattan O'Leary, a Royal Commission was created to investigate the abuse of Canadian hospitality by American popular magazines, chiefly *Time* and *Reader's Digest*, which for the Canadian market had special editions carrying Canadian advertising. This practice was cultural branch-planting with a vengeance, and to solve it the O'Leary Commission looked to the less frequently used strategy within the nationalist arsenal: protectionism. It recommended that any foreign periodical containing advertising directed specifically at the Canadian market be denied entry into the country; and conversely, that any advertiser's expenses in such a periodical be ineligible for tax exemptions. The Diefenbaker government accepted the principal recommendations, but allowed *Time* and *Reader's Digest* special exemptions. It also failed to generate legislation, and the result was a controversy that would continue long after Diefenbaker had fallen from power.

By 1961, therefore, the federal government not only had implemented most of the Massey Report's major recommendations, but had experimented with all the possible strategies of a national cultural policy, from subsidies (the Canada Council) to protectionism (magazine policy) to regulated competition (the BBG). Of

these policies, subsidies unquestionably worked best. The Canada Council became a major success story, providing 'serious' Canadian artists, writers, scholars, and cultural organizations with a degree of support that was the envy of much of the Western world. As we shall see, the government also was prepared by 1961 to offer subsidies to other cultural areas, including sport. The main problem, of course, was that subsidies were expensive and created expectations that were hard to meet—even where high culture alone was concerned—in an era when cultural activity was expanding dramatically. By 1964, within less than 10 years of its creation, the Canada Council was spending well beyond its original endowment, and the Pearson government determined to fund the additional expenses out of annual parliamentary grants, which came to cover an increasing proportion of the Council's expenditures. In the process, the Council lost its independence of public control, at least over general policy.

SPORTS POLICY

Before 1961 Canadian governments showed little interest in Canadian sport. But in that year several distinct trends came together to produce Bill C-131, 'An Act to Encourage Fitness and Amateur Sport', which unanimously passed the House of Commons in September of that year.[28] In fact, none of Canada's political parties had on record any policy on sport or physical fitness. Nevertheless, the time was ripe for such legislation.

First, a number of Canadians had become concerned about declining physical fitness in Canada, and in June 1959 the Duke of Edinburgh, in a speech to the Canadian Medical Association, advocated taking steps to improve it. A second quite separate concern was the success of Canadian athletes in international competition, especially but not merely in hockey. Both the frequency and the intensity of international sporting competitions had grown enormously after 1945, not least because of the Cold War and the battle between the US (leading the 'Western democracies') and the USSR (leading the satellite states of Eastern Europe). By the 1950s Canadian hockey teams were getting beaten regularly by the Soviets, and in the 1960 Rome Olympics the entire Canadian Olympic team won but one silver medal. As internal political issues increasingly led Ottawa to seek out symbols of national unity, the performance (or lack of it) of Canadian teams at Olympics and in international competition became an obvious focus. In September 1961 Opposition leader Lester Pearson—who himself had played lacrosse and hockey while he was at Oxford—said that given

> all the publicity attached to international sport and the fact that certain societies, particularly the communist societies, use international sport, as they use everything else, for the advancement of prestige and political purposes, it is a matter of some consequence that we in Canada should do what we can to develop and regain the prestige we once had, to a greater extent than we now have in international competition.[29]

Finally, with the introduction of television, Canada's relative lack of success in international events for the first time became evident to large numbers of Canadians, many of whom would rather watch sports on the tube than actually play them. The 1961 legislation was designed to funnel $5 million annually to amateur sport and fitness—although the fitness element was mostly a smokescreen to cover the subsidies to sport.

Bill C-131 was phrased in general terms, because nobody involved had any clear policy in mind when the bill was passed, beyond encouraging the success of Canadian amateur athletes in international competition. The government turned direction over to a National Advisory Council established by the Act, mainly to distance itself from the various requests for financial support it was certain would come. By the later 1960s the Advisory Council had become unmanageable, especially as the public service

became increasingly involved in the funding. Federal–provincial cost-sharing programs got bogged down in constitutional haggling, and the governing bodies of the various sports simply did not have the expertise and experience to improve performance within their spheres.

By the later 1960s, national unity was front and centre on the Canadian agenda, and in 1968 Prime Minister Trudeau came to see sport in the context of culture and national unity. In the 1968 election campaign he had promised a task force to investigate amateur sport in Canada in the course of talking about culture and its connection to unity. Sport itself had changed by the end of the 1960s. Television's insatiable demand for programming had greatly increased the number of hours per week devoted to sports. The advantage of sport for national unity was that it did not cost a great deal of money to support, and it appeared to have a national audience. The report of Trudeau's task force emphasized 'how scant the previous involvement of the government [was] in encouraging the development of so potentially influential a psychological nation-builder'. The task force seemed mainly interested in professional hockey, of which it was highly critical. It did recommend the establishment of Hockey Canada to manage and finance Canada's national hockey teams. A subsequent Proposed Sports Policy for Canadians offered a whole section on national unity, as well as some new policies including direct assistance to sports governing bodies, increased subsidies for athletes, and the establishing of the Canada Games.

HOCKEY

Nothing could be more quintessentially Canadian than hockey. But that sport entered the post-war period in the hands of the American entertainment industry, and the script never really changed. The main function of organized hockey in Canada had been to supply players for the professional teams, which almost without exception were located in the largest North

OX VS. SWISS

■ Oxford University–Switzerland hockey game, *c.* 1922–3. Lester B. Pearson is at right front. LAC, PA-119892.

American cities. By 1950 Canadian teams had real representation only at the National Hockey League (NHL) level, with two of six teams: Toronto and Montreal. At the minor-league level, only Vancouver had a professional team. But in the two decades after 1950 two developments hit the game. In the 1950s the Europeans (especially the Soviets) became serious about hockey; in the 1960s the NHL expanded. Together these two developments finally forced Canadian governments to begin to develop a policy.

Hockey had been played internationally for many years, but in the early 1950s several European countries, particularly the USSR and Czechoslovakia, decided to enter the sport in a big way. Over the years Canada had occasionally participated in international tournaments. In 1930, for example, a team of University of Manitoba alumni won an international tournament

(without giving up a goal) and toured Europe afterwards, where it went undefeated. But in 1954 the USSR sent a national team to the international championships in Stockholm. The Canadian Amateur Hockey Association (CAHA) had sponsored a senior team from a Toronto suburb—the East York Lyndhursts—which had experienced trouble beating teams like the Ravina Ki-Y Flyers in its own league. The Lyndhursts were willing to pay their own expenses to play the Russians, Swedes, Finns, and Czechs, all of whom were heavily subsidized by their own governments and were regarded as instruments of national policy. Most of the few Canadians who knew anything about this tournament agreed that the Lyndhursts should be good enough—Canadians had invented the game, hadn't they? The Lyndhursts were indeed good enough to make the finals, but they were clobbered there 7–2 by the Soviet Union. The defeat electrified Canada, which had been so blasé about the game that no Canadian sportswriter had bothered to attend. In response to public outrage the Canadian government declared that it had no intention of interfering in, much less spending money on, hockey.[30]

Nevertheless, the Stockholm defeat put the world hockey tournament on the sports schedule for the Canadian public. Throughout the 1950s the CAHA sent teams—local senior amateur teams, but better than East York—that managed to win most of the time. The Penticton Vees revenged the 1954 defeat in 1955 with a 5–0 win over the Russians; the Whitby Dunlops beat the Russians 3–1 in Oslo in 1958, and the Belleville McFarlands defeated the Russians 3–1 in Prague in 1959. But these teams still had to finance their own way to Europe, and at best they were only semi-professional. Canadians told themselves that the pros would wipe the upstarts out. But the Europeans improved rapidly, and Canada did little to alter its own style of hockey to meet the growing challenge.

Two problems needed to be solved. The first was the organization of Canadian amateur hockey, designed mainly to produce players for the professionals. Most talented young players signed professional contracts, making them technically ineligible for international play. As later developments showed, the pro versus amateur distinction was probably less critical than the fact that the world tournament took place at the same time as the financially remunerative playoffs leading to the Stanley Cup, and American employers were not willing to lose their best players to a Canadian national team. Second, North American hockey had developed differently from the international game, although both had started from roughly the same Canadian rule book. North American audiences liked their hockey gladiatorial; they wanted it to be a contact sport, like American football. The Europeans, however, took soccer as their model: the rink was much larger, bodychecking was def-

initely limited, and the emphasis was on finesse and fast skating. Canadians trained for the professionally oriented game of bodily mayhem found it difficult to play by the international rules. They acquired reputations in Europe as goons and bullies; Canadian teams spent most of their European game time playing shorthanded because of penalties.

From hockey's perspective, the most important government action came when Hockey Canada was organized in 1972 to deal with the problem at the international level, including the organization of national teams (Team Canada had been created in the mid-1960s by Father David Bauer) and negotiations with the NHL for professional players. Spearheaded by lawyer and player agent Alan Eagleson, Hockey Canada—which made possible the 1972 Canada–Russia hockey series—was also a belated political response to major developments in the world of professional hockey. Among those developments was the decision by the NHL's Board of Directors (also the team owners) to expand beyond six teams in 1967. Other professional sports leagues in the US, such as those in baseball and football, had already expanded to new cities with new facilities. Sports events were exciting and photogenic, and—given television's need for program content—there was plenty of money to be made from American networks willing to bid against each other for exclusive broadcast rights.

Television may not have been the sole factor behind hockey expansion, but it clearly dictated the nature of that expansion, in which Canadian applicants such as Vancouver were turned down in favour of American cities such as Philadelphia, where there was no hockey tradition whatsoever. Despite public concern in Canada, no level of government wanted to tackle the corporate level of sport, and NHL expansion provoked little political response—except for the creation of Hockey Canada, which dealt only with contractual matters involving players and a national team.

Virtually all Canadians over the age of eight on 28 September 1972 know where they were and what they were doing on that day. Most—the largest television audience ever assembled in Canada—were glued to TV sets, hastily installed by factories, offices, shops, and schools right across the country. Others listened on radio, mesmerized by an unofficial sporting event, played for no historic trophy or recognized world title: the eighth and last game of the Canada–Russia hockey series. Only bragging rights were at stake. The first seven games had been played to a virtual standstill, Canada winning only one and drawing one of the first four games played on home ice, and then winning two of the first three played in Moscow. This final game was equally close. The Soviets took an early lead, the Canadians fought back, and Paul Henderson of the Toronto Maple Leafs scored the game—and series—winning goal with 34 seconds remaining in regulation time. Canadian national honour in Canada's national game was vindicated—if only barely. Given the country's pre-series expectations of an early victory by its finest professional players, who had never previously been allowed to compete against the Russians, the victory could also be interpreted as a defeat, insofar as Canada's assumptions about its hockey pre-eminence were shattered.[31]

In the long run, the 1972 series would completely alter the way Canadians played hockey and lead to reform of the rough style of play, the so-called 'goon' tactics, that had until then been standard. At the time, more than one observer wondered how Canada could allow its collective self-image to be placed at the mercy of a handful of professional athletes, most of whom collected their paycheques from foreign employers. The answer is that sport in general was a part of culture—popular culture—and hockey was an integral component of both the Canadian National Culture and the national psyche. Moreover, after 1945 hockey had shared many of the same problems and changes as other elements of culture in Canada. Considering the priority Canadians gave to hockey, the wonder was that it took Canadian governments so long to make it a subject of deliberate cultural policy.

OTHER NEW DIRECTIONS IN THE 1960s

At the same time that the federal government was defining and expanding a national cultural policy, devoted chiefly to fostering a distinctive Canadian identity in the face of the ubiquitous Americans, provinces and municipalities also became involved in cultural affairs in direct and indirect ways. The arts became a growth area everywhere for a variety of reasons. Cities and provinces, anxious to promote tourism and dispel foreign misconceptions of Canada as a cultural wilderness, built museums and auditoriums, often in conjunction with various anniversary celebrations. The most important new developments in cultural policy throughout most of the 1960s occurred below the national level and went relatively unheralded—though all levels of government greatly increased their expenditures on arts and culture, particularly during the Centennial celebrations of 1967.

FILM

The Pearson government's effort to encourage feature film production in Canada was taken over by the Trudeau government as the Canadian Film Development Corporation (CFDC), which was given $10 million, the cost of about five Hollywood movies of the late 1960s, to subsidize Canadian feature film production. The films it backed were supposed not only to make money but to articulate a Canadian cultural identity—two objectives not necessarily compatible. When push came to shove, the CFDC opted for the language of commerce, its executive director, Michael Spencer, emphasizing 'any film that has a chance of developing the Canadian film industry, even if that film is not particularly interpretive of Canada to Canadians, would still be considered and possibly invested in by us.'[32] Investment was a maximum of $300,000, and by October 1971 the CFDC had exhausted its fund, investing in 64 films, only three of which made a profit. Some of the films were quite good: Don

Shebib's *Goin' Down the Road*, Claude Jutra's *Kamouraska*, Peter Carter's *The Rowdyman*. With an average budget of just over $250,000, in Hollywood terms these films were made on a shoestring. Hollywood was not interested in distributing them. Claude Jutra confessed, 'Not making the films you should be making is awful, but making them and not having them shown is worse.'[33] When the money ran out, so, for all intents and purposes, did the CFDC program. It had demonstrated that good films could be made, but not that they would be seen. Canada proved unwilling to experiment seriously with either exhibition quotas or box-office levies, both of which were seen by the industry as unpopular with the general public.

CANADIAN CONTENT

In 1968–9 the 'new broom' of the Trudeau administration produced some fine-tuning adjustments to the existing federal system of cultural policy. It studied sport and fitness and produced a landmark report. The Social Sciences and Humanities Research Council was hived off from the Canada Council in 1968. The Broadcasting Act of 1968 replaced the BBG with the Canadian Radio-Television Commission (CRTC), which would regulate all broadcasting without having to deal with the CBC Board of Governors. The 1968 legislation insisted that Canadian broadcasting must be owned and operated by Canadians, and in 1970 the CRTC redefined its content rules so that 60 per cent of all television

■ A folk art festival during Canada's Centennial celebrations, Toronto, 18 Aug. 1967. Frank Grant/LAC E001098960.

programming (in prime time as well as overall) had to be Canadian in origin, and 30 per cent of all music played on radio had to have some Canadian involvement in the production. The rules encouraged new Canadian work, and Canadian music and musicians, although in television they led mainly to clones of cheap and outdated American shows. The CRTC also began to be concerned about a form of broadcasting that had been previously ignored: the Community Antenna Systems (usually known as 'cable television'). Cable TV had initially been developed in Canada to enable remote areas to receive Canadian transmissions, but its market success had come in the early 1960s in the populated urban regions, where it permitted viewers to receive a full menu of distant American stations for one monthly fee. North Americans had

debated 'pay television' for several decades, but here it was quietly operating away. By 1968 cable was increasing its market share without regulation, and the CRTC would not succeed in controlling it until the 1970s.

THE DISCOVERY OF FOLK CULTURE

A final addition to Canadian cultural policy came in the later 1960s with the government's discovery of folk culture, particularly within the ethnic communities of Canada. Though the Royal Commission on Bilingualism and Biculturalism was briefed to promote the ideal of bilingualism throughout Canada, the Commission had another mandate on which it reported in the volume entitled *Cultural Contributions of Other Ethnic Groups* (1970). It recognized the richness of other ethnic cultures, and in 1971 it led to a new federal policy on multiculturalism, in 1972 to a separate minister, and in 1973 to a Multiculturalism Directorate in the office of the Secretary of State. In this context, the concern of the B&B Commission, and of subsequent federal policy, was less to preserve culture in the anthropological sense than to maintain the 'cultural heritage' of ethnic groups—music, dance, costumes, foods, and celebratory traditions. Quite independent of government policy, in 1970 Winnipeg organized the first large-scale multicultural festival in Canada as part of Manitoba's Centennial celebrations. 'Folklorama' rapidly became a major tourist attraction, was imitated elsewhere, and ethnic culture in general became another way to promote Canada around the world.

Much of the 'ethnic' culture celebrated in the 1960s was associated with relatively recent immigrants—but not all. A resurgence of interest occurred in traditional folk culture in many provinces, notably in Quebec and the Atlantic region, especially Newfoundland. Significant collecting of traditional culture had begun early in the twentieth century, led by anthropologist Marius Barbeau and the National Museum, especially in Quebec and among west coast Aboriginal groups, and considerable work also had been done in the Maritimes and Newfoundland by American and British collectors, as well as by collectors such as Helen Creighton and Kenneth Peacock under National Museum auspices. Part of the renewed interest could be attributed to the counterculture's rejection of industrial capitalism in favour of rural, pre-industrial roots. In Newfoundland this movement had the additional political edge of preserving and celebrating the culture of the outports, which were under heavy pressure from the government of Premier Smallwood to modernize. The first full-fledged university folklore department in Canada—at Memorial University in St John's—conserved and studied Newfoundland song, legend, and language. One of its major achievements would be an extensive dictionary of Newfoundland English.[34] This interest in folk culture was simul-taneously progressive in its acceptance of diversity, conservative in its celebration of pre-modern traditions, and nationalistic in its search for historic justifications of separate cultures.[35] At the same time, some of the tradition of folk culture 'recovered' by the folklorists—such as Inuit art or Haida totemic sculpture—was really 'invented' or 'reintroduced' to the cultures in its new self-consciousness, as artists were not only encouraged but in some cases even taught to work in the older forms. The most important development in First Nations art, as we shall see in the next chapter, was the move out of an ethnographic context in museums into a new creative autonomy exhibited in art galleries.

QUEBEC CULTURAL POLICY

In Quebec, not surprisingly, cultural policy quickly became an important ingredient of the Quiet Revolution. The Liberal campaign platform of 1960 stressed national development and declared it 'the duty of the Government of this Province to evaluate what we possess . . . so that it may be developed in such a manner that Quebec may . . . grow in the path of its traditions, its spirit and its culture.'[36] The first section of the platform, titled 'La Vie nationale' in French, was called 'Education and Culture' in English. The Lesage team promised educational reform in a section that began by advocating the establishment of a 'Department of Cultural Affairs', which would be no simple agency but rather an umbrella ministry for various agencies concerned with the nationalist direction of cultural affairs. The nationalist rhetoric of the platform did not draw much attention from contemporaries, probably because it was not expected to be implemented. But within months of assuming office, the Liberal government began to implement the creation of a department of cultural affairs. Lesage's speech to the Quebec Legislative Assembly made reference to the need not only to safeguard the French fact but to 'improve and assert it'. It also insisted that French Canada's culture was part of the larger Canadian defence against the US: 'our English-Canadian brothers know that the French-Canadian collectivity, if it continues to assert itself, will aid them . . . to counter an exceptionally grave danger, a sickness already present in us which constantly menaces our Canadian identity: the American cultural invasion.'[37] The new agency was intended to promote a cultural revival of French Canada that would find expression both within Quebec and outside it. Among its concerns would be the protection and development of the French language. Almost all observers in Quebec thought that the appropriate agency to protect French-Canadian culture (however that was to be defined) was the government of Quebec, and thus favoured the legislation.

As might have been anticipated, deciding to promote and protect French-Canadian culture was far easier than deciding what that would entail. The legislation creating the Ministry of Cultural Affairs had defined the ministry's mandate in one sentence: 'The minister shall promote the development of arts and letters in the Province and their diffusion abroad.' High culture and the French language were at the heart of most people's definition of Quebec national culture, leading to the establishment of an arts council and a French language bureau. Most of the conceptual problems were familiar enough, although expressed in the particular context of French Canada. The subsequent debate over *joual* was symptomatic. For many in Quebec, like Frère Untel, *joual* was an abomination, an illustration of what happened when anglicized commercialization was allowed to contaminate the French language and civilization. For others, however, *joual* was the symbol of a living language that actually had some meaning for ordinary French Canadians. While the intellectuals attacked it, the writers and artists of the province embraced both *joual* and the new conception of a culture that it represented. The term 'French-Canadian culture' came increasingly to mean the values and beliefs of the society as a whole.

CONCLUSION

Cultural policy before 1970 was characterized by only the most imprecise considerations of financial cost. For the most part, cultural agencies were expected to keep expenses manageable by avoiding the arena of popular culture, where, most commentators agreed, Canadians could not afford to compete with Americans. Within the realm of 'serious' culture, Canadian governments at all levels were prepared to spend large amounts of money to meet international standards, and to a considerable extent they succeeded. Whether the culture that resulted was *Canadian* culture was, of course, another matter.

SHORT BIBLIOGRAPHY

Canada. *Report of the Royal Commission on National Development in the Arts, Letters and Sciences*. Toronto, 1951. The classic Royal Commission report.

Canada. *Report of the Royal Commission on Broadcasting*. Ottawa, 1957. A fascinating study of broadcasting and broadcasting policy in the mid-1950s.

Finlay, Karen. *The Force of Culture: Vincent Massey and Canadian Sovereignty*. Toronto, 2004. A full discussion of cultural policy and sovereignty in post-war Canada.

Handler, Richard. *Nationalism and the Politics of Culture in Quebec*. Madison, Wis., 1988. An excellent study of the origins of cultural politics in Quebec.

Litt, Paul. *The Muses, The Masses, and the Massey Commission*. Toronto, 1992. A useful analysis of the Massey Commission's work, suitably skeptical of its overall influence.

Macintosh, Donald, with Tom Bedecki and C.E.S. Franks. *Sport and Politics in Canada: Federal Government Involvement since 1961*. Montreal and

Kingston, 1987. The first and best study of the origins of sports policy in Canada, emphasizing how sport moved under the cultural umbrella in the 1960s.

McLuhan, Marshall. *Understanding Media: The Extension of Mass Man*. New York, 1964. McLuhan's most brilliant book, elusive, illusive, and allusive.

Magder, Ted. *Canada's Hollywood: The Canadian State and Feature Films*. Toronto, 1993. A first-rate account of Canadian film policy in the late 1960s and early 1970s.

Morton, W.L. *The Canadian Identity*. Toronto, 1961. A conventional effort in 1961 to understand the meaning of the Canadian identity.

Park, Julian, ed. *The Culture of Contemporary Canada*. Toronto, 1957. A collection of essays surveying Canadian culture in the 1950s, emphasizing mainly how out of step the academy was with what was going on in the nation.

Tippett, Maria. *Making Culture: English-Canadian Institutions and the Arts before the Massey Commission*. Toronto, 1990. A superb account of English-Canadian culture before Massey, emphasizing that the Royal Commission had a substantial foundation on which to build.

Young, Scott. *War on Ice: Canada in International Hockey*. Toronto, 1976. A useful survey of Canada in international hockey, by Neil's dad.

STUDY QUESTIONS

1. How many different sorts of culture can you readily identify?

2. Why was culture such a big issue in post-war Canada?

3. How does the Tremblay Commission on Constitutional Problems structure its argument that the constitutional problems between Quebec and Canada are fundamentally problems of culture?

4. In what ways was Vincent Massey an appropriate choice to chair the Royal Commission on the Arts, Letters and Sciences?

5. In what ways was the Massey Commission report elitist?

6. What were the three strategies that Canada used in the 1950s to advance Canadian culture?

7. How did sport become part of overall cultural policy in Canada?

8. Did Quebec have a vision of culture different from English Canada?

CHAPTER NINETEEN

The Making of Canadian Culture, 1945–1972

■ Between 1946 and 1972 Canada discovered that culture was important at the same time that Canadian culture came into its own. The extent to which those two developments were connected has never been entirely clear. In these years a fully elaborated infrastructure for elite culture was put into place, and Canadian cultural production in art, music, and letters began to receive international recognition. At the same time Canadian universities expanded dramatically and became hotbeds of cultural activity, providing employment for thousands of cultural producers. Even the production of popular culture in Canada began to flourish.

THE CULTURE OF THE ELITE

The term 'culture of the elite' comes from Quebec's 1954 Tremblay Commission report, which postulated an interesting relationship between the high or elite culture 'representative of humanity's greatest ideals' and the 'common culture which is that of the mass'. Unlike the majority of their contemporaries, for whom elite culture was synonymous with culture itself, the commissioners considered the common culture 'made up of knowledge, means of expression, and values blended into a tradition of life' to be the fundamental one. Furthermore, they identi-

fied a mutually beneficial relationship between the two kinds of culture:

> The level of the common culture tends all the more to elevate itself to the extent that an active élite, through its works, specific action and general influence, incites it to surpass itself. In return, there is all the more chance of the élite increasing in quality and number as the level of the common culture itself becomes more elevated.[1]

Nevertheless, until the 1960s most Canadians recognized only elite culture as a proper culture, either consigning mass or pop culture to a much lower level or ignoring them altogether. As fundraisers for the institutions of elite culture fully recognized, people, including successful business people, who had not been raised around elite culture often held it in very high esteem. Supporting elite culture became a major mark of status for an increasingly affluent and sophisticated society, and there were those who argued that by 1970 certain forms of elite culture (symphony orchestras, ballet, art museums, opera) had become so democratized as to have shifted over into the realm of popular culture. Whether or not such democratization made elite culture less elite, in some areas it militated against experimentation with new forms (atonal music, for example).

TIMELINE

1946
F.R. Scott attempts to organize a gathering of writers.

1947
Paul-Émile Borduas and 15 others issue *Refus global.*

1950
Canadian Co-operation Project founded in Hollywood.

1952
Canadian Broadcasting Corporation opens first television stations in Canada.

1953
Stratford Festival founded. Winnipeg Ballet renamed Royal Winnipeg Ballet.

1955
First Canadian Writers' Conference held at Queen's University. Les Plasticiens manifesto issued in Quebec.

1956
The *Tamarack Review* founded.

1958
Les Grands Ballets Canadiens established. The first of the regional theatres (the Manitoba Theatre Centre) is founded.

1959
Mordecai Richler publishes *The Apprenticeship of Duddy Kravitz.*

1960
Jock Macdonald retrospective at the Art Gallery of Toronto.

1961
Margaret Laurence publishes *The Stone Angel*. W.L. Morton publishes *The Canadian Identity*.

1965
Literary History of Canada, written collectively, first published.

1967
Mr. Dressup begins on CBC. NHL expands to 12 teams.

1968
Leonard Cohen's first record album, *Songs of Leonard Cohen*, is released.

1971
Alice Munro publishes *Lives of Girls and Women*.

1972
Margaret Atwood publishes *Survival: A Thematic Guide to Canadian Literature*.

Many contemporary artists were ignored by the public because they were too avant-garde, while millions of dollars were spent on lavish productions of nineteenth-century Italian operas.

THE LITERARY SCENE IN ENGLISH CANADA

After the war Canadian writers were published in ever-growing numbers, some earning both criti-cal acclaim and commercial success. Beginning to 'create' Canada in the way that Nathaniel Hawthorne, a century earlier, helped to create New England,[2] they described a nation of regional cultures, united perhaps above all by a feeling for the land. The list of the Governor General's Award winners in fiction in these years contains a number of Canadian novels that have become classics. But in spite of these successes, the market for—and interest in—works of literature by Canadian writers was not strong, especially outside the country. Only a few of the larger publishing houses—among them Ryerson Press, McClelland and Stewart, Macmillan Canada, Clarke, Irwin, and (for poetry) Oxford University Press—regularly published Canadian writers.

Apart from a group of poets centred in Montreal, there was almost no sense of a literary community in post-war English Canada. Among the reasons were the sheer size of the country across which writers were scattered and the absence of wider-circulation literary review journals and major academic journals concentrating on Canadian literature. This absence of community was first noticed by F.R. Scott, whose efforts to organize a gathering of writers in 1946 did not bear fruit until a three-day Canadian Writers' Conference was held at Queen's University in July 1955. In bringing together some hundred delegates—poets, novelists, publishers, editors, critics, librarians, and interested members of the public—this Kingston Conference was a milestone. The papers from the conference were published in *Writing in Canada* (1956), edited by the poet and scholar George Whalley, who organized them in three sections: 'The Writer', 'The Writer's Media', and 'The Writer and the Public'. Though no problems were solved, the first steps towards creating a literary community had been taken.

At the time of the Writers' Conference, the leading literary magazine was *Northern Review* (1945–56). But in 1956 its editor, John Sutherland, died, and Robert Weaver founded *Tamarack Review* (1956–82), which featured stories, poems, interviews, essays, and reviews. *Tamarack Review* published the early, sometimes the first, work of several leading Canadian writers. The second issue contained Alice Munro's well-known story 'Thanks for the Ride', and an interview (by Nathan Cohen) with Mordecai Richler, who was living in London, England. Some of Richler's remarks indicate the lassitude of Canadian publishers where fiction by young writers was concerned:

I have had one experience with a Canadian publisher. When *The Acrobats* had been accepted here I was in Canada, and André Deutsch wrote to me to visit the Canadian distributor. I spent a day in Toronto and went to visit him. And the first question from this man who distributes books for— well, a dozen very reputable publishers—the first question he asked me about my novel was 'It is a thick book?' Because Canadians like thick books. The second question he asked was are there any Communists in it and is it anti-Canadian? The whole thing was ridiculous. The system of publishing in Canada and the system of awards is just a joke.[3]

Richler specialized in sending up Canadian institutions. However, *The Apprenticeship of Duddy Kravitz* (1959) met with great popular success (though it did not win a Governor General's Award) and established Richler as a major writer. Duddy Kravitz entered Canadian folklore. Richler was not the first Canadian novelist to mine the rich vein of ethnicity, particularly Jewish, but he was the first to mythologize the urban ghetto, its inhabitants, and its way of life. In 1966 he confessed: 'No matter how long I continue to live abroad, I do feel forever rooted in Montreal's St Urbain Street. This was my time, my place, and I have elected to get it exactly right.'[4] *St Urbain's Horseman*, arguably his best novel, was published in 1971.

Margaret Laurence was another major new novelist of the period. Having lived with her husband in Somalia and Ghana from 1950 to 1957, she was living in Vancouver when her African novel, *This Side Jordan* (1960), appeared. Soon afterwards she completed the first of the four 'Manawaka novels' that brought her international acclaim. Laurence was arguably the first Canadian writer who made her way to the world stage, even being considered a suitable candidate for the Nobel Prize in literature. *The Stone Angel* (1961), *A Jest of God* (1966), *The Fire-Dwellers* (1969), and *The Diviners* (1974) could be read on many levels and were easily the most richly tex-

■ Earle Birney, E.J. Pratt, Irving Layton, and Leonard Cohen on Bloor Street in Toronto in the 1950s.

tured fiction ever produced by a Canadian writer. Like Richler, Laurence created a place out of what she knew. The mythical Prairie town of Manawaka was a strongly conceived entity in itself, linking some powerful female protagonists struggling against its hypocritical Scots-Canadian constrictions and their own past. Noting that she was not much aware that her writing was Canadian, Laurence once commented: 'this seems a good thing to me, for it suggests that one has been writing out of a background so closely known that no explanatory tags are necessary.'⁵

Also in this period Mavis Gallant, with *The Other Paris* (1956) and *My Heart Is Broken* (1964), and Alice Munro, with *Dance of the Happy Shades* (1968) and *Lives of Girls and Women* (1971), established the foundations of their present international standing among the best writers of short stories in English. With a much smaller readership than fiction commanded, poetry not only held its own but acquired a substantial audience. Irving Layton, Earle Birney, and Al Purdy were sent on reading tours by their publishers, and became almost as adept at performance as at writing.

Performance of a different kind took over the career of Leonard Cohen, who straddled the worlds of high and pop culture when he set some of his poems to music, wrote new songs, and sang them to his own guitar accompaniment. Cohen published his first book of poetry, *Let Us Compare Mythologies*, in 1956 at the age of 22. It was followed in the sixties by two novels, including the haunting *Beautiful Losers* (1966), and several poetry collections that were especially appealing to the younger generation in their imagery and themes. In 1968, the year he refused a Governor General's Award for his *Selected Poems*, his first record album, *Songs of Leonard Cohen*, appeared, to be soon followed by *Songs from a Room* (1969). A few of his songs had already been performed by Joan Baez and Judy Collins, but Cohen's own chanting baritone was the perfect vehicle for popularizing them. By 1970 he was competing successfully with other pop poet-singers like Bob Dylan, Donovan Leitch, and Paul McCartney, and songs such as 'Suzanne', 'The Master Song', 'It Seems So Long Ago, Nancy', and 'Bird on a Wire' entered the vocabulary of the counterculture. Cohen captured youth's scorn for hypocrisy, and his songs counselled survival by withdrawal from the contests of life into a private world of the artist, not in triumph but in endurance through ceremony and self-understanding. These were powerful messages for the Woodstock generation. Ironically, while Cohen's songs contained almost no Canadian references, his self-deprecation and self-abnegation were frequently seen as essentially Canadian traits deeply rooted in his persona.

Concurrently with all this new writing, the subject of Canadian literature came to be considered in terms of its history and long-neglected writings. McClelland and Stewart's enduring New Canadian Library series began in 1958, offering mainly reprints of classic novels but also some brief critical studies of individual authors. *Canadian Literature*, 'the first review devoted only to the study of Canadian writers and writing', was founded in 1959 by George Woodcock. The collectively written *Literary History of Canada* was published by the University of Toronto Press in 1965. At the beginning of his 'Conclusion' to the first edition of this work, Northrop Frye wrote:

> The book is a tribute to the maturity of Canadian literary scholarship and criticism, whatever one thinks of the literature. Its authors have completely outgrown the view that evaluation is the end of criticism, instead of its incidental by-product. Had evaluation been their guiding principle, this book would, if written at all, have been only a huge debunking project, leaving Canadian literature a poor naked alouette plucked of every feather of decency and dignity. True, the book gives evidence, on practically every one of its eight hundred odd pages, that what is really remarkable is not how little but how much good writing has been produced in Canada.

And at the end:

> For present and future writers in Canada and their readers, what is important in Canadian literature, beyond the merits of individual works in it, is the inheritance of the entire enterprise. The writers featured in this book have identified the habits and attitudes of the country, as Fraser and Mackenzie have identified its rivers. They have also left an imaginative legacy of dignity and of high courage.[6]

By 1970 virtually every Canadian university offered an undergraduate course in Canadian literature, and a critical canon had more or less been established, which naturally emphasized the 'distinctively Canadian' qualities of Canadian writing.

Without the new breed of scholarly critics

■ Margaret Atwood and Mordecai Richler, 1968.

who were prepared to take Canadian writing seriously—as well as the subsidies that helped sustain authors, critics, scholars, and journals—that writing would probably have developed far more slowly. Before the 1950s few scholars and critics in Canada were prepared to devote much attention to writing in their own country. The change was doubtless symbiotic, with both the writing and the critical approach improving and reinforcing one another simultaneously. One leading critic, George Woodcock, insisted on not 'getting caught in the trap of a narrow nationalism', maintaining that 'the study of Canadian literature is merely the study of writers who happen to live and work in Canada.'[7] But inevitably the bias of

Canadian literary scholarship and criticism was in favour of those who, in one way or another, interpreted the Canadian identity. Northrop Frye stated in a 1959 review of poetry that 'the centre of reality is wherever one happens to be, and its circumference is whatever one's imagination can make sense of.'[8] According to this logic, a Canadian-based writer would have to reflect Canada somehow. For many critics, the challenge was to reveal quintessential Canadian-ness in the imaginative element of the literature.

Some critical writing showed as much imagination as the literature. Notable in this regard was Margaret Atwood's *Survival: A Thematic Guide to Canadian Literature* (1972), which completely altered the traditional terms of debate over the Canadian character. Although others (such as Frye and Woodcock) had occasionally turned to Canadian literature to explain the nation's psyche, Atwood was the first to set such an analysis squarely in the writing itself. Her basic assumption was that in writing the reader saw 'not the writer but himself, and behind his own image in the foreground, a reflection of the world he lives in'. Atwood thus made the great leap from literary themes to the collective persona in positing the central patterns of Canada (and Canadian literature) as survival within the context of victimization. Among the exploiters of the Canadian victim, obviously, were the Americans, although Atwood preferred not to be very explicit on this point.

The Americans may have had a unifying symbol in the Frontier, while the British had The Island. But for Canada, wrote Atwood, the central symbol was Survival/Survivance. Outlining through literary examples what she called the 'basic victim positions'—from denial through interpreting victimization as fair through refusing to accept the victim's role as inevitable to becoming a creative non-victim—Atwood offered many seemingly unsystematic insights that added up to a new way of perceiving the Canadian psyche. Many of these insights involved contrasting Canadian literary perspectives with those in Britain and especially the US. In discussing immigrant novels, for example, she argued that while American immigrants could escape into a new identity, English-speaking Canadians had no alternative identity to assume. And, she suggested, whereas Americans wrote about Amerindians as either noble savages or inferior beings, Canadians treated Aboriginal people either as instruments of Nature the Monster or as victims. Atwood's accomplishment was impressive. Not only did she successfully link feminism, Canadian nationalism, and not-Americanism, but she also turned Canada's creative writers—rather than its politicians or historians—into its cultural makers and cultural arbiters.

In his 'Conclusion' to the *Literary History*'s much expanded second edition of 1976, Northrop Frye noted 'the colossal verbal explosion that has taken place in Canada since 1960'. It was this growth, as well as the nationalistic climate that developed before and after Centennial Year, 1967, that encouraged the establishment of small publishing enterprises across the country. As a result, Toronto would no longer be the power base for all English-language publishing. At the same time, certain established Ontario houses were facing a financial crisis. The oldest, Ryerson Press—supported by the United Church of Canada—was so much in debt that it was sold in 1970 to the American firm McGraw-Hill. In the same year, just as the Ontario government was appointing a Royal Commission on Book Publishing (1970), it was forced to rescue McClelland and Stewart from an American takeover.

Despite the financial support provided by both Ottawa (through agencies such as the Canadian Book Publishing Development Program and the Canada Council) and provincial governments (through agencies such as the Ontario Arts Council), Canadian publishing was in a chronically precarious state. Together, the relatively small market for English-language books, the enormous volume of American and British (as well as Canadian) books available, the dominance of foreign-owned publishers, and the policy of full return of unsold books put Canadian-owned publishers at a competitive disadvantage. Fortunately this did not discourage many more publishers from setting up business through the 1970s and 1980s as more and more Canadian writers emerged with publishable manuscripts. Even those writers who became successful in the US faced disadvantages, since the American publishers would sell their leftover books from large print runs (known as 'remainders') in Canada at a fraction of the price the Canadian publisher was still asking for the same book. Publishers in Quebec, on the other hand, experienced less difficulty than those in the rest of Canada, despite

■ Marie-Claire Blais.

the small market, for apparently the people of Quebec were more willing to buy books in order to read about themselves.

WRITING IN QUEBEC

The immediate post-war era was also a turning point in French-Canadian fiction, marking an end to the century-old tradition of the *roman de la fidélité* pledged to safeguarding the survival of the French-Canadian people by celebrating their customs, traditions, and faith. In 1945 Germaine Guèvremont struck one of the final blows at that tradition in her novel *Le Survenant*, in which the

arrival of a stranger initiates the disintegration of a rural family in a traditional community. Two other novels published around the same time made the break with tradition complete by focusing on underprivileged working-class characters in urban settings: Roger Lemelin's *Au pied de la pente douce* (1944) and Gabrielle Roy's *Bonheur d'occasion* (1945). All three novels were published in English translation—as *The Outlander*, *The Town Below*, and *The Tin Flute*, respectively—and were widely read in English Canada, as were the succeeding books of Roy and Lemelin. Another important novel of the period was *Poussière sur la ville* (1953) by André Langevin—translated as *Dust over the City*—which was set in the asbestos-mining town of Thetford Mines. But the sensation of the decade was *La Belle Bête*, published in 1959 by the 20-year-old Marie-Claire Blais, which astonished the reading public—no less in its English translation, *Mad Shadows*—and scandalized the clergy for its portrayal of characters representing various kinds of moral and physical ugliness, and for its powerful impressionistic scenes of betrayal, disfigurement, pyromania, murder, and suicide. With this novel Blais began a long and prolific career. Blais was 'discovered' outside Quebec by the American critic Edmund Wilson, who in his *O Canada: An American's Notes on Canadian Culture* (1964) observed that Blais showed herself 'incapable of allowing life in French Canada to appear in a genial light or to seem to embody any sort of ideal'.[9] A few years later the novelist Claire Martin published two books that were scathing indictments of the ways in which Quebec's traditional institutions—family and Church—abused the young.

The effect of the Quiet Revolution on Quebec writing was considerable, although in fact the influence was reciprocal: one fuelled the other. The literary transformation that began in this decade and continued through the 1970s and 1980s—the anger and violence of language and subject matter, radical changes in syntax and formal structure, the freeing of style and content from the constraints of tradition—both mirrored

CLAIRE MARTIN (1914–)

❖

One of the most influential Quebec writers of the 1960s, virtually unknown in English Canada, was Claire Martin. Born Claire Montreuil in Quebec City in 1914, she was educated in boarding schools run by the Ursulines and the Sisters of the Congrégation de Notre-Dame. In two autobiographical volumes published in the 1960s she described in detail the various abuses, emotional and physical, to which the nuns subjected their students, as well as the abuse she suffered at the hands of her despotic father. Punishment at home was always the same, she wrote:

> It began with openhanded blows which immediately became very heavy, then, getting into the swing of it, blows with the closed fist, and if he got really swinging he would finish off with kicks that sent us skidding from one room to the next all through the downstairs."

Martin eventually had a successful career as a radio announcer, and began writing seriously when she married and lived in Ottawa. In 1958 she published a book of short stories, *Avec ou sans amour*, which won immediate recognition and the Prix du Cercle du livre de France. Most critics feel that her best fiction was published during the 1960s. In 1966 she won a Governor General's Award for the first of her autobiographical volumes, *Dans un gant de fer* (translated as *In an Iron Glove*)— ironically, in the fiction category. Apparently the judges could not bring themselves to believe that Quebec fathers and church schools had ever engaged in the systematic terrorism of the young that Martin described.

The revisionist picture of traditional Quebec society that Martin presented fitted well into both the critical and liberationist currents of thought in the Quebec of the 1960s. In her fiction she reversed roles, presenting women as unfaithful companions and men as the submissive figures in relationships. *Quand j'aurai payé ton visage* (1962, translated as *The Legacy*) dealt with incest and other family issues that in the past had been subject to the strictest taboos. Martin typically wrote in the first person, often using a male voice to sustain the narration and multiple voices to enrich it. In her autobiography, which created something of a sensation at the time of publication, she employed a single female voice that spoke unremittingly of being different, abused, and misunderstood. Martin moved to France in 1972, where she translated the work of her English-Canadian colleagues Margaret Laurence, Robertson Davies, and Clark Blaise into French, before returning to Quebec in 1982.

and fostered the spirit of liberation and the new goals of Quebec society.[10] And this work was no longer called French-Canadian but Québécois fiction. The journal *Parti pris* (1963–8), founded just after the first wave of FLQ bombings with an *indépendantiste* and Marxist perspective, published in January 1965 a special issue entitled *Pour une literature québécoise*—giving a name, which was quickly adopted, to the current and future works of francophone writers in Quebec. That issue also there was a strong reaction, in Canada and elsewhere, among young painters against figurative and representational painting, even in the works of the modernist painters in France. This reaction took the form of abstractionism and had its first expression, during the war, in the surrealist paintings of several young Montreal artists, whose teachers were Alfred Pellan at the École des beaux-arts and Paul-Émile Borduas at the École du meuble. As early as 1942, Borduas had said that what was required was a kind of stream of consciousness—an 'automatic painting that permits the plastic expression of images, of memories assimilated by the artist and which make up the sum of his psychic and intellectual being'.[12] He attracted a group of young painters —including his own students Marcel Barbeau and Jean-Paul Riopelle, as well as Pierre Gauvreau and Fernand Leduc from the École des beaux-arts. This group came to be called Les Automatistes after a small group show in an apartment on Sherbrooke Street West in February–March 1947. The show included a Borduas canvas *Automatisme 1.47* (also known as *Sous le vent de l'île*), a classic surrealist painting that is now in the National Gallery of Canada. Before the end of the year, Borduas struck out against all the religious and political inhibitions that constrained his creative life by writing perhaps the single most important manifesto of modern Quebec, *Refus global*. Four hundred copies were put on sale in August 1948.

Written in late 1947 and signed by 15 members of his group, *Refus global* is a rambling series of passionate, almost poetic utterances attacking virtually everything in Quebec society at the time. Borduas described the province where he was born as 'a colony trapped within the slippery walls of fear, the customary refuge of the vanquished', condemned by the restrictive powers of the Church. He called for both the artist's personal liberation and a social revolution:

> Break permanently with the customs of society, disassociate yourself from its utilitarian values.

■ Paul-Émile Borduas, c. 1958, from Jacques Godbout's film *Paul-Émile Borduas*. Produced by Fernand Dansereau. © 1962 National Film Board of Canada. All rights reserved.

promoted the use of *joual* in creative writing. According to the poet Paul Chamberland, one of the founding editors, 'any language must be shaken to its very foundations through the disfigurement inherent in our common speech, and in the lives of all of us.' Most of this literary explosion went unheeded in English-speaking Canada, partly because of the scarcity (and difficulty) of translation, but also—one suspects—because the spirit behind it was so unfamiliar.

PAINTING: THE ASCENDANCY OF THE NON-OBJECTIVE

The Quiet Revolution of the 1960s had an interesting connection with the painting community of Montreal of a decade earlier. After the war

Refuse to live knowingly beneath the level of our spiritual and physical potential. Refuse to close your eyes to the vices, the frauds perpetrated under the guise of learning, favour, or gratitude. Refuse to live in the isolation of the artistic ghetto, a place fortified but too easily shunted aside. Refuse to be silent—make of us what you please, but you must understand us—refuse glory, honours (the first compromise): stigmata of malice, unawareness, servility. Refuse to serve, to be made use of for such ends. Refuse every INTENTION, pernicious weapon of reason. Down with them both, to second place!

MAKE WAY FOR MAGIC! MAKE WAY FOR OBJECTIVE MYSTERIES! MAKE WAY FOR LOVE! MAKE WAY FOR NECESSITIES!

. . . The self-seeking action remains with its author—it is stillborn. Passionate acts take wing by their own energy. We cheerfully take the entire responsibility for tomorrow. . . . In the meantime, without rest or cessation, in a community of feeling with those who thirst for a better existence, without fear of a long deferment, in the face of encouragement or persecution, we will pursue in joy our desperate need for liberation.[13]

The next month, Borduas was fired from the École du meuble on the instruction of Paul Sauvé, Minister of Social Welfare and Youth (and Duplessis's eventual successor as Premier in 1959). In 1953 Borduas moved to New York, where he was influenced by American abstract expressionists, and began his famous series of black-and-white paintings. In 1955 he moved to Paris, where his steady application to painting was rewarded by growing international recognition through numerous one-man shows. He died in 1960, too soon to witness the cultural liberation he had advocated, never realizing that he would become a hero of the 1960s counterculture, or that with his *Refus global* modern Quebec could be said symbolically to have come into being.

Automatisme gradually dissolved after *Refus global*, as its exponents moved on geographically and spiritually. Some young painters were not satisfied with the combination of spontaneity and traditional spatial perspectives advocated by Borduas. Led by Fernand Leduc, in 1955 they produced a manifesto, signed Les Plasticiens, that was not inflammatory, like *Refus global*, but which also insisted on artistic freedom. Acknowledging the importance of Borduas, they said that they were drawn to 'plastic qualities: tone, texture, forms, lines, and the final unity between elements'.[14] They came increasingly to appreciate the importance of structure in their painting, insisting that abstractionism constituted a more objective version of reality by probing beneath the superficial. When a famous 'Art abstrait' show was held in Montreal in 1959, the Plasticiens disappeared and a new group became prominent, with Guido Molinari and Claude Tousignant eventually joining the ranks of the leading painters of the country. Abstractionism was no longer regarded as particularly avant-garde, but had become part of the mainstream, not only in Quebec but in Canada generally.

In the 1940s the rest of country—even Toronto, although Borduas exhibited there frequently—was isolated from the energy and innovation of the French-Canadian painters in Montreal. But on the west coast one painter was attracted by non-objective art. Scottish-born Jock (J.W.G.) Macdonald came to Canada in 1926 to head the design department of the Vancouver School of Decorative and Applied Arts, and in 1930 took up painting. He soon began experimenting with automatic painting and was encouraged by Lawren Harris, who moved to Vancouver in 1940. In 1947—the year Macdonald exhibited 36 of his abstracts at the San Francisco Museum of Art—he moved to teach drawing and painting at the Ontario College of Art. There he became the mentor of William Ronald, encouraging him to study for six weeks with the renowned teacher Hans Hofmann in New York. Ronald was captivated by the abstract expressionism of the New York painters. In 1953 Ronald persuaded the Robert Simpson Company

■ Nine members of Painters Eleven, November 1957. *Seated*: Tom Hodgson, Alexandra Luke (above), Kazuo Nakamura, Hortense Gordon, Jack Bush. *Standing*: Harold Town, Jock Macdonald, Walter Yarwood, Ray Mead. William Ronald, who founded the group, had resigned in August 1957, and Oscar Cahén had died the previous year. The two canvases are by Cahén. Photo by Peter Croydon, courtesy The Robert McLaughlin Gallery, Oshawa.

in Toronto—where he had worked for a time in the display department—to host an 'Abstracts at Home' exhibition, which included the work of six painters besides himself. Out of this exhibition a group was formed—with the addition of four more painters—called Painters Eleven. The group had an opening show at the prestigious Roberts Gallery in Toronto. The initial reaction ranged from uncomprehending and cool to indifferent. But many other exhibitions followed, including one in New York in 1956, and despite internal wrangling, Painters Eleven gained acceptance and a number of its members went on to greater glory. In April 1960 Jock Macdonald was given a retrospective exhibition at the Art Gallery of Ontario—the first living Canadian outside of the Group of Seven to be paid this honour, and he died soon after, just two months after Painters Eleven was formally dissolved.[15]

THE DEVELOPMENT OF FIRST NATIONS ART

By the early 1970s many Canadians had come to agree that the most distinctive art in the country was being produced in the various First Nations communities. Much of that art was based on traditional forms and techniques that were many centuries old. European observers had long recognized the striking beauty of Aboriginal artifacts, collecting them mainly for ethnographic purposes and displaying them in museums (rather than art galleries) as illustrations of a vanishing way of life, often associated with spiritual observances. In the twentieth century, self-conscious European artists like Pablo Picasso began to imitate the colours and designs of so-called primitive art, usually from Africa, and the non-representational and non-realistic aesthetics became much more favourable to an appreciation of Aboriginal art. A few Canadian artists, notably Emily Carr in British Columbia, were strongly attracted to Aboriginal traditions (of wood carving, for example). Not until after World War II, however, did First Nations creations begin to move out of the museums into the art galleries. To some important extent, this shift was associated with the increasing separation of the art from its ritualistic and ceremonial origins and its repositioning as the autonomous product of an individual artist (or group of artists) capable of being located within a commercial nexus. These shifts from ethnographic artifact to aesthetically pleasing—and marketable—art object and from traditional craftsperson to self-conscious artist occurred simultaneously in many places in Canada in the post-war period.[16] In many cases time-honoured First Nations traditions were dying and had to be resuscitated by a new generation of artists. Although the popularity of First Nations art has doubtless been assisted in recent years by an increasing public awareness of Canada's Aboriginal heritage, the basic shift had occurred more or less simultaneously with the First Nations renaissance of the 1960s. By the time of Expo 67 and its 'Indians of Canada' pavilion, which featured a collection of commissioned works by contemporary First Nations artists, the transformation had been largely completed, although ethnographic standards would continue to bedevil First Nations art for many more years.

INUIT SCULPTURE AND PRINTMAKING

In the High Arctic regions of Canada, the Inuit had a long tradition of carving ivory and stone. In 1948 the classically trained artist James Houston headed to the Arctic searching for a new direction to his life. Learning the local language, Inuktitut, and becoming a government administrator on Baffin Island, he quickly realized that the Inuit needed a source of income, and in 1949 he convinced the Canadian Guild of Crafts in Montreal to display and sell examples of the people's carvings in their shop, where they quickly became best-selling items. Although Houston was a government employee, his early success was quite independent of government policy and patronage. A few years later, Houston taught some Inuit to transfer their traditional art of animal-skin appliqué to paper stencils and even studied printmaking in Japan to improve the techniques he was teaching to the Inuit. In 1958 Houston managed to get some of the prints being produced into a show at the summer festival in Stratford, Ontario, and to persuade the Hudson's Bay Company and the Canadian Guild of Crafts to display the works for sale. Again the public—including opposition leader Lester B. Pearson—responded immediately, and the numbers of sculptors and printmakers at work among the Inuit began to expand rapidly.

HAIDA ART IN BRITISH COLUMBIA

Among a large number of coastal tribes that shared a distinct art, the Haida are perhaps the best known, chiefly because of their totem poles. Like other tribes, the Haida had virtually lost their traditional arts and skills under the pressure of government assimilationism. The artist most associated with the revival of Haida art was Bill Reid. Born in Victoria in 1920 to an American father and a Haida mother, Reid began simultaneously to show an interest in his Haida heritage and to work for the Canadian Broadcasting Corporation as a radio broadcaster. His decision to become a full-time artist came in 1958, when he began work on the restoration of a Haida dwelling and totem pole for the University of British Columbia Department of Anthropology. Reid began from a European base by copying existing material, but gradually developed his

■ 'Owl', stonecut, 1964, by Pauta Saila (1916–), printed by Echalook Pingwartok (1942–).
Reproduced with the permission of the West Baffin Eskimo Co-operative Ltd, Cape Dorset, Nunavut;
on loan to the McMichael Canadian Art Collection.

own work based on an understanding of the conventions of Haida art, particularly those of two-dimensional design. One of his major breakthroughs was to use wood for carving instead of argillite, which made much larger forms possible. In the 1950s other Haida artists began to study with him, and in 1967 an exhibit dealing with Aboriginal material as art rather than as ethnographic artifact was presented at the Vancouver Art Gallery.[17] Entitled 'Arts of the Raven', this exhibition marked the movement of First Nations art into the mainstream.

NORVAL MORRISSEAU AND ANISHNABE PAINTING

Like Bill Reid, Norval Morrisseau, born in 1932 on an Ojibwa reserve in northern Ontario, was an artist who began by trying to preserve his people's traditions, eventually published as *Legends of My People, the Great Ojibwa* (with Selwyn Dewdney, 1965). In late adolescence Morrisseau was confined to a long-term tuberculosis hospital at Fort William, where he learned to paint and where he had a series of visions that led him to become a 'shaman-artist'. Morrisseau began painting 'x-ray' pictures of the feelings inside animals, employing a pictography and iconography taken from the writings of spiritual Midewiwin rites and rock petroglyphs and adding colours. He insisted that 'all my painting and drawing is really a continuation of the shaman's scrolls.'[18] Morrisseau had a successful show in Toronto in 1962, but was heavily criticized by his own people for revealing Aboriginal secrets. He later became especially popular in France and Germany.

The meteoric success of Canadian Aboriginal art can be attributed to two features: one is that it was not really folk art, but a mixing of Native traditions with modern perceptions and techniques. The second is that, by 1970, Native art had become internationally recognizable as distinctively 'Canadian' art. Visitors to Canada accepted Inuit soapstone carvings and Haida silkscreen prints as simultaneously beautiful and outside the classical European traditions, and brought them home in great numbers.

THE PERFORMING ARTS: BALLET, OPERA, THEATRE

At the end of the war Canada had a strong amateur tradition in the performing arts but little in the way of professional music, dance, or theatre. By 1970 fully professional companies in all three arts were operating from coast to coast.

In 1938 two English dance teachers, Gweneth Lloyd and Betty Farrally, started a ballet club in Winnipeg. In 1941 it became the Winnipeg Ballet, and in 1953 it became the first such company in the Commonwealth to be granted a royal charter. Under the directorship of Saskatchewan-born Arnold Spohr, the Royal Winnipeg Ballet went on to receive international acclaim, employing distinguished choreographers and creating a major star in Evelyn Hart. In 1950 the English dancer and choreographer Celia Franca was brought to Toronto by some ballet enthusiasts to form a national company, and the next year the National Ballet of Canada was born. In 1959 the company began training its own dancers—including Veronica Tennant and Karen Kain—at the National Ballet School, and by the early 1970s it was collaborating with such world-famous dancers as Rudolph Nureyev (who staged his celebrated version of *The Sleeping Beauty* for the National in 1972) and Erik Bruhn (who would be artistic director from 1983 until his death in 1986). In 1958 a company founded by the Latvian-born Ludmilla Chiriaeff in Montreal became Les Grands Ballets Canadiens.

Opera had always been part of Canada's musical life. In the nineteenth and twentieth centuries famous singers gave recitals in the main towns and cities, touring companies visited, and opera associations formed briefly in Montreal and Toronto. In the first half of the twentieth century, a number of distinguished Canadian opera singers achieved international reputations, despite the scarcity of infrastructure in the country. By 1970 there were opera associations in Vancouver, Calgary, Edmonton, Winnipeg, Hamilton, and Quebec City, as well as the Canadian Opera Company (COC), which grew out of the Opera Festival of the Royal Conservatory Opera Company (1950) and was formed in Toronto in 1958. Like all opera companies, they depended on the standard repertoire for their survival, but in Centennial Year 1967, the COC produced a Canadian opera, *Louis Riel*, by Harry Somers, to critical appreciation.

The gradual spread of artistic activity across English Canada was particularly notable in regional or 'alternative' theatre, which pursued a more experimental course than such mainstream organizations as the Stratford Festival. The Manitoba Theatre Centre (MTC) was formed—as an amalgamation of the Winnipeg Little Theatre and Theatre 77, co-founded by John Hirsch and Tom Hendry—in 1958 and became professional in the early 1960s. The MTC was encouraged in part by the success of Sir Tyrone Guthrie in establishing a regional theatre in Minneapolis. Across the country, nearly 50 other professional and semi-professional theatre companies were established between 1963 and the early 1970s. In this period English-Canadian plays were not often produced, although in 1967 George Ryga's *The Ecstasy of Rita Joe* was presented first at the Vancouver Playhouse to great acclaim and sold-out houses, thus helping to open the door for a number of other playwrights. Contemporary drama by Québécois playwrights had a much earlier start and a much stronger following, beginning with Gratien Gélinas's *Tit-Coq* in 1948 (see Chapter 16). Ten years later, Gélinas

■ Karen Kain dancing in the National Ballet of Canada's production 'Mirror Walkers', 1970. Ken Bell/LAC, PA-195686.

the National Arts Centre in Ottawa (1969). Another part was the creation of subscription series in all of the arts, which had the advantage of reducing dependence on walk-in attendance and permitting revenues to be predicted in advance—and the disadvantage of discouraging adventurous programming. Nevertheless, by 1970, Winnipeg—a middle-sized, geographically isolated urban centre with no particular tradition of cultural patronage—was supporting a fully professional symphony orchestra; the Royal Winnipeg Ballet and other dance companies; an opera association mounting several works each year; the Manitoba Theatre Centre, with an impressive main stage building opened in 1970; an active art gallery; and a major concert hall. To some extent the various organizations were mutually supportive—the musicians from the symphony orchestra played in the pit for the ballet and the opera, for example, as well as with various chamber groups and other orchestras.

Centennials of various kinds provided the occasion to create cultural facilities and institutions across Canada. By 1970 no important city or region was without its own professional theatre company, art gallery, and symphony orchestra. Created with substantial public funds from all levels of government, new institutions initially relied heavily on recent immigrants to Canada for professional expertise, and as had been hoped, many of these professionals became teachers and sponsors of spin-off activities. It was not long before highly qualified younger Canadians were ready to step into these companies and organizations, and a substantial local audience had been developed.

THE CURIOUS CASE OF CANADIAN HISTORY

Canadian scholarship, like other areas of elite culture, was expanded and strengthened in the postwar era, particularly beginning in the 1960s, when a combination of grants from the Canada Council, the Social Sciences and Humanities

founded the Comédie-Canadienne, which produced 11 Quebec plays between 1958 and 1961.

It came as a surprise to many Canadians to discover that it was possible to create stable conditions for the performing arts outside Toronto and Montreal. Part of the secret was the construction of world-class facilities, such as the Jubilee Auditoriums in Edmonton and Calgary (1955), Vancouver's Queen Elizabeth Theatre (1959), the Confederation Centre in Charlottetown and the Playhouse in Fredericton (both 1964), Edmonton's Citadel Theatre (1965), the Arts and Culture Centre in St John's (1967), and

Research Council of Canada (SSHRCC), and the National Research Council (NRC) and an increase in the number of Canadian universities added greatly to the numbers of both academics and research students. Canadian scholarship grew not only in volume but in reputation, achieving international recognition in many disciplines. In literature, for example, the first two books of Northrop Frye, *Fearful Symmetry: A Study of William Blake* (1947) and *Anatomy of Criticism: Four Essays* (1957), established his international reputation as a scholar and critic. And in chemistry the German-born Walter Herzberg of the National Research Council was the author of numerous publications and won the Nobel Prize in 1971 for his contribution 'to the knowledge of electronic structure and geometry of molecules, particularly free radicals'.

The arrival in the 1960s of so many Ph.D.s on the staffs of Canadian universities—mainly, but not solely, from American graduate schools —gave Canadian scholarship a new flavour that was simultaneously American and international in nature. The increase in activity was especially noticeable in the humanities and social sciences; the sciences, which had for many years enjoyed generous government support, particularly for research, were far less immediately affected.

One field that had great difficulty in coming to terms with the rapidly changing world of Canadian scholarship was Canadian history, which before the 1960s had arguably been the premier humanistic discipline. A Canadian historian almost by definition could not achieve an international reputation, since the history of Canada was of little interest to anyone outside the country. Within it, however, Canadian historians had served as the effectual arbiters of, and spokesmen for, Canadian nationalism (or in the case of Quebec historians, Quebec nationalism)—not merely in the academy but in the political arena as well. Since the 1920s the writing of Canadian history in English Canada, and the training of graduate apprentices to continue the project, was dominated by the University of

■ Northrop Frye (1912–91) was a distinguished scholar whose study of English literature led to international recognition for his critical insights. He was made a Companion of the Order of Canada in 1972. LAC, PA-182431/Harry Palmer/Harry Palmer fonds. © LAC. Reproduced with permission of LAC.

Toronto. That institution controlled not only graduate training but the *Canadian Historical Review* (1920) and the University of Toronto Press, founded in 1901, which was virtually the only Canadian academic publisher in English of non-commercial scholarly monographs. Even those historians who were not closely associated with Toronto shared its general view of the nature and shape of the Canadian historical experience.

For most historians of Canada working within the English-speaking tradition, Canadian History was National History. Confederation marked the break between colonial beginnings and the fulfillment of national destiny. The focus was political and constitutional and unremittingly progressive—the country was settled, adopted representative government, turned representative government into responsible government, turned responsible government into union of the provinces, and with union moved towards full nationhood. The direction was clearly suggested by the title of a popular history of Canada, *From Colony to Nation* (1948) by Arthur Lower, a Harvard-trained historian who had taught at Wesley College, Winnipeg, and was teaching at Queen's University when the book was published. The overall dynamic of Canadian history was dominated by the Laurentian School founded by Harold Innis and Donald Creighton in the 1930s, emphasizing the east–west waterways and the expansion of central Canada into the peripheries, an approach that turned both the Atlantic region and the West into marginal outposts. The post-Confederation perspective—on the development of and debates about national policy—was centred on Ottawa, which—as the home of the Public Archives of Canada—was also the place where historians did most of their research. Perhaps not surprisingly, this unofficial fraternity helped to confirm the Ottawa-centric paradigm of national development. Quebec, of course, had its own paradigm, equally nationalistic and political in nature.

For much of this period, the world inhabited by historians of Canada was cozy, congenial, and largely masculine. In English-speaking Canada, most historians shared similar small-town or rural Protestant Ontario backgrounds; sons of the clergy were conspicuous in the generation that was still dominant in the early 1960s. The number of works published in a single year was small enough that anyone could read all of them; and the writings of all historians working in Canada—whether in Canadian history or not—could be reviewed in the pages of the *Canadian Historical Review*.

Historiographical controversy was kept to a minimum by the consensus tradition of the politics studied, through informal principles of territoriality, and through the conviviality that held sway at the Public Archives and at the Learned Societies meetings held every June at a different host university. As most of these historians were men, the history they wrote was profoundly male-oriented, centred on politics, war, and public service. The Confederation era was the focus of two award-winning biographies in the 1950s, of John A. Macdonald (two volumes) and George Brown (the first of two volumes), by Donald Creighton and J.M.S. Careless, respectively, both of the University of Toronto.[19] These highly respected historians were secure in their epistemology, believing that truth was not only definable but attainable, and that historical objectivity, while perhaps not entirely possible, was still a goal worth pursuing. The high point of this version of Canadian history was perhaps the plan to publish the Centenary Series, 19 volumes synthesizing the existing historical literature, divided by region and period, to be written by the leading experts of their generation and to appear in association with the Centennial Year in 1967. Unfortunately, some of the volumes were late and others were written by younger scholars, which rather spoiled the effect.

Like the Centenary Series, the tidy world of the historians began to come apart during the 1960s, though it would not collapse until the 1970s. The University of Toronto was unable to supply enough graduate students to maintain its intellectual dominance, as other universities went into the graduate business themselves (the total number of graduate students in history more than tripled in the decade after 1966). The results were much the same as in other areas of culture: diffusion and regionalization. By and large, Canadian history was not directly invaded by non-Canadians so much as it was undermined by the other influences to which graduate students in Canadian history were exposed in their non-Canadian seminars. In truth, Canadian history as it was being taught and written was profoundly out of step with what was happening in the rest of the world, where non-political dimensions had been discovered and elaborated. Moreover, as the old political consensus reflected in the traditional historiography was undermined by a new set of issues that had never before been examined, more international and socially concerned approaches to the teaching and research of history made compelling sense.

Younger historians of Canada began asking new questions about race, class, ethnicity, and gender that emerged out of the political turmoil of the late 1960s, and about the traditional historians' glaring neglect of Aboriginal people, women, the working classes, and visible minorities. To these changes in perspective, historians of Quebec added their own, often influenced by the new European schools of historical analysis, particularly the French 'Annales' school. Requiring new methodologies and new theories, the economic and social history implicitly asked whether the old nation-building paradigm was flexible and capacious enough to accommodate the new discoveries. By 1970 it was becoming increasingly clear that the old framework could not hold, although mainstream Canadian historians had little idea of how to rebuild it. They tended to fall back on adding new material in the form of chapters tacked on the end of textbooks that continued to focus on the nation and the problems of nation-building. Those who held to a concept of national history would not give up easily.

By the early 1970s the writing of Canadian history had changed as much as had the milieu in which it was being researched and written, moving away from the biographical and narrative approach towards a more specialized and concentrated form. Young historians were indifferent to large, nebulous topics such as the national character or identity, preferring, for example, to study various well-defined topics from a feminist perspective, to focus on regional history, or to explore specific fields such as labour, industry, law, or medicine. Like many other branches of elite culture, Canadian history had experienced diffusion. The traditional synthesis had been broken, and there was no vision to replace it.

Moreover, the extent of the problem was partially disguised because university courses in Canadian history continued to be popular. Enrolments and attendance figures ran high, and few wanted to try fixing what did not yet appear to be broken.

POPULAR CULTURE

The post-war years were also critical for the popular culture of entertainment in Canada. While governments wrestled with aspects of a cultural policy intended to protect Canadian culture and the Canadian identity from 'foreign' (read American) influence, their focus before 1960 was almost entirely on high culture. Few Canadians appreciated that the Americans were making a massive cultural shift of their own, in marshalling the media as well as the entire entertainment industry as delivery systems for American popular culture. What happened is what the American scholar Michael Kammen has described as the shift from popular to mass culture.[20] The secret of the United States' post-war success was an extraordinarily prosperous home economy, based partly on the extension of technological innovation into nearly every domestic household. The result was a domesticizing of entertainment as it moved from the public arena into the home. Many of the new consumer goods, such as television sets and high-fidelity equipment, required the development of related cultural products—TV programs, recordings—to make the new gadgets essential to every family, and the American entertainment industry was clearly up to the challenge. Hollywood suffered initially under the impact of the shift to home entertainment, but by the end of the 1950s it had captured control of television programming and was well on its way to dominating popular music as well. All aspects of American popular culture, including sports, were systematically brought into the web of the new entertainment industry. The effect on Canada would be profound.

While Canadians had long been susceptible to American popular culture in the form of print, film, and radio, they were now being inundated with new technologies whose influence was becoming increasingly pervasive. To some extent, the readiness of Canadians to accept the new technological innovations and the American culture they purveyed was a product of positive attraction. As Melinda McCracken has pointed out in her autobiographical account of teenage life in Winnipeg in the 1950s, 'everything American was so desirable. America appeared to be the source of all good things, things that were magical and ingenious and fun.'[21] American popular culture had virtually no competition from the rest of the world until the mid-1960s, when the 'British invasion' of the Beatles and Carnaby Street struck North America—and the American entertainment industry soon co-opted the Brits. In the area of high culture, Canadians could distinguish a Canadian novel from an import in a way that was impossible with popular culture. Moreover, Canada's traditional leadership tended to disdain popular culture as degraded or meretricious or irrelevant and hence unworthy of government assistance.

In his influential *The Canadian Identity*, published in 1961, Manitoba historian W.L. Morton observed that it did not 'greatly matter that Americans and Canadians share the same popular culture; after reading the same comic strips, and the same periodicals, Canadians remain as distinct as they ever were. What differentiates the two people are things far deeper than the mass culture of North America, which both countries share and both created.'[22] Morton's comment was illuminating in several respects. In his reference to comic strips and periodicals, he demonstrated how out-of-date he was. Thinking no doubt of the O'Leary Commission on magazine publishing—and dismissing its concerns as trivial—Morton obviously shared the government's blinkered conception of culture, while remaining hopelessly unaware of what was happening in the culture of the 1950s. Similarly, although Harold Innis in *The Bias of Communication* (1951) clearly identified the rela-

tionship between technology and culture, he too failed to comprehend the new media of his day; for Innis, radio, not television, was the relevant technology. Not until Marshall McLuhan would a Canadian thinker attempt to come to terms with the present. McLuhan doubtless overstated the case when he argued in *The Gutenberg Galaxy* that print, the technology that had dominated modern history, was obsolescent (though he qualified this in private correspondence by saying, 'obsolescence never meant the end of anything'). But at least he understood the implications of the electronic age.

Thus most Canadian commentators lagged at least a generation behind American reality in their understanding of the technology of popular culture, and they also tended to underestimate its pervasiveness. Again, McLuhan made the leap in his aphorism 'the medium is the message'—an insight that was criticized for all the wrong reasons. Most commentators before 1960 would have agreed with Morton that—American-dominated mass culture notwithstanding—Canada's distinctiveness resided elsewhere, in 'things far deeper'. Morton did not attempt to identify those 'things' but Vincent Massey did so in his 1948 book, *On Being Canadian*. For both men, culture encompassed all the characteristic activities and interests of a people. In Massey's mind, Canada meant:

> A constable of the Royal Canadian Mounted Police—and Canada has no better symbol; a sheaf of Marquis wheat; Canadian landscape painting; a beaver-pelt; a silvered church spire in French Canada; a bar of nickel; a bush-pilot; a pair of moccasins; the Wolfe-Montcalm monument at Quebec; a tube of insulin; a totem pole; a calèche; a cake of maple sugar; a Hudson's Bay blanket; the song 'Alouette'; a hockey stick; the 'Canadian Boat Song'; a pair of snow-shoes; a roll of birch-bark; a silver fox; a canoe; a Canada goose; a grain elevator; a lacrosse stick; a boom of logs; a buffalo; the Quebec Citadel; a maple tree; the opening of Parliament in winter.[23]

'CANCULT: THE RIGHT THING FOR THE WRONG REASON'

In 1961 the columnist Robert Fulford wrote the following piece, reprinted in its entirety, for the Toronto Star.

Dwight Macdonald, the New York journalist and critic, tried to isolate mass culture and middlebrow culture by giving them the distinctive Orwellian names, 'Masscult' and 'Midcult'. In Canada we are all acquainted with a third force, peculiarly our own. It permeates our literature, our art community, our theatre. It can be usefully named 'Cancult'.

Cancult is not hard to spot but impossible to kill. It is a Canadian cultural process by which literature and art are demoted to the status of a crutch for Canadian nationalism. It is a process which makes culture into an artificial historical event, a part of an unending quest for Canadian identity.

Under the unwritten rules of Cancult, a dramatic festival like Stratford is not an essay in theatrical art, but 'a distinctive contribution to Canadian culture'. Thus Stratford is assessed not as Shakespeare, which it is, but as a contribution to nationhood, which it is not.

Similarly a book of stories by Morley Callaghan is 'a significant part of Canadian literature' but not a part of literature, which is what it is. In the same process a mural by Harold Town becomes 'a part of our heritage' before anyone notices that it is art.

A Cancult person is one who is interested not in art but in 'Canadian art'. Sometimes such a person will say, 'I collect Canadian art' or 'We should put more interest in Canadian art'. Other art is thus put in its proper, secondary place.

In the same way a Cancult person reads Canadian books out of an obscure sense of duty; he believes that true Canadian citizenship will elude him if he fails to do so. He may well read *The Tamarack Review*, though he takes no notice of

English or American literary magazines. He has read Mordecai Richler's novels, but so far he has not heard of Richler's American contemporaries. The reason he reads Brian Moore is that Brian Moore used to live in Montreal.

If the Cancult person is a publisher he will publish Canadian poetry, though he could not give you the names of a dozen non-Canadian poets. He is not interested in poetry—only in Canadian poetry, which is a different thing.

He regards cultural institutions in the same way that the Massey Commission regarded them: not as cultural institutions but as contributions to Canadianism. Thus the CBC is not judged on the quality of its dramatic productions or on the music it performs. It is judged on its contributions to Canadian unity. All other considerations are secondary.

Similarly the Canada Council cannot simply support the painting of pictures and the writing of novels. Rather it must support them in such a way as to encourage Canadian culture—not just culture.

Cancult exacts a price. The price is anti-Americanism—or, as some anti-American Canadians say, 'pro-Canadianism'. Most countries can support the arts through government simply because the arts are good things to have around and don't pay for themselves. Not Canada. Canada demands that we justify the tax money used on the CBC, the Film Board, and the Canada Council by saying that it prevents something from happening. That something is the further spread of American culture in Canada. In the service of this cause, Cancult enlists singers and playwrights, panelists and dancers, musicians—and critics.

> Cancult is what makes us do the right thing for the wrong reason. Essentially, Cancult, while seeming to support culture—is anti-cultural; in fact, Philistine. It is Philistine because it holds that in a contest between art and nationalism, nationalism is more important. That's Cancult.
>
> SOURCE: Robert Fulford, 'Cancult: The Right Thing for the Wrong Reason', *Toronto Star*, 19 Jan. 1961, reprinted in Robert Fulford, *Crisis at the Victory Burlesk: Culture, Politics and Other Diversions* (Toronto: Oxford University Press, 1968), 182–3. Copyright © Oxford University Press Canada 1968.

The strengths and limitations of such a list are readily apparent. To see popular culture as significant would simply not have been Canadian, since popular culture was American; one sought the Canadian identity elsewhere, often in material artifacts. This approach helps account for the difficulty of finding the Canadian identity. But it also helps explain much of the passivity with which Canadians accepted what was happening in aspects of their popular culture such as film and hockey.

The 1960s did bring a somewhat new government attitude, at least in the sense that willingness gradually emerged to bring segments of popular culture under the umbrella of government policy. The politicians were not often clear that they were expanding Canada's cultural policies, nor did they appear to recognize any appropriate relationship between culture and the marketplace. But they did begin to take action.

CANADIAN FILM

The tale of the Canadian film industry in the years immediately after 1945 offers an excellent introduction to the problems facing Canada in the context of popular culture. Film was one of the few arenas of popular culture in which the federal government of the immediate post-war era did attempt to act in the policy sense. Unfortunately, the government did so for all the wrong reasons, and its attempted intervention failed miserably.

Since the 1920s American corporations had dominated the motion picture business in Canada. Not only did they produce most of the films Canadians wanted to pay money to see at the cinemas, but to make certain that Canadians saw them they also controlled distribution. In 1951 more than 80 per cent of feature-film distribution was in the hands of Canadian subsidiaries of Hollywood's largest studios, including 20th Century-Fox, Paramount, Columbia, and Warner Brothers. Hollywood-owned theatre outlets (Famous Players and Odeon) held two-thirds of Canadian commercial cinemas, chiefly in the prime locations.[24] It must be emphasized that Canadians had not done much to alter this situation. Canada had little tradition of making full-length feature films, and feature film production was not on anybody's cultural agenda. Not surprisingly, therefore, Canada had an unfavourable international balance of payments in terms of motion pictures. At the end of 1947, when the general flow of currency to the US threatened the stability of the Canadian dollar and various restrictions were placed on American imports, the government discussed the possibility of imposing a quota system for American films in the name of austerity.[25]

C.D. Howe, the Minister of Trade and Commerce (including motion-picture imports), saw the problem as an economic one, although a few other Canadians hoped to use the currency crisis to begin a new Canadian film industry. M.J. Coldwell, leader of the CCF, proposed that 'Canada should set up the protective tariff restricting the amount of money that could be taken out each year by the American distributors to ensure that a portion of the film profits made in Canada each year would be used to stimulate a Canadian film industry.'[26] This suggestion was classic 'National Policy'. Ross McLean, commissioner of the National Film Board (1945–50), recommended that American companies be required to use part of their revenue to make films in Canada for international audiences, and that American distribution companies be 'induced' to distribute short subjects (but not feature films) produced by Canadian filmmakers, including the NFB. That organization was the logical place to turn for Canadian production—and therein lay part of the problem. During the critical period of government negotiation with Hollywood in 1947–8, the NFB was suffering from another American import known as 'Communist witch-hunting'. John Grierson's former secretary had been named by Igor Gouzenko as a Soviet spy, and the entire organization was under investigation for Communist sympathies.[27]

As for Hollywood, it saw the dangers to itself clearly enough. J.J. Fitzgibbons, the Canadian president of Famous Players, put the case succinctly on 31 May 1948 in a letter to the head of Twentieth Century-Fox:

> There are people in Canada—as in every other country where American films are released—who insist upon American companies building studios all over the world and scattering their production activities in an uneconomic fashion. If we are to avoid extreme pressure for expensive and expansive studio operations in Canada, then we must demonstrate to the Canadian government our capacity really to do a job for the Dominion.[28]

Ironically, within a few years the filmmakers would be making films on location all around the world, but in this period most films were being shot almost entirely in Hollywood studios. In any case, the studios responded to Fitzgibbons's challenge. In a whirlwind of activity such as only Hollywood could unleash, including celebrity luncheons and visiting Hollywood starlets, the movie moguls persuaded the Canadian govern-

ment that, rather than impose a quota system, it should use Hollywood's control of the industry to Canada's advantage. What Hollywood offered was to publicize Canada in the movies, thus encouraging tourist travel in the Dominion and improving the balance of payments. They offered more newsreel coverage, promised to screen more NFB films, and agreed to 'undertake a program designed to insure proper selection of product'. This last point was key, for after discussions with Canadian officials, the moguls (who were not fools when their own economic interests were at stake) decided that a significant Canadian concern was—as the president of the Motion Picture Association of American put it— 'to avoid dollar expenditure for gangster films or other pictures of a low-toned nature'.[29] In other words, the Canadian government was behaving in a typically elitist way, afraid of spending precious dollars on kitsch.

Thus the Canadian Co-operation Project (CCP), a Hollywood press agent's dream, was born. Not much actually happened, but somebody got paid for a number of years to document meaningless statistics. One of the few early beneficiaries of Hollywood's concern for Canada was flood-inundated southern Manitoba in 1950, which received even more newsreel coverage than the photogenic disaster might otherwise have attracted, and as a result collected more money in disaster relief than the administrators could figure out how to spend.[30] Whether such disaster coverage brought in tourist dollars was another question. In 1952 the official project report, while admitting that 'the amount of Canadian material shown in US newsreels during 1951 showed ten fewer sequences than last year', added that 'the material used was of a highly significant nature and included few items dealing with unfortunate floods, fires and airplane accidents.' Moreover, through the newsreels, '1,500,000,000 audience impressions about Canada were brought to US theatre audiences'.[31] Only a Hollywood press agent could create a statistic for 'audience impressions'.

The other major accomplishment of the CCP was—in the words of Blake Owensmith, its man in Hollywood—to 'get in what we called hidden advertising—in other words a plug for Canada without being too obvious'. Some of these tourist hooks were actually reprinted in the 1952 report. The 'plug' from the dialogue of a film entitled *This Is Dynamite* was typical:

> – I'll refresh your memory. In 1932 Peter Manzinates was a produce dealer who refused to pay the organization. He went to Canada and never came back. . . .
> – Maybe the guy liked to travel.
> – March, 1932. You took a leave of absence from the police force. Gone three weeks. . . .
> – A vacation.
> – Did you like Canada?
> – Didn't go there.
> – You and Jimmy Kchop went to Canada. You took Manzinates to Canada and murdered him.
> – I never went to Canada. I don't know Manzinates, I never heard of Jimmy Kchop.[32]

Five (count 'em) Canadian references, multiplied by the total theatre audience for the film meant millions of 'audience impressions' of Canada. In a later interview, Owensmith offered 'as a perfect example of what we tried to do over the years', the change in the dialogue of *New York Confidential*:

> The script read, 'They caught Louis Engleday in Detroit.' We thought that was a very good chance to put in a plug for Canada, so we changed the dialogue to read, 'They caught Louis Engleday on his way to Canada.' This was a very good example because it flowed in and didn't seem forced and it got our plug over.[33]

Whether the notion of Canada as a haven for escaped gangsters did more than newsreel footage of fires and floods for tourist revenues is an unanswerable question.

Blake Owensmith eventually moved on from the CCP to become producer of *Sergeant Preston of the Yukon* for television, a series he insisted 'was a hell of a good promotional scheme; unwittingly they were selling Canada.' And so, in Hollywood terms, they were. No matter that the series promoted a variety of erroneous or outdated stereotypes about Mounties, the Canadian climate, and the Yukon gold rush. As that former Canadian Lewis B. Mayer is alleged to have remarked, 'there is no such thing as bad publicity.'

As for Canadian filmmaking, it stuck with high-quality educational short subjects until the late 1950s, and began making feature-length films only when it appeared likely that the industry would succumb entirely to television. The first signs of the new pressures came from Quebec. An article in *Parti pris* in April 1964 concluded: 'The film board is an instrument of colonization. It is a gigantic propaganda machine whose role it is to put the public to sleep and to exhaust the creative drive of the filmmakers.'[34] The awakening in Quebec focused the cultural agenda, not so much because the Quebec government had much of a cultural agenda as because the Quiet Revolution released enormous creative forces in the private sector.[35]

POPULAR MUSIC

Until the 1960s popular music in Canada survived but did not flourish under the shade of the American behemoth. A handful of performers managed to become known, mainly by immigrating to the US. The Americans neither knew nor cared that such popular musicians as Hank Snow, Percy Faith, the Four Lads, or Gisele MacKenzie were really Canadians in disguise. Others—the Crewcuts, the Penguins—made a living 'covering' American popular hits. The first Canadian-born superstar undoubtedly was Paul Anka, whose hit 'Diana' in 1957 began a run of million-sellers. Anka could be slotted loosely under the rubric of rock 'n' roll, as could Jack Scott. Canada's best-known popular performers of the 1960s, Ian and Sylvia, Joni Mitchell, and

Gordon Lightfoot, along with Leonard Cohen, were usually regarded as part of the evolving American folk scene. A recording industry existed only in Quebec, which had its own stars and its own best-sellers quite independent of the North American market.

CANADIAN TELEVISION

In September 1952 the Canadian Broadcasting Corporation opened the nation's first two television stations in Toronto and Montreal, and over the next two years it extended its television coverage into seven other major metropolitan areas. Television was hardly a new technology. The British and Americans both had experimental television stations operating before the war, and the Americans had begun introducing comprehensive television broadcasting, with national network organization, in 1946. By 1952, *I Love Lucy*, American television's first nationally popular situation comedy show, had been running for over a year. At the time of the introduction of television broadcasting in Canada, only 146,000 Canadians owned receivers (or 'sets', as they were usually called), tuning to American border stations and using increasingly elaborate antenna systems to draw in distant signals. Thus, most Canadians missed the whole first generation of American television programs, broadcast live from the studio, and were able to tune in only as the US networks moved from live to filmed programs and from New York to Hollywood. But if Canada got a slightly belated start into life with the tube, it rapidly caught up. By December 1954 there were nine stations and 1,200,000 sets; by June 1955 there were 26 stations and 1,400,000 sets; and by December 1957 there were 44 stations and nearly three million sets. The rate of set proliferation in Canada was almost twice that in the US, and the market for new ones was virtually saturated within five years.[36]

Television's popularity has been an international phenomenon transcending national circumstances and socio-economic conditions.

Nevertheless, for Canada in the post-war years, television fitted perfectly into the overall social and cultural dynamics of the time. Perhaps more than the automobile, or even the detached bungalow on its carefully manicured plot of green grass, television symbolized the aspirations and emerging lifestyle of the new suburban generation. Unlike other leisure-time activities that required leaving the home, it was a completely domesticated entertainment package that drew families into the home. Until the late 1960s most families owned only one TV, usually located in the living room (the only alternative was the 'family room'). Particularly on weekend evenings in the winter, the only sign of life on entire blocks of residential neighbourhoods was the dull flickering glow of the black-and-white TV sets coming from otherwise darkened houses. The family could even entertain friends who were interested in the same popular programs, and everyone could enjoy snacks served on small metal 'TV tables' or even a meal taken from the freezer and heated (the 'TV dinner'). Some of what people watched was Canadian-produced, but most of it came from the Hollywood Dream Factory. Except for *Hockey Night in Canada*, first telecast in 1954, TV drew Canadians into the seductive world of American popular culture. Everyone watched TV but probably none were more influenced by it than the young, whose perceptions of the world were largely shaped by the endless flow of images it presented, many of which celebrated suburban life.[37]

The golden age of Canadian television was undoubtedly in the 1950s. The Canadian Broadcasting Corporation was the only producer in town, and the live television drama it produced was outstanding—until it was killed by the competition of Hollywood-made filmed programming and the exodus of the major creators into the larger markets of Britain and the US.[38] The CBC could not compete with Hollywood. For the Americans, the opportunity to sell their products in Canada was a bonus, whereas Canadian productions had to put up the money for the

■ Interior of a CBC-TV studio during broadcast, 1954. Gar Lunney/National Film Board of Canada. Photothèque/LAC, PA-169804

Canadian audience, with no guarantees of overseas sales. After the arrival of American filmed programming, Canadian content largely disappeared from prime time, with the exception of *Hockey Night in Canada*. The voices of the hockey play-by-play commentators—Foster Hewitt and Danny Gallivan—probably were familiar to more Canadians than any other Canadian television personalities. A new era seemed to begin with the introduction of the current affairs program *This Hour Has Seven Days* in 1964, but the CBC could not sustain the momentum. Probably the most popular performers in the 1960s were the highly literate comedy team of Johnny Wayne and Frank Schuster, who were (mysteriously) embraced by Ed Sullivan in the United States.

Canadian television increasingly moved into specialized niches, including children's programming. The Americans featured thousands of hours of cartoons, but very little non-animated and non-aggressive television content. The first really successful CBC kids' program was *The Friendly Giant*, which began in 1958 and ran until 1985. The star of *The Friendly Giant* was an American, Bob Homme, who chatted with his puppet friends Rusty the Rooster and Jerome the Giraffe. The show featured a good deal of music, but for some children the biggest attraction was the castle full of tiny furniture. In 1963 Fred Rogers came north to develop *Mister Rogers* at the CBC; he soon took it to the Public Broadcasting Service in the United States. But he left behind his colleague Ernie Coombs, whose *Butternut Square* program evolved into *Mr. Dressup* in

■ Members of the Scheifner family watch television at their farm near Milestone, Sask., in December 1956. Richard Harrington/National Film Board of Canada, Photothèque collection. LAC, PA-111390.

1967. Like Friendly, Mr. Dressup performed with a couple of endearing puppets (Casey and Finnegan). For most Canadians growing up since the 1960s, *The Friendly Giant* and *Mr. Dressup* were a large part of their childhoods. Ironically, of course, both were played by American refugees from the schlock south of the border.

CONCLUSION

Between 1946 and the early 1970s Canada achieved considerable maturity in the many ways in which its culture expressed itself. A fully elaborated regional infrastructure, essential for high culture, was put in place and helped move

Canadian arts production to a new level of international recognition. Canadian governments came to understand the need to support popular culture as well, and the importance of Canadian production and performance in all media was recognized. Culture in Quebec was increasingly accepted as a distinct entity.

SHORT BIBLIOGRAPHY

Atwood, Margaret. *Survival: A Thematic Guide to Canadian Literature*. Toronto, 1972. A fascinating tour de force of literary criticism, simultaneously combining feminism and nationalism.

Berger, Carl. *The Writing of Canadian History: Aspects of English-Canadian Historical Writing: 1900 to 1970*, 2nd edn. Toronto, 1986. A first-rate analysis of the growth of Canadian historical writing, strongest on 'national' histories.

Berlo, Janet Catherine, and Ruth B. Phillips. *Native North American Art*. New York, 1998. A richly illustrated work that puts Canadian First Nations art in a continental perspective.

Berton, Pierre. *Hollywood's Canada: The Americanization of Our National Image*. Toronto, 1975. A wonderfully rich and ironic study of Hollywood's relationship with Canada.

Crean, S.M. *Who's Afraid of Canadian Culture?* Don Mills, Ont., 1976. A fierce polemic in favour of Canadian culture, very influential in its day.

Davis, Ann. *Frontiers of Our Dreams: Quebec Painting in the 1940s and 1950s*. Winnipeg, 1979. An important catalogue for an important exhibition of Quebec art.

Frye, Northrop. *The Bush Garden: Essays on the Canadian Imagination*. Toronto, 1971. A collection of essays on Canada by the doyen of Canadian literary scholars.

Macnair, Peter L., et al. *The Legacy: Tradition and Innovation in Northwest Coast Indian Art*. Vancouver, 1984. A sumptuously illustrated account of the history and present practice of Northwest Coast art.

Rutherford, Paul. *When Television Was Young: Primetime Canada, 1952–1967*. Toronto, 1990. A detailed and sober study of the tiny screen.

Shek, Ben-Z. *French-Canadian and Québécois Novels*. Toronto, 1991. A useful reading of Quebec fiction.

Wilson, Edmund. *O Canada: An American's Notes on Canadian Culture*. New York, 1965. Comments on Canadian culture by America's leading literary critic.

STUDY QUESTIONS

1. Why is elite culture so much easier to foster and encourage than popular culture?
2. What breakthrough did Margaret Atwood make in her book *Survival*?
3. What did Marie-Claire Blais and Claire Martin have in common as novelists?
4. What was the main theme of *Refus global*?
5. What happened to Canadian history in the 1960s?
6. How did Hollywood prevent the introduction of a film quota system?
7. What was 'Cancult'? Argue for and against it.
8. In what ways did developments in hockey resemble developments in other areas of Canadian culture and cultural policy (see Chapter 18) between 1946 and 1972?

☐ A mother from Uganda with her two-year old daughter at citizenship proceedings following the grand opening of the Pier 21 National Historic site in Halifax, 1 July 1999. CP Photo/Tim Krochak.

PART FIVE

1972–2007

■ Life during the twentieth century seemed to swing between long periods of buoyancy and pessimism. The upbeat climate of the years between 1945 and 1972 had been based on a resurgence of Canadian nationalism, a strong central federal government, and a combination of private enterprise and state economic intervention, with a social safety net to ensure citizens' welfare. Such Keynesian policies were generally accepted throughout the Western industrialized world, regardless of the parties in power.

In Canada, however, the political and constitutional framework in which Keynesianism operated proved increasingly unstable. It began to weaken in Quebec in the early 1960s, came under attack from the left in the later 1960s, and fell apart in the 1970s under both international and domestic pressures. Eventually, a number of contradictions defied management and became 'crises'. Public trust in the nation's political system and leaders declined as the old consensus deteriorated and no new paradigm emerged to take its place. For a time 'monetarism'—an economic theory originally associated with the American economist Milton Friedman, in which inflation, unemployment, and production were allowed to float free—gained popularity, especially after it was espoused by Ronald Reagan and

Margaret Thatcher in the US and Britain, respectively. Friedman also insisted 'there is no such thing as a free lunch' and called for cutbacks in social welfare provisions. Rejecting the idea of the 'greatest good for the greatest number'—the classic liberal principle—Canadians came to prefer the programs of provincial leaders who, at least by implication, opposed sharing. Led by Quebec and Alberta—for quite different reasons—the provinces sought constitutional revisions that would reverse the trend towards centralization.

After the defeat of the separatists in the referendum of 1980, it seemed urgent that Quebec be appeased. Accordingly, Prime Minister Trudeau opened the Pandora's box of constitutional reform. The federal government offered a package calling for Canadian control of amendments to the British North America Act ('repatriation'), a Charter of Rights to protect minorities, and some concessions to the provinces. Ottawa got its constitutional reforms in 1982, but they were not formally accepted by Quebec, which led to a series of efforts by the Tory government of Brian Mulroney (Meech Lake, Charlottetown) to gain unanimous agreement for further concessions to the provinces. These initiatives failed.

Canadians in the late 1980s and early

1990s proved unwilling to accept further tinkering with the Constitution. They also objected to attempts to reverse the universality of social programs, especially in the health-care sector. On the other hand, Canada appeared to accept the Free Trade Agreement with the US—and the subsequent North American Free Trade Agreement—with a minimum of argument. The Mulroney government came unstuck over the Goods and Services Tax and general public suspicion of its motives. In 1993, a federal election revealed the extent of Canada's political problems as the right polarized regionally and left only the Liberal Party intact with a huge majority. This situation would continue into the twenty-first century.

On the social front, continuing revelations of institutional abuse and attempted cover-ups contributed to a growing mood of cynicism regarding those in positions of authority. Many of Canada's problems, particularly in dealing with the poor and the aged, seemed beyond immediate solution. Changes in immigration policy, encouraging the admission of people from the Third World, began to remake the ethnic composition of the nation. At the same time, Canada promoted multiculturalism and attempted to protect its homegrown culture within the context of free trade by defending its 'cultural industries'.

After 1970 Canada no longer attempted to maintain consistently an independent posture internationally and, as the Cold War ended, increasingly accepted integration under the American military umbrella, occasionally emerging to engage in international peacekeeping operations. Canadians were appalled at the terrorist attack on the US on 11 September 2001, but also distressed by the heavy-handed American response. Canada tried to distance itself from the American sword-rattling, and was surprised by the vehemence of the American response to its lack of support. The commitment by the ruling Liberals in 2002 of a small military force to Afghanistan may have eased the tense relations with the United States at the official level at least to a small degree; the shift of these Canadian troops from Kabul to the Taliban-infested Kandahar district in 2005 signalled a greater Canadian involvement in what was becoming much more like war than trying to maintain a fragile status quo. Then, in early 2006, with the election of a minority Conservative government Canada's military commitment grew, as did the number of deaths of Canadian soldiers.

CHAPTER TWENTY

The Collapse of the Liberal Consensus, 1972–1991

For roughly 25 years an overall consensus had prevailed in Ottawa centred on economic and social liberalism. Implicit in that consensus was the belief that the central government should be in charge of a single Canadian nation. Then quite suddenly, around 1972, that consensus collapsed. No single event or factor can be identified as responsible. Rather, a cumulation of problems that defied management—many of which reflected worldwide trends—came together to produce a series of what the media called 'crises'. Increasingly, politicians and the public alike came to feel that any policies proposed as solutions to such problems could be no more than band-aids placed over festering wounds.

At the same time a shift became evident in the overall public mood and mentality. During World War II almost everyone had accepted the idea of personal sacrifice for the greatest good of the greatest number—a classic liberal position. Thereafter, however, it seemed that self-sacrifice was gradually replaced by self-interest as the mainspring of human activity. Public trust in the nation's political leaders declined (helped along, no doubt, by the Watergate affair in the United States, as a result of which US President Richard Nixon chose to resign rather than face impeachment), and cynicism became entrenched at the core of the national psyche. Little by little,

Canadians were increasingly attracted to politicians who, whether by implication or by open statement, suggested that they should not have to share after all.

THE DEMISE OF POST-WAR VALUES

For most Canadians the years between 1945 and the early 1970s were a period of affluence, optimism, and nationalism based on the assumption that a strong central government would ensure the welfare of citizens. The relative ease of the post-war era was the product of policies grounded in twentieth-century small-'l' liberalism—a delicate balance of private enterprise, corporate capitalism, and public corporatism. Not all those policies were directly influenced by Keynesian economics, but many of them were, and the whole system was orchestrated by the same Keynesian assumptions accepted by governments around the Western industrialized world. All the major Canadian political parties, federal and provincial, from the Socreds to the Parti Québécois, were essentially exponents of liberalism with a small 'l'.

Yet if liberal economic assumptions combined with federal nationalism were generally accepted even by the Tories during their six years of power in Ottawa, between 1957 and 1963, in

TIMELINE

1970

Loto-Québec established. DREE expanded. White Paper on Unemployment Insurance published.

1971

Senate publishes its *Poverty in Canada* report.

1972

Liberals form minority government. FIRA put in place to deal with foreign ownership.

1973

Yom Kippur War raises oil prices. Parti Québécois makes gains in Quebec election.

1974

Western Canada Lottery Foundation founded. Fraser Institute established in Vancouver.

1975

Postal strike. Mandatory wage and price controls introduced.

1976

PQ comes to power in Quebec.

1979

Tories form government under Joe Clark in June but lose confidence vote over budget in House of Commons in December.

1980

Trudeau returns to power. Quebec referendum. National Energy Program introduced.

1984

John Turner replaces Trudeau as Liberal leader and Prime Minister, but soon after loses election to Tories led by Brian Mulroney.

1986

Federal government admits that large numbers of farmers are to be encouraged to leave agriculture. Northlands Bank fails.

1987

Free Trade Agreement successfully negotiated with the US.

1990

GST introduced.

the later 1960s the constitutional framework became a source of conflict. As we saw in Chapter 16, the consensus increasingly came under attack from some of the provinces. It began seriously unravelling in the 1970s, and by the 1980s it was in tatters.

The Canadian political arena seemed incapable of devoting the same energy to economic and constitutional problems simultaneously, and so in the period after 1972 the focus alternated between the economic issues discussed in this chapter and the Constitution (discussed in the next). The two issues were not entirely separate, of course, for one of the major arguments of the federalists was that strong national policies were required to deal with the country's economic problems. After the election of a Tory government under Brian Mulroney in 1984, both nationalism and federalism were jettisoned for the Free Trade Agreement and Meech Lake, while the principles of liberal economics were at least partially replaced by privatization, clawbacks, and deregulation.

THE LOTTERY MENTALITY

Symptomatic of the new mentality—in which the possibility of sudden wealth for a few replaced the modest but certain comfort shared by all in a welfare state—was the intense interest aroused by lotteries in the early 1970s.[1] The main attraction of lotteries, of course, is the chance—however statistically small—to win an enormous amount of money for a relatively small investment. Lotteries had been conducted informally in Canada for centuries but were generally prohibited by the Canadian Criminal Code until it was amended in 1969 to allow provincial governments and certain other organizations to conduct and manage them. By this time a number of American states had gone into the lottery business. The Société des loteries et courses du Québec (better known as Loto-Québec) began in 1970. In 1974 the four western provinces set up the Western Canada Lottery Foundation (later the Western Canada Lottery Corporation, with British Columbia setting up the British Columbia Lottery Corporation in 1985). The Ontario Lottery Corporation was begun in 1975, and the Atlantic Lottery Corporation started up in 1976. Desperate for new sources of revenue, the provinces seized on lotteries as a way of adding to their coffers. In some provinces, a portion of the profits was designated for specific purposes (often cultural), but in Quebec and the Atlantic region the profits were simply returned to the provincial governments as general revenue. Lottery revenue soon became a political football between the provinces and the federal government. Loto-Canada Inc. was created as a federal Crown corporation in 1976 to help pay for the Montreal Olympics, and Ottawa subsequently set up other lotteries to assist with sport in Canada. The provinces took the federal government to court in 1984, and in 1985 an agreement was reached whereby lotteries became solely a provincial matter.

Probably the most interesting part of lottery mania was the willingness of Canadians to buy tickets, even when they knew how the odds were stacked against them. For most lottery participants, the chance for a win big enough to retire on was irresistible. Many winning tickets were purchased by informal syndicates of bettors, and there were several ugly court cases over the final distribution of prizes. Not until the twenty-first century were there revelations of corruption in the administration of the lottery corporations, notably through wins by those selling the tickets far beyond random chance.

Objections to the provincial lotteries surfaced from time to time, but the most serious complaints concerned the video gaming machines (Video Lottery Terminals, or VLTs) installed in virtually every drinking establishment in the nation. These machines were regarded as highly addictive, and when they were used by people under the influence of alcohol the consequences could be disastrous not only for players themselves but for their families.[2] Another subject of dispute was the introduction of gambling casinos on Aboriginal reserves, where they were exempt from most regulation because of the autonomous status of First Nations.[3]

THE OIL CRISIS

On 6 October 1973—the Jewish holy day of Yom Kippur—the Arabs and Israelis went to war again, as they had done periodically for many years. On this occasion, however, events in the Middle East had an immediate impact on the world. The Arab oil exporters (who dominated the world market) embargoed shipments of oil to nations supporting Israel, including Canada. Shortly thereafter, the Organization of Petroleum Exporting Countries (OPEC), which for 13 years had been a toothless cartel, managed to agree on another price raise, more substantial than the modest one announced before the Yom Kippur War. The price of oil more than tripled in 1973, and all Western industrial nations were suddenly forced to recognize how much their economic prosperity had depended on a constant supply of cheap oil.[4]

■ A cartoon by Duncan Macpherson, *Toronto Star*, 19 Nov. 1974. Depicting the Canadian West as the sidekick of big US oil, the Toronto-based Macpherson did nothing to ease regional tensions. LAC, C-112956. Reprinted with permission—Torstar Syndication Services.

Perhaps more than any other single commodity of the post-war era, oil symbolized the North American economy in the age of affluence and the contradictions inherent in it. Cheap oil had made possible the development of the increasingly large, powerful, and comfortable automobiles—the 'Yank Tanks', as they were called in Canada before they became the 'Detroit Dinosaurs'—that sat in every suburban driveway and clogged every freeway. Many of these cars had V-8 engines producing more than 300 horsepower. The freeways had been paved with materials derived from petroleum. The manufacture and sale of instantly obsolescent gas-guzzlers, together with the construction of the roads connecting thousands of new suburban developments, were major components of post-war economic prosperity in both the US and Canada. Some saw the car as a symbol of post-war America; others saw it as a sex symbol. Either way, a 20-horsepower electric engine simply did not have the same symbolic value. In addition to consuming gas and oil as if there were no tomorrow, the typical automobile discharged harmful hydrocarbons that were a principal component of the air pollution increasingly affecting North American health. Not until the 1990s would 'global warming' be a phrase on many lips, with hydrocarbon pollution held responsible for much of the problem. In any case, Detroit engineering had never been renowned for its flexibility. By the time Detroit responded to the demand for fuel efficiency and began producing smaller vehicles, the Japanese had taken command of the North American market—in the process signalling the arrival of a new world trading order.

If petroleum fuelled—literally as well as symbolically—the contradictions of the North American economy, it also exposed a number of problems that were specifically Canadian. Some of these had already been newsworthy before OPEC pulled the plug, but they seemed more urgent and apparent as the nation searched for a viable energy policy. The Canadian petroleum industry, located chiefly in Alberta, was almost entirely owned and operated by multinational corporations, most—though not all—of them American-based. Oil, indeed, epitomized the problems of foreign ownership in the 1960s and the early 1970s. Moreover, although the petroleum still in the ground not tied up by the multinationals was a Crown resource, it was controlled by provincial governments rather than the federal state. When the issue of jurisdiction over offshore deposits was added to the provincial control of internal natural resources, oil became a key item of potential dispute in federal–provincial relations (as we shall see in Chapter 21).

Oil consumption in Canada was heaviest in the industrialized East, while most of the raw material was in the resource-based West—a discrepancy that exacerbated regional tensions. Finally, increases in petroleum prices had a ripple effect throughout the Canadian and world economies, raising an already steady inflation to new highs—and at a time when labour unions were establishing themselves in many key industries, especially in the public sector. Having achieved full recognition of collective bargaining, union organizers next moved for improved working conditions and higher wages to match the cost-of-living inflation facing their members. OPEC's price increases, with promises of more to follow, thus affected Canada in several critical areas: foreign ownership, federal–provincial relations, regional conflicts, and labour relations.

THE RISE OF THE PARTI QUÉBÉCOIS

Virtually the only long-standing problem that did not seem directly connected to oil was that of Quebec and the Constitution—and even that issue had an indirect link to oil through the interest that oil-rich Alberta now had in seeking greater constitutional autonomy for the provinces. On 29 October 1973, a bare three weeks after the first shots were fired in the Yom Kippur War, Quebecers went to the polls to elect a new provincial government. From the outset of the contest between Robert Bourassa's Liberals and René Lévesque's Parti Québécois, the central issue, on which both parties had worked to polarize the electorate, had been the desirability of a separate Quebec. The result, on the surface, was a resounding victory for the Liberals: 1,600,000 votes (54.8 per cent of the total) to 897,0000 for the PQ, and 102 seats in the legislature to 6 for the PQ and 2 for the Créditistes. Nevertheless, the Péquistes had improved their performance over the 1970 election in almost every riding, and did exceptionally well among younger voters in Montreal. Post-election studies confirmed that the majority of Liberal supporters

■ René Lévesque on provincial election night, 29 October 1973. Duncan Cameron/LAC, PA-115039.

had favoured federalism and the majority of PQ supporters wanted independence for Quebec, although there were also other reasons for the PQ's increase in popularity.[5]

The relationship between the Quebec question and Canada's economic problems after 1973 was difficult to determine. In 1976 the PQ won a somewhat unexpected victory, which was not necessarily to be interpreted as a mandate for independence in any form—although one of its campaign promises had been to hold a referendum on sovereignty-association. When the referendum was finally held in May 1980, the Nons—those opposed to negotiating for sovereignty-association—won by 60 per cent to 40. Yet the PQ was re-elected the next year. Especially after the referendum, the federal government of Pierre Elliott Trudeau shifted its focus from the

economy to constitutional issues. Trudeau himself was not only a federalist Quebecer but a constitutional lawyer far more comfortable with the intricacies of the BNA Act than with oil-price equalization or economic planning. Oil and the Constitution were hardly the only issues after 1973, but they were certainly front and centre for many years, and the various attempts to resolve the problems they posed (as well as the ones they ignored) precipitated the deterioration of the traditional consensus.

THE SHAPE OF FEDERAL POLITICS

In Ottawa the years between 1972 and 1991 fall into two very distinct periods. The dividing line was 1984. During most of the first period, the Liberals clung tenaciously to power in several very close elections (1972, 1974, 1980), although in 1979 they were briefly replaced in office by a minority Tory administration headed by Joe Clark. This period may be best characterized as one of gradual disintegration both for the Liberal Party itself and for the small-'l' liberal consensus of the post-war era. In 1984 the Tories under Brian Mulroney swept to power in the most decisive election since 1945, exceeding even the Diefenbaker sweep of 1958 in percentage of popular vote and number of seats. The change in Quebec was particularly critical, although it remained to be seen whether the shift in allegiance would be as lasting as the one made in 1896, when the province abandoned the Conservatives for the Liberals. The new government would make radical changes in Canada's economic policies.

THE LIBERALS

The fortunes of the federal Liberal Party between 1968 and 1984 became increasingly associated with Pierre Elliott Trudeau, its leader for most of that period.[6] The identification was partly a product of television's relentless search for visual images and Trudeau's brilliant mastery of the medium. But it was also a product of Trudeau's own political and administrative style; increasingly, he operated as a loner and did not encourage strong professional politicians to emerge around him. Some analysts also talked about the emergence of a new presidential-style politics in Canada, and, as we shall see, there was evidence of some strong American influences. But the 'arrogance' ascribed to Trudeau was personal, not political.

As a French Canadian who had always firmly opposed Quebec separatism, Trudeau had little scope for manoeuvre as public opinion polarized in that province. As a federalist, he had little time for claims to provincial or regional autonomy whether they came from Quebec or from the West. And as an urban intellectual from central Canada, he had no empathy to offer

■ Newly elected party leader Pierre Elliott Trudeau at the Liberal convention in Ottawa, 6 April 1968. LAC , PA-111213.

either Atlantic or western Canada. Eastern voters never deserted him (his worst electoral performance in Atlantic Canada was his first, against Stanfield in 1968), but the West gradually abandoned the Liberals, Trudeau, and Canadian federalism. By 1980 'western alienation' had reduced the number of Liberal MPs west of Ontario to two (both from Manitoba). Never a fervent party man, Trudeau did not cultivate the grassroots, and the powerful Liberal political organizations that had existed before 1970 were allowed to wither away in most provinces, surfacing when federal patronage was to be dispensed but not at federal election time.

Trudeau disturbed many Canadians with occasional forthrightness ('Just watch me'), vulgarity bordering on obscenity (one four-letter word in the House of Commons was transcribed as 'fuddle duddle', and a raised-finger gesture to a western crowd appeared in newspapers across the nation), and unconventionality (he married, separated from, and divorced Margaret Sinclair while in office, dating other women after the separation in 1977 and fathering a child out of wedlock in 1991). Perhaps most damaging of all was an increasing tendency to treat almost everyone (members of his own caucus as well as the opposition, reporters, and voters) as ill-informed if not foolish. Trudeau's public persona oscillated between that of an affable 'swinger' and that of a university professor faced with a particularly dense class.

Trudeau announced his intention of retiring to private life late in 1979, following the Liberals' unexpected electoral defeat in May of that year by the Tories under Joe Clark.[7] But Clark's minority government fell before a new Liberal leader could be chosen. The caucus persuaded Trudeau to lead the party into the unexpected election of 1980, which returned one of the largest Liberal majorities of the post-war period. He would remain in power for the next four years, becoming one of the longest-serving prime ministers in Canadian history and easily the veteran among contemporary world leaders. In 1984, however, he resigned again and this time made it stick. John Turner had for years been touted as the logical successor to Trudeau, and a Liberal leadership convention chose him on 16 June. Turner became Prime Minister two weeks later, and on 9 July dissolved Parliament for the fateful 1984 election.

John Turner was born in England, came to Canada as a child with his mother and stepfather, and was educated at the University of British Columbia, Oxford, and the University of Paris. Thoroughly bilingual, he entered Parliament in 1962, representing an English-speaking constituency in Montreal (he later moved to an Ottawa one), and first joined the cabinet in 1965. He ran against Trudeau for the leadership in 1968, and remained in the government as one of its most powerful ministers until September 1975, when he quit the cabinet and then left politics.

Turner had a difficult decision to make in 1984. The polls indicated that the Liberals were in serious trouble. Turner could either run as a fresh face, on the momentum of the publicity surrounding his selection as leader, or remain in office a few months and attempt to establish a record of his own with the existing Parliament. He chose the former option, then compromised it by making several appointments to accommodate members of the Trudeau team. With no new policies to offer, he had to campaign in the face not only of Trudeau's continuing popularity and the general deterioration of liberal nationalism, but of a well-orchestrated campaign by the Progressive Conservatives. To the surprise of almost everyone, Turner turned out to have a singularly inept media presence, particularly on television. Never really perceived by the voters as a fresh face, he went down to a disastrous defeat and the Liberals were reduced to 40 seats.[8] Four years later, in the 'free-trade' election of 1988, the Liberals did even worse in Quebec and not much better in the West or the Atlantic region; only a resurgence in Ontario prevented another utter disaster. Turner was viewed as a lame duck almost from the moment of the announcement of the results at the polls. Shortly thereafter he declared his intention to step down as Liberal leader, although a leadership convention was not held until the summer of 1990.

THE PROGRESSIVE CONSERVATIVES

Robert Stanfield led the Progressive Conservatives through three successive defeats at the hands of the Trudeau Liberals before retiring in 1976. He was perhaps the best federal leader of the century who never became Prime Minister. His strengths—common sense, compassion, and consensus-building—might have served him well if he could have persuaded the voters to elect his party.[9] Unfortunately, the Canadian electorate found him much too low-key. In his best chance, the election campaign of 1974, he called for wage and price controls, which Prime Minister Trudeau ridiculed—then introduced himself soon after his electoral victory. Stanfield spoke French badly, and—although that was not the only reason—the Tories were never able to mount a credible campaign in Quebec under his leadership: they won only four seats there in 1968, two in 1972, and three in 1974.

Stanfield was succeeded as Tory leader by Joe (Charles Joseph) Clark, one of the few federal leaders of the twentieth century who had no adult occupation other than that of politician.[10] He had been a student leader at the University of Alberta, and later worked for the PCs in Alberta and Ottawa until his election to Parliament in 1972. He persevered to improve his French, which became more than passable, if occasionally awkward. He had unexpectedly emerged as the compromise 'progressive' candidate at the 1976 leadership convention, defeating among others Brian Mulroney, who was easily the leading Tory in Quebec despite never having held public office. For many Canadians, Clark was 'Joe Who?' The PCs had not made much of a showing in Quebec since the Diefenbaker years, and by the late 1970s had virtually written off the province. The unpopularity of Trudeau's Liberals was well demonstrated in the 1979 election, when Clark's Tories received 136 seats to 114 for the Liberals and formed a minority government. The 1979 election, however, also illustrated the limitations of serious campaigning only in English-speaking Canada. The Tories won only 2 seats in Quebec to the Liberals' 67; anything resembling a decent showing in Quebec would have given Clark a clear-cut majority.

Despite his government's precarious minority status, Clark attempted to govern Canada as if he had a majority.[11] He believed that the other parties (especially the NDP) would not wish to fight another election too quickly, and thought that if

■ Joe Clark speaking at the 1976 Progressive Conservative convention where he won the party's leadership. Photo by John de Visser.

his government was forced to fight another election prematurely, the voters would give it a majority, as had happened with the Diefenbaker government in 1958. Clark quickly came up against one of the other verities of Canadian politics apart from the Quebec fact: the NDP could keep the Liberals in power (as it had in 1963–5 and 1972–4) but would not support a Tory government, particularly one committed to balanced budgets and the privatization of Petro-Canada. Moreover, Clark's public image did not improve in office. He received much criticism for seeking to implement his campaign promise of moving the Canadian Embassy in Israel from Jerusalem to Tel Aviv, and on television Clark—like US President Gerald Ford a few years earlier—often seemed to stumble. In December 1979 his government was

■ Prime Minister Brian Mulroney talks with Deputy Prime Minister Don Mazankowski prior to a cabinet meeting in Montreal, 4 September 1986. CP/Paul Chiasson.

defeated on a motion of non-confidence on John Crosbie's budget, particularly gasoline pricing, and in the ensuing election the Tories were beaten by a resurgent Pierre Trudeau.[12]

As leader of the opposition Clark played a constructive role in the constitutional reforms of the early 1980s, but neither the public nor his party showed any real confidence in him. Eventually he called a leadership convention in June 1983, and on the fourth ballot was defeated by 'the boy from Baie-Comeau', Brian Mulroney.[13] Whether Mulroney's Tories actually represented a different vision that could serve as the basis for an alternative consensus was an open question, especially during the party's first term in office. Certainly they tried to appeal to the centre, which was thought (on the basis of polls

and voting patterns) to have become dubious about many elements of the old liberal consensus. But there was no clear evidence that a new political paradigm was emerging from the ashes of the old one. Instead, the events of the mid-1980s strongly suggested that Mulroney, like Diefenbaker a generation earlier, had no true alternative to offer beyond free trade and friendship with the Americans.

Mulroney's Tories promised that they would not dismantle the existing social welfare state, although the likelihood of maintaining an equitable social system for all Canadians seemed dubious, given the party's insistence on 'fiscal responsibility'. The Tories gradually found some direction away from the old liberal-federalist-nationalist state, committing themselves to better relations

BRIAN MULRONEY (1939–)

❖

Born in 1939 in Baie-Comeau, a prosperous mill town in eastern Quebec on the north shore of the St Lawrence River, about 400 kilometres east of Quebec City, Martin Brian Mulroney grew up fluently bilingual. He attended a private high school in Chatham, New Brunswick, and then went on to St Francis Xavier University in Nova Scotia, where he studied political science and was active in student politics. He was a Conservative from his undergraduate days. After taking a law degree at Laval, he became a corporate lawyer with a specialty in labour negotiations. In sharp contrast to Joe Clark, who had never been anything but a politician, Mulroney entered politics at the highest level without ever having held public office, although he had been active in the backrooms of the party for years. By 1974, when he served on the Cliche Commission investigating violence in the construction industry in Quebec, he was arguably the most important Tory fundraiser in the province.

From his earliest days in politics, Mulroney was a controversial figure. Many critics thought he was manipulative and 'too slick'. Unlike Clark, whose public utterances were stumbling and delivered in a boyish tenor (he took elocution lessons to lower his voice), Mulroney was not only polished in performance and perfectly bilingual, but the possessor of one of the deepest and most mellifluous voices in Canadian public affairs. He was an experienced labour lawyer and corporation executive, proud of the fact that he had closed his Iron Ore Company's mine at Schefferville, Quebec, with a minimum of public reaction. Trained as a public conciliator, Mulroney understood about keeping promises vague and making deals. He also appreciated the Tories' need for success in Quebec, and as his major plank in the leadership contest he promised the party to deliver that breakthrough. Accordingly, he brought a number of Union Nationale politicians into federal politics and promised Quebec voters a new deal on the Constitution. In the 1984 election he successfully captured the centre of the Canadian political spectrum, which was considerably less liberal and interventionist than it had been 20 years earlier, with a brilliant election campaign against a lacklustre John Turner. By 1987 he appeared to have established two important new policies for Canada: a new constitutional arrangement for Quebec (Meech Lake) and the Free Trade Agreement with the US. A personal friendship with American President Ronald Reagan seemed to facilitate harmony between the two countries.

These triumphs led to an easy re-election in 1988, but in fact Mulroney's accomplishments were not as solid as they appeared. The collapse of Meech Lake in 1990 was damaging, but what really did him in was probably his unbending support of the Goods and Services Tax (GST), introduced by his government and in effect since January 1991. Public hostility to the tax itself was obvious, and if anything this hostility was greater after Mulroney made a number of extraordinary Senate appointments so the tax could be pushed through that body over the strong opposition of the Senate's Liberal majority. After his retirement from politics in 1993, he became the centre of a controversy over influence-peddling (the Airbus affair), which led in 1997 to a government apology for charges made against him. Although Mulroney was not solely responsible for the collapse of the Progressive Conservative Party in Canada in the early 1990s, he had to take the bulk of the blame.

between Canada and the US, a less insistent economic nationalism, and improved relations between Ottawa and the provinces (especially, but not exclusively, Quebec), which meant surrendering some federal power to the provinces. Once in office with an enormous majority—211 seats, of which 58 came from Quebec—Mulroney in 1987 negotiated two controversial agreements: the Free Trade Agreement with the US and the Meech Lake constitutional accord with the provinces. On the strength of those successes he was returned to office easily in 1988, with a smaller but still impressive majority, including 63 of the party's total 169 seats from Quebec.

THE NEW DEMOCRATIC PARTY

Throughout this period the New Democratic Party remained a constant third force. Its continuity was exemplified by the consistency both of its popular vote in federal elections (between 15 and 20 per cent) and of its policies, which were unquestionably federalist, nationalist, and liberal. The party had purged its radical, ultra-nationalist wing, the Waffle, in the early 1970s, in order to remain in the centre of the political spectrum, but it continued to be unable to make significant inroads in either Atlantic Canada or Quebec to establish a truly national presence. None of its leaders managed to establish credibility in Quebec. The NDP was always the biggest loser when the popular vote was translated into parliamentary seats, particularly in eastern Canada. In 1988, for example, it won nearly half a million votes in Quebec, but not a single seat. The party occasionally had influence beyond its numbers of MPs, however, especially during the Trudeau minority government of 1972–4 and the Clark minority government of 1979–80. In the first case the NDP pushed the Liberals to the left, and in the second its refusal to support the PCs led to the Clark government's demise.

From 1971 to 1975 the NDP was led by David Lewis. Born in Russia in 1909, he immigrated to Montreal as a child, graduated from McGill University, and was a Rhodes Scholar. On his return to Ottawa he practised law and in 1936 he joined the CCF as its national secretary. Lewis was also an active member of the League for Social Reconstruction. He had played a major role during the 1950s, fighting Communist influence in Canada's labour unions, and was an important figure in the creation of the NDP.[14] His selection in 1971 as leader, succeeding Tommy Douglas, came after a bitter contest with the Waffle candidate, James Laxer. In his first election campaign as leader in 1972, Lewis coined the phrase 'corporate welfare bums' to refer to Canadian businesses that exploited their tax advantages, and led the NDP to a position in the Commons that enabled them to hold the balance of power in the minority Liberal government until 1974. In that year, he and his party paid for their collaboration with the Liberals when the NDP won only 16 seats (its lowest total ever to that date), and Lewis himself was defeated in his Toronto riding.

David Lewis was succeeded in 1975 by Ed Broadbent, a former political science professor at York University who had built up a considerable constituency in his home town of Oshawa, Ontario. Despite his inability to improve the party's overall position in a series of elections, Broadbent was an increasingly popular leader. The only serious challenge to his position came in the early 1980s, when many party faithful objected to his support for Trudeau's constitutional repatriation formula. Broadbent and his NDP benefited from the Liberal Party's neglect of traditional economic nationalism in the elections of 1980 and 1984. For most of the years that John Turner led the Liberal Party, the NDP kept federal liberal nationalism alive in Ottawa, and Broadbent was frequently identified in public opinion polls as the most trustworthy political leader in Ottawa.[15] This ringing public endorsement for the man never did translate into gains for the party, however, and Broadbent retired in 1990, to be replaced by Audrey McLaughlin, a former social worker representing the Yukon

Territory in Parliament. Like both her predecessors, as well as her leadership rivals, McLaughlin spoke halting French and was hardly likely to appeal in Quebec. Nevertheless, her selection as the first female party leader in Canada marked the NDP as yet again in the vanguard, for feminist issues were vital parts of the unresolved agenda of Canadian politics entering the 1990s.

THE AMERICANIZATION OF CANADIAN POLITICS?

As early as 1968, when Trudeau was selected as Liberal leader, many observers had identified a trend in Canadian politics towards style over substance, image over intellectual content, and executive prime minister over party caucus and Parliament—all qualities typically associated with American politics. Many of the charges came from people who did not understand the past. Style and image had always mattered in Canadian politics, as the careers of John A. Macdonald, Wilfrid Laurier, and Mackenzie King attested. Strong prime ministers had always dominated party caucuses and even Parliaments. Canadian politicians had always been quite willing to adapt new technologies, particularly on the campaign trail. But the Americans, international leaders in both popular politics and popular culture, usually led the way in the exploitation of new technology to political ends, and Canada typically lagged behind. Moreover, the Americans had developed constitutional mechanisms that seemed much more responsive to the popular will than the Canadian parliamentary system, which was based on British principles that had never included much direct reference to the people.

Canadian political parties copied the formula for their leadership conventions from the Americans, particularly in using these events in the best interests of the television viewers rather than of the delegates. The Liberals had won the election in 1968 partly on the strength of the publicity accompanying their leadership convention, and by the 1970s it would have been unthinkable to choose a party leader except in the full glare of the television cameras. Parties came to see the leadership convention as a way to monopolize a few days of news coverage and provide a launching platform for a new leader. The television coverage of these periodic rituals was equally imitative of American models. Despite the introduction of televised parliamentary debates, most Canadians still got much of their political information from TV news.

Whether the American 'presidential style' had a significant influence in Canada is somewhat less clear. Television not only encouraged the public to perceive the chief executive as the embodiment of the entire government, but made it essential that he or she perform well on TV. (The Americans took this conjunction to its logical conclusion when they elected a professional actor as their president.) Certainly Pierre Trudeau and Brian Mulroney both benefited from their ability to project effectively on TV. A more obvious example of American influence was the idea that the Canadian Senate should be 'Triple E': equal, elected, and effective. The idea of electing senators and giving them a positive role in the legislative process is profoundly American, and would unquestionably disrupt the Canadian political tradition of British-style responsible government.

The referendum used in Quebec, in 1980, to measure the public support for sovereignty-association was widely regarded as an American innovation. It was true that the US had made frequent use of referendums since they were introduced as a populist reform in the early 1900s. But they were not unknown in Canada. The federal government had held a referendum in 1898 over prohibition and again in 1942 over conscription (although in that case it was called a plebiscite), and Newfoundland had used more than one referendum to decide on unification with Canada. In many ways, the most important new political tool of the post-1970 period was the computer, particularly when it was harnessed to the older device of the public opinion poll. The computer enabled political campaigns to target potential supporters for special attention, and made it possible to test policy alternatives with the public on a constituency-by-constituency basis. Politicians were now able to get regular feedback about how their policies would be popularly received and to target key ridings at election time. Both the software and the techniques used by pollsters were largely taken from contemporary market research, most of which was American, and the central assumption was that political policies could be sold to the electorate the same way that soft drinks were. In the 1984 election campaign, the Mulroney Tories pioneered in the sophisticated application of computerized marketing, obviously quite successfully. Once in power, the Mulroney government allegedly used similar techniques to market free trade and Meech Lake to the Canadian public.

THE FEDERAL CIVIL SERVICE

By the end of the 1960s, 200,000 Canadians were employed in the federal public service. That total grew by 37 per cent during the first half of the next decade, reaching 273,000 by 1976. Between 1970 and 1976 alone 241,000 new appointments were made to the service and 438,000 appointments within it.[16] Under Trudeau the government had made a serious effort to rationalize and control the bureaucracy. The result was initially a greatly increased prime ministerial staff, headed first by Marc Lalonde and then by Michael Pitfield—which was the source of many of the complaints about encroaching presidential style. Ultimately, an entirely new level of bureaucrats emerged whose task was to use contemporary systems analysis to plan, rationalize, and staff. Nine cabinet committees were created in the early 1970s to assist in the process, recruiting new 'super-bureaucrats'— young, male, and university-trained in public administration—who were attracted to Ottawa by the opportunities for involvement in power politics at the highest level.[17]

By the mid-1970s the federal service was

exhibiting many characteristics that would become entrenched over the succeeding years. There were very high rates of turnover, often leading to instability, in the lower rungs, and increasing tendencies towards centralization in Ottawa–Hull, particularly in senior management positions. By 1976, 70 per cent of senior managers were in the nation's capital. (One by-product was that Ottawa–Hull consistently had the country's highest average income per family.) The federal public service had always discriminated against women at the upper levels, but that tendency became even more pronounced after 1976, a year when half the male civil servants were managers and over 90 per cent of the females were non-managers.

No agency was more male-dominated than the Privy Council Office itself. The managers were also relatively young, and the federal bureaucracy—like other professional organizations of the post-1970 period—was unable to recruit new members into its upper ranks because of the large numbers already there. When the size of the bureaucracy was finally frozen in the early 1980s, it was an aging, male-dominated hierarchical structure that was almost totally unresponsive to either outside directives or official policy statements. Instead of serving as the instruments of centralized federal policy, the federal bureaucracy had become a symbol of its stagnation. As so often happens, once the system had come to full fruition, it was no longer a subject of current debate except as a target for complaints about the inertia and failure of government. This situation would continue through the end of the century—and into the next one.

THE ECONOMY IN THE 1970s

THE 'ECONOMIC CRISIS'

The so-called economic crisis of the mid-1970s did not arrive overnight, and it ought to have been expected. At the same time, the measurable components of the crisis did not square well with the liberal economics (*pace* Keynes) that had dominated Canadian thinking since World War II. Runaway inflation, high interest rates, high levels of unemployment, and substantial poverty—all visible economic indicators—were supposed to be things of the past, and in any event ought not to be occurring simultaneously. In traditional economics, unemployment and poverty represented an economic downturn, even a recession or depression. Nobody wanted a depression, but the system was supposed to be self-correcting, with inflation and interest rates falling in response to the economic slowdown. Instead, some sectors of the economy were behaving as if they were overheated, while others were giving quite contrary signals.

The reasons for the contradictory economic indicators were not easy to explain to the Canadian public, particularly since the experts themselves did not agree on interpretations. Several realities were, or ought to have been, clear. One was that the manufacturing economies of the rest of the industrialized (and industrializing) world had not only recovered from the devastation of World War II, but had modernized and jumped ahead of a laggard Canada, which was unable to compete either internationally or in its own domestic market. While there were many reasons for Canada's manufacturing decline relative to its competition, a key factor was unusually low output per worker, which meant relatively high costs per unit. Some Canadians blamed the decline on foreign ownership, others on inadequate research and development. For some years, beginning in the 1960s, Canada had protected its domestic market and industries with higher tariffs and import quotas, but such responses only made it more difficult to sell Canadian goods in the world market. Canada was now manufacturing in a far more competitive and cutthroat world than ever before.

At the same time that Canadian manufacturing—notably in traditional sectors such as steel, automobiles, textiles, and shoes—was in serious trouble, Canada seemed unable to take full advantage of what many thought ought to have been its principal economic card: access to cheap energy and raw materials. Here, of course, what was in the best interests of the manufacturing industries was not in the best interests of the possessors and producers of those raw materials. The international cost of many raw materials shot up markedly in the early 1970s, creating a boom in the resource sector of the Canadian economy just as the manufacturing sector was becoming increasingly flat. The federal government tried to balance matters out a bit—as with its complicated multi-tiered pricing system for petroleum—but it only angered the producers (led by the Alberta government) without receiving the gratitude of consumers. Higher prices for gas, oil, and coal not only enraged consumers in central Canada, but also encouraged producers to sell abroad.

THE RESOURCE SECTOR

To make matters worse, not all sectors of Canada's resource economy benefited equally from international inflation. On the whole, prices for raw foodstuffs—either internationally or domestically—did not increase commensurately with those for other materials. The price of wheat more than doubled during the early 1970s, to the benefit of western farmers, but the price of oil rose from $2 to $30 per barrel and the price of breakfast cereal more than tripled. Through a complicated system of protectionism and subsidization, federal and provincial governments succeeded in insulating both the Canadian farmer and the Canadian consumer from the worst consequences, but the pricing problems remained unresolved. The price of food in Canada stayed comparatively low, costing a lower percentage of family income in 1980 than it had in 1970.

Despite quotas and marketing boards, Canadian farmers continued to produce more than the market required, especially since that market was also being supplied by American farmers who could produce at even lower costs. High operating costs (including energy) and high interest rates combined with fluctuating, even declining, prices to squeeze many Canadian farmers. No Canadian doubted that farmers were the backbone of Canadian society, or that—despite the temporary prosperity provided by wheat production in the early 1970s—the agricultural system, along with Canadian society, was in serious trouble. Uneven rainfall made matters worse. Nevertheless, the preferred solution was government assistance for farmers rather than higher food prices. Not all farmers would be supported, however.[18]

In early June 1986 the leading bureaucrat in Agriculture Canada created an uproar in Parliament by admitting in an interview that the federal government intended to resolve Canadian 'farm problems' by encouraging thousands of marginal farmers to leave the business. 'To me, the basic dilemma of the next three years will be to ease, assist and support the transition without installing terribly uneconomic devices', he said. 'I think 15 to 20 percent [fewer farmers] is not unrealistic. The period is another matter.'[19] Rural depopulation was hardly a new phenomenon in Canada, and programs to eliminate uneconomic producers in the fishery, for example, went back many years. But to state openly that there were too many farmers was not only to play with political dynamite, but to provide a graphic illustration of how much the nation had changed since Confederation, which had been undertaken in part to allow Canada to open a new agricultural West.

Although the opposition in Parliament demanded to be told how the 'one-in-five' farmer to be eliminated would be chosen, there was little mystery about who were most vulnerable: younger farmers, new to the business, were at maximum risk, although any farmer heavily in debt was in trouble. In the early 1970s young entrants particularly had responded, with the usual optimism of the agricultural community, to higher grain prices (created by crop failures in

the USSR, India, and Argentina) by borrowing money to buy land and equipment. In the early 1980s a combination of high inflation and falling commodity prices led to disaster for many in the farm community, despite heavy subsidies, but that downward turn was a short-term factor in the farm crisis. Perhaps the most important long-term factor was the cost of farmland, which was being driven up by non-agricultural causes. In Ontario, for example, land prices averaged $795 per acre (0.4 hectares), and were obviously much higher in prime areas—even after the bottom had dropped out of a speculative market in 1984—and good wheat land in the West was worth nearly $1,000 per acre. Those farmers who did not inherit their land started out deeply in debt, and only buoyant prices would allow them to rise out of it.

Even so, the farmers' dilemma in the 1970s and 1980s was not as apparent as that of the fishing people. Not only were fish stocks being constantly depleted by overfishing on the part of both domestic and international fleets, but the price of fish was not entirely dependent on supply, for fish had to compete with other foods. Luxury items such as lobster could sustain greater price increases, but the market for them was limited at best. Were the price of fish to get distinctly out of line with wheat, beef, or chicken, consumers could stop buying it altogether. Canadian fishers demanded protection for their fish stocks, while repeated government investigations indicated that there were too many Canadian fishers as well as too much international fishing in Canadian waters, especially off the Atlantic coast. Many fishers and their families compensated for inadequate earnings by collecting unemployment compensation (made possible by changes in the Unemployment Insurance Act of 1971) and by working in other jobs much of the year. But these strategies offered no permanent solution.

A more promising way of dealing with the difficulties experienced by the Atlantic fisheries was to provide fishers with new forms of employment. Under the Trudeau government of 1968–72, regional economic development and the correction of long-standing economic disparities had assumed a high priority. Federal programs, spearheaded by the Department of Regional Economic Expansion (DREE), pumped large sums of money into the Atlantic region. Unfortunately, regional development turned into a contest between the federal government and the provinces, partly because Ottawa needed to justify expanding centralization in order to keep Quebec and the West from getting out of control. Nor was job creation a panacea for regional disparities. In the Atlantic region, for example, new jobs were created at rates above the national average in the early 1970s, but the regional rate of unemployment outpaced that of job creation, mainly because of population growth fuelled by the promise of new jobs; people remained at home rather than migrating to areas of higher employment.

THE TRUDEAU GOVERNMENT AND ECONOMIC POLICY, 1968–75

The first Trudeau government, focusing on what the Prime Minister called 'the Just Society', related the performance of the Canadian economy to the needs of the society. Thus, in the early 1970s critics argued that unemployment insurance was serving as a sort of public welfare or even income redistribution program. In 1970 the Trudeau government published a white paper entitled 'Unemployment Insurance in the 1970s', which recommended that unemployment insurance coverage be extended to most of the adult population, the benefit increased to 66 per cent of former earnings, the qualifying periods be shortened, and the benefit period lengthened. The new Unemployment Insurance Plan was introduced in 1971, allowing the government to avoid directly confronting the concept of a guaranteed minimum income for all Canadians.

In addition to 'discovering' the structural realities of regional economic disparities, the government drew attention to the structure of

A demonstration by the National Farmers Union at the Alberta legislature, Edmonton, 9 November 1974. *Edmonton Journal* photo, Provincial Archives of Alberta J.1579/3.

poverty in Canada. The two issues were not unrelated. The key document was the report of a special Senate Committee on Poverty (appointed late in 1968) entitled *Poverty in Canada*, which first appeared in November 1971 and was reprinted several times over the ensuing months. In many respects, this report represented the high point of official 'liberal' thinking in Canada. It recognized that not all Canadians had shared equally in the post-war prosperity. It also pointed out that Canada had the highest unemployment among industrially advanced nations and that it was not randomly distributed: rather, it was centred on a minority of the labour force in certain economic sectors and in certain regions.

In effect, poverty in Canada had become

structural, perpetuating itself despite the welfare system. Indeed, the report argued that the welfare system itself helped to perpetuate poverty by keeping recipients going but not improving their situation. The committee recognized that single mothers made up an important segment among the poor, and called for improved daycare facilities. Its radical conclusion was to recommend a guaranteed annual income for all Canadians and incorporation of 'the right to an adequate standard of living for all Canadians into the Canadian Bill of Rights'.[20] Although the social inadequacies of the existing welfare system were well documented, the idea of a guaranteed income was doubtless Utopian.

In 1972 the Canadian electorate decided that the Trudeau government did not deserve a majority, electing 109 Liberal, 107 Tory, and 31 NDP MPs. Trudeau continued to govern with the support of David Lewis's NDP. The Just Society was put on the back burner during much of Trudeau's minority term—despite pressure from the NDP—chiefly because of the oil crisis, which forced the government to concentrate on the economy itself. While the Foreign Investment Review Agency (FIRA) was put in place to deal with the problem of foreign ownership in Canada, the OPEC action put oil and its successor, inflation, at centre stage. As might have been expected, Canadians had difficulty understanding the complications of the intersection of international and domestic economic problems. In 1974 the Liberal government again went to the polls. Robert Stanfield's Tories wanted to deal with an escalating double-digit inflation by introducing wage and price controls, a policy the Prime Minister pooh-poohed from coast to coast. To Stanfield's disappointment, voters rejected the idea of controls, and Trudeau won a resounding victory that almost demolished the NDP.

The unholy trinity of economic problems—inflation, interest rates, and unemployment, all in the double digits—continued unabated. Those seeking explanations could have blamed the banks, for the interest rates, or the business sector, for the unemployment. Instead Canadians generally chose to fasten on the most visible and immediate of the three problem areas—inflation—and a single factor to explain it. Polls taken in 1975 indicated that the majority of Canadians blamed inflation on overly powerful labour unions demanding unreasonable wage settlements.

Organized labour in Canada had made its great gains after World War II, and especially after 1960, when it grew in total membership, in its percentage of the workforce, and in its penetration of new industries, particularly in the public sector. Labour unions sought to protect their members from the effects of the new economic conditions, particularly by demanding high wage settlements and opposing management efforts to rationalize and modernize their workforces through the traditional mechanisms: laying off or firing redundant workers.[21] Strikes in many industries—including a much-publicized postal strike in the summer of 1975—made the demands of labour appear unreasonable. The 'posties' not only disrupted a public service that Canadians had long taken for granted, but won a substantial wage increase and a significantly shorter workweek in the process. There was apparently little public sympathy for such public-sector employees as the postal workers, though their wages had systematically fallen behind those of the private sector and their civil service managers appeared incapable of dealing fairly with them. When police, fire fighters, nurses, and teachers began taking similar steps, Canadians became alarmed. Not only were key public services threatened with interruption by strikes, but wage settlements in the public sector would have to be financed through either higher taxes or deficit spending.

THE GROWTH OF GOVERNMENT SPENDING

The traditional Keynesian system—in which deficits were not considered a significant prob-

TABLE 20.1

TOTAL HEALTH-CARE SPENDING, CANADA AND THE UNITED STATES, 1960–1991, AS A PERCENTAGE OF GROSS DOMESTIC PRODUCT

Year	Canada	United States
1960	5.5	5.3
1965	6.0	5.9
1970	7.1	7.3
1975	7.3	8.3
1980	7.5	9.2
1985	8.7	10.5
1991	9.9	13.2

SOURCE: Canada, Department of National Health and Welfare, Health Information Division, Policy, Planning and Information Branch, *Health Expenditure in Canada, Summary Report, 1987-1991* (Ottawa: Health Canada Mar. 1993). Reproduced with permission of the minister of Public Works and Government Services Canada, 2007.

lem—had become conventional wisdom because it offered an alternative to the regressive measures undertaken in response to the Great Depression. Although political leaders in the 1930s had balanced their budgets, a great many people had suffered in the process. According to Keynes, balancing the budget was exactly the wrong thing to do in a time of depression. Instead, governments needed to spend money to stimulate the economy, correcting the deficits created in bad times by increasing revenues in good times. Some liberal economists held that deficits never did have to be retired—although the age-old problem with public deficits is that they represent government debt that has to be maintained through interest payments. High interest rates, such as those of the early 1970s, made the government debt much more expensive to service, and the economic problems of the period set in motion a number of automatic mechanisms, built into the welfare state's safety net, that greatly increased public expenditures. When particular government programs of the day were added to automatic spending, the result was such a rapid increase in deficits that they became a public issue in themselves. By 1992–3 federal and provincial deficits together were $57.9 billion for the year.

Two competing theories were developed to explain the growth of government spending. One saw increased spending as natural, inevitable, and incremental, the product of a modern economy and society facing new demands and expectations. For example, the increased public role in health care certainly increased the expenditures on health care in Canada between 1960 and 1991, not only in absolute terms but especially in terms of the percentage of the gross domestic product devoted to it, although the increase was not as great as in the United States (see Table 20.1). By 1991 the total annual health-care bill in Canada was about $2,500 per capita. Behind the increases in spending on health care were new medical technologies and treatments (including new pharmaceuticals), the aging of the Canadian population, and greater use of the system by its clients. Health-care insurance was by far Canada's most expensive social program and the largest single item in every province's budget.[22]

The other theory, rooted in the self-interest of collective decision-making, has usually been called 'public choice' theory. It argues that the self-interest of politicians for popularity and of civil servants for larger budgets coincide to produce constant pressure on budgets. Public choice theory lies at the heart of the British television series *Yes, Minister* (later *Yes, Prime Minister*) that was widely enjoyed in Canada in the 1980s.[23] It is far more cynical than the incremental interpretation, and encourages the suspicions that many Canadians harbour concerning their political leaders.

Most Canadians recognized that they could not run their own households forever on government-style spending principles, and a host of more conservative economists now emerged to confirm that recognition. At their head was Milton Friedman of the University of Chicago, who set against Keynesianism an economic theory usually called monetarism. Friedman rejected the concept of the welfare state, insisting on a close relationship between general price levels and the money supply and opposing deficit spending. The best policy was to control the stock of money (and therefore inflation) and otherwise leave the market to regulate itself.[24] Signs of the rise of conservative economics in Canada included the establishment of think-tanks such as the Fraser Institute of Vancouver (1974) and the introduction of departments and faculties of business and management at Canadian universities, a trend that really took off in the early 1970s. The establishment or expansion of these faculties was partly a response to the alleged failure of departments of economics (often dominated by the Keynesians or even Marxists) to serve the needs of Canadian business and industry.

TRUDEAU'S ECONOMIC POLICY

The net result of these developments was the about-turn executed by Prime Minister Trudeau on wage and price controls, as well as on public-service unions. The government's tinkering with policies of voluntary restraint is associated with Finance Minister John Turner, whose May 1974 budget was defeated, forcing an election. He resigned in September 1975 and left politics the next year. On Thanksgiving Day 1975—a day chosen to catch the largest possible number of Canadians at home—Trudeau announced in Parliament and on national television that mandatory controls were necessary on any private corporation with more than 500 employees and on every public civil servant employed by the federal government. Increases would be held to 10 per cent in the first year, 8 per cent in the second, and 6 per cent in the third year of the program. Provincial governments of all stripes (even NDP) accepted the policy. Even though the Anti-Inflation Board did more to limit wages than prices, Canadians did not object. They also seemed to approve of the government when it adopted a far more confrontational policy towards its public-service unions.

The economic crisis of the mid-1970s, brought about when the policies and principles of 30 years of prosperity all seemed to collapse together, called for new initiatives from government and people alike. Some members of the public recognized the deep-rooted nature of the problem, but most preferred to find scapegoats, blaming labour unions in particular for something that was everybody's responsibility. Like the public, Trudeau's Liberals talked about the need for structural reform of the economy, but they were satisfied with band-aid solutions. Trudeau himself preached the need to consume less, but did nothing to encourage or compel such a development. The crisis passed without significant economic changes at either the public or the private level. And with the PQ's victory in late 1976, Ottawa considered the problems posed by Quebec to be more urgent than economic issues. Thus the Trudeau government—like other governments in Canada and around the world—continued to spend more than it collected in taxes and revenue, with no apparent concern for the future.

Increasingly the energy crisis led to confrontations with the provinces, especially Alberta. After its return to power with a majority in 1980, the Trudeau government unilaterally introduced the National Energy Program (NEP), a typical pre-emptive strike designed to avoid the need to negotiate with the provinces. The NEP dealt with many of the controversial matters of the past few years. It encouraged oil exploration and drilling, as well as consumer conversion to gas or electric heat. It took an increased share of energy revenues in the form of taxes and a government stake in new discoveries. It expanded the role of the Crown corporation Petro-Canada. All these measures were predicated on the assumption that the energy crisis would continue and the international price of oil would remain high. OPEC could not maintain a unified front, however, and prices began to drop in 1982. Although most features of the NEP were discontinued after the Mulroney government took office in 1984, the oil-producing provinces remained suspicious of Ottawa and its energy policies for many years thereafter.

THE ECONOMY IN THE 1980S

The 1980s were spared economic crises such as those of 1973–5 until the very end of the decade. The Canadian economy, however, settled down to rates of unemployment, inflation, interest charges, housing costs, and taxation that would previously have been regarded as disastrous. Throughout the decade, the annual seasonally adjusted unemployment rate never went below 7.5 per cent, and it remained in double figures between 1982 and 1985. Inflation dropped below double figures in 1982, but consumer prices continued a constant increase throughout the rest of the decade, at rates ranging from a low of 4 per cent (1985) to a high of 5.8 per cent (1983). Interest rates dropped from 1981 highs close to 20 per cent for prime bor-

rowers, but the prime rate fell under 10 per cent only in 1987 and increased again substantially in 1989 and 1990. Taxes as a percentage of personal income ran at 18.9 per cent in 1980 and 22.0 per cent in 1990; in no intervening year was there anything but another small annual increase.[25]

Canadians soon became accustomed to the new situation, and stoically took even the worst of times in stride. An economic slowdown that started in 1980 and by 1983 saw unemployment climb to 11.8 per cent of the total workforce (19.8 in the under-25 group) received minimal attention from the media, perhaps because attention was focused on the Constitution debate. There were no major new public initiatives for dealing with the economy and its problems in this recession. The social welfare net clicked in automatically, and while more Canadian families fell below the poverty line, few actually starved —or demonstrated in the streets. Canadians recognized that jobs were becoming harder both to get and to keep. The young, in increasingly large numbers, responded to the new situation by pursuing higher education, especially in courses that promised an immediate economic payout on graduation. But they did not become radicalized in any serious way—perhaps because they were too busy working at part-time jobs to keep up the payments on their credit cards.

Despite the decline in the Keynesian liberalism that had dominated most of the twentieth century and the rise of a 'conservative' ideology based on private enterprise (confusingly, this was what the nineteenth century had called 'liberalism'), the 1980s set new records for mortgaging the future. Canadians everywhere—from Parliament to the universities—were living literally beyond their means. West Edmonton Mall—the world's largest shopping centre at the time of its completion, in 1986—could be seen as a symbol for this consuming society. The total debt of the federal government grew from $100 billion in 1981 to $380 billion in 1990, which on a per capita basis was an increase from $4,140 to

TABLE 20.2
UNEMPLOYMENT RATES, 1981–1990 (%)

Year	Rate	Female	Male	Under 25
1981	7.5	8.3	7.0	13.2
1982	11.0	10.9	11.0	18.7
1983	11.8	11.6	12.0	19.8
1984	11.2	11.3	11.2	17.8
1985	10.5	10.7	10.3	16.4
1986	9.5	9.8	9.3	15.1
1987	8.8	9.3	8.5	13.7
1988	7.8	8.3	7.4	12.0
1989	7.5	7.9	7.3	11.3
1990	7.9	7.9	7.9	12.5

SOURCE: Minister of Industry, Science and Technology, *Canadian Economic Observer: Historical Supplement, 1990/91* (Ottawa, 1991), 36.

■ The 'World Waterpark' in the West Edmonton Mall. Built in three phases from 1981 to 1986, the mall is a prime tourist destination—a massive complex of department stores, shops, restaurants, recreation areas, amusements, and services that also includes a luxury hotel. Courtesy West Edmonton Mall.

$14,317 per Canadian in only 10 years. (In 1970 the per capita figure had been a mere $795.60.) There had not been a budget surplus since the fiscal year 1972–3. Among developed nations only Italy—always regarded as the weakest country of post-war Europe—had a worse record of debt management.

At the same time, the Canadian consumer debt more than doubled from $46 billion to $101 billion in the eighties, increasing in small but steady increments from 18.7 per cent of post-tax personal income to 21.5 per cent. Much of that debt, of course, was incurred through the credit cards issued in profusion by banks, credit unions, stores, and just about every kind of business imaginable. In the last year of the decade, the number of bank credit-card transactions alone increased from just over 100 billion to over 150 billion. Residential mortgage debt nearly tripled (from $88 billion to $237 billion) and as a percentage of post-tax personal income grew from 35.4 per cent to 50.2 per cent. Over 10 years, Canadian personal consumer debt (including mortgages) had increased from 54.1 per cent of disposable personal income to 71.7 per cent, despite a larger tax bite and truly debilitating interest rates, which for individuals never dropped into single digits over the entire decade. Personal savings rates declined constantly over the 1980s, and personal consumption rates increased considerably faster than inflation. Given the amount of deficit financing, it was surprising that only two major financial institutions (the Northlands and Canadian Commercial Banks in Alberta) collapsed, although there were reports that several of the chartered banks were in some difficulty because of loans made to Third World nations.[26] In March 1992, it emerged that some of the chartered banks' diciest loans had been made (in 1990) to a Canadian corporation, Olympia & York Developments Ltd, for the construction of a major new office complex in the Docklands area of London, England.

Both the housing industry (nearly 2 million new housing starts) and the automobile industry (nearly 10 million new cars and more than 7.5 million trucks) boomed for most of the decade, as did manufacturers of big-ticket consumer items like furniture and household appliances. Many popular bumper stickers referred to consumer spending; one common slogan was 'We're spending our children's inheritance'. As always, Canadian secondary manufacturing relied on the domestic market (which was going ever deeper in debt) for its prosperity. In 1981 nearly 60 per cent of the value of Canada's exports was in primary and resource commodities, and that figure did not change appreciably over the decade, declining slightly towards the end of the period because of the softness of the international resource market. Despite the generally overheated nature of the Canadian economy (and perhaps because of it), not all Canadian corporations flourished. The early 1980s saw three corporate busts: Massey-Ferguson, the farm equipment manufacturers; Canadair Limited, the airplane manufacturers; and Dome Petroleum.[27] The first two succumbed to better-managed international competition, the last to a rapidly acquired debt load with chartered banks that represented a substantial proportion of its capital.

THE SAD FATE OF THE POST OFFICE

In May 1986 Michael Wilson, the federal Minister of Finance, labelled 'not acceptable' a review committee's recommendation that Canada Post be allowed a grace period until 1990 before becoming financially self-supporting. Wilson wanted quicker action. The episode symbolized the new political thinking. Whereas an earlier federalism had regarded the Post Office as an essential national service, now all that mattered was its 'financial self-sufficiency'.[28]

From the first Post Office Act of 1867, the Canadian government had emphasized the need for a cheap, accessible, and efficient postal system. In 1884 one politician summarized the public attitude when he argued in a House of

Commons debate that 'Post Offices are not established for the purpose of providing a revenue, but for the convenience of the people', adding that post offices, like public works, could be viewed from the standpoint 'that the general business of the country will be promoted by them'.[29] Even though the system continued expanding before World War I, it turned surpluses regularly, if not annually, between 1900 and 1958. Two factors made profitability possible: the extent to which the postal service dominated communications in Canada, and the government's accounting practices, which charged the costs of land, buildings, and furnishings to Public Works rather than the Post Office itself. In the 1960s the postal service became unionized and no longer ran at a profit, but it was not yet in danger of being dismantled.

Not until the early 1980s did many commentators become concerned with the Post Office's 'deficit', which increased substantially after the government ended the practice of burying postal costs in other departments. The deficit was regarded as shocking by those Canadians, chiefly businessmen, who no longer relied exclusively on the mail to conduct their business and who increasingly saw the government service less as an essential public service than as an antiquated communications business in competition with other delivery systems. Much of the competition (couriers, telex, fax) had developed in response to the interruption of mail delivery by a series of crippling postal strikes in 1965, 1968, 1975, and 1981 and to a general deterioration in service, some of which was the consequence of the Post Office's efforts to cut costs.

In 1980 the federal minister responsible for the Post Office, André Ouellet, threw his support behind the central recommendation of a 1978 study group that a Crown postal corporation be established, to 'give Canada Post the independence to function in the marketplace in a way that is not possible now'. In 1985 another review committee insisted that the continuing operating deficit of Canada Post had to be eliminated

quickly, and claimed that Canadians were prepared to accept far longer delivery times (which had already increased from one day coast-to-coast in 1962 to four days in 1985) and higher costs in return for some standard of reliability.[30] Although much older than the many other universally accessible national services created in the affluent period following the war, the postal system—like them—had also been sheltered by the pre-1972 consensus and was shattered by its collapse.

THE TRIUMPH OF THE PRIVATE ENTERPRISE MENTALITY

A key catchphrase for business in the 1980s was 'better management practices'—necessary if Canadian corporations were to compete in the dog-eat-dog world of international capitalism. But there were also some contradictory trends, such as the growth in the mystique of the swashbuckling entrepreneur. The dichotomies of the era were reflected in the titles of two popular books for business readers: *In Search of Excellence* and *The Money-Rustlers*. The favoured entrepreneurialism took two basic forms. One involved manipulation of billions of dollars of borrowed money (in an age of easy access to credit at all levels) by mega-speculators on the international level. Robert Campeau, perhaps the most notorious speculator, had begun as an Ottawa contractor and flourished in the dizzy world of real estate development from the sixties to the eighties, along with Albert, Paul, and Ralph Reichmann (Olympia & York) and E.P. Taylor (Cadillac–Fairview). Campeau eventually moved into the American market, obtaining a number of merchandising corporations (including Saks Fifth Avenue and Bloomingdale's) on his way to eventual collapse.[31] The other favoured entrepreneur was the small businessman, who became one of the darlings of government and the business journals in the late 1980s.

Of course the private enterprise mentality that emerged in the 1980s, at the political as well as popular level, was not merely a Canadian phenomenon. The Mulroney Tories were actually participants in a worldwide trend that was characteristic of the decade. It had begun in Britain with the election of Margaret Thatcher in 1979 and continued in the US with the triumph of Ronald Reagan in 1980.[32] (Even the Russians would get into the act, with Mikhail Gorbachev proving to be the most committed private-enterpriser of the lot). In the 1984 election campaign Brian Mulroney had sought the political centre, one commentator arguing that he promised 'what amounts to Liberalism with a Fresh Face'.[33] But his party had strong support from the Canadian business community, which wanted action on tax reform, deficit reduction, and a general cutback in the government's direct involvement in the economy.

In power, the Tories did manage to reduce the growth rate of the deficit, but balancing the budget was a difficult political task. Mulroney's first administration emphasized closer attention to spending rather than major budget cuts—and the beginning of privatization, such as the selling of the assets of the Canada Development Investment Corporation (CDIC). Still, the government avoided open confrontation with the principle of universality of social insurance services and chose instead to concentrate on increasing revenue through greater economic prosperity. This ambition led Canada in what was ostensibly a major new direction, for the main vehicle for prosperity was to be a new economic relationship with Canada's largest trading partner, the United States. The eventual Free Trade Agreement (FTA) —negotiated in secret during 1986 and 1987— ran to 3,000 pages of legal language and would take years to work out in detail. Tariffs would gradually be removed, although Canadians would discover, to their surprise, that the disparity between what goods cost in American and Canadian shops was largely attributable not to tariffs but to economic differences between the two counties, including costs and market sizes. They were equally surprised to find that 'free trade' did not

apply to ordinary people shopping in the US and returning to Canada with their purchases. The most important part of the Free Trade Agreement was allegedly the elimination of discrimination on the basis of nationality.

The national debate over the deal produced much more heat than light.[34] Not even the economic experts could safely predict the ultimate effects of the treaty, although most favoured it in principle. Critics complained that the Canadian negotiators had traded access to the American market for Canadian resources (including energy) in return for continental economic integration. But most of that integration had already been achieved through previous arrangements, and only a small percentage of total Canadian–American trade was actually affected by the treaty. The strongest nationalist argument against the deal was that Canada would no longer have complete control of its own social policies, since many of them could be interpreted as unfair subsidies in breach of the national treatment rule, according to which a state must treat services and service suppliers of another state no less favourably than its own. Some critics warned that the Americans would not give Canada fair access to markets in industries (such as softwood lumber) where there was a strong US lobby. But the most telling criticism that could have been advanced against free trade was that it would not revolutionize Canadian–American economic relations, that, in fact, it was merely a cosmetic overhaul of the existing continental arrangement. In effect, a government seeking accomplishments suitable for an election campaign oversold the deal to the Canadian electorate.

The election of 1988 was held before ratification of either the Free Trade Agreement or the Meech Lake Accord, so the victorious Tories got only the benefits of the putative advantages in both cases. In its second term, the Mulroney government ran into many more problems than in its first. As we shall see, it failed miserably with Meech Lake, and its response to the recession at the end of the decade—an anti-inflationary pol-

ALLAN GOTLIEB ON
THE FREE TRADE AGREEMENT

Allan Gotlieb was born in Winnipeg and educated at Oxford University. He served as Canadian ambassador to the United States between 1981 and 1988, keeping a private diary of these years. The diary was published in 2006. This is part of the entry for the final day of the free trade negotiations.

Our side cooled down in the early evening, and we met Baker and Yeutter [James Baker, Ronald Reagan's chief of staff, and Clayton Yeutter, US Trade Representative—the two chief American negotiators] again on the dispute settlement mechanism, only to have them completely reject our new proposal! I pressed Baker very hard. 'We can't do it,' he said. 'Congress would never agree to such a vague approach and any limits on its power.'

We adjourned and the Canadians caucused again. It was about 9 p.m. Those in the room were polled—Wilson, Carney, Burney, Gotlieb, and Hartt—and all agreed we could not go forward; the deal was off. The negotiations were over. Finished. Burney telephoned the prime minister in Toronto and Clark in cabinet. They accepted our conclusion that it was all over.

We then prepared to announce failure. Burney went back in to see Baker alone to convey the news that the grand game was terminated and that we had failed. Our decision seemed to come as a thunderbolt to Baker. He pulled back and asked to be given more time. Burney agreed. An hour later, with only a few hours to go, Baker came back to us with a *volte-face*. He accepted our earlier proposal on dispute settlement. He had gotten the US side to agree to meet our fundamental requirements. Unbelievably, we had a deal.

We ironed out the remaining issues in a wild atmosphere, everyone running up and down corridors trying to keep up with the speed of developments. Baker kept popping into our caucus room saying, fifty minutes to go, forty to go, and so on down to the wire. The deal was done and completed at ten minutes before midnight. Baker then dispatched a messenger, and notice was received in Congress at a minute before the deadline.

If it were not for Baker, there would be no agreement.

Midnight

The Canadians came back to the Residence. We drank. And we drank. The mood was ecstatic. The night was cold, so we had the first fire of the year. Everyone praised everyone for two hours non-stop, and we toasted the prime minister for his leadership and his courage.

SOURCE: Allan Gotlieb, *The Washington Diaries, 1981–1989* (Toronto: McClelland & Stewart, 2006), 493.

icy (through the Bank of Canada) that raised interest rates and only increased the size of the deficit—reflected the monetarist thinking that had become the conventional wisdom in Ottawa.

Under Mulroney the federal government seemed to be bringing the runaway economy under control on all fronts except interest rates. High interest rates also contributed to unemployment, which reduced income tax revenues and increased expenditures on unemployment insurance and welfare. One economist calculated that almost two-thirds of the 1992 deficit was caused by lost tax revenues from unemployment and increased costs for social assistance; the rest was the result of high interest payments to creditors.[35] Another team of economists at the University of Toronto who examined the reasons for the recession of 1989–92 concluded that the principal cause was the Bank of Canada's anti-inflation policy.[36] Certainly the obsession with inflation rather than poverty or unemployment benefited creditors more than debtors. In the Canadian context, it also benefited foreign investors, who profited from an artificially favourable exchange rate created by anti-inflationary policy.[37] Nevertheless, many Canadians remained convinced that the welfare state rather than monetary policy was the cause of the huge budget deficits, and the government's monetary policy seldom came under real public attack.

On the other hand, the Mulroney government did run up against public opposition over tax reform. Characteristically, the Tories focused on the business taxation system rather than the structure of the personal income tax system. They decided to replace lost tariffs and other existing levies with a single across-the-board value-added tax (called the Goods and Services Tax, or GST) of 9 per cent imposed at the cash register. Not surprisingly, the provinces refused to eliminate their sales taxes in favour of the new federal levy, which would be paid by consumers and administered by the business people who, despite the additional paperwork involved, were virtually the only supporters of the scheme. Finance Minister Michael Wilson responded to business pressure by reluctantly agreeing to reduce the amount of the tax from 9 to 7 per cent, but neither he nor the government was really prepared for the extent of the public opposition that emerged as the date for implementation came closer and the need to pass the necessary legislation became urgent. As with policies such as Meech Lake and free trade, the Mulroney government had allowed a long lead time between announcement of the policy and its ultimate implementation. The purpose of the delay was to allow the government to make minor concessions (such as the reduction in the rate charged)

and disarm the opposition. As Meech Lake had demonstrated, not until the deadline for ratification was approaching did opposition really crystallize, and then the government was in serious trouble.

The Mulroney government assumed that its overwhelming majority in the Commons would ensure passage of the GST, whatever the public or the Liberal-controlled Senate thought. Michael Wilson's department began instructing businessmen on the intricacies of the tax and its collection before the requisite legislation had received final parliamentary approval. The Liberal majority in the Senate dug in its heels, encouraged by public opinion polls indicating that a vast majority of Canadians were dead set against the GST. With the threat of deadlock looming between the two houses of Parliament, in late September 1990 the Tories used the power that governing parties have always held over the upper houses in a parliamentary system: they appointed eight new Tory senators, giving their party a majority in both houses. This action was in broad terms constitutional, but it may not have been politically wise. Inevitably, the government was charged with 'arrogance', and the bill was clearly so unpopular that no one could seriously accuse senators who opposed it of 'thwarting the will of the people'. By 1991 it was clear that the Mulroney government had lost virtually all of its popular support. Less clear was whether the change in public attitudes had anything to do with the Tories' private enterprise philosophy or was merely a product of some ill-advised tactics. In general, prime ministers create governments that in some mysterious ways reflect their own personalities. Among the characteristics that Mulroney shared with his government were tendencies towards secrecy, manipulation, and heavy-handedness.

DÉTENTE

By the early 1980s Canada's relations outside North America had a very low profile apart from the perennial concern over trade figures and the occasional international conference attended by the Prime Minister. Canadian diplomats quietly participated in various international meetings devoted to further freeing up of trade, especially in the context of the General Agreement on Tariffs and Trade (GATT), first signed by Canada at its inception in 1947. In 1976 Canada joined the Group of Six leading industrial nations a year after the inception of this summit group, making it the G-7, that met in periodic summits to discuss world economic problems, hosting its first summit in Ottawa–Montebello in 1981.[38] Some attempt was made to gain political mileage from Prime Minister Trudeau's international stature, particularly in comparison with Joe Clark's lack of it, but while Trudeau always performed well at international events, his heart was seldom in them. Canadians seemed to understand that Canada was not a major world player and to expect very little from foreign policy initiatives. The military gave rise to a joke ('How did Canada deal with the needs of a two-ocean navy and only one aircraft carrier?' 'It scrapped the aircraft carrier.') but was otherwise largely forgotten. After 1988, of course, the Free Trade Agreement made it clear that Canada was more closely bound to the Americans than ever before.

The key events of the 1980s were international. The first was 'glasnost', the process of liberation from repressive communism in the Soviet Union, associated with Mikhail Gorbachev. The Soviet regime had been gradually opening up for decades. Détente between the USSR and the US had been achieved in the early 1970s, but no one was prepared for the speed with which, in the later 1980s, the USSR and its satellites in Eastern Europe began to move in what could only be described as capitalistic and democratic directions. The most obvious symbol was the razing of the Berlin Wall, in November 1989, when the fall of the East German government cleared the way for German reunification in late 1990. It was perhaps still too soon to celebrate the death of communism, but the changes in Germany symbol-

ized a new European order. The Warsaw Pact disintegrated, and Canada's main formal link with Europe—NATO—underwent a rapid transformation as it ceased to focus on defence against the Soviet bloc. Canada signalled the abandonment of its bases in Germany in the 1992 budget, and by 1993 the Allies had pulled most of their troops out of Berlin, ending the occupation that was virtually the last remnant of the Cold War in Germany. Soon the European Community was besieged with applications from former Soviet client states.

A reduction of tensions in Europe did not necessarily mean that the world had been saved for democracy, however. As if to demonstrate the fragility of international peace, in the summer of 1990 the Iraqi army invaded Kuwait, one of the small oil-rich principalities on the Persian Gulf. The world witnessed not only a *coup d'état* in terms of the occupation itself, but the unusual spectacle of American–Russian co-operation against Saddam Hussein. With Russian approval, President George H.W. Bush sent American forces to the Gulf with the object of preventing the Iraqis from taking over more oil states and, eventually, forcing them out of Kuwait by military means. Canada contributed three ancient destroyers to the international force assembling in the Gulf—another 'three tokens'—although in fairness, the vessels were the best the Canadian forces could muster.[39] The Iraqi takeover of Kuwait caused the price of oil to increase almost instantly from $20 a barrel—a stable price in the 1980s—to $35.

CONCLUSION

Between 1972 and the early 1990s the old liberal consensus had plainly collapsed, along with its Keynesian economic rationale. Now free-market monetarism prevailed, accompanied by a private enterprise mentality. The monetary policy used to address the recession of 1989–92 greatly increased the deficit, which many Canadians still wrongly blamed on the social insurance programs put in place before 1972. At the same time Canada had moved to continental free trade, an action that in itself was not critical but could become so if the FTA became part of a larger pattern of global integration, and in significant ways became a lesser player in global affairs.

SHORT BIBLIOGRAPHY

Blomqvist, Ake, and David M. Brown, eds. *Limits to Care: Reforming Canada's Health System in an Age of Restraint.* Toronto, 1994. An excellent collection of monographs on the problems of health care.

Cook, Peter. *Massey at the Brink: The Story of Canada's Greatest Multinational and Its Struggle to Survive.* Toronto, 1981. The fascinating story of the demise of Massey-Ferguson.

Fossum, John Erik. *Oil, the State, and Federalism: The Rise and Demise of Petro-Canada as a Statist Impulse.* Toronto, 1997. A detailed and careful analysis of the NEP and the role of Petro-Canada.

Giangrande, Carole. *Down to Earth: The Crisis in Canadian Farming.* Toronto, 1985. A useful account of the problems of Canadian agriculture in the 1980s.

Gwyn, Richard. *The Northern Magus.* Toronto, 1980. Arguably the best biography of Pierre Elliott Trudeau, insightful and intelligent.

McQuaig, Linda. *Shooting the Hippo: Death by Deficit and Other Canadian Myths.* Toronto, 1995. A trenchant revisionist view of Canadian policy that cuts against the conventional monetary policy of the post-1970s.

Morgan, Nicole. *Implosion: An Analysis of the Growth of the Federal Public Service in Canada, 1945–1985.* Montreal, 1986. A fascinating study of one of the important trends of the post-war years.

Savoie, Donald. *The Politics of Public Spending in Canada.* Toronto, 1990. An analysis of the budgetary deficits, showing where the money went and why.

Sawatsky, John. *Mulroney: The Politics of Ambition.* Toronto, 1991. Perhaps the best of the Mulroney biographies, not terribly sympathetic.

Saywell, John. *The Rise of the Parti Québécois, 1967–1976.* Toronto, 1977. A straightforward narrative study of the first 10 years of the PQ.

Vance, Joan. *An Analysis of the Costs and Benefits of Public Lotteries: The Canadian Experience.* Lewiston, Queenston, and Lampeter, 1989. An important study of Canadian lottery policy, more general than its title suggests.

STUDY QUESTIONS

1. Why did public trust in the nation's political leaders decrease after 1970?

2. What does the legalization of lotteries tell us about Canada after 1970?

3. Why was the oil crisis so important?

4. Why was Pierre Trudeau such a controversial figure in Canadian politics?

5. Why did the personal popularity of Ed Broadbent not translate into more votes for the NDP?

6. What were the key ingredients of the economic crisis of the 1970s?

7. What does Allan Gotlieb's account of the last day of negotiations over the FTA tell us about those negotiations?

8. What accounts for the furor over the GST?

9. Why did public opinion turn against Brian Mulroney?

CHAPTER TWENTY-ONE

■ The Provinces, the Constitution, and the Charter of Rights, 1968–2007

■ Throughout Canadian history, the balance of power between the central government and the provinces has tended to swing in a kind of pendulum effect. This is not to say that Canada has alternated between centralization and decentralization, but rather that the pendulum has swung from strong central government to a relative standoff between the federal and provincial powers. Canada emerged from Confederation with what seemed to be a strong central government, but it progressively weakened under the weight of the provincial rights movement and the pro-province decisions of the Judicial Committee of the Privy Council, so that by 1914 the provinces seemed to stand on an equal footing with Ottawa. The Great War briefly restored central dominance, but by the 1930s the provinces again shared power. World War II sent the pendulum back in the direction of Ottawa, where it remained until the early 1970s, although federal dominance was never totally uncontested. Beginning around 1972, however, the provinces —building on Quebec separatism and their own economic grievances—recovered a good deal of their momentum, and despite constitutional repatriation, in the last quarter of the twentieth century they were again contesting with Ottawa on fairly equal terms.

THE SHAPE OF PROVINCIAL POLITICS

Before 1970 traditional political theory and political analysis in Canada did not devote much attention to the provinces or the political parties that governed them. Canada's political scientists, like most other Canadian intellectuals, were for the most part committed centralists who concentrated on the national arena. Thus the first edition (1963) of a very popular collection of university-level readings on Canadian politics, Hugh Thorburn's *Party Politics in Canada*, paid almost no attention to the provincial scene. Subsequent editions, however, did trace the increasing importance of the provinces, and in the latest editions the provinces appear to be at least as significant as the federal government.

Truly viable two-party or multi-party systems seemed even rarer at the provincial level than the federal. Instead, most provinces continued to be run by a single dominant party (often unconnected with the two major federal ones). In Alberta, according to C.B. Macpherson, this 'quasi-party' system satisfied voters and mediated local conflict by ensuring that the important battles were not internal; rather, they were waged against external forces, often the federal govern-

TIMELINE

1968
Ernest Manning retires in Alberta.

1972
Joey Smallwood leaves office. W.A.C. Bennett retires.

1973
OPEC oil crisis.

1976
Montreal Olympics held. Parti Québécois comes to power in Quebec.

1977
Jacques Pépin and John Robarts appointed to head Task Force on Canadian Unity.

1979
Quebec white paper on sovereignty-association.

1980
Ottawa unilaterally introduces National Energy Program and proposals for constitutional reform.

1981
Supreme Court rules on constitutionality of federal constitutional initiatives. Trudeau negotiates a deal with the nine anglophone premiers. Revised constitutional package passes Canadian Parliament.

1982
Constitutional package, including Charter of Rights, passes British Parliament.

1987
Mulroney government negotiates Meech Lake.

1990
Meech Lake agreement expires. Bob Rae and NDP come to power in Ontario.

1992
Charlottetown Accord negotiated, but rejected in national referendum.

1993
Daniel Johnson Jr replaces Robert Bourassa as leader of the Quebec Liberal Party.

1994
PQ wins in Quebec.

1995
Quebec referendum voters reject sovereignty-association by a narrow margin.

1997
Kyoto Protocol negotiated in Japan.

1998
Supreme Court of Canada issues opinion regarding the legality of a unilateral secession of Quebec.

2002
Romanow report on health care released.

2004
Jean Charest leads Liberals in Quebec to victory. Supreme Court issues opinion in *Re Same-Sex Marriage*.

2005
Canadian Supreme Court renders decision in *Chaoulli v. Quebec (Attorney General)*.

2007
Liberals reduced to minority status in Quebec in a three-way election.

ment.[1] Certainly, conflict with Ottawa had been a staple of provincial politics since Confederation. Promises to outdo the opposition in bashing Ottawa were standard fare in provincial elections, particularly highly contested ones. A provincial party associated with the governing party in Ottawa was always in trouble when provincial rights or interests were on the table.

The 1970s were particularly hard on dominant parties in the provinces, four of which went down to defeat: the Liberals in Newfoundland and Quebec, and the Socreds in Alberta and British Columbia. It was never clear whether the coincidence of these defeats was part of a much larger political shift, the product of changing economic circumstances, or mere accident. In Alberta, Ernest Manning had retired in 1968 after 25 years as Socred Premier, and his successor, Harry Strom, lost the 1971 election to the Tories. But in Newfoundland and British Columbia, voters plainly rejected two of the grand old men of Canadian politics, each of whom had dominated his province's politics for decades. Liberal Joey Smallwood, Newfoundland Premier since 1949, finally left office early in 1972 after an electoral defeat a few months earlier at the hands of Frank Moores and his Tories. W.A.C Bennett, Premier of British Columbia since 1952, lost to the NDP under Dave Barrett in 1972. Eventually, 'yesterday's men' were succeeded by younger leaders—Peter Lougheed in Alberta, Brian Peckford in Newfoundland, Bill Bennett (son of W.A.C.) in British Columbia—whose sense of federal–provincial relations was not conditioned by depression, war, or post-war prosperity, and who were ruthless in their pursuit of the their own province's interests.

FEDERAL–PROVINCIAL RELATIONS

THE 1970S

Throughout the 1970s discussions between the federal and provincial governments were dominated by two topics: Quebec and energy. Constitutional reform died away after the 1971 negotiations discussed in Chapter 16. Oil, energy, and resource management generally were subjects of continual tension between some of the provinces (led by Alberta) and the federal government. When OPEC pulled the plug in 1973, Alberta became Ottawa's chief opponent on resource management, as Quebec had been on social programs. As oil prices continued to increase, making new resources (such as tar sands and offshore fields) financially viable, and prices of other resources rose constantly, more provinces began to recognize the advantages of provincial autonomy. Traditional 'have-not' provinces—like Newfoundland, Nova Scotia, and Saskatchewan—joined the resource-rich provinces of Alberta and British Columbia and the simply rich provinces of Ontario and Quebec in discovering the evils of national policy. Only PEI, Manitoba, and New Brunswick continued to see their provincial self-interest as best served by a strong federal government. By 1980 the rich provinces, often led by hard-headed businessmen who insisted that they put balance sheets ahead of sentiment, were ready to contest the National Energy Policy adopted by the Trudeau government in an effort to centralize direction of the economy in Ottawa.

THE PARTI QUÉBÉCOIS AND THE CONSTITUTION

The victory of the Parti Québécois in 1976 did not immediately bring about new initiatives for constitutional reform. Although it came as a shock to English-speaking Canada, it could have been predicted, given the situation in Quebec. The Bourassa government had been badly shaken by charges of scandal and corruption on top of its seeming inability to handle either the separatists or Pierre Trudeau. It lost considerable face when the Canadian Airline Pilots Association went on strike in June 1976, ostensibly over safety but really over bilingualism—an issue that only the federal government could resolve. Meanwhile,

■ Claude Ryan, former editor of *Le Devoir*, succeeded Robert Bourassa as leader of the Quebec Liberals in 1978 and campaigned vigorously for the '*Non*' side in the 1980 referendum. LAC, PA-141501.

rumours of cost overruns and construction disasters in the preparations for the 1976 Summer Olympics in Montreal had been rife for years. Bourassa's government was not directly involved in those problems, which were the primary responsibility of Jean Drapeau's Montreal government. But Drapeau was a Liberal ally, Bourassa had waffled over stepping into the crisis, and the province took over the Olympic construction at only the last minute. Many Montreal residents blamed the disaster on both Drapeau and Bourassa, the latter for failing to control the profligacy of the former.[2] There were similar concerns over the control of James Bay hydroelectric

development, but in the summer of 1976 these were not so immediately apparent as was the Olympic fiasco. With a resurgent Union Nationale splitting the non-PQ vote, René Lévesque and his Péquistes defeated the Liberals. A popular vote of 41 per cent translated into 71 seats for the PQ in the 110-seat National Assembly.

Issues are never tidy in an election, and there was no evidence that the PQ, despite its resounding victory, had received a mandate for its well-publicized option for constitutional reform, which it called 'sovereignty-association'. The Péquistes had maintained that they would not act unilaterally on separation without a provincial referendum, so that voters could support the PQ's reformist social democratic zeal without signing on to its extremist constitutional position. English-speaking Canada, however, responded to the Quebec election by assuming that separatism had triumphed in Quebec and that the nation needed to be saved at any cost. Had Lévesque sought to renegotiate the Constitution in 1976 or 1977, he would probably have been offered some sort of two-nations construct. But his party was committed both to internal reform within Quebec and to a democratic approach to separation, and it did not press its case.

In office, Lévesque's PQ successfully pursued a policy of economic and cultural nationalism. Its most controversial piece of legislation was Bill 101, which went well beyond an earlier Bourassa law, known as Bill 22, in turning Quebec into a unilingual francophone province. Bill 101 made it necessary for the children of most Quebecers, regardless of their background or preference, to be educated in French-language schools. Only those temporarily resident in Quebec or whose parents had been educated in English-speaking schools in Quebec were exempted. The legislation also made French the only legal medium of communication for business and government, requiring the elimination of almost all English-language signs in the province; symbolically, the latter provision was especially important. Many anglophones in Quebec and especially Montreal began to think seriously about leaving the province. In 1979 the Quebec government issued a white paper detailing what it meant by 'sovereignty-association'. It wanted a 'free, proud and adult national existence', but in the context of a series of joint Quebec–Canada institutions, including a court of justice and a monetary authority. A totally independent Quebec, it insisted, would still have access to Canada and its economy. Outside the ranks of the converted, the scheme seemed far too lopsided in Quebec's favour. It should also be emphasized that the province had no agreement with Canada on the subject: the proposal was a unilateral Quebec initiative.

As promised, there was a referendum, eventually scheduled for 20 May 1980. Referendums are supposed to be more straightforward than elections as a means of determining the public will, but they are, in truth, notoriously tricky.[3] Often voters are encouraged to say 'no' regardless of the nature of the disagreement with the positive side. Certainly the non-francophones in Quebec (less than 20 per cent of the population), although vehemently opposed to sovereignty-association, were not numerous enough in themselves to defeat the proposal. Claude Ryan, the leader of the Quebec Liberal Party since 1978, campaigned vigorously for the *Non* side, with the less than secret support of Ottawa, led by Prime Minister Trudeau. But in the end, almost 60 per cent of the province's voters and even a bare majority (52 per cent) of its francophones voted '*Non*'—a fairly decisive result, although it did still leave 40.5 per cent of the Quebec population and just under half of its francophones in favour of sovereignty-association. Nevertheless, Quebec had publicly rejected separation from Canada. The nation responded by breathing a sigh of relief and calling for a new approach to federalism.

PATRIATING THE CONSTITUTION

Although no formal attempt had been made to reform the Constitution since the PQ victory in 1976, Canadians had debated national unity and constitutional change. Proposals for reform were in the air, many of them surfacing in the travelling road show known as the Task Force on Canadian Unity, chaired by Jean-Luc Pépin of Quebec and John Robarts of Ontario, that was sent across Canada in 1978. Among the myriad suggestions, three points became clear. One was that many Canadians—including a fair proportion of academics and lawyers—were prepared to support relatively major alterations in the country's current Constitution, the British North America Act. A second was that the vast majority

THE TASK FORCE
ON CANADIAN UNITY

The following excerpt is from the 1979 report of the Pépin-Roberts Task Force on Canadian Unity.

Widening the Issue

When the B&B [Bilingualism and Biculturalism] commissioners were preparing their reports in the mid-sixties they could assume certain facts about the country which can no longer be taken for granted. This change reflects the important ways in which the challenge to Confederation has been modified and amplified in the intervening years.

The most important new element in the equation is the growing strength of the other provinces and the regional loyalties that have formed themselves, primarily within the framework of the provinces. A decade ago it was possible for the B&B Commission to minimize the obvious regional differences in Canada and to stress instead the relative unity within each of the two Canadian realities, French and English-speaking Canada. But that is no longer possible. The international tendency toward local particularism and the broad process of modernization which are reflected in Quebec have also taken root in the rest of Canada, reviving the regional tensions which are an old feature of Canadian life but which had remained relatively muted between the Second World War and the 1960s.

The revival of regionalism was assisted by Quebec. By resisting the centralizing impulse of the federal government during the post-war generation, Quebec helped to open the door to a more general provincial renaissance in the sixties and seventies. But this new reality has also widened the issue originally posed almost exclusively by Quebec so that it now spans the Canadian union as a whole. The crisis which the country faces today is not one of Quebec or of French Canada only: it is a crisis of Confederation itself. In this sense, the challenge to the country differs from that of a decade ago and must be considered in much wider terms. To the fundamental challenge of Canadian duality must now be added the other important challenge of Canadian regionalism.

Another factor which also merits consideration is the growth in self-consciousness of Canadians who are of neither French nor British background, and who are sometimes regarded as the third element to be added to the historic fact of Canadian duality. It was indeed the very definition of the country in dualistic terms, both in the mandate and outlook of the B&B Commission, which helped to stimulate the assertiveness of these ethnic groups, an assertiveness which was consecrated in 1971 by the Trudeau government's policy of multiculturalism. Thus, partly as a result of the government's policy and the response to it in the ethnic communities, the Canadian reality has become more complex, and this complexity must be taken account of in a way that did not seem as necessary a decade ago.

Another social development since the 1960s is the increasingly articulate voice of Canada's native peoples. The dilemma of the native peoples has been a continuing but neglected feature of Canadian life, yet it has acquired a new urgency in recent years, and their place in Canadian society can no longer be overlooked as it frequently was in the previous decade. . . .

Another new factor concerns the central government itself. Fifteen years ago, it stood high in the minds of a large number of Canadians, and was widely regarded with respect and a feeling of loyalty. Even those who felt little loyalty to it at least respected its efficiency and competence. Today, that is much less true; 'Ottawa', as we found on our tour, is for many Canadians synonymous with all that is to be deplored about modern government—a remote, shambling bureaucracy that exacts tribute from its subjects and gives little in return. We recognize that this is an unfair stereotype, and that in another fif-

teen years the pendulum may have swung back to the other extreme; but the fact that this view has such a widespread appeal today is one of the significant elements that must be borne in mind in any attempt to improve our situation.

SOURCE: Task Force on Canadian Unity, *A Future Together: Observations and Recommendations* (Ottawa, Jan. 1979), 15-16.

of anglophone Canadians did not want separation and were prepared to make substantial concessions to keep Quebec within Confederation. A third point, perhaps the least well understood by the public, was that the anglophone provinces of Canada—led by Alberta, British Columbia, and Saskatchewan, and strongly supported by Nova Scotia and Newfoundland—had developed their own agenda for constitutional reform. These provinces had long-standing regional grievances against Ottawa's centralizing federalism, which they regarded as operating almost exclusively in the interests of Ontario and Quebec. They were quite prepared to take advantage of Quebec's pressures for greater autonomy, particularly if they reduced Quebec's influence within Confederation and allowed for constitutional change in the best interests of other provinces besides Quebec. What the other provinces wanted above all was unrestricted control over their own natural resources and reform of some of Ottawa's governing institutions, notably the Senate and the Supreme Court, to reflect regional interests. The Trudeau government had seemed on the verge of conceding much of this provincial program when it was defeated in 1979, and the Clark government had not time to deal with the issues when it, too, had failed at the polls.

The opportunity presented to Prime Minister Trudeau by the Quebec referendum, as he called a first ministers' conference for early June 1980, was simultaneously real and dangerous. From the federalist perspective it was necessary

to deal with Quebec's aspirations without conceding too much to the other provinces, none of which was controlled by a Liberal government and all of which had their own visions for change. The federal government's most consistent ally was Ontario, which confirmed that it had been the chief beneficiary of the old federalism by opposing most proposals for decentralization. Quebec was hardly prepared to take the lead in the new round of general discussions, nor could it afford to be churlish about them. Its best strategy was to allow the anglophone provinces to initiate the dismantling of Confederation; and indeed, one of the principal characteristics of this round of constitutional discussion was that Quebec's concerns were not perceived to be central. General consensus was developed on some economic issues, but other questions remained difficult to resolve. Ottawa wanted to entrench a charter of rights in any constitutional document, chiefly to guarantee francophone linguistic rights across the nation, but the majority of the provinces (including Quebec) objected to such a charter as threatening their own rights. The provinces, for their part, wanted an amending formula that would give all of them both the right of veto and the right to opt out of any amendments that they regarded as threatening to their powers. This round of discussions broke down in September 1980, and Ottawa prepared —as Prime Minister Trudeau had been threatening for months—to take unilateral action.[4]

Politically, the federal package was carefully

calculated. As an ardent federalist, a constitutional lawyer, and a self-confessed exponent of *realpolitik*, Pierre Trudeau was in his element. The new proposals were more than simply constitutional. Bill C-48—the Canada Oil and Gas Act (COGA)—emphasized the right of Parliament to control the oil and gas industry, at a time when both Newfoundland and Nova Scotia were preparing to move into offshore oil.[5] It allowed Ottawa to have a share of offshore revenues and called for minimum Canadian ownership of 50 per cent for companies applying for exploration licences. The bill was designed to give control of oil and gas operations to Ottawa rather than big industry.[6] As provocative as this legislation was, it attracted little controversy compared to the government's constitutional proposals. The Constitution Act 1980, made public in October of that year—Prime Minister Trudeau called it a 'people's package'—proposed elimination of recourse to the British Parliament for amendment of the British North America Act ('patriation').[7] It also contained a charter of rights, with a number of qualifications on their applicability, that included rights of other minorities, to prevent French Canadians from being treated as a distinctive case. The package also provided for a new method of amendment, through national referendum initiated by Ottawa in the event of provincial obstructionism.[8] The Trudeau government was prepared to pass the package in the federal Parliament and send it to Britain for approval without consulting either the Supreme Court or the provinces, although it clearly infringed on the 'right' of the provinces to consent to constitutional change. The federal NDP supported this position, leaving the Progressive Conservative minority in Parliament to oppose it and represent the provinces, all but one of which strongly objected at first (the exception, not surprisingly, was Ontario, which was later joined by New Brunswick). Parliamentary amendments dealt with some of the most troublesome features of the original proposal and introduced some new wrinkles, including the specific affirmation of 'aborig-

inal and treaty rights of the aboriginal peoples of Canada'. The Liberal government had neatly set in opposition two sets of rights, one the human rights protected in the entrenched charter and the other the provincial rights ignored in both the amending process and in the charter itself. Eight of the provinces (excluding Ontario and New Brunswick) joined forces as what the media called the 'Gang of Eight' to oppose Ottawa's unilateral action, even though Quebec and the seven English-speaking provinces had quite different interests on many issues.

The first major hurdle for the federal initiative was the Supreme Court of Canada, to which constitutional opinions from several provincial courts had gone on appeal. If the federal government won in the Supreme Court, the provincial claim that the package was unconstitutional would be hard to sustain. Before the Court began its deliberations, on 11 March 1981, Lévesque and the PQ won a resounding electoral victory in Quebec. The win did not, of course, resolve the contradiction that the PQ represented as a separatist party that had sworn not to move unilaterally towards separation, but it did reactivate Quebec on constitutional matters. Although the British government refused to deal officially with the provincial premiers (much as it had in 1867, when Nova Scotia sent Joseph Howe to London), members of a First Nations delegation set up their own lobbying office in London. They had some claim to direct treaty connections with the British Crown and a decent legal case as well.

The Supreme Court of Canada handed down its ruling on 28 September 1981. The decision was difficult to understand; as one constitutional expert commented, in legal terms it was 'complex and baffling and technically unsatisfactory'.[9] In a political sense, this was exactly what the Court had intended. Essentially, by a decision of 7 to 2, it declared the federal patriation process legal, since custom could not be enforced in courts, but it also held, by a decision of 6 to 3, that federal patriation was 'unconventional'. Since most of the legal arguments against the process revolved around violations of constitutional 'convention' (or custom), which required that the provinces be consulted on amendments, these two opinions were mutually contradictory. Nevertheless, in law Ottawa had won. What the politicians would make of that ambiguous decision was an open question.

In the end, the nine English-speaking premiers, including seven former members of the Gang of Eight, worked out a deal with Prime Minister Trudeau on 5 November 1981.[10] Trudeau made considerable concessions to his formulations—abandoning, for example, the proposal he made on 4 November for two referendums initiated by Ottawa to decide the constitutional changes. The formula for provincial approval called for resolutions of the legislative assemblies of a majority of provinces that also included every province with a population of at least 25 per cent of Canada's population, plus two or more Atlantic provinces and two or more western provinces. Ontario joined Quebec in agreeing to drop its right of veto in favour of a complex formula ensuring that either one or the other (but not both) would have to agree to an amendment, which represented more of a loss for the central provinces, especially Quebec, than it did for Ottawa. At the same time, however, the Prime Minister's greatest concessions involved the Charter of Rights, particularly the 'notwithstanding' clause, which allowed any province to opt out of clauses in the Charter covering fundamental freedoms and legal and equality rights (but not other categories of rights, such as language). There was disagreement over the intention of the negotiations regarding Aboriginal peoples, resulting in a temporary omission of the clause guaranteeing treaty rights that had to be restored subsequently by Parliament; a constitutional conference was to be held later to define those rights. The final compromise satisfied the nine English-speaking premiers and theoretically reinforced the right of the provinces to use the 'notwithstanding' clause to opt out of the Charter on critical issues, including both Native rights and

women's rights. Native and women's groups understandably vowed to fight on in opposition to the revised constitutional package. As for Quebec, all it had lost was some of what it perceived to be its distinctive status in Confederation —but that loss would prove crucial, for Quebec would consistently refuse to accept these constitutional reforms made without consulting one of Canada's two 'national wills'. Eventually, another attempt to achieve provincial unanimity would be made at Meech Lake in 1987.

The revised constitutional package passed the Canadian Parliament in December 1981 and the British Parliament early in 1982. The latter had resolutely refused to become involved in the various protests against the new package, in effect surrendering its role as a court of last resort against unconstitutional actions within Canada. Not many Canadians at the time appreciated what had happened constitutionally, or what the changes would mean. The principle of patriation had been won, but at considerable expense. It was true that the Charter of Rights offered safeguards for collective and individual rights not protected by the British North America Act. But whereas in the traditional British model the legislature itself was the source of protection, the Charter established the American principle that the court system was the ultimate source of protection, ready to ensure fundamental rights against the legislature if necessary. And in place of the earlier concept that Parliament (especially the federal Parliament) was supreme, the new Constitution introduced a new series of formal checks and balances limiting parliamentary supremacy.[11]

THE CHARTER OF RIGHTS AND FREEDOMS

The new Constitution not only gave new powers to the provinces, which were traditional political units, but also recognized newer and more amorphous political units in the Charter of Rights and Freedoms, which was somewhat less concerned

■ Prime Minister Trudeau looks on as Queen Elizabeth II signs Canada's constitutional proclamation in Ottawa, 17 April 1982. Robert Cooper/LAC, PA-141503.

than the American Bill of Rights to define the individual rights of Canadians and somewhat more concerned to define their collective rights. Thus, in addition to providing equality before the law for individuals facing discrimination 'based on race, national or ethnic origin, colour, religion, sex, age or mental or physical disability' (section 15[1]), the Charter also specifically permitted in section 15(2) 'any law, program or activity that has as its object the amelioration of conditions of disadvantaged individuals or groups', including (but not limited to) those disadvantaged by the factors of discrimination mentioned in section 15(1). In addition, Aboriginal

and treaty rights—although pointedly not defined—were entrenched, as were sexual equality and multiculturalism (as section 27 put it, 'This Charter shall be interpreted in a manner consistent with the preservation and enhancement of the multicultural heritage of Canadians'). Although at first glance these provisions seemed to represent the ultimate triumph of liberalism, in several respects they negated it. In the first place, they could be overridden by the provinces, which now had increased power to control their own resources and call their own shots regarding application of the Charter and any constitutional amendments. In the second place, the constitutional introduction of a series of new collectivities introduced further complications for an already overloaded political process, which in the end would help to limit the liberal impulse itself. The Supreme Court would eventually find its judicial wheels clogged with new cases.[12] Finally, the behaviour of the politicians involved in the constitutional reform process helped to reduce the esteem in which they were held by the Canadian public.

On the twenty-fifth anniversary of the Charter and the new Constitution in 2007, a number of retrospective analyses were published by journalists and lawyers. Almost without exception, they emphasized that while the Charter had not quite revolutionized Canadian jurisprudence and the Constitution had not quite overhauled Canadian political practice, they had made some difference in the way the law and government operated. Curiously enough, the most contentious element of constitutional reform in 1982—the so-called 'notwithstanding' clause—had proved to be almost invisible and totally insignificant over the first quarter-century of the Charter's existence.

THE CHARTER AND THE SUPREME COURT

The 1982 Charter, with its explicit and implicit recognitions of both collective and individual rights, was hardly the last word on the subject. An ongoing body of case law would have to be developed in the courts, especially the Supreme Court of Canada, which became the ultimate arbiter in disputes over interpretation of the Charter's sometimes vague terminology. Governments, however, could have dealt in more specific terms with some of the recognized collectivities, such as women and First Nations. The understanding that existing Aboriginal rights would be spelled out in more detail later was never seriously acted upon, although the Liberal government had some concrete proposals in hand when it was defeated in 1984. As for women's rights, a few cosmetic

changes were made administratively or legislatively. The key issue of abortion, however, remained unresolved throughout the 1980s. The Charter was merely a wild card that could be used by the Supreme Court of Canada on behalf of a woman's right to abortion through its clause in section 7 concerning the 'life, liberty and security of the person'. For women, as for Aboriginal people, the courts proved to be more open to change than Parliament.

The Supreme Court has been particularly diligent in employing the Charter to provide further protection from injustice for individuals convicted under the Criminal Code. One example was the *R. v. Ruzic* case, on which the Court passed its final judgement on 20 April 2001.[13] The accused had been tried by a judge and jury on charges of smuggling two kilograms of heroin into Canada and of using a false passport in the process. She admitted both charges were true, but insisted that she had been forced to smuggle by a man in Belgrade who threatened to injure her mother if she did not bring the drugs to Canada. The Court allowed her the defence of duress against the prosecution's insistence that under section 17 of the Criminal Code the threat has to be immediate and the person threatening physically present when the offence was committed. The accused thus challenged the constitutionality of section 17 of the Criminal Code under section 7 of the Charter of Rights and Freedoms, and was acquitted. The Crown appealed but the Supreme Court found that the 'underinclusiveness' of section 17 of the Code infringed section 7 of the Charter by imposing obstacles to relying on the duress defence in hostage and third-party situations. The Supreme Court thus found part of section 17 of the Criminal Code to be unconstitutional.[14] By and large, the Court has taken a constructive and generous approach to Charter rights.

One of the most interesting features of the Supreme Court's behaviour with regard to the Charter (and the Constitution) is its ability to answer constitutional questions submitted by governments. Thus, in 1998, it offered in *Reference re Secession of Quebec* an opinion on the unilateral secession of Quebec from Canada. It opined that Quebec could not secede unilaterally, but if Quebec clearly wanted to secede, negotiations with Canada should ensue to make this possible. Six years later, in 2004, the Court spoke on the constitutional validity of same-sex marriage in Canada, saying that proposed same-sex marriage legislation was within the authority of Parliament and was consistent with the Charter. In both of these cases it dismissed arguments that such questions were political rather than legal and thus beyond its jurisdiction.[15]

MEECH LAKE

In 1987 the Mulroney government fastened on one of the loose ends of the 1982 constitutional process: Quebec's refusal to accept the 1982 Constitution. By this time René Lévesque had retired,[16] and his party had been defeated at the polls (in December 1985) by the Liberals under a rehabilitated Robert Bourassa, who thus proved an exception to the rule that there is no coming back from a devastating electoral defeat. Once again in power, Bourassa offered to compromise, and Mulroney summoned a new 'Gang of Ten' to a closed-door session on 30 April 1987 at Meech Lake, where a revised constitutional arrangement acceptable to Quebec was worked out. While Quebec was to be constitutionally recognized as a 'distinct society' and given further concessions, including a veto over most amendments to the Constitution, inducements were also offered to the other provinces, which would share in some of the new autonomy offered to Quebec. All provinces would be compensated by the federal government for programs they refused to join, and each province was given a veto over future amending. There was to be regular discussion of Senate reform, although no particular formula was agreed upon. Nevertheless, there was a consensus among participants that the federal Parliament and the legislatures of all 10

provinces would have to hold all the public hearings and deal with all the feedback they required to approve the agreement by June 1990—otherwise the arrangement was dead.[17]

The three years between the Meech Lake meeting and the deadline for ratification later created difficulties. While the Mulroney government understandably insisted that no changes could be made in the agreement until it had been approved, not every provincial government felt bound by the particular terms of a controversial understanding accepted by whoever happened to be its premier in April 1987. The subsequent public debate made clear that not all Canadians agreed with what was perceived to be a further dismantling of the federal government's authority in favour not merely of Quebec, but of all the provinces. The poorer 'have-not' provinces—led by Manitoba, New Brunswick, and eventually Newfoundland—were particularly concerned that few new federal programs would be mounted if the richer provinces had the option of receiving federal funds for their own versions. Other collectivities, such as Aboriginal people and women, worried that their rights were being bartered away to the provinces. Across the country, suggested revisions to Meech Lake sprouted like grass, many of them offering structural reforms (to the Senate, for example). As the deadline for acceptance loomed, only the legislatures of Manitoba and Newfoundland held out, the latter having rescinded an earlier legislative endorsement after Brian Peckford's Tories were defeated by the Liberals under Clyde Wells. Prime Minister Mulroney tried the time-honoured tactics of the labour negotiator, calling the premiers into closed-door sessions designed to shame the reluctant into support on the eve of the deadline. This tactic appeared to work. But in Manitoba, the Cree leader and NDP MLA Elijah Harper objected to the Accord on the grounds that it neglected Aboriginal people. By delaying debate on the Accord, Harper prevented the legislature from ratifying it before the deadline. Since Manitoba was not going to approve,

NDP MLA Elijah Harper sits in the Manitoba legislature holding an eagle feather for spiritual strength as he continues to delay debate on the Meech Lake Accord, 19 June 1990. CP Picture Archive (CP/*Winnipeg Free Press*/Wayne Glowacki).

concept. The cause was not helped when, a month before the Meech deadline, a number of federal Conservatives from Quebec, led by Environment Minister Lucien Bouchard, resigned from the caucus to form the Bloc Québécois. But in fact most Canadians seemed willing to allow Quebec almost total autonomy; the problem was the prospect of extending similar autonomy to the other provinces—which would effectively balkanize the nation. Symbolically, Elijah Harper's action called attention to a related problem: Meech Lake's potential incompatibility with the collective rights recognized by the Charter. During the summer of 1990 the failure of Meech Lake was followed by an extremely volatile confrontation at Oka, Quebec, between the local Mohawk band and the federal armed forces.

A few weeks later, in September 1990, one of Meech Lake's biggest supporters, Premier David Peterson of Ontario, suffered a crushing defeat by the NDP led by Bob Rae. Whether there was a connection with the unravelling of the Mulroney program was debatable. Yet the fact that Ontario for the first time had elected the NDP—still the most liberal, centralist, and nationalist of Canada's political parties—suggested that the erosion of those principles might be coming to an end. Subsequent 1991 NDP victories in British Columbia and Saskatchewan provided further confirmation that the electorate was having second thoughts about conservative rhetoric—until the wheel started turning again in the mid-1990s.

THE CHARLOTTETOWN ACCORD

Mulroney's last attempt to recover some popular credibility was the Charlottetown Accord of August 1992, the result of a meeting of provincial premiers in the PEI capital. It came after more than a year of public hearings, weekend conferences, and other efforts to get some 'democratic input' into the process of constitutional revision. But Canada had no tradition of consultative reform. In the end, another series of

Newfoundland's Wells backed off a previous commitment to gain his province's legislative endorsement. In the end, without the two provinces' endorsement, Meech Lake failed.

In the post-mortems, a number of points stood out. One was that after 1987 the popular support for the Mulroney Tories and the Meech Lake Accord had declined together. Quebec understandably interpreted the mounting hostility to Meech Lake in English-speaking Canada as directed specifically against the 'distinct society'

SHARON CARSTAIRS (1942–)

❖

Sharon Connolly was born in Halifax in 1942. Her father was a Nova Scotia cabinet minister who became Premier of the province in 1954. She studied at Dalhousie University, where she was active in student politics, and obtained an MA in teaching (a fairly experimental degree at the time) at Smith College in Massachusetts in 1963. She began her teaching career at a private school there, but soon joined the separate schools system in Calgary, where she was constantly confronted about her faith in Catholicism. She met John Esdale Carstairs during her first year in Calgary and married him soon after.

With her husband's encouragement, Sharon Carstairs ran provincially for the Liberals in the Calgary constituency of Elbow in 1975, finishing a distant second. A year later she was elected president of the Liberal Party of Alberta, but moved with her husband to Winnipeg the following year. Almost immediately she became involved in Liberal politics on behalf of Lloyd Axworthy. The Carstairs family and Axworthy subsequently became estranged. Carstairs soon recognized that the Liberals in Manitoba were extremely short on experienced leadership. When she was unable to find another candidate to support at a leadership convention in 1984, she decided to run for the position herself and won easily. When she ran for the provincial seat in Fort Garry, she startled the media by announcing that she would finish second. She did. Two years later she ran in the River Heights constituency and performed well in a televised leadership debate, having muscled her way into the

debate because her party managed to run candidates in all 57 constituencies. Carstairs won the only Liberal seat in 1986, but two years later her party became the official opposition in the Manitoba legislature.

Carstairs opposed the Meech Lake Accord from the beginning. Convinced that the majority in her province agreed with her, she was one of the few prominent politicians anywhere willing to express her concerns. In the spring of 1990, however, she was heavily pressured by Ottawa to support the deal, and she agreed. Back in Winnipeg, before the debates over ratification in the Manitoba legislature, she admitted publicly to taking mild tranquilizers to help her through a difficult period and found that many people in Manitoba felt that she had both broken down and backed off. Although Carstairs had led the Manitoba opposition to Meech Lake for several years, in the end it was Elijah Harper who succeeded in killing the deal. She explained to the media that she supported Harper and the First Nations in killing the Accord, but it was probably not enough to spare her considerable public criticism. According to her memoir, *Not One of the Boys* (1993), her principal response to the entire Meech Lake business was 'disgust with the process of constitutional reform'. Her unhappiness was compounded by the failure of Tory Premier Gary Filmon to honour a written commitment not to go to the polls until the autumn of 1990. The Liberals were badly beaten in this election. Carstairs was appointed to the Senate in 1994.

TABLE 21.1

RESULTS BY PROVINCE OF THE REFERENDUM ON THE CHARLOTTETOWN ACCORD, 26 OCTOBER 1992

Province/Territory	'Yes'	'No'
Newfoundland	62.9	36.5
Nova Scotia	48.5	51.1
Prince Edward Island	73.6	25.9
New Brunswick	61.3	38.0
Quebec	42.4	55.4
Ontario	49.8	49.6
Manitoba	37.9	61.7
Saskatchewan	45.5	55.1
Alberta	39.6	60.2
British Columbia	31.9	67.8
NWT	60.2	39.0
Yukon	43.4	56.1
Total	44.8	54.2

closed-door meetings between Ottawa and the anglophone provinces, joined at the end by Quebec at Charlottetown, produced a revised package. This one offered Quebec a distinct society, the provinces a veto, the Aboriginal peoples self-government, and the country reform of both the Supreme Court and the Senate.[18] The nation voted on the package in a referendum on 26 October 1992, two days after the Toronto Blue Jays became the first 'Canadian' team to win baseball's World Series.[19] To the simultaneous amusement and consternation of Canadians, in the opening ceremonies of this series, the US Marine Corps inadvertently carried the Canadian flag upside down. The eventual victory produced an outpouring of Canadian nationalism across the country. Some commentators openly feared

for a nation that enjoyed its greatest togetherness celebrating the success of highly paid foreign athletes.

In any event, six provinces (including Quebec) voted 'no' in the referendum; the national totals were 44.8 per cent in favour and 54.2 per cent against (Table 21.1). Polls indicated that many voters apparently agreed with former Prime Minister Trudeau, who insisted that Charlottetown would polarize the nation. Poorer provinces favoured the deal, but among individuals, those who were poorer, younger, and less well-educated were more likely to oppose it. According to one poll, household income of $60,000 per year was the economic cut-off between 'yes' and 'no', while a university degree was the educational one. Most of those who voted 'no' believed that their vote would not have negative consequences for the nation. As a region, the four western provinces cast the most decisive negative votes.

THE QUEBEC REFERENDUM OF 1995

Any hope that the referendum defeat of the Charlottetown Accord had put a lid on the constitutional pot was ended by the 1994 PQ victory in Quebec. Led by Jacques Parizeau, the Péquistes moved inexorably towards another referendum on sovereignty. As usual, the Liberals (now under Daniel Johnson Jr) lost the election as much as the PQ won it, and in fact the two parties had virtually identical shares of the popular vote, but the PQ had more seats. Parizeau had initially wanted complete independence and opposed sovereignty-association, but he gradually came to see the latter as a way to attract soft nationalists. Realizing that one of the major problems with the 1980 referendum had been the uncertainty regarding both the question and consequent action, Parizeau sought to pin down the new question precisely and had legislation passed defining the terms. In June 1995 he and two other separatist leaders, Action Démocratique leader Mario Dumont (an ex-Liberal who advocated sovereignty-association) and Bloc Québécois leader Lucien Bouchard, agreed on a plan. Quebecers would be asked to authorize their government to open negotiations with Ottawa on sovereignty-association. If the province gave a mandate and if an agreement with Canada was not reached within a year, Quebec would unilaterally declare sovereignty. The co-operation of the three leaders was intended to allay fears that the Quebec government would, in Parizeau's words, 'jump the gun' on a declaration of sovereignty. The vote was soon set for 30 October 1995. The official question asked voters whether they agreed 'that Quebec should become sovereign, after having made a formal offer to Canada for a new Economic and Political

Partnership, within the scope of the Bill respecting the future of Quebec and of the agreement signed on June 12, 1995'.

In the beginning the federalist (or 'Non') forces seemed to be well in control of the situation. Experts expected the usual ballot bonus for the federalists, who would turn out a higher proportion of their supporters. They also expected the usual conservative response to uncertainty. For the most part, Ottawa kept its distance from the campaign, allowing Liberal leader Daniel Johnson to carry the 'Non' message to the electorate. The federal strategy was to do as little as possible to fuel the sovereigntist position. Then, with polls showing a marked advantage for the 'Non' side, Lucien Bouchard actively entered the fray. Bouchard had only recently recovered from a rare bacterial infection that cost him a leg and nearly his life. He had not been expected to be an important campaigner, but the province was clearly not excited by Parizeau and Dumont. Bouchard introduced a new level of emotion into the campaign, simplifying the issues considerably. For many Quebecers, the need to move forward on the constitutional front, rather than sovereignty, became the key question in the referendum—and the federalist forces realized they were in trouble. What had been a ho-hum campaign suddenly turned into a barn-burner. At the last minute, Prime Minister Chrétien reflected the panic in Ottawa by offering Quebec concessions, including yet another 'distinct society' constitutional proposal.

Virtually every eligible resident of Quebec cast his or her ballot. The final turnout—over 94 per cent of the electorate—was seldom matched except in police states with compulsory elections. Millions of Canadians remained tuned to their television sets until late in the evening, waiting for the definitive result. Finally, it became clear that the 'Non' forces had won a narrow victory. In the end, 2,362,355 Quebecers (50.6 per cent of the total) voted 'Non', while 2,308,054 (49.4 per cent) voted 'Oui'. Young francophones living outside Montreal led the way in support-

■ Mario Dumont, Jacques Parizeau, and Lucien Bouchard at a rally for Yes supporters in Longueuil, Quebec, 29 October 1995. The referendum vote was held the following day. CP/Paul Chiasson.

ing sovereignty. There were many informal complaints about voting irregularities, but the vote was allowed to stand. Premier Parizeau had prepared a gracious speech of conciliation to accompany a sovereigntist victory. In his bitter acknowledgement of failure on national radio and television, he blamed anglophones and 'the ethnic vote' for thwarting the aspirations of francophone Quebec. As Parizeau spoke, the cameras panned around the crowd of people gathered at 'Oui' headquarters. Many were in tears. Parizeau's impulsive attack turned much public

opinion against him, even within his own party. Within hours he announced his resignation. In February 1996 he would be officially replaced by Lucien Bouchard.[20]

In the wake of the referendum, the Chrétien government passed a unilateral declaration in Parliament that recognized Quebec as a distinct society, but almost everyone realized the gesture was too little and too late. French Canadians in Quebec had made clear their desire for a new constitutional relationship with Canada. Only two real questions remained. When would a sovereign Quebec finally emerge? And would it remain within some sort of Canadian federation? Post-referendum polls continued to emphasize that Quebecers wanted to stay in Canada, but not under the present Constitution. Canadians turned to debate the next step in the ongoing constitutional process. One of the most difficult tasks would be to design a new process for generating a new constitutional arrangement, since most of the previous approaches now appeared totally discredited.

ABORIGINAL RIGHTS

Quebec's aspirations were not the only ones that any new constitutional arrangement would have to address: the First Nations wanted constitutional entrenchment of their conception of Aboriginal self-government. In many ways this demand for sovereignty paralleled Quebec's (it also helps explain the insistence of the Quebec government in early 1996 that the province was 'indivisible'). The Constitution Act of 1982, while entrenching existing Aboriginal and treaty rights, had not really come to terms with the self-government issue, mainly because the First Nations and Ottawa were so far apart on the subject. The First Nations maintained that they had the inherent right to make laws and institutions for their people—a right that was never surrendered by treaty. Ottawa, by contrast, saw Aboriginal self-government as the equivalent of municipal government: a subordinate entity to which powers are merely delegated by the jurisdictions that claim true sovereignty under the Crown and Constitution of Canada—that is, Ottawa and the provinces. As sovereign governments, First Nations would deal on an equal footing with Ottawa, which they maintain still owes them a heavy debt of financial responsibility, whereas if they were treated as municipal governments, they would have only those powers allowed them by the senior governments (federal and provincial). Recognition of the First Nations (more than 500 bands) as sovereign

would be facilitated if the Constitution recognized Quebec as sovereign in the same way. For many Canadians, however, such recognition would serve only to balkanize the country and create independent jurisdictions that benefited from their position inside Canada but held no concurrent responsibilities.[21]

HEALTH CARE, FEDERAL–PROVINCIAL RELATIONS, AND THE LIMITS OF THE WELFARE STATE

In some ways federal–provincial disputes seemed to decrease after the Quebec referendum, but in fact the struggles merely changed their venue. One point often overlooked in discussions about health care is that it is fundamentally a provincial matter. The federal government can try to impose some authority by setting rules for the use of the money it transfers to the provinces for health care, but it is unlikely to have much success. What the provinces want is more money and fewer federal guidelines. The bottom line is that health care represents by far the largest single component of any provincial budget and is probably the single most important political issue in any province.[22]

Cost is the main reason that maintaining a system of universal health care was the liveliest area of social disagreement between the provinces and the federal government in the decades of the 1980s and 1990s. Critics contended that Canada's universal system was becoming too expensive to sustain, and several provincial premiers (notably Ralph Klein in Alberta and Mike Harris in Ontario) advocated allowing private clinics and hospitals to operate alongside the public system, as Margaret Thatcher had done in Britain. However, Canadians in general were not as taken with private enterprise as Klein and Harris, and were not keen to dismantle such a crucial component of the welfare state as universal health care.

A large part of the cost problem in health care had less to do with universality than with the special problems (and expenses) of extended health care for the elderly. Instead of considering the elderly as a separate item of overall health care, the politicians continued to insist that the elderly be treated (and funded) within the existing system, which as a result became overloaded. More than half of all health-care spending went to treating patients, most of them elderly, in their last six months of life. The reduction in transfer payments to the provinces in the 1990s, as the federal government tried desperately to balance its budgets, further contributed to the erosion of service.

In their effort to keep the costs from getting out of hand, most of the provinces closed some of their hospitals and cut the numbers of beds available in those that remained. The savings thus effected were debatable. What was not debatable was that such downsizing, in turn, led to increased waiting times for specialist consultations and surgery, and perhaps even to an exodus of medical practitioners to the US. Some affluent patients even went south themselves for faster treatment—at a price. The private enterprisers in government thought those who could afford it should be able to seek private treatment within Canada. Opponents insisted that introducing a private system would create a two-tier system in which the rich could obtain immediate treatment by paying extra while ordinary Canadians would have to wait in increasingly longer lines. Some even argued that health-care availability should be guaranteed under the Charter of Rights.[23] All the polls indicated that most Canadians wanted neither a two-tier system nor privatization; indeed, they wanted current levels of health care maintained or even enhanced—although not many also wanted to pay higher taxes. The privatizers insisted, usually erroneously, that escalating costs for public health care made it impossible to balance budgets.

In November 2002 a Royal Commission chaired by former Saskatchewan NDP Premier Roy Romanow presented a long-anticipated report on the health-care system.[24] To nobody's surprise,

Romanow gave the existing system a largely positive review and rebuked the privatizers:

> Some have described it as a perversion of Canadian values that they cannot use their money to purchase faster treatment from a private provider for their loved ones. I believe it is a far greater perversion of Canadian values to accept a system where money, rather than need, determines who gets access to care.[25]

Most of Romanow's recommendations were in fairly common currency across the country. Few were profoundly innovative. He recommended the creation of a National Health Council, with representation from the provincial, territorial, and federal governments, to monitor health-care spending through the Canadian Institute for Health Information and the Canadian Coordinating Office for Health Technology Assessment. This new agency would operate quite independently of the federal government. This proposal was rejected out of hand by Ralph Klein, speaking for the provinces, as 'an intrusion into our responsibility for health care'. Romanow also called for a new Health Act with new provisions for portability and accountability, more federal money (an extra $6.5 billion by 2005–6), and more attention to primary care through increased access to family physicians and more preventative programs. Critics complained that the report did not do enough to address the issue of the elderly or the need to train more doctors to handle increased responsibilities. Romanow argued for an expanded home care system, but the provinces insisted that they knew best how to meet their own needs. In short, the Romanow report provided a focus for subsequent debate, but failed to deliver a reform package acceptable to a broad range of the players involved.

A number of constitutional issues were involved in the health-care debate, but probably the principal one was whether long waiting lines and the absence of private health insurance violated the Canadian Charter of Rights and

Freedoms and the Quebec Charter of Human Rights. On 9 June 2005, the Canadian Supreme Court issued a decision touching on some of these matters in the case of *Chaoulli v. Quebec (Attorney General)*. As is often the case, the Court's decision was badly misunderstood by the media, the politicians, and the general public. The situation upon which the Supreme Court pronounced was relatively simple. The appellants—a doctor who sought to offer private health services and a patient who wanted to receive them—insisted that Quebec's legislation prohibiting private health insurance for treatment covered under the public health system violated their constitutional rights under both the Canadian and Quebec Charters. The final decision, frequently heralded by both sides in the health-care debate as opening the door for the introduction of private services and a two-tier health system, probably did no such thing. Read literally, the decision applied only to Quebec and involved only the Quebec Charter. Whether the Court's reasoning could be extended across Canada and to the Canadian Charter of Rights was quite another matter. But commentators on the case were quite correct in their understanding of the importance and complexities of the issues involved, which were hardly resolved by the decision. Most commentators recognized the potential conflict between laws prohibiting private health insurance (to prevent a so-called 'two-tier system') and the Charters, and called for its resolution.[26]

THE KYOTO PROTOCOL AND THE PROVINCES

Some observers have seen a replay of the 1970s federal–provincial controversies over energy policy in the issue of the Kyoto Protocol and the implementation of Canadian commitments. In 1997 an international summit meeting at Kyoto, Japan, agreed on a world protocol for reducing emissions of the hydrocarbon gases that many scientists blamed for the 'greenhouse effect' and

■ Prime Minister Jean Chrétien and Environment Minister David Anderson shake hands following the House of Commons' vote on ratification of the Kyoto Agreement, 10 December 2002. CP/Tom Hanson.

other pollution. The extent of the greenhouse effect was still being debated by the scientific community. But the larger question involved the economic costs of complying with Kyoto. The Kyoto Accord was largely a creation of the industrialized European nations, which for a variety of reasons had managed to go much further than North America towards reducing industrial pollution. Europe had been supported by less developed countries that had little polluting industry. But the US bowed out of the protocol on the grounds that implementation would be too expensive.[27] As one of the few nations in the world seriously affected by the Kyoto program, Canada debated whether it could afford to comply, and in typically Canadian fashion the issue got tied up in constitutional hassles between the federal and provincial governments over procedure.[28] Several provincial premiers questioned the federal government's judgement on Kyoto, claiming the costs to their provinces would be prohibitive and threatening to use the Constitution as a weapon against implementation.

The questions surrounding the greenhouse effect and the best way of combatting it have proved to be singularly complex. Even scientists disagree on how serious a threat it poses, and the questions regarding costs are clearly beyond the capacity of the average voter to decide. In any event, in December 2002 Prime Minister Chrétien decided that the Protocol should be implemented, as part of his lasting legacy to Canada and the world. Apparently the Prime Minister was prepared to risk unfavourable public opinion and constitutional opposition from the provinces in the process of implementation. This decision was not to be the final word on Kyoto, but it temporarily silenced the provinces, which were not much heard from again in this environmental debate.

PROVINCIAL POLITICAL DEVELOPMENTS, 1990–2007

Provincial politics did not suggest any particular trends between 1990 and 2007, except the incapability of the NDP to maintain popular support in Ontario and British Columbia and the continued ability of Quebec to surprise.

The NDP had experienced some temporary provincial electoral success in the early to mid-1990s, forming governments in five jurisdictions (Ontario, Manitoba, Saskatchewan, British Columbia, and the NWT); however, the governments of Bob Rae in Ontario and Glen Clark in BC both went down to overwhelming defeat, in 1995 and 2001, respectively. Provincial voters continued to prefer parties with no apparent links to the governing party in Ottawa. The tendency was to elect provincial Liberal or NDP governments during the Mulroney era and Tory or NDP governments after the accession to power of the federal Liberals under Jean Chrétien. Progressive Conservatives did considerably better provincially than federally, and by the end of the 1990s they controlled the governments of all the Atlantic provinces except Newfoundland, as well as the governments of Ontario and Alberta; in Manitoba a long-standing Tory government was defeated by the NDP only at the very end of the decade. The only Liberal government at the provincial level was in Newfoundland. Seven years later, 'red' Tories (not the same ideological variety as in the national party) controlled all the Atlantic provinces except New Brunswick, Liberals were in command in Ontario and British Columbia, and the NDP was still in power in Saskatchewan and Manitoba.

At the end of the twentieth century, several of the bigger and wealthier provinces turned to leaders with neo-conservative agendas. Ralph Klein became leader of the Alberta Progressive Conservative Party and Premier of the province in 1992. He won elections in 1993 and 1997 on campaign platforms that emphasized downsizing, balancing the budget, and creating jobs in the private sector, and was re-elected once again in 2001. Towards the end of the 1990s he became an outspoken advocate of privatization in health care, although many observers detected little ideological edge to his position.[29] The Ontario NDP under Bob Rae ran into financial problems and was massacred by Mike Harris's Tories in 1995; the victory marked a return to the historic pattern of Tory dominance in Ontario. Harris was another free-enterpriser, and his government devoted a

TABLE 21.2

QUEBEC ELECTION RESULTS, 2003 AND 2007

Party	Seats 2003	Seats 2007	Change in Number, 2003–2007	Popular Vote, 2007 (%)	% Change, 2003–2007
Liberal	76	48	–28	33.1	–12.9
ADQ	4	41	+37	30.8	+12.6
PQ	45	36	–9	28.3	–4.9

NOTE: Other parties, such as the Green Party, Québec Solidaire, Christian Democrats, and Marxist-Leninists, as well as independent candidates, combined to receive the remainder of the popular vote but elected no members.

SOURCE: Adapted from <en.wikipedia.org/wiki/National_Assembly_of_Quebec>.

good deal of attention to educational reform, rhetorically seeking a return to older values and standards but also engaged in fierce cost-cutting that led to a long war with teachers and parents. In BC, the Liberal government of Gordon Campbell also chose to confront the province's teachers, and undertook a highly publicized campaign to reduce the size of the civil service. Klein left office in 2006, by which time Mike Harris was long gone, his replacement, Ernie Eves, sunk over his brief government's disastrous public relations response to the massive power failure of 2003. Soon thereafter, the Liberals under Dalton McGuinty returned to power in Ontario. By 2007 probably the outstanding features of provincial politics were the emergence of a number of attractive young leaders—all of them male—and the unpredictability of Quebec.

In Quebec, an election in early 2007 returned the Liberals with a minority government. In a three-party race, the Parti Québécois—the only party supporting separatism—finished third. Some observers blamed the PQ defeat on the acknowledged homosexuality of its leader, André Boisclair, while others held that the party had run out of ideas. Closer to the truth, perhaps, was that Boisclair, who resigned the PQ leadership shortly after the election, lacked electoral and government experience. Everyone

agreed that the Liberals, under Jean Charest, had run a lacklustre campaign and that the real winner of the election was the ADQ (Action Démocratique du Québec) led by Mario Dumont, which had run on a right-of-centre populist platform and became the official opposition (see Table 21.2). Clearly, separatism did not carry the same cachet it once had, and in the election's aftermath Mario Dumont, who had moved away from his earlier separatist leanings, called for Quebec to sign on to the 1982 Constitution. Many editorialists coast-to-coast warned against becoming overly sanguine about the defeat of separatism, however. The furor in Quebec over rumours that the Queen might visit the province during its 400th birthday celebration was symptomatic of the volatility of the province. The public outcry to a potential visit from the Queen dragged out all of the old grievances, from the Acadian expulsion to the execution of Louis Riel. Premier Jean Charest had backtracked quickly from a suggestion he made in the campaign that Quebec might indeed have to subdivide.

CONCLUSION

The Task Force on Canadian Unity warned in 1979 that Canada's constitutional crisis would not be resolved in a stroke: the beliefs and attitudes involved were too deeply entrenched. Subsequent developments in the area of constitutional reform proved the accuracy of that observation. They also suggested that ultimate peace on the Quebec front would come only with Canada's acceptance of an independent Quebec: anything short of independence would have to be seen as merely a temporary resolution. Nor would a resolution concerning Quebec settle all the problems between the provinces and the federal government. The reactions to the Romanow report and the Kyoto issue confirm that federal–provincial controversy will continue so long as the nation exists as a federal state.

SHORT BIBLIOGRAPHY

Brownsey, Keith, and Michael Howlett, eds. *The Provincial State in Canada: Politics in the Provinces and Territories.* Peterborough, Ont., 2001. An excellent compilation of material on provincial politics in Canada.

Cairns, Alan C. *Charter versus Federalism: The Dilemmas of Constitutional Reform.* Montreal and Kingston, 1992. A wide-ranging set of essays on the Constitution by one of Canada's leading political scientists.

Cohen, Andrew. *A Deal Undone: The Making and Breaking of the Meech Lake Accord.* Vancouver, 1991. The best account of the Meech Lake fiasco.

Croisat, Maurice. *Le Canada, d'un référendum à l'autre: les relations politiques entre le Canada et le Québéc, 1980–1992.* Talence, 1992. An analysis of constitutional relations between Quebec and Canada from the vantage point of a French-Canadian scholar.

Flood, Colleen, Kent Roach, and Lorne Sossin, eds. *Access to Care, Access to Justice: The Legal Debate over Private Health Insurance in Canada.* Toronto, 2005. A collection of conference papers exploring all dimensions of this thorny issue.

James, Patrick, David Abelson, and Michael Lusztig, eds. *The Myth of the Sacred: The Charter, the Courts and the Politics of the Constitution in Canada.* Montreal, 2002. A recent compilation on Charter politics.

McFarlane, Laurie. *The Best-Laid Plans: Health Care's Problems and Prospects.* Montreal and Kingston, 2002. An excellent survey of the current problems of Canadian health care.

McKitrick, Ross. *The Kyoto Protocol: Canada's Risky Rush to Judgment.* Toronto, 2002. A negative assessment of the Kyoto Protocol.

McRoberts, Kenneth, and Patrick Monahan, eds. *The Charlottetown Accord, the Referendum, and the Future of Canada.* Toronto, 1993. A useful collection of essays on Charlottetown.

McWhinney, E. *Canada and the Constitution, 1979–1982.* Toronto, 1982. Still the best contemporary narrative and analysis of the period in question.

Mandel, Michael. *The Charter of Rights and the Legalization of Politics in Canada.* Toronto, 1992. An insightful investigation of the implications of the Charter of Rights.

Roach, Kent. *The Supreme Court on Trial: Judicial Activism or Democratic Dialogue.* Toronto, 2001. A balanced survey of the question of judicial activism.

Trépanier, Anne. *Un discours à plusieurs voix: la grammaire du oui en 1995.* Sainte Foy, Que., 2001. A fascinating French-Canadian analysis of the 1995 referendum.

Whyte, John, and Roy Romanow. *Canada . . . Notwithstanding: The Making of the Constitution, 1976–1982.* Toronto, 1984. A balanced narrative of the years of constitutional reform.

STUDY QUESTIONS

1. What issues dominated federal–provincial relations in the 1970s?

2. What was the Task Force on Canadian Unity? How did it analyze the constitutional problems facing Canada?

3. What unilateral actions did the federal government take when constitutional discussions broke down in September 1980?

4. Was the Supreme Court ruling on the constitutionality of the amending process a straightforward decision?

5. Why was the Charter of Rights so important?

6. What were the problems of Meech Lake?

7. Why did Charlottetown fail?

8. What are the most important post-1995 constitutional questions in Canada?

9. What is the problem with a health-care system that does not provide for private health-care coverage?

CHAPTER TWENTY-TWO

The Fragmentation and Reconsolidation of Conservatism, 1990–2004

If one listened to the media pundits, Canadians lived in a constant state of turmoil in the years after 1990, lurching from one crisis to another without any road map to the future. Certainly Canada faced problems, but it was hardly alone. Even the potential disintegration of Confederation was not unique. Movements of national liberation were everywhere, and as the problems of Bosnia, the USSR, and Sri Lanka—to name but a few—reminded us, at least in Canada the opposing sides had not yet taken up arms. People almost everywhere else in the world would gladly have traded places with the average Canadian—though not, perhaps, the average Aboriginal Canadian. Canada continued to rank at or near the top of everyone's standard-of-living table.

In retrospect, what seems most obvious about the political direction of the nation was a paradox: even though organized political conservatism was falling apart, Canadians refused to move back to the left. One result was that the Liberals returned to power, but without any consensus about how to govern or what policies to pursue. They remained in power because for 10 years there was no political opposition able to form a credible alternative. Arguably one of the most striking developments of the 1990s and beyond has been the growing trend towards litigation (both public and private), in which compensation for injury plays an increasingly important role.

PRELUDE TO THE 1993 ELECTION

THE LIBERALS

The Liberals finally replaced John Turner in the summer of 1990, selecting Jean Chrétien as their leader after a lacklustre campaign.[1] Like Turner, Chrétien was a veteran of the Pearson and Trudeau cabinets, but unlike Turner, he had remained in the government throughout the Trudeau years, serving loyally in a number of portfolios, including the difficult Finance post. He had finished second to Turner in 1984, and for some time had been the front-runner to succeed him. Chrétien had many strengths. He was a proven campaigner, particularly in French Canada, and his down-to-earth persona and speaking style worked exceptionally well in both French and English. Cultivating the image of a small-town French Canadian, more shrewd than clever, Chrétien managed to disguise his mastery of the political game. Never flashy, he was a loyal party man who understood the importance of the local Liberal organizations he had cultivated for many years. He also had some legitimate credentials in Quebec, which would prove of some

TIMELINE

1971

Donald Marshall arrested for murder of Sandford Seale in Sydney, Nova Scotia.

1973

Calder case establishes that Nisga'a have unextinguished Aboriginal title.

1975

James Bay Agreement in Quebec.

1983

Donald Marshall acquitted of murder of Sandy Seale.

1987

Reform Party organized by Preston Manning. Ukrainians ask for acknowledgement of mistreatment during and after World War I. Royal Commission begins hearings on Marshall case.

1988

Redress agreement between the National Association of Japanese Canadians and the Canadian government.

1989

Marshall Royal Commission releases final report.

1990

Japanese Canadians get cheques and acknowledgement of mistreatment from Prime Minister Mulroney. Jean Chrétien becomes Liberal leader. Lucien Bouchard defects from Mulroney government to form Bloc Québécois. Kenichi Omae publishes *The Borderless World*.

1993

Federal government agrees to settle Inuit land claims and form a new territory to be called Nunavut. Kim Campbell replaces Mulroney as Progressive Conservative leader and Prime Minister. Liberals win easy election victory. Anglican Church apologizes for residential school abuse. Roméo Dallaire becomes commander of UN peacekeeping forces in Rwanda.

1997

Liberals win 1997 election. This year is the OECD's target date for introduction of new world order of Multilateral Agreement on Investment (MAI). Student demonstrators at the Asia–Pacific Economic Co-operation (APEC) meeting in Vancouver are doused with pepper spray. Supreme Court rules on *Delgamuukw* case.

1998

Jean Charest becomes Quebec Liberal leader. Lucien Bouchard and Parti Québécois win Quebec election. Agreement signed between federal government, BC government, and Nisga'a people.

1999

United Alternative convention held at Ottawa. Territory of Nunavut in the eastern Arctic becomes a reality on 1 April. Supreme Court *Marshall* decision on Aboriginal fishing rights.

2000

Stockwell Day chosen as Alliance leader. Liberals win 2000 election.

2001
Alliance chooses Stephen Harper as new leader.

2002
Paul Martin leaves federal cabinet. Auditor General criticizes out-of-control costs of Ottawa's gun registration program.

2003
Creation of the Conservative Party of Canada.

value. His leadership opponents did their best to label him 'Yesterday's Man', and indeed Chrétien stood four-square for all the traditional political values he had helped to implement throughout his long career in Ottawa; he gave no evidence of any new directions. Chrétien might have lost the leadership to a rival candidate with a fresh vision or style, but neither Sheila Copps nor Paul Martin Jr was the charismatic newcomer that Trudeau had been in 1968. Under Chrétien, the Liberals prepared for the next election with a schizophrenic platform, committed to maintaining the welfare state and health-care programs while balancing the budget and reducing the deficit. They also promised to end the GST and revise parts of the (still not finalized) North American Free Trade Agreement negotiated by the Mulroney government, and hinted at a re-evaluation of the original Free Trade Agreement with the US. None of these promises was ever fulfilled.

THE PROGRESSIVE CONSERVATIVES

During Brian Mulroney's second term as Prime Minister, his popularity ratings had regularly fallen to levels lower than those associated with any of his predecessors. Mulroney's problems were many. The defection of Lucien Bouchard and several other MPs from Quebec in 1990 to form the Bloc Québécois had been a blow, and after 1987 the populist Reform Party nipped away at the Tories' strength in Alberta and BC. Free trade had not proved much of a breath of

fresh air, and the North American Free Trade Agreement (NAFTA) with the United States and Mexico had not excited anyone. The Bank of Canada's monetarist policies did nothing for the general economy while increasing the deficit significantly, and the GST had been a disaster, at least from a public relations standpoint, from beginning to end.

By the close of 1992 it was clear that Mulroney was unlikely to win back the electorate. At the inevitable leadership convention of June 1993, Kim Campbell, a British Columbian who had originally been associated with the BC Social Credit Party, was chosen the new party leader on the second ballot.[2] Although Canada's first female Prime Minister was still a relative newcomer to federal politics, she had more experience than Brian Mulroney had in 1984, having held two major cabinet portfolios since 1989. The Tories apparently hoped that her gender and 'candour' would be sufficiently refreshing to give them a chance against the Liberals, even though her credentials in French Canada were hardly up to those of the man she had beaten for the leadership, Jean Charest. Some observers, particularly among feminists, argued that Campbell had been chosen as a 'sacrificial lamb' to bear the brunt of the inevitable electoral defeat about to occur.

In any case, like John Turner a decade earlier, Campbell inherited the enormous unpopularity of her predecessor and his administration. She had little time to establish a new government image before having to call an election.[3] Worse still,

Campbell and her advisers committed a series of campaign blunders. Running on a platform of deficit elimination through reform of social programs, Campbell promised to 'completely re-think Canada's Social Security', but refused to discuss any details of the program during the campaign. The party's standing in the polls dropped immediately. The worst faux pas, however, came near the end of the campaign, when Campbell was unable to distance herself quickly enough from a negative campaign ad suggesting that Chrétien was physically handicapped. Negative media campaigns had become common in the US, but even there physical characteristics were generally considered out of bounds. The result of the Tory ad was a large wave of popular sympathy for the Liberal leader. Largely ignored in the media's concentration on Campbell and Chrétien were a series of fascinating regional campaigns featuring a variety of conservative third parties, of which the Reform Party and the Bloc Québécois proved on the day to be the most attractive to the voters. The Liberals did not so much receive a mandate as triumph over an otherwise badly fragmented opposition headed by the singularly unpopular and inept federal Tories.

THE REFORM PARTY

The Reform Party had been organized in October 1987 by a group of western conservatives centred on Preston Manning, the son of the great Alberta Social Credit leader, Ernest Manning.[4] After graduating from the University of Alberta with a degree in economics, he preached on his father's *Back to the Bible Hour* and eventually established his own management consultancy firm in Edmonton. The Reform Party's backbone was in traditional Alberta and BC Socred country, but it had some appeal as far east as Ontario, especially among retired people and first-time voters. Although Manning was a fairly colourless speaker, his lack of charisma was redeemed by a self-deprecating sense of humour rarely seen among major political leaders. His party stood

■ Prime Minister designate Kim Campbell with Brian Mulroney outside the official residence at 24 Sussex Drive, Ottawa, 14 June 1993. CP/Tom Hanson.

four-square for the traditional populist values of the Canadian West, increasingly alienated from the remainder of the country. It wanted to reduce federal spending, cut taxes in half, eliminate some social programs, reform Parliament to make it more responsive to the popular will, and ensure equal treatment of provinces and citizens alike. The party had no time for the sovereigntist aspirations of Quebec, and it liked multiculturalism little better than it did biculturalism.

■ Opposition leader Preston Manning at a post-election news conference in Calgary, 3 June 1997.
CP/Frank Gunn.

Manning indicated his willingness to contemplate new limitations on immigration to Canada, although he was not pressed to be specific on the issue. Reform had no Quebec candidates.

THE BLOC QUÉBÉCOIS

Inside and outside its home province, the Bloc was inseparable from its central goal, Quebec sovereignty, and its founding leader, Lucien Bouchard.[5] Bouchard had been a lawyer in Chicoutimi before Mulroney appointed him Canadian ambassador to France in 1985, and had sat in Parliament since 1988. Bouchard raised strong feelings inside and outside Quebec. While many Québécois found him compelling and charismatic in the traditional pattern of *le chef* (the best example of which had been Maurice Duplessis), anglophones within and without the province were not attracted to him in the slightest, and at least one 'Hate Bouchard' website was ceremoniously closed down by the RCMP in the late 1990s. The Bloc did not run candidates outside Quebec.

THE NDP

Now led by Audrey McLaughlin, the NDP had enormous difficulty positioning itself for the

TABLE 22.1
PARTY STANDINGS BEFORE AND AFTER THE 1993 ELECTION

Party	Before	After	Change
PC	176	2	-174
Liberal	80	177	+97
NDP	44	9	-35
Reform	1	52	+51
BQ	8	54	+46

1993 vote.[6] Some NDPers insisted that the party should plant itself squarely on the left as the only socialist and nationalist option, while others maintained that such a move would be political suicide because the electorate had turned against anything associated with the traditional consensus. With nothing new to offer, the NDP suffered a major defeat in the election, losing all but nine of its 44 seats (see Table 22.1), along with its official standing in the House (the minimum requirement is 12 seats).

The Tories' loss was even greater, reducing them to just two seats. Even so, the loss of official standing was particularly serious for the NDP, which—without the financial support enjoyed by the two traditional parties—relied heavily on its Commons stipend for its Ottawa infrastructure. With 54 seats to Reform's 52, the Bloc Québécois became 'Her Majesty's Loyal Opposition', anomalously committed to the destruction of the institution in which it sat. The Tories soon jettisoned Campbell and replaced her with Jean Charest (b. 1958).[7]

In power, the Liberals had a relatively easy time, since the opposition was unable to agree on anything and lacked numerical strength, in any case. The main challenge for the Chrétien government was to reduce federal spending and the deficit without doing serious damage to major social programs—or the party's small-'l' liberal image. Finance Minister Paul Martin was able to parlay a lengthy period of unprecedented national economic prosperity into a major success, balancing the budget and maintaining most social services. A review of the entire welfare and unemployment system, headed by Lloyd Axworthy, led to essentially cosmetic changes intended to reduce the time people stayed on social assistance or make it more difficult to use welfare to subsidize seasonal unemployment. Predictably, the government sought to save money mostly by cutting into cultural programs and the military, and by reducing the amount of transfer payments to the provinces for health and higher education.

THE ECONOMY

The Canadian economy had now been running for so long without a major correction that the new standards of performance had become the norm. In the 1990s some of the traditional indicators were positive for economic growth. Inflation was low, interest rates were low and still falling, and the Canadian dollar was low against other world currencies. While Canadians travelling abroad certainly noticed the unfavourable exchange rate, Canadian exporters found it a great competitive advantage. The resulting economic growth was slow but constant. Foreign trade continued to be buoyant, mainly in the resource sector and associated industries. On the other hand, construction starts were stagnant and sales of new automotive vehicles were lower than they had been since the early 1980s. Ominously, the US chipped away at the Free Trade Agreement whenever this worked to its disadvantage.[8] The booming real estate market of the 1980s was no more, even in the still overheated economy of British Columbia. Household debt was up to 89 per cent of disposable income. Most importantly, official unemployment rates ran over 10 per cent nationally, and some of the regional figures were alarming, with rates east of Ontario consistently above the national average. Official unemployment in Newfoundland in 1994 was 20.4 per cent, and in Quebec 12.2. Such figures, of course, include only the people who are still looking for work. Many of those previously employed in dead industries like the Atlantic fishery had simply given up, as had quite a few of the young.

Finding a job was not easy, especially at the entry level. Keeping one was even harder. Downsizing continued to be the order of the day. Governments at all levels were attempting to reduce their workforces, and almost every private enterprise was trying (with some success) to make do with less. Even those who still had jobs lived in fear of the next round of 'rationalization'. In addition to reducing the numbers of their workers, many corporations moved their operations away from Canada, sometimes to the US but often to places in the developing world, where labour costs were much lower. Increasingly, it seemed that downsizing was not self-limiting in the way that economic theorists had hoped when they suggested that the resulting profits would eventually be reinvested in expansion. This was at least part of the thinking behind the public move to keep business taxes low in what came to be known as 'Reaganomics', after the American President who had campaigned on this view. What often seemed

to be happening in the early 1990s, however, was that the increasing profits produced by downsizing were simply distributed to the shareholders. Nonetheless, governments hesitated to increase the tax rates, especially given business threats to leave the country if pressed too hard.

Also disturbing was the apparent absence of new career growth areas for young people. The education counsellors had run out of suggestions for viable alternative careers. The service industry was growing but most of its jobs were at the part-time unskilled (and badly paid) end of the spectrum. 'Working at McDonald's' became the catchphrase for jobs that offered no future and usually provided no fringe benefits. A promotion to unit manager was the best most could hope for, since the real executive positions in the service chains were quite separate from the workers in the trenches. The younger generation, faced with such employment prospects, accepted the media label of 'Generation X'—the post-baby boomers who, through no fault of their own, had arrived at adulthood after all the decent jobs had been taken.[9] With little to look forward to, members of Generation X might well be bitter. But there was little sign that they represented an important political force, certainly not on the left.

Economic growth continued to be strong in household appliances and electronic equipment. What had once been luxury items now became necessities, and new gadgetry was introduced almost every day. As had been the case for over a century, technological innovations led to reductions in price that allowed more and more households to buy new equipment. In 1980 a handful of Canadian homes had microwave ovens, but by the mid-1990s more than 80 per cent did. By 1994 more than half of Canadian households possessed a gas barbecue, and more than a quarter had some form of air conditioning. From a standing start in the late 1980s compact-disc players and home computers had made their way into more than 50 per cent of households by 1995. Before the end of the century Canadians were among the world's leading users of e-mail.

Most of the electronic household gadgetry was assembled abroad, however, and although some jobs became available in the service end of the business, it was often cheaper to throw away broken electronic equipment and buy new than to try to repair it. At the same time, there was obviously room for employment in the rapidly developing computer industry. Canadians established some reputation for software development, and some 'Silicon Valleys of the North' emerged, one in the Ottawa region. While there was clearly a future in computers, it was a highly technical industry that required special skills and aptitudes. Business publications were full of stories of Canadian entrepreneurs who made fortunes in the glitzy new technologies, but they never explained how those successes would translate into large-scale employment opportunities.

In the later 1990s the stock markets experienced another of their periodic booms, despite evidence of a decline in economic prosperity in Asia. The market mania was fuelled chiefly by high-tech stocks. Dozens of companies—mainly in software and the Internet—started on a shoestring by young entrepreneurs made their owners millionaires, and in some cases even billionaires. Only later did it emerge that in many cases the high profits reported by these companies were based on dubious if not fraudulent accounting practices. The inevitable market collapse did not come until the new millennium, but in the meantime the downturn in Asia substantially reduced the demand for Canadian resources. Particularly hard hit was British Columbia, which lost not only its markets but also the enormous infusions of capital that had been a staple of its economy from the early 1980s. Overall, however, despite the signs of trouble, North American consumer demand remained high, and the economy did very well in the last years of the century.

GLOBALIZATION

Scholarly studies in the 1970s and early 1980s often called the market view of industrial development into question, but regional economic integration (Canada–US free trade, NAFTA) had a distinct neo-classical configuration in the Adam Smith tradition and gave a new boost to convergence theories, which envisioned the gradual spread of similar patterns of economic life around the world once constraints were removed. The academic economists were careful to confine their theories strictly to the economic realm, but the business press and other popularizers brought together ideas about a variety of new liberating forces, such as new communications technology and the mobility of capital, and combined them to produce a theory that came to be called 'globalization'. The term first appeared sometime in the late 1980s. Kenichi Omae's *The Borderless World: Power and Strategy in the Interlinked Economy* (1990) was perhaps the key text here.[10] The globalizers argued that the international flows of capital, services, and goods in a world of instant communication and liberal trade packages were not being controlled, and indeed could not be controlled, by national agencies.[11]

The new order, in which a rampant international capitalism would sweep all before it, was epitomized by a proposed Multilateral Agreement on Investment (MAI) that would align the capital-exporting countries of the industrial West against the less developed countries. The Organization for Economic Co-operation and Development (OECD), which consisted of the 29 most highly developed nations in the world (including Canada), set a target date of 1997 for the introduction of the new world order. But the plan generated an enormous amount of opposition, not just from the less developed countries but within the developed nations as well. To a large extent, the consciousness-raising and organization of opposition to the MAI was made possible by the Internet—to the frustration of the bankers and international politicians who had deliberately tried to keep the details out of the public eye. The critics argued that the MAI gave multinational corporations a series of political powers that had for several centuries been the

■ Protestors march to demonstrate against the APEC meetings held in Vancouver in November 1997. CP/Chuck Stoody.

public demonstrations at various summit meetings of the leading industrial nations at the end of the twentieth century and the beginning of the twenty-first.

Perhaps the most publicized Canadian protest occurred at the Asia–Pacific Economic Cooperation (APEC) meeting in Vancouver in November 1997, when representatives from 18 nations met to discuss a free trade zone in the Asian region of the globe. Globalization was obviously one of the protestors' concerns; as student demonstrators from the University of British Columbia put it, 'If you thought NAFTA was scary, wait until you hear about APEC.' But many people were also concerned that some of the heads of state in attendance had questionable records on human rights, including Jiang Zemin of China and General Suharto of Indonesia. Many UBC students were unhappy that the meetings were being held on the UBC campus (at the Museum of Anthropology). Then, when student demonstrators did not move out of the way quickly enough, the RCMP doused them with pepper spray, resulting in what came to be called 'Peppergate'.[13] The RCMP maintained that they had only acted on orders from the Canadian government, while Prime Minister Chrétien's response was 'Pepper? I put that on my plate.' When a formal investigation of the affair finally reported, in the summer of 2001, its findings were inconclusive.

The MAI posed a somewhat different problem for Canada than did North American free trade. Both were seen by their critics as threatening the Canadian nation-state, but whereas free trade encouraged mainly American economic integration, globalization went much further. A number of journalists saw continental economic integration as leading inevitably to political and social integration (or convergence) as well, although most theories on the subject focused on the economy. Conrad Black's new national newspaper, the *National Post*, actively advocated North American integration in the late 1990s.

Not all economists believe that convergence is necessarily the way of the future. Most of the

prerogative of the nation-state. Under the MAI international corporations could be treated no differently from domestic ones, and the nation-state could impose no unusual performance requirements on them (for example, requiring that managers be citizens of the nation in which they were operating).[12] While the MAI was quietly abandoned in 1997, the threat of some form of multilateral agreement by the rich nations of the West remained in place, contributing to fierce doubters think that the national state is capable of resisting and adjusting to new pressures.[14] In the jargon of the economist, the 'border effect' (the influence of the border on trade patterns) continues to be a powerful retardant. Moreover, in many nations the explicit backlash against integration and globalization is producing new political alliances and new ways of preserving the power of the nation-state.

The terrorist attacks on the United States of 11 September 2001 had almost immediate implications for North American airline, travel, and technology industries; the meltdown of the stock market paralleled the physical collapse of the World Trade Center. Further economic trouble followed revelations that a number of major companies, on directions from their CEOs, had been cooking the books and reporting profits they were not really making. For Canada, the greatest problem was the collapse of inflated stock prices for technology firms, including the giant Nortel. Many Canadians discovered that the drop in stock prices threatened their financial planning for retirement. To the surprise of many observers, however, the Canadian economy did not follow the stock market in its decline. On the contrary, the Canadian economy remained far stronger than the American one, with high rates of job creation and economic activity until the end of 2002, when there was some evidence of a slowdown.

THE 1997 FEDERAL ELECTION

To a large extent, the inability of the right to get its act together permitted the Liberals under Jean Chrétien to win their second election, in the late spring of 1997.[15] There was little evidence of any groundswell of political enthusiasm for the government, and the only real expressions of hostility to Chrétien came from Manitoba, where many thought the election should have been postponed while residents of the Red River Valley were cleaning up from the 'Flood of the Century'. But Manitoba did not have enough seats to wield much influence, and the battle was fought essentially in

Ontario. Manitoba was only one of a number of highly publicized 'embarrassments' for Chrétien in the months before the election, but most of them seemed not to amount to very much. The Liberals and NDP did well in Atlantic Canada, the Reform Party did well in the West, especially west of Manitoba (although it won no seats east of that province), and the Bloc Québécois won a majority of seats in Quebec, although its numbers were down substantially from 1993. In Ontario, the right-wing vote was split between Reform and the Progressive Conservatives, allowing the Liberals to win a fair number of seats with less than a majority of the popular vote. The NDP recovered somewhat from its shellacking in 1993, returning to roughly its usual proportions of seats and popular vote. In several polls the NDP showed more popular support nationally than the Reform Party, but of course this support was not as concentrated as Reform's was. The result of this election was to produce a razor-thin majority of the seats in a badly divided House—155 of 301. With 60 seats, the Reform Party under Preston Manning formed the official opposition; the Bloc Québécois had 44, and the NDP and the Conservatives had 21 and 20 (see Table 22.2). Having won seats in most provinces, the Liberals insisted that they were still the only national party. Chrétien would have little difficulty with this Parliament so long so he did nothing that could serve to unite the fragmented opposition. At the same time, the pre-election polls suggested that there was more national agreement and less regionalism than one might have expected, given the result. The biggest single issue all across Canada was unemployment, with national unity and the deficit held to be about equally important. Few Canadians seemed very concerned about health care, probably because no federal party was openly challenging the status quo.

THE 1998 QUEBEC ELECTION

Quebec went to the polls late in 1998. Lucien Bouchard led the Parti Québécois against a resurgent Liberal Party, headed no longer by Robert

TABLE 22.2
1997 FEDERAL ELECTION RESULTS

Party	Number of Seats	% of Total Seats	% of Popular Vote
Liberal	155	51.5	38.4
BQ	44	14.6	10.7
Reform	60	20.0	19.4
NDP	21	7.0	11.0
PC	20	6.6	18.9
Others	1	0.3	1.6

Bourassa (who was terminally ill) but by Jean Charest, who gave up the leadership of the federal Conservative party to become leader of the Quebec Liberals. Bouchard had not been able to make much mileage out of a ruling from the Canadian Supreme Court on Quebec's right to secede, handed down in August 1998, in response to a request from private parties. The court decided that Quebec could separate unilaterally if a 'clear majority' of the province's people answered 'yes' to a clearly phrased referendum question and Quebec then succeeded in reaching an agreement with Ottawa and seven of the 10 provinces. Most observers thought the ruling was sufficiently even-handed to avoid providing Bouchard with an election issue, although Bouchard made it clear that he intended to call another referendum as soon as he thought there was any chance of success. Once again, the federalists had to accept that 'Non' was never permanent but only signified a deferral of separation until a more propitious moment.

Jean Charest did not have much time to prepare for this election. He was not thoroughly familiar with local issues, and apparently did not have a clear sense of the mood of the electorate. Early in the campaign he talked about cutting income taxes and increasing private enterprise,

as Mike Harris had in Ontario. Bouchard's response—'That's not what we like in Quebec, it's not what we'll do'—simultaneously labelled Charest as an outsider and himself as the defender of the province's existing social insurance programs. Prime Minister Chrétien for the most part stayed out of the campaign, but when he did step in, his comment that the Constitution was 'not a general store' was not well received. The electorate did not rush to support Charest's general message that Quebec was tired of constitutional hassle and wanted nothing more than stability and economic development.

The result was another PQ majority, though not an outstanding victory.[16] The final standing was PQ 74, Liberals 45, and Mario Dumont's Action Démocratique du Québec 1, with two independents and three vacancies. The ADQ took francophone votes from both the PQ and the Liberals, but in the larger sense very little had changed. The PQ won few votes from the anglophone minority, while the Liberals won few votes in the rural ridings. Bouchard and the Quebec electorate seemed willing to wait for an opportunity to launch another separatist initiative. Most analysts agreed that the election result, while not a victory for separatism, was not a victory for the status quo either.

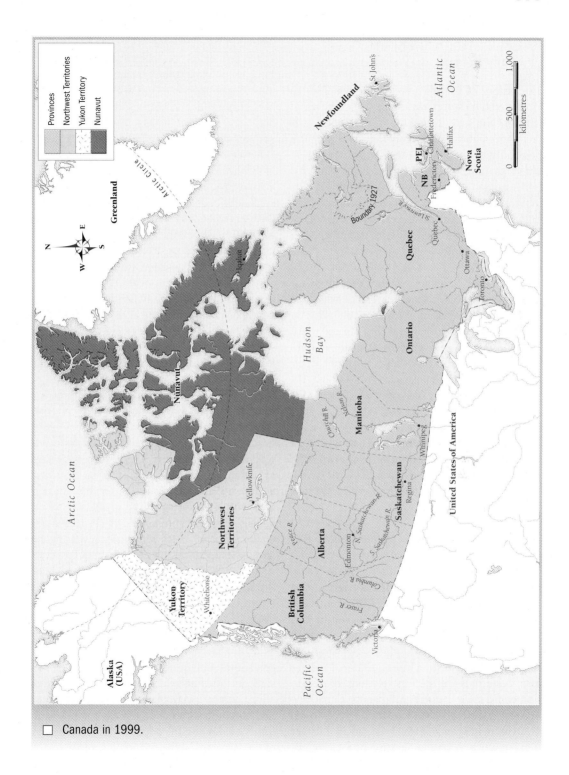

Canada in 1999.

Redressing Historical Mistreatment

The history of Canada is rife with examples of groups who have suffered unfair treatment at the hands of the state. Beginning in the 1960s various collectivities had begun talking about the possibility of redress in the form of apologies, compensation, or both. The First Nations, understandably, were in the forefront of this movement. But the Liberal government of Pierre Elliott Trudeau refused to deal with any collective grievances. As Trudeau told an audience in Vancouver in 1969:

> If we think of restoring aboriginal rights to the Indians well what about the French who were defeated at the Plains of Abraham? Shouldn't we restore rights to them? And what about . . . the Acadians who were deported—shouldn't we compensate for this? And what about the other Canadians, the immigrants? What about the Japanese Canadians who were so badly treated at the end or during the last war? What can we do to redeem the past? I can only say as President Kennedy said when he was asked about what he would do to compensate for the injustices that the Negroes had received in American society. We will be just in our time. This is all we can do. We must be just today.[17]

Trudeau made it clear that he did not believe in any sort of redress. The situation changed somewhat, however, when the courts began to recognize the existence of Aboriginal rights, and Trudeau himself admitted in 1973 that the First Nations may have had more rights than he had previously believed. Those interested in redress had two possible routes: to pressure government or go to court. The two most successful redress cases were those of the First Nations abused in residential schools and the Japanese Canadians mistreated during World War II.

The redress movement was part of a larger trend towards litigation seeking financial compensation for loss of property, health, and life. When the 'unsinkable' ship *Titanic* went down in 1912, more than 100 Canadians died. The literature on that tragedy has shown that it could have been prevented, and that responsibility for it was both systemic and widely distributed. What is perhaps often forgotten is that very few people, either among the survivors or among the families of the victims, ever seriously considered demanding a public inquiry, compensation from government, or class-action litigation in the courts. Disasters in Canada were traditionally regarded as acts of God. When the notion of public assistance for disaster losses began to take hold in Canada, after 1945, compensation was initially regarded as a matter not of right or reparation but, rather, of relief and generosity, which meant that it was not really compensation at all. Victims of the Manitoba flood of 1950 were assisted with reconstruction by the federal and provincial governments, as well as by a privately raised relief fund. How disaster relief gradually became translated into a right of compensation has not yet been carefully studied, but by the 1990s the concept of disaster compensation was well in place.

No doubt part of the shift was associated with the rise of insurance to cover a wide range of damages, from malpractice to accidental injury, and the increasing use of the courts to deal with such matters. The practice of seeking damages for injury from the civil courts escalated in the US after 1945 with juries awarding ever larger damage amounts, often exceeding the ability of the defendant ever to pay. In the process, the concept of liability has been transformed. In recent years, some damage suits have been conducted as class actions, in which a large group of plaintiffs sues for damages they have all suffered, as in the various suits brought against tobacco companies in recent years. The concepts that someone must be held responsible for every negative consequence and that every victim is entitled to compensation or redress for his or her injury are among the major social developments of the last third of the twentieth century.

THE JAPANESE CANADIANS

Early in 1990 thousands of Canadians received from the Minister of State for Multiculturalism and Citizenship a letter enclosing a substantial cheque and an 'acknowledgement signed by the Prime Minister'. The recipients of this material were individuals of Japanese background who had been uprooted from their homes in 1942 by the Canadian government. The cheque was for 'redress' (or compensation, as it was usually called), and the document from the Prime Minister acknowledged 'that the treatment of Japanese Canadians during and after World War II was unjust and violated principles of human rights as they are understood today'. Japanese Canadians had first organized to seek redress in 1977, the centennial of the first arrival of Japanese immigrants in Canada. The government of Pierre Trudeau had refused to consider action on this issue, but the leader of the opposition, Brian Mulroney, was more sympathetic. After the Tories swept to power in 1984, the Japanese renewed their efforts, and on 22 September 1988 Prime Minister Mulroney signed a Redress Agreement between the National Association of Japanese Canadians and the Canadian government.[18] The process mirrored a similar one in the US, and Mulroney's good friend Ronald Reagan had signed a similar arrangement only weeks earlier. Such agreements symbolized how attitudes towards both ethnicity and redress had changed by the end of the twentieth century.

OTHER EFFORTS AT REDRESS

Other campaigns for redress undertaken since the late 1980s have been less successful. In December 1987 the Civil Liberties Commission of the Ukrainian Canadian Committee presented a brief to the Standing Committee on Multiculturalism that called for Parliament to 'officially acknowledge the mistreatment suffered by Ukrainians in Canada during and after the First World War' and for the government to 'undertake negotiations with the Ukrainian Canadian Committee to redress these injustices'.[19] Despite media debate over this question through the early 1990s, nothing was ever done. The Chinese Canadian National Council sought redress for the damage done by Canadian immigration laws between 1885 and 1947, including the 'head tax' imposed on all Chinese immigrants arriving in Canada in the first half of the twentieth century. Finally, in 2006, the federal government made a formal apology to Canadians of Chinese descent, but compensation was offered only to the remaining handful of Chinese Canadians who had been required to pay the head tax. German Canadians, Italian Canadians, Canadian Sikhs, and the Canadian Jewish Congress all talked about restitution for past mistreatment of their people. The Mulroney government indicated a willingness to apologize for mistreatment, although not to provide cash, before it left office in 1993.

In 1992 the Manitoba Métis Federation went to court to attempt to recover lands promised to them by the federal government, which it claimed they had never received because of government manipulation. This case fell into the redress category rather than that of Aboriginal rights because Canada had never recognized the Métis as Aboriginal people. Sympathizers with the Métis also introduced several private members' bills into Parliament in an effort to rehabilitate Louis Riel. In 2002 the Acadians hoped that Queen Elizabeth II would issue an apology for British removal of the Acadians from the Maritimes in 1755. In June 2002 a class action suit was entered in a London (England) court on behalf of those young British immigrants who had been transported to Canada by the philanthropy of the Barnardo Homes at the turn of the century. The suit claimed that the children had been kidnapped and sold into slavery, and deserved to be compensated for their mistreatment.

ABORIGINAL PEOPLES

In 1996 there were some 554,000 status Indians in Canada. Two-thirds of them lived on about

2,300 reserves in nearly 600 registered bands, and the rest lived mainly in larger southern cities such as Winnipeg. In addition, there were 41,000 Inuit. The numbers of non-status Indians and Métis (officially 210,000) were harder to estimate, but probably totalled at least 500,000 across Canada. Despite increased levels of media attention, governmental expenditures, and Native self-awareness, the realities of Native life—while improving—continued to recall conditions in nations generally regarded as the most backward on the planet.

Between 1980 and 1985 infant mortality among First Nations ran at nearly three times the overall national average, at 19.6 deaths per 1,000 live births versus 7.9 per 1,000 in the population. Among the Cree-Ojibwa in northwestern Ontario, overall mortality rates in the early 1980s were twice the national average. Although infectious diseases among the Cree-Ojibwa accounted for only a small proportion of deaths, a Native person was more than four times as likely as an ordinary Canadian to die from them. Other diseases associated with industrialization, such as diabetes, increased markedly after 1950, suggesting that some Native people had 'caught up' with the worst features of civilization. Tuberculosis rates on Prairie reserves in the 1970s ran at 161 per 100,000, while comparable figures in the African nation of Tanzania were only 50 per 100,000. Native life expectancy continued to be 10 years lower, on average, than the overall Canadian figure, reaching an average of 66 years by 1990.

First Nations death rates from accidents and violence continued well above the national averages, and the percentages dying from such causes were on the increase. In 1964, for example, 22 per cent of First Nations deaths resulted from accidents and violence, and by 1990 the figure was up to 35 per cent (the national figure was 5 per cent). First Nations people were more than four times more likely to be murdered than Canadians in general. In the Sioux Lookout area of northwestern Ontario, for example, accidental

falls and motor vehicle accidents were the only categories in which Native people were no more likely than other Canadians to experience accidental or violent death. In other categories, such as house fires and drowning, the Native rates far outdistanced the overall Canadian rates. Native suicide rates, especially among young men, ran well above national norms and reached epidemic proportions in some communities. In one Alberta Cree community made relatively wealthy by oil, the suicide rate in the early 1980s was more than 80 times the national average. Alcohol and substance abuse also continued to be serious problems. Levels of smoking remained higher than national norms, and gasoline sniffing became 'a favourite form of mood alteration among socially deprived children' throughout the Canadian North.[20]

In the 1990s, the First Nations became for the first time popularly perceived as an important Canadian political 'problem', perhaps the most important of that decade and beyond. The immediate focus was not the horrifying demographics of Native life, although they continued to make headlines. Rather, four related issues came front and centre in the 1990s: Aboriginal land rights; self-government; reparations for past mistreatment, particularly in the residential school system; and, finally, the whole question of the bias of the Canadian justice system against Aboriginal people.

LAND RIGHTS

Aboriginal land claims come under two headings. First are what have come to be called specific claims, usually concerning either improper seizure of land or government failure to pay proper compensation for lands seized legally, filed by Aboriginal bands who previously accepted agreements or treaties with the Crown before Confederation or in the so-called numbered treaties 1–11 negotiated between 1871 and 1921. Second are comprehensive claims leading to modern treaties, the first of which was the James Bay and Northern Quebec Agreement of

1975, which are based on the concept of unextinguished Aboriginal title stretching back for many centuries. Comprehensive claims are negotiated between Native groups who never signed treaties or agreements and the federal and, in some cases, provincial governments. This distinction, and the contemporary process established to deal with land claims, evolved over the last decades of the twentieth century, starting from the federal government's aborted white paper on Indian policy in 1969.

The Trudeau government established the Indian Claims Commission to deal with land claims in December 1969, but the slow pace of negotiations soon led the Aboriginal peoples to turn to the courts for redress. A series of landmark decisions, many of them in the Supreme Court of Canada, gradually forced the federal and provincial governments to develop new policies. Over the ensuing years, a number of historic agreements would be reached with Aboriginal peoples, although the settlement process was slow and labyrinthian. Literally hundreds of land claims have been raised, and only a fraction of these have been dealt with, either through negotiations or through the courts. By and large, the courts have not so much settled land claims as they have maintained the Aboriginal right to negotiate them with government.

In 1973 the Supreme Court of Canada ruled in the *Calder* case that the Nisga'a of British Columbia had Aboriginal title to their land, which had never been extinguished. Mr Justice Wilfred Judson concluded: 'The fact is that when the settlers came the Indians were there, organized in societies and occupying the land as their forefathers had done for centuries. This is what Indian title means. What they are asserting in this action is that they had a right to continue to live on their lands as their forefathers had lived and that this right has never been lawfully extinguished.' Mr. Justice Emmett Hall added, 'What emerges from the . . . evidence is that the Nishgas in fact are and were from time immemorial a distinctive cultural entity with concepts of ownership indigenous to their culture and capable of articulation under the common law.'[21] In August 1973 Minister of Indian Affairs Jean Chrétien stated publicly that the federal government was committed to settling Aboriginal land claims.

Also in 1973 the Supreme Court ruled that the Quebec government could not continue with its James Bay hydroelectric project until it had resolved Aboriginal claims, which led to a historic agreement between the province and the James Bay Cree and Inuit in 1975—the first modern land claim agreement.[22] It provided for $225 million in financial compensation and established landownership and usage in the region of northern Quebec. Aboriginal rights and treaty rights were recognized in the 1982 Constitution Act, although they would have to be decided by the courts. In 1984, in a final ruling in *Guerin v. The Queen* (a case brought in 1975 by the Musqueam Indian band, whose traditional territory includes much of what is now Vancouver), the Supreme Court recognized that Aboriginal rights in Canada predated Confederation.

In 1984 a suit filed in the Supreme Court of British Columbia by 35 Gitksan and 13 Wet'suwet'en chiefs contested 58,000 square kilometres of land in the north of the province. The case (known as the *Delgamuukw* case) was heard from 1987 to 1990, and a decision was brought down on 8 March 1991. Before the *Delgamuukw* decision was handed down, the Supreme Court had ruled in 1990 in *Sparrow v. The Queen* that Aboriginal rights were protected under section 35 of the Constitution Act, 1982 and must be handled in a generous manner by the courts. In his decision in *Delgamuukw*, British Columbia Chief Justice Allan McEachern denied the plaintiffs the right to exclusive landownership and self-government, in large measure because he rejected the oral history on which the claims had been based, although he ruled that the plaintiffs had 'unextinguished non-exclusive aboriginal rights, other than right of ownership'. As a result of this case, the government of British Columbia and the First Nations agreed to a treaty-making process. The plaintiffs in *Delgamuukw* appealed, however, and were rejected again on their major points in 1993. Another appeal was heard by the Supreme Court of Canada, with a decision handed down on 11 December 1997.[23] The Supreme Court did not rule on title, indicating that the case would be better resolved through negotiations. But it did indicate that the courts must 'come to terms with the oral histories of Aboriginal societies, which for many Aboriginal Nations, are the only record of their past'.[24] On 16 July 1998, the federal and British Columbia governments signed a final agreement with the Nisga'a people, which granted them 1,930 square kilometres of land, self-government, and a large amount of cash. This agreement was finalized by an Act of Parliament in 2000.

ABORIGINAL SELF-GOVERNMENT

The question of self-government was another long-standing issue.[25] The First Nations insisted that the assertion of ultimate sovereignty over the land by the Crown did not extinguish either their land rights or their right to govern themselves according to their own laws in their traditional territories. Considerable historical evidence exists to indicate that in the past the Crown rarely attempted to assert direct political authority over Aboriginal land, but the legal relationship between the Crown and the First Nations was and is another matter entirely. In most instances, Aboriginal self-government follows the municipal model, with local councils ultimately responsible to the Crown, although several First Nations organizations insist that it must become something more.[26]

In May 1993 the federal government agreed to settle the Inuit land claims to the eastern Arctic and to establish a new territory, Nunavut, with a form of Aboriginal self-government. The demand for self-government had come from the Inuit, who had refused to surrender it in the years of discussion over land rights. The new territory, which was hived off from the previous Northwest Territories, came into existence on 1 April 1999, and its leg-islative assembly uses Inuktitut and English as its two official languages. However, some observers have argued that Nunavut is not so much an example of self-government as it is a highly traditional colonial situation, since Ottawa continues to have a strong presence through federal agencies, co-management boards, and equalization payments that comprise the larger portion of revenues for the territory.[27]

RESIDENTIAL SCHOOLS

The beginnings of the residential school system were put in place long before Confederation, usually in connection with the missionary activities of the churches, which sought to convert Native peoples to Christianity and especially to assimilate them into European society. The education of Aboriginal young people, especially in a milieu apart from their own culture, language, and families, was seen to be the best way to achieve these goals.[28] Residential schools came in a variety of forms (academic, religious, etc.), but in the twentieth century the most common were the so-called 'industrial schools'. They were located in almost every province and territory. The government of Canada shared in the administration of these schools from at least 1874. By the end of the nineteenth century, the schools had shifted from being church institutions partly funded by the government to being government institutions operated by the churches. Their purpose also shifted from assimilation to preparation for life on controlled reserves. From an early date, there was an undercurrent of abuse and intimidation associated with the system, which was by nature based on the (often forcible) removal of children from their families in order to 'civilize' them and 'convert' them to Christianity. In most of the schools, children were forbidden to speak their own languages or practice their spirituality, and the rules were typically enforced with corporal punishment. In 1969 the government of Canada took over the administration of the schools, and they gradually disappeared, the last closing in 1996. The churches

■ Cree children from the Lac La Ronge First Nation at an Anglican Church mission school in Saskatchewan, March 1945. On the blackboard at left is the commandment 'Thou shalt not tell lies.' Bud Glunz/LAC, PA-134110.

and government alike were slow to respond formally to the rising tide of complaints from the Aboriginal community about the residential schools, although stories of abuse were recounted to every commission that investigated the treatment of Aboriginal people in Canada, including the Royal Commission on Aboriginal Peoples, which was created in 1991 and reported in 1996. The Anglican Church formally apologized to the Aboriginal community for its part in the schools in 1993, and the federal government and the United Church followed suit in 1998.

Beginning in the 1990s, survivors of the resi-

dential schools began taking the federal government to court over their treatment. The government in its turn insisted on involving the various churches as co-defendants, in the process virtually bankrupting many churches, dioceses, and religious orders. By the end of the decade there were over 8,000 such cases pending. In January 1998 the federal government announced a program ('Gathering Strength—Canada's Aboriginal Action Plan') for dealing with past injustices, based on reconciliation and concrete action for the future. It also issued a Statement of Reconciliation acknowledging its part in the residential schools and apol-

The United Church Apology to First Nations People regarding Residential Schools, 26 October 1998

At the conclusion of a four-day meeting of the United Church's General Council Executive, the moderator of the United Church of Canada, the Right Reverend Bill Phipps, read the following announcement.

As Moderator of the United Church of Canada, I wish to speak the words that many people have wanted to hear for a very long time. On behalf of the United Church of Canada, I apologize for the pain and suffering that our church's involvement in the Indian Residential School system has caused. We are aware of some of the damage that this cruel and ill-conceived system of assimilation has perpetrated on Canada's First Nations people. For this we are truly and most humbly sorry.

To those individuals who were physically, sexually, and mentally abused as students of the Indian Residential Schools in which the United Church of Canada was involved, I offer you our most sincere apology. You did nothing wrong. You were and are the victims of evil acts that cannot under any circumstances be justified or excused.

We know that many within our church will still not understand why each of us must bear the scar, the blame for this horrendous period in Canadian history. But the truth is, we are the bearers of many blessings from our ancestors, and therefore, we must also bear their burdens.

Our burdens include dishonouring the depths of the struggles of First Nations peoples and the richness of your gifts. We seek God's forgiveness and healing grace as we take steps toward building respectful, compassionate, and loving relationships with First Nations peoples. We are in the midst of a long and painful journey as we reflect on the cries that we did not or would not hear, and how we have behaved as a church. As we travel this difficult road of repentance, reconciliation, and healing, we commit ourselves to work toward ensuring that we will never again use our power as a church to hurt others with attitudes of racial and spiritual superiority.

We pray that you will hear the sincerity of our words today and that you will witness the living out of this apology in our actions in the future.

SOURCE: '1998 Apology to First Nations' [online] by The Right Rev. Bill Phipps, former Moderator, posted January 8, 2007. Cited September 13, 2007. <http://www.united-church.ca/beliefs/policies/1998/a623> Reprinted with permission.

ogizing for its actions. It offered $350 million to help heal the injuries, but was not able to settle with the litigants. In late 2002 it accepted a proposal from the Anglican Church of Canada to limit the Church's responsibility; the Church was to contribute $25 million over five years towards a litigation settlement fund.[29] Further complicating matters, at least one recent court decision has ruled that the Anglican Church itself cannot not be held responsible for the behaviour of its Church Missionary Society, the body that signed the contracts with the federal authorities to administer the schools. By 2007 the residential schools business was not completely settled, although the bare bones of a settlement were in place, involving financial compensation, chiefly from the federal government, and apologies, chiefly from the church groups. Litigation would carry on for years.

THE CASE OF DONALD MARSHALL JR

On 28 May 1971, a 17-year-old black teenager named Sandford Seale left a church hall dance in Sydney, Nova Scotia, to make his way home before a midnight curfew. Walking through Wentworth Park at about 11:40 p.m., he met another 17-year-old, Donald Marshall Jr. Sometime between then and midnight, Sandy Seale was fatally stabbed, dying in hospital about 20 hours later. Although Donald Marshall had called the ambulance and reported to police that he and Seale had been assaulted by two older men (whom he described in considerable detail), the police investigation quickly focused on Marshall himself, who had a reputation as a 'troublemaker'. Witnesses were persuaded that Marshall had been the assailant, alternative evidence was ignored, and the young Mi'kmaq was arrested and charged with murder. Like the Sydney police, the Crown prosecutor ignored a file full of conflicting evidence and testimony. Marshall's counsel, although well-paid and competent criminal lawyers, did not bother to ask the Crown to disclose its case and thus expose the contradictions in it. Furthermore, the trial judge limited the cross-examination of witnesses and refused to permit other important testimony in Marshall's favour to be heard. Not surprisingly, Donald Marshall was convicted and sentenced to life imprisonment.

Within days of the conviction the Sydney Police Department was presented with evidence that Roy Ebsary (who fitted the description of the man Marshall said had attacked Seale and himself on 28 May) had committed the murder. A cursory police investigation of the new testimony was conducted, but its existence was not communicated to Marshall's lawyers before they appealed the conviction. For its part, the appeal did not properly represent the extent of the court's interference with the defence, and the junior counsel who researched the appeal in the Halifax office of the Department of the Attorney General—while he recognized judicial error—did not pursue the matter because defence counsel had not raised it. The appeal was summarily rejected.

Donald Marshall's case was re-examined at least three more times while he was in prison. On the third such occasion, in 1982, Marshall was interviewed in Dorchester Penitentiary by RCMP investigators after testimony had been received that Ebsary had boasted about stabbing young Seale. Marshall provided new details indicating that he and Seale had been involved in attempted robbery when the stabbing occurred. In the long run the RCMP investigation would lead to Marshall's release and acquittal, but in the short run it failed to examine the behaviour of the Sydney Police Department in its original investigation. Finally, on 29 July 1982, the Nova Scotia Court of Appeal permitted an application for bail for Donald Marshall, and he was released. Because he had never admitted culpability and was released on bail rather than paroled, the institutional structure of the justice system provided Marshall with absolutely no assistance or counselling as he emerged from 11 years of confinement.

Donald Marshall's lawyer in 1982 insisted that Marshall be acquitted rather than pardoned, and the Nova Scotia Court of Appeal decided on a procedure that literally forced Marshall to prove his innocence. It heard the evidence of seven witnesses in early December 1982, and re-examined older files and transcripts. On 10 May 1983, it reversed Marshall's 1971 conviction and entered a verdict of acquittal. The appeal court insisted that 'no reasonable jury', on the evidence before it, would find Donald Marshall guilty of the murder of Sandy Seale. The court had been asked only to deal with the conviction. But in its ruling it went on to comment that 'any miscarriage of justice' was 'more apparent than real', since Marshall's 'untruthfulness through this whole affair contributed in large measure to his conviction.' With these gratuitous comments the court absolved the Nova Scotia justice system of responsibility for Marshall's conviction and imprisonment. As a subsequent Royal Commission observed: 'Having concluded that Marshall was involved in a robbery attempt, the Court then took it upon itself to

■ Donald Marshall Jr, at a press conference in Dartmouth, NS, following his acquittal, 10 May 1983.
CP/Albert Lee.

blame him for not confessing to this criminal offence—one with which he had not been charged—in order to win his freedom on another charge, of which he was not guilty.'[30]

The case did not end with Marshall's acquittal. In 1983 concerned citizens asked the government of Nova Scotia to institute a public inquiry into the affair, but the request was rejected without serious consideration by the Deputy Attorney General. On a number of subsequent occasions the Nova Scotia Attorney General's Department refused to assist Marshall and his lawyers in obtaining the information and evidence they required to gain compensation, and worked actively to keep the compensation figure as low as possible. As a result, Marshall was awarded some $270,000 to drop all claims he might have against the government, a figure substantially lower than he might otherwise have received. After three trials, Roy Ebsary was finally convicted of Sandy Seale's death and was sentenced to three years in prison; in 1986 his sentence was reduced by the Court of Appeal to one year. Finally, on 25 October 1986 the Nova Scotia government appointed a Royal Commission to examine the Marshall case. It heard 67 witnesses over 36 days in Sydney, beginning in September 1987, and another 52 witnesses during 53 days of public testimony in Halifax. The public hearings produced nearly 17,000 pages of transcript evidence, and the Commission launched its own investigation of race and the criminal justice system in Nova Scotia, which resulted in findings paralleling those of similar studies in other provinces.

The final report of the Commission, released late in 1989, concluded:

> The criminal justice system failed Donald Marshall, Jr at virtually every turn from his arrest and wrongful conviction for murder in 1971 up to, and even beyond, his acquittal by the Court of Appeal in 1983. The tragedy of the failure is compounded by evidence that this miscarriage of justice could—and should—have been prevented, or at least corrected quickly, if those involved in the system had carried out their duties in a professional and/or competent manner. That they did not is due, in part at least, to the fact that Donald Marshall, Jr is a Native.[31]

The Marshall case had dragged on for nearly 20 years. It did not end even with the Commission report of 1989, which was criticized for pulling its punches about the extent of the 'cover-up' by provincial police officials and civil servants. The chairman of the Commission, the Chief Justice of Newfoundland, had been associated (although never personally involved) with another bureaucratic cover-up in his own province, connected with sexual abuse at the Mount Cashel orphanage. Above all, the Marshall case demonstrated that the judicial system of Nova Scotia not only discriminated against visible minorities, but was prepared to turn a blind eye to mistreatment until the evidence became overwhelming. The sadly consistent findings of other public inquiries across the nation—including the Aboriginal Justice Inquiry in Manitoba (1991)—suggested that the Canadian judicial system itself had become part of the problem.

Interestingly, the same Donald Marshall Jr became the focal point of another *cause célèbre* that served as a benchmark in the history of Canadian–Aboriginal relations. Several years later he was arrested for having caught and sold fish (eels) out of season. In court, his claim of an eighteenth-century treaty right to earn a modest living from the fishery was initially rejected, but when the *Marshall* case reached the Supreme Court the justices in 1999 determined otherwise and acquitted him. This acquittal led to sometimes violent confrontations in the Maritimes lobster fishery, particularly in Miramichi Bay in New Brunswick, the unprecedented action of the Supreme Court justices in their later attempt to qualify their initial judgement, and ultimately resulted in a small but viable Aboriginal lobster fishery in the region.

NATIONAL POLITICS IN THE LATER CHRÉTIEN ERA

UNIFYING THE RIGHT

During the Chrétien years, what the nation needed above all, politically, was a unified conservative opposition. This proved more difficult to find than might have been expected. In April 1998 Jean Charest stepped down as leader of the national PC Party to become leader of the Quebec Liberal Party. This shift of allegiance probably bothered the voters inside Quebec less than those outside the province. Into the national gap stepped Joe Clark, the former Prime Minister who in 1984 had been dismissed by his party in favour of Brian Mulroney. Clark was popular with backroom Tories in eastern Canada, but hardly anybody else. In early 1999, 1,500 delegates assembled in Ottawa at a conference designed to lay the groundwork for a new 'united alternative' on the right. Most of the delegates were members of the Reform Party, and neither the Tories nor the BQ showed much enthusiasm for this initiative. The result was the creation of the Canadian Reform Conservative Alliance.[32] Most Reform members shifted their allegiance to the new party, but Joe Clark's Conservatives stayed resolutely outside the new umbrella. Preston Manning ran for the leadership of the Alliance but was perceived to be unacceptable outside western Canada and in July 2000 he was rejected in favour of a relative newcomer named Stockwell Day.[33] Day proved to be less than compelling as a political leader. His first appearance

■ Two Mi'kmaq in a dory check out one of their boats that was rammed and sunk by a Department of Fisheries and Oceans boat, 29 August 2000. The clash occurred when Fisheries personnel sought to retrieve lobster traps set by Mi'kmaq off the coast of Burnt Church Reserve in northern New Brunswick. CP/Jacques Boissinot.

in the role, for which he donned a wetsuit and rode a jet ski to meet the media, was one embarrassment. Another was a lawsuit filed against him by a lawyer whom Day had criticized for defending an accused pedophile: not only did Day disregard the fundamental legal rights involved in that case, but he allowed the province of Alberta to assume the legal costs for his own defence in the libel suit. Although he eventually tried to make amends by mortgaging his house to pay the bill, the damage was done. Within a few

months of his selection, and before he had a chance to put his mark on the party platform or develop any popular new initiatives, Day was forced to lead the Alliance into an election.

THE 2000 FEDERAL ELECTION AND THE LIBERAL LEADERSHIP CONTROVERSY

In the 2000 federal election (see Table 22.3) the Liberals actually gained both in seats and in per-

TABLE 22.3

2000 FEDERAL ELECTION RESULTS

Party	Number of Seats	% of Total Seats	% of Popular Vote
Liberal	172	57.1	40.8
BQ	38	12.6	10.7
Alliance	66	22.3	25.5
NDP	13	4.0	8.5
PC	12	4.0	12.2
Others	0	0	2.3

centage of the popular vote.[34] The number of Liberal seats increased to 172 and the party's percentage of the popular vote grew to 40.8 per cent. Some of the increase came at the expense of the Bloc Québécois, which dropped from 44 to 38 seats, although the Tories and NDP both lost seats as well. The Alliance actually won six more seats than Reform had in 1997, but still exclusively in western Canada. Stockwell Day proved ineffective as leader of the opposition. Before long, prominent members of his caucus, including Deborah Grey and house leader Chuck Strahl, were expressing discontent. By April 2001, most of the caucus had turned against him, and 13 walked out (six of whom later returned). In late 2001 Day stepped down as Alliance leader, and although he ran in the leadership contest of March 2002, his party chose Stephen Harper instead. Harper was a well-known Alberta conservative with little track record either in the grind of daily politics or in leadership. The problem of the political right was that they seemed to have available as national leaders only unsuccessful old politicians (like Clark or Manning) or untested new ones (like Day and Harper).

Meanwhile, Prime Minister Chrétien came under increasing attack not only in the House and the media, but even in his own caucus. Much of the criticism was directed at his involvement with developers in his riding for whom he solicited government support, as well as over a wide variety of other ethically dubious interventions by Chrétien and others. In every case, the government's newly appointed ethics adviser ruled that no guidelines had been broken, but few in the opposition or the public were entirely convinced. One of the main issues within the Liberal caucus was succession politics. Chrétien was widely expected to step down soon after the 2000 election, and every potential leadership candidate tried to build up a financial war chest and support for the eventual contest. But the Prime Minister refused to announce a timetable for his retirement, and the arm wrestling among prospective leadership candidates became disruptive. Finally, by the summer of 2002 the leading contender was in open revolt against Chrétien's leadership. Paul Martin, whose father had been a key Liberal politician for many decades (see, for example, Chapter 13), had served for nearly 10 years as Minister of Finance and felt that he was ready to assume his rightful place as party leader. After a brief power struggle, Martin left the federal cabinet in June, and eventually seemed content with the Prime Minister's an-

SHEILA FRASER (1950–)

❖

Sheila Fraser was born in Dundee, Quebec, in 1950. She graduated from McGill University in 1972 with a Bachelor of Commerce degree and joined the Quebec City office of the accounting firm of Ernst & Young, becoming a partner in 1981. In Quebec City she worked closely with the Auditor General of Quebec on several projects. Fraser was involved in a good deal of professional activity, both provincial and federal, won several awards, and served as chair of several international auditing committees.

Fraser was appointed Deputy Auditor General of Canada in January 1999 and then Auditor General a little more than a year later. Her first report, tabled in Parliament in December 2001, was highly critical of government mismanagement, pointing out that the Department of Human Resources Development, which was responsible for a $16 billion budget, could not explain where many of its grants and contributions had gone. She was equally critical of cancer research programs in the Health Department and especially of Health Canada's HIV/AIDS program, which spent millions of dollars with no evidence of success in controlling disease. In her 2001 report, she emphasized that 'Canadians have a right to control how public funds are collected and used, and ultimately it is the members of Parliament we elect who carry out this control on our behalf.' Fraser returned to the attack in her 2002 report, this time gaining huge headlines for her revelations of massive cost overruns by the Department of Justice in connection with the Canadian Firearms Program, which appeared to be on the way to spending more than $1 billion without establishing a reliable database or reporting to Parliament.

nouncement that he would step down in February 2004. Most observers felt that Martin had lost considerable credibility as a consequence of the controversy, but no other leadership candidate seemed likely to beat him.

PARLIAMENTARY WEAKNESS AND EXECUTIVE IRRESPONSIBILITY

In her 2001 annual report, Auditor General Sheila Fraser referred to an alarming 'erosion of parliamentary control over how the government raises money and spends it'. This criticism was directed specifically at the huge surplus in the Employment Insurance Fund, but the problem was clearly widespread. One reason, of course, was the continuing political weaknesses of the post-2000 opposition, which lacked the unity (and the votes) to hold the government to account in any systematic way. Another, however, involved the long-term drift towards executive rather than parliamentary government. This began when the Privy Council Office (PCO) was formed early in World War II to manage affairs for a government that, because of wartime necessity, increasingly acted through Orders-in-Council rather than parliamentary resolution, and was reinforced in the 1960s, when the Prime Minister's Office (PMO) was established to manage party matters on behalf of the Prime Minister. The result was an enormous and increasingly complex bureaucracy whose job it was to manage the affairs of government.

Perhaps the best example of Parliament's loss

of control came in December 2002, when Fraser revealed that a gun control program originally expected to cost $119 million—with registration fees providing a return of $117 million, for a net cost of just $2 million—would end up costing more than $1 billion, and even then would be incomplete. The Canadian government had passed Bill C-68, the Firearms Act, in 1995 in response to several highly publicized incidents involving guns, including the massacre of 14 female engineering students in Montreal in 1989. Intended to replace earlier legislation controlling the purchase of firearms, it aimed to license all gun owners and provide a universal registry. Many Canadians opposed the bill, for a variety of reasons (including the suspicion that the law was unworkable), but many others supported it, some of whom took pride in Canada's willingness to adopt a measure that would be unthinkable in the US. The sheer technical problems involved in licensing and registration proved much more serious—and costly to address—than the proponents of the legislation had anticipated.[35] But the escalating costs were never submitted to Parliament and thus never publicly debated. In the wake of the Auditor General's comments, the Prime Minister admitted to his caucus that he had long known the costs were out of control, but he blamed the problem on the inevitable bureaucratization of any such endeavour, insisting that no single minister or group of ministers could be held responsible. For many Canadians, the gun control fiasco was just one more concrete example of the drift of the government, which seemed to lack not only direction but the will to establish it.

THE NEW CONSERVATIVE PARTY

Secret meetings between the Canadian Alliance and the Progressive Conservative Party in late 2003 resulted in the creation of the new Conservative Party of Canada (CPC), ratified by postal ballot among the Alliance membership and by regional conventions among the PCs. The 2000 election had made clear that the Liberals would govern forever if they continually faced a divided conservative opposition complicated by a sovereigntist party in Quebec. The two conservative parties had some difficulty in merging, since they represented different conservative traditions in Canada. The Progressive Conservatives, based mainly in eastern Canada at the provincial level, tended to be strong Canadian nationalists and supporters of state-run social programs, while the Alliance, as the heir to the western-dominated Reform Party, was more socially conservative, with strong roots in fundamentalist religion, and populist in its opposition to centralized federalism. The Alliance had moved increasingly to the centre, however, as it became clear that a truly right-wing party could not flourish electorally in Canada. A third conservative tradition in Canada, that in Quebec, was not much of a player in the new Conservative Party; the Bloc Québécois remained separatist. The new party was a neo-conservative one much like the Republican Party in the United States under George W. Bush. It was socially conservative, favourably disposed to the international use of military force, populist, and free-enterprising. It was also mainly anglophone. On 20 March 2004, Stephen Harper was elected leader of the CPC. Harper had succeeded Stockwell Day as leader of the Alliance in early 2003 and had helped engineer the merger of the two conservative parties. He was relatively young (b. 1959), articulate, and extremely self-assured; his French was passable and got better.

CANADA AND THE WORLD

PEACEKEEPING IN THE 1990S

The end of the Cold War opened a new era for peacekeeping. International co-operation at the United Nations facilitated the creation of 24 peacekeeping missions between 1991 and 1996. These missions reflected the increase in regional conflict and the favourable way the major pow-

- Peacekeeping in Cambodia: Corporal Corena Letandre of the Canadian Forces' 2 Service Battalion comforts a hospitalized child. Reprinted by permission of the *Canadian Military Journal*.

1991 ceasefire in Cambodia, monitored the demilitarized zone in Iraq and Kuwait beginning in 1991, and helped a UN special commission to inspect for biological and chemical weapons in Iraq. It became involved in the Balkans in 1992, the same year it entered Somalia under the United Nations Operation in Somalia (UNOSOM).

SOMALIA

The UN went to Somalia to ensure the distribution of food supplies to a population caught in a vicious civil war. The Canadian contingent consisted of the 900 members of the Canadian Airborne Regiment, a commando unit that modelled itself on the American Green Berets. When, in the spring of 1993, it was revealed that a small number of Airborne soldiers had tortured and killed a Somali teenager named Shidane Arone, Canadians were profoundly shocked, not only by the racist brutality of the murder but because it gave the lie to their treasured self-image as the world's good guys. Charges were laid against eight soldiers, and in 1995 the regiment was disbanded after videotapes surfaced that showed Airborne members participating in vicious hazing of new recruits. A subsequent inquiry demonstrated that the senior Canadian officers had attempted to cover up events in Somalia by altering documents; this was not the only case in which those in high command were implicated in a cover-up.[36]

THE BALKANS

Canada became involved in the Balkan civil wars with an enthusiastic commitment to peacekeeping that was soon eroded by the difficulty of finding any party in the region that was not guilty of some human rights abuse. The peacekeeping forces in 1994 found themselves caught between the Bosnian Serbs and the NATO high command. The latter attempted to employ bombing strikes; the former threatened to use human shields. In 1994–5 Canadian soldiers (including Captain Patrick Rechner, who was shown on videotape chained to an ammunition dump) were among

ers looked on peacekeeping as a means of managing conflict. Canada participated in many of these operations, contributing military contingents and RCMP units as well as civilians (from Elections Canada and the Canadian Red Cross). It provided observers in Haiti for the verification of the 1990 elections, helped to monitor the

ROMÉO DALLAIRE AND THE RWANDAN GENOCIDE

Rwanda is a mountainous country in central Africa. A German protectorate in 1899, it was mandated to Belgium in 1919 and became independent in 1962. The country has a long history of tribal conflict between a majority Hutu and a minority Tutsi, the latter entering the region in the sixteenth century and favoured by the European colonial powers. The Hutu controlled the country upon independence, and the first massacre of Tutsi occurred in the 1960s. By the early 1990s Rwanda was in the midst of civil war. In late 1993, Canadian General Roméo Dallaire (b. 1946) became force commander of UNAMIR, the United Nations military mission in Rwanda, which included a handful of Canadian peacekeepers (60 soldiers plus two Canadian CC-130 aircraft) along with Belgian, Ghanaian, Tunisian, and Bagladeshi soldiers. Not long after he took command, Dallaire discovered the likelihood that a massacre of moderate Hutus and Tutsis in Rwanda was in the works, but he was unable to prevent it. He called for more troops and supplies. Instead, the Belgians responded to the murder of 10 of their soldiers by withdrawing the remainder. The Americans refused to support the mission, and the UN Security Council reduced it to 260 men, a force too small to do anything more than create a safe zone around Kigali, the capital. Dallaire was able to use his handful of soldiers and their UN credentials to save a number of Hutus and Tutsis around Kigali, but could do very little for most of the victims in the countryside, many of whom were hacked to death in an orgy of killing that began on 6 April 1994. The nation was stabilized later in 1994 by the

Retired general Roméo Dallaire delivers a harsh review of the world's response to the genocide in Rwanda at the International Conference on War-Affected Children in Winnipeg, 14 September 2000. CP/*Winnipeg Free Press*/Ken Gigliotti.

United Nations after the murder of somewhere around one million people and the displacement of another 2 million.

Dallaire returned to Canada in total frustration, suffused with guilt for his inability to prevent the genocide, and after years of mental anguish he retired and began to lecture and write about his experiences. Dallaire's book, *Shake Hands with the Devil: The Failure of Humanity in Rwanda* (2003), written in collaboration with Major Brent Beardsley, won the Governor General's award for non-fiction in 2004.

the UN peacekeepers taken hostage by the Serbs on two occasions and used as human shields to prevent air strikes. Bosnian Serb leader Radovan Karadzic threatened to turn Bosnia into a

'butcher shop' if the UN used force to free the hostages. Rechner was eventually freed, and the court case against his abductors collapsed early in 2003.

Canada was not happy in Bosnia, and the major powers were not happy with Canada, which was opposed to the heavy employment of force in the Balkans and was known, moreover, to be attempting to reduce its commitment to the NATO alliance. A ceasefire in Bosnia late in 1995 enabled Canada to complete the withdrawal of over 1,500 troops from the former Yugoslavia.[37] Canada returned to the Balkans in 1997, however, as part of NATO's Stabilization Force in Bosnia-Herzegovina. It also became militarily involved in the UN mission in Haiti and in the UN Police Operation in Haiti, providing RCMP officers to help train local police.

Canadian involvement in overseas military activities was greatly curtailed in the late 1990s, for several reasons. One was the general downsizing of the Canadian military, which made it difficult for Canada to provide large numbers of troops for overseas activities and maintain its other commitments as well. Another was the sense of both the government and the public that peacekeeping in the context of civil war was thankless and impossible. Finally, there was an overall sense that the Canadian military was no longer sufficiently well trained and equipped to perform successfully abroad, although they did well in disaster relief activities at home, such as the Manitoba flood of 1997.

THE SPANISH FISHING CRISIS OF 1995

On 9 March 1995 the Spanish fishing vessel *Estai* was fishing in international waters when officials from the Canadian patrol vessel *Cape Roger* attempted to board it. Canada had earlier threatened to seize vessels fishing for turbot in the area on the grounds that the Spanish vessels had already taken their quota—only recently imposed by Order-in-Council—but Spain had argued that the quota of the European Community had not been exceeded and that its vessels were fishing in international waters. The *Estai* proceeded to take evasive action against the

boarding, and the *Cape Roger* was joined by another fisheries patrol vessel and a Canadian coast guard ship, the *Sir Wilfred Grenfell*, which allegedly shot water cannon against the Spaniards. Finally, the *Cape Roger* directed several bursts of machine-gun fire against the *Estai* and it was taken to St John's, where its captain was charged with breaches of the Coastal Fisheries Protection Act of Canada.

The incident might well have led to open hostilities between Canada and Spain if either nation had had a battle-ready navy. Spain applied for redress from the International Court of Justice at The Hague, and Canada answered that in 1994 it had added a new reservation to its general acceptance of the jurisdiction of the court that specifically excluded fisheries incidents over conservation. The International Court of Justice decided in Canada's favour. The Canadian government applauded the decision, adding that it preferred negotiation to litigation to resolve disputes. Although the Spanish incident was an isolated one, it suggested the global nature of the new world order in which Canada was operating.

CANADIAN STUDIES ABROAD

One of the few unqualified success stories involving Canadian policy abroad was the development of programs of Canadian Studies in many parts of the world. Before the 1970s the study of Canada was confined to a relative handful of academics, almost all of whom were based at Canadian universities. With the financial assistance of the government of Canada, the Association for Canadian Studies in the United States was founded in 1971, the British Association of Canadian Studies in 1975, and the French Association for Canadian Studies in 1976. The International Council for Canadian Studies was established in 1981 to serve as a central federation for what by 1990 had become 20 national and multinational Canadian Studies associations promoting research about and understanding of Canada in more than 30 foreign countries. Many of those associations have their own journals and sponsor their own academic conferences. A high proportion of the most active associations are in nations that have supplied many of Canada's more recent immigrants (such as Italy and India), and Canadian Studies programs at local universities provide sources for information about Canada for prospective newcomers. The sponsorship of Canadian Studies costs a mere pittance by comparison with other international programs, and it has provided very high returns on investment.

CONCLUSION

The years between 1990 and 2003 were confusing, with no clear replacement for the old paradigms that had collapsed in the last three decades of the century. At the federal level, the inability of those on the political right to agree on a single ideological vision gave the Liberal Party free rein to govern the nation without actually repudiating its old liberal principles while behaving in quite a conservative fashion. At the provincial level, several provinces supported liberalism (in the nineteenth-century sense) or conservatism (in the earlier twentieth-century sense). Socially, perhaps the most important development of the decade was the triumph of the principle of public compensation for historic abuse. In the realm of foreign affairs, Canada's long-cherished peacekeeping role was challenged and changed in the face of civil strife in various world regions and the altered global order that no longer could be clearly defined in the old Cold War terms. In other areas, such as the Spanish 'turbot crisis' of 1995 and the increasing extension of Canadian Studies abroad, the nation more than held its own.

SHORT BIBLIOGRAPHY

Dallaire, Roméo, in collaboration with Major Brent Beardsley. *Shake Hands with the Devil: The Failure of Humanity in Rwanda.* Toronto, 2003. An impassioned exposé of the world's failure in Rwanda.

Dobbin, Murray. *The Myth of the Good Corporate Citizen: Democracy under the Rule of Big Business.* Toronto, 1998. A provocative study of the growth of the MAI and its Canadian implications in the 1990s.

Flanagan, Thomas. *Waiting for the Wave: The Reform Party and Preston Manning.* Don Mills, Ont., 1995. An insider analysis of the development of the Reform Party.

Frizzell, Alan, et al., eds. *The Canadian General Election of 1993.* Ottawa, 1994. A useful study of one of the crucial national elections of our time.

Laycock, David. *The New Right and Democracy in Canada: Understanding Reform and the Canadian Alliance.* Toronto, 2002. An excellent analysis of the modern right in western Canada.

Lippert, Owen, ed. *Beyond the Nass Valley: National Implications of the Supreme Court's Delgamuukw Decision.* Toronto, 2000. A collection of essays that passes well beyond the ostensible topic.

McLeod, Ian. *Under Siege: The Federal NDP in the Nineties.* Toronto, 1994. A useful attempt to explain what happened to the NDP.

Martin, Lawrence. *The Antagonist: Lucien Bouchard and the Politics of Delusion.* Toronto, 1997. A revealing look at one of the most enigmatic figures of modern Canadian politics.

Mauser, Gary. *Misfire: Firearm Registration in Canada.* Vancouver, 2001. A well-informed and dispassionate dissection of the gun control business in Canada.

Miki, Roy, and Cassandra Kobayashi. *Justice in Our Time: The Japanese Canadian Redress Settlement.* Vancouver, 1991. An account of one of the most remarkable political stories of our era.

Miller, J.R. *Shingwauk's Vision: A History of Native Residential Schools.* Toronto, 1996. A careful academic history of a controversial topic.

Pue, Wesley, ed. *Pepper in Our Eyes: The APEC Affair.* Vancouver, 2000. The best source for 'Peppergate' and the controversy surrounding it.

Salisbury, Richard. *A Homeland for the Cree: Regional Development in James Bay, 1971–1981.* Kingston, 1986. An important study of Aboriginal affairs in the James Bay region.

Watson, William. *Globalization and the Meaning of Canadian Life.* Toronto, 1998. A pro-business analyst looks at the problems that international business trends create for Canada and the Canadian identity.

STUDY QUESTIONS

1. What does the phrase 'working at McDonald's' really mean?

2. How much of a threat to Canada is globalization?

3. Why has the policy of redress of historical grievances been so contested in recent years?

4. What did Donald Marshall's wrongful conviction for murder suggest about the Canadian judicial system?

5. In what ways is the gun-control fiasco representative of the state of Canadian politics in the new millennium?

6. How would you assess Jean Chrétien's record as Prime Minister?

7. Why were Reform and the Alliance not more successful, yet the new Conservative Party formed a minority government following the 2006 federal election?

8. What, to your mind, is the most important political development in Canada in the past decade?

CHAPTER TWENTY-THREE

Canadian Society and Culture, 1972–2007

In the last quarter of the twentieth century and the first years of the twenty-first, the social values that had been constructed in Canada, particularly since 1939, appeared to be falling apart, along with the liberal consensus that had made them possible. In truth, many (though not all) of the new realities had been present earlier, but had not been acknowledged. At the same time, not everything was doom and gloom. The new social order was more open than the old one. Canadians became far more cosmopolitan and receptive to new ideas from the outside world at the same time that they became more violent.

ABUSE AND SELF-INDULGENCE

Two disturbing social trends that began in the last quarter of the twentieth century were dramatic increases in abuse (often violent) of others and extreme self-indulgence. Reflecting a growing alienation among individuals, these trends may also have been symptomatic of a transitional period in society. As the Italian Marxist Antonio Gramsci wrote in another period of transition more than half a century earlier: 'The old is dying and yet the new cannot be born. In this interregnum, a variety of morbid symptoms appear.' In both cases, increasing incidence also reflected the power of the media, which in the one case pub-

licized what had long been occurring beneath the surface, and in the other promoted new consumer fads, fashions, and even needs, which in themselves could become powerful addictions.

SEXUAL AND PHYSICAL ABUSE

'Abuse' must be distinguished from the historic mistreatment for which, as we saw in the last chapter, various groups have sought redress. That mistreatment, in most cases the product of prejudice and war, was both systemic and systematic, and was imposed by the society on certain groups of people. Abuse, on the other hand, is a matter of violence, sexual and physical, inflicted on individuals by individuals in an unequal power relationship. Aboriginal children were mistreated by the institutions (the government and the churches) that placed them in residential schools because they were Aboriginal. But Aboriginal children in those schools were abused by individuals who preyed on them not because they were Aboriginals but because they were helpless children. The residential schools may have made abuse possible, but they were not intentionally or directly the agents of abuse.

Although the incidence of abuse of various kinds appeared to increase sharply, most professionals believed that what was increasing was not

TIMELINE

1973
Dr Henry Morgentaler reveals that he has successfully performed more than 5,000 abortions.

1976
Quebec government issues a Green Paper on cultural policy.

1978
First case of AIDS probably occurs (undiagnosed) in Canada.

1980
Terry Fox begins run.

1982
Laboratory Centre for Disease Control in Ottawa begins tracking AIDS.

1983
Suicide rate is 15.1 per 100,000. Paul Audley publishes *Canada's Cultural Industries*.

1985
HIV-antibody screening procedures become routine in Canadian blood banks.

1988
Ben Johnson loses Olympic gold medal for steroid use.

1989
Shootings at l'École Polytechnique in Montreal.

1991
Manitoba Aboriginal Justice Inquiry reports.

1993
Krever Commission appointed to inquire into the blood system in Canada.

1995
Canadian preference for SUVs (sports utility vehicles) well-established.

1996
RCMP charges Alan Eagleson with fraud.

1997
Sheldon Kennedy 'Skate Across Canada' held. Krever Commission reports on tainted blood.

1998
Canadian Red Cross transfers its blood services to new organizations.

2002
Canadian men's and women's hockey teams win gold at Salt Lake City Olympics.

2006
Pickton trial begins in New Westminster, British Columbia.

so much abuse itself as the reporting of it. Abuses that might have gone unreported in the past were now widely publicized by the media. The Canadian Charter of Rights and Freedoms also played an important role, encouraging collective minorities to seek equitable treatment for their members. In 1990 a schoolteacher in Alberta was removed from the classroom, after a controversial trial, for teaching racial hatred; in 1991 a teacher in New Brunswick was removed for similar reasons. Sexual abuse in junior hockey was exposed, and reports of organized sexual abuse reached as far as Maple Leaf Gardens in Toronto. And stories like that of Donald Marshall Jr, as seen in Chapter 22, demonstrated that both the social service and legal systems were, as visible minorities had always claimed, loaded against them.

In 1991 a provincial inquiry into Manitoba justice system's treatment of Aboriginal people was extremely critical of the police and the courts. In 1989 a Newfoundland provincial inquiry brought to light evidence of sexual abuse of children at an orphanage run by the Christian Brothers that had been ignored by the province's social service workers and covered up by its police and civil servants.[1] Across the country, hundreds of Canadians—many of them raised in institutions such as orphanages and residential schools—complained publicly that they had been abused (often sexually) by teachers and other authority figures. Sexual abuse of children, often incestuous in nature, was increasingly brought to light, sometimes by authors confronting experiences of childhood abuse in painful memoirs. Wife-beating—for decades the most common domestic crime on the police blotter—finally became a focus of public concern. In 1989, the year when a lone gunman killed 14 women students at the École Polytechnique in Montreal, apparently because 'feminists' had 'ruined [his] life',[2] the number of Canadian women who had been raped that year was estimated at 32,000.

■ Eleven years after the murders at the École Polytechnique, a man pays his respects at the school's memorial, Montreal, 6 December 2000. CP/Ryan Remiorz.

Not surprisingly, the abusers of the less powerful—children, women, Aboriginal people, visible minorities—often were traditional authority figures, from parents and pastors to teachers and policemen. On one level it was possible to take solace in the fact that such behaviour was now being exposed and addressed. On another level it was possible to argue that what had changed was not so much the behaviour of those in positions of authority but society's willingness to tolerate its worst extremities. Either way, however, both the extent of the abuse and the undermining of authority to which it contributed were distressing. Canadians could no longer believe that they were all 'good people' living in the 'Peaceable Kingdom'. Nor could they believe in the inherent benevolence of parents, priests and ministers, teachers, doctors, policemen—or even the judicial system. The revelations of the post-1972 period, particularly in the 1980s when they first became common, could only contribute to a

VIOLENCE AGAINST WOMEN

Violence against women in Canada was bookended in the last years of the twentieth century and the early ones of the twenty-first by two highly publicized occurrences. The first, on 6 December 1989, involved a lone gunman who calmly entered a classroom in l'École Polytechnique in Montreal, separated the men from the women, and systematically opened fire on the women. Fourteen died and many more were wounded. The nation responded with a spontaneous outburst of sympathy for the victims and their families and calls for gun control. In 1991 the Canadian Parliament established 6 December as the National Day of Remembrance and Action on Violence Against Women, to commemorate both the 1989 event and to call attention to the general problem. On 30 January 2006, in British Columbia Supreme Court in New Westminster, the trial of pig farmer Robert Pickton opened. Pickton was charged with 27 counts of first-degree murder against women who had gone missing from the Downtown Eastside of Vancouver and whose remains (among others)

were found at Pickton's pig farm in Port Coquitlam. A blackout on details of the trial in Canada was ignored by the American press. Many observers complained that the women murdered by Pickton were marginalized members of society, which meant that the authorities did not expend the same energy on their disappearances as they did for other women. Other observers of both the Montreal and Port Coquitlam cases emphasized that these highly publicized incidents were not typical of violence against women in Canada, because most such violence was domestic, usually beneath the purview of the media. Males are the perpetrators of most domestic violence, and the percentage of married women in Canada who have experienced such violence runs at about 30 per cent. Four in 10 women who have experienced spousal violence admit that their children have witnessed this violence. Three out of 10 women who sought refuge in shelters had reported the most recent incident of abuse to the police, who laid charges in only about one-third of the cases reported.

growing cynicism with regard to authority, which was not alleviated by the behaviour of the politicians discussed in the previous chapters.

NARCISSISM

Another striking characteristic of the period since the early 1970s, observed by many commentators, has been a strong tendency towards personal self-absorption. In its more benign form, this could be seen as a desire for self-fulfillment, but what was most often publicized was a more extreme manifestation, which the American historian and social theorist Christopher Lasch has labelled 'narcissism'.[3] Among the negative factors that contributed to this trend

were the economic conditions of the post-Keynesian period, including overheated short-term speculation, a fundamental lack of optimism, a lottery mentality, and a sense of the ultimate limits of growth. Opportunity did not exactly disappear—in the boom periods of the 1980s and the late 1990s it seemed to flourish—but its pursuit had to be quite ruthless and single-minded, and for relief from the stress of their working lives, many successful people relied on addictive drugs of various kinds.

Another factor in the trend was the effect of the baby boom on the job market. As this cohort progressed through life, entry-level employment became increasingly difficult to find in many fields, and later boomers often found the promotion lane clogged by large numbers of relatively equally qualified individuals. Job prospects were further limited by the fact that most employees could now expect to live to retirement age, and in a number of provinces the courts were striking down mandatory retirement at age 65 as discriminatory. Younger Canadians responded to the employment crunch by seeking further educational credentials, especially in financially remunerative professions such as accountancy, pharmacy, and computer programming. Contrary to predictions, university enrolments did not decline in the last two decades of the century, mainly because students were staying longer, some were taking more courses, and some needed more time to complete their studies because they had to maintain employment.

Those who succeeded in making their way to the top in many cases worked longer hours than ever before, and they rewarded themselves with expensive toys—'My Tastes Are Simple', read one popular bumper sticker; 'I Like the Best.' Several sizable groups emerged with money to spend on nice things: 'Yuppies' (Young Urban Professionals; the acronym developed about 1984), 'DINKS' (couples with double incomes and no kids), 'Empty Nesters' (aging boomers whose children had left home). Among the marketing strategies devised to appeal to these sorts of people were slick consumer magazines distributed free to homes in neighbourhoods with the appropriate demographics. Popular themes included home (re)decorating, gourmet foods, luxury travel, investment strategies, and planning for retirement. Many of the advertisements in these publications were for cars—increasingly, in the 1990s, four-wheel drive 'sports utility vehicles' (SUVs); by 2000 over half of the new vehicles being sold were in the truck rather than automobile category. A well-publicized flaw involving the tires on Ford Explorers may have cut slightly into sales in the late 1990s, but the market for four-wheel drive continued buoyant. Such vehicles guzzled gas and were seldom driven off the highways into the wilderness, but they gave their owners an illusion of rugged independence from the constraints of civilization. The high price of gas in 2006 actually made some dent in purchases of SUVs by Canadians and encouraged the sale of 'hybrid' vehicles that could run on alternate fuels, but these trends did not long continue.

The former assumption that in the normal course of events young Canadians would graduate from university and settle into lifetime careers was almost totally eliminated. Instead, a new category of non-career employment developed, involving work at a variety of low-paid part-time jobs in the service industry that provided no benefits beyond the minimum required by law. Only a handful of coffee shops (mainly in the Starbucks chain) provided fringe benefits for their full-time and part-time employees. Not surprisingly, people caught in such dead-end work sought their pleasure where they could find it. Smoking, for example, came to be both a class- and an age-related indulgence, far more in evidence among the young at the bottom of the social scale than among their elders at the top.

The first boomers began taking early retirement in the 1990s, and by the new century job opportunities were again opening in some fields. But the future remained problematic for many young Canadians, who had to seek fulfilling (or even just time-consuming) goals outside their careers.

BOOMERS, SANDWICHES, AND BOOMERANGS

The constraints of economic life in the twenty-first century led to an increased visibility in certain social phenomena relating to households and families: sandwiched parents and boomerang kids. Sandwiched parents, all members of the baby-boom generation, are those caring simultaneously for aging parents on the one hand and adult children on the other. In 2002, according to Statistics Canada, 2.6 million Canadians aged 45–64 had children under 25 living at home.[4] One-third of parents whose youngest child was between 20 and 34 had at least one child living at home, and one-quarter had an adult child who had returned to the parental home after leaving it at least once—the so-called 'boomerang generation'. At the same time, 27 per cent of the Canadians with children at home also provided elder care, and 21 per cent cared for two seniors. The reason for having to look after the elders is simple enough, but the 'boomerang' kids are a more complex business. Their numbers have increased significantly enough since earlier eras to represent a recognizable trend. Most adult children living at home do so because of a combination of high housing costs, high university tuition fees and/or high debts accumulated to attend university, and low wages after graduation. The probability of having adult children at home was substantially increased if parents lived in a single-family dwelling in one of the larger cities of Ontario. Only 17 per cent of parents in rural areas or in small towns were likely to have adult children living at home.

On the other hand, not all the factors contributing to the quest for self-fulfillment were necessarily negative, nor were all its manifestations. In the last quarter of the twentieth century Canadians enjoyed unprecedented personal freedom and opportunities for education, travel, self-expression, and spiritual growth. In the era of widely available birth control, young people could take their time before starting families. Relatively cheap plane tickets to anywhere in the world were now taken for granted, and even for those who stayed at home, immigration was making Canada an increasingly cosmopolitan place to live. In some cases, increasing openness to the world outside encouraged a heightened interest in spiritual exploration—though in many cases outside traditional religious institutions.

RELIGION

In some ways religious behaviour in Canada changed little during this period, although it seemed to be providing neither moral guidance nor solace for many Canadians, especially among the young. In the 1981 census, over 90 per cent of Canadians reported a religious affiliation, in almost all cases that of their parents. Nearly half (47.3 per cent) described themselves as Roman Catholic, 41.2 per cent as Protestant; only 7.3 per cent claimed to have 'no religion'. Only Alberta and British Columbia had more than 10 per cent of their population in the 'no religion' category, at 11.5 per cent and 20.5 per cent, respectively. Those figures were much the same in subsequent decades. Few Canadians displayed any interest in the various 'new' or 'alternative' belief systems that began emerging in the 1960s. In the 1980s the country contained only 700 Scientologists, 450 Hare Krishnas, perhaps 600 Moonies, and 250 Children of God.[5] Protestant sectarianism of the evangelical or Pentecostal variety made some gains, particularly in the suburbs. Third World immigration did not greatly increase the percentages of other religions (non-Christian and non-Jewish) among the Canadian peoples, at least before 1991, partly because many of the newcomers themselves came from Judeo-Christian backgrounds. At the same time, the fact that a large majority declared a religious affiliation to a census-taker did not necessarily say very much about the state of religion in the country.[6]

The most significant change in the area of religion was in the percentage of Canadians who regularly attended services. This figure declined precipitously in the major Christian denominations. The fall-off began with Protestants, but was visible among Catholics starting in the late 1960s. The situation was particularly evident in Quebec: whereas 88 per cent of Quebec Catholics in 1965 attended Mass at least twice a month, that percentage was down to 38 per cent in 1985, and it continued to fall. Figures for divorce, abortion, and the overall birth rate indicated that most Québécois paid little attention to Roman Catholic teachings. According to the surveys, most Canadians continued to believe in

God, the divinity of Christ, and the standard teachings of Christianity. But while nearly two-thirds asserted some belief in life after death, very few had any specific notion of what that life might be like.[7] In almost every religious denomination the young were less committed and knowledgeable about their churches' teachings than their elders, with the greatest discrepancies between young and old occurring among Quebec Catholics. Revelations of abuse did nothing to inspire faith in the clergy. But the real problem was simply that traditional Christian religion seemed less and less capable of providing a real sense of meaning. In 1980 a survey asking 'How sure are you that you have found the answer to the meaning of life?' found that fewer than one-third of respondents claimed to have any certainty at all.[8] From time to time a voice would appear in the media claiming that organized religion was making a comeback, but the revival usually proved as ephemeral as that of aging track stars or hockey players.

Some of the mixed messages about religion were especially confusing. Polls and studies persistently revealed that most Canadians believed in God and that many had enjoyed spiritual experiences, but regular church attendance in Canada, especially in the mainline churches, continued to fall off constantly. In 1946, 67 per cent of adult Canadians attended church regularly, but by 2001 that rate was down to 20 per cent. One poll taken in April 2006 indicated that regular attendance had decreased 4 per cent since 1996 and that less than half of the Canadians polled went to church more often than once a year; fewer than 20 per cent regularly attended church. Attendance was lowest in Quebec, but every province had pockets of high attendance rates and low attendance rates. Curiously enough, this attitude towards church attendance in Canada was quite different from that in the United States, where almost 40 per cent of Americans went to church at least once a week, a figure that has remained unchanged since 1900. The difference, many observers suggested, was that the Americans had many more evangelical congregations. In any event, these church-going statistics suggest a substantial difference in values between the United States and Canada in an important aspect of daily life, and provided a challenge to those who claimed that American and Canadian basic values were constantly converging.

That both Americans and Canadian Christians were questing for something spiritual they were not currently getting in church was well demonstrated by the bookstore success of fiction like Dan Brown's, *The Da Vinci Code*, which sparked a subgenre of religious literature dealing with alternate interpretations of early Christianity labelled as heresy and suppressed by the early Church in the fourth century. Most of this literature dealt with the Gnostic writings of early Christianity. Many of these writings offered a far more human Jesus and a far less dogmatic approach to belief. They marked the fruits of several generations of scholarship on early texts. How the mainline churches would respond to this evidence of interest in spiritual matters was another matter.

The exception to all the above trends was Islam, which grew in Canada by leaps and bounds and certainly seemed capable of inspiring many, often in extremist directions. Muslims were first counted in the 1981 census, when there were roughly 100,000 in Canada. By 1991 the total was 250,000 Muslims, and by 2000 it was estimated that well over half a million Muslims were living in the country. The situation for Canadian Muslims changed precipitously after 9/11, when many Muslims felt increasingly uncomfortable because of the suspicion against them manifested by both government and public opinion.

THE INTERNET

Canadians continued to demonstrate an extraordinary willingness to try and use new technologies. The nation was particularly advanced in

■ People praying in the mosque at the Islamic Society of North America Canada, in Mississauga, Ontario, 9 June 2006. CP/*Toronto Star*/Bernard Weil.

terms of the Internet, where Canadian broadband users were proportionally more numerous than in the United States and were continuing to increase. By 2004 almost 70 per cent of the adult Canadian population had access to and used the Internet and, by 2007, 81 per cent of on-line households would have broadband connections. This meant that Internet usage had penetrated more deeply into Canada than into the United States among the middle-aged, between the ages of 35 and 54, and among the older population. Only a few nations in Asia had higher rates of usage among the young than did Canada. The Internet was changing communications virtually overnight. On-line telephonic connections were growing rapidly, and radio listening via the Internet was cutting into normal patterns of radio use. The technology was so new that

nobody fully understood either its possibilities or its liabilities. The medium's capacity for being monitored was considerable. Canadian intelligence got on the trail of the alleged Toronto terrorists of June 2006 through the Internet.

CANADIAN POPULAR CULTURE

Despite continued dire predictions of the convergence of Canadian and American culture, most evidence suggested that Canadian identity and Canadian values were stubbornly holding their own against the onslaught of the American media. Canadian popular music, at least in English Canada, has become increasingly full of Canadian places and Canadian references, and the sitcom *Corner Gas*—with its setting in rural Saskatchewan—became very popular at home.[9]

The continued success of Tim Horton's restaurants proves that Canadian consumers can be very comfortable with American ownership of Canadian icons, and Tim Horton's management has accepted its responsibility by agreeing to open a branch in Afghanistan for Canadian troops.

NOSTALGIA AND NARCOTICS

By 2000 it was possible to find radio stations playing the hits of every decade from the 1940s onward: nostalgia for simpler, more stable times was widespread. At the same time, television became one of the narcotics of the age, joined after 1990 by video games and the Internet. Perhaps the most common narcotic of all, however, was shopping, which was increasingly recognized as an addiction for many people. The availability and use of drugs, including alcohol, increased steadily, while alcohol abuse continued unabated. Use of performance-enhancing drugs became common among athletes. Canada's most notorious example was the Olympic sprinter Ben Johnson, who was stripped of his gold medal at the Seoul Olympics in 1988 for steroid use that he initially denied but eventually admitted at a public inquiry.

Probably the most dangerous drug of all, however, was tobacco. By the end of the century, smoking was banned in most public places across the nation. The government put increasingly graphic health warnings on packets and continued to raise the taxes on cigarettes, hoping to cut consumption rates while profiting from those who were still addicted.[10] Canadians did lead the world in stopping smoking during the late 1980s, with a per capita decrease in tobacco consumption of nearly 30 per cent between 1984 and 1990. Yet, as late as 1986 nearly half a million Canadians under the age of 19 smoked over $260 million worth of cigarettes a year, undeterred by prices that rose to more than $6 a pack by 1990, where the price stabilized—and young smokers proved most resistant to the overall trend. The greatest increase in smokers in Canada occurred among those under 14, despite government attempts to ban the sale of cigarettes to minors. The young were obviously immune to evidence of the addictive dangers of tobacco presented to them in school and on television. According to one calculation, tobacco would ultimately kill eight times as many 15-year-olds as automobile accidents, suicide, murder, AIDS, and drug abuse combined. But although few Canadians would begin smoking after the age of 19, the non-smoking campaign—ostensibly aided by prohibitions against tobacco advertising, not very consistently enforced—was not winning. Young Canadians would continue to abuse themselves with addictive substances of all kinds.[11] And even if the cigarette companies were eventually to be put out of business, by 2002 many Canadians suspected they would only turn to selling legalized marijuana.[12]

GLIMMERS OF HOPE

Negative trends notwithstanding, there were occasional bright spots in the late twentieth century. Four of them were named Fox, Fonyo, Hansen, and Kennedy. Terry Fox, having lost a leg to cancer, originated the 'Marathon of Hope', in which he set out to run across Canada with one artificial leg to raise money for, and public awareness of, cancer research. Fox began in St John's, Newfoundland in April 1980 and ended at Thunder Bay on 1 September when tests revealed that his cancer had spread. In the process, he inspired the world as well as Canada, and the money he initially raised has increased substantially in annual commemorative runs since his death.

Like Fox, Steve Fonyo ran with an artificial leg. He finished his cross-country run on 29 May 1985, also raising millions for cancer research. Rick Hansen was a friend of Fox in wheelchair basketball whose 'Man in Motion' tour around the world in a self-propelled wheelchair began on 21 March 1985 and ended on 22 May 1987.

All three athletes raised public awareness of the courage and capabilities of people with physical disabilities. Then, in the late 1990s, hockey player Sheldon Kennedy joined those three heroes when he revealed the emotional damage he suffered as a result of sexual abuse at the hands of his junior coach in the 1980s and set out on a cross-Canada skate to raise money for sexually abused children. Like his predecessors, Kennedy encouraged other young Canadians to look beyond themselves.

DEMOGRAPHIC TRENDS

The most obvious demographic trend was the overwhelming influence of the baby boom generation as it moved through life's stages. Thus, in the early 1990s, when the first boomers were beginning to contemplate early retirement, the prospect of an aging population began to attract media attention. Meanwhile, the ongoing health problems of Canada's Aboriginal minorities received relatively little coverage. Overall, Canada's population continued to grow in size and its distribution to shift westward, while new immigrants came almost entirely from developing countries.[13] Poverty continued to be the most immediate problem for all too many Canadians, although it, too, was given a distressingly low profile. Markers of social instability of all kinds increased in incidence.

MARKERS OF INSTABILITY

The traditional indicators of social 'instability'—marital breakdown, divorce, suicide, rape, crime—all continued to rise through the 1980s. In 1974 a study had found that suicide was Canada's fifth-ranked cause of 'early death' (i.e., death before the statistical life expectancy), at a time when the annual rate of suicide per 100,000 Canadians was 11.9. By 1983 that rate had jumped to 15.1, although it gradually fell back to 12.3 by 1997. Suicide was much more common among males than females; in 1997 the distribu-

■ Terry Fox in Quebec City, 17 June 1980.
CP/Jacques Nadeau.

TERRY FOX (1958–1981)

❖

Terrance Stanley Fox was born in Transcona, Manitoba, a suburb of Winnipeg, on 28 July 1958. He attended school there until his family moved to British Columbia in 1966. (Curiously enough, the Transcona School Board has resolutely refused to name the school after Fox.) From his early days, Fox was distinguished by dogged determination and an interest in sports. In 1976 he enrolled at Simon Fraser University, where he was known as a politically committed student. In March 1977 he was diagnosed with cancer in his right leg, and the leg was amputated 15 cm above the knee. Within weeks he was walking on an artificial leg and within months he had joined the BC basketball team of the Canadian Wheelchair Sports Association, playing for the team in three national championship tournaments. By 1979 Fox had taken up marathon running, using a special prosthesis featuring a pogo stick, and he developed a plan to run across Canada to raise money for cancer research. He got corporate sponsorship from a number of national businesses and the Canadian Cancer Society, and began his Marathon of Hope in St.

John's, Newfoundland, on 12 April 1980. From the beginning, Fox received considerable local support, and his run was well publicized, but not until the Ontario wing of the Canadian Cancer Society put on a big campaign as he entered Ontario did the Marathon of Hope catch the nation's attention. Fox had raised $11.4 million by Sudbury, but his health was deteriorating, and the next few hundred miles were very difficult. Lung cancer was discovered as he reached Thunder Bay, and he was forced to give up the run after 3,339 miles. The Toronto Maple Leafs offered to finish his run for him, but he refused, wishing to complete the journey himself. Unfortunately, he died on 28 July 1981 in hospital in BC. A few months later, the first Terry Fox Run was held both nationally and internationally, with more than 300,000 people participating. It is now an annual event. In 2004 Canadian viewers of CBC television named him among the top 10 of greatest Canadians, and a photograph of him running on his prosthesis has become one of the most easily recognized iconic photographs around the world.

tion was 19.6 and 5.1 respectively. In 1984 the National Task Force on Suicide in Canada indicated that the causes of suicide were 'complex and multifactorial', but added that there appeared to have been 'a change in the contemporary fabric of society with lessened self-restraints and lowered morals (anomie). This coincides with a period of expanding economy, greater affluence as a whole, high-technology industrialization and increased unemployment.'[14] A similar explanation could have been

advanced for many of the nation's other 'morbidities'. Canada was hardly unique in this social trend. The American Surgeon General in 1998 labelled suicide a major 'public health hazard'.

The number of divorces in Canada was 32,389 in 1972 and 86,985 in 1987, representing a divorce rate of 649 per 100,000 among married women aged 15 years and over in 1972, and 1,372.2 per 100,000 in 1987. The great jump was caused by the liberalization of divorce laws in the late 1970s and early 1980s. The divorce rate would drop substantially by 1998, when the annual total was 69,086 divorces, but even so, nearly 4 out of every 10 marriages would end in divorce. The province with the highest divorce rate in 1996 was Quebec (46 per 100 marriages), followed by British Columbia (45 per 100) and Alberta (38 per 100). As early as 1986 it was being estimated that at least half of all Canadian children born after 1980 would at some point experience a broken home. Though not all marital separations and divorces left deep permanent scars on the children, all were at least temporarily traumatic and disruptive. Increasingly, international evidence became available indicating that divorce did enormous psychological and social damage to children, and suggesting that perhaps children were paying the price for their parents' personal self-fulfillment. At the same time, some argued that sustaining an unhappy marriage 'for the sake of the children' could be equally damaging.

Another set of rising statistics related to criminal activity, particularly involving crimes against the person. Between 1982 and 1987, for example, crimes against property increased 0.1 per cent, while crimes of violence increased 30.1 per cent. (On the other hand, between 1988 and 1996 the rate of motor vehicle thefts nearly doubled.) Much of the increase in the incidence of violence involved common assault, often in the context of domestic disputes. Data for 1971–82 suggested that in all categories of violent offences, rates had increased dramatically, including crimes of sexual violence.[15] In the closing years of the century, however, Criminal Code offences in general fell back in numbers and the violent crime rate declined annually beginning in 1993. The national homicide rate in the early 1960s was 1.5 per 100,000 people. The rate began increasing in the mid-1960s and peaked at over 3 per 100,000 people in 1975, declining to 2.1 per 100,000 in 1996. Guns were employed in about one-third of all homicides from 1979 onward, although increasingly after 1991 handguns replaced rifles and shotguns as the preferred weapons. People previously unknown to the victim were responsible for only a fraction of all homicides throughout the period.

THE BABY BOOMERS

Until 1970 the presence of the baby boomers was most evident in the educational system, but since then their influence has been felt in almost every aspect of Canadian society.[16] Canada had two million teenagers in 1960, and more than three million by 1975. The baby boomers, who hit the school systems in the 1950s and the universities in the 1960s, appeared in full force on the job market in the 1970s and early 1980s; thereafter, entry-level pressure on the job market was expected to ease, and did to some degree. The boomers were far better qualified educationally than previous generations, and the qualifications and expectations for females were little different than for males. Not surprisingly, not all were able to get the jobs for which they had prepared, particularly since hiring in both teaching and government had already peaked by the time the boomers reached the market, while changing ideas about aging and retirement kept many older employees in the workforce.

The largest cohort of baby boomers began their working lives in the 1970s, reaching mid-career in the 1980s. That fertility rates fell even further than forecasters had earlier predicted reflected the coincidence of several factors. Young women beginning careers were less willing to interrupt them to bear and raise children. Some of the successful women who did become mothers went back to work, leaving their husbands at home to look after the kids, and by the mid-1980s parent groups at nursery schools often included nearly as many fathers as they did mothers. Moreover, a tight job market combined with the increased consumer needs of the boomer generation to produce more childless working couples. The demands of parenting reduced what was regarded as the ideal number of children to two (or even one), and the increasing number of broken homes in the post-war years made adults fear divorce and its effects on any children they might have. In the later 1980s there was a slight resurgence of child-bearing in some sectors of the population, as childless women of the baby boom generation realized that their biological clocks would soon run out. Birth rates remained consistently lower in Quebec than elsewhere in Canada.

The baby boomers had a noticeable effect on housing markets, particularly in Toronto and Vancouver, which had attracted many newcomers after 1970. By the early 1980s the boomers had become sufficiently established in their lives and careers to consider home ownership—especially of a detached bungalow with a green lawn—essential. Given limited quantities of detached housing within easy commuting distance of cities, the real-estate market skyrocketed. Thus, in Scarborough, Ontario, the price of a typical three-bedroom detached bungalow rose from $71,700 in 1979 to $255,000 in 1989, while in Burnaby, BC, similar accommodation rose from $76,500 to $215,000 in the same period.[17] Although the upward spiral was temporarily broken by the recession of 1990, prices never returned to previous levels and by the mid-1990s it was estimated that in cities of premium-priced housing—almost all of Canada's major cities—fewer than one-quarter of those seeking to purchase their first house could qualify for a mortgage. Within a few years housing prices resumed their upward crawl, setting new records in 2001–2 in most markets. Commentators wrote of the 'New Suburbia', although suburban development was still driven by the old realities: lower prices and lower taxes.

A focus on carefully targeted audiences became a feature of market research and advertising campaigns beginning in the 1980s. Fearing that the days of profitable consumer mass-marketing were numbered, advertisers and retailers sought a market 'niche' by offering specialized goods and services for those who could afford them. As it turned out, the death knell for mass-marketing was premature, and in the 1990s the practice was resumed in several new guises. One took the form of the 'big box' store, often located in the outer suburbs, offering an enormous range of goods at the lowest possible prices. The market leader was the American chain Wal-Mart, but the 'big box' concept took hold in all retail areas, from books to drug stores to home improvement. Another new mass marketing technique was telephone solicitation, which took advantage of dramatic changes in the price structure of telephone service during the decade. Most Canadians could count on one or two telephone calls a night originating from anywhere on the continent. Finally, at the end of the 1990s 'on-line' marketing arrived with 'dot-com' companies setting up to do business on the Internet. Many failed rather quickly, perhaps because the nature of Internet selling was not yet sufficiently well understood.

The needs of those reaching mid-career and middle age were of special interest. One of the most common effects of aging is weakening vision. For those with normal eyesight, vision begins deteriorating only after the age of 40, but the deterioration is then fairly extensive, particularly at short range. One could thus safely predict an increased demand for eyeglasses, which suddenly became available in a wide variety of designer styles, some at luxury prices. But there was also a market for solutions to a host of other eyesight-related problems, such as large print books and special computer keyboards. Predictably, golf—which requires no great physical fitness and can be played by moneyed people of any age—became the growth sport of the end of the century. Finally, the boomers continued their fascination with the pop and rock music of their adolescence. Radio stations that had for decades tried to appeal to the teenage market suddenly shifted their programming to 'Golden Oldies' or 'Hits of the Seventies' in a blatant effort to capture the largest single audience segment in the market: middle-aged baby boomers who were no longer interested in anything new.

John Stackhouse on 'The New Suburbia'

The article excerpted here appeared in the *Globe and Mail* in October 2000.

What made David Suzuki, Canada's eco-guru, believe he could wade into the materialistic marshes of suburbia and win over the bourgeois crowd was not immediately clear.

But on a calm autumn day, just before the nation was to be plunged into a federal election campaign, there he was, on stage at the annual fair in Markham, north of Toronto, to implore the richest generation of middle-class homeowners Canada has ever known to consider . . . smaller houses.

In a suburban city where 2,000 square feet is billed as a cute starter home, the audience listened politely to the merchant of modesty and nodded as he spoke of downsizing their aspirations. Then they bolted to the display booths to survey the latest in interior palm gardens, back-yard irrigation systems and a $6,500 bathroom retrofit package that includes an oversized steam bath.

Such is the contradictory nature of suburban Canada today that homeowners who talk conservation also want to trade sprinklers for irrigation systems. And such is the contradictory nature of suburban politics that those who want better schools also want lower taxes.

Over the next four weeks, the suburban paradox will beguile politicians on both the left and right, perplex the national media and help determine Canada's fate, because the first election of the twenty-first century will be a knock-down fight for the suburbs, where a third of Canada's voters now live.

The suburbs have long been a political mystery, in part because Canada has yet to produce a truly suburban leader on the national stage. They are often stereotyped by the press as a cultural wasteland and assumed by the major parties to be bedroom bastions of parochialism.

Nothing could be more wrong. Many of today's suburbs are ethnically diverse, culturally ambitious, economically independent from the big city next door and politically angry. They have plenty of welfare cases (only more dispersed than downtown), crime (the latest example being the abduction and killing of 10-year-old Heather Thomas in Surrey, BC) and a growing number of single-parent families (divorced parents often have to settle for cheaper houses).

But if today's suburbs are a political enigma, they may not choose to be ignored for much longer.

According to custom builder Otto van Oosten, who has lived in the Markham area for 12 years, the suburbs' inherent contradictions—of people seeking city and country, of voters wanting liberalism and conservatism, of homeowners asking for size and manageability—stem from the important trait of suburban living. 'People here don't want to feel like they're regressing,' he says. . . .

When North America experienced its first suburban boom in the 1950s, most of its newcomers were white-collar workers looking for more and safer space for their families. In those days, the main income earner—a man, usually—was willing to commute by regional train. Today, the suburbs are much more diverse, demographically and economically. Most families have at least two income earners (but often more, with teenagers holding part-time jobs) and they tend to work in different locations. While one person may be able to take mass transit, the odds of two being in that position are much less. . . .

Not so long ago, unionized labour lived in bungalows, drove rusting sedans and wagons, and voted NDP. Now, you're just as likely to find them in a 2,500-square-foot house in a subdivision, driving a new sports utility vehicle and voting Alliance. . . .

Across Canada, immigrants and the grown children of immigrants are moving in record numbers to the suburbs, reflecting their increasing wealth, participation in the New Economy, which is largely suburban, and adoption of Canadian middle-class values that place a premium on space, schooling, and safety.

SOURCE: John Stackhouse, 'The New Suburbia', *Globe and Mail*, 28 Oct. 2000.

THE PREDICTABLE CRISIS: THE AGING OF CANADA

The progressive aging of the Canadian population—the 'process whereby a population is made up increasingly of older age groups'[18]—was neither a new development of the post-1970 period nor a distinctly Canadian one. If Canadians had been consistently living longer for nearly a century, this was a worldwide phenomenon among countries in a stage of advanced industrial development. By the year 2000 the percentage of Canada's population over 65 still had not reached Sweden's percentage in 1965 or that of the US in 1935.[19] Indeed, because of the baby boom and immigration, the percentage of the Canadian population over 65 had not changed as dramatically as might otherwise have been expected over the entire century, increasing from 5 per cent in 1901 to just under 12 per cent in 1996. What was new was the attention devoted to aging and the elderly, especially after 1976, when the Science Council of Canada published *Perceptions 2: Implications of the Changing Age Structure of the Canadian Population*. The resulting perception of a 'crisis' was primarily connected with what seemed to be the increased costs associated with the elderly in the welfare states of Europe, and which were rightly expected to arrive in Canada.[20]

While the numbers of elderly grew, change also occurred in the proportion of the population under age 14, a result partly of declining birth rates but mainly of declining death rates. From nearly 20 per cent in 1901, the proportion under 14 fell to less than 13 per cent in 1976. Thus, despite the rise in the over-65 age group, the total number of people assumed to be dependent on those still active in the labour force did not change as much as might have been expected. Such measures as 'dependency ratios' are not perfect indicators of demographic trends but are useful because they suggest the pressures on institutions and facilities in the social arena. When we consider the proportion of the Canadian population over 18 and under 65—younger children and older people being presumed not to be productive members of the workforce—at the begining of the twentieth century and at present, it is clear that there has been remarkably little change in the proportions of the traditional working-age population and their dependants over the last 100 years. While the number of children has declined, the number of the aged has increased, resulting in a great alteration in the meaning of dependency. In 1911 the dependency ratio for the elderly (the proportion of elderly to the proportion theoretically productive) was 8.8:100. By 1983 it was 18:100—and if birth rates do not alter, could reach 52:100 by 2031, meaning 52 people over the age of 65 and out of the workforce for every 100 between the ages of 18 and 64 within the workforce. Of course, not all of the 'elderly' will be dependent and non-productive, but many more will be so.

Population aging means that Canada's social responsibilities are shifting from providing for the young to providing for the elderly, a change that will require profound adjustments, both conceptual and physical. For example, the demand may be much higher for health-care than daycare facilities—but only to the extent that the very young are cared for in the home and the very old outside it, in institutions. Expenditures on health care for the elderly may be perceived as constantly escalating in a way that spending on the young is not—but only because society has never attempted to calculate the cost of caring for the young at home in the same way that it calculates the cost of hospitals and nursing homes. When one considers actual public spending on the young and old, it appears to cost much less to provide schools than health care for seniors. But if the total cost of raising a child is taken into account, the young cost substantially more than the old. Many experts have predicted major conflicts 'between groups which have catered to the needs of or benefited from a youthful population and those whose interests lie with the elderly'.[21] In fact the contest for funding between education and health care was already underway by the later 1980s and continued through the 1990s.

The actuarial basis of pension plans was threatened as early as the 1980s because they had always been based on the notion that the generation still in the workforce would support the one that had retired from it. Many governments, moreover, raided their own pension funds for ongoing expenses, and then were forced to replenish them through current levies. One study has argued that by the year 2021 the funds required for public pensions will be three and one-half times greater than in 1976, assuming continuation of the 1976 level of payments. Without a high level of pension support (and reform of the system to provide adequate pensions for segments of the population such as women who were not constantly formally employed throughout their working lives), the elderly—especially elderly women, who constitute a disproportionate number of the old because they outlive men by nearly a decade—would become an even greater proportion of Canadians below any defined poverty line. In 1986, for example, 46.1 per cent of unattached females over

the age of 65 were living below the poverty line as defined by the National Council on Welfare.[22]

Increased life expectancy has medical as well as social implications.[23] Many argue that improved health care may prolong life without improving its quality. Others predict an eventual 'compression of morbidity', whereby improved diet and exercise in earlier years—combined with better health care—will mean that the elderly will face fewer disabilities in old age. All these arguments, however, can be tested only over time. Meanwhile, the Canadian health-care system has had great difficulty responding to the new circumstances. Although Canadians have been more inclined to institutionalize their elderly than most European countries, only a small percentage of Canada's elderly can be accommodated in nursing homes, and far too many have been held in hospitals awaiting admission to underfunded chronic-care facilities.

To a considerable extent, the health-care 'crisis' at the end of the century, with complaints about 'hallway medicine' and the overcrowding of medical facilities, was really about the failure of the medical system to adjust to the needs of the elderly. Certainly the movement towards 'home care' has been slow in Canada, and has not produced the sorts of supportive mechanisms required if it is to replace public institutional care as a viable option for most Canadian families. In most provinces funding for home-care assistance for the elderly remains considerably less stable and generous than funding for chronic-care facilities, for example. Part of the difficulty is that a new category of care has emerged because of increased life expectancy, a category between the full independence of the healthy elderly and the total dependence of the chronically dependent. It has proved extremely difficult to persuade younger Canadians that the same energy and resources should be expended on the dependent old whose lives nearly have run their course, as on the dependent young, whose lives are before them. Moreover, increasing numbers of Canadians find themselves 'sandwiched' between the generations requiring care, with youngsters and oldsters competing for limited financial and emotional resources.

Although the problems posed by an aging population were predictable well in advance—demographers and other scholars saw it coming in the 1960s—Canada was very slow to face it seriously. By 2000 Canadians still had not come to terms with many of its implications. Except in certain limited areas associated with retirement, such as investment plans, housing, and travel, the elderly still are not perceived by most Canadian businesses as a separate market with distinctive needs. It could be argued that in a capitalist system nothing much will change until the nation's business people start paying attention to the aged. Most experts are persuaded that the aging of the population need not create serious problems in areas apart from health care until well into the twenty-first century. But while the nation may have a period of grace to work out new relationships, the scorecard at the end of the previous century was not encouraging. Canada will have to do better if it is to avoid a crisis involving the aging of its population.

THE UNANTICIPATED CRISIS: AIDS

Acquired immune deficiency syndrome, commonly known as AIDS, burst on the scene in the early 1980s without any warning. Since the mid-nineteenth century, numerous communicable diseases had proved susceptible to advances in medical science. Tuberculosis, pneumonia, diphtheria, scarlet fever, influenza, whooping cough, smallpox, and typhoid all were eliminated in northern North America from the list of major killers. Even polio had been conquered through vaccination. The first case of AIDS in Canada probably occurred in Montreal in 1978, but went undiagnosed because nobody knew what to look for. Not until 1981 did the Centers for Disease Control of the US Public Health Service begin receiving enough reports of cases to recognize a worldwide epidemic of an immunodeficiency disease caused by an infectious virus. In 1982 the Laboratory Centre for Disease Control in Ottawa began tracking the disease in Canada, and in 1983 the Institut Pasteur in France claimed to have isolated one of the new viruses involved.[24]

There are three major means of transmitting the immunodeficiency virus (HIV) that is believed to cause AIDS: sexual contact, parenteral means (such as blood transfusions or contaminated needles and syringes), and perinatal transmission (from infected mothers to infants). The majority of cases reported in North America have involved homosexual men, but increasing numbers of heterosexual men and women have contracted the disease as well. As of this writing, there is no cure for anyone who has contracted HIV, although two decades of desperate research have developed a number of drugs that can fend off the conversion of HIV to AIDS and prolong life. Nevertheless, avoidance remains the preventive strategy. Most of the unfortunate individuals infected with HIV through blood products were hemophiliacs. HIV-antibody screening did not become a routine procedure in Canadian blood banks until 1985, but since then the risk of medical transmission has been almost totally eliminated in this country. Unfortunately, needle contamination and unsafe blood transfusion remain common causes of transmission in many other countries of the world, where AIDS remains both prevalent and lethal.

In the early 1980s it was widely believed that only homosexual men could contract AIDS. Although AIDS spread quickly from the homosexual community to heterosexuals, people continued to associate AIDS with promiscuous sexuality of all kinds. This relationship was reinforced by the preventive campaign mounted by Canadian authorities, which emphasized the need for 'safe sex'. The continuing failure of industry to manufacture dependable condoms and the continuing failure of people to employ the available condoms effectively underscore the misleading quality of the term 'safe sex' and the inadequacy of the campaign. Indeed, as many social and religious commentators insisted, the only 'safe sex' was between a monogamous couple committed to each other for life.

It has been difficult to compile data on the extent of AIDS in Canada, partly because of its association with promiscuity and homosexuality. Evidence suggests that at the height of the epidemic, in the 1980s, about one-third of HIV-infected persons would develop AIDS within seven years, and there were some suggestions that certain lifestyles increase risk. But whether all HIV-infected persons would eventually develop AIDS was not clear in the 1980s, and the evidence is still not complete. Estimates in 1987 suggested that 30,000 Canadians were HIV-infected, and over 1,300 cases of AIDS had been reported. The per person annual hospital costs of dealing with AIDS patients varied in 1987 from $50,000 in Vancouver to $75,000 in Quebec, excluding the costs of drugs before hospitalization, and the total direct cost of HIV infection in 1987 was estimated at $150 million.

Because AIDS is mainly a sexually transmitted disease, with a high incidence among homosexuals and the sexually adventurous, it became a favourite target for moralists in the 1980s. Many concerns were expressed that AIDS would provoke judgemental responses to homosexuality and sexual freedom, but these were not borne out in the available survey literature. What surveys did show was widespread ignorance about AIDS and how to prevent it. Responses indicated far less fear of infection than one might have expected, given the media attention AIDS had received. In one Canadian study in 1989, 63 per cent of those questioned knew that sexual intercourse was the most common means of infection and about half identified homosexuals as the most likely people to become infected. Virtually everybody (90 per cent) knew that the best prevention was 'safe sex', with 40.5 per cent regarding condoms as 'very effective', while 77.5 per cent and 81.0 per cent regarded sexual abstinence and having sex with one partner in a long-term relationship, respectively, as 'very effective' means of prevention. At the same time, however,

only 54 per cent of male and 41 per cent of female respondents had changed their sexual behaviour because of the risk of AIDS infection; truly safe sex was far from the Canadian norm. Not only did many respondents take no precautions, but the study suggested a tendency, particularly among males, for people with more knowledge about AIDS to take greater risks.[25] Other studies suggested that only about half of those Canadians between 15 and 19 years of age thought they were at risk from sexually transmitted disease, and thus about half of this age group presumably took no precautions. Chlamydia became far more common than AIDS among the young.

As Canadians became more knowledgeable about infection, both individually and through the medical system, and as improved treatments for both the HIV-infected and for those who actually had AIDS were developed, HIV and AIDS ceased in the 1990s to become important public questions in the same way they had been a decade earlier. The problem did not disappear, but it was contained, at least in North America. It remained a serious one elsewhere in the world, especially in Africa. It could have been even better contained if more Canadians routinely had blood testing for HIV.

By the end of the century about 50,000 Canadians were living with HIV or AIDS, and over 4,000 new infections were occurring per year. Although men having sex with men and needle drug users were the most common victims, the number of females aged 15 to 29 who were infected increased dramatically. The greatest problem in Canada was that the need for caution came to seem less urgent. While the disease seemed to be under control in Canada, HIV infection and AIDS remained problems of epidemic proportions in much of the rest of the world.

THE TAINTED BLOOD SCANDAL

The AIDS epidemic of the early 1980s had a number of spinoff effects. One of the most important was on the blood transfusion service of the Canadian Red Cross, which had operated Canada's blood supply service since 1947. Initially the Red Cross had acted as a private agency, but over the years its blood service had been absorbed into the public medical system. By 1974 the blood service was completely supported by government, and in 1977 responsibility for that financial support was transferred to the provincial governments. The recruitment of blood donors had also come to receive some financial support from government. Because of the way the service had been moved into the public domain, the relationship between government and the Red Cross was never clearly defined. A Canadian Blood Committee had been created in 1981 to develop a national policy and define responsibilities within the blood service, but it still had not completed those tasks when troubles emerged in the system in the mid-1980s. As a result, it was not clear where the responsibility lay for ensuring that the blood supply was not tainted, and it was difficult for the system to respond to problems when they emerged. Moreover, a serious shortage of blood and donors in the late 1970s and early 1980s in some parts of Canada had made the Red Cross reluctant to introduce screening measures that might reduce the number of donors. As a consequence, the Canadian blood transfusion service in the early 1980s was routinely (if infrequently) using blood infected both with HIV and with hepatitis C. Much of the infected blood was given to hemophiliacs, who because of their medical condition required frequent transfusions.[26] Approximately 2,000 people were infected with HIV and 60,000 with hepatitis C through blood transfusions between 1980 and 1990.[27]

Another reason the system was slow in responding to the tainted blood problem had to do with financial considerations. At least this was the finding of a Royal Commission of inquiry headed by Mr Justice Horace Krever, which was appointed in 1993 and reported in November 1997. The controversy over the Krever report—which took years to complete and in the end did not recommend criminal action—was in some ways quite separate from the initial problems over blood transfusions, although in other ways it demonstrated some of the same problems and characteristics, chiefly about issues of responsibility.[28] For example, officials of the blood system maintained that consumers themselves were responsible for monitoring the distribution of the tainted product.

Victims of the tainted blood and their families had begun calling for a public inquiry from almost the first moment that the problem was made public. No doubt most of them wanted to be able to assign blame for the tragedy, not least so that they could sue for compensation. Both the government and the Red Cross were understandably less eager to fix responsibility, particularly since this was one of those situations in which ignorance and bureaucratic incompetence, rather than malice, appeared to be the chief culprits.

Justice Krever had enormous difficulty gathering all the necessary evidence and gaining the right to identify the individuals involved. He also had to fight a number of skirmishes, mainly generated by agencies that had been involved in the blood system. By the time all the legal cases had been dealt with and the report was issued, its findings were distinctly anti-climactic, partly because the question of compensation was already being discussed by many politicians and partly because many of the most pressing problems the Commission identified were already in the process of being resolved. The report was also anti-climactic because, in the end, it assigned no blame. Instead it documented what it described as a 'systemic' breakdown, a tale of individual and bureaucratic bungling and negligence, in which bureaucrats were reluctant to expose themselves by taking any action. The lines of failure extended quite broadly across an unregulated and unco-ordinated system. The report recommended that all recipients of tainted blood be offered compensation for their victim-

■ A man walks through a group of crosses representing Hepatitis C victims on the front lawn of Parliament Hill in April 1998. The crosses were left by protestors demonstrating against the government's compensation plan for tainted blood victims. CP/Tom Hanson.

ization, and 95 individuals connected with the Red Cross and the Canadian government were placed on notice of possible liability for misconduct. After the release of the report, many of the victims and their families called for criminal charges to be laid, and the RCMP indicated that it was investigating the possibility. Five years after the Krever report, an RCMP criminal investigation led to the laying of charges against a number of individuals connected with the Red Cross and the Health Protection Branch of Health and Welfare Canada.

In July 1998 the Canadian Red Cross agreed with the provincial and territorial governments to transfer its blood services to two new organizations. The Red Cross would be paid $132.9 million for its blood system assets. It would use any money left over after paying its debts for a fund to assist victims, who were also negotiating for compensation from the provincial governments. Those governments decided to limit compensation to victims who received tainted blood between 1986 and 1990, years in which the Red Cross might have screened their blood but did not do so. Victims were given until 2010 to claim compensation, and in 2002 most of the fund was still untouched. The Canadian Red Cross was pleased to be out of the blood business, which certainly had done great damage to an organization with an illustrious history of public service.

ABORTION

Undoubtedly the most hotly contested health-care issue of the 1970s and 1980s was neither AIDS nor aging but abortion. Abortion was a criminal offence in British North America under the Criminal Code of 1892, and was only partially decriminalized in 1969. Never an unequivocally feminist issue, abortion had a tendency to divide women in ways that daycare or equal pay did not. At the same time, pro- and anti-abortion positions on the issue of 'abortion on demand' became inextricably interwoven with larger feminist questions. By and large, feminists were pro-choice, while the anti-abortion faction, who preferred the more positive term 'pro-life', was largely made up of people who still believed that women's place was in the home. Those with traditional Catholic upbringing were more likely than Protestants to oppose abortion, even if they no longer went to church or obeyed the hierarchy on most social issues. There was also a division among Protestants, with members of non-traditional Pentecostal sects far less sympathetic to abortion than members of the old-line Protestant churches. Ironically, the individual who galvanized these positions was not a woman but Dr Henry Morgentaler, a Polish-Canadian Holocaust survivor who, as a general practitioner, by the late 1960s had made the provision of therapeutic abortions his life's work.[29]

A more liberal law introduced in 1969 permitted abortions in hospitals in cases where a committee of physicians decided that the pregnancy would endanger the life or health of the woman. But Dr Morgentaler operated outside the hospital setting, carrying out abortions in private Montreal clinics without the sanction of a committee. In 1973 he revealed that he had performed more than 5,000 abortions, and as a

result was charged in Quebec under Article 251 of the Criminal Code and found not guilty by a jury. He was imprisoned after the Quebec Court of Appeal overturned the jury verdict in 1974, but two further trials in Quebec also led to acquittal after the juries apparently accepted the argument that his actions were necessary because the law denied women equal access to abortion.[30] Protests by opponents of abortion spread as Dr Morgentaler opened clinics in other cities. In 1984 he and two colleagues were acquitted in Toronto of conspiring to procure a miscarriage, and when Ontario appealed, the Supreme Court of Canada in 1988 declared the abortion law to be in conflict with the Charter of Rights: 'forcing a woman, by threat of criminal sanction, to carry a fetus to term . . . is a profound interference with a woman's body and thus an infringement of security of the person.' The Court then refused to consider a case brought by former Manitoba cabinet minister Joe Borowski based on the claim that the fetus had a constitutional right to life— in effect avoiding judgement on whether the Charter of Rights was in conflict with the Charter of Rights.

The arguments of the anti-abortion faction came to centre on the rights of the fetus, an issue further complicated by new developments in reproductive technology. The ethical implications of in vitro fertilization and genetic engineering (including the cloning of animals) were not well understood. Equally worrying was the fact that the scientific advances were being made under conditions that showed little concern for either ethical or feminist apprehensions. In any event, by the later 1980s abortion had become such a divisive issue that Parliament was unable to pass new legislation, and a free vote on a bill to put abortion back in the Criminal Code failed in 1991 when the Senate produced a tie. Meanwhile, the incidence of therapeutic abortion had begun stabilizing in the early 1980s. While the rate of abortion had increased steadily from the 1969 liberalization, by the late 1980s it had steadied at around 10 per 1,000 and showed little sign of

■ Dr Henry Morgentaler at a press conference in Toronto marking the tenth anniversary of the Supreme Court's decriminalization of abortion, 28 January 1998. CP/John Lehmann.

moving.[31] By the last decade of the century, abortion rarely made the headlines except when abortion doctors were killed or wounded in a series of attacks mounted around Remembrance Day each year, or when someone laid a charge against Dr Morgentaler or one of his associates.[32]

POPULATION GROWTH AND SHIFTS

Demographic developments after 1971 continued long-term trends. Canada's total population continued to grow, from 21,568,311 in 1971 to 30,750,000 in 2000, while the annual rate of growth—which had reached its high point of 2.8 per cent in 1956—continued to slow, reaching less than 1 (0.08) per cent by 1986 and recovering to an average of just over 1 (1.19) per cent in 1992–7. Urban populations continued to increase faster than Canada as a whole: the average growth rate of the 25 largest metropolitan areas was more than six times that of the entire country in 1986 and almost as high in 2000. Most of the largest increases came in suburbia. The regional distribution of Canada's population also continued to shift westward. In 1971 the Atlantic provinces contained 9.54 per cent of the population. By 2000 the Atlantic provinces represented less than 8 per cent of the total. The big provincial gainers were Alberta and British Columbia, up from 17.7 per cent of the total in 1971 to just over 23 per cent in 1991. By 2000 Quebec's percentage of the total Canadian population had fallen from 29 per cent in 1971 to under 25 per cent.

IMMIGRATION

Population growth continued to depend largely on immigration, and most immigrants continued to

TABLE 23.1

IMMIGRANT ARRIVALS BY COUNTRY OF LAST RESIDENCE, 1974–1975 AND 1999–2000

Region	1974-1975		1999-2000	
	N	%	N	%
Europe	161,592	50.98	39,915	19.37
Africa	20,311	6.40	16,753	8.13
Australasia	4,768	1.50	867	0.42
North & Central America (incl. Caribbean)	91,455	28.90	15,905	7.72
South America	25,748	8.14	5,932	2.87
Asia	97,948	30.96	125,903	62.10
Oceania	4,468	1.47	774	0.37
TOTAL	316, 290		206,049	

come not from the highly industrialized Western nations but from Africa and Asia (see Table 23.1). Heading mainly for urban destinations in Ontario and the West, they brought new cultural influences along with the old social problems of poverty, slums, and ghettoization. In 1971 the top three non-official languages spoken in Canada were Italian, German, and Ukrainian; in 1996 the top three were Chinese, Italian, and Punjabi.

Like most prosperous industrial nations, Canada has faced an increasing problem of illegal immigrants from the less developed world, often smuggled in container ships, or in some cases literally dumped off the coast and left to make their own way ashore. These immigrants have created a dilemma both for immigration authorities and for Canadians generally. Humanitarian considerations suggest they should be allowed to remain, but the illegal immigration underworld should not be encouraged—not least because of the danger to which it exposes hopeful immigrants, often at very high cost.

CANADA'S 'NATIONAL GAME'

PROFESSIONAL HOCKEY

The National Hockey League was reluctant in the early 1970s to expand further into Canada. The result was the formation of a rival professional league, the World Hockey Association, which was dominated by successful Canadian franchises in Winnipeg, Edmonton, Calgary, and Quebec City. The WHA collapsed in 1979 because its American teams could not turn a profit. The NHL then allowed four new franchises in WHA cities, three of them in Canada: Edmonton, Winnipeg, and Quebec. The Atlanta Flames subsequently moved to Calgary, and an expansion franchise was voted to Ottawa (but none to Hamilton, the other Canadian applicant) in 1990. By this point the NHL had lost any vestige of Canadian control. The League's headquarters was moved from Montreal to New York, and a commissioner appointed who knew nothing

ALAN EAGLESON (1933–)

❖

Robert Alan Eagleson was born in St Catharines, Ontario, in 1933, graduated from the University of Toronto in 1954 and Osgoode Hall in 1957, and was admitted to the bar soon afterwards. He first came to prominence in 1966 when, as the pioneering agent for the Boston Bruins' rookie defenceman Bobby Orr, he negotiated a contract that paid Orr a considerably higher salary than any veteran in the league received. Eagleson's sense that hockey teams could and would pay more money to players, if properly approached, eventually brought him more than 150 clients, most of them hockey players.

In 1967 Eagleson helped found the National Hockey League Players' Association (NHLPA), and he served as its executive director until 1991. Almost from the beginning, some players complained that the association was not operating in their best interests and that they were not receiving very much money from their well-publicized contracts. Eagleson was well-known for having close ties to some of the owners and the NHL executive. The complaints were to some extent muted by Eagleson's success in arranging the 1972 series with the Russians. Rumours of fraud and embezzlement circulated for many years, but nothing much was done until 1989, when some players hired the former head of the National Football League Players' Association to report on Eagleson's activities as union president. Ed Garvey's conclusion was that Eagleson had been engaged in numerous conflicts of interest for years, and had been involved in a variety of improper deals with NHL management. Forced to step down as executive director of the NHLPA in 1990, Eagleson finally was indicted by a Boston grand jury in 1994 on various criminal charges, and the RCMP entered its own charges in 1996. Although he initially refused to appear in an American court, Eagleson ultimately pleaded guilty to fraud in Boston in 1998, and then to charges in Toronto. He was sentenced to 18 months in prison, eventually serving six. The government of Canada acted quickly to terminate Eagleson's membership in the Order of Canada, awarded him in 1989, and under considerable pressure he resigned from the Hockey Hall of Fame. A prominent Tory and friend of Brian Mulroney, Eagleson was for many Canadians emblematic of the era in which he operated.

about hockey but was regarded as a genius at packaging and marketing professional sports as entertainment. In the 1990s Canadian franchises in some smaller centres found it increasingly difficult to survive and particularly to prevent their operations from being moved to American cities able to offer owners better financial terms.[33]

The move of the Winnipeg Jets to Phoenix was symptomatic of the problems in the 1990s.[34] The Jets were not badly administered, nor were their on-ice teams uncompetitive, even if they seldom flourished in the 'second season' of the playoffs. Attendance at Winnipeg Arena was consistently good, although the arena was an older one with inadequate amounts of the more expensive facilities, such as corporate boxes. Popular support for the Jets was very high—considerably higher than could be expected in Phoenix, a city with no hockey background, however many Canadians were retiring there. The Jets moved to Phoenix chiefly because the province of Manitoba and the city of Winnipeg refused to build a new arena at public expense that, with all its collateral revenues, would in effect be turned over to the Jets' owners as a subsidy. Phoenix, a very wealthy growing city in the American Southwest, was prepared to offer such a deal. Additional contributing factors were the differential exchange rates of the Canadian and American dollar (which meant that Canadian clubs had to pay a premium to compete with the American ones), the absence of tax incentives for Canadian owners to do business in Canada, and the lack of a large television market. In economic terms, a Canadian city like Winnipeg simply could not compete with an American city like Phoenix, and insufficient numbers of people could be convinced that non-economic factors ought to be considered. At least Winnipeg had some opportunity to try to save the Jets; Quebec City lost its team the same year when its corporate owners simply transferred the franchise out of Canada. The story of hockey is symptomatic of the problems of North American integration for some Canadian institutions. Over the next few years only the very largest Canadian markets— Toronto, Montreal, possibly Vancouver—will be able to support NHL teams. Franchises in Edmonton, Calgary, and Ottawa all operated on shaky ground. A reform of the league's salary structure after the infamous strike/lockout ended in 2005 combined with the later achievement of near parity of the Canadian with the American dollar to make the Canadian franchises much more financially successful by 2007.

A generation ago, one team of sports historians suggested that 'If we cannot save hockey, we cannot save Canada.'[35] Recently, the federal government has indicated its willingness to add NHL hockey to that list of things that it is committed to protecting, although many critics would doubt

the value of such an exercise.[36] Exactly where hockey fits into the overall cultural picture is a bit difficult to determine, however. The very extent of the integration into the American entertainment industry is one problem, as was clearly demonstrated by the agonized discussion over the retirement in 1999 of hockey icon Wayne Gretzky, who in the course of his career slipped from Canada into American hands. But the chief difficulty comes from the conceptual jungle inherent in the term 'culture'.[37]

THE RISE OF WOMEN'S HOCKEY

Easily the most spectacular growth in Canadian hockey occurred among women. In its early years hockey had been very popular among female players, but participation fell off markedly after World War II and did not begin to recover until the 1960s. By the 1980s demands for equal treatment for women, especially in schools and universities, led to a spectacular rise in the number of female teams. This explosion of interest remained one of Canada's best kept secrets until 1990, when Canada fielded a team in the first Women's World Ice Hockey Championship in Ottawa. The women's national hockey team brought home gold medals from the first seven World Hockey Championships (in 1990, 1992, 1994, 1997, 1998, 2000, and 2001), although it had to settle for silver in the 1998 Olympics at Nagano. As with hockey in general, success at the elite level does not reflect the overall picture; however, it is true that international victories lead to enthusiasm at much younger levels. At the same time, it was not likely that Canada's early dominance could be long continued, and by the 2002 Olympics it was already clear that the days of easy wins were over.

THE INTERNATIONAL SCENE

Throughout the 1990s Canada's national team at the world championships was permitted to use NHL professionals, but the only ones available

■ Members of the Canadian women's hockey team pose with their coach, Danielle Sauvageau, and their gold medals after defeating the US team 3–2 at the Salt Lake City Winter Olympics, 21 February 2002. CP/COCl Mike Ridewood.

were those whose teams had been knocked out of the playoffs. In 1998, however, the NHL agreed to suspend competition to allow its professionals to play on national teams in the Winter Olympics at Nagano, Japan. By this time, at least half a dozen nations were capable of fielding championship teams, and Canadian-born players made up well under half of the NHL. These realities hit home to Canadians in 1998, when a Canadian team composed of NHL all-stars was completely shut out of the Olympic medals. In 2002 the Canadian team increased their efforts, under the management of Wayne Gretzky, and succeeded

in capturing the gold medal in a thrilling final game with the US. Completing Canada's satisfaction in 2002 was a rare double, with the women's hockey team also beating the favoured US team only a few days before the men's final.

By the new millennium, Canadians clearly understood that the spread of hockey, especially in Europe, made it impossible for Canada to dominate international tournaments on a regular basis, although the national junior team regularly outperformed expectations. Thus, it was particularly satisfying at the 2002 Winter Olympics when Canada's men's and the women's hockey teams both won gold medals. Nothing on the international level, however, prepared Canadians for 15 September 2004, the day the National Hockey League's commissioner, Gary Bettman, locked out the league's players after a protracted bout of unsatisfactory labour negotiations. The lockout lasted until mid-July of 2005. The 2004–5 season was finally cancelled on 14 February 2005. The NHL insisted that players' salaries had gotten out of hand; the NHL Players' Association replied that salaries had escalated because of greedy owners who couldn't resist signing high-priced free agents. The majority of Canadian fans found both sides at fault, trapped into positions from which they could not extricate themselves without losing face. The eventual deal included a salary cap and a mechanism relating salaries and revenue.

Canadians had watched in horror over the years as American big business messed around with a perfectly good game. Many observers agreed that the lockout was the ultimate by-product of the failure of the league to expand successfully into the southern United States and to convince Americans that they wanted to watch hockey on television on a regular basis. Empty seats in the South and the lack of a national American television contract spelled fiscal disaster for many owners. The league took advantage of the stoppage in play to study how the game could be made 'better', i.e., more exciting for fans, particularly those who did not understand the fine points of playing defence against the league's skilled superstars. A series of new rules were introduced to encourage more end-to-end rushes and to make the game more offence-oriented.

CANADIAN FICTION

Two quite disparate developments in Canadian fiction characterized the major trends in Canadian cultural production generally in the last quarter of the twentieth century and the opening years of the twenty-first. One was the increasing international recognition for the quality of Canadian writing. Beginning in the 1960s a number of Canadian authors—Margaret Laurence, Marie-Claire Blais, Robertson Davies—had achieved reputations outside Canada. But at the end of the century Canadian authors were basking in the glory of remunerative international prizes, including the Booker (for best English-language novel in the Commonwealth) and Pulitzer (for best novel published in the US). Major prize winners included Margaret Atwood, Yann Martel, Rohinton Mistry, Michael Ondaatje, Mordecai Richler, and Carol Shields. All wrote in the mainstream Anglo-American-Canadian narrative tradition, although only Richler and Atwood were native-born Canadians. Arguably the most feted of the lot was Rohinton Mistry, who was born in Bombay and immigrated to Canada in 1975. Both of Mistry's first two novels, *Such a Long Journey* (1991) and *A Fine Balance* (1995)—each a winner of many awards—focused on the complexities of East Indian life in the midst of socio-economic transformation. Obviously, the writing had internationalized as well. In 2007 the 15 nominees for the Man-Booker International Prize—an international award for lifetime achievement in writing open to citizens of any nation—included three Canadians, more than from any other nation. They were Margaret Atwood, Alice Munro, and Michael Ondaatje.

The other development was the appearance of Canadians in large numbers among the writers of popular genre fiction, such as mysteries and science fiction. The entry on 'Mystery and Crime' in the 1997 *Oxford Companion to Canadian Literature* opened by observing that 'Canada has no real tradition in the genre of mystery and crime fiction.'[38] Canadian crime writers operated either as Americans or as Brits, publishing and often setting their works abroad. But by 1982 a sufficient number of Canadians were active in the field—as Canadians—to justify the establishment of a genre organization, the Crime Writers of Canada, which today has a membership of more than 200 working writers, most of whom set their work in Canada. Eric Wright's well-known Charlie Salter was a cop in Toronto, L.R. Wright's policeman worked on BC's Sunshine Coast, and Joanna Kilbourne's amateur detective operated out of Saskatchewan. But others, such as John Brady (Dublin) and Peter Robinson (the north of England) have felt secure enough as Canadians to locate their criminal narratives overseas.

As for science fiction, the Canadian Science Fiction and Fantasy Association was founded in 1985, the same year that Margaret Atwood's *The Handmaid's Tale* was published. A year earlier, William Gibson had published *Neuromancer*, perhaps the most influential Canadian sci-fi novel ever written. Gibson not only popularized 'cyberpunk'—a dark futuristic place of corporate assassins, heavy-metal heroes, and cyberhackers—but also was among the earliest writers to explore seriously a new world of 'virtual reality' created by or made credible by computer technology. Although both Atwood and Gibson have won many literary awards for their work, most Canadian writers of genre fiction have little expectation of literary recognition. The fact that large numbers of Canadian writers accept their role as producers of mass entertainment—and are accepted as such—marks the cultural maturation of the nation.

THE 'CULTURAL INDUSTRIES'

The 1970s saw the development of 'cultural policy' as a major enterprise of state activity. There were probably almost as many experts analyzing cultural policy as there were artists actually making culture.[39] In 1970 Secretary of State Gérard Pelletier suggested in a speech to the First National Forum on Cultural Policy that the goals of federal cultural policy should be democratization, decentralization, pluralism, federal–provincial co-operation, and international co-operation. The office of the Secretary of State created an 'Arts and Culture Branch' to provide funding for projects in line with explicit government objectives. After the federal government added

'multiculturalism' to 'biculturalism' as a formal policy, the Secretary of State announced programs dealing with Canadian publication, museums, and film. The Heritage Canada Foundation was established in 1973 to preserve and show the nationally significant heritage of Canada.

The provinces also became interested in cultural policy. In 1976 Quebec's Minister of Cultural Affairs published a Green Paper, 'Pour l'évolution de la politique culturelle', laying out Quebec's reservations about federal policy and its ambitions to go it alone. Equally significant, the report reiterated Quebec's conviction that 'culture' meant more than just the arts. A further document, on a cultural development policy for Quebec, was published in 1978. At least three other provinces produced cultural policy reports in the late 1970s, and a number of municipalities also joined the bandwagon. When a cultural statistics program established by the Secretary of State in 1972 (and transferred to Statistics Canada in 1977) began to track and report on public expenditure on culture, it discovered that the cultural sector was one of Canada's major employers.

The policy people discovered the 'cultural industries'—television, sound recording, film, and publishing—in the early 1980s.[40] It was probably an inevitable development. Statisticians needed to be able to quantify culture and cultural expenditures, and governments had long been trying to develop policies for the mass media. Viewing cultural production strictly in economic terms—and culture as a commodity—was very attractive to policy-makers in an era when economic policy had triumphed over all other considerations. It came as a surprise to find that the cultural industries employed so many and were so important to the Canadian economy. It was now possible to discuss culture and government support for it quantitatively, in dollar terms.[41] But there were several real dangers in this approach, quite apart from the risk to the profits and jobs of the cultural industries inherent in the move to free trade.[42] One was that dealing with the cultural industries—and defending them in the free trade era—would come to dominate government policy at all levels at the same time that the activities of these industries would increasingly become identified, even in the public mind, with Canadian art and culture.[43] In 1985 George Woodcock referred in scathing terms to the government's 'modish inclination to equate with art the more mechanical and commercialized ways of filling leisure time'.[44] A related danger was that governments would quickly come to accept the claims of the cultural industries themselves that they were not simply employers of workers and producers of commercialized product in the marketplace, but the principal catalysts and defenders of the Canadian national identity as well.[45] In March 1981, for example, in its submission to the Cultural Policy Review Committee, the Canadian Broadcasting Corporation asserted, without documentation or detailed argument, that it played a 'central role as the pre-eminent catalyst in Canadian culture'.[46] It is important to distinguish between Canadian nationalism and the Canadian national identity. It is possible to support public broadcasting and state regulation of broadcasting, for example, without reference to cultural protectionism or the national identity—simply on the grounds that the nation-state is best equipped to deal equitably with these matters in order to provide all Canadians with

decent access to communications service.[47] While the cultural policy experts were in practice sharply delimiting the conception of Canadian culture, scholars in Canadian Studies were eagerly working to expand it and diffuse it in a variety of ways. For the most part the expansion has been within the traditional boundaries of the arts culture, of Canadian arts culture. But by the 1990s it was impossible not to recognize the presence of other cultures at work in Canada besides the French and the English. The literary canon has certainly been expanded to include languages other than the two official ones, and Aboriginal art has often been admired as the most original art in Canada. In a sense, Quebec's fears that multiculturalism would diminish the importance of French Canada as one of the 'two founding cultures' have been realized.

CONCLUSION

As the new century wore on, Canada's bookstores continued to offer a wide assortment of works dealing with the 'Canadian Question', which began with Goldwin Smith (see Chapter 7). Is there a Canadian nation? Is there a Canadian identity? Diagnosis varied more than prognosis. Not everyone could agree on exactly what ailed the nation, but there was much apprehension about the future.

SHORT BIBLIOGRAPHY

Bibby, Reginald W. *Fragmented Gods: The Poverty and Potential of Religion in Canada*. Toronto, 1987. *Unknown Gods: The Ongoing Story of Religion in Canada*. Toronto, 1993. Two useful attempts to explain the picture of organized religion in late twentieth-century Canada.

Dorland, Michael, ed. *The Cultural Industries in Canada: Problems, Policies, Perceptions*. Toronto, 1996. An important collection of monographs on the cultural industries.

Fischler, Stan. *Cracked Ice: An Insider's Look at the NHL*

in *Turmoil*. Toronto, 1995. A journalistic analysis of the problems of professional hockey.

Harris, Michael. *Unholy Orders: Tragedy at Mount Cashel*. Markham, Ont., 1990. An account of the sad story of abuse at Mount Cashel Orphanage in Newfoundland.

Novak, Mark W. *Aging and Society: A Canadian Perspective*, 4th edn. Scarborough, Ont., 2001. An excellent and up-to-date survey of aging in Canada.

Ornstein, Michael. *AIDS in Canada: Knowledge, Behaviour, and Attitudes of Adults*. Toronto, 1989. A fascinating study of what adults knew and did not know about AIDS at the height of the crisis.

Parsons, Vic. *Bad Blood: The Tragedy of the Canadian Tainted Blood Scandal*. Toronto, 1995. An account of the problems of the blood services in Canada.

Studler, Donley. *Tobacco Control: Comparative Politics in the United States and Canada*. Peterborough, Ont., 2002. A comparative study of tobacco policy, wider in its implications than the title suggests.

STUDY QUESTIONS

1. Do you think that the incidence of abuse in Canadian society actually increased in the last years of the twentieth century?

2. What happened to traditional Christianity at the end of the century?

3. In what ways did the baby boom influence social trends?

4. To what extent is the health-care 'crisis' a matter of caring for the elderly?

5. What was the relationship between AIDS and tainted blood?

6. Explain to what extent hockey could serve as a metaphor for Canada after 1972.

7. Why was the concept of the 'cultural industries' so important at the end of the century?

CHAPTER TWENTY-FOUR

Canada and the World after 9/11

On 11 September 2001, a series of events occurred that shook Americans—and the world—to their very core. A number of small cadres of terrorists prepared to die in the course of their actions hijacked four American commercial airliners. Two of the planes were flown directly into the World Trade Center towers in New York City, which subsequently collapsed in a literal inferno with the loss of close to 3,000 people, many of them firefighters. One of the planes was flown into the Pentagon, causing considerable damage, while the fourth crashed in a field in Pennsylvania after what was apparently an open confrontation between the hijackers and the passengers. The incidents demonstrated graphically how vulnerable the United States was to committed terrorists—many of those involved in 9/11 had even learned to pilot the airliners while living in the US—and the Americans became suddenly very security-conscious. It is doubtful that there was any connection between 11 September 2001 and 11 September 1973, the date upon which a CIA-sponsored coup brought down the Allende government in Chile. But the coincidence reminds us of the complications of the American role in the world in recent years.

Horrific as the events of that day were for Americans and Canadians alike, their true significance became apparent only as the shock waves continued to spread across the continent and the world. The United States government and its citizens understandably treated the successful terrorist attack as a national disaster and responded with a variety of extreme measures, in which Canada became inescapably entwined, even as the nation tried to stand apart from many of them. As a consequence, Canadian–American relations jumped to the front of the newspaper headlines and remained there.

THE WAR ON TERRORISM AND THE WAR IN IRAQ

Despite increasing evidence of internal economic and social integration between the United States and Canada at the beginning of the twenty-first century, the somewhat paradoxical truth was that, internationally, the political and philosophical gulf between the two nations was widening, especially in terms of their respective views of the world.[1] In the new era after the collapse of the Soviet Union and the end of the Cold War, the United States was left standing as the only superpower in the world, while Canada continued its long-standing policy of multilateralism and support of international co-operation combined with a skeptical view of the American unilateral use of power, partly an automatic reaction to dis-

■ Members of Alpha Company, 3rd Battalion, Princess Patricia's Canadian Light Infantry, in Afghanistan, 17 March 2002. Third from the rear is Sgt Marc Léger, one of the four Canadian soldiers killed early the next morning by American 'friendly fire'. CP/Stephen Thorne.

ports, Canada would have much difficulty with the Bush administration's 'with us or against us' position with respect to the 'war on terrorism' declared by President Bush, especially as the Americans widened the war to focus on Iraq. Canada recognized the need for increased border security and supported the United States in its naval operations in the Persian Gulf. It also contributed 850 troops to a military task force in Afghanistan in early 2002, the first deployment of Canadian ground troops in combat since Korea. After August 2003 it would become the largest single contributor to the United Nations' International Security Assistance Force (ISAF) in Afghanistan.

A willingness to join a military invasion of Iraq became the litmus test of any nation's friendship with the United States. Every nation allied to the Americans except Great Britain failed the test. President Bush and his administration began insisting that Iraq had 'weapons of mass destruction' (WMD) and was behind most international terrorism, while Canada insisted (according to External Affairs Minister Bill Graham) that 'Iraq under Saddam Hussein is clearly always a threat, but we have no evidence he is in possession of weapons of mass destruction or that he would intend to use them at this time.'[2] Moreover, Canada would join in military action against Iraq only in concert with the United Nations. Prime Minister Chrétien repeated these views before a meeting with President Bush on 9 September 2002. Three days later, Bush addressed the United Nations and continued his accusations that the Hussein regime possessed WMD and supported terrorists. Meanwhile, the Chrétien government supported action against Iraq in the UN but refused to get behind unilateral action, not long before the American Congress voted to allow Bush to use force in Iraq 'as he determines to be necessary and appropriate'.

Relations between the two nations were aggravated when a close associate of the Prime Minister, Françoise Ducros, accused President Bush of being 'a moron'. Chrétien was eventually

tance itself from the American juggernaut. The events of 9/11 heightened the gulf. While Canada's immediate response to the mass terrorism was enormous sympathy for the United States, combined with a spontaneous welcoming of thousands of American air travellers inadvertently forced out of the sky into Canadian air-forced to accept her resignation amid increasing international debate over the evidence for the existence of WMD and public opinion polls indicating that nearly two-thirds of the Canadian public opposed Canada's involvement in a war with Iraq without UN support; the opposition was even stronger in Quebec. Early in 2003, Chrétien told a journalist, 'If I have to say no, I will. If I have to say yes, I will. We are an independent country.' Canada proved unconvinced by the 'case' for Iraqi complicity in terrorism and possession of WMD that was delivered by Secretary of State Colin Powell to the UN Security Council on 5 February 2003. A spokesman for the Prime Minister's Office said it wanted not accusations, but hard evidence. Some Canadians, particularly those on the right of the political spectrum, became concerned that Ottawa was not being supportive of the United States, and Canada offered to send a battalion headquarters and soldiers to Afghanistan in order to free American troops for Iraq.

At the United Nations in February 2003, Canada sought to fill its traditional role as compromiser to break the log-jam between the American (and British) insistence on force in Iraq and other nations that were willing to go no further than a resolution calling for further arms inspection. Since Canada at this time did not have a seat on the Security Council, however, its influence was muted. In addition, the perception of the Canadian government's benevolence towards the United States was greatly weakened when Carolyn Parrish, a Liberal backbencher, said of the Americans, 'I hate those bastards.' She would apologize, but the damage was done; a State Department official called the comment part of a 'disturbing pattern'.[3] Canada continued to try to find a formula at the UN, calling at an open Security Council meeting for an authorization of war against Iraq if that nation failed to meet the UN's disarmament ultimatum by 1 April 2003. Leading protagonists on both sides rejected this plan, the Americans for allowing Saddam too much time, others for proposing a deadline at all.

In the end, the American President acted unilaterally and began the war. For its part, the Canadian House of Commons voted to remain out of the military action, although the Chrétien government said it would reconsider the decision if the Iraqis used weapons of mass destruction against the invaders. The American ambassador to Canada expressed his disappointment at the Canadian action, and President Bush pointedly cancelled an upcoming visit to Ottawa. Shortly after the initial 'shock and awe' bombardment of Baghdad by the Americans, the ambassador told the Economic Club of Toronto on 25 March that 'We [the United States] are at war to liberate Iraq, to protect the people of the United States and other countries from the devastating impact of Iraqi weapons of mass destruction being used by terrorists or the Iraqi government to kill thousands of innocent civilians.'[4] The trouble with this justification for the invasion, of course, was that it was not documentable. On 1 May 2003, the American President declared the war over. No weapons of mass destruction had been found.

The larger problem was that 'victory' did not bring peace to Iraq. The United States continued to have to commit large numbers of troops to occupation and attempted pacification of the country; the war increasingly came to look like another Vietnam, in which supposed victory had turned to defeat. Prime Minister Chrétien was forced from power in 2003 for reasons that had little to do with Iraq, and President Bush got a surprising (to many observers) endorsement for his war in the 2004 presidential election. But the Iraq invasion clearly damaged Canadian–American relations. Washington was understandably disappointed that a nation prospering under the American defence umbrella should adopt such an independent policy, while Canada became increasingly convinced that the Americans had made a terrible mistake in the invasion of Iraq. The Iraq War and attitudes towards the Bush administration demonstrated how far apart the American public was from the Canadian public, despite so-called convergence. Whether 9/11 and the Iraq War were solely responsible for the bad turn in Canadian–American relations in the early years of the new millennium was another question entirely, however. The answer was almost certainly not, for many of the problems were a product of the complexities of two thoroughly integrated economies in which the power relationships in a variety of ways were not equal.

HOMELAND SECURITY

The immediate response of the American government to 9/11 was to insist on improved security and safety, especially within the borders of the United States. President Bush proclaimed the 'war on terrorism', part of which involved much tighter security. The initial focus was on airports, where security had indeed gotten very lax, but it soon spread to border crossings from Canada into the United States. The result was long lines in airports and at border crossings. From the beginning, the American ambition—shared by most Western European nations—was for the total elimination of terrorist activity. This, of course, was quite impossible to achieve, given the democratization of technology and the willingness of the new breed of terrorists to sacrifice their own lives in the course of carrying out their attacks. As an earlier generation of terrorists had fully appreciated by the 1960s and even earlier, terrorist activity brought those involved enormous political power, much more than legitimate democratic protest. Few acts of terror were more successful than political kidnappings, although random bombings probably ran a close second. The public in Western democracies proved to have a very low pain threshold. Perhaps the worst feature of the search for unattainable total security was that each terrorist incident led to increased efforts to prevent the next one, often by singularly dubious methods and the sacrifice of basic human rights. The American security services before 9/11 underestimated the possibility of campaigns of terrorism within the American

homeland using essentially homemade weapons of mass destruction produced in kitchens, and, after 9/11, overestimated the possibility that the Iraqis had huge stockpiles of such weapons produced in laboratories and factories. No sensible person could possibly expect to advise either the American or Canadian publics to learn to live with a low level of terrorist fatalities on the grounds that the alternative would be far worse, but rationally such was probably the case.

Canadians have never faced the same level of terrorist threats as have the Americans (and perhaps their allies in the Iraq War, especially Great Britain), chiefly because Canada was not perceived as an important enough enemy to the terrorists. Despite the arrest of a number of alleged terrorists in the Toronto area in early June of 2006, the chief threat to Canada from terrorism was in the American security response, which greatly complicated the previously open border in terms of the movement of both people and goods, and would do the same after every major incident. The American media covered the terrorism arrests much more closely than did their Canadian counterparts. The Americans are unlikely to sacrifice economic prosperity through tightened security; it simply becomes another cost of doing business, added onto the final price. But the cost to Canadians is likely to be enormous, not least in terms of the end of the open border.

For nearly 200 years, Canadians and Americans had enjoyed a special relationship along their common border. That relationship has occasionally been difficult, but before 9/11 few observers would have conceived of a continent in which passports would be required to cross the border, as the United States by 2006 was uncategorically demanding. As originally envisioned, at the end of 2006, every Canadian entering the United States by air or sea would need a passport or other identity document establishing the bearer's identity and citizenship, and at the end of 2007 the requirement would be extended to land travel. In late May 2006 the United States

Senate extended the deadlines for the introduction of this policy another year. With this policy shift, regardless of the dates of final implementation, Canadians will cease to have a special travel status in terms of the United States but will be treated like all other visitors. Passport demand by Canadians rose significantly after 9/11. Less than 30 per cent of Canadians held a passport in 2000, and the figure was expected to rise to 50 per cent by 2008. Passport Canada had changed from producing travel documents to providing identity documents, including new passports with embedded digital chips. Any Canadian failure to pay serious attention to American security demands designed to produce that elusive goal of total security will doubtless cloud the Canadian–American relationship. At the same time, many recent immigrants to Canada come from countries that feel threatened by aggressive American security and are inherently anti-American.[5] Further complicating the border situation is the fact that the United States has been trying to decide how to deal with millions of illegal immigrants from Mexico. As Canadian politicians keep trying to tell the Americans, the two borders are quite different and cannot be treated with common policies, such as the construction of a wall along the border.

THE TALE OF TWO MAD COWS

Bovine spongiform encephalopathy (BSE), more commonly known as 'mad cow disease', is a neurological disorder found in cattle. How it is transmitted is not yet clear, although the suspicion is that the feeding of diseased animal meat-and-bone meal to live animals somehow plays a major part. Much evidence exists of a relationship between a serious if rare human disorder called Creutzfeldt-Jakob disease (CJD) and BSE in animals. CJD is a degenerative brain disease that is invariably fatal. It affects one in every million persons worldwide and is characterized by rapid progressive mental deterioration. The worst outbreak of BSE occurred in Europe in 1992 and

1993. In Great Britain thousands of herds were infected and many cattle were destroyed.

North America seemed to be amazingly free of BSE until early in the new millennium.[6] In May of 2003, Canada announced its first case of BSE, discovered in Alberta. A few months later the first case of BSE turned up in the state of Washington, and the infected cow was traced back to Canada. The Americans immediately responded by closing their border to Canadian cattle and kept it closed on health grounds until well into 2005. Therein was the problem. Farmers in western Canada, as a result of the removal of quotas and tariffs from the continental trade in beef and cattle by the FTA and NAFTA and flat prices for grain, had shifted much of their production activity into cattle in the 1990s, increasing exports of cattle from 500,000 head in 1988 to 1.5 million head in 2002, and raising beef exports from 200,000 metric tons to over 1 million metric tons. The three Prairie provinces (especially Alberta) contained most of the cattle producers and operators of feedlots. Beef cattle became western Canada's most important agricultural crop, and the nation's farmers after 2003 lost billions of dollars. The impact on Canada of the embargo was far more serious than in the United States, and both federal and provincial governments were forced to provide emergency aid for farmers. The increased beef exports from Canada after 1990 had not been greeted with enthusiasm in the cattle-producing states south of the border, where constant complaints were made of unfair practices and dumping. On the other hand, American cattle producers embraced the embargo and American state courts have supported its continuance, despite the further appearance of only a handful of cases of mad cow disease on either side of the border. At issue has been the establishment of an international agreement on a standard of minimal risk. Both nations agree on the need for scientific management of BSE, but they have disagreed over acceptable standards of infection. How many cases constitute an epidemic? Canada has introduced more stringent regulations on meatpacking and animal feed than have the Americans, but this does not seem to have affected the raising of the ban.

The situation over the international trade in cattle was exacerbated by several factors. One was the extent of inequality in a highly interdependent trade relationship. The Canadian farm industry was much more dependent on the cattle trade than were the Americans, especially since Canadians had restructured the beef industry to suit the new trade conditions by leaving more slaughterhouse and meatpacking functions to the Americans and concentrating more on the export of live cattle. Another was the difficulty of finding mechanisms of dispute resolution between the two nations under conditions as complex as these. The Canadians argued that the Americans had over-reacted, and were supported in this insistence by several international agencies, which had little effect on the policies of the United States Department of Agriculture. The best solution clearly was high-level bilateral negotiation between the two governments on an agreed standard of risk, and here the prevalent sense on both sides of the border of a deteriorating Canadian–American relationship undoubtedly complicated the diplomatic process. As the Americans continued to keep the border closed to Canadian cattle, the Canadians became increasingly convinced that they were somehow being punished for their failure to support the United States in Iraq. Canadian frustration with American policies was the result. Although the beef trade was reopened in 2005, it had still not returned to pre-mad cow levels by the summer of 2007.

SOFTWOOD LUMBER

Unlike the mad cow business, which emerged suddenly in 2003, the dispute over softwood lumber—the easy-to-saw lumber used in most building construction—is a long-standing one.[7] What has been chiefly at issue is whether Canadian timber practices constitute unfair subsidies for the Canadian lumber industry, as charged by the American lumber industry's Coalition for Fair Lumber Imports, a lobbying group heavily subsidized by the major American lumber producers. Interestingly enough, many consumer groups and advocates in the United States have been highly critical of the CFLI. Most Canadian timber is owned by the Crown and the fee for harvesting on public lands ('stumpage rights') is set by administrative practice rather than by open auction as in the United States.

In 1982 the CFLI petitioned the American Department of Commerce to apply countervailing duties on Canadian lumber imported to the United States, on the grounds that it was unfairly subsidized. Because the Canadian system was not confined to a single industry, countervailing duties were regarded as not applicable, and the CFLI did not appeal this ruling. But the American industry returned to its crusade in 1986 and won a decision for a tariff of 15 per cent. This action led Canada to agree to a Memorandum of Understanding and a phasing in of the tariff. In 1991 Canada withdrew from this agreement on the grounds that it had changed its practices, and the question of the tariff was referred to procedures instituted under the FTA. A binational panel of three Canadians and two Americans heard the case. The panellists voted strictly along national lines and found for Canada in a very controversial decision objected to by the United States on all sorts of procedural and substantive grounds. In 1996 the two nations came to an agreement limiting Canadian lumber exports to the United States from certain provinces (British Columbia, Alberta, Ontario, and Quebec) to 14.7 billion board feet annually. This understanding ended in 2001 and a replacement could not be negotiated. During the course of this agreement provinces that harvested lumber from private land (mainly in the Maritimes) greatly increased their market share in the United States because their lumber was not subject to tariff.

Another petition from the American lumber industry in 2001 asked for the imposition of countervailing duties and penalties against Canadian lumber exporters for dumping. Both requests were supported by the Bush administration. The United States Department of Commerce levied both charges on 25 April 2002, announcing a tariff of 18 per cent and combined levy of 27.22 per cent against Canadian lumber. Canada appealed to a NAFTA panel, which ruled in August 2003 that while the Canadian lumber industry was subsidized, the American tariff was much too high. Only weeks later a World Trade Organization panel also found the tariffs much too high. It also ruled that Canadian stumpage rights were clearly a 'financial benefit' to Canadian companies, but not enough to be a labelled a subsidy. The Americans insisted they had won because the panels had supported the American charge of subsidization and the concept of tariffs, while the Canadians maintained that they had won because the panels had found the subsidies much too high, almost punitive. The Americans appealed the NAFTA ruling to an 'extraordinary challenge panel' on the grounds that earlier decisions in favour of Canada ignored trade rules. On 10 August 2005 this panel sustained the earlier decision. The Canadian government called for the United States to stop collecting duties and to refund those collected over the years since 2002. The Americans rejected the NAFTA ruling and refused to scrap the duties. They subsequently agreed to comply with the cessation of collection, although whether they would refund anything remained unclear. Yet another NAFTA panel ruled in March 2006 that Canadian softwood exports were not subsidized.

By this time the Canadian election had resulted in a Conservative minority government. Prime Minister Stephen Harper sent friendly signals to the Bush administration and met with President Bush at Cancun at the end of March. Not long after this meeting, the United States and Canada announced they had reached an understanding for ending the softwood dispute. Under it, the Americans would return most (80 per cent) of the duties collected over the past four years, while Canadian lumber would be re-stricted to its present 34 per cent of the American market. Canada would levy an export tax on lumber exported to the United States if the price dropped under $355 per thousand board feet. This agreement was announced in Parliament on 27 April 2006. It was immediately criticized by the British Columbia lumber industry as a sellout to the Americans that compromised Canadian sovereignty.

The softwood lumber dispute is a perfect example of a legitimate disagreement between the United States and Canada that had little to do with 9/11, but a lot to do with internal politics and international law and most of all to do with power relationships. As in many disputes between the two nations under the FTA and NAFTA agreements, the American government found difficulty in accepting rulings that went against it under the conflict resolution provisions of the treaties, and Canada had no way of enforcing the favourable decisions it had received. As in most such cases, bilateral negotiation to resolve a dispute that should have been settled within the framework of the treaties was the ultimate outcome. In this case, the result of the bilateral discussions was almost certainly less satisfactory to Canada than the NAFTA rulings suggested.

ENERGY

On 14 August 2003, one of the hottest days of the summer, the lights went out for 50 million North Americans—10 million in Ontario and 40 million in eight American states. The cause of the blackout was not the heat, but rather a cascading failure in the transmission grid that supplied these regions, mainly involving automatic disconnects. Fingers were initially pointed at various culprits, the Americans blaming the Canadians, the Canadians denying responsibility, and much of the public fearful of a terrorist attack. As cooler heads prevailed, discussion centred on deregulation of the electricity market, which had reduced profits and hence incentives for new power lines and security backups. A joint working group commissioned by both the American and Canadian governments concluded after a lengthy investigation that many electric companies had not complied with voluntary reliability standards and recommended government regulation. For 50 million people, however, the immediate issue was loss of power and considerable personal inconvenience. Television cameras caught hundreds of thousands of commuters in New York City walking to their homes in New Jersey and Long Island, and they were only a small part of the commuters affected. Just as the loss cascaded across the grid, so, too, did its implications. Public transit ground to a halt, many gas stations were unable to pump fuel, and highways were crowded with automobiles that had run out of gas; oil refineries closed and were slow to open. Telephones mainly worked, but systems quickly overloaded. Cable television and the Internet were virtually shut down. Industrial closures were widespread, and 140 miners were stranded underground in the Falconbridge mine in Sudbury, Ontario. The eventual cost was estimated to be in the range of $6 billion on both sides of the border. Many political pundits claimed that the Ontario Tories lost a provincial election in October 2003 because of the blackout. It was clear that the Tories had not appropriately expanded the province's power facilities, and unlike other political leaders, Premier Ernie Eves was not visible on television for many hours after the disaster began (he was away from Toronto on holiday). The failure certainly highlighted the interdependence of the grid and emphasized, as well, its vulnerability to terrorist attacks. For the first time since blackouts in the 1960s, North Americans were made aware of their reliance on interdependent energy sources. Energy issues leaped to the fore and would remain there.

The interdependence of the Canadian–American energy relationship—in oil, natural gas, electricity generation and transmission, and even in water management (for water supplies much of Canada's electricity)—continued to grow throughout the early years of the twenty-first century.[8] Rises in energy prices, fears over security in the energy sector after 9/11, deregulation and market restructuring, and concern over the continuation of oil from the Middle East all played their part in increasing the complexity of the energy relationship and its problems. The economic pressures for oil from the Alberta tar sands caused unanticipated environmental damage as producers hastened to pump the oil south.[9] Continental co-ordination was increasingly required to manage energy matters.[10]

The Canadian–American energy relationship has been shaped in the early years of the twenty-first century by a number of factors. First, Canada within its own boundaries has had a surplus of energy in all three major energy sectors, while the United States saw demand exceed supply in both petroleum and natural gas. Canada's energy resources lie in less densely populated parts of the country, creating disagreement between energy-consuming provinces (Ontario and Quebec) and energy-producing provinces, as well as between developers and residents (often Aboriginal peoples) in the resource-rich regions. This means that internal Canadian energy policy is a hot political issue on several fronts. Second, American energy demands and energy policy are continual and extensive, thus shaping the continental market. The pressure is and will continue to be upon Canada to open up and develop its energy resources for the American market, perhaps more rapidly than is in Canada's best interests. This pressure will prove particularly intense if oil prices continue to rise and gas at the pumps remains at unprecedented high levels. Third, various trade agreements and other integrations have to some considerable extent limited the options of Canadian policy; Canada can no longer establish two-tier pricing policies as it did in the National Energy Program, for example, or attempt through federal action to control the amount of energy sold to the United States. Dealing with continental energy resources has become less a political issue and more a management issue, involving players from various levels of government and from the private sector. The Americans, moreover, would dearly love to add water (whether defined as energy or resource) to the existing package of complexity.

GLOBAL ISSUES

THE ENVIRONMENT

Many of the global questions that faced Canadians and their governments in the first years of the new millennium had continental implications that were in one way or another connected with international ones. Global warming, for example, was part of an environmental envelope that the United States government tended to downplay as much as possible. By 2007 many experts feared that increasingly unstable and extreme weather, including hurricanes and floods, were part of the warming problem that the United States refused to address. The global spread of epidemic disease, quite apart from its potential relationship to 'weapons of mass destruction', also suggested, as with terrorism, the impossibility of eradication in a modern world of international mobility. As for Canadian 'peacekeeping', which by 2006 had involved Canadian forces in a shooting war in Afghanistan, especially in Kandahar province, it was clearly a part of Canada's response to Iraq.

By 2007 two absolutely contradictory and irreconcilable conclusions had been reached about global warming.[11] On the one hand, almost all scientists and experts were agreed that global warming was for real and had to be addressed. The evidence was overwhelming, they said. A few skeptics (some in the pay of industry) still insisted that this was a natural process of the weather cycle, but most agreed that the greenhouse gases emitted by the industrialized nations —notably the United States and Canada—were indeed increasing the amounts of heat-trapping gases in the atmosphere. Since the eighteenth century, the average global temperature has risen

by 0.7 Celsius, and projections are that it will rise 2 degrees above pre-industrial levels by the middle of the twenty-first century. Unfortunately, global warming does not simply mean higher temperatures but a variety of other results: melting ice caps, higher sea levels, more frequent floods and hurricanes, and loss of biodiversity, as well as food shortages. The world, say most scientists, has already been subjected to the early harbingers of extreme global change. On the other hand, while scientists were convinced that something had to be done immediately, some world governments had reached the conclusion that little could be done practically to reduce significantly carbon dioxide pollution, at least by using the mechanism of the Kyoto Protocol. The chief problems were that too many nations did not buy into Kyoto and refused, as well, to cut emissions, insisting that the cost was too high for the gains. Distressingly, substantial publicity about the greenhouse effect and Kyoto had failed to penetrate very far into the Canadian public's consciousness. A poll conducted in the spring of 2006 indicated that two-thirds of Canadians knew nothing about the details of Kyoto.[12]

What may prove to be the final blow to Kyoto was struck by the Canadian government in May of 2006 when it called for the gradual elimination of Kyoto with no alternative suggested to replace it.[13] At the same time, the government also cancelled 'Project Green', the Liberal government's $12 billion seven-year plan to implement Kyoto. An independent study released after the project was terminated argued that it would 'fail dramatically to meet national objectives and yet will entail a substantial cost', with much of the money to be spent abroad.[14] While the Liberal government had been a strong supporter of Kyoto, the Conservatives had long been suspicious of it, concerned in part that it put Canada at odds with the United States, which was highly critical of the protocol, in part that adherence would be very expensive and damage Canada's global economic competitiveness. The extent to which the Conservatives were dependent for support on the oil and gas industry was an open question. The Harper government would subsequently indicate a more positive attitude towards environmental concerns, after Stéphane Dion became the Liberal leader, but remained hostile to Kyoto.

In April of 2007 the government announced its new 'green policy'. It spoke of a 20 per cent cut in greenhouse emissions by the year 2020, regulation of the production of greenhouse gases, and more demanding fuel-efficiency requirements for automobiles based on a standard not yet developed. The highest-profile facets of this announced policy were light bulbs, with incandescent bulbs to be phased out by 2012, and increased prices on many consumer items. The announcement of the policy provoked considerable controversy, with most environmentalists claiming that it was so unspecific and inadequate that it constituted an admission of failure. An international dimension was added to the criticism when former US Vice-President and presidential candidate Al Gore supported David Suzuki's claim on television that the new policy just wasn't adequate. 'In my opinion', Gore said, 'it is a complete and total fraud.' Gore added that much of the philosophy of the plan came straight from think-tanks financed by large oil companies. He admitted he had no right to speak out on Canadian decisions, but added that the world had looked to Canada for leadership on this issue.[15]

PANDEMIC DISEASE

While international co-operation on greenhouse gases seemed impossible to achieve, a much higher degree of agreement appeared to be possible on other fronts, including pandemic disease. Quick action by the authorities in 2003 kept under control a potentially serious outbreak of severe acute respiratory syndrome (SARS), apparently brought from Hong Kong to Toronto, although the advisory of the World Health Organization against unnecessary travel to Toronto had serious implications in the short run for the city's tourist industry.[16] Health authorities internationally seemed better equipped than usual to prevent local epidemics of highly contagious diseases (mainly of the influenza variety) from turning into pandemics. Canadian medical researchers have established themselves in the front lines of virus research. At the same time, experts warned that various communicable diseases, including H5NL (avian flu), could easily cripple the international economy, which requires the smooth transit of goods. In some ways the problems are related to the same ones that affect the environment and security. Most people (in Canada as elsewhere) would prefer to believe that a disaster won't happen and refuse to pay attention to the doomsayers, and most governments are as concerned with trade and tourism as they are with saving lives. Furthermore, most defence mechanisms are predicated on reducing the danger rate to its absolute minimum and contain few backup plans if any disease breaches the first line of protection.

THE WAR IN IRAQ AND PEACEKEEPING

As we have seen in earlier chapters, a series of Canadian governments dating back to the 1960s have engaged in 'smoke and mirror' operations to convince the Canadian public that a continually decreasing percentage of the federal budget being devoted to the military was compatible with both national security and Canadian international obligations. After 2003, and as a consequence of 9/11, the military illusion was finally breached. In 2002, Canada committed military forces to Afghanistan as a necessary gesture to its overall alliance with the United States. Those military forces were stepped up in number and their role increased by the new Conservative government in 2006.[17] Afghanistan was divided into military sectors and Canada given responsibility for the southeastern section of the country—Kandahar—in which the guerrilla fighting against the Taliban was the most

■ The coffin of Capt. Nichola Goddard arrives at the military cemetery for a full military burial ceremony in Ottawa, 7 June 2006. Goddard is Canada's first woman soldier to be killed in combat; she
died 17 May 2006 fighting Taliban insurgents in Afghanistan. CP/Tom Hanson.

intense. Few Canadians listened carefully as the Department of National Defence (DND) announced on 16 May 2005 that the Canadians would move from Kabul to Kandahar, a move that clearly implied a change in military policy. Newly elected Prime Minister Harper subsequently visited the Canadian troops on 12–13 March 2006, telling them that the government—and soldiers—would be there for a long time. At the same time, he refused to hold a parliamentary debate on Afghanistan, saying, 'In such a debate, such a lack of strength by any Canadian party would weaken our troops, and possibly place our troops in more danger.'[18] What the Liberal and then the Tory governments had done without actually saying so, of course, was to shift the role of its troops from peacekeepers to combatants. Canada was now committed to a new style of war, in which peacekeeping and humanitarian activities were combined with combat missions; the Canadian military command now had to think in terms of 'the enemy' rather than in terms of the minimum use of force. Moreover, that command was headed on the ground by a one-star general, with many senior military and civilian figures above him. Interestingly enough, all four parties in Parliament supported both the original mission and its refocusing. The result of the shift, of course, was a raised level of casualties, culminating in mid-May 2006 in the death of the first female Canadian soldier ever killed in combat. Canadians began to complain that soldiers were being killed without a clear rationale. On 17 May, in a tight vote of 149 to 145, the House of Commons extended for two years the mandate for a continued Canadian presence in Afghanistan.

One of the many casualties of the Afghan involvement was the virtual end of Canadian peacekeeping operations around the world. Canada could no longer continue its international role with 2,300 troops in Afghanistan. At the end of March 2006, the Canadian Forces made a final withdrawal of 190 soldiers from the Golan Heights, where a Canadian presence had been maintained since shortly after the Yom Kippur (October) War of 1973. After this withdrawal, Canada would have fewer than 60 peacekeepers serving under the United Nations flag, and most of those were policemen rather than soldiers. Few Canadians seemed aware—or cared very much—about what was happening.

CANADIAN POLITICS

THE MELTDOWN OF THE LIBERAL PARTY

While Canadian–American relations, and probably Canada's international relations, were perceptibly shifting, so, too, was domestic politics. The two shifts did not seem much connected, and probably were not. Few of the international dimensions of events after 9/11 seemed to have much impact on domestic politics, except for the public approval Prime Minister Chrétien enjoyed in refusing to support the United States in Iraq. Chrétien's substantial majority in the House of Commons in the 2000 election was, of course, largely illusive, caused by a plethora of parties with popular support combined with mechanical factors such as the Canadian electoral system. A true Liberal victory would have seen the popular support for the extra parties decline rather than increase. In any case, from the very beginning of the new Parliament, the Liberal caucus was full of squabbling as a number of contenders tried to position themselves to replace Chrétien, who

was perceived as on his way out. The Prime Minister was probably preparing to retire, but he wanted this to be on his terms and not those of the party. Having introduced a series of budgets that took advantage of a virtually unprecedented period of economic prosperity for Canada, which made both budget surpluses and many new policy initiatives possible, Finance Minister Paul Martin quickly emerged as the front-runner. He left the cabinet and ran a double campaign in 2002, both to force Chrétien out and to position himself to replace him. A smooth—some said 'slick'—bilingual businessman whose father had served in Liberal cabinets under four prime ministers, Martin's personal portfolio and its management would become problems for the Liberals, since he owned a shipping line that registered its vessels under flags of convenience that required little concern for safety. But his most serious problem was in distancing himself from Liberal corruption, particularly in Quebec, while still maintaining French-Canadian support. By 2002 it was clear that there were two Liberal parties in Canada, one led by Chrétien and the other by Martin. Liberal Party discipline was nearly non-existent, and various hopefuls floated policy balloons that often contradicted each other. The government was embarrassed by the gun control fiasco (see Chapter 22), and the revelations by the Auditor General in this regard were soon joined by further evidence of political incompetence and illegal behaviour at all levels.

By the time in November 2002 when Martin was chosen leader of the Liberal Party, a year of mudslinging had left virtually everyone in the party soiled, dirtied, and exhausted. The Canadian public had been exposed to more rumours and charges of wrongdoing than could possibly be swept under the rug. Many of the rumours involved a federal program in Quebec designed to counter separatism in the province by a judicious expenditure of money for federalist advertising. The corruption issue heated up in November 2003 when Auditor General Sheila Fraser introduced the sponsorship and advertising affairs in Quebec in her annual report to Parliament. Martin attempted to deal with the problem by appointing a Commission of Inquiry, headed by Mr Justice John Gomery of Quebec, and by firing the former head of the advertising program, Alfonso Gagliano, who subsequently became Canadian ambassador to Denmark. Other bureaucrats would later be fired. The Gomery Inquiry ordered by Martin to investigate the affair brought to the fore a number of associates of former Prime Minister Chrétien, each of whom denied any wrongdoing in not very convincing testimony. Several of these individuals were subsequently arrested by the RCMP for fraud. Chrétien called for Gomery to resign on grounds that he was biased. Gomery refused. When the Gomery Inquiry reported in the spring of 2004, Prime Minister Martin was not implicated in any wrongdoing (Gomery would later exonerate him completely), and Martin called an election for 23 May 2004.

THE RESURGENCE OF CANADIAN CONSERVATISM

By this time, as was detailed in Chapter 22, secret meetings between the Canadian Alliance and the Progressive Conservative Party in late 2003 had resulted in the creation of the new Conservative Party of Canada (CPC). Stephen Harper, an Albertan with roots in Toronto who formerly had headed the right-wing National Citizens' Coalition and had been leader of the Canadian Alliance, was elected as leader of this new yet old party.

The Canadian federal election of 28 June 2004 was a relatively quiet affair. Instead of five parties with hopes of electoral success there were only four. Most observers watched carefully the campaign performance of the recently united Conservative Party of Canada under its new leader. The Tories behaved responsibly and with considerable discipline. They suggested that they were pro-American and pro-business but did not actually say so. Their campaign platform called for high government expenditures and differed

■ Justice John Gomery arrives to make a statement on his first report on the sponsorship scandal in Ottawa, 1 November 2005. The sponsorship scandal centred on a program used to funnel money into the effort to stifle Quebec separatism. CP/Tom Hanson.

from the Liberals mainly on high-profile social issues—abortion, same-sex marriage, the death penalty—where it called for free parliamentary votes. Naturally, the Tories emphasized accountability and transparency in government. Unable to find a handle of attack in the Tory platform or campaign, Prime Minister Martin was reduced to charging that the Conservatives had a 'hidden agenda' (presumably to cut health care and social services as soon as possible). Canadians in a series of polls had made it quite clear that they

STEPHEN HARPER (1959–)

❖

Born in Toronto in 1959, Stephen Harper was educated at Richview Collegiate Institute in Etobicoke before moving to Alberta, where he worked as a computer programmer before attending the University of Calgary. He received a BA in 1985 and an MA (Economics) in 1991 from Calgary. A supporter of the Liberal Party in high school, he opposed the Trudeau government's energy policy and became chief aide to Tory MP Jim Hawkes in 1985 before leaving the PC Party in 1986.

Harper was quickly recruited by Preston Manning for the incipient Reform Party, made a speech at its founding convention in 1987, and served as Chief Policy Officer in 1988 at the time of the drafting of the 1988 election platform. He ran for Parliament in the 1988 federal election but was defeated by Hawkes. Harper subsequently became executive assistant to the well-respected Reform MP, Deborah Gray, in 1989 and wrote speeches for her until 1993. As Reform's policy officer to 1992, Harper argued that Reform needed to expand its regional base and criticized radical extremism.

■ US President George Bush and Prime Minister Stephen Harper listen as Mexican President Felipe Calderon (right) responds to a question during the closing news conference at the North American Leaders Summit in Montebello, Quebec, 21 August 2007. CP/Adrian Wyld.

He broke with Manning in 1992 over the Charlottetown Accord, which Harper wholeheartedly opposed, and defeated Hawkes in the 1993 election. In the Reform Party caucus, Harper quickly developed a reputation as a bright newcomer, opposed to centralizing federalism and socially conservative; he opposed same-sex marriage and gun control legislation, for example.

But Harper was never comfortable in the Reform Party or with Preston Manning's leadership, seeing both as too populist, and he resigned his parliamentary seat in early 1997 to become an officer of the National Citizens' Coalition. He opposed appeasement of Quebec separatism, arguing that 'Quebec separatists are the problem and they need to be fixed.'[19] After the Canadian Alliance was formed in 2000 and chose Stockwell Day as leader, Harper co-authored with a number of prominent Alberta politicians the 'Alberta Agenda', which called for the provincial government to 'build firewalls around Alberta' to prevent continued redistribution of Alberta's wealth to less affluent provinces.[20] He also insisted that Canada 'appears content to become a second-tier socialist country.' Harper ran for the Alliance leadership against Stockwell Day in March 2002 and won on the first ballot. He became leader of the opposition two months later, resigning the post early in 2004 to run for the leadership of the newly united Conservative Party of Canada. He won easily, but was unable to convince enough voters in the 2004 federal election that he and his party were ready for office.

After the defeat, Harper moderated the party platform and held the outspoken members of the party in check. In 2006 his party won power as a minority government. In office, Harper moved cautiously, but he was clearly determined to enhance American–Canadian friendship and to prosecute the war in Afghanistan with firmness. He also extended a full apology to Chinese Canadians for the nation's discriminatory treatment of them and supported Israel in the Lebanon crisis of the summer of 2006.

clung tenaciously to universal health-care coverage despite its cost. The leader of the NDP, a thoroughly bilingual and personally attractive Jack Layton, joined Martin in criticizing the phantom Tory campaign platform. The phantom platform may in the end have defeated the Conservatives. At the last minute, many voters had a sudden change of mind away from the Tories, leading to results considerably different from the last opinion polls taken, which had suggested a Conservative victory. The Liberals were returned instead with a minority government. The NDP won 38 seats, while the Bloc Québécois won 54 (all in Quebec) but had no place to go given the lack of support in Quebec for extreme measures.

MINORITY GOVERNMENTS, 2004–2006

The Liberal minority government of 2004 was an inherently unstable one. Its time in office was dominated by the findings of the Gomery Commission. The damaging testimony of Jean Brault, president of Groupaction—one of the leading actors in the sponsorship business—was eventually made public by Gomery in early April of 2005 and almost immediately hurt the Liberals in English Canada. Many in Quebec claimed that French Canada was being used as the 'fall guy' for a general government failure. Prime Minister Martin went on national television to insist that there would be a general election called within 30 days after Justice Gomery's final report. He requested to be allowed to govern until this time, but most of the opposition parties in Parliament were not prepared to wait. The NDP offered to keep the government alive in return for major concessions on the budget, although such a deal was a desperate gamble. On 17 May, Tory MP Belinda Stronach crossed the House and was immediately given a cabinet post. The Stronach affair replaced the Gomery Commission to some extent as a centre of media focus. On 19 May the government won two very close votes on the budget—the second by the casting vote of the Speaker of the House. When the preliminary Gomery report came down in early November, it cleared Martin on the grounds that as Finance Minister he did not have control over spending in the Prime Minister's Office. Gomery centred the Liberal problem within a small inner 'culture' of corruption in Jean Chrétien's office.

Political jockeying continued throughout most of 2005. A meeting of first ministers and Aboriginal leaders in Kelowna, British Columbia, led to the announcement by Prime Minister Martin on 25 November 2005 of a commitment of $5 billion in federal funds over the next five years to reduce the gap between the social conditions of Aboriginals and other Canadians. When the NDP tried to gain more social concessions as the price of its continued support, Martin refused, and the Liberal government fell 171–133 on a confidence motion in the House of Commons on 28 November 2005.

The election campaign of 2005–6, like the previous campaign, was relatively dull, not least because it was spread out over the holiday season. Many of the candidates, especially among the Liberals, appeared to be merely going through the motions. The buzz in the hundreds of Tim Horton's restaurants across the country (now owned by American interests but still regarded as where ordinary Canadians drank their morning coffee and 'rolled up the rim to win') was simple: 'it's time for a change.' The Liberals had been in

power for too long and had lost both their integrity and their links with the electorate. The Liberals, the BQ, and the NDP all lost seats to the CPC, as the threat of the 'hidden agenda' was less effective than in 2004. Harper managed to keep a lid on right-wing pronouncements from his more conservative candidates, and in the end he had sufficient parliamentary votes to become Prime Minister. As he had promised, Paul Martin resigned as party leader as soon as the votes were counted.

As a minority Prime Minister, Harper had a difficult task ahead of him. He apparently understood that he still did not have the complete trust of the electorate and would have to govern the nation in such a way as to avoid major outcries until he could eventually obtain a majority through another election. Many Canadians probably preferred a Harper government shackled in this way to another term with the free-spending Liberals. One action Harper took was to abandon the Kelowna Accord for Aboriginal peoples. He did so without raising much initial outcry, except from Aboriginal leaders, although western provincial premiers soon joined the chorus of those protesting the death of Kelowna.[21] One senior federal cabinet minister said, 'I'm convinced that actually delivering the goods is more important than 10-year plans that don't deliver anything.'[22]

Another action of the Prime Minister's was to continue to insist on tight control over communication between cabinet and caucus members and the parliamentary press corps. Within a few weeks Harper was complaining that the Ottawa journalists did not like him, while the national press chafed about 'managed news'. The Tories had to avoid becoming too dependent for their tenure on the BQ and had to pick the appropriate moment to go the nation for a new mandate; a huge lead in the polls could quickly disappear under the reality of an election or as a consequence of news that could not be managed. A surprise photo op for the newly elected PM in Kandahar might work, but when flag-draped coffins began to return regularly from Afghanistan, or when Harper called the heavy Israeli

■ Prime Minister Stephen Harper shakes hands with Kandahar elder Mulah Akibullah following their meeting in Kandahar, Afghanistan, 13 March 2006. CP/Tom Hanson.

bombing of Lebanon in the summer of 2006 a 'measured' response and a family of eight Lebanese Canadians from Montreal visiting in the country were killed, the news quickly became less manageable. The government would clearly be aided for some time by the disarray within the Liberal Party. No prominent Liberal—and precious few were about—came immediately forward to replace Martin. The result was a scramble among a number of lesser lights—as many as 11 or 12, briefly including Belinda Stronach—and some fairly ludicrous infighting, such as over the question of how bilingual some of the candidates truly were. For months, as a joke, ordinary Canadians went about their business announcing that they were not candidates for the Liberal leadership.

THE LIBERAL LEADERSHIP RACE

The Liberals spent most of 2006 gearing up for the leadership convention to be held on 2–3 December. Candidates strove mightily to sign up

■ Michael Ignatieff and Stéphane Dion at the Liberal Leadership Convention in 2006. CP/Ryan Remiorz.

members for the convention. Paul Martin continued briefly to lead the Liberal Party, but would not serve as Leader of the Opposition; Bill Graham of Toronto Centre became leader of the parliamentary opposition and then interim leader. The convention, meeting under the full scrutiny of the television cameras, turned out to be an exciting event, probably the best political show since Robert Stanfield had won the Progressive Conservative leadership in 1967.

By the time of the convention, there were two clear leaders who would garner most of the first ballot votes. One was Bob Rae, formerly the NDP premier of Ontario, the other Michael Ignatieff, the son of a prominent Canadian diplomat. Each had much ardent support, but each faced a hard core of delegates who would never

accept him. The principal complaints about Rae were that he was too opportunistic and not electable in Ontario, while the chief knock against Ignatieff was that he was a mercenary intellectual (who had been active in British and American politics) before coming home to Canada, where he had not lived for years and which he no longer fully understood. Moreover, Ignatieff had supported the Iraq war at the beginning. As often happens in such situations, the door was opened for a dark horse candidate more or less acceptable to all sides. In 2006 Stéphane Dion was the second choice of many delegates, and he overcame the disadvantages of being potentially the third consecutive Liberal leader from Quebec and of speaking English imperfectly (his English was at least as good as Prime Minister Harper's French)

STÉPHANE DION (1955–)

❖

Stéphane Dion was born on 27 September 1955 in Quebec City, the son of a Quebec federalist academic and a real estate agent born in France. He studied at Laval University and then spent four years in France, ending with a doctorate in sociology. He taught briefly at the Université de Moncton before taking an appointment at the Université de Montreal. In early years he had been a supporter of the Parti Québécois, but strongly supported federalism after Meech Lake and was recruited by Jean Chrétien to the Liberal Party in 1996, serving as Intergovernmental Affairs Minister and insisting that secession could only be achieved through negotiation rather than by unilateral action of Quebec. He became much disliked for his opposition to unilateral self-determination. In 1999 he refused to tolerate the antics of a group devoted to making political figures appear silly by throwing pies at them; he responded to his pie by pressing charges for assault. At the Gomery Commission hearings, he admitted that he knew about the sponsorship money being funnelled to Quebec but had no connection with the program. Dion lost his cabinet post when Paul Martin took over the government, but was restored to the front benches in July 2004 as Minister of the Environment. He saw the portfolio as a chance to rethink Canadian economic policy. At the time of the Liberal leadership convention he had not had much of an effect on the reduction of Canada's greenhouse emissions, but he insisted that economic change was more important than meeting targets. His campaign for the leadership focused on social justice, economic prosperity, and environmental sustainability. Although he was widely respected as a low-profile man of principle, he rapidly became involved in controversy. The first issue was over his dual Canadian and French citizenship, but Dion refused to be contrite and the criticism soon fizzled out. The second issue came in 2007 when Dion accepted a deal in which the Green Party leader, Elizabeth May, would not be opposed in Halifax in return for the Greens not opposing him in his riding. As Liberal leader, Dion concentrated on Kyoto with some success, but he failed to capture the imagination of the Canadian electorate in the early parliamentary rough and tumble.

---

to win easily on the fourth ballot. Dion was well-known mainly for being an ardent environmentalist, and his victory may have helped reshape the Canadian agenda on greenhouse gases.

THE CANADIAN ECONOMY

One of the factors mitigating and cushioning developments that would otherwise have been terrible blows was an extremely buoyant economy. Canada converted a protracted period of high commodity prices and high domestic construction demand into general employment growth that seemed to have no end. By 2007 the nation had seen 14 years of employment increases, with unemployment rates at a 30-year low. Over this period employment growth had averaged 2 per cent per year. That Canada was merely sharing in an international boom that seemed bottomless did not dampen Canadian enthusiasm for the situation. Construction was fuelled by a policy of low interest rates maintained by the Bank of Canada and by a rapidly rising demand for housing that inexorably drove up prices. Despite great increases in housing prices, inflation remained otherwise manageable. The Canadian government ran high surpluses and the Canadian international balance sheet saw substantial balances in the nation's favour as well. By October 2007 the biggest threat to Canadian prosperity was the weakening American dollar, which had fallen below the Canadian dollar for the first time in more than 30 years. Analysts warned that the high international value of the Canadian dollar was reducing the country's international competitiveness. The solution was higher interest rates, but if raised too high, these would take the steam out of housing. Greatly increased oil prices—gasoline at the pump reached over a dollar a litre in the spring of 2006—were also a danger to the continued smooth running of the Canadian economy.

Some weak spots had persisted in Canadian prosperity from the twentieth century. Farmers continued to suffer economic hardships, both from mad cow disease and from unusual weather conditions (drought and floods). Canada's share of international tourism was down, chiefly because American traffic across the international border decreased substantially. Americans stayed home because of security threats, because of perceived Canadian hostility to the United States, because of the lessening value of the American dollar, and because of increased Yankee boredom with what Canada had on offer for tourists: clean air, clean beaches, and attractive scenery. The decreased tourist trade had a significant effect everywhere in the country, but especially in the Maritime region, which had become almost totally dependent on visitors in the summer. Despite the problems of farmers, the three western provinces of British Columbia, Alberta, and Saskatchewan posted the most substantial rates of job creation and economic development. For many younger entrants into the job market, only part-time work without proper job security or fringe benefits was available, however.

Conclusion

The world of which Canada was but a small part was, according to the alarmists, teetering on the brink of catastrophe in the early years of the new millennium. The only question for many seemed to be which disaster would trigger Armageddon. Would it be world terrorism, or global warming, or pandemic disease, or some currently unsuspected difficulty? Amid all the predictions of doom and gloom, Canadians managed to carry on. The number of gardening centres and the sales of garden plants increased enormously in the new millennium, as did the sales of gourmet foods. Home renovation programs became extremely popular on TV and were reflected in the explosion of domestic reconstruction and redecorating projects across the country.

SHORT BIBLIOGRAPHY

Adams, Michael. *Fire and Ice: The United States, Canada, and the Myth of Converging Values.* Toronto, 2003. A study arguing that the United States and Canada were not becoming socially more alike.

Doern, Bruce, and Monica Gattinger. *Power Switch: Energy Regulatory Governance in the 21st Century.* Toronto, 2003. A careful analysis of how energy was and is regulated.

Drache, Daniel. *Borders Matter: Homeland Security and the Search for North America.* Halifax, 2004. A Canadian nationalist looks at the homeland security issue.

Koh, Tommy, et al., eds. *The New Global Threat: Severe Acute Respiratory Syndrome and Its Impacts.* River Edge, NJ, 2003. A multi-authored and international account of SARS.

Kolbert, Elizabeth. *Field Notes for a Catastrophe: Man, Nature, and Climate Change*. New York, 2006. A powerful vision of world disaster.

McDougall, John N. *Drifting Together: The Political Economy of Canada–US Integration*. Toronto, 2006. Argues the case for convergence.

McKinney, Joseph. *Political Economy of the U.S.– Canada Softwood Lumber Trade*. Orono, Maine, 2004. An analysis of the softwood lumber business, sympathetic to the American position.

McQuaig, Linda. *Holding the Bully's Coat: Canada and the U.S. Empire*. Toronto, 2007. A full-blown polemic against Canadian support of American policy at home and abroad.

STUDY QUESTIONS

1. Would Canadian–American relations in the early twenty-first century have been very much different without 9/11? Why or why not?

2. Why did the Liberal Party lose the 2006 election?

3. What was the 'mad cow' kerfuffle really about?

4. What do you think is the most important single issue facing Canada in the twenty-first century?

☐ Writing about Immigration and Ethnicity

■ The noun 'ethnicity' has come into common use only since about 1960. But the *Oxford English Dictionary* traces 'ethnic' to the fifteenth century—when it referred to 'nations not Christian or Jewish; Gentile, heathen, pagan'—and the notion that particular peoples or subgroups within a larger society have a distinctive cultural identity is very old. Over recent centuries that notion has been associated with both 'national' and 'racial' groupings. The study of ethnicity in Canada has changed substantially since 1907, when Howard Angus Kennedy published *New Canada and the New Canadians*—arguably the first serious effort at sorting out the various peoples in Canada. Focusing on the Canadian West, Kennedy referred to the subgroups he identified by national names, such as 'American' or 'Galician'. For him, the major question connected with the 'New West' was how its inhabitants would 'grow not only in material and moral prosperity, but in solidarity and brotherhood with the Motherland and all other lands now joined together under the British flag' (251). In his view, there was no reason to be concerned about an influx of Japanese 'and other Asiatics' provided they were of 'the right sort to make new homes for themselves within the borders of the Empire' (258). Immigrants who could fit into whatever vision of Canada was being propounded by the author were acceptable, while others

were not. Kennedy's book was soon followed by J.S. Woodsworth's *Strangers within Our Gates* (1909). Like most early writers on immigration to Canada, Woodsworth thought in terms of stereotyped racial categories, seeing foreignness—that is, non-Britishness—as a 'problem' for Canadian society, but favouring assimilation rather than exclusion. In the same year Ralph Connor published his novel *The Foreigner*, which also advocated assimilation.

Ideas about ethnicity have changed significantly since these early publications, but the process was slow. The 1920s and 1930s saw some systematic analysis of particular ethnic groups and their settlement in the West, but in most cases the categories as well as the theory behind them were still fairly simplistic. Helen Cowan's *British Immigration to British North America* (1928) was a quite competent historical study, though perhaps better on the immigration itself than its British origins. One honourable exception to simplistic theory was the sociologist C.A. Dawson's *Group Settlement: Ethnic Communities in Western Canada*, volume VII of the 'Canadian Frontiers of Settlement' series, published in 1936. Dawson's use of 'ethnic' in his title was one of the earliest in the Canadian literature, and his analysis was quite sophisticated, but even he referred to a need for patience regarding assimilation, suggesting that he thought it desirable. Like

Dawson, most commentators on immigration continued to believe implicitly in assimilation, while maintaining they were neither exclusionist nor coercive. As Robert England stated in his *The Central European Immigrant in Canada*, published in 1929:

> We start in this process of assimilation with an ideal of Canadian citizenship which would accept, from all the peoples who come to us, methods, customs or habits of life that tend towards progress, and we ask in return that our new Canadians correct their institutions, their habits of life, and if necessary, their language to make co-operation possible between us (169).

John Murray Gibbon's *The Canadian Mosaic: The Making of a Northern Nation* (1938) represented one step forward and one step back. It was refreshingly free from most assimilationist rhetoric. As its title suggested, it advocated acceptance of diversity among what the author called 'racial groups'. At the same time, the work was illustrated by a number of colour drawings of various 'types' that perpetuated racial stereotyping.

The various defences of the Japanese before and during World War II all insisted that, contrary to their critics, the Japanese were assimilating most rapidly. No one at this time tried to claim that the Japanese were entitled to choose not to join the majority culture.

After World War II studies of ethnic groups proliferated, and there were some pioneering attempts at serious theory. Most of the best work was done by sociologists, and much of the historical literature tended towards ancestor worship. But few Canadians inside or outside the universities took ethnicity seriously until the 1960s, when the study of immigration and ethnicity took off. One reason for the explosion of interest was the growth in numbers of academics, especially in the social sciences, capable of studying such questions in

Canada. A second was the general concern in the 1960s for minority groups and their aspirations. Finally, a third reason was related to the Royal Commission on Bilingualism and Biculturalism, which was surprised to discover that the cultural model implied by bilingualism and biculturalism—two founding nations and two founding cultures to which newcomers could become acculturated—bore no relation to the cultural reality that was Canada. Not only were there were more than two founding cultures, there were several vibrant non-founding cultures as well. The evidence was so overwhelming that Ottawa ended up adopting both bilingualism and multiculturalism as official policies. Adopted in 1971, official multiculturalism provided new subsidies for academic research and encouraged the further growth of ethnic studies.

Ethnic studies in Canada grew in sophistication as well as in quantity. There was a growing consensus that ethnicity had been badly misunderstood. The new scholarship recognized many new dimensions to ethnicity. While language remained critical, for example, scholars now appreciated that other aspects of culture, such as family, also contributed to ethnic identification, and that different groups stressed different aspects. Even more important, ethnic studies came to recognize that 'acculturation' and 'assimilation' were not necessarily the same thing, that it was possible to take on some (or even most) of the characteristics of the new society without losing all of one's ethnic identifications and identity, and that some degree of acculturation was inevitable, regardless of government policy or the attitude of the ethnic group in question. The old dichotomy between the Canadian mosaic and the American melting pot was broken down as scholars on both sides of the border came to understand that some aspects of ethnicity (including continuing ethnic identification) were able to survive assimilation into North American society.

Moreover, assimilation ceased to be the only conceivable outcome of immigration.[1] Ethnicity no longer was seen as an abstract reality set in statistical stone and became instead a living, evolving concept in which the most important factor was probably self-ascription.[2] Some students have also seen ethnicity (and race) as the product of unequal power relationships.[3] Not all students of ethnicity could agree on a definition, however.[4]

Many of the histories that have been written about Canada's ethnic groups have been intended to foster pride among group members and to persuade outsiders that the group had an important place in Canada. As a result, much attention has been devoted to 'firsts' and to major figures. This tradition continues. For many specialists, however, questions of change and persistence within and among immigrants and ethnic groups have become the main focus of attention— and disagreement.[5] Historians especially have been interested in placing the history of an immigrant or ethnic group within the overall historical pattern of Canadian development. Historians were relatively slow to move into the 'new ethnic studies', which were typically dominated by social scientists who have tended to focus on issues of the present and recent past.[6] Perhaps the earliest first-rate historical study of a Canadian ethnic group was Robin Winks, *The Blacks in Canada* (Montreal, 1971), which came out of a different historical tradition, that of American black history. Many of the best historical studies of the 1970s focused on ethnic-related topics of long-standing interest to historians, such as immigration, settlement, nativism, and racism. The most ground-breaking of these

works was probably Donald Avery's *'Dangerous Foreigners': European Immigrant Workers and Labour Radicalism in Canada, 1896–1932* (Toronto, 1979), which questioned many of the myths surrounding immigration in the post-1896 period. Some of the volumes in the series 'Generations: A History of Canada's Peoples', published by McClelland & Stewart (in co-operation with the Multicultural Branch of the Canadian government), beginning in the mid-1970s, were written by historians, although others tended to take a less academic approach. In the 1980s the Canadian Historical Association introduced a popular and influential series of pamphlets on ethnic groups, which was followed by a second series on related topics.

Finally, the new historical interest in ethnicity suggests two salient points. First, when historians began seriously to investigate the modern history of immigration and ethnicity in Canada, what they found was an almost universal pattern of government discrimination and duplicity. The findings of Irving Abella and Harold Troper regarding Canada's deliberate exclusion of Jewish refugees before and during World War II[7] were part of a general trend towards more critical assessments of Canada's history in the last quarter of the twentieth century. Second, it gradually became clear that multiculturalism and immigration policy after 1976 were combining to push a new (or at least greatly revised) master narrative of Canadian development to the fore. The new focus was less on national politics and policy than on the development of Canadian society and culture through the history of Canada's peoples.

■ Into the New Millennium

■ History texts that carry the story up to the present day sometimes conclude with an observation to the effect that nobody can know what the future will bring. To some extent, such observations are perfectly true. History is hardly a predictive science. Yet many of the issues that fill the newspaper headlines today trigger a strong sense of déjà vu. Often the specific event or issue seems quite new, even unique, but as the story unfolds, we realize that it is actually an expression of some unresolved question that has been with us for a long time, and is not about to disappear in the immediate future. The same four areas as in the last edition of this work contain important questions that remain unresolved: relations with the United States, Canadian identity, national governance, and the environment. One additional area has to be added: Canada's global responsibilities and commitments.

RELATIONS WITH THE UNITED STATES

In the spring of 2003, any Canadian newspaper reader would have had to regard relations with the US as the most important unresolved question facing Canada. Canadian–American relations seem today less menacing, but the need to come to terms with Uncle Sam is not likely to go away. Canada's place as the nearest neighbour of a superpower has been at issue for well over a century, and Canadian policy-makers have been performing a balancing act—trying to preserve Canadian autonomy while sheltering under the American military and diplomatic umbrella—at least since 1939. In recent years Canada has ceded its position as 'best buddy' to the United Kingdom, and many Americans are suspicious of Canada's reliability in times of crisis. Further complicating our situation, decades of relative neglect of our armed forces have left us particularly vulnerable and in possible need of American assistance should international events turn nasty at the very time when we are attempting to stand apart from what many Canadians regard as the excesses of American imperialism. Because of the complexities and intensities of the relationship, increased American suspicions regarding Canada's friendship will undoubtedly be reflected in further conflict over matters ranging from trade to culture. The extent to which the United States can no longer regard Canada as a 'good neighbour' remains uncertain. Whether either Canadians or Americans are prepared to tolerate such a situation for very long has never been tested. Moreover, most of a new continental accommodation would have to come from the United States.

Canadian Identity

Another constellation of unresolved questions has to do with the way Canadians perceive themselves and their nation. One example is the problem of constitutional change, which was not settled by either the national referendum on the Charlottetown Accord (1992) or the Quebec referendum on sovereignty (1995). In 2007, constitutional issues do not seem particularly urgent, but we know they could re-emerge at any time, since the underlying causes of discontent have never been removed, particularly where Aboriginal people and Quebec are concerned. Moreover, as a federal state made up of widely disparate regions, Canada may well face challenges from disadvantaged areas such as Atlantic Canada, which continues to lose population to the more prosperous provinces.

Quite apart from the constitutional questions they pose, the First Nations represent another series of unresolved policy issues for the federal government, the provinces, and the Canadian people. Aboriginal land claims have not been settled, any more than have the consequences of the residential schools on Native cultures, families, and individuals, the treatment of First Nations people living in urban areas, and the manifold problems of Aboriginal people in the Canadian justice system.

By the end of the twentieth century, most Canadians appeared to have accepted the principles of multiculturalism. But this acceptance can hardly be regarded as final. On 4 July 2002, for example, Statistics Canada announced that the Canadian fertility rate had fallen to 1.5 children per mother—far below the 2.1 level required to replace the existing population. This low fertility rate has not altered and will have several consequences for Canadian society in the future. For example, population maintenance—not to mention expansion—will depend on immigration, and high immigration from the less developed world will increase the speed at which the existing ethnic stock (chiefly of European origin) is replaced. Low fertility also means that the average age of the Canadian population will continue to rise, and a relatively small number of working-age Canadians will be obliged to support growing numbers of people retired from the workforce. Inevitably, an aging population will also place greater demands on the health-care system.

On the cultural front, maintaining a distinctively Canadian character (especially with respect to the United States) has continued to be a difficult exercise. The world of communications technology is changing almost daily, and in theory this technology should be encouraging cultural convergence. No doubt it is doing so in certain areas, such as popular music. Yet research in the area of public opinion over the last several generations suggests there has been less convergence than might have been expected.[1] As we have seen in this volume, the term 'culture' refers to a good many different matters, and this diversity probably encourages difference.

Canadian Governance

In the past few years Canada has managed to produce another national party to oppose the Liberals, both in Parliament and at the polls. But the nation is not yet out of the woods, since the electorate remains uncertain about where the Tories stand on major issues.

The Environment

The debate over the ratification and implementation of the Kyoto Accord has already raised the question of whether Canada can afford to adopt policies favourable to the conservation of natural resources and the prevention of environmental disasters. Part of the problem is that Canada does not exist in a vacuum and must compete economically in a world where not all nations can afford to have very much concern for the future. We do not know the extent to which Canadians are prepared to tighten their belts on behalf of the environment, especially when other nations are not doing the same thing. What we do know is that non-sustainable policies eventually lead to disaster. One example is the Atlantic cod fishery.

In the spring of 2003 Canadians became aware of other sorts of environmental problems in the form of two highly contagious diseases, one affecting humans and the other primarily animals but in rare cases humans as well (in the form of variant Creutzfeldt-Jacob disease). Severe acute respiratory syndrome (SARS) originated in the Guangdong province of China, and bovine spongiform encephalopathy (BSE, or 'mad cow disease') had earlier ravaged Great Britain, although its immediate Canadian origins remain unknown. The emergence of these diseases demonstrated the extent to which the entire world is now linked and therefore the necessity of taking the international context into account even in the case of issues that appear to be purely domestic. These outbreaks also demonstrated the many ways in which epidemiological disaster could affect Canadian society.

SARS was imported to Canada by travellers returning from Asia. A travel advisory issued by the World Health Organization (WHO) brought tourist traffic to a virtual halt in Canada, especially Toronto, where the outbreak seemed to be centred. Meanwhile, a more general decline in tourism and travel—begun with terrorist attacks, fuelled by the US invasion of Iraq in the early spring of 2003, and further encouraged by the SARS scare—had a severe impact on the airline industry. Air Canada, which had been teetering on the brink of bankruptcy for many months, was pushed into financial chaos by the new shortfalls in passengers and revenue.

As for BSE, the first announcement of its presence in Canada since 1993 (when one animal in Alberta had tested positive for the disease) brought embargoes on Canadian beef in the United States and threats of a rapid decline in beef consumption at home in Canada. One of the largest components of the agriculture industry was at risk. A major problem has been the lack of a test for living animals, which must be slaugh-

tered in order to be tested. Canadians were astounded to learn how many herds the affected cow had passed through in its lifetime.

In their responses to both diseases, Canadian authorities were initially slow to take decisive action and then had to scramble desperately to get on top of the situation. The suspected cow in Alberta was not actually tested until several months after its demise. In the case of SARS, infection control procedures were insufficiently rigorous in the first place, allowing the disease to spread through much of the Toronto hospital system; then, when the outbreak appeared to be over, precautions were relaxed too soon and a second outbreak followed, with even more serious consequences for the city's image abroad. These incidents demonstrate how complacency or inaction can lead to an interlinked chain of problems.

GLOBAL LEADERSHIP

Canadians are self-deprecating about many things, including the nation's role in the world. They frequently forget that while the nation is a mouse in the shadow of an elephant, it is in its own right an extremely rich and successful nation, all the more so given the current success of the Canadian dollar and economy. As one of the world's richest countries, Canada has a moral obligation to play an important role in the world, taking the lead in such matters as medical research and the pursuit of new ways of delivering foreign aid and assisting beleaguered nations. What is important is that Canada develop imaginative ways of assistance, perhaps by starting with its own Aboriginal peoples and working outward. Peacekeeping is not the only way of being useful.

CONCLUSION

The world is a far more complex place today than it was in 1900, or even 1950. The issues outlined in this epilogue may never be resolved

—certainly not to everyone's satisfaction—and difficult new questions seem to arise almost every day. Yet history can help us to face these uncertainties, and not only by telling us 'facts' about past events that we can use to guide our present actions. In addition, history can help us to appreciate points of view quite different from our own. It can also give us the perspective we need to cultivate a healthy skepticism about current 'crises', as well as an essential faith in the fact that change is constant—and life, in one form or another, does go on.

INTRODUCTION:
UNDERSTANDING HISTORY

1. Arthur Marwick, *The Nature of History* (London and Basingstoke, 1970), 144

2. E.H. Carr, *What Is History?* (Harmondsworth, UK, 1964), 103–4.

3. D.A. McArthur, 'The Teaching of Canadian History', *Ontario Historical Society Papers* 21 (1924): 207.

1 THE COMPLETION OF CONFEDERATION, 1867–1873

1. Quoted in J.M. Beck, *Joseph Howe*, vol. 2, *The Briton Becomes Canadian, 1848–1873* (Kingston and Montreal, 1983), 250.

2. Kenneth G. Pryke, *Nova Scotia and Confederation, 1864–1873* (Toronto, 1979).

3. *The Protestant*, 1 Oct. 1864.

4. George Coles's letter in the *Examiner*, 3 Dec. 1864.

5. *The Examiner*, 9 Dec. 1864.

6. Quoted in Francis Bolger, *Prince Edward Island and Confederation, 1863–1873* (Charlottetown, 1964), 139.

7. Quoted ibid., 156.

8. Ibid., 158.

9. *Islander*, 26 Oct. 1866.

10. Quoted in Bolger, *Prince Edward Island*, 199.

11. Ibid., 200–1.

12. Ibid., 218.

13. Quoted in Frank P. MacKinnon, *The Government of Prince Edward Island* (Toronto, 1951), 136.

14. Nobody ever seemed to conclude from various shortages of cod in the nineteenth century that the fishery might be a non-renewable resource.

15. Quoted in James Hiller, 'Confederation Defeated: The Newfoundland Election of 1896', in James Hiller and Peter Neary, eds, *Newfoundland in the Nineteenth and Twentieth Centuries: Essays in Interpretation* (Toronto, 1980), 75.

16. Musgrave to Buckingham, 17 Feb. 1868, Public Record Office, London, CO 194/177, 24.

17. *Journals of the House of Assembly*, 1869, 33–6.

18. J.M. Bumsted, *The Red River Rebellion* (Winnipeg, 1996), 11–15.

19. Quoted ibid., 45.

20. Ibid., 49.

21. Quoted in George F.G. Stanley, *Louis Riel* (Toronto, 1963), 63.

22. Ibid.

23. Quoted in Bumsted, *Red River Rebellion*, 71.

24. Macdonald to McDougall, 27 Nov. 1869, Public Record Office, London, CO 42/678.

25. Quoted in Bumsted, *Red River Rebellion*, 94.

26. What Scott's offence was has never been clear. See my 'Thomas Scott and the Daughter of Time', *Prairie Forum* 23: 2 (Fall 1998): 145–70, and 'Why Shoot Thomas Scott? A Study in Historical Evidence', in *Thomas Scott's Body and Other Essays in Early Manitoba History* (Winnipeg, 2000), 197–210.

27. *Preliminary Investigation and Trial of Ambroise D. Lepine for the Murder of Thomas Scott: being a full report of the proceedings in this case before the Magistrate's Court and the several Courts of Queen's Bench in the province of Manitoba* (Montreal, 1874).

28. The Métis leaders, including Riel, were eventually

granted amnesty in 1875. Riel's was conditional on his being banished from the country for five years.

29. Quoted in Bumsted, *Red River Rebellion*, 217.

30. Quoted in Cecil J. Houston and William J. Smyth, *The Sash Canada Wore: A Historical Geography of the Orange Order in Canada* (Toronto, 1980), 58.

31. Vancouver Island had incorporated the colony of Queen Charlotte Island in 1858, and British Columbia had annexed the colony of Stikine Territories in 1863.

32. Quoted in Margaret A. Ormsby, *British Columbia: A History* (Toronto, 1958), 217.

33. Quoted ibid., 219.

34. Ibid., 224.

35. Alexander Begg, *History of British Columbia from Its Earliest Discovery to the Present Time* (Toronto, 1894), 376.

36. Quoted ibid., 377.

37. Quoted in Ormsby, *British Columbia*, 228.

38. Quoted in Begg, *History of British Columbia*, 379.

39. Quoted in Isabel Bescoby, 'A Colonial Administration: An Analysis of Administration in British Columbia, 1869–71', *Canadian Public Administration* 10 (1967): 54.

40. Paul Phillips, 'Confederation and the Economy of British Columbia', in W. George Shelton, ed., *British Columbia and Confederation* (Victoria, 1967), 51–3.

41. Quoted in K.A. Waites, 'Responsible Government and Confederation', *British Columbia Historical Quarterly (BCHQ)* 6 (1942): 100.

42. Quoted ibid., 103.

43. Quoted in Derek Pethick, 'The Confederation Debate of 1870', in Shelton, *British Columbia*, 182.

44. Quoted in Ormsby, *British Columbia*, 245.

45. Willard E. Ireland, ed., 'Helmcken's Diary of the Confederation Negotiations, 1870', *BCHQ* 4 (1940): 111–28.

46. Quoted in Waites, 'Responsible Government', 118.

47. Ibid., 248.

48. Quoted in Ormsby, *British Columbia*, 250.

49. W.N. Sage, 'From Colony to Province: The Introduction of Responsible Government in British Columbia', *BCHQ* 3 (1939): 1–14.

2   ENVISIONING THE NEW NATION, 1867–1885

1. A.I. Bloomfield, *Patterns of Fluctuation in International Investment before 1914* (Princeton, NJ, 1968), 42–4.

2. M. Simon, 'New British Investments in Canada 1865–1914', *Canadian Journal of Economics* 3 (1970): 241.

3. Quoted in Jonathan Swainger, *The Canadian Department of Justice and the Completion of Confederation* (Vancouver, 2000), 112.

4. Ibid., 121.

5. Quoted in W.T. Easterbrook and M.H. Watkins, eds, *Approaches to Canadian Economic History* (Ottawa, 1962), 238.

6. R. Craig Brown, 'The Nationalism of the National Policy', in Peter Russell, ed., *Nationalism in Canada* (Toronto, 1966), 155–63; John H. Dales, *The Protective Tariff in Canada's Development* (Toronto, 1966).

7. J.R. Miller, 'Unity/Diversity: The Canadian Experience: From Confederation to the First World War', *Dalhousie Review* 55 (Spring 1975): 63–81.

8. *Parliamentary Debates on the subject of the Confederation of the British North American Provinces* (Ottawa, 1951), 511.

9. Quoted in Ramsay Cook, *Provincial Autonomy, Minority Rights and the Compact Theory 1867–1921* (Ottawa, 1969), 10.

10. Ibid., 11.

11. Ibid., 13. See also Donald Swainson, ed., *Oliver Mowat's Ontario* (Toronto, 1972).

12. Ibid., 31.

13. Ibid., 33.

14. *Toronto Globe*, 4 Aug. 1870.

15. Quoted in A.W. Rasporich, 'National Awakening: Canada at Mid-Century', in J.M. Bumsted, ed., *Documentary Problems in Canadian History*, vol. 1 (Georgetown, Ont., 1969), 225.

16. *Manitoba Free Press*, 7 May 1874.

17. Quoted in Carl Berger, *The Sense of Power: Studies in the Ideas of Canadian Imperialism, 1867–1914* (Toronto, 1970), 58–9.

18. Ibid.

19. The federal power that probably touched most Canadians immediately after union was control of the postal service. In 1867 the Dominion took over the operation of 3,477 post offices, which became 13,811 by the Great War in 1914. It almost immediately lowered rates from 5.5 cents to 3 cents per half-ounce on letters; by 1899 the rate was 2 cents per ounce. Post office patronage greased the wheels of party patronage, and Canadians saved their money in the postal savings banks. Throughout the first half-century of Confederation, the Canadian post office made money, while providing efficient public service to every inhabitant of the Dominion.

20. Bourinot, *The Intellectual Development of the Canadian People: An Historical Review* (Toronto, 1881).

21. Quoted in Neil McDonald, 'Canadianization and the

Curriculum: Setting the Stage, 1867–1890', in E.B. Titley and Peter J. Miller, eds, *Education in Canada: An Interpretation* (Calgary, 1982), 97.

22. Ibid., 100.

23. An anthology of their work and critical comment upon it, edited by Tracy Ware, is in *A Northern Romanticism: Poets of the Confederation* (Ottawa, 2000). See also Malcolm Ross, ed., *Poets of the Confederation: Carman/Lampman/Roberts/Scott* (Toronto, 1960); George Woodcock, ed., *Colony and Confederation: Early Canadian Poets and Their Background* (Vancouver, 1974).

24. Ware, *Northern Romanticism*, 79.

25. Quoted in Moncrieff Williamson, *Robert Harris 1849–1919: An Unconventional Biography* (Toronto, 1970), 64.

26. For a further discussion of this theme, see Dennis Reid, *Our Own Country Canada: Being an Account of the National Aspirations of the Principal Landscape Artists in Montreal and Toronto, 1860–1890* (Ottawa, 1979), 298ff.

27. Carl Berger, *Honour and the Search for Influence: A History of the Royal Society of Canada* (Toronto, 1996).

28. Quoted in The Royal Society of Canada, *Fifty Years' Retrospect, 1882–1932* (Toronto, 1932), 91–2.

29. For a detailed account of the negotiation of Treaty No. 6, see Deanna Christensen, *Ahtahkakoop: The Epic Account of a Plains Cree Head Chief, His People, and Their Struggle for Survival, 1816–1896* (Shell Lake, Sask., 2000), esp. 217–312.

30. Quoted in D.N. Sprague, 'The Manitoba Land Question, 1870–1882', in J.M. Bumsted, ed., *Interpreting Canada's Past*, vol. 2 (Toronto, 1986), 4.

31. David Lee, 'The Métis: Militant Rebels of 1885', *Canadian Ethnic Studies* 21, 3 (1989): 1–19.

32. Quoted in the *Dictionary of Canadian Biography* (*DCB*), XI, 746.

33. Quoted in Hartwell Bowsfield, *Louis Riel: The Rebel and the Hero* (Toronto, 1971), 116. Other studies of Riel—who has been the subject of more biographical attention than any other figure in Canadian history—include George Stanley, *Louis Riel* (Toronto, 1963); Thomas Flanagan, *Louis 'David' Riel: Prophet of the New Land* (rev. edn, Toronto, 1992); and my *Louis Riel v. Canada: The Making of a Rebel* (Winnipeg, 2001).

34. Bowsfield, *Louis Riel*, 121.

35. Ibid., 122.

36. The best survey of the rebellion is Bob Beal and Rod Macleod, *Prairie Fire: The 1885 North-West Rebellion*, 2nd edn (Toronto, 1994).

37. Bruce Tascona and Eric Wells, *Little Black Devils: A History of the Royal Winnipeg Rifles* (Winnipeg, 1983), 25–53.

38. See my 'Louis Riel and the United States', *American Review of Canadian Studies* 29, 1 (1999): 17–42.

39. A transcript of the trial is in Desmond Morton, ed., *The Queen v. Louis Riel* (Toronto, 1974).

40. Rev. edn (Toronto, 1998). For the other side, consult George R.D. Goulet, *The Trial of Louis Riel: Justice and Mercy Denied* (Calgary, 1999).

41. Blair Stonechild and Bill Waiser, *Loyal till Death: Indians and the North-West Rebellions* (Calgary, 1997).

42. Bowsfield, *Louis Riel*, 153.

43. Quoted in Barbara Robertson, *Wilfrid Laurier: The Great Conciliator* (Toronto, 1971), 50–1.

44. Quoted in Peter Li, *The Chinese in Canada* (Toronto, 1988), 29.

45. Quoted in A.I. Silver, *The French-Canadian Idea of Confederation, 1864–1900* (Toronto, 1982), 147.

46. In general, consult ibid.

3 THE FIRST TRIUMPH OF INDUSTRIALISM, 1885–1914

1. Argentinian scholar Domingo Cavallo, in his book *La Argentina que pudo ser* (*What Argentina Could Have Become*, 1989), argued that Canada and Argentina remained very similar economically until 1930, after which Argentina turned to protectionism—and stagnated—while Canada profited from American foreign investment—and flourished. See, in this regard, Carl E. Solberg, *The Prairies and the Pampas: Agrarian Policy in Canada and Argentina, 1880–1930* (Stanford, Calif., 1987).

2. Angus Maddison, *Dynamic Forces in Capitalist Development: A Long-Run Comparative View* (Oxford, 1991), 49–51.

3. Quoted in Michael Bliss, 'Canadianizing American Business: The Roots of the Branch Plant', in Ian Lumsden, ed., *Close the 49th Parallel: The Americanization of Canada* (Toronto, 1972), 58.

4. Gregory P. Marchildon, *Profits and Politics: Beaverbrook and the Gilded Age of Canadian Finance* (Toronto, 1996). See also Anne Chisholm and Michael Davie, *Beaverbrook: A Life* (London, 1992).

5. Quoted in Marchildon, *Profits and Politics*, 15.

6. Bliss, 'Canadianizing', 38.

7. Ibid., 30.

8. Ibid., 27.

9. Now Brascan Ltd, which in 1983 controlled assets of $3.3 billion from its headquarters in Toronto.

10. J.C.M. Oglesby, *Gringos from the Far North: Essays in the History of Canadian–Latin American Relations, 1866–1968* (Toronto, 1976), 111–12. See also Christopher Armstrong and H.V. Nelles, *Southern Exposure: Canadian Promoters in Latin America and the Caribbean, 1896–1930* (Toronto, 1988).

11. Robert Armstrong, *Structure and Change: An Economic History of Quebec* (Toronto, 1984), 233.

12. William L. Marr and Donald G. Paterson, *Canada: An Economic History* (Toronto, 1980), 384.

13. Craig Heron, *Working in Steel: The Early Years in Canada, 1883–1935* (Toronto, 1988).

14. Eric W. Sager and Gerald E. Panting, *Maritime Capital: The Shipping Industry in Atlantic Canada, 1820–1914* (Montreal, 1990).

15. See Kris E. Inwood, 'Maritime Industrialization from 1870 to 1910: A Review of the Evidence and Its Interpretation', *Acadiensis* 21, 1 (Autumn 1991): 132–55; T.W. Acheson, 'The National Policy and the Industrialization of the Maritimes', *Acadiensis* 1, 2 (Spring 1972): 3–28.

16. Quoted in Acheson, 'The National Policy'.

17. Gustavus Myers, *History of Canadian Wealth* (New York, 1914), ii.

18. Ibid.

19. R.T. Naylor, *The History of Canadian Business, 1867–1914*, vol. 1 (Toronto, 1975), 74–5; see also his *Bankers, Bagmen and Bandits: Business and Politics in the Age of Greed* (Montreal, 1990).

20. Ronald Rudin, *In Whose Interest? Quebec's Caisse Populaires, 1890–1945* (Montreal and Kingston, 1990).

21. W.F. Ryan, *The Clergy and Economic Growth in Quebec, 1896–1914* (Quebec, 1966).

22. Naylor, *History of Canadian Business*, vol. 1, 74ff., especially 161.

23. Jeremy Mouat, *Metal Mining in Canada, 1840–1950* (Ottawa, 2000).

24. Pierre Berton, *Klondike: The Last Great Gold Rush*, rev. edn (Toronto, 1972).

25. Jeremy Mouat, *Roaring Days: Rossland's Mines and the History of British Columbia* (Vancouver, 1995), 23–46.

26. Patricia Marchak, *Green Gold: The Forest Industry in British Columbia* (Vancouver, 1983).

27. See, for instance, Robert Chodos, *The CPR: A Century of Corporate Welfare* (Toronto, 1973).

28. John Eagle, *The Canadian Pacific Railway and the Development of Western Canada, 1896–1914* (Montreal and Kingston, 1989).

29. For one example, see Brian Young, *Promoters and Politicians: The North-Shore Railways in the History of Quebec, 1854–85* (Toronto, 1978).

30. Morris Altman, 'Railways as an Engine of Economic Growth? Who Benefited from the Canadian Railway Boom, 1870–1910?', *Histoire Sociale/Social History* 21, 42 (1988): 269–81.

31. John H. Dales, *Hydroelectricity and Industrial Development: Quebec, 1889–1940* (Cambridge, 1957); Merrill Denison, *The People's Power: The Story of Ontario Hydro* (Toronto, 1960).

32. Jeremy Mouat, *The Business of Power: Hydro-Electricity in Southeastern British Columbia 1897–1997* (Victoria, 1997).

33. Quoted in H.V. Nelles, *The Politics of Development: Forests, Mines & Hydro-Electric Power in Ontario, 1849–1941* (Toronto, 1974), 217.

34. E.W. Rathbun, *The Conference and the Lumber Question from a Canadian Standpoint* (Deseronto, Ont., 1898), quoted ibid., 77.

35. Quoted ibid., 18.

36. Quoted ibid., 147. See also Michael Bliss, *A Living Profit: Studies in the Social History of Canadian Business, 1883–1911* (Toronto, 1974).

37. Nelles, *Politics of Development*, 149.

38. T.W. Acheson, 'The Social Origins of the Canadian Industrial Elite, 1880–85', in David S. Macmillan, ed., *Canadian Business History: Selected Studies, 1497–1971* (Toronto, 1972), 144–75; 'Bourgeoisie and Petty Bourgeoisie', in Paul-André Linteau et al., *Quebec: A History 1867–1929* (Toronto, 1983), 399–407.

39. David Monod, *Store Wars: Shopkeepers and the Culture of Mass Marketing, 1890–1939* (Toronto, 1996).

40. Joy L. Santink, *Timothy Eaton and the Rise of His Department Store* (Toronto, 1990), 122.

41. Jeremy L. Stein, 'Dislocations: Changing Experiences of Time and Space in an Industrialising Nineteenth-Century Ontario Town', *British Journal of Canadian Studies* 14, 1 (1999): 115–30.

42. Morris Zaslow, *Reading the Rocks: The Story of the Geological Survey of Canada, 1842–1972* (Toronto, 1975).

43. J.J. Brown, *Ideas in Exile: A History of Canadian Invention* (Toronto, 1967); Bruce Sinclair et al., eds, *Let Us Be Honest and Modest: Technology and Society in Canadian History* (Toronto, 1974).

44. Clark Blaise, *Time Lord: The Remarkable Canadian Who Missed His Train and Changed the World* (Toronto, 2000).

45. Robert E. Ankli, 'Missed Opportunities: The Early Canadian Automobile and Machine Tool Industries', *American Review of Canadian Studies* 19, 1 (1989): 275–87.

4 URBAN CANADA, 1885–1914

1. Quoted in Judith Fingard, *The Dark Side of Life in Victorian Halifax* (Porter's Lake, NS, 1989), 18.
2. Stephen Leacock, *Arcadian Adventures with the Idle Rich* (London, 1914), 3.
3. Reprinted as Herbert Brown Ames, *The City Below the Hill*, with an introduction by P.F.W. Rutherford (Toronto, 1972).
4. Robert J. McDonald, *Making Vancouver: Class, Status, and Social Boundaries, 1863–1913* (Vancouver, 1996).
5. Quoted in Barry Potyondi, 'The Town Building Process in Minnedosa', in A.F.J. Artibise, ed., *Town and City: Aspects of Western Canadian Urban Development* (Regina, 1981), 130–1.
6. W. Peter Ward, *A History of Domestic Space: Privacy and the Canadian Home* (Vancouver, 1998).
7. Nancy B. Bouchier, 'Idealized Middle-Class Sport for a Young Nation: Lacrosse in Nineteenth-Century Ontario Towns, 1871–1891', *Journal of Canadian Studies* 29, 2 (Summer 1994): 89–110.
8. *Spokane Review*, 3 July 1891, as quoted in Jeremy Mouat, *Roaring Days: Rossland's Mines and the History of British Columbia* (Vancouver, 1995), 112.
9. Ibid., 119–20.
10. Bruce Ramsay, *Ghost Towns of British Columbia* (Vancouver, 1963).
11. Quoted in Terry Copp, *The Anatomy of Poverty: The Condition of the Working Class in Montreal, 1897–1929* (Toronto, 1974), 33.
12. Gregory Kealey, *Hogtown: Working Class Toronto at the Turn of the Century* (Toronto, 1974), 25; see also Michael Piva, *The Condition of the Working Class in Toronto, 1900–1921* (Ottawa, 1979); Bettina Bradbury, *Working Families: Age, Gender, and Daily Survival in Industrializing Montreal* (Toronto, 1993).
13. Kealey, *Hogtown*, 22.
14. Quoted in A.F.J. Artibise, *Winnipeg: A Social History of Urban Growth, 1874–1914* (Montreal, 1975), 241.
15. Kealey, *Hogtown*, 24.
16. Mariana Valverde, *The Age of Light, Soap, and Water: Moral Reform in English Canada, 1885–1925* (Toronto, 1991).
17. Quoted in Marilyn Baker, *The Winnipeg School of Art: The Early Years* (Winnipeg, 1984), 21.

5 RURAL CANADA, 1885–1914

1. Edward J. Chambers and Donald F. Gordon, 'Primary Products and Economic Growth', *Journal of Political Economy* 74 (1966): 315–32.
2. Wendy J. Owen, ed., *The Wheat King: The Selected Letters and Papers of A.J. Cotton, 1888–1913* (Winnipeg, 1985).
3. David J. Spector, *Agriculture on the Prairies, 1870–1940* (Ottawa, 1983); Vernon C. Fowke, *The National Policy and the Wheat Economy* (Toronto, 1957).
4. Simon Evans, *The Bar U and Canadian Ranching History* (Calgary, 2004).
5. David J. Breen, *The Canadian Prairie West and the Ranching Frontier* (Toronto, 1983).
6. Owen, *The Wheat King*, 70.
7. Ibid., 68.
8. Quoted in R. Douglas Francis and Howard Palmer, eds, *The Prairie West: Historical Readings* (Edmonton, 1985), 344.
9. Kenneth Sylvester, *The Limits of Rural Capitalism: Family, Culture and Markets in Montcalm, Manitoba, 1870–1940* (Toronto, 2000).
10. Quoted in David C. Jones and Ian MacPherson, eds, *Building Beyond the Homestead: Rural History on the Prairies* (Calgary, 1985), 117.
11. Quoted in Paul Voisey, *Vulcan: The Making of a Prairie Community* (Toronto, 1988), 158.
12. Marjorie Griffin Cohen, *Women's Work, Markets, and Economic Development in 19th-Century Ontario* (Toronto, 1988), 93–117.
13. Quoted in Veronica Strong-Boag and Anita Fellman, eds, *Rethinking Canada: The Promise of Woman's History* (Toronto, 1986), 99.
14. Novels by Robert J.C. Stead (*The Bail Jumper*, 1914, and *The Homesteaders*, 1916), Martha Ostenso (*Wild Geese*, written in 1921 but published in 1925), and Frederick Philip Grove (*Our Daily Bread*, 1928, and *Fruits of the Earth*, 1933) all feature an insensitive farmer controlling and subjugating his family—especially the women, who smoulder in unfulfilled rebellion. The rural patriarch, who had probably always existed, was now under attack for his acceptance of the values of modern industrial society, particularly the 'cult of Mammon'.
15. C.H.-P. Gauldrée-Boilleau, *Paysans de St-Irenée de Charlevoix en 1861 et 1862*, quoted in Gérard Bouchard, 'Family Structures and Geographic Mobility at Laterrière, 1851–1935', *Journal of Family History* 2 (1977): 364–5.
16. Ibid., 365.
17. Francis H. Early, ed., *Immigrant Odyssey: A French-Canadian Habitant in New England* (Orono, Maine, 1991).
18. Quoted in Jones and MacPherson, *Building Beyond the Homestead*, 126.
19. Quoted in Mary Rubio and Elizabeth Waterston, eds,

The Selected Journals of L.M. Montgomery, vol. 1, *1889–1910* (Toronto, 1985), 116.

20. Paul-André Linteau et al., *Quebec: A History, 1867–1929* (Toronto, 1983), 470.

21. Sarah Carter, *Lost Harvests: Prairie Indian Reserve Farmers and Government Policy* (Montreal and Kingston, 1990), 15.

22. Quoted ibid., 15.

23. Ibid., 20.

24. Quoted ibid., 210.

25. Quoted ibid., 129.

26. Rubio and Waterston, eds, *The Selected Journals of L.M. Montgomery*, vol. 1, 235.

27. Ibid., 178.

28. Ibid., 236.

29. See, e.g., Voisey, *Vulcan*.

30. Quoted in Brian Young, 'Conscription and Ontario Farmers', *Canadian Historical Review* 53 (1972): 293.

31. Ibid., 294.

6 IMMIGRATION POLICY, IMMIGRATION, ETHNICITY, AND RACIST EXCLUSION, 1882–1914

1. The best overall study of immigration for the earlier years of this period remains Norman Macdonald, *Canada: Immigration and Colonization 1841–1903* (Toronto, 1970). But see also Valerie Knowles, *Strangers at Our Gates: Canadian Immigration and Immigration Policy, 1540–1997* (Toronto and Ottawa, 1997), 47–99; Ninette Kelley and Michael Trebilcock, *The Making of the Mosaic: A History of Canadian Immigration Policy* (Toronto, 1998), 61–164; Donald Avery, *Reluctant Host: Canada's Response to Immigrant Workers, 1896–1994* (Toronto, 1995).

2. See David J. Hall's two-volume biography, *Clifford Sifton* (Vancouver, 1981, 1985).

3. Quoted in Knowles, *Strangers at Our Gates*, 68, but one of the best-known quotations in Canadian history.

4. There is no good biography of Frank Oliver.

5. Quoted in Knowles, *Strangers at Our Gates*, 81–2.

6. In general, see Paul Robert Magosci, ed., *Encyclopedia of Canada's Peoples* (Toronto, 1999).

7. For a useful discussion of the origins of racism in Canada, see Patricia Roy, *A White Man's Province: British Columbia Politicians and Chinese and Japanese Immigration, 1858–1914* (Vancouver, 1989). Roy argues for socio-economic explanations. W. Peter Ward, *White Canada Forever: Popular Attitudes and Public Policy towards Orientals in British Columbia* (Montreal, 1990), on the other hand, suggests that inherent prejudice is at the base of racism in Canada.

8. Peter Li, *The Chinese in Canada*, 2nd edn (Toronto, 1998).

9. Quoted in Magosci, *Encyclopedia of Canada's Peoples*, 359.

10. Toyo Takata, *Nikkei Legacy: The Story of Japanese Canadians from Settlement to Today* (Toronto, 1983).

11. Tamato Makabe, *Picture Brides: Japanese Women in Canada* (Toronto, 1985).

12. Ruth Klein and Frank Dimant, eds, *From Immigration to Integration: The Canadian Jewish Experience* (North York, Ont., 2001).

13. Jaroslav Petryshyn, *Peasants in the Promised Land: Canada and the Ukrainians, 1891–1914* (Toronto, 1985).

14. George Woodcock and Ivan Avakumovic, *The Doukhobors* (Toronto, 1968).

15. Quoted in Harold Martin Troper, *Only Farmers Need Apply: Official Canadian Government Encouragement of Immigration from the United States, 1896–1911* (Toronto, 1972), 12.

16. R. Bruce Shepard, *Deemed Unsuitable* (Toronto, 1997), 72.

17. Quoted ibid., 100.

18. Quoted in Avery, *Reluctant Host*, 30.

19. Baha Abu-Laban, *An Olive Branch on the Family Tree: The Arabs in Canada* (Toronto, 1980), is mainly about the Lebanese. See also 'The Lebanese', in Magosci, ed., *Encyclopedia of Canada's Peoples*, 919–29.

20. W.D. Scott, *Canada and Its Provinces: A History of the Canadian People and Their Institutions by One Hundred Associates*, Adam Shortt and Arthur C. Doughty, general eds (Toronto, 1914), vol. 7.

7 POLITICS AND THE NATIONAL QUESTION, 1885–1914

1. André Siegfried, *The Race Question in Canada*, edited and with an introduction by Frank M. Underhill (Toronto, 1966), 113.

2. Quoted in John English, *The Decline of Politics: The Conservatives and the Party System, 1901–20* (Toronto, 1977), 74.

3. Quoted in Gordon T. Stewart, 'Political Patronage Under Macdonald and Laurier, 1878–1911', in J.M. Bumsted, ed., *Interpreting Canada's Past*, vol. 2 (Toronto, 1986), 33.

4. Quoted in Christopher Armstrong, 'The Mowat Heritage in Federal–Provincial Relations', in Bumsted, *Interpreting Canada's Past*, vol. 2, 54. See also Paul Romney, 'The Nature and Scope of Provincial Autonomy: Oliver

Mowat, the Quebec Resolutions and the Construction of the British North America Act', *Canadian Journal of Political Science* 25, 1 (Mar. 1992): 2–28.

5. One excellent example of the new trend is Paul Romney, *Getting It Wrong: How Canadians Forgot Their Past and Imperilled Confederation* (Toronto, 1999).

6. Quoted in J.M. Bumsted, ed., *Documentary Problems in Canadian History*, vol. 2 (Georgetown, Ont., 1969), 1.

7. Disagreement over the settlement of the considerable property and seigneuries that had once been owned by the Jesuits in Quebec was resolved—with the help of Pope Leo XIII, who acted as arbiter—in July 1888 when the Jesuits' Estates Act was passed by the legislative assembly of Quebec, providing payments to the Jesuits and several educational institutions. Papal involvement angered the Orange Order and other Protestant extremist groups in Ontario.

8. Quoted in Bumsted, *Documentary Problems*, vol. 2, 78.

9. Ibid., 76.

10. Quoted in Carl Berger, *The Sense of Power: Studies in the Ideas of Canadian Imperialism, 1867–1914* (Toronto, 1970), 58–9.

11. Ralph Connor, *The Major* (London, 1917), 130–1.

12. Quoted in Bumsted, *Documentary Problems*, vol. 2, 72.

13. Goldwin Smith, *The Political Destiny of Canada* (London, 1878), 130.

14. Goldwin Smith, *Canada and the Canadian Question* (London, 1891), 191.

15. Siegfried, *The Race Question*, 28.

16. John S. Ewart, *The Kingdom of Canada: Imperial Federation, the Colonial Conferences, the Alaska Boundary and Other Essays* (Toronto, 1908), 6.

17. Ibid., 364.

18. Ibid., 80.

19. Quoted in Denis Monière, *Ideologies in Quebec: The Historical Development* (Toronto, 1981), 189.

20. Ibid., 190.

21. Quoted in Ramsay Cook, ed., *French-Canadian Nationalism: An Anthology* (Toronto, 1969), 147.

22. C.P. Stacey, ed., *Records of the Nile Voyageurs, 1884–1885: The Canadian Voyageur Contingent in the Gordon Relief Expedition* (Toronto, 1959); Roy McLaren, *Canadians on the Nile, 1882–1898: Being the Adventures of the Voyageurs in the Khartoum Relief Expedition and Other Exploits* (Vancouver, 1978).

23. Desmond Morton, *The Last War Drum: The North West Campaign of 1885* (Toronto, 1972).

24. Quoted in John Kendle, *The Round Table Movement and Imperial Union* (Toronto, 1975), 29.

25. Quoted in Mason Wade, *The French Canadians, 1760–1945*, vol. 1 (Toronto, 1968), 479.

26. Carman Miller, *Painting the Map Red: Canada and the South African War, 1899–1902* (Montreal, 1993).

27. Wade, *The French Canadians*, vol. 1, 480.

28. Robert Macdougall, *Rural Life in Canada: Its Trends and Tasks* (1913; reprint Toronto, 1973, with an introduction by Robert Craig Brown), 34.

29. Siegfried, *The Race Question*, 96.

30. Smith, *Canada and the Canadian Question*, 10.

31. Quoted in Bruce Hodgins and Robert Page, eds, *Canada Since Confederation* (Georgetown, Ont., 1976), 322–3.

32. Ibid., 326.

33. Quoted in Wade, *The French Canadians*, vol. 1, 509.

34. Quoted in Cook, *French-Canadian Nationalism*, 133.

35. Quoted in Siegfried, *The Race Question*, 184.

36. Ibid., 186.

37. Ibid., 243.

38. George Parkin, *Imperial Federation, the Problem of National Unity* (London, 1892), 15.

39. George Parkin, *The Great Dominion: Studies of Canada* (London, 1895), 5.

40. Goldwin Smith, *Loyalty, Aristocracy and Jingoism* (Toronto, 1896), 92.

41. Quoted in Valerie Knowles, *Strangers at Our Gates: Canadian Immigration and Immigration Policy, 1540–1997*, rev. edn (Toronto, 1997), 50.

42. These remarks based on Donald K. Pickens, *Eugenics and the Progressives* (Nashville, 1968); Angus McLaren, *Our Own Master Race: Eugenics in Canada, 1885–1945* (Toronto, 1990); Ian Robert Dowbiggin, *Keeping America Sane: Psychiatry and Eugenics in the United States and Canada, 1880–1940* (Ithaca, NY, 1997).

43. Quoted in Carol Bacchi, 'Race Regeneration and Social Purity: A Study of the Social Attitudes of Canada's English-Speaking Suffragists', in Bumsted, *Interpreting Canada's Past*, vol. 2, 195.

8 THE ERA OF SOCIAL REFORM, 1885–1914

1. Quoted in A.F.J. Artibise, *Winnipeg: A Social History of Urban Growth, 1874–1914* (Montreal, 1975), 57.

2. The best survey of the moral reform movement is Mariana Valverde's *The Age of Light, Soap, and Water: Moral Reform in English Canada, 1885–1925* (Toronto, 1991).

3. Desmond Morton, *Mayor Howland: The Citizens' Candidate* (Toronto, 1973).

4. Carolyn Strange, *Toronto's Girl Problem: The Perils and*

Pleasures of the City, 1880–1930 (Toronto, 1995).

5. Richard Allen, *The Social Passion: Religion and Social Reform in Canada, 1914–1928* (Toronto, 1971); Brian J. Fraser, *The Social Uplifters: Presbyterian Progressives and the Social Gospel in Canada, 1875–1915* (Waterloo, Ont., 1988).

6. See Allan Mills, *Fool for Christ: The Political Thought of J.S. Woodsworth* (Toronto, 1991).

7. Theodore Roosevelt in the United States called the progressive city reformers the 'goo-goos', and Stephen Leacock wrote a scathing chapter—easily one of his best satiric pieces—in *Arcadian Adventures* on 'The Great Fight for Clean Government'.

8. G. Frank Beer, 'A Plea for City Planning Organization', (1914), in Paul Rutherford, ed., *Saving the Canadian City: The First Phase, 1880–1920* (Toronto, 1974), 233.

9. Quoted in Walter Van Nus, 'The Fate of the City Beautiful Movement in Canada, 1893–1930', in Gilbert A. Stelter and Alan F.J. Artibise, eds, *The Canadian City: Essays on Urban History* (Toronto, 1977), 171.

10. Artibise, *Winnipeg*, 202.

11. Linda Ambrose, *For Home and Country: The Centennial History of the Women's Institutes in Ontario* (Erin, Ont., 1996).

12. Carol Bacchi, 'Race Regeneration and Social Purity: A Study of the Social Attitudes of Canada's English-Speaking Suffragists', in J.M. Bumsted, ed., *Interpreting Canada's Past*, vol. 2 (Toronto, 1986), 196.

13. Bryan D. Palmer, *Working-Class Experience: Rethinking the History of Canadian Labour, 1800–1991*, 2nd edn (Toronto, 1992) is the best introduction to this subject.

14. Craig Heron and Bryan Palmer, 'Through the Prism of the Strike: Industrial Conflict in Southern Ontario', *Canadian Historical Review* 58 (Dec. 1977): 433.

15. Michèle Martin, 'Feminization of the Labour Process in the Communications Industry: The Case of the Telephone Operators, 1876–1904', *Labour/Le Travail* 22 (1988).

16. Ibid.

17. Robert Babcock, *Gompers in Canada: A Study in American Continentalism before the First World War* (Toronto, 1974).

18. Quoted in Ross McCormack, *Reformers, Rebels, and Revolutionaries: The Western Canadian Radical Movement, 1899–1919* (Toronto, 1977), 54.

19. Ibid.

20. Gregory Kealey and Bryan D. Palmer, *Dreaming of What Might Be: The Knights of Labor in Ontario, 1880–1890* (Toronto, 1982).

21. 'Preamble and Declaration of Principles of the Knights

of Labour of America' (Philadelphia, 1885).

22. A.M.C. Waterman, 'The Lord's Day Act in a Secular Society: A Historical Comment on the Canadian Lords' Day Act of 1906', *Canadian Journal of Theology* 21 (1965): 108–23.

23. Carol Bacchi, 'Divided Allegiances', in Linda Kealey, ed., *A Not Unreasonable Claim: Women and Reform in Canada, 1880s–1920s* (Toronto, 1979), 89–108.

24. Wayne Roberts, 'Rocking the Cradle for the World', in Kealey and Palmer, *Dreaming of What Might Be*, 15–46.

25. Louise Carbert, *Agrarian Feminism: The Politics of Ontario Farm Women* (Toronto, 1995).

26. Quoted in Constance Backhouse, *Petticoats and Prejudice: Women and Law in Nineteenth-Century Canada* (Toronto, 1991), 294.

27. Joy Fielding, 'Sisters in Law', *Weekend Magazine*, 26 Aug. 1978.

28. Sharon A. Cook, 'Through Sunshine and Shadow': The Woman's Christian Temperance Union, Evangelicalism, and Reform in Ontario, 1874–1930 (Montreal, 1995).

29. Quoted in Ramsay Cook and Wendy Mitchison, eds, *The Proper Sphere: Women's Place in Canadian Society* (Toronto, 1976), 230ff.

30. Quoted in J.M. Bumsted, ed., *Documentary Problems in Canadian History*, vol. 2 (Georgetown, Ont., 1969), 191.

31. Quoted in Kealey, ed., *A Not Unreasonable Claim*, 73.

32. Social Service Congress, *Report of Addresses and Proceedings* (Toronto, 1914).

9 THE GREAT WAR AND ITS AFTERMATH, 1914–1919

1. For more on Hughes, see R.G. Haycock, *Sam Hughes: The Public Career of a Controversial Canadian, 1885–1918* (Toronto, 1987).

2. Bruce Tascona and Eric Wells, *Little Black Devils: A History of the Royal Winnipeg Rifles* (Winnipeg, 1983), 63.

3. These paragraphs are based on Desmond Morton, *When Your Number's Up: The Canadian Soldier in the First World War* (Toronto, 1993); Bill Rawling, *Surviving Trench Warfare: Technology and the Canadian Corps, 1914–1918* (Toronto, 1992); John Ellis, *Eye-Deep in Hell* (London, 1976).

4. Quoted in Ellis, *Eye-Deep*, 54.

5. Diary, vol. 1 (1914–16), 28 December 1915, Macphail Papers, Library and Archives Canada.

6. Tascona and Wells, *Little Black Devils*, 83–8.

7. *Le Devoir*, 5 August 1916.

8. Elizabeth Armstrong, *The Crisis of Quebec, 1914–1918*

(Toronto, 1974).

9. Ibid. 177–9.

10. David E. Smith, 'Emergency Government in Canada', *Canadian Historical Review* 50 (1969): 429–48.

11. Allan L. Steinhart, *Civil Censorship in Canada during World War I* (Toronto, 1986).

12. Gregory Kealey, 'State Repression of Labour and the Left in Canada, 1914–20: The Impact of the First World War', *Canadian Historical Review* 73, 3 (Sept. 1992): 281–314.

13. Quoted in John Herd Thompson, *The Harvests of War: The Prairie West, 1914–1918* (Toronto, 1978), 101.

14. *Grain Growers' Guide*, 1 August 1917.

15. Thompson, *The Harvests of War*, 59.

16. Ibid., 67.

17. Quoted in A.R. McCormack, *Reformers, Rebels and Revolutionaries: The Western Canadian Radical Movement, 1899–1919* (Toronto, 1977), 144.

18. Quoted in Thompson, *Harvests of War*, 157.

19. Maria Tippett, *Art at the Service of War: Canada, Art, and the Great War* (Toronto, 1984).

20. D.C. Masters, *The Winnipeg General Strike* (Toronto, 1950); David Bercuson, *Confrontation at Winnipeg: Labour, Industrial Relations, and the General Strike*, rev. edn (Montreal, 1990); J.M. Bumsted, *The Winnipeg General Strike: An Illustrated History* (Winnipeg, 1994).

21. Harry Gutkin and Mildred Gutkin, *Profiles in Dissent: The Shaping of Radical Thought in the Canadian West* (Edmonton, 1997).

22. Donald Avery, 'The Radical Alien and the Winnipeg General Strike of 1919', in J.M. Bumsted, ed., *Interpreting Canada's Past*, vol, 2 (Toronto, 1986), 227.

23. Ibid., 231–2.

24. Ibid., 234.

25. Desmond Morton and Glenn Wright, *Winning the Second Battle: Canadian Veterans and the Return to Civilian Life, 1915–1930* (Toronto, 1987), 200.

26. *Canada Year Book*, 1934.

10 ECONOMY, POLITY, AND THE 'UNSOLVED RIDDLE OF SOCIAL JUSTICE', 1919–1939

1. Eileen Pettigrew, *The Silent Enemy: Canada and the Deadly Flu of 1918* (Saskatoon, 1983).

2. Alan Bowker, ed., *The Social Criticism of Stephen Leacock: The Unsolved Riddle of Social Justice and Other Essays* (Toronto, 1973), 74.

3. Ibid., 79.

4. Paul MacEwan, *Miners and Steelworkers: Labour in Cape Breton* (Toronto, 1976); David Frank, 'Class Conflict in the Coal Industry: Cape Breton, 1922', in Gregory Kealey et al., eds, *Essays in Working Class History* (Toronto, 1970).

5. J.E. Crerar, *T.A. Crerar: A Political Life* (Montreal, 1997).

6. Quoted in David Jones, *Empire of Dust: Settling and Abandoning the Prairie Dry Belt* (Edmonton, 1987), 175.

7. Ernest R. Forbes, *The Maritime Rights Movement, 1919–1927: A Study in Canadian Regionalism* (Montreal, 1979).

8. Quoted in Ernest R. Forbes, 'The Emergence of the Campaign for Maritime Rights, 1921–2', in J.M. Bumsted, ed., *Interpreting Canada's Past*, vol. 2 (Toronto, 1986), 243.

9. Susan Mann Trokimenkoff, ed., *Abbé Groulx: Variations on a Nationalist Theme* (Toronto, 1974); Susan Mann Trofimenkoff, *Action Française: French-Canadian Nationalism in the Twenties* (Toronto, 1975).

10. Quoted in Mason Wade, *The French Canadians, 1760–1945* (Toronto, 1955), 880, 869.

11. In April 1660 Dollard and 16 other Frenchmen, and some Huron and Algonquin, set out from Montreal to ambush Iroquois hunters coming down the Ottawa River, but at the foot of the Long Sault rapids they were discovered by some 300 Iroquois. They were besieged for a week before all the Frenchmen lost their lives. The cult portrayed Dollard as a national saviour.

12. Quoted in Ramsay Cook, ed., *French Canadian Nationalism: An Anthology* (Toronto, 1969), 193.

13. Quoted in Wade, *The French Canadians*, 880.

14. James Gray, *The Roar of the Twenties* (Toronto, 1975), 312–13.

15. Margaret A. Ormsby, *British Columbia: A History* (Toronto, 1958), 439.

16. Peter C. Newman, *The Bronfman Dynasty: The Rothschilds of the New World* (Toronto, 1978), 74–96.

17. Doug Fetherling, *Gold Diggers of 1929: Canada and the Great Stock Market Crash* (Toronto, 1979).

18. Bettina Bradbury, 'Municipal Unemployment and Relief in the Early Thirties: Burnaby, North Vancouver City and District, and West Vancouver', MA thesis, Simon Fraser University, 1974.

19. Hansard, Feb. 1930, 55.

20. James Gray, *The Winter Years* (Toronto, 1966).

21. Denyse Baillargeon, *Making Do: Women, Family and Home in Montreal during the Great Depression* (Waterloo, 1999), 150.

22. Quoted ibid., 145.

23. Quoted ibid., 163–4.

24. Ibid., 153. See also Andrée Lévesque, *Making and Breaking the Rules: Women in Quebec, 1919–1939* (Toronto, 1994).

25. Barry Broadfoot, *Ten Lost Years, 1929–1939: Memories of Canadians Who Survived the Depression* (Toronto, 1973), 6.

26. A.E. Safarian, *The Canadian Economy in the Great Depression* (Toronto, 1959).

27. Michael Bliss and L.M. Grayson, eds, *The Wretched of Canada: Letters to R.B. Bennett, 1930–1935* (Toronto, 1971).

28. J.H. Wilbur, ed., *The Bennett New Deal* (Toronto, 1968).

29. Alvin Finkel, *Business and Social Reform in the Thirties* (Toronto, 1979).

30. Quoted ibid., 31–2.

31. Quoted in Alvin Finkel, 'Origins of the Welfare State in Canada', in Bumsted, ed., *Interpreting Canada's Past*, vol. 2, 298.

32. Ibid., 300.

33. John A. Irving, *The Social Credit Movement in Alberta* (Toronto, 1959); C.B. Macpherson, *Democracy in Alberta: The Theory and Practice of a Quasi-Party System* (Toronto, 1953); John L. Finlay, *Social Credit: The English Origins* (Montreal, 1972).

34. Conrad Black, *Duplessis* (Toronto, 1977); Hubert Quinn, *The Union Nationale: Quebec Nationalism from Duplessis to Lesage*, 2nd edn (Toronto, 1979).

35. Quoted in Gregory Baum, *Catholics and Canadian Socialism: Political Thought in the Thirties and Forties* (Toronto, 1980), 179.

36. This slogan of small businessmen (translated as 'buy from our own') had an anti-Semitic subtext that lost its currency in the late 1930s when fascism became so threatening.

37. Quoted ibid., 184.

38. Alex Laidlaw, ed., *The Man from Margaree: Writings and Speeches of M M. Coady* (Toronto, 1971).

39. The Research Committee of the League for Social Reconstruction, *Social Planning for Canada* (Toronto, 1935, reissued 1975), x, ix.

40. The Fabian Society assisted in the formation of the Labour Party, which elected 29 members to the British Parliament in 1906. In 1922 Labour became the official opposition, and in 1924 it formed its first ministry.

41. Michiel Horn, 'Frank Underhill's Early Drafts of the Regina Manifesto 1933', *Canadian Historical Review* 54 (1973): 393–418. See also Horn's *The League for Social Reconstruction: Intellectual Origins of the Democratic Left in Canada, 1930–1942* (Toronto, 1980), esp. 36–53.

42. Kenneth McNaught, *A Prophet in Politics: A Biography of J.S. Woodsworth* (Toronto, 1959); Allan Mills, *Fool for Christ: The Political Thought of J.S. Woodsworth* (Toronto, 1991).

43. Quoted in Ormsby, *British Columbia*, 453.

44. S.M. Lipset, *Agrarian Socialism: The Cooperative Commonwealth Federation in Saskatchewan: A Study in Political Sociology* (Berkeley, 1968).

45. Lita-Rose Betcherman, *The Little Band: The Clashes between the Communists and the Political and Legal Establishments in Canada, 1928–1932* (Ottawa, 1982).

46. William Beeching, *Canadian Volunteers: Spain, 1936–1939* (Regina, 1989).

47. Ormsby, *British Columbia*, 463–4; David Ricardo Williams, *Mayor Gerry: The Remarkable Gerald Gratton McGeer* (Vancouver, 1986).

48. John T. Saywell, *'Just Call Me Mitch': The Life of Mitchell F. Hepburn* (Toronto, 1991).

49. Donald Smiley, ed., *The Rowell-Sirois Report: An Abridgement of Book One of the Rowell-Sirois Report on Dominion–Provincial Relations* (Toronto, 1963).

50. C.P. Stacey, *Canada and the Age of Conflict: A History of Canadian External Policies*, vol. 2, *1921–1948* (Toronto, 1981), 51.

51. Ibid., 25.

11 CANADIAN SOCIETY AND CULTURE BETWEEN THE WARS, 1919–1939

1. By far the best study of Canadian society in this period, now almost 20 years old, is John Herd Thompson with Allen Seager, *Canada 1922–1939: Decades of Discord* (Toronto, 1985). But see also Pierre Berton, *The Great Depression, 1929–1939* (Toronto, 1990); Barry Broadfoot, *Ten Lost Years, 1929–1939: Memories of Canadians Who Survived the Depression* (Toronto, 1973); and the essays in Association for Canadian Studies, *Canadian Society and Culture in Times of Economic Depression* (Montreal, 1987).

2. James G. Snell, *In the Shadow of the Law: Divorce in Canada, 1900–1939* (Toronto, 1991).

3. E. Palmer Patterson II, *The Canadian Indian: A History since 1500* (Don Mills, Ont., 1972); J.R. Miller, *Skyscrapers Hide the Heavens: A History of Indian–White Relations in Canada*, 3rd edn (Toronto, 2000); Olive P. Dickason, *Canada's First Nations: A History of Founding Peoples from Earliest Times*, 3rd edn (Toronto, 2002).

4. A. Romaniuk and V. Piché, 'Natality Estimates for the Canadian Indian by Stable Population Models, 1900–

1969', *Canadian Review of Sociology and Anthropology* 9 (1972): 1–20.

5. Ibid., 19, 7.

6. M.G. Hurlich, 'Historical and Recent Demography of the Algonkians of Northern Ontario', in A.T. Steegman, ed., *Boreal Forest Adaptations: The Northern Algonkian* (New York, 1983), 143–99.

7. A. Romaniuk, 'Modernization and Fertility: The Case of the James Bay Indian', *Canadian Review of Sociology and Anthropology* 11 (1974): 344–59.

8. Grey Owl, *Pilgrims of the Wild* (Toronto, 1982), 163. For recent biographies of Grey Owl, see Jane Billinghurst, *Grey Owl: The Many Faces of Archie Belaney* (Vancouver, 1999), and Armand Ruffo, *Grey Owl: The Mystery of Archie Belaney* (Regina, 1997).

9. Valerie Knowles, *Strangers at Our Gates: Canadian Immigration and Immigration Policy, 1540–1997* (Toronto, 1997), 112.

10. Marjory Harper, *Emigration from Scotland between the Wars: Opportunity or Exile?* (Manchester and New York, 1998), xi.

11. Ibid., 35.

12. Geoffrey Bilson, *The Guest Children: The Story of the British Child Evacuees Sent to Canada during World War II* (Saskatoon, 1988).

13. A.R. Allen, *The Social Passion: Religion and Social Reform in Canada, 1914–1928* (Toronto, 1971).

14. See Claris E. Silcox, *Church Union in Canada: Its Causes and Consequences* (New York, 1933).

15. John Webster Grant, *The Canadian Experience of Church Union* (London, 1967).

16. Patricia Roy, *A White Man's Province: Politicians and Chinese and Japanese Immigrants, 1858–1914* (Vancouver, 1989).

17. Irving Abella and Harold Troper, *None Is Too Many: Canada and the Jews of Europe, 1933–1948* (Toronto, 1982).

18. Frank Peers, *The Politics of Canadian Broadcasting, 1920–1951* (Toronto, 1969).

19. Margaret Prang, 'The Origins of Public Broadcasting in Canada', *Canadian Historical Review* 44 (1965): 1–31.

20. Shirley Render, *Double Cross: The Inside Story of James A. Richardson and Canadian Airways* (Vancouver, 1999).

21. Peter Pigott, *Flying Colours: A History of Commercial Aviation in Canada* (Vancouver, 1997).

22. Rose would also later be among those exposed by Igor Gouzenko's documents as a Russian spy during the war.

23. See Bryan D. Palmer, *Working-Class Experience: Re-thinking the History of Canadian Labour, 1800–1991*, 2nd

edn (Toronto, 1992), 246–7.

24. Irving Abella, *Nationalism, Communism and Canadian Labour: The CIO, the Communist Party of Canada and the Canadian Congress of Labour, 1935–1956* (Toronto, 1973).

25. M. Urquhart and K.A.H. Buckley, eds, *Historical Statistics of Canada*, 2nd edn (Ottawa, 1983), D8–55.

26. Quoted in Ruth Roach Pierson, 'Gender and the Unemployment Insurance Debates in Canada, 1934–1940', *Labour/Le Travail* 25 (1990): 77–103.

27. Quoted in Denyse Baillargeon, *Making Do: Women, Family and Home in Montreal during the Great Depression* (Waterloo, Ont., 1999), 150.

28. Ibid.

29. See also Veronica Strong-Boag, *The New Day Recalled: Lives of Girls and Women in English Canada, 1919–1939* (Toronto, 1988).

30. Quoted in Norah Lewis, 'Physical Perfection for Spiritual Welfare: Health Care for the Urban Child, 1900–1939', in Patricia Rooke et al., eds, *Studies in Childhood History: A Canadian Perspective* (Calgary, 1982), 135.

31. Pierre Berton, *The Dionne Years* (Toronto, 1977).

32. Quoted in Nancy M. Sheehan, 'Indoctrination: Moral Education in the Early Prairie School House', in David Jones et al., eds, *Shaping the Schools of the Canadian West* (Calgary, 1979), 226.

33. Quoted in Thompson with Seager, *Canada, 1922–1939*, 158.

34. Mary Vipond, 'Canadian Nationalism and the Plight of Canadian Magazines in the 1920s', *Canadian Historical Review* 58 (Mar. 1977): 43–63.

35. An unrepresentative footnote to the period is provided by the surprising career of Canada's best-selling fiction writer, 'Frederick W. Dixon' (Leslie McFarlane, 1902–77), who, beginning in 1927, wrote for the Stratemayer Syndicate of New Jersey 89 books in the voluminous Hardy Boys series, the sales of which had reached some 50 million copies by 1982.

36. Quoted in Carl F. Klinck, *Literary History of Canada*, 2nd edn, vol. 2 (Toronto, 1976), 242.

37. Betty Lee, *Love and Whisky: The Story of the Dominion Drama Festival* (Toronto, 1973), 85–7.

38. Toby Gordon Ryan, *Stage Left: Canadian Theatre in the Thirties* (Toronto, 1981).

39. The theatre of the left is virtually ignored in the standard historical work on the DDF, for example.

40. Helmut Kallmann et al., eds, *Encyclopedia of Music in Canada* (Toronto, 1981), 118.

41. Peter Mellen, *The Group of Seven* (Toronto, 1970).

42. Quoted ibid., 174.

43. Ramsay Cook, 'Landscape Painting and National Sentiment in Canada', in *The Maple Leaf Forever: Essays on Nationalism and Politics in Canada*, new edn (Toronto, 1977), 158–79.

44. Laura Brandon, 'The Shattered Landscape: The Great War and the Art of the Group of Seven', *Canadian Military History* 10, 1 (Winter 2001): 58–66.

45. Angela Davis, 'Mary Riter Hamilton: An Artist in No-Man's Land', *The Beaver* 69, 5 (1989): 6–16.

46. Maria Tippett, *Emily Carr: A Biography* (Toronto, 1979); Doris Shadbolt, *Emily Carr* (Toronto, 1990).

47. Quoted in Barry Lord, *The History of Painting in Canada* (Toronto, 1974), 152.

48. Quoted in Harold Kalman, *A History of Canadian Architecture* (Toronto, 1994), 757.

49. Quoted in J. Donald Wilson et al., *Canadian Education: A History* (Scarborough, Ont., 1970), 363.

50. For a good description of the life of a Frontier College teacher in a slightly earlier period, see E.W. Bradwin's *The Bunkhouse Man: A Study of Work and Play in the Camps of Canada, 1903–1914* (Toronto, 1972).

51. Quoted in A.B. McKillop, *Matters of Mind: The University in Ontario, 1791–1951* (Toronto, 1994).

52. Paul Axelrod, *Making a Middle Class: Student Life in English Canada during the Thirties* (Montreal and Kingston, 1990).

12 WORLD WAR II, 1939–1945

1. The best general studies of the war and its aftermath, both fairly old, are Donald Creighton, *The Forked Road: Canada 1939–1957* (Toronto, 1978), and C.P. Stacey, *Arms, Men and Governments: The War Policies of Canada, 1939–1945* (Ottawa, 1970).

2. J.L. Granatstein, *The Ottawa Men: The Civil Service Mandarins 1935–1957* (Toronto, 1982). See also Douglas Owram, *The Government Generation: Canadian Intellectuals and the State, 1900–1945* (Toronto, 1986).

3. Granatstein, *Ottawa Men*, 195–6.

4. On this visit to London, the Prime Minister had the first discussions about the royal tour of George VI and Queen Elizabeth in Canada, which took place in May and June 1939 (with a brief visit to the United States) and greatly strengthened emotional ties to Britain on the eve of war.

5. Irving Abella and Harold Troper, *None Is Too Many: Canada and the Jews of Europe, 1933–1948* (Toronto, 1982), 18.

6. Quoted ibid., 32.

7. Quoted ibid., 46.

8. J.M. Pickersgill and D.F. Forster, eds, *The Mackenzie King Record*, vol. 2 (Toronto, 1968), 90–1.

9. Quoted in Susan Briggs, *The Home Front: War Years in Britain, 1939–1945* (London, 1975), 131.

10. C.P. Stacey, *A Very Double Life: The Private World of Mackenzie King* (Toronto, 1976).

11. Peter Neary, *Newfoundland in the North Atlantic World, 1929–1949* (Kingston and Montreal, 1988), 144–213.

12. Robert Bothwell and William Kilbourne, *C.D. Howe: A Biography* (Toronto, 1979), 152–3.

13. Quoted in F.J. Hatch, *Aerodrome of Democracy: Canada and the British Commonwealth Air Training Plan, 1939–1945* (Ottawa, 1983), 14.

14. Ibid., 15.

15. Stacey, *Arms, Men and Governments*, 488.

16. Ernest Forbes, 'Consolidating Disparity: The Maritimes and the Industrialization of Canada during the Second World War', *Acadiensis* 15 (1986): 3–27.

17. H.D. Woods and Sylvia Ostry, *Labour Policy and Labour Economics in Canada* (Toronto, 1962).

18. Michael D. Stevenson, *Canada's Greatest Wartime Muddle: National Selective Service and the Mobilization of Human Resources during World War II* (Montreal and Kingston, 2001).

19. C.P. Stacey, *Canada and the Age of Conflict: A History of Canadian External Policies*, vol. 2, *1921–1948* (Toronto, 1981), 332–3.

20. See, for example, J.P. Campbell, *Dieppe Revisited: A Documentary Investigation* (London, 1993); B. Greenhous, *Dieppe* (Outrémont, Que., 1993); Brian Villa, *Unauthorized Action: Mountbatten and the Dieppe Raid* (Toronto, 1989).

21. Serge Durflinger, *Fighting from Home: The Second World War in Verdun, Quebec* (Vancouver, 2006).

22. Quoted in J.L. Granatstein and J.M. Hitsman, *Broken Promises: A History of Conscription in Canada* (Toronto, 1979), 221n.

23. J.L. Granatstein, *The Politics of Survival: The Conservative Party of Canada, 1939–1945* (Toronto, 1967), 212–13.

24. Peter Hennessy, *Never Again: Britain, 1945–1951* (London, 1992), 72–7, 122–9.

25. Harry M. Cassidy, *Social Security and Reconstruction in Canada* (Toronto, 1943), 5.

26. Special Committee on Social Security, *Report of the Advisory Committee on Health Insurance* (Ottawa, 1943), 48.

27. Ibid., 2.

28. Reprinted Toronto, 1975.

29. Quoted in Robert Boyce, *Maturing in Hard Times:*

Canada's Department of Finance through the Great Depression (Kingston and Montreal, 1986), 120.

30. Quoted in John C. Bacher, *Keeping to the Marketplace: The Evolution of Canadian Housing Policy* (Montreal and Kingston, 1993), 177.

31. Ibid., 169.

32. Ibid., 172.

33. Ruth Roach Pierson, *'They're Still Women After All': The Second World War and Canadian Womanhood* (Toronto, 1986).

34. Carolyn Gossage, *Greatcoats and Glamour Boots: Canadian Women at War, 1939–1945*, rev. edn (Toronto, 2001).

35. M. Susan Bland, '"Henrietta the Homemaker" and "Rosie the Riveter": Images of Women in Advertising in *Maclean's* Magazine, 1939–50', in Laurel Sefton MacDowell and Ian Radforth, eds, *Canadian Working Class History* (Toronto, 1992), 595–619.

36. Thomas Socknat, *Witness Against War: Pacifism in Canada, 1900–1945* (Toronto, 1987), esp. 211–58.

37. R. Douglas Francis, *Frank H. Underhill: Intellectual Provocateur* (Toronto, 1986), 109–27.

38. Quoted in Ann Sunahara, *The Politics of Racism* (Toronto, 1981), 23.

39. Ken Adachi, *The Enemy That Never Was: A History of the Japanese Canadians* (Toronto, 1976).

40. F.W. Gibson and Barbara Robertson, eds, *Ottawa at War: The Grant Dexter Memoranda, 1939–1945* (Winnipeg, 1994).

41. Quoted in Ted Magder, *Canada's Hollywood: The Canadian State and Feature Films* (Toronto, 1993), 55.

42. Quoted ibid., 55.

43. William R. Young, 'Academics and Social Scientists versus the Press: The Policies of the Bureau of Public Information and the Wartime Information Board, 1939 to 1945', Canadian Historical Association *Historical Papers* (1978): 217–40. For information on Grierson, see Gary Evans, *John Grierson and the National Film Board: The Politics of Wartime Propaganda* (Toronto, 1984).

44. CBC War Effort (1943), quoted in Knowlton Nash, *The Microphone Wars: A History of Triumph and Betrayal at the CBC* (Toronto, 1994), 186.

45. Ibid., 190.

46. Ibid., 191.

47. Quoted in Wilfrid Eggleston, *National Research in Canada: The NRC, 1916–1966* (Toronto, 1976), 125.

48. *Globe and Mail*, 14 Sept. 2002, F9.

49. Quoted in Robert Bothwell, *Nucleus: The History of Atomic Energy of Canada Limited* (Toronto, 1988), 73.

50. United States Department of Agriculture War Food Administration, *Food Consumption Levels in the United States, Canada and the United Kingdom* (Washington, 1944).

51. Quoted in Nash, *Microphone Wars*, 204.

52. Quoted in John Gilmore, *Swinging in Paradise: The Story of Jazz in Montreal* (Toronto, 1988), 92.

53. Quoted ibid., 91.

54. Quoted in Gerald Bedford, *The University of Winnipeg: A History of the Founding Colleges* (Toronto, 1976), 238.

55. Quoted in J.M. Bumsted, *The University of Manitoba: An Illustrated History* (Winnipeg, 2001), 99–100.

56. Quoted in Maria Tippett, *Making Culture: English-Canadian Institutions and the Arts before the Massey Commission* (Toronto, 1990).

57. Ibid., 158–9.

58. See, for example, Alex Colville, *Diary of a War Artist* (Halifax, 1982).

59. Molly Lamb Bobak, *Double Duty: Sketches and Diaries of Molly Lamb Bobak, Canadian War Artist* (Toronto, 1992).

60. Ibid., 166.

61. Quoted in John Holmes, *The Shaping of Peace: Canada and the Search for World Order, 1943–1957*, vol. 1 (Toronto, 1979), 35.

13 CANADA AND WORLD, 1946–1972

1. House of Commons *Debates*, 22 Oct. 1945, 1, 334–7.

2. Quoted in Robert Bothwell and John English, 'Canadian Trade Policy in the Age of American Dominance and British Decline, 1943–1947', *Canadian Review of American Studies* 8 (Spring 1977): 54.

3. Hume Wrong to Vincent Massey, quoted ibid.

4. Quoted in Andrew Rettig, 'Canada's Limited Options, 1943–48: How International and Domestic Factors Shaped a Lesser Power's Policies on Post-War Europe during the Transition to a New World Order', Ph.D. dissertation (Freie Universitat Berlin, 1995), 212.

5. Tom Keating, *Canada and World Order: The Multilateralist Tradition in Canadian Foreign Policy* (Toronto, 1993).

6. John Sawatsky, *Gouzenko: The Untold Story* (Toronto, 1984).

7. Robert Bothwell and J.L. Granatstein, eds, *The Gouzenko Transcripts: The Evidence Presented to the Kellock-Taschereau Royal Commission of 1946* (Ottawa, 1982).

8. C.D. Howe to Combined Policy Committee on 20 Sept. 1949, quoted in James Eayrs, *In Defence of Canada*, vol. 4, *Growing Up Allied* (Toronto, 1980), 236.

9. David J. Bercuson, *Canada and the Birth of Israel: A Study in Canadian Foreign Policy* (Toronto, 1985).

10. Robert Cuff and J.L. Granatstein, 'The Rise and Fall of

Canadian–American Free Trade, 1947–8', *Canadian Historical Review* 58 (Dec. 1977): 459–82.

11. Quoted in Eayrs, *In Defence*, vol. 4, 63.

12. Ibid.

13. Ibid.

14. Document 1 in Eayrs, *In Defence*, vol. 4, 369–70.

15. Quoted ibid., 70.

16. Escott Reid, *Time of Fear and Hope: The Making of the North Atlantic Treaty, 1947–1949* (Toronto, 1977).

17. Ibid., 219–20.

18. L.B. Pearson, *Diplomacy in the Nuclear Age* (Toronto, 1958).

19. L.B. Pearson, *Mike: The Memoirs of the Rt. Hon. Lester B. Pearson*, vol. 2, *1948–1957* (Toronto, 1973), 60.

20. John Holmes, *The Shaping of Peace: Canada and the Search for World Order, 1943–1957*, vol. 2 (Toronto, 1982), 145.

21. Desmond Morton, *A Military History of Canada*, rev. edn (Edmonton, 1990), 234–5; H.F. Wood, *Strange Battleground: The Operations in Korea and Their Effects on the Defence Policy of Canada* (Ottawa, 1966); Denis Stairs, *The Diplomacy of Constraint: Canada, the Korean War, and the United States* (Toronto, 1974).

22. Donald Creighton, *The Forked Road: Canada, 1939–1957* (Toronto, 1976), 233.

23. James Barros, *No Sense of Evil: Espionage, the Case of Herbert Norman* (Toronto, 1986); Roger Brown, *Innocence Is Not Enough: The Life and Death of Herbert Norman* (Vancouver, 1986).

24. Richard Organ et al., *Avro Arrow: The Story of the Avro Arrow from Its Evolution to Its Extinction* (Erin, Ont., 1980); Craig Stewart, *Arrow through the Heart: The Life and Times of Crawford Gordon and the Avro Arrow* (Toronto, 1998); Craig Stewart, *Shutting Down the National Dream: A.V. Roe and the Tragedy of the Avro Arrow* (Toronto, 1988).

25. Knowlton Nash, *Kennedy and Diefenbaker: Fear and Loathing across the Undefended Border* (Toronto, 1990).

26. James Eayrs, *In Defence of Canada*, vol. 5, *Indochina: Roots of Complicity* (Toronto, 1983).

27. Quoted in J.L. Granatstein and Robert Bothwell, *Pirouette: Pierre Trudeau and Canadian Foreign Policy* (Toronto, 1990), 27.

14 PROSPERITY AND GROWTH IN THE POST-WAR WORLD, 1946–1972

1. The two volumes in the Canadian Centenary Series covering this period are Donald Creighton, *The Forked Road: Canada 1939–1957* (Toronto, 1976) and J.L. Granatstein, *Canada 1957–1967: The Years of Uncertainty and Innovation* (Toronto, 1986). Both are much stronger on politics, diplomacy, and constitutional matters than they are on economic ones. But see also Robert Bothwell, Ian Drummond, and John English, *Canada since 1945: Power, Politics and Provincialism*, rev. edn (Toronto, 1989).

2. David Kwavnick, ed., *The Tremblay Report* (Toronto, 1973), 183–4.

3. On Royal Commissions and economic policy, see Barry Anderson, 'Royal Commissions, Economists, and Policy: A Study of the Economic Advisory Process in Post War Canada', Ph.D. dissertation (Duke University, 1978).

4. Canada, Royal Commission on Canada's Economic Prospects, *Report* (Ottawa, 1958), 15.

5. Ibid., 19.

6. James Marsh, ed., *The Canadian Encyclopedia*, 2nd edn, vol. 3 (Edmonton, 1985), 1603.

7. Ed Gould, *Oil: The History of Canada's Oil and Gas Industry* (Saanichton, BC, 1976).

8. Keith Chapman, 'Public Policy and the Development of the Canadian Petrochemical Industry', *British Journal of Canadian Studies* 4, 1 (1989): 12–34.

9. Robert Bothwell, *Nucleus: The History of Atomic Energy of Canada Limited* (Toronto, 1988).

10. Canada, Royal Commission on Canada's Economic Prospects, *Report*, 209.

11. Statistics Canada, *Manufacturing Industries of Canada, 1957* (Ottawa, 1957), section D, 31–206, 5–6. In general, see K.J. Rea, *The Prosperous Years: The Economic History of Ontario, 1939–1975* (Toronto, 1985).

12. For information on Bennett, see David Mitchell, *W.A.C. Bennett and the Rise of British Columbia* (Vancouver, 1983).

13. Jennifer Sussman, *The St. Lawrence Seaway: History and Analysis of a Joint Waterhighway* (Montreal and Washington, DC, 1978).

14. Ironically, the completion of this linkage coincided almost exactly with the ending of the wide acceptance of the Laurentian interpretation of Canadian historical development.

15. David W. Monaghan, *Canada's New Main Street: The Trans-Canada Highway as Idea and Reality, 1912–56* (Ottawa, 2002).

16. H.D. Woods and Sylvia Ostry, *Labour Policy and Labour Economics in Canada* (Toronto, 1962).

17. Canada, *Annual Report on Labour Organization in Canada*

in 1972 (Ottawa, 1973), xxiv–xxv.

18. That asbestos was commonly used (in insulation and roofing) without concern for the very serious health hazards associated with it (especially lung disease) was indicative of attitudes towards health and environment in these years.

19. Fraser Isbister, 'Asbestos 1949', in Irving Abella, ed., *On Strike: Six Key Labour Struggles in Canada, 1919–1949* (Toronto, 1974), 163–96.

20. See André Langevin's novel translated as *Dust over the City* (1953), which gives a graphic description of the hazards in another city, Thetford Mines.

21. Quoted in Susan Mann Trokimenkoff, *The Dream of Nation: A Social and Intellectual History of Quebec* (Toronto, 1982), 292. See also Pierre Elliott Trudeau, ed., *La Grève d l'amiante: Un Étage de la revolution industrielle au Québec* (Montreal, 1956), translated as *The Asbestos Strike* (Toronto, 1974).

22. Wallace Clement, *Hardrock Mining: Industrial Relations and Technological Changes at Inco* (Toronto, 1981).

23. John Stanton, *Life and Death of a Union: The History of the Canadian Seamen's Union, 1936–1949* (Toronto, 1978).

24. Irving Abella, *Nationalism, Communism, and Canadian Labour* (Toronto, 1973).

25. Quoted in Bryan D. Palmer, *Working-Class Experience: Rethinking the History of Canadian Labour, 1800–1991* (Toronto, 1992), 317.

26. Canada, *Annual Report on Labour Organization in Canada in 1946* (Ottawa, 1948).

27. Trevor Levere, 'What Is Canadian about Science in Canadian History?' in R.A. Jarrell and N.R. Ball, eds, *Science, Technology, and Canadian History* (Waterloo, Ont., 1980), 14–23.

28. James Guillet, 'Nationalism and Canadian Science', in Peter Russell, ed., *Nationalism in Canada* (Toronto, 1966), 221–34.

29. G. Bruce Doern, *Science and Politics in Canada* (Montreal and London, 1972), 6.

30. C. Freeman and A. Young, *The Research and Development Efforts in Western Europe, North America and the Soviet Union* (Paris, 1965).

31. Canada, Royal Commission on Government Organization, vol. 4, report no. 23, 'Scientific Research and Development' (Ottawa, 1963).

32. Canada, House of Commons, *Debates*, vol. 3 (1966), 2849.

33. J.J. Brown, *Ideas in Exile: A History of Canadian Invention* (Toronto, 1967), 287–9.

34. Kari Levitt, *Silent Surrender: The Multinational Corpor-*

ation in Canada (Toronto, 1970), 127–35.

35. Canada, Royal Commission on Canada's Economic Prospects, *Report*, 403.

36. Quoted in Walter Gordon, *A Political Memoir* (Toronto, 1977), 64.

37. Kwavnick, *The Tremblay Report*, 45.

38. It could be argued that the bilingualism and biculturalism policies of the federal government in the 1960s were a belated response to a somewhat outdated French-Canadian analysis of federalism that emphasized cultural rather than economic autonomy.

39. Ibid., 166.

40. In 1961 the Columbia River Treaty was signed by Canada and the United States for the co-operative development of the Columbia River. The federal government initially opposed the terms of the sale, agreed to by British Columbia, of power benefits to the US, and the treaty did not come into effect until 1964.

41. W.T. Easterbrook and Hugh G.J. Aitken, *Canadian Economic History* (Toronto, 1956).

42. In general, see Stephen Azzi, *Walter Gordon and the Rise of Canadian Nationalism* (Montreal and Kingston, 1999).

43. Gordon, *A Political Memoir*, 57.

44. Ibid., 64.

45. Ibid., quoting Irving Brecher and S.S. Reisman, 'Canada–United States Economic Relations', a draft report prepared for the Commission.

46. See Levitt, *Silent Surrender*; see also Gordon Laxer, *Open for Business: The Roots of American Ownership in Canada* (Toronto, 1989).

47. Cited in Robert Laxer, *Canada's Unions* (Toronto, 1976).

15 THE ERA OF LIBERAL CONSENSUS, 1946–1972

1. R.M. Campbell, *Grand Illusions: The Politics of the Keynesian Experience in Canada, 1945–75* (Peterborough, Ont., 1988).

2. Robert Bryce, *Maturing in Hard Times* (Montreal and Kingston, 1986).

3. Despite the Mulroney/Campbell interlude from 1984–93, it is at least arguable that the national tendency still remains.

4. Generally useful on the shape of modern Canadian politics is David Bell and Lorne Tepperman, *The Roots of Disunity: A Look at Canadian Political Culture* (Toronto, 1979). For the recent period, see also Richard Simeon and Ian Robinson, *State, Society and the Development of Canadian Federalism* (Toronto, 1990), and Sylvia Bashevkin, *True Patriot Love: The Politics of Canadian*

Nationalism (Toronto, 1991).

5. Federal election results to 1968 are available in J. Murray Beck, *Pendulum of Power: Canada's Federal Elections* (Scarborough, Ont., 1968).

6. *Ottawa Citizen*, 4 April 1963.

7. Trudeau managed this feat of public image despite the fact that he was almost 50 years old and only five years younger than his main opponent.

8. *Toronto Star*, 29 June 1968.

9. J.E. Hodgetts and O.P. Dwivedi, 'The Growth of Government Employees in Canada', *Canadian Public Administration* 11 (1969): 224–38.

10. J.E. Hodgetts, 'The Changing Nature of the Public Service', in L.D. Musolf, ed., *The Changing Public Service* (Berkeley, 1968), 7–18.

11. Pierre Elliott Trudeau, 'The Practice and Theory of Federalism', in Michael Oliver, ed., *Social Purpose for Canada* (Toronto, 1961).

12. Richard Simeon, *Federal–Provincial Diplomacy: The Making of Recent Policy in Canada* (Toronto, 1972).

13. Philip Resnick, *The Politics of Resentment: British Columbia Regionalism and Canadian Unity* (Vancouver, 2000).

14. As the United States so well demonstrated in the 1950s and 1960s, 'civil rights' cases, decided by courts instead of legislatures, could produce major revisions in the fabric of the nation's legal and social systems.

15. Quoted in Peter Neary, *Newfoundland in the North Atlantic World, 1929–1949* (Montreal and Kingston, 1988), 314.

16. On the ideological complexities of Canadian politics, see W. Christian and C. Campbell, *Political Parties and Ideologies in Canada*, 3rd edn (Toronto, 1990).

17. Campbell, *Grand Illusions*.

18. J.R.H. Wilbur, ed., *The Bennett New Deal* (Toronto, 1968).

19. Frederick W. Gibson and Barbara Robertson, eds, *Ottawa at War: The Grant Dexter Memoranda, 1939–45* (Winnipeg, 1994), 405–6.

20. Alvin Finkel, 'Paradise Postponed: A Re-examination of the Green Book Proposals of 1945', *Journal of the Canadian Historical Association* 4 (1993): 120–42.

21. For the Regina Manifesto, see Michiel Horn, 'Frank Underhill's Early Drafts of the Regina Manifesto 1933', *Canadian Historical Review* 54, 4 (1973): 393–418.

22. Jeff Keshan, 'Getting It Right the Second Time Around: The Reintegration of Canadian Veterans of World War II', in Peter Neary and J.L. Granatstein, eds, *The Veteran's Charter and Post-World War II Canada* (Montreal and Kingston, 1998), 67–8.

23. Peter Neary, 'Canadian Universities and Canadian Veterans of World War II', in Neary and Granatstein, *The Veteran's Charter*, 139.

24. Robin Harris, *A History of Higher Education in Canada, 1663–1960* (Toronto, 1976), 459–60.

25. John C. Bacher, *Keeping to the Marketplace: The Evolution of Canadian Housing Policy* (Montreal and Kingston, 1993), 179–86.

26. Kenneth Bryden, *Old Age Pensions and Policy-Making in Canada* (Montreal and London, 1974).

27. Dennis Guest, *The Emergence of Social Security in Canada* (Vancouver, 1980), 157.

28. Robin F. Badgley and Samuel Wolfe, *Doctors' Strike: Medical Care and Conflict in Saskatchewan* (Toronto, 1967).

29. C. Howard Shillington, *The Road to Medicare in Canada* (Toronto, 1972).

30. Gerald J. Black, *Canada Goes Metric* (Toronto, 1974).

31. For example, Pierre Vallières's *White Niggers of America* (Toronto, 1971).

32. For a contemporary discussion of minorities, see Jean Leonard Elliott, 'Minority Groups: A Canadian Perspective', in Jean Leonard Elliott, ed., *Native Peoples* (Toronto, 1971), 1–14.

33. Quoted in E. Palmer Patterson, *The Canadian Indian: A History Since 1500* (Toronto, 1972), 177.

34. H.B. Hawthorn, ed., *A Survey of the Contemporary Indians of Canada: Political, Educational Need and Policies*, vol. 1 (Ottawa, 1966).

35. James Walker, 'The Indian in Canadian Historical Writing', Canadian Historical Association *Historical Papers* (1971): 21–47.

36. J. Rick Ponting and Roger Gibbons, *Out of Irrelevance: A Socio-Political Introduction to Indian Affairs in Canada* (Toronto, 1980).

37. Canada, *A Statement of the Government of Canada on Indian Policy* (Ottawa, 1969), tabled in the House of Commons on 25 June 1969.

38. Quoted in Patterson, *The Canadian Indian*, 178.

39. Derek G. Smith, ed., *Canadian Indians and the Law: Selected Documents, 1663–1972* (Ottawa, 1973); Sally M. Weaver, *Making Canadian Indian Policy: The Hidden Agenda, 1968–70* (Toronto, 1981); Bradford Morse, ed., *Aboriginal Peoples and the Law: Indian, Métis, and Inuit Rights in Canada* (Ottawa, 1989).

40. Canada, *A Statement*, 5.

41. Quoted in R.J. Macdonald, *Native Rights in Canada* (Toronto, 1970), Appendix 8.

42. Harold Cardinal, *The Unjust Society: The Tragedy of*

Canada's Indians (Edmonton, 1969), 170.

43. Donald H. Clairmont and Dennis William Magill, *Africville: The Life and Death of a Canadian Black Community* (Toronto, 1974).

44. Canada, *Report of the Royal Commission on the Status of Women in Canada* (Ottawa, 1970), vii.

45. Quoted in Myrna Kostash, *Long Way from Home: The Story of the Sixties Generation in Canada* (Toronto, 1980), 169.

46. Ibid., 171.

47. Gary Kinsman, *The Regulation of Desire: Sexuality in Canada* (Montreal, 1987).

48. John Sawatsky, *Men in the Shadows: The RCMP Security Service* (Toronto, 1980), 124–32; the 'fruit machine' was supposed to do this by recording the eye movements of people viewing a series of images, some of which were pornographic.

49. John Saywell, *Quebec 70: A Documentary Narrative* (Toronto, 1971), 152.

16 QUEBEC AND CONFEDERATION, 1945–1972

1. Jean-François Cardin, *Comprendre Octobre 1970: le FLQ, la crise et le syndicalism* (Montreal, 1990); John Saywell, *Quebec 70: A Documentary Narrative* (Toronto, 1971).

2. Quoted from Mordecai Richler, 'The North American Pattern', in Al Purdy, ed., *The New Romans: Candid Canadian Opinions of the U.S.* (Edmonton, 1967), 15.

3. *La Presse*, 3 Oct. 1970, quoted in Michel Vastel, *Bourassa*, trans. Hubert Bauch (Toronto, 1988), 49.

4. Quoted from transcript reprinted in Saywell, *Quebec 70*, 73.

5. Ibid., 152.

6. Louis Fournier, *FLQ: histoire d'un mouvement clandestin* (Montreal, 1982).

7. Herbert Quinn, *The Union Nationale: Quebec Nationalism from Duplessis to Lesage*, 2nd edn (Toronto, 1979).

8. *Le Devoir*, cited in Michael D. Behiels, 'Quebec: Social Transformation and Ideological Renewal, 1940–1976', in Michael D. Behiels, ed., *Quebec since 1945: Selected Readings* (Toronto, 1987), 22.

9. José E. Igartua, *The Other Quiet Revolution: National Identities in English Canada, 1945–1971* (Vancouver, 2006).

10. Horace Miner, *St. Denis: A French-Canadian Parish* (Chicago, 1939); Horace Miner, 'A New Epoch in Rural Quebec', *American Journal of Sociology* 56, 1 (July 1950): 1–10.

11. Quoted in Gérard Dion, 'The Church and the Conflict in the Asbestos Industry', in Trudeau, ed., *The Asbestos Strike*, 211.

12. The unexpected resignation of Mgr Charbonneau shortly after the strike was widely interpreted as one forced by his superiors because of his stand in favour of the strike. This interpretation was given wider circulation by John Thomas McDonough's well-known play of 1971, *Charbonneau et le Chef*, which characterized the strike as a power struggle between Duplessis and Charbonneau, in which the archbishop was betrayed by the Church (to audience cries of 'Judas!').

13. Pierre Trudeau, who edited an account of the strike, translated in 1974 as *The Asbestos Strike*, saw the strike as evidence of the evil of traditional Quebec nationalism.

14. Michael D. Behiels, *Prelude to Quebec's Quiet Revolution: Liberalism versus Neo-Nationalism, 1945–1960* (Montreal and Kingston, 1985).

15. For an example, see Pierre Vallières, *White Niggers of America* (Toronto, 1971).

16. Quoted in Behiels, *Prelude*, 109.

17. Pierre Elliott Trudeau, 'Politique fonctionnelle I', *Cité libre* 1 (June 1950), quoted in Behiels, *Prelude*, 69.

18. Dale C. Thomson, *Jean Lesage and the Quiet Revolution* (Toronto, 1984).

19. Mark Renaud, 'Quebec's New Middle Class in Search of Social Hegemony: Causes and Political Consequences', in Behiels, *Quebec since 1945*, 48–79.

20. For information on Laurendeau, see Philip Stratford, ed., *André Laurendeau, Witness for Quebec: Essays* (Toronto, 1973); Denis Monière, *André Laurendeau et le destin d'un people* (Montreal, 1983).

21. Jean-Paul Desbiens, *The Impertinences of Brother Anonymous* (Toronto, 1962), 29.

22. Jean-Paul Desbiens, *For Pity's Sake: The Return of Brother Anonymous* (Toronto, 1965), 72ff.

23. Ralph Peter Guntzel, 'The Confédération des Syndicats Nationaux (CSN), the Idea of Independence, and the Sovereigntist Movement, 1960–1980', *Labour/Le Travail* 31 (Spring 1993): 145–73.

24. The Clio Collective, *Quebec Women: A History* (Toronto, 1987), 304–7.

25. Quebec, *Report of the Commission of Inquiry on the Position of the French Language and on Language Rights in Quebec*, 3 vols (Quebec, 1972).

26. See, for example, the pieces collected in Pierre Elliott Trudeau, *Federalism and the French Canadians* (Toronto, 1980).

27. Frank Scott and Michael Oliver, eds, *Quebec States Her Case* (Toronto, 1964).

28. The characterization is Gérard Bergeron's in 'The Québécois State Under Canadian Federalism', in Behiels, *Quebec since 1945*, 178.

29. Fulton offered to entrench all existing provincial powers, as well as language, education, and the amending procedure itself, but Quebec wanted unemployment insurance included as well. Fulton-Favreau offered further concessions to Quebec and pension schemes provided an additional element of controversy.

30. Pierre Godin, *Daniel Johnson*, 2 vols (Montreal, 1980); Robert Comeau et al., eds, *Daniel Johnson: Rêve d'égalité et projet d'indépendance* (Sillery, Que., 1991).

31. See D.V. Smiley, 'Canadian Federalism and the Resolution of Federal–Provincial Conflict', in Frederick Vaughan et al., eds, *Contemporary Issues in Canadian Politics* (Scarborough, Ont., 1970), 48–66; W.R. Lederman, 'The Limitations of Co-operative Federalism', *Canadian Bar Review* 45 (1967).

32. G.F.G. Stanley, *The Story of Canada's Flag: A Historical Sketch* (Toronto, 1965).

33. Robert Fulford, *This Was Expo* (Toronto, 1968). See also Helen Davies, 'The Politics of Participation: A Study of Canada's Centennial Celebration', Ph.D. dissertation (University of Manitoba, 1999); Pierre Berton, *1967: The Last Good Year* (Toronto, 1997).

34. See J.F. Bosher, *The Gaullist Attack on Canada, 1967–1997* (Montreal, 1999).

35. Canada, *Report of the Royal Commission on Bilingualism and Biculturalism*, vol. 4 (Ottawa, 1970), Appendix I.

36. The use of the term 'British' in this context was, of course, incorrect, since Great Britain did not exist before 1707.

37. Canada, *Report of the Royal Commission on Bilingualism and Biculturalism*, vol. 4, 4.

38. Ibid., vol. 1, xxvii.

39. Ibid., vol. 4, 10.

40. Chantal Hébert, *Le Burlesque au Québec: un divertissement populaire* (Montreal, 1981).

41. Quoted in Jonathan M. Weiss, *French-Canadian Theater* (Boston, 1986), 25.

42. Published in English in Vancouver in 1974. See Renate Usmiani, *Michel Tremblay* (Vancouver, 1982).

43. Quoted ibid., 149.

44. Jean Daigle, ed., *The Acadians of the Maritimes* (Moncton, 1982).

45. Among the useful works about Quebec are: Alain G. Gagnon, ed., *Quebec: State and Society* (Toronto, 1984); Denis Monière, *Ideologies in Quebec: The Historical Development* (Toronto, 1981); Dominique Clift, *Quebec:*

Nationalism in Crisis (Montreal and Kingston, 1982); Léandre Bergeron, *Petit manuel d'histoire du Québec*, translated into English as *The History of Quebec: A Patriote's Handbook* (Toronto, 1971); Herbert Guindon, *Quebec Society: Tradition, Modernity, and Nationhood* (Toronto, 1988); Marcel Rioux and Yves Martin, eds, *French-Canadian Society*, vol. 1 (Toronto, 1964); Marcel Rioux, *Quebec in Question* (Toronto, 1971); various works by Kenneth McRoberts.

46. Sheila McLeod Arnopoulos and Dominique Clift, *The English Fact in Quebec* (Montreal, 1980).

17 THE NEW SUBURBAN SOCIETY, 1946–1972

1. Veronica Strong-Boag, 'Home Dreams: Women and the Suburban Experience in Canada, 1945–60', *Canadian Historical Review* 72 (1991): 471–504; S.D. Clark, *The Suburban Society* (Toronto, 1966).

2. In general, see Doug Owram, *Born at the Right Time: A History of the Baby-Boom Generation* (Toronto, 1996).

3. Alison Prentice et al., *Canadian Women: A History* (Toronto, 1988), 311.

4. M.C. Urquhart and K.A.H. Buckley, *Historical Statistics of Canada* (Toronto, 1965), 42.

5. Ben Wicks, *Promise You'll Take Care of My Daughter: The Remarkable War Brides of World War II* (Toronto, 1992).

6. Anthony Richmond, *Immigrants and Ethnic Groups in Metropolitan Toronto* (Toronto, 1967), 4.

7. T. Kue Young, *Health Care and Cultural Change: The Indian Experience in the Central Subarctic* (Toronto, 1988).

8. John Porter, *The Vertical Mosaic: An Analysis of Social Class and Power in Canada* (Toronto, 1965).

9. Canada, *Report of the Royal Commission on Bilingualism and Biculturalism, Book III* (Ottawa, 1969), Part 1, Chapters 1 and 3.

10. Richard J. Joy, *Languages in Conflict: The Canadian Experience* (reprinted Toronto, 1972), 9.

11. One threatened demolition, that of Toronto's Old City Hall, was stopped in the 1960s as a result of a public outcry.

12. Quoted in Clark, *The Suburban Society*, 68.

13. Ibid., 110.

14. Robert Fischman, *Beyond Utopias: The Rise and Fall of Suburbia* (New York, 1987), 9.

15. Paul-André Linteau, 'Canadian Suburbanization in a North American Context: Does the Border Make a Difference?', *Journal of Urban History* 13 (May 1987): 252–74.

16. For earlier suburbs, see John C. Weaver, 'From Land Assembly to Social Maturity: The Suburban Life of Westdale (Hamilton), Ontario, 1911–1951', in G. Stelter and A. Artibise, eds, *Shaping the Urban Landscape: Aspects of the Canadian City Building Process* (Ottawa, 1982), 321–55; David B. Hanna, 'Creation of an Early Victorian Suburb in Montreal', *Urban History Review* 9 (1980): 38–64.

17. Valerie Kovnick, *Roughing It in the Suburbs: Reading Chatelaine Magazine in the Fifties and Sixties* (Toronto, 2000).

18. Terrence Murphy and Roberto Perin, eds, *A Concise History of Christianity in Canada* (Toronto, 1996), 353–5.

19. John Webster Grant, *The Church in the Canadian Era: The First Century of Confederation* (Toronto, 1975), 155.

20. John R. Seeley, R. Alexander Sim, and Elizabeth W. Loosley, *Crestwood Heights: A North American Suburb* (Toronto, 1956), 139.

21. Quoted ibid., 148.

22. Canada, Department of National Health and Welfare, *Canadian Mother and Child*, 3rd edn (Ottawa, 1968), 35–6.

23. Ibid., 37.

24. Benjamin Spock, *The Pocket Book of Baby and Child Care* (New York, 1948), 195.

25. Melinda McCracken, *Memories Are Made of This: What It Was Like to Grow Up in the Fifties* (Toronto, 1975), 72.

26. Seeley et al., *Crestwood Heights*, 111.

27. Pierre Vallières, *White Niggers of America* (Toronto, 1971), 98.

28. Ibid., 100.

29. J. Donald Wilson et al., *Canadian Education: A History* (Scarborough, 1970); C.E. Phillips, *The Development of Education in Canada* (Toronto, 1957).

30. Owram, *Born at the Right Time*; John Kettle, *The Big Generation* (Toronto, 1980), esp. 56–89.

31. See, for example, the arguments in C.E. Phillips, *Public Secondary Education in Canada* (Toronto, 1955).

32. J.E. Cheal, *Investment in Canadian Youth: An Analysis of Input-Output Differences among Canadian Provincial School Systems* (Toronto, 1963).

33. Kettle, *The Big Generation*, 61.

34. Seeley et al., *Crestwood Heights*, 241.

35. Ibid., 226.

36. *Living and Learning: The Report of the Provincial Committee on Aims and Objectives of Education in the Schools of Ontario* (Toronto, 1968), 75.

37. Ibid., 47.

38. Paul Axelrod, *Scholars and Dollars: Politics, Economics,* and the Universities of Ontario, 1945–1980 (Toronto, 1982), 177–202.

39. Seeley et al., *Crestwood Heights*, 241.

40. Verner Smitheram, 'Development and Debate over School Consolidation', in Smitheram et al., eds, *The Garden Transformed: Prince Edward Island, 1945–80* (Charlottetown, 1982), 177–202.

41. Robert T. Handy, *A History of the Churches in the United States and Canada* (New York, 1977), 409–27; Terrence Murphy and Roberto Perin, eds, *A Concise History of Christianity in Canada* (Toronto, 1996), 361–70.

42. Canada, Commission of Inquiry into the Non-Medical Use of Drugs, *Interim Report* (Ottawa, 1970), especially 503–26.

43. Canada, *Proceedings of the Special Joint Committee of the Senate and House of Commons on Divorce* (Ottawa, 1967), 1515–16.

44. Myrna Kostash, *Long Way from Home: The Story of the Sixties Generation in Canada* (Toronto, 1980).

45. Quoted in Dennis Forsythe, ed., *Let the Niggers Burn: The Sir George Williams University Affair and Its Caribbean Aftermath* (Montreal, 1971), 9.

46. Quoted in Kostash, *Long Way from Home*, 250.

18 THE BEGINNINGS OF MODERN CANADIAN CULTURAL POLICY, 1945–1972

1. David Kwavnick, ed., *The Tremblay Report: Report of the Royal Commission of Inquiry on Constitutional Problems* (Toronto, 1973), 8.

2. Canada, *Report of the Royal Commission on Bilingualism and Biculturalism*, vol. 1 (Ottawa, 1969), xxi.

3. Kwavnick, *The Tremblay Report*, 12.

4. Harold Innis, *Empire and Communications* (Toronto, 1950); Innis, *The Bias of Communication* (Toronto, 1951).

5. Harold Innis, *Changing Concepts of Time* (Toronto, 1952), 18–19.

6. *Explorations: Studies in Culture and Communication* 2 (Apr. 1954): 6.

7. It first appeared in book form in McLuhan's *Understanding Media: The Extension of Mass Man* (New York, 1964), in which he discusses how life and culture were being shaped by the new electronic communications technologies.

8. Kwavnick, *The Tremblay Report*, 14.

9. For example, W.L. Morton, *The Canadian Identity* (Toronto, 1961); Malcolm Ross, ed., *Our Sense of Identity: A Book of Canadian Essays* (Toronto, 1954).

10. J. Russell Harper, *People's Art: Native Art in Canada* (Ottawa, 1973); Harper, *A People's Art: Primitive, Native, Provincial, and Folk Painting in Canada* (Toronto, 1974).

11. See, for example, the critics in Julian Park, ed., *The Culture of Contemporary Canada* (Toronto, 1957).

12. Betty Lee, *Love and Whisky: The Story of the Dominion Drama Festival* (Toronto, 1973).

13. Quoted in Maria Tippett, *Making Culture: English-Canadian Institutions and the Arts before the Massey Commission* (Toronto, 1990), 176.

14. Ibid., 180–1.

15. John Archer, *Saskatchewan: A History* (Saskatoon, 1980), 290–2.

16. Quoted in Tippett, *Making Culture*, 182.

17. Ibid., 184.

18. Canada, *Report of the Royal Commission on National Development in the Arts, Letters and Sciences* (Toronto, 1951), 8. In general, see Paul Litt, *The Muses, The Masses, and the Massey Commission* (Toronto, 1992).

19. *Report of the Royal Commission on National Development*, 305.

20. Ibid., 163.

21. Ibid., 64.

22. See J.M. Bumsted, 'Canada and American Culture in the 1950s', in J.M. Bumsted, ed., *Interpreting Canada's Past*, vol. 2 (Toronto, 1986), 401–2.

23. Dallas W. Smythe, 'Canadian Television and Sound Radio Programmes', Appendix 14 to Canada, *Report of the Royal Commission on Broadcasting* (Ottawa, 1957).

24. Bumsted, 'Canada and American Culture', 405 (table).

25. Canada, *Report of the Royal Commission on Broadcasting*, 8.

26. Ibid., 10, 11.

27. E. Austin Weir, *The Struggle for National Broadcasting* (Toronto and Montreal, 1965), 372.

28. Donald Macintosh, with Tom Bedecki and C.E.S. Franks, *Sport and Politics in Canada: Federal Government Involvement since 1961* (Montreal and Kingston, 1987).

29. Quoted in Don Morrow et al., *A Concise History of Sport in Canada* (Toronto, 1989), 328.

30. Scott Young, *War on Ice: Canada in International Hockey* (Toronto, 1976).

31. Jack Ludwig, *Hockey Night in Moscow* (Toronto, 1972); Harry Sinden, *Hockey Showdown: The Canada–Russia Hockey Series* (Toronto, 1972); Scott Morrison, *The Days Canada Stood Still: Canada vs USSR* (Toronto, 1989). See also Neil Earle, 'Hockey as Canadian Popular Culture: Team Canada 1972, Television and the Canadian Identity', in Joan Nicks and Jeannette Sloniowski, eds,

Slippery Pastimes: Reading the Popular in Canadian National Culture (Waterloo, Ont., 2002), 321–43.

32. Quoted in Ted Magder, *Canada's Hollywood: The Canadian State and Feature Films* (Toronto, 1993), 133–4.

33. Ibid., 149.

34. G.M. Story et al., *Dictionary of Newfoundland English*, 2nd edn (Toronto, 1990).

35. James Overton, 'Towards a Critical Analysis of Neo-Nationalism in Newfoundland', in R. Brym and R.J. Sacouman, eds, *Underdevelopment and Social Movements in Atlantic Canada* (Toronto, 1979), 219–49.

36. Quoted in Richard Handler, *Nationalism and the Politics of Culture in Quebec* (Madison, Wis., 1988), 103.

37. Quoted ibid., 105.

19 THE MAKING OF CANADIAN CULTURE, 1945–1972

1. David Kwavnick, ed., *The Tremblay Report: Report of the Royal Commission of Inquiry on Constitutional Problems* (Toronto, 1973), 12.

2. Hugo McPherson, 'Fiction, 1940–1960', in Carl F. Klinck, ed., *Literary History of Canada* (Toronto, 1965), 694.

3. *Tamarack Review* 2 (Winter 1957): 13, 17.

4. Mordecai Richler, 'The Uncertain World', in George Woodcock, ed., *The Sixties: Writers and Writing of the Decade* (Vancouver, 1969), 27.

5. Margaret Laurence, 'Ten Years' Sentence', ibid., 9.

6. Northrop Frye, 'Conclusion', in Klinck, *Literary History*, 821, 849.

7. Woodcock, *The Sixties*, 8.

8. 'Letters in Canada, 1959', in Northrop Frye, *The Bush Garden: Essays on the Canadian Imagination* (Toronto, 1971), 126.

9. Edmund Wilson, *O Canada* (New York, 1965).

10. Ben-Z. Shek, *French-Canadian and Québécois Novels* (Toronto, 1991).

11. Claire Martin, *In an Iron Glove*, trans. Philip Stratford (Toronto, 1968).

12. Quoted in Ann Davis, *Frontiers of Our Dreams: Quebec Painting in the 1940s and 1950s* (Winnipeg, 1979), 18.

13. Translations are from Dennis Reid, *A Concise History of Canadian Painting* (Toronto, 1988), 234–5. The complete text of *Refus global* is reproduced in facsimile form in *Paul-Émile Borduas: Écrits/Writings* (Halifax, 1978), published by the Press of the Nova Scotia College of Art and Design.

14. Quoted in Davis, *Frontiers*, 35.

15. Reid, *Concise History*, 247–72.

16. I am indebted for the theoretical distinctions in this paragraph to Janet C. Berlo and Ruth B. Phillips, *Native North American Art* (New York, 1998).

17. Wilson Duff, *Arts of the Raven* (Vancouver, 1967). In general, see Peter L. Macnair et al., *The Legacy: Tradition and Innovation in Northwest Coast Indian Art* (Vancouver, 1984).

18. Quoted in Lister Sinclair and Jack Pollock, *The Art of Norval Morrisseau* (Toronto, 1979), 26.

19. For a different interpretation of this same development, see Carl Berger, *The Writing of Canadian History: Aspects of English-Canadian Historical Writing: 1900 to 1970* (Toronto, 1976; 2nd edn, 1986).

20. Michael Kammen, *American Culture, American Tastes: Social Change and the 20th Century* (New York, 1999).

21. Melinda McCracken, *Memories Are Made of This: What It Was Like to Grow Up in the Fifties* (Toronto, 1975).

22. W.L. Morton, *The Canadian Identity* (Toronto, 1961), 81.

23. Vincent Massey, *On Being Canadian* (Toronto, 1948), 31.

24. Kirwan Cox, 'Hollywood's Empire in Canada: The Majors and the Mandarins through the Years', *Cinema Canada* 22 (Oct. 1975).

25. Pierre Berton, *Hollywood's Canada: The Americanization of Our National Image* (Toronto, 1975), 169–70.

26. Quoted in S.M. Crean, *Who's Afraid of Canadian Culture* (Don Mills, Ont., 1976), 90.

27. Rick Salutin, 'The NFB Red Scare', *Weekend Magazine*, 23 Sept. 1978. For an extensive account of the NFB purge, see Mark Kristmanson, *Plateaus of Freedom: Nationality, Culture, and State Security in Canada, 1940–1960* (Toronto, 2003), especially 49–85.

28. Quoted in Berton, *Hollywood's Canada*, 172.

29. Ibid., 171.

30. J.M. Bumsted, 'Developing a Canadian Disaster Relief Policy: The 1950 Manitoba Flood', *Canadian Historical Review* 68 (1987): 347–73.

31. Berton, *Hollywood's Canada*, 187.

32. Quoted ibid., 190.

33. Quoted ibid., 191.

34. Quoted in Ted Magder, *Canada's Hollywood: The Canadian State and Feature Films* (Toronto, 1993), 101.

35. David Clandfield, *Canadian Film: Perspectives on Canadian Culture* (Toronto, 1987), 87ff.

36. J.M. Bumsted, 'Canada and American Culture in the 1950s', in J.M. Bumsted, ed., *Interpreting Canada's Past*, vol. 2 (Toronto, 1986), 405.

37. For Canadian television, see Paul Rutherford, *When Television Was Young: Primetime Canada, 1952–1967* (Toronto, 1990).

38. Mary Jane Miller, *Turn Up the Content: CBC Television Drama since 1952* (Vancouver, 1987); Mary Jane Miller, ed., *Rewind and Search: Conversations with the Makers and Decision-Makers of CBC Television Drama* (Montreal and Kingston, 1996).

20 THE COLLAPSE OF THE LIBERAL CONSENSUS, 1972–1991

1. Joan Vance, *An Analysis of the Costs and Benefits of Public Lotteries: The Canadian Experience* (Lewiston, Queenston, and Lampeter, 1989).

2. Brian Hutchinson, *Betting the House: Winners, Losers and the Politics of Canada's Gambling Obsession* (Toronto, 1999).

3. Robin Kelley, *First Nations Gambling Policy in Canada* (Calgary, 2001).

4. For a discussion of the beginnings of the energy crisis, see John Erik Fossum, *Oil, the State, and Federalism: The Rise and Demise of Petro-Canada as a Statist Impulse* (Toronto, 1997), 25–72.

5. John Saywell, *The Rise of the Parti Québécois, 1967–1976* (Toronto, 1977), 72–105.

6. Richard Gwyn, *The Northern Magus* (Toronto, 1980); other biographies and studies of Trudeau; Christina McCall-Newman, *Grits: An Intimate Portrait of the Liberal Party* (Toronto, 1983).

7. Jeffery Simpson, *Discipline of Power: The Conservative Interlude and the Liberal Restoration* (Toronto, 1980).

8. Charles Lynch, *Race for the Rose: Election 1984* (Toronto, 1984); Greg Weston, *Reign of Error: The Inside Story of John Turner's Troubled Leadership* (Toronto, 1988).

9. Geoffrey Stevens, *Stanfield* (Toronto, 1973).

10. David L. Humphreys, *Joe Clark: A Portrait* (Don Mills, Ont., 1979).

11. Werner Troyer, *200 Days: Joe Clark in Power* (Toronto, 1980).

12. Simpson, *Discipline of Power*.

13. Among recent political leaders in Canada, only Pierre Trudeau has drawn more attention from biographers than Mulroney. In Mulroney's case, most of the writing has been unflattering. See, for example, Linda McQuaig, *The Quick and the Dead: Brian Mulroney, Big Business, and the Seduction of Canada* (Toronto, 1992); Michel Grattan, *'So What Are the Boys Saying?' An Inside Look at Mulroney in Power* (Toronto, 1987); John Sawatsky, *Mulroney: The Politics of Ambition* (Toronto, 1991); Jeffrey Brooke, *Breaking Faith: The Mulroney Legacy of Deceit, Destruction*

and Disunity (Toronto, 1992); Claire Hoy, *Friends in High Places: Politics and Patronage in the Mulroney Government* (Toronto, 1987). But see also Rae Murphy et al., *Brian Mulroney: The Boy from Baie-Comeau* (Toronto, 1984), and L. Ian MacDonald, *Mulroney: The Making of the Prime Minister* (Toronto, 1984).

14. David Lewis, *The Good Fight: Political Memoirs, 1919–1958* (Toronto, 1981).

15. Judy Steed, *Ed Broadbent: The Pursuit of Power* (Markham, Ont., 1988).

16. Nicole Morgan, *Implosion: An Analysis of the Growth of the Federal Public Service in Canada, 1945–1985* (Montreal, 1986).

17. Colin Campbell and George J. Szablowski, *The Superbureaucrats: Structure and Behaviour in Central Agencies* (Toronto, 1979).

18. Carole Giangrande, *Down to Earth: The Crisis in Canadian Farming* (Toronto, 1985).

19. Quoted in Barry K. Wilson, *Farming the System: How Politicians and Producers Shape Canadian Agricultural Policy* (Saskatoon, 1990), 2.

20. Senate Committee on Poverty, *Poverty in Canada* (Ottawa, 1971), 175.

21. Peter Warrian, *Hard Bargain: Transforming Public Sector Labour–Management Relations* (Toronto, 1996).

22. Ake Blomqvist and David M. Brown, eds, *Limits to Care: Reforming Canada's Health System in an Age of Restraint* (Toronto, 1994), 399–400.

23. Donald Savoie, *The Politics of Public Spending in Canada* (Toronto, 1990).

24. William J. Frazer, *The Legacy of Keynes and Friedman: Economic Analysis, Money, and Ideology* (Westport, Conn., 1994).

25. *Financial Post* data.

26. Arthur Johnson, *Breaking the Banks* (Toronto, 1986); H.H. Binhammer, *Depository Institutions: Risks and Insolvencies* (Ottawa, 1987).

27. Peter Cook, *Massey at the Brink: The Story of Canada's Greatest Multinational and Its Struggle to Survive* (Toronto, 1981); Peter Foster, *Other People's Money: The Banks, the Government, and Dome* (Toronto, 1983).

28. Brian S. Osborne and Robert M. Pike, 'From "A Corner-stone of Canada's Social Structure" to "Financial Self-Sufficiency": The Transformation of the Canadian Postal Service, 1852–1987', *Canadian Journal of Communication* 13 (1988): 1–26.

29. Quoted ibid., 4.

30. Government of Canada, *Report of the Review Committee on the Mandate and Productivity of Canada Post Corpor-*

ation, 2 vols (Ottawa, 1985).

31. John Rothchild, *Going for Broke: How Robert Campeau Bankrupted the Retail Industry, Jolted the Junk Bond Market, and Brought the Booming Eighties to a Crashing Halt* (New York, 1991).

32. Donald Savoie, *Thatcher, Reagan, Mulroney: In Search of a New Bureaucracy* (Pittsburgh, 1994).

33. Richard Gwyn, *Edmonton Journal*, 22 Aug. 1984.

34. Randall White, *Fur Trade to Free Trade: Putting the Canada–United States Trade Agreement in Historical Perspective*, 2nd edn (Toronto, 1988); Mordechai Kreinin, ed., *Building a Partnership: The Canada–United States Free Trade Agreement* (East Lansing, Mich., 2000).

35. Linda McQuaig, *Shooting the Hippo: Death by Deficit and Other Canadian Myths* (Toronto, 1995), 107.

36. Thomas Wilson et al., 'The Sources of the Recession in Canada: 1989–1992', *Canadian Business Economics* 2, 2 (Winter 1994).

37. Lars Osberg and Pierre Fortin, eds, *Unnecessary Debts* (Toronto, 1996); D'Arcy Jenish, *Money to Burn: Trudeau, Mulroney and the Bankruptcy of Canada* (Toronto, 1996).

38. In 1998 Russia formally joined the G-7, making it the G-8.

39. Jean H. Morin, *Operation Friction, 1990–1991: The Canadian Forces in the Persian Gulf* (Toronto, 1997).

21 THE PROVINCES, THE CONSTITUTION, AND THE CHARTER OF RIGHTS, 1968–2007

1. C.B. Macpherson, *Democracy in Alberta* (Toronto, 1973). For the provinces generally, see Keith Brownsey and Michael Howlett, eds, *The Provincial State in Canada: Politics in the Provinces and Territories* (Peterborough, Ont., 2001). For an example of alienation, see Philip Resnick, *The Politics of Resentment: British Columbia Rejection and Canadian Unity* (Vancouver, 2000).

2. Nick Auf der Maur, *The Billion-Dollar Game: Jean Drapeau and the 1976 Olympics* (Toronto, 1976).

3. Françoise Coulombe, *The Pre-Referendum Campaign in Quebec* (Ottawa, 1980); Maurice Croisat, *Le Canada, d'un référendum à l'autre: les relations politiques entre le Canada et le Québec, 1980–1992* (Talence, 1992).

4. The entire political process outlined here may be followed in detail in John Whyte and Roy Romanow, *Canada . . . Notwithstanding: The Making of the Constitution, 1976–1982* (Toronto, 1984).

5. J.E. Fossum, *Oil, the State, and Federalism: The Rise and Demise of Petro-Canada as a Statist Impulse* (Toronto,

1997), 140 ff.

6. Quoted ibid., 146.

7. James Ross Harley, *Amending Canada's Constitution: History, Processes, Problems and Prospects* (Ottawa, 1996), 55.

8. For the complete text, see ibid., 215–19.

9. E. McWhinney, *Canada and the Constitution, 1979–1982* (Toronto, 1982), 80.

10. For the text of this accord, see ibid., Appendix C, 165–6.

11. For a contemporary view, see Brooke Jeffrey, *The Charter of Rights and Freedoms and Its Effect on Canadians* (Ottawa, 1982). For more recent analyses, see Patrick James, David Abelson, and Michael Lusztig, eds, *The Myth of the Sacred: The Charter, the Courts and the Politics of the Constitution in Canada* (Montreal, 2002); Christopher Manfredi, *Judicial Power and the Charter: Canada and the Paradox of Liberal Constitutionalism* (Toronto, 2001); Alan C. Cairns, *Charter versus Federalism: The Dilemmas of Constitutional Reform* (Montreal and Kingston, 1992).

12. In general, see Michael Mandel, *The Charter of Rights and the Legalization of Politics in Canada* (Toronto, 1992).

13. 2001 SCC 24. File No. 26930.

14. See Kent Roach, *The Supreme Court on Trial: Judicial Activism or Democratic Dialogue* (Toronto, 2001).

15. Ronalda Murphy, 'Same-sex Marriage and the Same Old Constitution', *Constitutional Forum* 14, 3 (2005).

16. Lévesque resigned in June 1985 and was succeeded as PQ leader by Pierre-Marc Johnson (b. 1946); he in turn resigned in November 1987, a week after Lévesque's death, and was succeeded by Jacques Parizeau (b. 1930).

17. Andrew Cohen, *A Deal Undone: The Making and Breaking of the Meech Lake Accord* (Vancouver, 1991); Patrick Monahan, *Meech Lake: The Inside Story* (Toronto, 1991).

18. Kenneth McRoberts and Patrick Monahan, eds, *The Charlottetown Accord, the Referendum, and the Future of Canada* (Toronto, 1993).

19. The World Series was originally named after the New York newspaper the *World* and had no international implications.

20. Anne Trépanier, *Un discours à plusieurs voix: la grammaire du oui en 1995* (Sainte Foy, Que., 2001); Wayne Reilly, ed., 'Theme Issue: The 1995 Quebec Referendum', *American Review of Canadian Studies* (1995).

21. For a further discussion, see Chapter 22.

22. The literature on health care and health-care reform is voluminous, and grows in size daily. Some of the best recent work includes: Laurie McFarlane, *The Best-Laid Plans: Health Care's Problems and Prospects* (Montreal and Kingston, 2002); David Gratzer, ed., *Better Medicine: Reforming Canada's Health Care* (Toronto, 2002); Terrence James Sullivan, *First Do No Harm: Making Sense of Canadian Health Reform* (Toronto, 2002); Maude Barlow, *Profit Is Not the Cure: A Citizen's Guide to Medicare* (Toronto, 2002).

23. Stanley Hartt, *The Charter and Health Care: Guaranteeing Timely Access to Health Care in Canada* (Toronto, 2002).

24. Roy Romanow, *Building on Values: The Future of Health Care in Canada* (Ottawa, 2002).

25. Ibid., xx.

26. See Colleen Flood, Kent Roach, and Lorne Bossin, eds, *Access to Justice: The Legal Debate over Private Health Insurance in Canada* (Toronto, 2005).

27. David Victor, *The Collapse of the Kyoto Protocol and the Struggle to Slow Global Warming* (Princeton, NJ, 2001).

28. Ross McKitrick, *The Kyoto Protocol: Canada's Risky Rush to Judgment* (Toronto, 2002).

29. See, for example, 'Mister Dress-up', *National Post Business* (Dec. 2002): 56–66.

22 THE FRAGMENTATION AND RECONSOLIDATION OF CONSERVATISM, 1990–2004

1. Lawrence Martin, *Chrétien* (Toronto, 1995); Jean Chrétien, *Straight from the Heart* (Toronto, 1994).

2. Murray Dobbin, *The Politics of Kim Campbell: From School Board Trustee to Prime Minister* (Toronto, 1993); Kim Campbell, *Time and Chance: The Political Memoirs of Canada's First Woman Prime Minister* (Toronto, 1996).

3. Alan Frizzell et al., eds, *The Canadian General Election of 1993* (Ottawa, 1994).

4. Frank Dabbs, *Preston Manning: The Roots of Reform* (Vancouver, 1997); Thomas Flanagan, *Waiting for the Wave: The Reform Party and Preston Manning* (Don Mills, Ont., 1995).

5. Manon Cornellier, *The Bloc* (Toronto, 1995); Lawrence Martin, *The Antagonist: Lucien Bouchard and the Politics of Delusion* (Toronto, 1997).

6. Ian McLeod, *Under Siege: The Federal NDP in the Nineties* (Toronto, 1994).

7. André Pratte, *Charest: His Life and Politics* (Toronto, 1998); Jean Charest, *My Road to Quebec* (Saint-Laurent, Que., 1998).

8. Binational Secretariat, Canada–U.S. FTA, *In the Matter of Certain Softwood Lumber Products from Canada* (n.p., 1994).

9. In his novel *Generation X* (1991), Douglas Coupland popularized the term 'McJob', which found its way into the *Oxford Canadian Dictionary* as 'a low paying, low status and usually unstimulating job with few benefits and little possibility for advancement, especially in a service industry'.

10. Published in New York.

11. Kenichi Omae, *The End of the Nation State: The Rise of Regional Economics* (New York, 1995).

12. See, for example, Murray Dobbin, *The Myth of the Good Corporate Citizen: Democracy under the Rule of Big Business* (Toronto, 1998); Tony Clarke, *MAI: The Multilateral Agreement on Investment and the Threat to Canadian Sovereignty* (Toronto, 1997)

13. Wesley Pue, ed., *Pepper in Our Eyes: The APEC Affair* (Vancouver, 2000).

14. For a Canadian example, see William Watson, *Globalization and the Meaning of Canadian Life* (Toronto, 1998).

15. Neil Neville, ed., *Unsteady State: The 1997 Federal Election* (Toronto, 2000).

16. James P. Allan et al., 'The Election Everybody Won? The Impact of Party System Change, Voter Turnout, and Strategic Voting in the 1998 Quebec Election', *American Review of Canadian Studies* 30, 4 (2000): 497–520.

17. Quoted in *Vancouver Province*, 9 Aug. 1969.

18. Roy Miki and Cassandra Kobayashi, *Justice in Our Time: The Japanese Canadian Redress Settlement* (Vancouver, 1991).

19. Quoted in Lubomyr Luciuk, *Time for Atonement: Canada's First National Internment Operations and the Ukrainian Canadians, 1914–1920* (Kingston, 1988), 28.

20. T. Kue Young, *Health Care and Cultural Change: The Indian Experience in the Central Subarctic* (Toronto, 1988); Geoffrey York, *The Dispossessed: Life and Death in Native Canada* (Toronto, 1988).

21. Quoted in Daniel Raunet, *Without Surrender, Without Consent: A History of the Nishga Land Claims* (Vancouver and Toronto, 1984).

22. Richard Salisbury, *A Homeland for the Cree: Regional Development in James Bay, 1971–1981* (Kingston, 1986); Donna Patrick, *Media Contestation of the James Bay and Northern Quebec Agreement: The Social Construction of the 'Cree Problem'* (Montreal, 1997).

23. Mary C. Hurley, *Aboriginal Title: The Supreme Court of Canada Decision in Delgamuukw v. British Columbia* (Ottawa, 1998); Owen Lippert, ed., *Beyond the Nass Valley: National Implications of the Supreme Court's Delgamuukw Decision* (Vancouver, 2000).

24. Chief Justice Lamar in CNLR, 48.

25. Diane Engelstad and John Bird, eds, *Nation to Nation: Aboriginal Sovereignty and the Future of Canada* (Toronto, 1992).

26. Canada, Royal Commission on Aboriginal Peoples, *Partners in Confederation: Aboriginal Peoples, Self-Government, and the Constitution* (Ottawa, 1993).

27. Denis Wall, 'Aboriginal Self-Government in Canada: The Cases of Nunavut and the Alberta Métis Settlements', in David Long and Olive Patricia Dickason, eds, *Visions of the Heart: Canadian Aboriginal Issues*, 2nd edn (Toronto, 2000), 143–67.

28. J.R. Miller, *Shingwauk's Vision: A History of Native Residential Schools* (Toronto, 1996); John Milloy, *A National Crime: The Canadian Government and the Residential School System, 1879 to 1986* (Winnipeg, 1999); Agnes Grant, *No End of Grief: Indian Residential Schools in Canada* (Winnipeg, 1996). For a first-person account of life in the schools, see Mary Fortier, *Behind Closed Doors: A Survivor's Story of the Boarding School System* (Belleville, Ont., 2002).

29. *Anglican Journal*, Dec. 2002, 1–2.

30. Nova Scotia, *Royal Commission on the Donald Marshall, Jr, 'Prosecution'*, vol. 1 (Halifax, 1989), 119.

31. Ibid., 'Digest of Findings and Recommendations 1989', 1.

32. David Laycock, *The New Right and Democracy in Canada: Understanding Reform and the Canadian Alliance* (Toronto, 2002).

33. Claire Hoy, *Stockwell Day: His Life and Politics* (Toronto, 2000); Trevor Harrison, *Requiem for a Lightweight: Stockwell Day and Image Politics* (Montreal, 2002).

34. André Blais et al., eds, *Anatomy of a Liberal Victory: Making Sense of the Vote in the 2000 Canada Elections* (Peterborough, Ont., 2002).

35. Gary Mauser, *Misfire: Firearm Registration in Canada* (Vancouver, 2001).

36. David Bercuson, *Significant Incident: Canada's Army, the Airborne, and the Murder in Somalia* (Toronto, 1996); Jean-Paul Brodeur, *Violence and Racial Prejudice in the Context of Peacekeeping: A Study Prepared for the Commission of Inquiry into the Deployment of Canadian Forces in Somalia* (Ottawa, 1997).

37. Nicholas Gammer, *From Peacekeeping to Peacemaking: Canada's Response to the Yugoslav Crisis* (Toronto, 2001).

23 CANADIAN SOCIETY AND CULTURE, 1972–2007

1. Michael Harris, *Unholy Orders: Tragedy at Mount Cashel* (Markham, Ont., 1990).

2. Heidi Athjan, *December 6: From the Montreal Massacre to Gun Control: The Inside Story* (Toronto, 1999); see also *Canadian Psychology* 33, 2 (1992; Special Issue: 'Violence and Its Aftermath').

3. Christopher Lasch, *The Culture of Narcissism: American Life in an Age of Diminishing Expectations* (New York, 1978).

4. Martin Turcotte, 'Parents with Adult Children Living at Home', *Canadian Social Trends* (Spring 2006): 2–9.

5. Reginald W. Bibby, *Fragmented Gods: The Poverty and Potential of Religion in Canada* (Toronto, 1987), 38.

6. *Maclean's*, 12 Apr. 1993.

7. Bibby, *Fragmented Gods*; Reginald W. Bibby, *Unknown Gods: The Ongoing Story of Religion in Canada* (Toronto, 1993). See also *Maclean's*, 12 Apr. 1993.

8. Bibby, *Fragmented Gods*, 38; see also Hans Mol, *Faith and Fragility: Religion and Identity in Canada* (Burlington, Ont., 1985).

9. David J. Jackson, 'Peace, Order, and Good Songs: Popular Music and English-Canadian Culture', *American Review of Canadian Studies* 35, 2 (2005): 25–44.

10. Donley Studler, *Tobacco Control: Comparative Politics in the United States and Canada* (Peterborough, Ont., 2002).

11. Health and Welfare Canada, *Special Study of Youth* (Ottawa, 1988).

12. Studler, *Tobacco Control*.

13. General demographic trends.

14. National Task Force on Suicide in Canada, *Suicide in Canada* (Ottawa, 1984), 9.

15. Statistics Canada, *Crime and Enforcement Statistics* (Ottawa, 1985).

16. Doug Owram, *Born at the Right Time: A History of the Baby-Boom Generation* (Toronto, 1996).

17. 1990 Royal Lepage Survey of Canadian House Prices; 2000 data.

18. Susan McDaniel, *Canada's Aging Population* (Toronto and Vancouver, 1986), 2.

19. Canada, National Advisory Council on Aging, *Seniors in Canada: A Report Card* (Ottawa, 2001).

20. L.O. Stone and S. Fletcher, *A Profile of Canada's Older Population* (Montreal, 1982).

21. Maureen Baker, *The Aging Canadian Population* (Ottawa, 1988), 23; K. Rockwood et al., eds, *Canadian Study of Health and Aging* (New York, 2002); M.W. Novak, ed., *Aging and Society: A Canadian Perspective*, 4th edn (Scarborough, Ont., 2001).

22. National Council of Welfare, *Poverty Profile 1988* (Ottawa, 1988). Another population experiencing dis-proportionate incidences of life below the poverty line consisted of children in female single-parent families. According to the Canadian Council on Social Development, the incidence of life below the poverty line for children of single mothers ranged from 56.1 per cent in PEI to 71.4 per cent in Manitoba, with the national average at 65 per cent.

23. Novak, ed., *Aging and Society*.

24. Royal Society of Canada, *AIDS: A Perspective for Canadians*, 2 vols (Ottawa, 1988).

25. Michael Ornstein, *AIDS in Canada: Knowledge, Behaviour, and Attitudes of Adults* (Toronto, 1989).

26. Vic Parsons, *Bad Blood: The Tragedy of the Canadian Tainted Blood Scandal* (Toronto, 1995).

27. *Globe and Mail*, 20 Nov. 2002.

28. Canada, *Report of the Royal Commission of Inquiry on the Blood System in Canada* (Ottawa, 1997).

29. Catherine Dunphy, *Morgentaler: A Difficult Hero* (Toronto, 1996).

30. Angus McLaren and Arlene Tigar McLaren, *The Bedroom and the State: The Changing Practices and Politics of Contraception and Abortion in Canada, 1880–1980* (Toronto, 1986); R. Tatalovich, *The Politics of Abortion in the United States and Canada* (Armonk, NY, 1997); T.G. Jelen and M. Chandler, *Abortion Policies in the United States and Canada: Studies in Public Opinion* (Westport, Conn., 1974).

31. Statistics Canada, *Women in Canada 2000: A Statistical Report*, 4th edn (Ottawa, 2000), 144.

32. Nancy Bowes et al., *Access Granted: Too Often Denied; A Special Report to Celebrate the 10th Anniversary of the Decriminalization of Abortion* (Ottawa, 1998).

33. David Cruise and Alison Griffiths, *Net Worth: Exploding the Myths of Pro Hockey* (Toronto, 1991); Stan Fischler, *Cracked Ice: An Insider's Look at the NHL in Turmoil* (Toronto, 1995).

34. Jim Silver, *Thin Ice: Money, Politics, and the Demise of an NHL Franchise* (Halifax, 1996).

35. Bruce Kidd and John Macfarlane, *The Death of Hockey* (Toronto, 1975).

36. See, for example, Morie Holzman and Joseph Nieforth, *Deceptions and Doublecross: How the NHL Conquered Hockey* (Toronto, 2002).

37. It is perhaps worth observing that the federal minister, in announcing the possibility of tax relief for Canadian NHL teams, called hockey a part of the 'fabric of Canadian society', but did not invoke the words 'Canadian identity' or 'Canadian culture' in his discussion. This is consistent with overall government policy,

which is to support sport in Canada but not on either cultural or identity grounds.

38. Eugene Benson and William Toye, eds, *The Oxford Companion to Canadian Literature*, 2nd edn (Toronto, 1997), 782.

39. Some notion of the extent of the enterprise can be gathered from Jill Humphries and D. Paul Schafer, comps and eds, *A Bibliography of Canadian Cultural Management and Policy* (Waterloo, Ont., 1997).

40. For a popular study, see Paul Audley, *Canada's Cultural Industries: Broadcasting, Publishing, Records, and Film* (Toronto, 1983).

41. See, for example, Statistics Canada, *Government Expenditures on Culture, 1992–93: Culture Statistics*, and *Artstats: Selected Statistics on the Arts and Culture in Canada* (Ottawa, 1993).

42. The late Harry G. Johnson, a distinguished Canadian economist of the pre-free trade generation who held an appointment at an American university, once described nationalism as 'typically concerned, not with developing and providing national competence, but with acquiring ownership of the symbols of accomplishment for nationals'. He added, 'This I view as an attempt to turn political power into undeserved economic rents for the minority at the expense of the majority of their fellow citizens.' Johnson, *On Economics and Society* (Chicago, 1975), 290–1.

43. This is the point emphasized by D. Paul Schafer in his *The Character of Canadian Culture* (Markham, Ont., 1990), 83–4.

44. George Woodcock, *Strange Bedfellows: The State and the Arts in Canada* (Vancouver and Toronto, 1985), 112.

45. CBC, *Culture, Broadcasting, and the Canadian Identity* (Ottawa, 1981), 14. For a general discussion of the relationship of Canadian television and national identity, which concludes that Canadian identity resides in major social and political institutions rather than in the Canadian Broadcasting Corporation or other media, see Richard Collins, *Culture, Communication, and National Identity: The Case of Canadian Television* (Toronto, 1990). During the time of the free trade debate, the argument against public support for the cultural industries was perhaps best made by Steven Globerman in his *Culture, Governments and Markets: Public Policy and the Culture Industries* (Vancouver, 1987), which to a large extent reiterated the views he expressed in his earlier *Cultural Regulation in Canada* (Montreal, 1983).

46. CBC, *Culture, Broadcasting, and the Canadian Identity*.

47. Michael Dorland, ed., *The Cultural Industries in Canada:*

Problems, Policies, Perceptions (Toronto, 1996); Tom Henighan, *The Presumption of Culture: Structure, Strategy and Survival in the Canadian Cultural Landscape* (Vancouver, 1996).

24 CANADA AND THE WORLD AFTER 9/11

1. Michael Adams, *Fire and Ice: The United States, Canada, and the Myth of Converging Values* (Toronto, 2003).

2. *Toronto Star*, 8 Aug. 2002.

3. *Calgary Herald*, 1 Mar. 2003.

4. *Globe and Mail*, 26 Mar. 2003.

5. Edna Keeble, 'Defining Canadian Security Continuities and Discontinuities', *American Review of Canadian Studies* 35, 1 (Spring 2005): 1–23.

6. Kate O'Neill, 'How Two Cows Make a Crisis: U.S.–Canada Trade Relations and Mad Cow Disease', *American Review of Canadian Studies* 35, 2 (Summer 2005): 295–319.

7. See Joseph S. McKinney, *Political Economy of the U.S.–Canada Softwood Lumber Trade* (Orono, Maine, 2004).

8. Monica Gattinger, 'From Government to Governance in the Energy Sector: The State of the Canada–U.S. Energy Relationship', *American Review of Canadian Studies* 35, 2 (Summer 2005): 321–52.

9. *Washington Post*, 31 May 2006.

10. Bruce Doern and Monica Gattinger, *Power Switch: Energy Regulatory Governance in the 21st Century* (Toronto, 2003).

11. See, e.g., Elizabeth Kolbert, *Field Notes for a Catastrophe: Man, Nature, and Climate Change* (New York, 2006); Patrick J. Michaels, ed., *Shattered Consensus: The True State of Global Warming* (Lanham, Md, 2005); Dave Reay, *Climate Change Begins at Home: Life on the Two-Way Street of Global Warming* (New York and London, 2005).

12. *Winnipeg Free Press*, 29 May 2006, 7.

13. *Globe and Mail*, 20 May 2006, 1, 5.

14. *Winnipeg Free Press*, 29 May 2006, 7.

15. Associated Press, 30 Apr. 2007.

16. Tommy Koh et al., eds, *The New Global Threat: Severe Acute Respiratory Syndrome and Its Impacts* (Singapore, 2003).

17. Agnan R. Khan, 'Canada's Kandahar Balancing Act', *Maclean's*, 26 May 2006.

18. Ibid.

19. Susan Delacourt, "Seeds Planted for Opposition to Unity Plan', *Globe and Mail*, 18 Sept. 1997.

20. Open letter to Ralph Klein, *National Post*, 24 Jan. 2001.

21. *Winnipeg Free Press*, 30 May 2006.
22. *Vancouver Province*, 3 May 2006.

WRITING ABOUT IMMIGRATION AND ETHNICITY

1. On the American scholarship, see Rudolph J. Vecoli, 'From The Uprooted to The Transplanted: The Writing of American Immigration History, 1951–1989', in Valeria Lerda, ed., *From Melting Pot to Multiculturalism* (Rome, 1990), 25–53.
2. See, for example, Frances E. Aboud, 'Ethnic Self-iden-tity', in R.C. Gardner and R. Kalin, eds, *A Canadian Social Psychology of Ethnic Relations* (Toronto, 1981), 37–56.
3. The classic study here is John Porter's *The Vertical Mosaic* (Toronto, 1965). A more recent analysis is Peter S. Li, *Ethnic Inequality in a Class Society* (Toronto, 1988).
4. Wsevolod W. Isajiw, 'Definitions of Ethnicity', *Ethnicity* 1 (1974): 111–24.
5. See, for example, Alan B. Anderson and James S. Frid-eres, *Ethnicity in Canada: Theoretical Perspectives* (Toron-to, 1981).
6. Howard Palmer, 'History and Present State of Ethnic Studies in Canada', in Wsevolod Isajiw, ed., *Identities: The Impact of Ethnicity on Canadian Society* (Toronto, 1973), 167–83; Palmer, 'Canadian Immigration and Ethnic History in the 1970s and 1980s', *Journal of Canadian Studies* 17 (1982): 35–50.
7. Irving Abella and Harold Troper, *None is Too Many: Canada and the Jews of Europe, 1933–1948* (Toronto, 1982).

EPILOGUE

1. See, for example, George Perlin, 'The Constraints of Public Opinion: Diverging or Converging Paths?' in Keith Banting, George Hoberg, and Richard Simeon, eds, *Degrees of Freedom: Canada and the United States in a Changing World* (Montreal and Kingston, 1997), 71–149; cf. Neil Nevitte, *The Decline of Deference: Canadian Value Change in Cross-national Perspective* (Peterborough, Ont., 1996).

nature/nurture debate, 174
Naval Service Bill, 171
navy, 170–1, 298, 301
Neatby, Hilda, 447, 465
New Brunswick: forestry in, 73; francophones in, 421; politics in, 378; *see also* Maritimes
New Canadian Library, 485
New Dealism, 241–2, 384
New Democratic Party (NDP), 375–6, 377; 454, 455, 641; labour and, 354; minority governments and, 642; in 1970s and 1980s, 521, 524–5, 530; in 1990s, 370–1, 575; popular vote and, 524; provincial politics and, 554, 562
Newfoundland: Confederation and, 8–9, 381; education in, 448; folk culture and, 478; Meech Lake and, 553–4; politics in, 378, 544; relocation program in, 361; sexual abuse in, 599; World War II and, 292
'new liberalism', 368
Newman, Peter C., 364
'new nationalism', 406–8
newspapers, 35, 65
New Theatre Group, 278
Niagara Peninsula, 121
9/11 September: effects of, 575, 627–35
Nisga'a, 581–2
Nobel Peace Prize, 333
Norman, Egerton Herbert, 334, 336
North: prospects for, 361
North American Air Defence Command (NORAD), 335, 338
North American Free Trade Agreement (NAFTA), 633, 568
North Americanists, 274
North American integration, 330, 364, 537, 573–5
North Atlantic Council, 331
North Atlantic Trading Company, 139, 144
North Atlantic Treaty Organization (NATO), 330–1, 350
North West Mounted Police, 42, 48
North-West Cattle Company, 112
North-West rebellion, 132, 169
North-West Territories, 19, 40–50
Noseworthy, Joseph, 304
notwithstanding clause, 550, 552
Nova Scotia: Antigonish Movement and, 246; 'better terms' and, 159; Confederation and, 4–6;

politics in, 378; *see also* Maritimes
Nova Scotia Steel and Coal Corporation, 69–70
nuclear bomb, 328–9, 335, 337–8
Nunavut, 582

O'Brien, Lucius, 40
October Crisis, 401–4, 455
Official Languages Act, 417
Ogdensburg Agreement, 292
O'Grady, J.W. de C., 206
oil and gas industry, 347, 515–17; control of, 549; foreign investment in, 350; offshore, 362, 517; prices and, 515, 527
Old Age Security Act, 384
O'Leary Commission, 457–9, 471
Oleskiw, Joseph, 143, 144
Oliver, Frank, 138–9, 147
Olympics, 472, 545, 605, 621, 622–3
Omae, Kenichi, 573
Ondaatje, Michael, 623
Onderdonk, Andrew, 140–1
Ontario: agriculture in, 121; cities in, 84; education in, 445; manufacturing in, 68, 349–50; politics in, 378, 554, 562–3; provincial rights and, 32, 159–60; resources in, 75–6; suffrage in, 191
Ontario Alliance for the Total Suppression of the Liquor Trade, 260
Ontario College of Physicians and Surgeons, 189–90
Ontario Housing Act, 100
Ontario Hydro-Electric Company, 76–7
Ontario Power Commission, 77
Ontario Society of Artists, 39
On-to-Ottawa Trek, 248
opera, 495
Orange Lodge, 18
Organization for Economic Co-operation and Development (OECD), 573
Organization of Petroleum Exporting Countries (OPEC), 515, 533
Otter, William, 48
Ouellet, André, 536
Ouellet, Fernand, 200
Owensmith, Blake, 504

Pacific Scandal, 30